Good Housekeeping
COOKERY
ENCYCLOPEDIA

Good Housekeeping
COOKERY ENCYCLOPEDIA

octopus

Compiled by
Good Housekeeping Institute

This edition first published in 1978 by
Octopus Books Limited
59 Grosvenor Street, London W1

© The National Magazine Company Limited, England, 1964

ISBN 0 7064 0253 7

Printed in Italy by New Interlitho SpA

ABERNETHY BISCUIT

A plain, sweet biscuit, flavoured with caraway.

ABRICOTINE (APRICOT BRANDY)

A liqueur made from brandy, sugar and apricots (or apricot kernels).

ABSINTHE

A bitter liqueur distilled from wormwood and flavoured with a number of herbs. As it is habit-forming and dangerous to health, it is now banned in many countries.

ACCELERATED FREEZE-DRYING (AFD)

This is a process which was once thought to have great potential as foods treated in this way are superior in quality to conventionally dried ones. However, expense has prevented its development on the scale that was once envisaged.

Frozen food is dehydrated under sufficiently high vacuum to remove the ice directly in the form of water vapour and not as water. Sufficient heat must be applied to the foodstuff to assist this removal without thawing it out and the food gradually dries from its surface inwards. Reconstitution consists of soaking in water for a few minutes, or by adding the product to a liquid, e.g. tea or coffee.

Freeze-dried foods are extremely light, as the water content of food accounts for 60 to 90 per cent of its weight, depending on the particular type. Foods so treated have a maximum storage life of 2 years; refrigeration is not required.

ACETIC ACID

The essential constituent of vinegar, amounting to not less than 4 per cent. A dilute solution of acetic acid (4 to 5 per cent.) is sometimes used as a cheap substitute for white wine vinegar for pickling pur-

poses. Acetic acid is also used in very small quantities in making some sweets. (See Vinegar.)

ACETO DOLCE

An Italian pickle, chiefly used as an appetizer.

ADDITIVE

Any substance added to foods to perform a special function: this may be to prevent food spoilage or to enhance texture, flavour or appearance. The purposes legally acceptable are:

Preserving
Colouring and flavouring
Emulsifying and stabilizing
Improving
Processing.

The use of additives is very strictly controlled to prevent the careless or criminally-intended inclusion of harmful substances. The Food Standards Committee, which advizes the Ministry of Agriculture, Fisheries and Food on such subjects, emphasises that proposed additives must be proved to be:

(a) of benefit to the consumer
(b) harmless to the consumer's health.

ADULTERANT

A substance which is added to another (usually a foodstuff) in order to increase the bulk and reduce the cost, with intent to defraud. The adulterant is usually similar in consistency and colour to the food in question and the flavour is either similar or neutral. Common instances of adulterants that were formerly used were: starch in spices, curry powder and cocoa; water in milk, butter and beer; turmeric in mustard; chicory in coffee.

Since the first Food and Drugs Act of 1860, control of the adulteration of foods has improved considerably and there are laws governing the preparation and labelling of food as well as the content. These laws are continually being revised. For many food products, the manufacturer must state on the container the ingredients in order according to the respective quantities.

ADVOCAAT

A Dutch liqueur, yellow in colour, made with brandy and eggs.

AERATED WATER

Strictly speaking, this is distilled water with purified air added. However, the term is usually used to denote carbonated water – that is, natural or manufactured 'fizzy' water. Many varieties are now widely available. Perrier, Evian, Vichy, Contrexeville and Vittel are French, San Pellegrino Italian, Appollinaris German. Many are claimed to have medicinal properties. Because of the law, mineral water is bottled at source, making costs high.

(See also Mineral Water, Soda Water entries.)

AGAR-AGAR

The gelatine-like product of a red seaweed, which used to be produced chiefly in Japan, China, Russia and the U.S.A. A type of agar is now produced in this country, from *gelidium algae* collected round the coast of Britain.

Agar-agar, which is marketed in sheet or strip form, is employed commercially in canning, in the making of jellies, creams and emulsions and as a medium for the laboratory culture of bacteria. It has strong setting properties, so a far smaller proportion (25 mg per 600 ml, 1/10 oz per pint of liquid) is required than with gelatine.

AGARIC

A family of fungi, containing many different types of both edible and poisonous mushrooms. (See also Mushroom entry.)

AGENE

Nitrogen trichloride, which was used for some time as a bleaching agent in flour. It was then discovered to be harmful if given to dogs in large quantities, so was considered unsuitable for human consumption and its use is now forbidden.

AITCHBONE

The aitchbone (sometimes erroneously called the edgebone) is cut from the upper part of the leg of beef. It is generally a low-priced joint, but because of the high proportion of bone is not particularly economical. It is usually roasted, but may be boiled or braised in the same way as a round of beef

and may also be used in a stew. Aitchbone is sometimes salted, in which case it is, of course, boiled.

Owing to its awkward shape, an aitchbone is a difficult joint to carve, the best method being as follows: Turn the joint towards the carver, as shown in the diagram and slice across from A to B, to level the joint. The upper side, seen in the diagram, is the most tender part, but is too fatty for some people, who prefer the leaner underside. The firm fat should be sliced horizontally at C; the soft fat lies below D, on the back.

ALASKA, BAKED

(See Ice Cream entry.)

ALBUMIN (ALBUMEN)

A soluble protein which forms part of blood, milk and egg white. When gently heated to 70°C/158°F., or when mixed with alcohol, it coagulates into a flocculent mass.

ALBUMIN POWDER

This can be used instead of egg whites when making meringues or royal icing. Royal icing made with albumin powder has the advantage of being softer than that made with egg whites.

ALBUMIN WATER

Sometimes prescribed for invalids, but is less often used nowadays.

ALDERMAN'S WALK

A name formerly given to the best cuts of haunch of mutton or venison or sirloin of beef.

ALE

An alcoholic drink brewed from malt and hops. The name is generally confined to the lighter-coloured malt liquors or beers, though before the introduction of hops it applied to all malt beer. (See Beer entry.)

ALECOST

A perennial herb with a minty flavour, which can be used as a winter substitute for mint.

ALEWIFE

A kind of herring.

ALGERIAN WINES

Various red, white and rosé wines are made in

Algeria, but with one or two exceptions they do not have the quality of the similar French wines and are therefore cheaper.

ALGINATE

See Seaweed.

ALLIGATOR PEAR

A common name in the United States for Avocado. (See Avocado entry.)

ALLSPICE

Kitchen name for Pimento (Jamaican pepper). (See Pimento entry.)

ALLUMETTES

Potatoes cut in 'matchsticks' and fried; sometimes called straw potatoes. The name is also given to narrow pastry fingers, sweet or savoury.

ALMOND

The kernel of the fruit borne by two similar trees – the sweet and the bitter almond. Among sweet almonds the two best types are Jordan and Valencia.

Almonds are used in making cakes, biscuits and sweets and sometimes in savoury dishes. Salted almonds are popular served with drinks. Ground almonds are used in marzipan, macaroons and ratafias.

Almonds contain a fair amount of protein, fat and minerals, but no starch.

Bitter almonds contain traces of prussic acid, which is very poisonous, but when this has been removed the almond oil can be used commercially as a flavouring agent.

To blanch almonds: Drop the shelled nuts into boiling water and leave for a few minutes. Squeeze

each one between thumb and first finger and the brown skin will come away easily. Rinse in cold water and dry on a cloth.

Almond Essence

The flavouring obtained from bitter almonds (after the extraction of almond oil) by fermentation and distillation. It is often added to cakes, biscuits and puddings. Nowadays a synthetic form is generally used. (See Essences entry.)

Almond Oil

The oil obtained by pressing almonds. It is very expensive and is therefore occasionally adulterated with oil from peach or apricot kernels; the addition is very difficult to detect.

Almond Paste (Almond Icing, Marzipan)

There are many variations of almond paste, but most are made from ground almonds and fine sugar, bound together with egg. It is important to use freshly ground almonds, as they quickly lose their flavour and sometimes become mouldy. The paste may be bound with either the yolk or the white of egg, or with both; when the yolk only is used, the paste is richer and more yellow in colour, while the white only makes a lighter and more brittle paste. The egg should be added very gradually and the paste kneaded well, to soften it and bring out the natural oil. Almond paste may be coloured and flavoured as desired for use in cake decorating and sweet-making.

Several brands of commercially manufactured marzipan are on the market. However, instead of the homemade proportions, which are approximately half ground almonds and half sugar, the commercial type has generally only 25 per cent. of ground almonds. It is thus both sweeter and cheaper than the homemade variety.

ALMOND PASTE

METRIC/IMPERIAL
225 g/8 oz icing sugar
225 g/8 oz caster sugar

To apply almond paste
1. Press the strip of almond paste onto the cake by rolling the cake on its side.

2. Invert the cake centering it exactly on the almond paste and press down firmly. Cut away any excess almond paste.

3. Loosen the paste from the board and turn the cake the right way up. Smooth the join using a palette knife.

450 g/1 lb ground almonds
2 standard eggs, lightly beaten
1 × 5 ml spoon/ 1 teaspoon vanilla essence
lemon juice

Sift the icing sugar into a bowl and mix with the caster sugar and almonds. Add the essence, with sufficient egg and lemon juice to mix to a stiff dough. Form into a ball and knead lightly. This makes 900 g/2 lb almond paste.

To apply almond paste: Trim the top of the cake if necessary. Measure round the cake with a piece of string. Brush the sides of the cake generously with sieved apricot jam. Take half the almond paste, form it into a roll and roll out as long as the string and as wide as the cake is deep. Press the strip firmly on to the sides of the cake, smoothing the join with a round-bladed knife and keeping the edges square. Brush the top of the cake with jam. Dredge the working surface generously with icing sugar, then roll out the remaining almond paste into a round to fit the top of the cake. Turn the cake upside down, centre it exactly on the paste, and press it down firmly. Smooth the join, loosen the paste from the board and turn the cake the right way up. Check that the top edge is quite level. Leave for 2 to 3 days before coating with royal icing.

ALMOND PASTE DECORATIONS
Simple but attractive decorations for an iced cake can be made from almond paste and they are particularly suitable for Christmas or birthday cakes. Draw the chosen shape on card and cut it out. (Stars, candles, holly leaves, Christmas trees, houses or engines make good designs, as they have bold outlines.) Colour some almond paste by working edible colouring in evenly; roll out very thinly on a board sprinkled with icing sugar, lay the pattern on it and cut round with a sharp-pointed knife. For holly berries, roll tiny balls of red-tinted paste. Leave the shapes on a plate till quite dry, then stick them on to the royal icing (which must be firm), using a dab of fresh icing.

ALPESTRA (ALPIN) CHEESE

A hard, dry, lightly salted cheese, golden in colour, made at Briançon and Gap in France.

ALSACE WINES

Wines made in the border province of Alsace. The climate, soil and grape varieties give the wine its individual characteristics of medium dryness and delicate flavour. The 'appellation controlée' is imposed by the type of grape rather than the vineyard: principal names are Riesling, Trominer and Sylvaner.

ALUMINIUM FOIL

Thin, pliable sheets of aluminium can be produced in different gauges, according to the intended purpose. This foil is used to wrap commercially produced foodstuffs and is sold in a roll for domestic use. It is useful for food wrapping, particularly for bread, sandwiches and cakes. Meat and poultry can be roasted in it, keeping the oven clean; the foil should be opened for the last 20 minutes to brown the meat. It can be used to line tins, is very malleable and does not need greasing. Heavy duty or Freezer foil should be used when wrapping food for the freezer.

AMBROSIA

Mythical food of the gods of Olympus.

AMERICAN FROSTING (OR ICING)

The special feature of this icing is that whilst it forms a crust on the outside, it never becomes really hard in texture like royal icing. Though it is mostly used on sponge mixtures and on walnut and cherry cakes, it can be applied to any type of cake. Any decorations (e.g. nuts, crystallized fruit) must be ready to put on immediately, before the icing has time to set.

1. Place sugar, water and cream of tartar into a saucepan. Stir over a gentle heat.

2. Without stirring, boil to 120°C/ 240°F. Remove saucepan from heat.

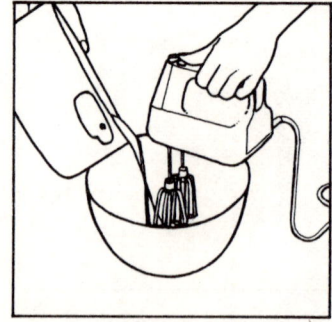

3. Beat egg whites stiffly, pour syrup onto egg whites in a thin stream.

AMERICAN FROSTING

METRIC/IMPERIAL
225 g/8 oz sugar
4 × 15 ml spoons/4 tablespoons water
pinch of cream of tartar
1 egg white

Note: To make this frosting properly, it is necessary to use a sugar-boiling thermometer.

Gently heat the sugar in the water with the cream of tartar, stirring until dissolved. Then, without stirring, boil to 120°C/240°F. Beat the egg white stiffly. Remove the sugar syrup from the heat and immediately the bubbles subside, pour it on to the egg white in a thin stream; beat the mixture continuously. When it thickens, shows signs of going dull round the edges and is almost cold, pour it quickly over the cake and spread at once evenly with a palette knife. The quantities given make sufficient frosting for an 18 cm/7 inch cake.

ANCHOVY

A small fish of the same family as the herring, which it resembles in colour and shape, though it is very much smaller. Anchovies are commonly canned in white oil or preserved in brine and are used (in small quantities only, as they are very highly salted) for savouries, hors d'œuvre and sauces and as a garnish and flavouring for meat and fish dishes.

To fillet whole anchovies: Salted anchovies should be soaked for several hours before use. If they are preserved in oil, remove this first by dipping them in boiling water. Wipe on a cloth or scrape to remove the skins and cut off the tails. Split the fish open with the finger and thumb, remove the bone and cut the flesh into two fillets or smaller pieces, which can be used for savoury pastries, e.g. Anchovy Twists.

ANCHOVY BUTTER
Mix 1 part of anchovies (boned and pounded to a paste) with 2 parts butter. A little spice or flavouring may be added.

ANCHOVY ESSENCE
This is a useful flavouring for many fish sauces and dishes; 1 × 5 ml spoon/1 teaspoon is enough to flavour 300 ml/½ pint white sauce.

ANCHOVY PASTE
This is commercially made by mixing pounded anchovies, vinegar, spices and water.

ANGEL CAKE (ANGEL FOOD CAKE)

An extremely light, feathery cake of the sponge type, containing egg whites; its success depends on the use of cake flour, which is not available in the U.K., the thorough beating of the egg whites and the careful folding in of the flour.

ANGELICA

A tall plant of the parsley family. It is chiefly cultivated on the Continent, especially in France, but it can be grown in this country and was at one time very popular because of its pleasant musk-like scent.

The hollow green stalks are candied and used for decorating cakes and desserts. They should be put in hot water for 2 to 3 minutes if necessary, to refresh the colour and remove the excess sugar. The seeds are incorporated in certain medicines and a tisane (tea) used to be made from them as a remedy for feverish colds.

ANGOSTURA

A herbal, spiritous compound invented in Venezuela during the last century for medicinal purposes. It is now made in Trinidad with a rum base. It is classed as a food flavouring therefore it does not carry excise tax. It is used in general cuisine and for making 'Pink Gin'.

ANISEED

The small seeds of the anise plant, cultivated in Malta, Spain, Russia and other places. They contain a volatile oil, with a warm, sweet, aromatic taste and odour. The extract oil of aniseed is used as a flavouring for sweets, pastries, liqueurs and cordials and has certain medicinal uses.

ANISETTE

An aniseed-flavoured sweet liqueur.

ANTI-PASTO

The dish served before the main course in Italy. This usually consists of an assortment of fish, cold meats and vegetables.

APERITIF

The French name for a drink taken before meals, differing from a cocktail in that it is fairly mild in character and often bitter in flavour. Vermouth and Sherry are the most popular aperitifs. There are many proprietary brands of aperitif such as Dubonnet, Amer Picon and St. Raphael.

APFEL STRUDEL

(See Strudel entry.)

APPLE

Apples are grown in most parts of the British Isles and in temperate climates throughout the world and there are very many varieties, both cooking and dessert.

From the strictly dietetic point of view, apples are not of great value. Most varieties have a low vitamin C content, though Bramley Seedlings have a higher proportion than other types. A crisp apple has the merit that it cleans the teeth satisfactorily. However, apples are one of the most popular and useful fruits.

In addition to their use as dessert, apples can be cooked in a large variety of ways to produce innumerable sweet dishes and they are sometimes used in combination with savoury foods, as in the case of apple sauce with pork and certain apple and cheese dishes. They can be baked, stewed, puréed or combined with pastry, milk puddings and many other foods; they can also be preserved in the form of jam, jelly, pickles, chutney, etc., and as dried apple rings and bottled fruit or pulp or frozen. Cooking apples are a rich source of pectin and are therefore useful in jam-making to combine with fruits that are poor in pectin. (See Jam entry.)

The following table shows some of the better varieties of home-grown and imported apples obtainable in this country, with the characteristic properties of each.

COOKING APPLES

Name	Country where produced	Description
EDWARD VII	England (December–April)	Large fruit, greenish-yellow with brownish-red flush; flesh hard, cream-coloured, juicy and acid; cooks dark red and transparent.
BRAMLEY SEEDLING	United Kingdom, Ireland (Late season)	Large, flat apple, green in colour, with dull red cheeks. Flesh firm and solid but tender, with an acid flavour. A good keeper; considered the best English cooking apple.
LANE'S PRINCE ALBERT	England (October–January)	Large round apple, green with crimson streaks. Good keeper.
LORD DERBY	England (September–November)	Very large apple, greenish-yellow and angular. Soft and tender flesh. Poor keeper.
MONARCH	England (December–April)	Large apple, green with crimson-red cheeks; resembles Newton Wonder but is considered superior. Good keeper.
NEWTON WONDER	England (November–June)	Large apple with solid, sweet flesh. Very good keeper.

DESSERT APPLES

Name	Country where produced	Description
BLENHEIM ORANGE	United Kingdom, New Zealand, Nova Scotia	Large apple, orange colour, streaked with red. Flesh crisp, acid and juicy.
COX'S ORANGE PIPPIN	England, Tasmania, Canada, Australia, New Zealand (Mid to late season)	Small to medium-sized round apple, greenish-yellow to orange in colour, streaked or shaded with red. Flesh tender, crisp and juicy; excellent flavour and aroma. Good keeper and best-known of English eating apples.
CRISPIN	England (December–April)	An apple with Japanese parentage which has recently been introduced. It is large, yellowy green with a good flavour.
DISCOVERY	England (August–September)	A new apple with a red skin. It is firm and juicy and keeps well.
DUNN'S SEEDLING	South Africa (March to May)	Crisp dessert apple (the larger size being also a good cooker). Green and russet with red streaks.
EGREMONT RUSSET	England (October–December)	A medium size crisp apple with a russet brown skin and an orange blush. It has a nutty flavour.

6

ELLINSON'S ORANGE PIPPIN	England (October)	Similar to Cox's.
GOLDEN DELICIOUS	South Africa (March to May), Australia, New Zealand (April to June)	Crisp, greeny-yellow, with characteristic five 'bumps' at the blossom end.
GRANNY SMITH	Australia, New Zealand, Tasmania, South Africa (Mid-season)	Medium-sized green apple. Flesh of good quality. A good keeper.
JAMES GRIEVE	England	Pale green to yellow, thin-skinned, soft, bruises rather easily.
JONATHAN	Canada, U.S.A., Australia, South Africa (Mid-season)	Small to medium-sized apple, yellow striped with red. Flesh crisp, sweet and juicy. Excellent keeper.
LAXTON'S SUPERB	England (Late season)	Medium-sized apple, round, yellow-shaded red cheeks. Flesh white, crisp and sweet. Excellent late apple.
RIBSTON PIPPIN	England, Tasmania, Canada (Mid-season)	Medium-sized, green to golden yellow with crimson-red cheeks. Flesh crisp, good flavour and aroma.
SPARKLING DELICIOUS	See Golden Delicious	Similar to Golden Delicious, but red in colour.
STURMER PIPPIN	England, Tasmania, Australia, New Zealand (Mid-season)	Small apple, green to russet-bronze. Flesh good quality, firm and sweet; an excellent keeper.
TYDEMAN'S EARLY	England (August-September)	A juicy, sweet scented apple similar to Worcester, but redder, larger and less conical.
WINTER PEAR-MAIN	South Africa (April-June)	Crisp, with a good flavour. Creamy-yellow flecked with russet colour.
WORCESTER PEAR-MAIN	England, Tasmania, New Zealand (Early September-October in England)	Medium-sized apple, conical shape and brilliant colour. Flesh soft, sweet and juicy, but poor flavour.

To stew apples: Wipe 0.5 kg/1 lb apples, peel thinly, core and cut into quarters and then into thin slices. Dissolve 100 g/4 oz sugar in 150 ml/¼ pint water and boil 5 minutes. Add fruit and simmer very gently until the apples are soft but not broken up.

For stewed dried apples, see Dried Fruit entry.

To bake apples: Wipe even-sized apples and cut through the skin round the centre. Remove the cores with an apple corer and stand the apples in a ovenproof dish or baking tin. Pour a few table-spoonfuls of water around and fill up the centre of each apple with demerara sugar and a knob of butter. Bake in a moderately hot oven (200°C/400°F, Gas Mark 6) – 45 minutes to 1 hour until tender. Serve hot or cold.

Alternatively, the apples may be stuffed with dried fruit or a mixture of chopped dates and nuts, a few shavings of butter being placed on top of the apples before baking. Apples can also be stuffed with a mixture of soft fruits, tossed in sugar and complementary spices.

TWO-CRUST APPLE PIE

METRIC/IMPERIAL
275 g/10 oz plain flour
pinch of salt
65 g/2½ oz lard or blended white vegetable fat
65 g/2½ oz margarine or butter
3–4 × 15 ml spoons/3–4 tablespoons water
1 kg/2 lb Bramley cooking apples
100 g/4 oz soft light brown sugar
2 × 15 ml spoons/2 tablespoons cornflour
1 piece stem ginger
milk to glaze
1 × 15 ml spoon/1 tablespoon caster sugar

Keep hands, utensils, working surface and ingredients cool. A special pastry blender with wooden handle and wire loops is good for those with warm hands. Self-raising flour can be used but gives pastry a more 'cakey' texture. For a richer pastry increase fats to 75 g/3 oz each. Soft tub margarines are best used only in specially evolved all-in-one pastry making methods.

7

Put flour and salt in a bowl, add firm, not hard, fat cut into small pieces; with fingertips rub in until it's of a fine breadcrumb texture. Shake bowl from time to time so that any larger crumbs can be seen. The hands should be lifted well up over the bowl so that air is incorporated in the mixture.

Allow about 1 × 5 ml spoon/1 teaspoon cold water for each ounce of flour – too much liquid gives a difficult-to-handle sticky dough which results in tough pastry.

Sprinkle liquid over the surface all at once. Gradual addition gives an uneven texture and this tends to cause blisters when the pastry is cooked. Once the liquid is added, use a round-bladed knife to distribute liquid as evenly as possible and draw crumbs together. When large lumps are formed, finish knitting dough together with fingertips into a ball.

With light fingertip handling, knead dough on sparsely floured surface (too much flour makes pastry tough). When pastry is smooth and free from cracks, divide in half, round up largest part. Dust rolling-pin with flour and roll lightly. Keep edges round. If they begin to break, pinch immediately. Keep pastry circular, turning frequently but not rolling sideways. Roll out to 2.5 cm/1 inch larger than plate.

Place 25 cm/10 inch inverted pie plate (foil or metal are ideal but ovenproof glass can be used) on pastry; cut round edge with a knife. Knead trimmings with rest of pastry and roll out to fit pie plate – about 2.5 cm/1 inch larger. Fold in half and transfer to dish. Unfold and ease into dish without stretching pastry. Shape into base with fingers and trim off any surplus.

Peel, core and slice apples to 5 mm/¼ inch thickness. To start cooking and enable more apple slices to be used, plunge slices into boiling water for 2 minutes. Drain at once and cool under running water. Drain again well. In a basin, combine sugar and cornflour, which thickens the juices as they are cooking.

Arrange the apple on the bottom of the pie, scatter the chopped ginger over and sprinkle with half sugar mixture. Repeat with rest of the fruit and sugar, keeping rim of dish clear. Apples should be kept level.

For more tartness add a little lemon juice to filling. Put a baking sheet in oven to pre-heat. This helps to boost initial sealing of pastry base and prevent a soggy base.

Using a soft pastry brush, moisten pastry rim with milk or beaten egg glaze. Loosely fold pastry round the rolling-pin and, with the support of one hand underneath, transfer to pie and guide pastry over filling. This prevents unnecessary stretching of dough. Gently press edges of pastry together with edge of finger to seal. Brush any surplus flour from pastry surface with a dry brush.

Place index finger, knuckle side down, on top of rim. Press lightly. Hold knife horizontally with back of blade towards edge. Beginning near rim of dish and working up towards finger, flake edges by knocking the back of the knife against cut edge.

For a scalloped edge, place thumb on top of pastry and index finger under rim. Press down lightly and, at the same time, move knife, held upright in other hand, up and in to make a small nick. The pressure of thumb against knife makes flute. Slit the centre.

Bake unglazed or glaze with milk and dredge with caster sugar. Place pie on pre-heated baking sheet and bake in centre of hot oven (220°C/425°F, Gas Mark 7) for 15 minutes. Reduce to (180°C/350°F, Gas Mark 4) for 30 to 35 minutes or until golden brown.

DEEP DISH APPLE-CHERRY PIE

1 kg/2 lb cooking apples
450 g/1 lb can pitted morello cherries
75–100 g/3–4 oz granulated sugar
2 × 15 ml spoons/2 tablespoons cornflour

PASTRY:
350 g/12 oz plain flour
pinch of salt
175 g/6 oz butter or block margarine
1 × 15 ml spoon/1 tablespoon caster sugar
3 × 15 ml spoons/3 tablespoons ground almonds
2 egg yolks
3 × 15 ml spoons/3 tablespoons water
egg white for glaze

Peel, core and slice apples and combine with the drained cherries, granulated sugar and cornflour blended with 2 × 15 ml spoons/2 tablespoons cherry juice. Turn into a 1.2 litre/2 pint pie dish. Sift together the flour and salt, rub in fat and stir in caster sugar and almonds. Combine yolks and water and use to form a manageable dough. Roll out pastry and use to cover the pie dish. Knock up and decorate the edges. Brush with egg white. Place on a baking sheet and bake in a hot oven (220°C/425°F, Gas Mark 7) for 15 to 20 min., reduce heat (180°C/350°F, Gas Mark 4) for a further 30 to 35 min. until apples are cooked. To serve, dust with caster sugar.

APPLE DUMPLINGS

METRIC/IMPERIAL
250 g/9 oz shortcrust pastry
4 even sized cooking apples
50 g/2 oz sugar
milk to glaze
caster sugar

Divide the pastry into four and roll out each piece into a round 20 cm/8 inches to 25 cm/10 inches across. Peel and core the apples, place one on each round and fill the centre with some of the sugar.

Moisten the edges of the pastry with water, gather the edges to the top, pressing well to seal them together, and turn the dumplings over. If you wish, decorate with leaves cut from any trimmings of pastry. Brush the tops with milk. Bake on a greased baking sheet in a preheated hot oven (220°C/425°F, Gas Mark 7) for 10 minutes. Reduce (160°C/325°F, Gas Mark 3) for 30 minutes, until the apples are soft. Dredge with caster sugar and eat hot or cold, with custard or cream.

APPLE SAUCE

METRIC/IMPERIAL
0.5 kg/1 lb apples
25 g/1 oz butter
sugar or lemon juice if required

Choose good cooking apples; peel and slice them with stainless steel knife and cook gently to a pulp in a covered pan. Beat with a wooden spoon until smooth, then add the butter. Sugar may be added, but to accompany goose, duck or pork the sauce should be fairly tart; if on the other hand the apples are sweet, a little lemon juice may be added.

DANISH 'PEASANT GIRL WITH VEIL'

METRIC/IMPERIAL
175 g/6 oz fresh breadcrumbs
75 g/3 oz brown sugar
50 g/2 oz butter
0.75 kg/1½ lb peeled, cored and sliced cooking apples
juice of ½ lemon
sugar to taste
150 ml/¼ pint carton double or whipping cream
50 g/2 oz grated chocolate

Mix the crumbs and sugar together and fry in the hot butter until crisp. Cook the apples in a very little water, with the lemon juice and some sugar to taste, until they form a pulp, – 10 to 15 minutes. Put alternate layers of the fried crumb mixture and the apple pulp into a glass dish, finishing with a layer of crumbs. When the pudding is quite cold, pour the cream on top and sprinkle with the chocolate.
Note: If you wish, spread a layer of raspberry jam between the last layer of crumbs and the cream.

APPLE GINGER PRESERVE

METRIC/IMPERIAL
1.75 kg/4 lb apples
600 ml/1 pint water
225 g/8 oz preserved ginger
3 × 15 ml spoons/3 tablespoons ginger syrup
grated rind and juice of 3 lemons
1.5 kg/3 lb sugar

Peel the apples and slice thinly; tie the cores and peel in muslin; add the water and simmer all in a

covered pan until soft. Remove the muslin bag and mash the apples with a spoon or whisk. Cut the ginger into neat pieces and add it to the apples, together with the ginger syrup, the grated lemon rind, the lemon juice and sugar. Bring to the boil, stirring constantly, test on a cold plate after 10 minutes boiling and as soon as the preserve sets, pot and cover immediately.

APPLE JELLY

METRIC/IMPERIAL
2.5 kg/5½ lb cooking apples
juice of 2 lemons
water
sugar

Windfalls or cooking apples can be successfully used, but dessert apples should not be used for jelly making. Wash the apples and remove any bruised or damaged portions, then cut them into thick slices without peeling or coring. Put them in a pan with the lemon juice and sufficient cold water to cover (about 1.75 litres/3 pints). Simmer until the apples are really soft and the liquid is well reduced (by about one-third), then strain the pulp through a jelly cloth. Measure the extract and return it to the pan, with 450 g/1 lb sugar to each 600 ml/1 pint of extract. Bring to the boil, stir until the sugar has dissolved and boil rapidly until a 'jell' is obtained on testing. Skim, pot and cover the jelly as for jam.

As the colour of apple jelly is sometimes unat- tractive, a few blackberries can be added with the apples; or, if preferred, some raspberries, red- currants, cranberries or loganberries may be used instead to give the preserve a better colour.

To preserve apples: In addition to their use in jellies, etc., cooking apples may be quartered, sliced or pulped and then bottled and sterilised. (For method see Bottling entry.) For directions for dried apple rings, see Drying Fruit and Veg- etables entry.

Apples can also be frozen in slices or as a purée. Slices should be blanched for 2 to 3 minutes and cooled in ice-cold water before packing; apples stewed for a purée should have very little water added and can be sweetened or unsweetened.

To store apples: Some good 'keeping' varieties of cooking and dessert apples may easily be preserved for winter and spring use. Among the best var- ieties for storing are Bramley Seedlings for cook- ing and Cox's Orange Pippin for dessert.

The apples are best left to mature on the trees until a light twist of the hand will detach them. Pick them carefully, taking care not to bruise them or pull the stalks out of their sockets, and place in baskets. Store only unblemished apples, placing them with the stalk upwards and not touching each other, on slatted wooden shelves in a cool, damp, frost-proof room. They should be looked over once a week and any that show signs of deterioration should be removed and used at once.

An alternative method of storing is to wrap the apples separately in oiled apple wraps (obtainable from most sundriesmen) and then pack them in boxes in a cool shed – not in a spare bedroom or dry, warm place.

Experiments have been carried out to investigate the effect of coating the varieties of apple that do not keep well and the most satisfactory results seem to be given by the use of wax or oil emulsions.

APPLE BRANDY (CALVADOS, APPLEJACK)

A spirit distilled from cider. It is very widely drunk in Normandy and the neighbouring apple-growing regions of France and is also popular in some parts of North America.

APRICOT

The fruit of a prunus tree, originally a native of China, which is now widely grown in the warmer temperate countries. Apricots are imported into this country from Spain, South Africa, Southern California and Australia, in fresh, canned and dried form.

The apricot somewhat resembles a small peach, being rounded in shape and yellow or orange in colour. It has a delicious flavour when ripe and is popular in all its forms, as a dessert fruit, in salads and other fruit dishes and in soufflés and similar confections. Jam is made from both the fresh and the dried fruit. The kernels, which are very like sweet almonds, are crushed to extract the oil for use in the fish-packing industry. The kernels and the fresh or dried fruit are used to flavour apricot brandy (abricotine).

The chief food value of apricots lies in their vitamin A content. Dried apricots are a valuable source of vitamin A, iron and calcium. They make excellent puddings and fruit 'compotes'.

For preparation and cooking, see Dried Fruit entry.

Apricots can be frozen although they may discolour unless ascorbic acid (Vitamin C) is added to the syrup.

The apricots should be plunged into boiling water for 30 seconds to loosen skins and then peeled. They can be sliced, cut in half, or left whole before packing in a syrup made with 0.5 kg/1 lb sugar to 1.2 litres/2 pints water. For each 0.5 kg/1 lb pack add 200 to 300 mg ascorbic acid.

APRICOT JAM
(Made from fresh fruit)

METRIC/IMPERIAL
1.75 kg/4 lb fresh apricots

450 ml/¾ pint water
juice of 1 lemon
1.75 kg/4 lb sugar

Wash the fruit, cut in half and remove the stones. Crack a few stones to remove the kernels and blanch them by dipping in boiling water. Put the apricots into a pan with the water, lemon juice and blanched kernels and simmer until they are soft and the contents of the pan well reduced. Add the sugar, stir until dissolved and boil rapidly for about 15 minutes, or until setting point is reached. Pot and cover in the usual way. Makes about 3 kg/6 lb.

APRICOT JAM
(Made from dried fruit)

METRIC/IMPERIAL
450 g/1 lb dried apricots
1.75 litres/3 pints water
juice of 1 lemon
1.5 kg/3 lb sugar
50–75 g/2–3 oz shelled and blanched almonds,
  optional

Wash the apricots thoroughly, cover with the water and soak for 24 hours. Put the fruit into a pan with the water in which it was soaked, add the lemon juice and simmer for 30 minutes, or until soft, stirring from time to time. Add the sugar and blanched almonds, stir until dissolved and boil rapidly until setting point is reached, stirring frequently, as the jam tends to stick. Pot and cover in the usual way. Makes about 2.25 kg/5 lb.

AQUAVIT

A Scandinavian liqueur, distilled from a variety of substances, including potatoes, grain and sawdust; it is colourless, unsweetened and usually flavoured with caraway seeds.

ARMAGNAC

A French brandy of excellent quality, named after the district where it is produced.

ARRACK

Also known as Raki or Rakia, it is a spirit made in the Near and Far East. It is made from fermented palm sap (toddy) but other bases such as dates, grapes and milk are used. Arrack may be flavoured, particularly with aniseed.

ARROWROOT

A pure starch powder obtained from the pith of the roots of the maranta plant, which is grown in Bermuda and the West Indies. As purchased in this country, it is a light, white, odourless powder, which will keep for a considerable time if stored in a dry place.

When mixed with boiling water, arrowroot forms a clear jelly and can be used for thickening fruit juices intended to cover or glaze flans and similar dishes. Mixed with milk, it may be used instead of flour or cornflour for puddings and sauces. Arrowroot also makes a popular thin crisp biscuit. It should always be blended with a cold liquid before heating.

Arrowroot Glaze

Measure 150 ml/¼ pint of sweetened fruit juice. Blend 1.5 × 5 ml spoon/1½ teaspoons arrowroot with the juice and pour into a saucepan. Bring to the boil, stirring. When glaze is clear take off heat and leave to cool a little before using to coat fruit etc.

ARROWROOT MADE WITH WATER

METRIC/IMPERIAL
7.5 g/¼ oz arrowroot
300 ml/½ pint cold water
1 × 5 ml spoon/1 teaspoon sugar

This is useful for those suffering from diarrhoea or gastric upsets.

Put the arrowroot into a small basin, add to it 1 × 15 ml spoon/1 tablespoon of the water and mix with a wooden spoon until quite smooth. Add the rest of the water, mix well and pour into a saucepan. Heat gently until it boils and thickens, stirring constantly. Cook for about 10 minutes, sweeten to taste and serve in a cup or basin.

ARTICHOKE

The name is applied to plants belonging to three different genera: (1) The true or globe artichoke; (2) the Jerusalem artichoke; (3) the Chinese (or Japanese) artichoke or Stachys.

Globe Artichoke

If allowed to reach full maturity, resembles a large thistle. The part eaten is the bud of the flower, which is cut off at the point where it joins the stem. The fond or bottom of the artichoke is particularly highly prized, while the choke, the thistly part, is discarded. Globe artichokes are in season from June to September. They supply a small amount of Vitamin C.

To cook Globe Artichokes: Choose young, fresh heads and allow at least one for each person, as they are not easy to divide. Cut off the stalks, level with the leaves; remove the hard bottom leaves and cut about 1 inch/2.5 cm off those at the top (using scissors). Wash them in several waters and soak in fresh cold water for at least 1 hour, then place them points downwards in a saucepan of fast-boiling water, slightly salted and sharpened with a little vinegar or lemon juice; a small bunch of herbs may be added to give flavour. Let the artichokes boil uncovered until the leaves can be detached quite easily when pulled – 30 minutes to 1½ hours. Drain well and serve piled up on a hot dish, with a sauce served separately.

Melted butter with a dash of vinegar or lemon juice is the best accompaniment for hot artichokes, or they may be served cold with French dressing or vinaigrette sauce. In either case they form a course by themselves, usually the starter to a meal.

The correct way to eat globe artichokes is to pull out the leaves one at a time with the fingers, dip each in the sauce and suck the soft end. When the centre is reached, remove the choke or soft flowery part and eat the bottom, which is the chief delicacy, with a knife and fork. The choke forms the basis of many main meal dishes as well as appetizers and vegetable dishes.

Jerusalem Artichoke

A member of the sunflower family. The tubers are cooked and eaten as a vegetable during the autumn and winter. The plant is native to the American continent, but is now grown extensively in Europe.

To cook the tubers, first scrub them, then peel quickly and drop them at once into clean, cold water, using a stainless knife or peeler and keeping them under water as much as possible to prevent discoloration. A little salt and a squeeze of lemon juice may be added to the water to help them keep a good colour. Place in boiling salted water to which a little lemon juice has been added, cook until tender (about 30 to 40 minutes) drain well and serve with a white sauce.

They are easier to peel if cooked first and then allowed to cool.

Artichokes give an excellent flavour to casseroles and are also very good baked in dripping to serve with roast meat.

The Chinese or 'Japanese' Artichoke (Stachys)

Rather a rarity in this country; the tubers, which are the edible portion, resemble Jerusalem artichokes in flavour.

To cook the tubers, first scrub them, then peel quickly and drop them at once into clean, cold water, then rub off the skins in a clean cloth. Put at once into cold water, adding a little salt and a squeeze of lemon juice to preserve the colour. Cook in boiling salted water until tender – 15 to 20 minutes. Drain well, then return the artichokes to the pan and toss with a piece of butter, a sprinkling of salt and pepper and a little chopped parsley. Serve very hot.

Stachys can also be served creamed or au gratin and are very good cold, in a salad.

ASCORBIC ACID

The scientific name for Vitamin C . (See Vitamins entry.)

ASPARAGUS

This is the cultivated form of a plant of the lily family which originally grew near the sea-shore. It has been popular for many centuries and there are therefore many varieties, some of them pale green, some almost white and some with purple tips. The green asparagus grown out of doors in England is in season from April until the end of June. Asparagus has very little nutritive value, but is prized as a delicious food. To extend its rather brief season, it may be bottled or frozen and it is also sold canned. It makes a good soup and both canned and packet soup preparations are available.

To cook asparagus, cut off the woody end of the stalks and scrape the white part lightly, removing any coarse spines. Tie in bundles and place upright in a saucepan of boiling salted water. Boil for 10 minutes, then lay flat and continue cooking until tender – a further 10 to 15 minutes. Drain very well and untie the bundles before dishing. Serve with melted butter or Hollandaise sauce.

Asparagus may also be served cold, with a vinaigrette dressing or with mayonnaise. It may also be served plain as a vegetable accompaniment.

CREAM OF ASPARAGUS SOUP

METRIC/IMPERIAL
1 large bundle of asparagus
½ onion, skinned and sliced
600 ml/1 pint white stock
50 g/2 oz butter
3 × 15 ml spoons/3 tablespoons flour
salt
pepper
300 ml/½ pint milk
3 × 15 ml spoons/3 tablespoons cream

Wash and trim the asparagus, discarding the woody part of the stem which is tough and inedible, and cut the remainder into short lengths, keeping a few tips for garnish. Cook the tips for about 5 to 10 minutes in boiling salted water. Put the rest of the asparagus, the onion, 150 ml/¼ pint of the stock and the butter in a saucepan, cover and simmer for about 20 minutes until the asparagus is soft. Blend the flour and the remaining stock to a smooth cream. Stir in a little of the hot soup and return this mixture to the pan; bring to the boil, stirring until it thickens. Cook for a further 2 to 3 minutes. Season to taste with salt and pepper and sieve the soup or purée it in an electric blender. Stir in the remaining milk and the cream, re-heat and garnish with asparagus tips.

ASPIC

An amber-coloured savoury jelly, deriving its name from a herb called 'spike' which was at one time used to flavour it. Aspic is made from clarified meat stock, fortified if necessary with gelatine and flavoured with vegetables, herbs and sometimes sherry. Prepared aspic jelly may be bought ready-made in jars, or in the form of crystals in packets or jars. As a quick alternative, stock (or water) and gelatine may be used.

Aspic jelly is used to set meat, game, fish and vegetables, etc., in a mould and as an exterior coating for decorating cold game, hams, tongues, raised pies, galantines, poultry, fish and so on. Chopped aspic jelly is used for garnish.

HOME-MADE ASPIC JELLY

METRIC/IMPERIAL
rind of 1 lemon
1 carrot
1 turnip
1 onion
a little celery
2–3 × 15 ml spoons/2–3 tablespoons lemon juice
2–3 × 15 ml spoons/2–3 tablespoons tarragon or chilli vinegar
2–3 × 15 ml spoons/2–3 tablespoons sherry
6 peppercorns
1 × 2.5 ml spoon/½ teaspoon salt
40 g/1½ oz gelatine
900 ml/1½ pints good stock
shells and whites of 2 eggs

Wipe the lemon and peel or grate the rind. Prepare the vegetables, cutting each into about 4 pieces, and place them in a large saucepan with the lemon rind and juice, the vinegar, sherry, peppercorns, salt, gelatine and stock. Wash and crush the egg-shells and add them, with the egg whites. Put over a low heat, begin to whisk vigorously and bring nearly to boiling point, whisking meanwhile. Stop whisking and allow the froth to rise to the top of the pan, then draw it aside and leave in a warm place for 5 minutes. Strain the liquid through a clean scalded cloth or jelly bag, passing it a second time through the cloth if not absolutely clear.

ASTI SPUMANTE

The best-known Italian sparkling wine; it is usually a sweet wine best served with dessert but drier types are available. Asti Spumante is becoming increasingly popular to serve at wedding receptions.

ATHOL BROSE

A Scottish drink, made of water in which oatmeal has been steeped, mixed with whisky and honey.

AU GRATIN

For this and similar phrases, see Menu Glossary entry.

AUBERGINE (EGGPLANT)

This plant is a member of the nightshade family a native of S.E. Asia. Its fruit, usually egg-shaped, is somewhat akin to the tomato; it varies in colour from a yellowish-white to violet.

Aubergines can be sliced and then fried, grilled or sautéed; baked with a savoury stuffing; made into fritters; used in soups and casseroles.

To prepare them cut off the stalk and peel or wipe the skin carefully. Slice or cut in half, according to the dish being made, and sprinkle with salt. Leave them for 20 to 30 minutes to 'dégorge' before rinsing and wiping. This helps to remove any bitterness and bring out the flavour. While exposed to the air the aubergine will discolour slightly.

BAKED STUFFED AUBERGINE

METRIC/IMPERIAL
*2 large, well-rounded aubergines – about 350 g/12 oz
    each*
salt
6 × 15 ml spoons/6 tablespoons vegetable oil
50 g/2 oz onion, skinned
2 × 15 ml spoons/2 tablespoons tomato paste
freshly ground black pepper
4 standard eggs
chopped parsley to garnish

Wipe the aubergines and trim off the stalks. Halve lengthwise and score the cut surface well. Sprinkle with salt and leave to stand for about 20 minutes to draw out the indigestible bitter juices. Pat the aubergines dry using kitchen paper and fry the aubergine halves gently in the hot oil, adding more oil if necessary, turning once, until just tender. Remove from the pan. Chop the onion finely and fry to a golden brown in the residue oil. Meanwhile scoop out the aubergine flesh leaving a good edge on the skin. Chop the flesh roughly and stir into the pan with the tomato paste and seasoning. Simmer gently until well combined. Pack the aubergines into a shallow ovenproof dish. Break the eggs, individually, into a cup and pour carefully into the aubergine shells. Spoon the pan ingredients along each end of the aubergines. Bake in a moderate oven (180°C/350°F, Gas Mark 4) for about 20 minutes or until the eggs are just set. Sprinkle with chopped parsley for serving.
Note: when the eggs are a little large for the shells allow the white to overflow and set in the bottom of the dish.

AUBERGINE FIESTA

METRIC/IMPERIAL
450 g/1 lb aubergines
boiling water
400 g/14 oz can tomatoes, drained
25 g/1 oz butter
1 clove garlic, skinned and crushed
a pinch of salt
freshly ground black pepper
350 g/12 oz can sweet corn
50 g/2 oz Parmesan cheese, grated
chopped parsley for garnish

Peel the aubergines, cut into 2.5 cm/1 inch slices and cut each slice into 4 triangular chunks. Put in a saucepan, cover with boiling water and boil gently for 5 minutes; drain well. Roughly chop the tomatoes. Butter the inside of an ovenproof dish and put in the aubergines, tomatoes, garlic, seasoning and corn. Sprinkle evenly with the cheese. Bake uncovered in a moderately hot oven (200°C/400°F, Gas Mark 6) for about 20 minutes, until the sauce is bubbly and the cheese has melted. Garnish with the chopped parsley.

AUDIT ALE

A strong ale, originally brewed at Oxford and Cambridge Universities and drunk at the 'Audit day' feasts.

AVOCADO

The fruit of a tree grown in the Americas, Middle East and parts of Africa. When ripe it is dark purple or green with soft flesh rich in oil, vitamins A, B, C, D, E and calcium. The flesh has a distinctive bland flavour and buttery texture.

Avocados are usually eaten as hors d'œuvre. To prepare them, make a lengthways cut around the centre, entirely encircling the fruit and reaching down to the large stone. To separate the two halves, twist them in opposite directions. Discard the stone and sprinkle the flesh with lemon or lime juice to prevent it from turning brown. The centre hollows may then be filled with mayonnaise, cream cheese, flaked salmon or tuna fish, or indeed any desired savoury mixture.

AVOCADO DIP

METRIC/IMPERIAL
2 medium avocados
2 × 15 ml spoons/2 tablespoons milk
225 g/8 oz cream cheese
1 × 5 ml spoon/1 teaspoon salt
a pinch of cayenne pepper
a dash of Worcestershire sauce
1 × 15 ml spoon/1 tablespoon finely grated onion
2 × 15 ml spoons/2 tablespoons lemon juice

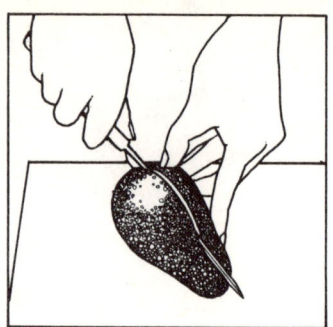

1. Using a stainless steel knife cut the avocado lengthwise to entirely encircle the stone.

2. Separate the halves by gently rotating them in opposite directions, and discard the stone.

3 Brush the cut surfaces of the avocado liberally with lemon juice to prevent discoloration.

Peel and stone the avocados and mash to a smooth purée with the milk. Cream the cheese until soft and beat into the avocado with the remaining ingredients. Serve with biscuits and pieces of vegetable to dip.

DRESSED AVOCADOS

METRIC/IMPERIAL
avocados (allow half per person)
lemon juice
French dressing
lettuce leaves (optional)

Cut open the avocados lengthwise, using a stainless steel knife and making a deep cut through the flesh, up to the stone and entirely encircling the fruit. Separate the halves by gently rotating them in opposite directions and discard the stone. Brush the cut surfaces with lemon juice. Serve with one of the following dressings spooned into the hollow of each avocado-half, or fill the hollow with shelled shrimps, prawns, flaked crab or lobster meat, moistened with thin mayonnaise or well seasoned soured cream. If you wish, serve the avocados on lettuce leaves. If liked, avocodos can be served filled with fresh fruits for a different type of appetizer.

BABA

A rich but light-textured cake, made from a yeast mixture and baked in a dariole or individual mould; it is usually soaked in rum syrup after baking and may be served hot or cold as a sweet.

BABA AU RHUM

METRIC/IMPERIAL
25 g/1 oz fresh yeast or 1 × 15 ml spoon/1 tablespoon
   dried yeast
6 × 15 ml spoons/6 tablespoons tepid milk
225 g/8 oz strong plain flour
1 × 2.5 ml spoon/½ teaspoon salt
2 × 15 ml spoons/2 tablespoons caster sugar
4 eggs, beaten
100 g/4 oz butter, soft but not melted
100 g/4 oz currants
whipped cream

FOR THE RUM SYRUP
8 × 15 ml spoons/8 tablespoons clear honey
8 × 15 ml spoons/8 tablespoons water
rum to taste

Lightly grease sixteen 8.5 cm/3½ inch ring tins with lard. Put the yeast, milk and 50 g/2 oz of the flour in a bowl and blend until smooth. Allow to stand in a warm place until frothy – about 20 minutes. Add the remaining flour, the salt, sugar, eggs, butter and currants, and beat well for 3 to 4 minutes. Half-fill the tins with the dough and allow to rise until the moulds are two-thirds full.

Bake in a moderately hot oven (200°C/400°F, Gas Mark 6) for 15 to 20 minutes. Cool for a few minutes, then turn out on to a wire tray.

While the babas are still hot warm together the honey and water and add rum (or rum essence) to taste. Spoon over each sufficient rum syrup to soak it well. Leave to cool. Serve with whipped cream in the centre.

BACON

The sides and back of the pig preserved by salting either in brine or in a mixture of salt and saltpetre.

(Ham is the thigh, removed and cured separately.) (See Ham entry.)

Bacon varies in quality according to the breed, age and feeding of the animal and also the curing and cut. English bacon differs in flavour and cut from that imported from abroad and also varies from county to county. Much of the bacon eaten in this country is imported from Denmark.

Bacon which is cured but not smoked is called 'green', 'fresh', 'white' or 'plain'; it has a white instead of a brown rind and a milder flavour than smoked bacon. It is more popular in the North of England than in the South.

Good quality, correctly cured bacon should have a pleasant smell, the rind should be thin and smooth, the fat firm and free from any yellow marks and the lean of a good deep pink colour and adhering closely to the bone; the parts with little or no gristle are preferable.

The choicest rashers for frying or grilling are those from the back – 'prime', 'long' and 'top back'; they are easily recognized by the fact that the fat and lean are not intermixed. Next in popularity comes streaky bacon, both 'wide' and 'thin' – narrow rashers with alternate streaks of lean and fat. 'Middle' or 'through-cut' rashers consist of streaky and back together. Collar, which gives a wider rasher with more lean than fat, is sometimes rather coarse for grilling and frying, but is suitable for using in pies and made-up dishes. Gammon rashers and steaks have considerably more lean than fat and are good fried or grilled; they are cut thicker than the other types of rasher, which are usually fairly thin. 'Oyster' and 'flank' rashers are fatty, but useful for larding poultry.

For boiling and braising joints, these are the various possibilities, with the approximate average weights:

WHOLE GAMMON
(6 kg/14 lb).

HALF-GAMMON
(3 kg/7 lb to 3.5 kg/8 lb): either prime end and shank or gammon hock.

BAC

MIDDLE GAMMON
(2.75 kg/6 lb): lean, boneless and most popular cut.

CORNER GAMMON
(up to 1.75 kg/4 lb): boneless and easy to carve.

GAMMON SLIPPER
(1 kg/2 lb): chumpy, lean, inexpensive.

GAMMON HOCK
(1.75 kg/4 lb): cheapest, because it includes some bone.

WHOLE FORE-END
(7 kg/16 lb).

COLLAR
(3.5 kg/8 lb): if sub-divided, choicest part is called prime collar. Boneless, with good proportion of lean, but less expensive than gammon.

FOREHOCK
(3.5 kg/8 lb): includes bone and knuckle, which can be used for soup, while rest can be employed in various ways; the meat is of good flavour but coarser-textured than gammon or collar. Often sold boned, rolled and sub-divided.

Packaged Bacon

There is a growing trend among bacon producers to package both rashers and joints in various ways. The 'vacuum pack', one of the commonest forms, usually contains rather thin-cut rashers, often de-rinded, and is always marked with a date stamp showing how long the contents will keep when unopened and in good storage conditions. Once the pack is opened, any rashers not cooked at once should be removed and re-wrapped in foil or cling film and used fairly quickly. Cellophane-wrapped rashers keep no longer than ordinary unwrapped bacon.

Ready frozen bacon is available from freezer centres, but once thawed this should be treated in the same way as fresh bacon.

Small joints of bacon may be presented in various types of plastics film wrapping. Unless there are any specific accompanying directions, treat them as plain bacon. Anyone who dislikes salty bacon is probably better advised to remove the joint from the wrapper to soak before cooking, although the printed instructions sometimes state that the wrapping can be left on for the cooking process.

COOKING AND SERVING

Fried or grilled bacon forms an essential part of the traditional English breakfast, being served either by itself or more usually with eggs, kidneys, tomatoes, mushrooms or potatoes. Boiled bacon may be served either hot or cold as a luncheon or supper dish or as a hot accompaniment to turkey, chicken and veal. Bacon is also used to give added flavour to made-up dishes, stews, stuffings and so

on. Its food value lies chiefly in its protein and fat content, but it also contributes a fair amount of the B vitamin thiamine.

To fry bacon: Cut off the rind thinly with scissors or a sharp knife, trim off any 'rusty' or discoloured parts on the under-edge and cut out any bones or gristle; the fat may be snipped at intervals to prevent the rashers from curling. Place in a heated frying pan without added fat (except in the case of collar or gammon rashers, which are best cooked in fat) and cook gently until the bacon fat loses its transparency, turning the rashers frequently to ensure even cooking.

To grill bacon: Lay the bacon in the grill pan under a hot grill and cook, turning it frequently, until the fat loses its transparency. Lean bacon should be brushed over with fat before being grilled, otherwise it tends to dry up during the cooking. Serve with grilled tomatoes or mushrooms, fried bread and/or fried egg, cooked in the fat from the bacon.

To boil bacon: Soak the bacon in tepid water for 3 to 4 hours, changing the water once or twice. Place it in a saucepan of cold water, bring to the boil, removing any scum that rises, and simmer very gently until thoroughly tender, allowing 20 minutes to the 0.5 kg/1 lb, plus 20 minutes. Leave to cool in the water for about 2 hours; it should then be quite easy to remove the skin. To remove the skin: place the bacon joint on a wooden board or secure on a spiked carving board, skin side facing uppermost. Ease the skin away from the fat by starting it off with a sharp knife. Carefully pull the skin upwards and away from the fat, scraping the fat down if it should stick. Sprinkle the surface with fine bread raspings and serve the bacon hot, with parsley sauce, young broad beans or peas and boiled potatoes; alternatively serve it cold, either with salad for lunch or dinner or unaccompanied as a breakfast dish. (See Boiled Ham under Ham entry.)

To bake bacon: Soak for 3 to 6 hours, changing the water once or twice. Simmer as above for half the cooking time, then remove from water and wipe dry. (This gives a moister result than when the bacon is cooked entirely in the oven.) Cover with a flour-and-water dough, made with 0.75 kg/1½ lb to 1 kg/2 lb plain flour and rolled out 2.5 cm/1 inch thick. Place on a rack in a greased tin and bake in a moderately hot oven (190°C/375°F, Gas Mark 5), allowing 25 minutes per 0.5 kg/lb. Remove and discard paste and any strings, peel off the skin and finish as described under Baked Ham (See Ham entry).

If preferred, bake for the whole time either in paste or in foil; in this case, soak for at least 8 hours.

BRAISED BACON
(See recipe under Braising entry.)

BACON AND EGG PIE

METRIC/IMPERIAL
175–225 g/6–8 oz shortcrust pastry
225 g/8 oz bacon
2 eggs
1 × 5 ml spoon/1 teaspoon chopped parsley
pepper

Cut the pastry in two pieces, roll out each to fit a 20 cm/8 inch pie plate and line the plate with one of them. Cut up the bacon into small pieces and mix it with the beaten eggs, parsley and pepper. Pour this filling into the lined plate, damp the edges of the pastry and cover with the other piece. Bake in a hot oven (220°C/425°F, Gas Mark 7) for about 10 minutes. Reduce to (180°C/350°F, Gas Mark 4) for 20 minutes.

To make bacon rolls: Take some thin, narrow pieces of lean or streaky bacon about 5 cm/2 inches long, roll loosely and string them closely together on a metal or wooden skewer. Grill or fry and serve as a garnish with chicken, veal, etc.

Savoury bacon rolls can be made by stuffing the rolls with a veal forcemeat, placing them in an ovenproof dish and baking in a moderately hot oven (190°C/375°F, Gas Mark 5) for about 20 minutes. Turn the rolls once to crisp the underside.

BACON STEWPOT

METRIC/IMPERIAL
0.75 kg/1½ lb unsmoked collar joint
40 g/1½ oz butter or margarine
225 g/8 oz leeks, sliced and washed
1 small onion, skinned and chopped
2 × 15 ml spoons/2 tablespoons plain flour
450 ml/¾ pint unseasoned stock
100 g/4 oz carrots, pared and sliced
pepper
215 g/7½ oz can butter beans
1 × 15 ml spoon/1 tablespoon chopped fresh parsley

Remove rind and any excess fat or gristle from the bacon. Cut meat into 1.5 cm/¾ in cubes. Place in a pan of cold water and bring slowly to the boil. Drain well. Melt butter in a saucepan, add leeks and onion and cook gently until soft but not brown. Stir in the flour and cook for a minute. Off the heat gradually add the stock. Bring to the boil, stirring. Cook for a further minute. Add carrots, bacon and pepper. Cover pan and cook gently for 1¼ hours. Drain butter beans and add to the stew with the parsley. Heat through for about 5 minutes before serving.

BAIN-MARIE

A device for keeping foods very hot without actually boiling. A large pan is filled with boiling water and placed over a gentle heat; one or more sauce-pans or basins can then be put in it, either to keep their contents hot and ready to serve, or to continue cooking very gently. (A double saucepan, though smaller, serves the same purpose.) This is a good way of cooking such things as Hollandaise sauce, Zabaglione and so on.

BAKED ALASKA

A sweet consisting of ice cream mounted on sponge cake and entirely covered with meringue, which is cooked in a hot oven for so short a time that the ice cream remains unmelted. (See Ice Cream entry.)

BAKEWELL TART

An open plate tart with a pastry base and a cake-type filling, originating at Bakewell in Derbyshire.

METRIC/IMPERIAL
100 g/4 oz flaky or rough puff pastry
1–2 × 15 ml spoons/1–2 tablespoons raspberry jam
50 g/2 oz butter or margarine
50 g/2 oz caster sugar
grated rind and juice of ½ lemon
1 beaten egg
75 g/3 oz cake crumbs, sieved
75 g/3 oz ground almonds

Roll out the pastry thinly and line a deep 18 cm/7 inch pie plate. Spread the bottom of the pastry with the jam. Cream the fat and sugar with the lemon rind until pale and fluffy. Add the egg a little at a time and beat after each addition. Mix together the cake crumbs and ground almonds, fold half into the mixture with a tablespoon, then fold in the rest, with a little lemon juice if necessary to give a dropping consistency. Put the mixture into the pastry case and smooth the surface with a knife. Bake in a hot oven (220°C/425°F, Gas Mark 7) for about 15 minutes, until the tart begins to brown; reduce to 180°C/350°F, Gas Mark 4 for a further 20 to 30 minutes until the filling is firm to the touch. Serve hot or cold, with cream or custard.

BAKING

This method of cooking in the oven by dry heat is used for a large variety of foods.

To bake meat: The term generally used for cooking meat in the oven. (See Roasting entry.)

To bake fish: Baking is a good way of cooking both whole fish and large steaks or cutlets; round fish may be stuffed with a savoury forcemeat.

To bake vegetables: Generally speaking, baking is not a satisfactory method of cooking vegetables, but potatoes, marrow, parsnips, Jerusalem artichokes, carrots and turnips are excellent when baked in dripping round a joint of meat; potatoes are also delicious when baked in their skins. (See Potato entry.)

To bake fruit: Fruit contains a high percentage of water, so can be cooked satisfactorily in the oven. Pour in a little water to start the process and to prevent shrivelling, add sugar as required and cook slowly in a covered ovenproof dish.

To bake cakes, pastries, biscuits, bread: Baking is the method of cooking for almost all these. (See individual entries.)

Times and temperatures for baking are regulated according to the particular food and the necessary details are given in each recipe. (See the Temperatures for Cooking entry.)

BAKING BLIND

A term applied to a method of baking pastry cases for flans, pies, tarts, etc. Line the flan ring, pie-plate or other container with the pastry and decorate the edges. Put in a piece of greased greaseproof paper, greased side down, and half-fill with baking rice, dried beans or small crusts (which may be used again and again). Bake in a hot oven (230°C/450°F, Gas Mark 8) until the pastry is almost cooked and the edges lightly browned – about 15 minutes, or 10 minutes for tartlets. Remove the paper and filling and return the case to the oven for 5 to 10 minutes, to dry it off and complete the cooking. If the filling requires cooking place in the case and return to the oven on a lower temperature. If the flan is to be served hot, add the hot filling; otherwise put the case on a wire rack, allow it to cool and then fill as required.

BAKING POWDER

A raising agent used to make a baked mixture light. Commercial baking powder is made from sodium bicarbonate (alkali) plus acids with dried starch or flour to absorb the moisture. The acid determines the speed with which carbon dioxide is given off when the mixture is moistened and heated.

Manufacturers agree to standardize the strength of baking powders at 12 to 13 per cent but by law they should not yield less than 8 per cent of available carbon dioxide.

All baking powders should be kept in an air-tight tin in a cool, dry place, to prevent the moisture present in the air from liberating the gas prematurely. When using the powder, see that it is free from lumps and mix it evenly by first stirring it well into the dry ingredients and then sieving the mixture.

A homemade baking powder can be made with 1 part bicarbonate of soda, 2 parts cream of tartar and 3 parts ground rice. The ingredients should be mixed carefully, sieved and stored in an airtight container.

For proportions of baking powder to use in different mixtures, see Raising Agents entry.

BALM

A fragrant herb, the leaves of which have a flavour and scent resembling those of lemon. Balm is used in punches, fruit drinks, etc., and may also be added to stuffings, soups, sauces, meat and salads. The leaves may be dried. (See Herbs entry.)

BAMBOO SHOOTS

In many parts of the East the ivory-coloured shoots of a particular variety of bamboo are eaten. They are cut while they are still young, tender and crisp – about 5 cm/2 inches in diameter – and before they become large, hollow and woody. Canned bamboo shoots are on sale in this country and are popular with those who like to try Chinese cookery.

Young shoots may be treated in the same way as asparagus. Larger ones are chopped and may be incorporated in a made-up dish or pickled and candied.

BANANA

The fruit of a tropical tree. The two chief varieties are the Jamaica or Plantain Banana, which is long, fairly large, has flesh of a creamy colour and is somewhat insipid in flavour, and the Canary or Dwarf Banana, which is smaller and shorter, with flesh that is more pink in colour and has a more aromatic flavour.

The 'hands' of bananas are exported to Great Britain while still green; the fruit is ripened in large heated warehouses and then dispatched to the shops. When buying bananas, avoid those with skins turning black, as the fruit will ripen too quickly and must be eaten immediately. If they are slightly under-ripe and green at the tip, they can be kept in a warm atmosphere until they are yellow all over and even slightly speckled with brown.

Bananas contain a high proportion of starch, which turns to sugar as the fruit ripens. One banana supplies about half the day's requirements of Vitamin C and a small amount of other vitamins.

Bananas may be used as a fruit or vegetable, and are delicious served with sugar and cream. As the fruit browns quickly on exposure to the air it should be prepared just before serving, or sprinkled with lemon juice to prevent discoloration; this also helps to bring out the flavour.

The fruit can be used in a variety of ways in cookery, in trifles, jellies, salads, etc. Bananas may also be baked or fried, as a sweet or cooked with ham and cheese as a savoury. A cooked banana has a very different flavour to the uncooked fruit. Chartreuse of bananas (See Chartreuse entry) and banana flan are delicious cold sweets.

Dried (dehydrated) Bananas
These are imported in small quantities and are on sale at Health Food Shops, etc. Although most unattractive in appearance, they have a good flavour.

Banana Flour
This is prepared from dried bananas and is useful for flavouring cakes, buns and biscuits; it is fairly expensive.

BANANA GONDOLAS

METRIC/IMPERIAL
4 medium bananas
50 g/2 oz butter
25 g/1 oz icing sugar
25 g/1 oz shelled walnuts, chopped
1 × 2.5 ml spoon/½ teaspoon ground cinnamon
grated rind and juice ½ lemon

Place the whole bananas, with their skins on, under a pre-heated grill for about 15 minutes, turning frequently until the skins turn brown. Cream the butter and sugar, then beat in remaining ingredients. Split the bananas along the upper surface and press gently at each end to form a hollow in the centre. Spoon walnut butter into each hollow and return to the grill for 5 minutes until the butter is melted. Serve at once.

FLAMBÉ BANANA IN ORANGE SAUCE

METRIC/IMPERIAL
8 large firm bananas
25 g/1 oz butter
3 × 15 ml spoons/3 tablespoons light soft brown sugar
2 × 15 ml spoons/2 tablespoons rum
3 medium oranges
2 × 15 ml spoons/2 tablespoons lemon juice
pouring cream to serve

Peel the bananas and cut into four even sized pieces. Heat the butter in a large frying pan. Toss in the bananas and sprinkle over the sugar. Fry gently, turning the bananas occasionally until golden brown and beginning to soften. Pour over the rum and set alight. Shake the pan gently until the flames subside. Coarsely grate in the rind and add strained juice of two oranges with the lemon juice. Cover the pan and simmer for 5 minutes to thoroughly heat through. Run a canelle knife around the third orange at 1 cm/½ inch intervals working downwards from stem end, not round, to remove a narrow strip of rind free of pith. Slice the same orange thinly discarding the pips. Serve the

bananas really hot with the juices. Decorate with orange slices and serve at once, pouring cream separately.

BANBURY CAKE

An oval flat cake originating from Banbury, Oxfordshire. It is made of flaky pastry filled with dried fruit.

BANBURY CAKES

METRIC/IMPERIAL
215 g/7½ oz puff pastry
50 g/2 oz currants
50 g/2 oz raisins, stoned
1 × 15 ml spoon/1 level tablespoon flour
25 g/1 oz chopped mixed peel
50 g/2 oz demerara sugar
1 × 2.5 ml spoon/½ teaspoon powdered nutmeg
1 × 2.5 ml spoon/½ teaspoon powdered cinnamon
25 g/1 oz melted butter

FOR THE GLAZE
beaten egg white
1–2 × 15 ml spoons/1–2 tablespoons caster sugar

Mix the fruit, flour, peel, sugar and spices with the butter. Roll out the pastry thinly and cut into six to eight 13 cm/5 inch rounds. Place 1 × 15 ml spoon/1 tablespoon of fruit mixture in the centre of each pastry round. Brush the edges of the pastry with the egg white and draw them up to the centre. Press well to enclose the filling. Turn the cakes over and roll lightly until the fruit just shows under the pastry and the cakes are oval in shape.

Make several cuts in the top of each cake, forming a criss-cross pattern. Brush the tops with egg white and sprinkle with caster sugar.

Place on a baking sheet and bake in a hot oven (220°C/425°F, Gas Mark 7) for about 20 minutes, or until the pastry is golden brown. Cool on a wire rack.

BANNOCK

A large round scone containing oatmeal, or barleymeal, baked on a girdle and usually served at breakfast or high tea, particularly in Scotland. There are many variations, including a thin biscuit type and a sweet bannock. (See Oats for recipe.)

BAP

A Scottish type of breakfast roll, eaten hot, which is made from a yeast dough, containing a little fat. Baps are usually made in a flat oval shape, brushed over with milk and water, then dusted with flour to give them their characteristic floury finish.

19

This word – derived from the French barbe-à-queue, literally beard to tail – originally denoted the roasting or broiling of a whole animal, which was fixed to a spit and cooked over a solid bed of glowing coals. Nowadays it is considered an informal way of entertaining. The food at a barbecue party is more likely to be steaks, chops, pieces of chicken, sausages, kebabs, hot dogs, previously made hamburgers and so on. Meat is often marinated beforehand (especially if there is any doubt as to its tenderness) and it may be basted during the cooking with a piquant sauce.

The simplest plan is to have a portable barbecue outfit, obtainable from most of the large stores at various prices, and to use ready-made charcoal as fuel (for a meal for 6 to 12 people you would need 1 kg/2 lb to 1.5 kg/3 lb charcoal). If you prefer to improvize your own fireplace you will need a few bricks and some iron bars (or the grid shelves from your oven). Arrange 14 to 16 bricks side by side in two rows, to form a rectangular base. Pile more bricks at each side to support the bars, then build the fire on the brick base, using either charcoal or wood – the former takes less time to produce a glowing fire.

Let the fire burn slowly for about 30 minutes; when the coals have burned to a greyish ash, shot with a red glow, the fire is ready for you to start cooking. If you need to add more fuel, place this round the edge of the fire, gradually drawing it into the centre as it ignites. Keep a sprinkler bottle handy to quench any flames which might char the food.

The food may be placed directly on the rack (which should be several inches above the fire) or it can be put on aluminium foil or cooked in a thick, strong old frying pan or saucepan. When cooking such things as a chicken on a spit, you will need some arrangement for collecting the juices and fat which will fall from it.

You will also need a table for food and equipment, tongs, long skewers and thick oven gloves.

Accompaniments to serve with meats and kebabs can include a variety of salads, vegetable stew such as ratatouille, jacket potatoes, crisps, crusty bread, rice or pasta salads. Sauces help to moisten the food so a good tasty one or two should be offered. Serve a variety of salad dressings.

It is a good idea to serve a starter as this can be eaten while food is cooking on the barbecue. If the meal is taken outside it should be something simple such as mugs of soup, slices of melon, dips or filled vol-au-vents.

Suitable desserts include fresh fruit, individual mousses, fruit fools or trifles, or slices of fruit cake followed by coffee. Alternatively a cheese board can be served with biscuits, crisp celery and dessert apples.

To barbecue steak and chops: Prepare the food as for grilling, skewering chops if necessary to keep them a good shape, season and brush over with oil. Place on the greased grid and cook over glowing hot coals for about the same time as for grilled meat. (See Grilling entry.)

Alternatively, fry in a heavy frying pan.

BARBECUE SAUCE

METRIC/IMPERIAL
50 g/2 oz butter
1 large skinned and chopped onion
1 × 5 ml spoon/1 teaspoon tomato paste
2 × 15 ml spoons/2 tablespoons demerara sugar
2 × 15 ml spoons/2 tablespoons vinegar
2 × 5 ml spoons/2 teaspoons dry mustard
2 × 15 ml spoons/2 tablespoons Worcestershire sauce
150 ml/¼ pint water

Melt the butter and fry the onion for 5 minutes, or until soft. Stir in the tomato paste and continue cooking for a further 3 minutes. Blend the remaining ingredients to a smooth cream and stir in the onion mixture. Return the sauce to the pan and simmer uncovered for a further 10 minutes.

Serve with chicken, sausages, hamburgers or chops.

BARBERRY

The fruit of various species of Berberis which grow in different parts of the world. They are used mostly for preserves, tarts, sauces and flavouring purposes.

BARCELONA NUT

A type of hazelnut from Spain, usually kiln-dried to make it keep well.

BARDING

To cover the breast of a bird with slices of fat before roasting it, to prevent the flesh from drying up.

BARLEY

A cereal grass with a wide climatic range grown for its seeds. These are used in cooking, for the production of breakfast cereals and for cattle food. The grain is also malted and used for the brewing of beer and the distillation of whisky.

Pot Barley, Scotch or Hulled Barley
The most nutritious form, as only the outer husk is removed. It is used in soups and stews and requires 2 to 3 hours' cooking to make it tender.

Pearl Barley

For this the grain is steamed, rounded and polished in the mill, after the removal of the husks. This barley, too, is used for thickening soups and stews (See Scotch Broth under Broth entry), also for making barley water and puddings. It requires rather less cooking time – 1½ to 2 hours.

Barley Meal

A wholemeal flour made by grinding barley coarsely; it is the crudest ground form and it is still used in some districts for porridge and gruel (See Gruel entry), also as an addition to a certain kind of bread.

Barley Flour

Is ground and powdered pearl barley. Blended with cold water, it makes a good thickening for soups and sauces made with milk.

Barley Flakes

Are pressed and flattened barley grains. They are used for making milk puddings and gruel.

Patent Barley Preparations

Are obtainable either as ground barley or as partially cooked flakes (see above); in using them, the manufacturers' instructions should be carefully followed.

To blanch pearl barley: This is often done to improve the colour of the pearl barley used for barley water or for thickening soups. Wash the barley, put it into a saucepan with sufficient water to cover, bring to the boil, strain and finally rinse the barley.

BARLEY WATER

METRIC/IMPERIAL
2 × 15 ml spoons/2 tablespoons pearl barley
400–600 ml/¾–1 pint cold water
½ a lemon
sugar (optional)

Blanch the barley as described above, put it back into the saucepan with the water and the lemon rind (peeled off very thinly) and simmer for 1½ to 2 hours, adding more water if it boils away. Then strain, add the lemon juice and a little sugar if desired and serve hot or cold.

BARLEY SUGAR

A hard toffee flavoured with lemon. It was formerly made with a decoction of barley (hence its name), but plain water is now used. (See recipe in Sweets entry.)

BARM (BREWER'S YEAST)

(See Yeast entry.)

BARON OF BEEF

The two sirloins of beef, left uncut at the bone and roasted.

BASIL

An aromatic annual herb of the mint family with a pungent aroma. There are two varieties, sweet and bush basil. Both are good used with tomato, eggs and fish, or added to soups, salads and curries. Basil can be used fresh or dried.

BASS

Many varieties of this fish are found in both fresh and salt water. The European variety is in season from May to August; it is not unlike salmon in shape, but the flesh is very white and delicate in flavour. Large bass has an excellent flavour and may be cooked according to any recipe for salmon. Small bass can be grilled, fried or cooked in any way suitable for trout; they may also be baked.

BASTING

To ladle hot fat (or liquid) over meat, poultry, etc., at intervals while it is baking or roasting, in order to improve the texture, flavour and appearance. A long-handled spoon is usually employed for the purpose.

Basting is not necessary for fatty joints, especially if the fat side can be placed uppermost.

BATH BUN

A type of yeast bun originally made in the city of Bath around 1700 A.D. A distinguishing feature is the coarse sugar crystals sprinkled on top.

BATH BUNS

METRIC/IMPERIAL
450 g/1 lb strong plain flour
25 g/1 oz fresh yeast
150 ml/¼ pint tepid milk
4 × 15 ml spoons/4 tablespoons tepid water
1 × 5 ml spoon/1 teaspoon salt
50 g/2 oz caster sugar
50 g/2 oz butter, melted and cooled, but not firm
2 eggs, beaten
175 g/6 oz sultanas
2–3 × 15 ml spoons/2–3 tablespoons chopped mixed peel

TOPPING
beaten egg
crushed sugar lumps

Grease two baking sheets. Put 100 g/4 oz of the flour in a large mixing bowl. Crumble the yeast

21

into a small basin, pour over the liquid and stir until dissolved. Add to the 100 g/4 oz flour and mix well. Set aside in a warm place until frothy – about 20 minutes. Sift together the remaining flour and salt and add the sugar. Stir the butter and eggs into the yeast mixture, add the remaining flour mixture, sultanas and peel and mix well. The dough should be fairly soft. Turn it out onto a floured surface and knead until smooth. Place in a bowl and cover with oiled polythene and leave to rise until doubled in bulk. Beat well by hand. Place in about eighteen spoonfuls on the greased baking sheets, cover with oiled polythene and leave to rise. Brush with egg and sprinkle with crushed sugar. Bake in the oven preheated to moderately hot (190°C/375°F, Gas Mark 5) for about 15 minutes, until golden. Cool on a wire rack and serve buttered.

BATH CHAP

(See Pig's Cheek entry.)

BATTENBERG CAKE

A two-coloured oblong cake, usually covered with almond paste.

BATTENBERG CAKE

METRIC/IMPERIAL
175 g/6 oz butter or block margarine
175 g/6 oz caster sugar
vanilla essence
3 beaten eggs
175 g/6 oz self-raising flour
15 g/½ oz cocoa
milk to mix, if necessary
raspberry jam or jelly
350 g/12 oz ready-made almond paste
caster sugar

Grease and line a Swiss roll tin measuring 30 × 20 × 6 mm/12 × 8 × ¾ inch and divide it lengthwise with a 'wall' of greaseproof paper or kitchen foil. Cream the fat and sugar together until light and fluffy and add a little essence. Gradually add the eggs a little at a time, beating well after each addition. When all the egg has been added, lightly fold in the flour, using a metal spoon. Turn half of the mixture into one side of the tin. Fold the sifted cocoa into the other half, with a little milk if necessary, and spoon this mixture into the second side of the tin. Bake in a moderately hot oven (190°C/375°F, Gas Mark 5) for 40 to 45 minutes, until well-risen. Turn out and cool on a wire rack.

When the two parts of the cake are cold, trim them to an equal size and cut each in half lengthwise. Spread the sides of the strips with jam and stick them together, alternating the colours.

Press the pieces well together, then coat the whole of the outside of the cake with jam. Roll out the almond paste thinly on caster sugar or between sheets of non-stick paper, forming it into an oblong about 35.5 × 25 cm/14 × 10 inches. Wrap the paste completely round the cake, press firmly against the side and trim the edges. Pinch with the thumb and forefinger along the outer edges and score the top of the cake with a sharp knife to give a criss-cross pattern.

BATTER

A thick liquid mixture, consisting essentially of flour, milk and eggs, but often combined with other ingredients. It forms the foundation for pancakes, drop scones and Yorkshire pudding. A thicker coating batter is used for making fritters and kromeskies and for coating fish for frying.

It used to be the custom to make batters at least 1 hour before cooking, the mixture being beaten or whisked to incorporate the air and then allowed to stand in a cool place. Recent experiments, however, show that equally good results are obtained when the batter is beaten just long enough to mix it and does not stand before cooking. Batter can successfully be made in a liquidizer.

In America the term is used for a mixture which contains fat and other ingredients, e.g. cake and biscuit recipes.

BASIC RECIPE FOR BATTER

METRIC/IMPERIAL
100 g/4 oz plain flour
a pinch of salt
1 egg
300 ml/½ pint milk and water

Sieve the flour and salt into a bowl. Make a well in the centre and add the egg. Add half the liquid, a little at a time, mixing with a wooden spoon from the centre outwards and gradually drawing in the flour. Mix until smooth and stir in the remainder of the milk.

For batter pudding, melt a little lard in a tin, then pour in the batter and bake in a hot oven (220°C/425°F, Gas Mark 7) for about 40 minutes. The mixture may also be steamed. Serve with butter and golden syrup or jam.

Savoury batter puddings may be made by adding herbs, finely chopped onions, grated cheese, etc.

BASIC COATING BATTER
For fritters

METRIC/IMPERIAL
100 g/4 oz plain flour
pinch of salt

1 egg
150 ml/¼ pint milk or milk and water

Mix together the flour and salt, make a well in the centre and break in the egg. Add half the liquid and beat the mixture until smooth. Gradually add the rest of the liquid and beat until well mixed.

LIGHT BATTER
For fritters

METRIC/IMPERIAL
100 g/4 oz plain flour
pinch of salt
1 × 15 ml spoon/1 tablespoon oil
150 ml/¼ pint water
2 egg whites

Mix together the flour and salt, make a well in the centre and add the oil and half the water. Beat until smooth and add the remaining water gradually. Just before using, whisk the egg whites stiffly and fold them into the batter, then use the mixture straight away.

Batter Cases
These require a special iron made in the shape of a basket, which is first heated by being dipped in hot fat, then dipped into pancake batter, plunged into hot deep fat and left for a few minutes, until the batter is golden-brown. The batter case is then slipped off the iron and returned to the fat to finish cooking inside. The cases are filled with a savoury mixture and served as an entrée or as a hot hors d'œuvre.

(See Fritters, Pancakes, Yorkshire Pudding and Popovers entries.)

BAVAROIS

A hot drink, said to have been invented in Bavaria towards the end of the seventeenth century, which used to be served at evening parties. It was made with eggs, sugar, boiling tea and boiling milk and flavoured with a liqueur or coffee, chocolate, orange, vanilla, etc.

BAVAROIS (SWEET)

A cold sweet consisting of a rich custard made with egg yolks and cream, set with gelatine.

BAY LEAF

The aromatic leaf of the sweet bay tree, a species of laurel originally grown in the Mediterranean zone. (Note: Ordinary laurel leaves cannot be substituted for bay leaves.)

Bay leaves are used fresh or dried for flavouring soups, stews and sauces and as an essential part of a Bouquet Garni. (See separate entry.)

BAY SALT (SEA SALT)

Common salt obtained from sea water by evaporation. It is less pure than that obtained from the brine from salt wells.

BEAN

A leguminous plant of which there are many varieties. The seeds and sometimes the pods are used as a vegetable. The mature seeds, when dried, are called pulses; they are a valuable food, containing more protein than is found in cereals and in fact are the best vegetable source of this nutrient. They are also a good source of the vitamin B group. Pulses are, therefore, important in countries where animal foods are in short supply, (also for vegetarians). Although they do not contain any vitamin C, they start producing it when they sprout, so sprouting peas and beans (eaten in China, for example) are a good source. Fresh green beans contain vitamins C and A.

BEANS

The edible seeds of leguminous plants grown in various parts of the world. Some varieties are used as green vegetables whereas others are more suitable for drying (pulses).

Broad bean (Windsor bean)
This is also known as Field bean, Horse bean, Scotch bean, Flava bean, Shell bean (and in the United States as Fava bean). It is considered to be the original bean and was first grown in North Africa. The beans are encased in a thick, tough pod with a furry lining. When very young and tender, the pods can be cooked whole, but usually they are shelled. As the plant matures the beans develop a grey outer skin which gradually becomes tougher. This can be removed before cooking by blanching for a few minutes in boiling water. The beans can be served with parsley sauce or tossed in melted butter. In season, early June to end July.

Runner bean
Also known as Scarlet runner, String bean or Stick bean. It was introduced into Europe from Mexico in the mid seventeenth century. It is a perennial, fast climbing plant but usually grown as an annual. Bush varieties are also available. The beans are at their best when picked young and should be finely sliced for cooking. In season early June to end of September.

French bean
Also known as Dwarf bean, Kidney bean (in the United States as Snap or Green bean.) It is an annual plant of South American origin. The beans are picked when they are 5 cm/2 inches to

23

10 cm/4 inches long and topped and tailed before being cooked whole or halved. In season July to October.

Flageolet bean

A yellow variety of French bean. The beans are allowed to develop fully allowing the seeds to become larger and harder and the pods tougher. These are shelled and the beans which are pale green in colour and long and thin in shape are eaten fresh or dried.

Haricot bean

The name given to a wide range of bean plants, the best known being the French or Kidney bean (see above). Haricot beans can be of various sizes and colours. Fresh haricot beans are not often seen in this country but dried ones are widely available. They can be stored for several months in a cool, dry place and are a useful standby for soups, casseroles and salads. Flavouring such as onions, herbs, or bacon can be added while cooking.

Lima bean

Also known as Butterbean. This is a bean of the haricot type, originally grown in South America. The seeds are short, flat, slightly kidney shaped and used dried as a vegetable.

Navy bean

Also called Boston bean: a variety of Haricot bean.

Soya (Soy) bean

Grown originally in China, Japan and India, but now extensively cultivated. Soya beans have many different varieties and uses. (See Soya entry.)

To cook dried beans: Beans should be bought from a store where there is a regular turnover as stale beans never soften however long they are cooked. Pick over the beans and soak overnight in clear cold water. Do not leave too long in a warm atmosphere as they can start to ferment. As a short cut to soaking bring the beans to the boil, remove from the heat and steep for 1 to 2 hours. To cook pour off the water and cover with fresh water. Add salt 2–3 × 5 ml spoons/1–1½ teaspoons to 600 ml/1 pint water. A pinch of bicarbonate of soda also helps especially in hardwater areas. Bring to the boil, skim off any foam and boil gently for 1 to 3 hours. Dried beans are not easily digested unless well cooked.

PORK AND BEAN CASSEROLE

METRIC/IMPERIAL
0.5 kg/1¼ lb belly of pork
0.5 kg/1 lb dried white beans, soaked overnight
1 × 15 ml spoon/1 tablespoon olive or corn oil
1 clove of garlic, crushed
1 × 156 g/5½ oz can tomato purée

1 × 15 ml spoon/1 tablespoon soft brown sugar
1 small bayleaf
salt and pepper

Remove any bones from pork and cut meat into 2.5 cm/1 inch squares. Drain beans and rinse under cold running water. Place in a large saucepan. Add the bones from the pork and a little salt. Cover with cold water. Bring to the boil and remove any scum with a slotted draining spoon. Cover and simmer for one hour, or until tender. Discard the bones. Heat the oil in a large frying pan. Add the cubes of pork and cook turning until golden-brown. Add the remaining ingredients and 300 ml/½ pint liquid from beans. Simmer gently for 10 minutes. Put a deep layer of drained beans in a large casserole. Cover with meat mixture and then the remaining beans. Add sufficient bean stock just to cover. Bake in a moderate oven (160°C/325°F, Gas Mark 3) for 1½ to 2 hours.

Preserving Beans

Apart from frozen broad beans, beans preserved in these ways are not so successful as peas, but they add variety to the menu. For Bottling, Canning, Drying and Freezing, see separate entries.

To salt French and runner beans: This is a simple and excellent way of preserving French and runner beans for winter use. You will need a glass or stoneware jar or crock (glazed earthenware is not suitable, as the salt impairs the glaze and makes the vessel porous).

Choose small, young beans and make sure that they are clean and dry. Break them in two if very long, but do not slice them if very small. Place alternate layers of beans and cooking salt in the jar, allowing about 0.5 kg/1 lb salt to 1.5 kg/3 lb to 1.75 kg/4 lb of beans. Finish with a layer of salt, press down firmly and leave for a few days to settle down. More beans may be added as they become ready, but always finish with a layer of salt and add an extra thick layer when the crock is full. Cover closely with a lid or several layers of paper.

To use the beans, rinse well in cold water or soak for a few minutes only. Cook and serve as for fresh beans, omitting the salt when boiling.

BEAN CURD

(See Soya entry.)

BEAN SPROUTS (MUNG)

A Chinese bean whose young, tender sprouts are famous in Chinese cooking. Fresh sprouts are rich in B vitamins and vitamin C. They can be cooked as a vegetable, added to soups and casseroles just before serving, or eaten raw in salads.

Soak beans overnight in cold water. Drain. Place a few layers of blotting paper, flannel or absorbent kitchen paper in a shallow dish or plastic tray. Sprinkle enough cold water over to moisten well. Sprinkle beans over the surface, spreading evenly. Slide dish or tray into a large polythene bag to retain moisture and keep in a warm, dark place such as a cupboard or drawer. Ready to eat when they're about 3 cm/1½ inches long, about 3 to 4 days after germination.

BÉARNAISE SAUCE

A rich sauce with a basis of eggs, served with grilled meat or fish. There are several variations.

SIMPLE BÉARNAISE SAUCE

METRIC/IMPERIAL
2 small onions
3 sprigs of tarragon
3 × 15 ml spoons/3 tablespoons tarragon vinegar
2 × 15 ml spoons/2 tablespoons malt vinegar
1 × 15 ml spoon/1 tablespoon water
2 egg yolks
50 g/2 oz melted butter

Chop or mince the onions and the tarragon leaves finely and cook them in the vinegars until reduced by half, then add the water. Strain into the egg yolks and stir over hot water until the mixture thickens. Remove from the heat, gradually beat in the melted butter and keep hot until ready to serve.

BEATING

To agitate an ingredient or a mixture by vigorously turning it over and over with an upward motion, in order to introduce air; a spoon, fork, whisk or electric mixer may be used.

To beat raw meat is to hit it briskly all over the surface with a rolling pin or something similar for the purpose of breaking down the fibres and making the meat more tender when cooked.

BÉCHAMEL SAUCE

A rich white sauce of coating consistency, used in many recipes for savoury dishes, especially with fish and as the foundation of a number of other sauces. Formerly (especially in restaurant cookery) white stock was sometimes used to replace all or part of the milk, for extra flavour.

BÉCHAMEL SAUCE

METRIC/IMPERIAL
300 ml/½ pint milk
1 skinned and sliced shallot, or a small piece of skinned onion
small piece of carrot, pared and cut up
½ stick scrubbed and sliced celery
½ bayleaf

3 peppercorns
25 g/1 oz butter
3 × 15 ml spoons/3 tablespoons flour
salt
pepper

Put the milk, vegetables and flavourings in a saucepan and bring slowly to the boil. Remove from the heat, cover and leave to infuse for about 15 minutes. Strain the liquid and use this with the butter and flour to make a roux sauce. Season to taste before serving.

This sauce is the basis of many other sauces.

BEECH NUTS

The small nuts extracted from beech mast, which may be eaten as they are or salted like almonds. (See Nuts entry.)

BEEF

The meat of the ox, cow or even bull, the best (and most expensive) meat being obtained from an ox about 2 years old. (See Veal entry.) The flesh of beef should be deep red – not purple or pale pink – the fat soft and cream-coloured. Prime meat is firm, fine-textured and slightly moist, having no gristle (which is an indication of age). Home-killed beef is the choicest, but imported frozen or chilled beef of good quality comes from Australia, New Zealand, the Argentine and other countries.

Beef, like all meat, is a source of protein of good value. It also supplies energy; particularly if there is a lot of fat. The amount of fat in different cuts varies considerably and it is impossible to give exact figures for the nutrients. It is a good source of the B vitamins and a fair source of iron.

Beef is cut in various ways, according to the region or country, but the diagram on page 245 gives a general idea of the method of dividing up the carcass.

How to Cook Cuts of Beef

SIRLOIN
(Can be boned and rolled) – Roast

RIBS
(Can be boned and rolled) – Roast

TOPSIDE
(Lean joint) – Roast, braise or pot roast

BRISKET
(fatty joint) – Slow roast or braise

BRISKET
(If salted) – Boil

SILVERSIDE
(often salted and boneless) – Bone or braise

25

AITCHBONE
(Large bone and fatty) – Roast

AITCHBONE
(If salted) – Boil or braise

FLANK
(Coarse flesh) – Stew, braise, pot roast

LEG AND SHIN
(Cheap cuts) – Stew

CHEEK
(Large amount of bone) – Soup

RUMP STEAK
(Next to the Sirloin) – Grill or fry

FILLET
(Undercut of Sirloin) – Grill or fry

TOURNEDOS
(Part of fillet) – Grill or fry

FILET MIGNON
(Small round end of fillet) – Grill or fry

CHATEAUBRIAND
(Thick slice from middle or fillet) – Grill or fry

PORTERHOUSE
(From thick end of fillet) – Grill or fry

MINUTE
(From upper part of Sirloin) – Grill or fry

ENTRECOTE
(From Sirloin rump) – Grill or fry

CHUCK OR BLADE
(A cheaper cut without bone from the shoulder) –
use any slow cooking method for stews, pies and
casseroles.

ROAST BEEF

Wash or wipe the meat, weigh it and calculate the
time needed for cooking. For the quick method, it
is usual to allow 15 minutes per 0.5 kg/1 lb and 15
minutes over for small joints; 20 minutes per
0.5 kg/1 lb and 20 minutes over for thicker joints;
and 25 minutes per 0.5 kg/1 lb plus 25 minutes over
for larger joints without bone (since the dense
tissues require longer cooking).

For the slow method, the times to allow are 20
minutes per 0.5 kg/1 lb plus 20 minutes; 27 minutes
per 0.5 kg/1 lb plus 27 minutes; and 33 minutes per
0.5 kg/1 lb plus 33 minutes, respectively.

Frozen meat can be thawed overnight in the
refrigerator and cooked as above. It is also possible
to cook joints from frozen provided care is taken to
cook the inside. A meat thermometer should be
used to check the internal temperature. For
medium cooked meat this should register
71°C/160°F. First seal the joint in hot fat in a pre-
heated hot oven (230°C/450°F, Gas Mark 8) for 20
minutes, turning once. Reduce the temperature to

moderate (180°C/350°F, Gas Mark 4) cover the
meat and cook for 50 minutes to the 0.5 kg/1 lb.
(See Roasting entry.)

Serve the meat with Yorkshire pudding, horseradish sauce and thin gravy.

To boil beef: (See entry under Boiling.) Allow 25
minutes per 0.5 kg/1 lb and 25 minutes over.

To cook salt beef: Put the meat in cold water, bring
to the boil and discard the water. Then cook but
without adding any salt. (See Boiling entry.)

To grill beefsteak: Cook as described in Grilling
entry.

BEEF (BROWN) STEW

METRIC/IMPERIAL
50 g/2 oz dripping
2 onions
0.75 kg/1 ½ lb stewing steak
40 g/1 ½ oz flour
salt
pepper
bunch of herbs
2–3 sliced carrots
900 ml/1 ½ pints stock

Melt the fat in the frying pan (or casserole), slice
the onions, fry them until light brown, then lift out
on to a plate. Trim the meat, cut into small pieces
and fry in the fat until lightly browned on all sides.
Add to onions, stir in flour and cook, stirring until
it is brown. Add the other ingredients and simmer
for about 2 hours, or until the meat is tender;
re-season if necessary. Take out the herbs and
serve the stew garnished with parsley and vegetables – a mixture of small whole carrots and peas
may be used.

BOEUF STROGANOFF

METRIC/IMPERIAL
0.75 kg/1 ½ lb thinly sliced rump steak
3 × 15 ml spoons/3 tablespoons seasoned flour
50 g/2 oz butter
1 skinned and thinly sliced onion
225 g/½ lb mushrooms, sliced
salt
pepper
300 ml/½ pint soured cream

Beat the steak, trim it, cut it into strips
0.5 cm/¼ inch by 5 cm/2 inch and coat with the
seasoned flour. Fry the meat in 25 g/1 oz butter till
golden brown – about 5 to 7 minutes. Cook the
onion and mushrooms in the remaining 25 g/1 oz
butter for 3 to 4 minutes, season to taste and add to
the beef. Warm the soured cream and stir it into the
meat mixture.

CARBONNADE OF BEEF

METRIC/IMPERIAL
1 kg/2 lb stewing steak, cut into 1 cm/½ inch cubes
salt
pepper
50 g/2 oz fat or oil
75 g/3 oz lean bacon, rinded and chopped
4 × 15 ml spoons/4 tablespoons plain flour
300 ml/½ pint beer
300 ml/½ pint stock or water
2–3 × 15 ml spoons/2–3 tablespoons vinegar
450 g/1 lb onions, skinned and chopped
1 clove garlic, skinned and chopped
bouquet garni

Season the meat and fry in the fat or oil until brown – about 5 minutes. Add the bacon and continue cooking for a few minutes. Remove the meat and bacon from the pan, stir in the flour and brown lightly. Gradually add the beer, stock and vinegar, stirring continuously until the mixture thickens. Fill a casserole with layers of meat, bacon, onion and garlic. Pour the sauce over and add the bouquet garni. Cover and cook for 3½ to 4 hours in a cool oven (150°C/300°F, Gas Mark 2). Add a little more beer while cooking, if necessary. Just before serving, remove the bouquet garni. Serve with plain boiled potatoes.

BEEF OLIVES

METRIC/IMPERIAL
8 thin slices of topside
seasoned flour
2 × 15 ml spoons/2 tablespoons oil
400 ml/¾ pint stock or water
2 onions, sliced

FOR THE STUFFING
50 g/2 oz shredded suet
50 g/2 oz ham or bacon, chopped
100 g/4 oz fresh breadcrumbs
2 × 5 ml spoons/2 teaspoons chopped parsley
a pinch of mixed dried herbs
grated rind of ½ lemon
salt
pepper
beaten egg to mix

Combine the ingredients for the stuffing and bind with the egg. Spread each slice of meat with stuffing, roll up, secure with fine string and toss in seasoned flour. Heat the fat or oil in a frying pan and brown the beef olives lightly, remove and place in casserole. Add 2 × 15 ml spoons/2 tablespoons of the seasoned flour to the frying pan, brown well, gradually add the stock and bring it to the boil; season to taste and pour over the olives. Add the onion slices, divided into rings, cover and cook in a moderate oven (180°C/350°F, Gas Mark 4) for 1½ hours. Remove the strings to serve.

STEAK AND KIDNEY PUDDING

METRIC/IMPERIAL
225 g/8 oz suetcrust pastry made with 225 g/8 oz
*   flour etc.*
225–350 g/½–¾ lb stewing steak, cut into
*   2 cm/¾ inch cubes*
100 g/¼ lb kidney
2 × 15 ml spoons/2 tablespoons seasoned flour
1 onion, skinned and chopped
water

Half fill a steamer or large saucepan with water and put it on to boil. Grease a 900 ml/1½ pint pudding basin. Cut off a quarter of the pastry to make the lid and roll out the remainder into a round large enough to line the basin. Coat the meat with the seasoned flour. Remove the skin and core from the kidney, cut into slices and coat with seasoned flour. Fill the basin with the meat, kidney, onion and 3 × 15 ml spoons/3 tablespoons water. Roll out the pastry for the lid to a round the size of the top of the basin and damp the edge of it. Place on top of the meat and seal the edges of the pastry well. Cover with greased greaseproof paper or foil and steam for about 4 hours.

VARIATION
The meat can be prepared and stewed with the onion for about 2 hours earlier in the day or the previous night before being used for the filling. In this case reduce the steaming time to 1½ to 2 hours.

Beef tea: Chop 0.5 kg/1 lb lean beef very finely, add 600 ml/1 pint cold water and place in a double saucepan (or a stone jar) over cold water. Heat very slowly, stirring occasionally; it must not go over 54°C/130°F – if it changes colour, this shows that it has been heated to too high a temperature. Strain through a coarse strainer and season. If necessary, reheat the beef tea over warm water before serving it.
   If desired, the meat may be soaked in the water for 1 hour before it is heated.
   (See Steak and Kidney Pie under Pie entry, and Goulash entries.)

BEEFBURGER (BURGER)

A meatcake of American origin. It is made from minced beef, onion and seasoning then fried in shallow fat or baked. By law any beefburger that is sold must contain at least 80 per cent meat. It is usually served inside a soft white bread bun and may also include cheese, nuts, anchovy, liver sausage, salad ingredients or a piquant sauce. In recent years burgers have become popular in this country with many special restaurants opening solely to sell this fare. They are also popular as a 'take away' food.
   In America they are called hamburgers

(although made from beef) because they originally came from Hamburg. (See Hamburger entry.)

BEER

An alcoholic beverage produced by the fermentation of malted barley and hops; the barley is wetted, allowed to germinate and then dried. It is next ground and mixed with water and hops are added; yeast is added to the resulting wort and fermentation takes place. The beer is then filtered and casked or bottled. Taste, colour and strength vary with type, brewing and bottling, but it generally contains 3 to 7 per cent alcohol. Pale beers are known as ales though before hops were used the name applied to all malt beers.

Beer is sometimes used in cookery (especially in country districts) and may replace part of the stock or water used in stews, hot-pots, meat ragoûts, etc. It also helps to mature dried fruit puddings and cakes, though owing to its relatively low spirit content it is not used as much as rum or brandy. Beer is a source of riboflavin and nicotinic acid.

Making beer at home is becoming an increasingly popular pastime. There are many preparations and kits on the market to make it an easy task. It is illegal to sell beer or wine made at home.

BEESTINGS

The first milk drawn from a cow after calving.

BEET, BEETROOT

Many varieties of this easily grown root vegetable are cultivated in Great Britain and beets are available during most of the year. They contain a fair amount of sugar – one type is in fact the source of much of the sugar we use in this country.

Small, young beetroots are best for cooking and are generally boiled or steamed. They may be served hot as a vegetable or cold, usually in a salad. They can also be preserved in vinegar. The leafy tops are sometimes cooked and served as a green vegetable.

To boil beetroot: Shorten the leaves but do not cut or damage the root or it will 'bleed'. If a root is accidentally cut it may be sealed by singeing. Wash the roots in cold water, taking care not to damage the skin. Put into a saucepan of boiling water with a little salt and vinegar and simmer with the lid on the pan until quite tender (2 hours or longer), then drain. A well-cooked beetroot may be easily skinned with the thumb and forefinger. Slice or cube and serve hot with melted butter, or with white sauce; alternatively, serve cold, either plain or with vinegar.

To bake beetroot: Prepare the beet as above, place in a greased ovenproof dish, sprinkle with salt and cook very gently in a cool oven (150°C/300°F, Gas Mark 2) until tender. Peel and serve as above.

Bortsch (Beetroot Soup)
(See Bortsch entry.)

BEL PAESE

An Italian cheese, rather mild in content and creamy in flavour.

BÉNÉDICTINE

One of the most popular of all liqueurs, sweet and aromatic with a base of cognac. It was devised by the Bénédictine monks at Fécamp in Normandy in the 16th Century and is still made by them.

BEURRE NOIR (BLACK BUTTER)

A type of sauce in which butter is browned and combined with vinegar and seasoning. It is served with eggs, fish and some vegetables.

To make it, melt 50 g/2 oz butter in a small saucepan and cook until nut-brown. (If literally cooked until black, it would be burned.) Allow to cool slightly, then add 1 × 15 ml spoon/1 tablespoon vinegar, 1 × 15 ml spoon/1 tablespoon chopped parsley and seasoning. Pour over the food and serve at once. Capers are sometimes included.

BEURRE NOISETTE

Butter browned to a nut-brown colour and combined with lemon juice and seasoning.

BEVERAGE

Any liquid, other than water, which is consumed as a drink. (See individual entries.)

BICARBONATE OF SODA

Bicarbonate of soda (also known as baking soda) is used by itself as a raising agent in recipes where one of the ingredients is an acid and also where a darkening effect is desired, as with gingerbread or chocolate cake. (See Raising Agent entry and Baking Powder entry.)

At one time bicarbonate of soda was used fairly generally to conserve the colour of boiled green vegetables, but this was gradually discontinued when it was found to have a destructive effect on the vitamin C content.

Bicarbonate of soda added to the water used for cooking very acid fruit (e.g. rhubarb) in the proportion of 1 × 2.5 ml spoon/½ teaspoon to 0.5 kg/ 1 lb fruit, helps to save sugar, as it neutralizes some of the fruit acid and this takes away the sour taste.

BILBERRY

(Also known as blueberry, whortleberry, whinberry and in Scotland as blaeberry.)

A small, dark-blue berry which grows wild, mostly on moors and hillsides; the fruit ripens in August or September. The berries have a distinctive and delicious sharp flavour and are excellent for tarts, jams and jellies. They are quite a good source of vitamin C, a serving giving about half the day's requirements.

To make bilberry fritters: Make a fritter batter and add enough bilberries to make it quite thick. Drop spoonfuls into hot shallow fat, fry until golden-brown, drain and coat with caster sugar.

BILBERRY JAM

METRIC/IMPERIAL
1.25 kg/2½ lb bilberries
150 ml/¼ pint of water
3 × 15 ml spoons/3 tablespoons lemon juice
1.5 kg/3 lb sugar
250 ml/8 fl oz bottle of commercial pectin

This is rather an expensive jam to make unless you can pick the bilberries yourself, but it has a delicious flavour.

Pick over the fruit, removing any leaves and stalks, wash it lightly and put in a pan with the water and lemon juice. Simmer gently for about 10 to 15 minutes, until the fruit is soft and just beginning to pulp. Add the sugar, stir until dissolved bring to the boil and boil for 3 minutes. Take off the heat, add the pectin, boil for a further minute and allow to cool slightly before potting and covering in the usual way.

Makes about 2.5 kg/5½ lbs.

BILTONG

Strips of meat dried by a method developed in South Africa which enables it to keep for years. The strips can be grated or sliced and eaten raw.

BINDING

To add a liquid, egg or melted fat to a mixture to hold it together.

BIOTIN

One of the B vitamins. (See Vitamins entry.)

BIRD'S NEST SOUP

This Chinese speciality is made from part of the nest of a small species of swallow found on the coasts of Eastern countries. The edible part is a glutinous material that forms the outer supporting 'skin' of the nest; it gives a rich, spicy, aromatic flavour. The soup is imported into this country in dried form. It is available in cans from specialist shops.

BISCUIT

Originally, as the name implies, biscuit dough was baked twice to give the characteristic crispness. There are innumerable kinds of biscuit, both sweet and savoury. The commercial types cannot be imitated at home, as they demand special ovens and ingredients but many good home-made biscuits can be produced in a domestic situation.

Biscuit Making

To mix: Follow the particular recipe carefully. It is important to make the mixture only just moist enough to bind together – too much or too little liquid makes the dough difficult to handle. It may be necessary to finish the mixing with the fingers. To do this, gently press the mixture together until it forms a ball. Continue to press the mixture against the side of the bowl until a smooth, crack-free dough is formed.

To roll: Roll the dough out thinly and evenly, so that the biscuits will all be of the same thickness, otherwise they will not brown evenly. Prick the surface with a fork (unless the recipe directs otherwise).

To cut: Various fancy cutters are available but if you want a shape for which no cutter is available, make a pattern in thin cardboard, place it on the dough and cut round it with a sharp knife; the rim of a tumbler or wine glass may be used as a round cutter. Flour the cutter and stamp out the biscuits, working from the edge of the dough towards the middle and using the dough as economically as possible. Any remaining dough may be lightly kneaded and rolled out again, although biscuits from this second rolling are never as 'short' as the first ones.

To bake: A moderate to moderately hot oven (180°C–200°C/350°F–400°F, Gas Mark 4 to 6) is usually required, but the richer types of biscuit need a lower temperature. The biscuits should be put on to a greased baking sheet and cooked at the top of the oven.

To cool: Most biscuits may be removed at once with a palette knife on to a wire cooling rack. A few varieties, however, are soft when they come from the oven and should be allowed to cool slightly before being moved.

To store: Biscuits must be quite cold before they are put away; they should be stored in an airtight tin and never in the same container as a cake. Soft biscuits may be re-crisped by being put into a moderate oven for a few minutes.

BISCUIT PIE CRUST

METRIC/IMPERIAL
175 g/6 oz wheatmeal or plain biscuits
75 g/3 oz melted butter

Grease a shallow 18 cm/7 inch to 20 cm/8 inch pie plate or tin. Crush the biscuits and bind together with melted butter. Line the plate or tin with the mixture, pressing it firmly into place. Chill until set. When set, this pie crust makes a popular alternative to a pastry crust or sponge flan, particularly for recipes such as cheesecakes and pies made with fruit.

Any variety of sweet biscuit can be used.

Sugar and other flavourings may also be added.

Piped Biscuits

Decorative fancy biscuits may be made with a special biscuit-forcer. This consists of a tube which holds the mixture and a plunger to force it out through one or other of several perforated discs (which can be easily fitted and changed). The mixture must be fairly rich, sufficiently soft to come easily through the tube when pushed by the plunger and yet stiff enough to retain its shape on the tin and during the cooking; the flavouring can, of course, be varied to suit your own taste. You will need a little practice in manipulating the biscuit-forcer.

If preferred, the biscuit mixture may be piped with an ordinary forcing bag and a fluted nozzle.

PIPED BISCUIT MIXTURE

METRIC/IMPERIAL
225 g/8 oz butter or margarine
50 g/2 oz icing sugar
175 g/6 oz plain flour
50 g/2 oz cornflour
flavouring as desired

Cream the fat and sugar together till smooth. Work in the flavourings and flours, mixing thoroughly. Put the mixture into the forcer and fit the required disc on the end, hold it over a greased tin and press the plunger downwards, making each biscuit a neat, even shape. Decorate as desired and bake in a moderately hot oven (190°C/375°F, Gas Mark 5) for about 10 to 15 minutes until the biscuits are lightly browned at the edges.

BISHOP

A favourite drink during the Middle Ages, composed of wine (usually port), sweetened, spiced and flavoured with oranges.

It is a popular hot beverage in northern European countries. Bishop can also be prepared with Champagne or any other wine.

THE BISHOP

METRIC/IMPERIAL
2 lemons
12 cloves
1.2 litres/2 pints port
600 ml/1 pint water
1 × 5 ml spoon/1 teaspoon ground mixed spice
50 g/2 oz lump sugar

Stick 1 lemon with the cloves and roast it in a moderate oven (180°C/350°F, Gas Mark 4) for 30 minutes. Put the port into a saucepan and bring to simmering point. In another saucepan boil the water with the spice; add to the hot wine with the roasted lemon. Rub the sugar over the rind of the remaining lemon to remove the zest, put the sugar into a bowl, adding the juice of half the lemon, and pour on the hot wine. Serve as hot as possible.

BISMARK HERRING

A whole herring, pickled and spiced; generally served as an appetizer.

BISQUE

A thick, rich soup, based usually on a white stock made from fish, often shellfish.

BITTERS

An essence or liqueur made from bitter-flavoured aromatic herbs, spices, roots barks, etc. Bitters are used in apéritifs and cocktails and occasionally as a flavouring.

BLACK BUN

(See Scotch Bun entry.)

BLACK BUTTER

(See Beurre Noir entry.)

BLACK COCK (GAME)

(See Grouse entry.)

BLACK PUDDING

A kind of sausage, popular in the Midlands and North of England, which is made of pig's blood, suet, breadcrumbs and oatmeal, usually sold ready boiled. It is fried and served with mashed potatoes or bacon.

BLACKBERRY (BRAMBLE)

Blackberries, both wild and cultivated, grow extensively in this country. The cultivated varieties (e.g. Himalayan Giant) are often larger and more juicy than the wild, but slightly different in flavour. Blackberries are a good source of Vitamin C, supplying the day's requirements (20 mg) in an average helping.

Ripe blackberries are very good eaten raw and served with sugar and cream; the fruit should be carefully picked over and washed. When cooked, blackberries are often combined with apples. Apples are also added to blackberry jam and jelly to supply the acid and pectin necessary for a good set. As blackberry seeds are very hard, many people use the fruit only in dishes in which it is sieved, as in blackberry fool, blackberry conserve and bramble jelly. The fruit, and also the young shoots, make a good wine. (See Wines entry.)

BRAMBLE JELLY

METRIC/IMPERIAL
1.75 kg/4 lb blackberries (slightly under-ripe)
juice of 2 lemons or 1.5 × 5 ml spoons/1 ½ teaspoons
  citric or tartaric acid
450 ml/¾ pint water
sugar

Wash the blackberries and pick them over. Put them with the lemon juice (or acid) and water into a pan and simmer gently for about 1 hour, or until the fruit is really soft and pulped. Strain through a jelly cloth, measure the extract and return it to the pan with 450 g/1 lb sugar to each 600 ml/1 pint of extract. Stir until the sugar has dissolved and boil rapidly until a 'jell' is obtained on testing. Skim, pot and cover in the usual way.

BLACKBERRY AND APPLE JAM

METRIC/IMPERIAL
1.75 kg/4 lb blackberries
300 ml/½ pint water
0.75 kg/1 ½ lb sour apples, prepared weight
2.75 kg/6 lb sugar

Pick over and wash the blackberries, put them in a pan with 150 ml/¼ pint of the water and simmer slowly until soft. Peel, core and slice the apples and add the remaining 150 ml/¼ pint water. Simmer slowly until soft and make into a pulp with a spoon or a potato masher. Add the blackberries and sugar, bring to the boil and boil rapidly, stirring frequently, until setting point is reached. Pot and cover in the usual way.

Makes about 4.5 kg/10 lb.

BLACKCURRANT

When really ripe, this small juicy fruit can be served raw as a dessert, but it is more often used in pies, tarts, mousses, fools, cheesecakes and as a flavouring for ice cream or cordials. Blackcurrants can be frozen loose or in a purée form; they can also be preserved as jam, jelly or syrup.

Cassis is a liqueur made from the fruit, and is particularly popular in France.

Fresh blackcurrants are a rich source of vitamin C which makes them a useful food for convalescents and children.

BLACKCURRANT JAM

METRIC/IMPERIAL
1.75 kg/4 lb blackcurrants
1.75 litres/3 pints water
2.75 kg/6 lb sugar

Remove the stalks from the fruit, wash the currants and put them into the preserving pan with the water. Simmer gently until the fruit is tender and the contents of the pan reduced considerably. As the mixture becomes thick, stir frequently to prevent burning. Add the sugar, bring to the boil and boil hard for 10 minutes and test for jelling. As soon as a set is obtained pot and cover immediately.

Makes about 4.5 kg/10 lb.
Note: As the skins of blackcurrants are often very tough, it is important to cook the fruit thoroughly before adding the sugar or the skins will toughen and cause the jam to be inedible.

BLACKCURRANT BRÛLÉE

Crack through the sweet top crust to the sharp-tasting fruit below.

METRIC/IMPERIAL
225 g/8 oz stemmed blackcurrants
150 ml/¼ pint water
75 g/3 oz demerara sugar
1.5 × 5 ml spoon/1 ½ teaspoons arrowroot
1 × 15 ml spoon/1 tablespoon water
150 ml/¼ pint soured cream
soft light brown sugar
a pinch of ground cinnamon

Place the blackcurrants and water in a saucepan. Cook gently until the fruit is almost tender, add the demerara sugar, return to the boil and cook for a few minutes longer. Blend the arrowroot with 1 × 15 ml spoon/1 tablespoon water, stir it into the blackcurrants and gently boil, stirring, for 1–2 minutes. Cool and spoon into individual oven-proof dishes. Top with soured cream and cover with a layer of soft light brown sugar, to which is added a pinch of ground cinnamon. Flash under a hot grill until bubbling then chill. Serve with sponge fingers.

BLAEBERRY

(See Bilberry entry.)

BLANCHING

To treat food with boiling water, in order to whiten it, to preserve its natural colour, to loosen its skin, to remove a flavour which is too acid, rank or otherwise too strong, or (in the case of vegetables which are to be bottled, frozen etc.) to kill unwanted enzymes.

The two usual ways of blanching food are:
1. To plunge it into boiling water – use this method for tomatoes and nuts which are to be skinned.
2. To bring it to the boil in the water – used to whiten sweetbreads or veal or to reduce the saltiness of such things as pickled meat or kippers, before cooking them in a fresh lot of water or stock.

BLANCMANGE

A sweet made from milk, which is flavoured, sweetened and stiffened either with starch (usually cornflour) or with gelatine. The hot mixture is poured into a wetted mould to set and is turned out before serving. (See Cornflour entry for recipe.)

BLANQUETTE

A white stew of chicken, lamb, veal or sweetbreads, enriched with egg yolk or cream and flavoured with a bouquet garni, onion and lemon juice. It is served hot, with a garnish of croûtons of bread or fleurons of pastry, button mushrooms and onions. (See Blanquette of Veal under Veal entry.)

BLEAK

A small European river fish of the carp family, which may be cooked like the sprat.

BLENDING

To mix flour, cornflour, rice flour and similar ground cereals to a smooth paste with a cold liquid (milk, water or stock), before a boiling liquid is added, in the preparation of soups, stews, puddings, gravies, etc., to prevent the cereal from forming lumps. Use a wooden spoon and add the liquid by degrees, stirring all the time. Experience will soon show the right amount of liquid to use – too little makes hard lumps which are almost impossible to disperse and too much causes smaller, softer lumps which are also difficult to smooth out.

BLENNY

A small European and American sea fish; it may be prepared like whitebait.

BLEWIT

A variety of edible fungus.

BLINIS

Small Russian yeast pancakes, made of buckwheat flour, which are served with smoked salmon, caviare, etc.

BLOATER

A herring which has been immersed in brine, smoked and cured by a special process, perfected at Yarmouth. Unlike kippers, bloaters are not split open and the curing process is not carried so far as with kippers, therefore bloaters do not keep well (except in the form of commercially prepared bloater paste).

To cook, cover the bloaters with boiling water and soak them for 1 to 2 minutes, then drain them. Remove the head and fins with scissors, cut the fish open, remove the roes and backbones and wipe the fish well. Put the bloaters on a greased grill pan, flesh side down, place under a hot grill and cook on both sides for about 10 minutes. Dish skin side down on a hot plate, place a little butter on each and garnish with parsley.

Alternatively, the bloaters may be baked in greased paper or poached in hot water. The roes should be cooked separately and served as a garnish.

BLUE DORSET

A cheese made in Dorset, white and crumbly with a blue vein through it; it does not travel well. It is only found in parts of Dorset.

BLUEBERRY

(See Bilberry entry.)

BOILED SWEETS

A wide variety of hard-textured sweets is made commercially by boiling sugar, glucose, an acid and a fruit or other flavouring to 146°C/295°F, and putting the mixture through a 'drop machine', so that round or fancy shapes are obtained.

(See entry on Sweets for lollipops, barley sugar and peppermint humbugs).

BOILING

To cook in liquid – usually stock or water – at a temperature of 100°C/212°F. Vegetables, rice, pasta and suet puddings, together with syrups, etc., that are to be reduced, are the chief foods that are actually boiled. Although meat, poultry and

fish are put into boiling water, the heat is then lowered and the food is simmered or stewed at a temperature just below boiling point – fast boiling during the whole cooking time causes meat, poultry, etc., to shrink and lose flavour and it also tends to become less digestible.

To boil meat: Wipe the meat thoroughly and remove any superfluous fat. (This may be rendered down and used for frying and roasting purposes.)

A large joint such as silverside of beef should be tied securely to prevent it from losing shape during the cooking.

Put fresh meat into salted boiling water (2 × 5 ml spoons/2 teaspoons salt per 0.5 kg/1 lb of meat). Allow it to simmer gently (i.e. the water should bubble slightly on one side of the pan only) for the required length of time.

In the case of salt meat, place it in cold water, bring quickly to boiling point, throw away this water and commence again with cold. When boiling point has been regained, allow the water round the meat to simmer gently as for fresh meat. Add no extra salt at this stage.

Onions or leeks, carrots and a little turnip may be added to the pot, also herbs and spices (e.g., clove or mace), according to taste.

The liquor in which meat is cooked contains nourishment and flavour, so some of it can be used to make a sauce or gravy to accompany the meat and any that remains should be used as a basis for soup.

Time to Allow
MUTTON
20 minutes per 0.5 kg/1 lb, plus 20 minutes.

SALT BEEF AND SALT PORK
25 minutes per 0.5 kg/1 lb, plus 25 minutes.

BACON AND HAM
Bacon and small pieces of ham, 20 minutes per 0.5 kg/1 lb, plus 20 minutes; whole hams, 6 kg/13 lb upwards, 15 minutes per 0.5 kg/1 lb, plus an additional 15 minutes.

To boil fowl, fish, vegetables and puddings: (See Chicken, Fish, Vegetables, Suet Puddings, and similar entries.)

BOLETUS

A genus of fungi, including both poisonous and edible varieties, the best-known member of the family being the edible Cèpe de Bordeaux, which is much esteemed in France.

BOLOGNA SAUSAGE

A large Italian smoked sausage of finely chopped pork, veal and cereal, seasoned and flavoured. Also known as Polony.

BOMBAY DUCK

A fish found in Indian waters, which is dried and often served with curry. It has a delicate flavour and is very nutritious.

BOMBE

The name given to a mould, usually made of copper with a tightly fitting lid which is mostly used for shaping different flavours of ice cream and sometimes, fruits. (See Ice cream entry.)

BONBON

A general name for various kinds of sugar confectionery.

BONDON

A small soft, whole-milk cheese made in Normandy; shaped in the form of a bun.

BONE

Bones contain anything from 20 to 70 per cent of mineral elements, 15 to 50 per cent gelatine-producing material (cartilage, etc.), 5 to 50 per cent of water and from ½ to 20 per cent fat.

In cookery, both raw bones and those taken from cooked meat are used in the preparation of stock which can form the basis of many soups, stews and sauces. A good flavour and a certain amount of gelatine are obtained from the bones, but stock has practically no nutritional value. (For method of making see Stock entry.)

The fatty substance in the interior of marrow bones is considered by some to be a delicacy and may be served as a savoury supper dish or used to replace suet in dumplings.

To make savoury marrow: Select large, fresh marrow bones and if possible get the butcher to saw them in half. Scrape and wash the bones and cover the end of each with a paste made of flour and water, in order to prevent the marrow escaping during the cooking. Tie each bone in a small pudding cloth, stand it upright in a pan of boiling salted water and simmer for 1 ½ to 2 hours, then remove the cloths and paste. Pin a small serviette around each bone and send to table upright on a hot dish, accompanied by dry, crisp toast. Alternatively, extract the marrow and serve it already spread on the toast. Salt and cayenne pepper are the only flavourings required.

BONNE-BOUCHE

A small savoury tit-bit served as appetizer or at the savoury course.

33

BONNE FEMME

This term means cooked in a simple or house-wifely style, with a garnish of fresh vegetables or herbs usually including mushrooms. It is generally applied to cream soups or fish dishes, e.g., Potage à la Bonne Femme – a purée or cream soup garnished with lettuce, tarragon and chopped chervil; Sole à la Bonne Femme – usually garnished with mushrooms in a sauce flavoured with shallots and white wine; Oeufs à la Bonne Femme – hard-boiled eggs, with the yolks pounded with chopped tarragon and butter, then replaced and garnished with beetroot.

BORAGE

A herb the young leaves of which are used to flavour claret cup, iced drinks and occasionally vegetables and as an addition to salads. They have a cucumber flavour which is particularly refreshing. The blue flowers may be used as a garnish.

BORDEAUX WINES

Bordeaux is the largest fine wine district of France. As a wine region it has the advantages of a stable climate, a position near the sea and many rivers and forests on the ocean side to protect it from strong salt winds and reduce the rainfall. Although the top soil is often poor the bed rock is rich in minerals. The wines are made from a mixture of grape varieties the proportions varying according to each proprietor. The main Bordeaux 'rouge' districts are Medoc, St. Emilion, Pomeral and Graves. There are many hundreds of Chateaux making and bottling excellent wines. Most of these will be vintage wines which those bottled overseas are not. The minimum age for a vintage wine is 5 years and some can live for 50 years or more.

Bordeaux white wines are usually medium sweet or sweet. The sweetest are the Barsacs whereas some Graves are quite dry. The best white Bordeaux wines are considered to be the Sauternes. Those of the best vintage will improve for at least 15 years, and even moderate vintages are worth keeping as they gain an added depth of flavour.

BORECOLE

(See Kale entry.)

BORTSCH (BORSHCH, etc.)

A Russian or Polish soup made originally from duck, other meat and beetroot; nowadays the duck is frequently omitted. The soup may be served hot or cold.

BORTSCH

METRIC/IMPERIAL
6 small raw beetroot, peeled, about 1 kg/2¼ lb
2 medium sized onions, skinned and chopped
2.25 litres/4 pints seasoned beef stock
2 × 15 ml spoons/2 tablespoons lemon juice
6 × 15 ml spoons/6 tablespoons dry sherry
seasoning
soured cream
chives (optional)

Grate the beetroot coarsely and put it together with the onion in a pan with the stock. Bring to the boil and simmer without a lid for 45 minutes. Strain and add the lemon juice and sherry. Adjust seasoning. Serve either well chilled or hot with a whirl of soured cream and chopped chives.

BOTTLING

A method of preservation by killing or inhibiting the moulds, yeasts, enzymes and bacteria which are normally present in the tissues of foodstuffs and by maintaining conditions in which new organisms cannot reach the sterilized foodstuffs. Provided it is adequately sterilized and hermetically sealed, bottled produce keeps indefinitely and provides a delicious supply for use in wintertime.

Fruits are most suitable for bottling as they contain less harmful bacteria than vegetables or meat. These are not recommended for bottling without a pressure cooker for health reasons.

Equipment

Elaborate equipment is not essential, but if you intend to do a large amount of bottling you will probably like to equip yourself with such apparatus as a sterilizer fitted with a thermometer, a pair of tongs for lifting the hot jars, a long-handled wooden packing spoon and a bottle brush. To bottle vegetables, a pressure cooker is essential, owing to the high temperatures necessary; it may also be used to sterilize bottled fruit.

The Bottling Jars, etc.

In principle, all bottling jars are the same – that is, they are fitted with a rubber ring and a lid of glass or metal and are provided with some means of holding the lid firmly in position; this may be a metal screw-band, a clip or a metal spring cap.

The jars are made in two sizes. It is a good idea to choose at least some jars with wide necks, for they are easier to pack (especially with large fruits such as Victoria plums or pears) and also easier to empty.

If you already have a stock of bottles, it is well to review them before the preserving season starts. This entails pairing them up with their lids and screws or clips, testing rubber bands, examining lacquered lids and making any necessary replacements or additional purchases.

As a general rule it is advisable to buy new rubber rings each season, but good quality ones may be used several times if necessary. As soon as they show signs of perishing or if they become in any way damaged they must be discarded.

Metal lids are lacquered on the inside to protect them from fruit acids, so when using this type of lid it is important to make sure that the lacquer film is intact. Lids with imperfections in the lacquer coating should not be used again.

Several types of covers are designed for jam jars; carefully used these are most satisfactory. The jars must be standard size with rims free from chips or imperfections. Follow the manufacturers' directions. Coffee jars can also be used in conjunction with special sealing rings.

Preparation of Jars
Check as above, then wash them thoroughly in warm soapy water and rinse well. It is better not to dry the jars with a cloth, but just to shake them to remove excess water or place them upside-down to drain.

Soak rubber bands in warm water for 15 minutes, then dip them in boiling water.

The Syrup or Liquid
Fruit may be bottled satisfactorily in plain water, but the flavour is much better if syrup is used. A suitable one for most fruits is made with 0.5 kg/1 lb sugar to 1.2 litres/2 pints water, but as much as 1 kg/2 lb to 1.2 litres/2 pints may be used for very acid fruits. To prepare it, put the sugar and water into a saucepan, cover and bring to the boil; boil for 1 minute, then strain the syrup through muslin. If any syrup is left over after all the jars have been filled, it may be strained, poured into a jar, sealed and sterilized at the same time as the fruit.

For tomatoes, use water with 2 × 5 ml spoons/2 teaspoons salt and 1 × 5 ml spoon/1 teaspoon sugar in each 1 kg/2 lb jar. Alternatively, use tomato juice (prepared by rubbing stewed tomatoes through a sieve).

The Fruit
Choose firm, dry fruit that is just ripe. When possible, it should be picked on a dry day. Bottle it as soon as possible after gathering.

Prepare fruit as for stewing, i.e., top and tail gooseberries, remove stalks from currants, hull loganberries, blackberries, strawberries and raspberries, halve and stone plums, if very large; cut rhubarb into convenient-sized lengths. When necessary, wash the fruit gently in plenty of cold water.

Tomatoes may be left whole, if small; large ones are better quartered or sliced. It is best to skin them before bottling; to remove the skins easily, first put the tomatoes into boiling water for a few seconds, until the skins start to split.

Apples, pears, peaches and some other fruits tend to discolour unless ascorbic acid tablets are added. Dissolve the tablets in the covering liquid and proceed in the usual way. For each jar use 125 mg., i.e., 1¼ tablets of 100 mg.–2000 i.u. potency or 2½ tablets of 50 mg.–1000 i.u. potency or 5 tablets of 25 mg.–500 i.u. potency.

Apples and pears may, if preferred, be peeled into a bowl of salted water, 25 g/1 oz salt to 2.25 litres/4 pints cold water, to prevent discolouring. The fruit must be well rinsed before it is packed into the bottling jars.

Colouring for Bottled Fruit
The addition of a little suitable colouring to the syrup used for rhubarb, strawberries, cherries, etc., gives a better appearance to the fruit.

General Procedure
Whenever possible, grade the fruit according to size and ripeness. Pack it tightly into the jars, without bruising; use a packing spoon or the handle of a wooden spoon if necessary to push the fruit gently into place. Shake the fruit down by striking the bottom of the jar smartly with the palm of the hand. Now follow the detailed instructions for either the under-water or oven method of sterilization.

Testing for a Seal
When the jars are quite cold, i.e., the next day, remove screw-bands or clips. You should be able to lift the jars by the lids, which will show that a vacuum has formed as they cooled and that the jars are now hermetically sealed.

Any jars that are not sealed must be re-sterilized before storing, or the contents must be used up within a day or so.

Storing
Bottled fruit should be stored in a cool, dry place. It is wise to re-check the seal a week or so after putting the bottles away and at intervals during the storage period. If, as sometimes happens, sterilization is not complete or if a breakdown in the seal occurs, fermentation or mould growth will set in. If this is noticed at once, while the fruit in the jars is still wholesome, it can be used up at once and need not be wasted.

Slight over-cooking, the use of a heavy syrup, or loose packing will cause fruit to rise in the jars during storage, which sometimes worries novices. It is often difficult to avoid over-cooking, especially when the oven method of sterilization is used, but it does not affect the keeping quality of the fruit – provided that sterilization is complete and the jars are hermetically sealed, the fruit should keep.

35

Sterilization under Water

This is on the whole the most reliable method of bottling fruit. A sterilizer or deep bath fitted with a thermometer is very convenient, but any deep receptacle such as a large saucepan, fish kettle or clothes-boiler will do quite well. It should be deep enough to enable the jars to be covered with water or for the water to be at least up to the neck of the jars and it must be fitted with a false bottom, which may be made of wire – such as the rack of a grill pan or a small cake rack or of slatted wood. Failing these, several thicknesses of cloth or newspaper can be used, but a rack is better as it allows the steam to escape and prevents excessive rattling. Pack a cloth or a pad of crumpled paper between the jars to prevent them touching.

Packing and Processing

Prepare, wash and grade the fruit and pack it tightly into clean jars. Fill the jars to the top with cold syrup, water or juice and put on the rubber rings, lids and clips or screw-bands. Loosen the screw-bands a very slight amount, by about one half-turn.

Place the bottles in the sterilizer or container with cold water to cover them or to come well up to the neck and cover with a lid to prevent evaporation. Heat very gently, so that after 1½ hours the water reaches the appropriate temperature for sterilizing, then adjust the heat and maintain this temperature for the time stated in the chart. If no thermometer is available, heat very gradually to a slow simmering temperature and maintain the water at this heat for 15 to 20 minutes.

Lift the jars out on to a wooden surface or folded newspaper. Tighten the screw-bands immediately and again after a few minutes' cooling. Leave undisturbed to cool. The next day, test the seals.

To seal bottles when no patent mixture is available, particularly useful for small bottles, make a cement out of 225 g/8 oz black resin, 20 g/¾ oz beeswax, 225 g/8 oz red sealing wax and one tallow candle. Heat all the ingredients except the tallow candle together in an iron or earthenware pot. When the mixture froths up, before all the solids have melted and before the mixture begins to boil up, stir it with the candle, which will settle the froth until the ingredients are melted and ready for use.

Quick Method of Sterilizing under Water

The following method is useful when time is short, though the finished appearance of fruit sterilized in this way is slightly less good than when the more usual method is followed.

Prepare and grade the fruit and pack it into warmed jars. Fill up the jars with syrup, water or brine (for tomatoes) heated to 60°C/140°F, then put on the rubber rings, lids and clips or screw-bands. Loosen screw-bands by about one half-turn.

Place the bottles in the pan or sterilizer on a rack, folded cloth or paper, and just cover with warm water 38°C or 100°F. Cover the pan and raise the temperature of the water to 88°C/190°F or simmering point in 25 to 30 minutes. Maintain this temperature for the following times:

Fruit	Time in minutes
Soft fruits (including gooseberries and rhubarb) for pies; apple slices (average pack)	2
Soft fruits (including gooseberries and rhubarb) for dessert; most whole stoned fruit (tight pack)	10
Apples (solid pack); nectarines; peaches; halved plums	20
Figs; pears	40
Tomatoes: whole	40
solid pack	50

Note: Allow extra time if using jars which are over 1 kg/2 lb in capacity.

Fruit	Temperature	Minutes
Apples, sliced	74°C/165°F	10
Apricots, Peaches	82°C/180°F	15
Blackberries, Loganberries	74°C/165°F	10
Cherries	82°C/180°F	15
Currants (black, red or white)	74°C/165°F	10
Gooseberries	82°C/180°F	15
Grapefruit	82°C/180°F	15
Grapes	82°C/180°F	15
Mulberries	74°C/165°F	10
Oranges	82°C/180°F	15

Fruit	Temperature	Minutes
Tangerines, Lemons	82°C/180°F	15
Pears	88°C/190°F	30
Pineapple	82°C/180°F	15
Plums, Greengages, Damsons	82°C/180°F	15
Quinces	88°C/190°F	30
Raspberries, Strawberries	74°C/165°F	10
Rhubarb	74°C/165°F	10
Whortleberries	74°C/165°F	10
Tomatoes	88°C/190°F	40

Sterilizing in the Oven

This simple method, which is useful when no deep receptacle is available for sterilizing under water, can be used for all fruits except those mentioned below. It is quicker than the water sterilizing method.

There are two ways of carrying it out:

1. STANDARD OR DRY PACK METHOD

The covering liquid is added to the jars when they are removed from the oven.

Prepare, wash and grade the fruit as described above and pack it fairly tightly into clean jars. Do not add any syrup or water and do not put on the rubber rings, clips or screw-bands, but either cover each jar with a patty-pan or other lid to protect the top fruit from scorching or put a baking tin over all the jars.

Put jars on a baking sheet in a very cool oven (110°C/230°F, Gas Mark ¼) and keep them at this temperature until the fruit begins to shrink and appears cooked and the juice begins to run – three-quarters to 1¼ hours (1½ hours for tomatoes). If the shrinkage is considerable, use the contents of one jar to fill up the others, replacing them in the oven for another 5 to 10 minutes to complete sterilization.

Have ready some fast-boiling syrup, water or brine (for tomatoes) and the rubber rings, lids, screw-bands or clips, which should be dipped into boiling water before being placed in position. Remove one jar at a time from the oven and place it on a wooden surface or folded newspaper. Fill up with the boiling liquid, place the rings and lid in position and secure immediately with the screw-band, clip or cap, according to type. Reboil the liquid and proceed with the next jar. Tighten the screw-bands again after a few minutes' cooling, then leave the jars undisturbed to cool. The next day, test the seal as already described.

This method is not recommended for apples (sliced or solid pack), whole stone fruit, citrus fruit, nectarines, peaches, pineapple, pears or solid-pack tomatoes.

The times given are for 0.5 kg/1 lb to 1.25 kg/4 lb in either 0.5 kg/1 lb or 1 kg/2 lb jars, and should be increased by up to 25 minutes for larger amounts. (See the following chart).

Fruit	Time in minutes
Soft fruits (including gooseberries and rhubarb) for pies	45 to 55
Soft fruits (including gooseberries and rhubarb) for dessert; most whole stoned fruit (tight pack)	55 to 70
Stone fruits – dark (whole cherries, damsons and plums)	55 to 70
Figs	80 to 100

2. QUICK OR WET PACK METHOD

Prepare and grade the fruit and pack into hot jars. Fill up with boiling syrup, water or brine (for tomatoes) to within 2.5 cm/1 inch of the top and put on the rubber rings and covers, but do not put on the screw-bands.

Place the jars 5 cm/2 inches apart on a baking sheet lined with newspaper and put them in the centre part of the preheated cool oven (140°C/275°C, Gas Mark 1). Keep the heat at the same level and process for the time given in the following chart:

Fruit	Time in minutes
Soft fruits (including gooseberries and rhubarb) for pies; apple slices (average pack)	30 to 40
Soft fruits (including gooseberries and rhubarb) for dessert; most whole stoned fruit (tight pack)	40 to 50
Apples (solid pack), nectarines, peaches, halved plums	50 to 60
Figs: pears	60 to 70
Tomatoes: whole	60 to 70
solid-pack	70 to 80

After processing is complete, remove the jars, put on the screw-bands and leave to cool. Test the seal the next day.

Note: The times given are for 0.5 kg/1 lb to 1.75 kg/4 lb (in either 0.5 kg/1 lb or 1 kg/2 lb jars) – for larger quantities increase the processing time by up to 20 minutes.

Re-sterilizing Bottled Fruit

If any jars of fruit have failed to seal, remove the tops and rubber rings and wipe off any pips or fruit fibres which may be adhering to them. 'Top up' the jars with syrup or water. If the rubber rings are hard, replace with new rings, after first treating these as described on page 35, under 'Preparation of Jars'.

Re-sterilize by the under-water method, timing carefully. The water should not be allowed to boil, as this causes the fruit to taste stewed.

Bottling Pulped Fruit

Preserving fruit in the form of pulp is quick and easy. It can be stored more compactly in this way and the pulp can either be used for puddings or made into jam at a later date. The pulp can be bottled either with or without sugar, as preferred.

First stew the prepared fruit in the minimum amount of water. When it is thoroughly cooked and mashed and still boiling hot, pour at once into hot sterilized jars and seal at once, as when bottling. Deal with one jar at a time and re-heat the pulp before filling the next jar. When cold, test the seal in the usual way.

Provided that the fruit is boiling hot when poured into the jar and the filling and sealing are quickly and carefully carried out, the pulp should keep satisfactorily without further sterilization. As an extra precaution, however, the filled and sealed jars may be sterilized. Loosen screw-bands by a half-turn, immerse the bottles in hot water, standing them on a rack or folded cloth, and bring the water to the boil. Boil for 5 minutes, then remove from the water, cool and test as for bottled fruit.

For fruit purée, cook the fruit until tender, liquidize or pass it through a nylon, hair or stainless metal sieve, then bring it back to the boil.

To make tomato purée: Cut up the tomatoes and put into a saucepan with 2 × 5 ml spoons/2 teaspoons salt to every 1 kg/2 lb tomatoes. Bring to the boil, stirring frequently, and cook gently until a thick pulp is obtained. Sieve or liquidize this and pour into warmed jars. Cover as for bottled fruit. To sterilize, put the filled jars into a pan of hot water, bring to the boil and boil for 10 minutes. Test the seal in the usual way.

This pulp is useful for soups and sauces in the winter months.

A quicker method, which dispenses with sieving or liquidizing, is to skin, cut up and stew the tomatoes and bottle them while still boiling hot, as for pulped fruit.

Fruit Juices and Syrups

Sweetened and unsweetened juices make good winter sweets, sauces and drinks. The best fruits to use are loganberries and blackcurrants, blackberries, raspberries and strawberries, while rose-hips, see recipe, make a syrup rich in Vitamin C. The fruit must be really ripe and fresh.

Have ready some small jars and covers suitable for fruit bottling or some bottles with screw caps and corks. Heat the jars in a cool oven or by bringing them to the boil in water; boil caps or corks for 10 minutes.

Put the fruit in a pan with little or no water (but for blackcurrants add 300 ml/½ pint water per 0.5 kg/1 lb, and for blackberries 300 ml/½ pint water per 2.25 kg/5 lb to 2.75 kg/6 lb). Bring to the boil, stirring and crushing frequently, and boil for 1 to 2 minutes. Strain the pulp through a jelly bag.

For a very clear liquid, allow the juice to stand for several hours, to let any sediment settle.

For fruit syrup, add 225 g/8 oz to 350 g/12 oz sugar per 600 ml/1 pint of the strained juice, dissolving it well. Strain through muslin.

Pour the liquid into the bottles to within 5 cm/2 inches of the cork or stopper and seal tightly, fixing with wire if necessary. Put into a deep pan on a false bottom and fill with cold water up to the base of the corks. Heat to 77°C/170°F and maintain this temperature for 30 minutes. (If no thermometer is available, raise to simmering point and maintain for 20 minutes.) Remove the bottles and dip the corks into melted paraffin wax when partly cooled. If no screw caps are used, wire the corks on. Store in a cool, dry place, as for Bottled Fruit.

To make rose-hip syrup: The hips should be fresh, fully ripe and deep red. Crush or grate and put at once in boiling water, allowing 1.75 litres/3 pints to 1 kg/2 lb hips. Bring back to boiling point, then set aside for 10 minutes. Strain through a jelly bag and when it ceases to drip, return the pulp from the bag to the pan, with a further 900 ml/1½ pints boiling water. Bring back to boiling point, leave for 10 minutes, then strain as before. Mix the two extracts, and reduce by boiling until the juice measures 900 ml/1½ pints. Add 0.5 kg/1 lb sugar and stir until dissolved. Bottle, sterilize and seal.

To make tomato juice: Simmer ripe tomatoes until they are soft, then rub through a sieve. To each 1.2 litres/2 pints of pulp add 300 ml/½ pint water, 15 g/½ oz sugar, 2 × 5 ml spoons/2 teaspoons salt and a shake of pepper. Put into jars or bottles and sterilize as for tomato pulp, above. Use for making tomato juice cocktails; a little lemon juice or Worcestershire sauce may be added to the juice when it is served as an appetizer, etc.

Bottling Fruit in a Pressure Cooker

This has the advantage of shortening the time and ensuring exact control of the temperature. Any pressure cooker will take 0.5 kg/1 lb bottling jars but for larger ones a pan with a domed lid is required.

METHOD

1. Prepare fruit as for ordinary bottling.
2. Pack into clean, warm bottles, filling them to the top.
3. Cover with boiling syrup or water to within 5 mm/¼ inch of the top of the bottles.
4. Put on the rubber bands and heat resisting discs and screw bands, screwing these tight, then turn back a quarter turn. As an extra precaution heat the jars by standing them in a bowl of hot water.
5. Place the inverted trivet on the pressure cooker and add at least 900 ml/1½ pints water plus 1 × 15 ml spoon/1 tablespoon vinegar or lemon juice to prevent the pan becoming stained (unless it is non-stick). Bring water to the boil.
6. Pack bottles into the cooker, making sure they do not touch by placing newspaper between them.
7. Fix the lid in place, put the pan on the heat and heat until steam comes steadily from the vent.
8. Put on the low (5 lb) pressure control and continue heating gently to take about 3 minutes to reach pressure. Reduce the heat and maintain pressure for the time given in the chart on the opposite page. (Any change in pressure will cause liquid to be lost from the jars and under processing may result.)

9. Remove the pan carefully from the heat and reduce the pressure at room temperature for about 10 minutes, before taking off the lid.

10. Lift the jars out one by one, tighten the screw bands and leave to cool.

Fruit	Processing time at Low (5 lb) pressure
Apples (quartered)	1 minute
Apricots (whole)	1 minute
Blackberries Loganberries Raspberries	1 minute
Cherries (whole)	1 minute
Red and Black currants	1 minute
Damsons	1 minute
Gooseberries	1 minute
Pears (eating)	5 minutes
Pears (cooking) (very hard ones can be pressure cooked for 3 to 5 minutes before being packed in bottles)	5 minutes
Plums (pricked if whole, stoned if halved)	1 minute
Rhubarb (in 5 cm/2 inch lengths)	1 minute
Strawberries (not recommended)	—
Soft Fruit (solid pack) Place fruit in a large bowl, cover with boiling syrup (175 g/6 oz sugar to 600 ml/1 pint water) and leave overnight. Drain, pack jars and cover with the same syrup. Process as usual.	3 minutes
Pulped Fruit (e.g. apples) Prepare as for stewing Pressure cook with 150 ml/¼ pint water at High (15 lb) pressure for 2 to 3 minutes, then sieve or liquidize. While still hot, fill jars and process	1 minute

Bottling Vegetables

This should only be carried out in a pressure cooker. (See Pressure Cookery entry.)

BOTULISM

A form of food poisoning (often fatal) caused by a toxin produced by a bacterium known as *Bacillus Botulinus*, which is fortunately rare in this country. It has been known to develop in such foods as home-canned fruits and vegetables (not cooked under pressure), meat, pies, fish and meat pastes, canned and smoked meat, raw and salted fish.

Frequently there is no indication of the presence of toxins and the food may appear, smell and taste quite normal. Boiling for not less than 10 minutes destroys the toxin and renders any contaminated food safe.

BOUCHÉE

A small pastry case in the shape of a vol-au-vent, filled with a mixture of finely chopped meat, poultry, fish or game, usually in a thick sauce. Bouchées are served as hot appetizers, after-dinner or cocktail savouries and at buffet parties.

Typical fillings are: Fish with mayonnaise sauce; chopped cooked mushroom, ham, tongue, prawn and chicken moistened with Béchamel sauce; sardine with diced tomato, lemon juice and a little mayonnaise.

BOUILLABAISSE

A renowned Southern French fish stew, made of various kinds of fish peculiar to the Mediterranean, cooked with olive oil, spices and herbs. Saffron is usually included as a flavouring.

BOUILLON

Plain unclarified meat or vegetable broth, served as a soup. It is made in a similar way to Pot-au-Feu. (See Pot-au-Feu entry.)

BOUQUET GARNI

A bunch of herbs, used in soups, stews and sauces to give flavour. Usually a sprig each of parsley and thyme, a bay leaf and sometimes other herbs or a piece of celery and leek are bound together as a faggot, or better still tied in a piece of muslin and cooked in the pot with the liquid and other ingredients. The bouquet garni is lifted out before serving.

There are many variations. In parts of Southern France a strip of dried orange peel is included, which gives an excellent flavour to some dishes. Some cooks add marjoram, others, winter savory or lemon thyme.

When fresh herbs are not available, a pinch or so of mixed dried herbs may be used instead. If the dish calls for spices such as cloves, peppercorns and mace, these are usually included in the bag of herbs.

Ready prepared Bouquets Garni are available from large supermarkets, grocery, cookery and gift shops.

BOURGUIGNONNE

A red wine sauce containing onion and sometimes mushrooms. It is also the name for a garnish which

39

incorporates mushrooms, small onions and grilled bacon in a red wine sauce.

BRAINS

The brains of calf, sheep or pig, which are sold either with the head or separately, are considered a delicacy, calves' brains being generally the most popular. The same recipes can be used for all types of brains.

The brains must be very fresh. Wash them in cold salted water, removing the loose skin and any clots of blood, then let them lie in fresh cold water for at least an hour. When they are thoroughly cleansed, put them into a small saucepan with cold water to cover, a pinch of salt and a good squeeze of lemon juice. Add a small bunch of herbs (parsley, thyme and bay leaf), and simmer slowly for 15 minutes, then strain, coat and fry or sauté or else serve in one of the following ways:

To make calf's brains on toast: Cook the brains as above. Make a good white sauce and add to it the yolk of an egg and a good squeeze of lemon juice. Place the brains on 2 rounds of toast, strain the sauce over and garnish with lemon, a few potato balls or green peas.

To make scalloped calf's brains: Cook as above, then arrange the brains in scallop shells, cover with white sauce and sprinkle breadcrumbs and grated cheese on the top. Brown under the grill.

BRAISING

This combination of stewing, steaming and roasting is suitable for various meats and vegetables; it gives a delicate flavour and a tender, moist consistency. Meat is first lightly browned in hot dripping and then laid on a bed of prepared vegetables, with just enough liquid to cover these. It may be cooked either in a moderate oven (180°C/350°F, Gas Mark 4) or on top of the stove; in this case, bake or roast in the oven for the last 30 minutes of cooking, to give a better flavour to the finished dish.

Preparation
Prepare the meat according to kind, boning and stuffing if liked. Weigh it to gauge the cooking time and allow 25 to 30 minutes per 0.5 kg/1 lb, plus 30 minutes. Then prepare the bed of vegetables, e.g., 1 onion, 1 carrot, 1 small turnip, 2 stalks of celery and a bouquet garni, with seasoning. Peel and trim the vegetables as usual and cut into pieces.

Cooking
If possible, choose a fireproof casserole or a pan with two handles which may be placed in the oven. Place about 25 g/1 oz of dripping in the pan, together with a few bacon rinds, and fry the veg-

etables lightly in the hot fat. Then add the bouquet garni, fresh herbs such as thyme and parsley and sufficient stock or water to half-cover the vegetables. Bring to the boil, then place the meat on top, cover and simmer gently, basting every 15 to 20 minutes with the liquor, for half the cooking time; remove the lid and complete the cooking in a hot oven (220°C/425°F, Gas Mark 7), basting frequently. Lift the meat on to a hot plate and pour round it a good sauce (made from the liquor). Garnish, if liked, with the vegetables, after removing the bacon rinds and the bouquet garni.

Alternative Method
Prepare the meat by coating it with seasoned flour. Melt a little dripping and when it is smoking hot fry the meat, turning it so that it is brown all over, then remove it from the pan. If necessary, add a little more dripping and in this fry a mixture of vegetables (onions, carrots, celery, etc) until lightly browned. Put the vegetables into a meat tin, place the meat on top and add enough stock or water just to cover the vegetables. Add more salt and pepper if necessary and some chopped herbs. Cover and cook in a warm oven (160°C/325°F, Gas Mark 3) until the meat is tender. Lift it on to a hot dish, arrange the vegetables at each end and pour the liquor round.

Cooking Time
For joints suitable for roasting, allow half as long again as for roasting; for stewing meat (scrag end of neck, etc.), 2 to 3 hours; rabbits, 1 to 2 hours; chicken, 1 hour; fowl, 2 hours.

BRAISED BACON

METRIC/IMPERIAL
piece of gammon, collar or forehock bacon
1 onion, skinned and sliced
4 carrots, pared and sliced
½ turnip, pared and sliced
2 sticks of celery, trimmed and sliced
3 × 15 ml spoons/3 tablespoons oil
stock
bouquet garni
salt
pepper

Soak the bacon or gammon for 1 hour (or overnight if you think it is likely to be very salty). Boil it for half the cooking time, allowing 20 to 25 minutes per 450 g/1 lb plus 20 minutes over. Lightly fry the vegetables in the hot fat or oil for 3 to 4 minutes. Put them in a casserole, put the bacon on top and add enough stock to cover the vegetables. Add the bouquet garni and the seasoning, cover and cook in a moderate oven (180°C/350°F, Gas Mark 4) for the remaining cooking time. Thirty minutes before the bacon is cooked, carefully remove the rind and continue cooking, uncovered, for the final thirty minutes. Remove the bouquet garni.

BRAISED CELERY

METRIC/IMPERIAL
4 small heads celery, trimmed and scrubbed
50 g/2 oz butter
well flavoured stock, preferably home-made and jellied
salt
pepper

Tie each head of celery securely to hold the shape. Fry lightly in half the butter for five minutes, until golden brown. Put in an ovenproof dish, add enough stock to come halfway up the celery, sprinkle with salt and pepper and add the remaining butter. Cover and cook for 1 to 1½ hours in a moderate oven (180°C/350°F, Gas Mark 4). Remove the strings and serve with the cooking liquid poured over; if the stock is home-made reduce it first to a glaze by fast boiling.

BRAMBLE

(See Blackberry entry.)

BRAN

Recent medical research has shown that roughage plays an important part in preventing diseases of the bowel and colon.

About 13 per cent of a grain of wheat is bran, which forms the outer layer of cells (pericarp and aleurone). Bran contains cellulose or roughage, which is not digested by the body but has a useful laxative action. The aleurone layer of bran is rich in protein, mineral elements and nicotinic acid, but also contains phytic acid, which tends to prevent the absorption of calcium.

BRANDER

Scottish name for a gridiron or grill.

BRANDY

A spirit distilled from wine. Brandy is colourless at first, but darkens in the cask as it matures. The quality of the brandy depends upon the type of wine used, the manner of distillation and the method and time of storage. The French Cognac and Armagnac brandies are considered the best. V.S.O.P., meaning 'very special old pale', denotes a brandy that is 18 to 25 years old, while V.V.S.O.P. applies to one 25 to 40 years old.

Brandy may be flavoured with apricots, cherries or other fruits.

Brandy is frequently found in recipes for celebration cakes and for flambé dishes.

BRANDY BUTTER (HARD SAUCE)

METRIC/IMPERIAL
75 g/3 oz butter
75 g/3 oz caster sugar
2–3 × 15 ml spoons/2–3 tablespoons brandy

Cream the butter until pale and soft. Beat in the sugar gradually and add the brandy a few drops at a time, taking care not to allow the mixture to curdle. The finished sauce should be pale and frothy. Pile it up in a small dish and leave to harden before serving.

Traditionally served with Christmas pudding and mince pies.

Note: If you prefer a less granular texture, use sifted icing sugar or half icing and half caster sugar.

To make rum butter: Make this as brandy butter, above, but use soft brown sugar, replace the brandy with 4 × 15 ml spoons/4 tablespoons rum and include the grated rind of half a lemon and a squeeze of lemon juice.

To make brandy sauce: To 300 ml/½ pint sweet white sauce add 1 to 2 × 15 ml spoons/1 to 2 tablespoons brandy.

BRANDY SNAP

A crisp rolled biscuit served at tea-time; when

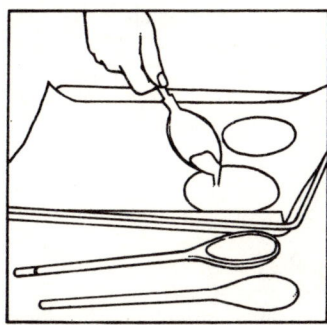

1. Drop small spoonfuls of mixture onto a lined baking sheet, allowing plenty of room for spreading.

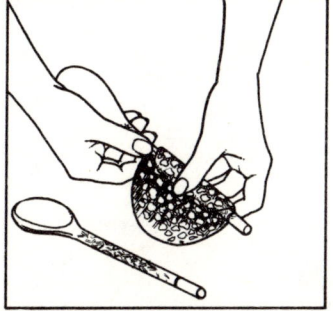

2. Roll warm Brandy Snaps round the greased handles of several wooden spoons, leave to cool slightly.

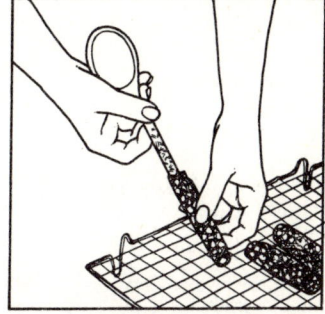

3. When Brandy Snaps are set and crisp transfer to a cooling rack.

given a cream filling it is sometimes used as a luncheon or dinner sweet.

BRANDY SNAPS

METRIC/IMPERIAL
50 g/2 oz butter or margarine
50 g/2 oz caster sugar
50 g/2 oz golden syrup (about 2 × 15 ml spoons/2 tablespoons)
50 g/2 oz plain flour
1 × 2.5 ml spoon/ ½ teaspoon ground ginger
1 × 5 ml spoon/1 teaspoon brandy, optional
grated rind of ½ lemon
whipped cream

Grease the handles of several wooden spoons and line 2 to 3 baking sheets with non-stick paper.

Melt the butter with the sugar and syrup in a small saucepan over a low heat. Remove from the heat and stir in the sifted flour and ginger, brandy and lemon rind. Drop small spoonfuls of the mixture about 10 cm/4 inches apart on the lined baking sheets, to allow plenty of room for spreading. Bake in rotation in a moderate oven (180°C/350°F, Gas Mark 4) for 7 to 10 minutes, until bubbly and golden. Allow to cool for 1 to 2 minutes, then loosen with a palette knife and roll them round the spoon handles.

BRAWN

True brawn is a preparation of boned meat made from pig's head and is eaten cold. Sheep's head, veal and other meats may be used to make an economical brawn.

The meat is stewed with spices and seasoning until very soft then picked from the bone and finely chopped. It is then set in moulds with some of the stock which is reduced sufficiently for the mixture to set to a jelly. Brawn is served cold and thinly sliced.

BRAWN

METRIC/IMPERIAL
½ pickled or fresh pig's head or calf's head
bouquet garni
6 peppercorns
1 large onion
pieces of carrot and turnip, pared
salt
freshly ground black pepper
ground nutmeg
1 hard-boiled egg, sliced

Wash the head thoroughly, making sure the ear and nostrils are clean; soak it in salted water for about 1 hour. Cut off the ear and remove the brains. Scald the ear, scrape it free of hair and wash well. Place the head in a large pan with the ear,

bouquet garni, peppercorns, vegetables and 1 × 5 ml spoon/1 teaspoon salt if the head is pickled, 2 × 5 ml spoons/2 teaspoons if it is fresh. Cover with water, bring to the boil, skim, cover and allow to cook very slowly until the meat is tender – about 2 to 3 hours. Strain off the liquid, remove the meat from the bones and cut it into small pieces. Skin the tongue and slice it thinly. Cut the ear into strips. Skim off the fat from the remaining liquid, add the brains, tied up in muslin, then boil uncovered until the liquid is reduced to half. Chop the brains and add to the meat. Season the mixed meats well with salt, pepper and nutmeg. Garnish the bottom of a mould or cake tin with sliced hard-boiled egg, pack the meat in tightly and pour some of the liquid over. Put a saucer and a weight on it and leave till cold and set. When the brawn is required for use, dip the mould into hot water and turn the brawn out onto a dish.

BRAZIL NUT

The edible seed of a large tree native to Brazil. The fruits are borne in large numbers high on the trees and each contains 12 to 22 nuts, with a distinctive tough, angular shell. The white kernels are eaten plain or used in confectionery and cakes. Like other nuts, they contain fat and protein.

BREAD

As long ago as 2000 BC bread was an important part of the Egyptian diet. In this country there is evidence that it was baked and eaten in the Stone and Iron Ages. Today, bread, with other cereal based foods provides more than a quarter of the total energy, protein, carbohydrate and iron in the average household diet. Bread also provides a good source of calcium, nicotinic acid and thiamine. Although some of these nutrients are lost during the milling of flour, calcium, iron and B Vitamins are added to white flour to make good the loss.

There is often controversy as to whether white or brown bread is better nutritionally. It is now accepted by most nutrition experts that both are a valuable source of nutrients in the diet as white bread is enriched in Britain. Brown bread is favoured by many because of its higher roughage content.

Varieties of Bread

WHITE BREADS
Bread made from white flour (See Flour entry) has the light texture which most people like. The nutritive value is high, owing to the additions already mentioned.

Many different varieties and shapes of loaf are made. The most widely sold, because of its convenience, is the wrapped, sliced loaf, although connoisseurs prefer crusty, unsliced bread, which should always be served as fresh as possible. Whatever your usual choice, it is a good idea to try some of the scores of varieties now available.

WHITE BREADS MADE FROM UNENRICHED DOUGH
These are the 'everyday' white breads, obtainable in a number of shapes.
70 cals/oz (265 kJ/25 g).

Tin, long tin, sandwich, sliced tin.	Baked in a rectangular tin. May be wrapped or unwrapped. Can be sliced.
Pistol, musket, rasp, barrel or landlady's loaf	Baked in a cylindrical corrugated tin.

CRUSTY WHITE BREADS
Coburg	Round, cut on top to form a cross.
Cottage	Made of two rounds, smaller on top of larger.
Long split tin	Cut deeply down the centre before baking.

MADE FROM ENRICHED DOUGH
Milk, eggs and/or fat and sometimes other ingredients are added.
70 to 73 cals/oz (265 to 275 KJ/25 g).

Farmhouse: enriched with milk and sometimes fat.	Baked in a tin; floury top with a lengthwise split. ·
Bloomer: enriched with milk, fat and sugar.	Long loaf, with slashes along the top.
Milk: according to regulations must have a minimum of 6.3 per cent by weight of whole milk solids.	Variety of shapes, some egg-washed; usually baked in a tin.
Cholla: Jewish bread with added oil, eggs and sugar, producing a soft texture.	Generally plaited; sometimes sprinkled with poppy seeds.
American: Enriched with soya flavour, producing a soft texture.	Baked in a tin.
Bun loaves: Enriched with milk, fat, sugar and fruit – similar mixture to that used for *Buns* (See Currant Bread entry.)	Various shapes, but generally baked in a tin.

SPECIALITY WHITE BREADS
Several of these types of loaf are Continental in origin.

Poppy seed plait.	Crusty plaited loaf, with top sprinkled with poppy seeds.
Caraway: contains caraway seeds.	Baton-shaped.
Vienna: enriched with milk, soft and light crumb, but the glazed crust is very crisp.	Baked under steam, which keeps crust moist until maximum expansion takes place, giving light, open texture; steam is then withdrawn and crust baked crisp. Various shapes.
French: made from an unenriched dough; very crisp crust.	Made like Vienna bread; long shape with a slashed top, which is sometimes sprinkled with poppy seeds.

PROTEIN AND GLUTEN BREADS
These have extra protein in the form of added gluten. This gives a lighter texture, but the Calorie (Kilo Joule) value is much the same as for other breads and the addition of protein to bread is of no particular nutritional importance in this country.

Regulations specify that before these names can be used:

Protein or high-protein bread must contain not less than 22 per cent protein by weight.

Gluten bread must contain not less than 16 per cent protein by weight.

(The protein content of bread is normally about 8 or 9 per cent.)

BROWN BREADS
The term covers a wide variety of wheatmeal and wholemeal types.
65 to 70 cals/oz (245 to 265 KJ/25 g).

WHEATMEAL
Made from a mixture of white and wholemeal flours. (See Flour entry.) Various finishes and shapes, for example:

Dusty wheatmeal	Baked in tin; floury top.
Norwegian or cracked wheat	Cob-shaped, baked on oven bottom; sprinkled with cracked wheat.

WHOLEMEAL
Made from wholemeal flour (See Flour entry); as digestible as white. Tin, long tin and cob shapes, some decorated with cracked wheat. Stoneground has same nutritive value.

WHEATGERM
Made from white flour to which extra wheat germ has been added, for example, Hovis, Turog, Vitbe. Baked in a tin.

MALT BREADS
Made of various flours and mixtures of flours. Malt extract is often added to bread dough to make a malt loaf. Dried fruits are by tradition, added to such loaves.

Plain or Fruit Malt: Dark colour, sticky when new. — Various shapes, but usually baked as 'square tins'.

Granary: Malted grains mixed with wheatmeal flour. — Baked in a tin or as a cob.

Bermaline: Malt and wheatgerm added to white flour. — Baked in a tin.

RYE BREADS

Made from a mixture of rye and wheat flours in varying proportions, so that the colour varies from white to black. They have a closer texture than wheat bread and a slightly sour taste. Various shapes.

Pumpernickel is a particularly dark and slightly sour-tasting rye bread.

CRISPBREADS

Flat, crisp wafers, made from rye or wheat flour or a mixture of the two; the wholemeal flour, sometimes quite coarsely ground, is generally used. Several commercial varieties are sold here and many more in Scandinavia.

UNLEAVENED BREADS

Made from flour derived from various grains, salt and water. The dough is kneaded to lighten it somewhat, but when baked it is flat, crisp and hard. Matzos – the Jewish unleavened bread – is the best-known one in this country. Chapattis and many other breads made in different parts of the world are also unleavened.

SODA BREAD

(See Soda Bread entry.)

TYPES OF ROLLS

Dinner: Soft crust, round or long shape.

Vienna: Made from Vienna bread dough; crisp crust, various shapes, with or without poppy seeds.

Brown: Made from brown bread dough; various shapes.

Bridge: Dinner roll dough, enriched with eggs; small, slim rolls.

Scotch Baps: Soft crust, floury top; round, slightly flattened shape.

Croissants: Made from a yeast dough into which butter is folded, as in puff pastry; crescent-shaped. (See Croissant entry.)

Starch-reduced Rolls: (See Rolls entry.)

Ingredients used in Breadmaking

YEAST

You can now buy fresh yeast from health stores and some bakers (those who bake their own bread are your best bet) and dried yeast can be found in chemists, supermarkets and grocers as well as health food stores. Which is best, dried or fresh? Both have their pros and cons. There is nothing to choose between the two as far as taste and texture of the end result is concerned. Fresh yeast is rather like putty in colour and texture and should have a faint 'winey' smell. There should be no discoloration and it should crumble easily when broken. Although it will store for up to a month in a screw-topped jar or wrapped in cling film or foil in the refrigerator, the best results are obtained when it is absolutely fresh, so buy it in small quantities when required.

Fresh yeast is usually blended with a liquid, it is then ready to be added to the flour all at once. It can also be rubbed directly into the flour or else added as a batter. This batter is known as the sponge batter process where only some of the ingredients are mixed, forming a sponge that is allowed to ferment and is then mixed with the remaining ingredients to form a dough.

Using sugar to cream the yeast before adding the liquid is not advised as concentrations of sugar kills some of the yeast cells and thus delays fermentation. The resulting bread has a strong yeasty taste. Fresh yeast is easiest measured by weight. According to the richness of the mixture, 25 g/1 oz fresh yeast is sufficient to raise 1.5 kg/3 lb white flour.

Dried yeast is sold in granulated form and is very convenient as it can be stored in an airtight container in a cool place for up to six months. Take care when buying it that it is bakers' yeast and not tonic or brewers' yeast as these have no rising powers. Dried yeast requires sugar and liquid to activate it. The sugar, in the proportion of 1×5 ml spoon/1 teaspoon to 300 ml/ ½ pint of tepid liquid, is dissolved in the liquid. The yeast granules are then sprinkled over the surface of the liquid and the mixture left to froth for about 15 minutes before being ready for use. Dried yeast is easiest measured as 1×5 ml spoon/1 teaspoon or 1×15 ml spoon/1 tablespoon. As it is more concentrated than fresh yeast, generally half the amount of dried yeast is required to fresh. 1×15 ml spoon/1 tablespoon dried yeast is equivalent to 25 g/1 oz fresh yeast.

FLOUR

Wheat, before it is made into flour, is either hard or soft. Hard wheat when milled produces a strong flour, rich in protein, which contains a sticky, rubber-like substance called gluten. When combined with the other essential ingredients used in breadmaking, the gluten stretches like elastic and as it is heated, it expands and traps in the dough the carbon dioxide released by the yeast. The gluten then sets and forms the 'frame' of the bread. A strong plain flour should have a gluten content of 10 to 15 per cent. It is the gluten content in a strong flour that gives the volume and open texture of baked bread.

Soft wheats when milled produce a flour with different gluten properties, more suited to the making of cakes, pastries etc. where a smaller rise and closer, finer texture are required.

For most bread the best results are obtained by using a strong plain flour. If this is not available, soft plain flour can be used instead but it will give a smaller rise and closer textured bread with a pale, hard crust and a generally disappointing result.

It is the flour used that gives each bread its characteristic flavour and texture. Nowadays there are many different flours readily available, from health food stores if not from your local supermarket or grocer.

Generally bread made with brown flour has a closer texture and a stronger, more distinctive taste than white bread. As brown flour does not store as well as white, it should be bought in smaller quantities.

Wholemeal flour contains 100 per cent wheat. The entire grain is milled, and bread made with this flour is coarse textured and has a nutty taste.

Wheatmeal flour contains 80 to 90 per cent wheat (i.e. some of the bran is removed) and it is more absorbent than white flour, giving a denser textured bread than white but not as coarse as wholemeal. Stoneground refers to the specific process of grinding the flour which heats it and gives it a slightly roasted, nutty flavour. Both wholemeal and wheatmeal can be stoneground.

Granary flour contains malt and crushed wheat, giving a crunchy, rough texture.

Rye flour used on its own produces rather dense, heavy bread as rye lacks sufficient protein for the formation of gluten. Finely milled rye flour gives the densest texture and bread made with coarsely milled rye flour is rougher and more open-textured. The traditional German pumpernickel is made from coarsely ground rye flour. The best results for baking at home are obtained by combining the rye flour with a strong wheat flour.

SALT
Salt is added to improve the flavour. It is essential to measure it accurately, as too little causes the dough to rise too quickly and too much kills the yeast and gives the bread an uneven texture. Salt is used in the proportions of 1 to 2 × 5 ml spoons/1 to 2 teaspoons to 0.5 kg/1 lb flour.

FAT
The addition of fat to the dough enriches it and gives a moist, close-textured loaf with a soft crust. It also helps keep the bread fresh and soft for a longer time.

LIQUID
Water is most suitable for plain bread, producing a loaf with an even texture and a crisp crust. Milk and water, or milk alone, will give a softer golden crust and the loaf will stay soft and fresh for longer.

The amount of liquid used will vary according to the absorbency of the flour, as too much will give the bread a spongy and open texture. Brown flours are more absorbent than white.

The liquid is generally added to the yeast at a tepid temperature i.e. 43°C/110°F.

GLAZES AND FINISHES
If a crusty finish is desired for bread or rolls, they can be brushed before baking with a glaze made by dissolving 2 × 5 ml spoons/2 teaspoons salt in 2 × 15 ml spoons/2 tablespoons water.

For a soft finish the surface should be brushed with oil and dusted with flour, or alternatively brushed with beaten egg or beaten egg and milk.

Some breads and yeast buns are glazed after baking to give them a sticky finish. To achieve this brush with warmed honey or a syrup made by dissolving 2 × 15 ml spoons/2 tablespoons sugar in 2 × 15 ml spoons/2 tablespoons water; bring to the boil.

There are many ways of adding interest and variety to bread and rolls. After glazing and before baking, lightly sprinkle the surface with one of the following:
1. Poppy, caraway, celery or fennel seeds.
2. Sesame seeds. Particularly good sprinkled on to the soft baps and eaten with hamburgers.
3. Cracked wheat or crushed cornflakes. Sprinkle them on top of wholemeal bread or baps.
4. A mixture of crushed rock salt and caraway. This is particularly good on rolls to be eaten with cheese or smoked sausage.

Step-by-Step Processes in Breadmaking

The processes used in making yeast mixtures form the basis of the method followed for nearly all yeast cooking.

1. MIXING THE DOUGH
Measure all the ingredients carefully and sift the dry ingredients (flour, salt, etc.) into a large bowl.

Add the yeast dissolved in the liquid all at once and mix the dry ingredients, using a wooden spoon or fork, until blended. Extra flour (taking care not to upset the balance by adding too much), can be added at this stage if it is too slack. Beat the dough by hand until the mixture is completely smooth and leaves the sides of the bowl cleanly.

2. KNEADING THE DOUGH
Kneading is essential to strengthen the gluten in the flour, thus making the dough elastic in texture and enabling it to rise more easily. To do this:

Turn the dough on to a floured working surface, knead the dough by folding it towards you and pushing down and away from you with the palm of the hand. Give the dough a quarter turn and continue kneading for about 10 minutes until it is firm, elastic and no longer sticky.

45

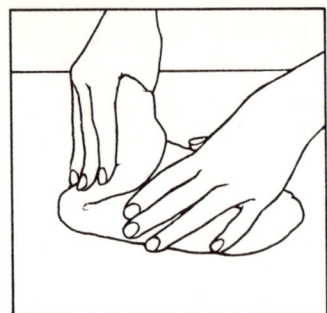

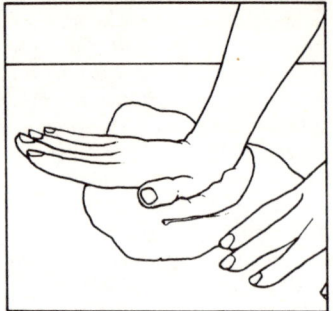

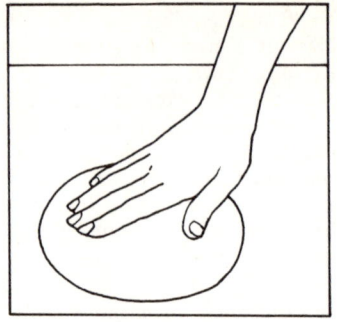

1. Knead dough by using the palm of one hand to fold the dough towards you.

2. Push down and away from you with the palm of the hand. Give the dough a quarter turn and repeat.

3. Continue kneading for about 10 minutes until the dough is firm, elastic and no longer sticky.

If you have a mixer with a dough hook attachment it can take the hard work out of kneading. Follow manufacturer's instructions; working with small amounts of dough is more successful than attempting a large batch all at once. Place the yeast dissolved in the liquid in the bowl, add the dry ingredients and begin at lowest speed and mix to form dough. Increase the speed for the recommended time.

3. RISING

The kneaded dough is now ready for rising. Unless otherwise stated, place in a greased bowl and cover with a large sheet of polythene brushed with oil, to prevent a skin forming during rising.

Rising times vary with temperature. As only extreme heat kills the yeast and extreme cold retards the growth of yeast the method of rising can be arranged to suit yourself.

The best results are obtained by allowing the covered dough to rise overnight or up to twenty-four hours in the refrigerator. The refrigerated dough must be allowed to return to room temperature before it is shaped.

Allow about 2 hours for the dough to rise at room temperature, 18°C/65°F. The dough can be made to rise in about 45 minutes – 1 hour if placed in a warm place such as an airing cupboard or above a warm cooker. The risen dough should spring back when gently pressed with a (floured) finger.

4. PREPARING TINS

While the dough is rising, prepare the tins or baking sheets by greasing and lightly flouring them. Whenever reference is made to a 0.5 kg/1 lb loaf tin, the approximate size to use is 20 × 10 × 6 cm/8 × 4 × 2½ inch top measurements. When reference is made to a 1 kg/2 lb loaf tin, use one with 23 × 13 × 7.5 cm/9 × 5 × 3 inch top measurements.

5. KNOCKING BACK

The best texture is obtained by kneading the dough for a second time after rising. Turn the risen dough on to a lightly floured working surface and knead for 2 to 3 minutes to 'knock' out any large bubbles and ensure an even texture. The dough is shaped as required and placed in tins or on baking sheets at this stage, then covered with polythene.

6. PROVING OR SECOND RISE

This is the last process before baking. The shaped dough should be allowed to 'prove', that is, left until it is doubled in size and will spring back when lightly pressed with a (floured) finger. This is done at room temperature. The dough is now ready.

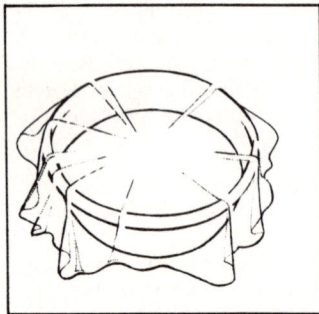

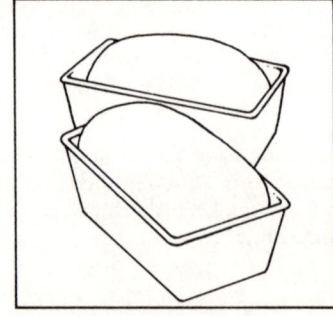

1. Rise the dough by placing the dough in a bowl and covering with an oiled polythene bag.

2. Knock back and shape bread dough to fit tin.

3. Allow the shaped dough to prove until it has doubled in size.

7. BAKING

Basic breads are baked in a hot oven (230°C/450°F, Gas Mark 8).

When cooked the bread should be well risen and golden brown and when tapped underneath with the knuckles it should sound hollow. Allow the bread to cool on wire racks before storing.

8. STORING

Bread should be stored in an airtight tin or frozen. Dough must be stored frozen.

9. REFRESHING BREAD

Wrap the bread in aluminium foil and place in a hot oven (230°C/450°F, Gas Mark 8) for 5 to 10 minutes.

Allow the bread to cool in the foil before unwrapping. For a more crusty loaf omit the foil and bake as above.

To Make Traditional Bread and Roll Shapes

Bread Shapes

TIN LOAF

Roll out dough to an oblong and roll up like a Swiss roll. Tuck the ends under and place in the prepared tin. Before baking score the top of the loaf with a knife if wished.

BATON

Shape into a long roll, with tapering ends, about 20 cm/8 inches long.

COB

Knead dough into a ball by drawing the sides down and tucking underneath to make a smooth top.

CROWN

Divide the dough. Knead into small pieces and place together in a greased round sandwich tin. It is usually pulled apart into rolls when served.

COTTAGE

Divide the dough into two, making one piece twice as large as the other. Knead both pieces well and shape into rounds, place smaller round on top of the larger one, and place on baking sheet. Make a hole through the middle of both pieces using the handle of a wooden spoon. Cover and leave to rise. Glaze with salt water before baking.

BLOOMER

Flatten the dough and roll up like a Swiss roll. Tuck the ends under and place on baking sheet. When proved to double in size make diagonal slits on top with a sharp knife. Brush with beaten egg or salt glaze (salted water) before baking.

PLAIT

Divide the dough into three and shape into three long rolls each about 30 cm/12 inches long. Pinch

the ends together and plait loosely crossing each strand alternately. Pinch the ends together. Place on a baking sheet and allow to prove. Before baking brush with beaten egg and sprinkle with poppy seeds.

Roll Shapes

ROLLS

Can be made in any of the traditional bread shapes by dividing the basic white dough into 50 g/2 oz pieces and shaping as for bread. Other variations are:

KNOTS

Shape each piece into a thin roll and tie into a knot.

ROUNDS

Place the pieces on a very lightly floured board and roll each into a ball. To do this, hold the hand flat almost at table level and move it round in a circular motion, gradually lifting the palm to get a good round shape.

RINGS

Make a thin roll with each piece of dough and bend it round to form a ring; damp the ends and mould them together.

Home Freezing Bread and Dough

FREEZING BAKED BREAD

Baked loaves and rolls, both commercial and home baked, can be home frozen, and it is a successful way of storing bread for up to about one month. There are three points to remember:
1. Only freeze freshly baked bread.
2. Freezer bags are the best containers. Make sure all the air is excluded before sealing the bag tightly.
3. Label to indicate the date of freezing.

STORAGE TIMES

The length of storage depends on the crust, but generally bread stores well for four weeks. Bread with any form of crisp crust only stores well for about a week, then the crust begins to 'shell off'. Enriched breads and soft rolls store well for up to six weeks.

THAWING BREAD

Leave to thaw in the sealed freezer bag (to prevent drying out) at room temperature, or overnight in the refrigerator.

TO MAKE THE CRUST CRISP

Remove the freezer bag and place the thawed loaf or rolls in a hot oven (230°C/450°F, Gas Mark 8) for 5 to 10 minutes, until the crust is crisp.

Freezing Bread Dough

All bread dough can be home frozen, but the storage time varies with the type of dough – plain or enriched.

Remember these four points:

47

1. The best results are obtained if the quantity of yeast used in the recipe is increased, for example, increase 15 g/½ oz yeast to 20 g/¾ oz.
2. Freeze the unrisen dough in the quantities you are most likely to use.
3. The most successful containers for dough are freezer bags. Oil them lightly and seal tightly. (The sealing is most important – see note below on 'skinning'.)
4. Label to indicate the date of freezing and type of dough frozen.

'SKINNING'

To prevent the dough forming a skin it should be tightly sealed in the freezer bag to exclude air, but, if there is a chance of the dough rising slightly before it is frozen, leave 2.5 cm/1 inch of space above the dough. A very marked skin will crack when the dough is handled, and the baked crust will have a streaked appearance. The degree of skinning also depends on the storage time: the longer the dough is kept, the more marked the skin.

STORAGE TIMES – UNRISEN DOUGH

Plain white dough will keep up to eight weeks; enriched white dough up to five weeks. Dough kept longer than these times gives poor results. Loss of resilience and difficulty in 'knocking back' the dough begins after about three weeks' storage; the dough is also slower to prove.

THAWING DOUGH

Thaw dough at room temperature: 18°C/65°F to 22°C/72°F. Dough can be thawed overnight in the refrigerator, but if left overnight at room temperature it will be over-risen. Thaw the dough in the freezer bag to prevent a skin forming, but first unseal the bag and then reseal it loosely at the top, to allow space for the dough to rise.

WHITE BREAD

This is a basic household bread recipe which lends itself to all sorts of variations.

METRIC/IMPERIAL
675 g/1½ lb strong plain flour
2 × 5 ml spoons/2 teaspoons salt
knob of lard
15 g/½ oz fresh yeast
450 ml/¾ pint tepid water

Grease a 900 g/2 lb loaf tin. Sift the flour and salt into a large bowl and rub in the lard. Blend the yeast with the water. Make a well in the centre of the dry ingredients and add the yeast liquid all at once. Stir in with a wooden spoon or fork. Work it to a firm dough, adding extra flour if needed, until it will leave the sides of the bowl clean. Do not let the dough become too stiff as this produces heavy 'close' bread.

Turn the dough on to a lightly floured surface and knead thoroughly until the dough feels firm and elastic and no longer sticky – about 10 minutes. Shape it into a ball and place in a large bowl.

Cover the dough with lightly oiled polythene to prevent a skin forming and allow to rise until it is doubled in size and will spring back when pressed with a floured finger. Turn the risen dough on to a lightly floured surface, flatten it firmly with the knuckles to knock out the air bubbles, then knead again well. Stretch the dough into an oblong the same width as the tin, fold it into three and turn it over so that the 'seam' is underneath. Smooth over the top, tuck in the ends and place in the greased 900 g/2 lb loaf tin.

Cover the tin with lightly oiled polythene and leave to rise until the dough comes to the top of the tin and springs back when pressed with a floured finger.

Remove the polythene, glaze and finish as desired. Place the tin on a baking sheet and place in the oven.

Bake in a hot oven (230°C/450°F, Gas Mark 8) for 30 to 40 minutes until well risen and golden brown. When the loaf is cooked it will shrink from the sides of the tin, and will sound hollow if you tap the bottom of it. Turn out and cool on a wire rack.

TO MAKE ROLLS

After knocking back the dough, divide it into about eighteen 50 g/2 oz pieces. Place on greased baking sheets about 2.5 cm/1 inch apart to allow room for expansion during baking.

QUICK WHOLEMEAL BREAD

METRIC/IMPERIAL
15 g/½ oz fresh yeast
about 300 ml/½ pint tepid water
1 × 5 ml spoon/1 teaspoon sugar
450 g/1 lb wholemeal flour or 225 g/8 oz wholemeal
   and 225 g/8 oz strong plain flour
1–2 × 5 ml spoons/1–2 teaspoons salt
25 g/1 oz lard

Grease two baking sheets. Blend the yeast with the water. Mix the sugar, flour and salt and rub in the lard. Add the yeast liquid and remaining water and mix with a wooden spoon to give a fairly soft dough, adding more water if necessary. Turn it on to a floured surface and knead well. Divide the dough into two, shape into rounds and place on the greased baking sheets. Cover with lightly oiled polythene and leave to rise until the two rounds have doubled in size. Bake in a hot oven (230°C/450°F, Gas Mark 8) for about 15 minutes, reduce to 200°C/400°F, Gas Mark 6 for a further 20 to 30 minutes. Turn out and cool on a wire rack.

WHOLEMEAL BREAD

METRIC/IMPERIAL
50 g/2 oz fresh yeast
900 ml/1 ½ pints tepid water
1.5 kg/3 lb plain wholemeal flour
2 × 15 ml spoons/2 tablespoons caster sugar
4–5 × 5 ml spoons/4–5 teaspoons salt
25 g/1 oz lard

Grease two 900 g/2 lb or four 450 g/1 lb loaf tins. Blend the yeast with 300 ml/ ½ pint of the water. Mix the flour, sugar and salt together; rub in the lard. Stir the yeast liquid into the dry ingredients, adding sufficient of the remaining water to make a firm dough that leaves the bowl clean. Turn it out on to a lightly floured surface and knead until it feels firm and elastic and no longer sticky. Shape it into a ball, place in a large bowl and cover with lightly oiled polythene to prevent a skin forming. Leave the dough to rise until doubled in size. Turn it out on to a floured surface and knead again until firm. Divide into two or four pieces and flatten firmly with the knuckles to knock out any air bubbles. Knead well to make it firm and ready for shaping. Shape to fit the tins. Cover with lightly oiled polythene and leave until the dough rises almost to the tops of the tins – about 1 hour at room temperature.

Brush the tops with salt glaze and bake the loaves in a hot oven (230°C/450°F, Gas Mark 8) for 30 to 40 minutes. Turn out and cool on a wire rack.

POPPY SEED PLAIT

METRIC/IMPERIAL
450 g/1 lb strong plain flour
15 g/ ½ oz fresh yeast
225 ml/8 fl oz tepid milk
1 × 5 ml spoon/1 teaspoon salt
50 g/2 oz butter or block margarine
1 egg, beaten

FOR THE GLAZE AND TOPPING
beaten egg
poppy seeds

Lightly grease a baking sheet. Put 150 g/5 oz of the flour into a large bowl. Crumble the yeast, add the milk and stir until dissolved. Add to the flour and mix well. Set aside in a warm place until frothy – about 20 minutes. Mix the remaining flour with the salt and rub in the fat. Add the egg and the flour mixture to the yeast batter and mix well to give a fairly soft dough that will leave the sides of the bowl clean. Turn the dough on to a lightly floured surface and knead until smooth and no longer sticky – about 10 minutes (no extra flour should be necessary). Place in a bowl, cover with lightly oiled polythene and leave to rise until doubled in size. Knead the dough again lightly on a floured working surface, divide in half and roll each half

into an oblong. Cut each half into three strips lengthwise, pinching the dough together at the top. Plait the strips, damp the ends and seal together. Place on the lightly greased baking sheet. Brush with the egg and sprinkle with poppy seeds. Prove again until doubled in size. Bake in a moderately hot oven (190°C/375°F, Gas Mark 5) for 45 to 50 minutes. Cool on a wire rack.

CHEESE PULL-APARTS

METRIC/IMPERIAL
225 g/8 oz strong plain flour
1 × 2.5 ml spoon/ ½ teaspoon salt
1 × 5 ml spoon/1 teaspoon dry mustard
50 g/2 oz Cheddar cheese, grated
25 g/1 oz butter or block margarine
50 g/2 oz celery or onion, finely chopped
15 g/ ½ oz fresh yeast
150 ml/¼ pint milk

FOR THE GLAZE
beaten egg

Grease an 18 × 24.5 × 4.5 cm/7 × 9¾ × 1¾ inch tin. Mix together the flour, salt, mustard and cheese. Heat the fat and sauté the celery or onion gently until soft. Add to the dry ingredients. Blend the yeast with the milk, add to the dry ingredients and work to a firm dough. Knead for 10 minutes. Place in a bowl, cover with lightly oiled polythene. Leave to rise until doubled in size. Turn out and knead again. Cut into eight equal-sized pieces, shape into finger-shaped pieces.

Cut down the length of each with a sharp knife to 5 mm/¼ inch depth. Place side by side in the tin, not quite touching. Cover with lightly oiled polythene and leave to rise in a warm place – about 45 minutes. Brush with beaten egg and bake in a moderately hot oven (190°C/375°F, Gas Mark 5) for about 25 minutes. Cool on a wire rack. Break apart and serve buttered.

SWEDISH TEA RING

METRIC/IMPERIAL
½ quantity of risen enriched white bread dough
15 g/ ½ oz butter, melted
50 g/2 oz brown sugar
2 × 5 ml spoons/2 teaspoons powdered cinnamon
glacé cherries, angelica and/or flaked almonds

FOR THE GLACÉ ICING
100 g/4 oz icing sugar, sifted
water
lemon juice

Grease a baking sheet. Roll the dough to an oblong 30 × 23 cm/12 × 9 inches. Brush with the butter, then sprinkle the mixed brown sugar and cinnamon over the dough. Roll up tightly from the long edge and bend round to form a ring and seal the ends together. Place on the baking sheet; using scissors, cut slashes at an angle 2.5 cm/1 inch apart and to within 1 cm/½ inch of the inside edge. Twist the cut sections to overlap each other. Cover with lightly oiled polythene and put to rise in a warm place for about 30 minutes. Bake in a moderately hot oven (190°C/375°F, Gas Mark 5) for 30 to 35 minutes. Ice and decorate (see below) and cool on a wire rack.

To make the glacé icing, blend the icing sugar with a good squeeze of lemon juice and just enough water to give a thick coating consistency. While the ring is still warm dribble icing over it with a spoon. Decorate with cherries, angelica 'leaves' and/or nuts.

WHEATMEAL FLOWERPOTS

Grease two clean clay flowerpots well and bake them empty in a hot oven before use. This will prevent the loaves sticking.

METRIC/IMPERIAL
450 g/1 lb wheatmeal flour or 225 g/8 oz each brown and white plain flours
2 × 5 ml spoons/2 teaspoons each salt and sugar
knob of lard
15 g/½ oz fresh yeast
300 ml/½ pint warm water
milk to glaze
cracked wheat

Grease two 10 cm/4 inch to 13 cm/5 inch flowerpots. Mix the flours, salt and sugar in a bowl, rub in the lard. Blend the yeast with the water and add to the flour, mixing to a soft dough that leaves the bowl clean. Knead the dough thoroughly on a floured surface for about 10 minutes and divide between the two greased flowerpots. Cover with lightly oiled polythene and leave to rise until doubled in size. Brush the tops lightly with milk or water and sprinkle with cracked wheat. Bake in a hot oven (230°C/450°F, Gas Mark 8) for 30 to 40 minutes. Turn out and cool on a wire rack.

MALT BREAD

METRIC/IMPERIAL
25 g/1 oz fresh yeast
350 ml (¾ pint less 4 × 15 ml spoons/4 tablespoons) tepid water
450 g/1 lb plain flour (not strong plain flour)
1 × 5 ml spoon/1 teaspoon salt
3 × 15 ml spoons/3 tablespoons malt extract
2 × 15 ml spoons/2 tablespoons black treacle
25 g/1 oz butter or margarine
225 g/8 oz sultanas

Grease two loaf tins with 20 × 10 cm/8 × 4 inch top measurements. Blend the yeast into the water. Sieve the flour and salt together. Warm the malt, treacle and fat until just melted. Stir the yeast liquid

and malt mixture into the dry ingredients and combine well. Stir in the sultanas and beat thoroughly for about 5 minutes. Turn the mixture into the two 20 × 10 cm/8 × 4 inch top measurement loaf tins. Cover and leave to rise in a warm place for about 45 minutes, or until the dough almost fills the tins. Bake in a moderately hot oven (200°C/400°F, Gas Mark 6) for 40 to 45 minutes. When cooked the loaves may be brushed with the sugar glaze made by dissolving the sugar in the water, and heating gently.

To pull bread: Using two forks, pull the crumb from the inside of a loaf while it is still hot and bake in small pieces in a moderate oven (180°C/350°F, Gas Mark 4) until crisp. Serve with soup, etc.

BREAD PUDDING

METRIC/IMPERIAL
225 g/8 oz white bread, preferably stale
300 ml/½ pint milk
100 g/4 oz currants, sultanas or stoned raisins
50 g/2 oz mixed peel, chopped very finely
50 g/2 oz shredded suet
50 g/2 oz demerara sugar
1–2 × 5 ml spoons/1–2 teaspoons ground mixed spice
1 egg, beaten
a little milk to mix
nutmeg, optional

Butter a 900 ml/1½ pint pie dish. Remove the crusts from the bread and break the crumb into small pieces; pour the 300 ml/½ pint milk over it and leave to soak for 30 minutes, then beat out the lumps. Add the cleaned dried fruit, the peel, suet, sugar and spice and mix well. Add the egg, with a little extra milk if required to make the mixture of a dropping consistency. Pour it into the pie dish, grate a little nutmeg over if you wish and bake in a moderate oven (180°C/350°F, Gas Mark 4) for about 1½ to 2 hours. Dredge with sugar before serving.

The peel may be replaced by an extra 50 g/2 oz dried fruit, if you prefer.

BREAD AND BUTTER PUDDING

METRIC/IMPERIAL
3–4 thin slices of bread and butter
50 g/2 oz currants or sultanas
1 × 15 ml spoon/1 tablespoon caster sugar
450 ml/¾ pint milk
2 eggs
ground nutmeg

Cut the bread and butter into strips and arrange, buttered side up, in layers in a greased ovenproof dish, sprinkling the layers with the fruit and sugar. Heat the milk, but do not allow it to boil. Whisk the eggs lightly and pour the milk on to them, stirring all the time. Strain the mixture over the bread, sprinkle some nutmeg on top and let the pudding stand for fifteen minutes. Bake in a moderate oven (180°C/350°F, Gas Mark 4) for 30 to 40 minutes, until set and lightly browned.

OSBORNE PUDDING
Use brown bread and butter, spread with marmalade; omit the dried fruit.

BREADCRUMBS

Both fresh white crumbs and browned dried crumbs (raspings) are used in cookery, as an ingredient in puddings and savoury dishes and as a topping or coating. Fried crumbs are served with game. Ready-prepared crumbs may be bought to save time, but they are of course more expensive.

Fresh Breadcrumbs
(Used for puddings and for bread sauce):
   Choose bread that is one or two days old. Remove the crusts and rub the crumbs through a wire sieve or use a grater (though this will not give such fine or even-sized crumbs). The quickest and simplest method is to place the bread in a liquidizer for a few seconds. If new bread has to be used, it will be more difficult to handle and will weigh appreciably more than dry bread in proportion to its bulk because of the higher moisture content.

Raspings
(Browned Breadcrumbs used for coating ham, etc, topping scalloped dishes, coating the inside of a mould used for réchauffés, and coating fish and other foods before frying):
   Put stale pieces of bread or crust on an old baking sheet or in a meat tin at the bottom of a very cool oven (lowest setting) and let them brown very slowly for several hours, until they are quite crisp and pale golden-brown. Cool, then crush them into fine crumbs with a rolling pin or pass them through a mincing machine. Sieve and store in an airtight jar. Alternatively use a liquidizer.

Fried Crumbs
(Served with roast pheasant, partridge, etc):
   Mix 100 g/4 oz breadcrumbs and 15 g/½ oz melted butter and fry over gentle heat until golden-brown, stirring constantly or they will brown unevenly and burn.

BREADSTICK

(See Grissini entry.)

BREAKFAST

As the name suggests, breakfast is the breaking of the fast, that is, the first meal of the day. Lack of a satisfactory breakfast can affect dietary intake and nutritional status, particularly in children. Research has shown that to meet the requirements for maintaining alertness throughout the morning, and to maintain general physical fitness, breakfast should provide a quarter to a third of the daily protein and energy intake.

   The word 'breakfast' was first used in the fifteenth century, the meal usually including strong meat and ales. The meal gradually became more important and in the nineteenth century enormous breakfasts were served: These usually included savoury dishes, fruit, rolls and tea. After the First World War the traditional 'British Breakfast' of cereal, bacon, eggs, bread, marmalade and tea became popular. With changes in life-style this type of breakfast has declined considerably, speed and simplicity now being an important consideration. More popular today are fruit juices, cereals, simple egg dishes, cheese, bread, toast and coffee: these foods can still provide sufficient nutrients for maximum efficiency.

BREAKFAST CEREALS

There is an enormous choice of breakfast cereals on the market today. These have been developed from dietary research of the nineteenth century. Corn Flakes were first made as a dietetic food in Michigan. They were so popular that commercial production was started in 1895. At about the same time Dr Bircher-Berner was developing a cereal food mixed with nuts and fruit for patients of his Zurich Clinic. Muesli was the name given to this cereal of which there are many variations.

   Most breakfast cereals are based on maize, rice, wheat or oats which are modified to make them immediately ready to eat. Some varieties are sugar coated and others have additives for health purposes: these include bran, high protein and low calorie cereals.

   Although cereals contain some nutrients the milk taken with them is more important in the diet.

BREAM

The fresh-water bream is of rather coarse texture and flavour, but the sea bream has white, delicate-flavoured flesh and is at its best from June to December. Both varieties are best served baked with a savoury stuffing, but they may also be boiled, fried or grilled.

BRESSE BLEU

A rich, soft, blue-veined cheese, made near Lyons and somewhat resembling Gorgonzola. It is made in small cheeses about 15 cm/6 inches across and 5 cm/2 inches high with a thin rind.

51

BREWER'S YEAST

(See Yeast entry.)

BRICK CHEESE

An American cheese, of medium firm texture, with many small holes. It has a somewhat sweet taste and may be either mild or strong. Brick may be eaten raw and used in cooking.

BRIDE CAKE

(See Wedding Cake entry.)

BRIDGE ROLL

(See Bread entry.)

BRIE

A soft-textured, creamy mould-inoculated farm cheese made in the north of France from whole milk. The best variety is that made in the autumn.

BRILL

A European flat fish very similar in flavour and texture to turbot. It may be served boiled whole; filleted and fried like sole; filleted and poached in a white wine sauce; or cut into steaks and baked with a little fat, seasoning and milk. Brill is in season all the year, but at its best from April to August.

BRINING

To immerse food (mainly meat or fish which is to be pickled and vegetables which are to be pre-served) in a salt-and-water solution. (See Pickling entry.)

BRIOCHE

A fancy sweet bread or yeast cake, sometimes containing currants and candied fruit. In France both large and small types are made, but in this country we are more familiar with the small type served instead of rolls.

BRIOCHES

METRIC/IMPERIAL
15 g/½ oz fresh yeast
1.5 × 15 ml spoons/1½ tablespoons warm water
225 g/8 oz strong plain flour
a pinch of salt
1 × 15 ml spoon/1 tablespoon caster sugar
2 eggs, beaten
50 g/2 oz butter, melted

52

FOR THE GLAZE
beaten egg

Oil twelve 7.5 cm/3 inch fluted patty tins. Blend the yeast with the water. Mix together the flour, salt and sugar. Stir the yeast liquid into the flour, with the eggs and butter. Work to a soft dough, turn out onto a lightly floured surface and knead for about 5 minutes. Place the dough in a bowl and cover with oiled polythene. Leave to rise until it is doubled in size and springs back when gently pushed with a floured finger. Knead the risen dough well on a lightly floured surface. Divide the dough into 12 pieces. Shape three-quarters of each piece into a ball and place in the patty tins. Press a hole in the centre of each. Shape the remaining 12 pieces of dough into knobs and place in the holes. Press down lightly. Cover the tins with oiled polythene and leave at room temperature until the dough is light and puffy and nearly reaches the top of the tins. Brush lightly with the egg glaze and bake in a preheated hot oven (230°C/450°F, Gas Mark 8) for about 10 minutes, until golden. Turn out and cool on a wire rack.

BRISKET

Brisket is the meat covering the breast-bone of any animal eaten for food, but usually the term refers to beef. As it is rather a tough and fat cut of meat, it is usually cheap. Brisket is best boiled, braised or stewed: it is also good when stuffed, rolled and roasted. It is often salted and boiled and is then served cold; if pressed and glazed, it is known as Pressed Beef.

BRISLING

The Norwegian name for sprats, large quantities of which are canned and exported. Brisling are used like sardines.

BROAD BEANS

(See Bean entry.)

BROCCOLI

White broccoli is the winter type of cauliflower and is cooked and served in the same way. It is coarser in flavour with open florets. There are several other varieties, including purple sprouting, available in March and April. Green sprouting is known as calabrese, the spears being cooked like asparagus. Broccoli is a good source of vitamin C, supplying a half-day's needs in an average helping.

BROILER

(See Chicken entry.)

BROILING

An American term for grilling.

BROSE

A Scottish dish, somewhat resembling gruel, made by pouring boiling water over oatmeal or barley, stirring well and adding salt. A richer version has additional milk and butter or cream. Fish, meat or vegetables may be added to make mussel, beef or kale brose, etc. When made with whisky it is called Athol Brose.

BROTH

Used in a strict sense, this term applies to a stock made from beef, mutton, veal or chicken, but it has been extended to cover such substantial soups as Scotch broth, which are usually thickened by the addition of a little pearl barley.

SCOTCH BROTH

METRIC/IMPERIAL
0.75 kg/1 ½ lb shin of beef
2.25 litres/4 pints water
salt
pepper
1 carrot and 1 turnip, peeled and chopped
1 onion, skinned and chopped or diced
2 leeks, thinly sliced and washed
3 × 15 ml spoons/3 tablespoons pearl barley
1 × 15 ml spoon/1 tablespoon finely chopped parsley

Cut up the meat and remove any fat, put it in a pan, cover with the water, add some salt and pepper, bring slowly to boiling point, cover and simmer for 1 ½ hours. Add the vegetables and the barley. Cover and simmer for about 1 hour until the vegetables and barley are soft. Remove any fat on the surface with a spoon or with kitchen paper and serve the soup garnished with parsley.

Traditionally, the meat is served with a little of the broth and the remaining broth is served separately.

Mutton Broth
Make as for Scotch Broth, using neck of mutton.

CHICKEN BROTH

METRIC/IMPERIAL
1 small boiling chicken
2 litres/3 ½ pints cold water
2 × 5 ml spoons/2 teaspoons salt
a pinch of pepper
1 onion, skinned and halved
50 g/2 oz each carrot and celery, diced
2 × 15 ml spoons/2 tablespoons long grain rice
chopped parsley

Wash the bird, cut it in half, put it into a large pan, cover with water and add the seasoning and vegetables. Bring to the boil, cover and simmer for 3 to 3½ hours, adding more water if necessary. Strain, then remove any grease from the top of the broth with a metal spoon or by drawing a piece of kitchen paper across the surface of the liquid. Return the broth to the pan, bring to the boil, sprinkle in the rice and simmer for 15 to 20 minutes, until the rice is soft. Serve sprinkled with chopped parsley. Some of the meat can be finely chopped and added to the broth, the rest being used in made-up dishes (e.g., fricassée).

The broth can also be made with a chicken or turkey carcass instead of a whole chicken, when it will need to be simmered for about 2 hours.

BROWN SAUCE

(See Sauce entry.)

BROWNING

To give a dish (usually already cooked) an appetizing golden-brown colour by placing it under the grill or in a hot oven for a short time.

BROWNING, GRAVY

A colouring matter used to darken soups, gravies, etc. There are many proprietary brands on the market, but browning may be made at home in one of the following ways: (1) Heat sugar until it is dark brown and add water (See Caramel entry). (2) Spread some flour on a baking sheet and heat it in the oven until it is brown, stirring it frequently. Keep in a covered jar.

BRUSSELS SPROUT

A member of the cabbage family. Brussels sprouts are best eaten when young and they should be firm, round and about the size of a walnut. As they are in season during the winter months, when other green vegetables are scarce, and contain a fair amount of Vitamin C they are a useful vegetable.

To cook
Wash well, removing any discoloured leaves, and cut a little cross in the base of the stalk to enable this part to cook through quickly. Cook in boiling salted water until they are just tender for 10 to 20 minutes, drain thoroughly, return them to the pan and re-heat with salt, pepper and a knob of butter.

To make brussels sprouts and chestnuts: Prepare the sprouts in the usual way and shell the chestnuts. Put in separate pans and boil them hard for 10 minutes, then strain both free from moisture and remove the thin brown skin from the chestnuts. Melt some butter, allowing 50 g/2 oz to about 0.5 kg/1 lb of chestnuts and Brussels sprouts, and sauté them in it until both are thoroughly tender – about 15 minutes. Serve very hot, in a border of creamed potatoes.

BRUT

A French word applied to the driest type of champagne.

BUBBLE AND SQUEAK

A traditional English dish, originally made from cold boiled beef (thinly sliced, diced or minced), mixed with cold cooked potatoes and finely chopped cabbage or other greens and then fried; it derived its name from the noises made while it was frying. The cooked dish was sometimes sprinkled with vinegar. In the modern version of bubble and squeak the meat is usually omitted and the dish consists of vegetables only. It is a good way of using up left-over food.

BUCKLING

A smoked herring; generally served as an appetizer with thinly sliced brown bread and butter.

BUCK

The male of the roe and fallow deer. (See Venison entry.)

BUCK RAREBIT

A savoury snack served for high tea or supper, consisting of a Welsh rarebit topped with a poached egg.

BUCKWHEAT (SARACEN CORN)

A cereal, a herbaceous plant which will grow on poor soil, used in Russia, Brittany and in the U.S.A. Buckwheat is used to make a kind of porridge, also griddle cakes, etc. Commercial preparations of buckwheat can be bought for pancakes.

BUFFET

The word used to describe a method of serving a meal. Buffet parties provide an easier way of entertaining a number of people than a formal dinner party. The buffet may be a fairly grand display of cold dishes or a simpler mixture of hot and cold foods. When no tables are provided, finger or fork foods should be served as these can easily be eaten while standing. The word also applies to an informal self-service restaurant.

BULLACE

The name given to wild forms of damson plums. They are not suitable for use as dessert fruit, but make good preserves; use any recipe suitable for damsons.

BULL'S EYE

A peppermint-flavoured boiled sweet, striped black and white.

BULLY BEEF

(See Corned Beef entry.)

BUN

Buns should strictly speaking be made from a mixture containing yeast. They are similar in texture to bread, but contain sweetening and usually some fat, currants and spice. Typical examples are Currant, Chelsea, Bath and Hot Cross buns. (See individual entries.)

The term is often applied to little cakes, quickly made and containing no yeast like Rock or raspberry runs and to cream buns, which are made of choux pastry.

BURGERS

(See Hamburger and Beefburger entries.)

BURGUNDY

A French province containing several vineyards that produce fine wines. The most important area for red and white wines is the Côte d'Or which includes the Côte de Nuits and the Côte de Beaune. Other areas are Chablis, Beaujolais and Mâconnais.

Much burgundy wine is exported as the wine of a district rather than a specific grower. It is bought in barrels from the grower and blended with other wines from the area to achieve certain standards. Most of the 'Appellations Controllées' in Burgundy refer to the geographical areas, but built into these is also a quality classification. Vintage wines do not improve with very long keeping and many are made for drinking almost immediately. Ten years is usually the maximum time for improvement.

Red Burgundy, which is usually served with roasts or game, should be drunk at room temperature. Well-known types include Vougeot, Chamberton, Volnay, Pommard and Beaujolais.

White Burgundy is served slightly chilled. The best-known are Meursault, Montrachet, Corton and Chablis (the last name is, however, frequently given in error to other white wines).

BUTTER

It is made from the fat of milk by churning cream in special conditions of temperature. The cream is flash heated to 91°C/195°F to 97°C/206°F to destroy enzymes and bacteria, then rapidly cooled. Sweet cream butter is then left to age in tanks for 12 hours before churning. To make lactic butter, after the initial heating, the cream is heated to 18°C/65°F to 21°C/68°F allowing lactic bacteria to develop: this produces diactyl, a flavouring substance. After ripening the cream is churned. This is the method used for most continental butters.

Regulations state that British butter must contain nothing other than milk fat, salt, lactic acid cultures and natural colouring materials.

Composition must be at least 78 per cent milk fat, 20 per cent other milk solids and not more than 16 per cent water. Countries that produce butter for sale in U.K. markets have national schemes of quality control.

British butters are of the sweet cream variety and have varying amounts of salt added according to the areas where they are to be sold. New Zealand and Southern Irish butter is also of this type, salted as a preservative as well as for flavour. Danish butter is traditionally a lactic butter available salted or unsalted, but a sweet cream variety is also available. German, French and Dutch butter may be of either variety, salted or unsalted.

Storing Butter

Butter should be kept covered in a cool, dark place such as a refrigerator or larder. Butter can be frozen, the unsalted varieties keeping longer than the salted: up to 3 months is recommended for salted butter and 6 months for unsalted. The butter can be left in its retail packaging as long as it is over-wrapped with freezer polythene or foil and freezer tape. Alternatively the butter can be removed from the packing and frozen only in freezer polythene. Foil is not recommended as the only packaging as it imparts flavour to the butter.

Clarified Butter

Butter which has been heated and strained to remove salt, water and solids. This pure butter is used in omelette making, Genoese sponge mixtures and pâtés. (See Fats entry.)

Melted (Drawn) Butter

This is a form of dressing served with asparagus, corn on the cob, seakale, globe artichokes and some fish dishes.

Place the required amount of butter in a sauce boat, allowing 20 g/¾ oz to 25 g/1 oz per person, and stand the boat in a warm place or in hot water;

this avoids waste and prevents the butter becoming brown through over-heating.

BUTTER BEAN

(See Bean entry.)

BUTTER ICING OR CREAM

A soft, creamy icing, made with almost equal quantities of butter and icing sugar and used for decorating the tops of cakes and as a filling.

VANILLA BUTTER ICING

METRIC/IMPERIAL
100 g/4 oz butter or margarine
175 g–225 g/6–8 oz sieved icing sugar
vanilla essence
colouring if required

Cream the butter, add the sugar by degrees, beating until smooth and creamy, then add the essence and any colouring.

Chocolate Butter Icing: Add 25 g/1 oz to 50 g/2 oz melted chocolate to the creamed butter and sugar.

Coffee Butter Icing: Add 1–2 × 5 ml spoons/1–2 teaspoons coffee essence.

Orange or Lemon Butter Icing: Add 1 × 5 ml spoon/1 teaspoon of the grated rind and 1 × 15 ml spoon/1 tablespoon of the juice and omit the vanilla essence.

Hungarian Icing: Add 50 g/2 oz melted chocolate, 2 × 5 ml spoons/2 teaspoons coffee essence and 2 × 15 ml spoons/2 tablespoons chopped walnuts.

BUTTERMILK

The liquid left from the cream which has been used for butter-making. It is composed of water, mineral salts, protein and milk sugar; its sourness is due to lactic acid.

Buttermilk is also made commercially by adding a culture to skim milk. It can be used in any dish to replace milk if a piquant refreshing taste is required. Buttermilk is often used in scones in conjunction with bicarbonate of soda as a raising agent. Fruit purée can be added to buttermilk to make it into a refreshing drink with a slightly acid flavour.

BUTTERSCOTCH

A variety of toffee, made from butter, sugar and water. (See Sweets entry.)

CABBAGE

There are many varieties of cabbage, the most important being the white and red types, spring greens, Savoy cabbage, turnip tops and kale. (Brussels sprouts, broccoli and cauliflower, which belong to the same family). Cabbages are further divided into winter-grown types, available for eating in the spring and early summer, and those planted in the spring to be eaten during the late summer, autumn and winter.

Cabbage contains vitamin A, iron and calcium and a very variable amount of vitamin C.

To cook: Remove the stumps and any very thick stalks or leaf ribs, wash the leaves thoroughly in cold water and shred them coarsely with a sharp knife just before cooking. Boil them in a small amount of salted water (150 ml/¼ pint water and 1 × 5 ml spoon/1 teaspoon salt to 0.5 kg/1 lb cabbage) for the minimum time – about 10 to 15 minutes. Drain thoroughly, press lightly to remove excess water and if desired re-heat with a knob of butter.

Cabbage is used in various made-up dishes such as Bubble and Squeak and Colcannon; it may be served in the same way as Cauliflower au Gratin (See Cauliflower entry) or pickled (See Pickling entry).

BEAN STUFFED CABBAGE ROLLS

METRIC/IMPERIAL
175 g/6 oz foule or other dried beans, soaked
175 g/6 oz garlic sausage
1 × 225 g/8 oz can drained tomatoes
100 g/4 oz onions
75 g/3 oz butter
1 × 15 ml spoon/1 tablespoon tomato paste
salt
freshly ground pepper
8 large cabbage leaves, e.g. Savoy
2 × 15 ml spoons/2 tablespoons chopped parsley

Drain the beans and cook in boiling, salted water until very tender – about 1¼ hours. Drain. Finely chop the garlic sausage and mix with the beans and tomatoes. Skin and finely chop the onion. Sauté in 25 g/1 oz of the butter until soft. Add to the bean mixture with the tomato paste and seasonings. Wash the cabbage leaves and trim out any tough centre stalk, blanch in boiling salted water for about 4 minutes. Drain. Divide the stuffing between the leaves, roll up securely and place in a buttered oval ovenproof dish. Cover closely with foil and bake in a moderate oven (180°C/350°F, Gas Mark 4) for 30 to 35 minutes. Beat the remaining butter with a wooden spoon to soften, then mix in the parsley. Serve with the cabbage rolls.

CABINET PUDDING

A simple moulded pudding made from bread and butter. A richer version is made with sponge cakes and glacé cherries, with an extra egg.

SIMPLE CABINET PUDDING

METRIC/IMPERIAL
50 g/2 oz stoned raisins
4 medium-sized slices of bread
2 eggs
300 ml/½ pint milk
1 × 15 ml spoon/1 tablespoon sugar
vanilla essence

Grease a basin and decorate it with some of the raisins by sticking them to the side of the basin. Cut the bread into 1 cm/½ inch dice. Beat the eggs, add the milk, sugar, a few drops of vanilla essence and the rest of the raisins. Pour onto bread and leave to soak for ½ hour. Pour into basin, cover with greased paper and steam for about 1 hour.

CACAO

(See Cocoa entry.)

CACCIO-CAVALLO

An Italian cheese made from skimmed cow's milk.

CAERPHILLY CHEESE

One of the nine traditional cheeses of the British Isles. It dates from about 1830 and was originally a full cream Welsh cheese made from the milk of Hereford cows. It is now mainly manufactured in the West country. It has a mild flavour and close texture: a whitish cheese which is only matured for about two weeks.

CAFFEINE

A white crystalline substance obtained from coffee, of which it is the active principle. Its main use is as a non-intoxicating stimulant.

CAKE

The three main types of cake are Plain 'rubbed in' mixtures (with Gingerbread as a subsidiary class), Rich and Sponge; they are classified according to the proportion of fat, sugar and eggs they contain and the method by which they are made. A so-called 'plain' cake can contain fruit or nuts, etc. A 'one-stage' mixed cake is classed as a rich cake. Given here are a typical example from each category. The finished cake may be left as it comes from the oven or iced and/or decorated according to taste. Some types are associated with traditional kinds of decoration – for example, Simnel cake.

Cake Ingredients

FLOUR

Choose a reliable brand of flour and store it in a dry place. Self-raising flour may be used for plain cakes made by the rubbed-in method, but for richer cakes and sponges, which need varying quantities of raising agent, or none, it is better to use plain. The flour should always be sieved before use. Be sure to use the type of flour stated in the particular recipe.

FAT

Butter is usually considered most suitable for cake-making as it gives a good flavour and texture and the cakes made with it keep well. Margarine is the best substitute and can be used alone, mixed with butter, or mixed with an equal amount of lard or vegetable shortening. Soft luxury margarines are particularly suitable for 'one-stage' mixtures. Lard, although a pure fat, has not a very good flavour in cakes and is best used in conjunction with butter or margarine; vegetable shortening or cooking fat is useful, but has little flavour, so this also is best combined with butter or margarine. Mild-flavoured dripping is suitable for plain cakes; it must always be clarified. (See Fats entry.) For certain mixtures (e.g., Genoese sponge) butter also needs to be clarified.

A proportion of oil (generally not more than 1 part oil to 2 parts fat) can be used in certain mixtures such as sandwich cakes. (See Oil entry.)

SUGAR

Granulated sugar is satisfactory for plain cakes, but it is better to use fine caster sugar for creamed and sponge mixtures to give a better texture. Moist brown, Barbados and Demerara sugars are good for gingerbreads, as they give a treacly flavour.

RAISING AGENT

Use a reliable make of baking powder, measure it accurately and sift it with the flour before use.

Bicarbonate of soda and cream of tartar or bicarbonate of soda and vinegar are sometimes used in place of baking powder. When soured milk is used in conjunction with cream of tartar and bicarbonate of soda, the amount of cream of tartar should be reduced, or it may in some cases be omitted, as the soured milk contains acid.

EGGS

Eggs improve the flavour of a cake and also help to make it light; like the gluten in flour, they also act as a structural material, helping to support the cake after it has risen. Sponge cake mixtures contain a high proportion of egg and the whisking method incorporates air, so very little, if any, extra raising agent is needed. Eggs are also beaten into a creamed cake mixture and again comparatively little additional raising agent is required, unless the fat and sugar content is low. In a plain cake, where beaten egg is added together with the liquid, the egg helps to bind and support the mixture, but has little effect as a raising agent.

Fresh hens' eggs are best, but fresh duck, goose or turkey eggs may be used.

Use size 3, 4 or 5 (standard) eggs, unless otherwise stated in the recipe. However, if larger or smaller eggs are used, adjust the number or the amount of the other ingredients accordingly.

FRUIT AND NUTS

All fruit must be carefully picked over and cleaned before use and it must be quite dry. (See Dried Fruit entry.) Candied peel, nuts and large fruit such as dates – and sometimes raisins – are cut up or chopped before use. These can also be purchased ready prepared.

Note: Spoon measurements in this book are always level, not rounded. To measure a level spoonful, first heap the spoon with the ingredient, then scrape off the surplus with a knife, making the contents level with the edges of the spoon. The spoons used are the normal, average-sized household teaspoon and tablespoon and metric standard spoons.

Preparing Cake Tins

An unsalted fat or oil (e.g., lard, unsalted butter, olive oil or salad oil) should be used for greasing cake tins and lining papers. If margarine is used, it should be clarified. (See Fats entry.)

1. Draw a circle using base of tin as a guideline and then cut out a round of greaseproof paper.

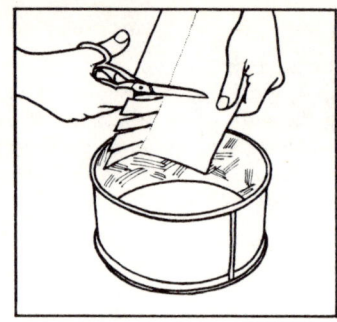

2. Cut a strip of greaseproof paper. Cut the greaseproof paper along fold at intervals.

3. Line greased tin with paper strip, overlapping at the join. Press round into base of tin.

Many recipes, particularly where the baking time is prolonged, require that the cake tin should be lined before the cake mixture is put in and greased greaseproof or kitchen paper or silicone paper should be used for this purpose. The lining should be done accurately, so that the surface of the finished cake is smooth and unmarked.

When lining tins for rich mixtures (e.g., wedding and birthday cakes) which require a long cooking period, use double greaseproof paper; in addition it is often advisable to put a double strip of thick brown paper round the outside of the tin, fixing it with a pin – this prevents any overcooking of the outside of the cake.

TO LINE A SWISS ROLL TIN
Cut a piece of paper about 5 cm/2 inches larger all round than the actual tin. Place the tin on the paper, and make a cut from each corner as far as the corner of the tin, remembering to allow for the thickness of the tin. Grease the tin and put the paper in it so that it fits closely, the cut pieces overlapping at the corners. Hold these overlapped pieces firmly in place by greasing each layer. Grease the complete inside of the paper lining.

TO LINE A ROUND TIN
First draw and cut out a round of paper to fit the bottom of the tin; allow for the thickness of the sides when cutting out. Now cut a strip long enough to reach round the tin and overlap about 2.5 cm/1 inch to 5 cm/2 inches and high enough to extend about 5 cm/2 inches above the top edge. Fold up the bottom edge 2 cm/¾ inch and with kitchen scissors make slanting cuts up to the fold at frequent intervals. (The smaller the tin, the closer together the slits should be to obtain a good fit). Grease the tin and place the strip in position round the inside, overlapping at the join. Grease the bottom overlapping edge. Put the round paper in position and thoroughly grease all paper surfaces.

TO LINE A SQUARE TIN
This may be done in the same way as for Swiss roll tin. This method is generally used for shallow tins,

e.g., for gingerbread. Alternatively, if the tin is deeper, line in the same way as for a round tin, making sure that the paper is well greased and fitted into the corners.

SPONGE AND SANDWICH TINS
These are used for cakes which do not require a long cooking time and therefore it is not necessary to line them completely. However, a greased round of paper may be used in the base, to facilitate turning out the cake; this also applies to the raised circle in a sponge flan tin. Grease the tins well. The quickest way is to use a pastry brush dipped in the melted fat. As an additional precaution, dust the tins out with a mixture of equal parts of flour and caster sugar. Place dusting mixture into the tins and shake to coat thoroughly.

FOIL AND PAPER BAKING CASES
These may be used in place of tins for small cakes, etc. They require no preparation. They may be put straight on a baking sheet, but the resulting shape is often better if the cases are placed in bun tins. Foil may be used to line cake tins and does not require greasing.

SILICONE PAPER
Silicone lining or baking paper has been found suitable for mixtures containing fat, but not for whisked sponges such as a Genoese mixture. It can be used to line a tin in exactly the same way as greaseproof paper, but is not greased with fat. It is not suitable for lifting a cake out of the tin, as it is rather slippery. When it is peeled off the cake, silicone paper leaves a smooth, shiny finish, not the characteristic rough surface. Clean carefully for re-use. Silicone paper makes no difference to the cooking time.

Plain Cakes (Rubbed-in Mixtures)
The amount both of fat and of sugar may be up to half the quantity of flour. Common examples are rock cakes, raspberry buns, scones and large flavoured cakes. The recipe below shows the general proportions of ingredients.

A TYPICAL 'RUBBED-IN' CAKE

METRIC/IMPERIAL
225 g/8 oz self-raising flour
1 × 5 ml spoon/1 teaspoon baking powder
a pinch of salt
100 g/4 oz butter or margarine
100 g/4 oz sugar
100 g/4 oz sultanas
50 g/2 oz currants
2 eggs
4 × 15 ml spoons/4 tablespoons milk

Sieve the flour, baking powder and salt together. Rub in the fat lightly, using the fingertips, until the mixture resembles breadcrumbs; lift the mixture while rubbing in the fat, to aerate it as much as possible. Add the sugar, prepared fruit and beaten eggs, together with sufficient liquid to make a soft dough. The consistency varies according to the recipe, but in general the finished cake will be dry, crumbly and close in texture if too little liquid is added, while too much makes it heavy and sodden. For a large cake, place the mixture in the greased and lined tin, three-quarters filling it, and bake for the time specified in the actual recipe; turn out and cool on a rack, after removing the paper carefully.

Small cakes are usually mixed to a stiff consistency (e.g., rock buns) or a fairly firm dough using one egg only and very little milk. They are then shaped and cooked on a greased baking sheet.

CAKES MADE BY THE CREAMING METHOD
RICH FRUIT CAKE – BASIC RECIPE

METRIC/IMPERIAL
225 g/8 oz butter
225 g/8 oz dark soft brown sugar
4 eggs
225 g/8 oz plain flour
225 g/8 oz currants
225 g/8 oz sultanas
225 g/8 oz stoned raisins
100 g/4 oz halved glacé cherries
100 g/4 oz mixed peel
50 g/2 oz almonds, chopped
1–2 × 15 ml spoons/1–2 tablespoons brandy

Cream the fat and sugar together in a large basin, using the back of a wooden spoon and working the ingredients until they resemble whipped cream in appearance and texture, or use electric mixer. If the fat is very hard, let it stand at room temperature or warm it very slightly before use, but on no account allow it to become oily through over-heating or the mixture will be heavy and close in texture. If by any mischance the fat has become too soft, stand the basin in a bowl of cold water or on a cold plate for a short while for the fat to solidify somewhat, then continue the creaming operation.

Break the eggs one at a time into a small basin, beat well, add gradually to mixture and again beat vigorously, keeping the texture smooth and creamy. The addition of too much egg at a time or insufficient beating may result in the curdling of the mixture. In this case, sprinkle in about 1 × 5 ml spoon/1 teaspoon of the measured flour before continuing to add the eggs.

Using a metal spoon, gradually mix in the sieved flour very lightly, together with the prepared fruit and add the brandy and any necessary liquid alternately with the flour to give a soft dropping consistency (i.e., the mixture should just drop from the spoon without shaking). While creaming the fat and sugar and beating in the eggs, beat as vigorously as you like, but once you have started to add the flour, handle the mixture as lightly as possible, folding or stirring it – never beating.

When using an electric mixer for creaming a cake mixture, first soften the fat at room temperature before putting it into the basin. Then switch on the current at the speed recommended and beat the fat until soft; add the sugar and beat for the required time. Now add the eggs one at a time, and allow about 1 minute's beating for each. Mix in the flour by hand with a metal spoon, or on a very low speed.

Three-quarters fill the prepared tin or tins and bake as directed in the recipes. Cool on a rack.

Small cakes are made by the same method but a less rich recipe and cooked in greased patty tins or in paper cases placed on a baking sheet.
(See Victoria Sponge Sandwich, Queen Cakes, Madeira Cake, etc., for recipes.)

Fatless Sponge Cakes (Whisked Mixtures)
An ordinary or 'true' sponge contains no fat, but a high proportion of eggs and sugar. These are whisked together and the flour is folded in very lightly. Swiss rolls, sponge cakes and sponge fingers and drops are familiar examples. (See Sponge Cake and Swiss Roll entries for recipes.)

The same whisking method is used for making a Genoese sponge, except that some melted butter is added alternately with the flour. (See Genoese Sponge entry.)

STANDARD SPONGE CAKE RECIPE

METRIC/IMPERIAL
100 g/4 oz plain flour
3 eggs
100 g/4 oz caster sugar

Take a sponge tin 15 cm/6 inch in diameter, or a Swiss roll tin 23 cm/9 inch by 30 cm/12 inch, and prepare it by greasing it and lining the base with greased greaseproof paper. When making sponge fingers dust the greased tins with a mixture of equal quantities of sugar and flour; this should also be used on the sides of large sponge cake tins.

Put the measured flour on a sheet of kitchen paper and stand it in a warm place to dry it.

Place the eggs and sugar in a basin standing over a saucepan half-filled with hot water and whisk briskly together until the mixture is creamy and sufficiently stiff to retain the impression of the whisk for a few seconds. The lightness of the cake largely depends on beating the eggs and sugar really stiffly. Remove the basin from the heat as soon as the mixture is whisked sufficiently.

When using an electric mixer, put the eggs and sugar into the basin and whisk at the recommended speed until of the required texture. Putting over hot water is not necessary.

Sift in all the flour over the mixture and fold in very lightly with a large metal spoon. If the recipe calls for any water, it is added at this stage; pour it in down the side of the bowl. It is important to agitate the mixture as little as possible when incorporating the flour, so choose a large spoon and fold very lightly with bold strokes. Stirring or beating at this stage will break down the air bubbles and thus spoil the texture of the cake, making it close and tough. Do not use an electric mixer.

Pour the mixture into the prepared tins, allowing it to run over the whole surface, or pipe it out in rounds or fingers. Bake in the oven (190°C/375°F, Gas Mark 5) 25 to 30 minutes for sponge sandwich, (220°C/425°F, Gas Mark 7) 7 to 10 minutes for sponge fingers and (220°C/425°F, Gas Mark 7) 7 to 9 minutes for Swiss roll.

All types of sponge, except Swiss rolls (see Swiss Roll entry) should be turned out and cooled on a rack.

If you use a soft margarine or a whipped-up white cooking fat, you can make a cake without rubbing in or creaming the fat first. Mix the ingredients very thoroughly, scraping round the sides of the bowl frequently. Do not overbeat.

ONE-STAGE FRUIT CAKE

METRIC/IMPERIAL
225 g/8 oz self-raising flour
2 × 5 ml spoons/2 teaspoons mixed spice
1 × 5 ml spoon/1 teaspoon baking powder
100 g/4 oz soft tub margarine
100 g/4 oz soft brown sugar
225 g/8 oz dried fruit
2 eggs
2 × 15 ml spoons/2 tablespoons milk

Grease an 18 cm/7 inch round cake tin and line the base with a round of greased greaseproof paper. Sift the flour, spice and baking powder into a large bowl, add the rest of the ingredients and beat until thoroughly combined. Put into the tin and bake in a moderate oven (160°C/325°F, Gas Mark 3) for

about 1¾ hours. Turn out to cool on a wire rack.

Baking Cakes

MANAGING THE OVEN
Before starting to make a cake, adjust the shelves to the position required. Modern ovens do not need to be preheated for long, but an older one should be turned on at this stage.

Small plain cakes, scones and Swiss rolls, all of which are baked at a high temperature, are placed near the top of the oven. Small rich cakes, sandwich cakes and biscuits, which require more moderate temperatures, are placed just above the centre of the oven, where the heat is even and steady. Put very rich ones and shortbreads near the bottom.

To maintain a correct temperature, avoid opening the oven door too often or too suddenly while the cake is cooking and see that no draught blows directly on to the oven from door to window. Allow the full cooking time given in the recipe.

OVEN TEMPERATURES
It is difficult to generalize about the different oven heats for baking cakes, but obviously the larger and deeper the cake, the longer it will take to cook and the cooler the oven will have to be to avoid over-cooking the outside before the cake has completely cooked through. In addition, rich mixtures need to be cooked at lower temperatures than plainer ones. The chart will act as a general guide.

The table below indicates the oven temperatures corresponding to descriptions in the chart and also the setting for the standard thermostats fitted to modern cookers.

EQUIVALENT OVEN SETTINGS

Oven Description	Approximate temperature; Electric setting	Standard gas thermostat
Very cool	110°C/225°F	mark ¼
	120°C/250°F	mark ½
	140°C/275°F	mark 1
Cool	150°C/300°F	mark 1–2
Warm	160°C/325°F	mark 3
Moderate	180°C/350°F	mark 4
Fairly hot	190°C/375°F	mark 5
	200°C/400°F	mark 6
Hot	220°C/425°F	mark 7
Very hot	230°C/450°F	mark 8
	240°C/475°F	mark 9

TO TEST WHEN A CAKE IS COOKED
Small cakes should be well risen, golden-brown in colour and firm to the touch, both on top and underneath. On being taken out of the oven, they should begin to shrink from the sides of the tin.

For larger cakes, the oven heat and time of cooking give a fairly reliable indication, but the following tests are also a guide:

1. Press the centre of the top of the cake very

Type	Oven	Time
Plain Cakes		
Small (e.g., Rock Cakes)	Hot	15 to 20 minutes.
Large	Moderate	Approx. 1 hour per 0.5 kg/1 lb of mixture (varying with depth of tin).
Rich Cakes		
Small (e.g., Queen Cakes)	Fairly hot	15 to 20 minutes.
Sandwich Cake	Moderate	15 to 35 minutes (depending on depth).
Large (e.g., Madeira)	Moderate	Approx. 1 hour per 0.5 kg/1 lb (varying with depth of tin).
Large (e.g., Fruit)	Moderate to cool	1 to 1¼ hours per 0.5 kg/1 lb of mixture (according to richness).
Sponge Cakes		
Large	Moderate	Depending on size and depth.
Swiss Roll	Very hot	7 to 9 minutes.
Sponge Sandwich	Hot	9 to 12 minutes.
Miscellaneous		
Gingerbread	Moderate	Depending on size and depth.
Scones	Very hot	8 to 10 minutes.
Biscuits	Moderate to cool	15 to 20 minutes.

lightly with the finger-tip. When done, the cake will be spongy, giving only very slightly to the pressure and rising again immediately, leaving no impression.

2. Insert a fine heated skewer or knitting needle (never a cold knife) in the centre of the cake. It should come out perfectly clean; if any mixture is sticking to it, the cake requires longer cooking.

3. In the case of a fruit cake, lift it gently from the oven and listen to it, putting it fairly close to the ear; a continued sizzling sound indicates that the cake is not cooked through.

Cooling and Storing

Allow the cake a few minutes to cool before turning it out of the tin; during that time an unlined cake will shrink away from the sides so that it is more easily removed. Turn it out very gently on to a clean towel held in the hand and remove any paper. Invert a wire cake rack over the cake, then turn it right way up and leave to become quite cold, keeping it in a place away from draughts.

Store cakes in a tightly covered tin or in a crock covered closely with a lid. Most cakes are nicest eaten quite fresh, but gingerbread and some rich fruit cakes are improved by keeping.

Rich fruit cakes which are to be kept for any length of time should be wrapped in double greaseproof paper before being put in the tin and left to mature.

Cake-making Faults

1. IF YOUR CAKE SINKS IN THE MIDDLE
It may be for any of the following reasons:
(a) The cake is not cooked through. Check up on the baking time and temperature and be sure that

the cake responds to the test before removing it from the oven.

(b) A sudden drop in the oven temperature at a critical stage of the cooking. Avoid opening the oven door too often or too suddenly and do not alter the position of the cake while it is still soft. See that no draught blows directly on to the oven from the kitchen door or window.

(c) Too much raising agent, causing the mixture to 'over-work' itself.

(d) Mixture made too wet. Test the consistency of the cake mixture carefully before putting it in the tin.

(e) Too much sugar in proportion to the other ingredients.

2. FRUIT SINKS TO THE BOTTOM OF A CAKE
For these reasons:
(a) The mixture is too slack to support the fruit.
(b) The fruit is not properly dried after washing.
(c) The baking temperature is too low.
(d) The fruit is left in too large pieces.

3. A CAKE THAT BOILS OUT THROUGH A CRACK IN THE TOP
Was put into too hot an oven. If the initial temperature is too high, the outside of the cake sets and forms a crust before the cake starts to cook in the centre; then instead of rising evenly, the mixture has to force its way out of the top of the cake through a crack.

4. IF YOUR CAKE IS HEAVY AND STICKY INSIDE
It may be due to any of the following:
(a) Baking at too high a temperature and for too short a time, so that the outside cooks too quickly, leaving the centre slightly raw. Reduce the heat

next time you use the recipe or place the cake lower in the oven. Be sure to allow the full baking time.

(b) Making the mixture too wet, so that the cake does not dry out in the centre.

(c) Cooling too suddenly. See that the cake is not put in a draughty place when first taken from the oven.

(d) Putting away while still warm. Make sure the cake is absolutely cold before putting it away in the cake tin.

5. A CLOSE OR HEAVY TEXTURE
May be caused by any of the following:

(a) Not enough raising agent. Check up on the recipe and measure baking powder accurately. If the cake is raised by air beaten into the mixture, perhaps you are not beating sufficiently thoroughly.

(b) Heavy handling. Cakes require a very light touch, especially when mixing in the dry ingredients.

(c) Too dry a mixture. If not moistened enough, the cake is likely to be close and dry when baked.

(d) Too wet a mixture. Too much liquid when mixing causes the cake to have a close, heavy texture.

Cake Fillings

Sponge sandwiches, pastry slices and similar cakes are often split open and spread with a sweet, well-flavoured mixture such as butter icing or confectioner's custard. (See individual and Mock Cream entries.) Given here are some typical cake fillings.

RICH BUTTER CREAM
CRÈME AU BEURRE

METRIC/IMPERIAL
175 g/6 oz sugar
2 × 15 ml spoons/2 tablespoons water
2 egg yolks
75 g/3 oz fresh butter
flavouring

Put the sugar and water in a small saucepan, place over heat and dissolve the sugar. When the syrup is perfectly clear, bring to the boil and boil without stirring until it will make a good thread on the end of skewer. Set it aside for a few minutes. Beat the egg yolks in a basin, then pour on the syrup in a thin stream, whisking all the time. (If the syrup is added too quickly or too hot, the eggs will curdle.) Beat until cool. Cream the butter and whisk a little at a time into the egg mixture. Flavour, and use very cold.

BANANA FILLING

METRIC/IMPERIAL
2 bananas
50 g/2 oz caster sugar
a little lemon juice
grated rind of half a lemon
2 × 15 ml spoons/2 tablespoons double cream

Purée the bananas, add the sugar, lemon juice and rind and finally add the stiffly whisked cream. Whisk the whole together for a minute, then use as required.

RUM BUTTER

(See Rum entry.)

CAKE ICINGS

(See Icing, Piping and also individual entries, e.g., Almond Paste.)

CAKE MIX

A prepared dry mix to which only water, milk or egg is added before baking. Various types are available for making a plain sponge, scones, layer cakes, gingerbread and other cakes.

The product generally contains flour, sugar, fat, raising agent and flavourings. The flour may be a weak cake flour or a high-ratio flour, depending on the type of cake, or even a stronger flour for gingerbread. The fat has to be of a special quality to resist rancidity. Sometimes milk powder is added and occasionally preservatives of some sort.

A prepared mix is more expensive than a home-made cake, but saves preparation time and is especially handy when unexpected visitors arrive.

CALCIUM

The most abundant mineral in the body which is the chief component of bones and teeth. It is of particular importance for children and for expectant and nursing mothers. A deficiency of calcium in the diet of children leads to rickets – badly shaped bones and poor growth. Expectant and nursing mothers pass calcium on to their babies and if there is not enough in their food, will deplete their own stores.

The suggested daily requirement for an adult is 500 mg. Pregnant women and nursing mothers require more. A child needs as much as an adult and an adolescent perhaps more.

Milk and cheese are the best sources of calcium. Vegetables (particularly the pulses) and cereals supply a fair amount. Calcium is added to all flour by law and since flour and bread are eaten each day, generally they are a good source. Fish and eggs supply calcium to some extent. Drinking water in hard-water districts also provides a little.

Acid calcium phosphate is present in some baking powders.

It is essential to have enough vitamin D to permit both the absorption and the use of the calcium in the body. Without it little is absorbed, whereas 20 to 30 per cent can be absorbed with adequate vitamin D.

CALF'S FOOT JELLY

A jelly that was at one time often served to invalids. It has little food value but is easily digested. It takes two days to make, as the stock must be made the first day and the jelly finished the second. A ready-made preparation can be bought.

To make the stock: Cut 2 calf's feet into pieces and wash and scrape them well. Put the pieces into a saucepan, cover with cold water and bring quickly to the boil, then pour off the water, rinse the pieces and return them to the saucepan. Cover again with 2.25 litres/4 pints to 2.75 litres/5 pints cold water, put on the lid and simmer slowly for 4 to 5 hours, until the liquid is reduced by half. Strain and leave until cold, when the stock should be a stiff jelly.

TO CLEAR THE JELLY

To 600 ml/1 pint calf's foot stock allow the following:

METRIC/IMPERIAL
100 g/4 oz loaf sugar
150 ml/¼ pint sherry
a 3.5-cm/1 ½-inch stick of cinnamon
3 cloves
3–4 lemons
2 egg whites and shells
2 × 15 ml spoons/2 tablespoons brandy

Remove all grease from the stock, measure 600 ml/1 pint of it into a saucepan and add the sugar, sherry, cinnamon stick and cloves. Wipe the lemons with a damp cloth and peel the rind very thinly off 2 of them. Squeeze and strain the lemon juice, measure 150 ml/¼ pint and add this to the stock, together with the lemon rind, the egg whites and the well-washed and crushed shells. Continue to clarify as described in the Jelly entry, repeating the straining process until the jelly runs perfectly clear. The straining should be done in a warm place and out of all draughts; should the jelly stiffen in the cloth before it has all run through, place a small basin or cup in the centre of the jelly and fill it with boiling water. If this fails to melt the jelly, it must be returned to the pan, whisked up again and strained as before. Finally, add the brandy.

Notes: In hot weather, it may be necessary to add a little gelatine to stiffen the stock. On the other hand, if it is too stiff, it must be diluted with a little water.

The amount of sugar used can be altered to suit different tastes and it can be omitted altogether if desired. The amount of wine used can also be altered; if less is included, more lemon juice should

be added. A little orange juice may be substituted for some of the lemon juice.

CALF'S HEAD, LIVER, ETC.,

(See Head, Liver and similar entries.)

CALORIE

The term used in dietetics for measuring the heat and energy-producing quality of goods. One Calorie (spelt with a capital letter) is defined as the amount of heat needed to raise the temperature of 1,000 grams of water by 1 degree Centigrade. (Spelt with a small 'c' a calorie is a term used in physics to denote the amount of heat needed to raise the temperature of 1 gram of water by 1 degree Centigrade.)

Foods vary very much in their calorific content; fats yield about 250 Calories per oz, but vegetables and fresh fruit only 5 to 10. A cup of milk, an average-sized slice of bread, 8 to 12 small lumps of sugar or 2 medium-sized potatoes each yield about 100 Calories.

Calorie requirements vary very widely, but it is usual to quote average figures. A moderately active woman or an adolescent girl needs about 2,200 Calories per day; a nursing mother or a boy of 13 to 15 years needs 3,000 and an adolescent youth even more. Men need rather more than women. The exact needs depend of course on the activities and weight and metabolic rate of the individual. For instance, when sitting at rest the average person needs 14 Calories per hour, whereas walking up stairs one uses them at the rate of 900 per hour.

After food has been eaten the body's digestive and metabolic processes are increased, owing to the specific dynamic action of the proteins, fats and carbohydrates; this results in increased production of heat, proteins producing most and carbohydrates least heat. About a seventh of the Calories consumed by a sedentary person is used up in carrying out physical activities, the remainder being converted into heat, which maintains the bodily temperature.

(See Diet and Joule entries.)

CALVADOS

(See Apple Brandy entry.)

CAMEMBERT CHEESE

A soft French cheese, made from the curd of cow's milk, which is inoculated with a white mould. The best Camembert cheeses are obtained during the summer months, when the milk is at its richest.

This cheese should be eaten soft; it is ready to serve when it will yield to gentle pressure of the fingers; if allowed to become over-ripe, it develops an unpleasant smell. It should be kept at room temperature, away from draughts.

CAMOMILE

A daisy-like plant with an aromatic scent and bitter flavour. The dried flower-heads were used to make a tisane, said to be a mild tonic, popular in the 19th Century. It is also used as a rinse for hair.

CANADIAN FRUIT PIE

(See Crumble Topping for Pies entry.)

CANAPÉ

Canapés are mouthfuls of savoury food, served on small pieces of bread, toast or biscuits. They are eaten hot or cold, as an hors d'œuvre, as cocktail snacks or as savouries at the end of a meal.

The base may be made of buttered bread (close-textured brown or white bread, thinly sliced and cut into rounds or fancy shaped pieces); fingers or shapes of toast or fried bread (if the canapés are to be served cold, the bread should be fried in butter, which gives a better flavour); neat fingers of rye bread, savoury biscuits or strips of pastry. The topping may be any kind of meat, poultry, fish, egg, cheese, vegetable or a mixture, suitably decorated, and is often held in place by aspic jelly.

PÂTÉ WHIRLS

FOR THE BASE
METRIC/IMPERIAL
10 slices from a small white loaf
75 g/3 oz butter

FOR THE TOPPING
225 g/8 oz smooth pâté
100 g/4 oz butter, softened
½ small garlic clove skinned and crushed
salt
pepper
parsley

Remove the crusts from the bread, squaring up the slices, and cut each into 4 small squares (giving 40 in all). Melt the 75 g/3 oz butter. Brush 2 baking sheets with butter and put the bread on to them. Brush the bread squares with the remaining butter and bake in a hot oven (220°C/425°F, Gas Mark 7) for 15 minutes until golden brown. Leave to cool on a wire rack.

Cream the pâté with the butter and garlic and adjust the seasoning. Using a forcing bag fitted with a large star vegetable nozzle, pipe whirls of the pâté on to the crisp squares. Garnish each with a minute piece of parsley.

Note: If you wish, use garlic pâté and omit the crushed garlic; use Ritz-type crackers instead of home-made crisp squares. If using crackers, prepare within 1 hour of serving, to prevent them softening.

SARDINE PYRAMIDS

METRIC/IMPERIAL
2 × 106 g/3¾ oz cans sardines, drained
lemon juice
salt
pepper
20–24 small cracker biscuits
chopped parsley or paprika to garnish

Remove the sardine tails, then mash the flesh with a little of the sardine oil, and with lemon juice and seasoning to taste. Mound some sardine mixture on to each cracker biscuit and make a cross on the top, using a skewer dipped in the finely chopped parsley or the paprika.

ANCHOVY TOASTS

METRIC/IMPERIAL
2 slices of bread
knob of butter
a squeeze of lemon juice
5 fillets of anchovy, chopped
a little pepper
a pinch each of ground nutmeg and ground mace
parsley

Toast the bread and cut it into fingers. Melt the butter, add a squeeze of lemon juice, the anchovies, pepper, nutmeg and mace. Beat well and rub through a sieve. Spread this mixture on the fingers of toast and decorate with sprigs of parsley.

Similar savouries can be made with sardines or herrings.

DEVILLED CRAB CANAPÉS

METRIC/IMPERIAL
1 × 15 ml spoon/1 tablespoon finely chopped onion
knob of butter
1 × 92 g/3¼ oz can crab meat
1 × 5 ml spoon/1 teaspoon Worcestershire sauce or a good dash of Tabasco sauce
pinch of dry mustard
2 × 15 ml spoons/2 tablespoons white sauce or double cream
parsley or paprika for garnish

Fry the onion lightly in the butter for 5 minutes, until golden brown. Drain and add to the crab meat; stir in the seasonings and sauce or cream. Use as a topping for 24 croûtes of fried bread. Decorate each with a sprig of parsley or sprinkle with paprika.

CANARY PUDDING

A steamed sponge pudding, which may be varied by adding different flavourings or fruit. Make a mixture as for Victoria Sponge, using 100 g/4 oz each self-raising flour, fat and sugar, with 2 eggs, and flavour with vanilla. Put into a greased basin, two-thirds filling it, cover with greased grease-proof paper and steam for 1½ hours. Turn out and serve with jam sauce.

Variations can be made by decorating the basin with canned pineapple, fresh or canned apricots, raisins, glacé cherries, jam, etc, before putting in the mixture. By varying the flavouring ingredient and accompanying sauce, many different sponge puddings can be made – for example:

Coffee Sponge Pudding
Add 2 × 15 ml spoons/2 tablespoons coffee essence and 1 to 2 drops of vanilla essence to the standard mixture, adding the essences to the creamed mixture after beating in the eggs and reducing the quantity of milk if necessary. Serve with coffee custard sauce.

Lemon or Orange Sponge Pudding
Omit vanilla and include the grated rind of 1 lemon or orange, adding it to the creamed mixture after the eggs. Serve with a sauce made with the juice of the fruit.

Chocolate Sponge Pudding
Add 25 g/1 oz cocoa sifted with the flour and adding the vanilla essence to the creamed mixture before incorporating the dry ingredients; use extra milk if necessary to bring the mixture to a soft dropping consistency. Serve with chocolate or custard sauce.

CANARY WINES

These wines, made in the Canary Isles, comprise both sherry types (also known as Sack) and port types. The best-known is Tenerife or Vidonia, a dry, full-bodied wine produced around Las Palmas. Malvoisie is made from a very sweet grape called Cabosa, which grows in the Canary and Madeira Isles. Canary Sack is a white wine of full flavour, rather similar to a Portuguese Madeira.

CANDY

Strictly speaking, candies are sweets made from crystallized sugar, but in America the term is used to cover all confectionery. (See Sweets entry.)

CANNED FOOD

The method of preserving foods in special cans serves the double purpose of making seasonal crops available all the year round and of enabling the housewife to keep a reserve stock for use in emergencies. Fruits, vegetables, soups, cereals, meats, fish, milk and many other products are available in this form.

Canning was first used as a form of preservation in the early nineteenth century. Canned foods did not reach the shops until 1830, but sales were slow mainly because of the high prices. However, by the end of the century certain canned foods were becoming an accepted part of our national diet.

Canning has no practical effect on proteins, carbohydrates, or fats, and, in general, vitamins are well retained.

Types of Can Available
(a) Open top cans are the most common and are made in a variety of sizes. These usually contain foods such as strained baby foods, baked beans, soups, animal food, fruit, vegetables and fish.

(b) Flat oval tins are used for meat and fish. Small sardine cans usually have a key for opening.

(c) Beverage cans are slimmer than the open top ones. Up to 440 ml volume they usually have a pull top for easy opening.

(d) Rectangular cans are used for meat such as corned beef and luncheon meat. These are opened with a key.

(e) Casserole cans are flat and round, used for ready meals.

(f) Pie and pudding cans are made in the shape of a pie or pudding and can contain fruit or meat fillings.

(g) Aluminium cans are made with pull tops and contain pâté, meat spreads and desserts.

(h) Cans with lever lids are made for coffee, malted drinks, cocoa, dried milk and skimmed milk. The advantage of these cans is that the lids can be replaced as the contents are not all used at once.

(i) Larger cans with open tops are made with a tongue then scored to give a less sharp edge when the top is removed. Foods stored in these are cod roes and fruit cake.

(j) A roltop jam can is made for fruit preserves.

Can sizes and descriptions are likely to change with more metric packaging. It is also possible that more cans will be available with pull off lids in the near future, thus avoiding the need for a can opener.

Follow the manufacturer's directions, as given on the cans, for heating and serving the contents.

Buying and Storing Canned Food
Canned foods should be examined for faults and any cans with bulging ends, leaks, etc., should not be bought. Such faults may have been caused by imperfect sterilization, inefficient sealing or subsequent damage to the cans due to careless handling. If cans develop these faults after purchase, they

must be discarded and it is wise to look over your stores from time to time, for a bulging can may burst and scatter its contents. Bulging may be due to the presence of bacteria which form gases or other harmful products, so the contents of such cans should never be eaten. It is also unwise to eat any canned food which has an unusual smell or colour, even though the can itself appears sound.

The life of a can of food depends not only on the contents but also on the kind of lacquer, if any, used inside the can and the temperature and humidity of the storage place. Generally speaking, the quality of the food processed under modern scientific conditions is very good and a reputable manufacturer takes care to use good-quality cans and suitable lacquer, so reliable brands, stored in a cool, dry place, should keep well. (Damp causes rusting, which may eventually lead to perforation of the metal.) When a can of food is bought for storage, it is a good idea to write the date of purchase on the label.

Research has shown that the nutritive value of canned food is generally satisfactory. Vitamin C and thiamine are less affected by length of storage than by temperature, while for riboflavine and nicotinic acid the reverse is the case. Carotene (source of vitamin A) is not severely affected; other nutrients are not affected at all.

Canned Fruits: One year is the usual time for storing, provided the cans are kept in a cold, dry place. If they are kept longer, the food value is not impaired, but the fruit may appear less attractive. The natural acidity of the fruit may attack any scratch or otherwise damaged parts of the lacquer; in this case, a metallic flavour develops and a gas (hydrogen) is produced which will eventually cause the can to bulge and the fruit will be very unpalatable if not actually unwholesome.

Honey and Jam should keep at least 3 years in lacquered cans.

Vegetables will store well for at least 2 years. If kept longer they may become less attractive in appearance, but the food value remains unchanged.

Fish and Meat will keep in good condition for several years. Hams present a special problem in food preservation and the packer's guarantee is usually only for 6 months. If, however, after longer storage the can has not bulged, the contents are sound.

Unsweetened Evaporated Milk keeps in good condition for about 3 years.

Sweetened Condensed Milk remains unchanged for 6 to 9 months, after which time it may become sugary, though this is not objectionable.

Dried Milk Powder in cans should be used within a few weeks. It tends to form hard lumps and develop a rancid flavour on long storage.

CANNING

The preservation of food by canning is now only carried out on a commercial scale. It is not recommended in the home from a health and hygiene point of view; also the equipment is no longer available to the individual.

Traditionally the canning process was carried out by placing the food in the can, sealing it and heating to a high temperature to achieve sterility. In recent years a new method known as aseptic canning has been developed. The food is sterilized by a higher heat treatment for a few seconds before it is placed in a sterilized can and closed with a sterilized lid. The food has a better flavour and a higher nutritional value. The higher shorter heat treatment also means that the food is sterilized without being overcooked. Many foods are now packed by this method although not all are suitable for the treatment.

CANNELONI

These are numbered among the largest of the stuffed pasta in Italy. They are large squares of pasta cooked in boiling salted water, then stuffed, rolled up and browned in the oven. Sometimes they are baked with butter and sprinkled generously with Parmesan cheese or else, as in Tuscany, they are covered with a sauce and baked until the top is a golden brown.

CANTALOUP

(See Melon entry.)

CAPE GOOSEBERRY

The berry of the plant which in England is commonly called 'Chinese Lanterns' and grown for decoration, as the fruit does not ripen well in our climate. In parts of Africa, America, India, etc., it ripens fully and the fruit may be made into jam or jelly or eaten raw as a dessert. To make attractive petits fours, bend back the orange calyx of each berry, dip the fruit into melted fondant and place in tiny paper cases to serve.

Tinned Cape gooseberries are imported from South Africa (usually under the name of 'golden berries') and these are useful for fruit salads and fruit cocktails.

CAPER

The pickled flower buds of a low-growing deciduous shrub native to the south of Europe. The fresh buds are picked each day during the flowering season, left to dry for 24 hours and put into a cask of pickling brine. They are then bottled in good quality vinegar. Capers are used to flavour a sauce which is traditionally served with boiled mutton and are also sometimes added to mayonnaise, etc. (See Sauce and Mayonnaise entries.)

CAPERCAILZIE

A game bird, also called cock o' the wood or wood-grouse with a distinctive flavour. It is similar in size to grouse and may be cooked in the same way. For roasting, choose a hen bird and be sure it is very young. Hang it well, then pluck, draw and truss; bard well with bacon and cook for 30 to 45 minutes in a moderately hot oven (200°C/400°F, Gas Mark 6), basting it well. The accompaniments may include gravy, bread sauce, fried crumbs, chipped potatoes, watercress, salad.

CAPILLAIRE

An infusion of maidenhair fern syrup with orange-flower water, used as a flavouring for punches and cocktails. It can also be made from water, eggs and orange-flower water or lemon essence.

CAPON

The term used for a castrated cockerel, specially reared for table purposes and killed at 6 to 9 months old.

CAPSICUM

The family name for a number of varieties of pepper. There are two main types: hot, such as the chilli, and sweet, like the ones eaten as a vegetable. Capsicums can be green or red, sometimes round, sometimes long, and they vary considerably in size. (See Chilli and Pepper entries.)

CARAMEL (BURNT SUGAR)

A substance prepared by heating sugar very slowly in a thick pan until it is dark brown in colour; when water is added it produces a dark brown liquid. Commercially it is used for colouring gravy, fruit cakes, wines, beers, vinegars, soups, sauces, etc.

If the caramel is heated for a shorter time, it will retain its sweet taste, instead of becoming bitter and it then makes an agreeable flavouring for cakes, puddings, custards and sauces.

CARAMEL CUSTARD

METRIC/IMPERIAL
115 g/4½ oz sugar
150 ml/¼ pint water
600 ml/1 pint milk
4 eggs

Put 100g/4oz of the sugar and the water into a small pan and dissolve the sugar slowly; bring to the boil without stirring until it caramelizes, i.e., becomes a rich golden brown colour. Pour the caramel into a 15 cm/6 inch cake tin which has been heated slightly, turning the tin until the bottom is completely covered. Warm the milk, pour on to the lightly whisked eggs and remaining sugar and strain over the cooled caramel. Place the tin in a shallow tin of water and bake in a moderate oven (160°C/325°F, Gas Mark 3) for 1 hour until set. Leave in the tin until quite cold (preferably until the next day) before turning out.

Note: Individual custards are easier to turn out. Divide the above mixture between 6 × 150 ml/¼ pint caramel coated tins. Cook for about 45 minutes.

CARAMEL (SWEET)

A type of sweet made in somewhat the same way as toffee, but not boiled to so high a temperature. Caramels may be either soft or hard in texture, according to the temperature to which they are boiled, and the mixture is usually enriched with butter, cream, condensed milk, etc., which necessitates stirring it occasionally during the cooking.

CARAWAY SEED (CARVIE)

The caraway plant originated in the East and was used as a spice by the Greeks. Though it can be grown in this country, the seeds – the only part used to any extent – are usually imported from Holland. They have a peculiar pungent, aromatic flavour. Caraway seeds are used for flavouring cakes (see Seed Cake entry), biscuits, bread, cheese, pickles and the liqueur kümmel. The essential oil distilled from them is used in various medicines, wines and condiments, while the root is cooked and eaten as a vegetable in some parts of Europe.

CARBOHYDRATE

As the name implies, a carbohydrate consists of carbon, hydrogen and oxygen (the two latter in the proportions in which they are found in water). Carbohydrates exist as glucose and other simple sugars and also as a number of glucose units combined into one substance. They provide most of the energy of the human diet. Carbohydrates are the cheapest foods, so therefore poor countries and the poorer classes in rich countries eat far more of them than of proteins and fats. They include:

Sugars: Glucose (sometimes called dextrose), fructose, sucrose (better known as the ordinary domestic sugar), lactose, maltose and others. These are not of any nutritional value, except as a source of energy.

67

CAR

Starchy Foods: Cereals (grains) and some vegetables store food for the new plant in the form of starch. Cereals include wheat, rice, barley, oats, rye and corn and their products, flour, cornflour, pasta, semolina, bread and many others. Vegetables include pulses, potatoes and other roots. Most of these foods have other important nutrients such as protein and minerals, besides carbohydrates.

Starch is a more complicated carbohydrate than sugar, being several glucose units linked together.

Cellulose: The cell structure of fruits, vegetables and grains. Unlike the sugars and starches, cellulose does not provide energy. It is useful to the body as roughage.

Other Carbohydrates: There are many others – for example, glycogen (found in most tissues, particularly of liver and shellfish) and pectin (found in fruit).

The carbohydrates, except cellulose, are broken down in the digestive system and absorbed into the blood stream as glucose. This is stored in the muscles and liver as glycogen, which is converted back into glucose when needed to provide energy.

The energy is the same whether sugar or starch is eaten, but since most starchy foods also provide other materials, they are more valuable. When more carbohydrate is eaten than the body needs, the excess is converted into fat and stored in the tissues, causing obesity.

Some carbohydrate should be eaten at the same time as protein, or some of the protein will be used to produce energy instead of body-building. The habit of eating such combinations as bread and cheese and meat and potatoes is therefore nutritionally sound.

A certain amount of the vitamin thiamine is necessary to make use of the carbohydrate and this is found in most cereals, if they have not been too refined. It is now added to white flour in this country, to make up for that removed during milling.

CARBONNADE

Originally this was a French culinary term referring to meat grilled over hot coals. Nowadays, however, it generally means a stew or braise of meat, usually incorporating beer.

CARDAMOM

The spicy, bitter seeds of a reed-like plant belonging to the ginger family, grown largely in Malabar; they are dark brown in colour and similar in size to mustard seeds. Cardamoms are used in the preparation of sauces, curry powders, cordials and for spicing cakes and confectionery. As they lose their flavour quickly once ground, they should be ground just before they are used.

CARDINAL SAUCE

A red sauce served with fish dishes. To make it, prepare some lobster butter (See Lobster entry), using about 15 g/½ oz coral and 25 g/1 oz butter. Make 300 ml/½ pint Béchamel sauce (See Béchamel entry), beat it well and season it with salt, pepper, a little grated nutmeg and a squeeze of lemon juice. Beat in the lobster butter and lastly add 2 × 15 ml spoons/2 tablespoons cream or a little butter. Pass the sauce through a tammy cloth and re-heat it without boiling.

CARDOON

A plant of the thistle family resembling the globe artichoke; the leaf-stalks and roots can be eaten as a vegetable. The blanched stalks are cooked like celery, while the fleshy main root is boiled and served cold or in salads.

CARMINE

A carnation-red colouring derived from cochineal.

CAROTENE

The yellow-orange pigment present in yellow and green vegetables and fruit. It is the precursor of vitamin A, being converted into that substance in the body. (See vitamin A in Vitamins entry.)

CARP

This fresh-water fish, found in rivers and ponds, sometimes lives to a great age. Carp is not valued much as food in England, but is popular in Chinese cooking and on the Continent and the French make several delicious dishes with it. It needs washing well in running water or salted water to remove the muddy flavour. It can be grilled or fried and is particularly good when stuffed and baked or cooked in red wine.

CARRAGEEN (OR IRISH) MOSS

A dark purple or green seaweed, *Chondrus crispus*, found on many coasts of northern Europe. When dried and bleached it can be used as a substitute for gelatine. Commercially, it is used as a thickening agent.

CARRAGEEN MOSS PUDDING

METRIC/IMPERIAL
10 g/¼ oz carrageen moss
750 ml/1¼ pints milk
5 × 15 ml spoons/5 tablespoons sugar
1 egg, separated
vanilla pod

68

Soak the moss in lukewarm water for 10 minutes. Drain and put in a saucepan with the milk and vanilla pod. Bring to the boil and *simmer* (do not boil) for 20 minutes. Pour through a sieve into a large bowl and rub the jelly-like moss through the sieve using a wooden spoon. Whisk in the sugar and egg yolk. Whisk the egg white stiffly and fold into the milk mixture – it will rise to the top. Pour into a serving dish and chill. Serve with a fresh fruit.

CARROT

Known since Elizabethan times, a useful root vegetable available all the year round. There are two main types; the long rooted and the shorter or round rooted. Carrots give flavour to stews, casseroles and soups, or they may be cooked in a variety of ways to serve as a vegetable. They can also be grated and served raw in salads. Carrots are a good source of Vitamin A (in the form of carotene) and contain a little of the B vitamins, calcium and sugar.

To Cook: Scrub the carrots and scrape lightly; large old carrots will require peeling thinly and cutting into strips or rounds. Cook in boiling salted water until tender – from 20 minutes for young carrots to 1 hour for coarser ones. Glaze with butter and toss in chopped parsley or coat with a creamy white sauce. Alternatively, mash and re-heat with salt, pepper and a knob of butter.

Carrots may also be cooked in a casserole in a very little water; place in a cool oven (150°C/300°F, Gas Mark 2) for at least twice the usual time. Add a little butter and just before serving sprinkle generously with freshly chopped parsley; serve in the casserole.

CARVIE

A Scottish name for caraway.

CARVING

Skilful carving makes the most of food, enabling one to obtain the maximum number of neat, appetizing portions and leave the joint looking attractive enough to serve cold. To serve the portions fairly, it is advisable to know something about the structure of the different joints and birds and where the lean and the fat, or the dark and light meat, are to be found. Good carving tools are essential.

KNIVES
For most joints, a carving knife with a fairly long and broad blade, slightly curved and pointed at the end, is generally satisfactory. Some modern stainless steel carving knives have a hollowed-out grooved blade which does not require sharpening and these knives are perhaps easier for an inexperienced carver to use, though a skilful carver generally prefers a blade with a plain edge.

For carving poultry and game, a knife with a short, straight, stiff blade, pointed at the end and with a comparatively long handle, gives more purchase and makes it easier to sever the joints. When a special game carver is not available use a sharp, pointed kitchen knife in preference to an ordinary carver.

For carving boned hams, pressed tongue, pressed brisket and brawn, the most practical knife is one with a very long, thin, straight and slightly flexible blade; this is usually rounded at the end, for the cuts are invariably made horizontally and a sharp point is unnecessary.

Whatever type of carving knife is used, it should always be very sharp.

FORKS
A carving fork has two sharp prongs, so that it will enter the meat easily, and a guard to prevent the hand from being cut should the knife slip. Forks for carving hams, tongues, etc., generally have a square or circular guard, similar to that of a sword.

FISH SERVERS
These consist of a blunt-edged knife, with a short, wide, slightly pointed blade, and a wide fork with short, broad prongs. They are generally silver, silver-plated or stainless; ordinary steel should not be used, as it gives the fish an unpleasant taste.

Rules for Carving
1. If necessary, secure the joint before cooking with skewers or string (or both), so that it keeps its shape. This is particularly important when the joint is boned (as in rolled rib or beef or boned sirloin) or stuffed (as with breast of lamb). Take care when trussing birds to give them a good shape.
2. Always use metal skewers, which can be removed with ease when the meat is cooked; wooden skewers swell during cooking, making it very difficult to remove them neatly.
3. Get the butcher to chine joints such as loin or neck of lamb, mutton, veal or pork, rather than having them chopped. (See Chining entry.)
4. Bone and stuff a joint such as loin of lamb or pork, as it can then be carved much more easily.
5. Score the crackling of pork before cooking – it is difficult to carve if left in thick pieces.
6. Any game birds that require cutting in half should be carved in the kitchen on a board before they are dished up.
7. Choose a large enough dish for the joint and keep the garnishes small; if any gravy or sauce is placed on the dish with the meat, use a small amount only, the rest being served separately in a sauce-boat.

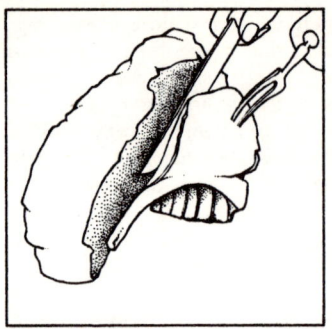

Carving a Wing Rib of Beef
1. Loosen meat from the narrow ribs.
Carve the meat downwards.

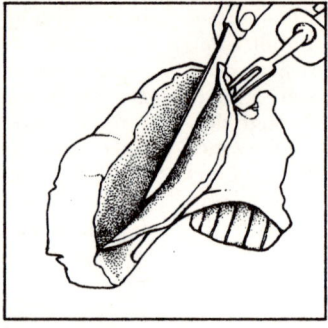

2. Continue to carve thin slices of the
meat, cutting down to the rib bones until
you have cut halfway through the joint.

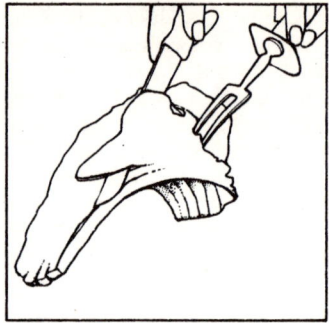

3. Turn the joint and continue carving
from the outside to the centre of the joint.

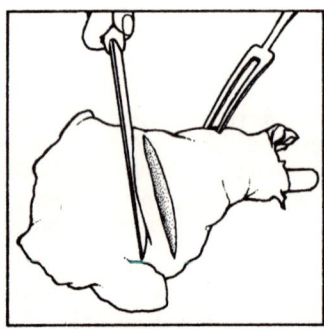

Carving a Leg of Lamb
1. Using a sharp carving knife, cut two
slices from the centre of the leg, cutting
down to the bone.

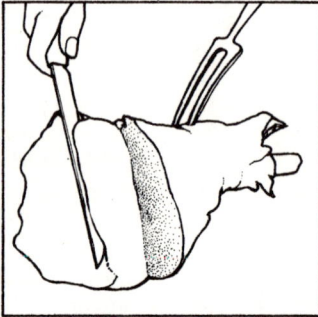

2. Continue carving slices from both sides
of the first two cuts and gradually carve
longer slices. Carve all the meat from this
side.

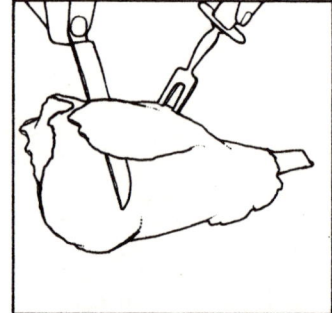

3. Turn the joint over. Cut away any
unwanted fat then carve horizontally
along the leg for longer slices. Continue
carving down to the bone.

8. Arrange for carving to be done at the side table if the carver is inexperienced or if the dining-table tends to be crowded. Place a carving cloth or napkin under the dish, to protect the table.

9. Have everything ready and the knife sharpened before beginning to carve and see that the guard of the fork is up.

Carving Meat

Meat is almost invariably carved across the grain, as this makes it more tender to eat. Generally speaking, beef is sliced very thinly (especially when cold); mutton and lamb should be fairly thick, while a medium thickness is best for pork and veal. Slice ham, tongue and brawn thinly.

Carving Poultry and Game

CHICKEN
As for turkey.

TURKEY
Loosen the legs from the body without removing them, then carve thin slices of breast the whole length of the bird. Remove the legs and separate the thigh from the drum-stick at the joint. Serve a piece of leg with a piece of breast and portions of the stuffings.

DUCK
Cut through the skin with the point of the knife and cut the meat from each side of the breast in long slices, parallel with the breast bone. Cut through the legs and wings at the joint. Serve a piece of leg with a piece of breast.

GOOSE
A goose is carved in the same manner as a duck, but the meat is generally sliced from the legs and wings, these joints being rather large for individual portions.

GAME BIRDS, ETC.
A pheasant or other game bird, if large, is carved in the same manner as a chicken. Partridges, pigeons and birds of similar size are generally cut in half; if very small, the whole bird may be served as one portion. Special scissors (rather like small secateurs) are designed for cutting birds in half, but it can be done with the game carver or with a short, pointed kitchen knife, by inserting the point of the knife in the neck end of the breast and cutting firmly through the bird in the direction of the breast bone.

Woodcock, snipe, quail and other small birds are served whole. They can however be cut into two for presentation.

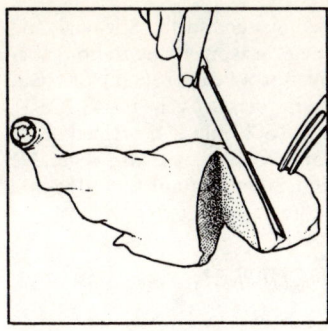

To Carve a Shoulder of Lamb
1. Cut a long slice from the centre of the joint right down to the bone.

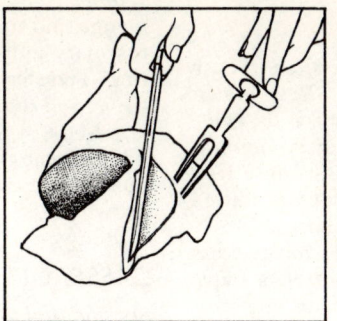

2. Continue to carve thick slices from either side of first slice. Turn the joint and carve from the other side in thin slices.

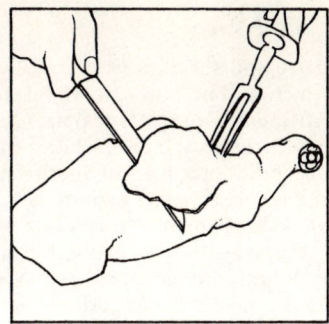

3. Turn the joint so that the shank end is facing you again and cut horizontal slices from the top.

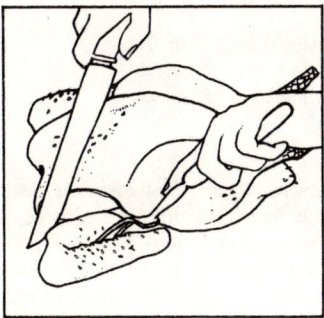

Carving a Chicken
1. Loosen the wings from body then press out and away from body to dislocate. Cut wings through joint.

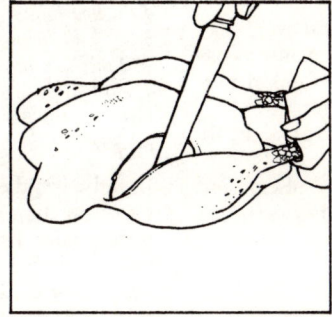

2. Loosen then cut legs from the body. Separate the thigh from the drumstick at the joint by cutting through ball and socket.

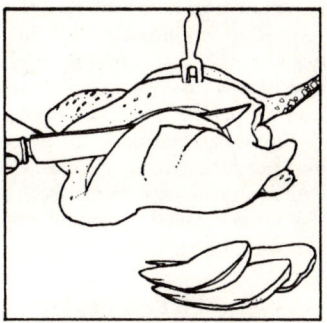

3. Carve slices of the white breast meat in long, thin downward slices from either side of the breast bone.

Carving Fish

The aim in carving fish is to serve it in neat portions without breaking up the flakes or mixing them with the bones or skin. The fish is laid flat on the dish, a round fish like cod being placed on its side. For a large fish, run the knife through the middle of the flesh from head to tail and cut slices of flesh from each side of the cut. Remove the backbone and cut the lower half similarly. To serve plaice and sole, first cut the head off, then cut right through the bone into sections across the fish. In the case of salmon, cut lengthwise through the middle of the flesh and carve the thick part of the fish (the back) in lengthwise slices; include a portion of the thin part (the belly) with each serving, cutting these slices widthways.

CASEIN

A substance produced from milk by precipitation. It results through the action of rennin on the milk protein caseinogen. This reaction takes place in the stomach as a course of normal digestion; it also occurs in the making of junket when rennet is added to warm milk. The milk sets, but when cut a liquid (whey) separates from the solids (curd); the casein is contained in the curd. The precipitation also takes place when an acid is added to milk although a less firm curd is formed.

The fermentation of casein is the origin of all cheesemaking as the milk is always clotted with rennet and/or acids. The casein clot traps the fat leaving much of the water to be drained off. Cheese is therefore a concentrated form of milk nutrients. (See Cheesemaking under Cheese entry.)

Casein has a high biological value as a protein which makes milk and cheese valuable foods in the diet.

CASHEW NUT

A kidney-shaped nut produced by a plant grown in the East and West Indies and in other tropical regions. The kernel of the nut has a pleasant taste and is popular roasted and served with cocktails and other drinks. It is used in the making of chocolate and sometimes in madeira wine.

CASSATA

An Italian frozen sweet, consisting of ice cream with chopped nuts, candied fruit, etc., in the centre.

A tropical shrub, a native of Central and South America, but now grown in the West Indies, Africa and some parts of Asia. Cassava is the name used in the West Indies, while the plant is known as manioc in some parts of South America and Africa and as yucca in other regions. The tubers produce a food also known as cassava or manioc.

Cassava is easy to grow, but unfortunately has very little protein and is not as valuable a staple food as wheat; in fact, protein deficiency is a great danger if the cassava is not accompanied by enough foods containing protein.

The large tubers contain hydrocyanic acid, which is removed by washing, exposure to the air, grating, heating and pressing the tubers; the resultant mass is ground into a coarse meal. This is used to produce a kind of cake, which, however, does not rise at all as it contains no gluten. Some variation of this cassava cake is the staple food of millions of people in many tropical countries.

Tapioca and farina, both almost pure starch, are also produced from cassava.

The juice expressed from the tubers and flavoured is called cassareep; it is used as a sauce in the West Indies.

CASSEROLE COOKERY

The term used to denote the very slow cooking of food placed in the oven in a covered heat-proof dish; very often the food is served in the same casserole. It is a simple method, excellent for cooking meat (particularly inferior cuts) fish and vegetables, as the food becomes very tender and all the nutriment is conserved. The process is economical on fuel; although it takes longer than ordinary methods, only a very low heat is required. The new slow cookers are particularly suitable for this method of cooking. (See separate entry.)

FLEMISH BEEF IN BEER

METRIC/IMPERIAL
1 kg/2¼ lb chuck steak or thick flank
3 × 15 ml spoons/3 tablespoons melted
    dripping or oil
200 g/7 oz button onions, skinned
2 × 15 ml spoons/2 tablespoons flour
finely grated rind and juice of 1 orange
150 ml/¼ pint water
300 ml/½ pint pale ale
1 × 2.5 ml spoon/½ teaspoon dried rosemary
pinch grated nutmeg

Cut the meat into 5 cm/2 inch cubes. Heat dripping or oil in a frying pan or flameproof casserole; fry meat quickly until browned on all sides. Remove meat and cook whole onions in remaining fat until browned. Stir in flour; return meat to pan. Add orange rind and juice, water and ale. Stir well, add rosemary and nutmeg. Season. Bring to boil, stirring. Transfer to ovenproof casserole if pan-fried. Cover and cook in a moderate oven (160°C/325°F, Gas Mark 3) for 1½ to 2 hours. If wished serve with a potato 'collar'. With a large rose vegetable nozzle pipe creamed potato round the edge and brown under a hot grill.

CASSEROLE OF CHICKEN

METRIC/IMPERIAL
2 medium sized onions, skinned, sliced
2 sticks celery, trimmed and chopped
100 g/4 oz mushrooms, sliced
50 g/2 oz bacon, rinded and chopped
1 × 15 ml spoon/1 tablespoon oil
4 chicken joints
3 × 15 ml spoons/3 tablespoons flour
450 ml/¾ pint chicken stock
1 × 425 g/15 oz can tomatoes, drained
salt
pepper

Lightly fry the onions, celery, mushrooms and bacon in the oil and butter for about 5 minutes, until golden brown. Remove them from the pan with a slotted spoon and use them to line the bottom of the casserole. Fry chicken joints in the oil and butter for 5 minutes until golden brown. Put the chicken in the casserole on the bed of vegetables. Stir the flour into the remaining fat and cook for 2 to 3 minutes; gradually stir in the stock and bring to the boil. Continue to stir until the mixture thickens then add the tomatoes, with salt and pepper to taste. Pour this sauce over the chicken joints, cover and cook in a moderate oven (180°C/350°F, Gas Mark 4) for 45 minutes to 1 hour, until the chicken is tender.

RICH RABBIT CASSEROLE

METRIC/IMPERIAL
1 rabbit, jointed
300 ml/½ pint dry cider
150 g/5 oz dried prunes
100 g/4 oz streaky bacon, in one piece
25 g/1 oz butter
200 g/7 oz button onions, skinned
2 × 15 ml spoons/2 level tablespoons flour
150 ml/¼ pint chicken stock
salt
freshly milled pepper
1 large cooking apple

Place rabbit in a bowl and pour cider over. Cover prunes with water. Leave both overnight. Drain and dry rabbit, reserving marinade. Drain and stone prunes. Cut bacon into 2 cm/¾ inch dice. Melt butter in a frying pan and fry rabbit with bacon and onions until brown. Place in casserole.

Stir flour into fat and cook for 1 minute. Blend in stock and cider. Simmer 3 minutes. Season and pour over rabbit, cover and cook in a cool oven (150°C/300°F, Gas Mark 2) for 1 to 1½ hours. Thirty minutes before end of cooking time, peel core and slice apple and add with the prunes. Cover and continue to cook. Garnish with triangles of fried bread.

RAGOÛT OF OX HEART WITH LEMON

METRIC/IMPERIAL
0.5 kg/1 lb ox heart
25 g/1 oz lard
1 medium onion, skinned and sliced
1 × 15 ml spoon/1 tablespoon flour
100 ml/4 fl oz beef stock
rind of 1 small lemon, finely grated
1 × 5 ml spoon/1 teaspoon lemon juice
1 × 2.5 ml spoon/ ½ teaspoon dried fines herbs
salt
freshly milled pepper
150 ml/¼ pint carton soured cream
1 ×15 ml spoon/1 tablespoon chopped parsley

Trim the heart discarding any little pipes and gristle and cut into strips about 1 cm/½ inch wide. Melt the lard in a frying pan or a flameproof casserole and sauté the sliced onion until golden. Fry the strips of heart quickly in the fat, to seal on all sides. Stir in the flour and cook for 1 minute, then gradually blend in the stock with the lemon rind, juice and herbs. Bring to the boil and add salt and pepper to taste. Transfer to an ovenproof casserole if pan-fried. Cover and cook in a cool oven (150°C/300°F, Gas Mark 2) for about 2 hours. To serve, adjust seasoning, stir in the soured cream and sprinkle with freshly chopped parsley.

CASSIA

The inner bark of a type of cinnamon tree grown in the East, particularly in China. Cassia resembles cinnamon in flavour, colour and aroma and may be used in the same way, but it is coarser and less expensive.

CASSIS

A French liqueur made from black-currants, drunk with chilled dry white wine as Kir (five parts wine to one part Cassis).

CASSOLETTE

An individual dish, china or glass, made to hold one portion of a savoury mixture (such as creamed chicken or mushrooms, game in sauce, etc.) which is to be served as an hors d'œuvre, entrée or after-dinner savoury. The container is sometimes lined with duchesse potato or puff pastry before the mixture is put in. Occasionally a sweet mixture is prepared and served in the same way.

CASSOULET

A haricot bean stew originating in the Languedoc region of France. It is prepared from pork, mutton and goose (or duck) and is made in an earthenware utensil known as the cassole d'Issel; this name has evolved into the word cassoulet.

CASSOULET

METRIC/IMPERIAL
225 g/8 oz dried haricot beans
225 g/8 oz streaky salt pork
225 g/8 oz lean shoulder lamb
0.5 kg/1 lb onions
25 g/1 oz lard
600 ml/1 pint bone stock
1 bay leaf
1 clove garlic, skinned
100 g/4 oz garlic sausage
1 × 15 ml spoon/1 tablespoon fresh chopped winter
  savory
salt
freshly ground pepper

Soak the beans overnight. Drain well. Remove rind from the pork and cut into strips with the lamb. Skin and slice the onions and sauté in the fat in a 2.75 litre/5 pint flameproof casserole until soft. Add the meats and cook to seal. Add stock, beans, bay leaf, skinned and crushed garlic, sliced garlic sausage, savory and seasonings. Bring to the boil, cover and simmer gently for 1½ to 2 hours or until the beans and meat are tender.

CASTLE PUDDING

A rich sponge mixture, baked or steamed in small dariole moulds or cups. Make a creamed mixture as for Victoria sandwich (see separate entry). Two-thirds fill greased dariole moulds with the mixture, cover with greased paper and steam for 30 to 40 minutes, or bake in a moderately hot oven (190°C/375°F, Gas Mark 5) for 30 minutes. Turn on to a hot dish and serve with jam sauce.

CATERING

The term usually applies when preparing food for large numbers. (See weddings, parties, etc., entries.)

CATFISH

A name applied to various fish in different parts of the world. The American catfish is called dogfish in England.

CATSUP

(See Ketchup entry.)

CAUDLE

A hot spiced wine drink, resembling mulled wine, which was popular in earlier centuries as a cure for a cold. It was sometimes made with water in which oatmeal had been soaked, or with gruel.

CAUL

A thin membrane covering the lower portion of an animal's intestines. At one time it was always used commercially for sausage-making and it is still used for home-made sausages and faggots. Pork caul is the best type.

CAULIFLOWER

A member of the cabbage family, available in summer and autumn. It has a compact white head (i.e., flowers, often called the curd), surrounded by green leaves.

The 'flower' or curd should be firm and close and protected by young leaves which curl over the flower naturally. Some of the inner green leaves should be kept on the flower when cooked as these add to the appearance of the vegetable. Cauliflower can be served as a vegetable, as part of a main dish (Cauliflower au gratin) or raw as part of a salad. It is also tasty made into soup or pickles. Cauliflower is quite a good source of vitamin C, an average helping supplying over half a day's requirements. To cook: Trim off any unwanted leaves, wash the cauliflower and cut a cross in the stalk to enable this thick part to cook through. Since the stalk takes longer to cook, it is best to place the cauliflower stem downwards in the pan. Cook whole in boiling salted water until tender – 20 to 30 minutes. Drain and serve with a white or cheese sauce. Alternatively, the cauliflower can be divided into sprigs or flowerets before cooking, to save time.

CAULIFLOWER AU GRATIN

METRIC/IMPERIAL
1 cauliflower, trimmed
40 g/1½ oz butter
3 × 15 ml spoons/3 tablespoons flour
300 ml/½ pint milk
100 g/4 oz cheese, grated
salt
pepper

Cook the cauliflower in fast-boiling salted water until just tender, drain and place in an ovenproof dish. Melt the butter, stir in the flour and cook for 2 to 3 minutes. Remove the pan from the heat and gradually stir in the milk; bring to the boil and continue to stir until it thickens. Stir in 75 g/3 oz of the cheese and season to taste. Pour over the hot cauliflower, sprinkle with the remaining cheese and brown under a hot grill. Cauliflower can also be served with an egg sauce.

CAVIARE

The salted roe of the sturgeon, considered a great delicacy because of its rare flavour, though it is an acquired taste and not appreciated by everyone. Most prized are the Russian varieties: – the processed roe of the sterlet from the Caspian Sea. It consists of a mass of black eggs each about the size of a pinhead. Caviare is also imported into this country from Germany and America, the latter type being less expensive.

Caviare should be kept very cold (preferably on ice). It is served either from its jar or from a small barrel placed on a folded napkin and is accompanied by crisp toast or brown bread and butter; or it may be sprinkled with lemon juice if desired. Caviare may also be made into canapés, included in hors d'œuvre, spread on croûtes of fried bread or served in blinis (small Russian pancakes).

CAYENNE

A very hot, pungent variety of pepper, bright red in colour, made from the dried seeds and pods of various capsicums. It originated in the district of Cayenne, in South America, from which it takes its name, but it is now grown fairly extensively in other tropical countries. Cayenne is used for flavouring curries and to season cheese and fish dishes.

CECIL

Old name for a type of fried meat ball.

CELERIAC

A variety of celery, available from November to February which is cultivated for its turnip-like stem base. The root only is served as a vegetable, made into a cream soup or grated raw in salads.

Peel it fairly thickly; the small roots may be cooked whole, but larger ones should be sliced thickly or cut into dice. Cook in boiling salted water or stock until tender 20 to 60 minutes or even longer. Drain well and serve with melted butter or with a good white sauce such as Béchamel or Hollandaise.

CELERY

A vegetable of the carrot family widely grown in

temperate regions. English celery is in season from October to March but imported celery is available all the year round. It is eaten either raw or cooked and also used as a decoration. (See Garnish entry.) Celery Cream Soup (made like the potato soup in the Soup entry) is well-flavoured and popular, while Celery Sauce goes well with poultry.

To prepare raw celery: Wash well to remove any grit and soil and take off the outside stalks and leaves. (Stalks can be used to flavour stews and soups.) Cut the centre part across into halves or quarters, according to the size of the head, the root being scraped and shaped to a point and left on each portion. The celery will keep well if put in a tall glass of water. It is often served in this way with a cheese board.

The raw stalks can also be chopped or cut up for use in salads.

To boil celery: Wash, cut into even lengths and tie in bundles. Cook in boiling salted water until tender, 30 to 45 minutes, depending on the coarseness of the stalks. Drain carefully and serve with a brown, white or cheese sauce.

Braised celery: This has a better flavour than the boiled vegetable. (See Braising entry for method.)

To stuff celery: Cut the prepared stalks into convenient pieces, spread thickly with seasoned cream cheese and garnish with coralline pepper. These make good cocktail snacks.

APPLE AND CELERY STUFFING

METRIC/IMPERIAL
50 g/2 oz bacon, rinded and chopped
25 g/1 oz butter
2 onions, skinned and chopped
2 sticks of celery, trimmed and chopped
*4 medium sized cooking apples, peeled, cored and
    sliced*
75 g/3 oz fresh white breadcrumbs
2 × 15 ml spoons/ 2 tablespoons chopped parsley
sugar to taste
salt
pepper

Fry the bacon in the butter for 2 to 3 minutes until golden brown and remove from the pan with a slotted spoon. Fry the onions and celery for 5 minutes and remove from the pan with the slotted spoon. Fry the apples for 2 to 3 minutes, until soft. Mix all the ingredients together.

Use with duck or pork, or make double the quantity and use for goose.

CELERY SALT

Salt flavoured with dried and powdered celery, used in stews and so on.

CELERY SEED

The ground aromatic seeds of a plant related to vegetable celery. It is used as a flavouring in stews, pickling spices and salads, with fish and meat dishes, etc.

CELLULOSE

(See under Carbohydrate entry.)

CÈPE

A fungus Boletus edulis of the mushroom family. They grow in this country although rarely recognised. They look similar to mushrooms but are a yellowish colour. Cèpes can be used in any of the ways appropriate for mushrooms. They are particularly popular in the Bordeaux regions of France.

CEREAL

Cereals are grasses cultivated for food. They grow all over the world, even in the Arctic Circle, and generally form the staple food of the population, being a cheap source of energy, protein, some vitamins and minerals.

The kind of cereal grown depends mainly on climate and soil; wheat and rice are the most widespread.

In general, cereals give economical energy and provide a good accompaniment to protein and stronger flavoured foods. e.g., rice with curry, bread with cheese.

Here is a list of the most important cereals. (See individual entries for details.)

WHEAT
In dry, temperate climates. It is ground into flour which is made into bread and cakes.

RICE
In damp, tropical climates. The grain is generally eaten whole (apart from the husk) and it goes with many dishes, both savoury and sweet.

RYE
In cold climates, particularly Northern Europe. It is the only cereal besides wheat from which true bread can be made. In the United Kingdom it is used mainly for cattle fodder.

MAIZE
In parts of America, Africa and India. Ground into cornflour for puddings and cakes or eaten as the whole kernel or on the cob.

BARLEY
One of the oldest cereals, but not often used as food now. It is ground for patent barley preparations and flaked for puddings; pearl barley can be added to soups and stews.

OATS

This cereal also is less used than formerly. It is ground into various grades of oatmeal for porridge, soups, biscuits and scones; rolled oats are also used.

MILLET

In dry, hot climates, mainly in Africa, Asia and Latin America. It will thrive on poor soil.

PREPARED CEREALS

These are specially treated to make them ready to eat. With milk and sugar, syrup or fruit, they make a good breakfast. (See Breakfast Cereals entries.)

CHABLIS

A light, dry white Burgundy wine, from the vineyards round Chablis. It is served slightly chilled, with fish or white meat.

CHAFING DISH COOKERY

A chafing dish is a vessel which is used at table for cooking and for keeping food warm. The classic chafing dish consists of two pans, an upper part (called the 'blazer'), which holds the food and a lower one which contains hot water. The chafing dish is really the equivalent of a double boiler and is suitable for foods which are normally cooked in that way, for example, Scrambled Eggs or Lobster Newburg. Swiss Fondue can be cooked in the blazer alone. (See Eggs, Lobster and Fondue entries for recipes.)

The modern electric skillet or frypan, which is becoming increasingly popular, may also be used at table, though the cooking is by dry heat. These skillets are usually sold with a comprehensive book of instructions, giving notes about temperatures and settings, etc., and in some cases, a selection of recipes. Here are some rules to help you make a success of chafing dish cookery:
1. Know your recipe thoroughly, making it up several times.
2. Study the manufacturer's instructions for regulating the heat of your cooker.
3. Have everything ready beforehand – food, seasoning, accompaniments, plates, etc.
4. Plan a first course that will occupy the guests while the second course is being cooked in the chafing dish.

CHAMPAGNE

A sparkling wine made from grapes grown within the boundaries of the ancient French province of Champagne. Champagne is always blended, firstly because the wines from different vineyards, although similar in type, are different in style and it is only by judicious blending that the individual wines are improved, the special qualities being merged into a harmonious whole; secondly, because the quantity of wine made each year from individual vineyards is so small that shippers must blend the wine of a number of vineyards in order to have sufficient champagne of uniform style to meet the demands of their customers.

Unlike other wines, champagne is bottled before fermentation is finished, so that the carbonic acid gas remains in solution and escapes when the cork is removed, giving a sparkling effect. A vintage champagne is one bearing the date of an outstanding year. These are not sold until 5 years old but the best will improve for another 5 years.

At formal dinners, champagne is served with the game and entremets. It may also be served as the only wine and this is more usual nowadays. It is the traditional wine for serving at wedding receptions for drinking the health of the bride and bridegroom. It is often served at other celebrations and chilled champagne is sometimes served before a meal. Champagne should be served thoroughly cool, but not icy, or the flavour will be lost.

CHAMPAGNE CUP

METRIC/IMPERIAL
1 bottle champagne
25 g/1 oz sugar
2 oranges sliced
a bunch of balm
a bunch of borage
1.2 litres/2 pints bottle soda water (optional)

Put all the ingredients except the soda water into a jug, cover and chill for 2 hours, then decant free from herbs and add the soda water, if used.

CHAMPAGNE COCKTAIL

(See Cocktails entry.)

CHAMPIGNON

French name for the button mushroom.

CHAPATTI (CHUPATTY)

An Indian unleavened bread or pancake, baked on a griddle and served with curry. A paste of flour and water is blended and rolled thinly.

METRIC/IMPERIAL
225 g/8 oz plain wholewheat flour
1 × 2.5 ml spoon/½ teaspoon salt
about 150–200 ml/5–7 fl oz water

Sift the flour and salt. Add enough water to make a soft dough, knit together with fingertips. Knead well for 10 minutes. Leave covered with a damp cloth for at least one hour. Knead well again and then divide into 6 pieces. Roll each out on a generously floured surface to make 10–13 cm/4–5 inch rounds. Heat up a griddle or a heavy based frying pan, very lightly greased and then cook two chapattis at a time until pale brown on each side. Serve hot, brushed with butter or ghee, to accompany any Indian dish.

CHAR

A freshwater fish with a red underside and pink oily flesh, found in some Scottish lochs and English lakes. It is cooked like trout.

CHARD

(See Swiss Chard entry.)

CHARLOTTE

A pudding made with stewed fruit and layers (or a casing) of bread or cake crumbs, sponge cake, biscuits, etc. In a Charlotte Russe, there is a centre of a cream mixture surrounded by cake. A savoury type of charlotte can also be made.

CHARLOTTE RUSSE

METRIC/IMPERIAL
600 ml/1 pint lemon jelly (135 g/4¾ oz tablet)
few diamonds of angelica
300 ml/½ pint milk
1 vanilla pod
3 × 15 ml spoons/3 tablespoons water
2 × 5 ml spoons/2 teaspoons powdered gelatine
3 egg yolks
2 × 15 ml spoons/2 tablespoons caster sugar
10–12 soft sponge fingers
150 ml/¼ pint carton double cream

Pour a little jelly into a 13 cm/15 in 900 ml/1½ pint sloping-sided russe tin. Allow to set. Arrange a pattern of angelica over and set carefully with a little more jelly. Place remaining jelly in a basin and leave to set.

Heat the milk in a saucepan with the vanilla, do not boil; leave to infuse for 10 minutes.

Put the water in a small bowl, sprinkle the gelatine over and leave to swell up. Beat the egg yolks and sugar, pour the strained milk over and return it to the pan. Cook gently to a coating consistency. Add the gelatine and stir until dissolved, then cool until beginning to set.

Arrange the sponge fingers (trimmed down each side) side by side round the tin. Lightly whip the cream until floppy and fold it into the custard. Turn it at once into the tin. Trim the fingers level with the mixture and place the trimmings over the top. Chill until set. Turn out as for jelly and decorate with the remaining jelly, chopped.

RHUBARB BETTY

METRIC/IMPERIAL
0.75 kg/1½ lb rhubarb, trimmed and wiped
100 g/4 oz fresh white breadcrumbs
75 g/3 oz demerara sugar
75 g/3 oz shredded suet
grated rind of 1 lemon, or
1 × 5 ml spoon/1 teaspoon ground ginger or cinnamon
knob of butter

Grease a 900 ml–1.2 litre/1½–2 pint ovenproof dish. Cut the rhubarb into short lengths and place half in the prepared dish. Mix together the crumbs, sugar, suet, and lemon rind, cinnamon or ginger and sprinkle half over the fruit. Add the remaining fruit and top with the remaining crumbs. Dot with the butter and bake in a moderate oven (180°C/350°F, Gas Mark 4) for 45 minutes.

CHARTREUSE (DESSERT)

A type of sweet dish made of fruit in a moulded jelly, with cream in the centre.

BANANA CHARTREUSE

METRIC/IMPERIAL
300 ml/½ pint lemon jelly
4 bananas, thinly sliced
1 × 15 ml spoon/1 tablespoon pistachio nuts finely chopped
300 ml/½ pint carton double cream, half whipped
25 g/1 oz caster sugar
2 × 5 ml spoons/2 teaspoons lemon juice
1 × 5 ml spoon/1 level teaspoon powdered gelatine
2 × 15 ml spoons/2 tablespoons cold water

Mask a plain 600 ml/1 pint soufflé dish or cake tin with a thin layer of lemon jelly. Line the mould entirely with half the sliced banana, dipping each piece in a little cold jelly. Fill the spaces with the nuts and coat the inside with another thin layer of jelly. Sieve the remaining banana and add to the half-whipped cream, together with the sugar and lemon juice. Dissolve the gelatine in the water over a gentle heat and add to the cream mixture; pour into the prepared mould and allow to set.

CHARTREUSE (LIQUEUR)

One of the most famous French liqueurs, made by Carthusian monks. There are two chief types, the yellow and the green; a third type is called Elixir.

CHASSEUR SAUCE

A rich, highly-seasoned brown sauce, usually containing white wine, mushrooms and shallots; it is served with meat, game or venison, etc. There are a number of different versions, but here is a popular one.

CHASSEUR SAUCE

METRIC/IMPERIAL
125 g/4 oz chopped mushrooms
butter
salt
1 × 15 ml spoon/1 tablespoon shallot finely chopped
150 ml/¼ pint white wine
150 ml/¼ pint Espagnole sauce (see Espagnole entry.)
150 ml/¼ pint tomato sauce
a little chopped parsley, chervil, tarragon

Sauté the mushrooms in butter and season with salt; when they are nearly cooked add the shallot. Stir in the wine, boil in an open pan until reduced by half, then stir in the Espagnole sauce and the tomato sauce and boil for a minute or two. Just before serving add 25 g/1 oz butter and some chopped parsley, chervil and tarragon.

CHATEAUBRIAND STEAK

A thick steak cut from the fillet of beef and served with maître d'hôtel butter. (See Steak entry.)

CHAUDFROID

A sauce used to coat cooked meat, fish, poultry galantine, etc., which are served as cold entrées.

A sweet chaudfroid (made by combining equal quantities of melted lemon jelly and half-whipped cream) is used to coat fruit to serve as a cold sweet.

CHAUDFROID SAUCE (WHITE)

METRIC/IMPERIAL
2.5 × 15 ml spoons/2½ tablespoons aspic jelly powder
150 ml/¼ pint hot water
2 × 5 ml spoons/2 teaspoons powdered gelatine
300 ml/½ pint béchamel sauce
100–150 ml/⅛–¼ pint single cream
salt
pepper

Put the aspic jelly powder in a small basin and dissolve it in the hot water. Stand the basin in a pan of hot water, sprinkle in the gelatine and stir until it has dissolved, taking care not to overheat the mixture. Stir into the warm béchamel sauce, beat well and add the cream and extra salt and pepper if necessary. Strain the sauce and leave to cool, stirring frequently so that it remains smooth and glossy. Use when at the consistency of thick cream, for coating chicken, fish or eggs.

CHEDDAR CHEESE

A traditional English cheese originally made in the late fifteenth century near Cheddar Gorge in Somerset. It is now made in other parts of the country. 'Cheddar type' cheeses are also made in other countries and are often imported from Ireland, Canada, Australia and New Zealand.

It is a firm smooth textured cheese with a clean unbroken rind. It is a straw colour and can be mild or strong in flavour. English Farmhouse Cheddar is made from whole milk from a single herd of cows. It is allowed to mature for at least 6 months to produce a rich mellow flavour. Other Cheddar cheese is made from a mixture of ripened and unripened milk; the close texture is obtained by pressing for 3 to 4 days with the pressure increased each day. The cheese can be left to ripen from 3 to 6 months depending on the flavour required. Cheddar is good served alone with bread or in cooked dishes.

CHEESE

Originally a method of preserving milk, cheese became very popular for its own sake at an early stage in man's history and has remained so ever since, for it is a very palatable and versatile food.

It is made by separating the curds from the whey (usually by the action of rennet) and ripening them in some way. The milk can be that of the cow, goat, ewe, camel, mare, llama or even buffalo, according to the part of the world; in Europe it is usually cow's, goat's, or ewe's milk.

The process used, the climate and vegetation help to widen the variety of cheeses. Some types cannot be imitated outside their own districts or under factory conditions. Others, such as Cheddar cheese, etc., are made world wide.

Cheese is eaten raw and is also cooked in a large number of savoury dishes, from cocktail snacks to main meals. (See selection of recipes given in this entry.)

Cheesemaking Process

These are the basic principles for cheesemaking, especially the hard Cheddar types. Different flavours and textures are determined by variations in times and temperatures, in the weight of pressing and the length of maturing.

1. Pasteurised milk is soured or ripened by a 'starter' culture or lactic acid bacteria which converts some of the milk lactose into lactic acid. Throughout the cheesemaking process the development of acid is carefully controlled to ensure that a good cheese results.

2. Rennet is added to coagulate the milk, and then the coagulum cut to allow the whey to separate from the curd.

3. The curd is scalded or heated to cause shrinkage and release more whey. It is then left to settle

which allows further shrinkage and drainage.

4. The curd is broken down and salt added as a preservative and for flavouring.

5. The curd is then pressed in moulds for varying times then removed as a whole cheese.

6. The cheese is then left to mature in a speciel ripening room which is kept at a certain temperature and humidity.

Food Value

Cheese is valuable protein food and plays an important part in the normal diet. The different types vary in composition, but approximately one-third of the weight of a typical English cheese is protein and one-third fat. 25 g/1 oz gives about one-third of the day's requirement of calcium, also some Vitamins A and D and some riboflavin. Bread and cheese are an excellent combination from the nutritional point of view as proteins in the bread enhance those in the cheese.

Cheese Classification

Cheese is classified in several ways. Sometimes it is grouped according to the type of processing – whether the cheese is heated and whether it is hard-pressed and so on. The classification here given is according to the general appearance and texture.

Type	Example
Very hard cheese	Parmesan
Hard cheese	
(a) without 'eyes'	Cheddar
	Cheshire
	Derby
	Double Gloucester
	Lancashire
	Wensleydale
	Leicester
	Cantal
	Dunlop
(b) with 'eyes'	Emmenthal
	Gruyère
Semi-hard	Caerphilly
	Edam
	Gouda
	Port du Salut
	Tomme
Blue-veined	Roquefort
	Gorgonzola
	Bresse Bleu
	Stilton
	Danish Blue
	Blue Dorset (Blue Vinny)
Semi-soft	Brick
	Munster
	Limburger
	Samsoe
	Mozzarella
Soft	
(a) Ripened	Brie
	Camembert
	Fromage de Monsieur
	Pont l'Evêque
	Bel Paese
(b) Unripened	Coulommier
	Cambridge
	Cottage
	Ricotta
Goat cheese	Chevret
	Saint Maure
	Valençay

CHEESES FOR TABLE USE

The nine British cheeses are described under individual entries.

Cheddar	Gloucester	Wensleydale
Cheshire	Leicester	Lancashire
Caerphilly	Derby	Stilton

SOFT CHEESES (Curd Cheeses)

These are characterised by their small size, high moisture content (50 to 70 per cent) and quick ripening properties. They have a mellow, slightly acid flavour and soft spreadible texture. Soft cheeses do not keep as long as the harder varieties, therefore they should be eaten while fresh.

Cream Cheese is made from fresh cream and usually has a fat content of 70 to 80 per cent. Cream Cheese may be designated as full fat soft cheese, medium fat soft cheese (curd cheese) or low fat soft cheese.

Cottage Cheese is a skimmed milk soft fat cheese. It is an acid curd cheese made from pasteurised fat free milk. It has a mild flavour which makes it suitable to serve with sweet or savoury foods. It is often used as part of slimming or low fat diets. (See Cottage Cheese entry.)

Packet and Processed Cheeses, usually sold wrapped in foil, are made by various processes, the ripening being halted at a selected stage. They are generally soft-textured and milky and are sometimes flavoured with tomato, onion, etc.

Foreign Cheeses

Supplies available in this country vary from time to time, and from one locality to another. Many shops and supermarkets now stock a comprehensive range. Here are some which should be available:

ALPESTRA (ALPIN)
Hard, dry cheese made in the French Alps.

AUSTRIAN SMOKED CHEESE
Cylindrical, with sausage skin covering; close-textured and with distinctive smoky flavour; good with wine.

BEL PAESE
Italian; soft, creamy and rich, very mild in flavour; texture slightly rubbery, but nonetheless agreeable. Good for cooking certain Italian dishes.

BONDON
Small, cylindrical, whole-milk cheese from Normandy. When ripe has a fairly pungent flavour.

BRESSE BLEU
A soft French blue cheese.

BRICK
American, usually made in shape of a brick; semi-soft, with small holes; rather less sharp in flavour than Cheddar.

BRIE
French; soft, with a crust rather than a rind; when in good condition, it is runny in texture, but a poor Brie is dry and chalky; well-flavoured.

CACCIOCAVALLO
Italian; name due to the fact that the roundish cheeses are strung together in pairs and dried suspended over a pole, as though astride a horse. If eaten fresh, the cheese has a tangy taste and firm, yet soft texture; if kept, it becomes hard and is then grated and used in cooking.

CAMEMBERT
French; soft, and with a distinctive flavour that strengthens as it ripens.

CANTAL
French; a hard strong cheese made in Auvergue.

CHEVRET
French; a Bresse cheese made from goat's milk.

COULOMMIER
French; soft cream cheese, eaten fresh after salting. White crust, creamy to the touch.

DANISH BLUE
Soft and white, with blue veins, sharp and rather salty in taste.

DEMI-SEL
French, a soft, mild cream cheese.

EDAM
Dutch; bright red outside, yellow inside; mild in flavour, close and fairly soft in texture.

EMMENTHAL
Swiss; hard, pitted with numerous fairly large irregular holes; like Gruyère, which it resembles, it has a distinctive flavour. Used in cooking, especially for cheese fondues.

DANISH EMMENTHAL
A good copy of the Swiss product.

FONTAINEBLEAU
French; creamy cheese, which is sometimes eaten with strawberries.

FROMAGE DE MONSIEUR
French; soft and slightly like Camembert, but milder.

GERVAIS
French; cream cheese, sold packed in boxes of 6 small portions.

GORGONZOLA
Italian; semi-hard, with a creamy texture. It is blue-veined and normally has a strong flavour. However, there are mild varieties of Gorgonzola, the Dolcelatte, made from a sweet milk, being much milder in flavour than the ordinary type; between the two comes the kind known as creamy Gorgonzola.

GOUDA
Dutch; creamier in taste and texture to Edam, and larger and flatter, and with a yellow outside coat. Smaller sizes are available.

GRUYÈRE
Swiss; hard, honeycombed with holes which are smaller and fewer than in Emmenthal; the cheese has a more creamy texture, and a distinctive, slightly acidulous flavour. Used in cooking, particularly for cheese fondues.
French Gruyère is also available.

HAVARTI
Danish; foil-wrapped; semi-firm texture, rather open; good full flavour.

KÜMMELKÄSE
German; caraway-flavoured; good with cocktails, etc.

LIMBURGER
Belgian or German; strong, ripe flavour and smell.

MARC DE RAISIN
French; semi-hard, with a crust of grapeskins and pips replacing the usual rind. A rather tasteless cheese.

MOZZARELLA
Italian; round, soft cheese, originally made from buffaloes' milk, but now also made from cows' milk. Should be used fresh. Eaten by itself it is somewhat tasteless, and it is more useful in making Italian dishes such as pizza.

MUNSTER
Alsation; semi-soft cheese, which is good for both cooking and table use; not unlike Pont l'Éveque in flavour.

MYCELLA
Danish; soft textured, creamy with green veins; strong flavour.

MYSÖST (GIETÖST)
Norwegian; whey cheese, principally made from goat's milk. Hard and dark brown, with a sweetish flavour.

NEUFCHÂTEL
French; whole-milk cheese; soft, dark yellow and with a flavour similar to that of Bondon.

PARMESAN
Italian; very hard, ideal for cooking and for grating to serve with pasta, etc. It is also available in packs, ready grated.

PETIT SUISSE
French; soft, creamy and unsalted cheese, made into little cylindrical shapes. Often eaten with strawberries or other fruit, accompanied by caster sugar.

POMMEL
French; a brand of double-cream cheese, similar to Petit Suisse.

PONT L'EVÊQUE
French, semi-hard cheese, sold in small square boxes; delicious mild flavour, somewhere between that of a Brie and a Camembert.

PORT-SALUT
French; semi-hard, with very good mild flavour.

RICOTTA
Italian; a fresh, moist, unsalted variety of cottage cheese.

ROQUEFORT
French; made of ewes' milk; white with blue veins, has a sharp, distinctive flavour; rather salty; creamy and rather crumbly in texture, somewhat like a Stilton.

SAINT MAURE
French; soft creamy goat's milk cheese. Samsoe: Danish; firm-textured, with regular holes, golden in colour; mild and sweet in flavour. Danbo is a small, square-shaped version; Fynbo, Elbo and Tybo are other variants, fairly similar in type; Molbo has a richer, more fruity flavour; Maribo is also more full-flavoured.

TOMME
French; semi-hard, covered with grape pips.

VALENÇAY
French; soft goats' milk cheese.

Cheeses for Cooking
Good British cheeses are Cheddar, Cheshire, Leicester, Lancashire, Derby and Dunlop, and the cream and curd cheeses. Suitable Continental cheeses are Parmesan, Gruyère, Emmenthal, Gorgonzola, Bel Paese, Mozzarella and Camembert.

Serving Cheese
When serving cheeses as a separate course, choose varieties which differ in style, flavour and consistency and arrange them attractively on a board or platter. To accompany them, serve any of the following: plain bread, biscuits (plain or very slightly sweetened), hot rolls, toast, rye bread, French bread and so on. Celery, radishes and watercress are popular accompaniments.

Cream cheese may be served plain with biscuits; alternatively, paprika, caraway seeds or chopped chives may be added and some people like chopped pineapple or other fresh fruits or nuts mixed with cream cheese, especially when it is served with salad.

Storing Cheese
Hard cheeses, such as Cheddar are best wrapped in aluminium foil, cling wrap or polythene and placed in a cool larder or the least cold part of a refrigerator. The ideal temperature for keeping cheese is 8°C/45°F to 12°C/55°F. However, the cheese should be brought to room temperature at least one hour before serving. Cheeses bought in vacuum packs are best re-wrapped once opened.

Soft cheeses can also be stored in a refrigerator but ideally they should be eaten as fresh as possible. Some of the soft French cheeses such as Camembert or Brie may be kept at room temperature for a few days to allow the flavour to develop further. Once ripe they are best eaten the same day.

Hard cheeses can be frozen for up to four months if packed in blocks of up to 0.5 kg/1 lb. Vacuum pack cheese can be frozen without repacking, but unwrapped cheese is best frozen in freezer polythene. Cheeses should be thawed in a refrigerator for 24 hours. In some varieties the texture changes and they may deteriorate more quickly than non-frozen cheese. Curd cheeses can be frozen successfully for up to three months. Cream cheese and cottage cheese do not freeze.

Drying and Grating
To make cheese become hard and dry, leave it exposed to the air in a dry but cool place; it is best hung in a muslin bag, as the air can then circulate completely. If the cheese is left on a plate or board to dry, stand it on its rind; a piece that has no rind should be turned occasionally, otherwise the underside will remain soft and will very likely mould.

Use a fine grater for a dry cheese; a soft or processed cheese should be shredded rather than grated. Very soft cheese can be sliced and added to sauces and so on, without first being grated or shredded.

Cooking
The less cooking cheese has, the better. Overheating tends to make it tough and indigestible, so when making a dish such as Welsh rarebit or cheese sauce, always heat the cheese very gently and do not cook longer than is necessary to melt it. A few recipes are given here. (See Welsh Rarebit and Cheese Sauce under Sauce entries).

To toast cheese: Lay a slice of cheese (Lancashire is excellent) on a round of freshly made buttered toast. A dab of mustard may be blended with the butter, if liked. Put under the grill and leave just long enough for the cheese to melt.

CHEESE PUDDING

METRIC/IMPERIAL
4–6 slices of white bread
4 × 15 ml spoons/4 tablespoons dry white wine,
  optional
25 g/1 oz butter, melted
2 eggs beaten
300 ml/½ pint milk
salt
pepper
100 g/4 oz mature cheese, grated

Cut the bread into cubes and place in a 900 ml/1½ pint greased ovenproof dish with the wine (if used) and the butter. Mix the eggs and milk, season well and pour over the bread mixture. Sprinkle with the cheese and bake in a moderately hot oven (190°C/375°F, Gas Mark 5) for 30 minutes, until golden and well risen. Serve at once.

COLD CHEESE SOUFFLÉ

Season this light and frothy soufflé mixture well to bring out the flavour.

METRIC/IMPERIAL
pinch each of salt, black pepper and cayenne pepper
1 × 2.5 ml spoon/½ teaspoon French Mustard
1 × 2.5 ml spoon/½ teaspoon tarragon vinegar
2 × 5 ml spoons/2 teaspoons gelatine, dissolved in
  300 ml/½ pint water
50 g/2 oz Parmesan cheese, grated
50 g/2 oz Gruyère cheese, finely grated
50 g/2 oz double cream, carton
300 ml/½ pint thick mayonnaise
150 ml/¼ pint toasted breadcrumbs
50 g/2 oz mustard and cress

Tie collars of greaseproof paper round 6 × 7 cm/2¾ inch diameter soufflé dishes, to extend 5 cm/2 inch above the rims of the dishes. Place the salt, pepper, cayenne and mustard in a bowl. Add the vinegar and gelatine, which should be cold but not quite set. Beat until frothy then add the cheeses and mix well. Whip the cream until almost stiff and fold it in, along with the mayonnaise. Blend the mixture thoroughly then spoon it into the prepared soufflé dishes and allow to set in a cool place. Remove the paper collars. Decorate each soufflé with toasted breadcrumbs pressed around the sides and a sprig of mustard and cress in the centre.

STUFFED CHEESE POTATOES

METRIC/IMPERIAL
4 large potatoes
25 g/1 oz butter, margarine or dripping
1 × 5 ml spoon/1 teaspoon chopped onion
1 ripe tomato
1 egg
a little milk

50 g/2 oz breadcrumbs
75 g/3 oz grated cheese
seasoning

Cut the potatoes in half lengthwise and scoop out part of the centres. Meanwhile, melt half the fat in a pan and add to it the chopped onion and the skinned tomato, cut in small pieces. Cook gently, shaking the saucepan frequently, for 10 to 15 minutes. Blend thoroughly, add the well-beaten egg, a little milk, the breadcrumbs and the cheese, season and place a portion of the mixture in each of the potato cases. Finish by baking in a little hot dripping in a moderate oven (180°C/350°F, Gas Mark 4) for 30 minutes.

CHEESE PASTRY AND STRAWS

METRIC/IMPERIAL
100 g/4 oz plain flour
pinch of salt
50 g/2 oz butter or block margarine and lard
50 g/2 oz Cheddar cheese, finely grated
little beaten egg or water

Mix the flour and salt together and rub in the fat, as for shortcrust pastry, until the mixture resembles fine crumbs in texture. Mix in the cheese. Add a little egg or water, stirring until the ingredients begin to stick together, then with one hand collect the dough together and knead very lightly to give a smooth dough. Roll out as for shortcrust pastry. Use as required. The usual temperature for cooking cheese pastry is in a moderately hot oven (200°C/400°F, Gas Mark 6).

Note: Use a well flavoured cheese with a bite when ever possible; a pinch of dry mustard added to the flour with the salt helps to bring out the cheese flavour.

CHEESE (PRESERVE)

This consists of fruit purée boiled with sugar to make it a stiff mixture; after it has matured in its pot, it can be turned out whole and cut with a knife. This is a particularly good method of using fruits which have a lot of pips or stones, such as black-currants and damsons or bullaces; other popular cheeses are made from quinces, cranberries, blackberries (good in combination with damsons), gooseberries, apples (often used in combination with other fruit) and medlars. Some fruit cheeses are eaten like jam, with bread and butter, while others are excellent with cold meat, cheese and other savoury foods; they are sometimes served as a cold sweet. A somewhat softer mixture is called Fruit Butter. (See separate entry.)

  The general method of making is as follows: Wash the fruit and put it in a preserving pan, barely covered with water. Simmer it very gently until soft, then sieve or liquidize and add sugar, the usual proportions being 350 g/12 oz sugar to 0.5 kg/1 lb of purée. After the sugar has dissolved, boil the mixture gently until it stiffens. Pot in small straight-sided jars or moulds, cover in the usual way and leave for a few months before opening.

DAMSON CHEESE

METRIC/IMPERIAL
1.5 kg/3¼ lb damsons
150–300 ml/¼–½ pint water
350 g/¾ lb sugar to each 0.5 kg/1 lb pulp

Wash the fruit, remove any stems, put the fruit and water in a covered pan and simmer gently until really soft. Sieve and weigh the pulp and return it to the pan with the sugar. Stir until dissolved, bring to the boil and boil gently until thick, stirring regularly. Pot as usual.

CHEESECAKE

Traditionally a mixture of local soft cheese, eggs and sugar baked in a pastry case. As it was made in Yorkshire it was known as 'Yorkshire Cheesecake'. The term now covers a wide variety of recipes which always include a soft cheese in the filling. It is usual to have a base of pastry, biscuit crust or sponge cake and a topping of fruit, nuts or another layer of the base. The continental type cheesecakes have a rich, creamy, smooth texture which is contrasted by the sharpness of a fruit topping. Chilled cheesecakes (originally from America) are usually set with gelatine and have a lighter texture. Both varieties are suitable for freezing.

POLISH CHEESE CAKE

METRIC/IMPERIAL
For the topping
225 g/8 oz cream cheese
6 egg yolks
50 g/2 oz butter, melted
225 g/8 oz caster sugar
little vanilla essence
glacé icing

For the pastry
100 g/4 oz butter
225 g/8 oz plain flour
50 g/2 oz sugar
1 egg yolk

Tie the cream cheese in muslin and squeeze out the moisture. When the cheese is dry, grate or crumble it into a mixing bowl. Add the egg yolks, melted butter, sugar and a little vanilla essence and beat thoroughly until the mixture is quite smooth. Rub the butter into the flour, add the sugar and work in

the egg, with a little water if necessary to give a firm but manageable dough. Roll out and use to cover the base of a 20 cm/8 inch square cake tin. Place the cheese mixture on top and bake in a moderate oven (180°C/350°F, Gas Mark 4) for 1 hour. Leave to cool in the tin until the topping is set. Turn out and coat with glacé icing. When set cut it into squares.

LEMON CHEESECAKE

METRIC/IMPERIAL
1½ pkts of lemon jelly
4 × 15 ml spoons/4 tablespoons water
2 eggs, separated
300 ml/½ pint milk
grated rind of 2 lemons
6 × 15 ml spoons/6 tablespoons lemon juice
0.5 kg/1 lb cottage cheese
1 × 15 ml spoon/1 tablespoon caster sugar
150 ml/¼ pint carton double cream whipped
glacé cherries and mint sprigs

For the crumb base
100 g/4 oz digestive biscuits
50 g/2 oz caster sugar
50 g/2 oz butter, melted

Put the jelly and water in a small pan and warm gently over a low heat, stirring until dissolved. Beat together the egg yolks and milk, pour on to the jelly, stir and return the mixture to the heat for a few minutes without boiling. Remove from the heat and add the lemon rind and juice. Sieve the cottage cheese and stir it in to the jelly or put jelly and cottage cheese in an electric blender and purée until smooth; turn the mixture into a bowl. Whisk the egg whites stiffly, add the 15 ml spoon/1 tablespoon sugar and whisk again until stiff; fold into the cool cheese mixture.

Fold in the cream. Put the mixture into 20 cm/8 inch spring-release cake tin fitted with a tubular base.

Crush the biscuits and stir in the sugar and butter. Use to cover the cheese mixture, pressing it on lightly; chill. Turn the cheesecake out carefully, and decorate with cherries and mint sprigs.

CHELSEA BUNS

These were an 18th-century speciality of the Old Chelsea Bun House in Pimlico which was then in the Borough of Chelsea.

METRIC/IMPERIAL
225 g/8 oz strong plain flour
15 g/½ oz fresh yeast
120 ml/4 fl oz tepid milk
1 × 2.5 ml spoon/½ teaspoon salt
about 15 g/½ oz butter or lard
1 egg, beaten

melted butter
75 g/3 oz dried fruit
2 × 15 ml spoons/2 tablespoons chopped mixed peel
50 g/2 oz soft brown sugar
clear honey to glaze

Grease an 18 cm/7 inch square cake tin. Put 50 g/ 2 oz of the flour in a large bowl. Blend together the yeast and milk until smooth. Add to the flour, mix well and set aside in a warm place until frothy 15 to 20 minutes. Mix the remaining flour and salt; rub in the fat. Mix into the batter with the egg to give a fairly soft dough that will leave the sides of the bowl clean after beating. Turn the dough out on to a lightly floured surface and knead until smooth about 5 minutes. Put in a greased bowl. Cover with oiled polythene and leave to rise for 1 to 1½ hours.

Knead the dough and roll out to an oblong 30 × 23 cm/12 × 9 inch. Brush with melted butter and cover with a mixture of dried fruit, peel and brown sugar. Roll up from the longest side like a Swiss roll, and seal the edge with water. Cut into nine equal sized slices and place these, cut side down, in the prepared cake tin. Prove until the dough has doubled in size and feels springy to the touch. Bake the buns in a moderately hot oven (190°C/375°F, Gas Mark 5) for 30 minutes. While they are still warm, brush them with a wetted brush dipped in honey.

CHERRY

The fruit of the Prunus Cerasus, some varieties of which are cultivated in most countries.

Eating Cherries

The best types grown in this country are the large, sweet White Heart and Black Heart, both of which ripen in June and July.

Cherries are delicious eaten raw, either for dessert or in fruit cocktails, fruit salad and other cold sweets, but they can also be cooked and may be bottled or canned, the red or black varieties being rather more suitable for this purpose, as the white ones turn a somewhat unappetizing fawnish colour when bottled.

Cherries for Cooking

The Morello and the May-duke are the best-known varieties; they ripen about August. Being very sharp in taste they are not suitable for eating raw, but are delicious when sweetened and cooked. For making preserves, the cooking variety should be chosen (dessert cherries have insufficient acid and pectin). Red Cherry Soup (See Fruit Soups entry) is an unusual way of using this fruit.

Glacé Cherries

These are prepared in the same way as other glacé fruits and are widely used in cakes, biscuits, puddings, sweets, etc., both as an ingredient and as a decoration.

Maraschino Cherries

Cherries which have been stoned, cooked in sugar syrup and flavoured with Maraschino liqueur: they are used as a decoration for cocktails, cakes, etc., and occasionally as an ingredient in puddings, cakes, etc.

To make cherry compote: Wash the fruit carefully and remove the stalks. If a cherry stoner is not available, make a slit down one side of the cherry and remove the stone from the centre, using a pointed knife.

To each 0.5 kg/1 lb of cherries allow 100 g/4 oz sugar and the juice of 1 lemon. Put the prepared fruit, sugar and lemon juice into a non-stick pan, without adding any water, cover and stew slowly until the fruit is tender without being broken. Lift out the cherries, boil the juice a few minutes longer and pour it over them. Cherries cooked in this way are delicious and retain their pretty red colour.

CHERRY JAM

METRIC/IMPERIAL
1.75 kg/4 lb cherries (Morello, May Duke)
1.5 × 5 ml spoons/1½ teaspoons citric or tartaric acid
  (or the juice of 3 lemons)
1.5 kg/3½ lbs sugar

Stone the cherries, crack some of the stones and remove the kernels. Put the cherries, kernels and acid (or lemon juice) in a pan and simmer very gently until really soft, stirring from time to time to prevent them from sticking. Add the sugar, stir until dissolved and boil rapidly until setting point is reached. Pot and cover in the usual way.

As cherries are lacking in pectin, this jam will give only a light set.
Makes about 2.25 kg/5 lb.

CHERRY CAKE

METRIC/IMPERIAL
100 g/4 oz butter or margarine
225 g/8 oz self raising flour
pinch of salt
100 g/4 oz sugar
100–175 g/4–6 oz glacé cherries, washed, dried and
  quartered
1 egg, beaten
1 × 2.5 ml spoon/½ teaspoon vanilla essence
about 5 × 15 ml spoons/5 tablespoons milk

Grease and line the base of a loaf tin measuring 21 cm by 11 cm/8½ inch by 4½ inch across the top, 1.25 litres/2¼ pint capacity. Rub the fat into the flour and salt until the mixture resembles fine bread crumbs. Stir in the sugar and the cherries. Make a well in the centre, pour in the egg, essence and some of the milk and gradually work in the dry ingredients, adding more milk if necessary to give a dropping consistency. Put the mixture into the tin and level the top. Bake in a moderate oven (180°C/350°F, Gas Mark 4) for about 1¼ hours, until well risen, golden brown and firm to the touch. Turn out and cool on a wire rack.

CHERRY AND ORANGE CAKE

METRIC/IMPERIAL
120 ml/4 fl oz vegetable oil
2 eggs, beaten
2 × 15 ml spoons/2 tablespoons milk
150 g/5 oz caster sugar
275 g/10 oz self raising flour
pinch of salt
225 g/8 oz glacé cherries, quartered
grated rind of ½ orange

Lightly oil and line an 18 cm/7 in round cake tin. Whisk together the oil, eggs, milk and sugar. Sift flour and salt, add cherries and grated orange rind. Gradually beat flour mixture into liquid ingredients, using a wooden spoon. Turn mixture into the prepared tin and bake in a moderate oven (180°C/350°F, Gas Mark 4) for 1 to 1¼ hours. Turn out on a wire rack to cool.

CHERRY BRANDY

A liqueur distilled from fermented cherries and their crushed stones.

CHERRY PLUM (MYROBALAN)

A small, round plum, golden-yellow or red in colour, which is grown in various parts of Europe, including this country, and ripens in July and August. In France, it is known as the Mirabelle and a liqueur of the same name is made from the fruit.

Cherry plums are rather mealy and uninteresting when eaten raw, but are excellent stewed or made into tarts and are also good for preserving. The skins are tough, but they can be slipped off quite easily from the cooked plum.

CHERVIL

Chervil is one of the most common herbs in French cookery, always to be found in the mixture of 'fines herbes' for omelettes. It is a garden herb of the carrot family with feathery leaves which turn almost purple in the autumn; the whole plant has an aroma of aniseed. It is often used for salads (sometimes with tarragon) and in soups and stews.

The bulbous roots of a different plant also called chervil are eaten as a vegetable in France and Italy.

CHESHIRE CHEESE

Probably the oldest English cheese. Like Cheddar, it is a hard type, but rather more crumbly in texture. There are two varieties of Cheshire cheese, the red, which is artificially coloured with the dye annatto and the white. Occasionally, more by accident than by design, a red Cheshire cheese will turn blue, that is to say, will develop a system of blue veins which spread all over the cheese and give it a very fine, rich texture and flavour.

CHESTNUT (MARRON)

The edible fruit of the Spanish or Sweet Chestnut tree. When the fruit ripens the prickly green husks fall to the ground, releasing the reddish-brown nuts. These can be roasted in front of the fire (or in a special chestnut roaster) and eaten with a pinch of salt, or they can be stewed and served as a vegetable. Chestnuts may also be dried and ground into flour, or cooked, sieved and used to make a variety of cakes, sweets and savouries.

CHESTNUT SOUP

METRIC/IMPERIAL
0.5 kg/1 lb chestnuts
25 g/1 oz butter
1 small onion
900 ml/1 ½ pints good stock
salt
pepper
15 g/½ oz flour
150 ml/¼ pint milk
pinch of sugar
2–3 × 15 ml spoons/2–3 tablespoons cream

Make a slit in the chestnuts at one end with a sharp knife (this facilitates removing the skins), boil them for about 10 minutes in boiling salted water, then remove a few at a time and skin them. Melt the butter in a saucepan and sauté the chestnuts and the sliced onions for a few minutes. Add the stock, salt and pepper, cover and simmer until the chestnuts are quite tender about 1 hour then rub through a sieve. Blend the flour with the milk and add to the purée. Bring to the boil, stirring, and cook for 2 to 3 minutes then re-season if necessary and add the sugar. Lastly, stir in the cream.

CHEWING GUM

A type of sweetmeat usually made of chicle (the coagulated latex of the sapodilla tree), to which syrup, sugar and flavouring are added.

CHIANTI

The best-known Italian red wine, light and fairly dry. There is also a White Chianti of good quality.

A young cock or hen for table use, although the term is used more loosely to apply to a fowl of any age. The poultry is classified according to its age and size:—

1. POUSSIN
Very small chicken of 4 to 6 weeks old. 0.5 kg/1 lb to 0.75 kg/1½ lb in weight. One bird should be allowed for each serving.

2. DOUBLE POUSSIN
8 to 10 weeks old and 1.5 kg/3 lb to 1.75 kg/4 lb in weight.

3. SPRING CHICKEN (BROILER)
Young chicken up to three months old weighing 1 kg/2 lb to 1.5 kg/3 lb. It is particularly suitable for frying and grilling when jointed.

4. ROASTING CHICKEN
Up to 1 year old 1.5 kg/3 lb to 1.75 kg/4 lb in weight.

5. BOILING FOWL
An older bird of 15 to 18 months. It is usually a hen bred to lay eggs then killed once her useful laying life is completed. As the meat is tougher than other birds it should be braised or stewed.

6. COCKEREL (CAPON)
A male bird which has been neutered. It has been specially fattened for table use to give a lot of flesh and good flavour. 1.5 kg/3 lb to 2.25 kg/5 lb in weight.

Chicken, like all meat, is a good source of protein and B vitamins. It contains very little fat. For the choice and preparation of a fowl, see Poultry.

Frozen Chicken

There has been a rapid increase in the sale of frozen chicken, which are generally of the broiler type; in fact, the production of thousands of broilers and the freezing of them has become a large industry. The freezing does not affect the flavour, texture or food value in any way, although, because the broilers are so young when killed, they have very little natural flavouring; they should therefore be well seasoned or dressed in a well-flavoured sauce. Frozen chicken joints and drumsticks are also available.

To roast chicken: This method of cooking is suitable only for younger birds.

Prepare the chicken, stuff it if desired with veal forcemeat and truss neatly. Lay a rasher of fat bacon over the breast or put a few dabs of dripping over it. A lemon or a bunch of fresh tarragon can be placed inside the bird for extra flavour. Place the bird in a roasting tin containing dripping and cook it in a fairly hot oven (200°C/400°F, Gas Mark 6) allowing 15 minutes per 0.5 g/1 lb, and basting

occasionally; if necessary, cover the breast with greaseproof paper or aluminium foil to prevent over-browning. If the slow method is preferred, cook in a moderate oven (160°C/325°F, Gas Mark 3) for 20 to 22 minutes per 0.5 kg/1 lb. Colourless roasting bags are suitable for chicken as they allow the bird to brown without splashing the oven.

Serve with vegetables and accompanied by bacon rolls, forcemeat balls, small chipolata sausages, bread sauce, brown gravy and green salad.

An older bird should be steamed or boiled first for about 2 hours, to make it tender; it is best to do this the previous day, so that it gets cold before it is stuffed. Then roast for 30 to 45 minutes, to make it crisp and brown.

To boil chicken: Boiled chicken gives you the basis for salads or any other recipes calling for cooked chicken – lots of lovely broth, too. Simply wash and dry chicken, leave whole or cut in serving pieces. Put in a large pan with tight-fitting lid. Add about 600 ml/1 pint water, a small sliced onion, cut-up celery top, 2 bayleaves and 1 × 5 ml spoon/1 teaspoonful salt. Bring to the boil, reduce heat and simmer for about 1 hour. The heat should be turned down so the liquid barely ripples.

To fry chicken: Young and tender chickens can be fried raw, but older birds are best partly cooked fresh first. Prepare the bird in the usual way. Cut a small bird in halves or quarters and a larger one into neat joints. Season with salt and pepper and coat all over with flour. Then fry in hot fat, turning the pieces so that they brown on all sides, then reduce heat allow 15 minutes on each side. Serve with brown gravy.

Alternatively, season the joints, then dip them in egg, coat with soft breadcrumbs and fry in deep fat. Serve with fried parsley and accompanied by a cream sauce or gravy. Alternatively, pile the pieces in a nakpkin-lined basket and garnish as desired.

To grill chicken: Young and tender chickens are suitable for grilling. Split the bird down the back but without cutting through the skin of the breast and flatten the bird out, removing the breast bone and breaking the joints where necessary. Skewer the legs and wings closely to the body, keeping it flat. Brush over with olive oil or melted butter, sprinkle with salt and pepper and place on a greased grid, skin side up. Grill under moderate heat for 20 minutes then turn and grill on the underside for about a further 20 minutes, or longer if necessary, basting. Serve plain with a clear gravy made from the giblets and garnish with watercress.

An alternative method is to sprinkle the chicken with a mixture of finely chopped onion, parsley and breadcrumbs, after brushing it with oil or butter; when it is cooked, garnish it with watercress and serve with brown or tomato sauce.

CHICKEN MARENGO

METRIC/IMPERIAL
4 chicken joints
3–4 × 15 ml spoons/3–4 tablespoons oil
2 carrots, pared and sliced
1 stick celery, trimmed and chopped
1 onion, skinned and chopped
50 g/2 oz streaky bacon, rinded and chopped
3 × 5 ml spoons/3 tablespoons flour
300 ml/½ pint chicken stock
1 × 425 g/15 oz can tomatoes
2 × 15 ml spoons/2 tablespoons sherry
salt
pepper
bouquet garni
100 g/¼ lb mushrooms, sliced
chopped parsley

Fry the chicken joints in the oil for about 5 minutes, until golden brown, remove them from the pan and put into a casserole. Fry the vegetables and bacon in the oil for about 5 minutes until golden brown; remove them from the pan. Stir the flour into the remaining fat, cook for 2 to 3 minutes and gradually stir in the stock; bring to the boil and continue to stir until it thickens. Return the vegetables and bacon to the pan and add the tomatoes, sherry, salt and pepper. Pour this sauce over the chicken joints, add the bouquet garni and sliced mushrooms and cook in a moderate oven (180°C/350°F, Gas Mark 4) for 45 minutes to 1 hour, until the chicken joints are tender. Remove them to a warm serving dish. Strain the sauce from the casserole over them and sprinkle with chopped parsley.

CHICKEN MARYLAND

METRIC/IMPERIAL
1–1.5 kg/2–3 lb oven-ready chicken, jointed
3 × 15 ml spoons/3 tablespoons seasoned flour
1 egg, beaten
dry breadcrumbs
50 g/2 oz butter
1–2 × 15 ml spoons/1–2 tablespoons oil
4 bananas
sweet corn fritters
4 rashers of streaky bacon

Divide the chicken into fairly small portions, coat each joint fairly liberally with seasoned flour, dip in beaten egg and coat with breadcrumbs. Fry the chicken in the butter and oil in a large frying pan until lightly browned. Continue frying gently, turning the pieces once, for about 20 minutes, or until tender. Alternatively, fry them in deep fat for 5 to 10 minutes. The fat should be hot enough to brown 2.5 cm/1 inch cube of bread in 60 to 70 seconds. Serve the chicken with fried bananas, corn fritters and bacon rolls.

COQ AU VIN

METRIC/IMPERIAL
75 g/3 oz bacon, rinded and chopped
175 g/6 oz mushrooms, wiped and sliced
16 button onions, skinned
knob of butter
1 × 15 ml spoon/1 tablespoon oil
1 roasting chicken, jointed
4 × 15 ml spoons/4 tablespoons brandy
3 × 15 ml spoons/3 tablespoons flour
450 ml/¾ pint red wine
150 ml/¼ pint stock
1 × 15 ml spoon/1 tablespoon sugar
bouquet garni
pinch of nutmeg
salt
pepper

Fry the bacon, mushrooms and onions in the butter and oil for about 3–4 minutes, until lightly browned; remove from the pan. Fry the chicken for 8 to 10 minutes, until golden brown and sealed all over. Pour brandy over the chicken, remove the pan from the heat and 'flame' it by igniting the liquid in the saucepan with a match. Remove the chicken when the flames have died down and place it in a casserole. Stir the flour into the fat remaining in the pan and cook for 2 to 3 minutes. Stir in the wine and stock gradually, bring to the boil and continue to stir until the mixture thickens; add sugar, herbs and seasonings. Add the browned vegetables to the casserole and pour the sauce over the chicken. Cover and cook in a moderate oven (180°C/350°F, Gas mark 4) for 45 minutes to 1 hour, until tender. Before serving, remove the bouquet garni.

CHICKEN LIVER PILAU

METRIC/IMPERIAL
225 g/8 oz chicken livers, cut in strips
50 g/2 oz butter
2 onions, skinned and finely chopped
25 g/1 oz shelled peanuts or almonds
175–225 g/6–8 oz long grain rice
salt
pepper
pinch of mixed spice
50 g/2 oz currants
2 tomatoes, skinned and chopped
750 ml/1¼ pints chicken or meat stock, boiling
little chopped parsley

Fry the livers lightly in the butter for 2 to 3 minutes and remove it from the fat with a slotted spoon. Fry the onions for 5 minutes in the same fat until soft but not brown. Add the nuts and rice and fry for a further 5 minutes, stirring all the time. Add the seasoning, spice, currants, tomatoes and stock, stir well, cover with a tightly fitting lid and simmer for about 15 minutes until all the liquid has been absorbed. Stir in the livers and parsley, cover again and before serving leave for 15 minutes in warm place (but without further cooking).

CHICKEN BRICK

An earthenware cooking utensil shaped to take a whole chicken. It is in two parts and unglazed giving a cooking result comparable to that done in clay. The chicken is cooked in the brick at a high temperature without fat or liquid. The brick should be soaked in cold water for 10 minutes before use.

CHICKEN LIVER

The livers are often served as a separate dish, frequently as an after-dinner savoury. They are also used to make simple pâtés.

CHICKEN LIVERS ON TOAST

METRIC/IMPERIAL
75–100 g/3–4 oz chicken livers
seasoned flour
butter for frying
4 rounds of bread about 5 cm/2 inch in diameter
½ glass of sherry or Madeira
50 g/2 oz sliced mushrooms, optional

Wash and dry the livers, cut them in small pieces and coat with the seasoned flour. Melt some butter in a frying pan and fry the bread for 2 to 3 minutes, until golden; remove it from the pan. Add more butter, put in the prepared livers and stir them over the heat until browned. Add the sherry or Madeira mix well and cook slowly for 10 to 15 minutes. Serve the livers on the croûtes of fried bread. If the mushrooms are used, cook them with the livers.

CHICORY

A group of plants cultivated for their leaves, the two principal types being wild chicory and garden chicory. The wild plant, which grows in meadowlands, is eaten only in salads; the bitter-flavoured leaves are cut into strips and eaten raw.

Garden chicory (also known as Belgian endive), has fleshy, tender leaves. It may be eaten raw in salads or braised and served with butter.

The large roots of one type of chicory are roasted, ground and used to blend with coffee, to which they impart a bitter flavour.

Note: There is some confusion between the use of the names chicory and endive. In this country they are used as shown in separate entries, but in France and the U.S.A. what we know as chicory is called endive or Belgian endive, while our endive is called chicory in the States and chicoree in France.

CHILDREN'S MEALS

The feeding of children has to cover several periods of transition, stretching from infancy to adolescence, but the emphasis throughout must lie on giving an ample supply of protein and the protective foods – that is, milk, meat, fish, eggs, cheese, fruit and vegetables, bread and butter.

Infants

During the first few months a baby has milk only. Breast feeding is now considered the best way to feed the baby during this early and important stage of development. It ensures that the baby is receiving the correct quantity of each nutrient and provides the right conditions for the digestive system to give maximum protection against infection. Antibodies from the Mother are passed to the baby through the milk. Breast milk is made up of similar constituents to cow's milk but contains less protein and more sugar. Vitamin drops should be given as a supplement from the age of 4 weeks until mixed feeding starts.

If, for any reason, it is not possible to breast feed, or there is a strong reaction against it, modified cows' milk preparations provide an excellent alternative. These are modified to reduce protein content and make them as near to breast milk as possible. They are also fortified with vitamins, making vitamin supplements unnecessary. When bottle feeding it is important to ensure that the bottles and teats are carefully sterilized.

3 to 4 months: Additions may be made to the diet such as cereal, sieved vegetables or fruits.

5 months: Strained meat, fish and lightly cooked eggs can be introduced into the diet. Rusks, toast, raw apple and carrot pieces can be given at this stage to help the baby with teething problems and to teach the process of chewing.

6 to 8 months: Most foods can be given if made to a soft manageable consistency. It is important to give the baby plenty of finger foods to encourage self feeding and chewing.

New foods should be introduced gradually so that by 1 year the baby will be enjoying a mixed diet similar to that of an adult with the exclusion of rich, spicy or greasy foods.

The Older Child

Children vary enormously in the amount of food they need. There is no need to worry if one child eats less than another as long as he is healthy.

Provide three good meals a day and a mid-morning drink. The meals should be based on the protein foods, vegetables and sometimes fruit. Bread and potatoes should be used as 'fillers', as they supply protein, vitamins and minerals as well as energy. Iron to maintain healthy condition of the blood, and calcium for the development of the teeth and bones are two important minerals. Adolescent girls should have food rich in iron to minimise the risk of anaemia.

It is a mistake to allow children to eat too many of the less nutritious foods. Obesity in children must be avoided as this can lead to trouble in later life, such as high blood pressure and varicose veins.

CHILLI

The dried, small red pod of a type of Capsicum. Chillis are very hot in flavour and are used in pickles, sauces, chutneys and for flavouring vinegar. Cayenne pepper is produced from chillis.

CHILLI CON CARNE

METRIC/IMPERIAL
0.75 kg/1 ½ lb raw minced beef
1 × 15 ml spoon/1 tablespoon fat or oil
1 large onion, skinned and chopped
1 green pepper, seeded and chopped
1 × 425 g/15 oz can tomatoes
salt
pepper
1 × 15 ml spoon/1 tablespoon chilli powder
1 × 15 ml spoon/1 tablespoon vinegar
1 × 5 ml spoon/1 teaspoon sugar
2 × 15 ml spoons/2 tablespoons tomato purée
1 × 425 g/15 oz can kidney beans

Fry the beef in the fat or oil until lightly browned, then add the onion and pepper and fry for five minutes, until soft. Stir in the tomatoes, add the seasoning and chilli powder blended with the vinegar, sugar and tomato paste. Cover and simmer for 2 to 2½ hours. Add the drained kidney beans ten minutes before the cooking time is completed.

CHINE BONE

A joint of meat, usually beef, consisting of part of the backbone of an animal, and some of the surrounding flesh. It is an uneconomical joint, owing to the quantity of bone, and is difficult to carve; it is best jointed and stewed or braised with vegetables.

CHINING

To sever the rib bones from the backbone by sawing through the ribs close to the spine. Joints such as loin or neck of lamb, mutton, veal, pork are best chined, instead of merely being chopped through the backbone, as this makes them easier to carve into convenient sized chops or cutlets.

CHINESE OR JAPANESE ARTICHOKE

(See Artichoke entry.)

CHINESE CABBAGE (CELERY CABBAGE)

This type of cabbage looks like a very long cos lettuce. It may be eaten raw or cooked.

CHINESE GOOSEBERRY

A delicious fruit with a brownish hairy skin and green flesh; also called Carambole.

CHIPOLATA

A very small sausage, made of ordinary sausage-meat filled into a narrow casing. Chipolatas are used to garnish meat dishes and to serve with roast fowl; they are also served on sticks as cocktail savouries. They may be baked, fried or grilled.

CHIPPED POTATOES ('CHIPS')

(See Potato entry.)

CHITTERLINGS

These are the intestines of ox, calf and pig; the latter being probably the most popular. They are not much eaten nowadays except in country districts, but are used in manufactured meat products. The chitterlings are cleaned and usually boiled before being sold and if fresh will be free of any unpleasant smell. If the chitterlings have not been boiled, wash them very thoroughly and simmer gently for about 2 to 3 hours, until tender.

CHIVE

A very small variety of onion; the leaves grow as slender hollow like needles and have a delicate onion flavour. Minced or chopped, chives are excellent for flavouring salads, omelettes, sauces, vegetables and as a garnish for cold savoury dishes and for soups. Use very fresh.

CHOCOLATE

A product of the cocoa bean (see cocoa entry), the three parts of which (nibs, germ and shells) are separated from each other and treated in various ways to give different products.

Types of Chocolate
POWDERED OR DRINKING CHOCOLATE
Cocoa nibs and sugar ground together and mixed with flavourings. Drinking chocolate was first manufactured in this country as long ago as 1728, over a century before the introduction of eating chocolate.

EATING CHOCOLATE
This is produced by adding sugar and cocoa butter

89

to cocoa-cake. The extra cocoa butter is needed to increase the fat content to approximately 32 per cent. – without this, chocolate does not mould satisfactorily. Flavourings such as vanilla, almond, cinnamon, cloves and cardamom are added in varying proportions.

Plain chocolate has some sugar added.

Bitter or unsweetened chocolate is mostly used commercially although a bitter dessert chocolate can be bought. Milk chocolate is sweetened, and powdered or condensed milk is also added.

Chocolate making is a highly skilled process, the quality and price varying according to manufacture.

Chocolate is useful nutritionally as a concentrated form of energy. It is thus of value (e.g., for expeditions) as a compact energy food, easy to carry and to eat.

COUVERTURE CHOCOLATE
A special type of good quality eating chocolate used for coating sweetmeats. It is made from selected cocoa beans, mixed with the finest sugar and cocoa butter; the exact proportions depend on the purpose for which the couverture is required and the type of centre to be covered. Couverture chocolate retains a high gloss after melting and cooling and is very smooth to eat. A type of couverture can be bought for home use, for cooking and icing purposes, but it is not of the same high quality as that supplied to sweet manufacturers.

Use of Chocolate in Cooking
Many so-called chocolate dishes are actually made with cocoa and some with sweetened drinking chocolate powder. However, slab cooking chocolate is used for certain things, especially icings, cold sweet dishes and home-made sweets; if necessary, it may be replaced by plain eating chocolate.

Cocoa, when used in a cake, etc., is usually sieved with the dry ingredients. Cooking chocolate is grated and melted down before being added to other ingredients. Eating chocolate may be grated or flaked and used as a decoration to cold sweets, but is not normally melted down.

CHOC-AU-RHUM

METRIC/IMPERIAL
175 g/6 oz plain chocolate
3 large eggs, separated
1 × 15 ml spoon/1 tablespoon rum
150 ml/¼ pint carton double cream, whipped
grated chocolate or finely chopped nuts

Melt the chocolate in a bowl over a pan of hot water. Beat the yolks into the melted chocolate and add the rum. Whisk the whites until stiff and carefully fold into the chocolate mixture. Chill and serve in small sundae glasses, topped with whipped cream and grated chocolate or chopped nuts.

CHOCOLATE CAKE

METRIC/IMPERIAL
75 g/3 oz self raising flour
2 × 15 ml spoons/2 tablespoons ground rice
100 g/4 oz plain chocolate, grated
100 g/4 oz butter or margarine
75 g/3 oz caster sugar
1–2 × 5 ml spoons/1–2 teaspoons vanilla essence
2 eggs, beaten
chocolate butter icing
chocolate glacé icing
crystallized violets

Grease and line a 15 cm/6 inch cake tin. Mix the flour and ground rice. Put the grated chocolate into a small basin, place over a saucepan of hot water and heat gently to melt the chocolate. Cream the fat, sugar and essence until pale and fluffy. Add the melted chocolate (which should be only just warm) to the creamed mixture and mix lightly together. Beat in the egg a little at a time. Fold in the flour, put into the tin and bake in a moderate oven (180°C/350°F, Gas Mark 4) for 1 to 1¼ hours. When cold, split in half and fill with butter icing. Ice with glacé icing and decorate with violets. Alternatively, fill and decorate with coffee butter icing and coarsely grated chocolate.

CHOCOLATE SAUCE

METRIC/IMPERIAL
1 × 15 ml spoon/1 tablespoon cornflour
1 × 15 ml spoon/1 tablespoon cocoa powder
2 × 15 ml spoons/2 tablespoons sugar
300 ml/½ pint milk
knob of butter

Blend the cornflour, cocoa and sugar with enough of the measured milk to give a thin cream. Heat the remaining milk with the butter until boiling and pour on to the blended mixture, stirring all the time to prevent lumps forming. Return the mixture to the pan and bring to the boil, stirring until it thickens; cook for a further 1 to 2 minutes. Serve with steamed or baked sponge puddings.

RICH CHOCOLATE SAUCE

METRIC/IMPERIAL
175 g/6 oz plain chocolate
large knob of butter
3 × 15 ml spoons/3 tablespoons milk
3 × 15 ml spoons/3 tablespoons golden syrup
1 × 15 ml spoon/1 tablespoon coffee essence

Put the broken up chocolate in a basin over a pan of hot water. Add the rest of the ingredients and heat gently until melted and warm. Beat well.

CHOCOLATE CRUMB PUDDING

METRIC/IMPERIAL
50 g/2 oz chocolate
75 g/3 oz butter or margarine
75 g/3 oz caster sugar
1 egg, separated
1 × 2.5–5 ml spoon/½–1 teaspoon vanilla essence
100 g/4 oz fresh white breadcrumbs
50 g/2 oz self raising flour
4–5 × 15 ml spoons/4–5 tablespoons milk

Half-fill a steamer or large saucepan with water and put on to boil. Grease a 900 ml/1½ pint pudding basin. Melt the chocolate in a basin over hot water. Cream the fat and sugar until pale and fluffy and beat in the chocolate, egg yolk and vanilla essence. Mix the breadcrumbs and flour and fold half into the creamed mixture, with 2 × 5 ml spoons/2 teaspoons milk. Fold in the remaining crumbs and flour and sufficient milk to give a fairly soft dropping consistency. Whisk the egg white until it stands in stiff peaks when the bowl is inverted and fold into the mixture. Turn it into the prepared basin, cover with greased greaseproof paper or foil and secure with string. Steam for 1½ to 2 hours over rapidly boiling water. Turn out and serve with hot chocolate sauce poured over the pudding or served separately.

CHOCOLATES

For chocolate-dipping, special couverture chocolate is required; even with this it is not possible for the amateur to attain results like those produced by the commercial firms. However, some very delicious sweets can be produced at home, using toffee, fudge, marzipan, fondant, nuts and dried fruit, etc., for the centres. (See chocolate recipes under Biscuits, Butter and Glacé Icings, Canary Pudding, Soufflé, Sweets, entries.)

CHOP

A slice of meat 2.5 cm/1 inch to 3.5 cm/1½ inches thick, usually mutton, lamb, pork or veal. A chop generally includes, a rib, but may also be cut from the chump or tail end of the loin, and is then known as a chump chop. Neck chops are usually referred to as cutlets.

To fry chops: When the meat is really tender, this is a very satisfactory method. Fry slowly in a little fat (dripping or lard), turning frequently, until they are well cooked 10 to 15 minutes. Alternatively, the chops may be first egg-and-breadcrumbed and then fried. Pork chops should be allowed at least 20 to 25 minutes.

To grill chops: Remove the skin and trim off some of the fat from the chops, wipe them with a damp cloth, then brush over with salad oil or butter.

Heat and grease the grill grid and place the chops in position under a pre-heated glowing red gas or electric grill. Cook on one side for about 2 to 3 minutes, until the outside is browned, then turn and cook on the other side. Continue to cook, turning frequently, until the meat is just cooked through 8 to 10 minutes. Use tongs or two spoons for turning, to prevent piercing the meat. Place the chops on a hot dish, and garnish lamb chops with grilled tomatoes, mushrooms or green pepper rings; for pork chops use grilled apple or pineapple rings. Serve with vegetables and accompanied by a well flavoured sauce or gravy.

CHOP SUEY

The name literally means bits and pieces and the dish is the Chinese way of dealing with leftovers in a type of stew, it originated in the United States.

Chop Suey can be made up of thin strips of raw chicken, pork or beef, cooked with onions in a little oil, with bean sprouts, mushrooms and other vegetables; chicken stock, soy sauce, sugar and salt are added to taste and the whole is thickened, if necessary, with cornflour. It should be served in a shallow bowl with a flat omelette on top. This omelette is intended as a cover to keep the food hot (you lift back this 'lid', help yourself to the chop suey, then pull the 'lid' forward again). It is usually served with rice or noodles.

CHOPPING

To divide food into very small pieces. The ingredient is placed on a chopping board and a very sharp knife is used with a quick up-and-down action.

CHOUX PASTRY

A paste prepared by beating eggs into a thick panada of flour, fat and liquid. The eggs cause the pastry to swell in cooking. It is used chiefly for éclairs and cream buns, rich fancy cakes and savoury or sweet fritters. For basic recipe, see Pastry entry. (See also Cream Bun, Eclair and Profiterole entries.)

CHOW-CHOW
A Chinese preserve of ginger and orange peel and other fruits in syrup. Also a mixed vegetable pickle, containing mustard and spices.

CHOWDER

A type of dish which originated in France, but is now associated with New England and Newfoundland. It is a thick soup or stew made of shellfish (especially clams) or other fish, with pork or bacon.

FISH CHOWDER

METRIC/IMPERIAL
1 onion, skinned and sliced
2 rashers of bacon, rinded and chopped
knob of butter
3 potatoes, peeled and sliced
0.5 kg/1 lb fresh haddock, skinned and cubed
1 × 425 g/15 oz can tomatoes
600 ml/1 pint fish stock
salt
pepper
1 bayleaf
2 cloves
chopped parsley to garnish

Lightly fry the onion and bacon in the butter for about 5 minutes, until soft but not coloured. Add the potatoes and the fish. Sieve the tomatoes with their juice, add them to the fish stock, combine with the fish mixture and add seasoning and flavourings. Cover and simmer for 30 minutes, until all the fish is soft but still in shape. Remove the bayleaf and cloves and sprinkle with parsley before serving.

CHRISTMAS CATERING

In Great Britain custom varies a little in different districts, but most households hold a family re-union at which the traditional fare is eaten. A typical menu for Christmas dinner is given here. Roast beef, pork, goose or chicken may be served instead of the turkey. Recipes for Christmas Pudding and Cake are given also. (See Mincemeat, Mince Pies, Turkey, entries.)

Roast Turkey
Gravy, bread sauce, stuffing
Brussels sprouts   Roast potatoes
Christmas pudding
Rum butter or Hard sauce
Mince pies
Coffee

Christmas Cookery Time-table

THE DAY BEFORE CHRISTMAS EVE
Prepare breadcrumbs for the stuffing and bread sauce.

CHRISTMAS EVE
1. Make stock from the turkey giblets
2. Make rum butter and leave it in a cool place or refrigerator
3. Stuff the bird
4. Make the mince pies
5. Make the soup (if any served)
6. Prepare the bacon rolls, if required

CHRISTMAS DAY
Programme based on a 5.5 kg/12 lb turkey cooked by the slow roasting method (i.e., roasting in a warm oven (160°C/325°F, Gas Mark 3) and allowing 20 minutes per 0.5 kg/1 lb plus 30 minutes).
6 hours before the meal: Put the pudding on to steam. Make the bread sauce.
5½ hours before the meal: Put the bird in preheated oven.
2 hours before the meal: Lay the table, prepare wines.
1½ hours before the meal: Put potatoes into oven to roast.
During last hour before meal:
1. Remove trussing strings from turkey and return it to warm oven on dish, with potatoes.
2. Make gravy.
3. Put on sprouts (or other vegetable) to cook.
4. Grill bacon rolls.
5. Heat soup (if any served).
6. Heat bread sauce and put into sauce-boat.
7. Garnish bird.
8. Turn out pudding.

CHRISTMAS PUDDING

METRIC/IMPERIAL
350 g/12 oz fresh white breadcrumbs
350 g/12 oz plain flour
1 × 5 ml spoon/1 teaspoon salt
1 × 2.5 ml spoon/½ teaspoon ground mace
1 × 2.5 ml spoon/½ teaspoon ground ginger
1 × 2.5 ml spoon/½ teaspoon ground nutmeg
1 × 2.5 ml spoon/½ teaspoon ground cinnamon
350 g/12 oz shredded suet
225 g/8 oz caster sugar
225 g/8 oz soft brown sugar
225 g/8 oz mixed candied peel, chopped very finely
350 g/12 oz currants
225 g/8 oz sultanas
550 g/1 lb 4 oz stoned raisins
175 g/6 oz almonds, blanched and chopped
225 g/8 oz apples, peeled and chopped
grated rind and juice of 1 lemon
grated rind and juice of 1 orange
4 × 15 ml spoons/4 tablespoons brandy
3 large eggs, beaten
about 150 ml/¼ pint milk

Mix together in a large mixing bowl all the dry ingredients, the almonds, apples and orange and lemon rind. Mix the lemon and orange juice and the brandy with the beaten eggs and add to the dry ingredients, with enough milk to give a soft dropping consistency.

Cover the mixture lightly and leave overnight. Half-fill 3 saucepans with water and put them on to boil. Grease 3 pudding basins, 600 ml/1 pint, 900 ml/1½ pints and 1.2 litres/2 pint, capacities. Stir the mixture before turning it into the prepared basins, cover with greased greaseproof paper and with a clean dry cloth or foil.

Steam over rapidly boiling water as follows:
600 ml/1 pint pudding   5 hours

900 ml/1½ pint pudding	7 hours
1.2 litres/2 pint pudding	9 hours

When the puddings are cooked, remove them from the pans and allow to cool. Remove foil or cloth but leave the paper in position. Recover with a fresh cloth or foil and store in a cool place.

On the day of serving steam the pudding as follows:

600 ml/1 pint pudding	2 hours
900 ml/1½ pint pudding	3 hours
1.2 litre/2 pint pudding	3 hours

Turn out on to a hot dish and serve with brandy or rum butter or a sweet white sauce flavoured with rum.

Note: Do not put the aluminium foil directly on to the pudding, as the fruit eats into it after some weeks; this does not harm the pudding, but the foil ceases to be watertight.

CHRISTMAS CAKE

METRIC/IMPERIAL
225 g/8 oz currants
225 g/8 oz sultanas
225 g/8 oz stoned raisins, chopped
100 g/4 oz mixed chopped peel
100 g/4 oz glacé cherries, halved
50 g/2 oz nibbed almonds
225 g/8 oz plain flour
pinch of salt
1 × 2.5 ml spoon/½ teaspoon ground mace
1 × 2.5 ml spoon/½ teaspoon ground cinnamon
225 g/8 oz butter
225 g/8 oz soft brown sugar
grated rind of 1 lemon
4 large eggs, beaten
2 × 15 ml spoons/2 tablespoons brandy

Line a 20 cm/8 inch cake tin, using two thicknesses of greaseproof paper. Tie a double band of brown paper round the outside. Clean the fruit if necessary. Mix the prepared currants, sultanas, raisins, peel, cherries and nuts. Sift the flour, salt and spices. Cream the butter, sugar and lemon rind until pale and fluffy. Add the eggs a little at a time, beating well after each addition. Fold in half the flour, using a metal spoon, then fold in the rest and add the brandy. Lastly fold in the fruit. Put into the tin. Spread the mixture evenly, making sure there are no air pockets and make a dip in the centre. Stand the tin on a layer of newspaper or brown paper in the oven and bake in a cool oven (150°C/300°F, Gas Mark 2) for about 3¾ hours. To avoid over-browning the top, cover it with several thicknesses of greaseproof paper after 1½ hours. When the cake is cooked, leave it to cool in the tin and then turn it out on to a wire rack.

To store, wrap it in several layers of greaseproof paper and put it in an airtight tin. If a large enough tin is not available, cover the wrapped cake entirely with aluminium foil. If you like, you can prick the cake top all over with a fine skewer and slowly pour 2–3 × 15 ml spoons/2–3 tablespoons brandy over it before storing.

CHUB

A fresh-water fish resembling carp, rather tasteless in flavour, which when fully grown may weigh 1.7 kg/4 lb to 3.5 kg/8 lb. It is seldom used in cookery.

CHUPATTY

(See Chapatti entry.)

CHUTNEY

A pickle or relish of Indian origin. Chutneys vary in type, but are usually composed of fruits (especially mangoes), vegetables, spices, acids and sugar. Tomatoes, apples, gooseberries, raisins, plums and marrow are frequently used for home-made chutneys.

Chutney is served with cold meat, cheese, etc., and with curry and is sometimes mixed with butter to make a savoury accompaniment to fish, etc., or a sandwich filling.

A good chutney should be smooth to the palate, with a mellow flavour. The amount of salt and other seasonings can, of course, be adjusted as required to suit individual tastes. Three points to remember are:

1. Slice or mince the ingredients finely.
2. Allow long, slow cooking. This softens the fruit and blends the flavours. Cooking should be continued until the chutney is of a jam-like consistency.
3. Put into hot jars and use the correct type of covers – (See Pickling entry.)

APPLE CHUTNEY

METRIC/IMPERIAL
1.5 kg/3 lb cooking apples, peeled, cored and diced
1.5 kg/3 lb onions, skinned and chopped
0.5 kg/1 lb sultanas or stoned raisins
2 lemons
700 g/1½ lb demerara sugar
600 ml/1 pint malt vinegar

This is a light chutney, fruity but not spiced, which is good with pork and poultry. Put the apples, onions and sultanas or raisins in a pan. Grate the lemon rind, strain the juice and add both to the pan, with the sugar and vinegar. Bring to the boil, reduce the heat and simmer until the mixture is of a thick consistency, with no excess liquid. Pot and cover. *Makes about 1.75 kg/4 lb.*

GREEN TOMATO CHUTNEY

METRIC/IMPERIAL
0.5 kg/1 lb apples, peeled and cored
225 g/ ½ lb onions, skinned
1.5 kg/3 lb green tomatoes, sliced thinly
225 g/8 oz sultanas
225 g/8 oz demerara sugar
2 × 5 ml spoons/2 teaspoons salt
450 ml/¾ pint malt vinegar
4 small pieces dried whole root ginger
1 × 2.5 ml spoon/ ½ teaspoon cayenne pepper
1 × 5 ml spoon/1 teaspoon dry mustard

A lightly spiced, smooth textured chutney. Mince the apples and onions and put in a pan with the rest of the ingredients. Bring to the boil, reduce the heat and simmer until the ingredients are tender and reduced to a thick consistency, with no excess liquid. Remove the ginger, pot and cover. *Makes about 1.5 kg/3 lb.*

PEAR CHUTNEY

METRIC/IMPERIAL
1.5 kg/3 lb pears, peeled, cored and sliced
0.5 kg/1 lb onions, skinned and chopped
0.5 kg/1 lb green tomatoes, wiped and sliced
225 g/8 oz stoned raisins, chopped
225 g/8 oz celery, finely chopped
675 g/1 ½ lb demerara sugar
a pinch of cayenne pepper
a pinch of ground ginger
2 × 5 ml spoons/2 teaspoons salt
5 peppercorns, in a muslin bag
1 litre/1 ¾ pints malt vinegar

A very dark, smooth, sweet and spicy chutney that is slightly hot.
  Put all the fruit and vegetable ingredients into a pan, with no added liquid, and simmer gently until tender. Add the remaining ingredients and simmer until of a thick consistency, with no excess liquid. Remove the bag of peppercorns, pot and cover. *Makes about 1.75 kg/4 lb.*

MARROW CHUTNEY

METRIC/IMPERIAL
1.5 kg/3 lb marrow, peeled and seeded
salt
225 g/8 oz shallots, skinned and sliced
225 g/8 oz apples, peeled, cored and sliced
12 peppercorns
2 cm/¾ in piece dried whole root ginger
225 g/8 oz sultanas
225 g/8 oz demerara sugar
900 ml/1 ½ pints malt vinegar

Cut the marrow into small pieces, place in a bowl and sprinkle liberally with salt; cover and leave for 12 hours. Rinse and drain, then place in a pan with the shallots and apples. Tie the peppercorns and ginger in muslin and put in the pan with the sultanas, sugar and vinegar. Bring to the boil, reduce the heat and simmer till the consistency is thick, with no excess liquid. Pot and cover. *Makes about 1.75 kg/4 lb.*

MAJOR MARSHALL'S CHUTNEY

METRIC/IMPERIAL
0.75 kg/1 ½ lb freestone plums
1.5 × 15 ml spoons/1 ½ tablespoons pickling spice
2 cloves garlic, skinned and crushed
350 g/12 oz onions, skinned and sliced
1 kg/2 lb tomatoes, skinned and sliced
900 ml/1 ½ pints malt vinegar
1 kg/2 lb cooking apples, peeled, cored and chopped
225 g/8 oz dried apricots, chopped
225 g/8 oz golden syrup
225 g/8 oz demerara sugar
4 × 5 ml spoons/4 teaspoons salt

Wipe the plums, halve and discard the stones. Tie the pickling spice in a muslin bag. Put the plums and all the other ingredients in a large pan, bring to the boil, reduce the heat and simmer uncovered until the ingredients are soft and well reduced. Remove the muslin bag. Pot and cover. *Makes about 2.25 kg/5 lb.*

RHUBARB AND ORANGE CHUTNEY

METRIC/IMPERIAL
2 oranges
1 kg/2¼ lb prepared rhubarb
3 onions, skinned and chopped
900 ml/1 ½ pints malt vinegar
900 g/2 lb demerara sugar
450 g/1 lb raisins
1 × 15 ml spoon/1 tablespoon mustard seed
1 × 15 ml spoon/1 tablespoon peppercorns
1 × 5 ml spoon/1 teaspoon allspice

Squeeze the juice from the oranges and finely shred the peel. Place in a large preserving pan with the rhubarb, onions, vinegar, sugar and raisins. Tie the spices in a piece of muslin and add to the ingredients in the pan. Bring to the boil and simmer until thick and pulpy, about 1 ½ hours. Remove the muslin bag, pot and cover. *Makes about 3.5 kg/8 lb.*

CIDER (OR CYDER)

A bright, honey-coloured liquid, the fermented juice of the apple. Cider usually contains 3 to 8 per cent. of alcohol, though this varies. Commercially manufactured cider is made by crushing special cider apples and squeezing out the juice; this is poured into casks, where it is left to ferment and to clear.

APPLE CIDER CUP

METRIC/IMPERIAL
2 dessert apples
juice and thinly pared rind of 1 lemon
8 cloves
4 × 15 ml spoons/4 tablespoons sugar syrup
1 litre/2 pints dry cider
½ syphon soda water

Peel, core and slice the apples and put into a bowl with the lemon juice and rind and the cloves. Heat the sugar syrup with about 300 ml/ ½ pint of the cider; when boiling, pour over the ingredients in the bowl and leave to cool. When cold, add the rest of the cider and the soda water.

HOT SPICED CIDER

METRIC/IMPERIAL
1 litre/ ¾ pint cider
100 g/4 oz sugar
12 whole cloves
4 sticks cinnamon about 5 cm/2 in long
8 whole allspice

Put all the ingredients in a saucepan and heat until the sugar has dissolved. Strain to serve.

CINNAMON

The bark of a tropical tree of the laurel family, used for flavouring sweet dishes, cakes, fruit, sweet pickles and mulled wine. The finest quality is a pale yellowish-buff colour and has an aromatic flavour; it is sold both in scrolls (or quills) and in powder form. It should not be confused with cassia, which although similar, is inferior in flavour.

CITRIC ACID

An acid obtained from citrus fruits, particularly lemons. The crystals are clear and colourless, with a pleasant, rather sour taste.

Commercially prepared citric acid is used to give a lemon flavour to drinks, fruit dishes, home-made wines, etc.; it is also used to ensure a good set in jams and jellies, especially with fruits such as pears and strawberries which have a low acid content.

CITRON

A fruit which resembles the lemon, but is rather longer and larger. The rind is used in crystallized form in cookery, being chopped and added to cakes, puddings and biscuits: a slice of citron peel is the traditional decoration on Madeira cake. The peel is usually bought ready prepared, but it can be made quite successfully at home (See the recipe in the Candied Fruit and Peel entry.)

CLAM

A bivalvular shellfish. There are many varieties, varying in size and shape, and nearly all are edible. The commonest forms are those caught on the North Atlantic coasts of America – the hard or round clam and the long or soft clam. Clams are available in Great Britain. They are best eaten in a casserole made with alternate layers of clams, sliced potatoes, chopped onion and chopped bacon. In the U.S. they are eaten in various ways, especially in chowder and clam bake. They can also be eaten raw like oysters.

CLARET

In England the name given to the red wine from the Bordeaux district of France. The term may also be used for other red wines, but in this case the country of origin should be given, e.g., Australian Claret.

Claret jelly, made with half claret and half water, flavoured with lemon and suitably coloured, makes a good party sweet. (See Bordeaux Wines entry.)

CLARET CUP

METRIC/IMPERIAL
150 ml/¼ pint sugar syrup
juice and thinly pared rind of 1 lemon and 2 oranges
2 bottles claret
4 'splits' tonic water
few thin slices of cucumber
sprigs of borage, if available

Put the syrup and the lemon and orange rind in a saucepan and simmer together for about 10 minutes. Cool and add the strained juice of the lemon and oranges, together with the claret; chill. Just before serving, add the tonic water, cucumber and borage (if used).

CLARIFYING

To clear or purify. The term is used mainly to denote the freeing of fat from water, meat juices, salt, etc., so that it may be used for frying, pastry-making and so on. The process of cleaning jellies and consommés is also sometimes called clarifying. (See Fats entry.)

CLEMENTINE

(See Tangerine entry.)

CLOVE

The dried unopened flower-bud of an evergreen shrub which grows in the Moluccas and in other countries with a similar hot, moist climate. When

95

freshly gathered, the flower buds are reddish, but they become dark brown – almost black – when dried; they then resemble a small tin tack in appearance. Cloves contain 16 to 20 per cent. of a volatile oil, which is of medicinal value and has a characteristic hot, spicy, aromatic taste and smell. Whole cloves are used in cookery for flavouring both sweet and savoury dishes and their flavour blends particularly well with that of apples. Ground cloves are used in some cakes and biscuits. For some purposes, as in bread sauce, the flavour of the cloves is obtained by infusion.

COBBLER

A sweetened cooling drink, usually made of a mixture of fruit and wine or liqueur, with ice. The name also applies to meat or fruit dishes which have a topping of scone rounds. The scones can be flavoured with herbs, cheese, spices or dried fruits to add addition of flavour or to complement the basis of the dish.

SHERRY COBBLER

METRIC/IMPERIAL
Ice
150 ml/¼ pint sherry
1 × 5 ml spoon/1 teaspoon sugar
2 × 5 ml spoons/2 teaspoons orange juice
Orange sections and a few strawberries

Put a few pieces of ice in a tumbler, add the sherry, sugar and orange juice and stir well. Put the fruit on top as decoration and serve with a drinking straw.

COBNUT

A type of hazel nut. Kentish cobs are considered the best, being very large and well-flavoured. The nuts are gathered when fully ripe, before they drop from the husks; they are then dried in the sun and should be stored in a cool, dry, airy place. Cobnuts are good as a dessert, but are not greatly used for cookery purposes.

COBURG CAKES

Small cakes containing syrup and usually flavoured with spices.

COCHINEAL

A red colouring matter obtained from a small beetle, originating in Mexico, which is dried and ground. Cochineal is used to give various shades of pink and red to sweetmeats, cakes, buns, biscuits, cold sweets and so on and also to improve the colour of jams and bottled fruits.

COCK-A-LEEKIE SOUP

A popular Scotch soup made from a fowl boiled with leeks.

METRIC/IMPERIAL
a boiling fowl
1 kg/2 lb neck of mutton or knuckle of veal
3.5 litres/6 pints cold water
salt
pepper
2 cloves
4 leeks
25 g/1 oz rice

Wash the fowl well and put it with the meat into a saucepan, then add the water and seasonings. When boiling, add the cut-up leeks and simmer for 1¼ hours. Wash the rice, sprinkle it into the soup, add additional seasoning if necessary and continue to simmer for 45 minutes. The chicken and meat can be served separately, with a parsley sauce made with a little of the broth, or with the soup.

COCKLE

A small bivalvular shellfish found in large numbers round the coasts of Britain.

Cockles must be washed to free them of sand, then soaked in slightly salted water for an hour or two. To cook, put them in a stewpan with about 2 × 15 ml spoons/2 tablespoons water at the bottom, cover with a clean cloth and heat gently, shaking the pan to prevent burning. As soon as the shells open (after about 5 minutes) they are done. Serve very hot on a napkin, with bread and butter, or use instead of mussels or oysters in fish sauces and similar recipes.

COCKTAIL

A short alcoholic drink, consisting of a variety of ingredients so well blended together (by shaking in a cocktail shaker, usually with cracked ice) that no one flavour predominates.

Cocktails, which are offered before lunch or dinner, are served in a small glass and are often decorated with a stuffed olive, a curl of lemon peel or a Maraschino cherry; they should be served very cold.

Cocktails are rather less popular than formerly, the current fashion being for the simpler drinks such as dry vermouth, Dubonnet, gin and tonic or whisky and water.

Making Cocktails

Follow the recipe carefully. The total quantities can of course be increased at will, but any variation in the proportions will change the flavour of the drink. It is not normally necessary to follow any particular order in adding ingredients for cocktails,

as they are shaken up well before being poured into the glasses.

Recipes for a few of the best known cocktails appear below. In some cases there is more than one accepted recipe and the version you use is a matter of individual taste.

SWEET MARTINI

1 part gin
2 parts Italian vermouth
a dash of orange bitters (optional)
Cracked ice

DRY MARTINI

2 parts gin
1 part French vermouth
Lemon rind
Cracked ice

MIXED MARTINI (DEMI-SEC)

2 parts gin
1 part Italian vermouth
1 part French vermouth
Cracked ice and lemon rind

PINK GIN

Use gin with a dash of Angostura bitters, diluted with iced water. This cocktail must not be shaken.

DAIQUIRI

Sugar for glass
2 parts Bacardi rum
1 part fresh lime juice

Dip dampened edge of glass in sugar. Shake rum and lime juice well together and serve in the glass.

BRANDY COCKTAIL

1 glass brandy
2 dashes of Curaçao
Crushed ice
A lemon rind curl

Shake the brandy and Curaçao with some crushed ice, pour into a glass and serve with a curl of lemon rind.

SIDECAR COCKTAIL

2 parts brandy
1 part Cointreau
Juice of ¼ lemon for each cocktail

Shake well with cracked ice and strain into cocktail glasses.

HARVEY WALLBANGER

1 part vodka
1 part Galliano
Orange juice
Orange slice and cherry

Shake vodka and Galliano together, pour into a glass and top up with orange juice. Serve with an orange slice and cherry.

MANHATTAN

2 parts whisky (rye, if possible)
1 part French vermouth
A dash of Angostura bitters
A dash of Curaçao
Cracked ice

Decorate with Maraschino cherries.

CHAMPAGNE COCKTAIL

4 dashes Angostura bitters
1 small lump sugar
Lemon
1 glass champagne

Pour the bitters over the sugar and put into a glass. Add the strained juice of a quarter-lemon and fill up with chilled champagne.

COCKTAIL (APPETIZER)

Various kinds of non-alcoholic appetizers served at the beginning of a meal are called cocktails. The best-known are made of fish, fruit and fruit juices and vegetable juices; here are some representative recipes.

FISH COCKTAIL

METRIC/IMPERIAL
100–175 g/4–6 oz peeled prawns or shrimps or flaked crab or lobster meat
½ lettuce, washed and shredded
2 × 15 ml spoons/2 tablespoons mayonnaise
2 × 15 ml spoons/2 tablespoons tomato ketchup
2 × 15 ml spoons/2 tablespoons single cream
salt
pepper
squeeze of lemon juice or a dash of Worcestershire sauce
cucumber slices, capers or lemon wedges to garnish

Use either fresh or frozen prawns or shrimps; crab meat may be either fresh or canned – if fresh, use only the white meat; lobster may be either fresh or canned. Line some small glasses with shredded lettuce. Mix the remaining ingredients to make a dressing. Combine the fish and dressing, pile into the glasses and garnish.

TOMATO JUICE COCKTAIL

METRIC/IMPERIAL
300 ml/½ pint tomato juice
1 × 15 ml spoon/1 tablespoon lemon juice
1 × 2.5 ml spoon/½ teaspoon salt
1 × 5 ml spoon/1 teaspoon granulated sugar
1 small onion (finely sliced)
1 bay leaf
1 piece of celery
2 × 5 ml spoons/2 teaspoons chopped parsley
1 × 5 ml spoon/1 teaspoon Worcestershire sauce
2 × 5 ml spoons/2 teaspoons grated horseradish

Combine all the ingredients and chill for several hours. Strain and serve in glasses.

COCKTAIL SAVOURIES

(See Savoury and Patty entries.)

COCO BEAN

A variety of French bean. (See Bean entry.)

COCO YAM

(See Taro entry.)

COCOA

The cocoa tree is native to the tropical countries of America, but now grows in other parts of the world, notably Africa, the West Indies and South America. The fruit is a large pod (ranging in colour from purple to yellow, according to variety) containing the seeds or beans. These are allowed to ferment until the pulp drops off. They are then dried and the hard outer skin is removed. Next the beans are roasted and shelled, leaving the kernels or 'nibs'. These nibs are ground and crushed between giant rollers, giving a brown paste. Some of the fat (known as cocoa butter) is then pressed out and the remaining dry cake is reduced to a fine powder, sieved and blended, to become the cocoa powder of commerce.

Nutritionally, cocoa is of no great value, since only 1 × 5 ml spoon/1 teaspoon is used per cup; it does, however, encourage many people to drink milk and the resulting beverage is of good food value. Cocoa is used to give a chocolate flavour to various puddings and cakes. (See Chocolate entry.)

COCONUT

The fruit of the coconut palm, growing in most tropical climates, though linked mostly with the Pacific Islands. When fully grown, a tree yields upwards of 100 coconuts a year. The fresh nut contains a thick jelly and a clear liquid called coconut milk, both of which are delicious. The milk is sometimes fermented to make palm wine.

The flesh is dried (when it is known as copra) and exported to many countries; the coconut oil is expressed from the copra and used in the manufacture of margarine and soap. Desiccated coconut is used in cakes, biscuits and sweets.

COCONUT PYRAMIDS

METRIC/IMPERIAL
2 egg whites
150 g/5 oz sugar
150 g/5 oz desiccated coconut

Grease a baking sheet and cover with rice paper. Whisk the egg whites stiffly and fold in the sugar and coconut, using a metal spoon. Pile in small pyramids on the baking sheet, press into neat shapes and bake in a cool oven (140°C/275°F, Gas Mark 1) until pale fawn – about 45 minutes to 1 hour. If you wish, the mixture can be tinted pink or green.

COCONUT 'CREAM'

This is made from the flesh of the coconut and is not to be confused with the coconut milk, the thin liquid found inside a ripe coconut. Coconut cream is very widely used throughout the East and in the Pacific islands; it is added to curries, fish and vegetables are cooked in it, and it is served (sometimes iced) with fruit salads and so on.

To make rich coconut cream: Grate the white flesh of a ripe coconut, pour a cupful of hot water over, then squeeze through a piece of muslin or cheese cloth, producing a thick, creamy liquid. To make a thinner cream, use more water.

Commercially made creamed coconut is also available.

COCONUT ICE

(See Sweets entry.)

COD, CODLING

One of the most important edible fishes in the world. It belongs to the same family of bony white fish as haddock, whiting, hake, etc. The cod is usually olive-green on the back and sides sprinkled with small dark spots and grows quite long, averaging about 1 metre/4 feet in length and weighing anything up to 30 kg/70 lb to 36 kg/80 lb. Codling is the young fish. Cod is caught in areas round Great Britain, the chief of which are Dogger Bank, off the Shetlands and the Orkneys and is obtainable all the year round, though it is at its best from October to May.

Cod is sold fresh, salted and in frozen form. As it

has only a delicate flavour, it is best baked with stuffing, fried in batter or steamed or poached and coated with a well-flavoured sauce; it is often made into fish cakes or pies.

The liver is used to produce cod liver oil. (See separate entry.)

MINT AND CUCUMBER FISH SALAD

METRIC/IMPERIAL
1 kg/2 lb fresh cod fillet (the thick end is the best choice)
juice of ½ lemon
salt
½ cucumber
2 × 15 ml spoons/2 tablespoons freshly chopped mint
2 × 15 ml spoons/2 tablespoons freshly chopped parsley

FOR FRENCH DRESSING
6 × 15 ml spoons/6 tablespoons olive oil
2 × 15 ml spoons/2 tablespoons vinegar
salt
freshly ground black pepper
mustard

FOR GARNISH
25–50 g/1–2 oz peeled prawns
lemon wedges
sprigs of mint

Wash and skin the fish and cut it into three or four pieces. Sprinkle with lemon juice and salt. Steam or gently poach until just cooked (the flakes should separate easily and look milky white all through). Leave the fish covered until quite cold. Flake the fish very coarsely into a large bowl, removing any stray bones. Wash the cucumber, cut it into small dice and add to the fish. Tip in the chopped mint and parsley. Stir the French dressing ingredients together in a basin and pour over the salad. Using two spoons, lift and turn the salad until all the ingredients are combined and coated with dressing. Take care not to break up the natural flakes of fish. Pile the mixture into individual dishes and garnish each one with prawns, lemon wedges and sprigs of mint. Alternatively, serve in a large salad bowl accompanied by mayonnaise, tossed green salad and French bread.

STUFFED COD STEAKS

METRIC/IMPERIAL
4 cod steaks (or cutlets)
½ onion, skinned and finely chopped
100 g/4 oz streaky bacon, rinded and chopped
knob of butter
2 tomatoes, skinned and chopped
50 g/2 oz fresh white breadcrumbs
salt
pepper
about 150 ml/¼ pint milk

Wash and wipe the fish, trim off the fins and remove the central bone with a sharp-pointed knife; place the fish in a greased ovenproof dish. Fry the onion and bacon gently in the butter for about 5 minutes, until soft; stir in the tomatoes and crumbs. Season well and add enough milk to bind the mixture. Fill the centre of each steak with this stuffing, and fix the flaps of fish with wooden cocktail sticks to secure the stuffing. Pour 2–3 × 15 ml spoons/2–3 tablespoons milk round the fish, cover with a lid or foil and bake in a moderate oven (180°C/350°F, Gas Mark 4) for about 20 minutes.

As an alternative filling use veal forcemeat made with 50 g/2 oz breadcrumbs or the following mixture.

CHEESE AND TOMATO STUFFING FOR COD

METRIC/IMPERIAL
2 lare tomatoes, skinned and chopped
75 g/3 oz cheese, grated
50 g/2 oz fresh white breadcrumbs
1 × 5 ml spoon/1 teaspoon dried mixed herbs or sage
salt
pepper
milk to bind

Mix all the ingredients together.

SALT COD

Salt cod requires soaking to remove the salt and must be very carefully cooked to make it really palatable. Choose thick fillets with firm, close flesh, avoiding stringy or yellow pieces. To prepare it, soak it in cold water for 24 hours, changing the water several times, and place the fish skin side uppermost in the water, to allow the salt to drain out. To cook the cod, put it into a pan with enough cold milk (or milk and water) to cover, bring just to the boil, then draw the pan aside and cook slightly below boiling point until tender. Drain thoroughly and use as required. It may be served with maître d'hôtel butter or a well-flavoured sauce, or better still dressed with a sauce and served au gratin, creamed, curried, as a fish pie, etc.

SMOKED FILLET ('PAINTED LADIES')

Fillets of cod, smoked and dyed yellow. These fillets somewhat resemble smoked haddock in appearance, though they are without skin or bone, but do not have so good a flavour.

COD'S ROE

(See Roe entry.)

99

COD LIVER OIL

An oil which is extracted from the fresh liver of the cod by heating and then cooled and processed. When sold, it is pale yellow in colour. The oil can be relatively tasteless if it is prepared from the fish liver when this is absolutely fresh and if it is kept from contact with the air; for this reason the plants for extracting the oil are now sited at or near to ports.

Cod liver oil contains large though varying amounts of vitamins A and D, the approximate figures being vitamin A, 29,000 i.u. per 25 g/per oz; vitamin D, 6,000 i.u. per 25 g/per oz.

The oil used to be given to infants to supply these vitamins, but specially prepared vitamin drops are now available.

CODDLING

A method of soft-boiling eggs. They are put into boiling water; the pan is then removed from the heat and allowed to stand with the eggs in it for 8 to 10 minutes.

COFFEE

A shrub, originally African, which produces greenish beans. These are roasted, ground and used to make a drink. Many varieties are now cultivated in Brazil (which produces about half the world's coffee), Venezuela, Costa Rica, the East and West Indies, India, British East Africa and other countries. Costa Rica, Kenya and Jamaican coffees are particularly good, the Jamaican Blue Mountain having an especially high reputation.

When ripe the berries are red; they contain 1 or 2 seeds. The berries are usually cleaned and graded before being exported. They must then be roasted, and on this depends to some extent the quality of the coffee. They should be roasted evenly, to a light or dark colour as desired, and should be cooled rapidly. The aroma and flavour develop during this process.

The beans should preferably not be ground until just before the coffee is needed, or they will lose their flavour and soon become stale. Buy ground coffee in small quantities only. Use it quickly once opened.

The caffeine in coffee generally has a mildly stimulating effect, but people vary in their reactions and some find it relaxing.

INSTANT COFFEE
Coffee which has been ground, dried and packed as a powder or in granules. It makes quite a good cup of coffee, although not comparable with that produced by the freshly ground product.

DECAFFEINATED COFFEE
A powdered coffee with the caffeine extracted.

COFFEE ESSENCE
A sweetened, concentrated preparation useful for flavouring cakes, etc.

To make Coffee
There are several methods, but the most important point is to use enough coffee – too little produces a tasteless brew. Allow at least 2–3 × 5 ml spoons/2 to 3 teaspoons per person – more for strong, black, after-dinner coffee.

INFUSION
Put 4 × 15 ml spoons/4 tablespoons coffee in a hot jug and pour on 600 ml/1 pint boiling water, stir, then stand it in a warm place for 10 minutes. Pour the coffee gently through a strainer into a heated jug or coffee pot. Special jugs are available with a strainer included, which make it easier to make coffee by this methd.

PERCOLATOR COFFEE
The water circulates through the grounds, extracting the flavour and falling through a strainer. Ideally the liquid should be kept at just under boiling point, as boiling spoils coffee.

FILTER COFFEE (CAFÉ FILTRE)
A perforated filter (sometimes used with a filter paper) is filled with finely ground coffee, which is pressed down firmly. Boiling water is poured on and the coffee drips slowly through into the cup or jug. Electric filter coffee pots are now available. They have the advantage of keeping the coffee hot once it has passed through the filter.

SUCTION METHOD
A special apparatus must be used, with water in the lower container and a funnel fitted carefully into its neck and filled with coffee grounds. On heating, most of the water is sucked up the funnel, remaining there for about 3 minutes. When the heat is withdrawn, the coffee filters down the lower container, leaving the grounds in the funnel.

EXPRESSO COFFEE
In coffee bars, etc., coffee is prepared under pressure, producing a strong, rather bitter brew.

TURKISH COFFEE
This is said to be the only coffee which should actually be boiled. Finely ground coffee, sugar and cold water are brought to the boil, stirred and allowed to stand away from the heat. The liquid is then reheated and the process repeated two or three times. A few drops of rose-water are added and the thick, syrupy brew is served in small quantities.

BLACK COFFEE (CAFÉ NOIR)
Should be strong, clear and very hot. It is generally served alone, but cream, hot milk or sugar may be served with it if desired.

COFFEE WITH MILK (CAFÉ AU LAIT)

This is strong, black coffee to which hot (but not boiling) milk is added, generally in the proportion of 2 to 3 parts milk to 1 part of coffee.

To make gaelic (Irish) coffee: Heat a goblet or claret glass and put in 2 lumps of sugar. Pour in a jigger of Irish whiskey and fill up two-thirds of the way with hot, strong black coffee. Dissolve the sugar, then carefully add some double cream, pouring it in over the back of a spoon, so that it lies on top. Do not mix, but drink the coffee and whiskey through the layer of cream.

To make iced coffee: Make some strong black coffee, using 50 g/2 oz ground coffee to 900 ml/1½ pints water. While it is still hot, sweeten to taste. Cool and chill. Pour into glasses, add a cube of ice and top with whipped cream.

COFFEE SAUCE

METRIC/IMPERIAL
25 g/1 oz butter
4 × 5 ml spoons/4 teaspoons cornflour
300 ml/½ pint black coffee
25 g/1 oz sugar
vanilla essence
1 egg yolk

Melt the fat in a small saucepan and mix in the cornflour. Add the coffee gradually and stir until boiling. Simmer slowly for 5 minutes, add the sugar and a little vanilla and just before serving stir in the egg yolk. Do not boil again.

COFFEE SANDWICH CAKE

METRIC/IMPERIAL
100 g/4 oz butter or margarine
100 g/4 oz caster sugar
2 large eggs, beaten
100 g/4 oz self raising flour

FILLING
75 g/3 oz butter
175 g/6 oz icing sugar, sifted
1 × 15 ml spoon/1 tablespoon coffee essence
1 × 15 ml spoon/1 tablespoon top-of-the-milk

Grease two 18 cm/7 inch sandwich tins and line the base of each with a round of greased greaseproof paper. Cream the fat and sugar until pale and fluffy. Add the egg a little at a time, beating well after each addition. Fold in half the flour, using a metal spoon, then fold in the rest. Place half the mixture in each tin and level it with a knife. Bake both cakes on the same shelf of a moderately hot oven (190°C/375°F, Gas Mark 5) for about 20 minutes, or until they are well risen, golden, firm to the touch and beginning to shrink away from the sides of the tins. Turn out and cool on a wire rack. For the filling, cream the butter until soft, but not oily, and gradually beat in the sifted icing sugar with the coffee essence and top-of-the-milk. When the cakes are cold, sandwich them together with half the filling. Top with the rest of the filling, level and mark in lines with the prongs of a fork.

COGNAC

Brandy of high quality based on the wines made in the Charente and Charente Maritime *départements* of France, lying round the town of Cognac. The best Cognac brandy is made from Grande Champagne wine. Cognac as sold is generally a blend of Charente brandies – the higher the proportion of best brandy, the finer the Cognac.

One Star Cognac is 3 years old, Two Star 4 years old and Three Star 5 years old. The initials V.S.O.P., meaning Very Special Old Pale, refer to older brandy.

Cognac is about 72 per cent alcohol.

COINTREAU

A French Curaçao, used as an after-dinner liqueur and to flavour punches and cocktails. It has a sweet orange flavour.

COLA

A tropical African tree, the seeds or 'nuts' of which have stimulating properties. It is used in making apéritifs, etc. It is also the name given to certain fizzy soft drinks.

COLCANNON

A mixture of potatoes and cabbage boiled together and mashed. It may also be made up with leftover cooked potatoes and cabbage, mixed together and fried in a pan. The dish is very similar to the one known as bubble and squeak.

COLEY

A fish of the cod family: it is available all the year round and has a coarse greyish flesh when raw. When cooked this turns white. Coley is more economical than cod but does not have such a good flavour. Coley is sometimes referred to as Coalfish, or Saithe.

COLESLAW

A salad with a base of finely shredded raw white cabbage dressed with cream or mayonnaise. Ingredients that can be added to this type of salad include grated carrot, chopped apple, chopped onion, nuts, dried fruit, cooked sweetcorn, chopped celery and chopped green pepper. The salad may be served in a bowl or in a hollowed out cabbage. It can be served with any savoury dish but usually accompanies cold meats and savoury flans.

COLESLAW

METRIC/IMPERIAL
½ hard white cabbage, washed and finely shredded
1 large carrot, pared and coarsely grated
small piece of onion, skinned and finely chopped
1 × 15 ml spoon/1 tablespoon chopped parsley,
    optional
about 5 × 15 ml spoons/5 tablespoons salad cream or
    mayonnaise
1 × 5 ml spoon/1 teaspoon sugar
salt
pepper
few drops of vinegar or lemon juice

Combine the cabbage, carrot, onion and parsley (if used) in a large bowl. Mix the salad cream or mayonnaise with the sugar, salt and pepper and add enough vinegar or lemon juice to sharpen the flavour. Toss with the salad in the bowl until lightly coated, adding a little more salad cream if necessary.
Note: Coleslaw may be garnished by sprinkling with chopped herbs.

RAINBOW COLESLAW

(See colour plate page opposite page 384)

METRIC/IMPERIAL
225 g/8 oz red cabbage
225 g/8 oz white cabbage
1 large carrot, pared
½ green pepper, seeded
150 ml/¼ pint soured cream
2 × 15 ml spoons/2 tablespoons mayonnaise
1 × 15 ml spoon/1 tablespoon lemon juice
1 × 2.5 ml spoon/½ teaspoon caraway seeds
1 × 2.5 ml spoon/½ teaspoon celery seeds
salt
freshly ground black pepper

Trim and finely shred the red and white cabbage. Wash and dry them well and put them in a large bowl. Grate the carrot on a coarse grater straight into the cabbage. Slice the green pepper finely and add it to the cabbage. Mix together the soured cream, mayonnaise, lemon juice, caraway seeds, celery seeds, salt and pepper. Pour this dressing over the coleslaw and mix thoroughly. Chill before serving.

COLLARED

Pickled or salted meat which is rolled, boiled with suitable seasonings and served cold.

COLLEGE PUDDING

A baked or steamed suet sponge pudding, containing dried fruit and spice.

STEAMED COLLEGE PUDDING

METRIC/IMPERIAL
100 g/4 oz plain flour
1 × 5 ml spoon/1 teaspoon baking powder
a pinch of salt
1 × 5 ml spoon/1 teaspoon mixed spice
75 g/3 oz finely chopped suet
100 g/4 oz breadcrumbs
75 g/3 oz caster sugar
50 g/2 oz currants
50 g/2 oz sultanas
1–2 eggs
150 ml/¼ pint milk

Sift together the flour, baking powder, salt and spice into a mixing bowl. Add the suet, breadcrumbs, sugar, currants and sultanas and mix well together. Beat the eggs well and add to the dry ingredients, then mix to a soft dropping consistency, adding milk as required. Half-fill a greased basin with the mixture. Cut a circle of greaseproof paper 2.5 cm/1 inch larger all round than the top of the basin. Place the greaseproof paper on a flat surface and form a pleat across the centre. Cover basin with greased paper and secure with string under rim. Steam for 35 to 40 minutes. Turn out and serve with custard or jam sauce.

COLLOP

A term derived from the French *escalope*; it is used (chiefly in Scotland) for a small boneless piece of meat and now often means a savoury dish made of finely minced meat.

SCOTS COLLOPS

METRIC/IMPERIAL
0.5 kg/1 lb braising beef cut very thinly
25 g/1 oz butter
225 g/8 oz onion, skinned and very finely chopped or
    minced
25 g/1 oz flour
small cooking apple
salt
milled pepper

Beat the meat out until wafer thin. Melt the butter and slowly brown the onion, meat, flour and apple. Season well and pour in enough hot water to just cover. Put the lid on the pan and simmer gently until tender – adding more hot water as needed to keep the contents from getting too thick. Serve with creamed potatoes.

MINCE COLLOPS

METRIC/IMPERIAL
0.5 kg/1 lb lean minced beef
1 × 5 ml spoon/1 teaspoon flour
150 ml/¼ pint stock
salt
milled pepper
1 small onion, skinned
toasted croûtons

Brown the mince in a heavy based pan separating it with a fork. This is best done over a low heat to ensure that the mince does not burn. Sprinkle in the flour and mix well. Heat the stock and pour in. Bring to the boil, reduce heat. Season with a generous shake of salt and freshly milled pepper. Add the whole onion. Simmer, covered, for about 1 hour, stirring often. Remove onion. To serve, pile on a hot dish, garnish with croûtons.

COLOURINGS

Domestically, colours may be used to tint sweets, icings, cakes and so on. Commercially, they are used to replace the natural colours lost during the processing of foods.

All prepacked foods must by law include on the label a list of ingredients in descending order by weight; this should include any colouring. It is an offence to mislead the public by the use of food colouring.

A few natural food colours are available, including the well-known cochineal but in general natural colours are not very strong and are so variable that no two batches are the same; they also tend to fade, being less stable than synthetic colours.

Synthetic colours are mostly coal-tar derivatives. There is some doubt about the safety of some of these products and in 1957 a list of permitted food colours (i.e., those that have been shown to be harmless) was drawn up and included in the Food Regulations. No colour not on this list may now be used in foods on sale in this country.

COMPOTE

Fruit stewed with sugar; a compote can be prepared from a single fruit or a mixture and can be served either hot or cold. The name is also occasionally given to a brown stew of small birds, such as pigeons.

To make compote of pears: Make a syrup of sugar and water; for 1 kg/2 lb of stewing pears 100 g/4 oz to 175 g/6 oz sugar, 300 ml/½ pint water, the juice of ½ lemon, 2 to 3 cloves, 2.5 cm/1 inch cinnamon stick and a few drops of carmine. Put all the ingredients, except the pears, into a thick saucepan, bring slowly to the boil, and boil for 10 minutes.

Peel the pears with a stainless knife, halve and core, taking care not to break the pieces and putting them into cold salted water to prevent discoloration. Stew slowly in the prepared syrup until tender, then lift out carefully with a spoon. Reduce the syrup, allow it to cool slightly and then strain. Unless the compote is to be used for children, a little red wine may be added to the syrup when stewing the pears. The pears may also be cooked in a covered dish in a moderate oven (180°C/350°F, Gas Mark 4) for 30 minutes to 2 hours, according to hardness.

Apples may be cooked in the same way. (See Cherry Compote under Cherry entry.)

CONDÉ

A sweet consisting of creamed rice combined with fruit and a red jam sauce.

PEAR CONDÉ

METRIC/IMPERIAL
50 g/2 oz rice
600 ml/1 pint milk
1 × 15 ml spoon/1 tablespoon sugar
1 × 5 ml spoon/1 teaspoon gelatine
2 × 15 ml spoons/2 tablespoons water
4 × 15 ml spoons/4 tablespoons raspberry or other red jam
4 ripe dessert pears or cooked stewing pears

Cook the rice in a double saucepan with the milk and sugar until it is creamy – about 2 hours. Soak the gelatine in 2 × 5 ml spoons/2 teaspoons of the water and boil the jam with the remainder of the water, then add the soaked gelatine. Divide rice between four individual dishes and arrange 2 cored pear halves on top of each. When the jam mixture is cool and of a syrupy consistency, pour it over the pears.

Apricot or Peach Condé may be made in the same way, with fresh, bottled or canned fruit.

CONFECTIONER'S CUSTARD

A thick, sweet white sauce with egg yolks added. It is used as a filling for cakes and sweet pastries, e.g., vanilla slices.

VANILLA CONFECTIONER'S CUSTARD

METRIC/IMPERIAL
1 whole egg, separated
1 egg yolk
50 g/2 oz caster sugar
2 × 15 ml spoons/2 tablespoons plain flour
2 × 15 ml spoons/2 tablespoons cornflour
300 ml/½ pint milk
vanilla essence

Cream the egg yolks and sugar together until really thick and pale in colour. Beat in the flour and cornflour and a little cold milk to make a smooth paste. Heat the rest of the milk in a saucepan until almost boiling and pour on to the egg mixture, stirring well all the time. Return the mixture to the saucepan and stir over a low heat until the mixture boils. Beat the egg white until stiff. Remove the custard mixture from the heat and fold in the egg white. Again return the pan to the heat, add essence to taste and cook for a further 2 to 3 minutes. Cool before using.

CONFIT

Old French name for a preserve.

CONGER EEL

A scaleless sea fish, greyish or dusky brown on top and silver underneath, up to 2.25 metres/8 feet long, which is often found off the south coast of England. Conger eels are cooked like fresh-water eels when small; when large they are somewhat coarse. They can be fried, boiled or baked and make good soup.

CONGRESS TARTS

These are small pastry cases, spread with jam and filled with a mixture of ground almonds, sugar and egg; they are often decorated with a cross made of pastry strips or topped with glacé icing. Congress tarts are normally bought from a baker, but can be made at home by the following recipe.

CONGRESS TARTS

METRIC/IMPERIAL
100 g/4 oz shortcrust pastry
raspberry jam
50 g/2 oz butter
50 g/2 oz caster sugar
50 g/2 oz ground almonds
grated rind and juice of ½ lemon
1 egg, separated

Roll out the pastry thinly and use to line 12 patty tins. Put a little jam in the base of each pastry case. Place the butter and caster sugar into a bowl and cream together using a wooden spoon, cream until light and fluffy. Add the ground almonds, lemon rind and juice, then the egg yolk; mix well. Stiffly beat the egg white and fold into the mixture. Divide between pastry cases. Roll out the pastry trimmings and cut into strips, use to make a pastry cross on top of each tart. Bake in the centre of a hot oven (220°C/425°F, Gas Mark 7) for 10 minutes, reduce heat (180°C/350°F, Gas Mark 4) and cook for a further 25 minutes. Cool on a wire rack.

CONSERVE

A preparation of fruits in sugar, very similar to jam, the chief difference being that a conserve is usually a 'whole-fruit' jam. The whole fruit (or pieces) should be unbroken and retain the original shape, though permeated with sugar and suspended in a highly concentrated syrup or jelly.

STRAWBERRY CONSERVE

METRIC/IMPERIAL
1.75 kg/4 lb strawberries
1.75 kg/4 lb sugar
4 × 15 ml spoons/4 tablespoons lemon juice

Select fruit which is just ripe, red and firm. Alpine strawberries are excellent for this preserve. Prepare and wash it in the usual way and drain it well, then put it in a basin with layers of sugar. Leave for 24 hours for the sugar to extract the juice and 'firm' the berries. Place in a preserving pan with the lemon juice and bring to the boil; boil for 5 minutes, then return the mixture to the basin and leave for a further 8 hours. Boil again, this time until the syrup is thick or a set is obtained. Allow to cool slightly before putting into hot jars (to ensure even distribution of the fruit), then pot and seal down.

CONSOMMÉ

A clear soup, made with the stock from fresh meat, chicken or even fish. Consommé can be served hot or cold and is usually garnished. Various commercial consommés are available.

BROWN STOCK FOR CONSOMMÉ

METRIC/IMPERIAL
0.5 kg/1 lb marrow bone or knuckle of veal, chopped
0.5 kg/1 lb shin of beef, cut into pieces
1.75 litres/3 pints water
bouquet garni
1 carrot, pared and sliced
1 medium onion, skinned and sliced
1 stick celery, sliced
1 × 2.5 ml spoon/½ teaspoon salt

To give a good flavour and colour, brown the bones and meat in the oven (exact temperature not important) before using them. Put in a pan with the water, herbs, vegetables and salt, bring to the boil, skim and simmer covered for 5 to 6 hours. Makes about 1.5 litres/2½ pints.

Note: For a more economical brown stock, use 1 kg/2 lb bones, omit the shin of beef and fry the onion until well browned.

CLASSIC CONSOMMÉ

METRIC/IMPERIAL
1.2 litres/2 pints brown stock (cold)
100 g/4 oz lean beefsteak, e.g. rump
150 ml/¼ pint cold water
1 carrot, pared and quartered
1 small onion, skinned and quartered
bouquet garni
1 egg white
salt
2 × 5 ml spoons/2 teaspoons dry sherry, optional

A completely clear, well flavoured broth, made from good brown stock. Both the stock and the utensils must be quite free from any trace of grease, to prevent droplets of fat forming on the surface of the soup.

Remove any fat from the stock. Shred the meat finely and soak it in the 150 ml/¼ pint water for 15 minutes. Put the meat and water, vegetables, stock and bouquet garni into a deep saucepan; lastly add the egg white. Heat gently and whisk continuously until a thick froth starts to form. Stop whisking and bring to the boil. Reduce the heat immediately, cover and simmer for 2 hours. If the liquid boils too rapidly, the froth will break and cloud the consommé.

Scald a clean cloth or jelly bag, wring it out, tie it to the four legs of an up-turned stool and place a bowl underneath. Pour the soup through, keeping the froth back at first with a spoon, then let it slide out on to the cloth. Again pour the soup through the cloth and through the filter of egg white.

The consommé should now be clear and sparkling. Re-heat it, add salt if necessary and if you like a little sherry to improve the flavour, but add nothing that would make the liquid cloudy.

CONTACT GRILLS (INFRA RED)

A fast method of cooking which is a fairly recent domestic development. Heat rays are carried by convection and radiation so they are transmitted to food almost immediately. The waves penetrate the water vapours which surround foods when heated, and enter the food to the depth of a few millimetres. The grills can be heated by gas or electricity and need to be pre-heated for 8 to 10 minutes. Food is cooked between two hotplates which are normally ridged and covered with a non stick coating. Some models can be opened out flat to form a griddle.

Foods most suitable to cook in the contact grill are steaks, chops, toast and sandwiches. Frozen foods such as fish steaks, beefburgers and fish fingers can also be cooked in this way but are best wrapped in oiled foil. Food should be of a regular shape with no protruding bones or the plates will not touch and cook it evenly.

As a mini oven with the baking tray, the grill can be used for eggs, sausages, fish, tomatoes, mushrooms and for baking small cakes, scones, pizzas, pies, flans, biscuits and puddings. It is also good for reheating foods. Instruction books are given with all models and should be consulted for food preparation and cooking times.

The main advantages of the grills are speed, economy (cheaper than electric cooker grills) and the need for very little fat; this means they are useful for people on low-fat diets. Disadvantages include the fact that the grills become very hot, tend to produce smoke and fumes and need very regular, careful cleaning.

CONTREFILET

(See Steak entry.)

COOKIE

American term for sweet biscuits. They are made to a variety of recipes. Some, like brownies are softer than the traditional crisp English biscuit.

Cookie also has the Scottish meaning of an enriched yeast dough with the addition of dried fruit. The dough is shaped like bread rolls and glazed with sugar and water.

NUT REFRIGERATOR COOKIES

METRIC/IMPERIAL
90 g/3½ oz butter or block margarine
90 g/3½ oz demerara sugar
1 egg, beaten
175 g/6 oz self raising flour
75 g/3 oz walnuts or almonds, finely chopped

Cream the butter with the sugar and beat in the egg gradually. Stir in the flour and chopped nuts to give a fairly firm dough. Shape into a long roll, wrap in a polythene bag or in aluminium foil and put in a cool place or in a refrigerator for several hours to chill thoroughly.

To finish, grease 2 baking sheets, cut the roll into 5 mm/¼ inch slices, place the biscuits widely spaced on the sheets and bake in a moderately hot oven (200°C/400°F, Gas Mark 6) for 10 to 12 minutes. Cool on a wire rack.

ORANGE GLAZED MELTAWAYS

METRIC/IMPERIAL
225 g/8 oz butter
50 g/2 oz icing sugar
grated rind of 1 orange
225 g/8 oz plain flour
2 × 15 ml spoons/2 tablespoons apricot jam, sieved
3 × 15 ml spoons/3 tablespoons icing sugar
1 × 15 ml spoon/1 tablespoon orange juice

Cream the butter until soft. Sift in the icing sugar and beat until light and fluffy. Stir in the orange rind and flour until well blended. Place the mixture in a nylon forcing bag fitted with a large star vegetable nozzle. Pipe about 40 shell shapes on to greased baking sheets. Chill for 30 minutes. Bake in a moderate oven (160°C/325°F, Gas Mark 3) for 20 minutes. Remove from the oven, brush each cookie with a little sieved apricot jam. Combine the sifted icing sugar with orange juice and brush over the jam. Return the cookies to the oven for a further 5 minutes, or until the sugar glaze begins to go slightly crystalline. Cool on a wire rack.

OAT COOKIES

METRIC/IMPERIAL
75 g/3 oz plain flour
1 × 2.5 ml spoon/½ teaspoon bicarbonate of soda
75 g/3 oz caster sugar
75 g/3 oz rolled oats
75 g/3 oz butter or margarine
1 × 15 ml spoon/1 tablespoon milk
1 × 15 ml spoon/1 tablespoon syrup

Grease 2 baking sheets. Sift the flour and bicarbonate of soda and stir in the sugar and oats. Heat the butter, milk and syrup together until melted, pour on to the first mixture and mix well. Roll into small balls and place 10 cm/4 inches apart on the baking sheets. Flatten slightly and bake in a cool oven (150°C/300°F, Gas Mark 2) for about 25 to 30 minutes. Cool on the sheets for 2 to 3 minutes then transfer the cookies to a wire rack to cool completely.

CORDIAL

Originally a spirit sweetened and infused with fruit or other agent to add flavour and scent. It was supposed to have some stimulating effect on the heart hence the name, meaning of or belonging to the heart. This product is now more often called a liqueur and the word 'cordial' is applied to a sweet fruit drink with no alcoholic content or to a concentrated fruit drink (as in lime juice cordial).

BLACKCURRANT CORDIAL

METRIC/IMPERIAL
0.75 kg/1 ½ lb blackcurrants
225 g/8 oz sugar
juice of 2 lemons
600 ml/1 pint boiling water
thin slices of lemon

Cook the blackcurrants slowly with the sugar (reserving 1 × 15 ml spoon/1 tablespoon of the berries); mash well, strain and measure the juice, adding water to make up to 600 ml/1 pint. Add the strained lemon juice and the boiling water. Allow to become cold, then chill and add the fresh blackcurrants and some thin slices of lemon.

CORING

To remove the central membranes, pips, etc., from apples, pears and so on, either by quartering the fruit and cutting out the core or by using a special apple-corer on the whole fruit. Also to remove the central membrane from kidneys which is tough and inedible.

CORIANDER

An Eastern spice, which was introduced into Europe by the Romans. The strongly scented plant has leaves similar to those of parsley and the flowers grow round the stem in tassels. The fragrant dried seeds are used as a flavouring for gin and in dishes such as curry, pickles and gingerbread; they are also used to flavour medicine. The flavour resembles a mixture of sage and lemon peel and therefore may be added to savoury stuffing.

CORN

A general term applied in England to all kinds of grain, such as wheat, rye, oats, barley, maize, etc. In Scotland the word usually denotes oats, while in America it mostly refers to maize. As a cooking term also it usually means maize or sweet corn. (See Corn On The Cob entry.)

CORN ON THE COB

Special varieties of maize are grown for use in this way, the yellow type being the most popular. Corn of good quality has a fresh-looking green husk, with brown 'silk', and the cob should be filled with plump, milky kernels, firm but not hard. Corn with yellow or dried-out husks or a cob full of very small, immature seeds should be rejected.

Choose the cobs when they are plump, well formed and of a pale golden yellow colour and cook them while still really fresh. Remove the outside leaves and silky threads, put the cobs into boiling unsalted water (salt toughens corn) and cook for 12 to 20 minutes, depending on their size – overcooking also makes them tough. Drain well and serve with plenty of melted butter, salt and freshly ground pepper.
Allow 1 to 2 cobs per portion.

Corn Fritters: Make up a batter from 100 g/4 oz flour, a pinch of salt, 1 egg and 150 ml/¼ pint milk. Fold in 1 × 300 g/11 oz can sweetcorn, drained. Fry in spoonfuls in a little hot fat until crisp and golden, turning them once. Drain well on crumpled kitchen paper.

CORN OIL

The germ of the maize or corn contains an oil, which is expressed and then refined. It is used for frying, in salad oils and in the manufacture of some cakes and biscuits. It has a high percentage of unsaturated fats. (See Fats and Oil entries.)

CORN SALAD

(See Lamb's Lettuce entry.)

CORN SYRUP

This product, which varies in colour from clear white to amber, is manufactured from corn starch by treatment with an acid. It may be used as a table syrup or as a sweetening agent, but is not as sweet as ordinary cane sugar. It is also possible to use corn syrup in preserving, brewing and cake making, but some additional sugar is needed for certain of these purposes and less liquid should be used, as the syrup contains 20 per cent water.

CORNED BEEF

A canned preparation of cooked pickled beef, usually imported from countries such as the U.S.A., the Argentine and other big cattle-producing regions of the world. Ways of using corned beef are very numerous, the simplest being to slice it and serve it cold with salads, but many people prefer it in cooked dishes, such as ragoûts, stews, curries, fritters, etc.

Corned beef has approximately the same protein and fat content as fresh meat, but contains less of some of the B vitamins.

CORNED BEEF HASH

METRIC/IMPERIAL
225 g/8 oz corned beef
1 kg/2 lb cooked potatoes
1 onion
50 g/2 oz dripping
salt
pepper
Worcestershire sauce
parsley

Cut the corned beef into small cubes, mash the cooked potatoes and chop or slice the prepared onion very thinly. Heat the dripping in the frying pan and fry the onion until golden-brown. Add the meat and potatoes and season with the pepper, salt and sauce. Combine well, then smooth out the mixture and cook very slowly until piping hot and nicely browned underneath – about 30 minutes. Turn onto a hot dish, brown side uppermost, garnish with parsley and serve immediately.

This may be varied by adding 3 to 4 cooked mashed apples and omitting the onion and Worcestershire sauce.

CORNET

A hollow conical biscuit, made of thin, crisp wafer pastry, used to hold ice cream.

CORNFLOUR

Cornflour is the inner part of the kernel of Indian corn or maize, very finely ground. It consists mainly of starch and is used for making milk puddings and cornflour moulds and for thickening soups, sauces and stews; it is also used in a few cakes, biscuits, etc.

CORNFLOUR MOULD

METRIC/IMPERIAL
600 ml/1 pint milk
4 × 15 ml spoons/4 tablespoons cornflour
a thin strip of lemon rind
50 g/2 oz sugar

Take three-quarters of the milk, add the lemon rind (or other flavouring) and bring slowly to the boil. Mix the cornflour and sugar to a smooth paste with the remaining cold milk and strain the boiling milk on to the paste, stirring well. Return the mixture to the saucepan, stir and boil for 5 minutes, then pour into a wetted mould. Turn out when set and serve with fruit or jam and cream.

Chocolate Mould: Omit the lemon rind, replacing it by a few drops of vanilla essence, and add 1 × 15 ml spoon/1 tablespoon blended cocoa (or 50 g/2 oz chocolate dissolved in milk) to the mixture.

Rich Cornflour Pudding: Mix as given for Cornflour Mould, but add an egg and bake the mixture for about 20 minutes in a moderate oven (180°C/350°F, Gas Mark 4). Alternatively, add yolk of egg only and top the pudding with meringue.

CORNFLOUR SAUCE

(See White Sauce (Blended Method), under Sauce entry.)

CORNISH CREAM, PASTY, SPLIT

(See Cream, Pasty and Split entries.)

COTTAGE CHEESE

A low fat soft cheese with a mild flavour and granular texture. It can be used in sweet or savoury dishes, or it may be served with salad. Cottage

107

cheese is also available with flavouring additions such as chives and pineapple. (See Cheese entry.)

COTTAGE PIE

A homely dish usually made with leftover cooked meat, often thought to be identical with Shepherd's Pie (See separate entry). Some people, however, assert that while Cottage Pie may be made with any meat, only lamb or mutton should be used for Shepherd's Pie. Other people say that whereas the Cottage Pie is made with minced meat, that used for Shepherd's Pie should be sliced.

COTTON SEED OIL

(See Oils entry.)

COUPE

A combination of fruit and ice cream served in a glass goblet.

Coupe Jacques: Half-fill some glass goblets with fruit salad, flavoured with Kirsch, cover this with a layer of vanilla ice cream and then add a layer of strawberry ice. Decorate with a glacé cherry.

COURGETTES

These are a variety of small vegetable marrow. They are normally cooked unpeeled, being either left whole or cut into rounds. They may be boiled in a minimum of water (allow 10 to 15 minutes), steamed or fried and are served with melted butter and chopped parsley or tarragon. Alternatively cook, dress with French dressing while still warm, then leave to go cold and serve as a salad. Courgettes are an essential ingredient in the vegetable dish, ratatouille, and can be added to casseroles, soups and stews.

Allow 100 g/4 oz per portion, when served as an accompaniment.

BUTTERED COURGETTES WITH LEMON

METRIC/IMPERIAL
0.5 kg/1 lb courgettes
salt
freshly ground black pepper
200 ml/⅓ pint water
25 g/1 oz butter
1 × 15 ml spoon/1 tablespoon chopped parsley
   or chives
lemon juice

Trim the courgettes and thinly slice. Cook in boiling salted water for 5 minutes, drain well. Finish cooking the courgettes in melted butter and when tender but still slightly crisp add the herbs, lemon juice and freshly ground pepper to taste.

COURGETTES WITH TOMATOES

METRIC/IMPERIAL
0.5 kg/1 lb courgettes, cut into 0.5 cm/¼ inch slices
salt
75 g/3 oz butter
225 g/8 oz tomatoes, skinned and chopped
1 × 15 ml spoon/1 tablespoon chopped parsley
1 small clove garlic, skinned and crushed
pepper
1 × 2.5 ml spoon/½ teaspoon sugar
50 g/2 oz cheese, grated
7 × 15 ml spoons/7 tablespoons fresh white
   breadcrumbs

Put the courgette slices into a colander, sprinkle with salt and allow to drain for about an hour; dry them well. Melt 50 g/2 oz butter in a frying pan and put in the courgettes. Cook gently until soft and slightly transparent and put them in an ovenproof dish. Melt the remaining butter and cook the tomatoes, parsley, garlic, pepper and sugar until a thickish purée forms. Re-season the mixture if necessary and pour it over the courgettes. Sprinkle with the cheese and breadcrumbs and grill until golden brown.

COURT-BOUILLON

A fish stock used instead of plain water to cook fish which is inclined to be flavourless. There are various types of court-bouillon, some containing white wine, claret, vinegar or milk.

To each 1.2 litres/2 pints water (or water and white wine mixed), allow:

METRIC/IMPERIAL
1 onion
1 clove of garlic
1 carrot
a small stalk of celery
a bunch of herbs
a small clove
1 × 15 ml spoon/1 tablespoon vinegar
1 × 5 ml spoon/1 teaspoon salt
freshly ground black pepper

Put all the ingredients together in a pan, cover and simmer for 30 minutes or longer. Strain this liquor and use for cooking the fish.

COUSCOUS

A North African culinary speciality made with millet flour or fine semolina made from wheat germ, cooked in water until fluffy and served with mutton stew.

COW-HEEL

The feet of cows and oxen, which are very gelatinous, are chiefly used to make jelly or soup, though stewed cow-heel is sometimes served. The washed cow-heel is boiled for 2 to 3 hours in milk and water with a sliced onion. The meat is removed and the liquid thickened with flour, then well seasoned and flavoured with lemon juice, nutmeg and some chopped parsley; this sauce is poured over the meat.

COWSLIP

These sweet-scented flowers can be used to decorate salads and also to make syrup, vinegar or wine. (See Home-made Wines entry.)

CRAB

Crabs should be eaten as soon as possible after cooking. Choose one of medium size, heavy in weight for its size, with large claws, a good red-coloured shell and bright eyes.

A crab is usually bought cooked and many fishmongers will also dress and prepare them. If it is bought uncooked, it should be still alive. Place it in cold water and very gradually raise the temperature to boiling point, then cook for 10 to 20 minutes, according to size; if over-cooked, crab becomes hard and 'thready'.

To prepare a Crab: Lay it on its back, hold the shell firmly with one hand and the body (to which the claws are attached) in the other hand, then pull apart.

The edible portion of the crab consists of two main parts; the white flesh of the claws and body, and the liver, or soft yellow substance, which almost fills the shell.

Take the shell part; using a spoon remove the stomach bag (which lies just below the head) and discard it. Then carefully scrape all the 'brown meat' from the shell into a basin and reserve it. Wash and dry the shell, then knock away the edge as far as the dark line.

Take the body and remove the legs and the greyish-white, frond-like pieces – the so-called 'dead men's fingers,' which are inedible. Remove the white flesh. Crack the claws (except the very tiny ones) with nut crackers or a weight and take out all the flesh. Use a skewer to get into the crevices and take great care not to get splinters of shell amongst the meat.

Crab Simply Dressed: Add 1 × 15 ml spoon/1 tablespoon fresh breadcrumbs to the brown meat, season with salt, pepper, lemon juice and a little chopped parsley and pack it into the sides of the prepared shell, leaving a space in the middle. Season the white flesh with salt, pepper, cayenne and lemon juice and pile it into the centre of the shell.

Decorate with parsley. Dip the back of a knife into cayenne pepper and mark diagonal lines across the dark meat. Alternatively, decorate with sieved egg yolk and chopped egg white. Lay the crab on a dish and garnish with the small claws.

SCRAMBLED CURRIED CRAB

METRIC/IMPERIAL
hot buttered toast
50 g/2 oz butter
1–2 × 5 ml spoons/1–2 teaspoons curry powder
1 can flaked crab
4 eggs
4 × 15 ml spoons/4 tablespoons cream or milk
celery salt or salt
a little black pepper

Have ready some hot buttered toast. Melt the fat and stir in the curry powder and the flaked crab. When it is thoroughly hot, pour in the beaten eggs mixed with the cream or milk; season and cook quickly, scrambling in the usual way. Serve piled on to the buttered toast.

CRAB-APPLE

A wild variety of apple. In this country the common crab-apple often grows in hedgerows. The fruit both of the common crab-apple and the Japanese and Siberian crab-apple makes an excel-

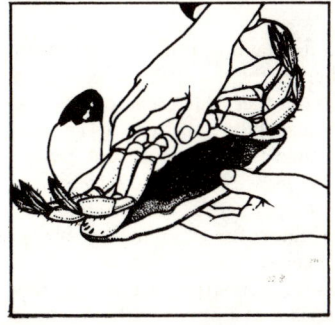

1. *To prepare a crab: Hold the shell firmly in one hand and the body in the other hand, pull the shell and body apart.*

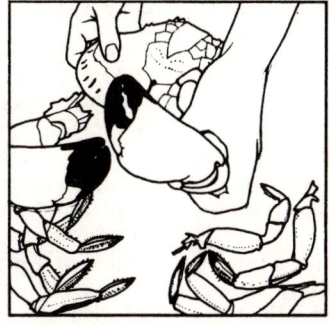

2. *Remove the stomach bag, found just below the head and discard. Remove and discard the 'dead men's fingers'.*

3. *Crack the claws, except the very tiny ones. Take out all the flesh from the legs using a skewer.*

lent jelly, which can be served as a tea-time preserve or with roast mutton as a substitute for redcurrant jelly.

CRAB-APPLE JELLY

METRIC/IMPERIAL
2.5 kg/5 ½ lb crab-apples
1.75 litres/3 pints water
cloves or bruised root ginger, optional
sugar

Wash the crab-apples and cut into quarters, without peeling or coring. Put into a pan and add the water. Bring to the boil and simmer for about 1 ½ hours, or until the fruit is mashed, adding a little more water if necessary. A few cloves or some bruised root ginger may be added while the apples are cooking, to give extra flavour. Strain through a jelly cloth, measure the extract and return it to the pan with 450 g/1 lb sugar to each 600 ml/1 pint of extract. Stir until the sugar has dissolved and boil rapidly until a 'jell' is obtained on testing. Skim, pot and cover in the usual way.

CRACKER BISCUIT

Various plain, hard biscuits suitable for eating with cheese are known by this name. In America the term is used for any type of biscuit.

CRACKLING

The crisp brown rind on a joint of pork after baking: the rind is usually scored before cooking, to prevent it pulling the joint out of shape, and is rubbed with salt, then brushed with fat or oil to make it crisp.

CRACKNEL

A type of plain biscuit made of paste which is boiled before being baked; this causes it to puff up.

CRAKEBERRY

(See Crowberry entry.)

CRANBERRY

The red berry fruit of a small low-growing evergreen shrub, which occurs wild on peaty soil in hilly northern regions of Great Britain. It is also extremely cultivated in America.

Cranberries, which are very sour, are usually used in conjunction with another fruit, such as apple, for making fruit pies and tarts. They can also be bottled whole and made into jams and jellies; a good jam is made with equal quantities of cranberries and apples. Cranberry sauce is a traditional accompaniment to roast turkey; the fruit can also be used in relishes and puddings.

Cranberry Sauce: Pick and wash 0.5 kg/1 lb cranberries and put them into a stewpan with 300 ml/½ pint water. Stew them until reduced to a pulp, bruising them well with the back of a wooden spoon, then add 225 g/8 oz to 350 g/12 oz sugar, stirring until dissolved, and a little port wine (if desired). Serve as an accompaniment to roast game or turkey.

CRAYFISH (CRAWFISH)

These variants of the same word are used almost indiscriminately to denote the two different shellfish described below, although, strictly speaking, only the first of them is entitled to the name.
1. The freshwater crayfish (French écrevisse), which is like a miniature lobster, but inhabits rivers and lakes; slightly different varieties are found in many parts of the world and the crayfish sold in this country are usually imported. When caught, they are a dull green or brown, but they turn a brilliant red on being boiled. Crayfish have a very delicate flavour and are used extensively in France. Small ones are used for soup and garnishes, while the larger ones can be boiled and served hot in a good cream sauce, or cold with brown bread and butter.

To prepare crayfish, wash them well and with a pointed knife remove the intestinal tube under the tail, as it has a bitter flavour. Place them in salted water or court-bouillon and cook for about 10 minutes after the liquid has reached boiling point.
2. The spiny lobster, sometimes called the 'sea crayfish' (French langouste), which resembles a lobster, but without the big claws, and is found off the shores of Europe, America, Africa, etc. It is prepared and cooked like lobster. In the British Isles, it is frequently seen in the canned form, being imported from South Africa and other countries, usually under the name of 'crawfish'.

CREAM

Cream is produced from whole milk by separation and can be described as the fat of the milk with a varying proportion of other milk constituents and water. These differ according to the type of cream.

As fat is lighter than the rest of milk it can be separated by gravity. However, in modern manufacture, the cream is separated by centrifugal force in a mechanical separator, the action being similar to that of a spin dryer.

All cream sold as fresh cream is pasteurised; this kills harmful bacteria and improves the keeping quality without affecting the flavour. The cream is heated to 79.5°C/175°F for 15 seconds then cooled to 4.5°C/40°F before packing.

The Cream Regulation 1970 specifies requirements for the description and composition of cream sold in England and Wales. The label should bear one of the following descriptions, and the fat content and heat treatment must comply with the regulations. The use of certain additives, including sugar, stabilizers and emulsifiers, is now permitted in specified types of cream, but this must be declared on the label.

HALF CREAM
Minimum 12 per cent butterfat; may be called top-of-the-milk or pouring cream.

SINGLE CREAM
Minimum 18 per cent butterfat; a pouring cream which will not whip.

WHIPPING CREAM
Minimum 35 per cent butterfat, usually 38 to 42 per cent. Will whip to at least double its volume. Suitable for piping and decorating.

DOUBLE CREAM
Minimum 48 per cent butterfat; a rich pouring cream, which can also be whipped or floated on top of coffee and soups.

DOUBLE CREAM 'THICK'
Minimum 48 per cent butterfat; heavily homogenised. Rich spoonable cream that will not whip.

The above creams have a keeping quality of two to three days in summer or three to five days in winter in a domestic refrigerator.

DOUBLE CREAM 'EXTENDED LIFE'
Minimum 48 per cent butterfat; homogenised spoonable cream, may whip lightly and will keep two or three weeks refrigerated. Sold in bottles.

STERILIZED HALF CREAM
Minimum 12 per cent butterfat, pouring cream in cans.

STERILIZED CREAM
Minimum 23 per cent butterfat; spoonable cream, will not whip. Packed in cans.

Both sterilized creams will keep for two years unopened; once opened they should be used as fresh cream.

ULTRA HEAT TREATED CREAM
Minimum 18 per cent butterfat; pouring cream, aseptically packed in foil lined containers. Will keep without refrigeration for several weeks.

CLOTTED CREAM
Minimum 55 per cent butterfat; a thick cream made chiefly in Devon, Cornwall and Somerset. Keeps 2 to 3 days in summer, 3 to 4 days in winter refrigerated.

SOURED CREAM
Made from single cream to which a culture has been added. It has a piquant refreshing flavour.

WHEY CREAM
Whey left from cheese-making contains lactose, fat and other milk constituents; it can be separated to make whey cream and butter. (See Mock Cream entry for a less expensive imitation.)

Freezing Cream
Only double and whipping creams can successfully be frozen. Whipping cream can be frozen for up to two months, but double cream gives better results if only frozen for up to one month. Both creams benefit by being semi-whipped before freezing then whipped to the desired consistency after thawing.

CREAM (COLD SWEET)
There are three main kinds of creams: 'whole', in which cream is the main ingredient; custard, made from a combination of cream and custard; and fruit, made from fruit purée and cream and sometimes including custard.

The general proportion of gelatine to use for creams is 15 g/ ½ oz (or more, according to the type used) to 600 ml/1 pint of the mixture. Use slightly more if the mixture is thin and slightly less if thick.

WHOLE CREAM – BASIC RECIPE
METRIC/IMPERIAL
2 × 5 ml spoons/2 teaspoons powdered gelatine
2–3 × 15 ml spoons/2–3 tablespoons water
50 g/2 oz sugar
1 × 5 ml spoon/1 teaspoon vanilla essence
600 ml/1 pint double cream, half-whipped

Use a 900 ml/1½ pint jelly mould or a basin. Sprinkle the gelatine over the water in a small basin, stand this in a pan of hot water and heat gently until the gelatine is dissolved. Fold the sugar and vanilla essence into the cream. Add a spoonful or two of cream to the gelatine, then quickly fold it into the bulk of the cream. When the mixture is just on the point of setting, pour quickly into the mould and leave to set. Unmould to serve.

Variations
Replace the vanilla essence by one of the following:

ALMOND
1 × 2.5 ml spoon/ ½ teaspoon almond essence.

COFFEE
3–4 × 5 ml spoons/3–4 teaspoons instant coffee, dissolved in 2 × 5 ml spoons/2 teaspoons hot water.

CHOCOLATE
50–75 g/2–3 oz chocolate, melted.

CUSTARD CREAM – BASIC RECIPE

METRIC/IMPERIAL
300 ml/ ½ pint pouring egg custard
1–2 × 5 ml spoons/1–2 teaspoons vanilla essence
2 × 5 ml spoons/2 teaspoons powdered gelatine
2 × 15 ml spoons/2 tablespoons water
1 × 300 ml/ ½ pint carton double cream, whipped

Use a 900 ml/1 ½ pint jelly mould (or a basin). Make up the custard in the usual way, using extra sugar to make a well sweetened mixture, add the vanilla essence and stir occasionally as it cools. To prevent a skin forming, press a piece of wetted greaseproof paper down on to the surface of the custard. Put the gelatine and the water in a basin, stand this in a pan of hot water and heat gently until the gelatine is dissolved; allow to cool slightly. Pour into the custard in a steady, thin stream, stirring the mixture all the time. Fold in the cream, check the sweetness and when the mixture is just on the point of setting, pour into the wetted mould and leave to set. Unmould just before serving.

GINGER CREAM
Add 50 g/2 oz preserved ginger, chopped

ITALIAN CREAM
Omit the vanilla and add 1 × 15 ml spoon/1 tablespoon brandy or curaçao.

STRAWBERRY CREAM

METRIC/IMPERIAL
0.5 kg/1 lb fresh strawberries or 2 × 432 g/15¼ oz cans, drained
sugar to taste
2–3 × 15 ml spoons/2–3 tablespoons water or fruit juice
2 × 5 ml spoons/2 teaspoons powdered gelatine
1 × 300 ml/ ½ pint carton double cream, whipped, or 1 × 150 ml/¼ pint carton cream and 150 ml/¼ pint custard

Use a 900 ml/ ½ pint jelly mould or a basin. Sieve the strawberries to make 300 ml/ ½ pint pureé; add sugar as necessary.

Put the gelatine and the water or fruit juice in a basin, stand this in a pan of hot water and heat gently until the gelatine is dissolved. Allow to cool slightly. Pour it into the purée in a steady stream, stirring the mixture all the time. Fold in the cream (and the custard if used). When the mixture is just on the point of setting, pour it quickly into the wetted mould and leave to set. Unmould just before serving.

CREAM BUN

A popular confection made of choux pastry (see Pastry entry) with a filling of whipped cream or confectioner's custard.

CREAM PUFFS

METRIC/IMPERIAL
choux paste, made with 8 × 15 ml spoons/8 tablespoons flour
150 ml/¼ pint double cream, whipped with 4 × 15 ml spoons/4 tablespoons single cream, or 300 ml/ ½ pint whipping cream, whipped
melted chocolate or icing sugar

The characteristic light, crisp texture and crazed tops of cream puffs are achieved by baking the pastry in its own steam. For this you will need a large, shallow tin with a tightly fitting lid. If this type of tin is not available, use a heavy, flat baking sheet and invert a roasting tin over it, sealing the join with a flour and water paste if necessary.

Pipe the paste into bun shapes 4 to 5 cm/1 ½ to 2 inches in diameter 7.5 cm/3 inches apart on 2 damp baking sheets and cover. Bake in a moderately hot oven at (200°C/400°F, Gas Mark 6) for 45 to 50 minutes. It is very important not to remove the covering tin during the cooking or the puffs will collapse; to test them, shake the tin gently – if the puffs move about freely, they are cooked. Split them and cool on a rack. When they are cold, fill with whipped cream and dip the tops in melted chocolate or dust with icing sugar.

CREAM CHEESE

A cheese made from cream which has been allowed to sour and then drained in muslin, e.g., Demi-sel and Petit-Suisse. The suggested standard butterfat content of the commercial product is 45 per cent. (See Cheese entry.)

A soft home-made 'cream' cheese can be produced from soured milk, the clot being strained through muslin to remove the whey. Pasteurized milk does not sour as satisfactorily as untouched milk; it is better to clot it with rennet or lemon juice and let it stand 12 hours or overnight. When the milk is strained, add seasonings such as salt, pepper or chopped chives. Alternatively, serve as Fromage à la Crème.

CREAM HORN

A favourite pastry confection, which may be made large or small and may be filled with any suitable sweet or savoury mixture.

CREAM HORNS

METRIC/IMPERIAL
225 g/8 oz puff pastry – ready made weight
1 egg, beaten
raspberry jam
150 ml/¼ pint carton double cream
4 × 15 ml spoons/4 tablespoons single cream
icing sugar

Roll out the pastry to a strip 66 cm/26 inches by 10 cm/4 inches to 11.5 cm/4½ inches. Brush with beaten egg. Cut eight 1 cm/½ inch ribbons from the pastry with a sharp knife. Wind each round a cream horn tin, glazed side uppermost; start at the tip, overlapping fractionally, and finish neatly on the underside. The pastry should not overlap the metal rim. Place on a damp baking sheet, join-side down. Bake near the top of a hot oven (220°C/425°F, Gas Mark 7) for 8 to 10 minutes. Cool for a few minutes. Carefully twist each tin, holding the pastry lightly in the other hand, to ease it off the case. A clean teatowel helps if the tin proves too warm to hold. When cold, fill the tip of each horn with a little jam. Whip together the two creams, and fill horns. Dust with icing sugar.

CREAM OF TARTAR

(See Tartaric Acid entry.)

CREAMING

The beating together of fat and sugar to resemble whipped cream in colour and texture. This method of mixing is used for cakes and puddings with a high proportion of fat.

Put the fat and sugar into a bowl and mix them with a wooden spoon. (The bowl may be slightly warmed to make the process easier.) Now beat the fat and sugar hard until the mixture is light and creamy. An electric mixer can be used to make the task easier and quicker.

CRÈME DE CAÇAO

A very sweet French liqueur, chocolate in colour, with the flavour of cocoa.

CRÈME DE MENTHE

A pale-green liqueur, made of wine or grain spirit flavoured with peppermint and sweetened.

CRÊPE SUZETTE

A French sweet pancake. The pancake is very thin, traditionally made from an orange-flavoured batter and re-heated in a mixture of butter, orange juice, sugar, orange liqueur and lemon juice and flamed with orange liqueur or brandy. Served in high class restaurants and usually for very special occasions.

CRÊPES SUZETTE

METRIC/IMPERIAL
butter for frying
300 ml/½ pint rich pancake mixture
50 g/2 oz sugar
50 g/2 oz butter
juice of 2 oranges
grated rind of 1 lemon
3 × 15 ml spoons/3 tablespoons Cointreau
2 × 15 ml spoons/2 tablespoons brandy

Heat a little of the butter in a 15 to 18 cm/6–7 inch thick-based frying pan, pour off the excess and cook the pancakes in the usual way, keep them flat between 2 plates in a warm place. Clean the pan, put in the sugar and heat gently, shaking the pan occasionally until the sugar has melted and turned golden brown. Remove the pan from the heat and add the butter and the orange juice. Fold each pancake in half and then in half again to form a quarter-circle. Add the Cointreau to the fruit juice, replace all the crêpes in the pan and simmer for a few minutes until reheated, spooning the sauce over them. Warm the brandy, pour it over the crêpes, ignite it and serve at once.

CRÉPINETTE

Crépinettes are savoury minced meat cakes resembling little sausages, wrapped in strips of fat bacon or pig's caul, which are baked or fried and served on a bed of spinach or potato. Leftovers or trimmings of poultry, game or veal can be used.

CRESS

This popular salad plant is native to Great Britain; it grows very quickly and easily on any damp patch of ground. Cress appears to be a fairly rich source of vitamins A and C, but the amount consumed at a serving is too small to contribute much of value to the diet.

Cress should be washed very carefully, as grit and soil cling firmly to its stalks. It can be used as a garnish for roast game and poultry, hot and cold entrées, meat, cheese, fish, etc.

CRISPBREAD

Bread made from crushed whole grains, such as rye and wheat, and prepared in large, thin, brittle biscuits.

Crispbread is often served at breakfast instead of toast, offered with the cheese course and used as a base for cocktail savouries. Crispbreads are of course very popular in Scandinavia, where they originated, and always appear on the Smörgasbord; they may also form the base of Smørrebrød (See separate entry).

CROISSANT

Croissants are the classic crisp, flaky rolls served for a Continental breakfast, and are best eaten hot.

They reheat quite well if lightly wrapped in foil. The secret of success in making them lies in layering the fat well, chilling the pastry while it is standing, to keep it firm, and working quickly so that the dough does not become too warm and soft through overhandling. The pastry is only allowed to rise at a warmer temperature after shaping.

CROISSANTS

METRIC/IMPERIAL
25 g/1 oz fresh yeast
300 ml/½ pint water less 4 × 15 ml spoons/4 tablespoons
450 g/1 lb strong plain flour
2 × 5 ml spoons/2 tablespoons salt
25 g/1 oz lard
1 egg, beaten
100–175 g/4–6 oz butter

FOR THE GLAZE
1 egg
about 2 × 5 ml spoons/2 teaspoons water
1 × 2.5 ml spoon/½ teaspoon caster sugar

Blend the yeast with the water. Sift together the flour and salt and rub in the lard. Add the yeast liquid and egg and mix well together. Knead on a lightly floured surface until the dough is smooth, 10 to 15 minutes. Roll the dough into a strip about 51 × 20 × 0.5 cm/20 × 8 × ¼ inch taking care to keep the edges straight and the corners square.

Soften the butter with a knife, then divide into three. Use one part to dot over the top two-thirds of the dough, leaving a small border clear. Fold in three by bringing up the plain (bottom) third first, then folding the top third over. Turn the dough so that the fold is on the right-hand side. Seal the edges with a rolling pin.

Re-shape to a long strip by gently pressing the dough at intervals with a rolling pin. Repeat with the other two portions of butter. Cover the dough with oiled polythene to prevent it forming a skin or cracking. Allow to 'rest' in the refrigerator for 30 minutes. Roll out as before, and repeat the folding and rolling three more times. Place in the refrigerator for at least 1 hour.

Roll the dough out to an oblong about 55 × 33 cm/22 × 13 inch. Cover with lightly oiled polythene and leave for 10 minutes. Trim with a sharp knife to 55 × 30 cm/21 × 12 inch and divide in half lengthwise. Cut each strip into six triangles 15 cm/6 inch high and with a 15 cm/6 inch base. To make the glaze beat the egg, water and sugar together. Brush glaze over the triangles then roll each one loosely from the base. Finishing the tip underneath. Curve into a crescent shape.

Put the shaped croissants on to ungreased baking sheets. Brush the tops with egg glaze, cover each baking sheet inside lightly oiled poly-thene and leave it at room temperature for about 30 minutes, until light and puffy. Brush again with egg glaze before baking in a hot oven (220°C/425°F, Gas Mark 7) for about 20 minutes.

CROQUETTE

A light entrée or garnish made from cooked and finely divided meat, fish, eggs, mushrooms, etc., mixed with a panada or thick binding sauce, formed into cylinders or balls, egg-and-crumb coated and fried.

SAVOURY CROQUETTES

METRIC/IMPERIAL
200 ml/7 fl oz milk
piece of onion
1 bayleaf
blade of mace
40 g/1½ oz butter
40 g/1½ oz flour
225 g/8 oz peeled prawns
75 g/3 oz grated cheddar
salt
ground white pepper
1 egg, beaten
a whole egg
breadcrumbs
sauce tartare

The thickness of the panada (basic sauce) is critical. Its proportions are carefully balanced to ensure that the finished filling will set firmly enough for shaping and yet not be heavy and stodgy to eat. Place the milk in a saucepan with the onion, bayleaf and mace. Bring slowly to just below boiling point, then remove from the heat and cover with a lid. Infuse for 10 minutes. In a separate pan, melt the butter and stir in the flour. Cook gently, stirring, until the mixture bubbles like honeycomb. Take off the heat to strain in the milk. Bring to the boil, stirring continuously for smoothness. Cook for about 2 minutes over a gentle heat – it is important to cook the sauce well or the filling will taste raw. Take pan from the heat and cover with a lid or place buttered greaseproof paper on the sauce to stop a skin forming.

Choose ready peeled cooked prawns for convenience, otherwise allow about 600 ml/1 pint cooked prawns in the shell to yield 100 g/4 oz peeled weight. Chop the peeled prawns fairly finely with a sharp knife. Grate the cheese and add with the prawns to the sauce, beating well to combine evenly. Season generously with salt and freshly milled white pepper, tasting as you go to ensure a lively flavour. Whisk the egg lightly with a fork and beat into the filling. (For added richness, use 2 egg yolks in place of the whole egg.) Leave in the pan, covered, for the flavours to mingle.

When cool, but not cold, turn out the prawn mixture on to a buttered plate or dish. Spread it evenly with a palette knife to give a thickish layer – about 1 cm/½ inch. Brush the surface with a little melted butter and cover with a second plate or cover with buttered greaseproof paper to prevent a skin forming. Allow to cool completely before shaping, preferably in the refrigerator. When quite cold divide the mixture into 8 to 10 equal parts. On a lightly floured surface neatly mould each piece into a cork shape ready for coating, making sure that the ends are kept square. For this stage use a small palette knife and the tips of the fingers lightly floured.

Break the second egg into a shallow dish or plate and beat lightly with a pinch of salt and a teaspoonful of oil for a really crisp coat. Put the breadcrumbs ready on a sheet of greaseproof paper. Lightly flour croquettes first, then place in the beaten egg. With the help of a small palette knife and fork, gently turn to coat thoroughly. Lift out carefully, one at a time, allowing the surplus egg to drain off. Transfer the croquette to the crumbs and with the aid of the paper gently roll croquettes to and fro until well and evenly coated, pressing crumbs in with palette knife. Coat all the croquettes before starting to fry. If time permits, put the coated croquettes in the fridge for an hour to 'set'. Alternative coatings to breadcrumbs are finely chopped nuts, crushed cornflakes or rolled oats.

In a deep, heavy based pan heat enough oil or lard to give a depth of 7.5 cm/3 inches. If a fat thermometer is available heat the oil/fat to 190°C/375°F. Otherwise test the temperature by dropping in a small cube of white bread – it should turn golden in about 20 seconds. The number of croquettes fried at one time should not be more than will cover the base of the pan. Either place the croquettes in a frying basket if you have one and lower into the pan or slide in one at a time with the aid of a fish slice or tongs. Fry until crisp and golden: this will take 3 to 4 minutes. Lift croquettes out in the basket or use a draining spoon. Transfer to absorbent kitchen paper. Whilst frying the next batch, keep hot on a baking sheet in a cool oven (150°C/300°F, Gas Mark 2). Serve with parsley sprigs, lemon wedges and sauce tartare.

CROUSTADE

A case (usually small) made of fried bread, pastry, duchesse potato, etc., used to serve a savoury or sweet mixture.

Fried Bread Croustades: Use bread which is at least 2 days old. Cut it into fingers or rounds about 1.5 cm/¾ inch thick and scoop out the centre part, then fry the cases in deep fat until they are golden-brown.

Fill with a hot mixture such as chopped ham or chicken and mushroom in sauce.

Butter Croustades: Divide some fresh butter into even-sized pieces, 100 g/4 oz will make about 8 croustades, and shape these into balls. Leave them to become cold and firm, then brush them over with beaten egg and coat with breadcrumbs, pressing these well into the butter. Repeat 3 to 4 times until a thick, substantial coating is made. Using a very small round cutter, cut half-way into each ball, but do not remove the cut portion. Put the balls into a frying basket and fry in deep fat from which a faint blue smoke is rising, until the breadcrumbs are golden-brown. Remove and drain the croustades, take off the lid and pour out the melted butter from inside. (This may be used for other cookery purposes.) Fill the croustades with the savoury mixture, handling them gently, as they are fragile, then replace the lids. These croustades may also be made in the shape of small flat rounds or cylinders.

Croûtons to Serve with Soups: Cut the slices of bread 5 mm/¼ inch to 1 cm/½ inch thick, remove the crust and cut into 5 mm/¼ inch dice. Fry these in smoking hot fat and drain, or bake or toast until golden-brown and crisp. Sprinkle with chopped parsley. Alternatively, fry or bake the slices of bread before cutting them up.

CROWBERRY

A heath-like wild plant bearing black berries, which may be used like cranberries.

CROWDY

Scottish for oatmeal gruel or cream cheese.

CROWN OF LAMB OR PORK

A handsome roast dish for a party, consisting of (1) two pieces of best end of neck of lamb each with 6 to 7 cutlets or (2) half a dozen ribs from each side of a loin of pork. The cutlet bones are partially separated and neatly trimmed and scraped, then the joints are bent round and secured in a circular shape, the centre being filled with stuffing. Protect the tips of the bones with greased paper caps to prevent burning. After roasting, the 'crown' is decorated with small white onions, balls of potato or cutlet frills stuck on the end of the cutlet bones. Serve with gravy and a suitable accompaniment such as a red-currant jelly with lamb or an apple sauce with pork.

CRULLER

An American fancy-shaped bun made from a baking powder dough and fried in fat; crullers are very similar to doughnuts.

115

CRUMBLE TOPPING FOR PIES

A rubbed-in plain cake mixture, used instead of pastry as a topping over fruit. A savoury mixture can be made to top meat by omitting the sugar and adding cheese and seasoning.

FRUIT CRUMBLE

METRIC/IMPERIAL
0.75 kg/1½ lb raw fruit, e.g., apples, plums,
   gooseberries, rhubarb, blackcurrants
granulated sugar
75 g/3 oz margarine or butter
175 g/6 oz plain flour

Prepare the fruit as for stewing and layer it in a 750 ml/1½ pint to 1 litre/2 pint ovenproof dish with 100 g/4 oz to 175 g/6 oz sugar, depending on the sharpness of the fruit. Rub the fat into the flour until the mixture is the texture of fine crumbs; stir in 50 g/2 oz sugar. Sprinkle the mixture on top of the prepared fruit and bake in a moderately hot oven (200°C/400°F, Gas Mark 6).

CRUMBS

(See Breadcrumbs entry.)

CRUMPET (PIKELET)

A soft cake made of yeast mixture, which is baked on a griddle in special metal rings. The underneath is smooth and brown and the top is full of small holes.

CRUMPETS

METRIC/IMPERIAL
350 g/12 oz strong plain flour
15 g/½ oz fresh yeast
300 ml/½ pint warm water
about 200 ml/7 fl oz milk
1 × 2.5 ml spoon/½ teaspoon bicarbonate of soda
1 × 5 ml spoon/1 teaspoon salt
oil or lard for greasing

Place half the flour in a bowl with the yeast and warm water. Blend until smooth, cover and leave until frothy, about 20 minutes. Stir in the remaining ingredients gradually, beating until smooth. Add more milk if necessary to make a pouring batter. Grease a griddle or heavy shallow frying pan, and about six crumpet rings or metal cutters, 7.5 cm/3 inches in diameter. Heat thoroughly. Pour about 2 × 15 ml spoons/2 tablespoons of the batter into the rings on the hot griddle. Cook until set and holes are formed before removing rings and turn crumpets over to brown lightly on the other side. Cool on a wire rack. Toast lightly on both sides and serve hot and buttered.

CRUST

The commonest meaning of this term is the crisp or outer part of a loaf, pie or other baked dish. As applied to wine, crust means the deposit of organic salts which wines throw off as they age.

CUBEB

A kind of pepper, native to the East Indies. The grey beans when dried somewhat resemble peppercorns. They have a pungent, spicy flavour like camphor and are used in Eastern cookery and also in some medicines.

CUCUMBER

The fleshy fruit of the gourd family originally from northern India. Cucumbers are eaten raw, sliced thinly and served as a salad vegetable or as an accompaniment to cold entrées, fish dishes, etc.; they also make an attractive decoration. (See Garnish entry.) They can also be cooked in a variety of ways and are then somewhat similar to marrow, with a distinctive but delicate flavour. Braised, stuffed or made into soups, are popular ways of serving cucumber. Small varieties of cucumber, known as gherkins, are often pickled. When buying cucumbers, choose those with a firm smooth skin.

Cucumber has little food value.

BUTTERED CUCUMBER

1 large plump cucumber
water
salt
knob of butter
freshly ground black pepper

Thinly pare the skin from the cucumber using a potato peeler. Cut the cucumber into about 5 cm/2 inch lengths and each piece into 4 lengthwise; remove some of the seed area. Place cucumber sticks in a saucepan with just enough water to barely cover, add salt and cook for about 7 minutes, making sure they remain crisp. Drain off the liquid and, just before serving, add a knob of butter and some freshly ground pepper.

MINTED CUCUMBER AND CELERY

METRIC/IMPERIAL
½ medium cucumber, finely diced
3 to 4 sticks celery, trimmed and finely sliced
150 ml/¼ pint natural yogurt
large pinch celery salt
a pinch of dried mint or 1 × 5 ml spoon/1 teaspoon
   fresh chopped mint
grated rind of ½ lemon
freshly ground black pepper

Put the cucumber and celery into a bowl. Add the yogurt, celery salt, mint, lemon rind and pepper. Mix them well together and chill before serving.

RAITA

A cool fresh tasting accompaniment to Indian dishes which can be made from a variety of fresh raw vegetables.

METRIC/IMPERIAL
half a cucumber about 225 g/8 oz
1 onion, skinned and finely chopped
1 clove of garlic, skinned and crushed
300 ml/½ pint natural yogurt
1 × 2.5 ml spoon/½ teaspoon salt
a pinch of black pepper

Dice the cucumber finely. Combine with the other ingredients and chill thoroughly for one hour before serving.

CULLIS (COULIS)

Originally this meant the juices that ran out of meat in the natural way while it was cooking. It then came to mean various sauces, but especially a rich gravy or concentrate made from meat and/or poultry, used in making sauces, soups and stews, etc. Veal stock is also sometimes called by this name.

The French term *coulis* is also used for a thickened type of soup made with a purée of game, poultry, fish or shellfish (though some authorities say that the last-named should be called a bisque).

CUMBERLAND SAUCE

METRIC/IMPERIAL
1 orange
1 lemon
4 × 15 ml spoons/4 tablespoons redcurrant jelly
4 × 15 ml spoons/4 tablespoons port
2 × 5 ml spoons/2 teaspoons arrowroot
2 × 5 ml spoons/2 teaspoons water

Pare the rind thinly from the orange and lemon, free of all the white pith. To pare, use either a very sharp, small vegetable knife or a special knife used solely for paring and called a cannel knife. Cut it in fine strips, cover with water and simmer for 5 minutes. Squeeze the juice from both fruits. Put the redcurrant jelly, orange juice and lemon juice in a pan, stir until the jelly dissolves, simmer for 5 minutes and add the port. Blend the arrowroot and water to a smooth cream and stir in the redcurrant mixture. Return the sauce to the pan and reheat, stirring until it thickens and clears. Drain the strips of rind and add to the sauce.

Serve with ham, venison and lamb.

CUMIN

A plant of the carrot family native to Egypt, Asia and the Mediterranean, its strong, spicy seeds are used to flavour liqueurs, cordials, cheese, breads, sauces, curries and pilaffs.

CUMQUAT

(See Kumquat entry.)

CUP

A type of drink usually made from claret or light white wine diluted with ice or soda water, and with sprigs of herbs, fruit and flavourings added. (See Champagne, Cider and Claret Cups, entries.)

CUP CUSTARD

Egg custard served in individual custard cups and decorated with ratafia biscuits.

CUP MEASURE

A special cup used for measuring ingredients in cookery. It is the standard method of measuring in U.S.A., Canada and Australia, all recipes quoting ingredients in cups. The standard American cup contains 250 ml/8 fl oz. There are British Standard cup measures which are as follows:

250 ml
150 ml
100 ml
75 ml
50 ml (optional in a set)

CURAÇAO

A sweet liqueur made of wine or grain spirit, sugar and orange pulp and peel. It is usually white or red and there are also some orange, green and blue types. Cointreau and Grand Marnier are both Curaçao liqueurs.

CURD

(See Lemon Curd entry.)

CURD CHEESE

(See Cottage Cheese and Cheese entries.)

CURDS

Curds are formed by milk when it coagulates – either naturally or because acid or rennet have been added. They consist of the proteins plus other constituents trapped with them. They may be eaten as they are or pressed to form cheese.

To Make Curds: Put 600 ml/1 pint milk into a saucepan with a squeeze of lemon juice and heat very slowly until a curd has formed; the milk must not be allowed to boil. Turn on to a sieve lined with muslin and leave until the whey has drained away and the curd is dry. Serve with cream and caster sugar. (See Cheesecakes entry.)

CURING

The process of salting and smoking fish or meat to preserve it. (See Salting and Bacon entries.)

CURLY KALE

(See Kale entry.)

CURRANT

This term is used both for an imported dried fruit and for a group of fresh fruits known as black, red and white currants. (See separate entries.)

Currants are dried seedless grapes, very small, deriving their name from Corinth, the Greek region from which they originally came. Supplies arrive here in the autumn. The best quality, known as Vosdizy currants, are fleshy and have a fine bloom, rich colour and soft skin. Currants are also imported from Australia, the shipments arriving here in Spring.

Currants are used in fruit cakes, biscuits, mincemeat, puddings and breads. They are widely available in a ready to use condition.

To Clean Currants: (See Dried Fruit entry.)

Currant Bread and Buns: (See Bread and Bun entry.)

CURRY

A savoury dish of Eastern and particularly Indian origin; it is highly flavoured with a mixture of condiments and spices, many of which are grown in India and similar regions. The main characteristics are that it is spicy, often hot and both sweet and acid in taste.

Mutton, chicken, fish and vegetables are the foods most usually served in the form of a curry. The cooking time naturally varies with the ingredients used: uncooked fish needs 15 to 20 minutes; uncooked meat or chicken 1 to 2 hours and vegetables about 30 minutes to 1 hour, according to type. All curries and curry sauces should be thoroughly cooked, to develop the flavour and blend the ingredients.

The flavourings may be varied to suit individual tastes and they should be so skilfully blended that no individual flavour predominates. Great variety may be achieved by adding, for example 1 × 2.5 ml spoon/½ teaspoon of powdered mixed spice, mace, cinnamon or allspice, or a very little garlic vinegar (vinegar in which a few chopped cloves of garlic have been steeped) or 1 × 15 ml spoon/1 tablespoon of preserved tamarinds instead of the lemon juice. Small quantities of freshly shredded coconut and a little coconut milk, or grated almonds, walnuts or Brazil nuts, give soft, mellow flavour.

The coconut milk mentioned in many recipes means an infusion of the coconut flesh, not the liquid found in the newly-opened fresh nut. (See Coconut entry.)

Curry Powder and Paste

Curry powder is a commercially prepared mixture of finely ground spices and different makers have their own recipes. Curry paste sometimes contains spices that are not included in the powder form. Both can be bought in prepared form and if you get a reliable brand and use it while it is still fresh, you can make very palatable but not true Indian curries.

Connoisseurs of Eastern cooking usually prefer, however, to use fresh spices of which these preparations are composed; they are chiefly cayenne, coriander, turmeric, cumin seed, ginger, mace, cloves, cardamom, fenugreek and pepper. Spices should be freshly ground if possible, so the best plan is to buy them in seed or 'whole' form and pound them in a mortar or electric grinder. To prevent deterioration, keep them in a dry place in well-corked bottles or tins. If you prefer, you can grind sufficient to make up a small supply of curry powder.

Making and Serving Curries

The cooking of many curries starts with the frying of the spices. Generally, begin with the mustard seed (which has a disconcerting habit of jumping, so don't be startled); add fenugreek last, as it burns rather easily. Fry the spices gently, turning them frequently, and avoid overcooking, which makes a dish taste pungent and bitter. If you are using curry powder, this too is often fried, to get rid of the raw taste.

The amount of either curry powder or individual spices and condiments can, of course, be varied to suit your own taste when you make a particular curry.

Here are some other notes about the art of curry-making:
1. Always cook curries slowly to extract the richness which is so characteristic of the dish.
2. Curries are rarely thickened with flour – the long cooking should give the sauce the required consistency.
3. In many Eastern recipes a sealed casserole is recommended. A thick flour-and-water paste is put round the rim of the casserole to reduce the amount of moisture escaping as steam and the cooking is done in a very little liquid.

4. If onions and garlic are fried as a preliminary step, do not allow them to brown unless this is specifically mentioned – to prevent browning, cover the pan with a lid and fry very slowly.

5. Although in this country we sometimes include apples (as a substitute for mangoes), sultanas, almonds, etc., these are not used in a true Indian curry, though they may appear in the accompanying rice or in pilaus and similar dishes.

6. Another British habit which is not known in India is that of garnishing a dish of curry with rice – the two are always served separately.

7. The main ingredients of a curry should be so prepared that the curry can be eaten with a spoon.

Accompaniments for Curries

Dry boiled rice (see Rice entry for method of cooking) is the almost invariable main accompaniment. Unpolished rice is more nutritious than polished and Patna rice is better than Carolina for curries, though either can be used.

Many types of side dish or titbit are served with curry in different Eastern countries and these accompaniments are known by such names as *sambals*, *santals*, *agram-bagrams* and *toulimoulis*. They may include tomato, sweet peppers, chutneys, cucumbers, mangoes, sliced hard-boiled eggs, grated fresh coconut topped with a sprinkling of red chilli, young French beans fried in oil and garnished with fried onion and many other attractive and colourful titbits. Serve each separately. Chapattis and poppadums are types of Indian breads often eaten with curries. (See separate entries.)

A suitable drink to serve with the curry would be an iced lager.

VINDALOO

From Western India a dish traditionally based on pork. The marinade imparts a characteristic hot and sharp flavour. You can use other meats, duck or here we introduce prawns.

METRIC/IMPERIAL
1 × 5 ml spoon/1 teaspoon coriander seeds
1 × 5 ml spoon/1 teaspoon cumin seeds
1 × 5 ml spoon/1 teaspoon mustard seeds
2.5 cm/1 inch piece of fresh root ginger, peeled and chopped
1 × 5 ml spoon/1 teaspoon ground cloves
1 × 2.5 ml spoon/½ teaspoon ground turmeric
150 ml/¼ pint white vinegar
3 cloves of garlic, skinned and crushed
2 onions, skinned and chopped
0.5 kg/1 lb prepared fresh prawns or frozen, thawed
3 × 15 ml spoons/3 tablespoons oil
2 tomatoes, skinned and chopped
1 × 5 ml spoon/1 teaspoon salt
1 × 2.5 ml spoon/½ teaspoon black pepper

Grind the seeds, ginger and spices in an electric mill or mortar. Blend this to a paste with the vinegar adding the garlic and half the onion. Add to the prepared prawns and leave for an hour to marinade. Heat the oil and gently fry the rest of the onion and gradually add the marinaded prawn mixture. Continue to cook for 2 to 3 minutes, stir in the tomatoes. Season with salt and pepper. Simmer gently for 5 to 10 minutes.

ROGAN JOSH

A popular richly spiced Northern Indian curry which tends to be drier than some. Mutton is the traditional choice but lamb is perfectly acceptable.

METRIC/IMPERIAL
3 × 15 ml spoons/3 tablespoons oil
1 onion, skinned and sliced
3 cloves of garlic, skinned and crushed
2 × 5 ml spoons/2 teaspoons ground ginger
2 × 5 ml spoons/2 teaspoons paprika
1 × 15 ml spoon/1 tablespoon ground coriander
1 × 5 ml spoon/1 teaspoon ground cumin
1 × 5 ml spoon/1 teaspoon ground turmeric
1 × 2.5 ml spoon/½ teaspoon cayenne pepper
large pinch of the following: ground clove, nutmeg, mace and cardamom
0.75 kg/1½ lb boned lean mutton or lamb, cubed
300 ml/½ pint natural yogurt
1 × 5 ml spoon/1 teaspoon salt
4 tomatoes, skinned and chopped
chopped parsley for garnish

Heat the oil in a large pan and brown the onion. Add the garlic and all the other spices with the meat and gently fry for 5 minutes. Stir in the yogurt, salt and tomatoes. Bring to the boil, simmer, reduce heat and stir occasionally, until the meat is tender and the sauce thick, about 1½ hours. If the sauce thickens too much before the meat is cooked, add some extra water or tomato juice. Serve hot, garnished with chopped parsley and accompanied by plain rice.

SAMOSAS

These are deep fried pastries containing a spicy filling which can be meat or vegetables. The little extra effort required in their making is worthwhile, they are delicious as an appetizer or snack.

METRIC/IMPERIAL
PASTRY
225 g/8 oz plain white flour
1 × 2.5 ml spoon/½ teaspoon salt
25 g/1 oz butter
4–6 × 15 ml spoons/4–6 tablespoons water

FILLING
1 onion, skinned and finely chopped
2 garlic cloves, skinned and crushed

1 green chilli, seeded and finely chopped
2.5 cm/1 inch piece of fresh ginger, peeled and
   chopped
25 g/1 oz butter
1 × 2.5 ml spoon/½ teaspoon ground turmeric
1 × 2.5 ml spoon/½ teaspoon chilli powder
1 × 5 ml spoon/1 teaspoon salt
2 × 5 ml spoons/2 teaspoons garam masala
350 g/12 oz raw minced lean meat

Make pastry as for shortcrust, then knead for about 5 minutes, until smooth and elastic. Leave covered with a damp cloth whilst making the filling. Gently fry the onion, garlic, fresh chilli and ginger in the hot pot for 5 minutes. Stir in the seasonings and the meat, mix well and fry for 15 minutes. Remove from the heat, allow to cool whilst shaping the pastry. Divide the pastry into 15 equal pieces. Roll out each to form a 10 cm/4 inch round. Cut each round in half and lightly dampen the edges of these semi-circles. Shape each up to form a cone and fill each with some of the mixture. Seal the edges well and set aside in a cool place for 30 minutes. Deep fry in hot oil, a few at a time, for 2 to 3 minutes until a golden brown. Drain and serve hot.

AVIAL (AVIYAL)

A mild vegetable curry with coconut and yogurt. The choice of vegetables is wide open, a variety is best. Indians always include okra (ladies fingers) to this or any other vegetable dish whenever they get the chance.

METRIC/IMPERIAL

1 × 5 ml spoon/1 teaspoon mustard seeds
1 onion, skinned and finely chopped
1 green chilli, seeded and finely chopped
1 × 5 ml spoon/1 teaspoon ground turmeric
1 × 15 ml spoon/1 tablespoon ground coriander
4 × 15 ml spoons/4 tablespoons oil
0.5 kg/1 lb mixed vegetables, prepared and sliced
   (choose from aubergine, carrots, beans, cauliflower,
   green pepper, okra, potatoes, tomatoes)
1 × 5 ml spoon/1 teaspoon salt
100 g/4 oz fresh grated coconut
150 ml/¼ pint carton natural yogurt
25 g/1 oz butter, melted

Gently fry the mustard seeds, onion, chilli and spices in the hot oil. Toss in the prepared vegetables, season with the salt, and simmer with sufficient water to just keep the vegetables moist. Cook until the vegetables are virtually cooked though still crunchy (the time will depend on the choice of vegetables used, those needing a little longer cooking can be started first). Stir in the coconut and simmer for a further 5 minutes. Remove from the heat, stir in the yogurt and melted butter and then serve.

TANDOORI CHICKEN

A hot, but not fiery, spiced chicken which is marinated overnight and then baked in a Tandoor oven. Here it is adapted for roasting and basting in a gas or electric oven.

METRIC/IMPERIAL

1.5 kg/3 lb oven-ready chicken, washed and dried
1 × 5 ml spoon/1 teaspoon salt
2 × 5 ml spoons/2 teaspoons chilli powder
1 × 2.5 ml spoon/½ teaspoon ground black pepper
2 × 15 ml spoons/2 tablespoons lemon juice

MARINADE

3 × 15 ml spoons/3 tablespoons natural yogurt
4 cloves of garlic, skinned and chopped
5 cm/2 inch piece of fresh root ginger, peeled and
   chopped
1 × 5 ml spoon/1 teaspoon cumin seeds
1 × 15 ml spoon/1 tablespoon coriander seeds
1 × 5 ml spoon/1 teaspoon paprika
1 × 2.5 ml spoon/½ teaspoon ground turmeric
1 × 2.5 ml spoon/½ teaspoon ground cinnamon
50 g/2 oz ghee or butter

Pierce all the flesh of the chicken with a sharp, thin skewer or needle. Sprinkle salt inside the bird. Stir together the chilli powder, seasonings and lemon juice. Rub this well into the chicken flesh and leave for 20 minutes. Prepare the marinade by blending all the ingredients to form a smooth paste. (Grind the spices first in an electric mill or mortar.) Place the chicken on a wide shallow plate or dish and spread over the marinade, again rubbing well into the flesh. Cover and leave for 24 hours in the refrigerator. Place the chicken on a rack (i.e., small cooling rack or small grill pan rack) and place this over a roasting tin containing 2.5 cm/1 inch cold water. Spoon over any remaining marinade from the bowl. Cover the chicken with small dabs of softened ghee or butter. Roast the chicken in a moderately hot oven (200°C/400°F, Gas Mark 6) for about 1 hour until tender, baste frequently with the liquid in the tin.

BIRYANI

A dish from the Moglai area in which rice is layered with spicy meat and onions. Originally made with lamb but adapts well to chicken pieces. May also be served as a vegetable dish.

METRIC/IMPERIAL

350 g/12 oz long grain rice
1 × 5 ml spoon/1 teaspoon saffron fronds
4 × 15 ml spoons/4 tablespoons oil
2 cloves of garlic, skinned and crushed
2.5 cm/1 inch piece fresh ginger, peeled and chopped
0.75 kg/1½ lb boned lean lamb, cubed
a pinch of cayenne pepper
1 × 5 ml spoon/1 teaspoon ground cumin

1 × 5 ml spoon/1 teaspoon ground coriander
1 × 5 ml spoon/1 teaspoon black pepper
1 × 5 ml spoon/1 teaspoon salt
1 × 5 ml spoon/1 teaspoon ground cloves
1 × 5 ml spoon/1 teaspoon ground cinnamon
300 ml/ ½ pint natural yogurt
2 onions, skinned and sliced
25 g/1 oz flaked almonds
25 g/1 oz sultanas
25 g/1 oz butter

Soak rice in cold water to cover. Put saffron fronds to soak in 4 × 15 ml spoons/4 tablespoons hot water. Leave both for about 30 minutes. Heat the oil and lightly fry the garlic and the ginger. Add the prepared meat and fry for 5 minutes. Stir in the spices and yogurt, blend well together and simmer for about 35 minutes. Meanwhile bring to the boil 900 ml/1½ pints lightly salted water. Drain the rice and plunge into the boiling water, bring back to the boil and boil for 2 minutes. Drain well and then divide into three portions. Place one third of the rice in a 1.5 litre/2½ pint casserole dish. Soak another third of the rice in the saffron water to colour it yellow. Place half of the lamb on top of the rice in the casserole and top with half the onion. Next add the drained saffron rice and repeat with the rest of the lamb and onion, with the remainder of the rice as the top layer. Cover the casserole with aluminium foil and then the lid of the casserole and bake in a moderate oven (180°C/350°F, Gas Mark 4) for 30 minutes. Sauté the almonds and sultanas in the butter and sprinkle on top of the biryani to garnish.

CURRY SAUCE

METRIC/IMPERIAL
2 medium sized onions, skinned
25 g/1 oz dripping or butter
1 × 15 ml spoon/1 tablespoon curry powder
1 × 5 ml spoon/1 teaspoon curry paste
1 × 15 ml spoon/1 tablespoon rice flour or ordinary
  flour
1 clove garlic, skinned and crushed
200 ml/7 fl oz stock or coconut milk
salt
little cayenne pepper
2 × 15 ml spoons/2 tablespoons chutney
1 × 15 ml spoon/1 tablespoon single cream, optional

Slice the onions and chop them finely. Melt the fat, fry the onions golden brown and add the curry powder, paste and rice (or ordinary) flour. Cook for 5 minutes, then add the garlic, pour in the stock or coconut milk and bring to the boil. Add the seasonings and chutney, cover and simmer for 30 to 40 minutes. This sauce is improved by the addition of the cream immediately before use and less curry powder may be used for those who prefer a mild dish.

Note: The rice flour and ordinary flour can be omitted, since a curry is thickened by reduction of the liquid and by long, slow simmering.

CUSHION

The cut nearest the udder in lamb or beef.

CUSTARD

A mixture of eggs and milk, with a characteristic somewhat jelly-like consistency due to the way in which eggs coagulate when heated. Special care is needed when making egg custards to heat the mixture only sufficiently to cook the eggs, as overheating results in curdling. The use of a double saucepan helps to control the temperature. Mock custards, which are often served as a sweet sauce with puddings or sweets, can be made with cornflour or with the various proprietary custard powders on the market; follow the manufacturer's instructions. The mixture is usually sweetened (though savoury versions of egg custards are sometimes served) and it may be flavoured.

Custards can be served alone or as an accompaniment to other dishes and often form part of cold sweets, such as trifles, fruit fools and moulds.

Canned custards are now available; they are more expensive than the home-made variety but are useful when speed is important.

BAKED CUSTARD

METRIC/IMPERIAL
600 ml/1 pint milk
3 eggs
2 × 15 ml spoons/2 tablespoons sugar
ground nutmeg

Warm the milk in a saucepan but don't boil it. Whisk the eggs and sugar lightly in a basin; pour on the hot milk, stirring all the time. Strain the mixture into a greased ovenproof dish, sprinkle the nutmeg on top and bake in a moderate oven (160°C/325°F, Gas Mark 3) for about 45 minutes, or until set and firm to the touch.

Note: The dish containing custard can be stood in a shallow tin containing water – this helps to ensure that the custard does not curdle or separate through overheating. Bake in individual dishes if preferred.

EGG CUSTARD SAUCE

METRIC/IMPERIAL
1½ eggs or 3 yolks
1 × 15 ml spoon/1 tablespoon sugar
300 ml/ ½ pint milk
few strips of thinly pared lemon rind or vanilla pod,
  split

Whisk the eggs and sugar lightly. Warm the milk and lemon rind and leave to infuse for 10 minutes. Pour the milk on to the eggs and strain the mixture into the top of a double boiler or into a thick-based saucepan. Stir over a very gentle heat until the sauce thickens and lightly coats the back of the spoon. Do not boil.

Serve hot or cold, with fruit sweets.

EGG CUSTARD TART

METRIC/IMPERIAL
150 g/5 oz shortcrust pastry i.e., made with 150 g/
5 oz flour etc.
2 eggs
2 × 15 ml spoons/2 tablespoons sugar
300 ml/½ pint milk
a little grated or ground nutmeg

Roll out the pastry, use it to line a fairly deep 18 cm/7 inch pie plate or flan case and decorate the edge. Place on a baking sheet. Whisk the eggs lightly with the sugar; warm the milk and pour on to the egg mixture. Strain the custard into the pastry case and sprinkle the top with nutmeg. Bake in a hot oven (220°C/425°F, Gas Mark 7) for about 10 minutes, until the pastry begins to brown. Reduce the oven temperature (180°C/350°F, Gas Mark 4) and continue cooking for a further 20 minutes, or until the custard is just set. Serve cold.

Note: If you have trouble with the crust rising when making a custard tart, this is probably due to a small break in the pastry. To avoid this (1) don't stretch the pastry when lining the pie plate; (2) brush the lined pie plate with raw egg white before adding the custard mixture to 'seal' the pastry.

CUSTARD APPLE

The fruit of a tree grown in the West Indies and South America. The large sweet fruit resembles a small pineapple; the flesh is yellow and of a pulpy nature.

CUSTARD MARROW

A member of the squash family, native to Mexico and now grown in various hot regions. The fruits may be used like pumpkin or marrow.

CUT-AND-FOLD

(See Folding-in entry.)

CUTLET

A term applied to a chop cut out from the best end of neck of lamb, veal (see Escalope) or pork. Cutlets may be grilled, fried or braised.

FRIED LAMB CUTLETS

Use small, lean cutlets cut from the best end of neck, remove the skin and any excess fat and scrape the end of the bone for at least 2.5 cm/1 inch, giving the cutlets a good shape and a neat appearance. Prepare some breadcrumbs and beat an egg in a shallow dish. Season each cutlet, brush over with the egg and cover it with crumbs. Wipe all crumbs off the exposed bone and fry the cutlets in smoking fat for 10 minutes, turning them once or twice. When golden-brown, drain on soft paper and dish up with a cutlet frill on the end of each cutlet. Pour brown or tomato sauce round and garnish the dish with green peas or pieces of carrot and celery.

LAMB CUTLETS PAPRIKA

METRIC/IMPERIAL
12 lamb cutlets
100 g/4 oz butter
1 × 5 ml spoon/1 teaspoon paprika pepper
1 × 2.5 ml spoon/½ teaspoon ground ginger
2 × 15 ml spoons/2 tablespoons capers, chopped
watercress for garnish

Trim the cutlets or get the butcher to do this for you. Place in a single layer in a baking dish and cook in a hot oven (220°C/425°F, Gas Mark 7) for about 20 minutes. Meanwhile, cream together the butter, paprika, ginger and capers. Drain the juices from the cutlets, spread the seasoned butter over them and return the dish to the oven to cook the cutlets for a further 10 to 15 minutes until they are crisp, golden and bubbly. Serve garnished with sprigs of crisp watercress.

BUTTERY LAMB GRILL

METRIC/IMPERIAL
25 g/1 oz butter
1 × 15 ml spoon/1 tablespoon corn oil
1 × 5 ml spoon/1 teaspoon each fresh chopped mint
and rosemary
1 clove garlic, optional
fresh ground black pepper
1 × 15 ml spoon/1 tablespoon lemon juice
8 lamb cutlets, trimmed
salt

In a small pan, melt the butter and add the oil, mint, rosemary, clove of garlic cut in half, a few turns of pepper and the lemon juice. Turn the cutlets in this marinade and leave for about 1 hour. Discard the garlic. Grill cutlets for about 5 minutes on each side under a fast grill, brushing with the excess marinade as needed. Towards the end of cooking, season with salt. Serve barbecue-style with paper napkins for easy handling, or as a main meal with buttered new potatoes, grilled tomato halves and sliced beans.

LAMB CUTLETS NAVARRE

METRIC/IMPERIAL
4 lamb cutlets
salt
pepper
25 g/1 oz lard
225 g/8 oz slice of gammon, diced
1 onion, chopped
0.5 kg/1 lb tomatoes, skinned and chopped
225 g/8 oz chipolata sausages

Season cutlets with salt and pepper and fry in the lard. When browned transfer to a casserole dish. Fry gammon and onion in the same fat. When onions are golden, add tomatoes, season and cook for 10 minutes. Pour sauce over cutlets, cover casserole and cook in a moderate oven (180°C/350°F, Gas Mark 4) for 20 to 30 minutes. Fry sausages. Place cutlets in a hot dish and garnish with sausages.

LAMB CUTLETS SAUTÉS

METRIC/IMPERIAL
75 g/3 oz butter
8 lamb cutlets, trimmed
2 × 5 ml spoons/2 teaspoons caster sugar

Melt the butter in a frying pan, add the cutlets and brown on each side for 2 to 3 minutes. Sprinkle with sugar, turn and cook for a further 3 to 4 minutes. Sprinkle the second side with sugar and cook again. Serve with a cutlet frill on the end of each bone.

CUTLETS, MOCK

Savoury mixtures of meat, fish, eggs or vegetables are often shaped like cutlets, egg-and-crumbed and fried. The bone at the thin end is imitated by inserting a short piece of macaroni.

CUTTING-IN

To combine one ingredient (usually fat) with others, by means of a knife used with a repeated downward cutting motion.

CYGNET

(See Swan entry.)

CYANOBALAMIN

One of the B vitamins. (See Vitamins entry.)

DAB

A small flat fish of the plaice and flounder species. It is light brown in colour, with small dark spots and white underside and has close-set scales. Generally 100 g/4 oz to 175 g/6 oz in weight. Dabs, which are considered to be the sweetest-flavoured fish of the plaice family, are excellent when egg-and-crumbed and either fried or baked. (See Plaice entry for general method of preparation and cooking.)

DABCHICK

A small moorhen or waterfowl.

DACE (DARE, DART)

A small freshwater fish of the carp family. It is not often used as food, as it does not grow to any size and has coarse, rather tasteless flesh. It can, however, be fried, grilled or baked whole, with or without a stuffing.

DAIQUIRI

A Cuban rum, also a drink made with the rum and fresh lime juice.

DAMASCENE

An inferior type of damson.

DAMSON

A very small variety of plum, dark blue in colour and slightly pointed at one end, which ripens in late August-September. It grows wild in some parts of Great Britain, but is also cultivated in country gardens.

If absolutely ripe, damsons can be eaten raw, but they are much better cooked in such dishes as damson pie and pudding. They also make delicious jam, jelly and cheese – having a high acid and pectin content, damsons give a very good set in these preserves.

DAMSON JAM

METRIC/IMPERIAL
2.25 kg/5 lb damsons
900 ml/1 ½ pints water
2.75 kg/6 lb sugar

Wash and pick over the damsons, put in a pan with the water and simmer for about 30 minutes, until the fruit is really soft. Add the sugar, stir until dissolved and boil rapidly until setting point is reached, removing the stones as they rise with a slotted spoon. Pot and cover in the usual way. *Makes about 4.5 kg/10 lb.*

(See also Blackberry and Damson Cheese in Cheese entry.)

DANDELION

The flowers of this wild plant may be used for making wine, while the leaves may be eaten raw in salads or boiled and served as a vegetable. If they are to be cooked, wash them well and cook them like spinach; when they are quite tender, sieve them, season well and add a knob of butter.

(For Dandelion wine, see Wines, Home-made entry.)

DANISH BLUE CHEESE

A soft white cheese made from full cream cows milk and veined with blue mould. It is produced in Denmark and has a sharp, strong flavour.

DARIOLE

Originally the name of a small cake, the word now means a small, narrow mould with sloping sides, used for making madeleines and individual sweets and savouries.

DARTOIS

A small, light pastry, suitably filled or flavoured, which is served as an hors d'œuvre or occasionally as a sweet. Puff pastry is generally used.

CHEESE DARTOIS

METRIC/IMPERIAL
1 egg, beaten
25 g/1 oz butter, melted
50 g/2 oz Cheddar cheese, grated
salt
pepper
100 g/4 oz flaky pastry, or 215 g/7½ oz pkt frozen
   puff pastry, thawed
beaten egg to glaze

Mix the beaten egg, butter and cheese to a smooth paste and season well. Roll out the pastry thinly into a 33 cm/13 inch square, cut it in half and place one half on a baking tray. Spread the cheese mixture over the pastry to within 5 mm/¼ inch of each edge. Damp the edges with water and cover with the remaining pastry. Glaze with the beaten egg and mark the pastry into fingers. Bake in a moderately hot oven (200°C/400°F, Gas Mark 6) for about 10 to 15 minutes, until well risen and golden brown. Cut into fingers before serving.

DATE

The fruit of the date palm which is cultivated in Northern Africa, Western Asia and South California. The best-quality dates, which come from Tunis, are large, tender and very sweet, with unwrinkled skins of a golden-brown colour. Dessert dates are usually dried before they become very ripe and are loosely packed (often on the stem) in long boxes. Other less expensive varieties, quite suitable for cooking, are stoned when they are quite ripe, pressed into a block and sold in bulk. Fresh dates are becoming more readily available.

Dietetically, dates are primarily of value for their sugar content (about 50 per cent), which means that they are useful as a concentrated source of energy.

DATE BRAN MUFFINS

METRIC/IMPERIAL
90 g/3½ oz plain flour
1 × 2.5 ml spoon/½ teaspoon salt
1 × 15 ml spoon/1 tablespoon baking powder
50 g/2 oz bran
275 ml/9 fl oz milk
2 × 15 ml spoons/2 tablespoons whipped-up white
   cooking fat
3 × 15 ml spoons/3 tablespoons caster sugar
1 egg, beaten
100 g/4 oz dates, chopped

Grease 12 to 16 6 cm/2½ inch deep muffin tins. Sift the flour, salt and baking powder. Soak the bran in the milk for 5 minutes. Meanwhile, cream the fat

and sugar until light, add the beaten egg and mix until smooth. Add to the bran mixture and stir. Add the flour mixture and dates, stirring only until just mixed. Fill the muffin tins two-thirds full and bake in a moderately hot oven (200°C/400°F, Gas Mark 6) for 20 to 25 minutes, until golden and well risen. Cool on a wire rack.

DATE SCONE BARS

METRIC/IMPERIAL
225 g/8 oz plain flour
1 × 2.5 ml spoon/½ teaspoon bicarbonate of soda
1 × 5 ml spoon/1 teaspoon cream of tartar
pinch of salt
50 g/2 oz butter or block margarine
25 g/1 oz sugar
75 g/3 oz dates, stoned
about 150 ml/¼ pint milk

Preheat a baking sheet. Sift together the dry ingredients. Rub in the fat until the mixture resembles fine breadcrumbs; add the sugar. Using kitchen scissors, snip the dates into small pieces and add to the mixture. Mix to a light dough with the milk. Roll out the dough into an oblong 30.5 × 10 cm/12 × 14 inches. Brush with milk and place on the baking sheet. Mark into eight bars, using the back of a knife. Bake in a hot oven (230°C/450°F, Gas Mark 8) for about 15 minutes. Break apart and cool on a wire rack. Eat on day of making.

STEAMED DATE SUET PUDDING

METRIC/IMPERIAL
100 g/4 oz chopped dates
175 g/6 oz self raising flour
pinch of salt
75 g/3 oz shredded suet
2 × 15 ml spoons/2 tablespoons caster sugar
grated rind of a lemon
about 150 ml/¼ pint milk

Half-fill a steamer or large saucepan with water and put on to boil. Grease a 900 ml/1½ pint pudding basin. Mix the dates, flour, salt, suet, sugar and lemon rind. Make a well in the centre and add enough milk to give a soft dropping consistency. Put into the greased basin, cover with greased greaseproof paper or foil and secure with string. Steam over rapidly boiling water for 1½ to 2 hours. Serve with lemon sauce, custard or pouring cream.

VARIATIONS
For a lighter pudding use 75 g/3 oz self raising flour and 75 g/3 oz fresh white breadcrumbs. For a richer pudding, use 1 beaten egg and about 6 × 15 ml spoons/6 tablespoons milk instead of the 150 ml/¼ pint milk.

PICKLED DATES

METRIC/IMPERIAL
1.5 kg/3 lb dates
1.5 litres/2 ½ pints vinegar
350 g/12 oz brown sugar
40 g/1 ½ oz mixed pickling spices

Stone and halve the dates. Boil the vinegar, sugar and spices together until a syrup is formed. Place the dates in a jar, pour the hot syrup over them and allow to get cold. Tie down and keep for 3 months before use.

STUFFED DATES
(See Sweets entry.)

DATE-MARKING

This applies to two methods of coding food to indicate its shelf life:

(a) Most packaged, canned and prepared foods are coded by the manufacturer to indicate the date of delivery. The retailer has a key to the code and can therefore place food on the shelves in rotation.

(b) Sell-by-dates are stamped on certain short life foods (yogurt, cream, butter etc.) for the benefit of the customer. The food should still keep for 2 to 3 days after this date. Neither such coding or marking is compulsory but an E.E.C. system may be introduced to make it so in the future.

DAUBING

(See Larding entry.)

DECANTING

Pouring wine carefully from a bottle into a wine jug or decanter, leaving any sediment in the bottle. It is only necessary with fine wines which have been long aged in the bottle, such as old clarets and ports. However, younger wines can also benefit from being exposed to the air before serving. Decanting is also done for aesthetic reasons.

DEEP FRYING

(See Frying entry.)

DEHYDRATED FOODS

Foods commercially dried to preserve them as spoilage organisms cannot thrive without moisture. They keep well if stored in an air-tight container – they have the advantage of taking up less storage space than most other preserved foods.

Due to entirely new methods of processing, foods can now be reconstituted to resemble the fresh product quite closely, unlike those treated by previous drying methods. The food value is also well preserved; the only nutrients affected are vitamins B and C, the small losses of these being no more than in fresh vegetables and fruit when cooked and eaten a day or two after picking.

The process can be applied to vegetables, fruit, meat, soups, salad dressings and other foods. Quite frequently, dehydrated foods are included as ingredients in mixes, e.g., dehydrated onion in onion sauce mix, packet stuffings or soups.

The reconstitution rarely takes more than 30 minutes soaking depending on the size of particles, but exact instructions are given on the packet.
(See Accelerated Freeze-Drying entry.)

DELICATESSEN

The name given to ready-to-eat foods such as cold meats, Continental sausages, poultry, pickled and smoked fish, potato salad, coleslaw, olives etc. The name usually indicates the store where this type of food is sold. Such shops, also tend to sell rather more unusual and specialist foods.

DEMERARA SUGAR

Originally the cane sugar produced in British Guiana, but the phrase now refers to all crystallized cane sugars from the West Indies and nearby countries.

A little of the colour from the cane juice remains in the sugar, with traces of minerals and other impurities; this gives it a honey colour. There is, however, no difference in food value between Demerara and other sugars and like them it is purely a source of carbohydrate.

DEMI-GLACE (HALF-GLAZE) SAUCE

Espagnole sauce to which has been added meat glaze, meat extract or, if preferred, brown or white stock or clear soup. The sauce must then be well reduced; finally, sherry or Madeira may also be added, if desired. Demi-glace is served with high-class meat dishes.

To make it, put about 600 ml/1 pint Espagnole sauce in a pan and add 75 ml/⅛ pint liquid meat glaze. Boil for 20 minutes, skimming frequently to remove all the fat, then strain.

DEMI-SEL

A soft, whole-milk French cheese.

DERBY CHEESE

A British cheese originally made in the North of England where it is still more widely available than in the South. It is a mild, moist cheese with a honey colour. As it darkens in colour and sharpens in taste with age there is a tendency to sell Derby when it is young. A sage Derby is made by flavouring and colouring the cheese with chopped sage leaves. This cheese is traditionally associated with Christmas.

DESSERT

Originating from the French 'le desert'. The last course of a formal dinner, usually consisting of fresh, dried and crystallized fruit of various kinds and sometimes in addition ices, petits fours or fancy biscuits. The fruit may be placed on the table in dishes, as part of the decoration scheme, or it may be handed separately (after the table has been cleared of all unwanted dishes, glasses and cutlery and a dessert knife, spoon and plate have been set in front of each guest). The fresh fruits offered are usually tangerines, oranges, apples, pears, peaches, pineapple, bananas or black and white grapes. In addition dates, raisins, pulled (dried) figs, almonds, crystallized fruits and preserved ginger may be served. If ices and similar sweet dishes are to be included, they should be served before the fruit. Nowadays the term is used with reference to any sweet course which may include tarts, mousses, pies, trifles, cheesecakes, fruit compote, meringues, pancakes and profiteroles.

DEVILLING

The process of applying a highly flavoured paste, or a mixture of dry condiments, to legs of poultry, game, fish roes, etc., and then grilling them, or coating them with breadcrumbs and frying them. Various mixtures of condiments are used, but they usually include some very hot ingredients and something piquant; made mustard is often used. Turkey legs and similar foods are slashed in several places so that the mixture may be inserted or rubbed in; roes etc., are just brushed over with devilling mixture.

DEVILLED BUTTER

METRIC/IMPERIAL
50 g/2 oz butter
a squeeze of lemon juice
a little cayenne pepper
a pinch of white or black pepper
1 × 5 ml spoon/1 teaspoon curry powder

Blend all the ingredients thoroughly with a wooden spoon and use as required.

DEVILLED GAMMON

Make some devilled butter as above, adding a pinch of ginger and substituting Worcestershire sauce for the lemon juice. Spread gammon steaks fairly generously with the mixture, place them

under a hot grill and cook slowly, turning once. Serve immediately.

DEVILLED POUSSINS

METRIC/IMPERIAL
4 poussins
little cayenne pepper
1 × 2.5 ml spoon/ ½ teaspoon black pepper
2–3 × 5 ml spoons/2–3 teaspoons Worcestershire sauce
2–3 × 5 ml spoons/2–3 teaspoons made mustard
2–3 × 5 ml spoons/2–3 teaspoons vinegar
3–4 × 15 ml spoons/3–4 tablespoons oil

Split the birds down the back and open them out. Blend all the remaining ingredients and when smooth spread the mixture on the poussins. Place them under a medium heat and grill, turning them once or twice, for about 20 minutes, until tender.

DEVILLED TURKEY DRUMSTICKS

Cut the drumsticks from a cooked turkey. (Other fair-sized portions can be used in the same way.) Score with a sharp knife, then brush with melted butter. To prepare the devilled mixture, mix on a plate 1 × 5 ml spoon/1 teaspoon each of French and English mustard, 2 × 5 ml spoons/2 teaspoons finely chopped chutney, a pinch of ground ginger and a little pepper, salt and cayenne. Spread this mixture over and into the cuts and leave the turkey legs for 1 hour or longer. Grill them on a greased grid under a medium heat until crisp and brown, turning them regularly to ensure even cooking. Serve garnished with watercress.

Devilled Nuts: (See Nuts entry.)

DEVONSHIRE OR CORNISH CREAM

Name sometimes given to clotted cream. (See Cream entry.)

DEVONSHIRE SPLIT

(See Split entry.)

DEWBERRY

A type of trailing blackberry, which may be used in the same way as that fruit.

DEXTROSE

Another name for Glucose. (See Glucose entry.)

DHAL

A pulse vegetable grown in India. It is used to make a dish similar to kedgeree or stew; or it can be

127

made into a purée to serve with curry. In this country it is made from lentils and split peas and seasoned with ginger or curry powder.

LENTIL PURÉE (DHAL)

METRIC/IMPERIAL
100 g/4 oz red lentils
300 ml/ ½ pint cold water
pepper
salt
1 medium onion, skinned
fat for frying
25 g/1 oz butter or dripping

There is no need to soak the lentils. Wash them, put them into the cold water, add pepper and salt and let them cook steadily for about 1 to 1 ½ hours, adding more water if they get too dry. Meanwhile, chop the onion finely and fry it. When the lentils are tender, remove them from the heat and stir vigorously. Add the butter or dripping and the fried onion and stir over the heat to blend well. Serve with curry.

DIABETIC FOODS

Specially prepared foods containing reduced amounts of carbohydrate. Diabetic squashes, jams and marmalades, chocolates and sweets may be bought. Saccharin is also available to replace sugar. On the whole, however, it is considered better for the diabetic to get accustomed to doing without sweet foods and to build his diet on the foods he is allowed, rather than to perpetuate his sweet tooth by buying expensive substitutes. These foods may be useful in certain circumstances – the squashes, for example, for children or during illness.

DIET

The food eaten regularly, or the pattern of eating. A diet also means, in a narrower sense, a special régime, generally followed for medical reasons.

The normal diet should provide sufficient protein, carbohydrates, fats, vitamins, minerals and water. Actual requirements of these nutrients are difficult to assess and can at best only be a rough estimate, for individual requirements vary enormously. (See individual entries and nutrition.)

People on special diets need the same nutrients, so it is important to check the diet and, if certain foods have to be omitted, to make sure the missing nutrients are made up in some other way.

Slimming Diet

Overweight (obesity) is becoming more of a problem in this country as today's lifestyle encourages over-eating with less exercise. There are many ways of cutting down on intake of food, but it is important that a régime suits the individual.

Snacks and between-meal nibbles of carbohydrates are a cause of obesity and should be rigorously avoided. If in any doubt about diets, medical advice should be obtained before starting one. (See Slimming entry.)

Diabetic Diet

A correct diet is of great importance in keeping the diabetic healthy. It resembles a slimming diet in that carbohydrate foods are cut down, but the essential point is that the carbohydrate content should be kept at the same level from day to day, depending on the doctor's orders.

Light Diet

Frequently ordered for a patient in bed. It may occasionally be a fluid or soft diet, if the patient has difficulty with swallowing. Otherwise, it simply means avoiding rich, highly spiced or fried foods.

Gastric Diet

The many specialized gastric diets have largely disappeared, leaving in use a fairly simple diet, rather like the light diet. Foods with pips and skins should be avoided and so should the spiced and fried items. As this means no fruit or vegetables (unless sieved), fruit juice or vitamin C tablets should be taken instead. But more important than the diet are the following principles:

Do not worry
Eat slowly and rest after meals
Eat small meals at regular intervals.

Other Diets

The doctor may in certain cases prescribe a low-fat, low-salt or low-protein diet. There are also other diets that control disorders in metabolism. None of these should be attempted except on specific medical orders.

Vegetarian Diet

(See Vegetarian entry.)

DIGESTION

With one or two exceptions, foods cannot be absorbed straight into the blood stream as they are. They have to be broken down, first physically into a soft mass and then chemically by the digestive juices into soluble products which can pass through the wall of the intestine into the blood stream. The cellulose in fruit and vegetables, together with the skins and pips, the coarse fibres and other indigestible material, are passed on and evacuated.

In the mouth, the food is ground to small pieces and mixed with saliva, which starts the process. Very little digestion takes place in the stomach, the gastric juice being mainly hydrochloric acid; the stomach acts as a food reservoir, makes the food

more fluid and allows it to pass gradually into the small intestine. There the digestive juices break down proteins to amino acids, fats to fatty acids and starches to sugars. They are then absorbed into the blood stream, along with the mineral salts, vitamins and water. The indigestible material is moved on to the large intestine.

The word 'indigestible' in this context merely applies to the coarse residue that the body cannot absorb, but which is useful roughage. The popular idea of 'indigestible' food means food that causes pain or discomfort. There are very few foods indeed which are in themselves indigestible, apart from poisonous fruits and fungi. The indigestion is caused by other circumstances, such as eating too quickly, too much or while very worried, or it may be caused by an individual idiosyncracy or by swallowing air. Psychological considerations of stress and overwork have far more effect on digestion than the food itself. In fact, over 95 per cent of the digestible parts of foods (i.e., excluding fibres and skins) is normally digested. Contrary to popular belief, foods that are disliked are apparently digested as thoroughly as those which are liked.

Foods vary in the time they take to pass from the stomach into the intestines, but this does not appear to have any practical importance, apart from the fact that the quick passage of food leaves you feeling hungry sooner, so for slimmers it may be advisable to eat foods that are not digested quickly.

DILL

An aromatic plant similar to fennel; it originated in Spain, but is now also grown in Britain. The seeds are used for flavouring soups, sauces and pickles. Oil of dill, used in the manufacture of dill water for infants, is distilled from the seeds. The leaves have a strong flavour and can be used sparingly fresh or dried, in soups, salads and fish dishes. Dill seeds make an unusual but interesting addition to a salad. They can be mixed into a coleslaw-type salad, sprinkled over a cucumber and yogurt salad or even mixed with yogurt or a vinaigrette dressing to add an interesting flavour variation.

DINNER

The name usually given to the main meal of the day when served in the evening. (If it is eaten at mid-day, it is more often called luncheon or lunch.) The accepted plan for a dinner in this country is soup or hors d'œuvre (melon, grapefruit, shrimp cocktail, pâté, etc.), a main savoury dish plus vegetable accompaniments and a sweet (which can be hot or cold). A popular alternative plan is main course, sweet course and cheeseboard. For simple family dinners, two courses only may be served,

Veal Goulash
Boiled Rice   Runner Beans
Apple Pie & Custard

Steak and Kidney Pudding
Mashed Potatoes   Brussels Sprouts
Caramel Custard

Liver Casserole
Scalloped Potatoes
Leeks in White Sauce   Peas
Pancakes and Lemon

Grilled Steak
Jacket Potatoes
Grilled Tomatoes   Salad
Queen of Puddings

Tomato Soup
Hamburgers
Chips   Fried Onions
Fruit Crumble and Custard

Sample Formal Dinner Menus

Cold Consommé
Grilled Salmon   Sauté Potatoes
Peas   Cucumber Salad
Baked Alaska Pudding
Dessert

Hors d'Œuvre
Sole Véronique
Roast Loin of Lamb
Roast Potatoes
Creamed Spinach   Carrots
Charlotte Russe

Grapefruit
Chicken Maryland   Fried Bananas
Sweet Corn Fritters   Grilled Tomatoes
Crème Chantilly
Cheese and Biscuits

Prawn Cocktail
Asparagus with Melted Butter
Grilled Lamb Cutlets   Duchesse Potatoes
Mushrooms   Watercress
Lemon Meringue Pie

Dinner Party
(See Party entry.)

DIP, SAVOURY

A dip is a fairly soft well flavoured mixture, often served at a cocktail or wine and cheese party or similar occasion; guests help themselves by dip-

129

ping or 'dunking' small savoury biscuits, potato crisps, short sticks of celery or something of the kind into a bowl of the mixture. Cheese, soft cheese, whipped cream and yogurt form ideal bases for the mixtures.

BLUE CHEESE DIP

METRIC/IMPERIAL
100 g/4 oz Danish Blue or Roquefort cheese, softened
75 g/3 oz cream cheese, softened
1 × 15 ml spoon/1 tablespoon lemon juice
pinch of salt

Blend all the ingredients to a smooth cream and serve with chunks of French bread or vegetable dunks.

This dip can form the basis of an interesting relish to serve at Barbecues with grilled meats and hamburgers.

HOT MUSTARD DIP

METRIC/IMPERIAL
1 × 15 ml spoon/1 tablespoon French mustard
2 × 5 ml spoons/2 teaspoons made English mustard
2 × 15 ml spoons/2 tablespoons vinegar
25 g/1 oz butter
3 × 15 ml spoons/3 tablespoons flour
300 ml/½ pint stock
1 × 15 ml spoon/1 tablespoon cream, optional

Blend the mustards and vinegar together. Melt the butter in a pan and stir in the flour. Cook for 2 to 3 minutes, stir in the stock, bring to the boil and stir until the mixture thickens. Remove from the heat and add the prepared mustard. Serve hot. If a milder flavour is preferred, stir in the cream just before serving with chipolatas, meat balls or potato crisps.

DOG-FISH

A name given to various fishes of the shark family found in different parts of the world; some types can be eaten.

DOLCELATTE

A mild creamy blue veined Italian cheese. It is a variety of Gorgonzola.

DOLMAS

A Turkish or Arabian dish prepared by stuffing vine, fig, cabbage or other edible leaves with a savoury mixture, usually minced lamb and cooked rice, then braising the rolled-up leaves. The term is sometimes applied in the Middle East to stuffed aubergines, courgettes, etc.

Dolmades is the name given to stuffed vine leaves in Greece.

DOUBLE GLOUCESTER CHEESE

A traditional British cheese with a smooth mature flavour and open buttery texture. Its light orange colour is achieved with the addition of the dye annatto.

Until the end of the Second World War there was a Single and Double Gloucestershire cheese. Both were made by similar methods but the Single Gloucester was smaller in size and less acid: this cheese is no longer made.

DOUGH

A thick mixture of uncooked flour and liquid, often combined with other ingredients. The term is not confined to the typical yeast dough, but is also applied to mixtures such as pastry, cakes, biscuits and scones. In pastry-making the dough is termed 'stiff' when only sufficient liquid is added to bind the ingredients together (e.g., shortcrust pastry), whereas in cake-making a stiff dough contains sufficient liquid to make it too sticky to handle, though it is still stiff enough to hold its shape when dropped from a spoon (e.g., rock cake dough). A 'firm' dough is slightly softer, though still fairly stiff – for example, the mixtures for scones, raspberry buns, biscuits; a 'soft' dough contains an amount of liquid that makes it only just firm enough to handle, e.g., suetcrust pastry, bread dough and other yeast mixtures. (See Bread entry.)

Refrigerated fresh dough is a live dough product in pressure-packed cylinders found in the cold cabinets in shops. Once purchased, store in the coolest part of the refrigerator and use by the date stamped on the can. Do not freeze refrigerated fresh dough. For use follow manufacturer's instructions on the pack.

DOUGHNUT

A cake made of slightly sweetened dough cooked in hot fat and dredged with sugar. Doughnuts can be made with either yeast or baking powder as a raising agent. They can be filled with jam, preserve or cream.

DOUGHNUTS

METRIC/IMPERIAL
15 g/½ oz fresh yeast
about 4 × 15 ml spoons/4 tablespoons tepid milk
225 g/8 oz plain flour
1 × 2.5 ml spoon/½ teaspoon salt
knob of butter or margarine
1 egg, beaten
thick jam
deep fat for frying
sugar and ground cinnamon to coat

Blend the yeast with the milk. Mix the flour and salt and rub in the fat. Add the yeast liquid and egg and mix to a soft dough, adding a little more milk if necessary. Beat well until smooth, cover with oiled polythene and leave to rise until doubled in size. Knead lightly on a floured surface and divide into ten to twelve pieces. Shape each into a round, put 1 × 5 ml spoon/1 teaspoon thick jam in the centre and draw up the edges to form a ball, pressing firmly to seal them together. Heat the fat to 180°C/350°F or until it will brown a 2.5 cm/1 inch cube of bread in 1 minute. Fry the doughnuts fairly quickly until golden brown (for 5 to 10 minutes, according to size). Drain on crumpled kitchen paper and toss in sugar mixed with a little cinnamon (if you like). Serve the same day.

SIMPLE DOUGHNUTS

METRIC/IMPERIAL
225 g/8 oz plain flour
1 × 2.5 ml spoon/½ teaspoon bicarbonate of soda
1 × 5 ml spoon/1 teaspoon cream of tartar
pinch of ground cinnamon
25 g/1 oz butter
50 g/2 oz caster sugar
1 egg, beaten
milk
deep fat for frying

Sift the flour, bicarbonate of soda, cream of tartar and cinnamon and rub in the butter until the mixture resembles fine breadcrumbs. Stir in the sugar. Make a well in the centre, pour in the egg and gradually work in the dry ingredients, adding a little milk if necessary to give a soft dough. Heat the fat so that when a 2.5 cm/1 inch cube of bread is dropped in it takes 60 to 70 seconds to brown. Drop small balls of the mixture into the fat and fry until a light brown colour, turning them frequently. Lift out, drain on crumpled kitchen paper and sprinkle with sugar. Alternatively, the dough may be made stiffer, turned out on to a floured board and lighly kneaded until free from cracks, then rolled out until 1 cm/ ½ inch thick and cut into rings using two lightly floured round cutters. The rings can then be dropped into the hot oil and fried in the same way.

DOVE

(See Pigeon entry.)

DRAGÉE

A French sweet made of fruit, nuts, etc., coated with a hard sugar icing; sugar almonds are the best-known example. In Greece, it is traditional to serve sugar almonds at weddings, festive occasions and parties.

DRAGON'S EYES

A fruit, found in the Far East, which somewhat resembles the lychee.

DRAINING

The two main methods of removing surplus liquid or fat from foods are by means of a sieve or colander or by placing them on crumpled absorbent kitchen paper.

DRAMBUIE

A Scotch liqueur, golden in colour, made of whisky and heather honey.

DRAWN BUTTER

Melted butter, used as a dressing for cooked vegetables, etc.

DREDGING

The action of sprinkling food lightly and evenly with flour, sugar, etc. Fish and meat are often dredged with flour before frying, while cakes, biscuits, pancakes, etc., may be sprinkled with fine sugar to improve their appearance. A pierced container of metal or plastic (known as a dredger) is usually used.

DRESS, TO

To prepare for cooking or serving in such a way that the food looks as attractive as possible. The term sometimes denotes a special method of preparation, as in dressed crab.

DRIED FRUIT

This term includes both small and large fruits, such as currants, sultanas, raisins, dates, prunes (plums), apricots, peaches, figs, pears and apples, which are used in cakes, puddings, fruit salads and other dishes.

Their chief food value lies in their sugar content. Apricots and prunes have a useful amount of vitamin A, but no dried fruit retains its original vitamin C.

Cake Fruit (Currants, Sultanas, Raisins and Dates)

Most dried fruit is available ready prepared, but fruit not pre-packed must be carefully cleaned before being used. A small quantity of currants, etc., which is required in a hurry may be cleaned by mixing the fruit with a little dry flour and rubbing on a sieve to remove the stalks, etc. If the fruit is really dirty, however, it must be washed.

Place it in a colander resting in a bowl and pour cold water over, shaking the fruit in the colander meanwhile. Drain the fruit well, spread it out on a cloth and leave to dry overnight; if necessary finish the drying in a very cool oven. Finally, pick the fruit over and pack it into clean, dry jars. It is most important that the fruit should be quite dry before it is stored or it will not keep, while if it is wet when used in a cake or pudding, it will sink to the bottom.

Raisins (unless seedless) need to be stoned before use: do this by hand, dipping the fingers into hot water after dealing with every 2 to 3 raisins. Dry the fruit and if necessary cut it up before use.

Dates which are to be used in cakes or puddings need to be cut up.

Prunes, Apricots, Peaches, Figs, Pears and Apples

These need to be washed and then soaked in cold water overnight; they should be cooked in the same water. They swell considerably and 225 g/8 oz will provide average-sized portions for 4 to 6 people, except in the case of apple rings, which will give about 12 servings per 225 g/8 oz. The cooking time ranges from 20 to 30 minutes for figs and pears to 30 to 40 for apricots and apples and 40 to 60 for peaches and prunes. About 25 g/1 oz to 100 g/4 oz sugar per 225 g/8 oz fruit (unsoaked weight) is required; figs and prunes usually need less sweetening, apricots and apples more.

Stewed Dried Fruit

Apricots, prunes and figs should be washed, then soaked for some hours (or overnight) in fresh water. Cook them in this water, adding 100 g/4 oz to 175 g/6 oz sugar and a piece of lemon rind per 600 ml/1 pint. Stew gently till soft and serve cold.

DRIED VEGETABLES

(See Dehydrated Foods, Drying, Pulses entries.)

DRINKS

(See individual headings – Tea, Coffee, Lemonade, Spirits, Wine, Cocktail entries etc.)

DRIPPING

The fat which melts and runs out from meat when it is roasted, or from pieces of fat which are rendered down (as described under Fats entry). It should be poured into a basin and allowed to harden. The stock, which forms a dark jelly underneath, can be used in gravy, while the fat can be clarified for use in frying and occasionally for making plain cakes. Strong-flavoured dripping (e.g., pork) should not be used for cake-making and is better reserved for savoury dishes.

DRIPPING CAKE

METRIC/IMPERIAL
450 g/1 lb plain flour
175 g/6 oz dripping
225 g/8 oz stoned and chopped raisins
75 g/3 oz candied orange peel
175 g/6 oz brown sugar
2 eggs
300 ml/½ pint milk (approx.)
40 g/1½ oz black treacle
2 × 5 ml spoons/2 teaspoons bicarbonate of soda

Grease a 900 g/2 lb loaf tin. Sieve the flour and rub in fat until no lumps remain and the mixture resembles fine breadcrumbs. Add the dried fruit, chopped peel and sugar and mix well together. Make a well in the centre of the flour and pour in the beaten eggs and sufficient milk to give a stiff consistency. Warm the remainder of the milk with the treacle, add the sieved bicarbonate of soda and stir into the flour mixture to give a soft dropping consistency. Put into a prepared tin and bake in a moderate oven (180°C/350°F, Gas Mark 4) for 1½ to 2 hours. When the cake is well risen and golden-brown, turn it on to a cake rack.

DROP SCONE

(See Scone and Girdle Cookery entries.)

DROPPING CONSISTENCY

The term used to describe the texture of a cake or pudding mixture before cooking. To test it, well fill a spoon with the mixture, hold the spoon on its side above a basin and count slowly – the mixture should drop in about 5 seconds without your having to jerk the spoon.

DRYING

One of the most natural ways of preserving fruits and vegetables. If the sun is hot enough the process can be done in the open air over several days. As the climate is not alway suitable in this country it is best to alternate sessions between sun and artificial heat (low oven, airing cupboard, top of boiler or warming trolley). The temperature should be between 50°C/120°F to 70°C/150°F.

Prepared fruit or vegetables should be spread out so that air can circulate freely. Slatted frames or large sieves are ideal, although some method can usually be improvised. It is also important to protect the food from dust and insects by covering with cheesecloth or muslin. When drying is complete, the fruit or vegetables should be left for 48 hours to cool completely. They can then be stored in a cool, dry, well ventilated place within jars, tins, or boxes. Unlike most foods they do not need to be in airtight containers. Food stored in this way should keep for about a year as long as the containers are moisture free.

Fruits Suitable for Drying

APPLES
Prepare the fruit by peeling, coring and slicing in rings about 5 mm/¼ inch thick, using a stainless steel knife or peeler. Put the sliced fruit in a solution of 50 g/2 oz salt to 4.5 litres/1 gallon water, leave for 5 minutes, then dry on a cloth. Spread the rings on trays or thread on thin sticks and dry in a very cool oven (lowest setting) until leathery in texture – about 6 to 8 hours.

PEARS
These should be nearly ripe. Peel, core and cut into halves or quarters, dip into salted water, spread on trays and dry.

STONE FRUIT
Dry these whole; large fruits, such as plums or greengages, can be cut in half and stoned. Dry them until no juice comes out when the fruit is squeezed.

GRAPES
Spread out, and continue drying until the grapes are no longer juicy.

Vegetables Suitable for Drying

ONIONS
Drying is an excellent way of treating onions which are unsuitable for ordinary harvesting. Peel them, slice into rings, then steam for 1 to 2 minutes or blanch in boiling water for ½ minute. Plunge the rings into cold water, drain and spread out to dry until crisp.

MUSHROOMS
Choose young and tender mushrooms, skin them and cut or slice if very big. Spread out or string (with knots between) and dry until leathery.

RUNNER BEANS
String and slice the beans, then blanch them in boiling slightly salted water for 3 to 5 minutes. Plunge them into cold water, drain and spread out to dry until crisp.

BROAD BEANS
Shell them and blanch in boiling water for 3 to 5 minutes. Plunge into cold water, drain and spread out to dry.

PEAS AND HARICOT BEANS
These are best left upon the plants until the pods become yellow. Gather the pods, shuck them and spread the seeds out to dry before storing. Late crops (especially haricots) should be pulled up bodily and hung in a dry, airy place to ripen before shelling.

To cook home-dried vegetables: Soak them for at least 12 hours before use and then cook in the same water; season, bring to the boil and simmer until tender.

Herbs are also suitable for drying. (See separate entries.)

DUBLIN BAY PRAWN

The largest and best of the prawn family, obtainable fresh during the summer months. They can also be bought frozen or canned. To prepare prawns, break off and discard the head, take the flesh intact from the shell and remove the black filament in the back. Serve the prawns on a bed of lettuce, garnished with cucumber or with their own claws, with mayonnaise as an accompaniment.

DUBONNET

A well-known and popular quinine-flavoured French apéritif. A fortified wine which may be drunk neat, with ice and lemon, or made into a cocktail with vodka or gin.

DUCHESSE POTATOES

(See Potato entry.)

DUCK

A web-footed bird, of which there are various wild and domestic varieties. The flesh is dark, and though ducklings have more fat than chicken, there is little flesh on the bones, so it is necessary to allow about 350 g/12 oz dressed duck per person. Wild duck is classed as game and is only in season for a short time (See Wild Duck entry). It is served roasted and undercooked. Domestic duckling bred for the table is classed as poultry and is readily available frozen. It can be roasted and served with stuffing, apple sauce or orange sauce. When choosing fresh duckling for the table, select a young bird, as the flesh is more tender. The bill should be yellow and the webbing of the feet easily torn. The bill and feet become darker and redder as the domestic birds grow older; with wild ducks, however, the feet are reddish even when the birds are quite young.

Preparation and roasting: The bird is plucked, drawn and trussed in the usual way (see Poultry entry), except that the wings are not drawn across the back. A young duckling does not require stuffing, but it is usual to stuff an older one with sage and onion stuffing at the tail end. Truss for roasting and sprinkle the breast with pepper and salt. Cook in a fairly hot oven (200°C/400°F, Gas Mark 6), allowing 15 minutes per 0.5 kg/1 lb and basting frequently. To cook by the slow method, put it in a

133

warm oven (160°C/325°F, Gas Mark 3) and allow 20 minutes per 0.5 kg/1 lb. Remove the trussing strings and skewers and serve the bird on a hot dish, garnished with watercress and accompanied by potatoes or other vegetables, apple sauce and thin brown gravy. Orange salad is also popular.

DUCK WITH BIGARADE SAUCE

METRIC/IMPERIAL
1 roasting duck
knob of butter
salt
pepper
150 ml/¼ pint white wine
4 oranges (use bitter oranges when available)
1 lemon
1 × 15 ml spoon/1 tablespoon sugar
1 × 15 ml spoon/1 tablespoon vinegar
2 × 15 ml spoons/2 tablespoons brandy
1 × 15 ml spoon/1 tablespoon cornflour
1 bunch watercress

Rub the breast of the duck with the butter and sprinkle with salt. Put the duck in the roasting tin with the wine and cook in a moderately hot oven (190C/375°F, Gas Mark 5) for 30 minutes per 450 g/1 lb, basting occasionally with the wine. Squeeze the juice from 3 of the oranges and the lemon and grate the rind from 1 orange. Melt the sugar in a pan with the vinegar and heat until it is a dark brown caramel. Add the brandy and the juice of the oranges and lemon to the caramel and simmer gently for 5 minutes. Cut the remaining orange into segments.

When the duck is cooked, remove it from the roasting tin, joint it and place the pieces on a serving dish. Drain the excess fat from the roasting tin and add the grated rind and the orange sauce to the sediment. Blend the cornflour with a little water, stir it into the pan juices, return the tin to the heat, bring to the boil and cook for 2 to 3 minutes, stirring. Season and pour the sauce over the joints. Garnish with orange wedges and watercress.

DUCK AND ORANGE CASSEROLE

METRIC/IMPERIAL
1 duck, jointed
seasoned flour
knob of fat
100 g/4 oz mushrooms, sliced
2 onions, skinned and chopped
25–50 g/1–2 oz flour
450 ml/¾ pint stock
150 ml/¼ pint orange juice
1 orange

Coat the duck joints with the seasoned flour. Fry the duck in the fat for 8 to 10 minutes, until well browned, and transfer to a casserole. Fry the mushrooms and onions lightly in the hot fat for about 3 minutes, remove from the pan and add to the casserole. Stir the flour into the remaining fat and brown it over a very low heat, stirring all the time. Remove from the heat, gradually stir in the stock and orange juice and bring to the boil; continue to stir until it thickens. Pour over the duck, cover and cook in a moderate oven (180°C/350°F, Gas Mark 4) for 1 hour, until the duck is tender.

Serve garnished with orange slices.

Duck Eggs
(See Eggs entry.)

DULSE

(See Seaweed entry.)

DUMPLING

A ball or outer casing of dough, usually boiled but occasionally baked. The dough may be a suetcrust or yeast mixture, or shortcrust pastry may be used, especially in making apple dumplings. Breadcrumbs are sometimes used to make a type of dumpling; for Sussex (or hard) dumplings flour, salt and water only are used; Norfolk dumplings are sometimes made of a milk, egg and flour batter, sometimes of a yeast mixture. When served with stews, dumplings are usually plain, but when they are used as a garnish to soups, etc., they can be flavoured with herbs or cheese.

SUET DUMPLINGS FOR SOUPS AND STEWS

METRIC/IMPERIAL
100 g/4 oz self-raising flour
50 g/2 oz chopped or shredded suet
a pinch of salt
water or milk

Put all the dry ingredients into a basin, mix well and make into a dough with water or milk. Form into small balls, using a little flour, and drop into the boiling soup or stew about 20 to 30 minutes before serving.

HERB DUMPLINGS

METRIC/IMPERIAL
100 g/4 oz self-raising flour
50 g/2 oz fine breadcrumbs
40–50 g/1½–2 oz chopped or shredded suet
1 × 5 ml spoon/1 teaspoon salt
1 × 2.5 ml spoon/½ teaspoon pepper
1 × 15 ml spoon/1 tablespoon chopped parsley
3 × 5 ml spoons/3 teaspoons chopped fresh herbs
   (thyme, marjoram, etc.) or pinch of dried herbs
1 egg (optional)
milk to mix

Mix the flour and breadcrumbs and add the chopped or shredded suet. Season with salt and pepper, add the parsley and herbs and stir in the beaten egg and sufficient milk to give a soft dough, mixing lightly. Form into small dumplings, flour these lightly and add them to the boiling stew or soup 20 to 30 minutes before serving.

DUNDEE CAKE

A fairly rich fruit cake, decorated with split almonds.

DUNDEE CAKE

METRIC/IMPERIAL
225 g/8 oz plain flour
pinch of salt
225 g/8 oz butter
225 g/8 oz caster sugar
4 large eggs, beaten
350 g/12 oz sultanas
350 g/12 oz currants
175 g/6 oz chopped mixed peel
100 g/4 oz small glacé cherries
grated rind of ½ lemon
50–75 g/2–3 oz whole blanched almonds

Grease and line a 20 cm/8 inch round cake tin. Sift together the flour and salt. Cream the butter, add the sugar and beat together until light and fluffy. Gradually add the beaten eggs one at a time. Fold in the flour, cleaned fruit, peel, cherries, lemon rind and 25 g/1 oz of the nuts, chopped. Turn the mixture into the prepared tin and level the surface. Split the remainder of the nuts in half and arrange neatly over the cake, rounded side uppermost. Bake in a cool oven (150°C/300°F, Gas Mark 2) for about 2½ hours. When quite firm to the touch, remove from the tin and cool on a wire rack.

DUNLOP CHEESE

A Scottish cheese, flat in shape, similar to Cheshire in taste and texture. It originated at Dunlop in Ayrshire, but is now made in other parts of Scotland.

DUTCH CHEESE

There are several varieties of Dutch cheese, the best-known being Edam and Gouda. (See individual cheese entries.) There are also some spiced Dutch cheeses.

EASTER

A number of traditional dishes are associated with the religious festival of Easter, particularly special biscuits, eggs and cakes. Simnel Cake is usually eaten on Easter Sunday or on Mothering Sunday (in mid-Lent), while Hot Cross Buns are by tradition eaten on Good Friday. (See separate entries for recipes.)

Pashka is a traditional Russian dish eaten at this time. It is a rich sweet mixture containing soft cheese, cream, peel and fruit.

EASTER BISCUITS

METRIC/IMPERIAL
100 g/4 oz butter
75 g/3 oz caster sugar
1 egg, separated
200 g/7 oz plain flour
pinch of salt
1 × 2.5 ml spoon/ ½ teaspoon ground mixed spice
1 × 2.5 ml spoon/ ½ teaspoon ground cinnamon
4 × 15 ml spoons/4 tablespoons currants
1 × 15 ml spoon/1 tablespoon chopped mixed peel
1–2 × 15 ml spoons/1–2 tablespoons milk or brandy
a little caster sugar

Grease 2 baking sheets. Cream together the butter and sugar and beat in the egg yolk. Sift the flour with the salt and spices and fold it into the creamed mixture, with the fruit and peel. Add enough milk or brandy to give a fairly soft dough. Knead lightly on a floured board and roll out to about 5 mm/¼ inch thick. Cut into rounds using a 6 cm/2½ inch fluted cutter. Place on the baking sheets and bake in a moderately hot oven (200°C/400°F, Gas Mark 6) for about 10 minutes. Remove from the oven, brush with beaten egg white and sprinkle lightly with caster sugar. Return to the oven for a further 10 minutes, until golden brown. Cool on a wire rack.

DECORATED HENS' EGGS

Boiled eggs can be painted or decorated. This is particularly popular with children.

CHOCOLATE EASTER EGGS

Tin moulds may be bought in various sizes. Use good quality couverture chocolate and break it up small. Melt over gently simmering water in a double pan, then remove half of it and stir until almost set. Return this chocolate to pan and mix well. Polish inside the moulds with cottonwool, half-fill with the chocolate and tilt so as to run the couverture to the edge of the mould quite evenly all round. Do this two or three times, then pour the surplus back into the chocolate pan. Run the finger round the edge of the mould, then turn it upside down on a cool, flat surface. As the shells cool, they will contract slightly and may be removed from the tins by pressing gently at one end. The outer glazed surface given by the contact with the bright metal must not be handled more than can be helped. The shells can be joined by lightly touching the two halves on to a warm, flat tin, so that just sufficient chocolate melts to enable them to set firmly together.

Wrap the eggs in foil, or decorate them with ribbon, icing, chocolate piping and so on.

ECCLES CAKE

A pastry with a filling of dried fruit moistened with melted butter and sugar.

ECCLES CAKES

METRIC/IMPERIAL
215 g/7½ oz puff pastry

FOR THE FILLING
25 g/1 oz butter, softened
25 g/1 oz soft brown sugar
25 g/1 oz finely chopped mixed peel
50 g/2 oz currants

FOR THE GLAZE
egg white
caster sugar

Roll out the pastry thinly and cut into 8.5 cm/3½ inch rounds. Bind the ingredients for the filling and place a small spoonful of mixture in centre of each pastry round. Draw up the edges together and reshape into a round. Turn it over and roll lightly until the currants just show through. Score with a knife in a lattice pattern. Allow the cakes to 'rest' on a baking sheet for about 10 minutes in a cool place. Brush them with egg white and dredge with caster sugar. Bake in a hot oven (230°C/450°F, Gas Mark 8) for about 15 minutes, until golden. Cool on a wire rack.

ÉCLAIR

A small finger-shaped cake prepared from choux pastry (see Pastry entry) and filled with cream or confectioner's custard; the top is iced with chocolate or coffee icing.

Small éclairs made in the same way, but with a cheese or other savoury filling, make a delicious titbit for cocktail parties.

ÉCLAIRS

METRIC/IMPERIAL
choux pastry, made with 8 × 15 ml spoons/8
   tablespoons flour
150 ml/¼ pint double cream, whipped with 4 × 15 ml
   spoons/4 tablespoons single cream, or 150 ml/¼
   pint confectioner's custard
chocolate or coffee glacé icing, made with
   100 g/4 oz icing sugar or
   50 g/2 oz melted chocolate

Put the choux pastry into a forcing bag fitted with a plain round nozzle of 1 cm/½ inch diameter and pipe in fingers 8.5 cm/3½ inches long on to the baking sheet, keeping the lengths even and cutting the paste off with a wet knife against the edge of the pipe. Bake in a moderately hot oven (200°C/400°F, Gas Mark 6) for about 35 minutes, until well risen, crisp and of a golden brown colour. Remove from the tin, slit down the sides with a sharp-pointed knife to allow the steam to escape and leave on a cake rack to cool. When the éclairs are cold, and shortly before serving, fill with whipped cream or flavoured custard, then ice the tops with a little chocolate or coffee glacé icing or dip them in melted chocolate.

SAVOURY ÉCLAIRS

METRIC/IMPERIAL
40 g/1½ oz butter or margarine
150 ml/¼ pint water
8 × 15 ml spoons/8 tablespoons plain flour
2 eggs, lightly beaten
fillings, see below

Use the fat, water, flour and eggs to make choux pastry. Using a 1 cm/½ inch plain vegetable nozzle, pipe about 24 small walnut-sized balls of paste on to greased baking sheets. Bake in a mod-

erately hot oven (200°C/400°F, Gas Mark 6) for 15 to 20 minutes, until golden brown and crisp. Remove from the oven and make a short slit in the side of each to let out the steam. If necessary, return the cases to the oven to dry out completely. Either spoon or pipe the filling into the cases.

FILLINGS
1. Cream together 100 g/4 oz cream cheese and 50 g/2 oz softened butter; add 1 × 5 ml spoon/1 teaspoon lemon juice and salt and pepper to taste.
2. Cream together 100 g/4 oz cream cheese, 50 g/2 oz softened butter and 2 × 5 ml spoons/2 teaspoons tomato paste, add a few drops of Worcestershire sauce and seasoning to taste.
3. Cream 175 g/6 oz to 225 g/8 oz butter with 2 × 5 ml spoons/2 teaspoons anchovy essence and pepper to taste.

EDAM CHEESE

A rounded, dark yellow Dutch cheese with an edible red skin made in Holland, Germany, Belgium, Yugoslavia and America. It is often used in cooking and is a pleasant cheese to eat with bread, biscuits and fruit.

EELS

A long, snake-like fish. There are several varieties, of which the best known are the Sharp-nosed, Broad-nosed and Snig types. In England, eels are at their best during the autumn and winter. The Thames eel is considered the best-flavoured of the freshwater types.

Eels can be jellied, fried, stewed or made into pies. Smoked eels are considered delicious by many people.

To prepare eels: First skin the fish: cut off the head, turn back the skin at the top and peel it off. Clean the fish thoroughly, wash it in salted water and cut into pieces 5 cm/2 inches to 7.5 cm/3 inches long.

STEWED EELS

METRIC/IMPERIAL
0.75 kg/1½ lb to 1 kg/2 lb eels, prepared
salt
pepper
squeeze of lemon juice
few sprigs of parsley
40 g/1½ oz butter
4 × 15 ml spoons/4 tablespoons flour
300 ml/½ pint milk
2 × 15 ml spoons/2 tablespoons chopped parsley

To prepare the eels: first they must be skinned; the fishmonger will usually do this for you as it should ideally be done when the eel is alive, but to do it yourself, cut off the head, turn back the skin at the head end and peel it off with a sharp pull. Split open the body and remove the backbone. Clean well and wash the eels in salted water.

COOKING

Cut the eels into 5 cm/2 inch pieces, cover with water and add the seasoning, lemon juice and sprigs of parsley.

Simmer for about 45 minutes, until tender. Drain and retain 300 ml/½ pint of the cooking liquid and keep the fish warm. Melt the fat, stir in the flour and cook for 2 to 3 minutes. Remove the pan from the heat and gradually stir in the cooking liquid from the fish with the milk. Bring to the boil and continue to stir until the sauce thickens. Remove from the heat, stir in the parsley, add seasoning to taste and serve the eels coated with this sauce.

FRIED EELS

Prepare the eels as above, dry the pieces, dip them in seasoned flour, coat with egg and breadcrumbs or batter and fry until crisp and brown.

EEL POUT

A freshwater fish of the cod family, resembling eel; it is cooked in the same way.

EGG

Usually refers to the hen's egg although those from other birds can be used.

A plentiful supply of eggs is one of the greatest aids when planning meals and cooking.

From the dietetic point of view, eggs provide protein and fat; one egg has a similar protein value to that of 25 g/1 oz of beef and rather more fat; it supplies calcium, iron and vitamins A, D, B1 and B2 in useful amounts.

Apart from their use as a main dish at almost any meal of the day, as an ingredient in savoury dishes and salads and as a garnish, eggs are employed in cookery for three purposes:

1. Emulsifying: The yolk only is used as in mayonnaise.
2. Thickening and binding: These properties are important in the making of sauces, custards, fish cakes, meat rissoles, meat loaves and as a coating for foods, which may disintegrate in cooking, e.g., croquettes, fritters.
3. Raising or 'foaming': Eggs are widely used as a raising agent in cakes and batters. Additional lightness is given by whisking the whites separately and folding into the mixture. Whisked egg whites are also used for meringues, soufflés and light foamy sweets.

The egg yolks alone are often added to pastry, almond paste, etc., to give extra richness and colour and sometimes to bind the mixture.

Egg grading

Since January 1978, to conform with EEC directives, eggs are graded in seven sizes:

NEW (*metric*)		OLD (*imperial*)
Size 1	70 g or over	
Size 2	65 to 70 g	Large 2³⁄₁₆ oz and over
Size 3	60 to 65 g	
Size 4	55 to 60 g	Standard 1⅞ to 2³⁄₁₆ oz
Size 5	50 to 55 g	
Size 6	45 to 50 g	Medium 1⅝ to 1⅞ oz
Size 7	40 to 45 g	Small 1½ to 1⅜ oz
		Extra small 1½ oz and under

Boxes of eggs must be marked with a quality classification: Class A eggs are as they come from the hen with a safeguard against cracks (4 per cent permitted) and blood spots (1 per cent permitted). Class B eggs are less fresh than A: They may have been washed, dry brushed, refrigerated or preserved. Class C are suitable only for food manufacture.

The box must also show the number of eggs inside, the size of eggs, the registered number of the UK packing station with the name and address, and a date code: This can either be the date of packing or the EEC week number which commences from the week including 1st January. A complete week starts on a Monday and runs from 1 to 52 or 53.

Accelerated Freeze-Dried Hens' Eggs

Eggs can also be preserved by AFD (see AFD entry).

Dried (preserved) Hens' Eggs

These are made by spraying pulped fresh eggs in hot air. The resulting powder (25 g/1 oz of which is equivalent to 2 fresh eggs) is similar in use to fresh eggs, though it does not aerate as well. Dried eggs can be of great help during times of food shortage, but are generally used only in commercial baking. They are not generally available.

Liquid Preserved Hens' Eggs

These also are used mainly for commercial purposes. The eggs are shelled, placed in cans, frozen and kept in cold storage.

Freezing eggs

Eggs can be frozen if the whites are separated from the yolks, each being stored in an airtight container. Whole eggs do not freeze as they will crack, and hard boiled eggs become very rubbery if stored in a freezer. However, beaten whole eggs can be frozen, providing they are mixed lightly together with a little salt or sugar.

Eggs from Other Birds

DUCKS' EGGS

These are similar in food value and cooking properties to hens' eggs, though they are larger and somewhat richer. As they are sometimes contaminated with bacteria which give rise to gastroenteritis, they should be cooked very thoroughly (14 minutes being allowed for boiling) and they should not be preserved or stored in any way, nor should they be used for making meringues as they will not give satisfactory results.

GOOSE EGGS

Any of the ordinary cooking methods may be used for goose eggs, which may also be used in cakes and puddings. As they are larger than hens' eggs, more time should be allowed for cooking – to soft-boil, allow 7 minutes. They should not be preserved unless they are known to have been laid under strictly controlled hygienic conditions.

TURKEY EGGS

Although larger than hens' eggs, turkey eggs are just as delicate in flavour. They may be cooked in all the same ways and can be used in all cakes and puddings. Allow longer time for boiling – e.g., about 7 minutes to soft-boil.

GUINEA FOWLS', GULLS' AND FULMARS' EGGS

These are not often sold nowadays, but when available they make a good hors d'oeuvre; hard-boil the eggs for 10 to 15 minutes, shell and serve on a bed of cress.

PLOVERS' EGGS

These used to be considered a great delicacy, but nowadays the taking and selling of the eggs of these birds are prohibited.

QUAILS' EGGS

These are available preserved in jars, or fresh.

To test eggs for freshness: These homely ways of testing freshness are based on the fact that there is always a small amount of air inside the shell of an egg, which increases as the egg ages, so the fresher the egg the fuller it is.
1. Place the egg in a tumbler of water. If fresh, it will remain resting at the bottom of the glass. If not quite fresh, it will rest with the large end higher than the small end; in this case it is probably not suitable for boiling, but will fry or scramble satisfactorily. The higher the large end is raised, the older the egg. If the egg floats, it is very likely bad; as an additional test, shake it – the contents will shift about if the egg is bad, because the shell is not full.
2. Make a brine, using 50 g/2 oz salt to 600 ml/1 pint water, and place the egg in it. If good it will sink, but if bad it will float.
3. Hold the egg to the light. If transparent in the centre it is good or new-laid; if transparent at the ends, it is bad. It is also bad if it does not look clear,

but appears watery or has dark spots or patches.

To separate eggs: Crack the egg sharply with a knife or on a sharp edge and open the crack only just enough to let the white slip out into a cup. Tip the yolk carefully from one half of the shell to the other to release all the white. There is also a special gadget available for separating eggs.

To store eggs: Eggs deteriorate unless special measures are taken to preserve them. They should be kept in a cool, airy place, although not necessarily in a refrigerator.

If eggs are kept in a refrigerator they should be taken out at least 30 minutes before they are to be used. Store eggs with the pointed ends down as the air cell is at the rounded end.

To preserve eggs: Eggs with very dirty shells and those with rough, uneven or very thin shells should not be preserved. Eggs are preserved by the exclusion of air. They can either be dipped into a proprietary solution and then stored, or they may be submerged in a solution of waterglass. Follow the manufacturer's instructions on the pack. It is not advisable to boil preserved eggs.

To pickle in spiced vinegar: This is a way of preserving hard-boiled eggs, which can be used as a snack or buffet dish or with salad.

PICKLED EGGS

METRIC/IMPERIAL
For every 6 hard-boiled eggs allow:
600 ml/1 pint white wine or cider vinegar
6 cloves garlic, skinned
25 g/1 oz pickling spice
small piece of orange peel
piece of mace

Boil all the ingredients (except the eggs) for 10 minutes in a heavy pan with a well fitting lid. When the mixture is cool, strain it into a wide-mouthed glass jar with a screw-lid or a tight cork. Put in the eggs (shelled but whole) and leave for at least 6 weeks before eating.

More hard-boiled eggs can be added as convenient, but they must always be covered by the liquid.

BOILED EGGS

Eggs should be simmered rather than actually boiled, or the shells may break. Put them into boiling water, lower the heat and cook for 3 to 4½ minutes, or put in cold water and bring slowly to the boil, when they will be lightly set.

Whatever method is used, fresh eggs tend to take a little longer to cook than those which are a few days old. The water in each case should be just sufficient to cover the eggs.

HARD-BOILED EGGS

Put in boiling water, bring back to the boil and cook for 10 to 12 minutes.

Hard-boiled eggs should be placed at once under running cold water until they are cold; this prevents the yolk discolouring on the outside and enables the shell to be easily removed – tap all round the egg with the back of a knife and draw off the shell.

CODDLED EGGS

These soft-boiled eggs are cooked as follows: place them in boiling water, cover, remove from the heat and keep in a warm place for 8 to 10 minutes.

POACHED EGGS

Eggs for poaching are at their best when about 2 days old; very fresh eggs and staler ones are both difficult to keep whole.

The eggs may be cooked in a special poaching pan or in a frying pan with the aid of round pastry cutters. To use an egg poacher, half-fill the lower container with water and place a small piece of butter in each cup. When the water boils, break the eggs into the cups, season lightly and cover the pan with the lid. Simmer gently until the eggs are lightly set and loosen them with a knife before turning out.

To use a frying pan, half-fill it with water, adding a pinch of salt (to lower the temperature at which the eggs coagulate). Bring the water to the boil and put in the required number of plain pastry cutters. Break an egg into each cutter, cook gently until lightly set, then lift out with a slotted spoon or slice. Drain the eggs and then serve them as desired – on hot buttered toast, or on spinach, etc., garnished with small sprigs of parsley.

Milk may be used instead of water and it is usually served with the eggs.

FRIED EGGS

If the eggs are to be served with bacon, cook this first, then remove the rashers and keep them hot. Break each egg separately into a cup, drop it carefully into the hot fat and cook gently, basting with the hot fat so that it cooks evenly on top and underneath. When the eggs are just set, remove them from the pan with a fish slice or broad palette knife and serve with the hot bacon.

SCRAMBLED EGGS

Beat eggs and add salt and pepper. A little milk can also be added. Pour into the saucepan and stir over a gentle heat until the mixture begins to thicken, then remove from the heat and stir until creamy. Pile it on to hot buttered toast and serve immediately.

Scrambled eggs can be flavoured by adding finely chopped fresh or dried herbs, small pieces of cooked bacon or ham, mushrooms, flaked cooked fish, etc. The toast may be spread with good dripping, meat or yeast extract or other pastes instead of butter.

BAKED EGGS

Use individual ovenproof dishes (ramekins). Place the dishes on a baking sheet, drop a knob of butter in each and put in a moderately hot oven (200°C/400°F, Gas Mark 6) for a minute or two. When the butter has melted, break a fresh egg into each dish, season with pepper and salt and return the dishes to the oven, leaving them until the eggs are just set, 4 to 5 minutes. Serve at once.

SHIRRED EGGS

Break the eggs into a dish, add some breadcrumbs and a little cream and cook in a moderately hot oven (200°C/400°F, Gas Mark 6) for a few minutes, until the eggs are set and the crumbs are brown.

FRAMED EGGS

METRIC/IMPERIAL
4 thick, large slices of white bread
lard or dripping
4 eggs

Remove the centre crumb from each slice of bread, leaving a 'frame' 1 cm/½ inch to 2 cm/¾ inch wide. Fry the frames in the hot fat until brown, turn them over and brown the second side. Break an egg into the centre of each frame and fry until the eggs are set. Lift out with a slice or palette knife, draining off any fat, and serve on a hot plate.

EGG CROQUETTES

METRIC/IMPERIAL
40 g/1½ oz butter
150 ml/¼ pint water
50 g/2 oz plain flour
1 egg, beaten
1 × 2.5 ml spoon/½ teaspoon mild curry powder
salt
pepper
2 eggs, hard-boiled and shelled
25 g/1 oz toasted chopped almonds
1 small egg, for coating
75 g/3 oz fresh white breadcrumbs
fat for frying

Melt the butter in the water and bring to the boil. Remove from the heat and quickly add the flour. Beat well until paste is smooth and forms a ball. Allow to cool for a few minutes and then beat in the egg. Season well with curry powder, salt and pepper. Chop the hard-boiled eggs and add with the almonds to the pan. Take heaped spoonfuls of the mixture and roll to a sausage shape on a floured surface. Pat the ends flat. Coat with beaten egg and breadcrumbs. Chill, then deep fry in oil at 150°C/300°F to 170°C/340°F for about 5 minutes until puffed and golden brown. Drain on kitchen paper. Serve immediately with tomato sauce.

EGG AND BACON PIE

METRIC/IMPERIAL
375 g/13 oz packet shortcrust pastry, thawed
225 g/½ lb boneless smoked bacon joint
100 g/4 oz spring onions
2 × 15 ml spoons/2 tablespoons vegetable oil
4 eggs
salt
freshly ground black pepper
beaten egg to glaze

Roll out two-thirds of the pastry and use to line a 23 cm/9 inch deep flan dish or sandwich tin. Bake blind until set but not coloured. Cut the bacon into fine strips discarding rind and excess fat. Cover with cold water bring to the boil, cover and simmer for 15 minutes, drain well. Wash and trim the onions, cut into 1 cm/½ inch lengths. Fry gently in the oil with the bacon until golden. Spoon into the pastry lined dish. Make four evenly spaced wells in the filling and carefully break an egg into each, season well. Roll out the remaining pastry to a round just slightly larger than 23 cm/9 inch. Cover the pie with pastry lid sealing the edges well, glaze. Decorate with pastry trimmings and glaze again. Bake in a moderately hot oven (200°C/400°C, Gas Mark 6) for 30 to 40 minutes or until the pastry is golden brown.

SCOTCH EGGS

METRIC/IMPERIAL
4 eggs, hard-boiled and shelled
2 × 5 ml spoons/2 teaspoons seasoned flour
Worcestershire sauce
225 g/8 oz sausage meat
1 egg, beaten
dry breadcrumbs
deep fat
parsley

Dust the eggs with the seasoned flour. Add a few drops of Worcestershire sauce to the sausage meat and divide it into 4 equal portions. Form each quarter into a flat cake and work it round an egg, making it as even as possible, to keep the egg a good shape and making sure there are no cracks in the sausage meat. Brush with beaten egg and toss in breadcrumbs. Heat the fat until it will brown a cube of bread in 40 to 50 seconds. (As the sausage meat is raw, it is essential that the frying should not

be hurried unduly, so the fat must not be too hot.) Fry the eggs for about 7 to 8 minutes. When they are golden brown on the outside, remove them from the fat and drain.

Cut the eggs in half lengthways, garnish each half with a small piece of parsley and serve either hot with tomato sauce or cold with a green salad.

STUFFED EGGS – HOT

METRIC/IMPERIAL
4 eggs, hard-boiled and shelled
50 g/2 oz mushrooms, chopped
1 onion, skinned and chopped
40 g/1½ oz margarine
300 ml/½ pint tomato juice
1 × 5 ml spoon/1 teaspoon sugar
salt
pepper
2 × 5 ml spoons/2 teaspoons cornflour

Cut the eggs in half lengthways and remove the yolks. Lightly fry the mushrooms and onion in the hot fat for 5 minutes, until golden brown. Put half the mixture in a basin. Add the tomato juice, sugar and seasoning to the remaining mixture in the pan and cook for 5 minutes. Blend the cornflour to a smooth cream with a little water. Stir in a little of the hot tomato juice and return it to the pan; bring to the boil, stirring until it thickens, and continue cooking for 1 to 2 minutes. Keep this tomato sauce hot. Meanwhile mix the egg yolks with the remaining onion and mushroom mixture in the basin and use to stuff the eggs. Place on a dish and pour the tomato sauce round.

PIPÉRADE

METRIC/IMPERIAL
2 × 190 g/6½ oz cans red peppers
0.5 kg/1 lb tomatoes
100 g/4 oz butter
1 large onion, skinned and finely chopped
3 cloves garlic, skinned and crushed
salt
freshly ground pepper
8 eggs
4 × 15 ml spoons/4 tablespoons milk
fried croûtons

Drain the peppers and shred finely. Skin the tomatoes, cut into halves, discard the seeds and roughly chop the flesh. In a medium sized pan, melt the butter; when it is frothy, add the onion and garlic and cook for 1 to 2 minutes, then add the peppers and simmer for 4 minutes. Add the tomatoes. Season well and leave to simmer while you beat the eggs, milk and seasoning with a fork. When the vegetables in the pan are well reduced, pour in the beaten eggs. Cook for 3 to 4 minutes, stirring continuously. When a soft scrambled egg is obtained, turn on to a hot serving plate, and surround with fried croûtons.

EGG NOG

METRIC/IMPERIAL
1 egg
1 × 15 ml spoon/1 tablespoon sugar
50 ml/2 fl oz sherry or brandy
300 ml/½ pint milk

Whisk the egg and sugar together and add the sherry or brandy. Heat the milk without boiling and pour it over the egg mixture; stir well and serve hot in a glass.

FRUIT FLIP

METRIC/IMPERIAL
1 egg
2 × 5 ml spoons/2 teaspoons caster sugar
juice of 1 orange
juice of 1 lemon

Whisk the egg and sugar together for a few moments. Add the strained orange and lemon juice, strain and serve chilled.

Curried Eggs

(See Curry entry; *Egg Sauce*: see Sauce entry; *Egg Custard*: see Custard entry; see also Omelette, Soufflé, etc. entries.)

Egg-and-crumbing

To dip food in beaten egg or egg and milk and then toss it in fine breadcrumbs: the breadcrumbs stick to the egg, forming a complete coating around the food. This coating is used for fish, cutlets, rissoles, croquettes and so on, which may then be either fried or baked.

Put the breadcrumbs on a piece of kitchen paper and the beaten egg (or egg and milk) on a plate or dish. Toss the food in a little flour (seasoned flour for a savoury dish), then put it in the egg, coating it well, dip it in the breadcrumbs, lift out and pass from one hand to the other until all loose crumbs have fallen off.

Some important points to remember are:
1. See that the food is completely coated with the egg before putting it into the crumbs. This is particularly important in deep fat frying, otherwise the flavour from the food will pass into the fat through the cracks in the coating. The food also becomes hard and spoilt.
2. Use a pastry brush to apply the egg and a knife to lift the food out of it.
3. Browned breadcrumbs (see Raspings entry) are suitable only when the food is cooked and merely requires heating through (e.g., fish cakes and rissoles). Raw foods, such as fillets of fish, require longer frying and must therefore be coated with light-coloured crumbs. Whichever method is used, excess crumbs should be removed to prevent contaminating the oil or fat.

EGG PLANT

(See Aubergine entry.)

ELDERBERRY

The fruit of a tree that grows wild in country hedgerows, etc., in most parts of Great Britain. It was formerly used for medicinal purposes, but today is only used in the home for making elderberry jelly and wine. (See Wines, Home-made entry.)

ELDERBERRY JELLY

METRIC/IMPERIAL
1 kg/2 lb elderberries
1 kg/2 lb cooking apples
600 ml/1 pint water
sugar

Wash the elderberries. Wash the apples and chop roughly without peeling or coring. Cook the fruits separately with just enough water to cover, until they are really soft and pulped. Strain the combined fruits through a jelly bag, measure the extract and return it to the pan with 350 g/12 oz sugar to each 600 ml/1 pint of extract. Stir until the sugar has dissolved and boil rapidly until a 'jell' is obtained on testing. Skim, pot and cover in the usual way.

ELDERFLOWER

The flowers of the elder tree are sometimes used to make wine. When infused they have a delicate flavour. They can also be used to flavour preserves, e.g., rhubarb jam, to which they impart a taste resembling that of muscat grapes.

ELECTRIC MIXERS AND THEIR USE

For anyone who does a fair amount of cooking, an automatic electric food mixer is likely to save both time and energy. The small portable ones (some held in the hand, some used with a stand) will carry out creaming, beating and whisking operations. The large mixers are normally used on a stand, but a few can also be hand-held for such jobs as whisking eggs and sugar for a sponge. These models will of course deal with bigger quantities of food and they have a wide range of optional attachments for carrying out such operations as grinding coffee, slicing and shredding, sharpening knives and so on. The machines known as liquidizers or blenders are primarily intended for pulverizing cooked foods and vegetables (especially for soup-making), for extracting juice from fruit and so on, but can also be used for mixing and in some cases for cake-making; the manufacturer's instructions must be closely followed.

Most of the attachments for a mixer have names that are self-explanatory and if you study the maker's leaflet or booklet you will be in no doubt as to when and how to use them.

An electric mixer can be used (with the correct attachments) for rubbing in (the fat must be at room temperature), for creaming fat and sugar, for whisking, for making icing, for kneading dough, and for whipping cream. Creaming of vegetables may be done using the beaters in a saucepan.

The lighter kind of mixing known as 'folding in' (for example when the flour is added to the whisked sugar and eggs in making a sponge), should only be done on a very low speed to avoid overbeating.

Blenders

Blenders, sometimes called liquidizers, chop and blend and are generally versatile in terms of simplifying and speeding up the preparation of food.

Blenders may be an independent unit or an attachment to a food mixer. All blenders perform the same functions, the difference lying in the power of the motor and the size of the blending goblet. A freestanding blender is useful for people who do not have a mixer or who have a small hand-held one with no blender attachment.

Blenders can be used for making breadcrumbs, mixing instant foods and drinks, making salad dressing, chopping raw vegetables, puréeing fruit and vegetables, making soups, batters and mixing flan fillings.

EMINCÉ

The French culinary name for a dish of meat cut into thin slices, put into an earthenware dish and covered with some suitable sauce, which can be sauce bordelaise, chasseur, italienne, poivrade, tomato or mushroom.

It is essential that the meat is simmered and not cooked quickly so that it remains tender.

ENDIVE

There are many forms of this plant, but in this country the name usually refers to one of the curly-leaved varieties. It is rather like lettuce, but its leaves are stronger and tougher, and the flavour is more bitter. The heart is usually blanched and made more tender by being covered with a tile during the plant's growth, so this part is more suited to eating in a salad. Endive may also be

cooked like spinach and served hot, as a vegetable accompaniment.

(See also the Chicory entry and the note there regarding the two names endive and chicory.)

ENRICHMENT

The addition of nutrients to food. This may be done to replace nutrients removed during processing (as when calcium, iron, thiamin and niacin are added to flour, which loses these nutrients during milling), or it may be to improve a substitute (as when vitamins A and D are added to margarine to make its food value comparable with that of butter). Occasionally the enrichment is to ensure a constant level of a particular nutrient in an otherwise variable food (as when vitamin C is added to fruit juice).

ENTERTAINING

(See Party entry.)

ENTRECÔTE

A steak cut from the middle part of the sirloin of beef; in France it means a steak taken between two ribs. (See Steak entry.)

ENTRÉE

A dressed savoury dish, consisting of meat, poultry, game, fish, eggs or vegetables, etc. (e.g., cutlets, fillets, croquettes, quenelles), served either hot or cold, complete with sauce and garnish. An entrée is always handed in its dish, however simple the meal. If there is a waiter, a hot or cold plate is placed at each cover, then the waiter hands the entrée dish on a folded napkin in the left hand, with serving spoon or fork. If there are two entrées, the hot one should be served first and the two should be quite different in both flavour and general appearance.

It was originally a dish forming a complete course in itself and in the days of long dinner menus the entrée followed the fish course and preceded the roast.

ENTREMETS

A light dish served between the roast and the dessert at formal dinners. Entremets may be divided into three classes:

DRESSED VEGETABLES
Any vegetables may be used if dressed in some way.

A SWEET
The most usual form of entremets nowadays: this may be either hot or cold.

143

A SAVOURY

Formerly this might have been a meat dish of almost any kind, but not a roast; nowadays it is likely to be a small, well-flavoured dish, usually hot, such as cheese fritters, devilled chicken livers, etc.

ENZYME

A catalyst (that is, a substance which induces a change in other substances without being affected itself), found in various foodstuffs and in the digestive juices. Enzymes are soluble proteins that are destroyed by heat, strong acid or alkalis; their effect is retarded by low temperatures. Examples are B vitamins (thiamin, riboflavin and nicotinic acid) which act as enzymes on carbohydrates, oxidizing them into sugars, etc., for absorption; oxidase in vegetables which destroys vitamin C; and the digestive enzymes in the alimentary tract which break down carbohydrates, fats and proteins into substances that can be absorbed into the body.

ESCALOPE

A thin slice of meat, usually veal, either round or oval-shaped, cut from the top of the leg – or fillet, in the case of veal. The word also means a thin slice of fish. Escalopes are egg-and-crumbed, then fried and served with a rich sauce. (See Veal entry.)

ESCAROLE

A name sometimes given to the broad-leaved chicory.

ESPAGNOLE SAUCE

A rich brown sauce, used in the preparation of many savoury dishes, entrées, etc.

ESPAGNOLE SAUCE

METRIC/IMPERIAL
1 rasher streaky bacon, rinded and chopped
25 g/1 oz butter
1 shallot, skinned and chopped, or a small piece of
  onion, chopped
4 × 15 ml spoons/4 tablespoons mushroom stalks,
  chopped
1 small carrot, pared and chopped
2–3 × 15 ml spoons/2–3 tablespoons flour
300 ml/ ½ pint beef stock
bouquet garni
2 × 15 ml spoons/2 tablespoons tomato paste
salt
pepper

This classic brown sauce is used as a basis for many other savoury sauces.

Fry the bacon in the butter for 2 to 3 minutes, add the vegetables and fry for a further 3 to 5 minutes, or until lightly browned. Stir in the flour, mix well and continue frying until it turns brown. Remove from the heat and gradually add the stock (which if necessary can be made from a stock cube), stirring after each addition. Return the pan to the heat and stir until the sauce thickens; add the bouquet garni, tomato paste and salt and pepper. Reduce the heat and allow to simmer very gently for 1 hour, stirring from time to time to prevent it sticking; alternatively, cook in a moderate oven (160°C/325°F, Gas Mark 3) for 1½ to 2 hours. Strain the sauce, re-heat and skim off any fat, using a metal spoon. Re-season if necessary.

1 × 15 ml spoon/1 tablespoon sherry may be added just before the sauce is served.

ESSENCE

Originally, an essence was a solution of essential oils or other flavouring ingredients in alcohol, the best-known examples being almond, anise, orange, lemon, citron, peppermint, vanilla, ginger, cinnamon and caraway, but nowadays many synthetic essences are prepared from esters (compounds of alcohol and an organic acid). They often resemble the natural flavouring fairly closely, but tend to lack the delicacy and richness of the natural substances; they have, however, the advantage of being decidedly cheaper. For family cooking, they make a suitable alternative to their more expensive counterparts.

Both natural and synthetic essences help to make food more palatable and varied. They should be used sparingly and when possible they should be added during the final stages of cooking, to prevent loss through volatilization.

The following are the most frequently used essences:

ALMOND
The essential oil obtained from pressed almonds after the almond oil has been extracted. An imitation almond essence almost identical with the natural product is produced synthetically from benzaldehyde.

FRUIT
Genuine essences are obtained from rind and pulp of various fruits, but they are difficult to make sufficiently concentrated and are often replaced by artificial essences made from esters.

VANILLA
The genuine essence is a dilute alcoholic extract of the vanilla bean; the synthetic type is produced by oxidation of a compound obtained from clove oil and has a somewhat crude flavour.

Other interesting flavourings available: Brandy, Butterscotch, Maple, Ratafia.

MEAT AND FISH ESSENCES
The term essence is also applied to the extractives of meat, poultry or fish, which may be used for flavouring, as in the case of anchovy essence, or as a food for invalids, e.g., chicken essence.

EVAPORATED MILK

(See Milk entry.)

EVERTON TOFFEE

A brittle sweet similar to butterscotch, but containing cream or evaporated milk. (See Sweets entry.)

EVE'S PUDDING

METRIC/IMPERIAL
450 g/1 lb cooking apples, peeled and cored
75 g/3 oz demerara sugar
grated rind of 1 lemon
1 × 15 ml spoon/1 tablespoon water
75 g/3 oz butter or margarine
75 g/3 oz caster sugar
1 egg, beaten
150 g/5 oz self raising flour
milk to mix

Slice the apples thinly into a greased 900 ml/1 ½ pint ovenproof dish and sprinkle the demerara sugar and grated lemon rind over them. Add the 1 × 15 ml spoon/1 tablespoon water. Cream the fat and sugar until pale and fluffy. Add the egg a little at a time, beating well after each addition. Fold in the flour with a little milk to give a dropping consistency and spread the mixture over the apples. Bake in a moderate oven (180°C/350°F, Gas Mark 4) for 40 to 45 minutes, until the apples are tender and the sponge mixture cooked.

EWE'S MILK

This contains a higher proportion of protein, fat and sugar than cow's milk; it is used in making a number of Continental cheeses, e.g., Roquefort, Brousses, Cachat.

EXTRACT

A preparation obtained from various foodstuffs, such as lean meat, by means of mincing, boiling and evaporation or some other process. Extracts are usually commercially manufactured and sold in concentrated form as proprietary brands.

Meat extracts consist of natural juices and mineral salts and are used to flavour soups and gravies. Yeast extracts, which are similar in flavour to the meat products, are often used to dilute them and also to flavour soups, etc. They are a useful source of B vitamins.

FAGGOT

A country-type savoury dish, the traditional accompaniment for which used to be pease pudding. Traditionally made of pigs' liver, lights, pork fat, onions, herbs and breadcrumbs.

The term can also apply to a bunch of herbs (bouquet garni).

FAGGOTS

METRIC/IMPERIAL
0.5 kg/1 lb pigs' liver
175 g/6 oz onion, peeled
275 g/10 oz fresh white breadcrumbs
75 g/3 oz shredded suet
salt
freshly milled black pepper
1 × 2.5 ml spoon/½ teaspoon chopped sage
1 × 15 ml spoon/1 tablespoon flour
600 ml/1 pint dark rich beef stock
chopped parsley

Mince the liver and onion together. Add the breadcrumbs and suet. Combine fully together. Season well with salt, pepper and sage. Bring together with the hands and shape into balls on a well-floured surface. Place each faggot in a small square of buttered foil. Loosely enclose and place on a baking sheet. Bake in centre of a moderate oven (180°C/350°F, Gas Mark 4) for about 30 minutes. After the cooking time remove faggots from foil, place in a flameproof container. To make the gravy, place the flour in a small bowl and blend to a cream with a little of the stock. Add remaining stock and pour round the faggots. Heat gently, turning faggots, until the gravy thickens. Cook for 5 to 10 minutes. Garnish with parsley.

Note: Foil takes the place of the original caul which is now difficult to buy.

FARCE

Another word for stuffing, from the French term. (See Forcemeat and individual stuffing entries.)

FARINA

The term used generally to denote the flour or meal produced fom any kind of corn or starchy root (e.g., cassava), but sometimes also used specifically in reference to 'English arrowroot', prepared from potato flour. Farina is also the name of a product made from wheat other than the durum type.

FARINACEOUS FOODS

Foodstuffs which consist very largely of starch – for example, bread (which contains 50 per cent), oatmeal, flour, pasta and semolina (which contain 70 to 75 per cent).

FARL

A Scottish oatmeal cake, similar to a bannock and triangular in shape.

FATS

Fats are compounds of fatty acids and glycerol. Like many organic compounds, they contain carbon, hydrogen and oxygen. They are valuable 'fuel' foods, supplying more than twice as many Calories (kilojoules) for heat and energy as in either protein or carbohydrates. If more fat is taken than is needed for these purposes, it is stored in the body. Some fats (though not vegetable fats nor mineral oils such as paraffin) also supply vitamins A and D.

The chief sources of fats are animal foods (meat, dairy produce and oily fish) and vegetable foods such as nuts, from which oil is extracted. The normal diet must contain a proportion of natural fats: an average of 75 g/3 oz daily for adults.

Oils

These are fats that are liquid at ordinary room temperature. (See separate entry.)

Fatty Acids

The three fatty acids which, when combined with

glycerol, make up a fat, can be of different kinds. In saturated fatty acids each link in the molecular chain of acids is single, but in the unsaturated fatty acids one or more is double.

In general, fats containing saturated fatty acids are more solid than those containing unsaturated fatty acids; animal fats contain mostly saturated fatty acids; while corn, olive and sunflower oils are mostly unsaturated. When fats such as groundnut, coconut, palm and whale oils are hardened to make margarine and cooking fats, hydrogen is added to 'take up' the extra links, thus converting unsaturated to saturated fatty acids. The resulting solid fat seems for some reason to be composed of even more saturated fatty acids than naturally solid fats.

There are three fatty acids which cannot be made within the body yet are required in small quantities for normal health: These are known as 'essential fatty acids'. However, a normal diet will contain enough of these fatty acids.

People who have a high blood cholesterol level should reduce the amount of fat in the diet, limiting it only to unsaturated fatty acids. It is believed by many medical experts, although not proved, that a high proportion of saturated fatty acids is a contributory factor to heart disease. It should, however, be emphasized that this is not a sole cause.

Fat in Cookery
Fats used in cooking are butter, lard, dripping, suet and various vegetable fats and oils, including margarine, which is a mixture of fats. Oils (chiefly olive, nut and vegetable) are mainly used for frying and for salad dressings, but may also be used for cakes and pastry.

PASTRY
Flavour and shortening power are the most important factors in pastry making. Butter or margarine provide flavour whereas lard has more shortening properties, hence for some pastries a mixture of the two fats is used. Block margarine is more suitable for pastry than soft margarine. Whipped vegetable fats and oil can also be used for pastry, but these are usually added to the flour with the water and mixed with a fork, rather than by the usual 'rubbing in' method.

CAKES
Butter is considered to give the best flavour although margarine is usually easier to cream. Softer luxury margarines are often preferred for cake making and certainly give a better result in the 'one-stage' method. Oils can also be used in cake making.

PUDDINGS
Many of these include pastry or cake mixture but the term also applies to suet puddings. Suet can be bought ready shredded or it can be obtained from the butcher and prepared at home.

FRYING
A good frying fat should be free from moisture, which makes it splutter when heated, and it should have a high 'smoking temperature', that is, it should be capable of being heated to high temperatures (not less than 182°C/360°F) before it smokes and burns. Butter is not suitable for general frying purposes, although good for cooking omelettes and certain vegetables; a mixture of butter and oil is sometimes used to give flavour and enable the use of a higher temperature. The best fats are olive oil, vegetable oil, lard and clarified dripping.

Rendering
To render means to extract the fat from pieces of meat, fat trimmings from the joint, bacon or suet. There are two methods of doing this:
1. Cut the fat in small pieces, place them in a pan and place in a cool oven (150°C/300°F, Gas Mark 2) until the fat has melted, leaving only crisp, brown pieces of tissue. Strain the fat into a clean basin.
2. Cut the fat into small pieces, place them in a pan with very little water and boil without a lid until the water has all been driven off. Continue to heat very gently until the fat has melted and left only crisp brown pieces of tissue. Strain as before.

Note: with both methods care must be taken not to have too fierce a heat, or the fat will burn and be spoilt.

Clarifying
Fats which are to be used for cake-making, frying and so on sometimes need to be freed of water, meat juices, salt and other ingredients that may be present.

To clarify dripping: Melt the fat and strain it into a large basin – this will remove any large fragments. Now pour over the fat 2 to 3 times its own bulk of boiling water, stir well and allow to cool. The clean fat will rise to the top. When it has solidified, lift it off, dab the underside dry with piece of muslin or absorbent kitchen paper and scrape off any sediment with a knife.

To clarify salted butter or margarine: Heat the fat gently until it melts, then continue to heat slowly without browning until all bubbling ceases – this shows that the water has been driven off. Remove it from the heat and let it stand a few minutes for the salt and any sediment to settle, then gently pour off the fat. If there is much sediment, the clarified fat may be strained through muslin, but this is seldom necessary.

Rancidity
This is due mainly to slight oxidization changes, whereby a fat acquires an unpleasant acrid taste and smell, though the condition is not necessarily

harmful. Hot weather, exposure to air and light and prolonged storage are the usual causes of rancidity, which occurs more quickly if there is much water present in the fat. To guard against fats turning rancid, they should be kept in a refrigerator or cold larder, or wrapped in aluminium foil.

The addition of a little bicarbonate of soda helps to neutralize slight rancidity and make butter or other fat more palatable. Put the fat in a saucepan, pour boiling water over it, melt it gently and allow it to cool. Strain off the liquid. Again melt the fat slowly in a pan with a very little hot water containing 1×2.5 ml spoon/½ teaspoon bicarbonate of soda to 600 ml/1 pint of water. Skim, allow to cool and strain off the liquid. Warm the fat up again with plain water, skim if necessary, allow to cool and finally strain off all liquid from the fat before using it.

FECULA (FÉCULE IN FRENCH)

Any of the starchy powders obtained from potatoes, rice, etc.

FENNEL

An aromatic plant, occasionally found growing wild in Great Britain. It is a hardy perennial, growing 1.25 m/4 ft to 1.5 m/5 ft high, with hollow, deep-green stalks and finely cut leaves of a rich green. The flower stems appear soon after midsummer and bear heads of bright yellow flowers, but as seed formation shortens the lives of the plants, gardeners generally remove the stems to prevent flowering. The stalks, leaves and seeds give a delicate liquorice flavouring. The feathery foliage is used like parsley for garnishing and for flavouring sauces to serve with salmon and mackerel. Fennel seeds can also be used for flavouring and in making liqueurs.

'Florence Fennel', which has become increasingly available in this country, is a different plant. It has solid white stems with a swollen base, rather resembling celery roots; they can be eaten raw as an hors d'oeuvre or with cheese or may be cooked in the same way as celery and served hot.

FENNEL SAUCE
(See Sauce entry.)

FENUGREEK

An aromatic, bitter sweet spice, the flavour resembling celery. It is an essential ingredient in many Indian dishes and is also used in Mediterranean cooking. It is a leguminous plant looking rather like a tall clover and is sometimes called bird's foot.

FERMENTATION

This term is used to denote chemical changes (deliberate or accidental) brought about by ferments – for example, the decomposition of carbohydrates, with the production of alcohol and carbon dioxide, caused by the action of yeast. This process is utilised in the making of breads, wines, etc. (See Yeast entry.)

Malt and wine vinegars are produced by a ferment action which converts alcohol into acetic acid. The souring of milk, with the formation of lactic acid, is another well-known example and there are many more. Jams sometimes show signs of fermentation when they are stored, if they have not been carefully made and covered: for preventive measures, see Jam entry. Fresh fruit, for example, cherries, sometimes ferment when kept and develop a slight alcoholic flavour. The change is entirely harmless and the fruit can be eaten with perfect safety. If, however, fermentation occurs in bottled or tinned fruit, it denotes incomplete sterilization and it is unwise to eat the fruit, since other undesirable changes may also have occurred.

FIG

Numerous species of fig are grown extensively in hot countries, including much of Southern Europe, the Near East and the Western States of the USA. The fruits have a fleshy exterior enclosing a large quantity of small, hard seeds. Both the green fig, which remains green or greenish-yellow inside even when fully ripe, and the purple fig, which ripens to a deep reddish purple in the centre, are grown to some extent in this country, though they seldom ripen fully out-of-doors. They can be purchased canned in syrup and are sometimes available fresh.

However, most figs are sold dried, the chief varieties used for this purpose being the Smyrna (the best-known kind) and the Adriatic fig. They may be dried in the sun or by artificial heat; after drying they are pressed flat and packed between laurel leaves.

Fresh figs make a delicious dessert fruit, while dried figs are used as a stewed fruit (either by themselves or in fruit salads), in various cakes and puddings (see Suet Puddings entry) and in some sweets. (See Dried fruit entry for the method of cooking them.)

FILBERT

One of the best species of English hazel nut, largely cultivated in Kent. Filberts are also imported from Italy, Spain and Palestine. The nuts, which may be recognized by their long fringed husks and elongated form, are in season from September to March. In England they are best left until October, when they will fall if the trees are shaken. After drying, they will keep for a long time.

Like all the nuts, filberts have a fairly high proportion of fat. They also contain a little protein, minerals and thiamine.

FILLED MILK

Milk from which the cream has been removed and replaced by other fat (vegetable oils). It is cheaper than full-cream milk. When sold dried or condensed it must be labelled 'skimmed milk with non-milk fat', not 'milk'. If it is used in a catering establishment to replace whole milk, the fact must be made clear.

FILLET

The undercut of a loin of beef, pork, etc., also the boned breast of a bird or the boned side of a fish. (See Steak entry and also Fish for method of filleting.)

FILTER

To strain a liquid through a special fine filter, as when making coffee, or through a cloth, as when making jelly preserves.

FINES HERBES

Fresh herbs (usually parsley, tarragon, chives, chervil, sweet marjoram and watercress), which are finely chopped and used to flavour omelettes, etc. It is quite common to only include parsley and chives.

FINGER ROLL

(See Grissini entry.)

FINNAN HADDOCK

(See Haddock entry.)

FISH

There are many varieties of fish and this country is particularly fortunate in the quality and quantity of its supply. The value of fish as a food has now been realised, hence the increase in fish farming.

Fish is an important source of protein, although it contains slightly less than meat. Fish oils – for example, cod and halibut liver oil – contain vitamins A and D in large quantities. Some of the small fish, such as sardines, may supply a useful amount of calcium when the bones are eaten.

Fish may be classified in more than one way. Sometimes they are grouped according to type of flesh, thus:

White fish: Cod, sole, turbot, coley
Fat fish: Herring, salmon, sardine
Shellfish: Crabs, prawns, lobsters, etc.
Another grouping is according to shape, thus:
Round fish: Cod, haddock, herring
Flat fish: Plaice, sole, skate
Shellfish: as above

Fresh fish is cheapest and best when it is in season and has the finest flavour just before spawning; during the spawning season it is poor in flavour and the flesh of white fish is inclined to be of a bluish tinge, watery and lacking in firmness. Some fish, such as cod, are available throughout the year, but for most there is a close season. (See individual fish entries.)

Fresh fish rapidly becomes stale and should be cooked as soon as possible after it is caught. When really fresh, it should have no unpleasant odour, the flesh firm and the body stiff, the gills red, the eyes bright and not sunken and the scales plentiful and sparkling. Fish of a medium size are superior in flavour and finer than over-large ones; a thick slice from a smaller fish is preferable to a thin slice cut from a large one.

A large percentage of fish in this country is sold from frozen food cabinets. Contrary to belief this does not mean that it is inferior in any way. As only the best quality fish are frozen it may be superior to fresh fish. Furthermore, as it is frozen as soon as it is caught (on the boat or on reaching land) all the nutrients are preserved. Other advantages of frozen fish are that they are usually gutted and boned, and sometimes coated ready for frying. Also it has less odour than fresh fish which makes storage in a refrigerator more acceptable. Ready prepared 'fish in sauce dishes', breaded or battered fish portions and smoked fish are all available frozen; these make serving quick and simple.

Also available frozen, are scallops, shrimps and prawns. The range of frozen fish is always increasing, and it is likely, with the closure of many fishmongers shops, that most of our fish will be sold from the freezer cabinets in years to come.

Canned fish is a good standby as the preservation is permanent and there are no inedible parts of the fish included; it is also ready to serve hot or cold. The oily fish are particularly suitable for canning, such as sardines, pilchards, herring, sild, roes, mackerel, sprats, brisling, anchovies, tuna and salmon. Also sold in cans are mussels, shrimps, prawns, kipper and herring fillets, lobster, crab, fish balls, quenelles, fish soups and chowders.

Preparation of Fish

Whole fish: Scrape off any scales on both sides of the fish using a knife and scraping from tail to head, with frequent rinsing to loosen the scales. To remove the entrails from round fish, make a slit

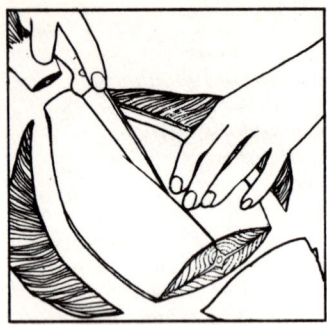 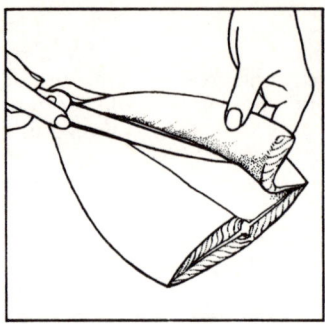 

1. Filleting flat fish: Place fish on a wooden board. Cut straight down the back, following the line of the bone.

2. Insert the knife under one side of the flesh and carefully cut it away from the bone, working from head to tail.

3. Turn fish over and fillet the other side of the fish in the same way so that you are left with four fillets of fish.

along the abdomen from the gills half-way to the tail, draw out the insides and clean away any blood. Rub with a little salt to remove black skin.

With flat fish, such as sole and plaice, open the cavity which lies in the upper part of the body under the gills and clean out the entrails as above. Cut off the fins and gills and remove the head and tail if desired. If the head is left on, the eyes must be removed. Finally, rinse the flesh thoroughly in cold water.

Cut fish, fillets and cutlets: Wipe with a damp cloth. Do not wash or leave lying in water, as this draws out the juices and impairs the flavour.

Skinning round fish (Haddock, Whiting, etc.): Round fish are skinned from head to tail. Cut across the skin just below the head and loosen the skin under the head with the point of a sharp knife, then dip the fingers in coarse salt and gently pull the skin down towards the tail, working very carefully. Skin the other side in the same way, dipping your fingers in coarse salt to prevent slipping.

Filleting round fish: Cut down the centre back to the bone with a sharp knife and cut along the abdomen. Remove the flesh cleanly from the bones, working from the head down, pressing the knife against the bones and working with short, sharp strokes. Remove the fillet from the other side in the same way. The fillets may be cut slantwise into two or three pieces if desired.

Skinning whole flat fish (Sole, Plaice, etc.): The black skin is usually removed, whatever the mode of treatment. A sole skins easily, so do this before filleting; a plaice is more difficult, so fillet it first and then skin the fillets. First wash the fish and cut off fins, then make an incision across the tail, slip the thumb between the skin and the flesh and loosen the skin round the sides of the fish. Now hold down the fish firmly with one hand and with the other take hold of the skin and draw it off quickly, upwards towards the head. The white skin can be removed in the same way, but unless the fish is large it is generally left on.

Filleting flat fish: With a sharp, flexible knife, cut straight down the back of the fish, following the line of the bone. Then insert the knife under the flesh and carefully remove it with long, clean strokes. Take the first fillet from the left-hand side of the fish, working from head to tail, then turn the fish round and cut off the second fillet from tail to head. Fillet the other side of the fish, in the same way. When the operation is finished, no flesh should be left adhering to the bone.

Skinning fillets of flat fish: Lay the fillet on a board, skin side down, salt the fingers and hold the tail end of the skin firmly. Then separate the flesh from the skin by sawing with a sharp knife from side to side, pressing the flat of the blade against the flesh. Keep the edge of the blade close to the skin while cutting, but do not press heavily or the skin will be severed. (See individual entries for preparation of shellfish.)

Methods of Cooking

Fish can be boiled, poached, steamed, stewed, baked, fried or grilled. Most fish requires a good sauce or special accompaniment to bring out the flavour.

We give below notes on the most usual methods of cooking, followed by a small selection of recipes; other recipes will be found under the names of the individual fish, e.g., Sole. (See Kedgeree, Soufflé, entries etc., also the Fish Paste given under Paste entry.)

Boiling: This is only to be recommended for a few fish such as salmon and large cuts of cod, etc. (Fish which is called 'boiled' is in fact often poached.)

Rub the cut surface of the fish with lemon juice to keep it firm and of a good colour, then put it in sufficient hot salted water or court-bouillon (see court-bouillon entry) to cover it. (A common fault is to put insufficient salt in the water.) If possible use a fish kettle, to enable the fish to be lifted out of the container without breaking; failing this, tie in muslin and place on a plate at the bottom of a saucepan. A small bunch of herbs and a little cut up

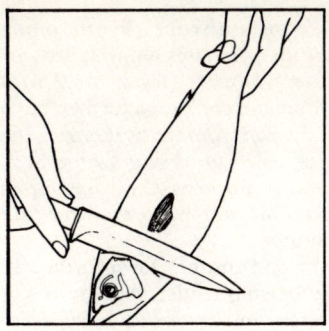
1. Skinning round fish: Lay fish on a board and cut across the skin just below the head to loosen the skin under the head.

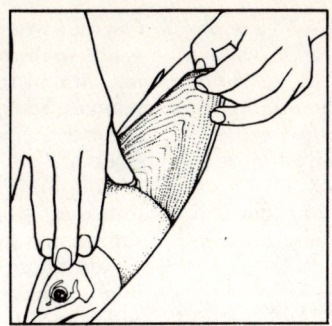
2. Dip the fingertips in coarse salt and grip the skin. Gently pull the skin towards the tail, working carefully.

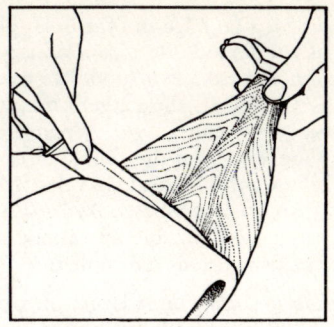
3 Skinning flat fish: Hold tail of fish and separate the flesh from the skin with a sharp knife.

carrot, onion and celery can be added to the water if the fish is of a tasteless kind. Bring the water to the boil and then simmer very slowly (removing any scum as it rises) until the fish is cooked, i.e., when the flesh comes away easily from the bone. The time depends on the shape and thickness of the fish, the average being 10 to 20 minutes per 0.5 kg/1 lb and 10 minutes over. Drain well, dish on a hot plate, garnish with parsley and lemon and serve with a suitable sauce.

(See Salmon entry.)

Poaching: Suitable for cuts of fish, particularly for small pieces and for small whole fish. Roll or fold the fish fillets to a convenient size. Heat sufficient milk and water in a saucepan or casserole to half-cover the fish. When this is simmering, lay the fish in the pan, season, cover and simmer very gently until tender, allowing 10 to 15 minutes to the 0.5 kg/1 lb according to the thickness of the cut, or about 20 minutes for a small piece. Lift out the fish, drain, place on a hot dish and serve coated with sauce made with the liquor in the pan.

Steaming: Prepare the fish as for boiling. Place large cuts or whole fish directly in the steamer; small fillets or thin cutlets will cook satisfactorily if laid on a greased deep plate with 1 × 15 ml spoon/1 tablespoon milk and some seasoning, placed over a saucepan of boiling water and covered with the lid or a second plate. For a large fish allow 15 minutes to the 0.5 kg/1 lb and 15 minutes over. Cook fillets for about 20 minutes. Serve with a sauce.

Frying: Almost any kind of fish is suitable for this method of cooking. Shallow frying is best for thick slices such as cod steaks and for whole fish such as soles, which require a fairly long time to cook through. Deep frying is better for fillets and small fish. (See Frying entry.) Small fish can be fried whole, while the large ones should be filleted and cut into convenient-sized pieces. The fish must be made quite dry and the outside coated so as to prevent the fat soaking into the fish itself. There are several methods of coating fish for frying:

Coating for shallow frying: The simplest method is to coat the fish with seasoned flour. Fine oatmeal may also be used, particularly for herring and mackerel.

A slightly more elaborate method is to dip the fish into seasoned flour, then into milk, and into flour again. Do not prepare the fish until just before frying it.

Coating for deep frying: Small pieces of fish may be dipped in batter. Season them with pepper, salt and a little lemon juice, then drop them into the batter and lift them out with a skewer, draining off any surplus batter before putting the fish into the frying fat. Do not coat the fish until just before frying it.

The fish may also be egg-and-crumbed which gives it a very attractive appearance when cooked. In this case the fish may be made ready beforehand, as the coating becomes drier on standing and the food fries all the better.

To serve fried fish: Garnish with lemon and parsley or maître d'hôtel butter and if desired with chipped potatoes. Any sauce should be served separately.

Grilling: Herrings, mullet, mackerel, plaice and sole are suitable fish to grill, as well as cuts of thick fish, such as halibut, cod, salmon, etc. (See Grilling entry.)

Baking: Weigh and wipe the fish, place it in a greased dish, sprinkle with salt and pepper and if desired a little lemon juice, then add a few dots of butter and cover fish with greased paper. Bake in a moderate oven (180°C/350°F, Gas Mark 4) until the flesh is white and firm, with a creamy curd between the flakes, and will come easily away from the bone.

Allow 6 to 10 minutes to the 0.5 kg/1 lb and 6 to 10 minutes over, according to the thickness. Thin fillets of fish will take about 15 minutes.

Fish baked in foil: Steaks of fish just need wiping over, but if the fish is to be cooked whole, clean it, leaving on the head, tail and skin. Place in the foil, dot with butter, sprinkle with salt, pepper and a little lemon juice and then completely enclose the fish in the foil. Place on a baking sheet or shallow dish and bake in a moderate oven (180°C/350°F, Gas Mark 4), allowing 15 minutes per 0.5 kg/lb, plus 15 minutes over. When the fish is cooked, remove it from the foil, skin carefully and serve hot or cold, garnished as desired.

Any fish can be cooked in this way, but it is particularly suitable for salmon and also for delicate fish such as red mullet.

Baking whole fish: A large sole or plaice or a small cod, hake or fresh haddock, served on a long platter and attractively garnished, makes a decorative dish. Wash the fish, remove any scales, clean it carefully, but leave the head on, removing the eyes. Stuff with a good forcemeat. (For example, one made from 50 g/2 oz or so of fresh breadcrumbs, salt and pepper, a little chopped fat bacon, some chopped parsley and a pinch of mixed herbs, moistened with beaten egg and a little milk.)

With a round fish, such as cod or hake, place the stuffing in the cavity from which the entrails have been removed. Roll any remaining stuffing into small balls and dust them with flour. Place the fish on a greased baking tin with some firm tomatoes (if desired) and the balls of stuffing.

In the case of a flat fish, such as plaice or sole, lay the fish on a board and cut through the flesh right down to the backbone; then, using the point of a sharp knife, loosen the flesh from the bone on each side as far as the fins, but not right through the skin. Fill the stuffing into the cavity thus formed, lay some small tomatoes along the centre of the fish and place it on a greased baking sheet.

Dot the stuffed fish with some shavings of butter, cover with greased paper and bake in a moderate oven (180°C/350°F, Gas Mark 4) for 45 minutes to 1 hour (according to size and thickness). Lift carefully on to a hot dish, using a palette knife and fish slice.

Garnish with lemon fans and fresh parsley or fennel and serve with parsley or fennel sauce.

CURRIED FISH

METRIC/IMPERIAL
0.75 kg/1 ½ lb filleted cod, coley, haddock or similar white fish, skinned
1 large onion, skinned and chopped
25 g/1 oz butter
1 × 5 ml spoon/1 teaspoon curry powder
4 × 15 ml spoons/4 tablespoons flour
300 ml/½ pint chicken stock
300 ml/½ pint milk
1 small apple, skinned, cored and chopped
2 tomatoes, skinned and chopped
25 g/1 oz to 50 g/2 oz sultanas
salt
boiled rice

Cut the fish into 2.5 cm/1 inch cubes. Fry the onion gently in the butter for 5 minutes without browning. Stir in the curry powder, fry it for 2 to 3 minutes, add the flour and cook for a further 2 to 3 minutes. Remove the pan from the heat, stir in the stock and milk gradually and bring to the boil, stirring until the sauce thickens. Add the apple, tomatoes, sultanas, salt and pepper; cover and simmer for 15 minutes.

Add the fish, stir and simmer for a further 10 minutes, or until the fish is tender. Add more salt and pepper if necessary and serve with boiled rice.

FISH CAKES

METRIC/IMPERIAL
225 g/8 oz fish, e.g., cod, haddock or coley
0.5 kg/1 lb potatoes, peeled and cut up
25 g/1 oz butter
1 × 15 ml spoon/1 tablespoon chopped parsley
salt
pepper
milk or beaten egg to bind
1 egg, beaten, to coat
dry breadcrumbs
fat for frying

Cook and flake the fish. Boil and drain the potatoes and mash with the butter. (Alternatively, use 225 g/8 oz leftover mashed potatoes or instant potato.) Mix the fish with the potatoes, parsley and salt and pepper to taste, binding if necessary with a little milk or egg. Form the mixture into a roll on a floured board, cut it into 8 slices and shape into cakes. Coat them with egg and crumbs, fry in hot fat (deep or shallow) until crisp and golden; drain well. Vary the flavour of the cakes by using smoked haddock, herrings, canned tuna or salmon instead of white fish.

As fish cakes tend to be dry, serve with a sauce such as tomato or parsley.

RUSSIAN FISH PIE

METRIC/IMPERIAL
225/8 oz white fish, e.g., cod, haddock
25 g/1 oz butter
3 × 15 ml spoons/3 tablespoons flour
150 ml/¼ pint milk
2 × 15 ml spoons/2 tablespoons chopped parsley
salt
pepper
1 hard-boiled egg, shelled and chopped
1 × 215 g/7½ oz packet frozen puff or 100 g/4 oz home-made flaky pastry, made with 100 g/4 oz flour, etc.
beaten egg to glaze

Cook and flake the fish retaining 150 ml/¼ pint of the cooking liquid. Melt the butter, stir in the flour and cook for 2 to 3 minutes. Remove the pan from the heat and gradually stir in the fish liquid mixed with the milk. Bring it to the boil and continue to stir until the sauce thickens. Mix half the sauce with the flaked fish, parsley, salt, pepper and chopped egg.

Roll out the pastry thinly into a fairly large square and place it on a baking sheet. Put the filling in the centre in a square shape, brush the edges of the pastry with beaten egg and draw them up to the middle to form an envelope shape. Press the edges well together and flake and scallop them. Brush the pie with beaten egg and bake in a moderately hot oven (200°C/400°F, Gas Mark 6) for about 30 minutes, until golden. Serve with the remaining parsley sauce.

FISH PROVENÇALE

METRIC/IMPERIAL
1 onion, skinned and chopped
1 small green pepper, seeded and chopped
50 g/2 oz to 75 g/3 oz streaky bacon, chopped
25 g/1 oz butter
0.5 kg/1 lb fillet of cod, haddock or whiting, skinned
seasoned flour
1 × 425 g/15 oz can tomatoes, drained
1 bayleaf
2 × 5 ml spoons/2 teaspoons sugar
salt
pepper

Fry the onion, pepper and bacon gently in the butter for 5 to 10 minutes, until soft but not coloured. Wash and dry the fish and cut it into 2.5 cm/1 inch cubes. Toss the fish in seasoned flour and fry with the vegetables for a further 2 to 3 minutes. Stir in the tomatoes, bayleaf, sugar and seasoning, bring to the boil, stirring gently, cover with a lid and simmer for 10 to 15 minutes, until the fish and vegetables are cooked. Serve with boiled rice.

FISH PIE

METRIC/IMPERIAL
0.5 kg/1 lb cod fillet or any other white fish
0.75 kg/1½ lb to 1 kg/2 lb potatoes
40 g/1½ oz butter
150 ml/¼ pint milk, plus 3 × 15 ml spoons/3
    tablespoons
3 × 15 ml spoons/3 tablespoons flour
2 × 15 ml spoons/2 tablespoons chopped parsley
salt
pepper
50 g/2 oz cheese, grated

Cook and flake the fish, retaining 150 ml/¼ pint of the cooking liquid. Boil and mash the potatoes in the usual way, add a knob of butter and 3 × 15 ml spoons/3 tablespoons milk and beat with a wooden spoon until creamy. Melt the remaining butter,

stir in the flour and cook for 2 to 3 minutes. Remove the pan from the heat and gradually stir in the fish liquid and 150 ml/¼ pint milk; bring it to the boil. When the sauce has thickened, remove it from the heat and stir in the flaked fish, the parsley and seasoning to taste. Pour the mixture into an ovenproof dish and cover with the creamed potatoes, sprinkle with the cheese and bake in a moderate oven (200°C/400°F, Gas Mark 6) for about 30 minutes, until the pie is well heated through and the cheese golden.

The parsley sauce can be replaced by a white sauce to which one of the following has been added:

METRIC/IMPERIAL
100 g/4 oz mushrooms, chopped and lightly fried or
100 g/4 oz peeled shrimps or
50 g/2 oz to 100 g/4 oz grated cheese

FLAGEOLET

(See Bean entry.)

FLAKY PASTRY

A rich pastry suitable for making meat and fruit pies, sausage rolls, jam puffs, Eccles cakes, etc. (See Pastry entry.)

FLAMBER

French term meaning to coat such foods as pancakes or Christmas pudding with a spirit, which is then ignited. The word also means to singe poultry before cooking. (See Poultry entry.)

FLANS

Flans are not only pretty and good to eat, but they also have the advantage that most if not all of the cooking can be done beforehand.

In addition to the conventional flan cases of pastry and sponge cake, uncooked flan cases can be made from mixtures based on crumbled biscuits, cornflakes and so on. (See recipes.)

Pastry Flan Cases
(See individual entries.)

Sponge Flan Cases
Grease 21 cm/8½ inch sponge flan tin and dust it with a mixture of flour and caster sugar. If you wish you can place a round of greased greaseproof paper on the raised part of the flan tin to prevent sticking. Make a fatless sponge cake mixture using 2 eggs, 50 g/2 oz caster sugar and 50 g/2 oz plain flour; pour it into the tin and bake in a hot oven (220°C/425°F, Gas Mark 7), for about 10 minutes, until well risen, golden and just firm to the touch.

Loosen the edge carefully, turn the flan case out on to a wire rack and leave to cool.

BISCUIT CRUST FLAN CASES

METRIC/IMPERIAL
175 g/6 oz wheatmeal or plain biscuits
75 g/3 oz melted butter

Grease a shallow 20 cm/8 inch pie plate, flan dish or sandwich cake tin. Crush the biscuits with a rolling pin and bind together with the melted butter. Spoon the crumbs into the plate, flan dish or tin, pressing it firmly into shape to make a shell. Chill or leave in a cool place until set.

VARIATIONS
1. Replace 25 g/1 oz of the crumbs by 25 g/1 oz desiccated coconut or chopped nuts.
2. Add the grated rind of 1 lemon.
3. Add 1 to 2 × 5 ml spoons/1 to 2 teaspoons ground ginger or mixed spice.
4. Bind the crumbs with 75 g/3 oz to 100 g/4 oz chocolate and a walnut-sized knob of butter, melted together.
5. Use gingernut biscuits and bind with melted plain chocolate.
6. Add finely grated orange rind from one orange
7. Use chocolate chip biscuits in place of wheatmeal or plain biscuits.

CORNFLAKE CRUST FLAN CASE

METRIC/IMPERIAL
75 g/3 oz cornflakes
50 g/2 oz butter
50 g/2 oz sugar
1 × 15 ml spoon/1 tablespoon golden syrup

Grease a shallow 18 cm/7 inch to 20 cm/8 inch pie plate or sandwich tin. Crush the cornflakes roughly in your hands. Heat the remaining ingredients until melted and bubbling, pour over the cornflakes in a basin and stir until well blended. Line the plate or tin with the mixture, pressing it firmly in place. Chill or leave in a cool place to set.

FRESH FRUIT FLAN FILLING

METRIC/IMPERIAL
225 g/8 oz fresh fruit, e.g., strawberries, raspberries
red-currant jelly or ½ packet red jelly

Pick over the fruit, wash it if necessary and arrange in the flan case. Make a glaze by melting 2 to 3 × 15 ml spoons/2 to 3 tablespoons red-currant jelly with about 1 × 15 ml spoon/1 tablespoon water or by making up ½ packet table jelly; pour the glaze over the fruit when it begins to thicken.

Note: Adapt the quantity to suit the size of flan case.

CANNED FRUIT FLAN FILLING

METRIC/IMPERIAL
1 × 425 g/15 oz can fruit
1 × 15 ml spoon/1 tablespoon cornflour
150 ml/¼ pint fruit juice

Arrange the drained fruit in the flan case, filling it well. Blend the cornflour with a little of the fruit juice to a smooth cream. Boil the rest and stir into the blended cornflour. Return this mixture to the pan and bring to the boil, stirring until a clear thickened glaze is obtained. Spoon over the fruit to coat it evenly.

Note: Adapt the quantity to suit the size of flan case.

Flan Pastry
A rich shortcrust pastry used for flans and tartlets. (See Pastry entry.)

FLAPJACK (SLAPJACK)

A biscuit made from a mixture of fat, sugar, rolled oats and usually syrup.

FLAPJACKS

METRIC/IMPERIAL
75 g/3 oz butter
75 g/3 oz demerara sugar
100 g/4 oz rolled oats

Grease a shallow 18 cm/7½ inch square tin. Cream the butter. Mix together the sugar and oats and gradually work into the creamed butter, until thoroughly blended. Press evenly into the prepared tin with a round-bladed knife. Bake in a hot oven (220°C/425°F, Gas Mark 7) for about 15 minutes, until golden brown; turn the tin half-way through, to ensure even baking. Cool slightly in the tin, mark into fingers with a sharp knife and loosen round the edge; when firm, break into fingers. The flapjacks may be stored in an airtight tin for up to one week.

FLAVOURING

Almost as old as the art of cookery itself is the practice of adding or enhancing taste, or disguising a poor flavour, by the use of extra ingredients. Herbs and spices (see separate entries) are added to innumerable dishes during the cooking to give flavour. Flavouring essences are also very widely used, especially in confectionery and in the making of wines, liqueurs and cordials. (See Essences entry for fuller details.)

Wines and liqueurs such as Madeira, port, sherry, Kirsch, Cointreau, etc., are much used in high-class cookery, as are the different types of brandy – Cognac, Calvados and so on.

FLEURON

A small fancy-shaped piece of pastry (usually puff, flaky or rough puff) used for garnishing entrées, ragoûts, mince, etc.

Roll the pastry thinly, then stamp it into crescents with a small round cutter; place the cutter about 1 cm/½ inch on to the edge of the pastry for the first cut, then move the cutter a further 1 cm/½ inch inwards and cut again, thus forming a crescent; continue the length of the pastry, moving the cutter 1 cm/½ inch each time. Alternatively, cut the pastry into rounds, squares, triangles, diamonds, etc. Place on a baking sheet, brush the tops lightly with beaten egg and bake in a hot oven (230°C/450°F, Gas Mark 8) until well risen, golden-brown and firm underneath – 7 to 10 minutes. Use at once, while crisp.

FLIP

A drink made with beaten egg and milk, wine, spirit or beer and sugar.

FLITCH

A side of pork, salted and cured.

FLOUNDER

A small flat sea-fish, resembling plaice, but of poorer texture and flavour. British flounders, which are found in the North Sea, are in season from February to September. Other species of flounders are found in the Baltic, the Mediterranean and off the Atlantic coast of America.

Flounders are best grilled or fried, but may be cooked in any way suitable for plaice.

FLOUR

Any fine, soft, white powder prepared from a grain, e.g., cornflour, rice flour and wheat flour. Unless otherwise indicated, however, the word usually implies wheat flour, obtained by milling the wheat grain. This is the staple food in most temperate climates and can be made into a wide range of products – breads, biscuits, scones, cakes, pastry, pasta, puddings. It is important as a thickening agent.

Types of Wheat Flour

The flour varies according to the type of wheat used. 'Hard' spring wheats, like those grown in Canada, produce 'strong' flours. These contain a large amount (10 to 15 per cent), of a protein forming substance, gluten. 'Soft' wheats, grown in milder climates such as those of England and Australia, produce a 'soft' or 'weak' flour, containing 7 to 10 per cent gluten. It is the gluten which

gives wheat flour its elasticity, so that it will rise if stretched by bubbles of gas produced by a raising agent and can then be set by baking. A strong flour is necessary to bake yeast goods, plain cakes and puff pastry. A weak flour is better for biscuits, rich cakes and shortcrust pastry, where the raising power is not so important as the ability to carry fat.

The British miller selects wheats from different parts of the world and blends them to produce different grades of flour. Most plain flours on the market, sold as 'general-purpose', are milled from a mixture of hard and soft wheats and are therefore of medium strength. Self-raising flour is generally a softer flour to which a raising agent has been added.

'High Ratio Cake Flour' is a special type, not yet readily available in this country but much used in the USA. It is made from a soft variety of flour from winter wheats containing about 7 per cent protein and is Patent Grade (i.e., a purer flour obtained early in the milling process). This flour is generally employed in cake mixes and commercial cake-making; a higher ratio of sugar, fat and liquid to flour is possible when it is used – hence the name.

Extraction Rates

When wheat is milled, it is crushed between rollers to split the husk and release the contents (including the wheat germ). The amount of bran and germ that remains determines the kind of flour. Wholemeal contains the whole of the cleaned wheat grain, nothing must be added to it or taken from it; white flour is produced from the inner endosperm and contains no bran or germ. The extraction rate of flour means the precentage of the whole grain that remains in the flour after milling, thus: Wholemeal and wholewheat flour is 100 per cent extraction of the cleaned wheat grain; Wheatmeal usually contains 80 to 90 per cent of the cleaned wheat grain; White flour usually contains 70 to 72 per cent of the cleaned wheat grain.

On the whole, millers prefer to make white flour, as it keeps better than wholemeal; the fat in the wheat germ goes rancid so wholemeal flour is best kept for up to 2 months.

According to the regulations for bread and flour which came into force in 1963, wheatmeal and wholemeal flour standards are as follows:

Wheatmeal flour must contain at least 0.6 per cent of fibre (husk) by weight, calculated on the dry weight.

Wholemeal flour must contain the whole of the product derived from milling the cleaned wheat.

Stone-ground flour is a 100 per cent extraction wholemeal flour, produced by grinding the wheat grains between stones instead of rollers.

Minerals and Vitamins

According to the Flour Composition Regulations,

155

all flours must contain not less than the following amounts per 100 g: Calcium, 235 to 390 mg; Iron, 1.65 mg; Thiamin, 0.24 mg; Nicotinic Acid, 1.60 mg.

This level of iron, thiamin and nicotinic acid is roughly what one would expect in a flour of 85 per cent extraction or over, so these substances are added to white flour, but are not normally needed with wheatmeal and certainly not with wholemeal flour. The calcium is at a higher level than one would expect in any flour and is added (as a pure form of chalk) not to restore the flour to the whole-grain level, but simply to increase the food value of the bread. It is not, however, added to wholemeal bread, in deference to the wishes of those who like the natural flour, untreated in any way except by milling or grinding.

In short, the position is this:

Wholemeal flour (100 per cent extraction) has no additions.

Wheatmeal flour (85 to 95 per cent extraction) has added calcium.

White flour (70 to 72 per cent extraction) has added calcium, iron, thiamin and nicotinic acid.

Bleaching and Improving Agents

Storage of flour in the quantities required today is a difficult matter, so the bleaching and improving which used to take place naturally, as the flour aged, are now carried out chemically. The 1972 Amendment to the 1963 regulations permit the use of ozodicarbonamide and L-Cysteine Hydrochloride as improving agents, offering technological and economic advantages of improvers previously permitted. Chlorine dioxide is now generally used as improver and benzoyle peroxide as a bleacher.

Self-raising Flour and Raising Agents

To make self-raising flour, 3 to 4 per cent of raising agent is added during manufacture and mixed in very thoroughly. According to current regulations there must be not less than 0.4 per cent of available carbon dioxide in this flour. The agents used are sodium bicarbonate and calcium acid phosphate or sodium pyrophosphate.

A homemade self-raising flour can be made by sieving together 1.5 kg/3½ lb flour, 25 g/1 oz tartaric acid, 40 g/1½ oz cream of tartar and 20 g/¾ oz bicarbonate of soda; the mixture should be sieved twice to ensure thorough mixing. It is difficult to obtain as good a result by this method.

Self-raising flour is considered to be more convenient by many housewives, so its use is increasing. It gives perfectly good results for most recipes, though strictly speaking it is not necessary for very rich creamed mixtures and whisked sponges, where eggs are sufficient raising agent, for biscuits and plain pastries (with the exception of suetcrust), which are not meant to rise, for bread, where yeast is the raising agent, and for batters, which are raised by steam.

Food Value of Wheat Flour

Flour is a cheap and valuable food. It supplies energy, protein, calcium, iron and vitamins of the B group. White flour has only about half the minerals and B vitamins contained in wholemeal flour, although it has much the same amount of protein and energy value. With the policy of enrichment of flour nutritionally, there is little difference in value between brown and white flour.

The higher extraction flours contain a substance called phytic acid which is thought to decrease the absorption of calcium to some extent, so probably enriched white flour supplies considerably more available calcium. In fact, odd though it seems, wholemeal flour is probably a poorer source of calcium than other flours.

To sum up, the advantages of white flour are that it has better baking qualities and produces a whiter loaf; it has less fat and therefore stores better; it has less phytic acid interfering with the absorption of calcium. On the debit side, as milled it contains less calcium, iron and vitamins of the B group, but since these nutrients are now added, this does not matter. It does not contain roughage as the bran has been removed. For this reason many people prefer to use wholemeal flour in bread and cooking.

Whatever kind of flour and bread is chosen, all types are easily digested, very nutritious and comparatively economical.

Flours from Other Cereals

RYE FLOUR

This ranks next to wheat flour as a bread-maker. It is not often used in this country, but in Europe it is extensively employed in 'black' bread such as pumpernickel. The flour is deficient in proteins as compared with wheat.

BARLEY FLOUR

It was formerly used in this country for bread-making, but the superior qualities of wheat and the increased supply from overseas led to a decline in its use.

RICE FLOUR

By itself this is unsuitable for bread- or cake-making, as it contains no gluten. Rice flour can, however, be combined with wheat flour to make bread and cakes and is used in small quantities in biscuit-making, to give additional 'shortness'.

CORNFLOUR

A maize or corn preparation which consists almost entirely of starch, since the proteins and fats are removed; in fact, in America it is known as corn starch. It is used for making blancmange and custard powders and for thickening sauces, gravies and soups; it may also be used for cake making in conjunction with wheat flour.

Flouring: To dredge flour over the surface of a food in order to dry it or coat it for frying, or to sprinkle flour over a pastry board before use.

FLUMMERY

An old English cold sweet made of a cereal (originally oatmeal), set in a mould and turned out. Other types were Dutch Flummery, made with gelatine or isinglass, egg yolks and flavourings, and Spanish Flummery, made of cream, rice flour, cinnamon and sugar.

GOOSEBERRY FLUMMERY

METRIC/IMPERIAL
350 g/12 oz gooseberries, topped and tailed
115 g/4½ oz caster sugar
grated rind and juice of 1 orange
300 ml/½ pint milk
50 g/2 oz semolina
3 × 15 ml spoons/3 tablespoons lemon juice
2 egg whites
whipped cream, chopped almonds or crystallized rose petals for decoration

Place gooseberries, 75 g/3 oz caster sugar, orange rind and juice in saucepan. Cook gently until soft. Either pass through a nylon sieve or liquidize to give a smooth purée. Allow to cool. Place milk in a clean pan and shower in semolina. When beginning to thicken add lemon juice and simmer for about 10 minutes, stirring continuously. Add remaining caster sugar and whisk well. Fold gooseberry purée through semolina, until light and fluffy. Allow to cool. Stiffly whisk egg whites, fold evenly into semolina mixture. Turn into six stemmed glasses. Chill and decorate with whipped cream and chopped toasted almonds or crystallized rose petals. Eat the same day.

FOIE GRAS

The liver of a goose which has been specially fed and fattened. These very large goose livers are esteemed a great delicacy on the Continent and are cooked in various more or less elaborate ways. They may be served hot or cold, as a savoury or hors d'oeuvre.

Fatted goose livers are also combined with pork, truffles and other ingredients to make the smooth rich paste known as pâté de foie gras, which is imported from France in terrines (small earthenware pots). This pâté is often eaten as an hors d'oeuvre and may be served in the terrine or cut into thin slices and garnished with chopped parsley and sliced lemon. Puréed foie gras may be served as a savoury dish and the pâté may also be used in making sandwiches, canapés and small savouries.

FOLDING IN (SOMETIMES CALLED CUTTING AND FOLDING)

A method of combining a whisked mixture with other ingredients so that it retains its lightness; it is used for mixing meringues, soufflés and certain cake mixtures. A typical example is folding dry flour into a whisked sponge cake mixture. First sift the flour on top of the whisked mixture. Using a large metal spoon, take up a spoonful of the sponge mixture from the bottom of the bowl, drawing the spoon across the base, then fold it over the top, enclosing the dry flour in between. Repeat until all the flour is incorporated, occasionally cutting through the mixture with the spoon held at right angles to the direction of the folding.

Important points to remember are that the mixture must be folded very lightly and that it must not be agitated more than is absolutely necessary, because with every movement some of the air bubbles are broken down.

FONDANT

This forms the basis of a large number of sweets and is also used for chocolate centres and for icing cakes, etc. True fondant is made by boiling sugar syrup to a temperature of 116°C/240°F to 118°C/245°F, but an unboiled version may be used for making simple sweets. (See Sweets entry.)

BOILED FONDANT

METRIC/IMPERIAL
150 ml/¼ pint water (good measure)
450 g/1 lb granulated sugar
3 × 15 ml spoons/3 tablespoons glucose or a good pinch cream of tartar

Put the water into a pan, add the sugar and let it dissolve slowly. Bring the syrup to the boil, add the glucose or cream of tartar and boil to 116°C/240°F. Sprinkle a little water on a marble slab or other suitable surface, pour on the syrup and leave for a few minutes to cool. When a skin forms round the edges, take the spatula and collect the mixture together, then work it backwards and forwards, using a figure-of-eight movement. Continue to work the syrup, collecting it into as small a compass as possible, until it changes its character and 'grains', becoming opaque and firm. Scrape it off the slab and knead it in the hands until of an even texture throughout.

Fondant Icing

Make the fondant as described above and prepare it for use as follows:

Put the required amount in a basin; the full amount given makes a generous coating for an 18 cm/7 inch cake; stand the basin over hot water and melt over a very gentle heat. Take care not to over-heat the fondant, as this makes the texture rough and destroys the gloss. Dilute the melted fondant with sugar syrup or with plain water to the consistency of double cream – or until the mixture will just coat the back of a wooden spoon. To make sugar syrup, dissolve 225 g/8 oz sugar in 300 ml/½ pint water, then boil without stirring to 110°C/225°F; cool before using. Cakes which are to be coated with fondant icing should be glazed completely with apricot glaze and then coated with almond paste, to give a really professional appearance. To ice small cakes or pastries, spear them on a fork or skewer and dip them in the prepared fondant.

To ice a large cake, put it on a wire tray with a plate below and pour the icing quickly all over the cake. Don't touch the icing with a knife or the gloss finish will be spoilt. Add any desired decoration and leave the cake to set.

UNBOILED FONDANT

METRIC/IMPERIAL
450 g/1 lb icing sugar
a pinch of cream of tartar
1 × 5 ml spoon/1 teaspoon lemon juice
1 egg white
colouring

Sift the icing sugar with the cream of tartar. Add the lemon juice and sufficient egg white to make a pliable paste, add a few drops of colouring as required. Knead thoroughly for 5 minutes, then set aside to 'mellow' for 1 hour before using.

Fondant Fruits: These make attractive petits fours. Prepare neat and fairly small pieces of crystallized ginger, glacé pineapple, clusters of raisins, etc., and dip them in liquid fondant (which may be coloured or plain, as desired).

Lift them out on to waxed paper and allow to dry. If the fruit is fresh and juicy, serve it within 2 to 3 hours, or the juice will spoil the fondant.

FONDUE

A speciality of Savoy and Switzerland, made basically of melted cheese, with wine and flavourings. There are many variations of cheese fondues which provide a popular way to entertain informally. Recipes for sweet fondues are also available. A French dish, Fondue Bourguignonne, consists of small cubes of tender steak impaled on a long fork and cooked in hot oil and served with a selection of sauces. Pieces of chicken, prawn and scampi may also be used.

FONDUE

METRIC/IMPERIAL
1 clove garlic, skinned and crushed
150 ml/¼ pint dry white wine and a squeeze of lemon juice
225 g/8 oz cheese, cut in thin strips (half Gruyère and half Emmenthal)
2 × 5 ml spoons/2 teaspoons cornflour
1 liqueur glass of Kirsch
pepper and grated nutmeg

Rub the inside of a flameproof dish with the garlic, place the dish over a gentle heat and warm the wine and lemon juice in it. Add the cheese and continue to heat gently, stirring well until the cheese has melted and begun to cook. Add the cornflour and seasonings, blended to a smooth cream with the Kirsch, and continue cooking for a further 2 to 3 minutes; when the mixture is of a thick creamy consistency, it is ready to serve.

Traditionally, fondue is served at the table in the dish in which it was cooked, kept warm over a small spirit lamp or dish-warmer. To eat it, provide cubes of crusty bread which are speared on a fork and dipped in the fondue.

An anglicized version of fondue can be made using a strong-flavoured Cheddar or Lancashire cheese, cider instead of white wine and brandy instead of Kirsch.

HOT CHEESE DIP

METRIC/IMPERIAL
150 ml/¼ pint medium dry white wine
1 × 5 ml spoon/1 teaspoon lemon juice
400 g/14 oz Gouda cheese, grated
1 × 15 ml spoon/1 tablespoon cornflour
1 × 5 ml spoon/1 teaspoon made English mustard
pepper

Put the wine and lemon juice into a heavy saucepan and heat until nearly boiling. Add the cheese and beat well with a wooden spoon.

Blend the cornflour with a little water and add to the cheese mixture, beating well. Stir in the mustard and season with pepper.

Serve at once with chunks of French bread.

Note: Serve as a traditional fondue for leisurely eating. Supply each guest with a fork for spearing the bread and then dipping into hot cheese mixture. Accompany with a well-tossed salad.

FONDUE DU RAISIN

A mild French cheese covered with grape pips which comes from the Province of Savoy. This cheese tends to be rather mild in flavour but it adds colour to a cheese board.

FONDUTA

A famous dish from Piedmont in Italy made with Fontina cheese and truffles.

FONTAINEBLEAU CHEESE

A French cheese of the cream type, soft and fresh, made in the country round Fontainebleau, mostly during the summer.

FONTINA D'AOSTA

One of Italy's great cheeses which comes only from the valley of Savoy.

FOOD

Food is essential for life. Plants can make their own from minerals, water and the gases in the air, but animals have to obtain their food ready-made. Basically, all animals get their food from plants, although many of them obtain it indirectly by eating other animals. The water, minerals and gases thus used are eventually returned to their original state through breathing, excretion and decay after death, and are then once more available to build new plants. This cycle is continuous and the total amount of food available to life on the earth remains constant. The human race is able to direct and improve the cycle, but it is not able to alter the basic principles or increase the amount of the basic ingredients.

All plant and animal life should theoretically be available as food for animals, but most species are restricted in their choice of foods. Sheep eat mainly grass and can get the necessary nourishment from it, whereas humans are so adapted that they could not be well-fed on grass. However, human beings are able to eat a very much wider variety of foods than most animals.

No single food eaten by humans supplies all that is necessary, although milk comes very near to doing so. Each food supplies nutrients of some kind in varying amounts and it is difficult to say that this food is more valuable than that one. What we can say is that the wider the choice of food, the more likely it is that all the necessary food factors will be obtained.

FOOD AND DRUGS ACT

A major act was passed in 1955, the legislation being made jointly by the Minister of Agriculture and the Secretary of State for Social Services. This only applies in England and Wales but there is similar legislation in Scotland and Northern Ireland.

Important provisions include the following although many detailed amendments have been made since 1955. The full regulations and amendments are obtainable from Her Majesty's Stationery Office, London.
1. General provisions regarding the composition and labelling of food.

(a) it is an offence to sell food under false pretences.
(b) labels or advertisements which falsely describe food or mislead as to its nature, substance or quality are not allowed.
(c) substances should not be added to or abstracted from food so as to make it injurious to health.
(d) it is an offence to sell unsound food of any kind.
2. Provisions for hygiene control in places where food is to be sold or prepared:
3. Regulations controlling markets, stalls, delivery vehicles, slaughter houses, and cold air stores.
4. Requirements to notify any type of food poisoning to authorities.
5. Special provisions are also made with regard to certain foods, such as ice cream, milk, other dairy products, shellfish, horseflesh, sausages, flour, meat pies, margarine, coffee, cocoa, soft drinks, spices and preserves.

FOOD POISONING

Any poison transmitted by food and drink is covered by this term, but it is generally used only for certain infections.

The number of cases due to natural poisons, such as deadly nightshade and certain fungi, and to artificial ones (such as insecticides, etc.) accidentally added to food, or lead derived from lead pipes, is not nearly so great as that due to bacterial infections.

A steady increase in these cases has led to food poisoning being made a notifiable disease, though many cases are still not notified, since a mild attack is easily overlooked and the doctor is not necessarily called in. Attacks are more frequent during the summer than in winter and they may set in within 6 to 24 hours after the infected food has been eaten. The symptoms are generally vomiting and/or diarrhoea. Such disorders, frequently dismissed as 'only a germ going about', are in fact due to a definite lack of hygiene somewhere.

The increase in food poisoning is probably due in part to changing food and eating habits. Much more use is made of communal feeding centres – restaurants, cafes, snack bars, school meal centres and industrial canteens. Practices that cause no harm in the home may be dangerous in the large-scale kitchen. Some of the possible causes are:
1. Lack of hygiene – poor personal hygiene, lack of washing facilities, unnecessary handling of food.
2. Lack of trained staff to instruct the workers, point out the dangers and supervise the preparation and storage of the food.
3. Lack of good cold storage facilities.
4. Cooked food not being reheated sufficiently.
The actual poisoning can be caused either by

159

bacteria or by toxins produced by bacteria. Bacteria thrive in warm, moist conditions, where there is a supply of food. Some of them produce poisons which cannot be destroyed except by thorough cooking, even though the bacteria themselves are killed.

Types of Food Poisoning

(A) SALMONELLA GROUP
Many varieties, producing mild or severe illness. Amongst them are the bacteria that cause gastroenteritis, typhoid fever and enteric fever.

Some of the foods that can be infected are meat dishes, milk and confectionery containing artificial cream. Raw oysters were formerly sometimes infected, but nowadays are generally farmed in a hygienic manner.

(B) STAPHYLOCOCCAL GROUP
These produce harmful toxins.

(C) BOTULISM
Caused by a powerful poison from *B. Botulinus*, but fortunately very rare.

(D) DYSENTERY
Particularly prevalent in tropical climates.

(E) CHOLERA
Very rare in Western countries.

FOOD STORAGE

Different kinds of food have different storage requirements. Here is a summary of the position:

Perishable Foods
Meat, fish, milk, fats, cheese, eggs, fruit and vegetables come into this group, since they all deteriorate fairly quickly owing to the action of bacteria and enzymes. Low temperatures slow down this action, so perishable foods should ideally be stored at a temperature low enough to delay such activity – that is, at about 4.5°C/40°F or just under. The domestic refrigerator, which is normally kept at 2°C/35°F to 7°C/45°F is thus suitable for storing fresh foods, milk, fats, etc. (See Refrigeration entry for further details.) In general, however, no attempt should be made to store these foods for a long period, even when a refrigerator is available, and most of them should be bought and used within a few days. Cream, yogurt and soft cheeses are usually marked with a date stamp which indicates the last day they can be sold by the shop. They will keep for a few days after this in a refrigerator. Failing a refrigerator, perishable foods should be kept covered in a cold, well-ventilated larder.

MEAT AND FISH
Raw meat and fish should be stored in the refrigerator covered lightly with foil, etc. Failing a refrigerator, meat should be placed on a rack standing on a plate and loosely covered with grease-proof paper or a meat cover; fish should be put on a plate and covered loosely. Both should, of course, be kept as cool as possible.

Cooked meat or fish should be wrapped in greaseproof paper or polythene or placed in a covered container.

MILK
Keep this in its bottle in the refrigerator or larder. If you have no refrigerator, milk can be kept cooler if you stand it in a bowl of water and cover it with a thick wet cloth, the ends of which are in the water.

Jugs of custard or cream should be covered.

BREAD
Air circulation is necessary, so keep bread in a ventilated metal or plastic bread bin or in a loosely wrapped plastic bag.

FATS AND OILS
Should be kept cool and if possible in the dark, since the light has a destructive effect on their vitamin content and tends to hasten rancidity.

CHEESE
For table use should be stored in conditions that prevent both mould growth and excessive drying. A cheese dish with a ventilated cover is good, provided it is placed in a cool, dry, airy place. Alternatively, wrap the cheese in cling film or aluminium foil or place it in a plastic container large enough to allow air circulation. Hard cheeses can be kept in a refrigerator, but soft ones should be kept in the larder or food cupboard. Cheese for cooking should be allowed to harden, especially if it is soft or immature when bought. (See Cheese entry.)

EGGS
Should be kept in a cool, airy place – not necessarily in a refrigerator.

FRUIT, VEGETABLES
Most of these foods contain some vitamin C and since the vitamin content diminishes rapidly during storage, they should be used fresh and stored for as short a time as possible in a cool and well-ventilated place. Root vegetables should be placed on a vegetable rack with slatted shelves. Green vegetables should be washed and put in the salad 'crisper' or a plastic container in the refrigerator; alternatively, put them in a cool larder, placing salad vegetables in a large bowl covered with a plate. Lettuce will also keep fairly well if put stem side down in a little water in an aluminium pan with the lid on.

FROZEN FOODS
(See separate entry.)

LEFTOVERS
Cool these rapidly by putting them in a cold place –

do not leave them on the stove or in a warm part of the kitchen. They are then best covered and stored in the refrigerator. Failing this, use them up as soon as possible, preferably the next day.

Storage Times for Perishables
(not Frozen Foods)

	IN COOL LARDER	IN REFRIGERATOR
Meat:		
Raw; roasts, chops	1 to 3 days	3 to 5 days
Offal, mince	A few hours	1 to 2 days
Cooked	1 to 2 days	2 to 5 days
Fish:		
Raw	A few hours	1 to 2 days
Cooked	1 day	2 days
Milk	1 day	3 to 4 days
Butter and Cheese	1 week	2 to 4 weeks

Dry Stores

Under this heading are included cereals, sugars, syrups, dried fruits, herbs, essences, flavourings, condiments and spices, etc. Deterioration during storage is not as a rule a serious problem, but most cereals are subject to attacks by weevils and mites and will mould if allowed to become damp. Oatmeal, since it contains an appreciable amount of fat, will become rancid if kept too long or in a warm place. In certain cases, notably with dried fruit, fermentation may set in after prolonged storage.

The dry goods cupboard should be cool and dry, well-ventilated but dustproof and the stores must be examined from time to time. A small cupboard or shelf near the cooker should be used for the stores which are constantly required, such as sugar, salt, pepper, tea and coffee.

Ideally, the shelving in the dry stores cupboard should be so arranged that the jars can be kept in single rows, and in any case not more than two deep, so that they can be easily seen. The shelves should be made removable and adjustable so that they can be adapted for jars and tins of different heights. Stepped shelves for small bottles, also shelves that slope backwards, economize on space.

Plastic or glass jars are excellent for cereals and dried fruits, etc., for quick identification and also to see immediately how much is in stock. Smaller plastic or glass jars with well-fitting lids are suitable for herbs and spices. Airtight containers are needed for cakes, biscuits, baking powder and coffee. A container with slight ventilation is needed for bread; an enamel bin is often used and a polythene bag is also suitable, if not wrapped too tightly round the loaf. Flour is best left in the packet and stored in a bin. Make sure the bin is kept clean by regular washing. Make sure to dry the bin thoroughly as a damp atmosphere should be avoided at all costs.

Storage Times for Dry Goods

Cereals, flour (*except wholemeal*) and pulses	Several months
Wholemeal flour	1 to 2 months
Sugar	Indefinitely
Preserves, pickles, bottled fruit and vegetables	1 to 2 years
Dried fruit	2 to 3 months
Canned foods:	
Fruit	1 year
Vegetables	2 years
Fish and meat (*except large hams*)	5 years
Evaporated milk	2 years
Soups	2 years
Packet foods, e.g., cake mixes	6 months

Larder Storage

A larder is usually only found in older houses, but these principles apply to any food cupboards.

If you have no refrigerator, arrange perishable foods on the lower shelves of the larder and dry stores on the higher ones. Clean the lower shelves frequently, wiping up spilt food and removing any used and dirty containers or plates. Clean the other shelves about once a month, washing them and allowing them to dry one by one. Wipe the containers as you return them to the shelves.

Refrigerator Storage

Allow hot foods to cool before putting them in the refrigerator.

Polythene, plastic containers or foil prevent food drying out.

All foods should be covered.

Wipe up spilt foods at once.

Cover any foods that are highly flavoured or strong smelling to avoid flavours from transferring from one food to another, for example, the strong smell of onion to milk.

Defrost according to the maker's instructions and wipe the inside of the refrigerator with a clean, damp cloth. Do not use soap, detergent or abrasive powder.

(See Refrigeration and Freezing entries.)

FOOL

A purée of fresh fruit or sometimes canned with cream and/or custard. (See recipe in Fruit entry.)

FORCEMEAT

Stuffing used for veal, chicken, hare, rabbit, hearts, fish, liver, etc. The mixture can also be rolled into small balls, fried or baked and used as a garnish. There are several types of forcemeat and the basic recipe can be altered according to the dish which it accompanies.

BACON OR HAM STUFFING

METRIC/IMPERIAL
¼ onion, skinned and chopped
1 × 15 ml spoon/1 tablespoon dripping
2 mushrooms, chopped
50–75 g/2–3 oz cooked bacon or ham, chopped
25 g/1 oz fresh white breadcrumbs
salt
pepper
little dry mustard
few drops of Worcestershire sauce
beaten egg or
milk to bind

Lightly fry the onion in the dripping for 1 to 2 minutes; add the mushrooms and bacon or ham and fry until the onion is soft but not coloured. Remove from the heat and add the crumbs, seasonings and sauce and bind with beaten egg or milk. Use as a stuffing for vegetables, tomatoes, small marrows, peppers, etc. This quantity is sufficient for a 1.5 kg/3¼ lb chicken and may be used to stuff poussin or capons.

VEAL FORCEMEAT

METRIC/IMPERIAL
100 g/4 oz lean veal
75 g/3 oz lean bacon, rinded
1 small onion, skinned and finely chopped
25 g/1 oz butter
75 g/3 oz fresh white breadcrumbs
1 large mushroom, wiped and chopped
1 × 5 ml spoon/1 teaspoon finely chopped parsley
salt
pepper
cayenne
ground mace
1 egg, beaten

Pass the mixed veal and bacon twice through a mincer, then beat them well in a bowl. Lightly fry the onion in a little of the butter, until soft but not coloured – 2 to 3 minutes; add to the meat. Add the breadcrumbs, mushroom, the remaining butter, parsley and seasonings and lastly the beaten egg. Mix well; if the mixture is too stiff, add a little milk.

Use for veal or lamb; double the quantities for a 6 kg/13 lb turkey.

NUT STUFFING

METRIC/IMPERIAL
50 g/2 oz shelled walnuts
3 × 15 ml spoons/3 tablespoons shelled cashew nuts
6 shelled Brazil nuts
50 g/2 oz butter
2 small onions, skinned and finely chopped
100 g/4 oz mushrooms, finely chopped

pinch of dried mixed herbs
1 × 15 ml spoon/1 tablespoon chopped parsley
175 g/6 oz fresh white breadcrumbs
1 large egg, beaten
giblet stock to moisten
seasoning

Finely chop the nuts. Melt the butter and sauté the onion for 5 minutes. Add the mushrooms and sauté for a further 5 minutes. Toss together the nuts, mixed herbs, parsley and breadcrumbs. Stir in the mushroom mixture with the beaten egg. If necessary, moisten with stock, season to taste with salt and freshly ground black pepper.

This is sufficient for a 4 kg/9 lb to 4.5 kg/10 lb turkey.

FOWL

An edible bird especially the domestic cock or hen. As a general term, the word can apply to a bird of any age, but it is often applied more particularly to an older tougher bird, suitable for boiling, steaming or casseroling.

For general directions regarding drawing, trussing etc., see Poultry entry. (For methods of cooking and recipes, see Chicken entry.)

FRANGIPANE (FRANZIPAN)

Originally frangipane was a jasmine perfume, which gave its name to an almond cream flavoured with the perfume. The term is now usually applied to a flan filled with an almond-flavoured mixture. It also applies to a type of choux pastry.

FRANGIPANE FLAN

METRIC/IMPERIAL
19 cm/7½ inch baked shortcrust pastry flan case
3–4 × 5 ml spoons/3–4 teaspoons cornflour
450 ml/¾ pint milk
4 egg yolks
2 × 15 ml spoons/2 tablespoons caster sugar
75 g/3 oz ground almonds
almond essence

FOR THE FRUIT LAYER AND TOPPING
100 g/4 oz white grapes, skinned, halved and seeded
2 oranges, peeled and segmented
1 banana, peeled and sliced
caster sugar
50 g/2 oz flaked almonds, toasted

Make the flan case in the usual way. Mix the cornflour to a smooth paste with a little of the milk. Put the remainder on to heat; stir in the cornflour paste and cook, stirring, until thick and smooth. Remove from the heat and beat in the egg yolks one at a time. Continue cooking over a gentle heat until the mixture thickens. Remove from the heat and stir in the caster sugar, ground almonds and a few drops of almond essence.

Cover, and leave until cold.

Arrange the fruits in the pastry case. Spread the frangipane cream mixture over and pile into a pyramid shape. Just before serving dust thickly with caster sugar. With a red-hot skewer, brand the sugar to caramelize it – reheat the skewer after marking each line. Sprinkle with the almonds.

FRANKFURTER

A Continental smoked sausage made from minced pork or beef and pork and often served with sauerkraut. In the USA, and to an increasing extent in this country, frankfurters are the sausage normally used to make Hot Dogs (See Hot Dog entry). Unless otherwise stated in the particular recipe, the frankfurters are usually boiled for a few minutes before being used.

FREEZER

Freezers are becoming increasingly popular and valuable pieces of equipment in the home. They are also invaluable in any establishment that has to cater for large numbers. The main advantages are:—
1. To make good use of abundant supplies of fruit, vegetables and other food.
2. To enable foods to be eaten when out of season.
3. To take advantage of bulk buying and thus reducing costs and shopping time.
4. To cook food in bulk to save on cooking time and fuel.
5. To be able to store meals and foods which can be used when shopping and cooking are not possible for various reasons.

Apart from the advantages, the cost of running the freezer must be taken into account. On top of the cost of the freezer, the cost of electricity, packing materials and insurance must be considered. Most people feel that the convenience of having a freezer outweighs these costs even if they do not save a great deal on the contents.

Types of Freezer
Freezers are of two main types – the upright kind (with a door) and the chest models (with a lift-up lid).There is also the combination refrigerator-freezer, which is useful for processing small quantities of food and where space is limited.

The type to choose depends on your requirements. It is reckoned that each 28 litres/1 cubic foot of space will store about 9 kg/20 lb of frozen food, depending on kind. A useful guide is to allow 56 to 84 litres/2 to 3 cubic feet space per person. Sizes range from 49.5 litres/1.75 cubic feet up to 707 litres/25 cubic feet.

UPRIGHT TYPE
This model takes up less floor space and the food is easier to get at. On the other hand, the cold air

inside tends to 'spill out' when the door is opened and warm, moist air enters. This kind of freezer frosts up more quickly for this reason, but the frost is easily scraped out. Size range from 49.5 litres/1.75 cubic feet to 566 litres/20 cubic feet.

CHEST TYPE
This type retains the cold better and is slightly cheaper to run. It is not so easy to see the contents nor to reach foods at the bottom. Most models are supplied with plastic covered wire baskets to hold the most often needed or delicate items, making them easier to find. De-frosting is required less frequently, but takes more effort to carry out. 113 litres/4 cubic feet to 707 litres/25 cubic feet include range of sizes.

COMBINATION REFRIGERATOR-FREEZER
This has two separate units, the freezer section being insulated from the refrigerator. The thermostat controls the refrigerator temperature without altering that of the freezer and the refrigerator can be defrosted without affecting the freezer.

It is important to distinguish between the refrigerator with a true freezer compartment and the one with a frozen food compartment; although the latter (and ice cube section) is often incorrectly called a freezer, it does not provide a sufficiently low temperature for freezing foods, but will store frozen food for a certain length of time, depending on the star rating (see Refrigeration entry). In many freezers a dial or switch can be set to give a lower temperature or fast freezing setting. This should be lowered before use, so that the freezing process is speeded up, quick freezing being important. Once the foods have been frozen the setting should be returned to 'normal' maintaining an internal temperature of −18°C/0°F.

A freezer is capable of freezing food without any change in the temperature of the food already being stored. It has the ability to freeze in 24 hours a specified quantity of fresh or cooked foods and to store them for periods of up to one year or more depending on the product.

It is an advantage to have a warning device (a light is the usual arrangement) which comes on when the temperature starts to rise above −18°C/0°F. Alternatively, a warning buzzer or light may be fitted to the plug which will come on when the current is cut off.

Looking after a Freezer
Most freezers are supplied with full instructions from the maker. Defrosting should be carried out every 9 to 11 months, or when the ice coating is about 5 cm/¼ inch thick on the sides of the cabinet. Defrost at a time when the freezer contains as little as possible. Remaining food can be placed in a refrigerator or wrapped in newspaper and blankets until the freezer is ready for use again.

163

Power Failure

If the power fails for any reason, do not open the freezer unless it is really necessary. The contents of the freezer will keep cold for at least 12 to 24 hours. When you do open the cabinet, inspect the packages; provided there are still ice crystals present in them it is safe to keep them in the freezer. If however the food has thawed it should be used as soon as possible, certainly within three days, and not refrozen. It is possible to have the contents of the freezer insured for a small premium per annum. Several insurance companies will handle such claims and some freezer centres offer cover if the freezer is purchased from them. Always check exactly what the policy covers.

Freezing

Although it has been known for thousands of years that cold retards the decay of food, only in the past few decades has the freezing and long-term cold storage of a variety of foods been widely developed.

It is the easiest and safest way of preserving food. It is a simple process of reducing food to a temperature at which bacteria become inactive. Freezing is carried out at a temperature of $-21°C/-5°F$.

Foods for Freezing

Most foods will freeze successfully, but it is important that they are of good quality: freezing does not change the quality of food. Particularly suitable for freezing are meat, fish, vegetables, fruit and dairy products. Any of these foods can be frozen raw or made into dishes and frozen: Bread, biscuits, cakes, pancakes, puddings, pastries and sauces can all be frozen and make useful standbys. If more convenient bread dough can be frozen uncooked: This also applies to pastry dough and cake mixtures.

The few foods which do not take kindly to freezing are whole eggs, hardboiled eggs, potato in cooked dishes, custards, mayonnaise, dishes containing a high proportion of gelatine and single cream. However, with correct treatment some of these can be frozen for short periods. Eggs can be separated and frozen in individual containers; they should be slightly whipped and a small amount of sugar or salt added to the yolks; potato is more satisfactory if mashed and custards can be frozen before being cooked.

Salad ingredients such as lettuce, watercress, celery, cucumber and chicory cannot be frozen successfully at all. The same applies to some fruits such as melon, bananas and pears (discolour badly).

Some frozen foods can be cooked from frozen such as meat for grilling or roasting, vegetables and fruits, but most need to be thawed first. Cooked dishes, such as stews and quiches can be cooked from frozen, but extra cooking time must be allowed. Slow thawing can be done in the refrigerator, which is most suitable for dairy products and dishes including them, or at room temperature for a shorter time. It is very important to allow frozen poultry to thaw thoroughly before cooking. It is possible to refreeze foods as long as there has been no risk of contamination: the quality will, however, be impaired slightly, so it is not advisable as a general rule.

General notes on Freezing

All food stored in a freezer must be carefully wrapped and sealed. There are many packaging materials available from supermarkets and freezer centres. These include heavy duty polythene, aluminium foil, rigid plastic boxes, wax cartons, foil dishes and basins and freezer tape. It is also possible to use yogurt and cottage cheese cartons provided they are carefully cleaned and sealed with freezer tape before being placed in the freezer. Food should be packed in portions to suit the family needs as this saves time and waste. When packing food, as much air as possible should be excluded, except with liquids when a space of 1 cm/½ inch should be left at the top to allow for expansion. All foods should be labelled with the content, date of packing and weight or number of servings. It is also advisable to keep an inventory of the contents of the freezer so that food can be used in rotation.

Freezing Fruits

PREPARATION

Clean, stem and sort the fruit, handling it carefully and working with small amounts to avoid bruising. Discard over-ripe parts, blemishes and green sections.

WASHING AND DRAINING

Use clean utensils and wash your hands before handling the fruit. Cold (or better still iced) water should be used for washing fruits, to firm them and prevent waterlogging and seepage of juice. Drain in a colander. Fruit to be frozen in a dry pack should be dried on absorbent paper towels.

PACKING

The flavour, colour and texture of most fruit will be better retained if it is frozen with sugar or syrup. The amount used depends upon personal taste, the tartness of the fruit and the way it is to be served. Fruits contain chemical substances called enzymes that are concerned with hastening chemical changes and go on working after the product is harvested. Instead of their being blanched to stop enzymatic action (as is done with vegetables), they are packed in sugar or syrup which protects them in two ways: the sugar retards the action of enzymes during frozen storage and the syrup (either prepared and poured over, or formed by the sugar and juice drawn from the fruit) keeps the air away and retards oxidation (browning).

Soft fruits may be packed without sugar or syrup but are usually preferred with one or the other. As already mentioned, some fruits, particularly pears, discolour badly when frozen, so they should either be blanched or packed in ascorbic acid solution or lemon juice; on the whole, they are perhaps better not frozen.

Method I – Dry pack: This method is used chiefly for fruits that are to be made into pies, jellies or preserves. It is satisfactory for cranberries, blueberries, currants and other small fruits that can be washed and prepared without breaking the skin and that do not darken easily upon exposure to the air. Carefully wash and sort the fruit, drain on absorbent towels, fill the containers full and freeze.

Method II – Free flow dry pack: This method is suitable for small fruit (or pieces of fruit) e.g., raspberries, cherries, grapefruit segments. Pick the fruit over, prepare as necessary; spread out on a baking tray and freeze until firm, then pack for storage.

Method III – Sugar pack: Use this method for juicy fruits that are sliced, crushed or puréed. The sugar draws the juice from the fruit, forming a natural syrup that covers and protects it. Allow 100 g/4 oz to 175 g/6 oz dry sugar to every 0.5 kg/1 lb fruit. The fruit must be mixed with the sugar until each piece is coated, so use a flour sifter to distribute the sugar and add alternate layers of fruit and sugar, shaking the contents after each addition to distribute the sugar and coat the fruit with natural syrup.

Method IV – Syrup pack: Syrup is used for packing fruits that have little free juice, e.g., peaches, apricots, greengages and plums. A syrup consisting of 225 g/8 oz caster sugar to 600 ml/1 pint water is sufficient for 0.5 kg/1 lb fruit. Stone and skin the fruit, place in the containers and cover with syrup. Leave 1 cm/½ inch to 1.5 cm/¾ inch head space for expansion during freezing. Keep syrup-packed fruits submerged by placing a piece of crumpled greaseproof or waxed paper under the cover of the container or in the top of the bag.

Method V – Fruit purées: Fruit that is not of prime quality can be made into a purée before freezing. This takes up less space and is useful for making mousses, fruit fools and sauces to accompany ice cream and other desserts. Some fruits such as rhubarb, apples, apricots, blackberries, raspberries, blackcurrants, gooseberries and plums will need to be stewed before puréeing. Softer fruits such as strawberries, can be puréed without cooking. Purées should be placed in rigid containers allowing 1 cm/½ inch headspace to allow for expansion.

If the fruit is to be served raw, thaw it slowly in the unopened container and eat while still slightly chilled. Fruits which tend to discolour, like peaches, should be thawed rapidly; stone fruit should be thawed in the syrup. Allow 6 to 8 hours to thaw in a refrigerator per 0.5 kg/1 lb of fruit, and 2 to 4 hours at room temperature. For quick thawing, place container in warm water for 30 minutes to 1 hour.

If the fruit is to be cooked, thaw until the pieces are just loosened. Cook as fresh fruit, adding sugar to taste (remember that it will be fairly sweet if packed in dry sugar or syrup).

Freezing vegetables
Most vegetables are suitable for freezing, except cucumber, radishes, lettuce, cress and other green vegetables that are eaten raw. New potatoes and onions do not freeze well; celery loses its crispness. Tomatoes are best frozen in purée form. Asparagus, sweet corn, peas, spinach, broad beans and cauliflower are very successful frozen.

PREPARATION
Speed is important here, for deterioration after harvesting is rapid at warm temperatures and vegetables lose some of their food value and 'garden freshness' if allowed to stand for even a few hours in a warm place. They must be frozen immediately after harvesting or refrigerated and frozen within 12 hours.

Carefully trim and wash the vegetables, i.e., prepare them as for cooking: large vegetables such as cauliflower and broccoli should be divided into pieces of the right size for serving. Small pieces of uniform size can be scalded and packaged more easily than large ones.

BLANCHING (SCALDING)
Fresh vegetables contain chemical substances called enzymes which help in the growing and ripening, but if the enzymes are allowed to continue working in harvested products, they will cause serious destruction of vitamins, texture and colour – even during storage at −18°C/0°F. Therefore all vegetables must be blanched to destroy these enzymes. Take a pan large enough to hold the colander, wire basket or net bag in which the vegetables are to be placed and put in about 4.5 litres/1 gallon water for each 0.5 kg/1 lb of vegetables. The food should be weighed into suitable quantities according to the number of portions needed at one time. Place in the colander or other container and immerse in fast-boiling water for the appropriate time, counting from the moment when the water returns to the boil. Put the colander into ice-cold water to cool, drain the vegetables, pack into containers, seal and label. It is best to blanch small amounts to ensure bringing the water back to the boil each time.

165

Freezing Cooked or Prepared Foods

FOOD	TYPES TESTED AND RECOMMENDED	PREPARATION AND FREEZING	PACKAGING	PREPARATION BEFORE SERVING
YEAST MIXTURES Storage time in freezer 4 weeks.	White and brown bread rolls. Chelsea buns. Fancy bread.		Polythene bags or foil.	Leave to thaw in sealed bag or wrapper 3 to 6 hours at room
Storage time up to 1 week in wrapper.	Bought bread.		Original wrapper or polythene bag or foil.	temperature or overnight in the refrigerator; or leave foil wrapped and crisp in oven (200°C/400°F, Gas Mark 6) for about 45 minutes.
Storage time up to 4 months.	Bought part-baked bread.	Freeze immediately.	Leave loaf in bag, rolls in polythene bag.	Follow packet instructions.
SANDWICHES Storage time in freezer 1 to 2 months.	Most types may be frozen but those filled with hard-boiled egg, tomato, cucumber or bananas tend to become taste-less and soggy.	Use freshly sliced bread; warm the butter so that it spreads easily; cut off the crusts.	Polythene bags or plastic boxes. Package in small amounts; do not pack too many layers. Seal.	Thaw in unopened package, 3 to 4 hours.
CAKES Storage time in freezer 6 months. Fruit cakes improve with keeping so may be stored longer; frosted cakes 2 months. Uncooked mixture 2 months.	Fatless sponges and sponge flan cases. Victoria sandwich Madeira cake. Chocolate buns, cup cakes, iced fancy cakes Fruit cakes.	Loaf and square cakes are easier to wrap and store than round ones. Make and bake as usual. Cool to room temperature. Cakes may be frozen iced or plain, filled or unfilled, though they keep longer and in better condition if not iced. Iced cakes are easier to pack if first placed in the freezer for 1 hour to harden the icing; butter icing freezes well.	Polythene bags, aluminium foil, waxed cardboard boxes, or plastic boxes. Seal. Wrap plain cake layers separately or together with waxed paper between layers.	Buns, cakes, un-iced layer cakes, 1 to 2 hours. Frosted layer cakes 4 hours.
BISCUITS Storage time in freezer 6 months for baked and unbaked.	Almost any type (preferably unfilled).	Make and bake as usual. If fragile, keep a day before packaging. Alternatively, freeze biscuit dough.	Waxed cardboard boxes; separate each layer with waxed paper. Seal. Biscuit dough may be moulded into a bar or roll and wrapped in poly-thene sheet.	Baked Biscuits: thaw for 15 to 30 minutes. To crisp up place them in a fairly hot oven for 3 to 5 minutes. Dough: thaw until it can be easily handled, about 30 minutes.

FOOD	TYPES TESTED AND RECOMMENDED	PREPARATION AND FREEZING	PACKAGING	PREPARATION BEFORE SERVING
PASTRIES Storage time in freezer. Baked: 3 to 6 months. Unbaked: 3 months.	Shortcrust: Pie crusts, jam tarts flan cases, etc. Flaky and Puff: Sausage rolls, vol-au-vent cases, cream horn cases, pie crusts. Choux: Éclairs (unfilled) and cream buns.	Make and bake as usual. If they are to be reheated, bake for slightly shorter time. Fruit pies which are to be served hot should be frozen unbaked, as this saves double cooking time. Puff, flaky and choux pastry cases should be frozen baked but not filled. Éclairs can be frozen filled for short periods only.	Pies: Aluminium foil dishes. Freeze before wrapping if they seem tender to handle. Seal. Bouchée Cases and Tartlets: Waxed cardboard boxes. Seal.	Pies, filled and baked: Thaw for 1 to 1½ hours. Heat in fairly hot oven (190°C/375°F, Gas Mark 5) for 30 to 50 minutes. Filled and Unbaked: Do not thaw, bake in hot oven for 40 to 60 minutes. Flan or Vol-au-vent Cases. Baked: Do not thaw, heat in fairly hot oven for 15 minutes. Unbaked: Do not thaw, bake in hot oven for 20 mins. Sausage Rolls, Bouchée Cases: Thaw, then reheat.
MEAT DISHES Storage time in freezer – 2 months.	Stews and casseroles. Meat balls, made with fresh meat. Meat croquettes, made with cooked meat. Note: Fried meats, pork and sausage-meats do not freeze well.	Make as usual but cook for slightly shorter time. Cool. Make and cook as usual, freeze in gravy. Freeze uncooked (if soft, freeze before packing).	1 litre/2 pint cardboard containers. Seal. Plastic boxes. Aluminium foil dishes covered with foil; polythene bags. Seal. Waxed cardboard boxes. Seal.	Reheat foods from cartons or bags in a pan for 30 minutes. Place in casserole, heat in moderate oven at (180°C/350°F, Gas Mark 4) for 1 hour. If in foil dishes, remove top cover and reheat in moderate oven for 40–50 minutes. Fry in deep fat 118°C/380°F until brown on all sides.
STOCKS AND SOUPS Storage time in freezer 2–3 months. Sauces – Savoury and Sweet. Storage time as above. If highly seasoned – 2 weeks.	Almost any type (e.g. tomato, chicken, etc.) but excluding onion and celery. Curry, barbecue, tomato, lobster. Butterscotch, chocolate. Highly spiced sauces should not be stored too long as some spices develop a musty flavour.	Make as usual, but blend the fat and flour in sauces particularly well to prevent separation during storage. Cool quickly to room temperature.	600 ml/1 pint or 300 ml/½ pint containers. Seal.	Thaw in container for 2 hrs. Pour into double boiler, Heat slowly, stirring all the time until really hot.
STEAMED PUDDINGS Storage time in freezer: Uncooked:	All types.	Make and steam as usual.	Aluminium foil dish, covered.	Uncooked: remove and re-cover with

167

FOOD	TYPES TESTED AND RECOMMENDED	PREPARATION AND FREEZING	PACKAGING	PREPARATION BEFORE SERVING
1 month. Cooked: 3 months.			Seal. Foil or polythene basin and lid.	greased foil, place frozen to steam 2½ hours. Cooked: re-cover as above and place frozen to steam for 45 minutes.
MOULDS, MOUSSES, CREAMS Storage time in freezer 2 to 3 months.	Honeycomb mould. Orange, lemon, mousse. Chocolate, coffee, vanilla cream. Dairy cream.	Make as usual.	Aluminium foil dishes covered with foil. Seal. Waxed carton.	Thaw slowly in refrigerator for 6 hours or at room temperature for 2 hours.
ICE CREAM Storage time in freezer: Commercial 3 months; Home-made 1 month.	All types.	Make as usual.	300 ml/½ pint or 600 ml/1 pint containers. Seal.	Freezing compartment of refrigerator for 6–8 hours. Some types may be used straight from freezer.

Notes:
1. Pies, Flans and tartlets: Fillings thickened with cornflour or gelatine freeze very well, but should be packaged separately from the pastry case. Custards may curdle. Jam, fruit and mince pie fillings all freeze satisfactorily in the pastry case.
2. All pastries are improved by reheating.
3. Cakes and Pastries: If you use waxed cardboard boxes, and wish to keep the foods for the maximum period, the boxes should be enclosed in polythene bags.
4. Particular care should be taken with the sealing of all meat dishes.

Scalding Times

Brussels Sprouts	3 to 4 minutes
Broad Beans	3 minutes
French and Runner Beans	2 to 3 minutes *according to size*
Peas	1 to 2 minutes
Asparagus: young thin stalks	2 minutes
thick stalks	up to 4 minutes
Cauliflower	3 minutes
Carrots	5 minutes
Broccoli	3 minutes

Freezing Fish

Freeze fish the same day as they are caught. Prepare as for cooking – scale, eviscerate, wash thoroughly, behead and cut off fins. Freeze small fish whole, but cut large ones into steaks or fillets.

PACKING
Pack in moisture-and-vapour-proof paper or sheeting, or put into shallow rectangular waxed cartons or aluminium foil. Seal carefully and label.

THAWING
Thaw slowly unopened in a cool place long enough to separate the pieces of fish (45 minutes at room temperature, 3 to 4 hours in refrigerator). Small fish may be cooked frozen; cook for a few minutes longer than usual.

FREEZING SHELLFISH
Freeze within 12 hours of being caught. Oysters and Scallops: wash outside of shell thoroughly, open carefully and drain, retaining the liquor. Wash in a brine solution 1 × 15 ml spoon/1 tablespoon salt to 600 ml/1 pint water. Drain and pack in small containers with reserved liquor. Prawns and shrimps: freeze raw, removing heads but not shells. Wash in brine solution, drain and pack. Crab and Lobster: cook before freezing; remove the meat from the shells and pack in small containers. The brown and white meat of crab should be packed separately.

Freezing Meat

If good quality meat is available from a farm or wholesale, freezing it is practical if the meat is selected carefully. Ready frozen meat is available from butchers, cash-and-carry and freezer centres in whole carcasses, halves and quarters. Beef and mutton should be hung 5 to 7 days before freezing, veal, lamb and pork for at least 24 to 48 hours. Always buy meat from reliable suppliers.

PREPARATION
Cut the meat into convenient pieces or joints; trim off excess fat and bone. Trim steaks and chops as usual and separate with greaseproof or waxed paper. Trim offal as required. Many butchers will prepare meat as ordered.

PACKAGING
Polythene bags or sheeting or aluminium foil; seal and label.

THAWING
Allow 6 hours per 0.5 kg/lb in the refrigerator or 3 hours at room temperature.

COOKING JOINTS FROM FROZEN
Place in cold oven set to required temperature and time from when this is reached. Always use a meat thermometer. (See Beef, Lamb, Pork entries for details.)

Freezing Poultry and Game

KILLING AND PLUCKING
Kill the bird and pluck; leave overnight in either refrigerator or cool larder. Game must be hung before freezing as for immediate use.

PREPARATION
Remove the head and feet (and the oil sac from ducks, geese and turkeys). Singe and trim the bird. Draw carefully, making sure that the lungs are completely removed. Wash well in cold running water, drain and discard the gall bladder. Clean and wash the gizzard, liver and heart.

PACKAGING WHOLE BIRDS
Truss the bird as for the table. Wrap the giblets in greaseproof paper, moisture-proof cellophane or polythene, and place by the side of the bird.

Package the bird in a moisture-and-vapour-proof container (a bag is the most suitable for quick handling) or in aluminium foil. If the bones of the legs are sharp and pointed, wrap small pieces of foil round them so that they do not pierce the bag. Label, marking the weight of the bird and the date when frozen.

The bag should then be sealed either by heat-sealing or with a bag fastener. With a large bird it is advisable to overwrap the bag with either mutton cloth or brown paper to prevent its being torn.

PACKAGING JOINTED BIRDS
Prepare as above but do not draw. Cut up the bird and remove the giblets. Clean the heart and gizzard. Wrap each piece of bird separately in either greaseproof paper or moisture-proof cellophane and package either in a waxed carton or moisture-and-vapour-proof bag, wrapping up the giblets separately. Label and freeze.

THAWING
Thaw the bird completely in its wrapping either under cold running water 30 minutes per 0.5 kg/1 lb or at room temperature 8 to 10 hours for 1.5 kg/3 lb bird or 15 hours in a refrigerator.

Freezing Dairy Products
With the exception of milk, cottage cheese and single cream (fat content under 35 per cent) dairy products can successfully be frozen.

CREAM
(See Cream entry.) Double cream can be frozen for up to 1 month and whipping cream for up to 2 months. They can be stored in retail cartons and sealed with freezer tape. However, better results are obtained if the creams are partially whipped then stored in rigid containers. 10 per cent sugar by weight can be added to the cream to act as a stabilizer but this limits its use to sweet dishes.

CHEESE
(See Cheese entry.) Cottage cheese does not freeze because of its high water and low fat content. Curd cheese can be frozen for up to 3 months, the best results being achieved when it is left in the retail carton. The higher fat content cream cheeses are not so successful as they produce a buttery granular texture on thawing.

Hard cheeses freeze for a considerable length of time; most for 4 months and Cheddar for up to 6 months. The texture may be more crumbly on thawing but still acceptable. Vacuum packs of cheese can be frozen without repacking, but unwrapped cheese should be packed in freezer polythene or cling wrap. (Aluminium foil tends to impart flavour to the cheese.) Grated cheese can be frozen in rigid containers or polythene bags with all air excluded.

YOGURT
(See Yogurt entry.) Fruit yogurts can be stored for up to 3 months with little or no deterioration. Some may separate slightly but this disappears on stirring. Nut yogurts can also be frozen for up to 3 months, but after this the nuts become soft.

The freezing of natural yogurt depends on the way it has been manufactured; those that have been heavily homogenized or have had stabilizers added are more successful than set type yogurts. There is a slight loss of flavour after 2 months.

The addition of sugar aids freezing but limits the use of the yogurt. Home-made yogurt does not freeze well.

Ideally yogurt is best frozen in the retail carton with freezer tape to secure the lid. Yogurt should be thawed in a refrigerator for 24 hours.

Freezing Cooked or Prepared Foods
Foods should be prepared and cooked in the normal way, taking care not to overcook them. It is also important not to season heavily as flavours tend to develop in the freezer. Some of the liquid may be reduced while the food is in the freezer but

169

this can be corrected on thawing and reheating.

Cooked food should be carefully packed, the container depending on the nature of the food. Many dishes and casseroles available are suitable for oven and freezer use, which means that food can be taken straight from the freezer and placed in an oven (not pre-heated). If it is not possible or desirable to freeze the dish it can be lined with aluminium foil, allowing enough to cover the top. When the food is frozen it can be removed from the dish and overwrapped with polythene. When it is required the food will then fit back into the dish.

Details of freezing prepared foods are given in the chart.

Approximate Storage Times in Freezer

Vegetables	10 to 12 months
Fruits	9 to 12 months
Beef	8 months
Lamb	6 months
Pork	6 months
Veal	6 months
Offal	3 months
Mince	3 months
Sausages	3 months
Chicken	12 months
Giblets	2 to 3 months
Turkey	6 months
Duck	4 to 5 months
Goose	4 to 5 months
Game birds	6 to 8 months
Fish	2 to 3 months

FREEZER CENTRES

These have become very much a part of life today with the increase of freezers in the home. They provide everything for the freezer including frozen food, packaging materials, freezers and information. Many also sell bulk quantities of dry goods, sauces and soft drinks. See entry on Frozen Food.

FRENCH BEAN

(See Bean entry.)

FRENCH BREAD

(See Bread entry.)

FRENCH DRESSING

(See Salad Dressing entry.)

FRICASSÉE

A stew of meat, poultry, eggs or vegetables served in a creamy white sauce. The main ingredients may be previously cooked, so a fricassée is an excellent means of using up left overs. In this case the cooked food should be added to the hot sauce and merely re-heated before serving.

(See Fricassée of Veal, in Veal entry.)

FRITTER

A portion of sweet or savoury food, coated with batter or (less often) egg-and-crumbed, then fried. Apple, banana, orange, cheese, corned beef and prawns are among the many fillings that may be used, and one of the mixtures given under Batter may be used for the coating. If desired, mixed spice or ground cinnamon may be added to the plain batter used to coat a fruit filling such as apple or pineapple.

To cook fritters: Prepare the filling and cut it into slices or small pieces. Apple should be peeled and sliced about 5 mm/¼ inch thick (keep the slices in the batter or under water to prevent discoloration). Bananas should be cut in half lengthwise, then halved crossways. Oranges are divided into sections, the pith being removed.

Prepare the batter and heat a pan of clean fat until a faint haze appears (approx 177°C/350°F to 191°C/375°F). Lift the fruit or other filling on a skewer one piece at a time and dip it into the batter, coating it well; allow it to drain and place it in the hot fat. When the fritters are brown on both sides, drain them on crumpled kitchen paper. Sprinkle sweet fritters with caster sugar. Serve immediately.

FIVE-MINUTE CURRANT FRITTERS

METRIC/IMPERIAL
100 g/4 oz self raising flour
1 × 5 ml spoon/1 teaspoon baking powder
25–50 g/1–2 oz currants
2 × 5 ml spoons/2 teaspoons olive oil
about 4 × 15 ml spoons/4 tablespoons milk
lard for frying
jam or sugar

Mix together the flour, baking powder and cleaned currants. Stir in the oil and enough milk to make a batter the consistency of thick cream. Place the batter in tablespoonfuls in the hot fat and fry quickly until golden-brown on both sides. Serve at once with jam or sugar.

FRITTO MISTO

An Italian dish consisting of a variety of small, thin pieces of meat, liver, etc., or vegetables, which are coated with either egg and breadcrumbs or batter and deep-fried.

FROG

Although it has never won general acceptance in

this country, the edible frog (*grenouille* in French) is of real gastronomic merit. Since frogs do not count as meat, they are regarded as a useful supplement to the diet during Lent. Only the hind legs are used, being either fried in butter, or cut up, stewed and served in a white sauce containing mushrooms. The meat is delicate in flavour, resembling the flesh of a young rabbit or a chicken.

FROMAGE À LA CRÈME (COEUR À LA CRÈME)

A French sour-milk cheese. The curd is drained, mixed with cream and again drained in heart-shaped moulds. It is usually turned out and served with fresh cream and sugar or salt. It can also be served with fresh strawberries or raspberries and sugar.

FROMAGE DE MONSIEUR

A soft French cheese made from cow's milk, milder than Camembert.

FROSTED FRUIT

Soft, juicy fruit such as grapes and redcurrants may be given a crisp, sparkling coating of fine sugar and served as a dessert or used to decorate puddings or cakes.

Wash the fruit if necessary, dry it carefully and divide into small clusters. Tie a short length of strong thread to each bunch. Either whip an egg white lightly, or make a syrup with 50 g/2 oz sugar and 2 × 15 ml spoons/2 tablespoons water and boil it for 2 to 3 minutes, then remove it from the heat. Dip the bunches one at a time in the egg white or syrup, toss them in the fine sugar and dry on a rack. Remove the threads before serving.

FROSTING

An American term for cake icing. In this country it generally denotes an icing made of sugar and white of egg, also known as American icing; it is sometimes applied to a coating of whipped egg whites, dredged with caster sugar to make it sparkle and dried out in a cool oven; this may be used on cakes or light sweet dishes. Frosting looks extremely attractive but very soon forms a crispy shell so it is best eaten the day it is made.

(See American Frosting entry.)

FROTHING

A very old practice of dredging meats or poultry with flour and salt just before taking them from the oven and applying a fierce heat to the bird or roast so that it appears encased in a crisp froth.

FROZEN FOODS

The first experiments in freezing foods were carried out by Lord Bacon who tried freezing foods in snow.

A very wide range of frozen foods is now available and the present high degree of technical skill results in the supply of excellent products. They include fruit, vegetables, fish, meat and poultry in bags and cartons; pies and complete meals in foil containers; made up dishes such as hamburgers, fish cakes and fish fingers; pastry dishes, sweet and savoury, raw and cooked; cakes, desserts, ice cream, sorbets; boil-in-the-bag range including such foods as curry and rice and spaghetti bolognese; fruit juices.

The three great assets of frozen foods are that they retain a high proportion of their vitamins and other nutrients, as well as their flavour, colour and good general appearance; they require very little preparation and entail no waste; they enable the consumer to enjoy out-of-season delicacies. They are thus particularly useful in menu planning.

(See Freezer and Freezing entries.)

Storage

The foods should be kept frozen and in their original packets until actually required; failing a refrigerator, keep them in a cool place, wrapped in a few layers of newspaper, for not more than 24 hours. The length of time they can be kept in the frozen storage compartment of a refrigerator depends on the 'Star Rating', as follows:

Star Rating	Max. Temperature of Frozen Food Compartment	Max. Storage time for:	
		Frozen Foods	Ice Cream
★★★	−18°C/0°F	2 to 3 months	1 month
★★	−12°C/+10°F	4 weeks	1 to 2 weeks
★	−6°C/+21°F	1 week	1 day

Thawing and Cooking

Follow meticulously any special directions on the packet.

FRUIT

Botanically speaking, a fruit is the ovary or seed-bearing part of any growing plant. In cookery it refers to those edible parts of a plant which are usually served at the dessert course of a meal. There are three main types of fruit used in cookery:
1. Stone (or hard) fruits, such as the apricot, plum, sloe and cherry.
2. Berries and other soft fruits, such as the gooseberry, strawberry, currant and grape, and those like the blackberry, which are actually made

171

up of a collection of tiny berries.

3. Citrus fruits (orange, lemon, grapefruit, etc.) and other large fruits, such as the apple, pear, banana and melon.

In addition there is rhubarb, which since it comes from the stems of a plant, is not strictly speaking a fruit, but is served as such.

The supply of fruit in this country is excellent, most of the usual varieties being available all the year round, either home-grown or imported from various parts of the world.

Food Value of Fresh Fruit

Fruit is particularly valuable for its pleasant flavour and wide variety and it does much to relieve the monotony of diets which otherwise might perhaps be rather dull. Fruits also supply some vitamins and minerals. They contain varying amounts of carbohydrates, in the form of sugar, cellulose and occasionally starch. Their protein and fat content is negligible. Pectin (see Jam entry) is present in most fruits in varying quantities.

Practically all fruits have a high proportion of water or juice (75 to 93 per cent), which contains the characteristic flavour and also much of the vitamins, mineral salts and acids.

The fruit acids (which the body converts into alkalis) and also the cellulose or fibrous framework of fruit, have a laxative effect. However, some unripe fruit which contains acids in a higher proportion is irritating to the digestive tract.

VITAMINS IN FRUITS

Although vitamins A, B1 and B2 and C are represented in some fruits, vitamin C is the most important and the most widely represented in fresh fruit. Of the winter fruits, the grapefruit, orange and lemon are richest in vitamin C; of the summer fruits, black-currants, strawberries, gooseberries, raspberries and blackberries are best, then come bananas, grapes, plums, pears and apples.

Oranges have the highest proportion of vitamin B1; apricots, bananas, blackberries, lemons, loganberries, peaches, plums, greengages and tomatoes contain a little vitamin A in the form of carotene; other fruits contain only a negligible amount.

Any of the following contains the day's quota of vitamin C for one person.

METRIC/IMPERIAL

1 small orange
½ a grapefruit
5 × 15 ml spoons/5 tablespoons orange, lemon or grapefruit juice
150 ml/¼ pint tomato juice or stewed tomatoes
50 g/2 oz raw strawberries
2 small raw tomatoes

Serving Fruit

Fruit may be eaten at any meal (except as a rule afternoon tea). It should be carefully looked over and wiped or washed as necessary before it is served. Some fruits, such as strawberries and melons, are usually accompanied by sugar and sometimes by cream (in the case of strawberries, raspberries, etc.) or by a flavouring such as powdered ginger (in the case of melon). Others, such as apples and pears, may be served just as they are.

Raw fruit also makes an effective garnish for all kinds of sweet dishes and for some types of savoury ones.

Cooked fruit may form a dish by itself or the basis of various more elaborate sweets and is also used as a decoration. Fruit soups are popular in some European countries particularly in Scandinavia.

Fruit may be preserved at home by bottling, freezing and drying and in jam, jelly and similar preserves; it may also be candied and crystallized. (More information will be found under the respective headings.)

The most usual way of cooking fruit is by stewing it, but it may also be baked (e.g., apples) or steamed and it is included in many baked puddings and pies and in boiled and steamed puddings. (See recipes under individual fruits, also Summer Pudding, etc.)

STEWED FRUIT

Peel, core or stone the fruit and if necessary cut up into neat pieces.

If you wish to keep individual pieces of fruit whole and of good shape (e.g., to serve as stewed fruit or to use in jelly, fruit trifle and so on) stew gently in a syrup made from sugar and water. The proportions will vary with the juiciness and sweetness of the fruit, but 150 ml/¼ pint to 300 ml/½ pint water and 50 g/2 oz to 100 g/4 oz sugar to 0.5 kg/1 lb fruit is the average. Lift out the fruit, simmer the juice until it is slightly syrupy and pour over the fruit. Serve warm or chilled with pouring cream.

If the fruit is required stewed to a purée (for fruit fools, creams and so on), it is better to cook it without sugar and in the minimum of water until tender and then to sweeten it, since the addition of sugar to the raw fruit toughens it and prevents it mashing properly.

Some fruits are improved by additional flavouring. Apples may be flavoured with lemon juice, grated lemon rind, cloves, cinnamon stick or marmalade (remove cloves or cinnamon before serving), pears are improved by cloves or cinnamon stick. Plums may be flavoured with their kernels or a few sweet almonds, rhubarb with root ginger, cinnamon stick or a strip of lemon or orange rind; remove before serving as all the flavour will have gone.

(See Dried Fruit entry.)

FRUIT SALAD

METRIC/IMPERIAL
100 g/4 oz sugar
300 ml/½ pint water
juice of ½ lemon
selection of fruit, e.g., 2 red-skinned apples, 2
  oranges, 2 bananas, 100 g/4 oz black or green
  grapes

To make a syrup dissolve the sugar in the water over a gentle heat and boil for 5 minutes; cool and add the lemon juice. Prepare the fruits as required and put them into the syrup as they are ready. Mix them all together and if possible leave to stand for 2 to 3 hours before serving, to blend the flavours. Any other combinations of fresh fruits can be used, such as dessert pears, strawberries, raspberries, cherries and melon.

To give additional flavour, add to the syrup:
1. a pinch of ground cinnamon or nutmeg or infuse a piece of cinnamon stick when preparing the syrup; this will avoid clouding the syrup.
2. 1–2 × 15 ml spoons/1–2 tablespoons fruit liqueur, brandy or rum.

Fruit salad can be served in a hollowed-out melon or pineapple; in either case the flesh which has been removed should be cut into chunks and used in the salad. Melon shells look particularly attractive especially when filled with melon balls of various colours, i.e. honeydew, Spanish water melon and Charentais.

Canned fruit such as apricot halves, peach slices and pineapple chunks can also be used in fruit salads, or the more exotic canned guavas and lychees. If you use canned fruit use some of the syrup from the can, sharpened with lemon juice, to replace sugar syrup. Liqueurs can also be added to complement the individual fruits.

WINTER FRUIT SALAD

METRIC/IMPERIAL
100 g/4 oz sugar
300 ml/½ pint water
pared rind and juice of 1 lemon
100 g/4 oz prunes, stewed and drained
100 g/4 oz dried apricots, stewed and drained
1 banana, skinned and sliced
2 oranges, skinned and segmented
1 grapefruit, skinned and segmented

Make a syrup by dissolving the sugar in the water over a gentle heat; add the lemon rind, heat and boil for 5 minutes. Add the lemon juice. If you wish, stone the prunes and halve the apricots, then strain the syrup over the prepared fruits and leave to cool.

Alternatively, use mixed dried fruit as a basis, cooking it in the usual way and adding any fresh fruit that may be available.

FRUIT FOOL

METRIC/IMPERIAL
0.5 kg/1 lb gooseberries, rhubarb, raspberries, etc., or
  a 1 × 575 g/1 lb 4 oz can, drained
100 g/4 oz sugar, optional
150 ml/¼ pint custard
150 ml/¼ pint carton double or whipping cream,
  whipped
chopped nuts

Stew the fruit in 2 × 15 ml spoons/2 tablespoons water, with the sugar (unless canned fruit is used). Purée the fruit, preferably using a nylon sieve or a liquidizer. Fold the purée into the custard and leave it until cold. Lightly fold in the cream. Pour into glasses and decorate with chopped nuts. Serve with shortbread, sponge fingers or a plain sweet biscuit. This sweet can also be made with apples, blackberries, apricots, rhubarb or raspberries (these should not be cooked, just sieve and sweeten).

Note: To prepare the custard use 150 ml/¼ pint milk, 1 × 15 ml spoon/1 tablespoon custard powder and 1 × 15 ml spoon/1 tablespoon sugar. Alternatively replace the custard and cream with a 300 ml/½ pint carton double or whipping cream.

Fruit Butter
A preserve which resembles a fruit cheese, but is softer, having the spreading consistency of butter.

QUINCE BUTTER

METRIC/IMPERIAL
1.75 kg/4 lb quinces, peeled and roughly chopped
water
1 × 5 ml spoon/1 teaspoon citric or tartaric acid
sugar

Put the quinces in a pan, almost cover with water and add the acid. Bring to the boil and simmer gently until the fruit is soft and broken down, then press it through a fine sieve and weigh the pulp. Return this to the pan, add 225 g/½ lb sugar to 0.5 kg/1 lb pulp. Dissolve, bring to the boil again and boil for 45 minutes to 1 hour, stirring continuously to prevent burning. The finishing point is determined by the consistency rather than by set or temperature – the butter should be thick but semi-soft, so that it can be spread. Pot and cover immediately.

FRUMENTY

A traditional Harvest Home dish, which used to be made from the new wheat. The grains were steeped in water and left in a warm place for hours, then husked and boiled with milk to make a kind of porridge, which was spiced and sweetened. It was sometimes enriched with cream or egg yolks.

173

The process of cooking food in hot fat or oil to seal in and give extra flavour (See Fats and Oils entries). There are two main methods of frying, as follows:

Shallow Frying

Only a small quantity of fat is used, in a shallow pan. This method is used for steak, chops, sausages, steaks of fish or white fish such as sole, and pancakes, which need only sufficient fat to prevent them from sticking to the pan. Made-up dishes, such as fish cakes or rissoles, require enough fat to half-cover the food. The fat should be heated until a faint haze rises before the food is added; take care not to overheat it. Sometimes the food is coated with a suitable covering. (See the individual entries e.g., Fish, for fuller details.) Cook it fairly quickly for a few minutes, until the surface is browned on each side, reduce the heat and finish cooking slowly. Turn the food carefully, to avoid destroying the coating, if used. When it is cooked, lift it from the pan, drain on absorbent paper to remove surplus fat and serve at once.

Deep Frying

This method is suitable for made up dishes such as croquettes and fritters, also for fish coated with batter and for whitebait, chipped potatoes, doughnuts, etc.

The food is cooked in sufficient fat to cover it completely. A deep pan and a wire basket are required, with enough fat to come about three-quarters up the pan; clarified beef fat, lard and oil are suitable. The fat should be pure and free from moisture, to avoid any spurting or boiling over, and it must be heated to the correct temperature (see table); if it is not enough, the food will be sodden with grease – if it is too hot, the food will burn.

Most deep-fried food (except potatoes, pastry, doughnuts, etc.) should be egg-and-crumbed or coated with a batter. Place the food in the wire basket and lower the basket slowly into the fat. When a large quantity of food is to be fried, cook it a little at a time to avoid lowering the temperature of the fat. As soon as the food is golden-brown, lift it out. Drain, using crumpled kitchen paper for fish, etc., and serve at once.

After use, strain the frying fat into a clean basin and keep it for further use; with care it can be used many times and will keep for months.

(See Fritter, Chipped Potatoes, under Potato entries.)

TEMPERATURES FOR DEEP FAT FRYING
For doughnuts, fritters and fish the temperature of the fat should be 177°C/350°F to 191°C/375°F.

For croquettes, the temperature should be 191°C/375°F to 196°C/385°F.

For French-fried or chipped potatoes, the temperature should be 190°C/385°F to 202°C/395°F.

If you have no thermometer, the temperature may be tested as follows: put one or two 2.5 cm/1 inch cubes of bread into the hot fat. If they take:
60 seconds to brown, the fat is at 177°C/350°F to 188°C/370°F
40 seconds, it is at 188°C/370°F to 195°C/380°F
only 20 seconds, the fat is at 190°C/380°F to 199°C/390°F

FUDGE

A sweet made from sugar, butter, milk and cream, in varying proportions. By using different flavourings and such additions as chopped nuts, glacé or dried fruit, many varieties of fudge can be made – chocolate, vanilla, honey, etc. The mixture is heated to a temperature of about 116°C/240°F and then it is 'grained', that is, stirred until minute crystals are formed. The mixture is also stirred during the cooking to prevent burning. Then while it is still liquid, the fudge is poured into an oiled tin, and cut as soon as it is firm.

(See Sweets entry for recipes.)

FUMET

French name given to a liquid used to give flavour and body to soups and sauces. It is prepared by cooking fish, meat, game or vegetables in stock or wine until reduced to a syrupy consistency.

FUNGUS

A mushroom, toadstool or similar plant. A large number of fungi are edible, but since some types are poisonous, it is essential to be able to distinguish between them or to buy only from a reliable source. A number of well-illustrated books on the subject have been published and will help one to recognize the main edible fungi, but it must be emphasized that if there is any doubt about a particular type, it should be rejected. All fungi should look fresh, not dried up or slimy, when picked or bought.

Mushrooms, blewits, morels and some species of boletus (cèpes) are the chief edible fungi. The field mushroom is the most widely known. This grows wild, as its name suggest, but is also cultivated to an increasing extent and indeed most of the mushrooms on sale in shops are in fact cultivated field mushrooms. (See Mushroom entry for recipes.)

The food value of fungi is negligible, apart from a little thiamine, and they are eaten for their excellent flavour. They may be used in many ways, either as the main ingredient of a dish or as a flavouring, accompaniment or garnish, particularly with fried foods.

GALANTINE

A cold dish made of poultry or white meat, which is boned, stuffed, then tied up tightly and cooked with herbs, vegetables, etc. The galantine is then formed into a neat shape and left to get cold before being covered with béchamel sauce, glazed and garnished with aspic jelly, etc.

CHICKEN GALANTINE

METRIC/IMPERIAL
1.5 kg/3¼ lb to 1.75 kg/4 lb oven-ready chicken
1 onion, skinned
1 carrot, peeled
3 parsley stalks
1 bay leaf
6 peppercorns
225 g/8 oz pork sausage meat
225 g/8 oz lean pork, minced
2 shallots, skinned and chopped
salt
pepper
4 × 15 ml spoons/4 tablespoons Madeira
75 g/3 oz cooked ham, sliced
75 g/3 oz cooked tongue, sliced
50 g/2 oz sliced bacon fat
15 g/½ oz pistachio nuts, blanched
6 black olives, stoned

FOR FINISHING
600 ml/1 pint aspic jelly, made from aspic jelly
  powder and chicken stock
450 ml/¾ pint béchamel sauce
salt
pepper
2–3 × 15 ml spoons/2–3 tablespoons double cream
7 g/¼ oz powdered gelatine
cucumber, radishes and black olives for garnish

Lay the bird on a board, breast side up. Using a sharp boning knife, cut off the wings at the second joint and the legs at the first. Turn the bird over and make an incision down the centre of the back. Keeping the knife close to the carcass and slightly flattened, to avoid damaging the flesh, carefully work the flesh off the rib cage – scrape just enough to expose both of the wing joints.

Take hold of the severed end of 1 wing joint. Scrape the knife over the bone backwards and forwards, working the flesh away from the bone. Continue until both wing and socket are exposed. Sever all the ligaments and draw out the bone. Repeat for second wing.

Carry on working the flesh off the carcass until the leg and socket are reached. Sever the ligaments attaching the bone to the body flesh and break the leg joint by twisting it firmly in a cloth. Hold the exposed joint firmly in 1 hand and scrape away all the flesh down to the broken leg joint. Working from the opposite end of the leg, ease out the bone, scraping off the flesh until the bone is completely exposed. Pull the leg bone free; repeat for the other leg. Continue working the flesh cleanly off the body and breast, being careful not to break the skin.

Lay the boned chicken, skin side down, on the board and turn the legs and wings inside out. Make a stock using the chicken bones, giblets, onion, carrot, parsley, bay leaf, peppercorns and enough water just to cover.

Work together the sausage meat, pork, shallots, salt and pepper in a bowl. Moisten with the Madeira wine. Slice the ham, tongue and bacon fat into long strips about 5 mm/¼ inch wide.

Spread half the farce over the boned out chicken. Lay along the bird, in alternate lines, strips of ham, tongue and bacon fat, pistachio nuts and the olives. Cover with the remaining farce. Draw the sides of the chicken together and sew up, using a trussing needle and fine string.

Wrap the galantine in a double thickness of muslin and tie the ends to make a neat shape. Strain the stock, pour it into a large pan and immerse the galantine in it. Cover well and simmer for about 2¼ hours. Drain, reserving the stock.

Place the galantine, still wrapped in muslin, on a plate; cover with another plate and top with a weight. When nearly cold, remove the muslin, and when thoroughly cold carefully remove the trussing string.

Make up 600 ml/1 pint aspic jelly using some of

175

the strained chicken stock. To make a chaudfroid sauce, make up 450 ml/¾ pint béchamel sauce, cover with wetted greaseproof paper to prevent a skin forming and allow to cool. Dissolve the gelatine in 120 ml/4 fl oz of the prepared aspic. Reserve 6 × 15 ml spoons/6 tablespoons and stir remainder into the cold béchamel sauce. Strain the sauce and beat well.

Place the chicken on a wire rack with a board or baking sheet underneath. When the chaudfroid sauce is on the point of setting, pour it over the chicken to coat it thoroughly.

When the chaudfroid sauce is set, decorate the galantine with cucumber, radishes and olives and spoon over the reserved aspic jelly. Put in a cool place to set.

GALLIMAUFRY

A hash or ragoût of poultry or meat.

GALLON

An imperial measure used for liquids, containing 4 quarts/8 pints. The standard gallon contains approx. 277 cubic inches and its weight is equal to 4.5 kg/10 lb of distilled water. Its metric equivalent is 4.55 litres.

GAME

Wild animals and birds hunted for food. British game animals are hares and deer (you need a licence for the latter). The seasons for game birds are given in the following list:

Bird	Shooting Season
Pheasant	1st Oct. to 1st Feb.
Partridge	1st Sept. to 1st Feb.
Grouse	12th Aug. to 10th Dec.
Black game	20th Aug. to 10th Dec.
Ptarmigan (in Scotland)	12th Aug. to 10th Dec.

There is also a list of birds which can be shot at certain seasons of the year, but which are not called 'game birds' although some of them are known by this term in the kitchen. They may be shot during the periods given below, but it is illegal to sell them between 28th February and 31st August.

Bird	Shooting Season
Teal, Widgeon, Mallard	1st Sept. to 30th Dec.
Ducks, including Pintail	Aug. to Feb.
Plover	20th Aug. to 10th Dec.
Snipe	12th Aug. to 20th Dec.
Wild Goose	Nov. to Dec.
Woodcock	1st Oct. to 20th Dec.

Fresh game can only be sold by a licensed dealer. It is possible to buy some game frozen.

Choosing and cooking Game Birds

1. Look for birds which have firm, plump flesh and weigh heavy for their size. Spurs should be short and round, flight feathers pointed and the feathers under the wing downy. As the bird gets older, the flight feathers become rounded and the spurs pointed. The feet should be supple and the vent firm.

2. Game birds are hung (by the neck) before they are plucked and cooked, the time varying with the bird, with individual taste and with the season: in hot weather they are hung for a shorter time than in winter, when the birds may be hung for as long as 2 to 3 weeks. For the average taste they are considered sufficiently mature when the tail or breast feathers can be plucked out easily. A green or bluish discoloration of the flesh shows that the bird has hung too long. Wild duck and other water fowl should be hung for a few days only, as the flesh tends to turn rank if kept too long.

3. All birds are plucked, but not all are gutted. Those types which are cooked with the entrails inside (snipe, woodcock, ortolans and quails) should not be hung for more than a few days.

4. Roasting is the best method of cooking game, as the full flavour is then retained, but if birds are old and likely to be tough, they are best braised or casseroled.

5. Game birds lack fat, so it is usual to cover the breast with pieces of fat bacon before roasting (i.e., to bard them) and to baste them frequently during the cooking. When they are half-cooked the bacon can be removed and the breast dredged with flour and basted: this is called 'frothing' and is done to brown the breast. Game birds are generally roasted in a hot oven (220°C/425°F, Gas Mark 7). Grouse and birds with the entrails left in should be placed on toast for roasting; this toast is served with the bird.

6. Accompaniments vary slightly for different birds (see individual entries) but thin gravy, game chips and fried crumbs are usual.

7. Game birds can also be used in pies, casseroles and soups.

GAME SOUP

METRIC/IMPERIAL
game carcase
1 onion
1 small carrot
1 small piece of turnip
butter or dripping for frying
1 × 15 ml spoon/1 tablespoon flour
600 ml/1 pint stock (approx.)
a bouquet garni
1–2 bacon rinds
salt
pepper
a little red wine (optional)

Cut or break up the carcase. Prepare and cut up the vegetables. Melt a little fat in a saucepan and fry the game and vegetables lightly, then stir in the flour and fry this also. Cover with stock and add the bouquet garni and bacon rinds. Season, cover and simmer gently for 1 to 2 hours, then strain the soup and return it to the pan with any meat from the bones, cut in neat dice. Add more seasoning if necessary; a little red wine may be added just before serving.

Game Pie: (See Pie entry.)

GAMMON

The hind-quarter of a side of bacon which has been wet-cured before the gammon is cut off. Gammon is either cooked whole and served as ham, or cut into large rashers, which have a high proportion of lean to fat and are usually cut thicker than bacon rashers. They are good grilled, fried or baked with a sweet spicy sauce (see those under Barbecue entry), or with pineapple. Gammon steaks are available, usually in vacuum packs. These consist only of the best lean meat, therefore there is no waste.

GAR (GARFISH, GARPIKE)

A slender fish, found off most European coasts; it has green bones. Garfish is usually skinned and may then be cooked in any way desired.

GARIBALDI BISCUITS

Square or oblong biscuits made by sandwiching dried fruit between two thin layers of sweet pastry. Some people prefer to mix the fruit into the pastry and to roll the dough out thinly before cutting.

GARLIC

A plant of the onion family, with long, flat leaves and a bunch of small white flowers at the top of each flower stalk. Each garlic 'bulb' is really a collection of several small bulbs, called 'cloves', which are bound together by the outer skin. The bulbs will keep for months in a dry place and are not impaired when some of the cloves are removed.

Garlic has a powerful acrid taste, due to the oil it contains. It gives a good flavour to soups, stews, re-heated savoury dishes, curries, gravies and sauces, while a mere suggestion of garlic in salad dressings is excellent.

Owing to its strong flavour, garlic should be chopped very finely before use and the addition of one or two cloves to a dish is usually enough for the English taste. For a salad it is often sufficient to rub the bowl round with a cut garlic clove.

A garlic press is a useful gadget as it extracts all the juice and flavour from a clove without leaving the flavour on kitchen equipment in general use.

GARLIC BREAD

Buy a loaf of French bread (or use rolls) and cut into 2.5 cm/1 inch slices almost through to the bottom crust. Mix some softened butter with a generous amount of chopped parsley and a very finely chopped clove of garlic (use a garlic crusher if available). Spread this savoury butter mixture between the slices, brushing the top of the loaf with any that is over. Wrap the whole loaf in aluminium foil, and place in a fairly hot oven (200°C/400°F, Gas Mark 6) for 15 to 20 minutes. Serve still in the aluminium foil, so that it keeps hot. This is very good with salads and savouries.

GARNISH AND DECORATION

Decorative touches are added to a dish to improve its appearance and to some extent its flavour and texture. All garnishes should be edible and must, of course, be chosen to suit the particular dish. Here are some general rules:

1. The garnish of any dish should be decided on beforehand, since the more elaborate ones take time to prepare.
2. As a rule, hot garnishes should be served with hot dishes and cold with cold dishes, though there are one or two exceptions. For hot food the decoration needs to be simple and quickly prepared, or the food may become lukewarm before it reaches the table.
3. The garnish should be comparatively small and must not obscure the main dish. It is often better to put the decoration round the edges of the dish rather than in the centre.
4. For soft food such as mince, a crisp garnish like fried croûtons or pastry fleurons is usually chosen, to provide a pleasant contrast in texture.
5. Colours should be chosen to tone with both the food and the serving dish. Two or at most three colours are sufficient.

Types of Garnish and Decoration

SALAD PLANTS

Probably the most commonly used for savoury dishes: parsley (in small sprigs, chopped or fried), watercress (small bunches, or groups of three leaves arranged to resemble clover), mustard and cress, green peas, spring onions, finely chopped chives, sliced gherkin, olives (whole or stuffed and sliced), young celery leaves or celery 'curls' (made by fringing a small length at each end and leaving in water till it curls), radishes (used whole or made into radish roses or lilies), tomatoes (sliced, quartered or made into 'lilies'), cucumber cones or slices (for decorative edges, slices, remove lengthwise strips of peel about 3 mm/⅛ inch wide

177

and 3 mm/⅛ inch apart, then slice the cucumber very thinly).

ROOT VEGETABLES
Carrots, swedes and turnips may be grated and used raw; cut into 'julienne' strips (matchlike sticks) about 3 cm/1¼ inch long, cooked and arranged in small piles; or cut into balls, which must be cooked carefully to keep them whole; fancy shapes may be stamped out of sliced root vegetables with small cutters.

POTATOES
Use as fried chips, crisps, lattice-work potatoes (a special cutter is required for these), curls or rounds. Mashed or Duchesse potatoes may be piped into fancy shapes or borders.

MUSHROOMS AND TRUFFLES
Cooked and used whole, sliced or chopped.

ONIONS
Usually cut into rings and fried.

HARD-BOILED EGG
Sliced or quartered and used to decorate salads, cold dishes or entrées. The white may be cut into fancy shapes or rounds and the yolk can be sieved, or the two combined to make 'marguerites'.

BREAD, PASTRY, ETC.
Toasted or fried bread croûtons are used with entrées and with soups; pastry fleurons are also used with entrées and so are noodles and fancy forms of pasta.

FRUITS
Strawberries, raspberries, cherries, grapes, sliced bananas, etc., may all be used to decorate sweet dishes. Melon, pears and apples can be used in small, thin slices or cut into balls with a scoop cutter. (These fruits turn brown if exposed too long to the air, but a coating of apricot jam or marmalade will prevent discoloration or they may be soaked in lemon juice.)

Oranges and lemons look well if peeled, quartered and skinned or thinly sliced. Lemons (and sometimes oranges) are used to garnish savoury dishes. To make lemon fans for use with fish, etc., cut slices 3 mm/⅛ inch thick and cut each in half, cut the rind in half again, leaving the centre membrane whole, and spread out the lemon into a fan shape.

ALMONDS, WALNUTS, PISTACHIO, HAZEL AND BRAZIL NUTS
After shelling and blanching, are used whole, or halved, chopped, sliced, shredded or grated. Almonds are sometimes tinted pale pink with carmine or lightly toasted. Chopped nuts are often used to decorate the sides of a cake.

JELLY
Can be roughly chopped and piled round a sweet, or stamped into fancy shapes. (Set a thin layer on wet paper for this purpose.)

DOUBLE OR IMITATION CREAM
Can be whipped until stiff, sweetened and flavoured, then piped on to sweets with a forcing bag and fancy nozzles.

MINIATURE MERINGUES
May be stuck round the sides of a sweet or meringue mixture piped through a fancy nozzle.

SWEETS AND BISCUITS
Chocolate drops, fruit gums, chocolate vermicelli, grated chocolate, marshmallows (whole or cut up), coloured sugar, hundreds and thousands, ratafias and other small biscuits, all make attractive decorations for such sweets as trifles, creams, whips and fools.

GLACÉ AND CRYSTALLIZED FRUIT, ANGELICA AND CRYSTALLIZED FLOWERS
Often used for sweet dishes and fresh flowers sometimes on salads.
Soup Garnishes: (See Soup entry.)

GÂTEAU

A term applied to various fairly elaborate cakes or sweets which are made by using a sponge, biscuit or pastry base and adding fruit, jelly, cream, etc., as decoration. Some of the best-known gâteaux, especially the professionally made ones, are of French, Austrian or Swiss origin.

STRAWBERRY GÂTEAU

Bake 2 sponge cakes (see Sponge entry) in round tins. (Alternatively, use 2 bought cakes.) Spread the bottom cake with crushed strawberries and whipped cream. Using a large pastry cutter, cut a circle out of the centre of the second cake and place the resulting 'frame' on the bottom cake. Pile more crushed strawberries and cream in the centre, decorate with a few choice berries and serve at once. The cream may be replaced by ice cream, if desired.

GÂTEAU ST. HONORÉ

METRIC/IMPERIAL
100 g/4oz shortcrust or flan pastry, made with 100 g/ 4 oz flour, etc.
choux pastry, using 8 × 15 ml spoons/8 tablespoons plain flour
1 egg, beaten, to glaze
2 egg yolks
50 g/2 oz caster sugar for filling
1.5 × 5 ml spoons/1 ½ teaspoons plain flour
4 × 5 ml spoons/4 teaspoons cornflour
300 ml/½ pint milk
1 × 5 ml spoon/1 teaspoon vanilla essence

3 egg whites, stiffly whisked
150 ml/¼ pint carton double cream, whipped
3 × 15 ml spoons/3 tablespoons caster sugar for syrup
3 × 15 ml spoons/3 tablespoons water
angelica and glacé cherries

Roll the shortcrust or flan pastry into an 18 cm/7 inch round, prick well and put on a lightly greased baking sheet. Brush a 1 cm/½ inch band round the edge with beaten egg. Using a 1 cm/½ inch plain nozzle, pipe a circle of choux paste round the edge of the pastry and brush it with beaten egg. With the remaining choux paste pipe about 20 walnut-sized rounds on to the baking sheet. Brush these with beaten egg and bake both the flan and the choux balls in a moderately hot oven (190°C/375°F, Gas Mark 5) for about 35 minutes or until well risen and golden brown. Cool on a rack.

Meanwhile prepare the pastry cream filling. Cream the egg yolks with the 50 g/2 oz caster sugar until pale, add the flours, with a little of the milk, and mix well. Heat the remainder of the milk with the vanilla essence almost to boiling point; pour on to the egg mixture, return this to the pan and bring to the boil, stirring all the time. Boil for a further 2 to 3 minutes, then turn the mixture into a bowl to cool. Whisk with a rotary beater till smooth, then fold in the egg whites. Pipe some whipped cream inside the cold choux buns, reserving a little for the top of the gâteau.

Dissolve the 3 × 15 ml spoons/3 tablespoons sugar in the water and boil until the edge just begins to turn straw-coloured. Dip the tops of the choux paste buns in this syrup, using a skewer or tongs to hold them. Use the remainder of the syrup to stick the buns on to the choux pastry border. Fill the centre of the gâteau with the pastry cream mixture and cover this with the remaining cream. Decorate with angelica and glacé cherries.

GAZPACHO

A famous Spanish soup which is served cold. It is a mixture of raw salad ingredients made into a purée.

GAZPACHO

METRIC/IMPERIAL
1 medium cucumber
0.5 kg/1 lb fully ripened tomatoes
100 g/4 oz green pepper, seeded
50–100 g/2–4 oz onions, skinned
1 clove garlic, skinned
3 × 15 ml spoons/3 tablespoons oil
3 × 15 ml spoons/3 tablespoons wine vinegar
1 × 425 g/15 oz can tomato juice
2 × 15 ml spoons/2 tablespoons tomato paste
pinch salt

Wash and roughly chop the cucumber, tomatoes, pepper, onion and garlic. Mix all the ingredients together in a basin. Purée them in a liquidizer in small portions. Return the purée to the bowl and add a few ice cubes. Serve the soup with very finely diced green pepper, and croûtons.

GELATINE

A protein substance made chiefly from calves' heads, cartilages, tendons, etc., which are boiled with acid and then submitted to various refining and purifying processes. Gelatine is equally satisfactory in powdered, flaked or sheet (leaf) form, though it is most commonly sold as a powder. It should be colourless and have no offensive smell. As the setting power of gelatine differs according to the make, it is essential to follow the manufacturer's instructions closely. The popular packets of table jelly consist of sweetened fruit-flavoured gelatine. When using commercial gelatine, always use according to the manufacturer's instructions.

(See Jelly entry.)

GENOA CAKE

A favourite rich fruit cake, generally decorated with almonds or brazil nuts.

GENOA CAKE

METRIC/IMPERIAL
225 g/8 oz sultanas
225 g/8 oz currants
50 g/2 oz chopped mixed peel
100 g/4 oz glacé cherries
40 g/1½ oz whole almonds
225 g/8 oz plain flour
pinch of salt
1 × 5 ml spoon/1 teaspoon mixed spice
1 × 5 ml spoon/1 teaspoon baking powder
200 g/7 oz butter or margarine
175 g/6 oz caster sugar
grated rind of 1 lemon
3 eggs, beaten
1–2 × 15 ml spoons/1–2 tablespoons milk

Grease and line the base and sides of an 18 cm/7 inch cake tin. Prepare the fruit and chop the peel. Halve the cherries and wash and dry them. Blanch and chop the almonds, reserving a few for decoration. Sift the flour, salt, spice and baking powder. Cream the fat, sugar and lemon rind together until pale and fluffy. Beat in the egg a little at a time and fold in the flour, followed by the fruit, adding milk if necessary to give a dropping consistency. Put into the tin, decorate with the remaining almonds, halved, and bake in a cool oven (150°C/300°F, Gas Mark 2) for 3 to 3¼ hours. Turn out and cool on a wire rack.

179

GENOESE SPONGE

A light, rich sponge cake, used as the basis for fancy cakes or petits fours which are to be coated with fondant or glacé icing; it can also be served as an undecorated sponge cake.

GENOESE SPONGE

METRIC/IMPERIAL
40 g/1 ½ oz butter
65 g/2 ½ oz plain flour
1 × 15 ml spoon/1 tablespoon cornflour
3 large eggs
75 g/3 oz caster sugar

Grease and line two 18 cm/7 inch sandwich tins. Heat the butter gently until it is melted, remove it from the heat and let it stand for a few minutes, for the salt and any sediment to settle. Sift the flour and cornflour. Put the eggs and sugar in a large bowl, stand this over a saucepan of hot water and whisk until light and creamy – the mixture should be stiff enough to retain the impression of the whisk for a few seconds. Remove from the heat and whisk until cool. Re-sift the flour and carefully fold in half with a metal spoon. Make sure the butter is cooled until it just flows and, taking care not to let the salt and sediment run in, pour the butter round the edge of the mixture. Then fold it in alternately with the rest of the flour. Fold very lightly or the fat will sink to the bottom and cause a heavy cake. Pour the mixture into the tins and bake in a moderately hot oven (190°C/375°F, Gas Mark 5) until golden brown and firm to the touch, 20 to 25 minutes. Turn out and cool on a wire rack. Use as required, for layered cakes and iced cakes.

Note: If you are using an electric mixer no heat is required during whisking.

GERMAN POUND CAKE

This is similar to Genoa Cake, but contains less fruit and no almonds.

GERMAN SAUSAGE

The general name given to many different varieties of sausage, usually eaten cold. They are made of pork, veal, beef, liver, bacon or blood, usually a mixture of two or more of these ingredients, suitably salted and spiced; garlic is a favourite addition. German sausages are often smoked and in fact all those imported into this country are so treated.

GERVAIS

A small, soft, delicately flavoured cream cheese made in France. The portions are generally sold packed in boxes of six.

GHEE

A type of fat or liquid butter made from cow or buffalo milk and used extensively in Eastern countries. It is allowed to go rancid and all the water is extracted. Salt is then added and when the ghee is bottled or canned it will keep for several years.

GHERKIN

The pickled fruit of a small variety of cucumber. The best gherkins are small and dark green and have a rough skin; large quantities are imported from France and Holland and are sold bottled in brine.

Gherkins are used as one of the ingredients in mixed pickles, as an accompaniment to cold meats and in savouries, sauces, etc., and they also make an attractive garnish for cocktail titbits and cold savoury dishes.

PICKLED GHERKINS

METRIC/IMPERIAL
0.5 kg/1 lb gherkins
brine
1 × 5 ml spoon/1 teaspoon whole allspice
1 × 5 ml spoon/1 teaspoon black peppercorns
2 cloves
1 blade of mace
600 ml/1 pint vinegar

Soak the gherkins in brine for 3 days. Drain them well, dry and pack carefully in a jar. Add the spices to the vinegar and boil for 10 minutes. Pour the vinegar over the gherkins, cover tightly and leave in a warm place for 24 hours. Strain the vinegar, boil it up and pour it over the gherkins; cover and leave for another 24 hours, repeating this process until the gherkins are a good green. Pack in wide-necked bottles, cover with vinegar, adding more if required, cork and store.

GIBLETS

The edible parts of the entrails of birds, consisting of the gizzard, liver, heart and also the neck. They are largely used in making gravy or soup, but the liver is often rolled in bacon and served with the bird or as a savoury. (See Poultry entry for preparation.)

To make giblet stock for gravy, cover the giblets with stock or water and simmer for 1 hour or longer.

Giblet soup is made in a similar way to Game Soup. (See Game entry.)

GILDING

(See Glazes for Pastry, under Glaze entry.)

GILL

An imperial measure rarely used nowadays. In the south of England it is interpreted as 150 ml/¼ pint but in other parts of the country particularly the North it often refers to 300 ml/½ pint.

GIN

A colourless spirit distilled from rye and barley or maize and flavoured with juniper berries. Gin is the purest of all spirits, being distilled at a high strength. It does not improve with keeping in the same way as brandy.

Two popular types in England are Dry or London gin and Old Tom or Plymouth gin, the former being dry and the latter slightly sweetened. Schnapps is a type of gin popular in Holland.

Gin is used as the basis of many cocktails, such as Martini, Gin Sling, Pink Gin and Bronx. (See Cocktail entry.) It is also used for various other long and short drinks, being diluted to the required strength with water, fruit juice, ginger ale or soda water.

GINGER

The underground stem of a reed-like plant which grows in Asia, the West Indies, South America, Western Africa and Australia. Both the knotty, fibrous roots and the stems have the characteristic hot flavour and are used in various forms in cookery and also in medicine.

The young green shoots are used fresh in the East. They are also preserved in syrup and often crystallized and served as a dessert; so are the roots and chippings, though these are fibrous and not so good. The dried roots are ground to produce powdered ginger for use as a spice in cakes, biscuits, puddings and curries, or may be used whole for pickling and jam-making. Jamaican ginger, which is generally considered the best variety, is buff-coloured and has a pleasant odour and pungent taste.

GINGER LOAF CAKE

METRIC/IMPERIAL
175 g/6 oz butter
75 g/3 oz soft brown sugar
75 g/3 oz golden syrup
3 eggs
225 g/8 oz self raising flour
2–4 × 5 ml spoons/2–4 teaspoons ground ginger
4 pieces of stem ginger, finely chopped
25 g/1 oz flaked almonds

Grease and base line a loaf tin with 23 cm/9 inch by 13 cm/5 inch top measurements. Cream butter, add sugar and syrup and continue creaming until

the mixture is light and fluffy. Add eggs, one at a time, beating well. Sift together the flour and ginger and fold into creamed mixture. Fold in chopped ginger. Turn mixture into prepared loaf tin. Sprinkle flaked almonds over the mixture, press in lightly and bake in a moderate oven (180°C/350°F, Gas Mark 4) for about 1 hour 10 minutes, until risen and firm to the touch. Turn out and cool on wire rack.

GINGERNUTS

METRIC/IMPERIAL
100 g/4 oz self-raising flour
1 × 2.5 ml spoons/½ teaspoon bicarbonate of soda
1–2 × 5 ml spoons/1–2 teaspoons ground ginger
1 × 5 ml spoon/1 teaspoon ground cinnamon, optional
2 × 5 ml spoons/2 teaspoons caster sugar
50 g/2 oz butter or block margarine
75 g/3 oz golden syrup

Grease two baking sheets. Sift together the flour, bicarbonate of soda, ginger, cinnamon and sugar. Melt the fat, and stir in the syrup. Stir these into the dry ingredients and mix well. Roll the dough into small balls, place well apart on the greased baking sheets and flatten slightly. Bake in a moderately hot oven (190°C/375°F, Gas Mark 5) for about 15 minutes. The gingernuts will have the traditional cracked tops. Cool for a few minutes before lifting carefully from the baking sheet.

Finish cooling on a wire rack and then store in an airtight tin.

If liked, these biscuits may be iced with lemon-flavoured glacé icing.

Ginger Ale
Coloured water aerated with carbon dioxide and flavoured with ginger. It is used as a soft drink, in punches, and in place of soda to dilute spirits such as whisky and brandy.

Ginger Beer
A slightly alcoholic effervescent beverage with a flavour of ginger. Ginger, cream of tartar and sugar are fermented with yeast, water is added and the liquid bottled before fermentation is complete. The legal limit is 2 per cent alcohol, but most ginger beers contain much less.

Ginger beer can be made at home once a 'ginger beer plant' has been established. This is made from yeast, sugar, ginger and water.

Gingerbread
This is a moist brown cake flavoured with ginger and containing treacle or golden syrup; it is usually served cut into squares, which may be decorated with preserved ginger. There are many different forms of gingerbread, varying in colour from light brown to a very dark shade, according to the

181

amount of bicarbonate of soda and the type of treacle used. (See Parkin entry.)

EVERYDAY GINGERBREAD

METRIC/IMPERIAL
450 g/1 lb plain flour
1 × 5 ml spoon/1 teaspoon salt
1 × 15 ml spoon/1 tablespoon ground ginger
1 × 15 ml spoon/1 tablespoon baking powder
1 × 5 ml spoon/1 teaspoon bicarbonate of soda
225 g/8 oz demerara sugar
175 g/6 oz butter or margarine
175 g/6 oz treacle
175 g/6 oz golden syrup
300 ml/½ pint milk
1 egg, beaten

Grease and line a 23 cm/9 inch square cake tin. Sift the flour, salt, ginger, baking powder and bicarbonate of soda. Warm the sugar, fat, treacle and syrup until melted, but do not allow to boil. Mix in the milk and the egg. Make a well in the centre of the dry ingredients, pour in the liquid and mix very thoroughly. Pour the mixture into the tin and bake in a moderate oven (160°C/325°F, Gas Mark 3) for about 1½ hours, or until firm to the touch. Turn out to cool on a wire rack. For a smaller cake, use half quantities, with an 18 cm/7 inch square tin; bake for about 1 hour.

If liked, ice the gingerbread with lemon glacé icing and walnut halves or slices of crystallized ginger.

SCOTTISH GINGER CAKE

METRIC/IMPERIAL
350 g/12 oz plain flour
1 × 2.5 ml spoon/½ teaspoon salt
2 × 5 ml spoons/2 teaspoons bicarbonate of soda
1 × 15 ml spoon/1 tablespoon ground ginger
50 g/2 oz sultanas
100 g/4 oz candied peel, chopped
50 g/2 oz preserved ginger, chopped
350 g/12 oz black treacle
175 g/6 oz butter or margarine
75 g/3 oz soft brown sugar
3 eggs, beaten
2–3 × 15 ml spoons/2–3 tablespoons milk

Line an 18 cm/7 inch square cake tin. Sift the flour, salt, bicarbonate of soda and ground ginger. Add the sultanas, peel and preserved ginger. Put the treacle, butter and sugar into a pan and warm gently, until melted. Mix with the eggs and milk, make a well in the centre of the dry ingredients, pour in the treacle mixture and beat very thoroughly. Pour into the tin and bake in a moderate oven (160°C/325°F, Gas Mark 3) for about 1¼ hours. Turn out to cool on a wire rack. This cake improves with keeping.

GIRDLE (OR GRIDDLE) COOKERY

A girdle is a thick, solid sheet of cast metal, usually round and slightly convex and provided with a half-hoop handle. It is largely used in Scotland and the North of England for the making of scones and teacakes. A heavy frying pan can take the place of a girdle.

How to use a girdle: 1. Rub the girdle over with salt and a piece of paper to ensure that it is smooth and clean. Dust off the salt with a dry cloth.
2. Heat the girdle thoroughly, so that the heat is spread evenly throughout. (If a frying pan is used on a gas cooker, put an asbestos mat underneath to distribute the heat more evenly.)
   The girdle is ready for use when it will turn flour a light brown in 2 minutes, or when drops of water will bounce off; with practice, the heat can be judged by holding the hand near the girdle – a comfortable but not fierce heat shows that it is ready.
3. For scones and teacakes it is enough to dredge the girdle with flour, but for cooking batters it needs to be greased either with a piece of suet held on the end of a fork, or failing this with a piece of lard wrapped in paper or muslin and rubbed lightly over the surface. Heavy greasing is not required and it is not always necessary to grease the girdle between the batches.
4. Scones, teacakes, crumpets, etc., to be cooked on a girdle should be less than 1.5 cm/¾ inch in thickness. The time varies according to the mixture and thickness, but is usually 3 to 5 minutes on each side. Turn them with a broad, flat knife. When ready, the scone will be light and spongy inside.
5. Wipe the girdle after cooking, but do not wash it. Keep it in a dry place.
   (See Scone and Potato Cake entries for recipes.)

GLACÉ FRUIT

Fruit which has been preserved by impregnation with a concentrated sugar syrup, giving a fairly firm texture and shiny, moist and sticky surface. This process is usually carried out commercially, the commonest glacé fruit being cherries, although almost any good quality eating fruit can be treated in this way. Glacé fruits are used in cakes and sweet dishes, as a cake decoration and as a dessert to serve at the end of a formal meal.

GLACÉ FINISH FOR FRUIT

This finish is given to fruit which has already been candied, whether commercially or at home.

Dissolve 0.5 kg/1 lb sugar in 150 ml/¼ pint water and stir carefully over a low heat. (The syrup remaining after the candying process must not be used for this purpose.) When the sugar is dissolved, bring it to the boil undisturbed and test the strength of the syrup with a hydrometer: it should register 35° Beaumé. If necessary, add water or sugar to bring to the correct strength. Have ready a clean cooling rack over a tin. Pour a little syrup into a cup, dip the pieces of fruit in one at a time, using a skewer or dipping fork, and put on the rack to dry. Keep the syrup in the pan warm and covered with a damp cloth. (A double pan will be found convenient for the purpose.) As the syrup in the cup gets cloudy, replace it with fresh. After dipping dry the fruit as before, turning it from time to time.

GLACÉ ICING

A simple glossy icing made from icing sugar and water, with flavouring added as desired.

GLACÉ ICING

Put 100 g/4 oz to 175 g/6 oz sifted icing sugar and (if you wish) a few drops of any flavouring essence in a basin and gradually add 1–2 × 15 ml spoons/1–2 tablespoons warm water. The icing should be thick enough to coat the back of a spoon. If necessary, add more water or sugar to adjust the consistency. Add a few drops of colouring if required and use at once.

For icing of a finer texture, put the sugar, water and flavouring into a small pan and heat, stirring, until the mixture is warm – don't make it too hot. The icing should coat the back of a wooden spoon and look smooth and glossy.

This amount is sufficient to cover the top of an 18 cm/7 inch cake or up to 18 small cakes.

ORANGE ICING
Substitute 1–2 × 15 ml spoons/1–2 tablespoons strained orange juice for the water in the above recipe.

LEMON ICING
Substitute 1 × 15 ml spoon/1 tablespoon strained lemon juice for the same amount of water.

CHOCOLATE ICING
Dissolve 2 × 15 ml spoons/2 tablespoons cocoa in a little hot water and use to replace the same amount of plain water.

COFFEE ICING
Flavour with either 1 × 5 ml spoon/1 teaspoon coffee essence or 2 × 5 ml spoons/2 teaspoons instant coffee powder, dissolved in a little of the water.

MOCHA ICING
Flavour with 1 × 5 ml spoon/1 teaspoon cocoa and 2 × 5 ml spoons/2 teaspoons instant coffee powder, dissolved in a little of the measured water.

LIQUEUR ICING
Replace 2–3 × 5 ml spoons/2–3 teaspoons of the

water with liqueur as desired.

When using flavourings of your own, do so carefully so as not to upset the basic consistency of the icing. Always add flavourings a little at a time rather than all at once.

To use glacé icing: Allow the cake to cool, see that any decorations are prepared and insert the filling if any. Cut small cakes to the required shape before icing them and make a large cake level on top by cutting off any peak; brush the surface free from crumbs. For a really smooth finish the cakes can then be given a thin coating of sieved apricot jam, which is brushed on and left to dry for a few hours. Place the cake or cakes on a wire rack over a piece of greaseproof paper.

When the icing is of the correct consistency pour it on to the centre of the cake and allow it to run down the sides; if it runs too much to one side, use a palette knife to divert the flow. Fill any gaps with icing from the tray, but try to avoid doing this as it often gives an untidy finish. If only the top surface is to be iced, pin a double band of paper round the cake to protect the sides, removing it with the help of a hot knife.

Small cakes can be coated in the same way or may be dipped into a bowl of icing, the cake being held in tongs or between the thumb and forefinger: this method is excellent for éclairs, when only a strip of icing is required on top. Any decorations should be put in place straight away, for the icing may wrinkle or crack if they are added when it is on the point of setting.

GLASSWORT

(See Samphire entry.)

GLAZE

A substance used to give a glossy surface to certain sweets and savouries. Different materials are used for different dishes. A glaze improves both appearance and flavour and many dishes (such as flans) are incomplete without it.

Some glazes, e.g., beaten egg or milk for pastry, are put on before cooking, while others are poured or brushed on after cooking.

MEAT GLAZE
(*For galantines, cutlets, brawns, etc.*)

Place 4.5 litres/1 gallon of good stock (made from meat and bones) in a strong saucepan, first skimming off any fat. Bring to the boil and continue to boil for several hours, until the stock is reduced and is of the consistency of glaze. It can then be brushed over hot or cold joints, galantines and so on. This quantity of stock should give approximately 150 ml/¼ pint of glaze.

183

QUICK MEAT GLAZE

METRIC/IMPERIAL
15 g/ ½ oz gelatine (or more according to type)
2 meat cubes
150 ml/¼ pint hot water

Dissolve the gelatine and meat cubes in the water. Use within 2 to 3 days, as this glaze will not keep.

ASPIC JELLY

(See Aspic entry for method of preparing.) This is used for glazing meat and fish moulds, cocktail savouries and open-type sandwiches.

Powdered or crystallized aspic jelly can be bought in packets and tins and provides a quick and useful standby.

ARROWROOT GLAZE
(For fruit flans, etc.)

METRIC/IMPERIAL
2 × 5 ml spoons/2 teaspoons arrowroot
150 ml/¼ pint strained fruit
juice or water
25–50 g/1–2 oz sugar
lemon juice (optional)
2 × 5 ml spoons/2 teaspoons red-currant jelly or
apricot jam (optional)
colouring, if required

Blend the arrowroot with a little of the fruit juice. Put the rest of the juice and the sugar into a saucepan to warm gently. Add the blended arrowroot and bring to the boil. Reduce heat and simmer until the syrup is quite clear and of a coating consistency. Add a squeeze of lemon juice, the jelly or jam and the colouring (if used). The syrup should be well flavoured and of a thick glazing consistency – if too thin, it will soak into the pastry and make it soggy. It must be used while still warm, as it sets quite quickly.

Other Types of Glaze

JELLY GLAZE (FOR MOULDS, FLANS, ETC.)
Any type of jelly can be used. For coating moulds, a thin 'lining' of jelly is set in the moulds or basin. For flans, etc., it is spooned over the food when it is about to set – it must not be poured on when liquid, as it is then absorbed by the material which it should coat. (See Jelly entry.)

SYRUP GLAZE (FOR FLANS, TARTLETS, GÂTEAUX)
A concentrated syrup made from sugar and water or fruit juice, suitably flavoured. It should be boiled until it coats the back of the spoon.

GLAZE FOR YEAST BUNS
Brush the buns over as soon as they come out of the oven with 50 g/2 oz sugar boiled in 2–3 × 15 ml spoons/2–3 tablespoons water.

SIEVED APRICOT JAM GLAZE (FOR SAVARINS, FRUIT FLANS, CAKES, ETC.)
Warm the jam in a pan of hot water before using.

GLAZES FOR PASTRY
Brush before baking with beaten egg or milk (this is sometimes called Gilding) or, for sweet dishes, with beaten egg white and sugar.

GLAZE FOR VEGETABLES
Toss the cooked vegetables in melted seasoned butter.

SAUCES AND ICING
These can be regarded as glazes when they are used to coat a dish. A sauce intended for this purpose should have a good sheen, which it acquires through thorough cooking and beating.

GLOBE ARTICHOKES

(See Artichoke entry.)

GLOUCESTER CHEESE

(See Double Gloucester cheese entry.)

GLOUCESTER PUDDING

A type of steamed suet pudding in which 100 g/4 oz finely chopped raw apple and 50 g/2 oz mixed peel are added to a standard pudding mixture containing an egg. (See Suet Puddings entry.)

GLUCOSE (DEXTROSE)

A simple sugar. It is a white, crystalline substance with a faintly sweet taste. Glucose is a constituent of ordinary cane sugar and of starch and when carbohydrates are digested, they are broken down to glucose, which is then absorbed by the blood stream. The level of glucose in the blood goes up after a meal, then returns to normal about an hour or so later, depending on the individual and on the kind of meal.

Commercially prepared glucose, which is made by heating a starchy food (often maize) with an acid, is used in sweet-making, because it does not crystallize to the same extent as other sugars, and also in the less expensive jams.

Glucose has no food value and is only taken for its energy value. It has no advantages over other sugars except that it is absorbed into the blood stream a little quicker. Medically, it is sometimes used for a patient who is too ill to eat properly, since it can be taken in greater quantities than other sugars as it does not taste so sweet.

GLUTEN

An insoluble protein which forms the major part

of the protein content of wheat flour. Gluten gives flour its elasticity and enables it to hold air or carbon dioxide, thus producing light, well-risen bread, cakes and puddings.

The strength and elasticity of gluten depends in the first place on the part of the world in which the wheat is grown. British wheat is 'soft' or 'weak', Canadian wheat 'hard' or 'strong', so most flour-millers blend flours to produce the strength they require. Bread needs a strong flour, rich cakes and biscuits a weak type. The flour sold on the retail market is usually a general-purpose one made by mixing strong and weak flours.

The 'strength' or toughness of gluten is modified by water, by handling and mixing and by very acid or alkaline conditions. Thus pastry becomes tough if the fat is not rubbed in sufficiently to prevent the water having access to the particles of flour; over-mixing of a cake or pastry makes it tough because it causes the gluten to develop too much; again, a cake mixture containing an excess of lemon juice or acid may be tough.

GLYCERIN(E) OR GLYCEROL

A sweet, colourless, oily liquid. It is a compound of carbon, hydrogen and oxygen, formed by the breaking down of fats and produced chiefly as a by-product of the manufacture of soap. Glycerine is occasionally added to royal icing to keep it moist.

GNOCCHI

An Italian dish, consisting of squares, rounds or other fancy shapes of semolina paste, used to garnish soup or other savoury dishes or served as a savoury dish with cheese sauce.

SEMOLINA GNOCCHI ALLA ROMANA

METRIC/IMPERIAL
600 ml/1 pint milk
100 g/4 oz fine semolina
salt
pepper
pinch of grated nutmeg
1–2 eggs, beaten
25 g/1 oz butter
75 g/3 oz grated Parmesan cheese
little butter
extra cheese for topping

Bring the milk to the boil, sprinkle in the semolina and seasonings and stir over a gentle heat until the mixture is really thick. Beat well until smooth and stir in the egg, butter and cheese. Return the pan to a low heat and stir for 1 minute. Spread this mixture, about ½ cm/¼ inch to 1 cm/½ inch thick, on

a shallow buttered dish and allow to cool. Cut into 2.5 cm/1 inch rounds or squares and arrange in a shallow greased ovenproof dish. Put a few knobs of butter over the top, sprinkle with a little extra cheese and brown under the grill or towards the top of a moderately hot oven (200°C/400°F, Gas Mark 6). Serve with more cheese and tomato sauce.

GOATS' MILK

Goats' milk has a higher percentage of fat and protein than some varieties of cows' milk and it has a somewhat stronger flavour. It is widely used for making cheeses (for example, Saint Maure) which are produced from May to November; in Scandinavia it is used for such cheeses as Gjetøst. Goats' milk can also be used for ordinary household purposes and in making milk puddings and similar dishes. It is useful for feeding babies who are allergic to cows' milk, though it must be adjusted to their needs.

GOLDEN BERRY

(See Cape Gooseberry entry.)

GOLDEN SYRUP

A light-coloured syrup produced by the evaporation of cane sugar juice. It contains various sugars, with some flavouring and colouring matter; it thus supplies energy but nothing else of nutritional value. Syrup is not quite so sweet as sugar, since it contains more water and glucose.

Golden syrup is used to sweeten and flavour cakes and puddings, to make sauces, as a filling for tarts and in gingerbreads.

(See Suet Pudding and Treacles, etc., entries for recipes using golden syrup.)

GOLDWASSER

A colourless, potent liqueur, flavoured with aniseed and orange, which contains minute particles of gold leaf or other yellow substance: these serve a decorative rather than a useful purpose.

GOOSE

A goose for the table should be young – not more than a year old. A 'green goose' is a bird up to the age of 3 to 4 months, a gosling one up to 6 months. When choosing a goose, see that the bill is yellow and free from hair and the feet supple; young geese have yellow feet, but these gradually turn red, so that the colour is some indication of age.

The season for home-killed geese lasts from September to February, but goslings are in season all the year round and foreign birds are available at

185

most times. Frozen birds are also available. The traditional time for eating geese in this country is Michaelmas, but they are also popular at Christmas time.

Geese are rather fat and when they are cooked the flesh is dark, with a rich, meaty flavour, therefore accompaniments should counteract this. Traditionally these are sage and onion stuffing and apple or gooseberry sauce.

ROAST GOOSE

Preparation: Pluck the bird (see Poultry entry) and remove all stumps from the wings. Cut off the feet and the wing tips at the first joint. Cut off the head, then, forcing back the neck skin, cut off the neck where it joins the back. Draw the bird in the same way as other poultry and clean the inside with a cloth wrung out in hot water. Put a thick fold of cloth over the breast-bone and flatten it with a mallet or rolling pin. Stuff with sage and onion stuffing.

Trussing: Working with the breast side uppermost and tail end away from you, pass a skewer through one wing, then through the body and out again through the other wing. Pass a second skewer through the end of the wing joint on one side, through the thick part of the leg and out the other side in the same way. Pass a third skewer through the loose skin near the end of the leg, through the body and through to the other side in the same way. Enlarge the vent, pass the tail through it and fix with a small skewer. Wind the string round the skewers, keeping the limbs firmly in position, but avoid passing the string over the breast of the goose. Tuck in the neck under the string.

Cooking: Sprinkle the bird with salt, put it in a roasting tin and cover with the fat taken from inside, then with greased paper. Roast in a moderately hot oven (200°C/400°F, Gas Mark 6) for 15 minutes per 0.5 kg/1 lb, plus 15 minutes, basting frequently. To cook by the slow method roast in a moderate oven (180°C/350°F, Gas Mark 4) for 25 to 30 minutes per 0.5 kg/1 lb. Remove the paper for the last 30 minutes, to brown the bird.

Serve with giblet gravy (made in the roasting tin after the fat has been poured off) and apple or gooseberry sauce. Apple rings which have been dipped in lemon juice, brushed with oil and lightly grilled, also make an attractive garnish. Cooked joints may be served in a rich espagnole sauce.

A Gosling is prepared in the same way as a duck, except that it is not usually stuffed. The bird should be roasted in the usual way for 45 minutes to 1 hour and garnished with watercress; hand brown gravy separately.

Goose Livers

Have an excellent flavour and are converted into

pâté de foie gras. (See Foie Gras entry.)

Goose Eggs
(See Eggs entry.)

GOOSEBERRY

The fruit of a prickly bush which was imported to this country from North Europe and Asia. The berries, which hang down from the underside of the stem, are green when first formed. There are many different varieties of gooseberries, round or long, hairy or smooth, cooking or dessert. The early varieties, usually ready in May, are among the first of the English fruits and make delicious pies and puddings, especially when they are young and small, with tender skins. Dessert types may be green, red or yellow.

Gooseberries have a good vitamin C content. The young fruit has a high percentage of acid and pectin and is useful in jam-making, but the riper fruit contain less. The juice can be bottled and stored for use with later summer and autumn fruits. (See Jam entry.)

Preparation and cooking: The stalk and the flowering end should be either pinched or cut off (often called 'topping and tailing') and the fruit should be thoroughly washed. They are stewed in the ordinary way (see Fruit entry), but being acid they require a fair amount of sugar – at least 100 g/4 oz per 0.5 kg/1 lb of fruit. Some of the acid can be counteracted by adding a pinch of bicarbonate of soda. If the fruit is soft, less water is required and sometimes less sugar.

GOOSEBERRY SAUCE

Sieve or liquidize slightly sweetened stewed gooseberries (fresh, canned or bottled) and re-heat with a knob of butter. Serve with goose, duck, mackerel, etc.

GOOSEBERRY JAM

METRIC/IMPERIAL
2.75 kg/6 lb gooseberries (slightly underripe)
1 litre/2 pints water
2.75 kg/6 lb sugar

Top, tail and wash the gooseberries and put them into a pan with the water. Simmer gently for about 30 minutes, until the fruit is really soft, mashing it to a pulp with a spoon and stirring from time to time to prevent the fruit sticking. Add the sugar, stir until dissolved and boil rapidly until setting point is reached. Pot and cover in the usual way. *Makes about 4.5 kg/10 lb.*

Gooseberry Fool
(See Fruit Fool, under Fruit entry.)

GORGONZOLA

A popular, semi-hard, blue-veined cheese of sharp flavour, made from cows' milk: it is named after the Italian town where it is produced. Gorgonzola is matured for 3 to 4 months in moist, draughty caves to encourage the formation of the blue veins. The cheese is made up in a small drum shape, weighing about 7 kg/15 lb and wrapped in foil. The white variety of Gorgonzola has a slightly bitter flavour appreciated by cheese connoisseurs.

GOUDA CHEESE

A wheelshaped Dutch cheese, not unlike Edam in taste and texture, but flatter in shape, with a yellow skin and very much larger, approximately 4 kg/9 lb in weight, and is an excellent cheese for cooking. There are also small Goudas, about 0.5 kg/1 lb in weight, known as Midget Goudas. Gouda has a smooth, mellow flavour, a yellow cheese with a deeper yellow coating.

GOULASH

A rich meat stew flavoured with paprika, Hungarian in origin, but found in several European countries. Soured cream can be stirred in or served separately.

GOULASH

METRIC/IMPERIAL
0.75 kg/1 ½ lb stewing steak, cut into 1 cm/ ½ inch
   cubes
3 × 15 ml spoons/3 tablespoons seasoned flour
2 medium sized onions, skinned and chopped
1 green pepper, seeded and chopped
2 × 15 ml spoons/2 tablespoons fat or oil
2 × 5 ml spoons/2 teaspoons paprika
3 × 15 ml spoons/3 tablespoons tomato paste
little grated nutmeg
salt
pepper
50 g/2 oz flour
300 ml/ ½ pint stock
2 large tomatoes, skinned and quartered
bouquet garni
150 ml/ ¼ pint beer

Coat the meat with seasoned flour. Fry the onions and pepper lightly in the fat or oil for about 3 to 4 minutes. Add the meat and fry lightly on all sides until golden brown – about 5 minutes. Add the paprika and fry for about a minute longer. Stir in the tomato paste, nutmeg, seasoning and flour and cook for a further 2 to 3 minutes. Add the stock, tomatoes and bouquet garni, put into a casserole and cook in a moderate oven (160°C/325°F, Gas Mark 3) for 1 ½ to 2 hours. Add the beer, cook for

a few minutes longer and remove the bouquet garni. Serve with sauerkraut and caraway-flavoured dumplings or with a green salad.

GOURD

This vegetable belongs to the same family as the marrow, pumpkin and squash. There are over 500 varieties, some of which are edible and in certain parts of the world form an important food, while the skins are dried and used as containers or just as decorations.

   The best gourds to eat are the 'Turk's Cap' and the 'Turban'; the flesh, which is yellow, sweet and floury, is used in the same way as that of the pumpkin. Among other edible gourds are the 'Calabash', 'Towel' and 'Snake'.

GRAHAM FLOUR, BREAD, CRACKERS

Graham flour, which is an American product, is becoming available in this country. It is ground from whole-wheat grain and is similar to whole-wheat flour. Bread made from it resembles a granary loaf.

   Graham crackers are crisp wholemeal biscuits, often flavoured with honey; digestive biscuits may be substituted for them if you wish to follow an American recipe.

GRANADILLA (PASSION FRUIT)

The fruit of the passion flower, of which there are numerous varieties bearing different-sized and coloured fruits. The type commonly grown in America is large and has seedy pulp similar to a pomegranate. Other types are grown in tropical climates, the smaller, darker ones often being more juicy. Although their appearance is unattractive, granadillas have a delicious and refreshing flavour. They are served as a dessert fruit, or made into ices, creams, jelly, etc. They are available fresh or canned in syrup.

GRAND MARNIER

A French liqueur based on cognac, light brown in colour and with the flavour of orange.

GRAPE

The fruit of the vine, of which there are many varieties in Europe and elsewhere. In warm countries, grapes are grown in vineyards in the open but in England most varieties will only ripen in greenhouses, though there are a few varieties which will ripen satisfactorily in the open.

   Dessert grapes are larger than the small wine grapes, which cannot be eaten, and have a better flavour and appearance; they bruise easily and

187

GRA

must be handled with care, so that the bloom on the fruit is not damaged. There are two main types – 'White' (actually a whitish-green) and 'Black' (actually dark purple). Both are good, but the skin of good black grapes is more tender than that of the white one. The black Hamburgs and the white Muscat are considered the best varieties. The small seedless grapes have a pleasant sharp flavour.

Dessert grapes are not washed before being served, but a bowl of water should be provided for each guest so that they may be washed at the table. For fruit salads and garnishes the skin is removed with a knife and the pips are taken out with a fine skewer or by slitting down the side of the fruit. The peeled grapes can be coloured pink by rolling them in a weak solution of water and cochineal.

Grapes are not easily made into jam, as their pectin content and acidity are both low and the flavour is usually too sweet for the average English taste, but a type of grape conserve made in other countries is sometimes imported. Grape cuttings (thinnings) can be stewed; their flavour closely resembles that of young green gooseberries.

In countries where grapes grow out-of-doors large quantities are of course used for wine-making and some special varieties are dried as raisins, etc. Grapes can be used in cooking certain meat and fish dishes.

The nutritional value of grapes is small.

GRAPEFRUIT

A large, yellow-skinned citrus fruit which originated in China and the East Indies. It is now grown in many hot countries. The fruit resembles an orange, but is more yellow in colour; it may even be tinged with pink. The grapefruit is larger than an orange, varying from the size of a large orange to types weighing several pounds. The thickness of the skin varies and most grapefruit contain a number of pips.

The juice of the grapefruit is more acid than that of the orange and it has a sharp flavour, which makes it a suitable appetizer for a meal. It is particularly popular served for breakfast. It is usually eaten uncooked, either alone or in fruit salads and other sweets, though it may be lightly grilled to serve as an appetizer. For more unusual dishes it can be mixed with vegetables and salad ingredients. Grapefruit cans and bottles well, but care must be taken to remove all the pith, otherwise it acquires a bitter flavour. It sometimes develops white spots due to a substance called 'naragin', which is quite harmless. Like all citrus fruits, grapefruit is a good source of vitamin C.

Grapefruit marmalade can be made either thick or clear; grapefruit can also be mixed with other citrus fruit. Grapefruit can be frozen in segments.

188 *To serve grapefruit*: 1. Peel the fruit, cutting off the

inner as well as the outer skin. Cut down the skin dividing the segments and remove the section of pulp. Remove the pips and place the sections of pulp in fruit glasses. Sprinkle freely with sugar and add 2 × 5 ml spoons/2 teaspoons of sherry to each glass. Place a Maraschino or glacé cherry in the centre and serve iced.

2. Cut the grapefruit in half across the sections. Using a grapefruit or other sharp knife, cut round the skin to loosen the pulp from the pith. Remove the centre pith and core and loosen each section from the surrounding skin. Put sugar in the centre, place a cherry on top and serve ice-cold. The edges of the grapefruit may be pinked with scissors if desired.

GRAPEFRUIT COCKTAIL

METRIC/IMPERIAL
2 Florida grapefruits
2 oranges
sugar
3 × 15 ml spoons/3 tablespoons lemon juice
maraschino cherries

Prepare the fruit in segments as described above. Add sugar and lemon juice to taste. Serve well-chilled in individual glasses, each garnished with a cherry.

GRAPEFRUIT SALAD

Place halved sections of grapefruit (prepared as in method 1 above) on a bed of lettuce leaves or watercress and serve with French dressing.

GRAPEFRUIT AND SHRIMP SALAD

METRIC/IMPERIAL
lettuce
1 grapefruit
½ a cucumber
150 ml/¼ pint prepared shrimps
French dressing

Prepare the lettuce and arrange a neat bed of the heart leaves in a shallow salad bowl. Peel the grapefruit, remove the pith and divide it into sections; cut each section into three and put the juice and grapefruit into a basin. Peel the cucumber, cut it into small dice and add it and the shrimps to the grapefruit. Pour on French dressing and mix lightly with a spoon and fork. Pile the mixture on the lettuce leaves and garnish with a few of the shrimp heads if they are available,

GRATING

To shave foods such as cheese and vegetables into small shreds.

Foodstuffs to be grated must be firm and cheese

should be first allowed to harden.

Food in grated form is often prescribed for invalids and babies, as it is more digestible; it is particularly important to serve it at once.

Some foodstuffs deteriorate in value when they are grated and thus exposed to the air, so such things as root vegetables for salads, etc., should be grated only just before serving.

GRAVES

The name given to the wines produced from the vineyards of the Graves district, west and south of Bordeaux. Both red and white wines are made, the red being the better of the two. The parishes which produce the best wines are Léognan, Martillac, Villenave d'Ornon and Mérignac. There are many famous château names for Graves: Château Haut-Brion is considered the best, followed by La Mission Haut-Brion, Pape Clément, etc. White Graves wines are usually sold under the name Graves and are often blended. The wine is medium-dry and is served with fish, poultry, veal, etc.

GRAVY

A type of sauce made from the juices and extractives which run out from meat during cooking. These juices are sometimes served as they are, but they can be thickened, diluted or concentrated; a little extra flavouring may be added, but too much tends to mask the true meat flavour.

The consistency and colour of gravy depend on the meat which it accompanies; gravy for beef and game should be thin and dark brown; for lamb, veal and poultry, medium brown and thickened; for mutton, pork and stuffed joints, thick and brown.

Thin Gravy

Pour the fat very slowly from the tin, draining it off carefully from one corner and leaving the sediment behind. Season well with salt and pepper and add 300 ml/½ pint hot vegetable water or stock (which can be made from a bouillon cube). Stir thoroughly with a wooden spoon until all the sediment is scraped from the tin and the gravy is a rich brown; return the tin to the heat and boil for 2 to 3 minutes. Serve very hot.

This is the 'correct' way of making thin gravy, but some people prefer to make a version of the thick gravy given below, using half the amount of flour.

Thick Gravy

Leave 2 × 15 ml spoons/2 tablespoons of the fat in the tin, add 1 × 15 ml spoon/1 tablespoon flour, (preferably shaking it from a flour dredger, which gives a smoother result), blend well and cook over the heat until it turns brown, stirring continuously. Slowly stir in 300 ml/½ pint hot vegetable water or stock and boil for 2 to 3 minutes. Season well, strain and serve very hot.

NOTES
1. If the gravy is greasy (due to not draining off enough fat) or thin (due to adding too much liquid) it can be corrected by adding more flour, although this weakens the flavour.
2. When gravy is very pale, a little gravy browning may be added.
3. Meat extracts are sometimes added to give extra taste; however, they do tend to overpower the characteristic meat flavour. A sliced carrot and onion cooked with the meat in the gravy will give extra 'body' to the taste without impairing it. 1 × 15 ml spoon/1 tablespoon cider or wine added at the last moment does wonders.

GRAYLING

One of the best fresh-water fishes, especially when it weighs between 275 g/10 oz to 350 g/12 oz. The season for grayling fishing starts about September, and the fish is best in November, but some young ones may be eaten in the summer, as they do not all spawn the first year.

Grayling can be cooked as for trout, but it is best fried, as follows: Remove the fins and tail, then clean, wash and dry the fish, but do not remove the head. Fry in hot fat, turning it over when the first side is cooked. Serve with a tartare sauce, lemon juice or melted butter.

GREEN BUTTER

A savoury spread used for biscuits, sandwiches, canapés, etc. Wash 50 g/2 oz watercress, drain and dry well, chop finely and pound it in a mortar. Cream 50 g/2 oz butter, mix with the chopped watercress and add salt and Cayenne pepper to taste: if necessary add a few drops of green colouring.

GREEN PEA

(See Pea entry.)

GREEN TEA

(See Tea entry.)

GREENGAGE

A type of plum, considered by many to be the finest flavoured of all. The fruit is round and green in colour, becoming yellowish when fully ripe – usually in September. There are several varieties, of which the most famous is the Reine Claude.

Other commonly grown types are the Cambridge Gage and Oullins Gage.

Greengages are chiefly used as a dessert fruit, but may also be stewed and they make excellent tarts and puddings. They bottle well and make good jam.

Preparation and cooking: Remove the stalks and wash the fruit. If it is required for salads, etc., remove the skin, cut the fruit in half and remove the stone.

Greengages may be stewed like other fruit and require about 75 g/3 oz to 100 g/4 oz sugar and 150 ml/¼ pint water for every 0.5 kg/1 lb of fruit.

GREENGAGE JAM

METRIC/IMPERIAL
2.75 kg/6 lb greengages
600 ml/1 pint water
2.75 kg/6 lb sugar

Wash the fruit, cut in half and remove the stones. Crack some of the stones to obtain the kernels and blanch. Put the greengages, water and blanched kernels in a pan and simmer for about 30 minutes, or until the fruit is soft. Add the sugar, stir until dissolved, and boil rapidly until setting point is reached. Pot and cover in the usual way. Makes about 4.5 kg/10 lb.

Note: Alternatively, cook the fruit with the stones in and remove them with a slotted spoon as the jam is boiling.

GRENADIN

A French term used for a small slice of fillet of veal. A grenadin is usually larded and braised, then served with a vegetable garnish, e.g., braised celery, chicory, or lettuce or buttered carrots.

GRENADINE

A French syrup made from pomegranate juice, red in colour; it is used as a sweetening and colouring agent in cocktails, fruit drinks, etc.

GREY MULLET

(See Mullet entry.)

GRIDDLE CAKES

(See Girdle Cookery entry.)

GRILLING

The process of cooking food by direct heat under a grill or over a hot fire. It is only suitable for cooking thin cuts of meat or fish of good quality. Best results are obtained by grilling over a charcoal fire,

but the special fittings on modern gas and electric cookers provide a quick and simple way of grilling.

The grill should be well heated before use; those with thin reflector plates generally need to be full on the whole time, otherwise the heat is uneven. The heat can be adjusted by raising or lowering the grill pan; some pans have a means of adjustment either on the pan itself or in the fitting in which it slides; failing this, the pan may be raised by placing a suitable tin under it. Unless the elements or burners, reflectors and grill plates are kept very clean, the grill will smell unpleasantly when heated. For open fire grilling, a gridiron with a channel for dripping is used, and the fire must be bright red and not smoking.

Browning Food under the Grill

Many dishes are improved by having the surface browned under a hot grill. A savoury dish is sprinkled with breadcrumbs (and often with grated cheese) and a few knobs of butter are dotted over the surface; a sweet dish may be sprinkled with sugar to give a caramelled finish. Put the dish under the hot grill and leave for a minute or two, until the surface has become a pleasing brown.

GRILLED MEAT AND POULTRY

Since grilling is a quick method of cooking, it is suitable only for the best cuts of meat – fresh, under-hung meat and poorer cuts will remain tough. Most meat is best marinated first, and rubbed with flavouring, although a first-class piece of fillet steak or loin of mutton chop merely requires sprinkling with salt and pepper and (if desired) brushing over with a little melted fat or oil. Kidney, tender liver, sausages, bacon and chicken joints are other foods suitable for grilling.

Steak: Wipe with a damp cloth and cut it into portions (not more than 3.5 cm/1½ inches thick), leaving where possible a rim of fat. Beat it well with a rolling pin (this breaks down some of the fibres and makes the meat more tender). Marinate it if desired, in a mixture of oil and vinegar.

Chops: Remove the skin and spinal cord and trim neatly. If they are unshapely, tie with string or fix with a skewer; alternatively, bone them first and then tie or skewer them into shape.

Liver: Wash, wipe and cut into slices 1 cm/½ inch thick.

Kidneys: Wash and skin them and cut them in half, removing the core, then thread them on a skewer so that they can be handled more easily.

Cook the meat under the red hot grill, turning at frequent intervals until cooked; to test, press with the bowl of a spoon – if it regains its original shape, it is ready. Steak is left rather under-done, but lamb and pork should be well grilled. Serve at once with an appropriate garnish.

Bacon or ham: Lean rashers, such as gammon, require brushing with fat; put them on the grid under the grill, and cook for 2 to 3 minutes – longer for thick rashers. As soon as the fat is transparent on one side, turn them and cook the other side. Ham may take 10 to 15 minutes if fairly thick. When eggs are cooked at the same time, place them in the fat in the base of the grill pan and cook till set.

Sausages: Prick the sausages and grill them rather slowly until well browned all over, turning them frequently.

Chicken joints: Wipe the joints with a damp cloth, season or rub with flavourings such as garlic, herbs or lemon. Brush with fat and cook slowly for 20 to 30 minutes.

Whole chicken: Young and tender birds (such as poussins or small broilers) are suitable for grilling. Split a whole bird down the back but without cutting through the skin of the breast; flatten it out, removing the breast-bone and breaking the joints where necessary. Skewer the legs and wings closely to the body, keeping the bird flat. A frozen bird should of course be allowed to thaw first.

Brush the chicken over with olive oil or melted butter, sprinkle with salt and pepper and place in the pan on a greased grid, skin side down. Grill under a moderate heat for 20 minutes, turn over and grill for a further 20 to 30 minutes, basting. Serve with a thin gravy made from the giblets and garnish with watercress.

Alternatively, sprinkle the chicken with a mixture of finely chopped onion, parsley and breadcrumbs, after brushing it with oil or butter; when it is cooked, garnish it with watercress and serve with brown or tomato sauce.

TIMES FOR GRILLING
The following table gives approximate times, which vary according to the thickness of the meat:

Steak 2.5 cm/1 inch thick:

Rare	6 to 7 minutes
Medium rare	10 to 12 minutes
Well done	15 minutes
Lamb or mutton chops	10 to 15 minutes
Pork Chops	15 to 20 minutes
Veal Cutlets	15 to 20 minutes
Liver	5 to 10 minutes
Kidneys	10 minutes
Bacon rashers	2 to 3 minutes
Ham	10 to 15 minutes
Sausages	10 to 15 minutes
(*Allow longer time for pork sausages*)	
Chicken Joints	20 to 30 minutes

MIXED GRILL
This may consist of a variety of the above meats.

Start by cooking those which require the longest time, so that all are ready together. Serve with grilled mushrooms, tomatoes, chipped potatoes and watercress and pats of maître d'hôtel butter.

KEBABS
A selection of small pieces of meat and vegetables are threaded onto a skewer, seasoned and brushed with fat. They should be cooked under a medium grill until the meats are cooked through. Turn frequently. The meats can be marinated for extra flavour. (See separate entry.)

FISH
Most fish can be grilled, though the dryer types are better cooked in other ways. The fish should be seasoned, sprinkled with lemon juice and (except for oily fish such as herring) brushed liberally with melted butter. Cutlets should be tied neatly into shape. Fillets and large fish should be cooked in the grill pan rather than on the grid.

Cutlets and fillets: Grill first on one side, then turn them over, brush the second side with fat and grill it. The time varies from 3 to 10 minutes on each side. Serve very hot, with a garnish and sauce.

Whole fish: Wash and scale the fish, then score it with a sharp knife in 3 to 4 places on each side, season and brush with melted fat. Place fish on the grid or in the pan and grill rather slowly, so that the flesh cooks thoroughly without the outside burning. Turn fish once or twice, handling it carefully to prevent breaking it. To test whether the fish is done, insert the back of a knife next to the bone to see if the flesh comes away easily. Serve with maître d'hôtel butter or melted butter, lemon wedges and chopped parsley.

VEGETABLES
Most vegetables contain a large proportion of cellulose, which does not soften in a fierce, dry heat, and only tomatoes and mushrooms can be grilled. Brush them well with fat and allow about 5 minutes for halved tomatoes, 10 to 15 minutes for mushrooms.

GRILSE

A young salmon.

GRINDING

The process of reducing hard foodstuffs such as nuts and coffee beans to small particles by means of a food mill, grinder or electric 'liquidizer'. When using a liquidizer add the foodstuffs through the top cap a little at a time. If the engine labours, empty the goblet and repeat.

GRISKIN

Chine of pork, also a thin, poor piece of loin.

GRISSINI (GRISTICKS)

These are also known as breadsticks; they are pencil-shaped rolls made from a dough similar to that used for French bread and baked until hard and crisp. They are usually eaten with cocktails.

GRISTLE

Gristle or tendon is part of the connective tissue of an animal body, forming the soft skeleton which supports the other tissues and organs. The principal constituent of gristle is collagen, which is converted into gelatine by prolonged cooking. It is usually inedible.

GROATS

The hulled and coarsely crushed grain of oats (or occasionally other cereals). Groats are used for making porridge, gruel and broths. For gruel, commercial preparations of finely milled groats are best and the manufacturer's instructions should be followed.

(See Oatmeal entry.)

GROG

A drink made with spirits, sugar and hot water.

GROUND MEAT

American term for minced meat.

GROUND RICE

(See Rice entry.)

GROUSE (MOOR FOWL)

There are several varieties of these game birds, but the word generally refers to the red or Scotch Grouse, which is at its best from August to October; the shooting season is from 12th August to 10th December.

The young birds make the best eating; they may be distinguished by the downy feathers under the wings, which have pointed flight feathers; the feathers on head and neck are of a rich brown colour.

Ptarmigan, which turns white in winter but is otherwise similar to the grouse, is often called 'white grouse', while black cock is called 'black grouse'.

Grouse is usually cooked by roasting and may also be made into a pie or removed from the bone and used for made-up dishes, though this is not recommended, as the distinctive flavour of the grouse is to some extent lost. As it is a small bird serve one bird per person.

ROAST GROUSE

After hanging, pluck, draw and truss the bird, season inside and out and lay some fat bacon over the breast. Put a knob of butter inside the bird and place it on a slice of toast. Roast in a moderately hot oven (200°C/400°F, Gas Mark 6) for 40 minutes, basting frequently. After 30 minutes, remove the bacon, dredge the breast with flour and baste well.

Remove the trussing strings before serving the bird on the toast on which it was roasted. Garnish with watercress and serve with thin gravy, bread sauce, fried crumbs and matchstick potatoes. A lettuce or watercress salad may also be served.

GRUEL

A drink or thin porridge, sometimes given to invalids or children, which is made with fine oatmeal or barley.

GRUYÈRE CHEESE

A large, flat, whole-milk cheese, originally made in the Swiss town of Gruyère, but now also made in France and elsewhere. It is easily distinguished by the large holes due to the production of a gas by the bacteria with which it is inoculated. Gruyère is firm and rather rough in texture, but it has a pleasant taste. Its flavour and its firm texture make it second only to Parmesan cheese in popularity for cooking. Unlike Parmesan, however, it also makes a good table cheese.

When buying Gruyère cheese, avoid any that have a very large number of irregularly shaped holes, or unduly small holes, as they are unlikely to be of good quality.

A considerable amount of Gruyère is pasteurized, compressed, shaped in small wedges, wrapped in foil and sold in boxes under the name of Petit Gruyère; these processed cheeses have the same flavour as the ordinary cheese, but are of a more creamy texture and therefore not so suitable for cooking.

GUAVA

The fruit of a tropical tree. It has pink flesh and numerous seeds. A delicately flavoured, stiff textured jelly and a cheese are made from guavas. Available in cans.

GUDGEON

A fresh-water fish similar to a carp, found in European rivers. It grows to about 20 cm/8 inch in length and has barbels at each corner of its mouth and black spots along the side of its body. Like all fresh-water fish, gudgeon needs soaking in salted water before cooking. It is best fried or grilled.

GUINEA FOWL

The guinea fowl is usually about the same size as a pheasant, 1 kg/2 lb but can be as large as a small chicken. It has grey plumage and white spots. The season lasts all the year round, but the birds are at their best from February to June. When in good condition they have a plump breast and smooth-skinned legs.

Guinea Fowl needs to be hung for some time after killing. All recipes for cooking chicken or pheasant are applicable, but take care to use plenty of fat when roasting, otherwise the flesh will be dry.

ROAST GUINEA FOWL

Singe, draw and wipe the bird (see Poultry entry) and truss it for roasting, tying a piece of fat bacon over the breast. Roast in a moderately hot oven (200°C/400°F, Gas Mark 6) for 30 minutes or longer, according to size, basting frequently with butter or dripping. Garnish with watercress and serve with gravy and orange or mixed green salad or with a celery or bread sauce.

Guinea Fowls' Eggs and Gulls' Eggs
(See Eggs entry.)

GUM

A sticky substance, which hardens somewhat on exposure to the air, obtained from various trees and plants. The two chief types used in cookery are gum arabic and gum tragacanth. The former, which is derived from Arabian and Indian species of acacia, is used in the manufacture of jujubes, pastilles and gumdrops, as well as in medicine; gum tragacanth, which is obtained from a spiny shrub grown in western Asia, is used for thickening creams, jellies and pastes, particularly the special stiff royal icing (pastillage) formerly employed to make ornaments for wedding cakes, etc.

The word is also used for sweets containing gum or an equivalent; they are of an elastic consistency, some being hard-textured and some soft, and they are transparent; gums are usually flavoured with fruit (and in the case of cough lozenges contain a medicinal ingredient as well). Commercially made gums consist of gum arabic, sugar, glucose and flavouring, with water; for clear gums agar-agar and glycerine are added. They are moulded and set in starch trays. A home-made type can be made with gum arabic, sugar and water, with suitable flavouring.

GUMBO

(See Okra entry.)

GURNET OR GURNARD

A small fish also known as Tubfish, Stickleback and Flying Fish. It has a large, angular, bony head and firm, white flesh of fairly good flavour. The red gurnet, which is better than the grey, is in season from July to April. Gurnets are best baked, but can be cooked by any recipe suitable for haddock or mullet.

GURNET WITH WHITE WINE

Remove the head and fins and score the skin on each side. Sprinkle fish with pepper and salt, cover it with some slices of tomato, lemon and onion and put a few pieces of butter on top of each fish. Pour about 150 ml/¼ pint white wine over the fish and cook in a moderately hot oven (200°C/400°F, Gas Mark 6) for about 20 minutes basting occasionally. Garnish with quartered potatoes.

GUTTING

To clean out the inside of a fish, removing all the entrails.

HADDOCK

A fish somewhat similar in appearance and colour to the cod, but with a more pronounced flavour; it may be identified by a black streak down the back and two black spots, one at each side above the gills. It can weigh from 750 g/1¾ lb to 1.5 kg/3¼ lb. Haddock is at its best from September to February. It may be cooked by any method suitable for white fish; small or medium-sized fish can be cooked whole, but larger ones should be filleted or cut into cutlets. The flesh tends to be dry, so the fish should be accompanied by a sauce.

Smoked Haddock

A considerable amount of haddock is smoked, especially in Scotland, and Findon, a village near Aberdeen, has given its name to the very delicious creamy-yellow smoked 'Finnan haddies' which are produced there. Smoked haddocks make a good breakfast, lunch or high tea dish and are excellent for kedgeree and for large and small savouries, such as fish soufflé, scalloped haddock, etc.

BAKED STUFFED FRESH HADDOCK

METRIC/IMPERIAL
1 fresh haddock
stuffing (see recipe)
flour
egg
breadcrumbs
cooking oil
parsley or watercress
anchovy sauce

Clean and dry the haddock. Make the stuffing, fill the fish, then sew it up with thin string and a trussing needle, tying the ends in a bow so that the string can easily be removed. Curl the fish round or shape it attractively. Flour, brush with egg and toss in breadcrumbs, place on a well-greased tin, cover with greased paper and bake for 30 minutes or longer in a moderately hot oven (200°C/400°F,

Gas Mark 6). Remove the string, serve garnished with parsley or watercress and hand the sauce separately.

STUFFING FOR BAKED HADDOCK

METRIC/IMPERIAL
2 × 15 ml spoons/2 tablespoons breadcrumbs
1 × 15 ml spoon/1 tablespoon chopped parsley
1 × 5 ml spoon/1 teaspoon mixed herbs
salt
pepper
1 × 5 ml spoon/1 teaspoon chopped onion
a few drops anchovy essence
a little beaten egg or milk to mix

Put all the dry ingredients and onion into a basin, add the anchovy essence, blend with a little beaten egg or milk and mix thoroughly.

HADDOCK JULIENNE

METRIC/IMPERIAL
0.75 kg/1 ½ lb haddock or cod fillet
25 g/1 oz butter
salt
pepper
ground coriander
juice of ½ lemon
50 g/2 oz onion, skinned
2 tomatoes, skinned and seeded
25 g/1 oz Cheddar cheese, grated
1 × 5 ml spoon/1 teaspoon arrowroot
chopped parsley

Remove the skin from the fillet. Cut the fish into 4 portions. Use half the butter to well grease a shallow ovenproof serving dish. Arrange the fish in a single layer, with salt, pepper and a little coriander. Pour over the lemon juice. Cut the onion thinly into rings. Cut the tomato flesh into strips. In a small frying pan, melt the rest of the butter; slowly fry the onion until soft and beginning to colour. Combine with the tomato and cheese.

Spoon the onion mixture evenly over each fillet. Cover and cook in a moderately hot oven

(190°C/375°F, Gas Mark 5) for 20 minutes.

In a small pan, blend the arrowroot with 1 × 15 ml spoon/1 tablespoon water, add the drained-off fish liquor and bring to the boil, stirring. Pour it over the fish and serve garnished with chopped parsley.

POACHED SMOKED HADDOCK

Cut the fins from the fish and if the fish is large, cut it into serving-sized pieces. Place in a frying pan (or large saucepan), barely cover with milk or milk and water, sprinkle with pepper and simmer gently for 10 to 15 minutes, or until tender. Alternatively, cook in the oven, adding a knob of butter. The haddock can be served topped with a poached egg.

SMOKED HADDOCK BALLS

Cook some smoked haddock, flake it thoroughly and mix to a fairly stiff paste with a little white sauce. Season well and leave to cool. Form the paste into small balls, egg-and-crumb them and deep-fry them to a golden brown. Serve hot, on cocktail sticks.

HADDOCK SOUFFLÉ

METRIC/IMPERIAL
225 g/½ lb smoked haddock (or white fish such as
   cod, haddock)
2 × 15 ml spoons/2 tablespoons cornflour
300 ml/½ pint milk
knob of butter
50–75 g/2–3 oz cheese, grated
1–2 eggs, separated
salt
pepper

Grease a 1 litre/2 pint ovenproof dish. Cook and flake the fish. Blend the cornflour with 2 × 15 ml spoons/2 tablespoons of the cold milk and boil the remainder with the butter; pour on to the blended cornflour, stirring well. Return the mixture to the pan and heat until boiling, stirring until the sauce thickens. Remove from the heat, add the cheese, fish and egg yolks and season well. Whisk the egg whites stiffly and fold into the fish mixture. Pour into the dish and bake in a moderately hot oven (200°C/400°F, Gas Mark 6) for about 20 minutes, until well risen and golden. Serve immediately, because the mixture sinks as it cools.

HAGGIS

A Scottish dish made from oatmeal, suet and the internal organs of a sheep, the stomach of the sheep being cleaned and used as a 'skin' to contain the mixture. A simpler type is made with liver and

cooked in a basin.

Haggis is available fresh or canned.

HAKE

A white fish, long and slender, with a pointed snout and large mouth; it has flesh of a close texture and a delicate flavour. Hake is available all the year round, but is at its best from June to January. It is cooked in any way suitable for cod.

HALIBUT

A very large flat fish found in the North Atlantic. The young fish, which weighs about 1.5 kg/3 lb is in season all the year round and has the best flavour. Larger ones, which can weigh up to 90 kg/200 lb, are best from August to April; they are sold in steaks or pieces.

Halibut can be grilled, steamed or served with a piquant sauce and can replace turbot or cod in many recipes.

BAKED HALIBUT WITH WINE

METRIC/IMPERIAL
4 pieces of halibut, about 1.75 kg/1½ lb
½ small onion, skinned and chopped
50 g/2 oz lean streaky bacon, rinded and chopped
25 g/1 oz butter
1 × 15 ml spoon/1 tablespoon flour
225 g/8 oz to 350 g/12 oz ripe tomatoes, skinned and
   chopped, or a 1 × 425 g/15 oz can of tomatoes,
   drained
3 × 15 ml spoons/3 tablespoons dry white wine
salt
pepper
a pinch of sugar
½ bayleaf
3–4 peppercorns

Rinse and dry the fish and place it in a greased ovenproof dish. Fry the onion and bacon in the butter until soft but not brown – about 5 minutes – and stir in the flour. Add the tomatoes, wine, seasonings and flavourings and pour over the fish. Cover with foil and bake in a moderate oven (180°C/350°F, Gas Mark 4) for about 20 minutes, or until the fish is tender. Remove the bayleaf and peppercorns before serving.

Halibut Liver Oil
This is a very good source of Vitamins A and D (containing a higher proportion than cod liver oil); it is generally taken in a capsule.

HAM

The thigh of the pig, specially prepared. The ham is cut off the untreated side of bacon and is dry-

195

cured in a mixture of salt and saltpetre. (Bacon, by contrast, is wet-cured, that is in a brine solution.) If the whole side is wet-cured and the hind leg is then cut off, it is called gammon, not ham.

The food value of ham is similar to that of all meat. It is a good source of protein, fat and thiamine.

There are many variations in the curing of hams. Some are smoked, some are not, the latter being known as 'green' or 'pale-dried'. Here are a few of the many varieties:

YORK
Pale-dried ham, with a mild, delicate flavour and a paler lean meat than in other varieties; the fat is a very faint pink colour. It is expensive because it is prepared by a special process which takes several months; when well matured, York ham should have a greenish mould on the outer surface. The ham keeps well.

BRADENHAM
Sweet-cured, almost black in appearance, processed in molasses instead of brine, needs long soaking and cooking.

SUFFOLK
Like Bradenham hams, but paler in colour.

VIRGINIAN PEACH-FED
Special spicing and smoking with hickory wood give these hams their individual flavour. As the name implies, peaches are fed to the pigs before they are killed.

DANISH
These hams are generally smaller in circumference but longer than the other types. They can be smoked or green.

PARMA
An uncooked, smoked ham served very thinly sliced, usually eaten as an hors d'œuvre with melon or fresh figs.

HONEY-BAKED
A ham that has been baked with a coating of honey, or honey and brown sugar and crumbs.

Choosing Ham
Select a plump ham, with a short shank and a thin skin. The lean should be firm and a deep pink in colour. The fat should look white (or pinkish in a York ham) and should not be soft and oily. There should be no yellow or green stains on the inside lean or fat, but there should be a greenish mould on the outside surface in York hams. If a knife inserted by the bone comes out clean and smelling sweetly, the ham is in good condition.

BOILING A HAM
Follow the usual method (see Boiling entry), allowing 20 minutes per 0.5 kg/lb and 20 minutes over for hams up to 5.5 kg/12 lb; above

5.5 kg/12 lb, allow 15 minutes per 0.5 kg/lb and 15 minutes over. Allow the ham to cool in the water, then remove the skin, sprinkle the fat with golden-brown breadcrumbs and place a frill round the knucklebone. Hams that are to be served hot are of course removed from the water immediately boiling is completed.

STEAMING A HAM
Mild-cured ham is particularly suitable for cooking in this way. Place it in a large steamer or fish kettle on a meat stand, in 5 cm/2 inches of water; allow 40 to 45 minutes per 0.5 kg/lb and 40 minutes over.

BAKING A HAM
First boil it for half the usual time, otherwise the flavour is apt to be strong. Meanwhile, make a soft dough with water and 0.75 kg/1½ lb flour (for a medium-sized ham), flour a board, roll out the dough until it is about 1 cm/½ inch thick and cover the cold part-cooked ham with it; if necessary, divide the ham so as to be able to get it in the oven.

Remove the grid shelves from the oven and see that the dripping pan is in position, then suspend the ham from a hook in the crown plate, if available, or place it on a meat stand in the baking tin. Bake in a fairly hot oven (190°C/375°F, Gas Mark 5) for the rest of the required cooking time. As the ham is covered with paste no basting is required. About 20 minutes before baking is completed, remove the pastry, skin the ham and return it to the oven. When it is cooked, cover with browned crumbs, brush over with glaze and serve it with cider sauce.

As an alternative the ham may be finished in the American way, as follows: While the ham is still hot, score the fat in squares or diamonds, then cover the surface with 175 g/6 oz brown sugar mixed with 50 g/2 oz flour and stud the squares with cloves. Return it to a moderately hot oven (200°C/400°F, Gas Mark 6) until it is golden-brown – 15 minutes.

GRILLED HAM
Slices from the knuckle or butt end are excellent cooked in this way. If the ham is very salt, the slices of meat may be soaked in water for 1 hour before grilling; after soaking, dry with a cloth and cook as described under Grilling.

HAMBURGER OR HAMBURG STEAK
A fried or baked cake of freshly minced and seasoned steak, very popular in the United States. Popularity is also increasing in Great Britain with many hamburger houses and restaurants now open. Hamburgers are usually served inside a soft bap or roll and may have varying garnishes such as cheese, egg, salad ingredients or coleslaw. They are very popular nowadays.

HAMBURGERS

METRIC/IMPERIAL

*0.5 kg/1 lb lean beef, e.g., chuck, shoulder or rump
  steak*
½ onion, skinned and grated, optional
salt
pepper
*melted butter or oil for coating or a little fat for
  shallow frying*

Choose lean meat and have it minced finely by the butcher. Mix well with the onion (if used) and a generous amount of salt and pepper. Shape lightly into 6 to 8 round flat cakes. To cook, brush sparingly with melted butter or oil and grill for 4 to 6 minutes turning once, or fry in a little fat in a frying pan, turning them once and allowing the same amount of time.

Hamburgers can be served rare or well done, according to personal preference, hence the variation in cooking time.

VARIATIONS

Traditionally, hamburgers contain no other ingredients, but they can be varied as follows:
1. Add any of the following when mixing the hamburgers:

METRIC/IMPERIAL

50 g/2 oz to 100 g/4 oz grated cheese
1 × 15 ml spoon/1 tablespoon sweet pickle
1–2 × 5 ml spoons/1–2 teaspoons made mustard
1 × 5 ml spoon/1 teaspoon dried mixed herbs
1 × 15 ml spoon/1 tablespoon chopped parsley
50 g/2 oz mushrooms, sliced

2. Make the hamburgers into thin cakes and wrap each with a rasher of bacon secured with a cocktail stick, then grill gently, turning them frequently.

HAND OF PORK

The fore-leg, which is usually salted and boiled.

HANGING

(See Meat, Poultry and Game entries.)

HARD SAUCE

A sauce served with Christmas and other rich puddings, which is made with butter and caster or brown sugar and flavoured with brandy or rum; as the name suggests, it becomes firm when cold. Ground almonds or stiffly beaten egg white are sometimes added and the sauce is usually sprinkled with grated nutmeg before serving. (See Brandy and Rum Butter entries for recipes.)

HARE

This wild animal resembles the rabbit but is somewhat larger and has flesh which is darker in colour and richer in flavour. Hares in England are in season from early August to the end of February, but are at their best from October onwards. The brown or English hare is usually more succulent and larger than the blue Scottish hare of similar age. A young hare should have small white teeth, smooth coat, claws well hidden by fur and should weigh between 2.75 kg/6 lb to 3 kg/7 lb. These are referred to as leverets. Hares lose about 40 per cent of their weight when dressed. A leveret of about 1.75 kg/4 lb dressed weight will feed four to six people.

Hares should be hung (without paunching) for about a week or longer in cold weather to improve the flavour; suspend them by the hind feet, with a bucket under the nose to catch the blood.

PAUNCHING

With a pair of scissors, snip the skin at the fork and cut it up to the breast-bone, taking care to cut the pelt only. Ease the pelt away from the skin on each side of the stomach. Place the hare on paper and open the paunch by cutting the inside skin in the same direction as the pelt was cut; draw out the entrails and dispose of them. Remove the kidneys and reserve them. Detach the liver, taking care not to puncture the gall bladder; cut out the gallbladder from the liver, keeping it intact, and discard it; cut away also the flesh on which the gallbladder rests, as this may have a bitter flavour. Draw out the lungs and heart and discard the former.

SKINNING

Cut off the feet at the first joint. Loosen the skin round the back legs, then, holding the end of the leg, bend it at the joint; the flesh can then be grasped and the skin pulled off. Do the same with the front legs. Then draw the skin off the head, cutting it through at the ears and the mouth. Cut out the eyes with a sharp knife. Wipe the whole of the body with a clean damp cloth to wipe away any blood or hairs.

JOINTING

First remove the legs. Cut the back into several pieces, giving the back of the knife a sharp tap with a hammer or weight to cut through the bone. Cut off the head and cut the ribs in two lengthwise. The head, split in two, may be included in the stew or casserole, but is not served as a portion.

Some butchers will prepare hares as requested; also they may sell joints of hare so that only the quantity required can be bought. If making Jugged Hare it is important to ask the butcher for the blood.

COOKING

Hare may be jugged, roasted, fricasseed, braised or made into pies and terrines; the best-known dish being jugged hare: hare soup is also very good.

JUGGED HARE

METRIC/IMPERIAL
1 hare
50 g/2 oz bacon, rinded and chopped
25 g/1 oz lard or dripping
1 onion, skinned and stuck with 2 cloves
1 carrot, pared and sliced
1 stick celery, trimmed and sliced
900 ml/1 ½ pints stock
bouquet garni
juice of ½ lemon
3 × 15 ml spoons/3 tablespoons flour
1 × 15 ml spoon/1 tablespoon red-currant jelly
150 ml/¼ pint port or red wine, optional
salt
pepper

Prepare the hare as described, retaining the blood; wipe and joint. Fry the joints with the bacon in the lard until they are lightly browned (about 15 minutes). Transfer to a deep casserole and add the vegetables, enough stock to cover the joints, the bouquet garni and lemon juice. Cover and cook in a moderate oven (160°C/325°F, Gas Mark 3) for 3 to 4 hours, or until tender.

A few minutes before serving, blend the flour with a little cold water to a smooth cream, stir in the blood of the hare and add to the casserole, with the jelly and wine (if used). Adjust seasoning. Reheat without boiling and serve with red-currant jelly, forcemeat balls, game chips and watercress or a green vegetable.

Roast Hare

Very young hares may be roasted whole like rabbits, but more usually the body of the hare alone is used, being known as saddle or baron of hare. Cut off the saddle close to the shoulders, reserving the legs, neck and head for jugging or to turn into a soup. Prepare some forcemeat, place this in the saddle, fold the skin over it and secure it well at the ends. Either lard the flesh of the back or lay slices of fat bacon over it. Cover with greased greaseproof paper, place in a roasting tin with some knobs of dripping and roast in a moderately hot oven (200°C/400°F, Gas Mark 6) for 1 to 1¼ hours, according to size. Baste frequently, as the flesh is very apt to taste dry. Serve with brown gravy.

HARICOT BEAN

(See Bean entry.)

HARICOT MUTTON

A thick meat stew, which originated in France and contained some dried haricot beans, though these are now often omitted. Neck of mutton with the breast attached is generally used for this dish. If it is to be served as an entrée, the cutlets only are used.

HARICOT LAMB

METRIC/IMPERIAL
100 g/4 oz haricot beans
1 kg/2¼ lb best end of neck or breast of lamb in a
  piece
2 × 15 ml spoons/2 tablespoons oil
2 onions, skinned and sliced
1 turnip, pared and sliced
1 × 5 ml spoon/1 teaspoon salt
pepper
1 × 15 ml spoon/1 tablespoon Worcestershire sauce

Soak the beans overnight in cold water. Cut the meat into serving-size pieces, trimming off any excess fat, and fry it in the hot oil for 2 to 3 minutes, until browned. Add the onions and turnip and fry for a further 2 to 3 minutes. Pour on just sufficient boiling water to cover the meat. Add the drained beans, salt and pepper, cover with a lid and simmer for 2 to 2½ hours, or cook in a moderate oven (160°C/325°F, Gas Mark 3) for 2½ to 3 hours. Stir in the Worcestershire sauce just before serving.

HASH

A dish of diced cooked meat re-heated in a highly flavoured sauce. Hash provides a good way of serving the last of a joint (the bones can be used to make stock as a basis for the sauce). It can be served with a border of creamed potatoes or savoury rice.

CORNED BEEF HASH

(See Corned Beef entry.)

HASLET

(See Pig's Fry entry.)

HASTY PUDDING

A very simple pudding, made by boiling milk, sprinkling in sufficient tapioca, sago, semolina or even flour to thicken it and stirring briskly. Sugar is added to taste and when thick the pudding is served hot with sugar, jam or treacle.

HAY BOX COOKERY

At one time this was quite a popular method, as it enabled food to be cooked slowly without requiring constant attention. A large wooden box was well padded with clean hay, in which were made two or three holes to fit saucepans. The food must first be brought to boiling point before being placed in the box and it needs to be reheated before it can be served, so very little fuel is actually saved. The hay box is very rarely used nowadays, except perhaps in makeshift versions for cooking porridge in camp and so on. A slow cooker is the modern way of leaving food to cook slowly. (See separate entry.)

HAZEL HEN

A game bird that used to be imported into this country in a chilled or frozen state, mainly from Scandinavia and Russia. The birds have white tender flesh of excellent flavour and are best roasted or prepared as for grouse.

HAZELNUT

The hazel tree is found all over Europe, but the best nuts come from Southern Europe, particularly Spain. Cultivated varieties include the Filbert, Cob and Barcelona. Hazelnuts are used in cooking for flavouring and decorating cakes, biscuits and desserts, etc.

HEAD

Heads contain a large amount of well-flavoured meat, the tongues and brains being especially good. The other meat can be removed and made into excellent pies, scalloped dishes, brawn, etc.

BOILED CALF'S HEAD WITH BRAIN SAUCE

METRIC/IMPERIAL
1 calf's head
2 carrots
2 stalks of celery
1 turnip
salt
pepper
12 peppercorns
a little mixed dried herbs
40 g/1 ½ oz butter
40 g/1 ½ oz plain flour
300 ml/½ pint milk
300 ml/½ pint calf's head stock
2 × 5 ml spoons/2 teaspoons chopped parsley
1 lemon
a little sherry

Remove the brains and wash the head thoroughly, paying particular attention to nostrils and ears. Soak it in cold water for 2 hours, dry and rub over with a cut lemon to whiten it. Cover the cleaned head with cold water, bring to the boil and skim. Add the chopped vegetables, seasonings and herbs and simmer for 2 hours.

Meanwhile prepare the brains (see separate entry). An hour before the head is ready, put them in a muslin bag and boil them with the head; remove the brains after 30 minutes boiling time and leave to cool.

While the head continues to simmer, make a sauce as follows: Melt the butter in a separate pan, add the flour and cook for two minutes, then add the milk, with 300 ml/ ½ pint of liquor from the head, stir together until boiling and simmer for 10 minutes. Chop the brains finely and add them to the sauce, with the chopped parsley, lemon juice, seasoning and sherry. Dish up the head as it comes from the stewpan and serve the brain sauce separately.

To serve, cut off all the meat, arrange it on a hot dish, coat with brain sauce and garnish with the sliced skinned tongue and with bacon rolls; sprinkle with grated lemon rind and chopped parsley.

Sheep's heads may be cooked in the same way.

HEART

Though somewhat neglected nowadays, hearts can be used to make a variety of economical and savoury dishes.

Bullock or ox heart is the largest and tends to be rather tough unless cooked long and slowly. It can be par-boiled whole and then roasted, or cut up and braised or used in stews, but in any case it needs strong seasonings and flavourings. When cooked whole, ox heart is often stuffed with a savoury forcemeat.

An ox heart may weigh about 1.5 kg/3 lb to 2 kg/4 lb and is enough for 4 to 6 people. It can also be bought sliced, for use in stews, casseroles and similar dishes.

Calf's heart is small and more tender, but still needs slow cooking to make it enjoyable. It may be roasted, braised or stewed.

One calf's heart will serve 2 people.

Lamb's heart: The smallest kind, one of which serves only 1 person. More tender than calf's or ox heart, it has a finer flavour and is usually stuffed and either roasted or braised.

STUFFED HEART CASSEROLE

METRIC/IMPERIAL
4 small lambs' hearts
100 g/4 oz fresh white breadcrumbs
1 medium sized onion, skinned and finely chopped
3 × 15 ml spoons/3 tablespoons melted butter
2 × 5 ml spoons/2 teaspoons dried mixed herbs
salt
pepper
2 × 15 ml spoons/2 tablespoons seasoned flour
25 g/1 oz fat or oil
600 ml/1 pint stock
1 onion, skinned and sliced
4 sticks of celery, trimmed and sliced
100 g/4 oz carrots, pared and sliced
1 × 15 ml spoon/1 tablespoon cider, optional

199

Wash the hearts, slit open, remove any tubes or gristle and wash again under cold, running water. Fill with a stuffing made from the breadcrumbs, onion, melted butter, mixed herbs and seasonings. Tie the hearts firmly into the original shape with string, coat with seasoned flour and brown quickly in the hot fat or oil. Place in a casserole with the stock, cover and bake in a moderate oven (160°C/325°F, Gas Mark 3) for 2½ hours, turning them frequently. Add the onion, celery, carrots and cider (if used) for the last 45 minutes of the cooking time.

RICH CASSEROLED HEART

METRIC/IMPERIAL
1 ox heart, weighing 1 kg/2¼ lb to 1.5 kg/3 lb
3 × 15 ml spoons/3 tablespoons oil
2 onions, skinned and sliced
3 × 15 ml spoons/3 tablespoons flour
300 ml/½ pint stock
salt
pepper
225 g/8 oz carrots, pared and grated
½ small swede, peeled and grated
rind of 1 orange
6 walnuts, chopped

Cut the heart into 1 cm/½ inch slices, removing the tubes, and wash it well. Fry the slices of meat in the oil till slightly browned and put into a casserole. Fry the onions and add to the casserole. Add the flour to the remaining fat and brown slightly. Pour in the stock, bring to the boil and simmer for 2 to 3 minutes, then strain over the slices of heart in the casserole; cover and cook for 3½ to 4 hours in a cool oven (150°C/300°F, Gas Mark 2) adding the carrots and swede after 2½ to 3 hours. Pare the rind from the orange, shred it finely, cook in boiling water for 10 to 15 minutes, then drain. Add the walnuts and orange rind to the casserole 15 minutes before the cooking is completed. Alternatively, replace the orange rind and walnuts by a 225 g/8 oz can tomatoes (chopped up).

HERBS

The addition of suitable herbs so greatly improves the flavour of soups, stews and other savoury dishes that a supply should be available in every kitchen. If it is not possible to have a small herb garden, flowerpots and window boxes can often be used to grow herbs.

Fresh herbs are superior to dried in cooking although dried herbs have a stronger flavour. It is therefore important to be more generous with fresh herbs. Fresh herbs can successfully be frozen.

Herbs are best used fresh, but can be dried for the winter months; a wide variety can·be bought ready dried. It is advisable to store each kind sep-arately, and useful to have also a jar of mixed herbs. The following are the most commonly used: (See individual entries.)

Balm	Fennel	Oregano
Basil	Garlic	Parsley
Bay	Horseradish	Rosemary
Borage	Lemon Thyme	Sage
Celery seeds	Lovage	Savory
Chervil	Marjoram	Sorrel
Chives	Mint	Tarragon
Dill	Nasturtium	Thyme

MIXED HERBS
Usually a mixture of equal quantities of parsley, chives, tarragon or chervil and thyme.

BUNCH OF HERBS OR BOUQUET GARNI
A bunch of herbs, including a sprig of parsley, thyme and marjoram and a bay leaf, is used for flavouring stews, etc. Fresh herbs should be tied together, dried ones tied in a muslin bag, so that they can be easily removed when serving.

TO DRY HERBS
Pick the herbs on a dry day shortly before they flower. Wash them and pick off any damaged leaves. Dry the herbs by hanging in the sun or by placing in a cool oven or in a warm airing cupboard. When the herbs are ready the leaves will crumble easily. Parsley and mint will keep green if dipped in boiling water for a minute and then dried fairly quickly. Crumble the leaves, put in jars and store in a cool, dry, dark place. Alternatively, tie them in bunches with a paper bag fastened over the leaves. Approximately 1 × 5 ml spoon/1 teaspoon dried equals 3 × 5 ml spoons/3 teaspoons fresh.

HERB VINEGAR
Using young, fresh, dry herbs (e.g., mint, tarragon), fill a jar three-quarters full, fill up with warm vinegar, put on the lid and leave for 3 weeks, shaking at intervals. Strain and bottle the vinegar. Store in a cool dark place.

HERB BUTTER
Fresh herbs such as chopped parsley, thyme, tarragon and chives can be added to creamed butter and used as a savoury sandwich spread, or, with the addition of lemon juice, as a sauce for fish or meat (see Maître d'Hôtel).

HERRING

A small, oily fish, caught in large quantities round the shores of Britain and in many other parts. Herrings are obtainable all the year round, but are at their best from June to December; when fresh, they are firm to the touch and covered with silvery scales. In America and Canada young herrings are frequently canned under the name of sardines.

The herring is economical and a good source of

first-class protein; it also contains nicotinic acid, vitamin A and some D, calcium and phosphorus. Fluorine, iodine, riboflavin and Vitamin B1 are present in small amounts.

Herrings can be served at any meal of the day and pickled herrings make appetizing savouries. The full flavour of the fish is best obtained when it is fried or grilled; grilled tomatoes and mustard sauce make good accompaniments. Herring roes have a delicate flavour and the soft ones make a delicious savoury.

The fish may be preserved as bloaters, kippers, red herrings, salt herrings, rollmops and Bismark herrings. (See individual entries.)

To prepare herrings, remove the head and entrails, which usually come away with it – if not they should be removed separately. Remove any black skin by rubbing with salt and wash the fish well. Scrape off the scales and trim off fins and tail with scissors. Score on each side, if the fish are to be grilled or fried whole.

HERRINGS FRIED IN OATMEAL

Prepare and bone the herrings, then sprinkle them with pepper and salt; dip each fish into coarse oatmeal, pressing it on to both sides. Fry the herrings on both sides in hot fat until a light golden colour, drain well and serve garnished with lemon wedges and parsley.

GRILLED HERRINGS

Score the skin across diagonally two or three times on each side, season the fish with pepper and salt and let them lie for a short time before cooking. Grill in the usual way, lowering the heat if the fish are large and thick, and cook for 7 to 10 minutes. Mustard sauce is a good accompaniment.

Alternatively, open and bone the herrings and arrange flesh side upwards on the grill rack. Cover with a few knobs of dripping or butter and cook till the fat melts. Sprinkle a few breadcrumbs or raspings over and replace the fish under the grill till they are brown and cooked. Serve with tomato or mustard sauce and garnish with parsley or watercress and lemon.

SOUSED HERRINGS

METRIC/IMPERIAL
4 large or 6–8 small herrings, cleaned and boned
salt
pepper
1 small onion, skinned and sliced into rings
6 peppercorns
1–2 bay leaves
few parsley stalks
150 ml/¼ pint malt vinegar
150 ml/¼ pint water

Trim off the heads, tails and fins, remove the bones and sprinkle the fish with salt and pepper. Roll up from the head end and secure with wooden cocktail sticks. Pack them into a fairly shallow oven-proof dish and add the onion, peppercorns and herbs. Pour in the vinegar and enough water to almost cover the fish. Cover with greaseproof paper or foil and bake in a moderate oven (180°C/350°F, Gas Mark 4) for about 45 minutes, or until tender. Leave the herrings to cool in the cooking liquid before serving as an appetizer or with salad. To serve as an appetizer, cut each herring into bite-sized pieces and secure on cocktail sticks. Alternatively, serve them whole or halved on slices of rye bread with a garnish of onion and green pepper rings.

Note: If you wish, the tails can be left on the fish; when the rolled fish are put in the dish, the tails are arranged pointing upwards. Herrings can also be soused whole.

HICKORY NUT

A type of walnut grown in North America, the best known being the pecan nut. (See separate entry.)

HIPPOCRAS

A mediaeval drink, heavily sweetened with honey and flavoured with herbs and spices. It is likely that soured wine was used up in this way.

HIPS, ROSE

(See Rose Hip entry.)

HOCK

The name given to white wines from the Rhine Palatinate and other parts of Germany. The original name, Hochheimer, was given to the wine made in the vineyards close to the town of Hochheim and this region still produces the best Hock, which is sold under a number of well-known names, e.g., Johannisberger, Steinberger, Liebfraumilch, Marcobrunner, Hochheimer.

A traditional Hock or Rhine wine glass is tall with a stout knobbled stem of brown or green glass which is intended to reflect the colour of the wine. All classic German wines are contained in slim-necked bottles, brown for Rhine wine and green for Moselle.

Hock is served with white fish, white meats and sweets, while the sparkling variety is used in place of champagne. It is also a good wine for making a cold refreshing cup to serve at buffet parties, etc.

The term also applies to meat taken from just above the foot of a pig, bullock or sheep.

HOCK CUP

METRIC/IMPERIAL
ice
1 bottle of hock
1 wineglass of brandy
1 × 15 ml spoon/1 tablespoon Curaçao
a few slices of lemon, orange and cucumber
a sprig of borage
300 ml/½ pint soda water

Place the ice in a jug. Add the hock, brandy, Curaçao, fruit, cucumber and borage and leave for about 20 minutes, then add the iced soda water, stir well and serve.

HOG PUDDING

A kind of sausage made of pork.

HOLLANDAISE SAUCE

A rich sauce made of egg yolks, butter and lemon juice and served with fish, asparagus, globe artichokes, or eggs.

HOLLANDAISE SAUCE

METRIC/IMPERIAL
2 × 15 ml spoons/2 tablespoons wine or tarragon
  vinegar
1 × 15 ml spoon/1 tablespoon water
2 egg yolks
75 g/3 oz to 100 g/4 oz butter
salt
pepper

Put the vinegar and water in a small pan and boil until reduced to about 1 × 15 ml spoon/1 tablespoon; cool slightly. Put the egg yolks in a basin and stir in the vinegar. Put over a pan of hot water and heat gently, stirring all the time, until the egg mixture thickens (never let the water go above simmering point). Divide the butter into small pieces and gradually whisk into the sauce; add seasoning to taste. If the sauce is too sharp add a little more butter – it should be slightly piquant, almost thick enough to hold its shape and warm rather than hot when served.

MOCK HOLLANDAISE SAUCE

METRIC/IMPERIAL
2 egg yolks
2 × 15 ml spoons/2 tablespoons cream
300 ml/½ pint Béchamel sauce
a little lemon juice or vinegar

Beat together the egg yolks and cream and add to the Béchamel sauce. Heat carefully in a double saucepan to cook the eggs, but do not allow it to boil. Add a very little lemon juice or vinegar drop by drop, to give a slightly sharp taste to the sauce.

Hollandaise Cream Soup
(See Soup entry.)

HOLLANDS

A type of gin distilled in Holland and highly prized by the Dutch. It is made from barley, malt, rye and juniper berries. The best-known type is Schnapps.

HOMINY

An American cereal, made from maize, which is split and coarsely ground after the hulls and germs have been removed. There are several different kinds – pearl lye, granulated and grits. Hominy may be served instead of oatmeal porridge for breakfast, but as it is coarsely ground it requires a long time to cook.

HONEY

This natural liquid sugar is prepared by bees from the flower nectar which they collect; the honey acquires the flavour of the flower predominantly used in its production, so that heather honey, for instance, has a different taste from that of garden flower honey.

Bees make from 9 kg/20 lb to 25 kg/50 lb of honey per year per hive, according to the size of the hive and the food available. They secrete an enzyme by which they convert the nectar sucrose they collect into invert sugar (dextrose and levulose), which represents 70 to 80 per cent of the total weight of the honey; water accounts for about 15 to 25 per cent and there is up to 8 per cent of unchanged sucrose. Honey is a good source of energy but has no other food value.

Natural honey is sold in various states:

In the honeycomb: The comb from a virgin hive (a hive from which the bees have not swarmed) is the whitest and best. It should be served by cutting or scooping horizontally, not vertically, as this keeps the honey from running out of the comb. Store in a warm, dry place and handle by the wooden casing.

Clear honey, which is extracted by hanging up the combs (after damaging the cells) and allowing the honey to drip out; it is then strained and bottled. Clear honey varies in viscosity, flavour and colour. The viscosity depends on the manner in which the honey is collected and extracted and the flavour on the flowers the bees have visited; these also affect the colour and it is generally considered that the light-coloured honey is better than the dark. Heather honey is light golden in colour and rather thick, with a bitter taste; clover honey is a clear greenish yellow and thin; mountain honey is the best type and has an exquisite flavour; it varies in colour though it is usually whitish.

Clear honey should be stored in a warm, dry place, otherwise it crystallizes out and this spoils the flavour. If it does crystallize, gentle warming will liquefy it.

Solid (thick) honey: This is merely clear honey which has solidified. The flavour is not generally considered so good as that of clear honey, but the texture is often preferred.

Use of Honey

Though honey is principally served as a preserve, which enables its full flavour to be appreciated, it has many other uses, especially in the preparation of sweets such as nougat. It can be substituted for sugar in the making of puddings, sweets and cakes, but a larger quantity of honey than sugar and less liquid will be required; thus 1 cup of honey will replace ¾ cup of sugar and ¼ cup of liquid. The texture of some mixtures (e.g., cakes made by the creaming method) is adversely affected if honey alone is used instead of sugar, but even in these a proportion of about 25 per cent can be used successfully. Clear honey is better for these mixtures. Honey also gives a delicious flavour to stewed fruit and hot drinks.

HONEY TEABREAD

METRIC/IMPERIAL
50 g/2 oz butter or block margarine
150 g/5 oz honey
150 g/5 oz demerara sugar
275 g/10 oz plain flour
pinch of salt
1 × 5 ml spoon/1 teaspoon bicarbonate of soda
1 × 5 ml spoon/1 teaspoon baking powder
1 × 5 ml spoon/1 teaspoon ground mixed spice
1 × 5 ml spoon/1 teaspoon ground ginger
1 × 5 ml spoon/1 teaspoon powdered cinnamon
50 g/2 oz to 100 g/4 oz finely chopped mixed peel
1 egg
150 ml/¼ pint milk
flaked almonds to decorate

Grease and line a loaf tin with 21 × 10 cm/ 8½ × 4 inch top measurements. Gently melt the fat in a pan. Remove from heat, stir in honey and sugar. Leave to cool. Sift flour, salt, raising agents and spices into a bowl. Add the chopped peel. Beat egg and milk together and mix thoroughly with the cooled honey mixture. Pour into the sifted flour, etc., and beat until smooth, Pour the mixture into the prepared tin and scatter flaked almonds over it. Bake in a moderate oven (180°C/350°F, Gas Mark 4) for 1¼ hours until well risen and firm.

Turn out the teabread and leave to cool on a wire rack. Keep for 24 hours before serving cut into slices and buttered.

HONEYCOMB MOULD

A light sweet consisting of an egg jelly with whisked egg white folded in. As it sets, it separates into a jelly layer and above this a fluffy-looking layer with a honey-comb appearance – hence the name.

HONEYCOMB MOULD

METRIC/IMPERIAL
2 large eggs, separated
600 ml/1 pint milk
3 × 15 ml spoons/3 tablespoons sugar
few drops vanilla essence
4 × 5 ml spoons/4 teaspoons powdered gelatine
2 × 15 ml spoons/2 tablespoons water

Make a custard with the egg yolks, milk and sugar and flavour with vanilla then leave to cool. Dissolve the gelatine in the water and add it to the custard. Whisk the egg whites very stiffly and fold lightly into the cool custard mixture. Pour into a glass dish or mould put in a cool place and turn out when set. Serve with chocolate sauce or with stewed fruit (or jam) and cream.

HONEYDEW MELON

(See Melon entry.)

HOPS

The ripened catkins or flowers of a climbing vine, the hop plant, which are used to impart a bitter flavour to beer. The tender shoots are eaten as a vegetable in France and Belgium.

HORS D'OEUVRE

Small cold or hot snacks served as an appetizer at the beginning of a meal. In some countries they are served in a different room, accompanied by wine or cocktails, but in this country the dishes are usually placed in the centre of the table or on a trolley or tray which is passed round. In the summer, a large hors d'œuvre makes a popular main course for a light meal. Hors d'œuvre should stimulate the appetite by their appearance as well as by their taste and seasoning.

There are two chief types of hors d'œuvre: (1) Single dishes (whether hot or cold), served by themselves; (2) Hors d'œuvre variés or mixed hors d'œuvre.

Single Hors d'œuvre

These are set at each place on individual plates. Their method of preparation will be found under their own names, but here is a brief list of such hors d'œuvre, with the usual accompaniments, if any: Stuffed olives, shrimps with dry toast and butter;

203

fillets of herring and mackerel; tunny fish; smoked salmon with lemon and brown bread and butter; oysters with brown bread and butter; caviare with lemon and freshly made toast and butter; sausages and cooked meats of various kinds, English and continental; pâtés of various types (sliced) with melba toast and butter; foie gras; grapefruit with cherry and sugar; iced melon with sugar and ground ginger; tomato juice with Worcestershire sauce or lemon juice and seasoning.

Hors d'œuvre Variés

Special dishes divided into sections are made for serving mixed hors d'œuvre. Small separate dishes can also be arranged on tray or trolley, or the hors d'œuvre may be set on a large platter, with the items separated by a garnish of small cress, watercress or parsley. The individual dishes (there should be at least four) can be chosen from meat, poultry, game, fish, eggs, cheese, nuts, vegetables, fruits. Cereals should be used with caution, as they are rather substantial, but a little savoury rice may be included. Serve hors d'œuvre very cold, accompanied by crisp rolls and butter, toast and butter or brown bread and butter.

The following is a list of suitable ingredients for mixed hors d'œuvre; unless otherwise stated, salad vegetables, etc., should be tossed in French or other dressing before being served.

Salad and Other Vegetables

LETTUCE
Crisp hearts or shredded leaves.

ENDIVE
Shredded, or torn into small pieces.

CHICORY
Sliced.

RADISHES
Left whole or cut into fancy shapes, or sliced, tossed in French dressing and sprinkled with chopped parsley.

CUCUMBER
Peeled, thinly sliced and laid in vinegar; or cut into small dice; or scooped out to form boats and filled with prawns in mayonnaise garnished with pineapple.

TOMATOES
Peeled, sliced, dressed and garnished with chopped parsley or onion or mixed with fine green beans and vinaigrette.

MUSHROOM CAPS
Fried and stuffed with a mixture of the chopped stalks, onion and bacon fried and mixed with breadcrumbs.

SPRING ONIONS
Left whole, cut into a uniform length, or sliced and tossed in dressing.

BEETROOT
Sliced or diced, sprinkled with finely chopped onion or chives.

CELERY
Usually sliced, tossed in dressing and garnished with chopped parsley. Alternatively, the celery stalks may be cut into short lengths and stuffed with cream cheese or other savoury filling. Cooked celery is sometimes served, sliced and dressed as above.

RED OR GREEN PEPPERS
Shredded or chopped and mixed with dressing or tomato ketchup.

POTATO
Cooked and sliced or diced, coated with mayonnaise and garnished with chopped parsley or chopped chives.

PEAS, FRENCH AND RUNNER BEANS
Cooked and tossed in dressing, or included in mixed vegetable mayonnaise.

ASPARAGUS TIPS
Cooked and dressed with vinaigrette dressing, or wrapped in smoked salmon.

CARROTS, TURNIPS AND ARTICHOKES
Cooked and diced, these are included in Russian salad or may be used alone in mixed hors d'œuvre. They are usually tossed in mayonnaise, but a simple dressing may be used if preferred.

CABBAGE
Shredded raw cabbage (possibly with caraway seeds) tossed in dressing, or pickled red cabbage served in its own liquor.

OLIVES
Whole, or stoned and stuffed. Chopped olives are sometimes mixed with other hors d'œuvres such as Russian salad, to give piquancy.

PICKLES
Pickled gherkins, mixed pickles, piccalilli, etc., served in their own liquor.

MUSTARD AND CRESS, WATERCRESS, PARSLEY
Used as garnishes.

HERBS
Chopped chives, tarragon, parsley or mint, etc., may be used to mix with, or sprinkle over, the hors d'œuvre.

Fish

SALTED AND PICKLED FISH, SUCH AS SARDINES, ANCHOVY FILLETS, ROLLMOPS, SOUSED HERRINGS AND SO ON
Usually served in their own liquor or with a simple dressing.

SHELLFISH

Shrimps, prawns, mussels, lobster, crab or crayfish – usually served dressed with mayonnaise dressing.

Other fish include: cold salmon, dressed with mayonnaise; cold smoked haddock with a creamy cheese sauce or mayonnaise, etc. White fish may be used, but the dressing should include a piquant ingredient such as capers or chopped pickled gherkins, or a dressing such as tartare sauce.

Meats

Cold cooked sausage; liver, breakfast or luncheon sausage, salami, garlic sausage and various other Continental types; usually served sliced and do not require dressing.

Cold cooked meats, such as roast beef, ham or tongue, chicken, game, etc.; usually cut up neatly and sometimes soaked in a marinade of oil and vinegar, with chopped parsley and perhaps chopped onion or chives.

Eggs

Hard-boiled eggs, sliced neatly, coated with mayonnaise and garnished with paprika or capers.

Pulses, Cereals, Pasta

Haricot Beans: cooked, mixed with tomato sauce or ketchup and garnished with chopped parsley or chopped chives.

Rice: dry boiled rice, mixed with chopped raisins with curry-flavoured dressing.

Macaroni: cooked, cut into short lengths, mixed with chopped ham and moistened with salad cream.

HORSEFLESH

This meat is not used for human consumption in the British Isles, although in many parts of Europe there is no prejudice against it and it is quite extensively eaten. In this country horseflesh serves as a valuable feeding stuff for domestic animals.

HORSERADISH

A plant with a pungent, acrid root, used as a condiment. The root is grated and made into a cream or sauce for serving with roast beef and some other meat entrées, and for adding to sandwiches.

HORSERADISH CREAM

METRIC/IMPERIAL
2 × 15 ml spoons/2 tablespoons grated fresh
  horseradish
2 × 5 ml spoons/2 teaspoons lemon juice
2 × 5 ml spoons/2 teaspoons sugar
pinch of dry mustard, optional
150 ml/¼ pint double cream

Mix the horseradish, lemon juice, sugar and mustard. Whip the cream until it just leaves a trail, then fold in the horseradish mixture.

Serve with beef, trout or mackerel. Horseradish cream may also be added to sandwich fillings to add a piquant flavour.

HORSE'S NECK

A long drink. Put 2 to 3 pieces of broken ice in a tall glass, fill up with ginger ale and hang a long curl of lemon peel over the side of the glass. A 'stiff Horse's Neck' is made by adding a dash of Angostura bitters and 75 ml/⅛ pint spirits.

HOT-CROSS BUN

A yeast bun traditionally eaten on Good Friday and around Easter time. The buns are flavoured with spice and as the name implies have a cross on top, which is made in one of the following ways: (1) by cutting the buns with a knife before putting them to prove; (2) by marking a cross with trimmings of pastry; (3) by forming a cross with candied peel.

HOT CROSS BUNS

METRIC/IMPERIAL
450 g/1 lb strong plain flour
25 g/1 oz fresh yeast
150 ml/¼ pint tepid milk
4 × 15 ml spoons/4 tablespoons tepid water
pinch of salt
1 × 2.5 ml spoon/½ teaspoon mixed spice
1 × 2.5 ml spoon/½ teaspoon powdered cinnamon
1 × 2.5 ml spoon/½ teaspoon grated nutmeg
50 g/2 oz caster sugar
50 g/2 oz butter, melted and cooled, but not firm
1 egg, beaten
100 g/4 oz currants
2–3 × 15 ml spoons/2–3 tablespoons chopped mixed
  peel
50 g/2 oz shortcrust pastry

FOR THE GLAZE
4 × 15 ml spoons/4 tablespoons milk and water
3 × 15 ml spoons/3 tablespoons caster sugar

Flour a baking sheet. Put 100 g/4 oz of the flour in a large mixing bowl. Crumble the yeast into a mixing bowl. Pour over the liquid, stir until dissolved. Add to the flour and mix well. Set aside in a warm place until frothy – about 15 to 20 minutes. Sift together the remaining 350 g/12 oz flour, salt, spices and sugar. Stir the butter and egg into the frothy yeast mixture, add the spiced flour and the fruit, and mix together. The dough should be fairly soft. Turn it out on to a slightly floured surface and knead until smooth. Place in a bowl and cover with oiled polythene. Leave to rise until doubled in size.

Turn the risen dough out on to a floured working surface and knead to knock out the air bubbles. Divide the dough into twelve pieces and shape into buns using the palm of one hand. Press down hard at first on the table surface, then ease up as you turn and shape the buns. Arrange them well apart on the floured baking sheet, and prove until doubled in size. Roll out the pastry thinly on a floured surface and cut into thin strips about 8.5 cm/ 3½ inch long. Damp the pastry strips and lay two on each bun to make a cross. Bake in a moderately hot oven (190°C/375°F, Gas Mark 5) for 15 to 20 minutes, until golden brown and firm to the touch. Meanwhile, heat the milk and water and sugar gently together. Brush the hot buns twice with glaze, then cool on a wire rack.

HOT DOG

METRIC/IMPERIAL
thin pork sausages or frankfurters
fat for frying
finger bread rolls
butter
mustard

Prick the pork sausages and fry them in the hot fat. Meanwhile heat some bread rolls and cut them half-way through; spread with butter and made mustard, insert a hot sausage in each and serve at once, with a paper napkin to hold them.
Frankfurters should be boiled for a few minutes, instead of being fried. A little tomato ketchup and chopped well-fried onion can be included.

HOT-POT

A baked stew or casserole dish made with meat or fish and finished on top with a layer of sliced potatoes. (To give these an attractive browned finish, the casserole lid is removed about 20 minutes before cooking is completed.)

LANCASHIRE HOT-POT

METRIC/IMPERIAL
8 middle neck chops
225 g/8 oz onions, skinned and sliced
2 lamb's kidneys, skinned and diced, optional
0.5 kg/1 lb potatoes, peeled and sliced
salt
pepper
300 ml/½ pint stock
25 g/1 oz lard or dripping

Remove any excess fat from the chops and put them in a casserole. Add the onions, the kidneys (if used) and lastly the potato; season well. Pour on the stock and brush the top of the potato with the melted lard or dripping. Cover and cook in a mod-erate oven (160°C/325°F, Gas Mark 3) for 2 hours, or until the meat and potatoes are tender. Remove the lid and brown the top layer of potatoes in a hot oven (220°C/425°F, Gas Mark 7) for 20 minutes.

Note: Some people prefer to use chunky pieces of potato for the topping instead of the slices suggested in this recipe.
Lancashire hot-pot is traditionally made containing oysters. Allow 1 shelled oyster to each lamb chop, putting the oysters on top of the chops in the casserole.

HOT-WATER CRUST

A type of pastry made by melting lard in boiling water and pouring the mixture onto the flour. It is kneaded to a dough and used for 'rasied pies'. The pastry is placed in a special mould, or moulded around a suitable container before being filled with veal, ham or a pork filling to make a traditional hot-water crust pastry pie.

HOTCH-POTCH

A thick soup or stew made of meat and vegetables.

HOWTOWDIE

A Scottish dish consisting of boiled chicken with poached eggs and spinach.

HUCKLEBERRY

A fruit found in most parts of the USA. It resembles the blueberry – in fact, in some parts blueberries go by this name. Huckleberries are used for pies, preserves and ice creams.

HUMBUG

A cushion-shaped boiled sweet, hard in texture and usually flavoured with peppermint, though other flavours may be used if preferred.
(See Sweets entry for recipe.)

HYDROMEL

A drink of honey and water, flavoured with herbs and spices to taste; when fermented, it becomes mead.

HYSSOP

A plant of the mint family with dark green leaves and deep blue flowers. Its pungent, aromatic leaves may be used in salads and soups. Honey made from hyssop flowers is said to be particularly good. The oil distilled from the leaves is used in liqueurs.

ICE

The chief domestic uses of ice are to keep food fresh; to chill food or drinks (which can either be stood on a block of ice or have chips or cubes of ice added to them); and to form a garnish to a dish or a table decoration.

Blocks of ice may be obtained from special suppliers or from fishmongers, though it is, of course, essential to obtain it from a clean and reliable source.

To retard the melting of a large block of ice, when there is no refrigerator available, wrap it in greaseproof paper, then in newspaper and finally in an old blanket or piece of flannel. An ice pick (if available) should be used to break it up; a pair of ice tongs or large sugar tongs is useful to handle small pieces.

Small blocks or cubes of ice can usually be made in the special ice-freezing compartment of a domestic refrigerator.

Ice made in the refrigerator may be tinted and flavoured before freezing, to give fancy cubes which look attractive in cold drinks. Decorated ice cubes for garnishing dishes or cocktails may be made by setting small well-washed flowers or petals, cherries, pieces of angelica, etc., in the ice-tray divisions before the water is added. To make a larger block to float on a bowl of punch, remove the divisions from the ice tray, place the decorations in position and pour in the water slowly and carefully.

ICE CREAM

This term covers a great variety of frozen sweets made with a foundation of rich milk, cream or evaporated milk and flavoured with fruit juice, etc. (A water ice – see separate entry – has a foundation of sugar and water syrup to which fruit juice or purée is added.) Delicious composite ices, iced puddings, sundaes and parfaits can be made from ice cream combined with whipped cream, fruit, fruit syrup, nuts and so on.

Various brands of commercially made ice cream

are available and strict hygiene regulations govern their manufacture. Legislation also strictly governs composition, labelling and advertising. New EEC regulations now control the names given to various types of ice cream. They are obtainable in a number of different flavours and also as Neapolitan blocks.

Making Ice Cream

Ice cream can be made with a cream or custard base; for both, the best results are obtained with rapid freezing and maximum agitation during the making process.

Electric or battery operated ice cream makers are available, and are useful if ice cream is made frequently. They usually give good results as the agitation is more thorough.

Although the best and smoothest-textured ice creams are made by means of a special freezer, quite satisfactory ices can be obtained by freezing a suitable mixture in a refrigerator. If the freezing compartment will accommodate only the ice trays, the ice cream must be made in these; if a larger space is available, iced puddings can also be moulded in suitable dishes, after the mixture has been semi-frozen.

IN A REFRIGERATOR

Set the dial at 'maximum' or 'coldest' about an hour or so before the mixture is prepared. Prepare the mixture, place it in ice trays and put the trays back into the refrigerator inside the freezing compartment. Large crystals or flakes of ice are apt to form when the ice cream is made under home conditions. This can be partly counteracted if the mixture is stirred at intervals of 10 to 20 minutes until it is half-frozen, then left undisturbed until it is sufficiently stiff; alternatively – and this is the better method – allow it to semi-freeze, remove the mixture to a cool bowl, whisk it thoroughly with a rotary or electric whisk, replace it in the freezing compartment in the trays and leave it for 1 to 4 hours, until frozen hard. (The time required for freezing varies greatly, according to the refrigerator and the mixture used.)

IN A PAIL FREEZER

First pack the bucket two-thirds full with ice (broken in small pieces or chipped), then use ice and coarse freezing salt in layers, in the proportion of 6 parts ice to 1 part salt or 4 parts ice to 1 part salt for quicker freezing), continuing until the cylinder is completely surrounded.

Fill the cylinder three-quarters full with ice cream mixture, insert the paddles and fix the lid and crank in position. Turn the handle of the crank slowly for the first 5 to 8 minutes, and when the mixture begins to freeze, i.e., to stiffen, turn more rapidly until it is of a mushy consistency – 15 minutes or more, according to the quantity. Then stop turning, remove the beaters and with a spoon collect the ice cream together, scraping it down from the sides of the cylinder. At this point, it can be moulded and the freezing completed by placing it in the cold compartment of a refrigerator; for a simple ice, the mixture is left in the freezer to 'ripen' for 1 to 2 hours without further agitation and it is then ready to serve. The bucket should be covered with a sack or old blanket and stood in a cool place during this time. If much of the ice has melted, refill the bucket before leaving the mixture to ripen.

RICH VANILLA ICE CREAM

METRIC/IMPERIAL
150 ml/¼ pint milk
3 × 15 ml spoons/3 tablespoons sugar
1 egg, beaten
0.5–1 × 5 ml spoon/½–1 teaspoon vanilla essence
1 × 150 ml/¼ pint carton double cream, half-whipped

Heat the milk and sugar and pour on to the egg, stirring. Return the mixture to the saucepan and cook it over a gentle heat, stirring all the time until the custard thickens; strain it and add the vanilla essence. Allow to cool, fold in the half-whipped cream, pour into a freezing container and freeze.

CHOCOLATE ICE CREAM
Add 6 × 15 ml spoons/6 tablespoons grated plain chocolate, melted.

COFFEE ICE CREAM
Add 2 × 5 ml spoons/2 teaspoons instant coffee, dissolved in 1 × 5 ml spoon/1 teaspoon hot water.

BANANA ICE CREAM
Add 2 small bananas, mashed or puréed.

GINGER ICE CREAM
Add 3 × 15 ml spoons/3 tablespoons chopped preserved ginger, and 1 × 15 ml spoon/1 tablespoon ginger syrup.

CHOCOLATE CHIP ICE CREAM
Add 100 g/4 oz chocolate chips or grated chocolate with up to 1 × 15 ml spoon/1 tablespoon orange juice or liqueur.

ORANGE ICE CREAM

METRIC/IMPERIAL
1 × 300 ml/½ pint carton double or whipping cream
300 ml/½ pint orange juice
caster sugar
segments of mandarin orange
wafers

Whip the cream until it holds its shape. Stir in 150 ml/¼ pint orange juice and add a further 150 ml/¼ pint a little at a time. Add sufficient sugar to make the mixture taste slightly oversweet. Half-freeze, stir well, then complete the freezing. Serve with mandarin orange segments and wafers.

To serve ice cream: Use an ice cream scoop to dish the ices (or, failing that, a soup spoon), dipping it in tepid water before scooping up the ice cream. Serve in any of the following ways:
1. Plain or topped with whipped cream, accompanied by wafer biscuits or fan-shaped biscuits.
2. In individual glasses, decorated with fresh or preserved fruits (cherries, angelica, etc.).
3. As an iced meringue, a spoonful of ice cream being placed between two meringue cases, piped with whipped cream and decorated with fruits.

FANCY ICES, SUNDAES, ETC.
These have a basis of ice cream of any flavour, combined with a fruit or other sweet sauce, fresh or canned fruit, chopped jelly, grated chocolate, chopped nuts or whipped cream. (See Parfait, Sundae, Knickerbocker glory and Peach Melba entries.)

NEAPOLITAN ICE CREAM
Use three or four kinds of ice cream, usually white (vanilla), green (pistachio or almond), brown (chocolate) and pink (raspberry). Use a square or oblong mould and pack in the half-frozen mixtures in layers; cover and freeze as above.

ICED BOMBES AND PUDDINGS
These are made by freezing ice cream mixtures in a decorated bombe mould. Numerous variations can be made by altering the flavouring and adding fruits or nuts.

Plain mixtures should be half-frozen, i.e., frozen to a mushy consistency, before being moulded. Mousse and parfait mixtures, being fluffy in texture, can be moulded when cold and then frozen. The preliminary freezing may be carried out by any method, but avoid freezing the mixture too hard, or it will not mould satisfactorily. Pack it into the chilled mould, filling this to the brim and taking care to leave no air spaces, press on the lid, and freeze in one of the following ways:
1. By freezing in a refrigerator. Place the filled and covered mould in the coldest part of the freezing unit and leave undisturbed, with the temperature

control set to 'coldest', for about 2 hours or longer.
2. By burying the mould in ice and salt. Either wind a piece of adhesive tape round the join of the lid or wrap the whole mould tightly in greased greaseproof paper, to prevent the salt seeping through to the mixture and spoiling the flavour. Bury the mould in a bowl or bucket of 4 parts crushed ice and 1 part freezing salt. Cover with a sack or blanket and stand it in a cool place for at least 2 hours, draining off the melted ice from time to time and adding more ice and salt if necessary.

To unmould the pudding: Brush a round of sponge cake with apricot jam and roll the sides in chopped nuts. Have ready some whipped cream in a forcing bag and any decorations, e.g., angelica or glacé cherries, etc. If the mould has been buried in ice and salt, rinse it in cold water. Dip in tepid water for a few seconds, then remove any adhesive tape and the lid and invert the ice cream onto the cake base. Pipe a border of whipped cream round the base, decorate and serve at once.

MAKING ICE PUDDINGS WITH TWO MIXTURES
Bombes and similar puddings may be made with two mixtures, one as the lining and the other as the filling. Chill the mould, then line it to a thickness of 1.5 cm/¾ inch to 2.5 cm/1 inch with one of the frozen mixtures, put the other frozen mixture in the centre and fill up with the first mixture. Cover and freeze as for a plain bombe. Good combinations are vanilla and raspberry ice cream, coffee and vanilla ice cream, chocolate and orange ice cream.

PRALINE BOMBE

METRIC/IMPERIAL
100 g/4 oz granulated sugar
150 ml/¼ pint hot water
4 egg yolks, beaten
100 g/4 oz almond toffee, crushed
1 × 5 ml spoon/1 teaspoon vanilla essence
pinch of salt
1 × 300 ml/½ pint carton double or whipping cream, whipped
600 ml/1 pint vanilla ice cream

Put the sugar into a saucepan and heat very gently until coffee-coloured: add the hot water, re-dissolve the caramel and cool. Put the egg yolks in the top of a double saucepan or in a bowl and pour on the caramel. If a bowl is used, stand it over a pan of hot water. Stir until the mixture is thick. Cool, add the crushed toffee, vanilla essence and salt and fold in the cream. Pour this praline mixture into a freezing container and freeze until half-set. Line a pudding basin or bombe mould with vanilla ice cream and fill it with the half-frozen praline mixture. (See making bombes entry.) Freeze, and turn out just before serving.

HOT ICED PUDDINGS
These delicious sweets are sometimes served at a dinner party as a surprise item. A block of ice cream is covered with a sweet omelette or meringue mixture, which is then browned for a few minutes in a very hot oven. A layer of sponge cake is put under the ice cream, to protect it from the heat of the oven.

BAKED ALASKA

METRIC/IMPERIAL
1 × 18 cm/7 inch round sponge cake
1 × 300 g/11 oz can fruit (e.g., raspberries), drained
1 × 450 ml/¾ pint block of ice cream
3/4 egg whites
100–175 g/4–6 oz caster sugar

Pre-heat a hot oven (230°C/450°F, Gas Mark 8). Place the sponge cake on a flat ovenproof dish and spoon over it just enough fruit juice to moisten the cake. Put the ice cream in the centre of the cake and pile the fruit on top. Whisk the egg whites stiffly, whisk in half the sugar, then fold in the remaining sugar. Pile this meringue mixture over the cake, covering the cake, ice cream and fruit completely and taking the meringue down to the dish. Place in the oven immediately and cook for 2 to 3 minutes, or until the outside of the meringue just begins to brown. Serve at once.

VARIATIONS
1. Use fresh crushed fruit, e.g., strawberries, when in season.
2. Sprinkle 1–2 × 15 ml spoons/1–2 tablespoons sherry or rum over the cake before the ice cream is added.
   (See Mousse, Parfait, Sherbet, Sorbet, Sundae and Water Ice entries.)

ICED DRINKS

These are prepared either by standing the bottle or jug in a refrigerator or in a bucket of ice, or by adding ice to the drink in the cocktail shaker or in the individual glasses. (See Cocktails, Punch, Iced Coffee and Iced Tea entries.)

ICELAND MOSS

A lichen closely resembling Carrageen Moss, but darker in colour, which grows on barren mountains in Iceland and other northern regions; it grows to about 1.2 metres/4 feet in height and has branched and flattened mycelium, with a dried appearance.

Iceland moss is sometimes used in cooking in the same way as Carrageen Moss (See Carrageen entry.) It has no particular food value.

The rather bitter flavour of the moss is removed by soaking it for 15 minutes in boiling water, to which a pinch of bicarbonate of soda has been added, repeating this once or twice and finally pouring on more boiling water and leaving it to soak overnight.

ICING

A sweet coating or covering for cakes, biscuits, pastries, etc., which improves their flavour and appearance and forms a good background for other decoration; icing also helps to keep a cake moist. The art of making and applying simple icing is easily learnt, and full directions for the following types are given under their individual names.

American frosting	for coating.
Almond paste	for coating and moulding into flowers, etc.
Butter icing	for coating and piping.
Fondant	for coating and simple decoration.
Glacé icing	for coating and simple decoration.
Royal icing	for coating and elaborate decoration.
Transparent icing	for finished coating.

INDIAN CORN

(See Maize entry.)

INDIAN TEA

(See Tea entry.)

INFRA-RED COOKING

(See Contact Grills entry.)

INFUSING

To extract the flavour from such things as spices by steeping them in a liquid, as when preparing milk to make Béchamel or bread sauce. Tea, coffee and lemonade are also infusions. The usual method of making an infusion is to pour on boiling liquid, cover and leave to stand in a warm place, without further cooking or heating.

INVALID DIET

(See Diet entry.)

IODINE

A minute amount of iodine is necessary to prevent goitre developing. Usually there is enough present in drinking water, in fish and some vegetables (watercress and onions). In some places, however, such as Switzerland and New Zealand and parts of England, there is evidence of a deficiency. Under these conditions, it is usually considered advisable to eat iodised salt (1 part in 100,000).

IRISH MOSS

(See Carrageen Moss entry.)

IRON

Nutritionally, iron is essential as a component part of haemoglobin – the substance which gives the red colour to blood. The amount contained in the body at birth is sufficient to last for the first six months of life; the level is gradually raised by the iron contained in the diet.

The daily requirement of iron varies from about 6 mg for babies under one year to about 15 mg for expectant or nursing mothers and during adolescence. Iron is lost from the body when any bleeding occurs and possibly as a result of the daily wear and tear of the tissues. Insufficient iron in the bloodstream will eventually lead to anaemia. General symptoms include tiredness, lassitude and loss of appetite.

Not all the iron contained in food is available to the body, but eggs, liver, other meat, green vegetables and dried fruits are useful sources. Iron is now added to flour, which makes this a good source.

ISINGLASS

This is a pure and practically tasteless form of gelatine prepared from the air-bladder tissue of fish, especially sturgeons. It is used commercially to clarify beer and wine and occasionally to replace gelatine in jellies and table creams. It is also used to preserve eggs.

ITALIAN PASTES

(See Pasta entry.)

JACKET POTATOES

(See Potato entry.)

JAGGERY

A brown sugar made from palm juice; also brown cane sugar.

JAM

Jam making is a useful method of preserving fruit and it always tastes superior to commercial varieties. Even if fruit is not available from the garden it can be bought when in season and at its cheapest. However, it is important that it is of good quality.

To obtain consistently good results – a jam that looks clear, has an attractive colour, is set but not stiff and will keep well – demands care, not guesswork, but the process is not difficult.

Jam sets because of a substance called pectin which is released when the fruit is boiled with sugar. The acid in the fruit and the added sugar are both important in the setting process. The correct amount of sugar will also prevent fermentation or crystallization. During the boiling, some of the water evaporates until the correct sugar concentration is obtained.

The Fruit

This should be of good quality, freshly picked, dry and under-ripe rather than over-ripe. Some fruits, such as cooking apples, currants and gooseberries, are rich in pectin and acid and easily set as jam. The following fruits are sufficiently rich in both pectin and acid for jam-making:

Apples (sour)
Blackberries
  (under-ripe)
Crab-apples
Cranberries
Currants (black, red,
  white)
Damsons
Gooseberries

Grapefruit
Greengages
Lemons
Limes
Oranges (Seville)
Plums (some varieties)
Quinces
Raspberries (slightly
  under-ripe)

Apricots, rhubarb and strawberries need added pectin; sweet apples, figs and peaches (also beets, carrots and turnips, which are sometimes mixed with fruit in jam-making) need added acid. Ripe blackberries and strawberries, sweet cherries, marrow and pears need both acid and pectin.

PECTIN

If there is any doubt as to whether a given fruit has sufficient pectin, test as follows: after simmering a small sample of the fruit in a little water until the skins are soft (and without adding any sugar), take 1×5 ml spoon/1 teaspoon juice, cool it and add 3×5 ml spoons/3 teaspoons methylated spirit; shake gently and leave for 1 minute. If there is plenty of pectin in the fruit, a transparent, jelly-like lump will form; but if there is very little pectin, the clot will be broken up into small scattered pieces. In this case, it will be necessary to do one of the following: use less water in making the jam and cook it longer; mix the fruit with some that is rich in pectin; add the juice of a fruit rich in pectin (see recipe); or add a proprietary pectin extract in liquid or powder form.

According to the type of fruit 150 ml/¼ pint home-made pectin extract may be needed with 1 kg/2 lb to 2.25 kg/5 lb of fruit. (If a proprietary extract is used, follow the maker's instructions as to quantities.) Boil the fruit for a short time, add the sugar and continue to boil for a little while, then remove the pan from the heat and add the pectin extract. Stir well, test for a set and pot and cover at once. The short boiling time conserves the fresh fruit flavour and considerably shortens the whole operation, so some people prefer to use pectin extract even when making jam with fruit of good pectin content.

GOOSEBERRY, RED-CURRANT OR APPLE JUICE (PECTIN EXTRACT)

Wash 3 kg/6 lb fruit (slice apples if used), and simmer it in a pan with 1.2 litres/2 pints water until tender, then mash well and strain through a jelly bag. Remove the pulp left in the bag, add enough water to make a mash and simmer again for 1 to 1½ hours, then strain again. Mix the two extracts, which should give a fairly thick liquid; if it is slightly watery, reduce it by boiling. When a good pectin clot is obtained on testing with methylated spirit, the juice may be bottled and sterilized for future use. Bring it to the boil and pour immediately into hot, clean preserving jars, filling them to the brim. Seal at once with hot lids, place the jars on a false bottom in a pan of hot water, just deep enough to cover them, bring the water to the boil and boil for 5 minutes.

ACID IN JAM-MAKING

A certain amount of acid is required to enable the pectin present to set the jam and convert some of the cane or beet sugar into invert sugar, which prevents the jam crystallizing. Some fruits (and vegetables) are lacking in acid and extra must therefore be added in the form of a more acid fruit juice or some tartaric acid. (To tell whether acid is required see list page 211.) To every 1.75 kg/4 lb acid-deficient fruit add one of the following:

METRIC/IMPERIAL
150 ml/¼ pint red-currant or gooseberry juice
2 × 15 ml spoons/2 tablespoons lemon juice
1 × 2.5 ml spoon/½ teaspoon tartaric or citric acid

Jam-making Processes

PREPARATION OF THE JARS
Wash them thoroughly, rinse in clear water and invert to drain. Dry in a warm oven.

PREPARATION OF THE FRUIT
Remove stalks, leaves and any damaged parts, then wash and drain the fruit. Remove stones from the large-stoned fruits with a knife and use a cherry stoner for cherries (tie the stones in a muslin bag to boil with the jam). Apricot and plum stones can be cracked and the kernels mixed with the fruit.

'BREAKING-DOWN' PROCESS
Water and/or acid are added, according to the par-

ticular recipe, and the fruit is simmered gently until it is completely cooked. With fruits rich in pectin, the yield of jam is increased by adding a fairly large quantity of water. Fruits lacking in pectin, such as strawberries, are simmered with acid alone. This cooking is best done in a preserving pan, but a large saucepan may be used. Aluminium, enamel, brass and copper pans are suitable; in the case of both brass and copper it is essential to see that the inside surface is immaculately clean and free from discoloration.

BOILING WITH SUGAR
Granulated and lump sugar are equally good. The quantity depends on the pectin strength of the fruit; if too little sugar is used, the preserve is apt to go mouldy on keeping – if too much is used, it may tend to crystallize. The sugar should form about 60 per cent by weight of the finished preserve, the amount varying according to the amount of water added, which in turn depends on the pectin content of the fruit. The following table shows the average proportions:

METRIC/IMPERIAL
575 g/1¼ lb sugar to 0.5 kg/1 lb fruit rich in pectin
450 g/1 lb sugar to 0.5 kg/1 lb fruit fairly rich in pectin
350 g/12 oz sugar to 0.5 kg/1 lb fruit weak in pectin

Warm the sugar before adding it, so that it dissolves more rapidly. Once it has dissolved, boil the jam quickly until setting point is reached. Too little boiling will not convert a sufficient proportion of the sugar into invert sugar and the jam will therefore crystallize, while over-boiling makes too much invert sugar, producing a syrupy consistency.

TESTING FOR THE SETTING POINT
There are several methods, number 1 being the simplest.
1. Place 1 × 15 ml spoon/1 tablespoon jam on a saucer and leave it to cool. If a skin can be seen on the surface when the little finger is pulled lightly

1. Place jam on a saucer and leave it to cool. It is ready if a skin can be seen on the surface when a finger is pulled lightly across the jam.

2. Dip a spoon into cold water then dip into the jam; if setting point has been reached the jam will drip slowly from the spoon.

3. Setting point is reached when the sugar boiling thermometer reaches a temperature of 104°C/220°F.

across, setting point has been reached.

2. Drop some of the jam from the side of a clean spoon that has been dipped in cold water; if it is at setting point it will not run off easily, but the drops will fall very slowly and run together.

3. Use a sugar-boiling thermometer: setting point is reached at a temperature of 104°C/220°F, provided the fruit has been cooked sufficiently, before the sugar is added.

POTTING JAM

Remove the scum from the surface. Strawberry jam, shred marmalade, etc., in which fruit or peel is likely to rise, should be allowed to cool until the jam thickens enough to hold the fruit throughout before it is potted. (Do not leave for too long, however, or mould spores may be introduced.) Other types, such as plum, can be put at once into the prepared jars. Pour the jam into a jug and fill the jars nearly to the top. Cover the jam immediately with a round waxed paper, making sure the disc touches the whole surface of the jam. Put on a round of Cellophane, wiping it with a damp cloth to make it stretch and ensure a good seal; when the jars are cold, label them with the name of the jam and the date.

(See various fruits, such as black-currant, raspberry, etc., for individual recipes.)

MAKING JAM FROM BOTTLED FRUIT

Drain the fruit in order to weigh it and calculate the sugar needed, but save the liquid, which should be used instead of water in making the jam. Otherwise, make in the usual way.

MAKING JAM FROM PULPED FRUIT

Fruit which has been preserved by pulping can be made into jam at any time convenient. To ascertain the amount of sugar required, use the pectin test; weigh the pulp and add sugar. (See boiling with sugar.) Add the sugar as soon as the excess water has been boiled off and finish the jam in the usual way.

(*Jam for Diabetics*: See Saccharin entry; *Jam Layer Pudding, Jam Roly-poly*: See Suet Puddings entries.)

JAM SAUCE

METRIC/IMPERIAL
4 × 15 ml spoons/4 tablespoons jam, sieved
150 ml/¼ pint water or fruit juice
2 × 5 ml spoons/2 teaspoons arrowroot
2 × 15 ml spoons/2 tablespoons cold water
squeeze of lemon juice, optional

Warm the jam and water and simmer for five minutes. Blend the arrowroot and cold water to a smooth cream and stir in the jam mixture. Return the sauce to the pan and heat, stirring, until it thickens and clears. Add the lemon juice before serving.

Serve hot with steamed or baked puddings or cold over ice cream.

Note: A thicker sauce is made by just melting the jam on its own over a gentle heat and adding a little lemon juice.

JAMAICA PEPPER

(See Pimento entry.)

JAPANESE ARTICHOKE

(See Artichoke entry.)

JAPONICA FRUIT OR APPLES

The fruits of the ornamental Japonica tree have no great culinary value, but they have a distinctive, somewhat scented flavour, so small quantities of the peeled and sliced fruit are sometimes included in such dishes as apple pie. They can also be made into jam or jelly, either alone or combined with apples and other fruit.

1. *Place the warmed jam jars on a wooden board to prevent them from slipping and, using a jug, pour jam into warmed jars.*

2. *Make sure that the jam reaches top of each jar before placing a waxed disc on top of the jam to completely cover the surface.*

3. *Place a round of dampened cellophane over top of each jar, secure with elastic band. When cold label giving date and content of jar.*

JAPONICA JAM

METRIC/IMPERIAL
1.75 kg/4 lb japonica fruit
3.5 litres/6 pints water
sugar
1 × 5 ml spoon/1 teaspoon powdered cloves or other
spice

Wash and slice the fruit, put it into a pan with the water, boil until tender and then sieve. Weigh the purée, add an equal weight of sugar, stir and bring to the boil. Add the powdered spice. Continue to boil for ten minutes and test for setting. As soon as it jells, pour into hot, dry jars and cover immediately.

JELLY (PRESERVE)

The principle of jelly-making is similar to that of jam-making, but it is even more important that the fruit should have a good pectin and acid content, since a 'runny' jelly is very difficult to manipulate. Most English fruits can be made into jelly, except a few that are poor in acid or pectin, such as strawberries and cherries.

There are two processes in jelly-making: firstly to extract the juice and secondly to set it, by boiling it with sugar. For the first, the fruit is put into a pan with water (the amount varying according to the pectin content) and is then cooked gently to a mash, so that the tissues are broken down and juice extracted; it is next strained through a scalded jelly bag, plenty of time being allowed for the juice to drip – it should not be squeezed through or the jelly will be cloudy. Fruits rich in pectin may be given a second boiling; the pulp in the bag is boiled again with more water, then strained and the two extracts are mixed together.

For the second stage the extract is weighed and an equal weight of sugar is added; or the juice can be measured and 575 g/1¼ lb sugar allowed for each 600 ml/1 pint. (Some authorities consider that 450 g/1 lb sugar to 600 ml/1 pint of juice gives a better set, less sugar being used if the pectin content is low and more if it is high.) Boil briskly until the preserve jells when tested on a cold saucer, taking off any frothy scum that is thrown up during the boiling process; if this is difficult to remove, strain the jelly through a muslin cloth into the pots. Cover in the same way as jam, and store in a cool, dry place.

(See individual fruits for individual recipes.)

JELLY (SWEET)

Under this heading come various popular sweets, including Fruit Jellies, Crèmes de Menthe, Turkish Delight, Marshmallows and Jujubes, some of which are quite simple to make at home. There are several methods of stiffening the sugar syrup which is used for making them – by adding gelatine, gum arabic, blended cornflour or arrowroot; by reducing the syrup by fast boiling, or by boiling an acid with cornflour to hydrolize it.

The sweets may be set in small moulds, in sweet rings or in tins. The more experienced worker can use starch trays or moulds, the liquid syrup being poured into the impressions.

Fruit jellies are usually tossed in caster or icing sugar. Turkish delight and marshmallows are both tossed and packed in a mixture of cornflour and icing sugar, while other sweets are tossed in icing sugar alone.

JELLY (TABLE)

A mixture, usually sweet, to which gelatine or a similar substance is added, so that it will set firm when it cools and can be turned out, keeping the shape of the mould in which it is made. Gelatine is occasionally replaced by Carrageen (Irish or Iceland) moss, which has the advantage that it may be eaten by vegetarians, or by isinglass, though this is more expensive than gelatine. For savoury dishes, an aspic jelly made from ordinary gelatine is usually used, but a very good jelly may also be made from calves' feet.

There are three main types of jelly:
1. Clear jellies, which should be of crystal transparency and good colour.
2. Whipped jellies (often called whips), which are whisked when they are on the point of setting, and so become opaque.
3. Milk, cream and egg jellies.

There is very little food value in jelly, unless made with fresh fruit juice, milk or eggs.

Proportion of Gelatine

If the jelly is being made in a refrigerator allow 15 g/½ oz to 20 g/¾ oz of standard gelatine to 600 ml/1 pint of a liquid such as fruit juice, milk or wine. This proportion will usually set the jelly so that it will mould without becoming too stiff, but in very hot weather and particularly if no refrigerator is available, the proportion of gelatine should be increased slightly. Certain proprietary brands of gelatine have a low melting-point, and a greater quantity must be used. In all cases the manufacturer's instructions should be meticulously followed.

To set 600 ml/1 pint fruit or other purée, use 15 g/½ oz gelatine; for very thick, well-aerated mixtures, such as cream and whipped egg whites, use 8 g/¼ oz to 15 g/½ oz to 600 ml/1 pint.

Method of Making Jelly

1. Measure the gelatine very accurately: 2 × 15 ml spoons/2 tablespoons of powdered gelatine weigh approximately 15 g/½ oz to 20 g/¾ oz.

2. Soak the gelatine in a little of the cold liquid for 10 to 15 minutes. (This is not essential but does help to make thorough mixing in easier.) Dissolve the soaked gelatine, preferably by placing the basin over a pan of hot water; the mixture must not be allowed to become hot.

3. Measure the correct amount of fruit juice, other liquid or purée, add flavouring, colouring and sugar if necessary. Add the lukewarm dissolved gelatine, pouring it through a strainer and stirring if necessary with a spoon or whisk.

When adding gelatine to very cold mixtures, make sure it is stirred in very quickly, to avoid 'roping'.

If a packet jelly is used, follow the directions carefully – many of them have to be made up to a total of 600 ml/1 pint of liquid, which does not mean adding an additional 600 ml/1 pint of hot water.

4. Clarify the jelly if necessary.

5. Pour the jelly into the wetted mould or other container or into small individual moulds and when nearly cold place in a refrigerator. Alternatively, if ice is available, stand the moulds in a dish and surround with chipped ice.

6. For milk jellies, the milk should be absolutely fresh and it must be only lukewarm when added to the jelly (which should be just beginning to set) – if it is hot, it is likely to curdle.

7. When solid ingredients (such as fruit and nuts) are included, they should be stirred in when the jelly is just beginning to set. Alternatively, proceed as directed in the recipe Fruit in Jelly.

8. When making a jelly from fresh pineapple juice, boil the juice for 2 to 3 minutes first. This kills an enzyme contained in the juice which would otherwise break down the gelatine and destroy its setting properties.

To Clarify Jelly

Use 1 egg shell and 1 egg white to 600 ml/1 pint of liquid jelly. Wash the eggshell well before breaking it, separate the egg very carefully and add the white and the crushed shell to the liquid. The pan should not be more than half-full, as the mixture is apt to boil over. Bring it nearly to boiling point, whisking all the time, then stop whisking and allow the froth to rise to the top of the pan. Draw the pan away from the heat, but leave it in a warm place for five minutes. Strain the jelly through a scalded jelly bag while it is still hot and repeat the process if it is not clear, using a fresh basin. Do not touch the bag during the straining.

To Unmould and Serve a Jelly

1. Half-fill a bowl with very hot water.

2. If a metal mould is used, hold it in the water for a few seconds, wipe with a clean cloth, dabbing the top of the jelly to dry it, then invert the mould on to the hand and give a good shake. As the jelly loosens, place it over the dish, slip the hand away, then lift off the mould.

3. If a china mould is used, stand or hold it in the hot water (which should just come to the top of the mould) for 1 to 2 minutes, according to the thickness of the mould. Then loosen round the edge with the fingers and turn it out as above.

4. Decorate with chopped jelly, whipped cream or fruit, etc. (To chop jelly, cut it up on wet greaseproof paper.)

TO MASK OR LINE A MOULD WITH JELLY

1. Fill a large basin with pieces of ice and nest the mould in it.

2. Pour 2–3 × 15 ml spoons/2–3 tablespoons cold but liquid jelly into the wetted mould and rotate this slowly until the inside is evenly coated. Continue pouring in and setting cold liquid jelly until the entire surface is lined with a thin coat of the jelly.

3. Dip the decoration (slices of pistachio nuts, cherries, angelica, etc.) in liquid jelly with the aid of skewers or a pointed knife, then place in position in the mould, allowing each piece to set firmly.

4. Finally, pour a thin coating of jelly over the whole and allow to set before pouring in the remainder of the jelly or the cream.

ORANGE JELLY

METRIC/IMPERIAL
75 g/3 oz lump sugar
1 lemon
3 oranges
4 × 15 ml spoons/4 tablespoons powdered gelatine
300 ml/½ pint cold water

Rub the lump sugar on the rind of the lemon and 1 of the oranges to extract the zest. In a saucepan, sprinkle the gelatine over the water, add the sugar and dissolve over a low heat, do not boil. Squeeze the juice from the fruit and strain it; if necessary, add water to make up to 150 ml/¼ pint. Add the strained juice to the gelatine mixture and strain through a piece of muslin into a wetted mould. Leave to set.

CLEAR LEMON JELLY

METRIC/IMPERIAL
4 lemons
whites and shells of 2 eggs
3 × 15 ml spoons/3 tablespoons powdered gelatine
175 g/6 oz lump sugar
900 ml/1½ pints cold water
3 cloves
2 cm/¾ inch stick cinnamon

Wash the lemons and the eggs. Pare the rind in thin strips from 3 of the lemons and squeeze the juice of

4, adding water if necessary to make up to 300 ml/½ pint. Put the lemon rind, lemon juice, gelatine, sugar and water, together with the cloves and cinnamon, into a large saucepan. Lastly, add the egg whites and the crushed eggshells, place over a gentle heat and start to whisk at once. Continue to whisk the mixture until nearly boiling, by which time there should be a thick froth on the surface. Stop whisking and allow the froth to rise and crack, then reduce the heat and simmer gently for 5 minutes.

FRUIT IN JELLY

Make some lemon jelly as above or with a packet jelly and prepare some fresh fruit such as grapes, cherries, raspberries, sections of oranges or sliced bananas (dip banana slices in lemon juice first to prevent discoloration) or well drained canned fruit such as peaches, apricots, mandarin oranges and pineapple. Pour about 2.5 cm/1 inch of jelly into the mould and arrange a few fruits in this; allow the jelly to set. Add more jelly and fruit and again allow to set. Continue until the mould is completely filled. It is essential that each layer of jelly poured into the mould be allowed to set before more is added, otherwise the fruit will move and the finished appearance will be spoilt.

MILK JELLY

METRIC/IMPERIAL
50 g/2 oz caster sugar
3 thin strips of lemon rind
600 ml/1 pint milk
20 g/¾ oz gelatine
3 × 15 ml spoons/3 tablespoons water

Add the sugar and lemon rind to the milk and allow to infuse for 10 minutes over gentle heat. Dissolve the gelatine in the water over gentle heat and add the cooled milk. Strain into a wetted mould and leave to set.

ORANGE SNOW

Follow the recipe for Orange Jelly, but when the jelly is just beginning to set, whip it until it is light and frothy, then fold in the stiffly whisked whites of 1 to 3 eggs. Set as usual.

JERKED BEEF

Beef cut into wafer-thin strips and dried or cured in the sun. The name is a corruption of a Spanish word used in South America.

JEROBOAM

A large bottle of wine. In champagne, it is equivalent to a double magnum.

JERUSALEM ARTICHOKE

(See Artichoke entry.)

JOHN DORY

A European sea fish, rather ugly, with a curiously shaped mouth and compressed body; the skin is an attractive golden colour and the flesh white with a delicious flavour.

Clean the fish in the usual way and remove the head and fins if it is to be cooked whole; otherwise fillet it. John Dory may be cooked whole by baking or by sautéeing in butter but it is usually filleted and cooked in any way suitable for sole.

JOINT

The carcasses of animals intended for human consumption are cut up into different parts, known as joints. The names of these joints and the methods of cutting the carcasses vary in different parts of the British Isles and still more so in other countries, but there is a fair amount of similarity between the general methods of cutting them up. (See Lamb and Beef entries for details.)

JOULE

A unit of energy or work; 4,186 joules of heat energy are required to raise the temperature of 1 kg of water through 1° celsius.

1 kilocalorie (k cal) equal to 1,000 calories, will supply the same heat. As joules are so small they are often expressed as kilojoules (kj) or megajoules (MJ). Under the Labelling of Food Regulations 1970 certain packaged foods must have the Calorie value of the contents on the label. With the change over to metric and to bring Great Britain in line with other countries using the International System (SI), this was to be quoted in joules from January 1977. Although the relevant Order still stands nothing has been enforced.

Food tables and labels may quote Calories and/or joules.

JUGGED HARE OR GAME

(See Hare entry.)

JUICE

The liquid part of fruit and vegetables; the word is also sometimes applied to the liquid from meat.

The juices of fruits and vegetables can be extracted to use as a drink or in cookery; some of them are especially valuable for their vitamin C content. They are most easily extracted by using an electric juice extractor, which obtains the liquid very rapidly, leaving the fibres behind. Alternatively, the whole fruit or vegetable can be pulped in a liquidizer. The pulp can then be strained to remove the fibres if desired, but for most purposes the pulp is sufficiently macerated to make straining unnecessary. Tomato, carrot, mixed vegetable, orange and many other juices obtained in this way make delicious drinks. Fruit juice can be extracted manually in a hand press or (with suitable types) on a lemon squeezer. Tomato juice can be obtained by putting tomatoes through a sieve.

The commercial canned products are very good and save time and trouble. Many of these consist of the natural juice and sometimes they are sweetened; certain permitted additives can be included but it must be obvious from the label that the juice is not in its natural state.

JUJUBE

Originally the name of a shrub of the buckthorn family growing in the East, the fruit of which is eaten candied or made into jelly. The name is also applied to a sweet made of gelatine or gum Arabic, water, sugar and flavourings. Jujubes are sometimes medicated or scented.

JULEP

A drink which was once popular in England, but is now better known in America.

MINT JULEP

METRIC/IMPERIAL
2 × 5 ml spoons/2 teaspoons caster or brown sugar
6 sprigs of mint
rye whisky or peach brandy
ice
lemon

Put the sugar and crushed mint into a glass, cover with the whisky or brandy and leave for 10 minutes. Add a little more whisky, the ice and a half-slice of lemon and stir briskly before serving.

JULIENNE

The name of a clear vegetable soup first made by a noted eighteenth-century French chef named Jean Julien. See Consommé entry for recipe.

The term is also used for Julienne strips – thin pieces of carrot and turnip, shaped like matchsticks, which are used to garnish soups, stews, etc. Cut the peeled vegetable into oblong-shaped blocks of equal size, cut these into very thin slices, place one on top of the other and slice down in the opposite direction, to give matchstick pieces. Cook in boiling salted water for about ten minutes until tender, then drain and add to the dish just before serving.

JUMBLE

A small rich biscuit flavoured with lemon, almond, etc., baked in the shape of an 'S' or in tiny rock-like heaps.

JUNIPER BERRY

The fruit of the juniper tree, which grows throughout Europe. The small, dark, purple-blue, aromatic berries (which take two years to ripen) are used to flavour sauces, stuffings, gin and medicines.

JUNKET

A dessert made of curds, produced by treating milk with rennet. The action of the rennet on the milk protein makes it easily digested, so junket is very suitable for children and invalids.

The important point to remember in making junket is that the milk should be only lukewarm, since the setting of the junket is obtained by the action of an enzyme in the rennet, which is destroyed by high temperatures. On the other hand, cold retards its action, so the junket should be allowed to set at room temperature, after which it may be chilled in a refrigerator or cold larder. Avoid shaking the dish, as the milk separates out easily. Follow the manufacturer's directions regarding the amount of rennet to use.

Pasteurized milk should be used but not homogenized. Long life milk is not suitable for junkets (see Milk entry).

Junket is excellent served with fruit, in place of custard. Any that is left over can be used to make curd cheese cakes (see recipe under Cheesecakes entry).

JUNKET

METRIC/IMPERIAL
600 ml/1 pint rich milk (not Long Life)
1–2 × 15 ml spoons/1–2 tablespoons caster sugar
1 × 5 ml spoon/1 teaspoon liquid rennet
flavouring

Heat the milk to blood heat 37°C/98°F and dissolve the sugar in it. Stir in liquid rennet. Pour the mixture at once into a glass dish or individual glasses and put in a warm place to set. Chill before serving.

Note: Rennet is sold as a liquid or in a tablet without added colouring; there are also commercial preparations of rennet in powder, tablet and liquid form, which are already coloured and flavoured. Store rennet in a cool, dry place.

NUTMEG
Sprinkle a little grated or ground nutmeg over the surface of the junket.

KAFFIR CORN

(See Millet entry.)

KALE (KAIL)

A green, curly-leaved vegetable of the cabbage family; unlike the cabbage, however, it does not form a head. There are several distinct types, one of the latest and best being known as 'Hungry Gap', because the crop arrives before the so-called 'spring' cabbages appear in fair quantities.

Kale has a good flavour when picked young and is a rich source of vitamin C. Prepare and cook it like cabbage.

KEBAB

Strictly speaking a kebab is a piece of meat, but what is generally referred to as a kebab is a Shish Kebab. It is a dish which originated in the East, particularly in Turkey and other Arabic countries. Basically, it consists of small pieces of meat (usually lamb or mutton) threaded on to skewers or swords and grilled. The meat is well seasoned and sometimes marinated beforehand and it may be combined with onions, mushrooms, tomatoes, peppers and so on.

They can be cooked under a grill or they are particularly popular for barbecuing. Kebabs are usually served on a bed of rice with sauces or relishes served separately. In recent years they have become popular 'take-away' foods, many Greek eating houses offering a variety of kebabs and accompaniments for this purpose.

(See Grilling and Barbecue entries.)

PORK AND PIMIENTO KEBABS

METRIC/IMPERIAL
0.75 kg/1 ½ lb fillet of pork
1 × 15 ml spoon/1 tablespoon grated onion
2 × 15 ml spoons/2 tablespoons parsley, finely chopped
a pinch of dried oregano

1 × 2.5 ml spoon/½ teaspoon each of ground cummin, ground coriander and ground mace
a pinch of ground ginger
a pinch of salt
pepper
a pinch of cayenne pepper
100 g/4 oz small onions
1 × 215 g/7½ oz can pimientos, drained
oil

Trim the meat, removing any excess fat. Prick all over with a fork. Cut into 2.5 cm/1 inch pieces. In a bowl combine the grated onion, herbs, spices and seasoning. Add the meat and turn to distribute the spices. Leave covered in a cool place for 3 hours. Pour boiling water over the small onions, stand for 2 to 3 minutes before draining off and peeling. Cut the pimiento into large pieces, fold over if necessary to give a neat shape. Thread eight skewers with meat, onion and pimientos alternately. Brush liberally with oil. Place under a pre-heated grill or rotary spit at full heat for 5 minutes to seal surface. Reduce to medium heat and cook for about 45 minutes until well browned, turning at intervals. Baste frequently using pan drippings to keep well moistened.

GINGER GLAZED LAMB NUGGETS

METRIC/IMPERIAL
0.5 kg/1 lb boned leg or shoulder lamb

MARINADE
3 × 15 ml spoons/3 tablespoons chopped stem ginger
1 × 15 ml spoon/1 tablespoon soy sauce
1 × 15 ml spoon/1 tablespoon tomato paste
2 spring onions, chopped
salt
freshly milled black pepper
6 × 15 ml spoons/6 tablespoons white stock

Cut the meat into bite-sized pieces. Place in a small shallow dish. Combine all marinade ingredients in a small pan using the white part only from the onion. Heat gently for 5 minutes, cool and pour over meat. Cover and leave to marinate overnight in the refrigerator. The next day, drain the meat, thread on four skewers and grill under a moderate heat for 30 minutes. Brushing over with a little of the marinade. Turn several times to ensure meat is cooked on all sides. Arrange skewers in a serving dish. Heat marinade, add any meat juices from grill pan, avoiding fat, and pour over the meat. Serve garnished with the snipped green of the spring onions.

VEAL KEBABS

METRIC/IMPERIAL
1 × 150 ml/¼ pint carton natural yogurt
salt
milled pepper
100 g/4 oz onion, skinned and grated
0.5 kg/1 lb shoulder veal
2 medium onions, peeled and quartered
3 firm tomatoes, halved
1 green pepper, deseeded and cut into squares
2 × 15 ml spoons/2 tablespoons oil
paprika
garlic salt

Combine the yogurt, salt, freshly milled black pepper and grated onion. Cut the veal into thirty 2.5 cm/1 inch cubes. Place in the yogurt marinade and leave for 2 hours for the flavours to infuse. Drain meat, keeping excess marinade, and thread on to six skewers alternating with onion quarters, halved tomatoes and green pepper pieces. Grill using a rôtisserie kebab attachment under a moderate to hot heat for 30 to 40 minutes or under a pre-heated grill, turning several times during cooking and brushing with oil. Sprinkle kebabs generously with paprika and garlic salt. Serve the cold marinade separately.

DEVILLED SWEET CORN

METRIC/IMPERIAL
2 medium-sized fresh corn cobs
100 g/4 oz butter, softened
4 × 15 ml spoons/4 tablespoons Branston Pickle
1 × 5 ml spoon/1 teaspoon lemon juice
1 × 5 ml spoon/1 teaspoon chopped parsley
salt
milled pepper

Remove the beard and outer leaves from the corn. Trim, if necessary. Blanch in boiling water for about 6 minutes, then drain. Combine butter, pickle, lemon juice, parsley and seasoning together. Divide mixture in half and spread on each cob. Wrap separately in kitchen foil and cook in a moderately hot oven (200°C/400°F, Gas Mark 6) for about 40 minutes until corn is tender. Roll back top of foil and serve.
NB – If frozen prepared cobs are used omit the blanching.

SHISH KEBAB

METRIC/IMPERIAL
0.5 kg/1 lb boned leg or shoulder of lamb
150 ml/¼ pint olive oil
1 clove garlic, peeled and crushed
50 g/2 oz onion, finely chopped
1 × 2.5 ml spoon/½ teaspoon salt
1 × 2.5 ml spoon/½ teaspoon milled pepper
2 × 15 ml spoons/2 tablespoons lemon juice
4 small courgettes, trimmed
bayleaves
8 small tomatoes
2 medium sized onions, skinned and quartered

Cut the lamb into 2.5 cm/1 inch pieces. Make the marinade by combining the olive oil, garlic, onion, salt, pepper and lemon juice. Add the meat, cover and allow to marinate overnight in a cool place. Cut the courgettes at an angle into small wedge shaped pieces, about 3.5 cm/1½ inches long. Blanch in salted water for 2 to 3 minutes before using. Drain meat, retaining the marinade. Alternate the meat, bayleaves and vegetables on eight skewers. Brush well, particularly the vegetables, with the remaining marinade. Place skewers under a preheated grill and grill for 15 to 20 minutes, turning frequently and basting to keep moist. Serve on a bed of boiled rice.
NB – If the tomato is added as the last item on the skewer then the cooking time can be adjusted; tomatoes, especially if ripe, take only 7 to 10 minutes.

KEDGEREE

A dish of Anglo-Indian origin, consisting of rice, cooked white or smoked fish and usually hard-boiled eggs. It is traditionally eaten for breakfast, but can be served for supper or a light lunch, accompanied by a fresh salad.

KEDGEREE

METRIC/IMPERIAL
450 g/1 lb smoked haddock
175 g/6 oz long grain rice
2 hard-boiled eggs
75 g/3 oz butter or margarine
salt
cayenne pepper
chopped parsley

Cook and flake the fish. Cook the rice in the usual way and drain if necessary. Shell the eggs, chop one and slice the other into rings. Melt the butter or margarine in a saucepan, add the fish, rice, chopped egg, salt and cayenne and stir over a moderate heat for about 5 minutes, until hot. Pile it on a hot dish and garnish with lines of chopped parsley and the sliced egg.

KEFIR

A cultured milk product which originated in Russia and Poland. It is made from whole or skimmed cows milk to which Kefir grain is added. It differs from yogurt in that additional cultures are introduced which produce alcohol. Kefir is a milky white, slightly greasy, homogenous product resembling liquid cream. It has a lactic flavour and usually no additional flavour is introduced. It should be kept in a glass container which is resistant to pressure as carbon chloride is produced during storage. To allow a slight escape of gas the jars usually have spring-loaded clip closures. (See Koumiss entry.)

KETCHUP (CATSUP)

A type of table sauce with one predominating flavour, e.g., tomato, mushroom, cucumber or walnut, etc. Ketchup is made by extracting the juice, boiling it down to a very concentrated form and seasoning it highly.

TOMATO KETCHUP

METRIC/IMPERIAL
5.5 kg/12 lb ripe tomatoes, sliced
450 g/1 lb sugar
600 ml/1 pint spiced vinegar
1 × 15 ml spoon/1 tablespoon tarragon vinegar
pinch cayenne pepper
1–2 × 5 ml spoons/1–2 teaspoons paprika pepper
2 × 15 ml spoons/2 tablespoons salt

Place the tomatoes in a pan and cook over a very low heat until they become liquid; reduce by boiling until the pulp thickens, then rub it through a nylon sieve. Replace it in the pan, together with the other ingredients, and boil until the mixture thickens. Pour into warm bottles, sterilize for 30 minutes and seal.

MUSHROOM KETCHUP

METRIC/IMPERIAL
1.5 kg/3 lb mushrooms, washed and roughly broken
75 g/3 oz salt
1 × 5 ml spoon/1 teaspoon peppercorns
1 × 5 ml spoon/1 teaspoon whole allspice
1 × 2.5 ml spoon/½ teaspoon ground mace
1 × 2.5 ml spoon/½ teaspoon ground ginger
a pinch of ground cloves
600 ml/1 pint vinegar

Put the mushrooms in a bowl, sprinkle with the salt, cover and leave overnight. Rinse away the excess salt, drain and mash with a wooden spoon. Place in a pan with the spices and vinegar, cover and simmer for about 30 minutes, or until any excess vinegar is absorbed. Press the mixture

through a nylon sieve and pour into warm bottles. Sterilize and seal.

KIBBLING

To grind or chop coarsely.

KID

A young goat. Kid is seldom eaten in this country, but is popular in some Mediterranean regions. The flesh is sweet and tender if properly prepared, but inclined to be dry and a little lacking in flavour, so it is either marinated in a mixture of vinegar, oil and seasonings before cooking, or is stuck with slices of onion or sprigs of herbs.

Kid is usually roasted whole, like sucking pig. Clean it, marinate for a few hours, if desired, then hang it for a day or two. Before cooking, lard well, pepper and dredge with flour. Roast as for lamb (see Lamb entry) and serve with mint sauce, fruit chutney or red-currant jelly, as desired.

KIDNEY

The kidneys of many different animals are eaten, from the small ones of rabbits and hares to the large ox kidneys. Like other forms of meat, they supply protein; they are rich in iron and contain a certain amount of other minerals and vitamin A and nicotinic acid.

Kidneys give a rich, distinctive flavour to steak pie or pudding; they also make good casserole dishes, stews, curries, soups, etc., as well as a savoury filling for omelettes. Grilled or fried sheep's, pig's and calf's kidneys may be served for breakfast or as part of a mixed grill (see Grilling entry). Ox kidneys require long, slow moist cooking.

Preparation: Remove excess fat (suet) surrounding the kidney, then remove the skin. Cut it through at the thickest part to the centre fatty 'core', peel off the outer skin and cut out the core, using kitchen scissors. Wash and dry.

KIDNEYS WITH SHERRY

METRIC/IMPERIAL
25 g/1 oz butter
1 onion, skinned and chopped
2 cloves garlic, skinned and crushed
2 × 15 ml spoons/2 tablespoons flour
300 ml/½ pint stock
2 × 15 ml spoons/2 tablespoons chopped parsley
1 bayleaf
2 × 15 ml spoons/2 tablespoons oil
8 lambs' kidneys, prepared
5 × 15 ml spoons/5 tablespoons dry sherry
salt
pepper

Heat the butter and sauté the onion until clear. Add the garlic, sprinkle in the flour and stir to blend. Gradually add the stock, stirring until thick and smooth. Add the parsley and bayleaf and leave over a low heat. Heat the oil, add the kidneys and brown evenly; transfer them to the sauce, draining carefully. Add the sherry to the pan drippings, and bring to the boil, add to the kidneys and mix all together. Simmer for 5 minutes, remove the bayleaf and adjust the seasoning.

CURRIED KIDNEYS

Lambs' kidneys may be cooked in the sauce given for Curried Beef but since they are very rich, a smaller quantity is required, and they should be served in a border of noodles or rice. Use 225 g/8 oz kidneys, finely chopped, and halve the quantities for the sauce ingredients; cook for about 30 minutes, or until the kidney is tender.

KIDNEY SOUP WITH DUMPLINGS

METRIC/IMPERIAL
225 g/8 oz ox kidney
seasoned flour
1 onion, skinned and finely chopped
40 g/1 ½ oz dripping
1 litre/2 pints brown stock
small bouquet garni
2 × 15 ml spoons/2 tablespoons flour
gravy browning, optional
herb dumplings

Skin the kidney, wiping it if necessary. Cut in half, discarding the fatty core, and toss in seasoned flour. Fry the prepared kidney and onion in the dripping for 5 minutes, or until lightly browned. Chop the kidney finely, return it to the pan and pour in the stock gradually, stirring well. Add the herbs, cover and simmer for 1½ hours, skimming and stirring occasionally. When the kidney is tender, blend the flour to a smooth cream with a little water. Stir in a little of the hot soup and add the mixture to the pan. Colour it if you wish with a little gravy browning. Re-boil, stirring, until the soup thickens. Add the dumplings and cook for a further 15 to 20 minutes, until the dumplings are cooked.

KIDNEY BEAN

(See French and Scarlet Runner Beans, under Bean entry.)

KILOJOULE

A unit of energy 100 times greater than a joule. (See Joule entry.)

KIPPER

A herring split, salted and dried in smoke. Kippers can be grilled, baked, fried or poached. If they are known to be very salty, trim them, place in a jug and pour boiling water over them, leave for 3 minutes, then finish as directed below, cooking the skin side first. Frozen kippers should be cooked as directed on the packet.

To grill: Cook slowly for 4 to 5 minutes on each side.

To bake: Cover with greased paper and cook for 15 minutes in a moderately hot oven (200°C/400°F, Gas Mark 6).

To fry: Cook in a very little fat for about 4 minutes on each side.

To poach: Place in a bowl, pour boiling water over and leave for 10 to 12 minutes. Alternatively, the kippers can be cooked in a frying pan of hot water: this method does away with the disagreeable odour accompanying the other methods.

For snacks: Filleted and boned kippers are sold canned and frozen and these make excellent savoury snacks, sandwiches, vol-au-vent fillings or fish pâtés. Cooked kippers can be freed from bone and used in the same way.

KIPPER PÂTÉ

METRIC/IMPERIAL
350 g/12 oz kipper fillets
6 × 15 ml spoons/6 tablespoons dry white wine
2 × 15 ml spoons/2 tablespoons lemon juice
100 g/4 oz butter, softened
black pepper
6 tomato slices
Melba toast

Remove the skin from the kipper fillets. Place the fish in a shallow dish and pour over the wine. Cover and leave to marinate for 4 hours. In a bowl, mash the fillets and wine together to a paste. Add lemon juice to make a softer mixture.

Beat in the softened butter and season with black pepper. Divide between six ramekin dishes. Smooth over the tops and mark with a fork. Top each with a tomato twist. Serve with Melba toast.

KIRSCH OR KIRSCHWASSER

A colourless liqueur made from black cherries, produced in Germany and Switzerland. The special flavour comes from the crushed stones of the fruit and glucose is added for sweetening. Kirsch is excellent for adding to fruit salads, trifles or other sweets.

KNEADING

Working dough with the hands to obtain a required consistency. This is done by stretching and folding on a floured surface. It is a particularly important process in bread making. It can be done in an electric mixer if there is a dough hook attachment.

KNICKERBOCKER GLORY

METRIC/IMPERIAL
¼ packet red jelly
¼ packet yellow jelly
1 × 215 g/7½ oz can peach slices, chopped
1 × 215 g/7½ oz can pineapple chunks
1 × 450 ml/¾ pint block of vanilla ice cream
1 × 150 ml/5 fl oz carton double cream, whipped
4 glacé cherries

Make up the jellies as directed on the packet, allow to set and then chop them. Put small portions of the chopped fruits in the bottom of tall sundae glasses. Cover this with a layer of red jelly. Put a scoop of ice cream on top and add a layer of yellow jelly. Repeat, then finish with a layer of cream and a cherry.

KNUCKLE OF VEAL

The lower part of the leg of the calf, next to the fillet or the shoulder. Knuckle is served either as a soup or as a stew; the former gives a more tender result.

STEWED KNUCKLE OF VEAL

METRIC/IMPERIAL
1.5 kg/3 lb knuckle of veal
1 onion
1 carrot
1 stalk of celery
a small piece of turnip
sprigs of thyme and parsley
salt
pepper

FOR THE SAUCE
50 g/2 oz butter
50 g/2 oz plain flour
150 ml/¼ pint milk
450 ml/¾ pint veal liquor from the knuckle
a little chopped parsley

Have the knuckle cut up into convenient-sized pieces, put into a pan with just enough boiling water to cover and boil gently for 2 to 3 minutes, removing any scum that rises. Add the cut-up vegetables, the herbs and seasoning, cover and simmer gently until the meat is tender, 2 to 3 hours. A few minutes before serving, make a sauce with the butter, flour, milk and the liquor from the knuckle, season well and add some chopped parsley. Lift the knuckle from the pan, drain well and place on a hot dish. Coat with the sauce and garnish with the cooked carrot.

KOHL-RABI

A stem vegetable, with a turnip-like globe (the enlarged stem), topped with curly green foliage, which grows above ground. It is primarily a summer vegetable, but keeps very well if the leaves are removed and the root left intact; it may be clamped for storage, like the potato.

To prepare and cook: Choose young, small globes. Wash, peel and cut into cubes or slices (very young ones can be scrubbed and left whole) and boil in a small quantity of salted water until tender – 30 to 50 minutes. Drain and toss in butter and chopped parsley or serve with a white sauce, garnished with chopped chives. Alternatively, steam for 30 to 50 minutes until tender. Kohl-rabi can also be served cold with vinaigrette sauce.

KOSHER FOOD

Food prepared especially for the Jewish community in accordance with their religious rules.

Certain foods are forbidden and restrictions govern the consumption of others.

Only fish which have fins and scales (not shellfish) may be eaten: Game birds and all pig products are forbidden. Milk and meat may not be cooked or eaten together. Separate and easily distinguishable sets of cooking utensils, china, cutlery, table linen, bowls and working surfaces are required for meat and milk. All manufactured products must be known to be free from non-kosher ingredients: These products are available to the community from specialist shops.

KOUMISS

A weak alcoholic sour beverage similar to Kefir (see Kefir entry). Koumiss is made from mares milk which has a fat content of 1.7 per cent. A culture and yeast are added to give the sour taste. It is a milky white mixture with a grey tinge: the texture is similar to that of cream except that it is permeated by small gas bubbles. A characteristic odour reflects the alcoholic content and sour taste.

In Russia, where Koumiss originated, there

were numerous sanitoria where Koumiss therapy was available for the treatment of tuberculosis. As this is no longer such a common illness, many of these institutions have now closed. Many cultured milk products were thought to have therapeutic value but there is no modern evidence of this.

KROMESKI

A Russian and Polish dish, consisting of a mixture of minced poultry, game or meat, bound to a stiff paste with sauce and wrapped in bacon, then coated with batter and fried.

KROMESKIES

METRIC/IMPERIAL
225 g/8 oz cooked lean meat – beef, lamb, pork

MARINADE
4 × 5 ml spoons/4 teaspoons cooking oil
5 × 15 ml spoons/5 tablespoons cider vinegar
6 peppercorns
1 bay leaf
pinch of mixed herbs

BATTER
175 g/6 oz plain flour
2 × 5 ml spoons/2 teaspoons salt
freshly ground pepper
1 large egg
200 ml/⅓ pint half milk half water
1 × 15 ml spoon/1 tablespoon HP fruity sauce
1 egg white
350 g/12 oz cooked vegetables – carrot, cauliflower,
  beans, peas, sweetcorn
oil for deep frying

Finely dice or chop the meat, place in a bowl with the marinade ingredients and leave for several hours. Drain meat, discard peppercorns and bay leaf. Make a batter with flour, whole egg, milk and water, salt, pepper and sauce. Finely dice or chop the vegetables and fold into the batter with the drained meat. Lastly fold in the stiffly whisked egg white. Drop the mixture in spoonfuls into hot deep fat and fry for about 5 minutes until crisp and golden. Drain well and serve at once with a dusting of grated Parmesan.

KÜMMEL

A sweet, colourless liqueur, originally made in the Baltic countries, which is flavoured with caraway seeds, cummin and fennel. It is now also distilled in England, France and Holland.

KÜMMELKÄSE

A German cheese, flavoured with caraway. Good with cocktails.

KUMQUAT (CUMQUAT)

A small sub-tropical fruit of a bright yellow colour, similar to the mandarin orange, with juicy pulp and a sweet though slightly bitter flavour. Kumquats are eaten raw as dessert and they can also be cooked or used in preserves. The Chinese make a delicious sweetmeat by preserving them in sugar. Kumquats may be baked as follows: cover the fruit with sugar syrup or pour a little golden syrup over them and bake in a moderate oven (180°C/350°F, Gas Mark 4) for about 50 minutes or until tender. Serve with whipped cream or ice cream.

KVASS

A Russian home-brewed drink made from rye, malt and yeast and often flavoured with mint.

LACTOSE

A type of sugar (disaccharide) found in milk. As it is very much less sweet in taste than cane sugar, it is sometimes used for invalids to make drinks with a high energy content without being sickly sweet. It is also used in milk feeds for babies.

Lactose aids the absorption of calcium in the intestine.

LADIES' FINGERS

An English name for okra (See Okra entry). The name is sometimes given to Boudoir biscuits or sponge fingers.

LAGER

A type of beer which can be dark or pale. For centuries it was made in Bohemia and for a long time in Germany and elsewhere. In many countries it is now produced on a massive scale in a lighter form. Although based on hops the process is slightly different from beer. Lager is a carbonated drink which is at its best when served chilled.

LAMB

The meat from a sheep under one year old. (For Mutton, see separate entry.) Lamb should be light in colour and firm in texture; the fat should be firm and white and there should be a fair proportion of it in the joints.

Joints of Lamb and Methods of Cooking

Joint	Method
Leg	Roast, boil.
Loin	Roast; fry or grill chops.
Best end of neck	Roast, braise; fry or grill cutlets.
Middle neck or scrag	Stew, braise, make into soups.
Breast	Roast slowly, stew.
Shoulder	Roast.

(See Mutton and Carving entries.)

Roast Lamb

Joint	Time When cooked at 180°C/350°F, Gas Mark 4.
Leg – plain	30 to 35 minutes per 0.5 kg/1 lb
boned and stuffed	40 to 45 minutes per 0.5 kg/1 lb
Shoulder – plain	30 minutes per 0.5 kg/1 lb
boned and rolled	40 to 45 minutes per 0.5 kg/1 lb
boned and stuffed	40 to 45 minutes per 0.5 kg/1 lb
Best end – plain	1 hour 15 minutes
Guard of honour	1 hour 15 minutes
Crown roast	25 to 30 minutes per 0.5 kg/1 lb
stuffed	30 minutes per 0.5 kg/1 lb
Loin – plain	1 hour 45 minutes to 2 hours
boned and rolled	40 to 45 minutes per 0.5 kg/1 lb
boned and stuffed	40 to 45 minutes per 0.5 kg/1 lb
Breast – boned and rolled	1 hour 30 minutes

NB *Always calculate the cooking time of stuffed joints by weighing them when stuffed.*

Frozen joints of lamb can be thawed overnight in a refrigerator and cooked as above. They can also be cooked from frozen provided care is taken to cook the inside. A meat thermometer is essential to check this: the temperature should reach 64°C/180°F when the meat is cooked through. Seal the joint in hot fat in a preheated oven (230°C/450°F, Gas Mark 8) uncovered for 20 minutes turning once. Reduce the temperature (180°C/350°F, Gas Mark 4), cover the meat and cook for 60 minutes per 0.5 kg/1 lb basting frequently.

COUNTRY LAMB POTAGE

METRIC/IMPERIAL
0.75 kg/1 ½ lb scrag of lamb
1.75 litres/3 pints water

bouquet garni
225 g/8 oz carrots, peeled
2 stock cubes
3 × 15 ml spoons/3 tablespoons oil
1 large onion, peeled and sliced
225 g/8 oz leeks, sliced and washed
1 large turnip, peeled and diced
50 g/2 oz pasta
salt and pepper
chopped parsley

Place lamb in saucepan, cover with cold water, bring to boil, drain, refresh under cold running water. Replace drained meat in pan; cover with the water. Add bouquet garni tied in muslin, carrots and stock cubes. Bring to boil, reduce heat and simmer, covered, for about 1 hour. Cool sufficiently to skim off fat.

Heat oil in large saucepan. Add onion, leeks and turnip; cook over gentle heat, covered, for about 10 minutes. Strain lamb stock over the vegetables. Strip meat off bones, slice cooked carrots and add to pan with pasta. Adjust seasoning. Simmer for about 45 minutes. Add chopped parsley to serve.

LAMB AND POTATO PASTIES

METRIC/IMPERIAL
1 × 15 ml spoon/1 tablespoon oil
225 g/8 oz potatoes, peeled and diced
1 small onion, skinned and diced
350 g/12 oz boned lean shoulder of lamb, coarsely
    minced
1 beef stock cube
salt
freshly milled pepper
375 g/13 oz packet frozen puff pastry, thawed
milk to glaze

Heat the oil in a frying-pan and gently fry the potato and onion for 3 to 4 minutes. Lift out using a draining spoon. Fry meat quickly to seal, then mix with potato, onion, crumbled stock cube, salt and pepper. Cool. Roll out pastry thinly and cut out four 18 cm/7 inch rounds, using a saucepan lid as a guide. Divide the filling between the rounds, brush the edges with milk, then bring the pastry up and seal on top by pressing together with fingertips. Place the pasties on a baking sheet, brush with milk and bake in a hot oven (220°C/425°F, Gas Mark 7) for 15 minutes then reduce the heat (180°C/350°F, Gas Mark 4) for a further 20 to 25 minutes.

SPICED LAMB WITH AUBERGINES

METRIC/IMPERIAL
1 kg/2¼ lb lean breast of lamb, boned
25 g/1 oz lard
225 g/8 oz onion, skinned and chopped
1 × 5 ml spoon/1 teaspoon turmeric
1 × 5 ml spoon/1 teaspoon chili seasoning
1 × 5 ml spoon/1 teaspoon ground cumin
1 × 5 ml spoon/1 teaspoon salt
2 × 15 ml spoons/2 tablespoons curry paste
3 × 15 ml spoons/3 tablespoons mango chutney
75 g/3 oz sultanas
2 × 15 ml spoons/2 tablespoons peanut butter
1 × 15 ml spoon/1 tablespoon Worcestershire sauce
300 ml/½ pint beef stock
0.5 kg/1 lb aubergines, sliced

Mince the lamb coarsely and fry in the melted lard to seal. Add next six ingredients and cook for 5 minutes stirring. Stir in the chutney, sultanas, peanut butter, Worcestershire sauce and stock. Bring to the boil, reduce heat and simmer for 1 hour. Sprinkle the sliced aubergines with salt and leave for 5 minutes to dégorge. Rinse and dry thoroughly and add to the pan. Simmer gently for a further 30 minutes and serve with boiled rice.

LAMB'S FRY

Lamb's liver, sweetbread, heart and some of the inside fat or 'leaf'.

LAMB'S LETTUCE

A hardy annual plant used in France and Italy for salads in winter and early spring.

LAMB'S WOOL

An old English drink, mentioned by Pepys, made by pouring hot ale over pulped roasted apples and adding sugar and spices.

LAMPERN

A fish resembling a small lamprey; cooked like eels.

LAMPREY

An eel-like fish, which can reach a considerable size, formerly considered a great delicacy. Lampreys may be prepared like eels, but require longer cooking.

LANCASHIRE CHEESE

A white crumbly cheese with a clean mild flavour after maturing for four to eight weeks. It has excellent toasting properties so is frequently used for cheese on toast and similar dishes. Traditionally it was sprinkled over Lancashire Hotpot. Lancashire cheese was made in farm kitchens right up until 1913 when the factory production of cheese was well established. A small amount of Farmhouse Lancashire is still available, this being made in the traditional cylindrical shape.

LANCASHIRE HOT-POT

(See Hot-pot entry.)

LANGOUSTE

French name for the spiny lobster. (See Crayfish entry.)

LANGUE DE CHAT

A sweet biscuit, flat and finger-shaped; also a piece of chocolate shaped in the same way.

LAPWING

(See Plover entry.)

LARD

The inside fat of a pig, which is melted down, freed from fibrous materials and stored in airtight containers for future use. The best-quality lard (sometimes called 'leaf' lard) comes from the abdomen and round the kidneys. Ordinary commercial lard comes from fat from all parts of the pig.

Lard is suitable for pastry making, but is inclined to make cakes heavy, so is better mixed with butter or margarine for this purpose. It is suitable for both deep and shallow frying. As pure lard is 99 per cent fat, it does not splutter when heated and it has a high 'smoking' temperature (i.e., it can be heated to a high temperature – not less than 182°C/360°F – before it smokes and burns).

LARDER

(See Food Storage entry.)

LARDING

To insert small strips of fat bacon into the flesh of game birds or meat before cooking, to prevent it from drying out when roasted. A special larding needle is used for the purpose.

LARDY CAKE

A type of cake made with bread dough, lard, sugar and dried fruit. It is mostly found in Sussex, Wiltshire and Oxfordshire.

LARDY CAKE

METRIC/IMPERIAL
*15 g/½ oz fresh yeast or 2 × 5 ml spoons/2 teaspoons
   dried yeast*
1 × 5 ml spoon/1 teaspoon caster sugar
300 ml/½ pint tepid water
450 g/1 lb strong plain flour

2 × 5 ml spoons/2 teaspoons salt
2 × 15 ml spoons/2 tablespoons cooking oil
50 g/2 oz butter
100 g/4 oz caster sugar
1 × 5 ml spoon/1 teaspoon powdered mixed spice
75 g/3 oz sultanas or currants
50 g/2 oz lard

Grease a tin measuring 25 × 20 cm/10 × 8 inches. Blend the fresh yeast with the water. For dried yeast, dissolve the sugar in the water, sprinkle the yeast over and leave until frothy. Sift the flour and salt into a basin and stir in the yeast mixture, with 1 × 15 ml spoon/1 tablespoon oil to give a manageable soft dough. Beat until smooth. Leave in a warm place, about 23°C/75°F, to rise until doubled in size.

Turn the dough out on to a lightly floured surface and knead for 5 to 10 minutes. Roll out to a strip 5 mm/¼ inch thick. Cover two-thirds of the dough with small flakes of butter and 3 × 15 ml spoons/3 tablespoons sugar, and sprinkle with half the spice and half the dried fruit. Fold and roll out as for flaky pastry. Repeat the process with the lard, 3 × 15 ml spoons/3 tablespoons sugar and the remaining spice and fruit. Fold and roll once more. Place the dough in prepared tin, pressing it down so that it fills the corners. Cover, and leave to rise in a warm place until doubled in size. Brush with oil, sprinkle with the remaining caster sugar and mark criss-cross fashion with a knife. Bake in a hot oven (220°C/425°F, Gas Mark 7) for about 30 minutes. Cool on a wire rack. Serve sliced, plain or with butter.

LARK

This small wild bird is seldom eaten in England now. Larks used to be served chiefly in pies, though they were also roasted, grilled and set in aspic. They are caught by nets and considered a great table delicacy on the Continent.

LASAGNE

Wide ribbons of pasta which can be plain or flavoured with spinach (lasagne verdi). It is cooked in salted boiling water until soft, then layered with cooked minced meat in a dish, covered with cheese sauce and browned in the oven. There are slight variations to this popular Italian dish. Green or mixed salad make excellent accompaniments.

LASAGNE AL FORNO

METRIC/IMPERIAL
2 × 425 g/15 oz cans tomatoes
1 × 58 g/2¼ oz can tomato paste
0.5–1 × 5 ml spoon/½–1 teaspoon dried marjoram
salt

pepper
1 × 5 ml spoon/1 teaspoon sugar
225 g/8 oz cooked veal or ham, diced
100 g/4 oz lasagne
175 g/6 oz Ricotta or curd cheese
50 g/2 oz Parmesan cheese
225 g/8 oz Mozarella or Bel Paese cheese

Combine the canned tomatoes, tomato paste, marjoram, seasonings and sugar, simmer gently for about 30 minutes and add the veal or ham. Cook the lasagne in boiling salted water in the usual way for about 10 to 15 minutes (or as stated on the packet) and drain well.

Cover the base of a fairly deep ovenproof dish with a layer of the tomato and meat sauce. Add half the lasagne, put in another layer of the sauce, then cover with the cheeses, using half of each kind.

Repeat these layers with the remaining ingredients, finishing with a layer of cheese. Bake in a moderately hot oven (190°C/375°F, Gas Mark 5) for 30 minutes, until golden and bubbling on top. Serve at once. The tomato and meat sauce can be replaced by a bolognese sauce (See Spaghetti Bolognese entry).

Note: If neither Ricotta nor curd cheese are available use a blend of half cream cheese and half cottage cheese.

LAVER

(See Seaweed entry.)

LAX

Norwegian smoked salmon, packed in oil.

LAYER CAKE

A sponge cake baked in two, three or more separate tins, the layers being put together when cold. Each layer can be spread with jam, cream, butter icing or other filling and the top or the complete cake may be iced. (See Sponge Cake and Victoria Sponge entries for method of making the cake; Cake Fillings, Butter Icing entries, etc., for suitable spreads.)

LEAVEN

A piece of sour dough, kept to ferment the next batch of bread; used in the days before yeast was generally obtainable.

LEEK

A vegetable belonging to the same family as the onion and garlic, although it does not form a bulb. The flavour is milder but distinctive. The lower part of the stem is earthed up and remains white.

Leeks are excellent in soups and stews and as a vegetable. They supply a small amount of vitamin C. In season November to March.

Preparation and cooking: Remove the coarse outer leaves and cut off the tops and roots. Wash the leeks very thoroughly splitting them down to within 2.5 cm/1 inch or so of the bottom, to ensure that all grit is removed; if necessary cut them through completely. Leave leeks whole or slice and cook them in boiling salted water until they are tender, 15 to 25 minutes. Drain very thoroughly. Serve coated with a white or cheese sauce.

CREAM OF LEEK AND POTATO SOUP

METRIC/IMPERIAL
4 medium-sized leeks, sliced and thoroughly washed
1 small onion, skinned and sliced
3 medium-sized potatoes, peeled and sliced
50 g/2 oz butter
1.2 litres/2 pints white stock
salt
pepper
3 × 15 ml spoons/3 tablespoons cream

Lightly fry the vegetables in the butter for 5 minutes, until soft but not coloured. Add the stock, cover and simmer for about 45 minutes until the vegetables are cooked. Sieve the soup or purée in an electric blender and return to the pan.

Re-heat, season to taste and stir in the cream just before serving.

LEEK AND POTATO BAKE

Choose a dish for baking that is suitable for the table. Serve golden and bubbling; it is especially good with a bacon joint or baked pork chops.

METRIC/IMPERIAL
450 g/1 lb potatoes, peeled and thinly sliced
450 g/1 lb leeks, sliced and thoroughly washed
50 g/2 oz strong Cheddar cheese
salt
pepper
300 ml/½ pint milk
1 egg

In a buttered ovenproof dish, layer the potatoes and leeks, sprinkling each layer with half the Cheddar and salt and pepper to taste. Mix together the milk and egg and pour over the dish. Sprinkle the remaining cheese on top. Bake, uncovered, in a moderate oven (180°C/350°F, Gas Mark 4) for 1¼ hours or until the potato is tender.

LEFTOVERS

The food remaining after a meal. Leftovers should be kept to the minimum by buying and cooking only as much food as required, but inevitably there will be some remaining and it is an important part of catering to use these to best advantage.

Leftovers should be stored with care and used as quickly as possible, before they deteriorate. Meat, fish and milk products, in particular, can become harmful if not treated correctly. Cooked meat and fish should be cooled rapidly and placed in a refrigerator or cool larder. If they are to be reheated, they should be brought rapidly to boiling point and allowed to simmer for at least 15 minutes or cooked thoroughly in some other way, and never just warmed through.

(For ways of using up leftovers, see Réchauffé entry.)

LEG OF MUTTON

(See Mutton entry.)

LEGUMES

These are the vegetables which consist of a bi-valved pod with seeds attached along one join and they include peas, beans and lentils. Unlike most vegetables, legumes are a good source of protein and when fresh, they also supply some vitamins A and C. Dried legumes, called pulses, are important in various parts of the world where animal protein foods are scarce. They are also important in a vegetarian diet.

LEICESTER CHEESE

A mild mellow cheese at its best for eating at twelve weeks; the texture is slightly flaky and the colour is a rich orange red due to the addition of annatto. The cheese is famous for its use in Welsh Rarebit; it is also a good dessert cheese.

LEMON

The fruit of the lemon tree, *citrus limonum*, which is now cultivated in most warm countries; the chief sources of British supply are Italy, Sicily, Spain and Australia. The lemons are usually gathered when green and are ripened in special storehouses. Although those which ripen on the tree have the finest flavour, they decay sooner than the ones ripened after being picked.

Lemons are an excellent source of vitamin C. Their acid and pectin content make them useful in jam-making and they are often included in marmalade. The rind and juice of lemons are used in small quantities to flavour many sweet and savoury dishes and in larger quantities to make such sweets as lemon meringue pie, lemon curd and lemonade. Lemon juice can be used instead of vinegar in salad dressings. The essential oil contained in the skin is extracted to make a flavouring essence; it may be obtained from a fresh lemon by rubbing lump sugar over the well-washed surface.

It is not usually necessary to preserve lemons, as they are on sale all the year round. However, the following methods may occasionally be useful.
1. Sound, fresh lemons may be stored for a few months by wrapping them in greaseproof paper or polythene.
2. To bottle, simmer the lemons for 10 minutes, then discard the liquid and proceed as usual. (See Bottling entry.)
3. Slices of lemon can be frozen and used in drinks, for decoration and garnishes.

LEMON CURD

METRIC/IMPERIAL
grated rind and juice of 4 lemons
4 eggs, beaten
100 g/4 oz butter
450 g/1 lb sugar

Put all the ingredients into the top of a double saucepan or in a basin standing in a pan of simmering water. Stir until the sugar has dissolved and continue heating, stirring from time to time, until the curd thickens. Strain into small pots and cover in the usual way. *Makes about 0.75 kg/1 ½ lb.*

LEMON MERINGUE PIE

METRIC/IMPERIAL
150 g/5 oz shortcrust pastry
3 × 15 ml spoons/3 tablespoons cornflour
150 ml/¼ pint water
juice and grated rind of 2 lemons
100 g/4 oz sugar
2 eggs, separated
75 g/3 oz caster sugar
glacé cherries and angelica

Roll out the pastry and use it to line an 18 cm/7 inch flan case or deep pie plate. Trim the edges and bake blind in a hot oven (220°C/425°F, Gas Mark 7) for 15 minutes. Remove the paper and baking beans and return the case to the oven for a further 5 minutes. Reduce the oven temperature (180°C/350°F, Gas Mark 4). Mix the cornflour with the water in a saucepan, add the lemon juice and grated rind and bring slowly to the boil, stirring until the mixture thickens, then add the sugar. Remove from the heat, cool the mixture slightly and add the egg yolks. Pour into the pastry case. Whisk the egg whites stiffly, whisk in half the caster sugar and fold in the rest. Pile the meringue on top of the lemon filling and bake in the oven for about 10 minutes, or until the meringue is crisp and lightly browned. Decorate before serving with glacé cherries and angelica.

LEMON BALM

A herb of the mint family, used for flavouring stuffing, etc., also in drinks. It has a pronounced lemon aroma and flavour.

LEMON SOLE

This fish, which is also known as French sole, inhabits the sea from the North of Scotland to the Mediterranean, but it is most abundant in the English Channel: it is in season all the year round. Lemon soles are smaller than ordinary soles (the largest on record being 36 cm/14 inches long) and they have not such a good flavour or texture.

Lemon soles may be cooked by any of the usual methods used for fish, particularly frying and grilling. Fillets are delicious when steamed, baked or poached and served with a rich cream, white wine or mushroom sauce.

LEMON SQUASH

(See Soft Drinks entry.)

LEMON THYME

A herb used for flavouring stuffings, etc.; its strongly flavoured leaves are sometimes used as substitute for lemon.

LEMONADE

A refreshing drink made from the juice of lemons, the essence of the rind, sugar and water. The name is also applied to many drinks tasting of lemon. In some commercial products the water is replaced by aerated water, the sugar by a cheap form of glucose and saccharine and the lemon by citric acid and yellow colouring.

A recent introduction is Bitter Lemon, a product of lemon juice, sweetening and aerated water, which much more nearly resembles true lemonade.

STILL LEMONADE

METRIC/IMPERIAL
1 lemon
50 g/2 oz sugar
300 ml/½ pint boiling water

Wash the lemon and peel the rind very thinly; put it with the sugar into a jug, pour on the boiling water, cover and allow to stand until cool, stirring occasionally. Add the lemon juice and strain the lemonade.

LEMON SYRUP OR SQUASH

METRIC/IMPERIAL
rind of 2 lemons
675 g/1½ lb sugar
450 ml/¾ pint water
300 ml/½ pint lemon juice

Wash the lemons and grate or pare off the coloured part of the rind very thinly free of all the white pith. Put the lemon rind, sugar and water into a pan and heat slowly until the sugar is dissolved; strain into a basin or jug, add the lemon juice and stir well. Pour into bottles and lightly screw on caps with an acid-resistant lining.

Place the bottles in a deep pan padded with newspaper and fill with water to the base of the caps. Heat the water slowly to simmering point, 75°C/170°F, and maintain this temperature for 20 minutes. Remove the bottles and screw the caps down tightly.

The syrup may be used diluted with water or soda water – allow 1 part syrup to 2 to 3 parts water, according to taste.

Do not keep home-made syrups from citrus fruits longer than 1 to 2 months, as the colour and flavour deteriorate.

LENTIL

A pulse vegetable, the seeds of a leguminous plant. Lentils are about half the size of a pea and have a characteristic flavour. In the East, especially in Egypt, they have been a staple item of diet for many centuries; they are now grown all over the South of Europe and also in the United States. Three main varieties are marketed: Egyptian or red lentils, grown in Arabia and Palestine as well as in Egypt; European or yellow lentils, grown chiefly in France and Germany; German lentils, a variety of European lentils, which are dark green and supposed to be more palatable than the yellowish-red variety.

Lentils are a cheap and useful source of protein, which they contain in a form known as legumin. They also supply carbohydrates, thiamine, iron and calcium.

Lentils are generally used in soups and stews. Bacon bones or fat should be added to the cooking liquid to give extra flavour.

To cook lentils: Use fresh lentils, as they go stale and hard very quickly and then even prolonged cooking will not soften them. Wash them thoroughly, cover with boiling water and soak for 6 hours (or overnight, if convenient). Cook the lentils in the water in which they were soaked, as this contains some of the mineral matter and other nutrients that have been extracted. Bring to the boil and simmer very gently until they are tender and the liquid is absorbed, adding more liquid if necessary; the time needed is about 30 minutes. The lentils may then be rubbed through a sieve or liquidized to give a purée; this renders them more digestible by removing their outer coat.

LENTIL AND BACON SOUP

METRIC/IMPERIAL
175 g/6 oz lentils
1.25 litres/2 ½ pints stock
1 clove garlic, skinned and crushed
1 clove
salt
pepper
200 g/7 oz lean bacon rashers, rinded and diced
1 × 225 g/8 oz can tomatoes
100 g/4 oz onions, skinned and chopped
0.5 kg/1 lb potatoes, peeled and diced
2 × 15 ml spoons/2 tablespoons lemon juice

For garnish: Crisply fried bacon rolls, chopped parsley, grated cheese or croûtons.

Wash the lentils and put them in a saucepan with the stock. Add the garlic, clove, salt, pepper, bacon, tomatoes and onion. Bring to the boil, cover and simmer for about 1 hour, until the lentils and bacon are soft. Add the potatoes and cook for a further 20 minutes. Remove the clove, pour the soup into a sieve or liquidizer and purée it until smooth. Add the lemon juice and re-heat to serving temperature.

LETTUCE

A green plant, first introduced into England in the 16th century, which is used chiefly as a salad, though it can also be cooked and served as a vegetable or made into soup. There are several species and about a hundred varieties, the best-known being the cabbage and the cos lettuce: the former is round in shape and has short, open leaves, while the latter has long, crisp leaves which are tied together in order to blanch them. The lettuce forms a good and decorative background for almost every type of salad and is pleasantly refreshing in hot weather.
Lettuce has very little food value.

Preparation: Remove any old or badly damaged leaves. Wash the lettuce quickly but thoroughly in cold running water and drain it well, then place the leaves in a salad basket or clean towel and shake with a smooth, swinging movement to remove the remaining moisture. Toss in French dressing or serve as desired.

LEVERET

A young hare (See Hare entry).

LIAISON

A thickening – for example, blended cornflour and milk used to thicken purée soups. Other liaisons include flour, eggs and blood. (See Thickening entry.)

LIGHTS

The lungs of sheep, bullocks or pigs, used for feeding pets and very occasionally for human food.

LIMA BEAN

(See Butter Bean, under Bean entry.)

LIMBURGER CHEESE

A semi-hard, fermented Continental cheese, of strong flavour and smell.

LIME

The fruit of the citrus lime tree, which requires the same climatic conditions as the orange tree and grows in the West Indies, Italy, Sicily, etc. The lime, which is oval and of a pale yellowish-green colour, is very acid, but makes a delicious marmalade and a good cordial. The rind and juice of limes are used in the same ways as lemon rind and juice. Limes contain about half the amount of vitamin C found in lemons. Long before the discovery of vitamins they were used by British ships to prevent scurvy among the crews – hence the nickname 'Limey' given to our sailors by other nations.

Lime Juice Cordial
This is made from fresh lime juice, which is obtained by crushing the whole lime and contains both the fruit pulp and the essential oils from the rind. The juice is then concentrated and citric acid, sugar, saccharine, a preservative and colouring matter are added to produce a standardized product. Lime juice is delicious with iced water and is popular in gin drinks and combined with rum to make various 'long' drinks.

LIME MARMALADE

METRIC/IMPERIAL
0.75 kg/1 ½ lb limes
1.75 litres/3 pints water
1.5 kg/3 lb sugar

For this recipe, weigh the empty pan before you start. Wash the limes and remove the stem end. Place the limes in a pan with the water and cover with a tight-fitting lid. Simmer for 1½ to 2 hours, until the fruit is really soft. Remove it, slice very thinly, using a knife and fork, and discard the pips. Return the sliced fruit and the juice to the liquid in the pan and weigh. If necessary, boil the mixture until it is reduced to 1.25 kg/2½ lb. Add the sugar and stir until it has dissolved. Boil until setting point is reached, allow to stand for about 15 minutes and pot and cover in the usual way.

LIME BLOSSOM

The dried flowers of the lime (linden) tree can be infused to make a pleasant, delicately flavoured tea or tisane, which used to be regarded as a medicinal drink for debility, indigestion and sleeplessness.

LIMPET

This small, single-shelled fish can be prepared, cooked and served like the cockle or periwinkle. Limpets may also be fried or used in soup and in scalloped dishes like mussels.

LING

A large fish of the cod family, which grows to about 2 m/7 feet in length and weighs about 54 kg/120 lb. It is found mostly in British waters. Ling is generally sold salted and sometimes passed off as cod. Salted ling should first be soaked to remove the salt and then requires careful cooking to make it palatable.

LIQUEUR

This name is applied to a variety of spirits or cordials sweetened with sugar, flavoured with essences and sometimes scented and coloured. In the preparation of liqueurs the fruits or herbs are first bruised and are then steeped in diluted grain spirits or rectified alcohol; after sufficient steeping the volatile constituents extracted by the alcohol are separated by distillation and the distillate is sweetened. The product is stored in wooden casks to mature and is finally bottled. Liqueurs are principally served as after-dinner drinks, though they are also used to flavour sweets and desserts.

Some of the best-known liqueurs are: Absinthe, Advocaat, Bénédictine, Brandy (also Apricot Brandy and Cherry Brandy), Chartreuse, Crème de Cacao, Crème de Menthe, Curaçao, Drambuie, Grand Marnier, Kirsch (or Kirschwasser), Kümmel, Maraschino, Noyau, Prunelle, Sloe Gin and Van der Hum.

(For details, see individual entries.)

LIQUORICE (LICORICE)

The black juice prepared from the roots of this plant is used to make various popular sweets, as well as in medicine.

LITCHI

(See Lychee entry.)

LIVER

The livers of calves, oxen, pigs and sheep, also those of poultry and game, are all used in cookery.

Calf's liver, which is regarded as the best, is popular when fried and served with bacon or mushrooms or in a mixed grill. Sheep's and lamb's liver can also be fried. Ox liver is coarse in texture (and therefore much cheaper) and it needs to be casseroled or cooked in some similar way to prevent its being hard and granular. Pig's liver is normally used in sausages of various kinds and in liver pâté. (See Pâté entry.)

Pâté de foie gras, made from the livers of specially fattened geese, is regarded as a great delicacy. Chicken livers have a good flavour and are used in pâté and toasted savouries.

The food value of liver is high. It contains protein, vitamin A, the vitamin B complex and iron in appreciable amounts. Liver eaten once a week supplies a good portion of the iron required.

LIVER AND ONIONS

METRIC/IMPERIAL
0.5 kg/1 lb onions, skinned and chopped
25 g/1 oz fat or oil
salt
pepper
1 × 2.5 ml spoon/½ teaspoon dried sage or mixed
    herbs, optional
0.5 kg/1 lb calf's or lamb's liver

Fry the onions lightly in the hot fat or oil until they begin to colour, then add the seasoning (and the herbs, if used). Cover the frying pan with a lid or large plate and simmer very gently for about 10 minutes until the onions are soft. Meanwhile wash and trim the liver and cut it into thin strips. Add to the onions, increase the heat slightly and continue cooking for about 5 to 10 minutes, stirring all the time, until the liver is just cooked. Remove it from the pan, drain and serve with freshly boiled rice and salad.

LIVER MARSALA

METRIC/IMPERIAL
0.5 kg/1 lb calf's or lamb's liver
lemon juice
seasoned flour
50 g/2 oz butter
3 × 15 ml spoons/3 tablespoons Marsala
150 ml/¼ pint stock
whole grilled tomatoes, matchstick potatoes and
    parsley to garnish

231

Wash and slice the liver. Sprinkle it with the lemon juice and coat with seasoned flour. Melt the butter in a frying pan and fry the liver quickly on both sides until lightly browned. Stir in the Marsala and stock and simmer until the meat is just cooked and the sauce syrupy. Arrange the liver on a serving dish and garnish with the tomatoes, potatoes and parsley.

RAGOÛT OF LIVER

METRIC/IMPERIAL
0.5 kg/1 lb lamb's liver
4 × 15 ml spoons/4 tablespoons seasoned flour
4 rashers bacon, rinded and chopped
25 g/1 oz fat or oil
400 ml/¾ pint stock
100 g/4 oz long grain rice
2 × 15 ml spoons/2 tablespoons sultanas
1 apple, peeled and grated
1 × 5 ml spoon/1 teaspoon tomato paste

Wash the liver, cut it into small pieces and coat with the seasoned flour. Fry the liver and bacon in the fat or oil until golden brown, for about 5 minutes. Add the stock to the pan and bring to the boil, stirring to prevent burning. Add the rice, sultanas, apple and tomato paste and simmer for 20 minutes, until the rice is cooked and all the stock is absorbed.

LAMB'S LIVER, CHINESE STYLE

450 g/1 lb lamb's liver
2 × 5 ml spoons/2 teaspoons cornflour
2 × 15 ml spoons/2 tablespoons sherry
3–4 slices of fresh ginger
1 small onion, skinned and finely chopped
25 g/1 oz dried mushrooms, or 4 fresh mushrooms
175 g/6 oz canned bamboo shoots
oil for frying
2 × 5 ml spoons/2 teaspoons soy sauce

Cut the liver up small and mix with the cornflour, sherry, ginger, and onion. If dried mushrooms are used, soak in hot water until soft, then cut them up small. Cut the bamboo shoots into strips. Heat the oil, fry the liver quickly over a strong heat and add the vegetables. Stir till every piece is golden, then pour in the soy sauce and serve hot.

LIVER PASTE

(See Paste entry.)

LOACH

A small British river fish of the carp family; it is prepared like the smelt.

LOAF

A neatly shaped mass of a foodstuff, such as bread, cooked meat, sugar, etc.

LOBSCOUSE

A sailor's stew of meat and vegetables.

LOBSTER

A shell fish belonging to the crab family, one of the two great divisions of crustacea. The common lobster is found abundantly along many European shores. Its natural colour is greenish-black, but changes to red on being boiled; it is obtainable all the year round, but at its finest from June to September.

Lobsters are best served quite simply, with an accompaniment of oil and vinegar dressing, mayonnaise or tartare sauce and salad. Lobster meat can also be served hot in the form of an au gratin dish, devilled, curried, scalloped, served as cutlets or used as a filling for patties or omelettes, etc.

CHOICE, BOILING AND PREPARATION
Lobsters are generally sold ready boiled. A medium-sized one is best; it should be heavy in proportion to its size and the tail should have plenty of 'spring'. For eating purposes, the male or cock lobster is superior to the hen and is more delicate in flavour; it does not grow to so large a size and is generally narrower in the back part of the tail. On the other hand, the hen lobster is prized for its red coral (the spawn), which is useful for garnishing and for making cardinal sauce.

If the lobster is bought alive, tie up the claws securely and wash it in clean water. Then place it in cold water, bring slowly to boiling point, and let it boil fairly quickly and without stopping for 15 to 20 minutes, according to size; allow it to cool in the water. If a lobster is boiled too long, the flesh becomes hard and thready. Remove any scum before lifting out the lobster and if the shell is to be used, rub it over with a little oil, to give a gloss.

First twist the large claws off the lobster and crack them without injuring the flesh. Remove also the smaller claws, which are only used for garnishing. Then split the lobster right down the middle of the back from head to tail, using a strong, pointed knife. Remove the intestine (which looks like a small vein running through the centre of the tail), the stomach, which lies near the head, and the spongy-looking gills. To serve, stand the head upright on a dish, arrange the cracked claws and split tail round it and garnish with parsley or salad. Serve the sauce or condiments separately.

LOBSTER MAYONNAISE

Cut the lobster meat into small, neat pieces and slice a hard-boiled egg. Line a salad bowl with lettuce and watercress, mix the lobster with mayonnaise sauce and pile in the centre. Decorate with lettuce heart, sliced egg and lobster coral (if available) or the lobster claws and head.

LOBSTER NEWBURG

METRIC/IMPERIAL
2 small cooked lobsters, weighing 225 g/8 oz each
25 g/1 oz butter
white, cayenne and paprika pepper
salt
4 × 15 ml spoons/4 tablespoons Madeira or sherry
2 egg yolks
150 ml/¼ pint carton single cream
buttered toast or boiled rice
chopped parsley to garnish

Cut the lobsters in half, carefully detach the tail meat in one piece and cut it into fairly thin slices. Crack the claws and remove the meat as unbroken as possible. Melt the butter in a frying pan, lay the lobster in the pan, season well and heat very gently for about 5 minutes, without colouring. Pour the Madeira or sherry over and continue to cook a little more quickly until the liquid is reduced by half. Beat the egg yolks with a little seasoning and add the cream. Take the lobster off the heat, pour the cream mixture over and mix gently over a slow heat till the sauce reaches the consistency of cream. Adjust the seasoning, pour at once on to hot buttered toast or boiled rice and sprinkle with parsley.

LOBSTER THERMIDOR

METRIC/IMPERIAL
2 small cooked lobsters, 225 g/8 oz each
50 g/2 oz butter
1 × 15 ml spoon/1 tablespoon chopped shallot
2 × 5 ml spoons/2 teaspoons chopped parsley
1–2 × 5 ml spoons/1–2 teaspoons chopped tarragon
4 × 15 ml spoons/4 tablespoons dry white wine
300 ml/½ pint béchamel sauce
3 × 15 ml spoons/3 tablespoons grated Parmesan cheese
mustard
salt
paprika pepper

Remove the lobster meat from the shells, chop the claw and head meat roughly and cut the tail meat into thick slices. Melt half the butter in a saucepan and add the shallot, parsley and tarragon. After a few minutes add the wine and simmer for 5 minutes. Add the béchamel sauce and simmer until it is reduced to a creamy consistency. Add the lobster meat to the sauce, with 2 × 15 ml spoons/2 tablespoons of the cheese, the remaining butter, in small pieces, and mustard, salt and paprika to taste. Arrange the mixture in the shells, sprinkle with the remaining cheese and put under the grill to brown the top quickly. Serve at once.

LOBSTER BUTTER

Remove the coral from a cooked lobster, wash it and dry it in a cool oven, without allowing it to change colour. Pound it in a mortar with double its weight in butter, season to taste and rub it through a hair sieve. Use to make lobster bisque or cardinal sauce.

LOCUST BEAN

The fruit of a Mediterranean shrub, much used in the Near East; also called carob. The whole pod, which is rather sweet and insipid, is used to make a kind of meal and also a syrup.

LOGANBERRY

A succulent aggregate fruit, larger and rather more acid than raspberries, with a hardish hull and when fully ripe of a dark purplish red. Really ripe loganberries are suitable for dessert and they also make good tarts, pies, wine and preserves; loganberry jam, which is made in the same way as raspberry jam, is particularly delicious.

LOIN

The name given to the back portion of various animals.

LOIN OF LAMB
The back portion of the sheep nearest to the leg. The loin is considered the choicest joint for roasting, but it is expensive on account of the large amount of bone and fat; the latter should, however, be well trimmed by the butcher. There are two cuts of loin:
1. The best end, consisting of the first 6 bones after the best end of neck, together with the kidney; this cut is roasted or baked, or used for chops.
2. The chump end next to the tail, which has more bone; from this part of the loin large chump chops are cut.

The double loin, undivided, is called the saddle and is a joint suitable only for very large households or when entertaining.

233

To prepare and cook: Remove the marrow from the chine bone; this should be well jointed by the butcher, as it is difficult to carve. Saw across the rib bones of the neck (if this has not already been done by the butcher) about 7.5 cm/3 inches from the tips; fold this flap under and tie the joint into a compact form. If the outer skin is tough, remove it. Roast as described under Lamb and serve with red-currant jelly or cranberry sauce.

LOIN OF PORK

The foreloin is cut with the spare-rib; the hind loin is the part containing the kidney. Both joints can be roasted. (See Pork entry.)

LOIN OF VEAL

This is cheaper than the fillet, but has a considerable amount of bone; the best end, which contains the kidney, is superior to the chump end and is a prime part for roasting; the loin is often braised, and chops are also cut from it. (See Veal entry.)

LOLLIPOP

A boiled sweet or toffee stuck on a small wooden stick. (See Sweets entry.)

LOQUAT

A Japanese species of medlar, with yellow fruit the size of a gooseberry. It is used for jams and jellies.

LOTE

(See Eel Pout entry.)

LOVAGE

A perennial herb similar to angelica in appearance. Every part is aromatic and can be used for culinary purposes. The seeds, leaves and stems all have a slightly celery flavour and fragrance which is retained when dried. The stems are thick and hollow and are often candied and used in confectionery. Lovage was known to the Greeks and Romans as a medicinal herb. In Tudor times the leaves were extensively used in salads and broths. Today it is used as an ingredient in some dried soup powders.

LOVE-APPLE

An old name for the tomato.

LUNCH CAKE

A fairly plain, substantial fruit cake.

LUNCHEON (LUNCH)

The midday meal. It varies so much in character according to taste and circumstance that no hard-and-fast description is possible, for the word may cover anything from the sandwich lunch taken by some office and factory workers to the fairly elaborate formal meal given when guests are entertained at a public function or private party.

LUTING

A strip of pastry placed round a dish to seal on the lid or pastry cover; used when preparing potted game, etc., in covered dishes.

LYCHEE (LITCHI)

The fruit of a tree of Chinese origin that grows in many parts of the East. Lychees have a scaly, reddish-brown outer covering, white, pulpy flesh and a hard brown stone; their flavour is very attractive, acid yet sweet. The fruit is obtainable in this country in cans, and fresh when in season.

MACARONI

The most widely known type of pasta. It is made from wheaten flour in the form of a long tube about 6 mm/¼ inch or less in diameter. It is also made into shapes such as the letters of the alphabet, shells, rings and stars etc. It is a staple food of Italy and it is said that the name derives from the Greek meaning of the word which is 'blessed bread'. This is an allusion to the ancient custom of eating it at feasts for the dead.

Macaroni can be served in innumerable ways, the simplest being with plenty of butter, pepper, salt and grated Parmesan cheese. In England it is generally eaten as macaroni cheese, but it can be served as an accompaniment or a garnish or added to soups and stews and is occasionally made into sweet puddings and salads.

To cook macaroni: When used as a main dish, an accompaniment or a garnish, macaroni is cooked in boiling salted water, stock or milk. Allow plenty of liquid (about 1.2 litres/2 pints to 100 g/4 oz) as the macaroni absorbs a great deal of fluid – for example 100 g/4 oz weigh about 400 g/14 oz to 450 g/16 oz when cooked. Bring the liquid to the boil and add salt with flavouring such as a small onion if desired. If not already in small pieces break the macaroni into 5 cm/2 inch lengths and boil for 20 to 30 minutes, stirring occasionally to prevent it sticking to the pan. Cook until the macaroni feels soft if pressed between the thumb and finger, then drain off the liquid. Toss in a little melted butter.

MACARONI CHEESE

METRIC/IMPERIAL
175 g/6 oz shortcut macaroni
40 g/1½ oz butter
4 × 15 ml spoons/4 tablespoons flour
600 ml/1 pint milk
pinch grated nutmeg or 1 × 2.5 ml spoon/½ teaspoon made mustard
175 g/6 oz mature cheese, grated
2 × 15 ml spoons/2 tablespoons fresh white breadcrumbs (optional)

Cook the macaroni in fast boiling salted water for 10 minutes only and drain it well. Meanwhile melt the fat, stir in the flour and cook for 2 to 3 minutes. Remove the pan from the heat and gradually stir in the milk. Bring to the boil and continue to stir until the sauce thickens; remove from the heat and stir in the seasonings, 100 g/4 oz of the cheese and the macaroni. Pour into an ovenproof dish and sprinkle with the breadcrumbs (if used) and the remaining cheese. Place dish on a baking sheet and bake in a moderately hot oven (200°C/400°F, Gas Mark 6) for about 20 minutes or until golden and bubbling. Quick macaroni can also be used – cook as directed on the packet.

VARIATIONS
Add to the sauce any of the following:

METRIC/IMPERIAL
1 small onion, skinned, chopped and boiled
100 g/4 oz bacon or ham, rinded, chopped and lightly fried
½ – 1 green pepper, chopped and blanched
½ – 1 canned pimiento, chopped
1 medium can of salmon or tuna, drained and flaked
50 g/2 oz mushrooms, sliced and lightly fried
1 medium can of sardines, drained and flaked
1 small can tomatoes

MACAROON

A cake made of ground almonds, sugar and egg whites and baked on rice paper; small macaroons can be served as petits fours and the mixture may also be used as a filling for tartlets. A similar mixture is made with coconut.

MACAROONS

METRIC/IMPERIAL
1 egg white
50 g/2 oz ground almonds
90 g/3½ oz caster sugar
1 × 2.5 ml spoon/½ teaspoon almond essence
few split almonds
little egg white to glaze

Line 1 to 2 baking sheets with silicone (non-stick) paper or rice paper. Whisk the egg white until stiff and fold in the ground almonds, caster sugar and almond essence. Place spoonfuls of the mixture on the baking sheets, leaving plenty of room for spreading. (Alternatively pipe the mixture onto the paper, using a piping bag and 1 cm/½ inch plain pipe.) Top each biscuit with a split almond and brush with egg white. Bake in a moderate oven (180°C/350°F, Gas Mark 4) for 20 to 25 minutes until just beginning to colour. Cool on a wire rack.

MACE

The husk of the nutmeg, which is used in both 'blade' and powder form. It improves the flavour of sauces, soups and stews and is usually one of the ingredients of curry powder. It is occasionally added to the other herbs forming a bouquet garni. One blade of mace is generally sufficient for most savoury dishes.

MACÉDOINE

This French term is commonly used in England to denote a mixture of vegetables or fruit, diced or cut into various shapes and served as a cocktail, a salad or a garnish.

Macédoine of Vegetables

Cut such vegetables as carrots, turnips and celery into dice or fancy shapes, add some peas and boil in salted water until tender. Serve plain, tossed in butter or in a Béchamel sauce. For Russian salad, mix with mayonnaise.

Macédoine of Fruit: See Fruit salad, in Fruit Entry.

MACKEREL

A round fish, in season from October to July, but at its best during April, May and June. Mackerel has distinctive blue-black markings on the back and silvery underside; when fully grown it may be 30 cm/1 foot in length. The flesh is oily and the flavour is best when the fish is eaten fresh from the sea. When buying mackerel make sure that it is perfectly fresh; choose a fish that has clear eyes, bright colouring and bright red open gills, it should also be stiff although this is not an infallible guide, as stiffness may be due to ice storage. Frozen and canned mackerel are also available.

Mackerel is a good source of protein and vitamins A and D; it also contains small amounts of minerals.

Preparation and Cooking

Remove the scales by scraping from tail to head, but handle carefully as the skin is delicate. Slit the belly from the head to the vent and remove the entrails. Wash the fish and cut off the fins and head (except for baking).

Mackerel may be steamed, grilled, fried or baked. Suitable accompaniments to serve with them include parsley, fennel, gooseberry, apple, caper and mustard sauce and maître d'hôtel butter. They are also delicious split in half, dipped in oatmeal and fried. Soused mackerel is prepared like Soused Herring (See Herring entry).

If desired the prepared and scored mackerel may be soaked in a marinade for 1 hour before grilling, then served hot or cold, garnished with lemon or parsley.

Smoked mackerel: serve grilled or fried.

Canned mackerel: serve cold in hors d'oeuvre and salads or hot with sauce. It can also be made into interesting dishes with potato or savoury crumble toppings.

BAKED MACKEREL

Score the mackerel 2 to 3 times on each side. Sprinkle lightly with salt and pepper and a squeeze of lemon juice and place on a greased tin, with a few pieces of dripping on top, then cover lightly with a piece of greased paper. Bake in a moderate oven, (180°C/350°F, Gas Mark 4) for 20 to 30 minutes, basting twice during the cooking. Serve with gooseberry or mustard sauce and garnish with parsley.

MACKEREL IN CREAM SAUCE

METRIC/IMPERIAL
4 mackerel
bunch of parsley
little butter
2 × 15 ml spoons/2 tablespoons flour
fat for frying
salt
150 ml/¼ pint water
150 ml/¼ pint soured cream

Wash the fish then fillet them and sprinkle with chopped parsley and a few flakes of butter. Roll up and tie with fine string. Toss in flour and fry in a saucepan until brown. Add salt to taste, the water and soured cream. Cover and simmer for 10 minutes. Remove strings and serve with sauce.

MADEIRA

A fortified wine from the Island of Madeira; the grapes are grown on the rich volcanic soil which gives an individual flavour. Before being fortified the wine is subjected to heat in the maturing casks. There are several types of Madeira with different flavours and characteristics. Malmsey is rich, sweet and dark and can be very old: there is some known to be over 100 years old. It is good served after dinner. Bual is a less expensive form of Malmsey and essentially a dessert wine; Sercial is a light dry Madeira and Verdels is medium sweet. These are more suitable to serve as an apéritif.

MADEIRA OR MARSALA SAUCE

Add up to 150 ml/¼ pint Madeira or Marsala to 300 ml/½ pint espagnole sauce (coating consistency) and re-heat but do not re-boil. The juice and extracts from the meat tin can also be reduced and added to give extra flavour.

Serve with any meat or game.

MADEIRA CAKE

A type of rich cake, often erroneously referred to as 'plain' because it contains no fruit and is flavoured only with lemon. The characteristic decoration consists of candied citron peel which is placed on top during baking.

MADEIRA CAKE

METRIC/IMPERIAL
100 g/4 oz plain flour
100 g/4 oz self raising flour
175 g/6 oz butter
175 g/6 oz caster sugar
1 × 5 ml spoon/1 teaspoon vanilla essence
3 eggs, beaten
about 1 – 2 × 15 ml spoons/1 – 2 tablespoons milk
2 – 3 thin slices citron peel

Grease and line an 18 cm/7 inch cake tin. Sift the flours together. Cream the butter, sugar and essence until pale and fluffy. Beat in the egg a little at a time. Fold in the flour, adding a little milk if necessary to give a dropping consistency. Put into the tin and bake in a moderate oven (180°C/350°F, Gas Mark 4). After 20 minutes put the citron peel on top of the cake and continue to cook for a further 40 minutes. Cool on a wire rack.

MADELEINE

A small fancy cake baked in a dariole mould and often coated with jam and coconut. Madeleines were originally made from a rich Victoria sponge mixture, but sometimes a Genoese sponge is used.

In France the name is applied to a sponge cake baked in a scallop-shaped mould.

MAGNUM

A large wine bottle, containing 1.6 litres/⅓ gallon.

MAISON

Such a description of a dish, e.g. Pâté Maison, should indicate that it is a speciality of a restaurant or house.

MAID OF HONOUR

These are small tartlets with a filling made from flavoured milk curds. They originated in Henry VIII's palace at Hampton Court, where they were popular with the Queen's Maids of Honour, and the recipe was a closely guarded secret. However, in George I's reign a lady of the court gave it to a gentleman who set up a shop in Richmond, where the tarts are still made. The recipe was made public in 1951 for a television programme about historic dishes of Britain.

MAIDS OF HONOUR

METRIC/IMPERIAL
600 ml/1 pint milk
pinch salt
1 × 15 ml spoon/1 tablespoon rennet
75 g/3 oz butter, softened
2 eggs
1 × 15 ml spoon/1 tablespoon brandy
3 × 15 ml spoons/3 tablespoons nibbed almonds
2 × 5 ml spoons/2 teaspoons caster sugar
215 g/7½ oz pkt bought puff pastry
few currants – optional

Warm the milk until it feels just warm to a finger, add the salt and rennet and leave to set; when firm put into a piece of fine muslin, secure with a piece of string and hang it up over a bowl. Allow to drain overnight. The next day rub the curds and butter through a sieve. Whisk the eggs and brandy together and add to the curds, with the almonds and sugar. Line about 12 6 cm/2½ inch deep patty tins with thinly rolled pastry, press it into the bases. Half fill with the curd mixture and if you wish sprinkle with currants over the top. Bake in a hot oven (220°C/425°F, Gas Mark 7) for 15 to 20 minutes. Turn out to cool on a wire rack.

MAÎTRE d'HÔTEL

Literally, Chief Steward's style; the name given to simply prepared dishes garnished with maître d'hôtel butter – for example Filet de Sole à la Maître d'Hôtel. The name is also given to a sauce.

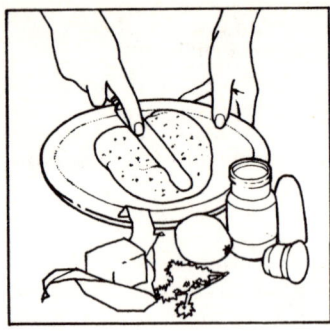 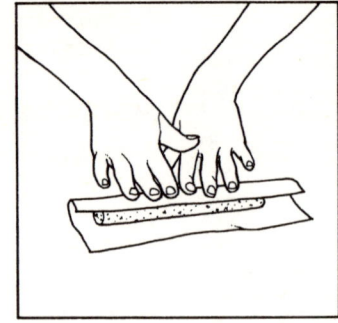 

1. Cream the butter, chopped parsley, lemon juice and seasoning together on a small plate.

2. Roll the butter into a sausage shape in a piece of greaseproof paper, wrap and refrigerate until hard.

3. Unwrap butter roll and cut into thin slices approximately 1 cm/½ inch thick.

MAÎTRE D'HÔTEL BUTTER

METRIC/IMPERIAL
25 g/1 oz butter
2 × 5 ml spoons/2 teaspoons finely chopped parsley
1 × 5 ml spoon/1 teaspoon lemon juice
salt
cayenne pepper

Warm and cream the butter, then work in the parsley, lemon juice and seasonings; leave to harden and cut into cubes or shape into pats. When served with hot food maître d'hôtel butter should be added only just before the dish is put on the table, otherwise it melts, losing its decorative appearance.

MAIZE (INDIAN CORN)

A cereal which is grown in enormous quantities on the American continent, where it is used both for animal feeding and for human consumption. It also grows well in Italy and other south European countries and in some parts of Africa and Asia.

Maize is used to produce corn syrup, alcoholic drinks, corn oil etc., is cooked as a vegetable and is ground into meal and flour – of various degrees of fineness – for use in the production of cornflour, custard powder, starch and cereal preparations of different types. Maize porridge, corn bread, hominy and corn mush in the U.S.A., polenta in Italy and stirabout in Ireland are some of the best known dishes made with corn meal. As it does not keep well it should be bought in very small quantities.

There are many varieties of maize, some of the best known being:—

SWEETCORN
This type has a particularly sweet flavour. The head grows about 15 cm/7 inches long. It is available fresh as corn on the cob when in season. Canned and frozen sweetcorn is always available. It is popular served as a vegetable or used in salads, flans and creamy sauces – particularly tasty with chicken dishes. (See Corn on the Cob entry.)

FLOUR CORN
Though slightly smaller than sweetcorn this is preferred by the Indian tribes, because it has soft, mealy kernels.

POPCORN
This type, which has heads about 10 cm/4 inches long is so named because when the hard kernels are heated, they burst with a pop as the moisture contained in the cells expands on turning into steam.

MALAGA

A sweet fortified Spanish wine. It is made from local wine to which Pedro Ximenez sherry and grape brandy are added.

MALLARD

(See Wild Duck entry.)

MALT

The substance produced by allowing barley to germinate to a certain stage under controlled conditions, the starch being converted into dextrin and malt sugar; when the correct stage of germination is reached the grains are dried by heating and become malt: which is largely used by brewers. To most housewives, however, the word suggests malt extract, a dark sticky syrup made by evaporating malted barley at a low temperature or in a vacuum. When malt extract is used in cakes, bread and puddings it imparts a distinctive flavour and a rather moist texture. Used in medicines etc., its flavour helps to mask unpleasant tasting ingredients such as cod and halibut liver oils.

MALT BREAD

METRIC/IMPERIAL
25 g/1 oz fresh yeast or 1 × 15 ml spoon/1 tablespoon
dried yeast and 1 × 5 ml spoon/1 teaspoon caster
sugar

about 150 ml/¼ pint tepid water
450 g/1 lb plain flour
1 × 5 ml spoon/1 teaspoon salt
4 × 15 ml spoons/4 tablespoons malt
1 × 15 ml spoon/1 tablespoon black treacle
25 g/1 oz butter or margarine
sugar and water glaze, optional

Blend the fresh yeast in the water.

For dried yeast, dissolve the sugar in the water, sprinkle the yeast over it and leave until frothy. Mix the flour and salt. Warm the malt, treacle and fat until just melted. Stir the yeast liquid and malt mixtures into the dry ingredients and mix to a fairly soft, sticky dough, adding a little more water if necessary. Turn onto a floured board, knead well until the dough is firm and elastic. Divide into two pieces. Shape both into an oblong, and roll up like a Swiss roll and put into two prepared 450 g/1 lb loaf tins. Leave to rise in a warm place (about 23°C/75°F) until the dough fills the tins; this may take about 1½ hours as malt bread dough usually takes quite a long time to rise. Bake in a moderately hot oven (200°C/400°F, Gas Mark 6) for 30 to 40 minutes. When cooked the loaves can be brushed with a sugar glaze of 1 × 15 ml spoon/1 tablespoon water and 25 g/1 oz sugar.

Serve cut into slices and buttered liberally.

RAISIN MALT LOAF

METRIC/IMPERIAL
225 g/8 oz plain flour
a pinch of salt
2 × 15 ml spoons/2 tablespoons soft brown sugar
1 × 5 ml spoon/1 teaspoon bicarbonate of soda
150 g/5 oz seedless raisins
50 g/2 oz golden syrup
2 × 15 ml spoons/2 tablespoons malt
about 150 ml/¼ pint milk

Grease and line an oblong loaf tin with 21 cm/8½ inch × 11 cm/4½ inch top measurements. Sift together the flour, salt, sugar and bicarbonate of soda, add raisins. Melt the syrup and malt in half of the milk. Make a well in the centre of the dry ingredients, pour in the malt mixture adding more milk to give a sticky, stiff consistency. Put into the tin and bake in a moderate oven (160°C/325°F, Gas Mark 3) for 1 to 1¼ hours. Turn out to cool on a wire rack and keep for 24 hours before serving, sliced and buttered.

Maltose (Malt Sugar)

This form of sugar is one of the intermediate 'break-down' products occurring when starch-splitting (diastatic) enzymes work on starches such as wheat (during the making of bread) also in the mouth and intestine, during digestion. Glucose is the final result.

MANDARIN ORANGE

(See Tangerine entry.)

MANGEL WURZEL, MANGOLD

A coarse beet, usually grown for cattle feed; it can be cooked like a turnip.

MANGO

A tropical fruit combining a distinctive, somewhat spicy flavour with slight acidity. The fruit varies considerably in size, ranging from the size of a plum to about 2.25 kg/5 lbs in weight; its colour also varies from green to yellow and red. Some varieties are delicious, others are most unpleasant in taste.

Ripe mango is eaten as a dessert fruit; green mango is also eaten in fruit salads etc.

MANGOSTEEN

A tropical fruit with a refreshing, pleasant flavour. It resembles an orange in shape but is dark brown with white spots and has rose-coloured pulp.

MANHATTAN COCKTAIL

(See Cocktail entry.)

MANIOC

(See Cassava entry.)

MAPLE SUGAR

As its name implies, this sugar is derived from the sap of various species of the maple tree. It has a characteristic flavour and may be used to replace part or all of the ordinary sugar in cakes, puddings etc. It is also used in confectionery (often mixed with brown sugar) and in sauces for ice cream, waffles, blancmanges etc. It is particularly popular in Canada and U.S.A.

Maple Syrup

A very sweet syrup, made from Maple sugar. It has a distinctive but delicate flavour, and is used in sweet dishes and as an accompaniment to ices, waffles, etc., as well as in the manufacture of confectionery.

MARASCHINO

A liqueur made from a type of small, sour, black cherry grown in Dalmatia, known as Marasca. The kernels are distilled together with the leaves and this distillate gives a bitter tang to an otherwise sweet drink. Maraschino is often used to flavour sweets, punches, cocktails etc.

MARC DE RAISIN

A French semi-hard cheese with a 'crust' of grapeskins and pips replacing the ordinary rind.

MARENGO

A chicken dish named after the Italian village of Marengo. Here the dish is said to have been invented by Napoleon's chef and cooked after the battle in 1800. Traditionally the chicken is sautéed in oil and flavoured with tomato, garlic and brandy and garnished with eggs and crayfish. There are variations to this original recipe.

MARGARINE

A manufactured fat, produced as an imitation of butter. It was invented by a Frenchman, Mèges Mouriés, in 1869 and was originally made from a mixture of animal fats.

Present day margarine includes vegetable and/or animal fats and cultured or sweet fat free milk, all blended together as an emulsion. A wide range of oils are used, most of which are imported; these include palm oil, groundnut, coconut, sunflower, cottonseed, soya bean, beef and mutton tallow, herring and pilchard oils. The blend varies according to the supply and cost of the ingredients at any given time.

As these fats have varying melting points, a suitable blend has to be calculated to give a margarine of the required consistency. Fortunately it is possible to modify the melting characteristics of the fats by one of the following processes:

Hydrogenation: Fats that are too liquid are hardened by incorporating hydrogen into the fatty acids.

Interesterification: The glyceride structure of the fat is altered resulting in a change of melting point.

Fractionation: A fat is separated into two parts, one of which contains a higher proportion of solid glycerides, thus hardening the oil.

The manufacture of margarine is a complicated process, but this is the sequence of operations carried out:—
1. Initial refining of oils.
2. Modification of melting points.
3. Final refining of oils.
4. Blending of oils and fats.
5. Addition of other ingredients (salt, vitamins, colouring, emulsifiers, flavouring agents).
6. Mixing with pasteurised, cultured milk.
7. Emulsification, chilling and texturing.
8. Packaging.

Margarine Legislation
This has been introduced to ensure that all table margarines conform to certain nutritional standards. Margarine must not contain more than 16 per cent water, nor may more than 10 per cent of the fat be derived from butter. No preservatives can be added with the exception of salt. Colouring is allowed in the form of vegetable dyes, the most common in Great Britain being annatto (derived from seeds of the roucou tree); beta carotene is also used. Margarine is enriched with vitamins A and D both of which can be synthesized. By law the following quantities must be included:
800–1000 international units Vitamin A per 100 g margarine.
(i.e., 230–280 mg Vitamin A per 1 oz margarine)
7.0–8.8 mg Vitamin D per 100 g margarine
(i.e., 2.0–2.5 mg Vitamin D per 1 oz margarine)

Margarine in the Diet
It is principally a source of energy, but also contributes a significant amount of Vitamins A and D to the daily diet. Margarine is eaten with other foods to make them more palatable.

Some margarines are high in polyunsaturated fats (always labelled as such) which are recommended for those wishing to keep blood cholesterol levels down. It is believed in some medical circles that a diet high in saturated fatty acids can lead to a high blood cholesterol level and subsequent heart disease. This is not considered the sole cause and has not been entirely proved.

Margarine in Cooking
Margarine is not suitable for frying at high temperatures but can be used for sautéing vegetables and cooking omelettes. Margarine can be used in pastry alone or combined with lard; it is particularly good for cakes, soft icings and sauces. Soft margarines which spread straight from the fridge are popular for cakes. They are best used in any of the one-stage recipes as they blend with the other ingredients more readily.

MARIGOLD

The flowers of this garden plant were formerly used to flavour and decorate salads etc., and to make a cordial.

MARINADE

A mixture of oil, wine, vinegar or lemon juice and herbs in which meat or fish is soaked before cooking to give it flavour and make it more tender. Marinating is especially useful for cuts of meat which are suitable for quick methods of cookery, but are not of the best quality; the meat should be beaten and then left to soak for at least 2 hours in the marinade. Marinades are also used for kebabs and meat to be stewed or casseroled; also used in making salads.

A SIMPLE MARINADE

METRIC/IMPERIAL
2 × 15 ml spoons/2 tablespoons salad oil
1 × 15 ml spoon/1 tablespoon lemon juice or vinegar
onion juice, chopped onion, shallot or chives
salt
pepper

Mix all ingredients and use as required.

WINE MARINADE

METRIC/IMPERIAL
1 sliced onion
150 ml/¼ pint dry white wine, red wine or cider
1 bay leaf
6 bruised peppercorns
4 bruised parsley stalks
2 × 15 ml spoons/2 tablespoons olive oil

Mix all the ingredients. Strain the liquid after use and add it to the gravy.

MARJORAM

A herb of the mint family. Sweet marjoram has a delicate flavour and should be treated as an annual. Pot marjoram is grown from seed and is a perennial. All types of marjoram are aromatic and have a scent similar to thyme. Marjoram is particularly good served with lamb, but is also used in soups, salads and meat dishes. Wild marjoram is known as oregano (See Oregano entry).

MARMALADE

This is the preserve traditionally served at breakfast in this country. The name derives from the Portuguese word marmalada, from the Latin word for quince, since the preserve was originally made from that fruit. In English the word now applies exclusively to a preserve made from Seville oranges (and sometimes other citrus fruits such as lemons, limes and grapefruit). In France, however, the term 'marmalade' means thick purée, made by stewing fruit until considerably reduced; many different fruits can be cooked in this way.

In addition to its use as a spread on toast or bread, marmalade is sometimes used in making puddings, tarts and sauces. As with other preserves the chief nutritional value of marmalade is as an energy provider.

Marmalade-making

The process is similar to jam-making except that the peel of the fruit requires longer to cook and during the cooking, which takes about two hours, a considerable amount of moisture is evaporated, so a larger quantity of water must be used in the first instance. If the peel is not softened before the sugar is added, it will remain hard – prolonged boiling after the sugar is added does not soften the peel but it darkens the colour of the marmalade and breaks down the pectin, causing it to lose its 'jelling' properties.

When large quantities of marmalade are made, a marmalade cutter is well worth buying. Failing this, the peel can be put through a coarse mincer, but the appearance and the texture of the finished marmalade are not so good. When slicing the fruit by hand it is essential to have a sharp knife to cut the rind thinly; if desired, the cutting can be made much easier by partially cooking the fruit first; cut the rind in quarters and cook it with the required amount of water until it is soft, then slice it and complete the cooking.

SEVILLE ORANGE MARMALADE

METRIC/IMPERIAL
1.5 kg/3 lb Seville oranges
juice of 2 lemons
3.5 litres/6 pints water
2.75 kg/6 lb sugar

Wash the fruit, cut it in half and squeeze out the juice and the pips. Slice the peel thinly and put it in a pan with the fruit juices, water and pips (tied in muslin). Simmer gently for about 2 hours until the peel is really soft and the liquid is reduced by about half. Remove the muslin bag, squeezing it well, add the sugar and stir until it has dissolved. Boil rapidly until setting point is reached – about 15 minutes. Leave to stand for about 15 minutes and then pot and cover in the usual way. Makes about 4.5 kg/10 lb.

MARMALADE MACE TEABREAD

METRIC/IMPERIAL
225 g/8 oz self-raising flour
pinch of salt
1.5 × 5 ml spoons/1½ teaspoons ground mace
100 g/4 oz butter or block margarine
100 g/4 oz demerara sugar
1 egg beaten
6 × 15 ml spoons/6 tablespoons chunky marmalade
4 × 15 ml spoons/4 tablespoons milk
3 crystallized orange slices, optional

Grease and line a loaf tin with 24 cm/9½ inch × 14 cm/5½ inch top measurements. Sift flour, salt and mace together into a basin. Rub in the fat until the mixture resembles fine breadcrumbs. Add the demerara sugar. Stir in the egg, 4 × 15 ml spoons/4 tablespoons marmalade and the milk. Turn the mixture into the prepared cake tin, level the surface and top with the halved slices of orange.

Bake in a moderate oven (180°C/350°F, Gas

Mark 4) for about 1 hour. Turn out onto a wire rack. Whilst still warm brush surface of cake with remaining marmalade. Cool. If wrapped in foil, this teabread stores well for up to a week.

MARMALADE SAUCE

METRIC/IMPERIAL
1 × 15 ml spoon/1 tablespoon marmalade
1 × 15 ml spoon/1 tablespoon caster sugar
150 ml/¼ pint water
2 × 5 ml spoons/2 teaspoons cornflour
a little lemon juice
colouring

Place the marmalade, sugar and water in a saucepan and bring to the boil. Add the cornflour, mixed with a little cold water, and boil up until the sauce is clear and the cornflour cooked – about 2 to 3 minutes. Add the lemon juice and a little colouring to improve the colour of the sauce if necessary.

CALEDONIAN CREAM

This syllabub, a good dinner party choice, is based on two of Scotland's best known exports – Drambuie and marmalade. A dark pungent marmalade enhances the flavour of the liqueur to make a rich, smooth dessert. It freezes well in freezerproof glasses or tiny soufflé dishes, and thaws in two to three hours at room temperature.

METRIC/IMPERIAL
6 × 5 ml spoons/6 teaspoons thin shred marmalade
25 g/1 oz caster sugar
4 × 15 ml spoons/4 tablespoons Drambuie
juice of one lemon
300 ml/½ pint double or whipping cream

Mix together the marmalade, sugar, Drambuie and lemon juice. Whisk the cream until it is just beginning to hold its shape. Gently whisk in the marmalade mixture until the cream stands in soft peaks – take care not to over whip the cream. Serve in small glasses.

MARMITE

French term for a covered cooking pot, and hence for a broth cooked in such a pot. The name is also given to a brand of yeast extract (See separate entry).

MARRON GLACÉ

A popular delicacy, made from chestnuts treated with syrup, which is served as a dessert or used as decoration on sweets; marrons glacés may also be seived and beaten into a meringue mixture or blended with cream as a sweet.

CHESTNUTS IN SYRUP

METRIC/IMPERIAL
225 g/8 oz granulated sugar
225 g/8 oz glucose or dextrose
150 ml/¼ pint plus 2 × 15 ml spoons/2 tablespoons water
350 g/12 oz whole chestnuts, peeled and skinned (weight after preparation) or 350 g/12 oz canned chestnuts, drained.
vanilla essence

Put the granulated sugar, glucose or dextrose and water in a pan large enough to hold the chestnuts and heat gently together until the sugars are dissolved; bring to the boil. Remove from the heat, add the chestnuts (drained if canned ones are used) and bring to the boil again. Remove from the heat, cover and leave overnight, preferably in a warm place. On the second day re-boil the chestnuts and syrup in the pan without the lid, remove from the heat, cover and again leave standing overnight. On the third day add 6 to 8 drops of vanilla essence and repeat the boiling process as above. Warm some 450 g/1 lb bottling jars in the oven, fill with the chestnuts and cover with the syrup. Seal in the usual way to make airtight.

Note: This recipe gives a delicious result, but the chestnuts are not exactly like the commercially prepared marrons glacés, which cannot be reproduced under home conditions.

MARROW

A member of the gourd family. There are several varieties, some being short and fat, others long and slender, some yellow and some green, while the type known as the custard marrow is of a flattened round shape, with fluted sides, and is particularly suitable for stuffing. The flavour of the marrow is best when it is young, though for preserves it should be used when full-grown. Marrows can be kept for several months if the stalk end is sealed with wax and they are hung in nets or arranged so that the air circulates round them.

As marrows consist chiefly of water, they have very little nutritional value, but their delicate flavour blends well with dishes of a more pronounced taste. They may be cooked in various ways and when stuffed form a good main dish. Marrow lends itself equally well to use in sweet dishes and may be used with apple in fruit pies, or preserved in the form of jam or chutney.

Preparation and cooking: Very young marrows may be cooked whole, but it is more usual to peel a marrow, remove the seeds and cut the flesh into cubes or slices.

Steaming: Place the prepared pieces of marrow in a container or tie them in muslin and cook for 20 to

40 minutes according to age and size. If a stuffed marrow is steamed it will need 1 hour or more.

Boiling: As marrows are so watery, this is not a very good method of cooking. Boil the vegetable for 15 minutes in salted water, drain well, dice, toss in butter and serve with white or cheese sauce.

Frying: Cut the marrow into 2.5 cm/1 inch cubes or slice and coat with seasoned flour; a little lemon juice may be added if desired. Sauté slowly in butter or good dripping. Fried marrow is good served with fried mushrooms.

Stewing: Cut the marrow into small pieces and sauté in butter with chopped onion. Add skinned chopped tomatoes and seasoning. Simmer until cooked.

Baking or roasting: Prepare the marrow and cook it around the joint, allowing about one hour.

STUFFED MARROW

METRIC/IMPERIAL
1 vegetable marrow about 1 kg/2¼ lb
350 g/12 oz minced meat
4 × 15 ml spoons/4 tablespoons fresh breadcrumbs
1 – 2 × 5 ml spoons/1 – 2 teaspoons mixed herbs or
  1 × 15 ml spoon/1 tablespoon chopped parsley
1 onion, finely chopped
salt
pepper
1 egg, beaten
tomato sauce

Wash the marrow, peel, cut in half and remove the seeds. Mix the meat, crumbs, herbs, onion and seasoning together with a fork and add enough egg to bind the mixture together. Put this stuffing into the two halves of the marrow and place them together again. Wrap in greased greaseproof paper, put in an ovenproof dish and bake in a moderate oven (180°C/350°F, Gas Mark 4) for about 1 hour until the marrow is done. Remove the paper and serve the marrow with a tomato sauce.

Alternatively, cut the marrow into slices about 4 cm/½ inch to 5 cm/2 inches thick, remove the seeds, stand the pieces on a greased ovenproof dish and fill each with the same stuffing as used above. Cover the dish with foil and bake at the same temperature for about 15 to 20 minutes.

MARROW AND GINGER JAM

METRIC/IMPERIAL
1.75 kg/4 lb marrow (prepared weight)
1.75 kg/4 lb sugar
25 g/1 oz root ginger
thinly peeled rind and juice of three lemons

Peel the marrow, remove the seeds and cut into

pieces about 1 cm/½ inch square. Weigh, place in a basin. Sprinkle with 450 g/1 lb of the sugar and allow to stand overnight. Press or 'bruise' the ginger with a weight to release the flavour from the fibres, tie up in a piece of muslin with the lemon rind and place in a pan with the marrow and lemon juice. Simmer for 30 minutes, add the remaining sugar and boil gently until setting point is reached and the marrow looks transparent. Remove the muslin bag and pot and cover in the usual way.

Makes about 2.75 kg/6 pounds.

MARROW BONE

(See Bones entry.)

MARSALA

An excellent white wine made from grapes grown around the town of that name in Sicily. It is usually served with dessert, though it sometimes replaces sherry.

MARSHMALLOW

A sweet of an elastic, spongy texture, which derives its name from the plant, since a gum formerly used in the cooking was obtained from its roots. Marshmallow may be tinted pink or other pale colours and is given various flavours; it is usually cut into 2.5 cm/1 inch cubes and these are rolled in icing sugar or occasionally coated with chocolate.

Marshmallows – either plain or toasted under the grill – are sometimes used as decoration for a cold sweet. They may also be chopped up and added to ice creams and jellies or dissolved in frosting and sauces.

MARSHMALLOW SAUCE

METRIC/IMPERIAL
100 g/4 oz granulated sugar
3 × 15 ml spoons/3 tablespoons water
8 marshmallows
1 egg white
a few drops of vanilla essence
carmine or cochineal

Dissolve the sugar in the water, then boil together for about 5 minutes. Add the marshmallows, cut into small pieces with scissors. Beat the egg white stiffly, then gradually fold in the marshmallow mixture. Add the vanilla and enough carmine or cochineal to give a pale pink tint. Serve poured over ice cream or fruit.

MARTINI COCKTAIL

(See Cocktail entry.)

MARZIPAN

Nowadays this term is generally used as equivalent to almond paste. The name is applied particularly to sweets made of this paste. (See Sweets entry.)

MASKING

To cover or coat a cooked meat or similar dish with savoury jelly, glaze or sauce; also to coat the inside of a mound with jelly.

MATÉ

(See Yerba Maté entry.)

MATZOTH (MOTZA)

A large, brittle, very thin biscuit of unleavened Jewish bread, eaten during the Passover.

MAY BOWL

A type of white wine cup, of German origin, also called May drink and May wine.

MAYONNAISE

(See Salad Dressing entry.)

MEAD

A drink made by fermenting honey with hops or yeast; cowslips or other wild flowers or spices are added for flavouring. It was drunk by Ancient Britons and also known as metheglin.

SPICED MEAD

METRIC/IMPERIAL
1.5 kg/3 lb honey
225 g/8 oz sugar
6.7 litres/1½ gallons hot water
juice of 2 lemons
rind of 1 lemon
8 cloves
1 piece stem ginger
a sprig of rosemary
15 g/½ oz yeast spread on a piece of brown toast

Dissolve the honey and sugar in the water and boil for 30 minutes removing the scum. Add the lemon juice and rind, spices and rosemary, put into a tub, leave to cool and add the yeast, then leave 3 to 4 days. Fill a cask with the liquid, leaving the bung loose. As it ferments the liquid will spill over and the cask must be refilled with more liquid from the tub. When fermentation ceases put in the bung and leave for 8 months before bottling. If a cask is not available allow the fermentation to take place in the tub and bottle the mead when it ceases.

MEALIE

The South African name for maize.

MEALY PUDDING

An oatmeal pudding which is served with grilled sausages, bacon, herrings, etc. If pudding skins are available, force mixture into these.

SIMPLE MEALY PUDDING

METRIC/IMPERIAL
450 g/1 lb coarse or medium oatmeal
225 g/8 oz beef suet
2 onions
salt
pepper

Toast the oatmeal in the oven turning it over frequently until it is golden-brown. Shred the suet finely and chop the onions very finely. Mix all the ingredients together and season well, tie in a cloth and boil for 1 hour.

If the mixture is put into pudding skins, cook in gently boiling water for 30 minutes.

MEASURES

In 1970, to take into account a change to the metric system of weights and measures, the British Standards Institution introduced a new specification for measuring spoons, measures and measuring jugs.

MEASURING SPOONS
To be one of the following: 20 ml, 15 ml, 10 ml, 5 ml, 2.5 ml, and 1.25 ml. The 20 ml and 1.25 ml are optional in a set.

MEASURING JUGS
The capacity of measuring jugs corresponding to the top graduation mark shall be as follows: 1 litre (1000 ml) marked at 7.5 dl, 5 dl, 2.5 dl, 1.25 dl, 1 dl, 0.5 dl, (500 ml) marked at 2.5 dl, 1.25 dl, 1 dl. Smaller markings are permissible. Many jugs are marked in millilitres only. (See Weights and Measures and Metrication entries.)

MEAT

The flesh of animals such as pig (pork), calf (veal), ox (beef), sheep (mutton), deer (venison), and rabbit. The flesh of many other animals is eaten in different parts of the world.

Meat is the muscle tissue of the animal and consists of bundles of fibres held together by connective tissue, in the meshes of which are a number of fat cells. The fibres vary in length according to the type of animal and the cut of meat but broadly speaking the longer fibres are tough and require

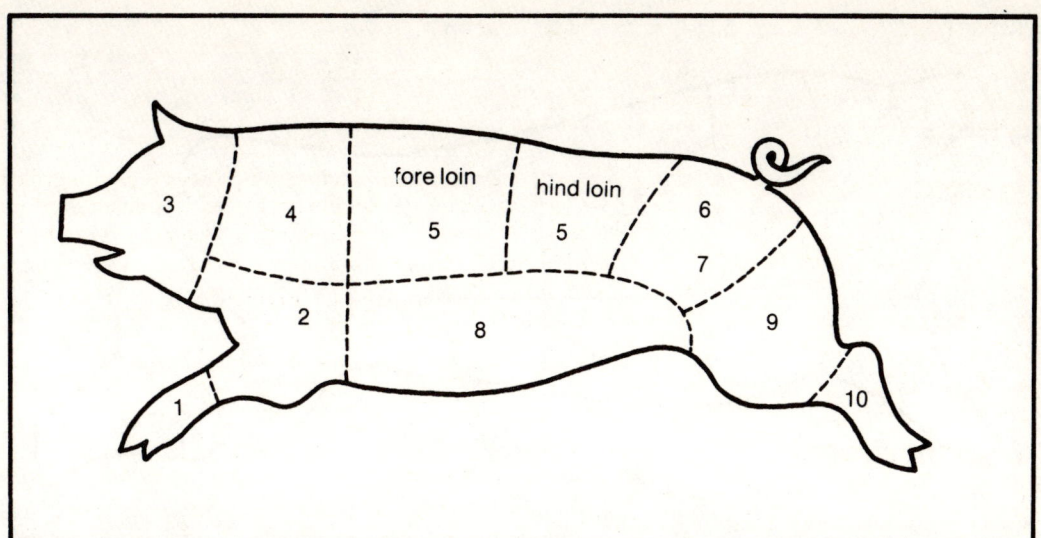

Pork *1. Trotter. They contain a large amount of natural gelatine and are a useful addition to pies set with a jelly. 2. Hand and spring. Sold fresh or salted it is an economical joint as the knuckle end can be salted for boiling, up to three steaks can be cut from the centre and grilled or fried, while the centre portion can be roasted whole. 3. Head. Economical and mainly used for brawn making. 4. Neck end and spare rib. Neck end can be boned and rolled and cut into joints or cubed and used for kebabs. Spare rib is suitable for roasting, braising or stewing. 5. Loin. A choice cut which can be roasted whole or cut into joints, hind loin, fore loin or the rib end. 6. Fillet. A choice cut for roasting whole or stuffed. 7. Chump chop. With the central bone removed they can be beaten and served as pork escalopes. 8. Belly. Serve roasted, boned and rolled, in stews or grilled. 9. Leg. Roast. 10. Knuckle. Can be roasted, boiled or stewed.*

Veal *1. Shoulder. This joint is also known as the oyster when the fore knuckle has been removed. It is extremely economical to bone and roast. 2. Scrag. Very inexpensive, sold mainly in one piece for stewing or boiling but there is a high percentage of bone to meat. 3. Middle neck. An inexpensive cut but again with a high percentage of bone. Usually sold in cutlets for stewing and braising or boned and sold for pie veal. 4. Best end of neck. A medium-priced cut sold on the bone which can be boned and stuffed for roasting. Sometimes sold in neck cutlets. 5. Loin. A prime cut sold on the bone or boned and stuffed. Loin can be roasted or cut into single bone portions to serve as cutlets. 6. Breast. An economical cut which can be roasted on the bone or boned, stuffed and rolled. Cut into thick strips and use for braising and stewing. 7. Fillet and knuckle. Fillet is roasted, knuckle for stews and casseroles or slow-roasting.*

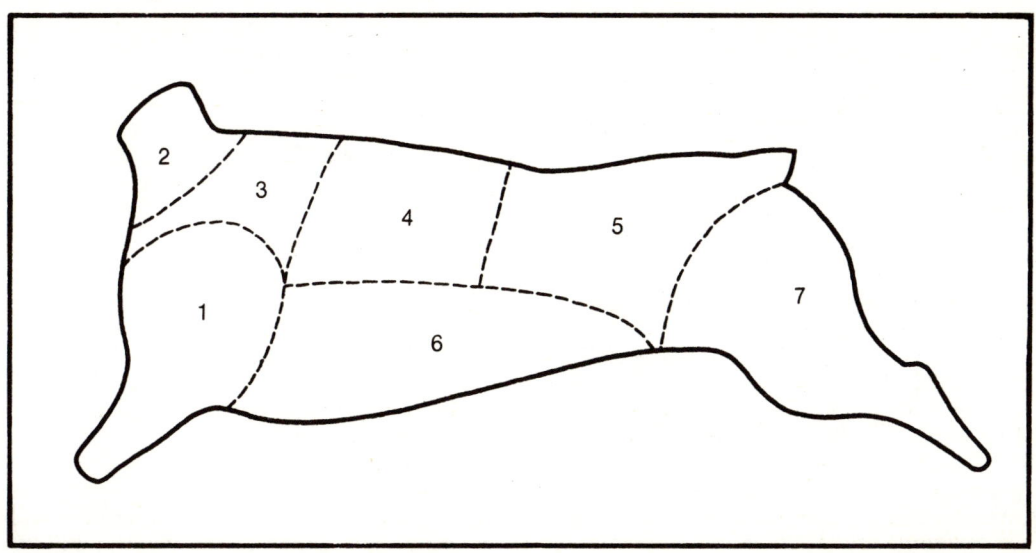

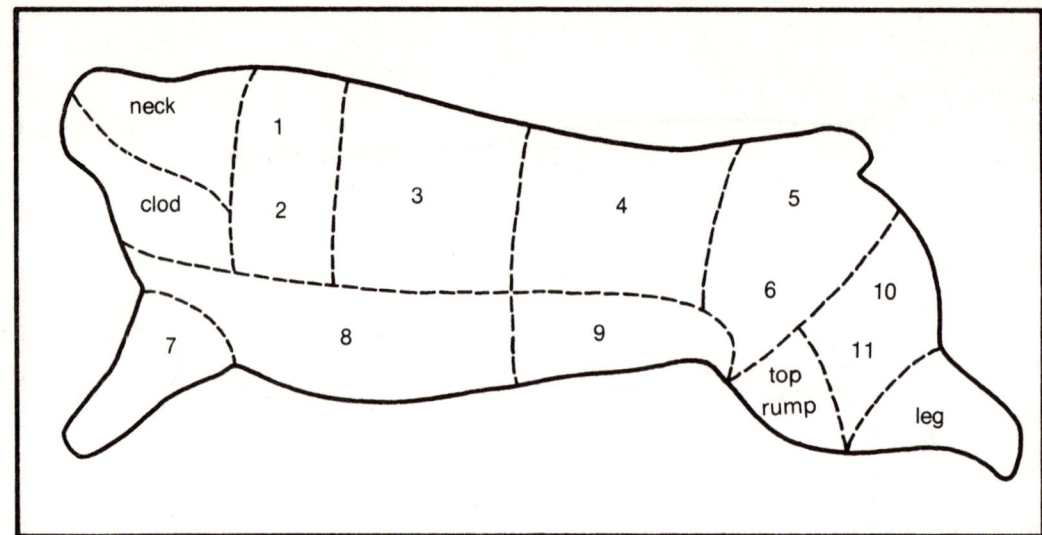

Beef 1. *Chuck. Best for stewing, braising or as pie and pudding filling. 2. Shoulder, known as blade is sold as braising steak. Lean shoulder can be used for slow-cooked casseroles and braises. 3. Best rib. A large joint to roast. 4. Sirloin. Ideal to roast and can be bought on the bone or boned and rolled. 5. Rump steak. Excellent for grilling, or frying. 6. Rump. Usually cut into two joints to pot-roast, also sold cubed for casseroles and stews. 7. Shin. A fairly gristly cut, sold for stews, casseroles and pies. 8. Brisket and Rolled Rib. On the bone for pot-roasting and braising and rolled rib for pressing and serving cold. 9. Flank. A fatty joint for pot-roasting, braising or boiling. 10. Topside. A lean boneless joint for pot-roasting, slow-braising, or roasting. 11. Silverside. A boned joint, spiced or salted for slow-boiling to press and serve cold. Unsalted, it can be pot-roasted or larded and slow-roasted.*

Lamb 1. *Neck. Sometimes sold in one piece which includes the Scrag. It contains a high proportion of bone and fat to meat and is best when used for stews. When boned it can be sliced and fried. 2. Scrag. Contains a high proportion of bone and gristle to meat. Sold chopped it can be used for stews, broths and soups. 3. Shoulder. Sweet in flavour and ideal for roasting. It can be boned and rolled or boned and stuffed before roasting. 4. Breast. An extremely economical cut, usually sold boned, stuffed and rolled for roasting or braising. Not a popular cut because of the high amount of fat to meat. 5. Rib. The complete rib is seldom sold whole but instead cut into three cuts, known as the best end of neck, middle neck and the scrag. 6. Loin. A prime cut sold whole or in smaller joints for roasting or boned. 7. Leg, fillet. A roasting joint sold on the bone or boned and rolled. The fillet is a separate joint which has lean meat and little bone.*

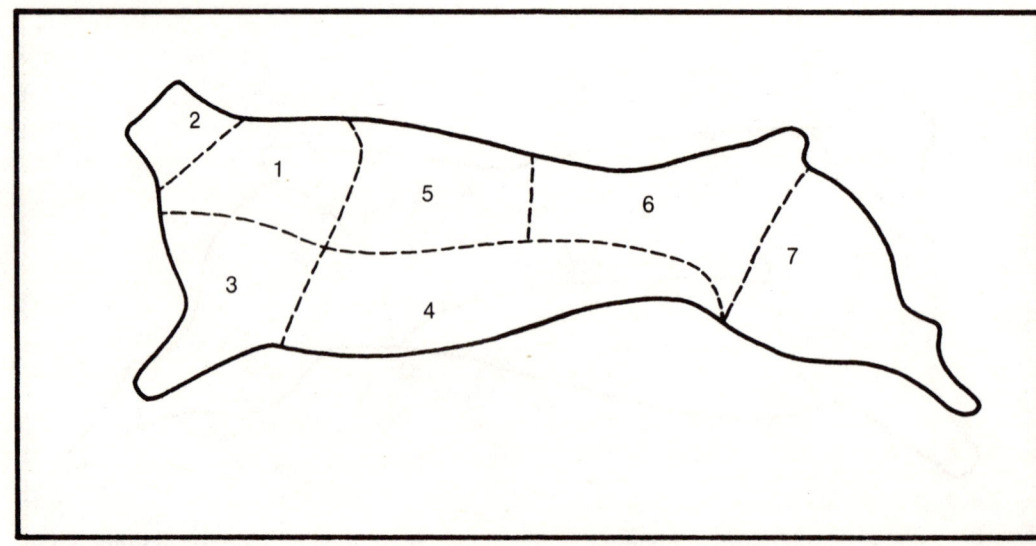

slow, moist cooking for best results.

Meat is an important source of protein; it also supplies valuable amounts of vitamins of the B group and a moderate amount of iron. The fat, which adds to the flavour, is of high energy giving value. The cheaper cuts of meat are just as nutritious as more expensive ones, provided that they do not contain a large proportion of bone or gristle.

Meat should not be eaten too fresh, for freshly killed meat lacks flavour and is likely to be tough. If it is kept for a while (the exact time varying with the kind of meat and the temperature at which it is kept) enzyme and bacterial action take place, breaking down the fibres, thus making the meat more tender and at the same time developing the flavour. This maturing process must not be allowed to continue beyond a certain point, otherwise the meat putrifies and becomes unwholesome.

A good butcher will usually advise with the selection of meat, but general rules are to choose meat which does not have an undue amount of fat; what fat there is should be firm and free from dark marks or discoloration. Lean meat should be finely grained with a marbling of fat, firm and slightly elastic.

Imported meat is less expensive than home-killed and while the quality and flavour may not always be quite so good, any defects can usually be overcome by skilful cooking.

Many supermarkets now have a large variety of meat ready packed and partially prepared; that is excess fat removed, and joints rolled or skewered.

Frozen Meat
This is also widely available from supermarkets and freezer centres. The latter sell meat in larger packs for the convenience of freezer owners. The only disadvantage of buying meat this way is that it is difficult to see the quality or how much fat etc., is included in the pack.

Many butchers sell meat ready frozen for customers with freezers, or on request they will prepare meat to order to be frozen at home. This is popular when whole or half animal carcasses are bought.

Storing Meat
Fresh meat should be kept covered in a refrigerator or cool place. It should not be stored for too long before cooking as deterioration may occur. Frozen meat can be kept in the ice compartment of a refrigerator for the time recommended by the star rating.

Cooking Meat
Best quality meat and cuts may be cooked by the quicker methods, such as roasting, grilling and frying. The coarser cuts are tougher and need a

slow, moist method of cooking, such as braising, steaming, stewing or casserole cooking; mincing or shredding breaks down the long fibres mechanically and so helps to shorten the cooking time. Salt meat also requires long, slow cooking. For more detailed information see Beef and Lamb entries, also Roasting, Boiling and Salting entries.

MEAT EXTRACT

Meat Extracts are made by cutting up meat, removing the tendons etc., mincing and boiling it; the mixture is then skimmed, filtered and evaporated. Meat extracts contain small amounts of protein, minerals and some of the vitamins, and also have a strong flavour. They are of value for their stimulating action on the gastric juice and their vitamin content. A teaspoon of extract contains approximately as much riboflavin and nicotinic acid as 50 g/2 oz of roast beef. They make a pleasant drink and the extracts can also be added to soups, stews and gravies.

MEDLAR

There are several varieties of this fruit, which is of Central European origin. Medlars are not unlike a rose hip in shape, but about the size of a plum, and of a russet-brown colour. They are gathered in November and should not be eaten until the fruit is soft and mealy; they usually need to be kept for two to three weeks after gathering until mellow and 'bletted' or softened. They may be eaten raw and also make good preserves.

MÉDOC

Red Bordeaux wines made in the Médoc district of France. The specific areas giving slight differences to the wines are St. Estèphe, Pauillac, St. Julien, Central Médoc, Margaux and Southern Médoc, the latter producing the finest wine.

The river Gironde stretches along the area, its gravel banks giving the area and its wines a character and quality. Although some of the Médoc wines are of excellent quality there are many lesser classed ones which are suitable for serving at family meals.

(See Bordeaux wines entry.)

MELBA SAUCE

A sweet sauce which is made from fresh raspberries and served with fruit sundaes, peach melba and similar desserts.

MELBA SAUCE

METRIC/IMPERIAL
4 × 15 ml spoons/4 tablespoons redcurrant jelly
75 g/3 oz sugar
150 ml/¼ pint raspberry purée from 225 g/8 oz
   raspberries, sieved.
2 × 5 ml spoons/2 teaspoons arrowroot or cornflour
1 × 15 ml spoon/1 tablespoon cold water

Mix the jelly, sugar and raspberry purée and bring to the boil. Blend the arrowroot with the cold water to a smooth cream, stir in a little of the raspberry mixture, return the sauce to the pan, bring to the boil stirring with a wooden spoon until it thickens and clears. Strain and cool.

MELBA TOAST

(See Toast entry.)

MELON

The fruit of a creeping plant grown outdoors in sunny moist climates or indoors in greenhouses. There are numerous varieties, which can be divided into two main groups, Musk and Water melons. Both consist mostly of water and have little nutritional value, but they provide a refreshing dessert; they can also be pickled.

CANTALOUPE MELON
This is one of the best known and best flavoured melons. It has a segmented exterior and flesh of pinkish-yellow, with a delicious flavour. When ripe it should have the characteristic melon fragrance and should yield to slight pressure at the blossom end.

CHARENTAIS MELON
These are small melons (suitable for 2 people) with yellowish-green skin, deep yellow flesh, a sweeter and somewhat more pronounced taste than some melons and a rather perfumed aroma.

TIGER MELON
This is also segmented and striped green and yellow in colour.

WATER MELON
These round or oval melons, which are imported from the continent and North Africa, have a light or dark green skin and flesh of various colours, frequently red, in which the seeds are embedded. They are watery and somewhat insipid, but cool and refreshing.

HONEYDEW MELON
When ripe, honeydews have a creamy yellow smooth skin and the blossom end yields to slight pressure. They are usually oval in shape and the flesh is greenish in colour, sweet and fragrant.

OGEN MELON
Oval melons from Israel with greenish yellow segmented skin. The flesh is greenish yellow, juicy but not too sweet. As they are small, one is served to each person.

To serve melon: Chill thoroughly, cut into wedges, remove seeds and serve with caster sugar and powdered ginger or a garnish of fresh fruit.
   A hollowed out melon may be filled with fruit salad or ice cream to make a decorative sweet.

MELON PICKLE

METRIC/IMPERIAL
1 kg/2 lb prepared melon, cubed
2 × 15 ml spoons/2 tablespoons salt dissolved in 2.25
   litres/4 pints water, for brine solution
450 ml/¾ pint water
150 ml/¼ pint distilled vinegar
1 small stick cinnamon
1 × 5 ml spoon/1 teaspoon ground cloves
450 g/1 lb sugar
225 g/8 oz cherries (see note)

Soak the prepared melon overnight in the brine solution. Drain. Combine the 450 ml/¾ pint water, vinegar, cinnamon, cloves and sugar and bring to the boil. When the sugar has dissolved, add the melon and cherries. Simmer, covered, for 30 to 40 minutes, until the melon is clear and tender. Pot and cover.
Note: Use either canned cherries or bottled maraschino cherries, well drained.

MELTING

To convert a solid into liquid by gently heating. Some food, such as chocolate, needs very careful handling and is best melted over hot water.

MENU

The list of dishes to be served at one meal. For a formal meal it is written on cards, placed on the table, the dishes being given in order of serving. (See Party entry.) Restaurants should provide a menu giving the choice of dishes available.
   In recent years dinner menus have been simplified, as it is unusual for people to spend as long over their meals as in the past. Even for a formal dinner not more than five courses are usually served, while lunch may consist of 2 or at the most 3 courses.

MERINGUE

A confection made from white of egg and sugar and baked in a very slow oven. Meringues are usually plain but a flavouring such as coffee, chocolate or chopped nuts may be included. When filled with whipped cream, ice cream, marshmallow or fruit, meringues make a delicious sweet and they are also popular for afternoon tea; small meringues or a piped or piled meringue mixture may be used as a topping for various sweets. Meringue can be made into flan cases and filled with fruit and cream.

Mixing: To each egg white allow 50 g/2 oz sugar. The best texture is obtained by using caster or icing sugar. Separate the egg whites carefully, place in a clean dry mixing bowl and whisk until stiff. Whisk in half the sugar, then fold in the remainder lightly, using a metal spoon.

Shaping: There are two satisfactory methods.
1. With two spoons; dip one into a jug of cold water, shake off excess drops and fill with the meringue mixture. Using a knife smooth the mixture along the sides of the spoon until it resembles the shape of a finished meringue case, with a ridge along the top. With the second wet spoon, half lift the mixture out of the first spoon, then, preserving its shape and keeping the ridge on the top, allow it to slide out on to the prepared tin or board, using the first spoon to free it from the second spoon.
2. With a forcing bag and plain 1 cm/½ inch nozzle, squeeze out the mixture into pyramids, rounds, fingers or ovals etc. Alternatively, place meringue into a forcing bag fitted with a fancy nozzle.

Baking: Ideally, meringues should be baked on hardwood boards, but failing these, tins can be used quite successfully; they should be smooth and quite free from grease or crumbs; line with greaseproof paper and oil very lightly with olive oil, rubbing it with the finger-tips.

Dredge the meringues lightly with caster sugar, put in very cool oven (110°C/225°F, Gas Mark ¼) until they are firm and crisp both on top and underneath, but not coloured. This may take 3 to 4 hours. As the meringues should not colour and to maintain the necessary low temperature the oven door can be left ajar.

MERINGUE À LA CHANTILLY

To 12 meringue cases (6 whole meringues) allow 150 ml/¼ pint double cream. Sweeten and flavour it with 2 × 15 ml spoons/2 tablespoons of sugar and a drop of vanilla essence and whip stiffly. Sandwich the meringue cases together in pairs with the cream (which may be either spread with a knife or piped) and place the meringues in paper cases. If the cream is forced, use a star pipe and finish with a row of stars where the meringues join. Sprinkle the cream with chopped nuts, crushed crystallized violets or flaked chocolate.

When the meringues are to be served as the sweet course for lunch or dinner they may, if desired, be accompanied by a chocolate sauce.

MERINGUE TOPPING FOR TARTS, ETC.

Allow up to 50 g/2 oz caster sugar to each egg white. Whisk the egg white until very stiff, then fold the sugar in lightly. Pile on top of the (cooked) tart or pudding and put into a cool oven (150°C/300°F, Gas Mark 2) for 30 minutes or in hot oven (220°C/425°F, Gas Mark 7) for about 10 minutes till crisp to the touch and very lightly coloured.

MESCAL

An alcoholic drink made in Mexico and South America from the Maguey or American sloe.

METABOLISM

The chemical reaction which takes place in the body and enables it to make use of food for energy, building and repair.

The carbohydrates are absorbed into the blood as sugars; these are then either used in the tissues to provide energy or else stored as glycogen in the liver or muscles. Any excess of sugar is converted into fat and leads to obesity. When energy is required, the carbohydrate is oxidized and broken down into carbon dioxide and water.

Fat is also used to produce energy and is a more concentrated source than carbohydrates. It is laid down in the body and supports certain organs such as the kidneys, acting as a kind of protection and energy store.

The amino-acids from proteins are built again into proteins and used for new tissue to repair the old – indeed proteins form part of every cell in the body. Some of the protein eaten is used to provide energy, if carbohydrate is not eaten at the same time. Eventually protein in the body breaks down and is excreted to be replaced by fresh protein.

People differ in their rates of metabolism. Some people can burn up energy and food much quicker than others and can therefore consume larger quantities of food without putting on weight. People with a slow metabolism can eat small quantities of food, yet still suffer from weight increase. Certain drugs can change body metabolism, but these should never be taken without medical advice.

METRICATION

The metric system of weights and measures which is exclusively decimal. The United Kingdom is now in the process of changing over to this system from Imperial weights and measures.

The target dates for completion are scheduled for 1980/81. All prepacked foods are to be in metric quantities by early 1980. Already there are many such foods sold in metric packs, but 1979 will see a big increase. Cans and packets are marked in metric but this is often a straight conversion from the imperial which gives an odd figure such as 119 g. Eventually all food packs will be marked in metric units such as 50 g, 100 g, 200 g, etc., and for a time the imperial equivalents will be shown.

The Metrication Board are often blamed for the slowness of the changeover plan, but they do not give orders or make definite decisions. They are there to inform and help manufacturers and the public. They encourage manufacturers to adopt round metric quantities where possible. As the changeover speeds up they will increase informative advertizing to help the public.

Foods sold by weight will be the last to change to metric. This should happen in late 1980 to 1981. The changeover is planned to take twelve months to enable weights and measures people to make necessary adjustments. The public will first familiarize themselves with buying meat and fish by the kilo, followed by fruit and vegetables and then other weighed foods such as cheese. This will be the greatest challenge to the shopper as retailers will show the unit price on produce in metric. Hopefully many shops will display comparison charts between metric and imperial with the relevant prices.

In cookery and recipes, many books and magazines are using the imperial and metric system, and some give only metric measurements. The exact conversions are too complicated to use in recipes, hence the approximate equivalent is used. The following tables show the equivalents used in this book and many others. Care is always taken to ensure that the recipes work, but if imperial and metric quantities are given, only one should be followed.

MICROWAVE COOKING

Microwave cooking utilizes electronic energy which passes through the mass of food, cooking it simultaneously throughout. It is important to note that the heat is produced within the food itself and not conducted from an outside source. Waves are then reflected by revolving blades and then by

LIQUID AND VOLUME MEASURES

Metric	Imperial
1 × 1.25 ml spoon (or pinch)	¼ teaspoon (or pinch)
1 × 2.5 ml spoon	½ teaspoon
1 × 5 ml spoon	1 teaspoon
1 × 15 ml spoon	1 tablespoon
1.5 × 15 ml spoons	1½ tablespoons
2 × 15 ml spoons	2 tablespoons
3 × 15 ml spoons	3 tablespoons
4 × 15 ml spoons	4 tablespoons
5 × 15 ml spoons	5 tablespoons
6 × 15 ml spoons	6 tablespoons
7 × 15 ml spoons	7 tablespoons
120 ml	4 fl oz
150 ml	¼ pint
175 ml	6 fl oz
200 ml	⅓ pint
250 ml	8 fl oz
300 ml	½ pint
350 ml	12 fl oz
400 ml	14 fl oz
450 ml	¾ pint
500 ml	18 fl oz
600 ml	1 pint
750 ml	1¼ pints
900 ml	1½ pints
1 litre	1¾ pints
1.2 litres	2 pints
1.25 litres	2¼ pints
1.5 litres	2½ pints
1.6 litres	2¾ pints
1.75 litres	3 pints
2 litres	3½ pints
2.25 litres	4 pints
2.5 litres	4½ pints
2.75 litres	5 pints

WEIGHTS

Imperial	Metric	Imperial	Metric	Imperial	Metric
½ oz	15 g	14 oz	400 g	4 lb	1.75 kg
1 oz	25 g	15 oz	425 g		
1½ oz	40 g	1 lb	0.5 kg	4¼ lb	2 kg
2 oz	50 g			4½ lb	
2½ oz	65 g	1¼ lb	0.75 kg		
3 oz	75 g	1½ lb		4¾ lb	2.25 kg
3½ oz	90 g			5 lb	
4 oz	100 g	1¾ lb	1 kg		
5 oz	150 g	2 lb		5¼ lb	2.5 kg
6 oz	175 g			5½ lb	
7 oz	200 g	2¼ lb	1.25 kg		
8 oz	225 g	2½ lb		5¾ lb	2.75 kg
9 oz	250 g			6 lb	
10 oz	275 g	2¾ lb		7 lb	3 kg
11 oz	300 g	3 lb	1.5 kg	8 lb	3.5 kg
12 oz	350 g	3¼ lb		9 lb	4 kg
13 oz	375 g	3½ lb		10 lb	4.5 kg

CENTIMETRES

⅛ inch	3 mm	6 inch	15 cm
¼ inch	5 mm	7 inch	18 cm
½ inch	1 cm	8 inch	20 cm
1 inch	2.5 cm	9 inch	23 cm
2 inch	5 cm	10 inch	25 cm
3 inch	7.5 cm	11 inch	28 cm
4 inch	10 cm	12 inch	30 cm
5 inch	13 cm	13 inch	33 cm

contact with the sides of the oven. Glass, porcelain, china, paper and plastic transmit microwaves and thus remain cool; avoid foil containers which shield the food.

This method of cooking is becoming much more widely used in the home as well as in restaurants and catering establishments. It is particularly valuable for cooking foods from frozen in a very short time. Also, they are cheaper to run than conventional cookers. One disadvantage is that food does not brown, so colourful decoration and garnishing are important. However, a browning dish is now available which acts as a griddle within the microwave; this helps to overcome the problem of browning with some dishes. Microwave cooking does not tenderize meat so good cuts are preferable. Other cuts can be tenderized by beating or marinating.

Poultry, white meats, fish, shellfish, most vegetables, chops and steaks cook excellently in a microwave oven. Cakes, particularly with a high fat and syrup level, are also good. Dishes that do not cook well are Yorkshire pudding, soufflés, meringues, éclairs, puff and flaky pastries.

Microwave Ovens

These are cabinets which can sit on top of a work surface without taking up too much room. The oven cavity is entirely metal and contains the microwaves which are deflected off the walls and base to be absorbed by the food. The door and surrounding frame is provided with special seals constructed to ensure that the microwaves are confined within. As the door is opened the power is automatically shut off.

Reputable manufacturers will ensure that the microwave oven is electrically safe and that the radiation leakage is insignificant. As with all electrical appliances, a further guarantee of safety is the BEAB approval label for household appliances, or the Electricity Council label for commercial catering equipment.

Manufacturers supply instruction books for their ovens and these should be carefully studied before use.

MILK

Milk is one of the most complete of all foods. In a mixed diet it is particularly significant as a source of protein, calcium and riboflavin. It is especially important for growing children, pregnant women, nursing mothers and the elderly. The latter find it particularly valuable as it does not require preparation and it can be delivered to their door.

Milk is a very versatile food as it can be taken as it is or made into many interesting and nutritious dishes.

Care of milk

As milk is a perishable food the following points should be remembered:
1. Do not leave milk in the sunlight as it destroys the B vitamins.
2. Keep milk in a cool place, preferably a refrigerator.
3. Milk should be kept in a clean container. The bottle is most suitable as it has been sterilized.
4. Milk should always be used in rotation. Pasteurized milk will keep for 2 to 3 days in a refrigerator, 1 to 2 days in a cool place.

Grading of milk

All milk sold in England and Wales is pasteurized, except for a small quantity of untreated milk sold from farms. A special licence must be obtained by the farmer. The Milk Marketing Board controls all other milk, buying it from the farmers and selling it to dairies and creameries. It also controls distribution over the country in relation to population. They are continually trying to help farmers to produce milk of better quality and in larger quantities.

Pasteurization is a process of heat treatment applied immediately before bottling destroys any pathogenic (disease-carrying) organisms. Milk is heated to 72°C/161°F for 15 seconds and then quickly cooled to below 10°C/50°F and bottled. The pathogenic organisms are destroyed and the milk souring organisms reduced in number.

PASTEURIZED MILK (SILVER TOP)
Milk is pasteurized as above.

HOMOGENIZED MILK (RED TOP)
Milk is warmed then passed through fine apertures to break down the fat globules. These remain evenly distributed throughout the milk, therefore there is no creamline. This gives the milk a whiter appearance than ordinary pasteurized milk. The milk is pasteurized after homogenization. As the fat globules are small and easily digested the milk is particularly suitable for young children, invalids and the elderly.

CHANNEL ISLANDS (GOLD TOP)
Milk from the Jersey or Guernsey Breed of cow. The high butterfat content gives it a rich creamy flavour and colour.

STERILIZED (BLUE OR CROWN CAP)
Milk is homogenized, sealed then heat treated to above boiling point, not less than 100°C/212°F for 20 to 30 minutes then cooled. Available in long necked glass bottles this milk has a slight caramel flavour.

ULTRA HEAT TREATED (FOIL LINED PACK OR PINK TOP)
Milk is homogenized, heated at an extended time at lower temperatures to stabilize protein, then

subjected to ultra high temperatures, not less than 132°C/270°F for 1 second. It is aseptically packed in foil-lined containers. Unless opened the milk will keep for several months. (Always check the date stamp.) It has a similar flavour to ordinary pasteurized milk.

UNTREATED MILK

This is available as ordinary (green top) and Channel Islands (green/gold top). No treatment is given to the milk and it is bottled under licence at farm or dairy.

SKIMMED MILK

Pasteurized milk which must by law contain less than 0.5 per cent fat. It is available sterilized in long neck glass bottles with a crown cap, or ultra heat treated in plastic bottles.

BUTTERMILK

Pasteurized skimmed milk which is treated with a specific bacteria culture to give a sour, refreshing taste. It is usually sold in cartons.

SOURED MILK

If pasteurized milk is allowed to go sour naturally, putrifactive rather than acid-producing bacteria tend to develop and the milk becomes unfit for use. It is therefore better to use artificial means to sour the milk if it is required. Add 2 × 15 ml spoons/2 tablespoons lemon juice or white vinegar to each 600 ml/1 pint of milk, allow the milk to stand in a warm room for 30 minutes and then return to a cold place for storage. This milk can be used in baking for soda bread and scones.

CONDENSED MILK

This consists of whole or skimmed milk reduced by evaporation and usually sweetened with cane or beet sugar (sucrose) in the proportion of 1 part sugar to six parts milk (by weight). This sweetened milk will keep indefinitely when the can is unopened and even after it is opened the milk will keep for a considerable time as the low proportion of water and high proportion of sugar do not favour bacterial growth.

Whole milk, when sweetened and condensed, contains an average of 9 per cent fat, 8 per cent protein and 55 per cent sugar, including both the lactose or milk sugar and the added sucrose. Skimmed milk treated in the same way contains practically no fat, but has about 9 per cent protein and 60 per cent sugar.

Apart from its obvious use as a substitute for fresh milk in beverages, canned milk may be used in milk puddings etc., and is good in caramels, fudges and similar sweets and in ice cream mixtures. It has a distinctive caramel flavour.

EVAPORATED MILK

The term 'evaporated' milk as distinct from 'condensed' is used to denote unsweetened canned milk, both full-cream and skimmed. During the process of manufacture the milk is reduced by evaporation to about one-third of its original bulk and then sterilized. Evaporated milk contains about 9 per cent fat, 12 per cent sugar and 8 per cent protein. It has a distinctive flavour although less sweet than condensed milk. It is useful for many cooking purposes and also as a substitute for cream with cold sweets and other dishes.

DRIED MILK

Dried milk is prepared from whole, partly skimmed or skimmed milk and may be either roller- or spray-dried. Roller-dried milk powder is not as readily soluble as the spray-dried in cold water, and when re-constituted has a somewhat 'heated' flavour. It keeps better than the spray-dried type but the flavour of the latter is nearer that of fresh milk.

The nutritive value of reconstituted full-cream dried milk is fully equal to that of ordinary milk; in addition it is sterile. It is therefore used extensively for infant feeding and many of the commercial brands of infant food consist of dried milk fortified with vitamins A and D, minerals such as iron, and sugar; malt extract and dextrinized flour are also sometimes added.

Skimmed milk powder is similar to full cream milk but lacks fat and fat soluble vitamins. This should not be given to infants.

For skimmed non-fat dried milk put 50 g/2 oz powder into a dry measure, top up with cold water to 600 ml/1 pint and stir well.

Dried milk in cooking: Reconstituted, dried milk may be used for many cooking purposes and in beverages. Bring liquid to the boil then allow liquid to cool slightly before adding the powder. Store in a cool, dry place with the lid firmly on; the contents of the can will keep in good condition for up to six months.

Damp, hot conditions cause deterioration with some loss of food value. Opened cans should be used up quickly as the powder can form hard lumps and develop a rancid flavour when in contact with the air.

Milk Jelly
(See jelly entry.)

Milk Pudding

A hot or cold sweet dish made with milk and a grain (whole, crushed or ground) which may be either baked or boiled. Milk puddings are easily made, nourishing and provide an excellent means of introducing plenty of milk into the family diet; for children and invalids they are invaluable as the body building and protective qualities of the milk are supplemented by the additional energy giving and protein food supplied by the grain.

Full cream or skimmed fresh milk or diluted canned milk may be used: dried milk can also be used for boiled milk puddings.

The cereals that can be used include various forms of barley, oatmeal, rice, cornflour, sago, semolina, tapioca, macaroni and similar products. Milk puddings may be enriched by the addition of beaten egg, cream, or undiluted evaporated milk, or by shavings of butter or margarine put on top of the pudding before it is baked. When eggs or cream are used they should be added towards the end of the cooking and care should be taken to avoid curdling due to overheating.

The flavour may be varied by the addition of fruit, spices etc., or a 'toffee' surface may be given by sprinkling the cooked pudding with sugar and caramelizing it under the grill.

PROPORTIONS TO USE

METRIC/IMPERIAL
For puddings allow:
40 g/1½ oz whole or small grain (e.g., rice, sago, semolina) to 600 ml/1 pint milk.
25 g/1 oz ground grain (e.g., ground rice) to 600 ml/1 pint milk.
For moulds allow:
50 g/2 oz whole or small grain (e.g., rice, sago, semolina) to 600 ml/1 pint milk
40 g/1½ oz ground or powdered grain (e.g., ground rice, cornflour) to 600 ml/1 pint milk

Several varieties of milk puddings are available in cans, which make valuable convenience foods. (See Cornflour and Rice entries.)

Milk Shakes

Mix the milk with strong coffee, chocolate powder, fruit juice or syrup, or use a special milk shake flavouring; blend until frothy either with a rotary whisk or in an electric blender. For an ice-cold milk shake add 1 to 2 × 15 ml spoons/1 to 2 tablespoons ice cream to each glass before serving.

MILLE-FEUILLE

Puff pastry split and filled with jam and cream; the top is iced with glacé icing. A savoury version can be made with cheese.

MILLE-FEUILLES SLICES

METRIC/IMPERIAL
215 g/7½ oz packet frozen puff pastry, thawed
2 – 3 × 15 ml spoons/2 – 3 tablespoons raspberry jam
150 ml/5 fl oz double cream, whipped
glacé icing
1 – 2 × 15 ml spoons/1 – 2 tablespoons chopped nuts

Roll the pastry into a strip 3 mm/¼ inch thick, 10 cm/4 inches wide, and 30 cm/12 inches long. Brush the baking sheet with water, lay the pastry on it and cut it from side to side in strips 5 cm/2 inches wide, but don't separate the slices. Bake in a

hot oven (230°C/450°F, Gas Mark 8) for about 10 minutes. Separate the strips and cool them; split each into two and sandwich them together in threes or fours with jam and cream. Cover the tops with glacé icing and sprinkle chopped nuts at each end.

Note: Ready-made pastry should be rolled thinner than home-made.

MILLE-FEUILLE GÂTEAU

METRIC/IMPERIAL
100 g/4 oz puff or rough puff pastry, made with 100 g/4 oz flour etc., or a 215 g/7½ oz packet frozen puff pastry, thawed
450 g/1 lb fresh raspberries
caster sugar
300 ml/½ pint double cream, whipped
pale green glacé icing
3 × 15 ml spoons/3 tablespoons roughly chopped walnuts

Roll out the pastry very thinly (this is easier to do if it is rolled between sheets of waxed paper) and cut into three 15 cm/6 inch rounds. Place on wetted baking sheets, prick and bake in a hot oven (230°C/450°F, Gas Mark 8) for 8 to 10 minutes, until crisp and golden brown. Cool on a cooling rack.

Reserve a few raspberries for decoration and then crush and sweeten the remainder. Sandwich the pastry rounds together with layers of cream and raspberries, cover the top with glacé icing and decorate with raspberries and nuts.

Any other soft fruit can be used in the same way.

MILLET

A cereal which is easily grown in dry regions and is the staple food of many people in Africa and in some parts of Asia. With the introduction of new methods of cultivation, including irrigation, millet tends to be replaced by wheat and is thought to be inferior. It is true that millet is not as pleasant to eat, but it has quite a high protein value.

There are many varieties and names including sorghum, kaffir corn and finger millet.

Like most cereals, millet is husked and is then made into a sort of porridge or ground into meal. It can also be fermented to produce an alcoholic drink.

MILT

The soft roe of fish, also the spleen of animals.

MINCE

The name given to meat which is finely divided by chopping or passing through a mincing machine.

The term usually refers to uncooked meat, but cooked meat is often minced before re-heating.

As the meat is finely divided it is easy to assimilate and is suitable for those with weak digestions and for young children. Mince is often mixed with cereals, vegetables and pulses, to make the meat go further while still retaining its appetizing flavour; these added ingredients also serve to give body to the dish. Mince needs careful serving if it is to appear appetizing; it may be served with potato rings and garnished with snippets of fried bread, tomatoes and mushrooms; or it can be made into meat rissoles, patties or pies.

SAVOURY MINCE

METRIC/IMPERIAL
1 onion, skinned and quartered
2 carrots, pared and quartered
2 sticks celery, scrubbed
450 g/1 lb cold cooked beef
1 × 290 g/10½ oz can oxtail soup or 150 ml/¼ pint beef stock
salt
pepper
2 × 15 ml spoons/2 tablespoons curry powder
50 g/2 oz raisins or sultanas

Mince together the vegetables and meat (or if preferred dice the vegetables and mince the meat). Put them into a pan and stir in enough of the soup or stock to give a really moist mixture. Add the seasoning, curry powder and raisins or sultanas, cover with a lid and simmer gently for 20 to 30 minutes, until the vegetables are soft and the flavours are well blended. Stir from time to time as the mixture tends to stick slightly; add more stock or soup if it becomes too thick. Serve with chipped or boiled potatoes, or as a sauce over pasta or rice.

CHILLI CON CARNE

METRIC/IMPERIAL
0.75 kg/1½ lb raw minced beef
1 × 15 ml spoon/1 tablespoon fat or oil
1 large onion, skinned and chopped
1 green pepper, seeded and chopped, optional
1 × 425 g/15 oz can tomatoes
salt
pepper
1 × 15 ml spoon/1 tablespoon chilli powder
1 × 15 ml spoon/1 tablespoon vinegar
1 × 5 ml spoon/1 teaspoon sugar
2 × 15 ml spoons/2 tablespoons tomato paste
1 × 425 g/15 oz can red kidney beans

Fry the beef in fat or oil until lightly browned, then add the onion and pepper and fry for 5 minutes, until soft. Stir in the drained beans and tomatoes and add the seasoning and chilli powder blended with the vinegar, sugar and tomato paste. Cover and simmer for 2 to 2½ hours, or until tender. Add the kidney beans 10 minutes before the cooking time is completed.

Note: Add chilli powder very judiciously; some of it is very hot. American chilli powder is generally a milder pre-mixed seasoning, based on ground Mexican chilli, so look for this type.

HUNGARIAN STEAKS

METRIC/IMPERIAL
50 g/2 oz salami
4 onions
2 tomatoes, skinned
2 small green peppers
0.5 kg/1 lb finely minced beef
1 × 15 ml spoon/1 tablespoon lemon juice
1 × 15 ml spoon/1 tablespoon tomato purée
salt
pepper
mustard
1 × 15 ml spoon/1 tablespoon plain flour
a little oil
creamed potato

Finely mince the salami, 1 onion and the tomatoes with the flesh of the green peppers and mix these with the beef. Add the lemon juice, tomato purée, seasonings and flour. Shape into 4 rounds and fry slowly in oil until thoroughly cooked. Meanwhile slice and fry the remaining onions. Pipe some potato round the edge of a dish and brown lightly under the grill. Place the steaks in the dish and put the fried onions on top of them.

MINCE PIES

(See Mincemeat entry.)

MINCING

To chop or cut into small pieces with a knife or, more commonly, in a mincing machine or electric mixer.

MINCEMEAT

The preserve used as a filling for mince pies, which are part of the traditional Christmas fare in Britain. As the name suggests, the original mincemeat included cooked lean beef, though today this is almost invariably omitted. There are numerous treasured family recipes, all differing slightly; for example some use Seville oranges and some use sweet oranges or tangerines, while others omit the orange flavour altogether.

A rich mincemeat is best allowed to mature for a month after it is made, but if a larger proportion of apple and no brandy are included it should not be kept more than a week or it may ferment.

Mincemeat is usually made into mince pies or mince tarts, but may also be used in steamed suet or sponge puddings. It is also tasty in less traditional desserts; it blends well with apples and pears.

MINCEMEAT

METRIC/IMPERIAL
0.5 kg/1 lb currants, cleaned
0.5 kg/1 lb sultanas, cleaned
0.5 kg/1 lb raisins, cleaned and stoned
0.5 kg/1 lb cut mixed peel
0.5 kg/1 lb cooking apples, peeled and cored
100 g/4 oz sweet almonds, blanched
450 g/1 lb soft brown sugar (dark)
225 g/8 oz shredded suet
1 × 5 ml spoon/1 teaspoon ground nutmeg
1 × 5 ml spoon/1 teaspoon ground cinnamon
grated rind and juice of 2 lemons

Finely chop the prepared fruit, mixed peel, apples and nuts. Add the sugar, suet, spices, lemon rind and juice and mix all the ingredients thoroughly together. Cover the mincement and leave to stand for 2 days. Stir well and put into jars. Cover as for jam and allow to mature for at least 2 weeks before using.

Note: For mincemeat that will keep well, use a firm, hard type of apple such as Wellington, a juicy apple, such as Bramley Seedling, may make the mixture too moist.

MINCE PIES

Shortcrust, rough puff, flaky or puff pastry can be used, but puff pastry is probably the most traditional type. Roll it out to 5 mm/¼ inch thickness and cut out rounds 7.5 cm/3 inches in diameter. Then roll out the trimmings of pastry and cut out an equal number of rounds only somewhat thinner. Line some patty tins with these rounds, fill up with mincemeat and moisten the edges with cold water or white of egg. Lay on the thicker rounds of pastry and press the edges together. Make a small hole in the top of each pie, brush over with white of egg and dredge with caster sugar. Bake in a hot oven (230°C/450°F, Gas Mark 8) for 20 minutes, or until the pies are well risen and nicely browned.

If wished, serve dusted with icing sugar.

MINERAL WATER

Natural mineral waters containing various minerals, and sometimes charged with aerating gas, spring from the earth in many places. A great many of these are claimed to have medicinal properties and at some places the waters are bottled and sold (e.g., Vichy and Seltzer water). In countries where the water supply is not fit for drinking these waters are served.

Commercially the name 'mineral water' is given to various aerated liquids, such as soda water, lemonade etc., intended for table use. (See individual entries for details.)

MINERALS

Various chemical substances which are necessary for the efficient working of the body, are referred to in dietetics as the 'minerals'. Those which are most likely to be deficient in the diet are calcium and iron and it is important to include food rich in these substances. Traces of other minerals – copper, iodine, colbalt, fluorine – are also important but these are not likely to be in short supply. Other necessary chemicals, such as sulphur, potassium, sodium, phosphorus and magnesium are present in a normal diet in an adequate amount for health.

MINESTRA

An Italian term for thick soup.

MINESTRONE

The most celebrated Italian soup, made from a variety of vegetables and pasta and served with grated Parmesan cheese. A number of different recipes exist.

MINESTRONE

METRIC/IMPERIAL
½ leek, shredded and washed
1 onion, skinned and finely chopped
1 clove garlic, skinned and crushed
25 g/1 oz butter
1 litre/1¾ pints white stock
1 carrot, pared and cut into thin strips
1 turnip, peeled and cut into thin strips
1 stick celery, trimmed and thinly sliced
3 × 15 ml spoons/3 tablespoons shortcut macaroni
¼ cabbage washed and finely shredded

3 runner beans, thinly sliced
3 × 15 ml spoons/3 tablespoons fresh or frozen peas
1 × 5 ml spoon/1 teaspoon tomato paste or 4 tomatoes
    skinned and sliced
1–2 rashers of bacon, rinded, chopped and fried
salt
pepper
grated Parmesan cheese

Lightly fry the leek, onion and garlic in the melted butter for 5 to 10 minutes, until soft. Add the stock, bring to the boil, add the carrot, turnip, macaroni and celery and simmer, covered, for 20 to 30 minutes. Add the cabbage, beans and peas, cover and simmer for a further 20 minutes. Stir in the tomato paste or tomatoes, bacon and seasoning to taste. Bring back to the boil. Serve the grated Parmesan cheese in a separate dish.

MINESTRA DI CAVOLFIORE

METRIC/IMPERIAL
1 large cauliflower
½ onion, peeled and chopped
3 × 15 ml spoons/3 tablespoons oil
50 g/2 oz butter
1.2 litres/2 pints chicken stock
175 g/6 oz rice
50 g/2 oz Parmesan cheese, grated

Remove green leaves from cauliflower, separate into florets and wash. Sauté onion in a large saucepan with all the oil and half the butter until browned. Add chicken stock, cauliflower and rice. Cover and simmer for 20 minutes. To serve, pour into soup tureen, stir in the remaining butter and sprinkle with Parmesan cheese.

MINT

An aromatic perennial plant used to flavour a number of dishes. A sprig of mint is cooked with new potatoes and peas, mint sauce is served with lamb or mutton and chopped mint may be added to salads. A sprig of mint can be added to lemonade, other drinks or sorbets to give a refreshing flavour, while a mint-flavoured syrup can be used to sweeten China tea.
  There are several kinds of mint which have varying uses:

SPEARMINT
The everyday garden mint used for flavouring vegetables and in mint sauce.

BOWLES MINT
Has a green furry leaf, a more delicate flavour, and does not revert to wild mint.

APPLEMINT
A delicate flavour with a round variegated leaf; used in fruit cups and chutneys.

EAU DE COLOGNE MINT
Has a reddish leaf and is highly scented, and therefore is not suitable for food. It is good used in flower arrangements.

PINEAPPLE MINT
This is used similarly to Eau de Cologne mint.

PEPPERMINT
This is used for flavouring chewing gum, toothpaste and for medicinal purposes. The flavouring, peppermint oil, is extracted from this herb.

MINT SAUCE

METRIC/IMPERIAL
small bunch mint, washed
2 × 5 ml spoons/2 teaspoons sugar
1 × 15 ml spoon/1 tablespoon boiling water
1–2 × 15 ml spoons/1–2 tablespoons vinegar

Put the mint leaves only with the sugar onto a board and chop finely. Put into the sauceboat, add the boiling water and stir until the sugar has dissolved. Stir in the vinegar to taste. The sauce should be left for one hour before being served.
  Mint sauce is served with lamb.

MINT SAUCE FOR BOTTLING

METRIC/IMPERIAL
600 ml/1 pint wine vinegar
150 ml/¼ pint young mint
25 g/1 oz sugar

This is prepared in the same general way but no water is added and the mint leaves must be completely dried before they are chopped. The sauce will then keep through the winter.

MINT JELLY

METRIC/IMPERIAL
2.5 kg/5½ lb cooking apples
1.25 litres/2¼ pints water
bunch fresh mint
1.25 litres/2¼ pints vinegar
sugar
6–8 × 15 ml spoons/6–8 tablespoons chopped mint
green colouring, optional

Wash and roughly chop the apples, put in a large pan with the water and bunch of mint and simmer until really soft and pulped. Add the vinegar and boil for 5 minutes. Strain through a jelly cloth.

Measure the extract and return it to the pan with 450 g/1 lb sugar to every 600 ml/1 pint extract. Stir until the sugar has dissolved and boil rapidly until a 'jelly' is obtained on testing. Stir in the chopped mint and a few drops of colouring if you wish. Skim, pot and cover in the usual way.

MINT JULEP

(See Julep entry.)

MIRABELLE

(See Cherry Plum entry.)

MIREPOIX

A mixture of carrots, celery and onion, often including some ham or bacon, which are cut into large pieces, sautéed in fat and used as a 'bed' on which to braise meat.

MIXED GRILL

(See Grilling entry.)

MIXED SPICE

A blend of ground or powdered spices chosen from the following: cinnamon, nutmeg, mace, cloves, coriander, caraway, cassia, ginger, cardamom and pimento. Mixed spice is used in flavouring puddings, biscuits and cakes.

MOCHA

A strongly flavoured coffee imported from Arabia. It is used mainly in blended coffee since most people find it too rich unless mixed with other coffee beans.

The word 'mocha' is often used to describe cakes and puddings flavoured with coffee and is sometimes applied to a mixture of coffee and chocolate flavourings.

MOCK CREAM

A mixture that can have a similar flavour to fresh cream and can be used as a substitute in certain dishes. Nothing can beat 'the real thing' but some mixtures are suitable for buns and cakes. A commercial imitation cream is available in powder form; this is reconstituted by whisking with milk. The mixture can then be used in the same way as cream to serve with puddings or to fill cakes etc. No mock cream mixture will have the whipping properties of fresh double and whipping creams.

Mock cream is also available in cartons, ready to use in a thickened form. This can be found in the refrigerated cabinets of most large supermarkets.

'CREAM' CAKE FILLING

METRIC/IMPERIAL
15 g/ ½ oz cornflour
150 ml/¼ pint milk
25 g/1 oz butter
25 g/1 oz sugar
vanilla essence

Make a white sauce with the cornflour and milk; when it is cool beat in the butter and sugar and flavour to taste with vanilla essence.

MOCK TURTLE SOUP

A brown soup made from calf's head which is supposed to resemble real turtle soup. After cooking, the pieces of meat from the head are preserved and left until cold, then cut into tiny pieces which are added to the soup at the last minute.

MOLASSES

The general term used for the thick, brown syrupy drainings from raw sugar or the syrup obtained from the sugar during the process of refinement. Molasses varies in texture, that drained from beet sugar being very bitter and disagreeable to taste. In America the term is sometimes used for treacle. Molasses has no nutritional value apart from a little sugar.

(See Golden syrup and Treacle entries.)

MONASTINE

A yellow liqueur made in France, which resembles yellow Chartreuse in flavour.

MONOSODIUM GLUTAMATE

(See Sodium Glutamate entry.)

MOORFOWL (MOORGAME AND MOORCOCK)

Terms used in Scotland for grouse; in England they sometimes denote black game.

MOORHEN

A small waterfowl.

MOREL

A succulent edible fungi which is greyish-yellow to black and has a sponge-like honeycombed cap. It grows in woods and hedgerows during the spring. Morel is used in cooking to garnish soups and sauces or as a vegetable stewed or fried in butter. It is available in a dried form to use as a flavouring for savoury dishes.

257

MORTADELLA

A large sausage made in Bologna, Italy; it consists of finely minced pork, ham and pork fat, flavoured with freshly ground white peppercorns, garlic and pistachio nuts.

Mortadella is mostly used for appetizers.

MOSELLE

The name given to wines made in the vineyards in the Moselle area. They resemble Rhine wine and hock, but of very fine flavour, dry and clear. They can be served as a drink without food or with light meals.

MOULD

A hollow dish which can be of varying shapes, used for making certain sweet and savoury dishes. Moulds can be made of plastic, metal, glass or china and usually have indentations which are printed on the food when it is turned out. The food is placed in the mould whilst in a liquid form then chilled or cooked to turn it to a solid mass. (See recipe below.)

The term also applies to a woolly, furry growth which consists of minute fungi. It will grow on meat, cheese, bread and sweet food if the correct conditions of warmth and moisture are present. The growth usually indicates that the food is not fresh. Although not harmful, the mould gives food an unpleasant taste and appearance.

Certain mould growths are responsible for the flavour and colour in cheeses such as Roquefort, Stilton and Camembert (outside skin). However, these are controlled and deliberately introduced.

VEAL, HAM AND TONGUE SALAD

METRIC/IMPERIAL
600 ml/1 pint aspic jelly
3 hard-boiled eggs
225 g/8 oz cooked veal
225 g/8 oz cooked tongue
225 g/8 oz cooked ham

Mask an oblong cake or bread tin with almost-setting aspic jelly, and decorate it with slices of hardboiled egg. Chop up any remaining egg and mix it with the diced meat. Put the mixture into the tin and cover with aspic. When set turn out and serve, cut into slices.

A colourful accompaniment is a salad of cooked asparagus and tiny red tomatoes stuffed with cubed cucumber and peas in mayonnaise.

MOULES MARINIÈRE

(See Mussels entry.)

MOUNTAIN ASH

(See Rowan Berry entry.)

MOUSSAKA

A savoury dish eaten in Balkan and near Eastern countries. There are many variations, but it generally contains meat (usually lamb) and aubergines.

AUBERGINE MOUSSAKA

METRIC/IMPERIAL
2 aubergines, sliced
3–4 × 15 ml spoons/3–4 tablespoons olive oil
4–5 medium sized onions, skinned and sliced
0.5 kg/1 lb minced beef or lamb, raw
4 tomatoes, peeled and sliced
150 ml/¼ pint stock
3 × 15 ml spoons/3 tablespoons tomato paste
2 eggs
3 × 15 ml spoons/3 tablespoons milk
3 × 15 ml spoons/3 tablespoons cream
salt and pepper

Fry the aubergines in half of the oil for about 4 to 5 minutes, then arrange them in the bottom of an ovenproof dish. Fry the onions and meat until lightly browned – about 5 minutes. Place layers of onion and minced meat on top of the aubergines and lastly add the slices of tomato. Mix the stock and tomato paste and pour into the dish. Bake in a moderate oven (180°C/350°F, Gas Mark 4) for about 30 minutes. Beat together the eggs, milk and cream, season well and pour this mixture over the meat. Put it back into the oven for 15 to 20 minutes, until the sauce is set and the mixture is firm and golden to touch.

MOUSSE

A mousse is a light creamy dish which may be hot or cold, sweet or savoury. It has as its base a white or custard sauce, or a fruit purée to which eggs and whipped cream are often added. A cold mousse can be frozen but when a gelatine mixture is used it is merely chilled.

RASPBERRY MOUSSE

METRIC/IMPERIAL
2 × 425 g/15 oz cans raspberries, drained or 450 g/
    1 lb fresh raspberries, sieved, to make 300 ml/
    ½ pint purée
caster sugar to taste
150 ml/5 fl oz double or whipping cream, whipped
4 × 5 ml spoons/4 teaspoons powdered gelatine
3 × 15 ml spoons/3 tablespoons water or raspberry
    juice
2 egg whites, whisked
whipped cream for decoration

Mix the raspberry purée, sugar and cream. Put the gelatine and the water or fruit juice in a basin, stand the basin in a pan of hot water and heat gently until the gelatine is dissolved. Allow to cool slightly. Pour into the raspberry mixture in a steady stream, stirring the mixture all the time, and fold in the whisked egg whites. Pour into a dish and leave in a cool place to set. Decorate with whipped cream.

SALMON MOUSSE

METRIC/IMPERIAL
2 × 215 g/7½ oz cans salmon
about 300 ml/½ pint milk
25 g/1 oz butter
3 × 15 ml spoons/3 tablespoons flour
2 eggs, separated
1 × 150 ml/5 fl oz carton double cream, lightly whipped
2 × 15 ml spoons/2 tablespoons tomato ketchup
1 × 5 ml spoon/1 teaspoon anchovy essence
1 × 5 ml spoon/1 teaspoon lemon juice
salt
pepper
4 × 5 ml spoons/4 teaspoons powdered gelatine
4 × 15 ml spoons/4 tablespoons warm water
slices of cucumber to garnish

Drain the juice from the salmon and make it up to 300 ml/½ pint with milk. Remove the skin and bones from the fish and mash the flesh until smooth. Melt the butter, stir in the flour and cook for 2 to 3 minutes. Remove the pan from the heat and add the egg yolks. Allow the sauce to cool slightly and stir in the cream, ketchup, essence, lemon juice and seasoning to taste and add it to the salmon. Dissolve the gelatine in the water by putting it in a small basin in a pan of hot water; stir into the salmon mixture. Whisk the egg whites stiffly and fold these into the mixture. Pour it into an 18 cm/7 inch soufflé dish and leave to set in a cool place. Garnish with slices of cucumber before serving.

MOUSSELINE SAUCE

Hollandaise sauce to which beaten egg white or whipped cream has been added just before serving, giving a frothy effect. Serve as soon as possible; it is a good accompaniment for fish (e.g., sole) or green vegetables such as asparagus.

A sweet mousseline sauce can be made from eggs, sugar and sherry beaten together over hot water; it is served with sponge puddings and fruit.

MOZZARELLA

A white Italian cheese made from buffalo milk. It is very soft and moist and should be eaten when freshly made and unripened. Mozzarella is often used in making pizzas. Smoked mozzarella has a golden skin.

MUESLI

A cereal which was first made in Switzerland for health reasons by D. Bircher-Benner towards the end of the nineteenth century. It consists of a mixture of raw cereals which includes some or all of the following: oats, wheat, rye, millet and barley flakes; to these are added dried fruit, nuts, sugar, bran, wheatgerm and apple flakes. Muesli has now become a popular breakfast cereal served with milk and sometimes yogurt or cream.

There are many commercial varieties on the market, most of which have a high sugar content. A homemade muesli can be made from a muesli base which merely requires the addition of flavouring and sweetening; alternatively it can be made by buying each cereal separately and combining them with flavouring ingredients. The cheapest and easiest method is to use rolled oats as a base, but these tend to be floury and soft compared to other cereal bases.

Whichever variety of muesli is served, additional ingredients such as fresh citrus fruit, extra nuts and sugar can always be added to suit individual tastes. (See Breakfast cereal entries.)

MUFFIN

A thick flat yeast cake made from a soft dough and baked in rings on a griddle or hot plate, usually served warm.

MULBERRY

A fruit similar to the blackberry but larger. The berries are red, ripening to a deep purple colour when ready for picking. Mulberries are eaten raw with sugar for dessert and they may also be stewed in syrup, made into pies or flans, bottled or made into wine. As mulberries have a low pectin content they do not make satisfactory jams or jellies when used alone, but should be combined with apple.

MULBERRY AND APPLE JAM

METRIC/IMPERIAL
1.5 kg/3 lb mulberries
600 ml/1 pint water
0.5 kg/1 lb apples (prepared weight)
1.5 kg/3 lb sugar

Wash the mulberries and simmer them in half the measured water until they are soft. Peel, core and slice the apples, weigh them and simmer gently in the remaining water until they are really soft and pulped. Combine the mulberries and the apples and add the sugar. Stir until this is dissolved and

259

then boil the jam until setting point is reached. Pot and cover in the usual way. Makes about 2.25 kg/5 lb.

MULLED WINE OR ALE

These are made by heating, spicing and sweetening the wine or ale. The hot liquor is sometimes poured over beaten eggs.

MULLED CLARET

METRIC/IMPERIAL
1.2 litres/2 pints claret
½ lemon, sliced
a piece of cinnamon stick
4 cloves or a pinch of grated nutmeg
50 g/2 oz sugar

Heat all the ingredients together but do not boil. Pour into a hot jug and serve at once.

MULLED ALE

METRIC/IMPERIAL
1.2 litres/2 pints ale
1 × 15 ml spoon/1 tablespoon caster sugar
a pinch of ground cloves
a pinch of ground nutmeg
a pinch of ground ginger
1 glass rum or brandy

Heat all the ingredients except the spirit to nearly boiling point. Add the rum or brandy with more sugar or flavourings if required, and serve at once.

MULLET

A salt water fish, which may be of two different types:

RED MULLET
This is a striking looking fish, bright pink in colour; one variety also has two to five bright yellow bands from head to tail. Red mullet are only 1 kg/2 lb to 1.5 kg/3 lb in weight when fully grown and are at their best from April to October. The flesh is firm and white and has a delicious but very delicate flavour, so it should be grilled or baked.

Clean the fish thoroughly, retaining and replacing the liver, which is regarded as a delicacy. The gills are pulled out and with them will come all of the entrails that it is necessary to discard. Wipe the fish and remove the fins, tail and eyes. Score the fish twice on each side, season well and sprinkle with lemon juice. Wrap in greaseproof paper, add a few pats of butter, lay in a greased, ovenproof dish and bake in a moderately hot oven (200°C/400°F, Gas Mark 6) for 15 to 20 minutes. To serve, arrange in a hot dish, still in the paper, which should be opened up to show the fish.

GREY MULLET
This has a greenish back, with a silvery underside. Grey mullets reach 4.5 kg/10 lb to 5.5 kg/12 lb in weight when fully grown. They are caught in shoals off the Cornish coast in early summer when they are not unlike a bass and are covered with large, broad scales. When large they are treated as cod; small ones may be cooked in the same way as red mullet, although the flavour is not so good. The flesh is white and firm and easy to digest.

MULLIGATAWNY SOUP

A curry-flavoured soup of Anglo-Indian origin, made with meat or chicken stock.

MULLIGATAWNY SOUP

METRIC/IMPERIAL
2 onions
1 carrot
a piece of turnip
a sour apple
a rasher of bacon
25 g/1 oz butter
1 × 15 ml spoon/1 tablespoon curry powder
1 × 5 ml spoon/1 teaspoon curry paste
50 g/2 oz plain flour
1.2 litres/2 pints stock
salt
pepper
a bouquet garni
a squeeze of lemon juice
1–2 × 15 ml spoons/1–2 tablespoons single cream

Prepare and cut up the vegetables, peel and chop the apple, rind and dice the bacon and fry it lightly to extract the fat, add the butter and when this has melted, fry the vegetables, apple, curry powder and paste. Stir in the flour, then gradually add the stock. Bring to the boil, stirring, add salt, pepper, bouquet garni, then cover and simmer gently for about one hour, skimming occasionally. Sieve the soup or purée in a blender, return it to the saucepan and boil up. Add more seasonings if necessary and stir in the lemon juice and cream. Serve accompanied by boiled rice.

MUM

A strong sweet ale made of wheat and malt, which was originally brewed in Brunswick.

MÜNSTER

A semi-hard cheese of German origin, often square in shape; it is yellow in colour and has a red outside. Münster is made from whole milk, flavoured with caraway or aniseed, and is good for both table and kitchen use.

MUSCADET

A fresh, dry white wine made from Muscadet grapes grown in the Loire vineyards. Also produced in Italy and Chile. It is often drunk as an apéritif and is also suitable to serve with light meals.

MUSCATEL

A type of fine, large, juicy, sun-dried raisin from Spain, served as a dessert, especially at Christmas time, and usually accompanied by blanched almonds; muscatels may also be used in cooking.

The name is also applied to sweet white wines made in France, Spain and Italy from Muscat grapes.

MUSH

A kind of maize porridge, resembling polenta, made in America.

MUSHROOMS

Several varieties of edible fungi are included under this name.

Mushrooms and other fungi should never be eaten if there is the slightest doubt about their identity and the only safe way of recognizing the edible types is to learn their botanical characteristics from a really reliable illustrated book or chart. There are various more or less superstitious beliefs – for instance, that cooked poisonous fungi will blacken a silver spoon, while edible ones will not, or that edible fungi all have a skin that peels easily; however, none of these methods of telling edible from poisonous mushrooms is reliable.

FIELD MUSHROOM

This grows wild in pastures during the summer and autumn. It is whitish to brown on top with thin gills underneath ranging from white and brownish-pink to dark purplish brown. It grows on a short stalk girded by a membranous ring towards the middle or top. When young, the small, very rounded 'button' mushrooms are similar to puff balls, but they can be distinguished by the gills.

HORSE MUSHROOMS

These are somewhat similar to the Field mushroom and are found growing wild in summer and autumn beneath scattered trees and sometimes in fairy rings. Like the Field mushroom it is ball-shaped when young and the cap flattens as it grows bigger but it attains a large size, about 12 cm/5 inches in diameter. It has a whitish silky skin and if damaged turns a yellowish-brown colour. The thick stem, which widens towards the base, is white, sometimes with brownish yellow stains,

and it has a double ring round the upper part. The gills are white, turning to a dark reddish brown; they remain dry as the mushroom ages. The flesh is firm and white, tinged with yellow.

FAIRY RING MUSHROOMS

Characteristic rings of these mushrooms grow in fields. The slightly humped cap, which is reddish-buff in colour and about 2.5 cm/1 inch to 5 cm/2 inches in diameter, is borne on a thin straight, firm stem of a pale colour. The thick, off-white gills are spaced slightly apart, long and short ones alternating. The flesh is yellowish with a pleasant smell. Only the caps should be used and they need long slow cooking.

CULTIVATED MUSHROOMS

These are grown on a very large scale and are available all the year round; they are graded into buttons, caps and flat.

Mushrooms in Cooking

The food value of mushrooms is negligible but their rich, appetizing flavour make them a good addition to stews, sauces, soups, omelettes or patties and they provide a quickly made snack when served on toast or combined with fried and grilled foods. They can also add interest served raw in a salad or marinated 'à la Greque' style. Button mushrooms are excellent for garnishing, mushroom sauce, or to serve whole or sliced raw. Caps: slightly riper mushrooms which are starting to open. Use for adding to stews or casseroles or for stuffing and baking whole. Open or flat: fully opened mushrooms with plenty of flavour used for grilling or frying; may be made into ketchup or pickles and also dried. Field mushrooms need to be washed well, drained, and if necessary, peeled. Trim stalks or remove completely; the stalks are useful in soups or stuffings.

Cultivated mushrooms need to be wiped with a damp cloth or washed and drained.

BAKED MUSHROOMS

Wash and drain the mushrooms, or wipe them, and place them, stalks uppermost, in a greased baking dish. Put a small pat of butter on each mushroom, season with salt and pepper and cover with greased greaseproof paper. Bake in a moderately hot oven (190°C/375°F, Gas Mark 5) for 15 to 30 minutes, or until cooked.

GRILLED MUSHROOMS

Wipe the mushrooms and trim the stalks level with the caps. Melt 50 g/2 oz butter for every 0.5 kg/1 lb mushrooms. Dip the caps in butter and then put them in the grill pan, cap uppermost. Grill for 2 minutes, turn them, sprinkle the gills with salt and pepper and grill for a further 2 to 3 minutes.

261

FRIED MUSHROOMS

Heat 50 g/2 oz butter per 0.5 kg/1 lb mushrooms. Put in the mushrooms, stalks uppermost, season with salt and pepper and if you wish add a squeeze of lemon juice. Cover the pan and cook over a moderate heat for 4 to 5 minutes. Do not turn the mushrooms over, and the juice will remain in the mushrooms.

MARINATED MUSHROOMS

METRIC/IMPERIAL
0.5 kg/1 lb mushrooms
juice of ½ lemon
salt
120 ml/4 fl oz vinegar
6 × 15 ml spoons/6 tablespoons olive oil
2 cloves of garlic, crushed
1 bay leaf
1 sprig thyme
1 × 15 ml spoon/1 tablespoon chopped parsley
8 cumin seeds

Remove and reserve mushroom stalks. Rinse and dry mushrooms, place in a saucepan, cover with cold water and add lemon juice and salt. Bring to the boil and simmer for 10 minutes. Drain and transfer to a bowl. Combine remaining ingredients in a saucepan and simmer over a low heat, covered, for 30 minutes. Pour marinade over the mushrooms and chill for 24 hours. Drain off marinade before serving.

MUSSEL

A greenish-black bi-valve mollusc, in season from September to March. Take care to gather mussels from a suitable source, as otherwise they are sometimes unfit to eat; those sold in shops are specially treated to ensure cleanliness. Mussels should be alive when bought – discard any with gaping shells as the fish inside will be dead.

Mussels can be purchased frozen, ready for use, or in jars. Before use the latter must be drained and the mussels soaked.

Preparation and cooking: Wash the mussels in several changes of water, scraping and scrubbing each shell separately until it is perfectly clean. Finally, lift them out of the water, leaving any sediment behind.

Put 1 cm/ ½ inch water in a saucepan and add the mussels. To improve the flavour, add a slice of onion, a bay leaf, some parsley stalks, thyme and pepper. Cover the pan tightly and cook over a gentle heat for about 5 to 6 minutes; shaking the pan frequently. When the mussels are cooked the shells will open. Drain well, reserving the liquor and with scissors remove the 'beard' and any foreign bodies. Serve plain with vinegar or lemon juice, salt and pepper and brown bread and butter, or accompanied by a white sauce made from the liquor. Mussels can also be added to fish soups and stews and are an important ingredient in the Spanish dish Paella.

MOULES MARINIÈRE

METRIC/IMPERIAL
4 dozen mussels, about 3.5 litres/6 pints
butter
4 shallots or one medium onion, skinned and finely
   chopped
½ bottle dry white wine
chopped parsley
2 sprigs thyme, if available
1 bayleaf
freshly ground black pepper
flour

Put the mussels in a large bowl and under running water scrape off the mud, barnacles, seaweed and 'beards' with a small sharp knife. Discard any that are open or even just loose (unless a tap on the shell makes them close) or any that are cracked. Rinse again until there is no trace of sand in the bowl. Melt a large knob of butter and sauté the shallots until soft but not coloured. Add the wine, a small handful of chopped parsley, the thyme, bayleaf and a generous shake of pepper. Simmer and cover for 10 minutes. Add the drained mussels a handful at a time. Cover and 'steam', shaking until the shells open; this will take about 5 minutes. Holding the mussels over the saucepan to catch the juices, remove the top shells and place the mussels in warm, wide soup plates. Keep them warm. Strain the liquor and reduce it by half by fast boiling. Thicken it a little by adding a small knob of soft butter creamed with 2 × 5 ml spoons/2 teaspoons flour. Pour over the mussels, sprinkle with more parsley and serve at once.

MUSTARD

There are three types of mustard seed which may be ground to make mustard – white, black and brown. The black and brown seeds contain myronic oil, which gives the true piquant flavour but makes them of poor keeping quality; the white seeds, although inferior in flavour, keep better. Manufactured mustard powder is usually a mixture of one or more varieties of mustard seed, with a cereal – wheat flour or some other type, added to absorb the oil and retard fermentation. Powdered black mustard is seldom on sale in this country.

To make up English mustard: Place a little powdered mustard in an egg cup and mix to a smooth, soft paste with the top of the milk or water. Transfer to the mustard pot.

It is also available ready-mixed in jars.

FRENCH MUSTARD

This is made from powdered dark mustard seeds, mixed with vinegar or wine that has been flavoured with garlic, tarragon, thyme, parsley, mace and other spices; salt is also added. Some French mustard is imported from France but a certain quantity is manufactured in this country.

DIJON MUSTARD
Mixed with the juice of unripe grapes.

BORDEAUX MUSTARD
Mixed with unfermented wine.

CREMONA MUSTARD
An Italian mustard mixed with wine vinegar with crystallized fruit added.

AMERICAN MUSTARD
Made from white seeds only and made as a very mild mustard.

Mustard can be used in cooking to bring out the flavour of an ingredient such as cheese or to counteract an oily taste as in salad dressing. It is also widely used as a seasoning with meals such as beef, pork, bacon and liver.

MUSTARD SAUCE

METRIC/IMPERIAL
300 ml/½ pint white sauce
1 × 15 ml spoon/1 tablespoon dry mustard
2 × 5 ml spoons/2 teaspoons sugar
1 × 15 ml spoon/1 tablespoon vinegar

Make the sauce using all milk or half milk and half stock from fish or a chicken bouillon cube. Blend the mustard, sugar and vinegar to a smooth cream and stir into the sauce. Serve with fish.

To vary the flavour, use some of the many different mustard mixes now available, adapting the amount added to taste.

MUSTARD AND CRESS

The hardy mustard plant is frequently grown in conjunction with cress for table use and is cut when still quite young and small. Wash well, to remove seed cases and any grit, then drain. Use in salads, as a garnish, or as a sandwich filling.

MUTTON

The flesh of a full-grown sheep, as opposed to lamb, which comes from an animal under a year in age. The best mutton comes from well fed sheep of good breed, about 2 to 3 years old and the meat should be hung in a cool, airy place for about two weeks after slaughtering, to improve the flavour and tenderness.

ROAST MUTTON
Cook as for Lamb. (See Lamb entry.)

BOILED LEG OF MUTTON WITH CAPER SAUCE

METRIC/IMPERIAL
1 small 1.5 kg/3 lb leg of mutton
2 × 5 ml spoons/2 teaspoons salt
water to cover
2 onions, skinned and halved
3–4 carrots, pared (halved if they are large)
1 small turnip, pared and quartered
1–2 sticks of celery, trimmed and halved
caper or onion sauce

Trim the joint, removing any excess fat, then weigh the meat and calculate the time required for cooking, allowing 25 to 30 minutes per 0.5 kg/1 lb plus 25 minutes over. Put the meat in a large saucepan with the salt and cold water to cover. Bring it to the boil, skim off any scum which rises, then add the vegetables; reduce the heat and cover the pan with a lid. Simmer until the meat is tender, drain the meat from the cooking liquid and serve it hot, coated with the caper or onion sauce. If preferred, the vegetables can be added to the saucepan about 45 minutes before the cooking is completed and may then be served as an accompaniment to the meat.

Middle neck of lamb can also be cooked this way.

NAARTJE

A small African tangerine.

NASTURTIUM

The round hot-flavoured leaves are occasionally eaten in salads, choose young leaves and use them either whole or shredded. The yellow, orange or red flowers may be used to garnish salads. The green, berry-like seeds are also edible and when pickled make a reasonable substitute for capers.

PICKLED NASTURTIUM SEEDS

METRIC/IMPERIAL
Nasturtium seeds
spiced white vinegar (to each 600 ml/1 pint allow 6 peppercorns, 2 bay leaves and 2 × 5 ml spoons/2 teaspoons salt

Pick the seeds on a dry day. Wash and drain them well, then dry them in a cool oven (140°C/275°F, Gas Mark 1) or in the sun for 3 to 4 days. Put the vinegar into a saucepan with the peppercorns, bay leaves and salt, bring to the boil, removing from the heat to infuse for 30 minutes, and then cool. Pack the seeds into jars, fill up with the cold spiced vinegar, cork and store as usual.

NEAPOLITAN

A name frequently given to sweets, cakes, ices etc., made with layers of two or more colours, e.g., white (or cream) pink, pale green and coffee or chocolate, each layer being appropriately flavoured. The layers are assembled before baking, setting or freezing or they can be sandwiched together afterwards, as is most convenient. Neopolitan dishes should be presented or cut so that the different colours show to the best advantage.

NEAT'S FOOT, TONGUE

(See Calf's Foot Jelly, Tongue entries etc.)

NECTARINE

The fruit of a type of peach tree, which is found in both free and cling stone varieties. The smooth, shiny skin is like that of a plum, but the flesh resembles that of a peach in appearance and flavour, indeed some people consider the ripe nectarine superior to the peach. They can replace peaches in any recipe, but are best eaten fresh as a dessert fruit.

NEGUS

A type of mulled wine, generally a mixture of port, claret or sherry, spice (such as nutmeg), lemon, sugar and hot water.

PORT WINE NEGUS

METRIC/IMPERIAL
1 lemon
75 g/3 oz loaf sugar
600 ml/1 pint port
ground nutmeg
1.2 litres/2 pints boiling water

Rub the skin of the lemon with the lumps of sugar until all the flavour is extracted. Crush the sugar in a clean cloth and pour over it the wine and lemon juice, mixed with the ground nutmeg. Add the boiling water, mix well and serve hot.

NESSELRODE PUDDING

A rich and elaborate dessert made from chestnuts, egg yolks, cream and sometimes candied fruits, which is moulded and frozen.

NETTLE

Young stinging nettles, which have a pleasant, slightly bitter taste, may be cooked as a vegetable. Like spinach, nettles shrink during cooking so allow a good 225 g/8 oz per person. Wear gloves, to protect the hands, sort the nettles out for weeds and remove the roots. Wash, drain and immerse in boiling water for 2 minutes, then pour off the water and cook very gently without water until they are tender, as for spinach. Drain and chop well, add seasoning, a nut of butter and 1 × 15 ml spoon/1 tablespoon cream or top of the milk for every 1 kg/2 lb of nettles.

YOUNG NETTLE SOUP

Wash about 0.5 kg/1 lb young nettle tops thoroughly, put them in a pan with a knob of butter and 1 × 15 ml spoon/1 tablespoon water and bring to the boil, then cook gently for 10 to 15 minutes, until tender. Meanwhile make 600 ml/1 pint thin white sauce and season it. Sieve or liquidize the nettles, add the sauce and gradually flavour to taste with sugar and nutmeg.

NEUFCHÂTEL CHEESE

A soft whole-milk cheese prepared in Normandy and other parts of France. It is usually made in rectangular shape, the pieces weighing about 75 g/3 oz.

NICOTINIC ACID (NIACIN)

B₂ vitamin. (See Vitamin entry.)

NOGGIN

A liquid measure, usually 150 ml/¼ pint; how-ever, the measure is variable and the term is often taken to mean simply a portion or ration of liquid.

NOODLES (NOUILLES)

A type of pasta, originating in Italy, but now widely eaten in this country. The paste, which is mixed with egg, is cut into long narrow, flat strips. Noodles can be served broken up in soups or as an accompaniment or garnish with the main dish instead of potatoes; they may also form a main dish in themselves when served with a meat sauce.

A somewhat different kind of noodle is a staple food in China, where they are made from wheat and rice flour, mixed with egg and water. The paste is shaped or 'thrown' by hand into the long thin 'strings', which vary in diameter from that of the Italian spaghetti to that of the finest vermicelli. Chinese noodles can be served in a sauce of meat and vegetables; in soup or fried. There is, how-ever, some difference in the preparation of fried noodles (Chow Mein). In the Chinese restaurants in this country the noodles are parboiled, rinsed in cold water, formed into a 'nest' and fried in deep fat until crisp; they are then served as an accompani-ment with many savoury dishes. In China the noodles are boiled, rinsed, then shallow-fried with meat, vegetables and seasonings and served as a complete dish.

NORFOLK DUMPLING

(See Dumpling entry.)

NORMANDY SAUCE

A white sauce served with fish; it is made with fish liquor and enriched with butter and egg yolk.

NORMANDY SAUCE

METRIC/IMPERIAL
300 ml/½ pint white sauce, made with fish liquor
1 egg yolk
15 g/½ oz butter
lemon juice

Make the white sauce in the usual way, cook and beat well. Cool slightly, then beat in the egg yolk and reheat carefully without boiling. Stir in the butter a little at a time and finally add lemon juice to taste.

NOUGAT

A hard sweet, usually white or pink, containing chopped glacé or dried fruits, nuts etc. (See Sweets entry.) Montélimar nougat is a famous white nougat made with boiled sugar, egg white, chop-ped nuts and cherries.

NOUILLES

(See Noodles and Pasta entries.)

NOYAU

A liqueur originally made in France, but now pro-duced in other countries. It is rather sweet and is flavoured with cherry stone kernels, which give a taste resembling bitter almonds; it may be white or pink in colour.

NUTMEG

The seed of a tall, evergreen tree, grown in various tropical countries. The fruit splits when ripe, to reveal a single seed, surrounded by a husk (which when dried is known as mace). When the seeds are dry they are opened and the light-brown kernels or nutmegs are removed. Small ones are used for the extraction of their oil (nutmeg butter or oil of mace), while the larger ones are usually left as they are for export as whole nutmegs. Ground nutmeg is more widely sold but some people prefer to buy whole nutmegs and grate them as required, since the flavour is better.

Nutmeg is used as a flavouring for various types of food – cakes, puddings, biscuits and milk pud-dings – as well as nutmeg cream which is good with baked apples, etc.

265

NUT

NUTRIENT

A chemical component of food (sometimes called a food factor). In the body the nutrients perform the following functions.

(a) Production of energy.
(b) Growth and repair of tissues.
(c) Regulation of body processes.

The nutrients are proteins, carbohydrates, fats, vitamins, minerals and water. Some of them carry out more than one of the above functions – for example, proteins can be used both for growth and repair and also to produce energy, while some of them are concerned with controlling body processes.

All food contains at least one and usually several nutrients. At one extreme, glucose contains only one – carbohydrate – but milk contains all six.

(See individual entries.)

NUTRITION

The science of food in all its aspects, from the growing of the foodstuffs to their use in the body by animals and humans. Usually the word is taken to mean human nutrition. Our knowledge of the subject has increased rapidly over the last half-century and during that time most of the essential food factors have been discovered and identified. The main factors, as mentioned in the preceding entry are: proteins, carbohydrates, fats, vitamins, minerals and water. Roughage is also supplied by food.

It is not possible to estimate exactly how much of these food factors is necessary or to state how much is contained in different foodstuffs, so average figures only can be quoted for any one individual's requirements or for the composition of any food. (See Diet, Metabolism, Protein and Vitamin entries.)

NUTS

There are many varieties of edible nuts, among them: Almond, Barcelona, Brazil, Cashew, Chestnut, Coconut, Filbert, Hazel, Hickory, Peanut, Pecan, Pistachio and Walnut. (See individual entries.)

Although nuts are not usually eaten in large enough quantities to play an important part in the diet, they are a valuable food and vegetarians are able to use them to a considerable extent as a substitute for meat. This is due to the fact that nuts contain a large proportion of vegetable protein. The fat content of the nuts is considerable. The fat is often extracted and used as oil. (See Almond Oil entry.) Carbohydrates (starch and sugar), are also present; the chestnut being the richest source of these factors.

Apart from their use as a dessert, nuts add flavour to many dishes. Salted nuts are served with cocktails and drinks, chopped nuts are used in sweets, savouries, salads, cakes and biscuits, while ground nuts make excellent pastes for confectionery and add richness to cakes, biscuits, etc. Some nuts, particularly the attractively shaped almond and walnut and the delicate green pistachio, make a good garnish.

To shell nuts: Use a well designed pair of crackers or strike the nut with a heavy hammer or weight, taking care not to crush the kernel.

To blanch nuts: Barcelonas may be blanched by heating in the oven for a short time, until the inner skins become brittle enough to rub off with the fingers. Chestnuts should have the skin slit at both ends with a sharp knife and can then either be boiled for about 10 minutes, or put in the oven for a few minutes, when it should be quite easy to strip off both the outer and the inner skin. For almonds, pour boiling water over and leave for about 2 minutes, when the skins may be slipped off.

SALTED NUTS

Almonds, walnuts, peanuts, cashew nuts etc., can be salted and a mixture of these nuts makes a very attractive appetizer for cocktail parties. To each 100 g/4 oz blanched nuts heat about 1 × 15 ml spoon/1 tablespoon fresh butter or oil in a frying pan. Distribute the nuts in a thin even layer over the surface of the pan and fry slowly, stirring continuously, until the nuts are a uniform delicate brown. Remove them from the pan and drain, then dredge the nuts generously with fine table salt, using a sprinkler, and spread them out to cool and become crisp before serving. A little paprika pepper may also be sprinkled over the nuts.

SPICED NUTS

Follow the same procedure as for salted nuts, including the browning stage; then to each 100 g/4 oz of nuts mix 1 × 2.5 ml spoons/½ teaspoon salt and 1 × 2.5 ml spoon/½ teaspoon mixed spice and sprinkle freely over the nuts. Allow them to become cool and crisp before serving.

DEVILLED NUTS

Fry the nuts until browned then add 1 × 5 ml spoon/1 teaspoon Worcestershire sauce, 1 × 15 ml spoon/1 tablespoon chutney and some cayenne pepper and salt to the pan; stir into the nuts and cook slowly for about 4 minutes. Serve on hot toast or biscuits.

NUT FORCEMEAT
(See Forcemeat entry.)

OATS

A cereal, 'Avena', which is widely cultivated throughout the world; it will grow in colder and wetter climates and poorer soils than any other cereal and also in hotter climates than wheat or rye. Oats used to be the staple food in Scotland, but are now replaced by wheat.

The seeds are husked and the grain ground or rolled in different ways to give the various grades of oatmeal and rolled oats. The latter are produced by treating the grains with heat while passing them between rollers; quick-cooking rolled oats are produced by the application of greater heat, which partially cooks the grain.

All types of oatmeal have much the same food value and contain carbohydrates, protein, fat, iron, calcium and Vitamin B. Oats have very little gluten and therefore they cannot be used for bread-making. Since oatmeal contains fat, it does not keep as well as some other cereals, so it should be bought in small quantities and stored in a tin in a dry place.

Oatmeal and rolled oats are used for making porridge, gruel, oatcakes, flapjacks, biscuits and occasionally pastry. The meal can also be added to puddings, scones, etc., in small quantities, as a rule, up to one-quarter of the total amount of flour normally used may be replaced by fine or medium oatmeal.

There are many brands of 'quick oats' which are specially treated to speed up the making of porridge; cooking directions will be found on the packet. The pinhead and coarse types of oatmeal need longer cooking, though some people contend that the time can be shortened if they are soaked overnight. (See Porridge and Gruel entries.)

Oatcakes

An unleavened form of bread found in the North of Britain. The ingredients include oatmeal, water, salt and fat. In Wales and Scotland the mixture is made with pinhead oatmeal, rolled thinly and cut into rounds or triangles, then cooked slowly on a girdle or in an oven. In Yorkshire the meal is finely ground and made into a thick batter, then a thin layer is poured onto a heated iron plate and cooked until it can be removed and hung over a line in a warm room to dry and become crisp. All oatcakes should be crisp when eaten, they are popular served with butter and cheese.

OATCAKES

Put 175 g/6 oz fine oatmeal in a basin with a little salt and a pinch of bicarbonate of soda. Add 1 × 15 ml spoon/1 tablespoon melted butter or bacon fat and make into a soft paste with hot water. Turn onto a board sprinkled with oatmeal, flatten out with the hand or with a rolling pin until very thin and rub over with more oatmeal. Cut the dough into a large round with a saucepan lid, then cut it across again into 4 to 6 pieces. Slide the cakes carefully onto a hot girdle and cook over a moderate heat until they begin to curl up, then toast in front of the fire or under the grill for a few minutes. Serve spread with butter and fruit preserve.

OATMEAL BANNOCKS

METRIC/IMPERIAL
175 g/6 oz plain flour
1 × 15 ml spoon/1 tablespoon baking powder
1 × 5 ml spoon/1 teaspoon salt
25 g/1 oz butter or margarine
50 g/2 oz medium oatmeal
1 × 15 ml spoon/1 tablespoon sugar
150 ml/¼ pint milk and water

Mix together the flour, baking powder and salt. Rub the fat in very thoroughly with the fingertips, then add the oatmeal and sugar. Make a well in the centre of the mixture and add enough liquid to form a soft, light dough. Form into flat, round cakes about 1 cm/½ inch thick and cook on an electric griddle or hot girdle until well risen and brown, turning the cakes when cooked on the underside. To serve, split and spread with butter and fruit preserve.

OATMEAL BISCUITS
(See Biscuits entry.)

OFFAL

The edible internal parts of an animal, which are cut out during the preparation of a carcass. Ordinary meat is composed mainly of muscle, but the structure of offal varies considerably according to the particular part; thus the heart, tongue and tail, which are used for active work, are very different from the liver, which is used for storage. (See individual entries.)

The following is a list of offals.

Brains
Chitterlings
Feet or trotters (calf's, pig's, sheep's)
Heads (calf's, pig's, sheep's)
Hearts (ox, sheep's)
Kidneys (ox, calf's, pig's, sheep's)
Ox palate
Ox-tail
Sweetbreads (calf's, sheep's)
Tongue (ox, calf's, pig's, sheep's)
Tripe

OIL

A fat of vegetable, animal or mineral origin, which is liquid at normal temperatures.

Oils are a chemical combination of three molecules of fatty acids and one molecule of glycerol. The fatty acids may be of different types and this leads to the difference in characteristics between, say, a firm fat such as mutton fat and a liquid one such as olive oil. Oils have a preponderance of unsaturated fatty acids which make them liquid instead of solid. Oils are used for frying, baking, roasting and in cake and pastry making.

Vegetable Oils

These are often used in place of other fats. The main varieties are:

ARACHIDE
Oil which is extracted from the kernel of the groundnut or peanut plant. Also sold under the names of groundnut and peanut oil.

COCONUT
The nut from the coco palm yields a variety of oils with a strong flavour; these require a lot of refining before they can be used for culinary purposes. It contains a high proportion of saturated fatty acids.

CORN OIL
This is extracted from the germ of the seed of the maize plant. It has a high percentage of unsaturated fats, and can be used for all culinary purposes.

COTTONSEED OIL
Extracted from the seeds of the cotton plant. This oil is much used in the United States particularly in the food industry.

OLIVE OIL
Extracted from the ripe olive.

SOYABEAN OIL
Taken from the soy bean which is a member of the leguminosae family. The oil is much used in commercial food processing. Its strong flavour makes it less suitable for salads.

PALM KERNEL OIL
Oil extracted from the nuts of palms. It is a white or pale yellow colour and used in the manufacture of margarine.

SUNFLOWER OIL
This is taken from the seeds of the Helianthus annis. It has a pleasant taste and can be used for all culinary purposes. It also has a high ratio of unsaturated fatty acids.

WALNUT OIL
Extracted from the nut of the walnut tree (Fuglans regia). It has a delicate but distinctive flavour, but does not keep well. Walnuts grow in abundance in the districts of Perigard and Dordogne in France, hence the oil is much used in these areas.

GRAPESEED OIL
An oil of delicate flavour.

Fish Oils

The oils extracted from cod and halibut liver are valuable sources of Vitamins A and D.

Mineral Oils

These are not normally eaten. Although liquid paraffin has certain medicinal uses, it is inadvisable to use it in cooking, as it tends to prevent the absorption of nutrients.

FORK-MIX PASTRY MADE WITH OIL

METRIC/IMPERIAL
2.5 × 15 ml spoons/2 ½ tablespoons oil
1 × 15 ml spoon/1 tablespoon cold water
100 g/4 oz plain flour
pinch salt

Put the oil and water into a basin and beat well with a fork to form an emulsion. Mix the flour and salt together and add to the mixture to make a dough. Roll this out on a floured board or between greaseproof paper.

This is a slightly more greasy pastry than one made with solid fat so it is more suitable for savoury dishes than sweet tarts. Bake in a moderately hot oven (200°C/400°F, Gas Mark 6).
Note: This pastry is best used as soon as it is prepared when it is a soft dough. If it has to be stored, wrap in a polythene bag and store in the refrigerator for no longer than 24 hours. Before using, remove from polythene bag and leave at room temperature for one hour before using.

VICTORIA SANDWICH CAKE MADE WITH OIL

Cakes made using oil are very easy to mix and successful. When using oil for making sandwich cakes it is essential to add extra raising agent or to whip the egg whites until stiff and to fold them into the beaten mixture just before baking. This helps to counteract the heaviness that sometimes occurs when oil is used.

METRIC/IMPERIAL
150 g/5 oz self raising flour
1 × 5 ml spoon/1 teaspoon baking powder
pinch salt
115 g/4½ oz caster sugar
7 × 15 ml spoons/7 tablespoons vegetable oil
2 eggs
2.5 × 15 ml spoons/2½ tablespoons milk
few drops vanilla essence
jam

Grease two 18 cm/7 inch sandwich cake tins and line the base of each with greased greaseproof paper. Sift the flour, baking powder and salt into a bowl and stir in the sugar. Add the oil, eggs, milk and essence and stir with a wooden spoon until the mixture is blended, beat until smooth – not less than 2 minutes. Put into the tins and bake in a moderate oven (180°C/350°F, Gas Mark 4) for 35 to 40 minutes. Turn out to cool on a wire rack. When cold, sandwich together with jam and, if wished, sprinkle the top with icing sugar.

OKRA (GUMBO, LADIES' FINGERS)

A vegetable grown in the East and West Indies, America, India and the Mediterranean countries. The young pods, which resemble immature cucumbers, are used as a vegetable and in soups.

OLIVE

The fruit of the olive tree, which grows in sunny, warm climates, particularly in the Mediterranean region. There are many different varieties. Each fruit contains a large, single stone to which the flesh clings. The size of the olive varies considerably, according to the variety. Olives may be picked when green or when fully ripe and black.

The flesh of the olive contains an oil which has many uses in cookery. The olive itself has a sharp flavour and is therefore popular as an appetizer. Olives can also be added to savoury dishes and when stuffed with pimientos are used for appetizers and as a garnish.

Both plain and stuffed olives are bought pickled in brine. To prevent turning the olives black take them out with either stainless steel or wooden tools. Serve the olives on cocktail sticks or piled in a dish. Any surplus may be put back into the brine.

Olive Oil

The oil obtained from ripe olives. There are three grades: the best or 'virgin' oil is almost colourless, the 'first quality' is yellowish and the 'second quality' faintly greenish. Most olive oil available in the shops is second grade. Olive oil is used in cookery extensively on the Continent, less so in this country. It makes excellent salad dressings and mayonnaise and can be used for frying, in marinades and batters and for greasing casseroles.

If olive oil is adulterated with other oils, it must be labelled 'salad oil' or some other name and not sold as olive oil.

To obtain the best results with many dishes it is considered essential to use pure olive oil because of its distinctive flavour, e.g., in mayonnaise. Olive oil has only a moderate amount of unsaturated fatty acids, so cannot be classed as cholesterol-lowering.

OLLA PODRIDA

A Spanish dish, consisting of a type of stew or hodge-podge, which usually contains meat or poultry, beans and sausages.

OMELETTE

With care anyone can master the art of omelette making. Delicate handling is needed but a little practice perfects the knack – do not be discouraged if your first two or three omelettes are not successful. Two points about omelettes that make them particularly convenient are the short time they take to make and the way they use up odds and ends – such as cooked meat, fish or vegetables – either in the omelette itself, as a filling or as an accompaniment.

Have everything ready before beginning to make an omelette, including the hot plate on which to serve it – an omelette must never wait but rather be waited for.

Omelette Pans

Special little omelette pans are obtainable and should be kept for omelettes only. If you do not own such a pan, however, a thick-based frying pan can equally well be used. Whether of cast iron, copper, enamelled iron or aluminium, the pan should be thick, so that it will hold sufficient heat to cook the egg mixture as soon as this is put in. Thus the omelette can be in and out of the pan in about 2 minutes – one of the essentials of success; slow cooking and over cooking both make an omelette tough. A 15 cm/6 inch to 18 cm/7 inch pan takes a 2 to 3 egg omelette.

To season an omelette pan put 1 × 15 ml spoon/1 tablespoon salt in the pan, heat it slowly, then rub well in with a piece of kitchen paper. Tip

269

away the salt and wipe the pan with kitchen paper. To clean the omelette pan after use, do not wash it but rub it over with kitchen paper, then with a clean cloth. Non-stick pans are ideal for omelettes and do not need seasoning.

A few minutes before you want to cook an omelette place the pan on a very gentle heat to ensure that it is heated evenly right to the edges – a fierce heat would cause the pan to heat unevenly. When the pan is ready for the mixture it will feel comfortably hot if you hold the back of your hand about 2.5 cm/1 inch away from the surface.

NOTE
Manufacturers of non-stick pans advise that heating the empty pan will damage the surface, so add the fat before heating the pan.

FAT FOR GREASING OMELETTE PANS
Undoubtedly butter gives the best flavour, but unsalted margarine can be used as a substitute. Bacon fat can also be used.

Types of Omelette
Basically, there are only two different kinds, the plain and the soufflé omelette, in which the egg whites are whisked separately and folded into the yolk mixture, giving it a fluffy texture. Plain omelettes are almost invariably savoury and soufflé omelettes are most commonly served as a sweet. There are, of course, many different omelette variations, achieved by the different ingredients added to the eggs or used in the filling.

PLAIN OMELETTE

Allow two eggs per person. Whisk them just enough to break down the egg; don't make them frothy as overbeating spoils the texture of the finished omelette. Season with salt and pepper and add 1 × 15 ml spoon/1 tablespoon water. Place the pan over a gentle heat and when it is hot add a knob of butter to grease it lightly. Pour the beaten eggs into the hot fat. Stir gently with the back of the prongs of a fork or wooden spatula, drawing the mixture from the sides to the centre as it sets and letting the liquid egg from the centre run to the sides. When the egg has set, stop stirring and cook for another minute until it is golden underneath and still creamy on top. Tilt the pan away from you slightly, and use a palette knife to fold over a third of the omelette to the centre, then fold over the opposite third. Turn the omelette out onto the warmed plate, with the folded sides underneath, and serve at once. Do not overcook or the omelette will be tough.

OMELETTE FILLINGS

Fines herbes: Add 1 × 5 ml spoon/1 teaspoon mixed dried herbs or 2 × 15 ml spoons/2 tablespoons finely chopped fresh herbs to the beaten egg mixture before cooking. Parsley, chives, chervil and tarragon are all suitable.

Cheese: Grate 40 g/1 ½ oz cheese and mix 3 × 15 ml spoons/3 tablespoons of it with the eggs before cooking; sprinkle the rest over the omelette after it is folded.

Tomato: Peel and chop 1 to 2 tomatoes and fry in a little butter in a saucepan for five minutes, until soft and pulpy. Put in the centre of the omelette before folding.

Mushroom: Wash and slice 50 g/2 oz mushrooms and cook in butter in a saucepan until soft. Put in the centre of the omelette before folding.

Bacon: Rind and scissor snip two rashers of bacon and fry in a saucepan until crisp. Put in the centre of the omelette before folding.

Kidney: Skin, core and chop 1 to 2 sheep's kidneys, add 1 × 5 ml spoon/1 teaspoon finely chopped onion and fry lightly in a little butter in a saucepan until tender. Put in the centre of the omelette before folding.

Ham or Tongue: Add 50 g/2 oz chopped meat and 1 × 5 ml spoon/1 teaspoon chopped parsley to the beaten egg before cooking.

Fish: Flake some cooked fish and heat gently in a little cheese sauce. Put in the centre of the omelette before folding.

Shrimp or Prawn: Thaw out 50 g/2 oz frozen shrimps or prawns and sauté in melted butter (or use the equivalent from a can) in a saucepan, with a squeeze of lemon juice. Put into the centre of the omelette before folding.

OMELETTE ARNOLD BENNETT

METRIC/IMPERIAL
100 g/4 oz smoked haddock, poached
50 g/2 oz butter
150 ml/¼ pint double cream
3 eggs, separated
2 × 15 ml spoons/2 tablespoons grated Parmesan cheese
salt
freshly ground black pepper

Flake the cooked fish, removing any skin and bones. Place the fish in a saucepan with half the butter and 2 × 15 ml spoons/2 tablespoons cream. Toss over a high heat until the butter melts then leave it to cool. Beat the egg yolks with 1 × 15 ml spoon/1 tablespoon cream, 1 × 15 ml spoon/1 tablespoon Parmesan cheese and seasonings. Stir in the fish mixture. Stiffly whisk the egg whites and fold into the fish. Melt the remaining butter in an omelette pan and cook the omelette in the usual way, but do not fold over. Slide onto a heatproof plate, top with the remaining cheese and cream blended together, then quickly bubble under a pre-heated grill.

SPANISH OMELETTE

METRIC/IMPERIAL
3 × 15 ml spoons/3 tablespoons olive oil
2 large potatoes, peeled and cut into 1 cm/ ½ inch cubes
2 large onions, skinned and coarsely chopped
salt
freshly ground black pepper
6 eggs, lightly beaten

In a medium-sized frying pan, gently heat the olive oil. Add the potatoes and onions and season with salt and pepper. Sauté, stirring occasionally, for 10 to 15 minutes until golden brown. Drain off excess oil and quickly stir in the eggs. Cook for five minutes, shaking the pan occasionally to prevent sticking. If you wish, place under a hot grill to brown the top. Turn out onto a warmed serving plate.

NOTE
This is the basic Spanish omelette, but other vegetables may be added, such as chopped fresh red pepper, tomatoes, peas, mushrooms, spinach. Either add them raw at the beginning or stir cooked vegetables into the eggs (peas and spinach should be added already cooked).

SOUFFLÉ OMELETTE

METRIC/IMPERIAL
2 eggs
1 × 5 ml spoon/1 teaspoon caster sugar (or salt and pepper to taste for a savoury omelette)
2 × 15 ml spoons/2 tablespoons water
knob of butter

Separate the yolks from the whites of the eggs, putting them in different bowls. Whisk the yolks until creamy. Add the sugar (or seasoning) and the water and beat again. Whisk the egg whites until stiff but not dry. At this point place the pan containing the butter over a low heat and let the butter melt without browning. Turn the egg whites into the yolk mixture and fold in carefully, using a spoon. Grease the sides of the pan with the butter by tilting it in all directions and then pour in the egg mixture. Cook over a moderate heat until the omelette is a golden brown on the underside. Put under the grill until the omelette is brown on the top. Remove at once as overcooking tends to make it tough. Run a spatula gently round the edge and underneath the omelette to loosen it, make a mark across the middle at right angles to the pan handle, add any required filling and double the omelette over. Turn it gently on to a hot plate and serve at once.

SOUFFLÉ OMELETTE FILLINGS

Jam: Spread the cooked omelette with warm jam, fold it over and sprinkle with caster or icing sugar.

Rum: Substitute 1 × 15 ml spoon/1 tablespoon rum for half the water added to the egg yolks before cooking. Put the cooked omelette on a hot dish, pour 3–4 × 15 ml spoons/3–4 tablespoons warmed rum round it, ignite and serve immediately.

Apricot: Add the grated rind of an orange or tangerine to the egg yolks. Spread some thick apricot pulp over the omelette before folding it and serve sprinkled with caster sugar.

Savoury: Any of the fillings already given for plain omelettes can be used for soufflé omelettes.

BAKED SOUFFLÉ OMELETTE

METRIC/IMPERIAL
4 eggs
2 × 15 ml spoons/2 tablespoons caster sugar
6 almonds, blanched and finely chopped
2 × 15 ml spoons/2 tablespoons water
pinch salt
knob butter
sugar for dredging
jam or stewed fruit, optional

Separate the yolks from the whites of the eggs and whisk the yolks thoroughly with the sugar. Add the almonds and the water. Whisk the egg whites and the salt stiffly and fold into the yolk mixture. Grease a shallow ovenproof dish with butter and put the omelette mixture into it. Bake in a moderate oven (180°C/350°F, Gas Mark 4) for 15 to 20 minutes, sprinkle with sugar and serve at once.

A little jam or some stewed fruit may be put at the bottom of the dish before the egg mixture is added.

ONION

A type of bulb, widely grown throughout the world, which is eaten as a vegetable and is also used to flavour soups, stews, rechauffés and sauces. The onion is often regarded as the most important vegetable in the kitchen, for its flavour improves almost every savoury dish. It has, however, little food value – a small amount of vitamin C and some minerals.

Onions are available all through the year but are at their best in the early autumn and winter. These are the main varieties of onion available:

ALL-PURPOSE ONION
Rather squat in shape with a dark or pale skin; it has a strong flavour.

SPANISH ONION
A large onion with a delicate flavour.

271

BUTTON ONION (PICKLING)

A small round onion with a brown skin and white flesh. It is used for pickling or to garnish dishes.

SILVERSKIN ONION

A small onion with white flesh and silvery skin; the most prized variety for pickling.

GREEN ONION

A Welsh onion which grows in clusters and has no bulb. It is a perennial and does not need to be lifted in the autumn. The green shoots are used in salads and for flavouring.

SCALLION (SYBOE OR SPRING ONION)

Both the green stalk and white bulb are edible and are mostly used for salads.
(See Shallots entry.)

Preparation

Cut the top from each onion but retain the root end for if this is cut the pungent vapour which attacks the eyes is released. Remove the skin.

To chop: Cut the onion in half from stem to root and place the cut side downwards on the board. Slice down through the onion lengthways (not cutting quite to the root) then slice across at right angles, first horizontally and finally vertically. The onion will fall into rough cubes which can be chopped finely if the dish requires it.

BOILED ONIONS

Cook in boiling salted water until tender, 30 to 45 minutes, according to size. Drain carefully and coat the onions in a white or brown sauce before serving.

BAKED STUFFED ONIONS

METRIC/IMPERIAL

4 medium sized onions, skinned
2 × 15 ml spoons/2 tablespoons fresh breadcrumbs
salt
pepper
50 g/2 oz cheese, grated
a little milk
a little butter

Cook the onions in boiling salted water for about 25 minutes, removing them before they are quite soft; drain and cool. Scoop out the centres, using a pointed knife to cut the onion top and a small spoon to remove the centres. Chop the centres finely, mix with the crumbs, seasoning and half the cheese and moisten with milk if necessary. Fill the onions and place them in a greased ovenproof dish. Put small knobs of butter on top and sprinkle with the remaining cheese. Bake in a moderately hot oven (200°C/400°F, Gas Mark 6) for about 35 minutes, till the onions are cooked and browned.

Serve with a white sauce, making it with equal quantities of milk and onion liquor, season well and flavour with grated cheese. A tomato sauce makes a good alternative.

FRIED ONION RINGS

These are often used as a garnish for savoury dishes. For preference make them with the large Spanish onions. Slice the onions and separate them into rings, dip in lightly beaten egg white, toss in seasoned flour and fry in hot fat. Alternatively, coat rings with a batter and then fry for about 5 minutes, until tender. Drain and serve hot.

Pickled onions
(See Pickling entry.)

ORANGE

The fruit of an evergreen tree which grows in hot climates in many parts of the world. There are two main varieties sweet and bitter (or Seville); the latter type, which comes chiefly from Spain, is used mainly for making marmalade. Sweet oranges include the China, Lisbon, Navel, Blood, Tangerine and Egg varieties. There are also mandarin oranges, which have a sweet flavour and a loose skin that peels off easily. The Kumquat is a dwarf orange. Oranges are available all the year round and are imported principally from Sicily, Spain, Portugal, Malta, Israel and South Africa.

Oranges have a high Vitamin C content – 1 orange providing well over the daily requirement.

Preparation: For fruit salads, prepare the orange as follows, working over a plate to catch any juice that escapes and using a sharp knife, remove all the skin, peeling the orange like an apple and cutting deep enough to disclose the pulp. Hold the orange in the left hand and remove the flesh of each segment by cutting down at the side of the skin and then scraping the segment off the skin on the opposite side; repeat the process for each segment.

ORANGE FLAVOURINGS FOR CAKES, SWEETS ETC.
Grate the rind, taking only the coloured part, not the underlying white pith. The juice can also be added to cakes and puddings in small amounts and is used for making jellies.

ORANGE RINDS
These may be dried and stored for future use and they may also be candied. Fresh orange skins may be made into baskets in which to serve orange jelly, cream or mousse mixtures etc.

SWEET ORANGE SALAD

Peel some oranges and remove the flesh in segments. Arrange these in the serving dish, sprinkle some caster sugar and Kirsch over them and chill for about 1 hour. Toasted almonds may be sprinkled over the salad just before serving or simply sprinkle with sifted icing sugar and omit the caster sugar.

SAVOURY ORANGE SALAD

METRIC/IMPERIAL
2 sweet oranges
a little chopped tarragon and chervil, if available
1 × 15 ml spoon/1 tablespoon salad oil
2 × 5 ml spoons/2 teaspoons vinegar
1 × 5 ml spoon/1 teaspoon lemon juice

Peel the oranges and remove all the white pith, then cut the fruit in thin slices, removing the seeds. Put the pieces in a salad dish and sprinkle with the tarragon and chervil, if used. Add the oil, vinegar and lemon juice and leave to stand for a short time. Garnish with watercress.

Orange-flower water
A flavouring distilled from orange blossoms, used in making sweets and pastries.

Orangeade
A drink made from fresh oranges and served cold. There are various proprietary brands on the market, but it can also be made at home.

ORANGEADE

METRIC/IMPERIAL
2 oranges
1 lemon
50 g/2 oz sugar
600 ml/1 pint boiling water

Wash the fruit and thinly pare off the coloured part of the rinds, free of all the white pith. Put the rinds and sugar into a bowl and pour the boiling water over. Leave to cool, stirring occasionally; add the strained juice of the oranges and the lemon.

ORGEAT

A beverage, originally made from barley, later from almonds and sugar.

ORIGAN (OREGANO)

This is a wild marjoram, which is a bushy herb of the mint family. It is much used in Italian cookery and as an ingredient in South American dishes such as Chilli con Carne on pizza, pasta dishes, and amalgamated with salad dressings.

ORTANIQUE

This citrus fruit is a cross between an orange and a tangerine and at present comes only from Jamaica.

ORTOLAN

A delicately flavoured wild bird, like the bunting in appearance and about 15 cm/6 inches long. At one time it was found in this country, but it is now extinct. On the Continent ortolans are caught in nets and fattened in captivity before being killed for the table.

To prepare: Pluck and singe the birds, but leave the trail inside. The crop may be drawn from the hole made in the back of the neck and the head and neck removed. For roasting, the breasts should be covered with vine leaves and wrapped in thin rashers of fat bacon. Roast in a very hot oven (230°C/450°F, Gas Mark 8) for 12 to 25 minutes, basting with butter. To serve, leave on the vine leaves and bacon and place each bird on a croûte of fried bread or buttered toast. Serve with thin gravy, fried crumbs and chipped potatoes.

OSSO-BUCCO

A popular dish in Italy, made from knuckle of veal which is cut into pieces, sautéed and then stewed with garlic, onion and tomato. The meat is served on the bone with spaghetti or rice.

OUZO

A Greek liqueur, flavoured with aniseed.

OVEN TEMPERATURES

(See Temperatures for Cooking entry.)

OX PALATE

This is usually boiled, skinned and made into a fricassée.

OXTAIL

When skinned and chined, this makes an excellent stew or soup, but as there is a large percentage of bone, one oxtail serves only about four people.

OXTAIL CASSEROLE

METRIC/IMPERIAL
1 oxtail, jointed
25 g/1 oz fat or oil
2 onions, skinned and sliced
3 × 15 ml spoons/3 tablespoons plain flour
450 ml/¾ pint stock
pinch of dried, mixed herbs
bayleaf
2 carrots, pared and sliced
2 × 5 ml spoons/2 teaspoons lemon juice
salt
pepper

273

Fry the oxtail in the fat or oil until golden brown, then place it in a casserole. Fry the onions and add to the meat. Sprinkle the flour into the fat and brown it, add the stock and gradually bring to the boil, then pour over the meat. Add the herbs, carrots and lemon juice, season, cover and cook in a moderately hot oven (190°C/375°F, Gas Mark 5) for 30 minutes, then reduce oven to cool (150°C/300°F, Gas Mark 2) and simmer very gently for a further 2½ to 3 hours.

FRIED OXTAIL

Wash and dry an oxtail and divide it at the joints. Put in a pan with about 900 ml/1½ pints stock, season and simmer for about 2 to 3 hours. Drain and leave till cold, then coat with egg and breadcrumbs and fry in hot oil until golden-brown.

OX TONGUE

If carefully prepared this makes a delicious dish. (See Tongue entry.)

OXYMEL

A drink or syrup made of four parts honey to one part vinegar.

OYSTER

A bivalve mollusc with a flat rough grey shell. They are in season from September to April. Oysters usually live in the mouth of a river or in a bay near the shore, the cultivated ones being reared in special beds. There are many varieties of oysters. In this country the smaller ones from the Essex and Kent beds are the best for eating raw, while the Portuguese types or the large American Blue Points (now also cultivated in the British Isles) are used for cooking.

When oysters are bought the shells should be firmly closed and should come from a reliable source.

Keeping and Opening Oysters: It is possible to keep oysters alive for a day or two until they are required. Place them in a deep pan with the deep shell on the bottom, cover with salt water, allowing 175 g/6 oz to 200 g/7 oz salt to 4.5 litres/1 gallon of water and keep in a cool place. Change the water daily and sprinkle fine oatmeal in the water after it has been changed.

When oysters are required scrub them, then open. Hold each in a cloth in the palm of the left hand, with the deep shell downwards, and prise open the shells at the hinge. (A special knife may be obtained for this purpose.) Cut the oyster from the flat shell and use as desired.

Serving Oysters: They should be served in the deep shell in their own liquid; the shell may be embedded in cracked ice. Thin brown bread and butter, slices of lemon and cayenne pepper are the correct accompaniments. Tabasco sauce or French wine vinegar may also be served if desired.

Oysters are occasionally cooked, usually to serve as a savoury.

ANGELS ON HORSEBACK

Simmer some oysters in their own liquor until the edges curl. Wrap each in a thin rasher of bacon, thread on a skewer and grill until the bacon is cooked. Prepare some small rounds of toast and place two bacon rolls on each round; garnish with parsley and serve very hot.

OYSTERS AU GRATIN

Place a layer of fine white breadcrumbs in some well-greased scallop shells or an au gratin dish. Put in a layer of oysters and season with pepper, salt and a pinch of mace. Add a layer of well flavoured white sauce and top with more breadcrumbs. Dot with butter and bake in a hot oven (230°C/450°F, Gas Mark 8) until the crumbs are a rich brown, 15 to 20 minutes. Serve with brown bread and butter and garnish with parsley.

PAELLA

A Spanish national dish, made from rice and a variety of ingredients according to taste and depending on what is available, although chicken and shellfish (especially crayfish and mussels) are regarded as traditional. Paella is cooked and served in a special large, shallow pan.

PAELLA

METRIC/IMPERIAL
6–8 mussels, fresh or bottled
50–100 g/2–4 oz Dublin Bay prawns or frozen
   scampi
1 small cooked lobster
1 small chicken
4 × 15 ml spoons/4 tablespoons olive oil
1 clove garlic, skinned and crushed
1 onion, skinned and chopped
1 green pepper, seeded and chopped
4 tomatoes, skinned and chopped
225–350 g/8–12 oz long grain rice
900 ml – 1.5 litres/1½–2½ pints chicken stock
salt and pepper
a little powdered saffron
100 g/4 oz frozen peas

The quantities given in this recipe should serve at least eight people.

   Shell or drain the mussels and peel the prawns, if fresh. Remove the lobster meat from the shell and dice it, retaining the claws for decorating. Cut the meat from the chicken into small pieces. Put the oil into a large paella or frying pan and fry the garlic, onion and green pepper for 5 minutes, until soft but not browned. Add the tomatoes and chicken pieces and fry until the chicken is lightly browned. Stir in the rice, most of the stock, the seasoning and saffron (blended with a little of the stock). Bring to the boil, then reduce the heat and simmer for about 20 to 25 minutes, until the chicken is tender and the rice just cooked.

   Stir in the mussels, prawns, lobster and peas and simmer for a final 5 to 10 minutes, until heated through. Serve garnished with a few extra pimiento or green pepper strips and the lobster claws. Mussels in their shells can also be used as a garnish.

PAIN PERDU (MOCK FRITTERS)

There are various forms of this simple sweet, which makes a good way of using up left-over bread. It is sometimes called 'Poor Knight's Pudding'.

PAIN PERDU

METRIC/IMPERIAL
a French roll or some stale bread or cake
milk
1 beaten egg
butter for frying
caster sugar
ground cinnamon or jam

Cut slices of bread 2.5 cm/1 inch thick and trim to a neat shape, then soak them in milk, adding flavouring such as ground cinnamon to taste. Melt the butter in an omelette pan, dip the bread in the egg, put it carefully in the pan and fry to a light brown on both sides. Sprinkle with sugar and cinnamon or serve with jam.

PALM OIL

The oil extracted from the pulp of the palm fruit (not to be confused with palm kernel oil). It is reddish in colour and fairly soft in consistency. It is also used in the manufacture of margarine.

PALM WINE

In many tropical countries a wine is made by fermenting the sap of various palms, particularly date and coconut palms.

PALMIER

A cake consisting of puff or flaky pastry, sandwiched together with cream or jam.

275

PALMIERS

METRIC/IMPERIAL
100 g/4 oz puff pastry, i.e., made with 100 g/4 oz
  flour etc., or 225 g/8 oz ready made puff pastry
caster sugar
sweetened whipped cream or jam
icing sugar

Roll the pastry out evenly until it is 3 mm/⅛ inch thick (2 mm/¹/₁₆th inch if bought pastry) and about 50 cm/20 inches long, then sprinkle generously with sugar. Fold the ends over to the centre until they meet and press down firmly. Sprinkle generously with more sugar and fold the sides to the centre again, press and sprinkle with sugar. Place the two folded portions together and press, then with a sharp knife cut into 5 mm/¼ inch slices. Place cut edge down on a baking sheet, allowing room to spread and bake in a hot oven (220°C/425°F, Gas Mark 7) for 6 to 7 minutes, until golden brown. Turn them and bake for a further 6 to 7 minutes. Cool on a rack and just before serving spread sweetened whipped cream on half the slices, sandwich with the remaining slices and dredge with icing sugar. (If preferred jam may be used instead of cream.)

PANADA

A very thick sauce, made from a roux, 50 g/2 oz butter and 50 g/2 oz plain flour to 300 ml/½ pint liquid. It is used to bind rissoles, fish cakes etc., and as a basis for such dishes as soufflés. Its flavour depends partly on the stock used and on whether or not the roux from which it is made is allowed to brown slightly. Seasoning and extra flavouring are added as required.

A panada based on breadcrumbs is often used for forcemeat balls, quenelles etc. To make this soak 225 g/8 oz bread (without crust) in 2–3 × 15 ml spoons/2–3 tablespoons milk or stock then squeeze it dry in a cloth. Melt 25 g/1 oz fat, add the bread and beat to a smooth paste. Season and flavour as required.

PANCAKE

There are two main kinds of pancake and many ways of serving each kind. The English pancake is made of batter cooked on both sides in a frying pan, giving a wafer thin cake which is served with lemon and sugar or filled with jam or some sweet or savoury filling. French pancakes are somewhat similar, but are made lighter by separating the eggs and beating the egg whites stiffly before adding them to the mixture.

A substantial main dish can be made by filling the pancakes with a savoury mixture. The pancakes can then be rolled or folded into parcel shapes and served with a complementary sauce.

PANCAKES

METRIC/IMPERIAL
300 ml/½ pint pouring batter
lard
caster sugar
lemon wedges

Make up the batter mixture. Heat a little lard in an 18 cm/7 inch heavy based flat frying pan until hot, running it round to coat the sides of the pan; pour off any surplus. Raise the handle side of the pan slightly, pour a little batter in from the raised side, so that a very thin skin of batter flows over the pan; move it to and fro until the base is covered. Place over a moderate heat and leave until the pancake is golden brown. Turn with a palette knife or by tossing and cook the second side until golden. Turn out onto sugared paper and sprinkle with sugar. Repeat, greasing the pan each time.

If you are cooking a large number of pancakes, keep them warm by putting them as they are made between two plates in a warm oven. Finally, sprinkle each pancake with lemon juice, roll up and serve at once, with extra sugar and lemon wedges. Cooked pancakes will keep for up to one week if wrapped in greaseproof paper and stored in a refrigerator. Re-heat them in a hot frying pan, without any fat, turning them over once.

ENRICHED PANCAKES

METRIC/IMPERIAL
100 g/4 oz plain flour
a pinch of salt
2 eggs
300 ml/½ pint milk
25 g/1 oz caster sugar
a grating of lemon rind

Sift the flour and salt, add the egg yolks and beat in about half the milk. Whisk thoroughly to aerate the mixture, then add the remaining milk. Whisk the egg whites until stiff, whisk in the sugar and lemon rind and fold this mixture into the batter. Cook immediately.

Pancake fillings

SWEET
Sugar and lemon juice.
Sugar and ground cinnamon.
Jam (with whipped cream if desired).
Fruit purée.
Cleaned sultanas, raisins or chopped dates.
Bramble jelly and apple purée.
Banana and sugar.
Rum or Brandy sauce.

SAVOURY
Diced meat or poultry in sauce.
Fried mushrooms or tomatoes.

Chopped fried sausage.
Asparagus tips.
Green peas and diced fried potato.
Canned salmon and cooked mushrooms, heated in
    white sauce.
Grated cheese, seasoning and chopped parsley.

CINNAMON-APPLE PANCAKES

Have a store of pancakes in the freezer; here's a way
to zip up purée of apples and enjoy a quick hot
pudding too.

METRIC/IMPERIAL

BATTER
100 g/4 oz plain or self-raising flour
pinch of salt
1 egg
300 ml/½ pint milk, approx

FILLING
100 g/4 oz fresh white breadcrumbs
80 g/3½ oz butter
grated rind and juice of 1 lemon
0.75 kg/1½ lb cooking apples, peeled and sliced
50 g/2 oz caster sugar
1 × 5 ml spoon/1 teaspoon ground cinnamon
icing sugar

Sift the flour and salt into a bowl. Break an egg into
the centre, add 2 × 15 ml spoons/2 tablespoons
milk and stir well. Gradually add the rest of the
milk, stirring continuously. Beat until the consistency of single cream. Heat an 18 cm/7 inch frying
pan, preferably one with slightly sloping sides.
Brush the surface of the heated pan with a little lard
or corn oil. Raise the handle-side of the pan slightly. Pour the batter in from the raised side, so that a
very thin skin of batter flows over the pan; move to
and fro to achieve this. Place the pan over a moderate heat and leave until the pancake is golden. Turn
pancake over and cook the second side until golden. Turn the pancakes on to a clean tea towel.
Repeat, greasing the pan each time.
For the filling: Fry the crumbs in 65 g/2½ oz butter
until golden, turning often. Place the remaining
butter, lemon rind, juice, apples, sugar and cinnamon in a pan, cover and cook gently until puréed.
Add the fried crumbs. Divide the mixture between
the pancakes and roll up. Place them side by side in
a single layer in a moderate oven at (160°C/325°F,
Gas Mark 3) for about 20 minutes. Dust heavily
with icing sugar before serving.

Freezing Pancakes

Pancakes freeze successfully. They should be
wrapped with greaseproof paper between each
pancake, then the pile overwrapped in foil and a
freezer bag. Use within 2 to 3 months.

PANTOTHENIC ACID

One of the B Vitamins. (See Vitamin entry.)

PAPAW

One of the varieties of custard fruit, grown in the
tropics and in the southern states of U.S.A. It is
green, with greenish-white flesh, and is generally
not pleasant to eat. There is, however, one edible
variety which when ripe turns brown, with yellow
flesh.
    Papaw is supposed to resemble the real paw-
paw which is a different fruit.

PAPAYA

(See Pawpaw entry.)

PAPRIKA

The red powder obtained from the fruit of a capsicum; the best comes from Hungary. The
strength of paprika varies greatly, some types
being quite mild; the best kind is that known as
Szegediner. The characteristic sweet, aromatic
taste of paprika makes it a very good addition to
many savoury dishes and it is indispensable in
Hungarian goulash; it goes well with tomato and
up to 1 × 5 ml spoon/1 teaspoon mild paprika may
be added to 300 ml/½ pint tomato sauce. When
paprika is used in appreciable quantities it gives a
pink colouring to a dish or sauce. To obtain maximum benefit from the flavour it should be
'sweated' with any vegetables or meat. It may also
be used as a garnish on savoury snacks, cocktail
biscuits and so on. As paprika does not keep well it
should be bought when needed.

PARBOILING, PARCHING

To part-boil, the food is boiled in the normal way,
but for only half the time until somewhat softened,
and is then finished by some other method.
Parch: To brown in dry heat.

PARFAIT

A type of frozen sweet, similar to a mousse, but somewhat richer; beaten eggs are usually included to give lightness.

FRUIT PARFAIT

METRIC/IMPERIAL
100 g/4 oz sugar
2 × 15 ml spoons/2 tablespoons water
1 egg white
300 ml/½ pint double cream
a few drops of lemon or other flavouring essence
fruit salad and whipped cream to serve

Boil the sugar and water to 110°C/225°F or until it makes a thread. (See Sugar Boiling entry.) Pour a thin stream on to the stiffly whisked egg white, beating meanwhile and continue to beat until thick. Cool, add the flavouring essence and the whipped cream and freeze in the usual way. (See Ice Cream entry.)

Meanwhile, prepare some fruit salad, then chill it. Divide over each serving of parfait and top with whipped cream.

PARING

To peel or trim.

PARKIN

A moist ginger cake usually served cut in squares. It originated in Yorkshire, where oatmeal is always used in its preparation.

OATMEAL PARKIN

METRIC/IMPERIAL
225 g/8 oz plain flour
2 × 5 ml spoons/2 teaspoons baking powder
4 × 5 ml spoons/4 teaspoons ground ginger
225 g/8 oz medium oatmeal
100 g/4 oz caster sugar
175 g/6 oz golden syrup
175 g/6 oz black treacle
1 egg, beaten
4 × 15 ml spoons/4 tablespoons milk

Grease and line a 23 cm/9 inch square cake tin or a shallow meat tin. Sift together the flour, baking powder and ginger. Rub in the fat and add the oatmeal and sugar. Heat the syrup and treacle over a very low heat; do not over-heat. Make a well in the centre of the dry ingredients and gradually stir in the liquid from the saucepan and the beaten egg and milk. Pour into the tin and bake in a moderate oven (180°C/350°F, Gas Mark 4) for 45 minutes to 1 hour. Allow to cool a little in the tin, then turn out to finish cooling. Serve, cut into squares or fingers.

PARMENTIER

The name of the man who introduced the potato into France in the eighteenth century. The name is now applied to a number of potato dishes.

POMMES PARMENTIER

Prepare 1 kg/2 lb potatoes and cut into 1 cm/½ inch dice. Fry in hot fat – shallow or deep – until crisp, golden brown and soft throughout. Season and serve at once.

PARMENTIER SOUP

METRIC/IMPERIAL
0.5 kg/1 lb potatoes
3–4 leeks
25 g/1 oz butter
600 ml/1 pint chicken or veal stock
seasoning

Fry the potatoes and leeks in the butter, stir in the stock and simmer until the potatoes are soft. Sieve the soup and re-boil then season to taste.

PARMESAN CHEESE

A hard Italian cheese made from partially skimmed milk. In Italy it is referred to as Grana owing to its granular texture. Parmesan has an excellent flavour and is used grated for cooking. It is expensive but only a little is required, owing to its strong flavour. It can be obtained ready grated in packets or drums or it may be bought in a piece, grated and stored in a jar. If carefully stored, Parmesan will keep for years.

PARSLEY

This herb, with its curled, bright green leaves, is invaluable as both flavouring and garnish. In addition to the ordinary parsley which has such names as 'Champion Moss' and 'Curled', there is a turnip-rooted type, grown for its large roots; the green foliage of this type can also of course be chopped and used for flavouring but it is inferior in flavour to ordinary parsley.

At one time parsley was said to be a good source of Vitamin C, but so little is eaten that it is not really significant.

To chop parsley: Wash the parsley to remove the grit, squeeze it dry in a cloth and chop it finely.

PARSNIP

This root vegetable, which is available from autumn to spring, has a characteristic strong flavour which appeals to many people. Parsnips may be boiled and then served either in pieces or mashed, with seasoning, a little cream or milk and butter, or they may be roasted round the joint. A less common way of cooking is to dip strips of boiled parsnip in batter and fry them in hot fat. A homemade wine may also be prepared from parsnips.

Parsnips, like all root vegetables, contain carbohydrates and therefore have a higher energy value than green vegetables.

Preparation and cooking: Wash, peel off the tough skin and remove the hard centre core. Cut in slices, strips or dice and leave in water till ready for cooking. Boil in a covered pan in a 2.5 cm/1 inch depth of salted water for 30 to 40 minutes, until tender. Drain and toss in butter, seasoning and grated nutmeg.

To roast parsnips, parboil for 5 minutes in salted water, drain, place in fat around the joint and roast for 1 hour.

PARSON'S NOSE

The tail of a fowl.

PARTRIDGE

A greyish-brown bird, which in this country is shot from September 1st to February 1st, but is at its best in October and November. When it is young the feet and legs are yellowish, the beak supple and the wing feathers pointed. Old birds have slatey-blue legs and feet, hard beaks and rounded wing feathers. The feathers are the best guide to age as the feet change colour more quickly. At the optimum age for eating, which is between two and four months the partridge weighs about 0.5 kg/1 lb. One bird per serving is usual.

Preparation, roasting and serving: As soon as possible after shooting hang the bird head downwards for 3 to 4 days in a cool, airy place. Pluck, singe and clean it, season the inside with pepper and salt and replace the liver. Stuffing may be added if desired (either a simple stuffing made of breadcrumbs, parsley etc., or a more elaborate one containing chopped mushrooms or truffles). Truss the partridge in the same way as poultry, pressing up the breast to give it a plump, rounded appearance.

During the cooking the bird must be well basted to prevent the breast from drying while the legs, which the heat takes longer to penetrate, are cooking. As an additional precaution the breast may be 'waistcoated' with vine leaves and bacon – trim a fine vine leaf to rectangular shape, spread it lightly with butter and lay it on the breast with a thin slice of bacon of the same size on top; fix it with a piece of string and remove it before the bird is served. Cook in a hot oven (220°C/425°F, Gas Mark 7); the average time is 25 minutes.

Remove the trussing strings and serve the bird at once with a good thin brown gravy made in the roasting tin in the usual way.

The choice of garnish and accompaniments is very much a matter of taste. Quarters of lemon and watercress, seasoned and sprinkled with a few drops of vinegar, are often served. Bread sauce and browned crumbs are liked by some, while potato crisps and a salad are indispensable additions. A crisp lettuce salad, sprinkled with a little chopped tarragon, is a favourite. A partridge can also be made into tasty dishes by grilling, poaching and stewing with other ingredients.

CASSEROLE OF PARTRIDGE

METRIC/IMPERIAL
2 medium sized onions, skinned and sliced
2 sticks of celery, trimmed and sliced
100 g/4 oz mushrooms, sliced
100 g/4 oz bacon, rinded and chopped
1 × 15 ml spoon/1 tablespoon oil
25 g/1 oz butter
2 partridges, plucked, drawn and jointed
3 × 15 ml spoons/3 tablespoons flour
400 ml/14 fl oz stock
400 g/14 oz can tomatoes
salt
pepper
150 ml/¼ pint red wine

Fry the onions, celery, mushrooms and bacon in the oil and butter for about 5 minutes, until golden brown. Remove from the pan and line the base of a casserole with them. Fry the partridge joints for about 5 minutes then place on the vegetables. Stir the flour into the pan and cook for 2 to 3 minutes. Gradually stir in the stock, bring to the boil and stir until it thickens. Add the tomatoes, salt, pepper and wine. Pour the sauce over the partridge, cover and cook in a moderate oven (180°C/350°F, Gas Mark 4) for 1 hour.

PARTRIDGE WITH GRAPES

METRIC/IMPERIAL
2 young partridges
2 × 15 ml spoons/2 tablespoons vegetable oil
175 ml/6 fl oz light stock
6 × 15 ml spoons/6 tablespoons dry white wine
salt
freshly ground white pepper
1 × 15 ml spoon/1 tablespoon cornflour
1 egg yolk
2 × 15 ml spoons/2 tablespoons double cream
100 g/4 oz white grapes, skinned, halved, pipped
chopped parsley to garnish

Halve the partridges and remove the back bones. Carefully pull off the skin. Heat the oil in a large frying pan and lightly brown the birds on both sides. Pour over stock and wine, season and bring to the boil. Cover tightly, cook gently on top of the stove for about 25 minutes or until tender. Drain partridges, keep warm on a serving dish. Blend together cornflour, egg yolk and cream. Add to pan juices with grapes, cook gently without boiling, until sauce thickens. Adjust seasoning. Spoon sauce over partridges and garnish.

TO FREEZE
Prepare to the end of stage three cooking for 20 minutes only, pack and freeze. To use, thaw, reheat, covered, on top of stove and complete as above.

PARTY

Whether a party is to be large or small, formal or simple, it will have a greater chance of success if you plan it beforehand.

Buffet Parties

These provide an easy way of entertaining a large number of people; they have become very popular, as they need less space than a formal dinner or lunch and are less expensive.

If possible, arrange the buffet table in the middle of the room and have smaller tables set at convenient points to prevent congestion. Try to provide sufficient chairs for guests to be seated if they wish.

All the food should be easy to eat (preferably without the use of a knife) and set out so that the guests can easily help themselves. Plates, forks, spoons and napkins should be placed near the dishes. Soup may be served at one end of the buffet table; coffee or other hot drinks may be served there or at a separate table. Cold drinks and glasses should, if possible, be placed on a third table, to avoid congestion.

(See Buffet and Wedding buffet entries.)

Cocktail and Sherry Parties

If a large number of people are invited, the room should be arranged as for buffet parties. (See Cocktail entry for some popular drinks recipes.) Sherry, also tomato juice or orange juice, should be offered as alternatives. To accompany the drinks, serve small hot or cold canapés and snacks, such as olives, salted nuts, stuffed prunes, salty biscuits and toast fingers spread with cream cheese, pâté, flaked sardines or other fish. Potato crisps accompanied by a savoury dip are also popular. Plain slightly sweet biscuits are good with sherry.

Wine and Cheese Party

The main requirements are an assortment of cheeses (say 3 to 4 types for a small party and 6 to 8 for a larger one), with a variety of breads, crispbreads and biscuits. Choose well contrasted cheeses but have one mild kind for the less adventurous; allow about 50 g/2 oz to 75 g/3 oz per person. The cheeses will look attractive arranged on a wooden board or platter; Cheshire or Cheddar cheese may be cut into cubes and served on cocktail sticks. Provide also titbits such as potato crisps, onions, olives, radishes, gherkins, salami and tiny sausages, with perhaps chutney or other relish.

Other savouries that can be served at a wine and cheese party include:

Welsh rarebit, cut into neat squares.
Smoked salmon and grape rolls on sticks.
Stoned green grapes, stuffed with cream cheese and speared on sticks.
Salted almonds.
Celery cheese boats or similar pastry savouries.
Cheese straws and assorted cocktail biscuits.
Cubes of cheese and pineapple.
Smoked fish cut into small pieces.

If you are serving both bread and biscuits allow 75 g/3 oz biscuits per person (more if they are large or weigh heavily) and the equivalent of 2 slices of bread. Thus, for a party of 20 get two large rye loaves, 2 long French ones, and 1.5 kg/3 lb to 2 kg/4 lb biscuits, 0.5 kg/1 lb butter gives about 40 small pats.

'Dunks' are popular; for these have bowls of one or two savoury mixtures, with breadsticks, chunks of crisp French bread, potato crisps or celery sticks.

Almost any drink can be served, from bottles of inexpensive wine to iced wine cup or hot punch. It is wise to also have soft drinks and hot coffee.

There is no strict rule as to what wine is best with each cheese, so a choice of red or white can be offered. Allow about half a bottle per person. Some port or sherry – the classic accompaniment to cheese – can be served, while for any guests that do not care for wine, cider, stout or beer make a welcome alternative.

Here are some suitable wines:

RED WINES
Claret (red Bordeaux), e.g., Médoc, St. Julien or
  St. Émilion
Burgundy, e.g., Mâcon, Beaune, Nuits St.
  Georges
Beaujolais
Red Chianti
Rhône wines, e.g., Châteauneuf du Pape

WHITE WINES
Bordeaux, e.g., Graves, Sauternes
Burgundies, e.g., Mâcon, Aligoté
Swiss Wines, e.g., Neuchâtel

ROSÉ WINES
Anjou, Tavel, Portuguese, e.g., Mateus Rosé

Informal Dinner Parties

The menu for these informal meals usually consists of three courses, followed by coffee. Anyone who has to be both cook and hostess should choose at least some dishes which can be prepared beforehand; here are two sample menus:

Spring or Early Summer

Crème Vichyssoise
Veal Cutlets
French Beans
Duchesse Potatoes
Cherries in Wine

Autumn or Winter

Moules Marinière
Tournedos with Béarnaise Sauce
Braised Chicory
Potato Parmentier
Rum and Chocolate Gâteau

Formal Dinner Parties

The number of courses at a formal meal may vary from three to five or more. Often menu cards are provided for each person or one to each small table if this is the seating arrangement.

At a large celebration dinner, place cards can be used on the table. At an informal dinner the hostess indicates where the guests are to sit. This begins with the senior lady guest who sits on the right of the host; the ladies are seated first and then the men are shown their places.

The full menu for a dinner or banquet in former times comprised these courses:

Appetizer
Soup (choice of clear and thick)
Fish
Entrée
Remove or Roast Joint of Meat (with vegetables)
Sorbet (only served at very formal meals)
Rôti (poultry or game, with game chips and salad)
Entremets: these may comprise one or more of the following:
    dressed vegetables, hot and cold sweets and a savoury
Glace (ice: only served in addition to a sweet entremets at very formal meals)
Dessert (fresh fruit, dried or crystallized fruit, bon-bons, petit fours etc.)
Coffee (black or white)

Simplified menus are now made up in one of the following ways:
1. Appetizer or soup; fish, meat, game or poultry, with vegetables; dessert, sweet or savoury; coffee.
2. Soup; fish; game; sweet; savoury.
3. Soup, game and sweet.
4. Appetizer, entrée, sweet and savoury.

NOTE
A first course of iced melon, melon cocktail, oysters, or any simple appetizer may be followed by soup, or the soup may be omitted altogether.

SERVING THE MEAL
1. The first course (appetizer, fruit cocktail, etc.) is usually placed ready on the table, either in individual dishes or (in the case of hors d'œuvre) grouped in the centre of the table.
2. Soup, fish and entrées are usually served at the table by the hostess. For a more formal occasion, they can be served at a side-table, and handed to the guests by a waitress. Food and plates are served and removed from the left, with the left hand, while drinks, with the glasses or cups, are served and removed from the right.
3. It is usually more convenient to carve joints and game at a side-table.
4. Sauces are served in a sauce-boat and other accompaniments in serving dishes.
5. Sweets are served at table or, if in individual dishes, they are handed round.
6. Savouries are handed round.
7. Cheese and biscuits are served on dishes so that the guests can help themselves.

Luncheon Parties

These are usually less elaborate than dinner parties, though a formal luncheon is served exactly like a formal dinner, the chief differences lying in the simpler menu and table setting; there is no formality when entering the dining room and place cards are not used, except for very large functions.

For informal luncheons it is increasingly the practice to serve two courses only, followed by coffee.

Children's Parties

These can be given for various occasions, although birthday parties are the most popular. As different age groups require different amusements and food it is advisable not to have too wide an age range. For older children a theme adds interest; this can be introduced with decorations and dress, then carried through to the food and games.

The food should be novel in presentation, but the actual tastes and textures should not be too unfamiliar. Include fancy sandwiches and open rolls, sausage rolls, hamburgers, cheese straws, savoury flans, toasted sandwiches and sausages on sticks and baked beans. For cakes, you can have meringues, éclairs, brandy snaps and small iced cakes, as well as gâteaux and fruit cakes. Jellies, trifles, fruit salad and ice cream are usually popular, but avoid having too many rich things, for some children are easily upset. As a centrepiece, make an attractively iced birthday or party cake. This can sometimes be based on a favourite object or character, such as a train, boat, or animal. Plan the table to look pretty, but keep it simple for young children.

Popular drinks for small children are orange and lemon squash, milk or milk shakes. School children may like these and also enjoy fresh lemonade, fruit cups and a not too heady cider cup.

Tea Parties
For light afternoon tea, serve a good Indian or China tea (or both) and offer such things as thinly cut bread and butter, open savoury scones, thin layer sandwiches or rolled sandwiches, assorted fancy pastries and gâteaux, fingers of fruit cake and assorted biscuits. In winter, fingers of hot, savoury toast or hot butter scones or teacakes can be included. Provide knives and forks for eating these, or pastry forks for the fancy types of cake.

Bridge Parties
These are planned to suit the time of day – for an afternoon party serve a light tea, if the guests arrive after dinner, serve coffee or tea, small sandwiches, pastries, petits fours or biscuits during an interval.

Wedding Reception
It is a matter of choice as to whether this is a very formal occasion, informal, large or small gathering. For a summer wedding a garden setting is delightful, but it is wise to have a marquee, or to make some alternative arrangements for bad weather.

Buffet refreshments are easy to arrange, especially for a large number of guests, and are suitable for any time of day. A sit-down meal, however, is especially appropriate after an early wedding and makes a more dignified setting for the ceremonies of cutting the cake and proposing the toasts.

Buffet Wedding Breakfast
For general arrangements (see Buffet Parties entry). Suggested menus are given below, the first one being for a midday reception and the second for an afternoon function. (For quantities required, see the list at end of entry.)

Tomato Juice Cocktail (or Iced Consommé)
Chaudfroid of Chicken
Salmon Fingers
Cocktail sausages
Bouchées
Shrimp Horns
Fruit Salad in Melons
Chocolate Soufflé
Meringues
Chocolate Éclairs
Wedding Cake
Champagne
Punch
Tea
Coffee

Lobster Salad
Chicken and Ham Bouchées
Asparagus Rolls
Salmon Éclairs
Shaped Sandwiches
Macaroons
Iced Petits Fours
Meringues
Fruit Tartlets
Wedding Cake
Champagne
Punch
Tea
Coffee

Sit-down Wedding Breakfast (Midday)
Either a hot or cold luncheon may be served; here are two suggested menus:

Consommé Julienne
Baked Salmon Steaks
Hollandaise Sauce
Asparagus Tips
New Potatoes
Syllabub
Strawberry Flan
Wedding Cake
Sherry
Champagne
Coffee

Iced Consommé
Smoked Trout
Horseradish Sauce
Cold Roast Duck
Orange and Lettuce Salad
Potato Salad
Raspberry Soufflé
Wedding Cake
Burgundy
Champagne
Coffee

Choose wines and beverages to suit the food served; champagne or sparkling white wine is best for the toasts – allow at least one glass per guest, more if possible. Cocktails and sherry may be served whilst the guests are being received. Fruit cups, punches or squashes should be available at either a buffet or a sit-down meal. Black and white coffee (hot or iced) are served at morning receptions and tea and coffee in the afternoons.

Special Occasion Parties

HALLOWE'EN
The decorations for this party are almost as important as the food, and should be carried out in the 'Devil's Colours' – orange, red and black. The lighting should be dim and mysterious so rely on

Sandwiches: A 1 kg/2 lb loaf gives 20 to 24 slices (10 to 12 rounds) 100 g/¼ lb butter required. Allow 3 to 4 small (quarter) sandwiches per person.

Sandwich fillings: For 10 to 12 rounds (i.e., 1 kg/2 lb loaf) allow one of the following ingredients (approximate quantities): 0.5 kg/1 lb tomatoes, 1 cucumber, 350 g/¾ lb cooked and sliced ham; 3 cans sardines; 3 small cans salmon; 3 scrambled eggs.

Cold meat, poultry: 50 g/2 oz per person etc. (without bone): when salad is served.

Chicken (in portions): 100 g/4 oz to 350 g/12 oz dressed weight per person with bone.

Turkey: 6 kg/14 lb bird gives about 25 portions.

Lobster: 1 average-sized lobster gives about 3 to 5 portions.

Smoked Salmon: 25 g/1 oz to 50 g/2 oz per person.

Sausage Rolls: 0.75 kg/1½ lb pastry and 1 kg/2 lb sausage meat give 50 small rolls.

Savoury Patties: 0.75 kg/1½ lb puff pastry makes about 75 small patties.

Lettuce: 1 large lettuce serves 6 to 8 people.

Creams, Jellies, Blancmanges: 1.2 litres /2 pints give 10 servings.

Ice Cream: 1.2 litres/2 pints give 12 servings.

Champagne: 1 ordinary bottle serves 5 persons.

Wine: 1 bottle serves four persons.

Sherry: 1 bottle gives 16 glasses

Spirits: 1 bottle gives 32 'singles'.

Teas for 100: (to serve 2 cups each you will need about 22.5 litres/5 gallons) in urns, allow approx. 75 g/3 oz tea per gallon water, i.e., 1 lb tea. In teapots, allow 100 g/4 oz per gallon, i.e., 600 g/1¼ lb tea. Allow 3.5–4.5 litres/6–8 pints milk and 1 kg/2 lb sugar.

Coffee for 100: (to serve 1–2 cups each you will need about 4 gallons, including milk) use 13.5 litres/3 gallons water and 4.5 litres/1 gallon milk, or half-and-half. Allow 100–350 g/¼–¾ lb coffee per gallon, i.e., 1–1.5 kg/2–3 lb coffee. Allow 1.25–1.5 kg/2½–3 lb sugar.

---

candles, turnip lanterns and if possible a wood fire. Decorate the walls with large silhouettes of cats, bats, owls and witches on broomsticks, cut out of paper and perhaps decorated with sequins.

A barrel or coal scuttle makes a good cauldron and when filled with colourful fruit and vegetables – apples, oranges, peppers – it is very effective, especially if you can contrive a model of a large cut-out witch to stand by it.

The food can be as for an ordinary buffet supper, with decorations in the Hallowe'en colours. For example, have cakes iced with orange icing and decorated with slices of orange; sandwiches and rolls garnished with black olives or mushrooms, fruit salad containing orange slices and black grapes. Roasted chestnuts (parboil them for 15 minutes to make them cook more quickly) will be welcomed, while bobbing for apples is a traditional pastime. Hot soup and potatoes are popular fare.

Guy Fawkes Party
Fireworks should be carefully supervised by adults because if mishandled they can be very dangerous.

Traditional fare to serve at Guy Fawkes parties includes, treacle toffee, parkin, potatos in their jackets, hot dogs, roasted chestnuts, hot pies and soup. If soup is not served a hot drink is essential.

PASHKA

A sweet dish originally made in Russia: it is made from curd cheese, cream, almonds and dried fruit and is set in a wooden mould. It can also be placed in an earthenware pot. It is a rich dish traditionally served at Easter with cake.

PASSION FRUIT

(See Granadilla entry.)

PASTA

Pasta, which originated in Italy, is now produced in many countries. It is made from the flour of a very hard wheat, 'durum' wheat, which grows particularly well in parts of Italy. Pasta constitutes the staple food in these parts, supplying energy, protein and some vitamins and minerals, like bread in other countries.

Basically, the paste or dough is made from flour, salt, oil and water. Occasionally butter is used instead of oil, while for some kinds of pasta (e.g., noodles) eggs are included; green, red or yellow colouring matter is sometimes added. The dough is next forced through perforations of various shapes, or rolled out and cut, then allowed to dry.

There is an immense number of different pasta shapes, each with its Italian name. Some of these are

283

familiar in England and often the name itself gives some indication of the size or shape. Here are a few.

Vermicelli	Macaroni
Spaghetti	Denti di Cavallo ('elbows')
Stellete (stars)	Ravioli (envelopes containing a meat or savoury mixture)
Alfabeto (Alphabet)	
Chiocciole (shells)	Cannelloni
Tagliatelle (noodles)	Lasagne

Pasta is sold in dried form and keeps quite well, but is really best used when fairly fresh. After cooking and draining it can be served in many different ways. In Italy, pasta is popular served quite simply tossed in butter and grated cheese: it is also served with a variety of tomato, meat and other sauces and as accompaniment to casseroles, grills and fried meat in place of potatoes, and in soups.

In this country, pasta dishes can be served as a single course, as a main dish for lunch or supper or occasionally to replace potatoes with a meat dish. Since it contains a fair amount of starch, it is not usual to serve another starchy food with it – macaroni cheese, for example, is better served with tomatoes than with potatoes.

(See Macaroni, Spaghetti, entries etc.)

Most pasta dishes can be frozen successfully but it is only really worthwhile for those that need more preparation. They can be cooked straight from frozen.

Cooking and serving pasta: The Italians serve 75 g/3 oz to 100 g/4 oz of pasta per person but in Great Britain 40 g/1½ oz to 50 g/2 oz is more usual. It should be cooked in a large quantity of fast boiling salted water until just resistant to the teeth (al dente); it should not be allowed to become mushy and slimy. When the pasta is cooked it should be drained immediately and served on a heated dish. A knob of butter or a little olive oil can be stirred in; grated Parmesan cheese can be mixed into the pasta or served seprately.

Pasta that has been stored for some time will require longer cooking time than a fresher product.

Vermicelli	5 minutes
Spaghetti	12 to 15 minutes
Macaroni	15 to 20 minutes
Fancy shaped	10 minutes
Ridged	20 minutes
Tagliatelle	10 minutes
Lasagne	10 to 15 minutes
Stuffed pasta	15 to 20 minutes

These cooking times give a softer pasta than that preferred on the Continent.

When used as an ingredient in soups and stews,

pasta is often added raw up to 30 minutes before the dish is ready to serve.

SPAGHETTI ALLA BOLOGNESE
(Using a traditional Italian meat sauce)

METRIC/IMPERIAL
225 g/8 oz spaghetti
grated Parmesan cheese to serve

FOR THE SAUCE
50 g/2 oz bacon, chopped
knob butter
1 small onion, skinned and chopped
1 carrot, pared and chopped
1 stick celery, trimmed and chopped
225 g/8 oz minced beef
100 g/4 oz chicken livers, chopped
1 × 15 ml spoon/1 tablespoon tomato paste
150 ml/¼ pint dry white wine
300 ml/½ pint beef stock
salt
pepper

Make the sauce first. Fry the bacon lightly in the butter for 2 to 3 minutes, add the onion, carrot, celery and fry for a further 5 minutes until lightly browned. Add the beef and brown lightly. Stir in the chopped chicken livers. After cooking them for about 3 minutes, add the tomato paste and wine, allow to bubble for a few minutes and add the stock and seasoning.

Simmer for 30 to 40 minutes, until the meat is tender and the liquid in the sauce is well reduced. Adjust the seasoning if necessary.

Meanwhile cook the spaghetti in the usual way in fast-boiling water for about 10 to 20 minutes. Drain and serve on a heated dish with the sauce poured over. Serve the cheese sprinkled over the sauce or in a separate dish.

CANNELLONI WITH CHEESE SAUCE

METRIC/IMPERIAL
8 large cannelloni or 32 rigatoni
salt
100 g/¼ lb mushrooms, chopped
50 g/2 oz butter
1 × 190 g/6 ½ oz can pimientos, drained
1 × 283 g/10 oz can garden peas, drained
2 cloves garlic, skinned and crushed
1 × 215 g/7 ½ oz can salmon or tuna steak, drained and flaked
50 g/2 oz fresh white breadcrumbs

FOR THE SAUCE
50 g/2 oz butter
4 × 15 ml spoons/4 tablespoons flour
600 ml/1 pint milk
175 g/6 oz Cheddar cheese, grated
salt
pepper

Cook the pasta in salted water for the time directed on the packet; drain well. Meanwhile sauté the mushrooms in the butter; add three-quarters of the pimiento, diced, the peas, garlic, fish and breadcrumbs. Cook over a low heat for 5 minutes, stirring.

Make up the sauce in the usual way, using 150 g/5 oz of the cheese. Stuff the pasta with the fish filling so that it protrudes slightly at each end. Arrange side by side in an ovenproof dish. Pour the sauce over. Garnish with the remainder of the pimiento, cut in strips, and scatter the rest of the cheese over. Bake in a moderately hot oven (200°C/400°F, Gas Mark 6) for 30 minutes, until bubbly and golden brown.

CANNELLONI AU GRATIN

METRIC/IMPERIAL
275 g/10 oz cannelloni
a chunk of bread the size of an orange
milk
1 hard-boiled egg, finely chopped
1 × 15 ml spoon/1 tablespoon chopped parsley
50 g/2 oz mushrooms, chopped
salt
pepper
1 egg, beaten
300 ml/½ pint cheese or tomato sauce
breadcrumbs
grated Parmesan cheese

Cook the cannelloni and drain. Make the stuffing by dipping the bread in milk and squeezing it dry, then add the hard-boiled egg, parsley, mushrooms, salt, pepper and beaten egg and mix together.

Stuff the cannelloni carefully and lay in a buttered ovenproof dish. Coat with sauce and sprinkle with breadcrumbs and cheese. Bake in a moderately hot oven (200°C/400°F, Gas Mark 6) for 15 minutes.

HOME-MADE NOODLES

METRIC/IMPERIAL
225 g/8 oz plain flour
1 × 2·5 ml spoon/½ teaspoon salt
25 g/1 oz butter
1 egg

Sieve the flour and salt and rub in the fat very thoroughly. Add the beaten egg and enough liquid to make a very stiff dough, then knead until smooth. Divide into two portions and roll out very thinly. Flour the surface, fold each piece up into a long roll and cut off pieces about ¼ inch wide with a sharp knife. Toss in a floured cloth to unroll the strips and leave to 'rest' in the floured cloth for 30 minutes–1 hour before cooking in the usual way. Any noodles which are not required

immediately should be hung in a warm, dry place (near the stove, or before the fire) until crisp and dry; they can then be stored for a short period.

TAGLIATELLE CON PROSCIUTTO

METRIC/IMPERIAL
225 g/8 oz tagliatelle
225 g/8 oz prosciutto ham, chopped
butter
grated Parmesan cheese

Cook the tagliatelle in fast-boiling water in the usual way for about 10 minutes. Meanwhile lightly fry the ham in a little butter for 2 to 3 minutes. Drain the pasta, mix with the butter and ham and serve on a hot dish, sprinkled with the cheese.

CREAMY CHEESE LASAGNE

METRIC/IMPERIAL
1.75 litres/3 pints milk
2 slices onion
2 slices carrot
bay leaf
6 peppercorns
100 g/4 oz margarine
100 g/4 oz flour
2 × 142 ml/5 fl oz cartons soured cream
225 g/8 oz cooked ham, finely diced
450 g/1 lb cheese, grated (mixture of Cheddar, Edam,
   blue cheese)
salt
pepper
350 g/12 oz lasagne

Place the milk, onion, carrot, bay leaf and peppercorns in a saucepan, bring to the boil, then remove from the heat. Cover the pan and leave to infuse for 20 minutes, then strain.

Melt the margarine in a saucepan and stir in the flour. Cook gently for 1 minute, stirring constantly. Gradually stir in the strained milk, stirring briskly until the sauce is smooth. Bring to the boil, then reduce the heat and simmer for 3 minutes. Remove from the heat; stir in the soured cream, finely diced ham, three-quarters of the cheese and salt and pepper to taste.

Arrange the uncooked pasta and sauce in layers (starting with pasta and ending with a good covering of sauce) in a lightly greased 3 litre/5 pint shallow ovenproof dish. Sprinkle with the remaining cheese.

Bake in a moderately hot oven (200°C/400°F, Gas Mark 6) for about 1¼ hours or until golden brown and the pasta just tender; cover if necessary.

NOTE
Any combination of cheese can be used but add salt sparingly if using much blue cheese.

285

PASTE (FISH AND MEAT)

Fish and meat, when pounded and mixed with other ingredients and flavourings, give a smooth paste which is good for sandwich fillings, canapé spreads and so on. Many commercially made brands are sold and these may be stored unopened for some time, as they contain preservatives. A list of ingredients in order of quantity must be shown on the label. Delicious fish and meat pastes may also be made at home, but these should be prepared as required and used up within a day or two as they do not store well.

HOME-MADE FISH PASTE

METRIC/IMPERIAL
1×115 g/4⅜ oz can sardines in oil
225 g/8 oz cottage cheese with chives
25 g/1 oz onion, skinned
4×5 ml spoons/4 teaspoons lemon juice
1×5 ml spoon/1 teaspoon tomato paste
salt
freshly ground black pepper
50 g/2 oz butter or block margarine

Halve sardines and discard backbones. Put in blender with cheese, sliced onion, lemon juice, tomato paste and seasoning (go lightly on salt). Blend together until puréed, dropping in small knobs of softened butter, and turn out into a bowl. Adjust seasoning, cover and refrigerate until needed. Serve with French bread or Melba toast.

LIVER PASTE OR PÂTÉ

METRIC/IMPERIAL
350 g/12 oz liver
25 g/1 oz plain flour
25 g/1 oz dripping
1 onion, sliced
300 ml/½ pint stock or water
salt
pepper
a bouquet garni
a little melted butter

Cut the liver into slices, removing the pipes, and coat with the flour. Melt the dripping in a saucepan or casserole and fry the liver lightly. Add the onion, sauté for a few minutes, then stir in remaining flour. Add stock and seasoning and bring to boil, add bouquet garni tied in muslin, cover and simmer gently until very tender – 45 minutes to 1 hour. Remove the bouquet garni, lift the liver from the sauce and pass it through a fine mincer, then sieve, or purée in an electric blender with a little of the cooking juices. Add more seasoning if necessary, with enough of the juices to make a soft paste consistency. Pack into small pots, cover at once with a little melted butter and leave to cool.

Keep in a cold place and use within a few days (or less in hot weather). Serve with freshly made toast and fresh butter, this makes an excellent appetizer and it is very good as a sandwich spread, combined with watercress or sliced cucumber.

PASTEURIZATION

A method of partially sterilizing a liquid by heat treatment, first discovered by Louis Pasteur when experimenting with wine. (See Milk entry.)

PASTILLE

A small gum lozenge, usually flavoured with fruit juice. (See Gum entry.)

PASTRIES

A name loosely applied to fancy cakes, usually iced or decorated. They include a vast assortment of different types, such as meringues, éclairs, mille-feuilles, rum babas, cream horns, various types of small iced cakes, etc. (See Individual entries.)

PASTRY

There are seven main types of pastry – shortcrust (both plain and flan), suetcrust, rough puff, flaky, puff, hot-water crust and choux. The chief difference between them is the method of introducing the fat; in the short pastries it is rubbed into the flour, in suetcrust the chopped suet is simply mixed in, without further manipulation, and in the puff and flaky types the fat is rolled into the dough; in hot-water crust and choux pastry the fat is melted in hot liquid before being added to the flour. There is also a shortcrust made with cooking oil and a pastry made from yeast dough.

Ingredients for Pastry-making

FLOUR
Plain flour should be used, though in suet pastry, where a raising agent is needed, self-raising flour may be used instead of plain flour and baking powder.

RAISING AGENT
Baking powder is generally used in suet pastry. Steam acts as the raising agent in puff and flaky pastries, in combination with the air enclosed between the layers of the paste. In choux pastry the raising agents are eggs plus steam.

FAT
Butter, lard and margarine used to be the fats most commonly used, but nowadays proprietary vegetable shortenings, both blended and whipped up, and pure vegetable oils are also used. Butter gives the best flavour and should always be used for puff

pastry. Lard is suitable for shortcrust and flaky pastry, used with butter or margarine, in the proportion of half butter or margarine to half lard. Suet (either fresh or packet type) is used for suetcrust pastry.

General Hints on Pastry-making
1. Coolness is important for good results. Handle the pastry as little as possible and always use the finger-tips for rubbing in the fat. Rich pastries are improved by being made on a cold slab and placed in a refrigerator between rollings so that the pastry remains firm.
2. Always sift the flour and salt together into the mixing bowl, as this helps to lighten the mixture. Additional air is incorporated by lifting the flour from the bowl with the finger-tips when rubbing in. Always rub in with a light, rather than a heavy hand.
3. The liquid should be very cold and must be added carefully; an excess causes a sticky, unmanageable dough and any extra flour then added will alter the proportions of the ingredients and cause the pastry to be tough. Chill the liquid in the refrigerator before use.
4. Rolling out must be done lightly and firmly; do not roll more than necessary. Always use firm, light strikes, rolling in one direction only.
5. Pastry requires a hot oven. Too slow an oven causes pale, hard pastry; see the pastry recipes given here and the individual recipes throughout the book.

Short Pastries
These include pastries which are of a crumbly rather than a flaky texture – shortcrust, flan pastry (also called biscuit crust) and suetcrust. Shortcrust is the most widely used type, being employed for a great variety of pies, tarts, turnovers and pasties, both sweet and savoury. Flan pastry is used for sweet tarts, etc., and suetcrust for sweet and savoury puddings, which may be steamed, boiled or baked.

SHORTCRUST PASTRY

METRIC/IMPERIAL
250 g/9 oz plain flour
a pinch of salt
115 g/4½ oz fat – half lard, half block margarine or butter
about 9 × 15 ml spoons/9 tablespoons water

Mix the flour and salt together. Cut the fat into small knobs and add it. Using both hands, rub the fat into the flour between finger and thumb tips. After 2 to 3 minutes there will be no lumps of fat left and the mixture will look like fresh breadcrumbs. So far as possible, add the water altogether sprinkling it evenly over the surface, (uneven addition may cause blistering when the pastry is cooked). Stir it in with a round-bladed knife until the mixture begins to stick together in large lumps. With both hands, collect it together and knead lightly for a few seconds, to give a firm, smooth dough. The pastry can be used immediately, but it is better when allowed to 'rest' for 15 minutes before use. It can also be wrapped in polythene and kept in the refrigerator for a day or two.

When the pastry is required, sprinkle a very little flour on a working surface and the rolling pin, not on the pastry, roll out the dough evenly in one direction only, turning it occasionally. The usual thickness is about 3 mm/⅛ inch; do not pull or stretch it. Use as required. The usual oven temperature is moderately hot to hot (200–220°C/400–425°F, Gas Mark 6–7).

This amount is sufficient to cover a 1 litre/2 pint pie dish, a 23 cm/9 inch flan dish, or to make a top and bottom crust for an 18 cm/7 inch pie plate.

Note: For a slightly richer pastry increase the fat to 150 g/5 oz.

CHEESE PASTRY
(See Cheese entry.)

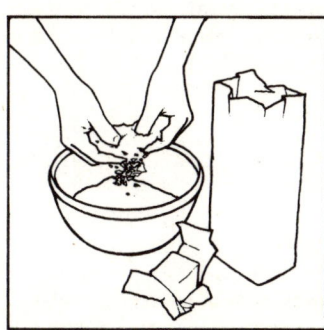

Shortcrust Pastry
1. Using both hands, rub the fat into the flour between the finger and thumb tips.

2. Add the water and stir in with a round-bladed knife until the mixture begins to stick together in large lumps.

3. Using both hands, gently knead the mixture together, to give a firm smooth dough.

FLAN PASTRY

METRIC/IMPERIAL
100 g/4 oz plain flour
a pinch of salt
75 g/3 oz butter or block margarine and lard
1 × 5 ml spoon/1 teaspoon caster sugar
1 egg, beaten

Mix the flour and salt together and rub in the fat with the fingertips, as for shortcrust pastry, until the mixture resembles fine crumbs. Mix in the sugar. Add the egg, stirring until the ingredients begin to stick together, then with one hand collect the mixture together and knead very lightly to give a firm, smooth dough. Roll out as for shortcrust pastry and use as required. This pastry should be cooked in a moderately hot oven (200°C/400°F, Gas Mark 6).

To adjust this recipe for various sizes of flan ring or loose bottomed fluted flan tin allow:
100 g/4 oz flour etc. for a 15 cm/6 inch ring
150 g/5 oz flour etc. for an 18 cm/7 inch ring
200 g/7 oz flour etc. for a 20 cm/8 inch ring
250 g/9 oz flour etc. for a 23 cm/9 inch ring
Adjust other ingredients in proportion.
These amounts also apply to shortcrust pastry.

SUETCRUST PASTRY

METRIC/IMPERIAL
200 g/7 oz self-raising flour
1 × 2.5 ml spoon/½ teaspoon salt
90 g/3½ oz shredded suet
about 7 × 15 ml spoons/7 tablespoons cold water

Mix together the flour, salt and suet. Add enough cold water to give a light, elastic dough and knead very lightly until smooth. Roll out to 5 mm/¼ inch thick.

This pastry may be used for both sweet and savoury dishes and can be steamed, boiled or baked; the first two are the most satisfactory methods, as baked suetcrust pastry is inclined to be hard.

This quantity is sufficient for a 900 ml/1½ pint to 1 litre/2 pint pudding basin.

Flaky Pastries

FLAKY PASTRY
Probably the commonest of the flaked types, it can be used in many sweet and savoury dishes; sausage rolls and pies are particularly popular. Good flaky pastry is judged by the evenness of the flakes when it is cooked, and the rolling and the even distribution of the fat are two important factors in achieving this result.

ROUGH PUFF PASTRY
Similar in appearance and texture to flaky although not quite so even. It is quicker and easier to make and can be used instead of flaky in most recipes (popular for Eccles cakes, mince pies).

PUFF PASTRY
The richest of all the pastries. It gives the most even rising, most flaky effect and crispest texture. It should be handled very carefully. It is used for bouchées, vol-au-vents and teatime pastries.

The following general hints apply to all flaky pastries:—
1. The fat should be the consistency of soft butter. Lard alone is too soft and margarine too hard, but a mixture of half lard and half margarine gives good results.
2. Make the flour dough of the same consistency as the fat, so that they mix easily together. Use a little lemon juice to make the pastry more pliable.
3. See that the air is evenly distributed during the rolling process and avoid bursting the air bubbles. Keep the edges of the pastry straight and the corners square.
4. Keep the pastry cool and allow it to rest between rollings and before baking, to avoid shrinkage.
5. Bake in a hot oven.

ROUGH PUFF PASTRY

METRIC/IMPERIAL
200 g/7 oz plain flour
a pinch of salt
150 g/5 oz butter or block margarine and lard
about 7 × 15 ml spoons/7 tablespoons cold water to mix
squeeze of lemon juice
beaten egg to glaze

Mix the flour and salt; cut the fat (which should be quite firm) into cubes about 2 cm/¾ inch across. Stir the fat into the flour without breaking up the pieces and mix to a fairly stiff dough with the water and lemon juice. Turn on to a floured board and roll into a strip 3 times as long as it is wide. Fold the bottom third up and the top third down, then turn the pastry through 90° so that the folds are at the sides. Seal the edges of the pastry by pressing lightly with a rolling pin. Continue to roll and fold in this way 4 times altogether. Leave to 'rest' wrapped in greaseproof paper for about 30 minutes before using. Roll out and use as for flaky pastry.

Rough puff gives a similar result to flaky pastry, but the flakes are not usually as even, so where even rising and appearance are particularly important, e.g., with patties and vol-au-vents, it is better to use flaky pastry. On the other hand, rough puff has the advantage of being quicker to make.

The usual oven setting for rough puff is hot (220°C/425°F, Gas Mark 7).

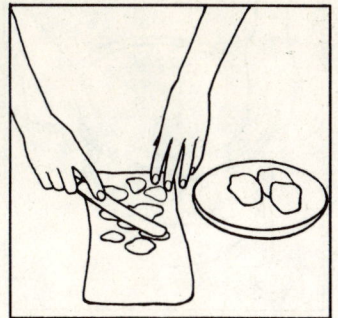

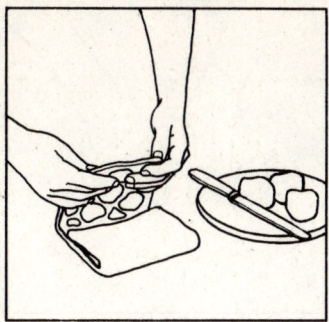

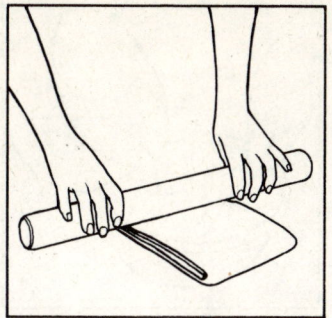

Flaky Pastry
1. Dab on one quarter of the fat over the top two-thirds of the pastry.

2. Fold bottom third of pastry up over centre third, then fold top third over.

3. Turn the pastry through 90° so that the folds are now at the side. Seal pastry edges.

FLAKY PASTRY

METRIC/IMPERIAL
200 g/7 oz plain flour
a pinch of salt
150 g/5 oz butter or a mixture of butter and lard
about 7 × 15 ml spoons/7 tablespoons cold water to mix
squeeze of lemon juice
beaten egg to glaze

Mix together the flour and salt. Soften the fat by 'working' it with a knife on a plate; divide it into 4 equal portions. Rub one quarter of the softened fat into the flour and mix to a soft, elastic dough with the water and lemon juice. On a floured board, roll the pastry into an oblong 3 times as long as it is wide. Put another quarter of the fat over the top two-thirds of the pastry in flakes, so that it looks like buttons on a card. Fold the bottom third up and the top third of the pastry down and turn it through 90° so that the folds are now at the side. Seal the edges of the pastry by pressing with the rolling pin. Re-roll as before and continue until all the fat is used up.

Wrap the pastry loosely in greaseproof paper and leave it to 'rest' in a refrigerator or cool place for at least 30 minutes before using.

Sprinkle a board or table with a very little flour.

Roll out the pastry 3 mm/⅛ inch thick and use as required. Brush with beaten egg before baking, to give the characteristic glaze.

The usual oven setting for flaky pastry is hot (220°C/425°F, Gas Mark 7).

PUFF PASTRY

METRIC/IMPERIAL
200 g/7 oz plain flour
a pinch of salt
200 g/7 oz butter, preferably unsalted
about 7 × 15 ml spoons/7 tablespoons cold water
squeeze of lemon juice
beaten egg to glaze

Mix the flour and salt. Work the fat with a knife on a plate until it is soft, then rub a knob of it into the flour. Mix to a fairly soft, elastic dough with the water and lemon juice and knead lightly on a floured board until smooth. Form the rest of the fat into an oblong and roll the pastry out into a square. Place the block of fat on one half of the pastry and enclose it by folding the remaining pastry over and sealing the edges with a rolling pin. Turn the pastry so that the fold is to the side, then roll out into a strip 3 times as long as it is wide. Fold the bottom third up and the top third down and seal the edges by pressing lightly with the rolling pin. Cover the pastry with waxed or greaseproof paper and leave to 'rest' in a cool place or in the refrigerator for about 20 minutes. Turn the pastry so that the folds are to the sides and continue rolling, folding and resting until the sequence has been completed 6 times altogether. After the final resting, shape the pastry as required. Always brush the top surfaces with beaten egg before cooking, to give the characteristic glaze of puff pastry.

The usual oven setting for puff pastry is hot (230°C/450°F, Gas Mark 8).

NOTE
Even without a freezer, uncooked home-made puff pastry keeps 2–3 days, wrapped in a cloth or foil in the refrigerator.

To freeze uncooked flaky and puff pastry: prepare up to the last rolling before freezing. Roll into an oblong shape, wrap in foil, then over-wrap in a freezer bag. Seal the bag and label it giving the date and quantity of pastry. To thaw, leave the pastry in the wrappings overnight in the refrigerator for best results, but if you are in a hurry it can be thawed at room temperature for 3 to 4 hours. This kind of pastry is time-consuming to make, and it is therefore well worth storing some in the freezer.

Hot-Water Crust Pastry
1. Beat in melted lard mixture quickly to form a soft dough.

2. Working quickly, lightly pinch the dough together and knead in the bowl until the dough is smooth.

3. Cover the dough in the bowl with a plate and leave to rest for 20–30 minutes.

HOT-WATER CRUST PASTRY

METRIC/IMPERIAL
450 g/1 lb plain flour
2 × 5 ml spoons/2 teaspoons salt
100 g/4 oz lard
150 ml/¼ pint plus 4 × 15 ml spoons/4 tablespoons milk or milk and water

Mix the flour and salt. Melt the lard in the liquid, then bring to the boil and pour into a well made in the dry ingredients. Working quickly, beat with a wooden spoon to form a fairly soft dough. Use hands to lightly pinch the dough together and knead until smooth and silky. Cover the dough in a bowl with a plate. Leave to rest for 20 to 30 minutes for the dough to become elastic and easy to work. Use as required.

CHOUX PASTRY

METRIC/IMPERIAL
50 g/2 oz butter or block margarine
about 150 ml /¼ pint water
8 × 15 ml spoons/8 tablespoons plain flour, sifted
2 eggs, lightly beaten

Melt the fat in the water and bring to the boil; remove from the heat and quickly tip in the flour all at once. Beat with a wooden spoon until the paste is smooth and forms a ball in the centre of the pan. (Take care not to over-beat or the mixture becomes fatty.) Allow to cool for a minute or two. Beat in the eggs a little at a time, beating vigorously – this is important – to trap in as much air as possible. A hand-held electric whisk is ideal for this and will also enable you to incorporate all the egg easily. Carry on beating until a sheen is obvious. Use as required. Some people prefer to chill a hand-made paste in the bag for about 30 minutes before piping. The usual oven setting is moderately hot to hot (200–220°C/400–425°F, Gas Mark 6–7).

NOTE
When beating by hand with a wooden spoon the arm tends to tire, the beating speed is reduced and the final consistency is often too slack to retain its shape. In this case a little of the egg may have to be omitted – and remember to use standard eggs for the hand method.

Choux Pastry
1. Melt the fat and water over a moderate heat. Bring slowly up to the boil and remove from the heat.

2. Tip in the flour all at once. Beat with a wooden spoon until the paste is smooth and forms a ball in the centre of the pan.

3. Beat in the eggs, a little at a time, beating well after each addition to entrap as much air into the mixture as possible. Carry on beating until a sheen is obvious.

STIR-IN PASTRY

(See Oil entry.)

ONE-STAGE SHORT PASTRY

METRIC/IMPERIAL
100 g/4 oz soft tub margarine
175 g/6 oz plain flour, sifted
1 × 15 ml spoon/1 tablespoon water

Place the margarine, 2 × 15 ml spoons/2 table-spoons flour and the water in a mixing bowl. Cream with a fork for about half a minute, until well mixed. Mix in the remaining flour to form a fairly soft dough. Turn on to a lightly floured board and knead until smooth. Roll out fairly thinly. One-stage pastry is usually baked in a moderately hot oven (190°C/375°F, Gas Mark 5).

This amount is enough to line a 20 cm/8 inch fluted flan ring.

PASTY

A shortcrust pastry case, usually of a torpedo shape, with a filling of raw meat and diced vegetables. The traditional Cornish pasty (see below) contains beef or mutton, onion, potato and sometimes turnip, but pasties can be made with a variety of savoury fillings such as cheese and onion, poultry and game.

CORNISH PASTIES

METRIC/IMPERIAL
350 g/12 oz chuck or blade steak
100 g/4 oz raw potato, peeled and diced
1 small onion, skinned and chopped
salt
pepper
350 g/12 oz shortcrust pastry made with 350 g/12 oz
   flour, etc.

Cut the steak into small pieces, add the potato and onion and season well. Divide the pastry into four and roll each piece into a round 20 cm/8 inches in diameter. Divide the meat mixture between the pastry rounds, dampen the edges, draw the edges of the pastry together to form a seam across the top and flute the edges with the fingers. Place on a baking sheet and bake in a hot oven (220°C/425°F, Gas Mark 7) for 15 minutes to brown the pastry, then reduce the oven to moderate (160°C/325°F, Gas Mark 3) and cook for a further hour. Serve hot or cold.

PÂTE

This French word literally means paste and is usually used to denote pastry, dough or batter; it is also used for Italian pasta.

PÂTÉ

Strictly speaking, this French term means a savoury pie (sweet ones being more usually called tourtes). By extension it is sometimes applied to a paste of the foie gras type, made from minced or pounded game, poultry, meat, liver, fish, etc., and shaped like a pie. A pâté of this type is usually served as an appetizer, accompanied by lettuce leaves, sliced lemon and toast and butter.

(See Paste and Foie Gras entries.)

CHICKEN LIVER PÂTÉ

METRIC/IMPERIAL
0.75 kg/1 ½ lb chicken livers
75 g/3 oz butter
1 medium sized onion, skinned and finely chopped
1 large clove garlic, skinned and crushed
1 × 15 ml spoon/1 tablespoon double cream
2 × 15 ml spoons/2 tablespoons tomato paste
3 × 15 ml spoons/3 tablespoons sherry or brandy
melted butter, optional

Rinse the chicken livers and dry thoroughly on kitchen paper. Fry them in the butter until they change colour. Reduce the heat, add the onion and garlic, cover and cook for 5 minutes. Remove from the heat and cool. Add the cream, tomato paste and sherry or brandy. Purée in a blender or press through a sieve. Turn into individual dishes. Cover tops with melted butter if you wish. Chill.

PETER'S PÂTÉ

METRIC/IMPERIAL
0.5 kg/1 lb pigs' liver
50 g/2 oz butter
1 onion, skinned and chopped
100 g/4 oz streaky bacon, rinded and diced
100 g/4 oz belly pork, diced
1 clove garlic, skinned and crushed
1.5 × 15 ml spoons/1 ½ tablespoons tomato paste
a good pinch black pepper
a good pinch garlic salt
a good pinch dried basil
a good pinch salt
4 × 15 ml spoons/4 tablespoons red wine
grated rind of ¼ lemon
2 bayleaves

Remove the skin and any gristle from the liver. Melt the butter in a saucepan and fry the onion. Add all the other ingredients, cover and cook slowly for about 1 ½ hours. Remove the bayleaves and drain the meat, retaining the liquor. Mince the meat finely and stir in the liquor. Press the mixture into a 700 ml/1¼ pint ovenproof dish. Cover and cook in a moderate oven (180°C/350°F, Gas Mark 4) for 30 minutes; remove from the oven and allow to cool.

THREE-FISH PÂTÉ

An ideal starter to mellow the meal of the evening.
There is no need to use top quality salmon.

METRIC/IMPERIAL
215 g/7 ½ oz can salmon
200 g/7 oz can tuna
100 g/4 oz peeled prawns
175 g/6 oz fresh white breadcrumbs
100 g/4 oz butter, melted
grated rind and juice of 2 lemons
3 × 5 ml spoons /3 teaspoons anchovy essence
300 ml / ½ pint single cream
salt
pepper

Flake the contents of the can of salmon, adding the
juices together with the contents of the can of tuna.
Roughly chop the prawns. In a bowl, combine
breadcrumbs, butter and lemon rind and juice.
Add to the flaked fish with the prawns. Stir in the
anchovy essence and cream and adjust seasoning to
taste. Divide between 8 150 ml/¼ pint individual
soufflé dishes, level off the mixture and chill. Serve
with fingers of freshly made toast.

SMOKED TROUT PÂTÉ

METRIC/IMPERIAL
225 g/8 oz smoked trout
50 g/2 oz butter
75 g/3 oz fresh white breadcrumbs
finely grated rind and juice of 1 lemon
salt and freshly ground black pepper
pinch grated nutmeg
150 ml/¼ pint single cream
150–300 ml/¼–½ pint aspic jelly

Remove the skin and bones from the trout and
finely chop the flesh. Melt 2 oz butter in a small pan
and pour it on to the breadcrumbs with the lemon
rind and juice. Season well with salt, pepper and
nutmeg. Add the fish to the breadcrumbs and fold
the cream through. Spoon the mixture into 6
ramekins. Make up aspic jelly and when it is on the
point of setting, spoon it over the fish mixture.
Chill.

PÂTISSERIE

When correctly used, this term applies to highly
decorated pastries, as produced by a French pâtis-
sier or pastry cook, e.g. mille-feuilles, palmiers,
cream horns and slices. In this country it is used
more widely to denote any small fancy cakes and
pastries.

PATTY

A case of flaky or puff pastry in the form of a
miniature pie or vol-au-vent. Small vol-au-vents
are called bouchées. When the patties are closed the
filling is put in before baking; it can consist of raw
or cooked meat, poultry or game, sometimes with
additional ingredients such as mushrooms. For
open patties, the filling is added after the pastry
cases are baked and consists of cooked meat,
poultry, game, shellfish, mushrooms or similar
ingredients, moistened with a savoury sauce: see
the recipes below.
To fill 24 bouchée cases:—

MUSHROOM
Melt a knob of butter in a small pan and sauté
75 g/3 oz button mushrooms, roughly chopped.
Put on one side, wipe the pan and melt a further
25 g/1 oz butter. Stir in 3 × 15 ml spoons/3 tablespoons flour and cook for 1 minute. Slowly beat in
150 ml/¼ pint milk and bring to the boil, stirring;
cook for about 2 minutes. Fold in the mushrooms
and enough single cream or top of the milk to give
a thick pouring consistency – about 3 × 15 ml
spoons/3 tablespoons. Season to taste with salt,
pepper and a dash of Worcestershire sauce.

PRAWN SAUTÉ
Use 100 g/4 oz shelled prawns to replace the mushrooms and add 1 × 5 ml spoon/1 teaspoon chopped
parsley and a little lemon juice instead of the
Worcestershire sauce.

CHICKEN SAUTÉ
Use 1 small onion, skinned and finely chopped to
replace the mushrooms; replace the Worcestershire sauce with Tabasco, and add 100 g/4 oz diced
cooked chicken meat before re-heating.

PAUNCHING

To remove the entrails of rabbits, hares, etc. (See
Hare entry.)

PAWPAW (PAPAYA)

A tropical fruit, originally found in South America, but now grown in most countries with a suitable climate; it forms an important food in some
regions. There are a number of varieties, differing
in colour and size. Ripe pawpaws can be eaten like
a melon, with sugar; when not quite ripe, they can

be boiled like a vegetable and served with an oil and vinegar dressing.

The fruit produces an enzyme, papain, which breaks down meat fibres and is therefore the basis of meat-tenderizing powders.

PEACH

The single-stoned fleshy fruit of the peach tree, which is grown chiefly in warm countries such as Italy, the South of France and California; it may also be grown in sunny, sheltered corners of English gardens, but in this country it is usually cultivated in glasshouses. The majority of the fresh peaches sold here are imported from the Continent; their flavour is not so delicate as that of home-grown ones, since they are picked before they are ripe, but they are very good in fruit salads and similar sweets. Dried and canned peaches are also available.

There are two main varieties of peach, the free-stone and the cling-stone. In the former the skin and stone separate easily from the golden flesh, but in the cling-stone type the flesh is firmer and is freed from the stone with difficulty. Peaches bruise readily and the bloom is easily rubbed off, so they should be handled gently and as little as possible.

Peaches have little nutritive value, though they contain some Vitamin C and some carotene. As the fruit contains little acid, extra must be added when it is used for jam-making.

Peaches can be frozen in syrup or as a purée. (See Freezing entry for methods.)

(See Bottling, Drying entries, etc., for methods of preserving; for dried peaches, see Dried Fruit entry.)

Serving Peaches: The fruits are usually served whole as a dessert fruit. They may, however, be cut up and used for fruit salads, flans, cold sweets, ices, etc. They look attractive when cut in halves and stoned; a glaze helps to keep them moist and prevents any discolouring. Peaches are sometimes stewed or puréed and used to make a delicious soufflé. Canned or bottled peaches may be made into party sweets such as peach condé or melba, meringue pie and 'poached eggs' (halved and glazed peaches on rounds of sponge cake, surrounded by a ring of whipped cream). Sieved peaches, sweetened and mixed with whipped cream, make a good cake or gâteau filling.

PEACH MELBA

METRIC/IMPERIAL
ice cream
halved peach
Melba sauce
whipped cream
chopped nuts

Place the ice cream in sundae glasses, then add a halved peach to each, hollow side downwards. Cover with the Melba sauce (see separate entry) and decorate with whipped cream and chopped nuts.

PEACHES IN LIQUEUR

Choose peaches which are not too ripe, plunge them into boiling water and leave for 3 minutes, then peel. Place the peaches in a serving bowl and cover with a light sugar syrup (see below), pouring it over while still hot; flavour with liqueur and leave to cool. Serve very cold, with fresh cream.

To make the light syrup, boil 600 ml/1 pint water and 175 g/6 oz sugar for 5 minutes, then skim. If desired, the syrup may be flavoured by adding a piece of lemon rind while it is being boiled.

PEANUT (GROUND NUT, MONKEY NUT)

The seed of a leguminous plant grown in hot countries. The flowers bury themselves in the earth when they wither and the pod containing the nuts is therefore formed underground (hence the name ground nut). The pod is pale yellow and crinkled and it cracks easily to reveal 2 to 3 brown nuts. The nuts are usually roasted for a few minutes and the brown skins may then be easily removed by rubbing them.

Peanuts are valuable on account of the oil they contain, which is used in the manufacture of margarine and other fats. They have a high percentage of vegetable protein and fat and also contain iron, nicotinic acid and thiamine, so they are a protective food and a good provider of energy. Both the nuts and peanut butter are a useful addition to the diet and in some countries they are very important.

Salted Peanuts
(See Nuts entry.)

Peanut Butter
A brownish-yellow, oily paste, with a somewhat rough texture, made from peanuts. It may replace butter for use with bread, water biscuits, etc., and it is most palatable when spread thickly and dusted with salt. Mixed with celery, onion or pickles, it can be used in sandwiches. It is used in making some cakes and biscuits.

PEANUT BUTTER COOKIES

METRIC/IMPERIAL
50 g/2 oz peanut butter
grated rind of ½ orange
50 g/2 oz caster sugar
3 × 15 ml spoons/3 tablespoons light, soft brown sugar

PEA

50 g/2 oz butter
1 standard or medium egg
2 × 15 ml spoons/2 tablespoons raisins, stoned and
   chopped
100 g/4 oz self-raising flour

Cream together the peanut butter, orange rind, sugars and butter until light and fluffy. Beat in the egg, add the raisins and stir in the flour to make a fairly firm dough. Roll the dough into small balls about the size of a walnut and place well apart on an ungreased baking sheet; dip a fork in a little flour and press criss-cross lines on each ball. Bake in a moderate oven (180°C/350°F, Gas Mark 4) for 25 minutes, until risen and golden brown. Cool on a wire rack.

PEAR

The fleshy fruit of a tree widely grown in most parts of the world, except the tropics. Many different varieties of dessert and cooking pear are grown and marketed in this country and large numbers are also imported. Some are very juicy and sweet and when absolutely ripe these make an excellent dessert fruit, though if allowed to become over-ripe they are woolly and insipid. They make good cold sweets when combined with other fruit, cream, ice cream, etc.

Pears ripen from the end of summer to the beginning of winter and some types will keep until Christmas; they should be stored well apart, on wooden shelves, in a temperature from 4°C/40°F to 16°C/60°F. The English dessert pears which are ready in late August, September and early October must be carefully watched and eaten as soon as they are ripe. Later varieties, which can be kept until Christmas or longer, and most of the imported pears, deteriorate less quickly, remaining in a ripe state for several days. A dessert pear which is ready for eating should yield to slight pressure at the stalk end.

Some of the most esteemed dessert pears are: William, Jargonelle, Duchesse, Marie Louise, Bon Chrétien, Louise Bonne, Doyenne de Comice, Durondeau and Beurre d'Amanlis. Good cooking pears are: Bartlett, Kieffer, Uvedales, St. Germain, Verulam and Catillac.

The Conference pear is a good all round fruit suitable for eating, cooking and bottling.

To cook pears: Peel, halve or quarter and remove the cores, then cook as described in Compote of Pears, under Compote. Pears usually require a little additional flavouring, such as clove, lemon, ginger or cinnamon and combine particularly well with a chocolate sauce. They are delicious poached in cider and brown sugar. Pears are also good with cheese: a simple appetizer can be made by halving a pear, removing the core and filling with a cheese mixture. (See Bottling entry.)

POIRE HÉLÈNE

Put some lemon or vanilla ice cream into sundae glasses, place one canned pear half in each, top with chocolate sauce (see recipe under Sundae entry) and decorate with shredded or chopped almonds or crystallized violets.

PEARS BRISTOL

METRIC/IMPERIAL
4 firm dessert pears
75 g/3 oz sugar
water
2 oranges
50 g/2 oz caster sugar

Peel the pears, cut into quarters and remove the cores. Dissolve the sugar in 12 tablespoons water in a small saucepan, bring to the boil and boil for 5 minutes. Add the pear quarters and simmer, covered, until the fruit is tender. Leave until cold. Using a potato peeler, pare the rind from ½ orange and cut into very fine strips. Cook in a little water until tender – about 5 minutes. Rinse the rind in cold water. Peel the oranges free of pith and cut into segments. Dissolve the caster sugar in a pan, shaking occasionally – do not stir. Bubble until golden, then pour it on to an oiled tin. When brittle crack with a rolling pin. Turn the drained pears into a serving dish and top with orange segments. Add the orange strips to the pear juice and pour over the fruit. Scatter caramel over and chill.

PEAS

Green peas are the seeds of a climbing plant, of which there are numerous varieties, ranging in height from 0.5 metre/1½ feet to 1.75 metres/5 feet. The seeds are contained in a green pod which is not usually eaten, except in the case of the sugar (or mange-tout) variety. The peas themselves vary in size from the small 'petits pois', with a diameter of about 3 mm/⅛ inch to large ones nearly 1 cm/½ inch in diameter.

Peas are one of the most popular vegetables in the country. The season for fresh peas lasts for only about 6 weeks, but they are sold preserved in various ways: frozen, canned, dried and dehydrated.

Frozen peas are very popular as they taste similar to fresh peas and there is no preparation required. Freezer owners have the advantage of being able to buy them in bulk packs. Processed peas, which are dried peas that have been soaked and then canned, are cheaper than canned garden peas, because they can be canned at the manufacturer's convenience at any time of the year, while garden peas can be canned only during the season. Dried peas add considerably to the protein in the diet. Nowadays, however, they have largely been replaced by frozen and canned peas.

Split peas are dried peas that have had the outer skin removed.

Dehydrated peas, which are dried by modern methods, retain many of the characteristics of fresh peas.

In addition to the protein already mentioned, peas supply a useful amount of Vitamin C and A. Dried peas do not contain any Vitamin C, but canned garden peas, dehydrated and frozen peas retain most of theirs, so their food value is very much the same as that of fresh peas.

Preparation and Cooking

FRESH PEAS

Shell and wash, place in boiling salted water with about 1 × 5 ml spoon/1 teaspoon sugar and a sprig of mint and cook until tender – 20 to 30 minutes.

PETITS POIS

This particularly small, sweet type of pea is much used on the Continent. They are generally cooked with the addition of a little chopped onion and butter.

SUGAR PEAS (MANGE-TOUT)

Wash the pods in salted water, then 'top and tail' them. Sauté with a finely chopped onion in a little fat for 10 minutes; season, add 1 × 15 ml spoon/1 tablespoon each of chopped parsley and chopped chives (sufficient for about 0.75 kg/1 ½ lb peas) and cover with water. Simmer until tender – about 40 minutes. Blend 15 g/½ oz flour with 150 ml/¼ pint milk and add to the peas, stir until the sauce thickens and simmer for 5 to 10 minutes.

DRIED PEAS

Soak overnight in hot water containing 1 × 2.5 ml spoon/½ teaspoon bicarbonate of soda for every 225 g/8 oz peas. Put into fresh cold water, add salt, a sprig of mint and an onion and boil gently until tender – about 2½ hours. Serve tossed in butter or a white, cheese or tomato sauce.

SPLIT PEAS

Prepare and cook in the same way as dried peas. They are used chiefly in soups and pease pudding and can also be substituted for lentils in various recipes.

PEA SOUP (USING DRIED PEAS)

METRIC/IMPERIAL
175 g/6 oz dried peas
1.2 litres/2 pints water
1 large onion
1 small carrot
a small piece of turnip
25 g/1 oz dripping
seasoning
a bouquet garni
150 ml/¼ pint milk

Wash the peas and soak overnight in the water. Fry the cut-up vegetables lightly in the melted dripping. Add the peas, the water in which they were soaked, seasoning and bouquet garni, then simmer gently for 1½ to 2 hours, until the vegetables are reduced to a pulp. Remove the bouquet garni, add the milk, re-heat and serve. If desired, the soup may be sieved before the milk is added.

PEASE PUDDING

METRIC/IMPERIAL
225 g/8 oz split peas
salt
1 ham bone or some bacon scraps
25 g/1 oz butter
1 egg, beaten
pinch of sugar
pepper

Wash the peas well, removing any discoloured ones, and soak overnight in cold water. Tie loosely in a cloth, place in a saucepan with a pinch of salt and boiling water to cover and add the bone or bacon scraps. Boil for 2 to 2½ hours, or until soft. Lift out the bag of peas, sieve or purée in a blender and add the butter, egg, sugar and pepper to taste. Beat until thoroughly mixed, then tie up tightly in a floured cloth and boil for another 30 minutes. Turn on to a hot plate to serve.

To give extra flavour, chopped onion or herbs may be added.

Pea-flour

This is made from dried ripe peas and is used to thicken sauces and as a basis for soup.

Pease Brose

A kind of Scottish porridge made with pea flour or meal.

PECAN

A nut grown in America, somewhat similar to the walnut in appearance, but with a brittle, reddish-brown shell, and thinner and longer in shape. Pecans are used like walnuts.

PECTIN

A jellying carbohydrate substance, occurring naturally in the cell walls of many plants, which in combination with sugar causes jam to set. (See Jam entry.)

PEMMICAN

Well-dried buffalo or deer meat, powdered and mixed with melted fat; a concentrated food used originally by North American Indians and then by trappers and other travellers. Modern explorers take a similar preparation of dried beef on expeditions.

PEPPER

There are several varieties of pepper, obtained by grinding the fruits of certain plants which have a hot, pungent taste.

WHITE PEPPER
This comes from the fully ripened berries of a climbing tree or tropical shrub. The outer skin is removed and the berries cleaned. It can be bought whole or ground and is less pungent and aromatic than black pepper. It is good to use in light sauces as it does not discolour them.

BLACK PEPPER
This comes from the berries picked while still green and left to dry in the sun until they shrivel and darken. It is available whole or ground but is at its best when freshly milled.

GREEN PEPPERCORNS
These are the unripe berries picked and canned without drying out. Their fresh pungent flavour is totally different from the dried varieties. Green peppercorns add an unusual tang to grilled meat or poultry. They can also be mashed and added to sauces.

CAYENNE PEPPER
A very hot and well-flavoured pepper made from certain powdered capsicums. It is useful for many cooking purposes (especially highly flavoured savouries), but is usually too 'hot' to serve as a table condiment.

CORALLINE PEPPER
A red variety, with a very mild flavour, useful for decorating savouries.

PAPRIKA PEPPER
This comes from the fruit of a Hungarian tree. It is red and has a fine aromatic taste and since it is not as hot as other peppers, can be used more liberally.

PIMENTO OR JAMAICA PEPPER
(generally called allspice)
This brown type is produced by grinding the seeds contained in the berries of the pimento tree. It is more aromatic than black or white pepper, but less pungent. See separate entry for fuller details.

PEPPER (VEGETABLE)

The fluted, pear-shaped fruit of the capsicum plant, available most of the year. The shiny skin is green, yellow or red, according to the degree of ripeness and the variety. Red peppers are often known by the Spanish name pimiento.

Fresh peppers have many uses in the kitchen: their sweet piquancy will enhance a salad if finely chopped, or cut in rings they make an attractive garnish. They give flavour to stews and casseroles or they may be stuffed and baked to serve as a main dish or vegetable. Suggested fillings are a mixture of some of the following: Cheese, cold meats, bacon, cooked rice, breadcrumbs, chopped nuts, onion, mushrooms, herbs, canned fish. They may be served with a sauce.

STUFFED PEPPERS

METRIC/IMPERIAL
4 green peppers, halved lengthways and de-seeded
1 onion, skinned and chopped
100 g/4 oz bacon, chopped
40 g/1 ½ oz butter
4 tomatoes, skinned and sliced
100 g/4 oz long grain rice, boiled
salt
pepper
4 × 15 ml spoons/4 tablespoons grated Cheddar cheese
50 g/2 oz fresh breadcrumbs
150 ml/¼ pint stock

Put the halved peppers in an ovenproof dish. Lightly fry the onion and bacon in 25 g/1 oz of the butter until golden brown. Add the tomatoes, cooked rice, seasoning and half the cheese. Mix the rest of the cheese with the breadcrumbs. Put the bacon stuffing into the cases and sprinkle with the breadcrumb mixture. Pour the stock round the cases, top each with a knob of butter and cook in a moderately hot oven (190°C/375°F, Gas Mark 5) for 15 to 20 minutes, or until the pepper cases are cooked. Carefully lift stuffed peppers out of the dish and serve on circles of deep-fried bread so that the bread can soak up the gravy.

SWEET PEPPERS WITH TOMATOES

METRIC/IMPERIAL
2 × 15 ml spoons/2 tablespoons cooking oil
½ onion, skinned and chopped
1 clove garlic, skinned and crushed
4 tomatoes, skinned and sliced
2 × 15 ml spoons/2 tablespoons tomato paste
150 ml/¼ pint dry white wine
4 peppers, de-seeded and thinly sliced, about
   0.5 kg/1 lb
salt
pepper

Heat the oil in a large frying pan or saucepan and lightly cook the onion and garlic for 5 minutes without colouring. Add the tomatoes, tomato paste and wine and simmer for 5 minutes. Add the peppers, cover and simmer gently for 30 minutes. Season if necessary. Serve as an accompaniment to grilled meats and fish.

ITALIAN PEPPER SALAD

METRIC/IMPERIAL
2 green peppers
2 red peppers
2 × 15 ml spoons/2 tablespoons red wine vinegar
2 × 15 ml spoons/2 tablespoons olive oil
1 × 5 ml spoon/1 teaspoon Worcestershire sauce
1 × 5 ml spoon/1 teaspoon tomato paste
1 × 2.5 ml spoon/½ teaspoon paprika
salt
pinch sugar
4 black olives, stoned and quartered

Slice the peppers, remove the core and de-seed.
Put the slices in a pan of cold water, bring to the
boil then drain and cool. Meanwhile, make the
dressing. Put all the remaining ingredients (except
the olives) into a bowl and whisk well together.
Arrange the cold peppers in a serving dish. Pour
the dressing over and leave for 30 minutes. Scatter
the olives over the top. Serve as a side salad.

PEPPERMINT

A European plant, similar to garden spearmint,
but with a more pronounced odour and taste. An
oil and a flavouring essence are made from the
plant, the oil being obtained by distilling the plant
with water and the essence consisting of the essential oil mixed with spirit. The oil has the stronger
flavour, while the strength of the essence varies
according to the degree of dilution.

Peppermint forms a popular flavouring for confectionery, drinks and occasionally for desserts and
it is also used medicinally. Sweets, jellies, etc., that
have been flavoured with peppermint are often
coloured green.

PERCH

A freshwater fish of delicate flavour which is in
season from the beginning of June to the end of
February. Perch are hardly ever seen in the
fishmonger's shop, so they are eaten chiefly by
anglers. Several varieties are found in English rivers, weighing from 0.5 kg/1 lb to 1.5 kg/3 lb. Perch
has a characteristic sharp front dorsal fin and is of a
greenish-brown colour on the back and a light
colour below. The Zander, a large variety of perch
caught in the Elbe, is considered a great delicacy.
Perch should be cooked as soon as possible after
catching.

Preparation and cooking: The scales are more easily
removed if the fish is plunged into boiling water
for 2 minutes. Trim, clean and wipe the fish, score
it on both sides and either grill or fry in a little
butter.

Alternatively, place it in a well buttered ovenproof dish, cover with pats of butter and then pour
over it white wine and fish stock in equal parts;
cover with foil or a buttered paper and bake for 20
to 30 minutes in a moderately hot oven
(200°C/400°F, Gas Mark 6). Drain off the liquid
and reduce by boiling. Add 50 g/2 oz butter, little
by little stirring constantly, and finally add
2 × 5 ml spoons/2 teaspoons finely chopped
parsley. Serve the fish with the sauce poured over
it and garnish with fried croûtons, lemon quarters
and parsley.

PERIWINKLE

(See Winkle entry.)

PERNOD

An apéritif that takes its name from a French firm
which used to distil absinthe. The modern Pernod
is based on aniseed and contains no absinthe,
which is now prohibited in France. Pernod is usually served with one part of pernod and three parts
water and topped up with chunks of ice.

PERRIER

A natural mineral water from the south of France,
colourless and tasteless.

PERRY

The fermented juice of a hard, astringent type of
pear (unsuitable for eating). Perry is made in a
similar way to cider, the pears being crushed between rollers; the resulting pulp is packed in cloths
between frames and the juice is pressed out and
collected in a cask, in which it is allowed to ferment.

PERSIMMON (DATE PLUM)

The fruit of a tree of Far Eastern origin, now also
grown in Mediterranean countries and in the
U.S.A. Persimmons are about the size of a small
plum, with a leathery skin covering a yellow or
orange-coloured pulp; some have seeds, but the
best varieties are seedless. The green fruit is very
astringent and even the ripe fruit is somewhat
acid and bitter, though at the same time sweet.
Persimmons are used for flavouring ices and jellies
and for making preserves.

PETIT FOUR

Petits fours are very small, rich, sweet cakes and
biscuits served as a dessert at the end of a dinner,
also with morning coffee or afternoon tea. A few
typical recipes are given here. (See Macaroon,
Meringue, Éclair, entries etc.) Candied fruits and
sweetmeats are sometimes served as petits fours.

ALMOND PETITS FOURS

METRIC/IMPERIAL
2 egg whites
175 g/6 oz ground almonds
75 g/3 oz caster sugar
few drops almond essence
glacé cherries and angelica to decorate

Line 2 baking sheets with silicone (non-stick) paper or rice paper. Whisk the egg whites until stiff and fold in the ground almonds, sugar and almond essence. Place the mixture in a piping bag fitted with a 1 cm/½ inch star pipe. Pipe in small stars, circles, whirls and fingers on to the baking sheets. Decorate each with a small piece of glacé cherry or angelica and bake in a cool oven (150°C/300°F, Gas Mark 2) for 15 to 20 minutes, until just beginning to colour. Cool on a wire rack.

ICED PETITS FOURS

Make some Genoese sponge (see Sponge entry), pour it into a shallow rectangular tin and bake in a moderate oven (180°C/350°F, Gas Mark 4) for 30 to 35 minutes, until firm and golden-brown. When it is cold, cut it into small fancy shapes – oblongs, squares, rounds, triangles, diamonds, crescents, etc., – and coat with warmed apricot jam.

Make some glacé icing in different colours and coat some of the cakes with it. Others may have a roll or knob of almond paste, or a complete layer, placed on top before the glacé icing is added. Decorate the petits fours with crystallized flowers, nuts, pieces of glacé cherry, silver and mimosa balls, piped butter icing and so on; when the icing and decorations are quite dry and set, place the cakes in small paper cases.

PETIT POUSSIN

The French name for a young chicken, of an average weight of 350 g/¾ lb to 0.5 kg/1 lb. Although petits poussins do not have such a high proportion of flesh to bone as the older birds, they make delicious eating, being usually roasted, fried, sautéed or grilled. (See Chicken and Poultry entries.)

PETIT SUISSE

A French cream cheese.

PETITS POIS

(See Peas entries.)

PETTITOES

(See Pig's Trotter entry.)

PHEASANT

A game bird which is at its prime in October and remains in season until February 1st; the actual shooting season is 1st October to 1st February. At its best, pheasant is one of the choicest game eaten in this country.

In the fields it is the cock bird, with its colourful feathers, which delights the eye, but on the table the duller brown hen is preferred. After being shot the birds should be hung for about a week. When buying pheasant, look for pointed flight feathers and downy under-wing feathers; in the case of a cock bird, the spurs should be short and blunt.

A pheasant will serve 2 to 3 people depending on size. Pheasants are available frozen.

Preparation and Roasting

Pluck the pheasant, taking care not to break the skin, which is often very delicate; keep the best tail feathers. Singe off any hairs with a lighted taper. Remove the crop by making an incision in the back of the neck. Cut off the head and neck close to the body, leaving sufficient of the neck skin to fold over the back and cover the opening. Then remove the inside through a slit cut in the vent and wipe the bird inside and out with a damp cloth – on no account must it be washed. Scald and skin the feet.

Put inside the bird a piece of butter seasoned with pepper, salt and lemon juice. (Alternatively, put inside 100 g/4 oz juicy beef, cut in small pieces, seasoned with pepper and salt, which will enhance the flavour and help to make the flesh more juicy.) To truss the bird, push the thighs back close under the wings and the body, then tie the second joints of the legs firmly together, making the feet stand up. Cut off the tips of the claws and either skewer or sew down the neck skin at the back. Tie 2 to 3 slices of fat bacon over the breast of the pheasant and roast in a hot oven (220°C/425°F, Gas Mark 7) for about 30 minutes to 1 hour, according to size, basting frequently with butter or bacon fat. Unlike most game, pheasant should be well cooked rather than slightly underdone.

The usual accompaniments are browned crumbs, bread sauce and thin gravy. Cranberry sauce, red-currant jelly, green salad, orange salad or stuffed oranges can also be served.

Pheasants may also be mixed with veal, ham and mushrooms in a pie, or cooked in a casserole with onion, tomato, bacon and sherry or other ingredients such as apple, celery, grapes, cream and wine.

BURGUNDY PHEASANT

METRIC/IMPERIAL

Prepare the bird as for roasting.

1 tender pheasant
3 shallots or 1 small onion, skinned

1 × 15 ml spoon/1 tablespoon oil
50 g/2 oz butter
6 small onions
2 × 15 ml spoons/2 tablespoons sugar
300 ml/½ pint red Burgundy
50 g/2 oz button mushrooms
1 × 15 ml spoon/1 tablespoon flour
salt
pepper

Chop the shallots finely and put inside the pheasant with its liver. Heat the oil and 30 g/1 oz butter in a heavy pan and sauté the pheasant gently until brown all over. Meanwhile, skin the onions, leave whole and boil them in salted water until just tender. Drain. Melt 15 g/½ oz butter in a separate pan, add 2 × 15 ml spoons/2 tablespoons sugar, stir, add the onions and cook slowly until colouring. Put the pheasant in a casserole with the onions. Add the wine and mushroom stalks to the juices in the pheasant pan and reduce by about half. Melt an additional 15 g/½ oz butter in the onion pan, sauté the mushroom caps and add them to the casserole. Work the flour into the juices and when bubbling gradually stir in the liquor from the other pan. Add seasoning, simmer to thicken and strain over the pheasant. Cover and cook in a moderate oven (180°C/350°F, Gas Mark 4) for about 30 minutes or until the pheasant is tender.

PHEASANT CASSEROLE

METRIC/IMPERIAL
1 pheasant
seasoned flour
fat for frying
100–175 g/4–6 oz mushrooms
2 rashers of bacon
salt
pepper
stock
a little port wine (optional)

Joint the bird and dip the pieces in the seasoned flour. Heat the fat in a frying pan and fry the pieces of pheasant until they are golden-brown, then put them in the casserole with the sliced mushrooms, chopped bacon, salt, pepper and sufficient stock to half-cover the pheasant; a little port wine may be added with the stock, if desired. Cook gently in a moderate oven (180°C/350°F, Gas Mark 4) for about 1 hour.

PHOSPHORUS

One of the essential minerals, used by the body for a number of vital purposes. It is one of the constituents of bones and teeth and is concerned in the life and structure of all the cells of the body. An ordinary balanced diet is unlikely to be deficient in this mineral, which is found in many foods.

PICCALILLI
(See Pickle entry for recipe.)

PICKLE

A pickle usually consists of a combination of vegetables or fruits, or both, preserved in spiced vinegar. Pickles add interest to a meal, especially to such foods as cold meat and cheese. They may be of many different types, sweet or salt, pungent or bland, extra thick, and so on.

A very wide range of foods may be preserved by pickling, including beetroots, cabbage, cauliflower, cucumber, onions, marrow and tomatoes (especially green ones), apples, damsons, lemons, pears, plums and walnuts. Salt meat and fish are sometimes referred to as 'pickled'.

Preparation for Pickling
Use a reasonably large aluminium, stainless steel or enamel pan – not copper or brass, as the acid in the vinegar will react with the metal to give traces of the very poisonous salt, copper acetate.

VEGETABLES
Choose sound, fresh vegetables and prepare as for cooking, cutting or breaking them into small pieces (except for such ingredients as small pickling onions and nasturtium seeds, which are left whole).

FRUIT
Treat according to kind – remove the stones and cores, top and tail gooseberries, etc., wipe lemons and slit the peel through in several places, as though the fruit were going to be quartered.

Brining
This is intended to remove some of the water present in vegetables, which otherwise would dilute the vinegar, so that it would look cloudy and the pickle would not keep well.

Fruit is not brined.

DRY BRINING
This is suitable for very watery vegetables, such as cucumber, marrow, tomatoes, etc. Place the prepared vegetables in a deep bowl, sprinkling salt between the layers, cover and leave overnight. Only a small amount of salt is needed – 2 × 5 ml spoons/2 teaspoons to 0.5 kg/1 lb of vegetables.

WET BRINING
This is suitable for vegetables such as cauliflower onions and shallots. Allow 50 g/2 oz salt to 600 ml/1 pint water (sufficient for about 0.5 kg/1 lb vegetables). Place the prepared vegetables in a deep bowl, cover with the brine and leave overnight.

Root vegetables such as artichokes and beetroot must be cooked in half-strength brine until they are tender.

After brining, rinse the vegetables thoroughly and drain them. If it is not possible to pickle them immediately, they may be placed in a fresh brine, made like the first one, and left until required.

SPICED VINEGAR

The vinegar used for pickling is usually flavoured with spices, including ginger and chillies. The flavour may be varied according to the fruit or vegetable to be pickled, but the following is a typical mixture:

METRIC/IMPERIAL
1 litre/1¾ pints vinegar
2 × 15 ml spoons/2 tablespoons blade mace
1 × 15 ml spoon/1 tablespoon whole allspice
1 × 15 ml/1 tablespoon cloves
18 cm/7 inch piece cinnamon stick
6 peppercorns

Put the vinegar and spices in a pan, bring to the boil and pour into a bowl. Cover with a plate to preserve the flavour and leave for 2 hours, then strain the vinegar and use as required.

An even better result is obtained if the spices are left to stand in unheated vinegar for 1 to 2 months.

NOTES
If the individual spices are not available, use 25 g/1 oz to 50 g/2 oz pickling spice. Different brands of pickling spice will vary considerably, e.g. some contain whole chillies, and give a hotter result.

For such things as cocktail onions, white (distilled) vinegar is usually used; it is occasionally replaced by dilute acetic acid.

Packing and Storing
Pack the fruit or vegetables into dry, wide-necked jars to within 2.5 cm/1 inch of the top and pour on the vinegar, leaving a 1 cm/½ inch space at the top to prevent it touching the lid of the jar. Cover fruit with hot vinegar and vegetables with cold.

Proprietary brands of synthetic skin are suitable for covering pickles. If metal covers are used, they must be lined with waxed paper or coated inside with melted paraffin wax so that the vinegar does not come into direct contact with the metal. Alternative coverings are corks wrapped in greaseproof paper; parchment paper covers; glass tops used with preserving jars; and calico dipped in melted paraffin wax or coated with melted candle grease.

The jars do not need sterilizing after filling and covering, as the growth of bacteria is prevented by the acid in the vinegar and by the salt and spices.

Pickles should be stored in a cool, dry, dark but airy place, as exposure to sunlight often spoils their colour, and they should always be left for 2 to 3 months before being eaten, otherwise the flavour is not fully developed. Cabbage is an exception, for it usually tastes better if it is eaten while it is still crisp.

PICKLED RED CABBAGE

Remove the outer leaves and shred the rest of the cabbage finely. Dry-brine for 24 hours, drain, pack loosely into bottles or jars, cover with cold spiced vinegar and cover as usual. Do not store for longer than 2 to 3 months or the cabbage will lose its crispness.

PICKLED CUCUMBER

Cut the cucumbers into quarters lengthwise, then into 2.5 cm/½ inch slices, and dry-brine them for 24 hours. Drain and pack into jars, cover with cold spiced vinegar and cover the jars.

PICKLED ONIONS

Use small pickling onions. Remove the skins carefully, without cutting the onions, wash and wet-brine for 24 hours. Drain, wash and dry, put into jars, fill up with cold spiced vinegar and cover the jars.

  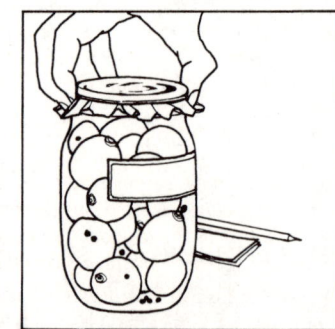

1. Pack fruit or vegetables into dry wide-necked jars to within 2.5 cm/1 inch of the top.

2. Pour on the vinegar, leaving 1 cm/½ inch space at the top to prevent it touching the lid of the jar.

3. Cover and label giving date and contents of the jar. Metal covers must be lined with waxed paper or coated with melted paraffin wax.

PICKLED WALNUTS

Walnuts should be pickled while still green and before the hard shell has formed. Wipe the nuts, prick them well, rejecting any that feel hard, and put them in a basin. Cover with brine and allow to soak for 8 days, then throw away the brine, cover with fresh brine and re-soak for 14 days. Wash and dry the walnuts and spread them out, exposing them to the air until they turn black. Have some hot spiced vinegar ready, put the walnuts into pickle jars, cover with the hot vinegar and tie down when cold. Allow pickled walnuts to mature for 5 to 6 weeks before using them.

PICKLED CAULIFLOWER (ITALIAN STYLE)

METRIC/IMPERIAL
2 cauliflowers
vinegar
1 × 15 ml spoon/1 tablespoon dried marjoram
seasoning
¼ of a red pepper
olive oil

Divide the cauliflower into florets, boil them in salted water for 5 minutes, drain well, put in a bowl and cover with boiling vinegar, then leave for 24 hours. Lift out the florets, drain well and put them in layers in a jar, sprinkling the marjoram, seasoning and chopped red pepper between the layers. Pour a mixture of two-thirds olive oil and one-third vinegar over the pickle until there is at least 2.5 cm/1 inch of liquid over the last layer. Cover with vinegar-proof paper and store in a cool place.

To serve, lift out the florets, pour over them some of the liquid from the jar and garnish with strips of red pepper and capers.

MIXED SWEET PICKLE

METRIC/IMPERIAL
¾ cucumber, washed
0.5 kg/1 lb tomatoes, halved and seeded
0.75 kg/1 ½ lb marrow, peeled and seeded
900 ml/1 ½ pints malt vinegar
300 ml/ ½ pint white vinegar
350 g/12 oz demerara sugar
4 × 5 ml spoons/4 teaspoons salt
2 × 15 ml spoons/2 tablespoons turmeric
1 × 2.5 ml spoon/ ½ teaspoon ground mace
1 × 2.5 ml spoon/ ½ teaspoon ground mixed spice
2 large pieces root ginger, bruised
1 × 2.5 ml spoon/ ½ teaspoon celery seed

Mince the vegetables coarsely. Add the vinegars, sugar, salt and spices and the ginger and celery seed tied in muslin. Stir, bring to the boil and simmer for 3 hours, until dark in colour and of a fairly thick consistency. Remove the bag of spices, pour into warm jars, seal and store in a cool place.

PICCALILLI

METRIC/IMPERIAL
2.75 kg/6 lb prepared vegetables (marrow, cucumber, beans, small onions, cauliflower)
0.5 kg/1 lb salt
4.5 litres/8 pints water
250 g/9 oz sugar
1 × 15 ml spoon/1 tablespoon dry mustard
1.5 × 5 ml spoons/1 ½ teaspoons ground ginger
1.7 litres/3 pints white vinegar
4 × 15 ml spoons/4 tablespoons flour
2 × 15 ml spoons/2 tablespoons turmeric

Dice the marrow and cucumber, slice the beans, halve the onions and break the cauliflower into small florets. Dissolve the salt in the water and add the vegetables. Cover and leave for 24 hours.

Remove the vegetables, rinse and drain. Blend the sugar, mustard and ginger with 1.5 litres/2½ pints vinegar in a large pan, add the vegetables, bring to the boil and simmer for 20 minutes. Blend the flour and turmeric with the remaining 300 ml/½ pint vinegar and stir into the cooked vegetables. Bring to the boil and cook for 1 to 2 minutes. Pot and cover.

PICKLED APPLES

METRIC/IMPERIAL
2 × 15 ml spoons/2 tablespoons whole cloves
18 cm/7 inch stick cinnamon
2 × 15 ml spoons/2 tablespoons whole allspice
600 ml/1 pint white vinegar
1 kg/2 lb sugar
1 × 2.5 ml spoon/ ½ teaspoon salt
1 kg/2 lb cooking apples, peeled, cored and cut into quarters

Put all the ingredients except the apples into a pan, heat gently to dissolve the sugar and then bring to the boil. Add the apples and cook gently until soft but not mushy. Drain the apple segments and pack in warm jars.

Boil the syrup till it is beginning to thicken; strain, pour over the apples and seal the jars.

This is a particularly popular way to eat a meal in the summer months. For some reason the food always tastes better eaten out of doors.

A picnic can be a highly organized affair to include plates, knives, forks and a three course meal, or an impromptu event with a few finger foods and paper napkins. Often the informal picnic is more enjoyable especially for children.

There is a great deal of equipment available to make transporting food more pleasant and simple. The amount and type purchased will depend on the form of transport used for the outing. Insulated bags or boxes which keep food hot or cold are popular and can be used to carry most of the meal. The bags or boxes are kept hot or cold by freezing or heating the sachets which are placed in the box. A cold sachet should be placed at the top and a hot one at the bottom for maximum effect. Also available are a wide range of packaging materials such as aluminium foil, cling film, greaseproof paper, polythene and plastic boxes. Plastic cups with fitted lids are also useful. Old yogurt and cottage cheese cartons can be used for making transportable sweets such as trifles, fruit fools, jellies and mousses. Wide neck vacuum flasks are useful for carrying ice cream, fruit salad or yogurt. An ordinary vacuum flask can be used for hot soup and hot or cold drinks. Other useful items to include are salt, pepper, can opener, bottle opener, sugar, paper napkins, damp cloths (keep in polythene bag) and a large plastic bag for rubbish.

The food eaten will depend on taste and the occasion. Many of the recipes in this book and other Good Housekeeping books provide suitable fare.

PIE

The name given to various large and small combinations of pastry with a sweet or savoury filling. In single-crust pies the filling is placed in a deep dish or plate and covered with pastry; in open-faced pies (usually called tarts or flans) a pastry shell is filled with the mixture. Some pies have both a top and a bottom layer of pastry; many of those having a pastry shell are given a topping of meringue or something similar.

Shortcrust, flan, flaky and hot-water crust pastry are the most usual types, but other kinds are sometimes used and occasionally a sweet pie has a shell made of biscuit crumbs or something similar. (See pastry entries.)

ONE-CRUST SPICED RHUBARB PIE

METRIC/IMPERIAL
0.75–1 kg/1½–2 lb pink rhubarb
50 g/2 oz preserved stem ginger
75–100 g/3–4 oz sugar
1 × 15 ml spoon/1 tablespoon cornflour

PASTRY
200 g/7 oz plain flour
pinch of salt
1 × 2.5 ml spoon/½ teaspoon ground ginger
100 g/4 oz butter or block margarine
water to mix
milk to glaze

Trim and thickly slice rhubarb. Chop ginger and add. Combine sugar and cornflour and toss with fruit. Turn into a 900 ml/1½ pint pie dish. Sift together the flour, salt and spice into a mixing bowl. Rub in the fat. Add just enough water, about 7 × 5 ml spoons/7 teaspoons, to give a manageable dough. Roll out and use to cover the pie dish, knock up and decorate edges. Brush pastry with milk. Place on a baking sheet and bake in a hot oven (220°C/425°F, Gas Mark 7) for 15 minutes; reduce oven to moderate (180°C/350°F, Gas Mark 4) and bake for a further 20 to 30 minutes until the crust is pale golden and the rhubarb tender. Dredge with caster or icing sugar to serve.

NOTE
For plum variation, replace rhubarb with halved stoned plums, stem ginger with a piece of cinnamon stick and the ground ginger with cinnamon.

To line a pie
1. Cut a strip of pastry to fit the rim of the pie dish. Gently press onto the rim.

2. Roll out the remaining pastry to fit the top of the dish, and press pastry edges together firmly.

3. Cut off any surplus pastry. Flake the pastry edges together with a knife and scallop edge.

STEAK AND MUSHROOM PIE

METRIC/IMPERIAL
0.5 kg/1 lb stewing steak
2 × 15 ml spoons/2 tablespoons seasoned flour
1 onion, skinned and sliced
water
100 g/4 oz mushrooms
215 g/7½ oz pkt frozen puff pastry, thawed
beaten egg to glaze

Wipe the meat, cut it into small, even pieces and coat with seasoned flour. Put the meat and sliced onion into a pan and just cover with water. Bring to the boil, reduce the heat and simmer for 1½ to 2 hours or until the meat is tender. Alternatively, the meat can be cooked for 2 hours in a covered casserole in a moderate oven (160°C/325°F, Gas Mark 3). Leave it to cool.

Put the meat and mushrooms into a 1 litre/2 pint pie dish with enough of the gravy to half fill it. Roll out the pastry 2.5 cm/1 inch larger than the top of the dish. Cut off a 1 cm/½ inch strip from round the edge of the pastry and put this strip round the dampened rim of the dish. Dampen the edges of the pastry with water and put on the top of the pie, without stretching the pastry; trim if necessary and flake the edges. Decorate if you wish and brush with beaten egg. Bake in a hot oven (220°C/425°F, Gas Mark 7) for 20 minutes. Reduce oven to moderate (180°C/350°F, Gas Mark 4) and cook for about a further 20 minutes.

GAME PIE

METRIC/IMPERIAL
225 g/8 oz veal
225 g/8 oz ham
seasoning
100 g/4 oz mushrooms
1 pheasant
225 g/8 oz hot-water crust
stock
egg to glaze

Mince the meats and season well; chop the mushrooms; remove the flesh from the pheasant and cut it up roughly. Line a pie mould with pastry and put a layer of minced meat at the bottom and round the sides. Put the pheasant and mushrooms in the pie and cover with the remaining minced meat. Cover with a pastry lid, decorate and cut a hole in the centre of the lid. Glaze the top and bake for about 1 hour in a hot oven (220°C/425°F, Gas Mark 7). Add some stock, reduce the oven to moderate (180°C/350°F, Gas Mark 4) and cook for a further hour.

PLATE PIE (DOUBLE-CRUST)

Prepare the meat or fruit filling. Make the pastry,

allowing 175 g/6 oz shortcrust or flaky pastry to a 23 cm/9 inch plate. Divide the dough into halves, then roll out one half and line the bottom of the pie plate, taking care to ease the pastry well into the curves of the plate; wet the rim of the pastry and place the filling in the centre. Roll out the other piece of pastry for the top, put it in position, easing it on to the rim, and press it down firmly. Cut off any surplus pastry as above, then press the edges of the pastry together, flake them with a knife and decorate with scallops. (Wide scallops are traditionally used on a savoury pie and close ones on a sweet pie). Brush a savoury pie over with beaten egg and a sweet pie with milk. Bake for 15 minutes in a hot oven (220°C/425°F, Gas Mark 7), then reduce the temperature to moderate (180°C/350°F, Gas Mark 4) and bake for another 15 to 20 minutes, depending on the filling. When cooked, a savoury pie can be garnished with parsley and a sweet pie can be dusted with caster or icing sugar.

OPEN-FACED PIES
(See Flan and Tart entries.)

Envelope Pie: For this type, the pastry (short or flaky) is usually rolled into a square and a filling of fish, meat or poultry, moistened with a sauce, is placed in the centre. Fold the corners to centre, brushing the edge of the pastry with egg or milk and pressing and crimping firmly together. Decorate with pastry leaves and bake the pie in a hot oven (220°C/425°F, Gas Mark 7) for 20 to 45 minutes, according to size.

Raised pies: (See individual entry for method of making.)

Pasties and patties: (See individual entries.)

Biscuit-crumb and cornflake crust: (See Flans for Biscuit Crust entry.)

DUTCH APPLE PIE

METRIC/IMPERIAL
700 g/1½ lb cooking apples, peeled, cored and
   quartered
4 × 15 ml spoons/4 tablespoons water
100 g/4 oz soft brown sugar
1 × 15 ml spoon/1 tablespoon cornflour or arrowroot
1 × 2.5 ml spoon/½ teaspoon salt
1 × 5 ml spoon/1 teaspoon ground cinnamon
2 × 15 ml spoons/2 tablespoons lemon juice
25 g/1 oz butter
1 × 2.5 ml spoon/½ teaspoon vanilla essence
250 g/9 oz shortcrust pastry
milk to glaze

Simmer the apples with the water until soft. Mix together the sugar, cornflour or arrowroot, salt and cinnamon and add to the cooked apples. Stir in the lemon juice and cook, stirring, until fairly thick. Remove from the heat, stir in the butter and

303

essence and cool. Roll out half the pastry and line a 22 cm/8½ inch greased pie plate; put the cooked apples in the pastry case. Roll out the remaining pastry to make a lid. Dampen the edges of the pastry on the plate and cover with the lid, pressing the edges well together; flake and scallop the edges. Make short slashes with a knife into the centre. Brush the top with milk, put the plate on a baking sheet and bake in a moderately hot oven (200°C/400°F, Gas Mark 6) for about 1 hour. Cover loosely with foil after 30 minutes to prevent it over-browning. Serve hot or cold, with cream or custard.

PECAN PIE

METRIC/IMPERIAL
100 g/4 oz blended vegetable fat
25 g/1 oz butter
175 g/6 oz plain flour
salt
3 × 15 ml spoons/3 tablespoons water

FOR THE FILLING
3 eggs
1 × 15 ml spoon/1 tablespoon milk
175 g/6 oz demerara sugar
150 ml/¼ pint maple or corn syrup
50 g/2 oz butter, softened
1 × 2.5 ml spoon/½ teaspoon vanilla essence
175 g/6 oz pecan or walnuts, halved

Cream together the white fat and butter. Gradually stir in the sifted flour and salt; cream well after each addition. Add the water and mix thoroughly with the hands. Knead lightly with extra flour, as this pastry is sticky to handle. Chill. Roll out the pastry and line a 23 cm/9 inch ovenproof flan dish; flute the edge. Chill this case while preparing the filling.

Beat the eggs and milk together. Boil the sugar and syrup together in a saucepan for 3 minutes. Slowly pour on to the beaten eggs and stir in the butter and essence. Use half the nuts to cover the base of the pastry case, spoon the syrup mixture over and cover with the remaining nuts. Bake in a hot oven (220°C/425°F, Gas Mark 7) for 10 minutes. Reduce the heat to moderate (170°C/325°F, Gas Mark 3) and cook for a further 45 minutes, until the filling is set. Serve warm or cold with unsweetened whipped cream.

PIGEON

Both wild and tame pigeons may be eaten. When selecting a bird, choose one with small eyes, soft, red feet, short rounded spurs and bright neck feathers, of the same colour as the body feathers. The wild birds (which can be recognized by their large feet) are excellent if hung for 2 to 3 days after shooting; tame pigeons should be starved for 24 hours before they are killed; pluck while still warm. Young pigeons may be roasted or grilled, while the older, tougher birds are excellent for making raised pies, rich stews and curries. Allow one pigeon per person as the largest weigh only 0.75 kg/1½ lb. Pigeons can be bought frozen.

Preparation: Pigeons are plucked, drawn, singed, washed and trussed like other poultry, except that the feet are not cut off but are scalded and scraped; the wings are not drawn across the back in trussing.

ROAST PIGEON

Prepare and truss the birds, allowing one for 1 to 2 people. Cover the breast with a slice of fat bacon, place a small shallot inside the bird and roast for 20 to 30 minutes in a moderately hot oven (200°C/400°F, Gas Mark 6). Serve each bird on a croûte of fried bread, garnish with watercress, etc.; serve with gravy.

If desired, the pigeons may be stuffed before roasting with a stuffing made as follows: Mix 2 chopped fried pigeon livers, 2 × 5 ml spoons/2 teaspoons chopped onion, 1 × 15 ml spoon/1 tablespoon chopped parsley, 3 × 15 ml spoons/3 tablespoons breadcrumbs, 1 cooked, chopped rasher of bacon, salt, cayenne pepper and a pinch of nutmeg; bind with beaten egg.

CASSEROLE OF PIGEON

METRIC/IMPERIAL
4 pigeons, plucked, drawn and jointed
2–3 × 15 ml spoons/2–3 tablespoons oil
50 g/2 oz bacon, rinded and chopped
2 carrots, pared and sliced
1 onion, skinned and chopped
3 × 15 ml spoons/3 tablespoons flour
600 ml/1 pint chicken stock
1 × 15 ml spoon/1 tablespoon tomato paste
salt
pepper

Fry the pigeon joints in the oil for about 5 minutes, until golden brown, remove from the pan with a slotted spoon and put in a casserole. Fry the bacon, carrots and onion in the remaining oil for about 5 minutes, until golden brown. Remove the vegetables from the pan with a slotted spoon and add to the casserole. Stir the flour into the remaining fat in the pan and cook for 2 to 3 minutes. Remove the pan from the heat and gradually stir in the stock. Bring to the boil, continue to stir until it thickens and add the tomato paste and seasoning. Pour the sauce over the pigeon joints, cover and cook in the oven at (160°C/325°F, Gas Mark 3) for about 1½ hours, or until the pigeons are tender.

PIGEONS À LA FRANÇAISE

METRIC/IMPERIAL
4 large pigeons
salt and pepper
4 × 15 ml spoons/4 tablespoons oil
6 × 15 ml spoons/6 tablespoons dry sherry
175 g/6 oz button onions, skinned
1 lettuce, washed and shredded
0.5 kg/1 lb frozen peas
1 × 1.25 ml spoon/¼ teaspoon mint essence
knob of butter
2 × 5 ml spoons/2 teaspoons flour

Halve the pigeons and season with salt and pepper. Fry in oil, flesh side down, until golden brown. Drain and place in a flameproof casserole. Pour over the sherry, add the onions, cover and place in a moderate oven (180°C/350°F, Gas Mark 4) for 1¾ hours. About 30 minutes before the end of the cooking time add lettuce, peas and mint essence. Thicken the juices with the butter and flour creamed together to make a paste. Serve.

TIPSY PIGEONS

METRIC/IMPERIAL
8 black olives
4 × 15 ml spoons/4 tablespoons dry sherry
2 pigeons, plucked and drawn
2 × 15 ml spoons/2 tablespoons oil
1 large onion, skinned and sliced
100 g/4 oz bacon, rinded and chopped
4 slices garlic sausage
3 × 15 ml spoons/3 tablespoons flour
300 ml/½ pint chicken stock
2 × 15 ml spoons/2 tablespoons brandy
salt and pepper

Marinade the olives in the sherry for 2 hours. Fry the pigeons in the oil until golden brown, about 5 minutes. Remove from the pan with a slotted spoon and put in a casserole. Fry the onion, bacon and garlic sausage in the remaining fat until golden brown, about 5 minutes. Remove from the pan with a slotted spoon and add to the casserole, with the sherry and olives. Stir the flour into the fat remaining in the pan and cook for 2 to 3 minutes. Gradually stir in the stock, bring to the boil and stir until it thickens. Add the brandy, season and pour the sauce over the pigeons. Cover and cook in a moderate oven (110°C/350°F, Gas Mark 4) for 1½ hours, until tender.

PIG'S CHEEK

This portion of the pig is usually pickled and may be dried and cured, when it is known as a Bath chap. It is usually sold ready cooked, but the cooking is quite a simple matter.

A pig's cheek which is fresh from the pickle only needs to be washed in 2 to 3 waters, but if it is a long-cured one, it must first be soaked for 6 hours. Place it in warm water, bring it to the boil, simmer for 2½ hours, skin, cover with browned breadcrumbs and bake it in a moderately hot oven (200°C/400°F, Gas Mark 6) for about 30 minutes.

PIG'S EAR

This part is now rarely eaten as a separate dish; it can be cooked with trotters, after being washed and cleansed, but it is generally used in sausages and other commercial preparations.

PIG'S FRY (HARSLET OR HASLET)

A country-type dish in which the heart, liver, lights and sweetbreads of a pig are cooked together. As the name suggests, it is usually fried, but may also be stewed, casseroled, or made into faggots (see faggot entry). Use when very fresh.

FRIED HARSLET

Wash the fry well, dry it and cut it into slices about 7 mm/⅓ inch thick. Dip the pieces in seasoned flour and fry them until lightly browned, together with a little minced bacon (optional), chopped onion and powdered sage.

PIG'S HEAD, TONGUE

(See Head and Tongue entries.)

PIGS IN BLANKET

(See Oyster entry.)

PIG'S TROTTERS OR FEET

A variety of delicious and nourishing dishes may be made from pig's trotters. After being boiled in water flavoured with herbs, they may be served hot, with an onion sauce, or cold; alternatively, they may be grilled (either plain or after being egg-and-breadcrumbed), stuffed, fricasséed or made into soup.

JELLIED PIG'S TROTTERS

Wash, trim and blanch the feet and put them into a saucepan with salt, a bunch of herbs, a blade of mace, a slice of onion and a small carrot. Just cover with cold water and simmer gently until the meat is tender. Strain the liquid into a basin. Cut the meat from the bones, dice it and add it to the stock with 2 ×5 ml spoons/2 teaspoons chopped parsley. Turn the mixture into a wetted mould and allow it to set, then use like brawn.

PIKE

A freshwater fish with a long head, scaly body and fins placed towards the tail end. It can grow to 13.5 kg/30 lb in weight, but those normally eaten average 2.25 kg/5 lb. Pike are not usually considered very palatable, as the flesh is dry and there are many bones, but they can be improved by baking with a highly flavoured stuffing or in a white wine and by serving a piquant sauce with them. They may also be fried or grilled. The flesh will be more tender if salt is put both inside and outside the fish as soon as possible after catching: it should then be left for several hours before washing and preparation.

In season October to January.

BAKED STUFFED PIKE

METRIC/IMPERIAL
4 mushrooms
100 g/4 oz fat bacon
3 anchovies, chopped
100 g/4 oz fresh white breadcrumbs
seasoning
1 × 5 ml spoon/1 teaspoon thyme, chopped
1 × 5 ml spoon/1 teaspoon parsley, chopped
1 × 5 ml spoon/1 teaspoon chives or onion, chopped
1 egg yolk
150 ml/¼ pint white wine

Remove the fins and scale and clean the pike, cut it in pieces, then skin and fillet the pieces.

Make a forcemeat as follows: Fry mushrooms with fat bacon, then chop them both; add chopped anchovies, breadcrumbs, some seasoning and chopped thyme, parsley and chives or onion; bind with egg yolk.

Spread the forcemeat over half the fillets, cover with the other fillets and pour over a little stock mixed with about 150 ml/¼ pint white wine. Bake for 1 hour in a moderate oven (180°C/350°F, Gas Mark 4). When the pike is cooked, place it on a dish and pour Hollandaise or anchovy sauce over it; garnish with baked tomatoes.

If preferred, chestnut, oyster or shrimp stuffing may be used.

PIKELET

A north country name for crumpets. The name pikelet is sometimes applied to drop scones and girdle scones. (See Crumpet entry.)

PILAF (PILAU, PILAW)

An Oriental and Levantine dish, consisting of rice flavoured with spices and cooked in stock, to which meat, poultry or fish may be added. There are many versions and the method of serving varies considerably, but a very common way of dishing a pilaf is to pile the rice on a dish and embed the meat or poultry in it. Fried onion rings, grilled tomatoes, seeded raisins and blanched almonds, etc., form a suitable garnish.

LAMB PILAU

METRIC/IMPERIAL
0.5–0.75 kg/1–1 ½ lb loin or best end of neck of lamb
900 ml/1 ½ pints chicken stock
175 g/6 oz long grain rice
pinch ground cinnamon
pinch ground cloves
salt
pepper
50 g/2 oz currants or stoned raisins
50 g/2 oz butter

Trim the meat and cut it into even-sized pieces. Cover with the stock and stew until tender, then lift out, drain and keep on one side. Wash the rice well and sprinkle into the liquid in which the meat was cooked; add the spices, seasoning and currants. Bring to the boil, then cover and simmer very gently for about 15 minutes, until all the liquid is absorbed and the rice is just soft. Remove from the heat and leave covered for about 15 minutes to dry out. Fry the meat in half the butter until lightly browned and stir the remaining butter into the rice mixture. Serve the rice piled on a dish with the meat in the centre. If liked, this dish can be garnished with wedges of tomato or fried onion rings.

PILCHARD

A small fish of the herring family, abundant off the shores of Devon and Cornwall, where it can be enjoyed from July to December. As fresh pilchards do not travel well, they are not often seen in other parts of the country. They are, however, canned fairly extensively, both in oil and in tomato sauce. Young pilchards, caught off the coasts of France, Portugal, etc., are known as sardines.

Pilchards, like all herrings, are economical and nutritious. They supply protein, fat, calcium and vitamin D.

Cooking: The fresh fish are prepared like herrings, and are best fried or grilled. Canned pilchards may be eaten without further preparation, accompanied by a green salad, or they can also be used as a sandwich filling or a topping for cocktail savouries; the fish may be heated in their liquor and served with mashed potato, or mashed mixed with other ingredients and baked.

PIMENTO (ALLSPICE, JAMAICA PEPPER)

The pea-like berries of an evergreen tree which grows in the West Indies and South America. The berries contain small seeds which are dried to a very dark brown colour and are used either whole or finely ground. Their flavour is said to resemble a combination of nutmeg, cloves and cinnamon and for this reason they are often known as allspice. In the powdered from they are also called pimento and Jamaica pepper (though they lack the hot, pungent taste of true pepper). Pimento is used to flavour pickles, meat dishes, soups, marinades and stock, and is an ingredient of curry powder; it is also used in such sweet dishes as fruit puddings, gingerbread and spicy cakes.

PIMIENTO

A red Spanish pepper with a sweet, pungent flavour, used in salads and as a vegetable. Also available canned. It is sometimes incorrectly called 'pimento'.

PIMMS

A proprietary drink marketed as 'Pimms No. 1 Cup'. It is gin based, and is served with ice and diluted with sparkling lemonade, garnished, if desired, with sliced fruit, cucumber, mint or borage.

PINE KERNEL

Small, oblong, delicately flavoured nuts obtained from pine cones. Pine kernels are rich in oil and protein.

PINEAPPLE

A tropical fruit, almost cylindrical in shape, which grows on a short stem from the middle of a tuft of grey-green pointed leaves. It has a hard, ridged skin of deep orange and firm but juicy flesh. There are many varieties which differ in size and colour, the three main ones being the Queen, Cayenne and Spanish; generally the best quality ones are of darker yellow, softer and sweeter than the other varieties. Fresh pineapples, which have a delicious flavour, are imported and tend to be expensive. Canned pineapple is more widely bought and is available in slices, cubes, chunks and whole, crushed and in other cuts such as 'fingers' and titbits. Pineapple juice is canned both sweetened and unsweetened. The quality is graded in various ways:

MALAYAN GRADES
'Golden' – well-coloured and ripe.
'G.A.Q.' – whiter and less ripe.

HAWAIIAN AND SOUTH AFRICAN GRADES
'Extras' – best quality.
'Standard' – whiter, less ripe and canned in a lighter syrup.
'Broken Slices' – poorer quality and lighter syrup.

AUSTRALIAN GRADES
'Fancy' – even slices, good colour.
'Choice' – other cuts, regular size and even colour.

Preparation of fresh pineapple: Peel the pineapple fairly thickly, removing the 'eyes'. When served as dessert, pineapple is usually cut in wedge-shaped slices from top to the base, but if preferred, it may be further cut into chunks.

Pineapple in Cookery

In both the fresh and the canned form, this fruit can be used in a variety of sweet and savoury dishes – en surprise, pineapple snow, hot or cold soufflé, fritters, to accompany pork, grills and so on. When crushed and mixed with cream it forms a good cake filling; when combined with cream cheese, tomato or cucumber and mayonnaise it makes an excellent salad.

Fresh pineapple should not be used in gelatine mixtures unless previously boiled, as it contains an enzyme which prevents the jelly from setting, but the canned fruit may be used without boiling.

The pineapple case can be cut in half lengthways and used to serve fruit mixtures or savoury dips.

COLD PINEAPPLE SOUFFLÉ

METRIC/IMPERIAL
1 × 425 g/15 oz can crushed pineapple
1.5 × 15 ml spoons/1 ½ tablespoons powdered gelatine
4 large eggs, separated
75 g/3 oz caster sugar
2 × 15 ml spoons/2 tablespoons whisky
150 ml/¼ pint single cream
150 ml/¼ pint double cream
chopped pistachio nuts and whipped cream for decoration

Prepare a 15 cm/6 inch, (900 ml/1 ½ pint) soufflé dish. Drain the pineapple. Reserve 4 × 15 ml spoons/4 tablespoons juice and pour it into a small bowl. Sprinkle over the gelatine. Place the bowl in a pan with hot water and dissolve the gelatine. Whisk the egg yolks, sugar and whisky in a large deep basin over a pan of hot water until they are thick and pale. Remove the basin from the heat and add the crushed pineapple. Add a little pineapple mixture to the gelatine and pour back into the soufflé mixture, whisking. Leave to cool, whisking occasionally.

When the mixture is not quite cold, whisk the creams together until thick. Fold into the cool, but not set, pineapple base. Whisk the egg whites until stiff but not dry, pour the pineapple cream base over the whites and fold in lightly. Turn the mixture into the prepared soufflé dish and chill. To serve, remove the paper collar, decorate the edges with pistachio nuts and top with piped cream.

PINEAPPLE SURPRISE

METRIC/IMPERIAL
1 pineapple
strawberries, grapes, etc.
caster sugar
ice cream

Remove the top of the pineapple with the leaves and keep for decoration. Scoop out the central part of the pineapple and cut it up into small pieces, mixing the flesh with some fresh strawberries, raspberries, skinned and stoned grapes or other fresh fruits as available. Add a little sugar and chill the mixture in a refrigerator. Put the fruit in layers in the pineapple shell, alternately with some well-frozen ice cream, replace the pineapple leaves on top and serve at once.

BAKED PORK CHOPS WITH PINEAPPLE

Trim off the excess fat from 4 pork chops and lay them in a baking tin. Cover with greased paper and bake the chops in a moderate oven (180°C/350°F, Gas Mark 4) for ¾ to 1 hour. About 10 minutes before the cooking time is up, open a small tin of pineapple slices, remove the paper cover and place a slice of drained pineapple on top of each chop; pour 150 ml/¼ pint of pineapple juice over and season. Return the chops to the oven to brown. Serve with the cooking liquid, which can be thickened slightly with cornflour.

PINK GIN

(See Cocktail entry.)

PIPING

The process of forcing a smooth, soft mixture (such as icing, creamed potatoes, etc.) into fancy shapes. The mixture is placed in a paper or fabric bag and forced through a special piping or forcing tube. There are many shapes and sizes to give different patterns. Piping forms an attractive way of decorating cakes, sweets and savouries – even the simplest piping helps to give a professional touch to an ordinary dish.

Mixtures for Piping

These must be free of all lumps, which might block the forcing tube. The sugar for glacé and royal icing, for instance, must be passed through a fine sieve before being used. During the final mixing, stir rather than beat the mixture to break down any large air bubbles. The mixture should be of such a consistency that it can be forced easily through the pipe, but will retain its shape. If it is at all runny in the bowl, it will be too soft for piping. Cream should be whipped until it holds its shape and loses the glossy look. Potato and biscuit mixture should be mixed to a soft not stiff consistency.

Filling the Forcing Bag

CLOTH BAG
Turn the bag so that the join comes to the outside and insert the forcing tube. Hold the bag in the left hand, turning the top hem back in the left hand, and fill with a spoon, pushing the mixture off the spoon with the covered thumb of the left hand. To leave both hands free to fill the bag, place it over a cylindrical grater or tall jug. When the bag is about two thirds full, turn up the top hem. Place the bag on a flat surface and press the contents towards the nozzle. Screw round with the right hand until the mixture shows through the forcing tube. At inter-

Raised Trellis
1. Pipe icing in straight lines, so that the icing falls onto the cake approximately 1 cm/½ inch apart.

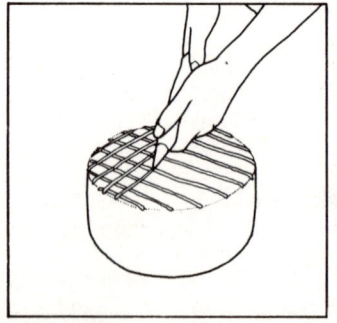

2. Pipe lines of icing approximately 1 cm/½ inch apart across the first set of lines.

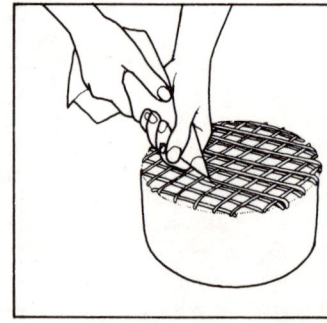

3. Pipe a third set of lines in the same direction as the first. Allow to dry out.

vals stop piping and repeat this screwing process, to keep the mixture in one mass.

PAPER BAG

1. Fold a 25 cm/10 inch square of greaseproof paper into a triangle.
2. Holding the right angle of the triangle towards you, roll over one of the other corners to meet it. Roll the second corner over in the opposite direction to meet the first at the back of the bag. Adjust the two corners over one another until a point is formed at the tip.
3. Fold over the corners several times to secure them in position.
4. Cut a small piece from the tip of the bag and drop in the required metal nozzle or pipe.
5. Place enough mixture in the bag to fill it about one third. (Any more than this will leak out of the top.) Fold over the top edges of the bag several times and press down.

Method of Piping

The usual rule is to press with the left hand and guide with the right, but some people manage better the other way round. For sugar icing stars and rounds, piped duchesse potatoes, etc., the bag must be held perpendicular to the surface, but for shapes like leaves the angle at which the bag is held, the movement of the hand and the speed of pressure may all be varied to alter the shape of the leaf.

Eclairs: Use a plain 1 cm/½ inch nozzle and pipe in finger lengths 5 cm/2 inches to 7.5 cm/3 inches on to a greased and damped baking sheet.

Meringues: Use a plain 1 cm/½ inch nozzle and pipe in mounds on to lightly oiled greaseproof paper laid on a baking sheet.

Swiss tarts: Use a large star pipe and force the mixture into paper cases; starting at the centre, pipe with a spiral motion round the sides, leaving a shallow depression in the centre.

CAKE ICING

The beginner is advised to draw the design for cake icing, etc., on greaseproof paper and then prick it out by pushing a pin through the paper (the piping later covers these lines). Freehand piping can only be done successfully when one has a good deal of experience.

Trellis piping: Either butter or royal icing may be used for trellis patterns that lie flat on the surface of the cake, but only royal icing is suitable for a raised trellis pattern.

To work trellis straight on to the cake, first prick out the pattern, then pipe the icing through a writing pipe, holding this about 2.5 cm/1 inch above the cake, so that the icing falls in straight lines. Allow the first set of lines to dry a little, then pipe across them to give the trellis effect. To make the pattern stand out well, a third set of lines can be piped over the first set, giving a raised effect.

To make a raised trellis shape, the lines must be piped over an icing nail or round a small boat-shaped patty tin. Lightly grease this support, then pipe the lines as described above. Leave the trellis to set hard (preferably for 24 hours) before removing it. Warm the support slightly and remove the trellis carefully, then fix it to the cake, using a little wet icing to hold it. It may be given a piped decorative border if desired.

Icing flowers: For these royal icing must be used; if desired it may be tinted, but the colours should be kept very delicate. The forcing bag should be fitted with a petal nozzle and an icing nail or flat-topped cork is needed, also some small squares of greaseproof paper. For each separate flower, stick a square of paper on to the nail or cork, using a tiny dab of icing.

To make a rose, pipe a cone of icing in the middle of the paper to form the flower centre, and allow this to dry for a minute or two. Pipe the first and second petals, holding the nozzle as upright as possible, with the thick side of the nozzle at the base. Turn the nail round very slowly to pipe the successive petals; do not make too many, as this gives a shapeless, crowded effect. For the final ring

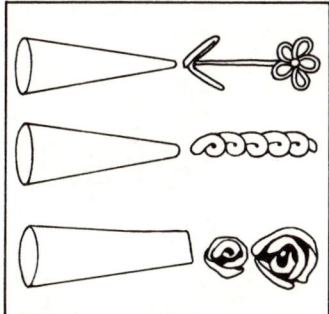
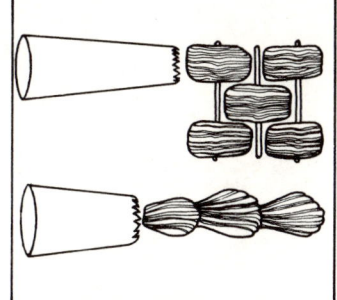
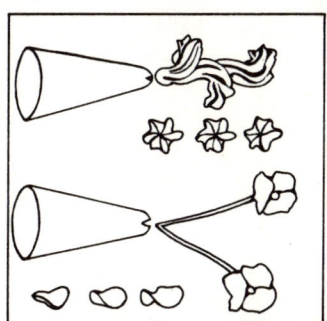

Icing tubes and nozzles
1. *Plain, small writing tube*
2. *Plain, medium-sized writing tube*
3. *Petal nozzle for icing flowers*

4. *Flat star nozzle*
5. *Star (or rosette) nozzle*

6. *Small star nozzle*
7. *Petal nozzle*

of petals, work the top edge outwards in a pleasing natural curve. When the flower is finished, remove it from the nail, on its paper, and leave it on a flat surface to dry for 24 hours. Attach the rose to the cake with a little freshly made icing.

To make pansies, narcissi and other flowers, use the same petal nozzle, holding it with the thick edge to the centre of the icing nail and the thin edge outwards. Pipe the petals to suit the particular flower. When the flower is hard and dry, pipe a spot of dark yellow icing into the little hole left in the centre between the petals.

Leaves are made in a similar way, with a leaf nozzle.

PIQUANT SAUCE

A well flavoured sharp sauce served with fish, re-heated meat dishes etc.

METRIC/IMPERIAL
2 shallots or a small piece of onion, skinned and finely chopped
knob of butter
150 ml/¼ pint wine vinegar
300 ml/½ pint espagnole or demi-glace sauce
2–3 gherkins, finely chopped
1 × 15 ml spoon/1 tablespoon chopped parsley

Fry the shallots or onion in the butter for about 10 minutes, until really soft but not browned. Add the vinegar and boil rapidly until reduced by about half. Stir in the sauce and simmer for 15 minutes. Add the gherkins and parsley and serve without further cooking.

Serve with pork or any cold meat.

PISSALADIÈRE

A savoury flan or tart filled with tomatoes, onions, black olives and anchovy fillets. It is said to have originated in Greece but is mainly found in the South of France.

PISSALADIÈRE

METRIC/IMPERIAL

PASTRY
150 g/5 oz plain flour
a pinch of salt
65 g/2½ oz butter
1 egg

FILLING
1 × 15 ml spoon/1 tablespoon olive oil
25 g/1 oz butter
0.75 kg/1½ lb onions, skinned and finely sliced
1 × 2.5 ml spoon/½ teaspoon salt
pinch of pepper
pinch of nutmeg
3 egg yolks

3 × 5 ml spoons/3 tablespoons milk
100 g/4 oz cream cheese
GARNISH
16 anchovy fillets
16 black olives

Make pastry adding sufficient egg to bind the mixture together. Wrap pastry in foil and chill for 2 hours. Heat the oil in a frying pan, add butter and onions. Cook, covered for 30 minutes until soft and pale golden. Add seasoning and nutmeg. Use the pastry to line a 23 cm/9 inch fluted flan tin placed on a baking tray. Line with greaseproof paper and baking beans. Bake 'blind' in a moderately hot oven (200°C/400°F, Gas Mark 6) for 20 minutes. Remove beans and greaseproof paper.

Blend together egg yolks, milk and cheese, then mix in the onion. Pour filling into pastry case and return to oven for a further 20 minutes or until set. Arrange anchovy fillets in a lattice over flan with black olives. Bake for 10 minutes.

PISTACHIO NUT

The fruit of a tree which is grown in Southern Europe, Western Asia and Mexico. The small, bright-green kernel, which is sweet and delicate in flavour, is covered with a yellowish-red skin and a bluish husk. The nuts are sold shelled and blanched. They can be chopped or sliced and used to decorate various types of sweets, cakes and ices or salted like almonds. They also make a flavouring for ice cream.

PIZZA

An Italian dish made from yeast dough, rolled into a flat round and covered with tomato, grated cheese, anchovies or other additions such as ham, egg, mushrooms, olives and onion.

It is brushed with oil and baked. They are best eaten straight from the oven with a mixed or green salad. Pizzas freeze very well and can be reheated from frozen in about 30 minutes.

Pizzas have become more popular in this country in recent years as they provide an economical, quick meal. Many Pizza restaurants have opened to provide this service: the Pizzas are usually available to take away or eat on the premises. At home pizzas are ideal for informal entertaining: a large one can be made and cut into slices or serve small individual ones.

PIZZA NAPOLETANA

METRIC/IMPERIAL
about 150 ml/¼ pint water
1 × 2.5 ml spoon/½ teaspoon sugar
1.5 × 5 ml spoons/1½ teaspoons dried yeast or
    15 g/½ oz fresh yeast

225 g/½ lb strong plain flour
1 × 5 ml spoon/1 teaspoon salt
small knob lard
cooking oil

FOR TOPPING
0.5 kg/1 lb onions, skinned and chopped
2 × 425 g/15 oz cans tomatoes, drained
2 × 5 ml spoons/2 teaspoons dried marjoram
salt
pepper
100 g/4 oz Bel Paese or Mozzarella cheese, cut into
    small dice
2 × 50 g/2 oz cans anchovy fillets, drained
black olives

Warm the water to blood heat and dissolve the
sugar in it. Sprinkle the dried yeast on and leave in
a warm place until frothy. If you are using fresh
yeast, blend it with the water and use at once; omit
the sugar. Mix the flour and salt, rub in the lard and
pour in the yeast mixture. Hand mix and beat until
the dough leaves the bowl clean. Knead on a
floured board until smooth and elastic. Put the
dough in an oiled plastic bag, leave in a warm place
until doubled in size. Turn the dough on to a
floured surface and roll to a long strip. Brush with
oil and roll it up like a Swiss roll.

Repeat 3 times. Grease a 30 cm/12 inch plain flan
ring on a baking sheet, and roll out the dough to fit
this (if no flan ring is available, roll out the dough
to a 30 cm/12 inch round and place on a baking
sheet). Brush with oil. Sauté the onions in a little
oil until soft but not coloured. Spread to within
1.5 cm/¾ inch of the edge of the dough. Arrange
the tomatoes on top, sprinkle with marjoram and
seasoning and bake in a hot oven (230°C/450°F,
Gas Mark 8) for 20 minutes. Scatter the cheese over
top, lattice with anchovy fillets and arrange olives
in the spaces between lattice. Cover loosely with
foil and cook for a further 20 minutes. Serve hot in
wedges, with a green salad.

QUICK PIZZA

METRIC/IMPERIAL

100 g/4 oz self-raising flour
1 × 2.5 ml spoon/½ teaspoon salt
5 × 15 ml spoons/5 tablespoons oil
4 × 15 ml spoons/4 tablespoons water
1 small onion, skinned and chopped
400 g/14 oz can tomatoes, drained and chopped
2 × 5 ml spoons/2 teaspoons mixed herbs
25 g/1 oz butter
100 g/4 oz cheese, cut into small cubes
few olives and anchovy fillets

Mix the flour and salt and stir in 1 × 15 ml spoon/1
tablespoon oil and enough water to mix to a fairly
soft dough. Roll out into an 18 cm/7 inch round
and fry on one side in the remaining oil in a large

frying pan. Meanwhile make the topping by frying the onion, tomatoes and herbs in the butter.
Turn the dough over and spread with the tomato
mixture, the cheese, and a few sliced olives and/or
anchovy fillets. Fry until the underside is golden
and place under a hot grill until the cheese is golden
and bubbling. Serve hot, cut in wedges – it goes
well with a green salad.

PIZZA SPECIAL

METRIC/IMPERIAL
50 g/2 oz onion, skinned and thinly sliced
2 × 15 ml spoons/2 tablespoons vegetable oil
0.5 kg/1 lb ripe tomatoes, skinned
4 × 15 ml spoons/4 tablespoons mango chutney
100 g/4 oz sliced cooked ham
salt
pepper
283 g/10 oz packet brown bread mix
175 g/6 oz St. Paulin cheese, chilled

Soften the onion in the heated oil in a frying pan.
Add the roughly chopped tomatoes and mango
chutney and cook to a pulp. Shred the ham
roughly and mix into the tomato mixture with
seasoning to taste. Cool.

Mix and knead the dough according to packet
instructions. Roll out to fit a foil-lined and lightly
greased 33 × 23 cm/13 × 9 inch Swiss roll tin.
Spread the tomato mixture over the dough. Grate
the cheese over it evenly. Leave to rise in a warm
place for about 1 hour. Bake in a hot oven
(220°C/425°F, Gas Mark 7) for about 25 minutes or
until golden brown and crisp.

PLAICE

A flat fish with characteristic red spots on the dark
side and with eyes of uneven size on the same side
of its head. Plaice vary in size from the small dab to
a fish weighing approximately 4.5 kg/10 lb. The
medium ones have the best flavour and the very
small ones not worth buying, as they are mostly
bone. When fresh, plaice has firm flesh and the
spots are bright, which dull upon keeping. Plaice
are in season all the year round, but are at their best
towards the end of May.

Preparation and cooking: Plaice may be cooked
whole or in fillets. (See Fish entry for method of
filleting, etc.) Small plaice (and also dabs) are fried
whole.

Frying is one of the most usual methods of cooking plaice. Fillet, skin and dry the fish, dip it in
seasoned flour or coat with egg and breadcrumbs
and fry in hot deep fat. Garnish with slices of
lemon and fried parsley and serve separately a
well-flavoured sauce such as anchovy, prawn, etc.,
or maître d'hôtel butter.

Plaice fillets may if preferred be egged-and-crumbed and then placed in a greased baking tin, covered with a knob or two of butter and a greased paper and baked for 20 minutes in a moderately hot oven (200°C/400°F, Gas Mark 6). Alternatively, the egging and crumbing may be omitted, in which case the fish should be coated with a sauce after baking – cheese, parsley, shrimp, vinaigrette, Hollandaise and Tartare are all suitable; use the bones (if available) to make stock for the sauce.

PLANKING

To cook (usually to serve) meat or fish on a special wooden board. The plank should be of well-seasoned hardwood, oblong or oval in shape. It is heated in the oven, then oiled with olive oil or melted butter and the meat or fish is placed on it, dabbed with pieces of butter or bacon and cooked in a hot oven or under a grill (provided it can be placed at a safe distance from the heat).

(See Planked Steak recipe in Steak entry.)

PLANTAIN

A tropical fruit resembling a banana – in fact some of the many varieties are almost indistinguishable from bananas, though rather bigger and coarser. The ripe fruit of the better types has sweet, soft flesh. The coarser varieties, and also the unripe fruit, can be cooked by baking or frying.

Plantain is also the name of a weed found in the British Isles, which used to be dried and made into a drink before tea was introduced.

PLOVER

A small wild bird, several varieties of which are eaten. The green plover, also known as the bustard plover or lapwing, is the most common, and is in season August to March. The golden plover, grey plover, stone curlew and ring-dotted plover are also found in the British Isles. Roasting is the most usual method of cooking – one per person should be allowed.

Preparation and roasting: Like snipe, plovers should not be kept long before they are cooked, especially if they are to be roasted without being drawn. Pluck and wipe the bird carefully and draw it or leave it undrawn, as preferred; in either case remove the gizzard and leave the liver in the bird. Skin the head and neck and remove the eyes. Twist the leg joints and bring the feet back on the thighs. Press the legs and wings together and draw the head round so that the beak may run through the wings and legs. Pass a string round the head and tip of the bill, and tie it securely. Place the bird in a roasting tin, on a round of buttered toast, if desired, and roast for 15 to 20 minutes in a moder-

ately hot oven (200°C/400°F, Gas Mark 6), basting it frequently.

PLOVERS' EGGS
(See Eggs entry.)

PLUCK

The liver, heart and lights of a sheep or other animal.

PLUCKING

(See Poultry entry.)

PLUM

A stone fruit of the genus *Prunus*, supposed to have developed originally from the sloe. Many hundreds of varieties of plum are grown throughout the world, ranging in colour from gold to very dark purple, and varying considerably in size. Some are suitable for dessert, some for cooking purposes and a few may be used in either way. In England the best plums are grown in Kent and the Vale of Evesham. The types known as gages are generally considered the best for eating. In France and California, special brands of plum are grown for drying as prunes (see Prune entry).

The skins of plums are inclined to be tough, and it is better to remove them when the raw fruit is used in fruit salads, etc.

Plums are used for all the usual fruit sweets, such as pies, baked and steamed puddings, flans, jelly whip, fruit salad, etc.; they may also be frozen, pickled, dried, bottled or made into jam.

PLUM JAM

METRIC/IMPERIAL
2.75 kg/6 lb plums
900 ml/1½ pints water
2.75 kg/6 lb sugar

Wash the fruit, cut in halves and remove the stones. Crack some of the stones and remove the kernels. Put the plums, kernels and water in a pan and simmer gently for about 1 hour, or until really soft. Add the sugar, stir until dissolved and boil rapidly until setting point is reached. Pot and cover in the usual way. *Makes about 4.5 kg/10 lb.*

NOTE
Alternatively, cook the fruit without stoning, removing the stones with a slotted spoon as the jam is boiling.

BOTTLED AND DRIED PLUMS
(See Bottling and Drying entries.)

PLUM PUDDING
(See Christmas Pudding entry.)

PLUM UPSIDE-DOWN PUDDING

METRIC/IMPERIAL
25 g/1 oz butter
2 × 15 ml spoons/2 tablespoons demerara sugar
350 g/12 oz red plums
25 g/1 oz whole unblanched almonds
100 g/4 oz caster sugar
2 eggs
100 g/4 oz self-raising flour
50 g/2 oz ground almonds
1 × 2.5 ml spoon/½ teaspoon almond essence

Butter an 18 cm/7 inch cake tin well, using all of the 25 g/1 oz. Sprinkle the base with the demerara sugar. Halve and stone the plums. Place each plum half face down in the base of the tin with a whole almond inside the stone cavity. Place all the remaining ingredients in a mixing bowl and beat well with an electric hand mixer or wooden spoon until light and smooth – 2 to 4 minutes. Turn the creamed mixture into the tin and smooth the surface. Bake in a moderately hot oven (190°C/375°F, Gas Mark 5) for about 1 hour until well-risen and golden brown.

POACHING

To simmer a food such as fish very gently in milk, water or other liquids. (See Fish and Egg entries.)

POLENTA

A substantial type of porridge eaten in Italy; in some parts of the country it is a staple food. It is used to make gnocchi and some bread and cakes; it is often used as a substitute for semolina. Polenta is usually made with maize; it is left to cool and is then cut up into pieces, fried and served with bacon, etc., as a breakfast or supper dish.

POLENTA

METRIC/IMPERIAL
750 ml/1¼ pints water
2 × 5 ml spoons/2 teaspoons salt
225 g/8 oz finely ground polenta
freshly ground black pepper

Bring the water and salt to a steady boil in a saucepan. Slowly pour in the polenta, stirring all the time with a wooden spoon until a smooth mixture is formed. Lower the heat and simmer, stirring frequently, for 20 to 25 minutes or until it resembles thick porridge. Add pepper to taste. If a thicker polenta is required, continue cooking over a very low heat until almost too thick to stir. Serve 'porridge' consistency polenta with a meat, tomato or mushroom sauce poured over, and hand grated Parmesan cheese separately. Thick polenta can be shaped on a wooden board to a flat cake when cold, cut into slices and fried, grilled or baked to serve with small roast birds or with a hot sauce.

POLLOCK (POLLACK, COAL FISH, ROCK SALMON)

Large white fish of various species caught off the Atlantic coasts of Europe and near Newfoundland. They resemble cod and may be used in the same ways.

POLONY

An Italian dry sausage made of partly cooked or smoked bacon, pork, veal and occasionally beef, with cereal, herbs and seasonings. It is generally packed in a bright red sausage casing. It is usually sold ready to eat without further cooking. Serve sliced with pickles or as a sandwich filling.

POMEGRANATE

The fruit of a tree grown in Southern Europe, the Eastern countries and South America, which reaches this country during the late autumn. Pomegranates are about the size of an orange, of a yellowish-red colour and contain a mass of pulpy red grains. The fruit can be squeezed to obtain the juice, which when strained free of pips is used in drinks and for flavouring ices. In Persia the fruit is made into wine; a Mexican liqueur called Aguardiente is also made from pomegranates.

POMELO

A type of grapefruit, with pinkish flesh.

POMMEL

Brand name of a type of French unsalted double cream cheese.

PONT L'ÉVÊQUE CHEESE

Originally made in Normandy, France. It is a semi-hard fermented cheese, yellow in colour with a very delicate flavour. It is a summer and autumn cheese made from whole or skimmed milk. The cheese is usually sold in flat wood chip boxes.

POOR MAN'S GOOSE

A casserole dish made from liver.

METRIC/IMPERIAL
225 g/8 oz liver
seasoned flour
2 large onions
25 g/1 oz fat
2 × 5 ml spoons/2 teaspoons sage
0.5 kg/1 lb potatoes, parboiled
300 ml/½ pint stock or water

Toss the liver in the seasoned flour. Lightly fry the onions in the fat and mix with the sage. Put alternate layers of liver and onion in a casserole and top

313

with a layer of sliced potatoes. Pour in just enough liquid to cover the contents and bake in a moderate oven (180°C/350°F, Gas Mark 4) for about 1½ hours. To brown the potatoes on top, put the casserole at the top of the oven and turn up the heat for the last 30 minutes.

POPCORN

Grains of Indian corn or maize which have been roasted, the best corn for the purpose being the small cob variety known as Non-pareil. The heat converts the water in the grain into steam and causes the grain to burst open with a 'pop'. The grain so treated often develops odd shapes and usually turns inside out. Flavoured popcorn, which is frequently sold at fairs, is very popular with children.

POPE

A fish resembling the perch.

POPE'S EYE

The small circle of fat found in the centre of a leg of pork or mutton.

POPE'S NOSE

(See Parson's Nose entry.)

POPOVER

An individual batter (Yorkshire) pudding, served with roast beef. Popovers can also be flavoured with grated cheese, a little chopped onion, bacon or herbs to serve for high tea or supper. A sweet variation can be made by adding a little finely chopped apple or some other fruit to the basic batter mixture.

PLAIN POPOVERS

Make some pancake batter as described under Batter entry. Prepare 6 popover tins, or small cup-shaped moulds, well greased and thoroughly hot, and fill them two-thirds full with the batter. Bake in a hot oven (230°C/450°F, Gas Mark 8) for 20 to 30 minutes until nicely browned, very light and hollow inside. Take them out of the tins and serve at once, while they are still really hot.

POPPADUM

An Indian biscuit or bread made from potato, rice or gram flour (the last-named ground from chick peas). Poppadums are thin, round, very light and crisp. If made from gram flour they are yellowish, but whiter if made from potato or rice flour. They are fried or grilled and served with curry and other savoury dishes.

POPPY SEED

The small deep-blue seeds of one type of poppy flower are sprinkled on top of rolls, milk bread and certain plain cakes as a decoration; they are also used as a filling for yeast cakes and strudels: they have a mild but distinctive flavour. Poppy seeds are much used on the Continent.

PORK

The meat of the pig eaten fresh, as distinct from bacon and ham, which are cured. The best pork comes from young animals and is recognized by its smooth, thin skin, firm flesh and white fat. Pork should be hung for a day or two only, as it does not keep longer, especially in hot weather. For this reason pig-killing for pork usually commences in the autumn. The meat can be bought fresh and frozen at home or it can be bought ready frozen. It can be stored for up to six months in a freezer.

Pork must be well cooked, to prevent the danger of infection by trichinosis, caused by worms which are present in the meat. When thoroughly cooked, pork should look white – pink-coloured pork should never be eaten. It requires long, slow cooking, but because of the large amount of fat it contains, roast pork seldom requires to have much extra fat added or to be basted during the cooking. To counteract its richness, roast, grilled or fried pork is usually accompanied by something sweet and tart, such as apple sauce.

Like other meats, pork is a good source of animal protein and also of vitamin B1 or thiamin.

We give a list of the most usual cuts and the ways of treating them.

(See Carving entry.)

Cuts of Pork and How to Cook Them

Leg (fillet, knuckle)	Roast
Shoulder (blade-bone)	Roast
Loin – in the piece	Roast
– cut into chops	Fry, grill or bake
Spare rib	Roast
Belly (usually pickled)	Boil or stew
Hand (usually pickled)	Boil
Pork pieces	Stew or use in pie

GRILLED PORK CHOPS OR CUTLETS

Cook as described under Grilling entry, allowing at least 20 minutes for a cutlet, 25 minutes for a chop. Serve with fried apples as a garnish and serve a thickened gravy separately. Chops may be served with a barbecue sauce, which goes very well with pork.

ROAST PORK

Prepare the meat in the usual way and stuff if desired. Do not remove the skin, but score it and rub with the salt to make the crackling. To cook by the quick method allow 25 minutes per 0.5 kg/1 lb plus 25 minutes for joints with bone and 30 minutes per 0.5 kg/1 lb plus 30 minutes for boned joints. For the slow method, allow 40 minutes per 0.5 kg/1 lb plus 40 minutes. (See Roasting entry for details.) To test whether the meat is done, run a skewer into the thickest part of the joint – no juice should flow out when the skewer is removed.

Pork can be cooked from frozen if a thermometer is used to check the inside temperature. This should read 70°C/190°F. Place the joint in a cold oven set at (220°C/425°F, Gas Mark 7) and allow 25 minutes per 0.5 kg/1 lb plus 25 minutes extra from the time the oven reaches the set temperature.

Serve with apple sauce, sage and onion or walnut stuffing and a thickened gravy.

Loin of pork should be chined before roasting. For a special occasion, it is usually bent into a 'crown' and the centre filled with sage and onion stuffing. Spare ribs are usually stuffed. Pork chops also can be baked in a moderate oven (180°C/350°F, Gas Mark 4) for 45 minutes to 1 hour and served with onions, apple or pineapple rings.

SWEET AND SOUR PORK

This is a Chinese method of cooking small pieces of pork in batter and serving it with a 'sweet and sour' sauce containing both vinegar and sugar, as well as soy sauce and other ingredients. There are various recipes, but here is a typical one:

METRIC/IMPERIAL
0.5 kg/1 lb belly of pork
oil or fat for frying
2 eggs
2 × 5 ml spoons/2 teaspoons flour
2 × 5 ml spoons/2 teaspoons cornflour

FOR THE SAUCE
50 g/2 oz pickles
1 carrot
2 onions
½ can pineapple slices
2 × 15 ml spoons/2 tablespoons oil or lard
3 × 15 ml spoons/3 tablespoons soy sauce
150 ml/¼ pint stock, water or pineapple juice
2 × 15 ml spoons/2 tablespoons sugar
2 × 15 ml spoons/2 tablespoons vinegar
1 × 15 ml spoon/1 tablespoon cornflour
1 × 5 ml spoon/1 teaspoon salt

First make the sauce. Fry the pickles with the shredded vegetables and pineapple in the oil for 10 minutes. Add the soy sauce, liquid, sugar and vinegar, then simmer for 15 minutes. Mix the

cornflour with 3 × 15 ml spoons/3 tablespoons cold water, stir into the sauce and simmer for 5 minutes longer, until the mixture is translucent. Season to taste and keep hot. Cut the pork into 2.5 cm/1½ inch cubes and fry until brown. Beat the eggs with the mixed flour and cornflour. Dip the pieces of pork into the egg mixture and fry in deep fat until golden-brown, then drain well. Pour the sauce over the pork.

FILLET OF PORK CHASSEUR

METRIC/IMPERIAL
1 kg/2¼ lb pork fillet
2 × 15 ml spoons/2 tablespoons oil
2 onions, sliced
75 g/3 oz butter
225 g/8 oz button mushrooms
3 × 15 ml spoons/3 tablespoons flour
150 ml/¼ pint bay stock
150 ml/¼ pint white wine
salt
black pepper
chopped parsley
croûtons

Cut the pork into 3 cm/1¼ inch to 4 cm/1½ inch pieces. Heat the oil in a frying pan, add the pork and cook quickly to brown and seal the surface. Remove from pan, transfer to an ovenproof casserole. Heat 50 g/2 oz butter in the frying pan, add the onions and cook slowly until soft. Add the mushrooms and quickly sauté. Remove while still crisp and place over the meat. Blend the flour into the remaining pan juices, adding remaining butter and gradually add the stock and wine. Blend to a smooth consistency. Bring to the boil and simmer for 2 to 3 minutes. Adjust seasoning and pour into the casserole.

Cover and cook in a moderate oven (180°C/350°F, Gas Mark 4) for about 1¾ hours until pork is fork tender. Serve sprinkled liberally with chopped parsley. Garnish with croûtons or sliced, toasted French bread.

PORK PIE
(See Raised Pie entry.)

PORRIDGE

An oatmeal breakfast dish which originated in Scotland but is now common all over the British Isles. The name is also sometimes given to a type of thick soup made from maize, buckwheat, etc.

There are many different ways of making and eating porridge. Fine, medium or coarse oatmeal, pin-point or quick porridge oats can all be used, with water or a mixture of milk and water. The true Scottish fashion is to eat it with milk and salt and some people like to accentuate the savoury touch with a few pieces of crisply fried bacon sprinkled on top. Others prefer milk or cream and sugar, syrup or honey.

Partially cooked porridge is available as a breakfast cereal. This just requires the addition of hot milk.

OATMEAL PORRIDGE

METRIC/IMPERIAL
2 × 15 ml spoons/2 tablespoons medium oatmeal
600 ml/1 pint water
salt

Measure out the oatmeal, bring the water to boiling point, then sprinkle in the oatmeal, stirring well. Continue to stir until boiling point is again reached and boil for a few minutes, then allow to simmer (in a double saucepan if possible) for 30 minutes to 2 hours, according to the size of the grains, until the oatmeal is well swollen and tender. More boiling water may be added if necessary to make the porridge of a good pouring consistency.

Commercially prepared oats or rolled oats can be cooked very quickly, according to the directions on the packet.

PORT

A fortified wine made from grapes in Upper Douro, Portugal. Not all of the wine made in this district is made into port, production being carefully restricted by the government. To make port, partially fermented red wine is run into the barrel a quarter full of brandy; this stops the fermentation. As the wine still contains at least half of its grape sugar a strong and sweet mixture results.

The grape skins are retained during the short fermentation by treading, so that they can be used to colour and preserve the port.

The port is left to rest in vats before being taken to Vila Nova de Gaia, where it is kept in warehouses known as lodapes. It is then shipped from the nearby port of Oporto.

1. VINTAGE PORT

The port made from one years wine without the necessity for blending. It is bottled not later than three years after the harvest and left to mature in the bottle. This means that a lot of deposit (crust) forms, therefore care must be taken when serving the port.

2. LATE VINTAGE PORT

A more recent variety of port approved by the authorities. It can be bottled up to six years after the vintage which means it has longer to mature in the cask. It therefore has less deposit (crust) than a Vintage port.

3. CRUSTED PORT

Made from a blend of wines of vintage quality which may be from several harvests. It is treated in the same way as Vintage Port, therefore it has a similar amount of 'crust'.

4. TAWNY PORT

Blended wines are matured in wood casks which is a much quicker process than for Vintage port. As some of the sugar is lost the port is comparatively pale and dry. It is given its name because of the colour.

5. WHITE PORT

Made from white grapes. It is often served chilled as an apéritif.

Port must be carefully poured, so as not to disturb the acid-tasting crust which forms during storage; it is often strained into a decanter before being served. This is particularly important with Vintage Port.

PORT-SALUT (PORT DU SALUT) CHEESE

A semi-hard cheese, made originally by Trappist monks in the west of France. It is made from rennetted cows' milk in a flattened round shape, weighing 1.5 kg/3 lb to 1.75 kg/4 lb. Port-Salut is very good when eaten plain, but its flavour is scarcely strong enough for it to be used in cooked cheese dishes. Serve with black grapes, crusty French bread or crisp cheese biscuits.

PORTER

A dark-brown beer, the colour and flavour being due to roasted malt and sometimes to added burnt sugar. Stout can be made by adding molasses to porter.

PORTERHOUSE STEAK

(See Steak entry.)

POSSET

A drink made of sweetened milk curdled with treacle, ale or wine, etc., which used to be given to anyone who had a cold.

POT-ROASTING

A method of cooking meat in a saucepan or casserole with fat and a very small amount of liquid; it is particularly good for small and less tender cuts of meat. It is an ideal dish to cook in a Slow Cooker (see entry).

POT-ROAST MEAT

METRIC/IMPERIAL
1.5 kg/3 lb joint
3 × 15 ml spoons/3 tablespoons fat
water
carrot
turnip
potato

Rub the meat over with seasoned flour, then brown it in hot fat (about 3 × 15 ml spoons/3 tablespoons for a 1.5 kg/3 lb joint). Slip a low trivet under the meat, add a cupful of water, cover tightly and cook gently until tender – about 1½ to 2 hours – turning the joint occasionally. One hour before serving, add some cut-up carrot, turnip and potato. Place the meat on a hot dish, with the vegetables, and serve separately a gravy made with the juices in the pan.

POTAGE

French name for a thick soup.

POTATO

This everyday vegetable, so widely used in this country, is one of the best and cheapest of the starchy foods. In Britain about 100 kg/220 lb potatoes are consumed per head annually. The edible part of the plant is the tuber or thickened stem.

The potato plant was originally a native of South America and was introduced into Europe during the 16th century. At first the potato was a curiosity, eaten only by the rich, but, by the 19th century it had become a staple article in the diet of the poorer classes; in the case of the Irish, it became their most important food, so much so that a failure in the potato harvest led to famine and disaster.

Potatoes contain more starch than other vegetables; their vitamin content is low, but as they are eaten in such large quantities, they are an important source of vitamin C. (This applies particularly to new potatoes and to potatoes cooked in their skins.) The protein content is not high, but may be important if large quantities of potato are eaten. Potatoes also contain small amounts of minerals.

The majority of potato growers are registered with the Potato Marketing Board who guarantee money to the growers and a set standard of potatoes to the consumer. The standards are as follows:

Potatoes should be excluded if they are:—
1. Afflicted by common scab on more than half the surface.
2. Unsound or not virtually clean.
3. Tainted, damaged or diseased.
4. Badly misshapen
5. Bruised or damaged by frost or pests.
6. Affected by greening, hollow heart or water logging.

The sacks in which potatoes are packed must be clean and free from anything which would taint the contents. As potatoes are taken from the earth it is impossible to spot every blemish as they pass over the grading machine: therefore a small number of faults are tolerated.

Potatoes are also graded for size: those sold to warehouses must pass through a 7.5 cm/3 inch square riddle and stand on a 4 cm/1⅜ inch square riddle. The sale of potatoes over 16.5 cm/6½ inches in length is usually banned. However there are special arrangements for the sale of extra small or extra large potatoes.

Here are some of the best varieties:

First Earlies

ULSTER PRINCE
Rarely available in Scotland. Very good in May, June, July, August. White flesh, rarely discolours after cooking. Waxy texture, becoming floury on maturity.

ARRAN PILOT
Very good in May, June, July, August. Flesh creamy white, soft but not mealy on cooking. Mild flavour. Very good boiled and for salad.

EPICURE
Popular in Scotland. Very good in May, June, July. Flesh creamy white. Cooks with a distinctive flavour. Rarely discolours and maintains its shape. Excellent boiled.

HOME GUARD
Very good in June, July, August. Flesh creamy white, close texture. Rarely discolours after cooking. Delicate flavour. Very good boiled and for salad.

Second Earlies

MARIS PEER
Very good in July, August, September. Flesh pale cream, firm texture. Rarely discolours on cooking. Very good boiled, salad and August-September for chips.

RED CRAIG ROYAL
Very good in July, August, September. Pale cream flesh of close texture. Rarely discolours after cooking. Very good for boiled and for salad.

Maincrop

Available from September and October onwards. Towards the end of the season, April to May, after long storage the red varieties tend to lose their skin colour.

DESIRÉE
A pale cream flesh, very rarely discolours after cooking. Mealy texture. Good for most methods of cooking.

GOLDEN WONDER
Generally only available in Scotland. Cream flesh of mealy texture. Mild flavour. Excellent for jacket baked.

REDSKIN
Pale lemon flesh of mealy texture. Popular in the North of England and Scotland. Very good mashed.

KERRS PINK
Usually only available in Scotland. Creamy white flesh. Some surface sloughing on boiling. Floury texture. Very good general potato.

KING EDWARD
Creamy white flesh of mealy texture. Very rarely discolour on cooking. Slight red marks on a smooth skin. Excellent general potato.

MAJESTIC
Creamy white flesh of mealy texture. A slight tendency to discolour on cooking. Good keeping quality. Very good for roast, chipped, jacket baked.

MARIS PIPER
Creamy white flesh of mealy texture. Rarely discolours on cooking. Very good boiled, mashed.

PENTLAND IVORY
White flesh of close texture. Very good boiled, mashed, jacket baked.

Potatoes are available all the year round, as they can be satisfactorily stored for winter use; they are best kept in a dry shed, between layers of dry earth, sand or ashes; avoid moist or over-warm conditions, as these induce sprouting, while extreme cold causes frost-bite.

Potatoes do not freeze successfully raw, but for convenience they can be frozen cooked or partially cooked. Partially cooked chips are more successful than cooked. Duchesse and croquette potatoes freeze successfully (open freeze then seal). New potatoes can be boiled with mint, cooled, and frozen to give an appearance similar to canned potatoes.

Potatoes are available in cans, both whole and diced. Dehydrated potato is available in flakes, granules and powdered form.

Preparation and Cooking

Potatoes should be peeled as thinly as possible, with either a special potato peeler or a sharp, short-bladed knife. New potatoes are scraped or brushed. The potatoes should be cooked as soon as possible after peeling or scraping, but if it is necessary to let them stand for a while, they should be kept under water, to prevent discoloration. There are literally hundreds of recipes for cooking potatoes. Here are some of the methods of using them.

BOILED

Scrape, brush or peel the required number of even-sized potatoes and place in enough boiling salted water to cover them, adding a sprig of mint to new potatoes. Boil them gently till cooked: the time varies according to age, type and size, from 15 to 30 minutes. Test with a skewer and drain when they are tender. If they have been cooked in their skins, hold each on a fork and remove the skin; otherwise shake them gently over a low heat to dry off. Potatoes may, if desired, be boiled in the oven; choose a pan with a well-fitting lid, place in the coolest part of the oven and allow about twice the usual time.

Very floury potatoes break up easily, so are best boiled slowly till nearly cooked. Strain them and leave with the lid on in a warm place, to finish cooking in their own steam. Old waxy potatoes should be put on to boil in cold water and sprinkled with chopped parsley when dished up. Toss new potatoes in melted butter and sprinkle with chopped parsley.

STEAMED

Scrub the potatoes and remove a 1 cm/½ inch strip of skin round the centre of each or peel completely. Steam for about 1 hour, or until tender.

MASHED

Boil or steam the potatoes in the usual way, drain and dry off over a low heat then mash with a fork or a potato masher.

CREAMED

Mash the cooked potatoes with a knob of butter, seasoning to taste and a little hot milk. Beat them well over a gentle heat till really hot and fluffy and serve in a heated dish, sprinkled with chopped parsley.

BAKED (OR 'JACKET')

Choose even-sized potatoes, scrub and dry, prick and bake in a moderately hot oven (200°C/400°F, Gas Mark 6) until they feel soft when pinched – about 45 minutes to 1 hour for small potatoes and 1 to 1½ hours for large. To serve, cut open and insert a knob of butter.

ROAST

There are two methods of roasting, the first giving a harder skin than the second. It is usual, though not essential, to peel potatoes before roasting.

First method: Cut the potatoes into suitable-sized pieces and dust with salt. Melt some dripping in a roasting tin, put in the potatoes, turn them over in the hot fat and bake in a hot oven (220°C/425°F, Gas Mark 7) for 1 to 1¼ hours, until tender and brown. Half-way through the cooking, turn the potatoes in the fat.

Second method: Peel and cut the potatoes into suitable-sized pieces and boil them for 10 minutes in salted water, then drain off the water thoroughly. Put the potatoes into a roasting tin containing hot fat and turn them over in the fat. Cook in a hot oven (220°C/425°F, Gas Mark 7) for 45 minutes, until brown and tender, turning them over once.

SAUTÉ

After boiling the potatoes until they are just cooked, cut into slices 7 mm/⅓ inch in thickness. Fry slowly in a little butter or other fat and turn when the first side is browned. Serve very hot, sprinkled with a little chopped parsley and chives.

FRIED

Chipped: Peel the potatoes, cut them into even 5 mm/¼ inch slices and then cut the slices into strips. Place them in cold water and leave for at least 30 minutes, then drain them and dry well in a cloth. Heat some fat to a temperature of 196°C/385°F, place the potatoes in a frying basket (not too many at a time), and lower them into the hot fat. Cook for a few minutes, stirring the chips to ensure even cooking, then remove the basket from the fat. When the fat has reached a slightly higher temperature, about 200°C/395°F, place the basket of chips in it again and fry them until they are golden-brown. Drain the potatoes on soft paper, season and serve very hot.

Crisps: Scrub and peel the potatoes, then slice them very thinly into rounds. Fry them in deep fat at 200°C/395°F until they are golden brown, shaking them frequently.

Curls: These are the same as crisps, but are cut in long strips round and round the potato and are fried in the curled form.

Potato rings: Slice the potatoes about 3 mm/⅛ inch thick, then cut into rings by using pastry cutters of two different sizes. Treat as for chips.

Soufflé potatoes: Choose waxy potatoes for these. Peel and cut them into 3 mm/⅛ inch slices, then soak in cold water for 1 hour or longer. Drain and dry the slices and fry them slowly in deep fat until a few of them begin to come to the top. Remove the potatoes and raise the temperature of the fat to 200°C/395°F then plunge the potatoes into the very hot fat, adding a few at a time, and they will puff out.

DUCHESSE POTATOES

METRIC/IMPERIAL

0.5 kg/1 lb cooked potatoes
25 g/1 oz butter
1 × 15 ml spoon/1 tablespoon cream or milk
1 egg
salt
pepper

Rub the potatoes through a sieve. Melt the butter in a saucepan and add the potatoes. When warm, add the cream and beaten egg (reserving a little for glazing), season well and mix together thoroughly. Turn out on to a floured board and divide into small squares, place these on a greased baking tin, brush over with the beaten egg and mark into lines with the back of a knife. Brown in a hot oven and pile neatly in a hot vegetable dish.

If preferred, this mixture may be forced on to the tin in rosettes through a large star pipe, or a fluted nozzle may be used to make rings or 'baskets'. The potato may also be piped round a savoury dish as a border. Glaze and bake as above.

POTATO SALAD

Choose waxy potatoes, cook them and cut into 1 cm/½ inch dice. Mix together some salad cream and chopped chives, spring onions or parsley. Pour this over the potatoes and toss gently until well combined.

POTATO CAKES

METRIC/IMPERIAL

0.5 kg/1 lb potatoes
2 × 5 ml spoons/2 teaspoons salt
25 g/1 oz butter
75–100 g/3–4 oz flour

Boil the potatoes, then drain and sieve them. Add the salt and butter and work in as much flour as the potatoes will easily absorb. Turn on to a floured board and knead lightly.

For thin cakes: Roll out 5 mm/¼ inch thick and cut into rounds or triangles. Cook on a hot greased girdle or in a thick frying pan until golden-brown on both sides, about 8 to 10 minutes. Spread with butter and serve hot.

319

For thick cakes: Form the dough into a roll as thick as a rolling pin, cut off slices about 1 cm/ ½ inch thick, dust with flour and cook on a hot greased girdle or in a thick frying pan until golden-brown on both sides, about 10 to 15 minutes. Serve hot with butter.

Cold cooked potatoes can be used, but the cakes will not be so light as when freshly boiled hot potatoes are used. A little grated cheese may be included if liked.

POT-AU-FEU

A traditional French dish of meat and vegetables.

POT-AU-FEU

METRIC/IMPERIAL
1 kg/2¼ lb lean beef (brisket, flank or topside)
3 litres/5¼ pints water
salt
pepper
1 carrot, pared and quartered
1 turnip, peeled and quartered
1 onion, skinned and quartered
1 parsnip, peeled and quartered
2 small leeks, quartered and washed
2 stalks of celery, trimmed and quartered
1 small cabbage, washed and halved
bouquet garni
2 × 15 ml spoons/2 tablespoons seed pearl tapioca

Tie the meat securely to keep it in one piece, put into a large saucepan, add the water and 2 × 5 ml spoons/2 teaspoons salt, cover and simmer for 2 hours. Add the vegetables (except the cabbage) and the bouquet garni and cook for another 2 hours. Put the cabbage into the pan and continue cooking for a final 30 minutes, or until it is soft. Strain off most of the liquid, put into a pan, bring to the boil, sprinkle in the tapioca and simmer for about 15 minutes, or until the tapioca clears. The meat can be served separately, with the vegetables and any remaining cooking liquid. Adjust seasoning before serving.

POTTAGE

A thick, well-seasoned meat or vegetable soup, usually containing barley or a similar cereal, or a pulse such as lentils. When cooked, the soup should be of the consistency of thin porridge.

POTTED FISH, MEAT AND CHEESE

Various types of cooked fish and meat may be turned into a paste and preserved for a few days. (See Paste, Fish and Meat entries.)

Shrimps and prawns may also be potted whole, as follows: Shell the fish and remove the black 'vein' down the back in the case of prawns. Season them with a little salt and cayenne pepper and a pinch of ground cloves and pack tightly into jars, with a knob of butter on top. Put into a moderate oven (180°C/350°F, Gas Mark 4) for 10 minutes, remove and cover with a layer of clarified butter at least 5 mm/¼ inch thick. Keep only a few days.

Potted shrimps and prawns may be served as an appetizer or placed on toast or plain biscuits to make attractive canapés; they are also good in sandwiches.

Cheese can be mixed with softened butter or margarine and other ingredients such as garlic, sherry and seasoning, then pressed into a small pot. It should be served chilled with toast or savoury biscuits.

POTTED BEEF

METRIC/IMPERIAL
0.5 kg/1 lb lean stewing beef or shin
1 beef stock cube
150 ml/¼ pint hot water
1 clove
blade of mace
salt
pepper
50 g/2 oz butter
bayleaves

Cut off gristle and fat from meat. Put in casserole with stock cube, crumbled and dissolved in hot water, the clove, mace and seasoning. Seal casserole well and cook in a moderate oven (160°C/325°F, Gas Mark 3) for 2½ to 3 hours or pressure cook for 20 minutes. Discard clove and mace. Drain off stock and reserve.

Mince cooked meat twice, add meat juice and 25 g/1 oz melted butter. Adjust seasoning. Press into ramekins or individual soufflé dishes. Cover with remainder of butter, melted. Garnish with bayleaf. Chill. (As potted meat contains no preservative it will keep only for a few days in refrigerator.)

NB
A tasty base for open type sandwich rolls with salad.

POTTED CHEESE

METRIC/IMPERIAL
225 g/8 oz mature cheese, finely grated
50 g/2 oz soft tub margarine
1 × 5 ml spoon/1 teaspoon dry mustard
50 g/2 oz butter, melted

Beat the cheese and margarine with the mustard until well blended. Spoon into small ramekin dishes. Cover with melted butter and refrigerate until set.

POTTEEN (POTHEEN)

An Irish whiskey illicitly made from barley. It is very crude and is injurious to health.

POULTRY

This term includes all the farmyard birds (as distinct from the edible wild birds, which are classed as game). General instructions regarding preparation, etc., are given here, but detailed information about the under-mentioned types of poultry, together with roasting instructions and recipes, will be found under the individual headings:

Chicken Guinea Fowl
Duck Pigeon
Goose Turkey

CHICKENS
The present-day classification is as follows:

Poussin: Smallest grade; 4 to 6 weeks old; 0.5 kg/1 lb to 0.75 kg/1½ lb.

Broiler: The most economical one produced; 12 weeks old 1 kg/2 lb to 1.5 kg/3 lb.

Large roaster: 1.75 kg/4 lb to 3 kg/7 lb.

TURKEYS
A small turkey is better than a large cockerel and can now be obtained as small as 2.25 kg/5 lb. Special broad-breasted ones are being bred to give more meat in proportion to bone and more white meat to dark.

DUCKS
Aylesbury and Muscovy ducks are both good breeds. The broiler industry has developed ducks in much the same way as broiler chickens.

GEESE
A Michaelmas goose is less fat than a Christmas one and is therefore preferred.

PIGEONS
Tame pigeons are generally smaller than wild pigeons. Unlike the latter, they do not need hanging.

Choosing Poultry

When selecting fresh poultry choose a bird which is fresh and plump, with a well rounded breast and thin, moist, tender skin. To tell whether it is young, test the breastbone, when held between the thumb and first finger, this should feel soft and flexible; in an older bird, the gristle turns to bone, which feels hard and rigid. Pliable legs and smooth feet, with small scales and short spurs and claws, also indicate a young bird.

Many butchers and fishmongers sell fresh poultry ready prepared and drawn.

Frozen poultry is widely available from butch-

ers, supermarkets and freezer centres. This is of good quality and prepared for immediate use once thawed. It may not have quite as much flavour as fresh poultry so extra should be added in cooking. It is essential to thaw frozen birds thoroughly before cooking.

Plucking and Singeing

The bird should, if possible, be plucked while it is still warm, as the operation is then much easier. Avoid draughts while working. Place a large sheet of paper on the table under the bird. Holding the bird firmly, take two or three feathers at a time and pull sharply towards the head, in the opposite direction to the way they lie. The large feathers on the wings should be plucked singly, with pliers if necessary. Pluck out all the feathers and lastly singe off the down with a lighted taper or by holding the bird over an open flame and swinging it gently until all the down is singed off.

Poultry should be hung by the feet for 2 to 3 days in a cold, airy larder, as this improves both flavour and texture. The bird can be hung unplucked, if preferred, but it should not be drawn until required for cooking. Always protect it by wrapping it round with muslin, if the larder is not flyproof.

Drawing

Except in the case of a very young bird, the sinews in the leg should be drawn, or the legs will be tough. With a sharp knife cut a small slit in the leg, just above the claw and in the direction of the leg bone, exposing the sinews, which usually number four or five in each leg. Slip a skewer underneath each sinew in turn, then holding the foot firmly, pull the skewer – this will draw out the sinew from the flesh of the leg. Do not try to draw all the sinews at once.

Unless the bird is very young, it is usual to cut off the feet. You will probably find it easier to sever the leg at the joint. Bend the foot back, insert the knife in the joint and cut through. (Keep the feet for the giblet stock; first wash and scald them, then remove the scales, nip off the claws and add the feet to the giblets.)

To cut off the head, first cut through the skin of the neck about 5 cm/2 inches from the body. Slip back the skin and cut off the neck close to the trunk. Keep the neck for stock and discard the head. Slit the skin of the neck a little way down the back of the bird – far enough to enable you to get your fingers inside to loosen the windpipe and gullet: this greatly simplifies the drawing process.

To draw the bird, cut round the vent at the tail end with scissors or a sharp knife, taking care to avoid puncturing the entrails. The hole should be large enough to slip your fingers inside the body, then, by taking hold of the gizzard, you can draw out all the entrails, including the lungs, windpipe

321

and gullet. Reserve the giblets (liver, gizzard and heart) and any fat; dispose of the remainder. Wipe out the inside of the bird with a clean damp cloth.

THE GIBLETS

Cut out the gall-bladder from the liver keeping it intact, and discard it; discard also the flesh on which the gall-bladder rests, as this may have a bitter flavour. If the gall-bladder has burst, discard the whole liver. Carefully cut through the flesh of the gizzard up to, but not through, the crop; then peel off the flesh and discard the crop, containing the stones. Wash the liver, gizzard and heart (cut away any blood vessels round the heart) and put them with the neck (scrape this well) and scalded feet into a pan, cover with water and stew gently for 45 minutes to 1 hour. The stock obtained is used for making the gravy.

Stuffing and Trussing

Turkey and fowls are stuffed at the breast end (though it is not usual to stuff very young chickens). Loosen the skin, pack the stuffing firmly and evenly over the breast and tuck the flap of skin under. Any stuffing that remains can be put into the tail end, or rolled into balls and cooked in the dripping in the roasting tin.

Ducks and geese are stuffed at the tail end.

The object of trussing is to keep the bird a good shape so that it will be easy to carve. A trussing needle (a long needle with an eye large enough to take fine string) is useful for the job, but if one is not available, a skewer and a length of fine string may be used.

Place the tips of the pinions towards the backbone so that they hold the neck skin in position. Then set the bird on its back and press the legs well into the side, thus raising the breast. Slit the skin of the vent and put the tail (the 'parson's nose') through this.

Insert the threaded trussing needle close to the second wing joint on the right side, passing it out so as to catch the corresponding joint on the left side. Insert the needle again in the first joint of the same wing (i.e. the left side), pass it through the flesh at the back, catch the tips of the pinions and the neck skin and pass it out near the first joint of the wing on the right side. Tie the two ends of the string in a bow. To truss legs, re-thread the needle and insert it through the gristle at the right side of

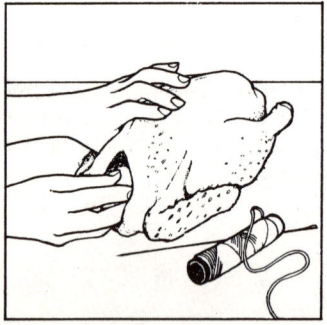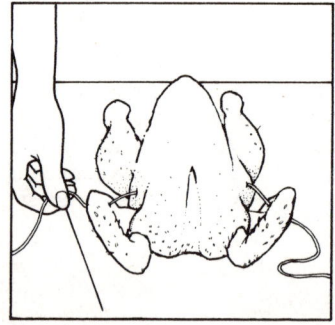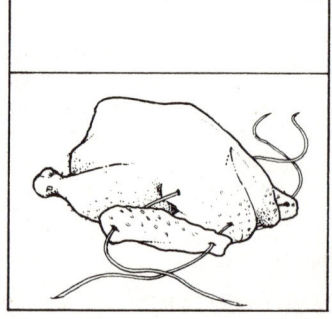

Stuffing and Trussing
1. Loosen the skin and pack the prepared stuffing firmly yet evenly into the breast cavity until no more stuffing will fit.

2. Insert the trussing needle close to the second wing joint (on the right side), passing it out through the corresponding joint on the other side.

3. Insert the needle again into the first joint of the same wing, pass needle through flesh at the back catching tips of pinions, neck skin and right wing.

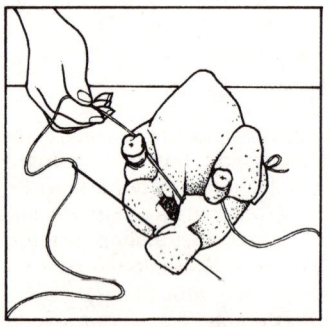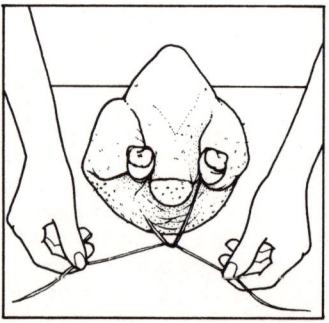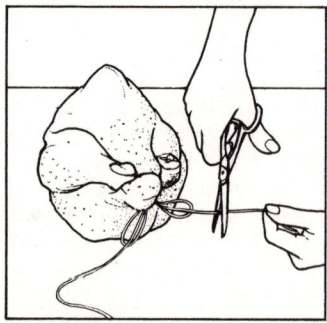

4. To truss legs, insert needle through gristle at right side of 'parson's nose', over right leg, through base of breast bone.

5. Carry thread over the left leg, through gristle at left side of 'parson's nose' then behind legs.

6. Tie together firmly to keep it in position.

the 'parson's nose'. Pass the string over the right leg, through the skin at the base of the breast-bone, over the left leg, through the gristle at the left side of the 'parson's nose', then carry it behind the legs and tie firmly to keep it in position.

Failing a trussing needle, insert the skewer right through the bird just below the thigh bone. Turn the bird on its breast. First, catching in the wing pinions, pass the string under the ends of the skewer and cross it over the back. Turn the bird over and tie the ends of the string together round the tail, at the same time securing the drumsticks.

Boning

For certain dishes, such as galantine of chicken, it is necessary to bone a fowl before cooking it. A boiling fowl is quite suitable to use in this way. First pluck, draw and clean. Cut off the tip of the wings and bone the bird carefully as follows. Using a small, sharp knife, slit down the centre back and separate the flesh from the bones, gradually turning the flesh inside out. Remove the bones, then continue working around the bird to the breast-bone. Work the flesh from the breast-bone and remove the carcass. Finally, turn the bird the right side out.

Cooking Poultry

The most traditional method is to roast poultry but interesting stews and casseroles can be made with the addition of vegetables, fruit, stock and wine. The birds may be left whole, jointed or first cooked and the flesh removed. The latter is popular for serving in a rich creamy sauce. Poultry is frequently used in Chinese and Indian dishes as it blends well with spices.

POUND CAKE

A fruit cake, so-called because all the ingredients used to be added in 1 lb quantities. A more practical version is the 'half-pound cake'. Despite the changeover to metrication no doubt this traditional cake recipe will continue to be used in old measures with the name remaining.

HALF-POUND CAKE

METRIC/IMPERIAL
225 g/8 oz butter or margarine
225 g/8 oz caster sugar
4 eggs, beaten
225 g/8 oz seedless raisins
225 g/8 oz mixed currants and sultanas
100 g/4 oz glacé cherries, halved
225 g/8 oz plain flour
1 × 2.5 ml spoon/ ½ teaspoon salt
1 × 2.5 ml spoon/ ½ teaspoon mixed spice
4 × 15 ml spoons/4 tablespoons brandy
few halved walnuts

Line a 20 cm/8 inch round cake tin with double greased greaseproof paper. Cream the fat and sugar together until pale and fluffy. Add the eggs a little at a time, beating well after each addition. Mix the fruit, flour, salt and spice and fold into the creamed mixture, using a metal spoon. Add the brandy and mix to a soft dropping consistency. Put the mixture in the tin, level the top and put on the nuts. Bake in a cool oven (150°C/300°F, Gas Mark 2) for about 2½ hours. Turn out and cool on a wire rack.

PRAIRIE OYSTER

A drink sometimes given to invalids and also to those suffering from a 'hangover'; it is made from an unbroken raw egg, and so slightly resembles an oyster in appearance and consistency.

METRIC/IMPERIAL
1 × 2.5 ml spoon/ ½ teaspoon Worcestershire sauce
a squeeze of lemon juice
a pinch of salt
1 egg

Put the sauce, lemon juice and salt into a wine glass and break in the egg.

PRALINE

A confection of nuts and caramelized sugar, often used as a centre for chocolates and to flavour and decorate puddings; also the name of a French sweet, an almond encased in sugar.

To make praline: Rinse 100 g/4 oz unblanched almonds in cold water. Place 100 g/4 oz sugar and 75 ml/⅛ pint water in a heavy based saucepan and heat gently until the sugar has melted. Bring to the boil, add the almonds and continue boiling, brushing the sides of the pan with a damp pastry brush to prevent sugar crystals forming. When the mixture is a rich brown caramel colour (i.e., at a temperature of about 193°C/380°F to 240°C/400°F, pour it on to an oiled baking sheet or marble slab. Allow to cool and set, then break it up roughly with a rolling pin and store in an airtight tin, to use as required.

PRAWN

Prawns, which resemble large shrimps, are obtainable all the year round, but are at their best during the spring and summer. They are usually sold ready boiled. When caught, they are of a greyish-brown colour, but after boiling they turn bright pink, which makes them a decorative addition to a salad, mayonnaise or appetizer. They have an excellent flavour and make a good stuffing for white fish, omelettes, patties, etc. Prawns are used in sauces, scalloped and curried dishes and savouries of various kinds, also in cocktails. The majority of prawns sold are frozen, these being of excellent quality; they are also available in jars and cans.

PREPARATION AND SERVING
For most purposes, prawns are taken out of the shells and the black 'vein' down the back is removed. The heads are usually kept for decoration.

To serve prawns simply, shell them, garnish with lemon and parsley and offer brown bread and butter as an accompaniment.

To boil freshly caught prawns: Wash the prawns thoroughly. Heat some water, adding salt in the proportion of 15 g/½ oz salt to 600 ml/1 pint of water; when it boils put in the prawns and cook for about 8 minutes. Skim off the scum during the boiling and drain the fish thoroughly.

(See Potted Meat and Fish entries.)

PRESERVATIVE

This term legally denotes any substance which is capable of inhibiting, retarding or arresting the process of fermentation, acidification or other decomposition of food or of masking any of the evidences of putrefaction. It does not include the traditional preservatives, salt, saltpetre, sugars, vinegars, acetic or lactic acid, alcohol or potable spirits, spices, herbs, hop extract, essential oils used for flavouring, glycerine, or any substance added by the process of curing known as smoking.

The only permitted preservatives are:

SULPHUR DIOXIDE, INCLUDING SULPHITES
This is the only preservative permitted in jam. It is also allowed in other foods, such as sausage and sausage-meat; fruit and fruit pulp (not dried); dried fruit; crystallized glacé fruit; sugar and syrup; cornflour; liquid glucose; gelatine; non-alcoholic wines, cordials and fruit juices, sweetened or unsweetened; beer, cider and alcoholic wines; sweetened mineral waters.

BENZOIC ACID
Pickles and sauces are permitted to contain benzoates. These are also permitted in non-alcoholic wines, fruit juices, soft drinks, sweetened mineral waters, brewed ginger beer and coffee extract.

SODIUM AND POTASSIUM NITRATE
These may be added to bacon, ham or articles of food containing bacon and ham.

DIPHENYL AND O-PHENYLPHENOL
Only some fruits may be preserved with these substances.

PROPRIONIC ACID AND SORBIC ACID
Used with flour products.

Preserving
One of the greatest advances in human nutrition

has been the discovery of various methods of keeping food in good condition from the season when it is abundant to the winter and spring seasons, when few cereal and vegetable crops are available and when it is correspondingly difficult to feed animals.

The main causes of deterioration of food are the micro-organisms, the moulds, bacteria and yeasts. Food is also spoiled by staling or drying and by being contaminated with dirt or pests, but preserving is generally directed against the above mentioned micro-organisms.

Moulds grow on many foods, but particularly on cheese, meat and sweet foods. They are not harmful and can be scraped off, but they do indicate that the food is old or has not been stored properly.

Bacteria attack many foods and some types are harmful. Acid foods are less likely to be infected by harmful bacteria than other foods. Bacteria can be destroyed by heat, some more quickly than others.

Yeasts grow in sugary foods, fermenting the food in the growing process and therefore producing alcohol.

To sum up, the micro-organisms are not always harmful (and are in actual fact important in many processes, such as the making of cheese and wine). However, to keep food for some time it must be protected from these organisms.

The methods are broadly speaking:
1. Heat treatment
2. Refrigeration
3. Drying (dehydration)
4. Treatment with chemicals.

Some methods have been in use for centuries. Drying, for example, was certainly applied to fish and meat 4,000 years ago. The addition of chemicals, particularly salt, sugar and vinegar, is also traditional. Canning, bottling and more recently, freezing and new methods of drying, are now widening the scope of preserving, so that it is possible to obtain an enormous variety of foods from all parts of the world and at all times of the year.

Some foods (e.g., grains, and such root vegetables as potatoes) require comparatively little special treatment, suitable storage conditions being sufficient, but the perishable foodstuffs such as meat and eggs require very careful preservation.

In the home, the chief methods used are freezing, bottling and the making of jam, jelly, marmalade and pickles, candied fruit and wines. Drying, salting and smoking are nowadays rarely carried out at home.

(See Bottling and Freezing entries.)

PRESSED BEEF

Boned brisket beef, which has been salted, cooked, pressed and glazed. It is served cold, with salad.

PRESSURE COOKERY

A pressure cooker cuts down lengthy cooking times and saves fuel and money. It is a great help for specific jobs like steaming puddings, cooking pulses, making stock, etc., which will otherwise be very time consuming.

There are a wide range of pressure cookers on the market today in varying sizes and finishes. Large families and freezer owners will find a big one most useful, otherwise, as a rough guide you'll need a 4.5 litre/8 pint model for a household of 2 to 3 people; a 5.5 litre/10 pint to 7.5 litre/13 pint model for 4 to 6 people. For preserving and steaming puddings you need a cooker with a 3 pressure control (usually low, medium and high, or 2.25 kg/5 lb, 4.5 kg/10 lb and 6.75 kg/15 lb), while for processing large bottling jars you will require one of the models with a domed lid. If the pan is to be used on a solid hotplate, check that it has a thick, heavy base.

Directions for use vary from make to make so you should read and follow the manufacturer's instructions carefully.

With most cookers the prepared food is put into the pan with the required quantity of liquid, the lid closed and fixed into position and the pressure cooker placed over high heat (unless otherwise stated). When steam flows from the valve on top, the weights are put into place and the contents brought to pressure – recognizable by the muttering noise produced. At this point the heat is reduced and the timing of the cooking period calculated from then.

To get the best from your pressure cooker there are a few points to note. Quantities and times here are for use with 4.5 litre/8 pint to 7 litre/12 pint models.
1. Do not overfill the cooker – it should never be more than two-thirds full for solid foods and half-full for liquids, cereals and preserves. Models with a domed lid may be filled with solids to within 2.5 cm/1 inch to 5 cm/2 inch of the pan rim.
2. Cooking times will vary according to the quality of the food and the thickness of the pieces. When in doubt (e.g. with root vegetables that seem particularly young and tender) cook for a slightly shorter time than stated in the table. If necessary you can always bring the cooker to pressure again for a minute or so but nothing can be done about overcooked food.
3. Before opening the pan, let the pressure drop to normal. This is done either quickly or slowly, according to what is being cooked. For example, cereals and pulses, which tend to froth up and clog the vent, should be allowed to reduce slowly.

To reduce pressure quickly, take the pan to the sink and run cold water over it for a few seconds without wetting the valve or the vent. Lift the weight gently with a fork to check there is no

hissing before removing the weight and the lid. If hissing persists, run more cold water until it stops. To reduce pressure slowly, leave the pan at room temperature until the weight can be lifted without hissing.
4. All pressure cookers should have a safety valve designed to operate and release steam if the pressure rises above 9 kg/20 lb. This may occur if the pan boils dry or the vent becomes blocked by dirt, grease or food. If the valve does blow, inspect the vent, clean it if necessary and see that there is sufficient liquid in the pan before replacing the safety valve, resetting the pressure and cooking again.
5. Pressure cookers should be kept completely clean. The vent should be inspected and washed after each use and the gasket or rubber ring round the lid kept free of grease and food particles. Store the pan with the lid upturned in it.

If steam escapes round the rim, remove the rubber gasket, rub it with oil, stretch it slightly and replace. Renew the gasket if steam continues to escape.

Stocks and Soups
Any recipe may be used though it may be necessary to reduce the liquid to conform with the maximum amount the pan can take. Put all ingredients into the cooker (the trivet should not be used), bring to the boil without putting the lid on, skim the surface and fix the lid. Lower the heat and bring slowly to high 6.75 kg/15 lb pressure then reduce the heat and cook for 45 minutes. Except when making soup from pulses reduce the pressure quickly using cold water.

Meat and Poultry
You have a choice of three methods.

Boiling: This is suitable for salt meat such as silverside or brisket. Soak the meat overnight in cold water. Drain, put the meat in the pan without the trivet and add 1 small onion, 1 carrot and a stick of celery and cover with water. Allow 15 to 20 minutes per 0.5 kg/1 lb, depending on the thickness and size of the joint.

Pot roasting: This is the nearest to pot roasting that can be achieved in a pressure cooker. It is suitable for lean cuts such as topside which go a little dry if roasted in the ordinary way in the oven, and fresh silverside or brisket.

Rub some seasoning into the meat and brown it all over in hot fat. Put the meat on the trivet and add water as follows: 300 ml/½ pint for a joint of 1.5 kg/3 lb or less; 150 ml/¼ pint extra for every further 1 kg/2 lb of meat. Allow 15 to 18 minutes per 0.5 kg/1 lb, depending on the size and thickness of the meat.

Braising: Prepare the joint of meat and a bed of

vegetables as for ordinary braising, add the normal amount of liquid and allow 15 to 18 minutes per 0.5 kg/1 lb, depending on the size and thickness of the joint.

Chops and liver can be prepared as for a large piece of meat, but are cooked for 7 to 8 minutes only.

BACON AND HAM

All boiling cuts of ham and bacon, particularly the cheaper cuts of bacon (e.g. collar, flank, streaky), can be treated in this way. Soak for 3 to 4 hours in cold water and drain. Put in the pan with 300 ml/ ½ pint of water for a joint weighing 1.5 kg/3 lb or less and an extra 150 ml/¼ pint for each extra 0.5 kg/1 lb above this weight. (It is unlikely that a joint above 2.25 kg/5 lb would fit in the cooker.) Cook for 12 minutes per 0.5 kg/1 lb. A few vegetables such as onion, carrot, celery or turnip, and a bouquet garni, improve the flavour considerably.

BOILING FOWL

Pressure cooking is ideal for softening older and tougher birds. Rub seasoning on to the outside, put the bird on the rack, add 300 ml/ ½ pint to 400 ml/¾ pint water, depending on the length of cooking, and cook for 10 to 12 minutes per 0.5 kg/1 lb, according to size and age. If you wish you can finish the bird by browning it in a hot oven (220°C/425°F, Gas Mark 7) for about 15 minutes.

Alternatively, brown the bird in hot fat, put it on a bed of browned vegetables, add just enough water to cover these and cook for 10 minutes per 0.5 kg/1 lb.

STEWS AND CASSEROLE DISHES

Most recipes for a stew or casserole can be adapted for use in a pressure cooker; reduce the cooking liquid if necessary so that it does not exceed 600 ml/1 pint and add any thickening (usually in the form of blended flour or cornflour) at the end of the processing in the pressure cooker.

Beef stew: The best flavour and colour are obtained if the meat is tossed in seasoned flour and browned lightly before cooking. Cook for about 20 minutes (depending on the quality of the meat).

Irish stew: Prepare in the usual way and cook for 15 minutes.

Veal stew: Prepare in the usual way and cook for 12 to 15 minutes. Steak and Kidney for a pudding or pie can receive their preliminary cooking in a pressure cooker. Allow 10 to 15 minutes (depending on the quality of the meat).

Ox-tail stew: Prepare in the usual way and pressure-cook for 40 to 45 minutes. Leave overnight, skim off the fatty layer and pressure-cook for a further 5 to 7 minutes before serving.

Stuffed sheep's hearts: Prepare in the usual way and allow about 30 minutes.

Tripe and onions: Cook the blanched and prepared tripe and onions for 15 minutes. Use the liquid to make the white sauce in the usual way.

Beef olives: Prepare in the usual way. Allow about 20 minutes.

Root Vegetables

1. Choose vegetables of the same size or cut them into even-sized pieces.
2. Cook at high 6.75 kg/15 lb pressure and time them accurately.
3. Use 300 ml/ ½ pint water for all vegetables except beetroot, which requires 600 ml/1 pint.

COOKING VEGETABLES

VEGETABLE	PREPARATION	TIME
Artichokes, Jerusalem	Peel and place in water containing lemon juice until required.	7 to 9 mins., depending on size
Beetroot	Wash and trim off the leaves.	20 to 35 mins., depending on size
Carrots – Old	Peel and dice or cut in rings.	3 to 4 mins.
Carrots – Young	Scrape and leave whole if small.	4 to 6 mins., depending on size.
Onions	1. Trim off root; skin and leave whole	5 to 10 mins., depending on size
	2. Chop or slice	3 to 4 minutes
Parsnips	Peel, core and cut in halves (quarters if large).	6 to 7 mins., depending on size and age.
Potatoes – Old	Peel. If medium-sized, leave whole.	8 to 10 mins., depending on size.
	If large, cut in quarters	6 mins.
Potatoes – New	Scrape and leave whole, unless large	7 to 9 mins., depending on size
Swedes, Turnips	Peel and dice	4 to 5 mins., depending on size
Pulses	Soak for 30 minutes; add 1.2 litres/ 2 pints cold water and 1 × 5 ml spoon/1 teaspoon salt	20 mins. for haricot beans, butter beans and dried peas. 15 mins. for split peas and lentils.

Sprinkle the actual vegetables with seasoning.
4. Bring quickly to pressure and reduce the pressure quickly.
5. Put in first the vegetables that require the longest cooking time. After the necessary period, reduce the pressure, open the cooker, add the other vegetables and continue cooking until ready.

PUDDINGS

1. Never fill a basin more than two-thirds full.
2. Cover the basin with double greaseproof paper.
3. Stand the basin on the rack in the pan and add 150 ml/¼ pint boiling water for every 15 minutes of the total cooking time, plus 300 ml/½ pint.
4. Cover the pan, heat until the steam flows and allow it to flow freely for the specified time.
5. Put on the weights, bring to pressure and cook for the required time.
6. Reduce the pressure slowly.

Pudding	Steam without pressure for:	Pressure	Time at pressure
Sponge: 600 ml/1 pint	15 mins.	Low 2.25 kg/5 lb	25 mins.
Sponge: individual	5 mins.	Low 2.25 kg/5 lb	15 mins.
Fruit Suet	15 mins.	Low 2.25 kg/5 lb	35 mins.
Jam or mince-meat roly-poly (wrap loosely to allow for expansion)	10 mins.	Low 2.25 kg/5 lb	25 mins.
Sponge suet	15 mins.	Low 2.25 kg/5 lb	35 mins.
Christmas Puddings: 0.5 kg/1 lb	15 mins.	High 6.75 kg/15 lb	1¾ hours
0.75 kg/1½ lb	30 mins.	High 6.75 kg/15 lb	2½ hours
1 kg/2¼ lb	30 mins.	High 6.75 kg/15 lb	3 hours

Before serving Christmas pudding, pressure cook at high 6.75 kg/15 lb pressure, without any preliminary steaming, for a further period: 0.5 kg/1 lb 20 minutes; 0.75 kg/1½ lb 30 minutes; 1 kg/2¼ lb 45 minutes.

Marmalades and Jams

Provided your cooker is one with a three-pressure gauge, it is a good idea to use it for preserving, as it saves quite a bit of time and the fruit retains its flavour and colour.

There are a few points to remember:
1. Always remove the trivet from the pressure pan.
2. Never fill the pan more than half-full.
3. Cook fruit at medium (4.5 kg/10 lb) pressure.

4. Reduce pressure at room temperature.
5. Only the preliminary cooking and softening of the fruit must be done under pressure – never cook a preserve under pressure after adding the sugar (and lemon juice, if used), but boil it up in the open pan.
6. You can adapt any ordinary marmalade or jam recipe for use with a pressure cooker by using half the stated amount of water and doing the preliminary cooking of the fruit under pressure. With marmalade, only half the required water is added when the fruit is cooked under pressure, the rest being added with the sugar. These are the times required for different fruits (all at medium (4.5 kg/10 lb) pressure):

Apples	5 minutes
Blackberries and apples combined	7 minutes
Black-currants	3 to 4 minutes
Damsons, plums and other stone fruit	5 minutes
Gooseberries	3 minutes
Marrow	1 to 2 minutes
Pears (cooking)	7 minutes
Quinces	5 minutes
Citrus fruits	20 minutes

NOTES
Soft fruits such as raspberries and strawberries need very little preliminary softening and are therefore not usually cooked in a pressure cooker.

When two fruits (e.g. blackberries and apples) are combined, the cooking times may vary.

JELLIES
The fruit used for making jellies can also be softened in the pressure cooker and this method is particularly useful for fruits which have hard skins, pips and so on.
1. Prepare the fruit according to any ordinary jelly recipe.
2. Place it in the cooker (without the trivet) and add only half the amount of water in the recipe.
3. Cook at medium 4.5 kg/10 lb pressure, then reduce the pressure at room temperature. (See note regarding times.)
4. Mash the fruit well and pour it into the prepared jelly bag. Finish in the ordinary way.

NOTE
Here are examples of the cooking times required when using fruit to make jellies.

Apples	7 minutes
Blackberry and apple	9 minutes
Black-currants	4 minutes
Damsons, plums and other stone fruit	5 minutes
Gooseberries	3 minutes
Pears (cooking)	9 minutes
Quince	7 minutes
Citrus fruits	25 minutes

PRETZEL

A brittle, hard, salted biscuit, originally made in Germany; it is formed into a looped shape resembling a letter B, sometimes said to be the initial of the alternative form, Bretzel. It is sprinkled with salt and sometimes cummin seeds.

PRICKLY PEAR

The watery, refreshing fruit of various types of cactus plants. It may be eaten raw or stewed. Often called 'Indian Fig'.

PRIMEURS

Early forced vegetables and fruit.

PROCESSED CHEESE

A medium-soft cheese manufactured by special processes from ordinary cheese of various kinds, e.g., Cheddar, Dutch, Gruyère. The rind is removed and the cheese is then ground, melted and mixed with emulsifiers and colourings, after which it is moulded into various shapes and wrapped in tin-foil. The heat to which it is subjected during the processing arrests the further growth of bacteria, therefore it keeps well.

Processed cheese has less food value than ordinary cheese as the percentage of water is higher and that of the other in-nutrients slightly lower. It creams well with butter for sandwich spreads and can be used in some cheese dishes; it has a mild uniform flavour which limits its use a little.

PROFITEROLE

This term originally meant a kind of light cake, baked on hot ashes and filled with cream or custard. Nowadays, it implies a case of choux paste, forced out into a small bun shape the size of a walnut; the cases are brushed over with beaten egg and milk and baked in a hot oven (220°C/425°F, Gas Mark 7) for 15 to 20 minutes. When the profiteroles are cooked, a hole is made in the side through which whipped cream can be inserted. Serve the profiteroles with a dark chocolate sauce poured over them.

A savoury filling can also be used for small puffs. Very small ones can be used to garnish consommé.

PROOF

(See Spirit entry.)

PROTEIN

A substance which is an essential constituent of animal and plant cells. In animals, all the muscular tissue of the body is composed of proteins, therefore protein is vitally necessary for the growth and repair of the human body, both for growing children and for adults; it also provides energy and heat.

Proteins are made up of a number of amino-acid units and there may be more than 20 different kinds of amino-acids in a single protein. The different kinds and different arrangements of the amino-acids differentiate one protein from another. In general, it can be said that animal proteins usually contain the essential amino-acids in proportions suitable for human needs, while vegetable proteins may be lacking in one or other of these acids and may therefore need to be supplemented by other protein foods, either animal or vegetable.

There is a continual turnover of protein in the body – it moves in and out of the tissues and is lost in various ways from the skin, hair, nails and other tissues. Protein is also used in producing hormones and enzymes. The amounts required vary enormously from individual to individual, so it is impossible to say exactly how much is required. Slightly more is needed by children and by pregnant and nursing mothers than by other adults. A man doing heavy work does not, however, require any more than a man in a sedentary occupation.

ANIMAL PROTEIN

The following are good animal protein foods: Meat of all kinds; game, poultry; fish; milk and milk products; cheese; eggs.

VEGETABLE PROTEIN

Plants can form their own protein from organic materials, and animals, which are unable to do this, can assimilate the protein made by plants. The foods providing vegetable protein are: soya beans (used in the form of flour); peanuts and other nuts; cereals, especially whole-grain; peas, beans and lentils.

PROVING

(See Bread entry.)

PRUNE

The purplish-black dried fruit of several special types of plum tree, the best known of which is the d'Agen plum, a native of France, but now also grown in California. The finest prune is the French Imperial, which has a thin skin, small stone and good flavour. Of the prunes grown in California, the Santa Clara is the best grade and the Californian the next. Prunes are also grown in South Africa and Australia.

The fruit is dried in various ways, some being sun-dried and some by a mixture of both methods.

Some are dipped in a caustic solution to help the drying.

Prunes supply energy and small amounts of carotene (vitamin A) and iron; they have a slightly laxative effect.

Stewed prunes (see dried fruit entry), may be served with junket, yogurt, custard, cream or ice cream, or with a cereal for breakfast. They can also be used in a variety of hot puddings: they can be sieved or liquidized to give a purée for use in cold sweets.

Prunes are sometimes included in meat dishes and savouries, as in the two recipes given here.

STUFFED PRUNES

Fill stoned prunes with anchovy butter, cream cheese with chopped nuts or other savoury stuffings, using a forcing pipe or a spoon. Serve on cocktail sticks, biscuits or toast, or in salads.

PORK AND PRUNE HOT-POT

METRIC/IMPERIAL
100 g/4 oz prunes
1 lemon
0.5 kg/1 lb pork
25 g/1 oz plain flour
salt
pepper
15 g/½ oz dripping

Cover the prunes with cold water, soak for a few hours, then stew them with the rind of a lemon until tender. Strain off the juice and reserve. Stone the prunes. Wipe the pork, cut it into neat pieces and coat in the seasoned flour. Melt the dripping in a frying pan and fry the pork until brown, then place the pork and prunes in alternate layers in a casserole. Make some brown gravy with the remaining fat, flour and about 300 ml/½ pint of the prune juice and pour this over the pork. Add the juice of the lemon, cover with the casserole lid or greased paper and cook in a moderate oven (180°C/350°F, Gas Mark 4) for about 1 hour. Serve in the casserole and accompany with new boiled potatoes and a green vegetable.

PRUNE AND APPLE ROLL

Make in the same way as a jam roly-poly (see Suet Puddings entry), substituting a mixture of soaked chopped prunes, chopped apple, sugar and marmalade for the jam. Serve with a custard sauce flavoured with vanilla.

PRUNELLE

A pale-green, sloe-flavoured French liqueur.

PTARMIGAN

A small wild bird of the grouse family, which is found in Northern Europe, including Scotland, and is in season from August 12th to December 10th; it turns white during the winter months. Other names for it are willow or rock partridge and mountain grouse. It is now rarely seen in shops.

The flavour of ptarmigan is not so good as that of grouse, but the bird may be treated in the same way; serve it with fried breadcrumbs, bread sauce and thin brown gravy and garnish with watercress. Allow one bird for 1 to 2 people.

PUDDING

A dish usually served as the sweet course of a meal (though there are some savoury ones like Steak and Kidney Pudding). The word often implies a cooked dish although nowadays, such cold sweets as soufflés, jellies and moulds are also classified as a pudding.

There are hundreds of different puddings, but most of them fall into one of the following categories:

BAKED PUDDINGS
This large class includes:
1. Pastry-based sweets, such as Fruit Pies and Flans, Bakewell Tart, Lemon Meringue Pie, Apple Strudel and sweet Vol-au-Vents.
2. Cake and yeast mixtures, such as Cottage Pudding, Eve's Pudding, Upside-down Pudding, Rum Babas and Savarin.
3. Scone mixtures, such as Fruit Crumble and Fruit Cobbler.

MILK PUDDINGS
1. Made from cereals such as rice, sago and semolina and either cooked on top of the stove or baked in the oven. They can be served hot or cold, alone or combined with eggs, fruit or other flavourings. Examples include Peach Condé, Glazed Pineapple Rice, Chocolate Semolina Whip, Tapioca, Sponge and Sago creams.
2. Junkets, made with milk treated with rennet.

STEAMED PUDDINGS
These popular puddings can be divided into:
1. Suet or rubbed-in cake mixtures, e.g., Ginger Pudding, Huntingdon Pudding, Christmas Pudding.
2. Suet pastry mixtures, e.g., Apple Suet Pudding, Syrup Pudding, Fruit Layer Pudding, Jam Roll.
3. Sponge mixtures, e.g., Castle Puddings, Chocolate and Duchess Pudding.
4. Custard and breadcrumb mixtures (cake crumbs can replace the bread), e.g., Cabinet and Saxon Puddings.

EGG PUDDINGS

These include puddings where eggs are the chief ingredients or are used as the raising or lightening agent.

1. Egg custards, which include Baked and Caramel Custard, Custard Tart; Bread and Butter Pudding and Queen of Puddings.
2. Sweet or Soufflé Omelettes, served with jam, fruit or cream.
3. Soufflés, which can be baked or steamed and served hot.
4. Meringues and meringue-based sweets, such as Meringue Baskets.

BATTER PUDDINGS

These are made from a thin mixture of milk, eggs and flour and include Fruit Batters (also Yorkshire Pudding), which are baked, Fritters or Pancakes, which are fried, Waffles, which are cooked in a special iron, and Steamed Batters.

JELLIES, CREAMS, MOUSSES, SOUFFLÉS AND MOULDS

Innumerable attractive cold sweets come into this group. They are usually set with gelatine or cornflour and can either be made in a mould and turned out before serving or made and served in sundae glasses, etc.

Examples are Table Creams, Jellies, Blancmange, Milk and Wine Jellies, Fruit Chartreuse, Fruit Creams, Honeycomb Mould, Charlotte Russe, Mousses flavoured with coffee, etc., Milanese Soufflé.

ICED SWEET PUDDINGS

These include Cream Ices, Water Ices, Sherbets and Sorbets, Parfaits, Splits, Sundaes and Bombes and desserts such as Baked Alaska, Pineapple Surprise, Fruit and Ice Cream Gâteaux and Refrigerator Cakes. A number of these may be made with bought ice cream, but if a refrigerator is available a wide variety of iced sweets can be produced.

FRUIT SWEET PUDDINGS

Fruits provide a very wide variety of flavours, colours and textures and form the basis of many delicious hot and cold sweets. Examples include Stuffed Apples, Fruit Charlotte, West Indian Pudding, Raspberry Meringue Pudding, Fruit Fool, Summer Pudding, Fruit Trifle, Bananas Flambées, Apricots in Brandy, Fruit Salad and Fruit Gâteaux.

(See individual entries for recipes.)

PUFF BALL, GIANT

The largest member of a family of fungi of rounded shape; it may grow to 30 cm/12 inches or more in diameter and while it is at the young stage, the flesh is white and cheesy, and can be eaten. To cook it, skin, slice 1 cm/½ inch thick, egg-and-crumb and fry.

PUFF PASTRY

(See Pastry entry.)

PULLET

A young hen or female fowl.

PULSES

The dried seeds of such plants as beans and peas. The most commonly used pulses are butter, haricot and soya beans, dried and split peas and lentils.

Generally speaking, pulses are useful on account of their protein content (when cooked, they have about a quarter of the protein content of cheese) and their calorific value, which in the cooked pulses is similar to that of boiled potatoes and one-third that of bread. They are particularly valuable in Eastern diets which might otherwise be short of protein. They also supply a certain amount of the B vitamins. Sprouting pulses (like the bean shoots eaten in China) also supply some vitamin C.

To cook pulse foods: Soak the pulses for 12 to 24 hours in warm water, to which a good pinch of bicarbonate of soda may be added. (This soaking is not essential for red lentils, though they soften more quickly if soaked.) Place the pulses in a pan, cover with fresh water, add seasoning and a bouquet garni and simmer gently for 2 to 3 hours, until tender: lentils take only 30 minutes to 1 hour.

See the individual entries for further details and recipes.

PUMPERNICKEL

A German black bread made of coarse rye flour.

PUMPKIN

A member of the gourd or marrow family, which can grow to a very great size. The sweet, orange-coloured flesh of the pumpkin is used in soups, meat and savoury dishes and in the popular American dish, pumpkin pie. Pumpkins have a pleasant flavour and make an interesting change in the menu. They should be allowed to mature before being eaten, the flavour is not at its best in the young vegetable.

The best method of cooking pumpkin is to peel, cut up and remove the seeds. It may then be roasted round the joint like potatoes.

Alternatively, cube and boil in water for 15 minutes, or until tender. (Add salt, if making a savoury dish.) Another method is to blanch the pumpkin in boiling water and finish the cooking in the oven, adding a knob of butter.

Cooked pumpkin may be served with cheese

sauce, added to meat in a meat pie, mixed with other vegetables in cream soups or cooked and mixed with apple for apple pie (it is better in this case to use cinnamon rather than cloves).

PUMPKIN PIE

The traditional Thanksgiving dessert in the United States.

METRIC/IMPERIAL
0.5 kg/1 lb pumpkin
200 g/7 oz shortcrust pastry
2 eggs, beaten
100 g/4 oz caster sugar
4 × 15 ml spoons/4 tablespoons milk
pinch ground nutmeg
pinch ground ginger
2 × 5 ml spoons/2 teaspoons ground cinnamon

Cut the pumpkin into pieces, remove any seeds and cottonwoolly inside part and cut off the outside skin. Steam the pieces of pumpkin between 2 plates over a pan of boiling water until tender, 15 to 20 minutes, and drain thoroughly. Mash well with a fork or purée in an electric blender.

Roll out the pastry and use it to line a 20 cm/8 inch flan case or deep pie plate; trim and decorate the edges. Beat the eggs with the sugar. Add the pumpkin, milk and spices. Blend well and pour into the pastry case. Bake in a hot oven (220°C/425°F, Gas Mark 7) for 15 minutes, then reduce the temperature to moderate (180°C/350°F, Gas Mark 4) and bake for a further 30 minutes or until the filling is set. Serve warm, with cream.

PUNCH

A drink made from a mixture of ingredients, one of which should be a spirit. It is said to derive its name from the Hindu word panch, meaning five, because it was originally made from five ingredients – the spirit arrack, sugar, spice, lemon juice and water. Punches became popular in this country in the seventeenth century. Nowadays a punch may have a base of white or red wine, cider, ale, lager, cold tea or champagne and small quantities of sherry, whisky, rum, brandy or a fruit liqueur may be added.

There are many types of punch, some served hot and some cold; they provide useful drinks for parties, as they are generally less expensive than spirits or fine wines. A glass of hot rum punch makes an excellent welcome to guests arriving on a cold winter's night and milk punch is a warming 'night-cap', while a refreshing cold fruit punch is a popular addition to a buffet party. Fruit punches can be made without any alcoholic ingredient, the sparkle being provided by ginger ale or soda water. Fresh fruits, cut in a decorative fashion are often served in a fruit-based punch.

HOT ALE PUNCH

METRIC/IMPERIAL
1.2 litres/2 pints mild ale
1 wineglass sherry
1 wineglass brandy
1 × 15 ml spoon/1 tablespoon sugar
peel and juice of 1 lemon or 2 × 15 ml spoons/2
*   tablespoons lemon squash*
a little grated nutmeg

Mix all the ingredients together in a medium-sized saucepan, bring to the boil stirring and serve piping hot.

RUM PUNCH

METRIC/IMPERIAL
1.75 litres/3 pints cold water
450 g/1 lb sugar
1 lemon
4 oranges
300 ml/½ pint strong tea
300–600 ml/½–1 pint rum

Put the water and sugar in a pan with the thinly pared rinds of the lemon and 1 orange. Stir until the sugar is dissolved, bring to the boil and boil for 5 minutes. Remove the pan from the heat and add the juice of the lemon and all the oranges, the tea and the rum. Strain and serve hot or cold.

BISHOP'S PUNCH

Stick an orange with cloves and toast it in a hot oven until soft and brown; cut into quarters and put into a saucepan. Pour 1.2 litres/2 pints port wine (heated) over the orange, add sugar to taste and allow to simmer for 30 minutes. Strain and serve.

MILK PUNCH

METRIC/IMPERIAL
½ wineglass rum
½ wineglass brandy
1 × 15 ml spoon/1 tablespoon sugar
hot milk
nutmeg

Mix the rum, brandy and sugar, place in a large glass and fill up with very hot milk. Serve at once, sprinkled with grated nutmeg.

COLD TEA PUNCH

METRIC/IMPERIAL
rind of 1 lemon
75 g/3 oz caster sugar
900 ml/1 ½ pints tea
150 ml/¼ pint rum
150 ml/¼ pint brandy

Grate the lemon rind and blend it with the sugar. Pour on the freshly made tea, stir well and set aside to become thoroughly cold. Strain carefully and add the rum and brandy.

PARTY PUNCH

METRIC/IMPERIAL
1.2 litres/2 pints cider
1 wineglass brandy
1 wineglass sherry
1½ bottles soda water
1 slice each of lemon, orange and grapefruit (or other fruit as available)
a sprig of mint

Mix all together and stand the punch on ice for 30 minutes before serving. Decorated ice cubes (see Ice entry) add a touch of colour.

PURÉE

Fruit, vegetable, meat or fish which has been pounded, sieved or liquidized (usually after cooking) to give a smooth, finely divided pulp. A soup made by sieving or liquidizing vegetables with a liquor in which they were cooked is also called a purée.

The thickness of the purée depends on the amount of liquid present before sieving; a purée of cooked green peas or potatoes, for example, is very stiff and can be piped for decoration. Tomato purée, on the other hand, is soft and runny and usually requires thickening before it can be used. When making a fruit purée for gelatine sweets,

it is advisable to use very little water for stewing the fruit, otherwise the purée will be too thin.

The food is usually sieved or liquidized while still warm; in the case of meat and fish, the bones and gristle must first be removed and the flesh can then be pounded in a mortar.

A wire sieve may be used for vegetables and meat, but a nylon or hair one is better for fruit, to avoid discoloration and a metallic taste.

PURI

A kind of Indian chapatti made on special occasions; it is fried in deep fat.

PURL

An old-fashioned English winter drink. One kind was made by gently warming 300 ml/½ pint of ale, adding a dash of bitters and finally a liqueur glass of whisky or brandy.

An alternative recipe was made by warming 600 ml/1 pint of ale with 300 ml/½ pint milk, sweetening to taste and finally adding a wineglass of gin, brandy or whisky.

PURSLANE

An annual herb grown and used as a salad vegetable or flavouring material.

PYRIDOXINE

One of the B vitamins. (See Vitamins entry.)

QUAIL

The quail, which used to nest in large quantities, in this country, was formerly treated as a game bird, but it has now become so scarce that it has been given complete protection under the Protection of Birds Act, 1954, and can no longer be classed as game. However, quails are now being cultivated as a domesticated bird on quail farms, and are available all year, fresh or frozen. The particular species used is the Japanese quail, which is slightly different from the common quail.

There are recipes for quails in aspic, stuffed quail, and braised quail, though probably the favourite recipe is for roast quail (see below). The eggs are also used in various ways. (See Eggs entry.)

ROAST QUAIL

Allow 1 bird per person. Pluck and singe and if necessary draw it from the neck end. Remove the head and neck, cut off the wings from the first joint, pick out the shot and wash the bird. Scald and scrape the feet. If desired, place a large oyster in the centre of each bird. Turn the wings under to hold the neck skin in place, push the legs forward towards the wings and secure in position with fine string, using a trussing needle. Wrap the bird in a vine leaf and a piece of fat bacon and roast in a hot oven (230°C/450°F, Gas Mark 8) for 15 to 20 minutes. Remove the string, vine leaf and bacon and place each bird on a round of fried bread or toast which has been spread with the pounded quail liver cooked in butter. Garnish with watercress and fried breadcrumbs and brown gravy.

QUASSIA

A tree found in South America and the West Indies, from which is extracted a bitter oil, used for medicinal purposes.

QUEEN CAKE

A small, light, rich cake, containing dried fruit and baked in patty tins or paper cases.

QUEEN CAKES

METRIC/IMPERIAL
100 g/4 oz butter or margarine
100 g/4 oz caster sugar
2 eggs, beaten
100 g/4 oz self raising flour
50 g/2 oz sultanas

Place 12 to 16 paper cases on a baking sheet, or for a better finished shape put them into patty tins. Cream the fat and sugar until pale and fluffy. Add the egg a little at a time, beating well after each addition. Fold in the flour and then the fruit, using a tablespoon. Two-thirds fill the cases with the mixture and bake in a moderately hot oven (190°C/375°F, Gas Mark 5) for 15 to 20 minutes, until golden.

VARIATIONS
Replace the sultanas by one of the following:

METRIC/IMPERIAL
50 g/2 oz chopped dates
50 g/2 oz chopped glacé cherries
50 g/2 oz chocolate chips
50 g/2 oz chopped or crystallized ginger

QUEEN OF PUDDINGS

A pudding made of custard and breadcrumbs, with a meringue topping. Usually it is flavoured with lemon rind and vanilla, but for variety, apricots or peaches may be placed on top of the custard mixture instead of jam when it is set and before it is covered with the meringue.

QUEEN OF PUDDINGS

METRIC/IMPERIAL
450 ml/¾ pint milk
25 g/1 oz butter
grated rind of ½ lemon
2 eggs, separated
50 g/2 oz caster sugar
75 g/3 oz fresh white breadcrumbs
2 × 15 ml spoons/2 tablespoons red jam

Warm the milk, butter and lemon rind. Whisk the

333

egg yolks and half of the sugar lightly and pour on the milk, stirring well. Strain over the breadcrumbs, pour into a greased 1.2 litre/2 pint ovenproof dish and leave to stand for 15 minutes. Bake in a moderate oven (180°C/350°F, Gas Mark 4) for 25 to 30 minutes, until lightly set; remove from the oven. Warm the jam and spread it over the pudding. Whisk up the egg whites stiffly and add half the remaining sugar; whisk again and fold in the remaining sugar. Pile the meringue on top of the jam and bake for a further 15 to 20 minutes, until the meringue is lightly browned.

QUENNELLE

Quennelles consist of fish or meat, cooked, liquidized, sieved or pounded to a forcemeat consistency and bound with beaten egg; this mixture is moulded into egg shapes with a spoon or dropped from a forcing tube straight into boiling stock or water. If made the size of a croquette, then egg-and-breadcrumbed and fried, quennelles may be served as an entrée.

FISH QUENNELLES

METRIC/IMPERIAL
225 g/½ lb cod or any similar white fish – pike is the classic choice
25 g/1 oz butter
3 × 15 ml spoons/3 tablespoons flour
4 × 15 ml spoons/4 tablespoons milk
1 egg, beaten
1 × 15 ml spoon/1 tablespoon cream
salt
pepper

Cook the fish and purée it in an electric blender. Melt the fat, stir in the flour and cook for 2 to 3 minutes. Remove the pan from the heat and gradually stir in the milk. Return the pan to the heat and stir until the sauce thickens. Remove from the heat and stir in the fish, egg, cream and a generous amount of salt and pepper. Mix together until thoroughly combined.

Grease a large frying pan, three-quarters fill it with water and heat to simmering point. Using 2 wetted spoons, make the fish mixture into egg-shaped or oval pieces, put into the pan and simmer for about 10 minutes, basting well, until the quennelles are swollen and just set. Remove them from the pan with a slotted spoon and serve coated with a well flavoured sauce.

QUETSCH

A pure white, potent liqueur distilled in France (chiefly in Alsace) from the type of plum of the same name and flavoured with the plum-stone kernels.

QUICHE

A savoury custard tart, a speciality of Lorraine and Alsace. There are many variations to the filling, as mushrooms, fish, celery, sweetcorn, ham or peppers can be included.

QUICHE LORRAINE

METRIC/IMPERIAL
150 g/5 oz shortcrust pastry, i.e., made with 150 g/ 5 oz flour, etc.
75–100 g/3–4 oz lean bacon, chopped
75–100 g/3–4 oz Gruyère cheese, thinly sliced
2 eggs, beaten
150 ml/¼ pint single cream or creamy milk
salt
pepper

Roll out the pastry and use it to line an 18 cm/7 inch plain flan ring or sandwich cake tin, making a double edge. Cover the bacon with boiling water and leave for 2 to 3 minutes, then drain well. Put into the pastry case with the cheese, mix the eggs and cream, season well and pour into the case. Bake in a moderately hot oven (200°C/400°F, Gas Mark 6) for about 30 minutes, until well risen and golden.

There are many variations on this traditional dish – it can be made with bacon or cheese or both as shown. The cheese and bacon given above may be replaced by 75 g/3 oz blue cheese mixed with 175 g/6 oz cream cheese.

In some recipes lightly boiled rings of onions or leeks are used instead of, or as well as, the bacon.

QUICK FREEZING

The commercial process of freezing food. It is a very much quicker process than freezing at home. The difference is that the temperature drops at great speed through the water-freezing zone (known as 'the zone of maximum crystal formation'). Between 0°C/32°F to −4°C/25°F, water freezes into ice crystals. If this happens slowly the crystals are large and tend to damage the cells of the food; if it takes place rapidly, the crystals are small, the cells remain undamaged and less deterioration takes place in the appearance and texture of the food.

Quick freezing is carried out in three main ways:
1. Plate freezing: the food is packed in rigid containers and placed between metal shelves in which a refrigerant, often liquid ammonia at −33°C/−26°F circulates, freezing the packed food in 2 to 3 hours.
2. Air Blast Freezing: the food is placed on metal trays and loaded onto trolleys, which then move slowly through a tunnel in which air at −30°C/−22°F is forced in the opposite direction. This takes 2 to 3 hours.

3. Flo Freezing: an ideal method for small foods, peas, sweetcorn. Cold air at −40°C/−40°F is forced upwards through perforated trays as the food moves along a tunnel and is frozen in 3 to 8 minutes. This method keeps individual items separate, they can then be packed in polythene bags.

After quick freezing the food is transferred to a cold store at −29°C/−20°F, until required for distribution. It leaves the factory in insulated lorries at −28°C/−18°F and is stored in the shop cabinet at less than −18°C/0°F. Freezing preserves the colour and flavour of foods better than other methods of preserving and also retains the nutritional value.

(See Freezing entry.)

QUINCE

The hard, dry-textured fruit of a tree belonging to the apple family, which grows in temperate climates. When ripe, in September or later, quinces become golden-yellow or slightly reddish in colour and resemble apples or pears in appearance. They have an unusual and powerful smell and are therefore best stored apart from other fruit.

Quinces are not suitable for eating raw, but are good when baked like apples and they make excellent jams and jellies, alone or mixed with apples, cranberries, pumpkin or marrow. In Portuguese the name for this fruit is Marmelo; from this came the word marmalade, which originally meant quince jam.

To ensure a good set when making quince jam or jelly, the juice of 2 lemons can be added to the water in which the fruit is cooked.

QUINCE JAM

METRIC/IMPERIAL
1 kg/2 lb quinces (prepared weight)
1 litre/1¾ pints water
1.5 kg/3 lb sugar

Peel, core and slice the quinces and then weigh them. Put them in a pan with the water and simmer very gently until the fruit is really soft and mashed. Add the sugar, stir until it is dissolved and boil the mixture rapidly until setting point is reached. Pot and cover the jam in the usual way.

QUINCE JELLY

METRIC/IMPERIAL
1.75 kg/4 lb quinces
rind and juice of 3 lemons
3.5 litres/6 pints water
sugar

Wash the quinces and chop. Simmer, covered, with 2.25 litres/4 pints water, the lemon rind and juice until tender – about 1 hour; strain through a jelly bag. Return the pulp to the pan and add the remaining water. Bring to the boil, simmer for 30 minutes, then strain. Mix the two extracts together and measure. Bring to the boil and add 450 g/1 lb sugar to each 500 ml/1 pint of extract. Return to the boil and boil vigorously until setting point is reached. Pot and cover in the usual way.

(See Quince Butter entry, under Fruit Butter entry.)

RABBIT

In this country both wild rabbits and those bred in captivity are eaten, the tame ones being considered to have the better flavour. Home-bred rabbits are in season during the winter, while imported frozen ones are available during much of the year. Both fresh and frozen rabbits are usually sold ready cleaned and skinned; if unfrozen, avoid any which have flesh of a bluish colour, as they will probably be stale.

Rabbits give a white meat which has a low fat content and a high percentage of animal protein, so they form an easily digested, nutritious food, especially suitable for those on a light diet. A really good rabbit has an excellent flavour, rivalling that of chicken.

Preparation and cooking: A rabbit should be paunched within a few hours of killing (see Hare entry for method of paunching and skinning). Before cooking, it should be washed and soaked in salted water for a time, to make the flavour less strong. It may then, if required, be jointed like a hare.

Rabbits may be cooked in almost any way suitable for other types of meat, though only young, tender ones should be roasted or fried. They are frequently used in a fricassée (see Fricassée entry), braised or jugged; they make a good pie filling and lend themselves well to such made-up dishes as jellied moulds and terrines. In casseroles the meat blends well with coriander, saffron, tomatoes, cider, prunes and vegetables.

POACHER'S PIE

METRIC/IMPERIAL
*200 g/7 oz shortcrust pastry, i.e., made with 200 g/
7 oz flour, etc.*
4 rabbit joints, chopped
2 potatoes, peeled
1 leek, trimmed and washed
3–4 rashers bacon, rinded and chopped
salt
pepper
1 × 15 ml spoon/1 tablespoon chopped parsley

a pinch of mixed dried herbs
stock or water
beaten egg to glaze

Make the pastry. Wash the rabbit pieces; slice the potatoes and leek. Fill a pie dish with alternate layers of rabbit, bacon and vegetables, sprinkling each layer with seasoning and herbs. Half-fill the dish with stock or water, cover with the pastry and make a hole in the centre to let the steam escape. Decorate with leaves made from the pastry trimmings and brush with egg. Bake in a hot oven (220°C/425°F, Gas Mark 7) until the pastry is set, then reduce the temperature to moderate (160°C/325°F, Gas Mark 3) and cook for about 1¼ hours, until the meat is tender.

NOTE
This recipe may be used for individual pies if you prefer.

ROAST RABBIT

Fill rabbit with veal stuffing (see Forcemeat entry) and sew it up. Truss it by tying the legs in a bent position, so that the rabbit is in a sitting attitude. Cover with bacon or a little fat and for the first 45 minutes cover with greased paper also. Bake in a moderate oven (180°C/350°F, Gas Mark 4) for 1 to 1½ hours, until tender. Serve with gravy and bacon rolls.

RADISH

This small red or white-and-red vegetable has a characteristic, slightly hot flavour which makes it a useful addition to many kinds of salad. It is available chiefly in summer, though it is marketed to some extent at other times.

Radishes should be eaten while young and tender and are best served raw. If they are to be eaten whole, cut off the tops, leaving 1 cm/½ inch of stalk, and remove any large roots, then wash them well. Larger radishes may be boiled (unpeeled) in salted water until tender, 15 to 20 minutes. Serve with a well-seasoned white or parsley sauce. When used as a garnish, radishes may be sliced thinly, or cut into 'roses' or 'lilies'. (See Garnish entry.)

Radish tops may be cleaned and cooked in salted water like other green vegetables.

RAGOÛT

A stew of meat or poultry and vegetables, browned in a little fat and then gently simmered. It can be flavoured with mushrooms, port wine, tomatoes, etc. A mutton ragoût is often known by the French name Navarin.

RAGOÛT OF POULTRY OR MEAT

METRIC/IMPERIAL
1 duck, chicken or rabbit or 225 g–0.5 kg/½–1 lb
   lean meat
seasoning
plain flour
dripping
900 ml/1½ pints stock
1 × 15 ml spoon/1 tablespoon vinegar
4 cloves
8 allspice
8 peppercorns
1 clove of garlic, chopped

Roast the bird or rabbit for 25 minutes, if it is young; otherwise joint it, dip in seasoned flour and fry until brown in the dripping; cut meat into small pieces and fry it. Place in a casserole and brown 25 g/1 oz flour in the remaining dripping. Add the stock, vinegar, spices (tied in muslin) and garlic, then pour into the casserole and cook in a moderate oven (160°C/325°F, Gas Mark 3) for 1 hour or longer, till tender (old birds will need 2½ hours). Alternatively, the ragoût may be simmered gently in a saucepan on top of the stove. If desired, include 100 g/¼ lb mushrooms or tomatoes or substitute a wineglass of red wine for the vinegar.

RAISED PIE

A pie made with hot-water crust pastry (see Pastry entry), which becomes firm during baking and retains its shape. Raised pies are usually served cold and after baking are filled up with stock which sets into a jelly.

There are two ways of shaping a raised pie: (1) by using a special raised pie mould or a greased cake tin; (2) by moulding the pie by hand, sometimes with a jam jar or small tin as a basis.

Making a Raised Pie
Pastry made with 0.5 kg/1 lb flour is required to fill a 15 cm/6 inch cake tin.

Cut off a quarter of the pastry, wrap it in greaseproof paper and leave it in a warm place. Mould the remaining pastry round a cake tin, jam jar or the hand; if a mould is used, press the pastry well into the mould. In both cases, take care to make the base and sides of the same thickness. Add the filling. Roll the smaller piece of pastry into a round and cover the pie, pinch the edges together and flute the border or cut with scissors and bend down alternate pieces. Pin a stiff paper band round pie to keep the shape, make a hole in the centre top and add a few leaves made from pastry trimmings. Brush over with beaten egg and place on a greased baking tin. Bake in a hot oven (220°C/425°F, Gas Mark 7) for 20 minutes, then reduce oven to cool (150°C/300°F, Gas Mark 2) and bake for a further 1½ hours, or until the meat feels cooked when tested with a skewer run through the centre hole. Allow the pie to cool for a few minutes, then remove it from the tin or mould. Fill the spaces in the pie with jelly stock made from the meat bones, with extra gelatine added if necessary.

RAISED PORK PIE

METRIC/IMPERIAL
0.75 kg/1½ lb pie pork, cubes
450 ml/¾ pint chicken stock, made from a cube
200 g/7 oz hot-water crust pastry
1 × 15 ml spoon/1 tablespoon chopped parsley
salt
pepper

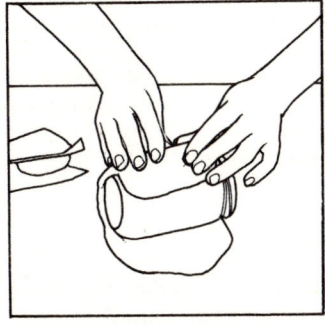  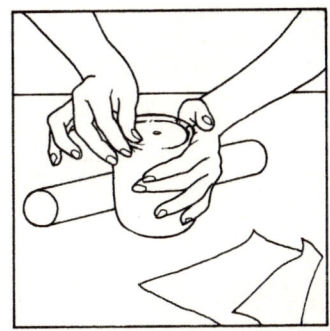

Raised Pie
1. Mould three-quarters of pastry round a jam jar to cover sides.

2. Ease pastry 'mould' out of jam jar and fill with pork mixture.

3. Cover top of pie and pinch edges together.

337

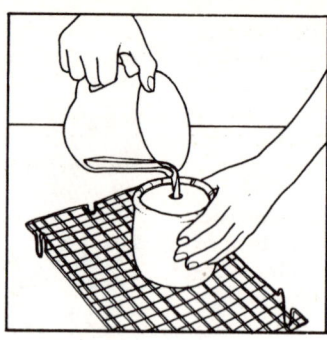

4. Secure with a stiff paper band around the pie. Make a hole in the centre.

5. Allow the pie to cool for a few minutes, add stock.

6. When cold top up with any remaining jellied stock.

THE DAY BEFORE
Put the meat in a pan with the stock, cover and simmer for 1 hour or until tender. Drain it and leave in a cool place until required. Boil the stock rapidly until it measures 300 ml/½ pint; cool.

THE NEXT DAY
Mould three-quarters of the pastry into a shell about 10 cm/4 inches in diameter. Put the cold cooked meat in the pastry case with the parsley and seasoning. Remove any fat from the top of the stock (which should have set to a soft jelly) and add a few spoonfuls of the liquid to the meat. Use the remaining quarter of the pastry to make the lid for the pie. Using a sharp knife make a small hole in the top of the pastry to pour the stock through when cooked. Bake it in a hot oven (220°C/425°F, Gas Mark 7) for 15 minutes, reduce the temperature to moderate (180°C/350°F, Gas Mark 4) and cook for a further 40 minutes. Remove the paper band and cook for another 20 minutes. Leave the pie until cold, then melt the remaining jellied stock and fill it up. If the stock does not set well, add 1–2 × 5 ml spoons/1–2 teaspoons powdered gelatine and dissolve it in the stock over a gentle heat. Leave the pie until quite set before cutting it.

RAISED VEAL AND HAM PIE

METRIC/IMPERIAL
0.5 kg/1 lb hot-water crust pastry
350 g/12 oz pie veal, diced
100 g/4 oz ham, chopped
1 × 15 ml spoon/1 tablespoon chopped parsley
grated rind and juice of 1 lemon
salt
pepper
little stock or water
1 hard-boiled egg
beaten egg to glaze
jelly stock

Make a pastry case. Mix the veal, ham, parsley, lemon rind and juice, season with salt and pepper and moisten with a little stock or water. Half fill the pastry case with this mixture, put the hard-boiled egg in the centre, add the remaining meat mixture, cover and decorate the pie. Make a small hole in the centre with a sharp knife, to allow you to test whether the meat is cooked and to fill with jelly stock when cooked. Glaze the top with a little beaten egg and tie a greaseproof paper band round the pie. Bake in a hot oven (220°C/425°F, Gas Mark 7) for 15–20 minutes, then reduce the heat to moderate (180°C/350°F, Gas Mark 4) and continue cooking for a further 1½ hours or longer, until the meat feels tender when tested with a skewer. When cold, fill the pie up with jelly stock made by dissolving 2 × 5 ml spoons/2 teaspoons gelatine in 300 ml/½ pint chicken stock. Leave to set.

RAISIN

Raisins are white or black grapes which have been dried either in the sun or by artificial means. There are seedless varieties, but the best flavoured type – the muscatel – has pips. Raisins come from various countries, including southern Spain, Greece, California, Australia, South Africa and Crete. From October onwards the new season's fruit is available in this country; the choice Malaga muscatels are usually sold at Christmas time. Raisins are mostly available dried, cleaned and pre-packed.

They are used in cakes, pies, puddings, chutneys, jam and mincemeat and a wine can be made from them. Their food value lies in the iron they contain and also in their sugar content; the total amount usually consumed is, however, so small that raisins contribute little to the diet beyond their agreeable taste.

RAISING AGENT

Any means whereby air or gas is introduced into bread, cake, pastry or pudding mixtures to make them rise during the cooking process. For example, in the making of sponge cakes, air is introduced by the whisking of egg and sugar over hot water, and this air acts as the raising agent. Batters, such as Yorkshire pudding, depend principally on the conversion of water into steam to make them rise, for the steam has 1,600 times the volume of the original water. The most usual raising agent, however, is carbon dioxide, produced either by the action of yeast or by chemicals.

For domestic use, the chemical agents most commonly employed to produce the carbon dioxide are (1) bicarbonate of soda and cream of tartar or tartaric acid, or (2) prepared baking powder. Soured milk is sometimes used instead of or in addition to cream of tartar: 300 ml/½ pint soured milk with 1 × 5 ml spoon/1 teaspoon bicarbonate of soda replaces 4 × 5 ml spoons/4 teaspoons baking powder; alternatively 4 × 15 ml spoons/4 tablespoons vinegar or lemon juice may be used with the same quantity of bicarbonate of soda. When tartaric acid is used instead of cream of tartar, the quantity of acid should be halved, as it releases twice as much carbon dioxide.

The following are the quantities (in level teaspoonfuls) of chemical raising agents required with 225 g/8 oz plain flour. (With self-raising flour, which is frequently used in home cooking, no extra raising agent is normally necessary.)

Very plain mixtures, scones, etc: 1 × 2.5–1 × 5 ml spoon/½–1 teaspoon bicarbonate of soda and 1–2 × 5 ml spoons/1–2 teaspoons cream of tartar. *or* 2–3 × 5 ml spoons/2–3 teaspoons baking powder

Creamed mixtures: 2 × 5 ml spoons/2 teaspoons baking powder

Very rich mixtures: 1 × 5 ml spoon/1 teaspoon baking powder, or none

NOTE
The amount of baking powder used varies considerably according to the richness of the mixture and whether any other raising agent is also being used, e.g., eggs, which introduce air in creamed mixtures.

(See Flour, Yeast and Baking Powder entries.)

RAMEKIN

A savoury or entrée served in a small fireproof china or glass container known as a ramekin dish or case. Sometimes, as in France, the name is given to cheese fritters or fingers. Ramekin also indicates a tartlet with a kind of cream cheese filling.

RANCIDITY

(See Fats entry.)

RAPE

A cabbage-like weed used in this country for ani-

mal fodder. The seeds yield an oil used for soap-making and also for lubrication purposes.

RAREBIT

(See Welsh Rarebit entry.)

RASPAIL

A French liqueur.

RASPBERRY

A wild or cultivated juicy fruit; it may be red or yellow in colour and cap- or thimble-shaped. The peak of the raspberry season is the end of June. Raspberries have quite a good vitamin C content.

The full flavour of raspberries is best appreciated when they are eaten immediately after picking, either alone or with cream and caster sugar. They also make excellent jam; for this purpose, use dry and slightly under-ripe fruit, as the pectin content is then at its highest; red-currant or gooseberry juice is sometimes added to assist the set. Raspberries have a good flavour when bottled by either the oven or the under-water method of sterilization, though the colour is not as a rule very good. (See Bottling entry.) Raspberries freeze well; the flavour is best preserved when they are frozen in sugar. The fruit may also be used for home-made wine, raspberry syrup and raspberry vinegar.

Raspberries are excellent for use in many made-up forms, including flans, ice creams, gâteaux, shortcakes, meringue tartlets, cold soufflés or moulds, fruit salads and fools. Raspberry jam with a little added lemon juice gives a good flavour to puddings, cakes, etc. Raspberry sauce is good with ices and cold sweets.

To prepare the fruit, remove the hulls. If the fruit is dirty, wash it in a colander, but avoid this if possible, as washing spoils both shape and flavour.

RASPBERRY FOOL

Sprinkle 0.5 kg/1 lb raspberries with sugar to taste and leave for 4 hours, then sieve. Mix the purée with 300 ml/½ pint double cream, custard or a mixture of both, colour if required, chill and serve.

RASPBERRY JAM

METRIC/IMPERIAL
1.75 kg/4 lb raspberries
1.75 kg/4 lb sugar

Wash and hull the fruit and simmer very gently in its own juice for about 15 to 20 minutes, or until really soft. Add the sugar, stir until dissolved and boil rapidly until setting point is reached. Pot and cover in the usual way. *Makes about 3 kg/7 lbs.*

RASPINGS

(See Breadcrumbs entry.)

RATAFIA

A liqueur or cordial flavoured with the kernels of cherries, almonds, peaches or other kinds of fruit, also a flavouring essence used in cookery.

The name is also applied to a type of sweet biscuit formerly eaten with the liqueur and now usually flavoured with ratafia essence. These biscuits somewhat resemble macaroons, but are smaller and browner; they may be served as a wine biscuit, used whole to decorate trifles and other cold sweets, or crushed up and mixed with cold sweets.

RATATOUILLE

A casserole or stew of vegetables, originating in Provence. It can be served hot as a vegetable or cold as an appetizer.

RATATOUILLE

METRIC/IMPERIAL
4 tomatoes
2 aubergines
a small green pepper
2 onions
3 courgettes
½ a cucumber
2 × 15 ml spoons/2 tablespoons oil
25 g/1 oz butter
seasoning
clove of garlic, crushed
chopped parsley

Skin and slice the tomatoes; wipe and slice the aubergines; prepare the pepper, removing the pips, then slice; skin and slice the onions; slice the courgettes; slice the cucumber. Heat the oil and butter in a flameproof casserole (preferably enamelled iron) and add the prepared vegetables, seasoning and crushed garlic. Stir well, cover tightly and place in a moderate oven (180°C/350°F, Gas Mark 4) for 1 to 1½ hours. Serve garnished with chopped parsley.

RAVIGOTE BUTTER

A green-coloured butter, made by adding fresh aromatic herbs to creamed butter, which is served with grilled meat, etc. To make it, take 1 × 15 ml spoon/1 tablespoonful each of tarragon, parsley, chives, chervil and, if available, burnet, wash them and squeeze them dry in muslin; chop the herbs finely, pound with a finely minced or chopped shallot and if desired a little garlic. Season, mix with 40 g/1½ oz to 50 g/2 oz creamed butter and let it harden before serving.

Ravigote Sauce

A French salad dressing containing pounded hard-boiled egg yolks and highly flavoured with chopped herbs and garlic.

A hot sauce of the same name is made by adding a generous amount of ravigote butter and some wine and vinegar (reduced by boiling) to a velouté sauce base. It is served with boiled poultry, etc.

RAVIOLI

Small squares of noodle paste, containing a well-seasoned, savoury minced mixture. They are cooked like macaroni and served with tomato sauce and grated cheese, or used as a garnish for soups. The filling may consist of cooked chicken or meat moistened with a sauce, or creamed or puréed vegetables. Ravioli may be bought ready for cooking in a can or frozen and they may also be made at home.

RÉCHAUFFÉ

A made-up dish of re-heated food. A variety of réchauffés can be made from leftovers of cooked food, so that they become appetizing dishes in their own right. In general, the aim should be to re-heat rather than re-cook the food and it is usually necessary to combine it with a well-flavoured sauce or other accompaniment. As cooked food does not absorb flavours this must come from other ingredients. It is often a good idea to heat and serve réchauffés in individual dishes or small pastry cases, etc., to make them look more attractive.

Take great care in storing leftover food that is going to be used in réchauffés. Meat, fish, milk products and vegetables in particular are easily contaminated with the germs that cause food poisoning. They should therefore not be left by the side of the cooker in a warm kitchen. Instead they should be cooled as rapidly as possible and placed in the refrigerator or in a cool larder. When the food is to be re-heated, this should be done quickly and the food should then be allowed to cook for 15 minutes – this will destroy any microbes that may have contaminated it.

Using Leftover Meat

Trim the meat from the bones, removing fat, gristle and any inedible parts. Cut or mince the meat finely and use for such dishes as beef croquettes, rissoles, hash, mince, cottage or shepherd's pie, meat flan and meat mould. Additional moisture in the form of a sauce or gravy is usually necessary – for example, a panada or thick binding sauce for croquettes and rissoles.

To season white meats (veal, poultry, rabbit), use lemon rind and juice, parsley, herbs, nutmeg and tomato; for other meats, use onion, tomato, mushroom, curry paste or piquant table sauces.

Meat may also be sliced and re-heated in a sauce. Use a white or light-coloured one for white meats and a brown one for red meat or game.

Using Leftover Fish

Free the fish from skin and bone and flake it – this is best done while the fish is still warm. (The bones and trimmings may be used for stock for sauce.)

Any sauce left over from the original dish should be used and may prove sufficient for binding and moistening the fish mixture, which can be served as fish cakes, croquettes, cutlets, scallops, fish pies and puddings or kedgeree. A mixture of white and smoked fish will sometimes make a better-flavoured dish than white fish alone.

Cooked fish, which tends to be rather insipid, needs to be very well seasoned and attractively flavoured; lemon, parsley and anchovy are the most popular additions. Lemon and parsley are also used for garnishing.

Using Leftover Vegetables

These can be mixed with cooked pasta or rice to serve as a salad or added to soups, sauces and savoury flans.

(See Cottage Pie, Croquettes, Hash, Rissoles, Fish Pie (under Fish), Russian Salad, Soup and Leftovers entries.)

RECIPE

The list of ingredients and the instructions for making a dish. With some types of dish it is possible to vary the nature and amount of the ingredients and the method of mixing and cooking, so that there are often many different recipes for one dish. With certain classic or specialized recipes, however, particularly those devised by the great chefs of the last century or so, there is only one really 'correct' or authentic version.

Beginners should follow recipes carefully and learn the basic methods for cakes, pastry, sauces, etc., before attempting too much in the way of variation. Basic recipes will be found under the appropriate headings throughout this book. These recipes are for four unless otherwise stated.

The quantities given in a recipe can usually be doubled or halved without further alteration, but when quantities are varied beyond this, the proportions of the ingredients often require modification: this applies particularly to such ingredients as raising agents, flavouring and mixing liquids, which need to be used in slightly smaller proportions when the quantities are increased. When you want to cook a large quantity of some particular mixture it is often better to make two moderate-sized batches rather than one very big one.

This ensures better quality results and ensures that you can use existing kitchen equipment.

RED CABBAGE

(See Cabbage and Pickling entries.)

RED-CURRANT

The fruit of a bush widely grown in this country, with small red, translucent berries which grow in clusters and are in season from June to August. When fully ripe, the currants may be eaten as a dessert. To counteract the somewhat acid taste, dip the clusters in fine sugar or frost them (see separate entry).

Red-currants contain an appreciable amount of Vitamin C.

Fresh, bottled and frozen red-currants make good pies, puddings, summer puddings, trifles, fools, moulds, etc., when mixed with other soft fruits; red-currant jelly is excellent with roast game and other meat. In jam-making, red-currants are usually mixed with another fruit, especially raspberries. They are rich in acid and pectin and therefore help preserves to set well, so they are often added to fruits with poor setting qualities. Strained red-currant juice may also be used for the same purpose; add 150 ml/¼ pint to 1 kg/2 lb to 2.25 kg/5 lb fruit.

White-currants are similar in flavour; they are usually eaten raw.

RED-CURRANT JELLY

METRIC/IMPERIAL
1.5 kg/3 lb red-currants
600 ml/1 pint water
sugar

Wash the fruit, but don't remove the stalks; put it into a pan with the water and simmer gently until the red-currants are really soft and pulped. Strain through a jelly cloth, measure the extract and return it to the pan with 450 g/1 lb sugar to each 600 ml/1 pint of extract. Stir until the sugar has dissolved and boil rapidly until a 'jell' is obtained on testing. Skim, pot and cover in the usual way.

RED-CURRANT FOOL

METRIC/IMPERIAL
0.5 kg/1 lb red-currants with stalks removed
2 × 15 ml spoons/2 tablespoons water
100 g/4 oz sugar
150 ml/¼ pint custard
150 ml/¼ pint double cream
red food colouring

Cook the red-currants with the water and sugar until the fruit is soft and well reduced, then sieve it. Whip the cream. Fold the custard and then the cream into the red-currant purée. Add a few drops of colouring and chill. Divide the fool between 4 sundae glasses.

RED HERRING

A smoked and salted whole herring.

RED MULLET

(See Mullet entry.)

RED PEPPER

(See Pepper, Condiment entry.)

REDUCE, TO

The process of boiling a mixture (especially when making a sauce, soup or syrup) in an uncovered pan to evaporate surplus liquid and give a more concentrated result.

REFORM (RÉFORME) SAUCE AND GARNISH

These are the accompaniments for a dish of breaded and fried lamb cutlets devised by the chef of the Reform Club in London. A brown sauce of the Espagnole type is enriched by the addition of port wine and red-currant jelly. The garnish consists of an assortment of the following, chosen to give a good colour contrast: cooked carrot, truffle or mushroom, lean ham or tongue, hard-boiled white of egg and gherkin. Cut into Julienne strips, heat and place in the centre of the dish of cutlets.

REFRIGERATION

This is a means of artificially cooling food in a special appliance called a refrigerator.

A domestic refrigerator, the cabinet of which is normally maintained at a temperature between 1.5°C/35°F and 7°C/45°F, chills but does not freeze food. This temperature enables perishable food to be stored under ideal conditions for the short period necessary between purchase and consumption – usually a matter of a few days at the most. It is a mistake to leave highly perishable food longer than this, for although deterioration is much slower than at ordinary room temperature or in a larder, the bacteria are not destroyed and slow changes occur if the food is kept too long in the refrigerator.

How to Use a Refrigerator

1. Since variations of storage temperature encourage the growth of microbes, the refrigerator should be opened as little as possible and hot food should never be placed in it.
2. Never pack food in too tightly, as this prevents the free circulation of the air.
3. As the air in the refrigerator is dry and will absorb moisture from any exposed food, see that everything (particularly moist food and uncooked cake and yeast mixtures, biscuit doughs and pastry) is covered before being put into the cabinet. Special refrigerator boxes are available, made from plastic, but china and glass bowls covered with a plate, with a lid of foil or with a piece of plastic film, are equally satisfactory. Foil and film can also be used to wrap items like cheese, and polythene bags are also very useful.
4. Stong-smelling foods such as fish should be stored for as short a time as possible. Remember to cover them closely, or else you may find the flavour is transferred to other foods.
5. Vegetables should be prepared before being stored in the special crisper or in a polythene bag or plastic box.
6. Pack the food in accordance with the temperature in the different parts of the cabinet. The coldest part is below the frozen food storage compartment, and as the air at the base gets warmer, it rises towards this compartment and is then re-chilled. Foods requiring the lowest temperature (e.g., meat, fish) should be placed directly under the frozen food storage comparment. Anything that is not wanted too cold, such as cooking fat, is best kept in the warmest position, so fats and eggs are generally stored in racks or compartments on the door.
7. Frozen foods should be stored only for the recommended length of time. This depends on the 'Star Rating' of the refrigerator. Recommended times are as follows:

Star Rating	Max. Temperature of Frozen Food Compartment	Max. Storage Time for: Frozen Foods	Ice Cream
★★★	−18°C/0°F	2 to 3 months	2 to 3 months
★★	−12°C/+10°F	4 weeks	1 to 2 weeks
★	−6°C/+21°F	1 week	1 day

8. The following foods, though they should not be stored in a refrigerator, may be chilled before serving: canned foods, e.g., fruit juice; wine and light beers; fresh pineapple and melon; sweets such as trifles which have been decorated ready for the table (leave these uncovered).
9. Sliced cooked meats, eggs and cheese should be removed from the refrigerator about 1 hour before being served. Fruit juices, salads, chilled sweets, etc., are usually best if served straight from the refrigerator.

Storage times in a Refrigerator

Dairy Produce

Butter, Fats, etc.	2 to 4 weeks
Milk, Cream	3 to 4 days

Custards, Milk Puddings	2 days
Hard Cheeses	1 to 2 weeks
Soft Cheeses	1 week
Eggs	10 to 14 days
Bacon	7 to 10 days

Meat and Poultry

Raw Meat:	
Joints	3 to 5 days
Chops, Steaks	2 to 4 days
Stewing Meat	2 to 4 days
Mincemeat, Liver,	1 to 2 days
Kidneys, etc.	
Fresh Poultry	2 to 3 days
Frozen Poultry	depends on star rating; 2 to 3 days in main cabinet
Cold Roast Meat	3 to 5 days
Meat Pies, Casseroles	2 to 3 days
Raw Poultry	2 to 3 days
Cooked Poultry	2 to 3 days

Fish

Raw Fresh Fish	1 to 2 days
Cooked Fish	2 days
Lightly Smoked Fish	1 to 2 days
Heavily Smoked Fish	2 to 3 months
Frozen Fish	depends on star rating

Fruit

Soft Fruit	1 to 3 days
Citrus Fruit	10 to 14 days
Other Fruit	3 to 7 days

Vegetables

Salad Ingredients	3 to 6 days
Greens	5 to 7 days
Frozen	depends on star rating

Yeast

Fresh, in loosely tied polythene bag	up to 1 month

RE-HEATED FOOD

(See Réchauffé entry.)

REINDEER

The meat of young reindeer, both cows and steers, resembles mild venison; the tongues are excellent when smoked. For method of cooking see Venison entry.

RELEVÉ

(See Remove entry.)

RELISH

A condiment, sauce or pickle taken with food to give added flavour. The name used to be applied to dishes of the appetizer type, served after the soup and fish, to stimulate the appetite.

RÉMOULADE SAUCE

Into 150 ml/¼ pint mayonnaise, fold 1 × 2.5 ml spoon/½ teaspoon each of French and English mustards, 1 × 5 ml spoon/1 teaspoon each of chopped capers, gherkin, parsley and chervil, and 1 anchovy fillet, finely chopped.

REMOVE (RELEVÉ)

The roast joint course in a formal meal. The phrase is seldom used nowadays as long dinner menus are no longer fashionable.

RENDERING

To extract fat from meat trimmings. (See Fats entry.)

RENNET

A preparation made from the stomach of a calf and containing the rennin, which possesses the property of coagulating the casein in milk to form a fairly solid, easily digested clot. When served as a dessert, this clotted milk is known as junket. Rennet is also used to form the curd in cheese-making.

Various rennet preparations are on the market, in liquid, powder and tablet form; when using them, follow accurately the directions given on the bottle or packet. As it deteriorates with age it is best to use rennet when fresh. (See Junket entry.)

RÉVEILLON

The name of a feast held in France on Christmas Eve after Midnight Mass. It consists of a very elaborate supper and is often provided by the wealthy members of the town or village. The chief dish is usually 'boudin noir' – black pudding. The name Réveillon is also applied to a feast held on New Year's Eve.

RHUBARB

Rhubarb is strictly speaking a vegetable, being the stalks of the plant, but since it is cooked and eaten like fruit, it is commonly included under that heading. The stalks, which vary in colour from green to red, are best picked when young; they are ready for eating in the spring and early summer, before the majority of home-grown fruits are available. Rhubarb has a pleasant, refreshing flavour, particularly when the better varieties are grown. It has little food value, but may add a small amount of Vitamin C to the diet. The leaves should be dis-

343

carded and no attempt should be made to use them as greens as they can be poisonous.

Preparation and cooking: Remove the leaves from the rhubarb, wash the stalks and 'string' them if they are old, then cut into 7.5 cm/3 inch lengths.

Rhubarb easily breaks down into an unattractive, stringy mass, so it needs to be cooked slowly and gently (preferably in a casserole or heatproof dish in the oven). Use a very small quantity of water and cook in a cool oven (150°C/300°F, Gas Mark 2) or simmer on top of the stove for a few minutes until tender; sweeten to taste with sugar or syrup. The addition of orange juice and rind gives a pleasant flavour.

As rhubarb cooks so quickly it is particularly suitable for baking under a sponge mixture, as in Eve's Pudding. Because of its sharp flavour, it makes a good fruit fool and it can be made into jam, preferably mixed with other fruits; when used alone, it is usually flavoured with ginger. Rhubarb may also be bottled. (See Bottling entry.) It can be frozen in syrup, dry pack or as a purée. (See Freezing entry.)

RHUBARB MOUSSE

This mousse has a hint of surprise – marmalade.

METRIC/IMPERIAL
0.5 kg/1 lb rhubarb, prepared weight
100 g/4 oz sugar
150 ml/¼ pint water
5 × 15 ml spoons/5 level tablespoons ginger marmalade
1 × 15 ml spoon/1 level tablespoon powdered gelatine
3 × 15 ml spoons/3 tablespoons water
1 egg white
150 ml/¼ pint double cream
1 × 15 ml spoon/1 tablespoon milk

Cut the rhubarb into 2.5 cm/1 inch lengths. Put the rhubarb, sugar, water and 4 × 15 ml spoons/4 tablespoons marmalade in a saucepan and cook until the rhubarb is tender. Purée it in a blender or put it through a sieve. Dissolve the gelatine in the water in a small bowl over a pan of hot water. Stir this into the rhubarb. When it is on the point of setting, fold in the stiffly beaten egg white. Divide between 6 stemmed glasses and chill. Whip the cream with the milk until it just holds its shape, fold in the remaining tablespoon of marmalade and use to top the mousse.

RHUBARB FOOL

METRIC/IMPERIAL
150 ml/¼ pint custard
350 ml/¾ lb rhubarb
4 × 15 ml spoons/4 tablespoons orange juice
grated rind of ½ orange
50 g/2 oz sugar
pink or red food colouring
2 × 15 ml spoons/2 tablespoons double cream

Make the custard. Cool until lukewarm. Slice the rhubarb, cook with the orange juice, rind and sugar until well reduced and with little liquid remaining. Cool. Purée the rhubarb with the custard in an electric blender, or sieve the rhubarb and combine it with the custard. Add colouring to tint an attractive pink. Divide between two bowls or glasses. Chill. When ready to serve, pour on the cream and feather with the handle of a teaspoon.

RIBOFLAVIN

One of the B vitamins. (See Vitamins entry.)

RICE

This cereal is extensively cultivated in hot, moist climates such as that of India, Java, China, Japan and parts of the USA and is the staple food of half the human race. In some parts of the world two harvests a year can be obtained.

After threshing, the rice grain is left in its tough husk; in the milling process, first this husk and then the inner skin are removed. Since most of the vitamins B are found in the inner skin, white 'polished' rice has less food value than 'unpolished' rice, though the latter has the slight disadvantage of taking longer to cook. Attempts are now being made to preserve more of the nutritive value of rice by steaming it before milling, so that the thiamine and nicotinic acid are absorbed by the white grain; this 'parboiled' or 'cured' rice is then polished and is greatly superior in nutritive value to ordinary white rice.

Shapes of Grain
There are three main kinds of rice grain – long, medium and short.

The long slender grains are fluffy and separate when cooked so they are ideal for made-up savoury rice dishes and for rice used as an accompaniment to savoury dishes such as curries and stews. Medium and short grain rice are more moist and sticky. The medium grains are very suitable for savoury dishes where the rice needs to be moulded or bound together (e.g., rice rings, stuffings and croquettes). Short grain rice is used for rice puddings and other sweet rice dishes.

Types of Rice
REGULAR MILLED, LONG GRAIN WHITE RICE
The hulls, germ, and most of the bran layers are removed. The rice is white in colour, with only a bland, very slight flavour when cooked.

344

BROWN RICE
Whole unpolished grains of rice with only the inedible husk and a small amount of bran removed. It takes longer to cook than white rice (about 40 minutes), and more liquid. Apart from its fawn colour when cooked, it differs from white rice by having a more chewy texture and a pleasant, nutty flavour. It is used in savoury dishes.

PAR-BOILED OR PRE-FLUFFED RICE
Cooked before milling by a special steam pressure process, which helps to retain the natural food value. It takes longer to cook than regular milled white rice (20 to 25 minutes), absorbs more liquid (2½ parts water to 1 part rice), but it more easily produces a perfect result, with grains that are fluffy, separate and plump when cooked.

PRE-COOKED OR INSTANT RICE
This is completely cooked and then dehydrated. It is useful when in a hurry as it only needs heating in boiling water for about 5 minutes or as directed on the pack. It is a very good stand-by for snacks and quick rice dishes, both savoury and sweet.

RISOTTO RICE
Known as Arborio, a plump Italian rice which gives risotto its essentially creamy texture, with each grain firm in the centre and slightly chewy.

WILD RICE
This is not actually rice, but seeds from a wild grass, used for savoury dishes. It is expensive and not widely available, but delicious for special occasions, particularly with game.

Preparing and Cooking Rice
Rice sold in unbranded packs or loose should be washed before it is cooked. Put it in a strainer and rinse it under the cold tap until all the loose starch (white powder) is washed off – it is this loose starch which prevents rice drying out into separate grains when cooked.

Storing and Re-heating Rice
The rice can be cooked in quite large quantities and any not required at once can be stored in a covered container in a refrigerator for up to a week without any deterioration, or for several days in a cool place. To re-heat it, place about 1 cm/ ½ inch water in a pan, add some salt, bring to the boil and add the rice. Cover tightly, then reduce the heat and simmer very gently for about 5 minutes. Place the rice in a strainer and rinse under a hot tap. Shake strainer to dry off rice and place over a saucepan of fast boiling water for five minutes to re-heat rice and separate the grains.

BOILED RICE
Place 225 g/8 oz long grain rice in a saucepan with 600 ml/1 pint water and 1 × 5 ml spoon/1 teaspoon salt. Bring quickly to the boil, stir well and cover with a tightly fitting lid. Reduce the heat and simmer gently for 14 to 15 minutes. Remove from the heat and before serving separate out the grains gently, using a fork. (The rice will not need draining.) If a drier effect is required, leave the rice covered for 5 to 10 minutes after it has been cooked. The grains should then be tender, but dry and quite separate. 225 g/8 oz rice gives 3 to 4 servings. Here are some points to remember when using this method:

Do not increase the amount of water or the finished rice will be soggy.

Do not uncover the rice whilst it is cooking or the steam will escape and the cooking time will be increased.

Do not stir the rice while it is simmering – it breaks up the grains and makes them soggy. When the rice is cooked, don't leave it longer than 10 minutes before serving, or the grains will stick together.

CURRIED RICE

METRIC/IMPERIAL
1 onion, skinned and finely chopped
25 g/1 oz butter
225 g/8 oz long grain rice
25–50 g/1–2 oz currants or stoned raisins
1 × 2.5 ml spoon/ ½ teaspoon curry powder
600 ml/1 pint chicken or beef stock
salt
pepper
25 g/1 oz blanched almonds, slivered and browned (optional)

Fry the onion in the butter for about 5 minutes, until soft. Add the rice and fry for a further 2 to 3 minutes, stirring all the time. Add the fruit, curry powder, stock and seasoning and bring to the boil. Stir and cover with a lid, reduce the heat and simmer gently for 14 to 15 minutes. Stir in the almonds (if used) and serve.

Good with meat or chicken.

FLAVOURED RICE

Although rice is most usually cooked in water, it can also be cooked in other liquids to give extra flavour and variety. The water may be replaced by any of the following:
Chicken or beef stock (fresh or made from a cube).
Canned tomato juice, undiluted or used half-and-half with water.
Orange juice – used half-and-half with water.

Alternatively, rice can be flavoured as in the following recipes:

SAVOURY RICE
Fry some chopped onion, pepper, celery or bacon in a little butter in the pan before adding the rice.

HERBY RICE
Add a pinch of dried herbs with the cooking liquid (e.g., sage, marjoram, thyme, mixed herbs).

RAISIN RICE
Add stoned raisins (or currants or sultanas) with the cooking liquid; a pinch of curry powder can also be added.

VARIETY RICE
When the rice is cooked stir in any of the following: diced pineapple, chopped canned pimiento, slivered brown almonds, grated cheese, chopped fresh herbs.

FRIED RICE

METRIC/IMPERIAL
100 g/4 oz long grain rice
2 eggs, beaten
4 × 15 ml spoons/4 tablespoons oil
1 × 2.5 ml spoon/½ teaspoon salt
½ onion, skinned and finely chopped
50 g/2 oz mushrooms, thinly sliced
2 × 15 ml spoons/2 tablespoons frozen peas
50 g/2 oz cooked ham, diced
2 × 5 ml spoons/2 teaspoons soy sauce

Boil the rice – which should be fluffy and dry. Make a plain omelette from the eggs, cut it into thin strips and set aside. Fry the drained rice preferably in a non-stick pan for about 5 minutes in 2 × 15 ml spoons/2 tablespoons very hot oil with the salt until light golden brown, stirring gently all the time; remove from the pan and set aside. Fry the onion in the remaining oil for about 3 minutes till lightly browned, add the remaining vegetables, rice and the ham and fry lightly for a further 3 minutes stirring gently. Stir in the soy sauce and shredded omelette; serve the mixture as soon as it is hot, to accompany chicken.

RICE PUDDING

METRIC/IMPERIAL
3 × 15 ml spoons/3 tablespoons short grain rice
2 × 15 ml spoons/2 tablespoons caster sugar
600 ml/1 pint milk
knob of butter
whole nutmeg

Wash the rice and put it into a buttered 900 ml/1½ pint ovenproof dish with the sugar. Pour on the milk, top with shavings of butter and grate some nutmeg on top. Bake in a cool oven (150°C/300°F, Gas Mark 2) for about 2 hours; stir it after about 30 minutes.

VARIATIONS
1. Add 50 g/2 oz dried fruit to the pudding.
2. Add 1 × 5 ml spoon/1 teaspoon ground cinna-mon or mixed spice to the pudding before baking it; omit the nutmeg.

(See Kedgeree, Pilaf and Risotto entries.)

RICE PAPER

A thin, semi-transparent, edible paper made from the pith of a plant grown in China. Macaroons and similar delicate cakes are often baked on rice paper, which need not be pulled away before the cakes are eaten.

RICE WINE

A potent wine made in China: it resembles sherry in appearance and flavour.

RICOTTA

An Italian curd cheese. It is used for filling ravioli, and in cannelloni or lasagne dishes; also used in cheesecakes.

RICKEY

An unsweetened long drink made from a liqueur or spirit and ginger ale; it is flavoured with fresh fruit.

RIESLING

A type of white grape used to make wines which are usually given this name. It is the classical German grape producing the best wines in this country. Most of the grapes are grown in the Mosel and Rheingau areas. The wines are comparatively expensive as the Riesling only gives about half as much wine per plant as other varieties of grapes. Good Riesling wines are also produced in Austria and Alsace. The grapes are also grown in Australia, South Africa, Chile and California but the climates are too hot for producing the excellent wine made in Germany.

A Riesling wine must be labelled with the country of origin.

RISOTTO

A famous Italian dish made by boiling rice in stock and flavouring it with onion, cheese, mushrooms, kidneys, white wine, etc., according to the type of risotto. Here are two typical recipes.

CHICKEN RISOTTO

METRIC/IMPERIAL
½ boiling chicken or 2–3 good-sized chicken portions, uncooked
75 g/3 oz butter
2 small onions, skinned and finely chopped

1 stick celery, scrubbed, trimmed and finely chopped
1 clove garlic, skinned and crushed, optional
1 green pepper, seeded and finely chopped
50 g/2 oz mushrooms, sliced
50 g/2 oz bacon or ham, rinded and chopped
150 ml/¼ pint dry white wine
chicken stock
salt
pepper
chopped fresh herbs as available (e.g., marjoram,
    thyme or basil)
225 g/8 oz long grain rice
grated Parmesan cheese

Skin the chicken, bone it and cut the flesh in strips. Melt 25 g/1 oz of the butter and fry half the chopped onion gently for 5 minutes, until soft. Add the chicken, the remaining vegetables and the bacon or ham and fry for a further few minutes, stirring all the time. Add the wine and let it bubble until well reduced; just cover with chicken stock and add the seasoning and herbs. Put on the lid and leave to simmer for about 1 hour, until the chicken is really tender. Drain off the juices and make up to 600 ml/1 pint with more stock if required.

Fry the remaining onion in 25 g/1 oz of the remaining butter for about 5 minutes, until soft. Add the rice and stir until transparent. Add the chicken stock and bring to the boil. Cover and simmer for 10 minutes. Fold in the chicken mixture, stir well and continue cooking until the two mixtures are well blended and the liquid all absorbed. Stir in the remaining butter and some Parmesan cheese and serve.

SHELLFISH RISOTTO

METRIC/IMPERIAL
1 onion, skinned and chopped
75 g/3 oz butter
225 g/8 oz long grain rice
150 ml/¼ pint dry white wine
900 ml/1 ½ pints chicken stock
salt
pepper
1 clove garlic, crushed, optional
225 g/8 oz scampi or prawns
grated Parmesan cheese

Prepare the risotto as above, using 50 g/2 oz of the butter. Just before the rice becomes tender, gently fry the garlic (if used) and the shellfish in the remaining 25 g/1 oz butter for 5 minutes. Stir into the risotto and serve with cheese.

A few sliced button mushrooms can be fried with the shellfish or a few frozen peas or strips of canned pimiento can be added to the risotto just before the rice is cooked. Other shellfish, such as crab or lobster meat (fresh or canned) may also be used; or a mixture of shellfish, with possibly a few mussels (canned or fresh).

RISSOLE

Nowadays this word is usually taken to mean a small roll or round cake, made of cooked minced meat bound with mashed potatoes, which is coated in egg and breadcrumbs and fried in hot fat. True rissoles, however, were enclosed in a thin envelope of pastry before they were fried.

Rissoles may be served as a supper or light luncheon dish, with a brown or tomato sauce.

RISSOLES

METRIC/IMPERIAL
225–350 g/8–12 oz cooked minced beef
½ small onion, skinned and grated
0.5 kg/1 lb potatoes, boiled and mashed
1 × 15 ml spoon/1 tablespoon sweet pickle or table
    sauce
salt
pepper
beaten egg
dry breadcrumbs for coating
shallow fat for frying

Mix the meat, onion and potatoes and add the pickle or sauce and a generous amount of seasoning. Stir until well blended. Turn on to a floured board, form into a roll and cut into slices about 2.5 cm/1 inch thick. Shape these into round cakes, coat with the beaten egg and then with crumbs. Fry on both sides in the fat until golden. Drain well on absorbent paper before serving.

VARIATIONS
1. Replace the minced meat by a can of corned beef, finely chopped.
2. Omit the pickle or sauce and season with 1 × 15 ml spoon/1 tablespoon chopped parsley, 1 × 5 ml spoon/1 teaspoon mixed dried herbs or 1–2 × 5 ml spoons/1–2 teaspoons curry powder.

ROACH

This small freshwater fish of the carp family is in season from September to March. It has white flesh, which turns red when cooked. To counteract the muddy flavour, rub it well over with salt (or hang it up with salt in its mouth) and leave it for a while. Clean and wash the fish thoroughly, then soak it in salted water for 2 to 3 hours before cooking.

Frying and grilling are the usual methods of cooking. Garnish with parsley and serve accompanied by anchovy sauce.

ROASTING AND BAKING

A method of cooking by radiant heat. True roasting is done on a spit in front of an open fire or on a rôtisserie. The meat turns continuously to cook it evenly throughout; to keep it succulent it should be basted frequently. (See Rôtisserie entry.)

The term roasting is usually applied to cooking meat in an oven although strictly speaking this is baking. Many cuts of meat are suitable for roasting (see individual meat entries). Poultry and game can also be roasted; younger birds only should be used, the older ones being more suitable for stewing and braising.

To cook joints from frozen, see individual Beef, Lamb and Pork entries.

Roasting Meat in the Oven

Meat is roasted either at the traditional high temperature in a hot oven (220°C/425°F, Gas Mark 7), when the joint is seared quickly on the outside, giving a good, meaty flavour, or in a moderately hot oven (190°C/375°F, Gas Mark 5) when the joint is more moist, there is less shrinkage and (since the fibres are broken down) the meat is more tender, though some people consider that the flavour is not quite so good.

Arrange the shelves in the oven so that the meat is in the centre. Put the joint in the roasting tin so that the largest cut surfaces are exposed and the thickest layer of fat is on top; this automatically bastes the joint. If the fat is rather meagre, top the meat with 50 g/2 oz dripping or lard. Do not prick the meat with a fork or anything sharp while it is cooking or you will lose some of the juices. If you turn or lift the joint, use two spoons.

BASTING
If the hot fat and juices from the tin are spooned over the joint several times during the cooking period, the flavour is improved and the meat is moist and juicy.

FROTHING
Sprinkling with flour and salt 15 minutes before the cooking is finished gives a crisp outside.

ROASTING ON A GRID
If the meat is cooked on a rack or grid standing inside a roasting tin, the finished result will be less fatty.

ROASTING IN A CLOSED TIN
Using a covered tin produces a moist joint (and incidentally keeps the inside of the oven clean). However, the meat is pale in colour and doesn't have such a good flavour as when it is roasted in an open tin. You can remove the lid during the last half-hour of the cooking time and brown the joint.

ROASTING IN FOIL
If the meat is wrapped in aluminium foil before it is put in the roasting tin it will be moist and tender and will not shrink so much. However, foil wrapping has the same effect as roasting in a closed tin and the meat will not develop so much flavour and colour. The foil should therefore be opened during the last 30 minutes of the cooking time, so that the joint can become crisp and brown.

ROASTING WRAPS AND BAGS
The main purpose of these is to keep the oven clean while the meat roasts. The bag or wrap also collects the meat juices together, and if a little flour is sprinkled inside the bag before inserting the meat, you have ready-made gravy at the end of the cooking time. The packets usually recommend cooking times and temperatures – usually up to a moderately hot oven (200°C/400°F, Gas Mark 6). Instructions suggest piercing or slitting the bag or wrap before cooking, to allow for expansion of air. To obtain crisp, browned meat, the wrap or bag should be opened during the last half-hour of the cooking time.

Roasting on a Spit
The latest roasting method is in effect a return to the older ways. Cookers are available with an attached spit roaster, or you can buy one separately. A joint roasted on an open spit has a much better flavour than oven-roast meat; spit-roasting in the oven, however, shows little difference from ordinary oven-roasting. (See Rôtisserie Cooking entry.)

Meat Thermometers
Some people find a meat thermometer a great help when roasting meat. Insert it into the thickest part of the joint before this is put into the oven. When the thermometer registers the required internal temperature (see chart), the meat will be correctly cooked. The thermometer is particularly useful with beef, ensuring that you can have it rare, medium or well-done, to your particular taste. (It is, of course, still necessary to work out the approximate length of cooking time, in order to know at what time cooking should be started). Make sure the thermometer does not touch the bone.

A thermometer is essential if you are cooking meat from frozen.

USING A MEAT THERMOMETER

Beef:

Rare	60°C/140°F	Very rare when hot, but ideal when cold.
	75°C/160°F	Brown meat, but bloody juices running from it, pale pinkish tinge when cold
Well done	77°C/170°F	Well cooked. Tends to be dry when cold.
Very well done	82°C/180°F	Fibres breaking up; fat rendered down.
Veal:	82°C/180°F	Moist, pale meat
Lamb:	82°C/180°F	Moist, brown meat
Pork:	89°C/190°F	Moist, pale meat

Pot Roasting

This method of cooking joints of meat in a covered pan is particularly suitable for small, compact pieces and for cuts which are inclined to be tough, such as breast of mutton (boned, stuffed and rolled); brisket; stuffed sheep's heart.

ROBERT SAUCE

A piquant sauce containing onion, dry white wine, vinegar, espagnole or demi-glace sauce and mustard. Serve with hot or cold meats, especially chops, steaks, pork and goose when the tangy sauce will liven up the bland flavour of the meat.

ROBERT SAUCE

METRIC/IMPERIAL
1 small onion, skinned and finely chopped
25 g/1 oz butter
150 ml/¼ pint dry white wine
1 × 15 ml spoon/1 tablespoon wine vinegar
300 ml/½ pint espagnole or demi-glace sauce
1–2 × 5 ml spoons/1–2 teaspoons mild made mustard
pinch of sugar
salt
pepper

Fry the onion gently in the butter for about 10 minutes without browning. Add the wine and vinegar and boil rapidly until reduced by half. Stir in the sauce and simmer for 10 minutes. Add the mustard, a little sugar and extra seasoning if necessary.
Serve with pork.

ROCAMBOLE

A kind of onion which bears 'fruits' at the top of the stem; these resemble garlic, but are not so pungent.

ROCK CAKE

Plain buns containing fruit and spice, which are baked in small heaps on a tin or baking sheet. The mixture must not be too wet or the buns will spread and lose their 'rocky' shape.

ROCK BUNS

METRIC/IMPERIAL
100 g/4 oz butter or margarine
225 g/8 oz plain flour
2 × 5 ml spoons/2 teaspoons baking powder
pinch of salt
1 × 2.5 ml spoon/½ teaspoon mixed spice, optional
grated rind of ½ a lemon
100 g/4 oz demerara sugar
100 g/4 oz mixed dried fruit

1 egg, beaten
about 1 × 5 ml spoon/1 teaspoon milk, optional

Grease two baking sheets. Rub the fat into the sifted flour, baking powder, salt and spices until the mixture resembles fine breadcrumbs. Stir in the rind, sugar and fruit. Make a well in the centre, pour in the egg and a little milk if necessary, to give a stiff crumbly consistency. Bind together loosely using a fork. Use two forks to shape the mixture together in rough heaps on the baking sheets. Bake in a moderately hot oven (200°C/400°F, Gas Mark 6) for 15 to 20 minutes.

VARIATION
Replace the dried fruit by 100 g/4 oz chopped stoned dates and 1 × 15 ml spoon/1 tablespoon chopped crystallized ginger.

ROCK SALMON

(See Pollock entry.)

ROE

The spawn or milt of a fish. In many cases it is only suitable for cooking as part of the fish, but the roes of herring and cod are often used to make separate savouries or made-up dishes. Sturgeon's roe, commonly called caviare, is an expensive delicacy used as an appetizer or for cocktail savouries.

COD'S ROE

This can be bought either cooked or raw. To cook raw roe, tie in muslin and boil gently in salted water with a few peppercorns, until it is tender (30 minutes to 1 hour, according to thickness). Lift it out and allow to cool. Cut the roe in slices, dip in seasoned flour or fine oatmeal or egg-and-crumb and fry in hot fat until golden-brown. Serve on toast or with sautéed potatoes, accompanied by sliced lemon or Tartare sauce.

SMOKED COD'S ROE
This can now be bought at most delicatessen shops. It may be served as an appetizer, accompanied by slices of lemon and toast or brown bread and butter. Smoked cod's roe also forms the basis for the famous Greek appetizer, Taramasalata.

ROEBUCK

(See Venison entry.)

ROLL (BREAD)

Rolls may be made in numerous shapes and from many kinds of dough: certain textures are traditionally associated with certain shapes, thus, finger-shaped sandwich or bridge rolls are soft;

349

Vienna rolls are crisp and very light; milk rolls (which may be made in various shapes) are soft, croissants are made from a dough with extra fat added.

Rolls become rather tough when stale, but this can be remedied by sprinkling with water and re-heating in a moderate oven, to crisp them up. This process cannot be repeated or the rolls become hard.

MILK ROLLS

METRIC/IMPERIAL
15 g/½ oz fresh yeast or 1.5 × 5 ml spoons/
   1½ teaspoons dried yeast and 1 × 5 ml spoon/
   1 teaspoon sugar
about 150 ml/¼ pint tepid milk
225 g/8 oz strong plain flour
1 × 5 ml spoon/1 teaspoon salt
25 g/1 oz margarine or lard

Blend the fresh yeast with the milk. For dried yeast, dissolve the sugar in the milk, sprinkle the yeast over and leave until frothy. Mix the flour and salt and rub in the fat. Add the yeast liquid and mix to a fairly soft dough, adding a little more milk if necessary. Beat well and knead on a floured board until smooth. Allow to rise in a warm place (about 23°C/75°F) until doubled in size, knead lightly on a floured board, divide into 8 pieces and shape in any of the following ways:

PLAIT:
Divide a small piece of dough into three, shape each into a long roll and plait together, joining the ends securely.

TWIST:
Divide a piece of dough into two, shape into long rolls, twist together and secure the ends.

COTTAGE LOAF:
Cut two-thirds off a piece of dough and make into a bun shape; treat the remaining one-third in the same way; damp the smaller one, place on top of the larger one and secure by pushing your little finger right through the centre.

KNOTS:
Shape each piece into a long roll and tie a knot.

ROUND:
Place the pieces on a very lightly floured board and roll each into a ball. To do this, hold the hand flat almost at table level and move it round in a circular motion, gradually lifting the palm to get a good round shape.

RINGS:
Make a long roll with each piece of dough and bend it round to form a ring; damp the ends and mould them together.

Put the shaped rolls on a greased baking sheet and allow to rise for 15 to 20 minutes. Bake in a hot oven (220°C/425°F, Gas Mark 7) for about 15 minutes, until golden brown and cooked. The rolls can, if you wish, be brushed with milk or beaten egg before cooking, to give a glazed finish.

QUICK WHOLEMEAL ROLLS

Use wholemeal dough given in Bread entry. Divide into 12 pieces, place on a floured baking sheet, cover with greased polythene and leave to rise until doubled in size. Bake at the top of a hot oven (230°C/450°F, Gas Mark 8) for 20 to 30 minutes.

ROLLS, STARCH-REDUCED
Several proprietary brands of starch-reduced rolls are available. The dough is treated to remove some of the starch and the protein is therefore in a higher proportion. These rolls are lighter and crisper than ordinary ones.

Starch-reduced rolls are sometimes advised for diabetics in place of bread, as their carbohydrate content is lower. They are also sometimes included in slimming diets.

ROLLMOP

An uncooked pickled herring fillet, sometimes rolled round a small gherkin and skewered together. Rollmops are usually sold packed in brine, in glass jars. They are served as appetizers etc.

ROLY-POLY

(See Suet Pudding entry.)

ROMAINE

(See Cos Lettuce in Lettuce entry.)

ROOT VEGETABLES

This term includes such vegetables as carrots, beetroots, turnips, swedes, parsnips, radishes and salsify; it is often used also for potatoes and Jerusalem artichokes, though these are actually tubers, also for kohlrabi and celeriac (which are swollen stems) and onions, which are bulbs. Most of these vegetables are cooked and eaten hot, though some, especially carrots, may be used raw in salads. Cold cooked beetroots, carrots, turnips, parsnips and of course potatoes may be included in salads. Radishes are seldom cooked, but are usually used raw as an appetizer or in salads.

Cooking: For the general preparation and cooking, see the individual vegetable entries. The most usual ways of cooking root vegetables are boiling, steaming and baking.

Frozen and dehydrated root vegetables should be treated according to the instructions on the container.

Serving: Boiled root vegetables are usually drained and tossed with seasoning and a little melted butter. Parsnips, turnips and swedes may be mashed with a little milk, seasoning and butter or cream. Carrots when old may be served with parsley sauce. Kohlrabi, salsify, celeriac, hot beetroot and radishes are usually served with white sauce. Potatoes may be treated in a multitude of different ways.

ROPE

A bacterial contamination of the dough, which can make bread turn 'ropy' in hot, moist conditions. In the tropics, it is sometimes necessary to add a little vinegar to the bread dough to prevent the infection.

ROQUEFORT

A cheese of a pale cream colour, with a blue mould; it originated in the South of France and is made with ewes' milk, which is often mixed with either cows' or goats' milk. The characteristic pungent flavour is acquired by storing the cheeses in the natural caves in the Roquefort district for about 40 days while they mature. The atmospheric conditions in this part of France make the French Roquefort superior to other Roquefort types produced elsewhere.

ROSE HIP

Hips, the fully ripe, dark red fruits of the wild rose, are valuable on account of their high vitamin C content, but they are not suitable for eating raw, as they are somewhat sour and have many hard seeds and irritating silky hairs. When cooked they may be made into an agreeable preserve or a pleasant-flavoured syrup, which may be taken by itself or used to add extra sweetness and food value to sauces and cold sweets.

ROSE-HIP SYRUP

METRIC/IMPERIAL
2.5 litres/4½ pints water
1 kg/2 lb ripe rose-hips
0.5 kg/1 lb sugar

Have ready 1.75 litres/3 pints of boiling water, preferably in an aluminium or unchipped enamel pan. Mince the rose-hips in a coarse mincer, place them immediately in the boiling water and bring this again to the boil. As soon as it re-boils remove the pan from the heat and leave it for 15 minutes, then pour into a scalded jelly bag and allow the

bulk of the juice to drip through. Return the pulp to the saucepan, add 900 ml/1½ pints of boiling water, re-boil and allow it to stand without further heating for another 10 minutes, then strain as before. Pour the juice into a clean saucepan, and reduce until it measures about 900 ml/1½ pints, then add 0.5 kg/1 lb sugar and boil for a further 5 minutes.

Pour the syrup while it is hot into clean hot bottles and seal at once. Process for 5 minutes. Cool, and dip the corks in melted paraffin wax.

It is advisable to use small bottles, as the syrup will not keep for more than a week or two once it is opened. 2 × 5 ml spoons/2 teaspoons of this syrup each day is recommended if the diet is lacking in vitamin C.

ROSE PETALS

(See Crystallizing entry.)

ROSE WATER

This is either distilled from rose petals or prepared from rose oil and is usually employed to give a pleasant flavour and aroma to such sweets as Turkish Delight.

ROSEMARY

A fragrant evergreen shrub of the mint family, native to the Mediterranean region and now widely cultivated as a flavouring herb. It has greyish leaves and blue flowers and the fragrance and taste are refreshing and somewhat piney.

In its fresh state, rosemary is generally used in chopped form, while the dry leaves are usually finely ground. It makes a good addition to stuffings, stews, roast meat, herb dumplings and many similar dishes, but must be used sparingly. It is particularly good with lamb, chicken or rabbit.

ROSOLIO

A bright red liqueur made in Italy and France; it is flavoured with either oil of roses or tangerine rind, orange juice and orange blossom.

RÔT, RÔTI

Literally, 'roast' or 'baked'. The poultry or game course in a formal dinner, as distinct from the remove, which is usually a meat roast.

RÔTISSERIE COOKERY

A method of cooking which has developed from the old fashioned spit over an open fire. The main advantages are that the meat bastes itself, there is little splashing, and the flavour, which some con-

351

sider to be better than oven-baked meat. Rôtisserie units are fitted on many gas or electric cookers, and separate electrically operated units are also available.

A rôtisserie attachment consists of:

A Shaft on which the food is impaled.

Holding Forks which slide on the shaft and can be secured by thumbscrews to hold the food firmly in place.

The Motor into which the loaded shaft is fitted.

The Tray placed under the revolving shaft to catch the drippings from the food as it cooks.

General Hints for using a Rôtisserie Unit:

1. Prepare the food in the usual way.

2. Push one end of the holding forks onto the shaft and secure it. Place the food on the shaft, pushing this through the centre of the food. Push on the second holding fork and secure.

3. Turn on the heat and allow the grill or oven to get very hot.

4. Place the loaded shaft in position (follow instruction booklet with cooker).

5. Turn on the rôtisserie motor and allow the shaft to revolve several times before leaving it, to make sure there is no obstruction and that it is turning evenly.

6. Turn down the heat and cook the food as instructed by the makers.

The food may be basted from time to time with the fat and juices in the tray or with any suitable flavouring. A slice of onion or garlic can be added to the dripping to give extra flavour.

Kebab cookery (see Kebab entry) has become more popular. Special kebab attachments are now supplied with some rôtisserie units. They consist of a number of skewers which are revolved by means of the rôtisserie motor.

ROULADE

French term for a meat roll.

ROUGH PUFF PASTRY

(See Pastry entry.)

ROUGHAGE

The name given to carbohydrate which is not available to the body as food, passing through without being assimilated. Most roughage consists of cellulose, the fibrous material which composes much of the stiffer structures of vegetables and cereal foods. Roughage is digested to a very small degree by bacterial fermentation in the intestines and makes a quite insignificant contribution to the diet, but it is of value in stimulating the contraction and evacuation of the bowels. There is some medical evidence to show that diseases of the bowel have increased in recent years due to food

becoming more refined. Hence, there is considerable publicity to encourage more roughage to be included in the diet.

In some types of illness roughage must be eliminated from the diet because its presence irritates the intestines.

ROUT CAKES AND BISCUITS

Confections somewhat similar to petits fours which were formerly served at 'routs' or evening parties. Many different types were made.

ROUX

This mixture, which forms the foundation of most sauces, is made by cooking together equal amounts of fat and (plain) flour. For white roux the mixture is cooked until it resembles a cream coloured paste; for blond roux it is cooked to a pale fawn colour and for brown roux to a rich golden-brown colour.

SIMPLE WHITE SAUCE – ROUX METHOD

POURING CONSISTENCY

METRIC/IMPERIAL

20 g/¾ oz butter or margarine
2 × 15 ml spoons/2 tablespoons flour
300 ml/½ pint milk or milk and stock
salt
pepper

Melt the fat, add the flour and stir with a wooden spoon until smooth. Cook over a gentle heat for 2 to 3 minutes, stirring until the mixture (called a roux) begins to bubble. Remove from the heat and add the liquid gradually, stirring after each addition to prevent lumps forming. Bring the sauce to the boil, stirring continuously, and when it has thickened, cook for a further 1 to 2 minutes. Add salt and pepper to taste.

COATING CONSISTENCY

METRIC/IMPERIAL

25 g/1 oz butter or margarine
3 × 15 ml spoons/3 tablespoons flour
300 ml/½ pint milk or milk and stock
salt
pepper

Make the sauce as above.

For a thick coating sauce increase the quantities to 40 g/1½ oz butter, 4 × 15 ml spoons/4 tablespoons flour.

BINDING CONSISTENCY (PANADA)

METRIC/IMPERIAL

50 g/2 oz butter or margarine

50 g/2 oz flour
300 ml/½ pint milk or milk and stock
salt
pepper

Melt the fat, add the flour and stir well. Cook gently for 2 to 3 minutes, stirring, until the roux begins to bubble and leave the sides of the pan. Off the heat, add the liquid gradually, bring to the boil, stirring all the time, and cook for 1 to 2 minutes after it has thickened; add salt and pepper to taste. This very thick sauce is used for binding mixtures such as croquettes.

ROWAN BERRY

The bright red fruit of the mountain ash. Rowan berries are occasionally used in making a jelly to serve with game and may also be sieved and added to apple sauce to vary the flavour.

ROWAN JELLY

Make in the usual way, using 2.75 kg/6 lb rowan berries, 1.5 kg/3 lb sharp apples and water to cover; allow 0.5 kg/1 lb sugar to each 600 ml/1 pint strained juice.

ROYAL ICING

The hard, white icing, made from egg whites and icing sugar, which is used for coating Christmas and other cakes that are to be decorated and kept for some time. It is usually applied over a coating of almond paste.

ROYAL ICING

Allow 4 egg whites to every 1 kg/2 lb icing sugar; 1 × 15 ml spoon/1 tablespoon glycerine may be added to give a softer texture. Sift the sugar twice. Separate the eggs, place the whites in a bowl and stir slightly – just sufficiently to break up the albumen, but without including too many air bubbles. Add half the icing sugar and stir until well mixed, using a wooden spoon; beat for about 5 to 10 minutes, or until the icing is smooth, glossy and white. Cover the bowl with a damp cloth or dampened greaseproof paper and leave to stand for at least 30 minutes, to allow any air bubbles to rise to the surface.

Gradually add the remaining icing sugar until the required consistency is obtained. When the icing is intended for flat work, stand a wooden spoon upright in it – if the consistency is correct it will fall slowly to one side. For rough icing, the mixture should be stiff enough for peaks to be easily formed on the surface when you 'pull' it up with the spoon. Add any desired colouring. If possible, leave the icing overnight in an airtight container in a cool place before use. To obtain a really smooth result, just before using the icing, remove 1 × 15 ml spoon/1 tablespoon of it and mix to a coating consistency with water, return it to the rest and mix until smooth.

NOTES
1. Royal icing can be made quite satisfactorily in an electric mixer; set the control on 'medium' speed and whisk the egg whites slightly. Now add the sifted sugar gradually until the mixture is of the required consistency. It is important to avoid over-beating and to allow the icing to stand for 24 hours before using it.
2. When using royal icing, it is advisable to keep the bowl and/or forcing bags covered with a damp cloth or a polythene bag, to prevent a crust forming on the icing.

To rough-ice a cake: Place 1 × 5 ml spoon/1 teaspoon of the icing on the cake-board and put on the cake firmly, centering it accurately. Spoon the icing on top of the cake. Working with a palette knife in a to-and-fro motion until the air bubbles are broken, cover the top and sides of the cake evenly. Now draw a clean ruler or palette knife across the top of the cake evenly and steadily, until the surface is

Flat Icing
1. Work icing with a palette knife in a to-and-fro motion across cake until evenly covered.

2. Draw a metal ruler across the top of the cake, then again at right angles to the first stroke.

3. Work the remaining icing onto the side of the cake then draw a baker's card round the side.

smooth. Using a round-bladed knife, draw the icing up into peaks round the sides and in a 3.5 cm/1 ½ inch border round the top of the cake – or as liked. Before the icing is set, you can put on one or two simple decorations.

If you want a very simply decorated cake, put almond paste on the top of the cake only and then royal icing on the top and down the sides for about 2.5 cm/1 inch, so that the almond paste is hidden. Rough-ice the sides and make a border round the cake as above. Decorate as desired and tie a ribbon round the cake below the icing. For this sort of decoration use half the suggested amounts of almond paste and royal icing.

To flat-ice a cake: Place the cake on the cake-board. Spoon about half the icing on top of it and with a palette knife work with a to-and-fro motion across the icing until the air bubbles are broken and the top of the cake is well and evenly covered. Some of the icing will work down the sides of the cake so return this to the bowl. Now draw an icing ruler or the palette knife across the top of the cake evenly and steadily. Draw it across again at right angles to the first stroke until the surface is smooth. If possible, leave the cake for 24 hours. (In this case, put the icing from the bowl into a polythene bag and store in a refrigerator.)

Put the cake and board on an upturned plate or a turn-table and work the remaining icing on to the sides of the cake. Draw a ruler, knife or baker's card round the sides until they are smooth. Smooth out the join between top and sides, then leave to set for at least 24 hours. Finally, remove any unevenness with a sharp knife.

If liked, apply a second layer of icing to give a really smooth finish. Save a little of the royal icing and mix it with a little water to give a coating consistency; pour on to the centre of the cake then, using a knife, spread it over the top and down the sides. Knock the board gently up and down on the table to bring any air bubbles to the surface, so that they can be burst with a pin before the icing sets. Leave to harden for 2 to 3 days.

ROYAL JELLY

The food given to certain bee larvae, which causes them to become queen bees.

It is claimed – without any scientific proof – to have certain magical effects on human health.

ROYAN

A delicately flavoured fish similar to a sardine. It is caught off the coast of France, near the town of that name.

RUBBING IN

A method of incorporating fat into flour, used in making shortcrust pastry, plain cakes and so on, where a short texture is required. First cut the fat into small pieces in the flour, then rub fat and flour between the thumbs and fingertips. Lift the hands well above the bowl – this helps to keep it cool and introduce air. Continue until the mixture is even throughout and resembles fine breadcrumbs. To test this, shake the bowl, when any large lumps remaining will be seen on the surface, while dry flour will collect at the bottom of the bowl.
1. Never try to rub in more than half as much fat as flour.
2. Have the fat cold and firm.
3. Do not cut short the rubbing-in process – it must be done thoroughly to ensure a short and even texture.

RUM

A spirit distilled from molasses and made chiefly in the West Indian and Caribbean region, especially in such sugar cane districts as Jamaica, Barbados, Trinidad, Demerara (Guyana), Martinique, Cuba and Puerto Rico. It can be sold as 'white rum', but is usually coloured with caramel and often flavoured with fruits such as prunes, raisins and guavas. Many hot and cold drinks may be made with it (see Punch entry, etc.) and it is also used for making rum butter and a syrup for Babas, also for flavouring cakes, omelettes, sauces, etc.

RUM BUTTER

METRIC/IMPERIAL
75 g/3 oz butter
75 g/3 oz soft brown sugar
2–3 × 15 ml spoons/2–3 tablespoons rum

Cream the butter until pale and soft. Beat in the sugar gradually and add the brandy a few drops at a time, taking care not to allow the mixture to curdle. The finished sauce should be pale and frothy. Pile it up in a small dish and leave to harden before serving.

RUM BABAS

METRIC/IMPERIAL
25 g/1 oz fresh yeast or 1 × 15 ml spoon/1 tablespoon dried yeast
6 × 15 ml spoons/6 tablespoons tepid milk
225 g/8 oz strong plain flour
1 × 2.5 ml spoon/ ½ teaspoon salt
2 × 15 ml spoons/2 tablespoons caster sugar
4 eggs, beaten
100 g/4 oz butter, soft but not melted
100 g/4 oz currants
whipped cream

FOR THE RUM SYRUP
8 × 15 ml spoons/8 tablespoons clear honey

8 × 15 ml spoons/8 tablespoons water
rum to taste

Lightly grease about sixteen 8.5 cm/3½ inch ring tins with lard. Put the yeast, milk and 50 g/2 oz of the flour in a bowl and blend until smooth. Allow to stand in a warm place until frothy, about 20 minutes. Add the remaining flour, the salt, sugar, eggs, butter and currants, and beat well for 3 to 4 minutes. Half-fill the tins with the dough and allow to rise until the moulds are two-thirds full.

Bake in a moderately hot oven (200°C/400°F, Gas Mark 6) for 15 to 20 minutes. Cool for a few minutes, then turn out on to a wire tray.

While the babas are still hot, spoon over each sufficient rum syrup to soak it well. Leave to cool. Served with whipped cream in the centre.

Rum syrup: Warm together the honey and water and add rum (or rum essence) to taste.

RUMP STEAK

(See Steak entry.)

RUNNER BEANS

(See Bean entry.)

RUSK

This may mean a type of sweetened tea biscuit, a piece of bread or cake crisped in the oven, or a commercially made product intended especially for young children and invalids. Both the last two types of rusk are frequently given to babies when they are teething and also to older children to keep their teeth in good condition. Plain rusks are sometimes served with cheese as an alternative to biscuits or bread.

RUTABAGA

A plant of the cabbage family, also known as the Swedish turnip, Russian turnip or swede. The stem swells underground to form a large fleshy root, orange-yellow in colour. (See Turnip entry for method of cooking.)

RYE

A hardy cereal which will grow in cold climates and in poor soil. The grain, which is brown and hard, with a slightly sour taste, is often mixed with other flours in bread-making, and is used on the Continent for making 'black' bread. It is also used for making special thin, dry, crisp biscuits.

The composition of rye flour varies with its source and the milling, the protein content being double and the calcium treble in the wholemeal flour, as compared with a low-extraction rye one: the calorific values of high-extraction rye flour are about the same as those of white flour (see Flour entry), but the calcium content is slightly higher in rye flour. The gluten content of rye flour is very poor and unless some other flour is mixed with it it makes a damp, heavy bread.

A whisky distilled from rye is popular in the USA and the Russian drink Kvass is also made from it.

SABAYON

This French version of the Italian word Zabaglione denotes a sweet sauce served with a rich sponge or fruit pudding (often steamed). It is a light frothy mixture made from eggs, sugar and wine or sherry; it is not quite as thick as Zabaglione.

SABAYON SAUCE (COLD)

METRIC/IMPERIAL
50 g/2 oz caster sugar
4 × 15 ml spoons/4 tablespoons water
2 egg yolks, beaten
grated rind of ½ lemon
juice of 1 lemon
2 × 15 ml spoons/2 tablespoons rum or sherry
2 × 15 ml spoons/2 tablespoons single cream

Dissolve the sugar in the water and boil for 2 to 3 minutes, until syrupy. Pour slowly on to the yolks, whisking until pale and thick. Add the lemon rind, lemon juice and rum or sherry and whisk for a further few minutes. Fold in the cream and chill well.
Serve with cold fruit sweets.

SACCHARIN

A white crystalline powder, manufactured from coal tar, which has remarkable sweetening properties. It has no food value and passes through the body unchanged: it is therefore used to sweeten food for people suffering from diabetes or other illnesses in which sugar is forbidden, or for those who are on a slimming diet. In times of sugar-shortage saccharin has been widely used in drinks, cakes, puddings, etc. There is some controversy over the addition of artificial sweeteners to food, as large doses have shown ill effects in animals. However, saccharin is permitted in certain foods, but it should be shown as an ingredient on the label.
The sweetening power of saccharin is about 550 times more than that of sugar. It is sold in the form of small white tablets, containing 0.2 grains of saccharin: ½ to 1 tablet is generally enough to sweeten a cup of tea or coffee. Saccharin tablets dissolve much more readily in hot liquids than in cold. The taste is improved if a little sugar is added with the saccharin.

Saccharin in Cooking

For sweetening fruit juice, jellies and moulds use 1 to 2 tablets to 300 ml/½ pint juice.
For junket and milk puddings use ½ to 1 tablet to 300 ml/½ pint milk.
For puddings and cakes use 3 tablets saccharin and 75 g/3 oz sugar to 225 g/8 oz flour.

NOTES
1. When saccharin is used for sweetening stewed fruit, milk puddings, etc., the tablets should be added after cooking or a bitter taste results.
2. Saccharin is not satisfactory for fruit-bottling, owing to a bitter flavour which develops. It is preferable to bottle the fruit in water and to add saccharin at the time of serving.
3. It is important to use some sugar with the saccharin in cakes and puddings, as this helps to give the desired texture.

JAM MADE WITH SACCHARIN
As saccharin has neither setting nor preserving qualities, it is necessary to add gelatine to obtain a good set. The jars containing the cooked jam must be sterilised and hermetically sealed, otherwise it will not keep satisfactorily. It is advisable to pot the jam in small jars, since it does not keep well once the jar is opened.

SACK

An old name for various white wines, particularly those from Spain and the Canaries; sherry is the only modern representative of the family.

SADDLE OF LAMB

This comprises the whole of the back of the animal, from the end of the loin to the best end of neck. It is usually divided into smaller joints.
Saddle of lamb is a prime roasting joint, an ideal choice for special occasion cookery or when cooking for large numbers.

SAFFLOWER OIL

An oil extracted from the seeds of a flowering plant. It is classed with other vegetable oils (such as corn oil and sunflower oil), as it contains a high proportion of poly-unsaturated fatty acids.

The dried and powdered flowers are also used as a colouring in foods and cosmetics.

SAFFRON

The yellow powder obtainable by drying the flower stigmas of the *Crocus Sativus*. It has an aromatic and slightly bitter taste and is used as a flavouring for certain cakes and buns and for bouillabaisse and for rice in various foreign dishes. It is also used to colour certain foodstuffs (e.g. alcoholic beverages). Saffron must not be kept more than about a year, as after that time the colour and flavour deteriorate. Always store in small air-tight containers.

It is expensive but weighs very light, and is usually bought from a chemist by the drachma. Before using saffron, soak a pinch in 2–3 × 15 ml spoons/2–3 tablespoons water, for ½–1 hour then strain.

SAFFRON CAKE

The Phoenicians introduced saffron to Cornwall where this cake is believed to originate and where it is still made today.

METRIC/IMPERIAL
25 g/1 oz fresh yeast
150 ml/¼ pint tepid milk
450 g/1 lb strong plain flour
1 × 5 ml spoon/1 teaspoon salt
50 g/2 oz butter
50 g/2 oz lard
175 g/6 oz currants
grated rind of ½ lemon
25 g/1 oz caster sugar
small packet (10 grains) of ground saffron, infused
    overnight in 150 ml/¼ pint boiling water

Grease a 20 cm/8 inch round cake tin. Crumble the yeast into a small basin, stir in the milk. Mix the flour and salt and rub in the butter and lard. Stir in the currants, lemon rind and sugar. Strain the saffron infusion into a pan and warm slightly; pour into the other ingredients, add the milk and yeast mixture and beat well. Turn the dough into the tin, cover with oiled polythene and leave in a warm place to rise until nearly at the top of the tin – about 1 hour. Bake in a moderately hot oven (200°C/400°F, Gas Mark 6) for 30 minutes, reduce to moderate (180°C/350°F, Gas Mark 4), and bake for a further 30 minutes. Turn out and cool on a wire rack.

SAGE

A strongly flavoured herb with a slightly bitter taste. There are several varieties, red and green sage being used for culinary purposes. The leaves, in both fresh and dried form, are used to flavour meat dishes, stuffings, cheese and lentil dishes, soups, salads and milk puddings; the flowers may be used in salads. Sage tea was drunk to a considerable extent in England before the introduction of China tea; it was thought to be a mild tonic and to soothe a sore throat. It was made by infusing 20 g/¾ oz fresh sage or 7 g/¼ oz dried sage in 600 ml/1 pint boiling water and served with sugar and lemon to taste.

SAGE AND ONION STUFFING

METRIC/IMPERIAL
2 large onions, skinned and chopped
25 g/1 oz butter
100 g/4 oz fresh white breadcrumbs
2 × 5 ml spoons/2 teaspoons dried sage
salt
pepper

Put the onions in a pan of cold water, bring to the boil and cook until tender, about 10 minutes. Drain well, add the other ingredients and mix well. Serve with pork.

SAGO

This pearly grain, obtained from the powdered pith of a type of palm-tree, is used for milk puddings and fruit moulds, in invalid dishes and for thickening soups. Sago contains little beyond starch, so it is essentially energy-giving food. (See Milk Pudding and Thickening entries.)

SAKÉ OR SAKI

A Japanese alcoholic drink made by fermenting rice. It is colourless and quite still and is usually served warm, in tiny porcelain bowls.

SALAD

The term 'salad', which is used in some form in most European languages, is derived from the Latin, *sal*, salt, since a salad originally meant merely something 'dipped in salt'. The most widely used kind is probably that made of uncooked green plants, but an infinite variety of vegetables and fruits can be used, either cooked or uncooked, to make delicious dishes, many of which form a meal in themselves when combined with a portion of a food such as fish, cheese, egg, cold meat, etc. Salads can also include cooked rice or pasta, nuts, dried fruit and herbs.

SAL

The nutritive value of salads obviously varies according to the foods used. Their vitamin C content is increased if the ingredients include a good percentage of raw fruits or vegetables, but the vitamin C in salad plants is quickly lost, so it is important to use them as soon as possible after they are gathered and to prepare them carefully.

Salads should be attractively presented, either in large dishes or salad bowls or individual plates or hors d'oeuvre dishes. They are usually served with French dressing, mayonnaise or something similar.

Salad plants and vegetables should be left uncut until required for use; then, using a sharp stainless knife, shred them coarsely rather than finely, to conserve the vitamins.

GREEN VEGETABLES
Wash quickly but thoroughly in running cold water, shake well over the sink and dry them by shaking in a salad basket or cloth. Shred lettuce with a stainless knife or break off the leaves with the fingers. Shred raw cabbage, Brussels sprouts, etc.

RAW CARROT
Peel or scrape and if not used at once, keep covered in cold water. Grate just before serving.

LEFTOVER COOKED ROOT VEGETABLES
Dice neatly.

POTATOES
Boil the potatoes and when cold mix with French dressing; mayonnaise may be added to hot or cold potatoes.

BEETROOT
Cook, then dice, cut into strips or slice. If desired, beetroot may be allowed to stand for a time in vinegar. Raw beetroot may be grated and added to salads in small quantities to add flavour and a crunchie texture.

PEAS AND BEANS
Cook and allow to cool before adding to the salad.

CAULIFLOWER
This may be added cooked or uncooked: in either case, break it into florets – very small ones, if raw.

CELERY AND CHICORY
Pull apart and wash or scrub each piece, then divide into suitable lengths.

CUCUMBER
Wipe and peel either completely, or in strips; slice thinly. The skin can be scored with a fork to give a decorative edge.

FRUITS
Prepare according to kind. The skins may if desired be removed – in the case of tomatoes, this is done more easily if the fruit is first dipped into boiling water for a moment.

358

CANNED VEGETABLES OR FRUIT
Any of these can be added to a salad. They should be well drained before use.

Garnishes for Salads
The following is a brief list; choose the garnish to contrast pleasantly with the salad.

Crimped slices of cucumber or lemon; celery curls; root vegetables cut into balls or fancy shapes; radish roses or lilies; diamond-shaped pieces of runner beans, etc.; sliced hard-boiled egg; sieved egg yolk; egg whites chopped or sliced and cut into fancy shapes; whole flowers or petals of nasturtium, wild rose or violet; balls of cream cheese, anchovy butter, etc.

It is important not to over-garnish a salad as it will not look appetizing.

Green Salads
These consist of one or more plants such as lettuce, cress, endive or watercress, tossed in a French or similar dressing. Prepare the salad plants, shake and dry them carefully and if they are not required at once, leave in a covered basin in a refrigerator or other cool place. Just before serving rub a clove of garlic or an onion round the inside of the salad bowl, put in the dressing and toss the salad in it. If a still more delicate garlic flavour is desired, rub a clove of garlic on a cut piece of bread, toss this with the salad and then discard it.

Salads containing just one dressed vegetable or fruit are quite common, e.g. tomato and orange salads. These are usually served as an accompaniment to savoury dishes.

Salads such as:
Tomato and onion salad.
Celery and walnut salad.
Watercress and orange salad.
Cucumber and onion salad.
Pepper and onion salad.

TOMATO SALAD

METRIC/IMPERIAL
4 tomatoes
a small piece of onion and ½ an apple (optional)
salt
pepper
2 × 15 ml spoons/2 tablespoons olive oil
2 × 5 ml spoons/2 teaspoons vinegar
chopped fresh basil or dried oregano to garnish
 (optional)

Remove the stalks from the tomatoes; if desired, the skin also may be removed by immersing in boiling water. Cut the tomatoes in slices, arrange neatly in a shallow dish and sprinkle on the chopped onion and apple, if using, and salt and pepper. Mix the oil and vinegar and pour over the salad. Garnish with herbs.

RUSSIAN SALAD – 1

(Using aspic jelly)

METRIC/IMPERIAL
1 small cauliflower, cooked
1–2 envelopes of aspic jelly powder
4 × 15 ml spoons/4 tablespoons cooked peas
2 × 15 ml spoons/2 tablespoons cooked diced carrot
2 × 15 ml spoons/2 tablespoons cooked diced turnip
3 potatoes, cooked and diced
1 small beetroot, cooked and diced
2 tomatoes, skinned and diced
50 g/2 oz ham or tongue, diced
50 g/2 oz shrimps or prawns cooked
50 g/2 oz smoked salmon, cut in strips, optional
3 gherkins, chopped
1 × 15 ml spoon/1 tablespoon capers
few lettuce leaves, shredded
2–3 × 15 ml spoons/2–3 tablespoons salad cream
4 olives
4 anchovy fillets

Divide the cauliflower into small sprigs. Make up the aspic jelly following the manufacturer's instructions. When it is cold, pour a little into a ring mould and turn this round until the sides are coated with jelly. Decorate with a little of the peas and diced vegetables and allow to set. Set layers of vegetables, meat, fish, gherkins and capers alternately with layers of jelly in the mould, but don't use up all the vegetables. When the mould is set, turn it out. Toss the lettuce and remaining vegetables in the salad cream and pile into the centre of the mould. Decorate with olives and anchovy fillets.

NOTE
Failing a ring mould, use an ordinary jelly mould; the remaining salad can be served in a border round the jellied salad.

RUSSIAN SALAD – 2

(Without aspic jelly)

Prepare vegetables, meat and fish as above; put layers of them in a salad bowl, season with salt, pepper and a pinch of caster sugar and cover each layer with salad cream. Decorate with beetroot, olives, capers, anchovies and salmon (if used).

TOSSED FRESH SPINACH SALAD

METRIC/IMPERIAL
4 × 15 ml spoons/4 tablespoons salad oil
2 × 15 ml spoons/2 tablespoons white wine vinegar
*1 × 2.5 ml spoon/½ teaspoon dried basil or 1 × 5 ml
  spoon/1 teaspoon fresh chopped basil*
1 × 2.5 ml spoon/½ teaspoon salad seasoning
2 × 5 ml spoons/2 teaspoons finely grated lemon rind
100 g/4 oz spinach

1 lettuce heart
6 radishes, trimmed and sliced
6 spring onions, trimmed and sliced

Put the oil and vinegar in a screw-top jar with the basil, salad seasoning and lemon rind. Shake well and leave to stand. Wash the spinach thoroughly, discarding any tough stems; then dry thoroughly. Wash and dry the lettuce. Using your fingertips, shred the spinach and lettuce into bite size pieces. Mix these with the sliced radishes and spring onions, toss the dressing through and pile into a serving dish. Serve as a side salad with grills or cold meats.

APPLE, RAISIN AND WALNUT SALAD

METRIC/IMPERIAL
2 × 15 ml spoons/2 tablespoons lemon juice
1 × 2.5 ml spoon/½ teaspoon apple pie spice
3 crisp, green eating apples
50 g/2 oz seedless raisins
50 g/2 oz walnuts, roughly chopped

Mix together the lemon juice and spice. Core the apples and slice them thinly. Toss the apple slices in the spiced lemon juice. Add the raisins and walnuts and toss well together. Serve as a side salad with pork, cooked bacon joint or chicken.

SALAD DRESSING

There are many recipes for salad dressings, but strictly speaking only two standard ones – French dressing and mayonnaise.

The success of a salad dressing depends very much on the quality of the ingredients. Pure olive oil is considered the best to use for dressings as it gives the most delicate and pure flavour. However, it is more expensive than salad oils which usually consist of a blend of oils. These will make a satisfactory dressing.

Use the finest mild-flavoured malt vinegar, or better still, a good French wine vinegar. Avoid crude or strongly flavoured brands, which are likely to make the dressing less palatable. Lemon juice can be used in place of some or all of the vinegar if desired and is preferred by some people. Herb-flavoured vinegars, such as tarragon, may be included, but only in small quantities, otherwise the flavour of the herb may predominate.

Seasonings, such as salt and pepper, should be measured carefully; their presence should not be accentuated in the finished dressing.

Using salad dressings: French dressing should be put on the salad shortly before serving, as such things as lettuce become limp after the dressing has been on any length of time.

Mayonnaise gives a better flavour if mixed with potatoes and other vegetables while they are hot.

359

When mayonnaise is intended to coat vegetables, etc, it is best put on just before serving, unless it is set with aspic jelly.

Salad dressings will tarnish silver, so wooden, glass, china or plastic utensils should be used.

FRENCH DRESSING (SAUCE VINAIGRETTE)

French dressing, consisting of oil and vinegar with seasonings, is the simplest of all and is usually preferred by the connoisseur. It may be varied by adding various flavouring ingredients such as chopped chives or herbs or piquant ingredients such as a relish or chopped pickles, olives and so on: a few of these variations are given below.

METRIC/IMPERIAL
pinch salt
pinch pepper
pinch dry mustard
pinch sugar
1 × 15 ml spoon/1 tablespoon vinegar
2 × 15 ml spoons/2 tablespoons salad oil

Put the salt, pepper, mustard and sugar in a bowl, add the vinegar and stir until well blended. Beat in the oil gradually with a fork. The oil separates out on standing, so if necessary whip the dressing immediately before use. If you wish, store it in a salad cream bottle, shaking it up vigorously just before serving.

The proportion of oil to vinegar varies with individual taste, but use vinegar sparingly. Malt, wine, tarragon or any other vinegar may be used.

VARIATIONS
To the above dressing add any of the following:

METRIC/IMPERIAL
clove of garlic, crushed
1–2 × 5 ml spoons/1–2 teaspoons chopped chives
1–2 × 2.5 ml spoons/½–1 teaspoon curry powder
2 × 5 ml spoons/2 teaspoons chopped fresh parsley
1 × 2.5 ml spoon/½ teaspoon dried marjoram and a pinch of dried thyme
1 × 5 ml spoon/1 teaspoon chopped fresh parsley
1 × 5 ml spoon/1 teaspoon chopped gherkins or capers, 1 × 5 ml spoon/1 teaspoon chopped olives
1–2 × 5 ml spoons/1–2 teaspoons sweet pickle
1 × 15 ml spoon/1 tablespoon finely sliced or chopped stuffed olives
1–2 × 5 ml spoons/1–2 teaspoons Worcestershire sauce
1–2 × 5 ml spoons/1–2 teaspoons chopped fresh mint
1 × 15 ml spoon/1 tablespoon finely chopped anchovies
pinch of curry powder, ½ hard-boiled egg, shelled and finely chopped, 1 × 5 ml spoon/1 teaspoon chopped onion (this is called Bombay dressing)
25 g/1 oz blue-vein cheese, crumbled
1 × 15 ml spoon/1 tablespoon finely diced pepper

Vinaigrette

There are many different interpretations of vinaigrette dressing; generally, it means a French dressing to which have been added one or more of the following: finely chopped gherkins, chives, shallots, capers, parsley and/or other herbs.

Some writers use the term to mean simply a plain French dressing.

Mayonnaise

This is essentially an emulsion of oil and raw egg yolks, with seasonings and vinegar or lemon juice to give piquancy. Occasionally whipped or soured cream is used to replace some or all of the oil.

The process of making mayonnaise is rather lengthy, unless a mixer is available. However, it may be made in fairly large quantities and stored for some weeks in a refrigerator or a cool place.

In addition to its use with ordinary salads, mayonnaise is served with such dishes as lobster mayonnaise, with certain vegetables (e.g., asparagus, globe artichokes) and to blend savoury fillings for cocktail snacks; it may also be stiffened with gelatine and used to mask chaudfroid savouries.

CLASSIC MAYONNAISE

METRIC/IMPERIAL
1 egg yolk
1 × 2.5 ml spoon/½ teaspoon dry mustard
1 × 2.5 ml spoon/½ teaspoon salt
a dash of pepper
1 × 2.5 ml spoon/½ teaspoon sugar
about 150 ml/¼ pint salad oil
1 × 15 ml spoon/1 tablespoon white vinegar

Put the egg yolk into a basin with the seasonings and sugar. Mix thoroughly, then add the oil drop by drop, stirring briskly with a wooden spoon the whole time or using a whisk, until the sauce is thick and smooth. If it becomes too thick add a little of the vinegar. When all the oil has been added, add the vinegar gradually and mix thoroughly. If liked, lemon juice may be used instead of the vinegar.

NOTES
To keep the basin firmly in position, twist a damp cloth tightly round the base – this prevents it from slipping. In order that the oil may be added 1 drop at a time, put into the bottle neck a cork from which a small wedge has been cut.

Should the sauce curdle during the process of making, put another egg yolk into a basin and add the curdled sauce very gradually, in the same way as the oil is added to the original egg yolks.

VARIATIONS
Using 150 ml/¼ pint mayonnaise as a basis, add a flavouring as follows:

Caper: Add 2 × 5 ml spoons/2 teaspoons chopped capers, 1 × 5 ml spoon/1 teaspoon chopped pimiento and 1 × 2.5 ml spoon/½ teaspoon tarragon vinegar. Goes well with fried or grilled fish.

Celery: Add 1 × 15 ml spoon/1 tablespoon chopped celery and 1 × 15 ml spoon/1 tablespoon chopped chives.

Cream: Add 4 × 15 ml spoons/4 tablespoons whipped cream. Goes well with salads containing fruit, chicken or rice.

Cucumber: Add 3 × 15 ml spoons/3 tablespoons finely chopped cucumber and 1 × 2.5 ml spoon/½ teaspoon salt. Goes well with fish salads, especially crab, lobster and salmon.

Herbs: Add 2 × 15 ml spoons/2 tablespoons chopped chives and 1 × 15 ml spoon/1 tablespoon chopped parsley.

Horseradish: Add 1 × 15 ml spoon/1 tablespoon horseradish sauce.

Piquant: Add 1 × 5 ml spoon/1 teaspoon tomato ketchup, 1 × 5 ml spoon/1 teaspoon chopped olives and a pinch of paprika pepper.

Tomato: Add ½ tomato, skinned and diced, 1 spring onion, chopped, pinch salt and 1 × 5 ml spoon/1 teaspoon chopped parsley.

Blue cheese: Add 25 g/1 oz crumbled Danish blue cheese.

All these variations can also be made using a basis of bought salad cream.

In small quantities, mayonnaise can only be made in a blender if the blades are set low enough to beat the egg yolk. It sometimes helps to add 1 × 15 ml spoon/1 tablespoon warm water or to use a whole egg. It is easier to make mayonnaise in large quantities.

SOURED CREAM DRESSING

METRIC/IMPERIAL
150 ml/¼ pint carton soured cream
2 × 15 ml spoons/2 tablespoons white vinegar
small piece of raw onion, skinned and finely chopped
1 × 2.5 ml spoon/½ teaspoon sugar
1 × 5 ml spoon/1 teaspoon salt
pinch of pepper

Mix all the ingredients thoroughly. Serve with jacket potatoes

YOGURT DRESSING

Yogurt can be used in salad dressings in the same way as soured cream. Use 1–2 × 5 ml spoons/1–2 teaspoons lemon juice or wine vinegar and flavour with chopped spring onions, chives, parsley or other fresh herbs, or a little curry powder.

SALAMI

A type of dry sausage produced in Italy, Hungary and various other European countries. It is made from finely chopped lean pork, pork fat, highly seasoned, flavoured with garlic and moistened with red wine. The sausages are air-dried or smoked and if properly stored will keep for a very long time. Salami is eaten as an appetizer or with other cold meats and salad. It can be filled with a savoury mixture and rolled up, used in open sandwiches or as a garnish.

SALLY LUNN

A plain type of teacake baked in cake tins of various sizes. Sally Lunns are served hot, split and buttered. Alternatively, they may be served cold, topped with glacé icing.

The name is said to have come from a pastry cook in Bath.

SALLY LUNN

METRIC/IMPERIAL
50 g/2 oz butter
200 ml/⅓ pint tepid milk
1 × 5 ml spoon/1 teaspoon caster sugar
2 eggs
15 g/½ oz fresh yeast
450 g/1 lb strong plain flour
1 × 5 ml spoon/1 teaspoon salt

FOR THE GLAZE
4 × 15 ml spoons/4 tablespoons water
2 × 15 ml spoons/2 tablespoons sugar

Thoroughly grease two 13 cm/5 inch round cake tins. Melt the butter slowly in a pan, remove from the heat and add the milk and sugar. Beat the eggs and add with the warm milk mixture to the yeast. Blend well. Add to the flour and salt, mix well and lightly knead. Put into the cake tins, cover with oiled polythene and leave to rise until the dough fills the tins – about 45 minutes to 1 hour. Bake in a hot oven (230°C/450°F, Gas Mark 8) for 15 to 20 minutes. Turn the Sally Lunns out of the tins on to a wire rack. Make the glaze by heating the water and sugar to boiling point and boiling for 2 minutes. Use at once to glaze the hot buns.

SALMAGUNDI

An old English supper dish of the eighteenth century consisting of meat, salad, eggs, anchovy, pickles and beetroot, diced and carefully arranged to form a pattern, and served on a bed of salad.

SALMI

A kind of ragoût, usually made from game or

poultry, which is cooked by a mixture of two processes, roasting and then stewing.

SALMI OF GOOSE

METRIC/IMPERIAL
1 goose, lightly roasted
1 shallot, skinned and chopped
1 orange, peeled and segmented
150 ml/¼ pint stock
300 ml/½ pint espagnole sauce
150 ml/¼ pint red wine
few white grapes, skinned and pipped
red-currant jelly

Remove the skin from the goose; cut off the leg and wing joints and put aside. Break the carcass into small pieces and put in a pan with the shallot, thinly pared orange rind and stock. Simmer together for 30 minutes. Strain the stock from the pan, put it with the espagnole sauce, wine and goose joints into a saucepan and simmer until the joints are heated through – about 10 minutes. Arrange the joints on a serving dish and boil the sauce until it is reduced to a syrupy consistency. Pour it over the goose and garnish with the grapes and sections of orange. Serve with red-currant jelly.

SALMON

A round fish, weighing 4.5 kg/10 lb to 13.5 kg/30 lb, caught in the rivers in this country from February to August. It is imported all the year round and is also obtainable in canned and smoked form.

Salmon is at its best when the head and tail are small and the neck thick; it should be stiff, red in the gills and covered with bright silvery scales; the flesh should be of a bright red colour.

Salmon is one of the oily fish and is thus digested more slowly than white fish, but it is a good source of vitamin D and has a higher energy value than white fish: it also provides animal protein and calcium.

Freezing: A whole salmon can be frozen with care. It must be really fresh (under 12 hours from catch). Wash, remove scales and gut. Wash thoroughly under running water. Drain and dry. Place the fish unwrapped in the freezer until solid. Remove and dip in cold water. This forms thin ice over the fish. Return to the freezer. Repeat the process until the ice glaze is 5 mm/¼ inch thick. Wrap in heavy duty polythene and support with a thin board.

To thaw, allow 24 hours in a cool place before cooking. Once thawed use promptly.

Salmon steaks and cuts freeze very well. They should be individually wrapped or interleaved. Salmon pieces are available ready frozen, and do not require thawing before cooking.

Preparation and cooking: Scale the fish, holding it by the tail and using a knife. Gut it, then scrape and wash all the blood away, but do not wash the fish more than necessary. Salmon may be cooked whole or cut across into large pieces or steaks and it may be served hot or cold. Boiling, grilling and baking are all good methods of cooking for this fish.

CANNED SALMON
The grade I type can be used in place of fresh fish, especially in scallops, moulds and similar dishes. Grades II and III salmon are best served in made-up dishes such as fish cakes, with a well-flavoured accompaniment like cheese or parsley sauce.

Red salmon is named 'Sockeye' on the can label, the best being the middle cut. Pink salmon has the name 'Cohoe' (silver).

SMOKED SALMON
This delicacy, which is sold ready to serve, is eaten as an appetizer (sliced very thinly and served with lemon and brown bread and butter). It may also be used in salads and sandwiches. Smoked salmon offcuts can be bought at a reduced price and used for pâtés and pastes.

POACHED SALMON

This may be done in a saucepan on the top of the stove or in a shallow covered casserole in a moderate oven (180°C/375°F, Gas Mark 4). Whole fish and large pieces are usually cooked on the top of the stove completely covered in liquid. A special fish kettle is required for this.

Prepare the fish and wrap in muslin or aluminium foil so that it is easy to remove, then place in the pan. Cover with salted water or court bouillon and simmer gently until the fish is tender. Allow about 10 minutes to the 0.5 kg/1 lb.

Smaller steaks or slices of salmon tend to break unless carefully cooked. Wrap in muslin, foil or greaseproof paper and poach very gently, allowing 10 minutes to the 0.5 kg/1 lb. If to be eaten cold allow the fish to cool in the cooking liquid before removing.

FOIL-BAKED SALMON

Line a baking sheet with a larger piece of foil, and butter the surface. Place the prepared salmon on the foil. Dot each steak with butter and season with salt, pepper and lemon juice. Package loosely and cook in a moderate oven (180°C/350°F, Gas Mark 4) for 20 to 40 minutes, according to the thickness of the fish. Serve with maître d'hôtel butter or hollandaise sauce or garnish with poached diced cucumber, sliced lemon and parsley sprigs. If it is to be eaten cold, leave it to cool still wrapped in the foil.

Foil-baked salmon can be prepared the day before it is required and stored in the refrigerator to cook just before serving. Cod steaks can also be cooked by this method.

SALMON MOUSSE

METRIC/IMPERIAL
2 × 215 g/7½ oz cans salmon
about 300 ml/½ pint milk
25 g/1 oz butter
3 × 15 ml spoons/3 tablespoons flour
2 eggs, separated
150 ml/¼ pint carton double cream, lightly whipped
2 × 15 ml spoons/2 tablespoons tomato ketchup
1 × 5 ml spoon/1 teaspoon anchovy essence
1 × 5 ml spoon/1 teaspoon lemon juice
salt
pepper
4 × 5 ml spoons/4 teaspoons powdered gelatine
4 × 5 ml spoons/4 teaspoons warm water
slices of cucumber to garnish

Drain the juice from the salmon and make it up to 300 ml/½ pint with milk. Remove the skin and bones from the fish and mash the flesh until smooth. Melt the butter, stir in the flour and cook for 2 to 3 minutes. Remove the pan from the heat and gradually stir in the salmon liquid and milk. Bring to the boil and continue to stir until the sauce thickens. Remove from the heat and add the egg yolks. Allow the sauce to cool slightly and stir in the cream, ketchup, essence, lemon juice and seasoning to taste and add it to the salmon.

Dissolve the gelatine in the water by putting it in a small basin in a pan of hot water; stir it into the salmon mixture. Whisk the egg whites stiffly and fold these into the mixture. Pour it into an 18 cm/7 inch soufflé dish and leave to set in a cool place. Garnish with slices of cucumber before serving.

SALMON TROUT

This sea fish is in season from March to August. It resembles salmon, but when cooked has slightly pinker flesh. The flavour is not quite as good making it cheaper than salmon. It is cooked whole with the same accompaniments as salmon. (See Salmon and Trout entries.)

SALPICON

The French name given to many different mixtures of chopped fish, meat and vegetables in a sauce, used as stuffings or fillings. It usually means minced or diced poultry or game, mixed with ham or tongue and mushrooms (or truffles) bound with sauce and used for croquettes, appetizers, bouchée fillings and canapés.

SALSIFY ('VEGETABLE OYSTER')

A white root vegetable similar to a parsnip in

shape. It has a slightly sweet flavour, supposed to resemble that of oysters, which accounts for its common name. It is ready for digging in September and will keep through the winter in the ground or stored in sand. There is a black variety known as Scorzonera: both have a long tapering root.

Salsify is used as a vegetable and to flavour steak pies, etc.; the flower stalks may be cooked like asparagus. It contributes a small amount of vitamin C to the diet.

Preparation and cooking: Wash the salsify carefully, cutting a small piece off the end of each stalk. Scrape it lightly and place it in cold water, adding a few drops of vinegar to prevent discoloration. Boil until tender in a small quantity of boiling salted water, with a few drops of vinegar added – 30 to 40 minutes. Serve with a white sauce. If preferred, it may be re-heated in a good sauce such as Béchamel.

Salsify may also be steamed – it will take about 40 to 50 minutes. Another variation is to coat the well-drained boiled salsify in batter and fry it until golden-brown.

SALT

Salt (sodium chloride) is a mineral deposit, found in different parts of the earth. It has always been an important substance and much involved in trade. At one stage in history people were paid in salt and this has given us the word 'salary', from the Latin word meaning money for the purchase of salt.

Salt is found in solid form, as rock salt, and in solution in both sea water and brine wells. Nowadays, salt for table and other purposes is usually produced from brine wells, although in Cheshire there is one rock salt mine still working which was an important source in the days of the Roman Empire. Most salt produced in this country comes from Cheshire, although a little is also found in Worcestershire and Lancashire.

To obtain the salt a well is sunk to the level of the brine and this is pumped out. As water seeps through the earth to the salt it forms more brine. The pumped-out brine is purified, evaporated and then dried. The residue eventually consists of over 99.8 per cent pure salt; the remaining fraction may consist of minute impurities and a little moisture.

Salt is essential to life, but it is so widely used in cooking and as a condiment that there is normally no difficulty in ensuring an adequate supply. When heavy manual work or high temperatures cause an unusual amount of perspiration, however, extra salt should be taken, either as a tablet or in water or in a lemon or barley drink, to prevent fatigue and cramp. On the other hand, low-salt diets are sometimes medically prescribed in certain conditions and illnesses, such as kidney and heart complaints.

TABLE SALT

Salt which is finely ground and usually mixed with a very small proportion of magnesium carbonate and calcium phosphate, to help keep it in a dry condition. Iodized table salt can also be obtained, to ensure a sufficient supply of iodine. Salt has a corrosive action on metals, so it should not be left in silver containers and any metal container should have a glass lining.

COOKING SALT

A cheap and less refined type which can be used for general domestic purposes. The more old-fashioned block salt is rarely obtained nowadays. These salts readily absorb moisture, so must be kept in a dry place in a covered container, preferably of stone or glass.

SEA SALT

This salt is obtained by evaporating sea water.

FREEZING SALT

A type specially sold for mixing with the ice used in ice cream freezing machines. (See Ice cream entry.)

Using Salt

The use of the correct amount of salt improves the flavour of most savoury dishes and of many sweet ones. A pinch of salt should always be added to cakes and puddings, to help make the gluten in the flour more elastic, so that the mixture will rise better.

Salt is added to the water used for cleaning vegetables, to remove grubs. Fish being skinned and filleted can be held more firmly if the fingers are dipped in salt.

SALT HERRING

Herrings preserved by salting. They are stored in barrels, covered with brine, for if they come into contact with the air, their oil turns rancid. Any fat that collects on the top must be skimmed off.

Preparation and cooking: Wash the fish very thoroughly to remove the brine, cut off the head and fins, clean out the inside and bone, if desired. Soak in cold water for 12 to 24 hours, then remove the skin and use the fish as required.

SALTED NUTS

(See Nuts entry.)

SALTING

This is one of the oldest methods of preservation and is still a useful way of keeping meat, fish, butter and some vegetables such as beans. There are two methods, wet and dry, and in both cases sea or common salt, brown sugar and saltpetre are used. Dry salting involves more work, but enables spices to be used, which give meat a better flavour.

WET SALTING (ALSO CALLED PICKLING)

Use a container of suitable size (not glazed earthenware, as the salt will injure the glaze) which can be stood on a shelf or on pieces of wood.

For a piece of pork or beef (usually silverside) weighing about 2.25 kg/5 lb, add 0.5 kg/1 lb to 0.75 kg/1½ lb sea or common salt, 175 g/6 oz brown sugar and 25 g/1 oz saltpetre to 4.5 litres/ 1 gallon water; bring to the boil, strain into the container and allow to become cold. Put the meat in the liquid, cover and leave for 5 days, turning it daily.

DRY SALTING

This is specially suitable for thin flank, aitchbone or round of beef. Rub a mixture of salt, sugar and saltpetre (in above proportions) into the meat. The following day rub in a mixture of 7 g/¼ oz black pepper, 15 g/½ oz powdered allspice, 1 × 5 ml spoon/1 teaspoon ground ginger, 1 × 2.5 ml spoon/½ teaspoon ground cloves and 1 × 2.5 ml spoon/½ teaspoon ground mace. Turn the meat daily for 1 to 2 weeks.

To cook salted food: Wash away surplus salt by rinsing the food in several changes of cold water, then cook in the usual way.

SALTPETRE (POTASSIUM NITRATE)

This is used extensively in conjunction with common salt for the preservation of meat, e.g., in pickling and preparing corned beef.

It gives an agreeable reddish colour to meat.

SAMBALS

Accompaniments to Indian and Pakistan dishes, particularly curries (see Curry entry).

SAMPHIRE

A piquant-flavoured succulent plant found along various rocky European coasts. The leaves can be pickled in vinegar or served fresh in salads or as a vegetable.

SAMSOE (SAMSØ)

A golden Danish cheese made on the island of Samsø. It is a cartwheel shape, about 40 cm/16 inches in diameter and weighs 14.5 kg/32 lb. It is often eaten fresh on the island but is stored for 5 months before being exported. (See Cheese entry.)

SAND CAKE

A Madeira-type cake containing cornflour, ground rice or potato flour.

CORNFLOUR SAND CAKE
A traditional tea-time cake.

METRIC/IMPERIAL
cornflour and caster sugar to prepare tin
100 g/4 oz butter
150 g/5 oz caster sugar
3 eggs
175 g/6 oz cornflour
grated rind of 1 lemon
1 × 5 ml spoon/1 teaspoon baking powder

Grease an 18 cm/7 inch ring mould tin and dust it with a mixture of 1 × 5 ml spoon/1 teaspoon cornflour and 1 × 5 ml spoon/1 teaspoon caster sugar. Beat the butter until soft, add the sugar and beat until white and creamy. Add the beaten eggs a little at a time, beating after each addition and adding a little of the cornflour if the mixture shows signs of curdling. Add the lemon rind and fold in the remaining cornflour, sifted together with the baking powder. Turn the mixture into the tin and bake in the centre of a moderate oven (180°C/350°F, Gas Mark 4) for about 1 hour. Leave the cake in the tin for a short time before turning it out.

SANDWICH

Two slices of bread enclosing some kind of filling. Sandwiches are said to have been invented by Lord Sandwich, from whom they take their name. A wide range of shapes and sizes can be made, to suit different occasions, ranging from a snack meal to afternoon tea, and the sandwiches can be served either hot or cold.

Preparing the filling: Meat should be minced or cut small and vegetables, apples, nuts, herbs, etc., should be chopped, shredded or grated and bound with softened butter, salad cream, etc. On occasions when sandwiches have to be made in advance, avoid very moist fillings, which soak into the bread or biscuits.

Cutting: If possible, use bread which is about 24 hours old. When making wafer-thin sandwiches for afternoon tea or for invalids, butter the slices before cutting, but for large numbers and for more substantial sandwiches, it is often quicker to slice the whole loaf before buttering. Providing the bread is not too new, the crusts may be removed before slicing, but they are usually left on when catering for children and teenagers or for informal occasions like picnics. When you are making large numbers of sandwiches, thinly cut sliced loaves are a great labour-saver. Malt and currant breads, provided they are not over-sweetened, may be used for sweet sandwiches.

Spreading: Sandwiches inevitably use a fair amount of fat, but the butter or margarine will spread much more easily and economically if it is slightly

warmed and softened beforehand.

Serving: To keep the sandwiches fresh, cover them with a basin until required, or wrap them in a damp cloth, aluminium foil or polythene film. If you have a freezer, sandwiches may be prepared a week or two in advance, wrapped and frozen. These should not contain hard-boiled egg or salad ingredients, as these are not suitable for freezing.

When several varieties of fillings are used, the type should be indicated by the garnish or by a sandwich flag.

Types of Sandwich

FANCY-SHAPED
Cut the slices lengthwise and shape them with special cutters, e.g., into hearts, diamonds, etc.

DECKER SANDWICHES
These are appetizing for snack meals, especially when made with toast and served hot. Place different fillings between three or more layers of any type of bread or toast.

HOT SANDWICHES
Use hot rolls, baps or bread toasted on one side.

OPEN SANDWICHES
Use a base of white or brown bread (cut into fancy shapes), small rolls, crispbread or biscuits. See Smørrebrød.

ROLLED SANDWICHES
Use moist bread; butter it, cut it thinly, spread with filling or insert asparagus tips, etc., and roll.

PINWHEEL SANDWICHES
Make large rolled sandwiches with slices cut lengthwise off the loaf, and then cut them across to give a Swiss roll effect.

NEAPOLITAN SANDWICHES
These are made of white and brown bread used alternately, with different-coloured fillings between the layers. Cut 3 mm/⅛ inch slices lengthwise across the loaves, sandwich three or more together and cut across the layers. Arrange the sandwiches on a plate to show the striped effect.

BREAD BARS
Cut 1 cm/½ inch slices of bread into bars and spread the whole outside surface with the sandwich mixture. Roll the bars in chopped parsley, chopped nuts or sieved egg yolks, etc.

SANDWICH LOAF
Cut a loaf horizontally into 4 slices, then remove all the crusts. Sandwich together, using a different filling for each layer – for example, flaked salmon, scrambled egg flavoured with cheese, shredded lettuce and chopped ham bound with mayonnaise. Coat the outside with cream cheese and garnish. To serve, cut down into slices.

Fillings

In addition to a single filling such as meat, egg, cheese, etc., many unusual and interesting fillings may be achieved by combining two, three or even more ingredients. Anything like gherkins, celery, olives, etc., should be chopped small. Here are some popular mixtures.

1. Beef with horseradish sauce, onion or gherkins and French mustard.
2. Chicken or other white meat with celery and mayonnaise or olives and tomato sauce.
3. Fish with tomato sauce and onion (or pickle), shredded cabbage and mayonnaise.
4. Salmon or smoked salmon with lettuce and lemon juice or cucumber and tomato sauce.
5. Crab, lobster and other shellfish with cress and cucumber or tomato and mayonnaise.
6. Smoked cod's roe with tomato, lettuce and lemon juice.
7. Various kinds of cheese with celery and pickles, chives and parsley or apple and chutney.
8. Egg (hard-boiled, scrambled or fried) with cream cheese and chives or capers and tomato sauce.
9. Vegetable mixtures such as fried mushrooms, tomato and parsley; cooked peas, mint and mayonnaise; olives, lettuce and vinegar; pickled onion, cucumber and piquant sauce.
10. Fruit mixtures such as apple, nutmeg and brown sugar; mashed banana, chopped raisins and orange juice; dried fruit, peanut butter and sliced orange; dates, ginger and chopped apple.

SANDWICH CAKE

(See Victoria Sponge, Sandwich Cake and Layer Cake entries.)

SARACEN CORN

(See Buckwheat entry.)

SARDINE

Originally this name was given to young pilchards caught off the shores of Sardinia; it is now applied to various somewhat similar fish in different parts of the world. French and Portuguese sardines are still chiefly young pilchards; in America and Russia they are usually young herrings; in Norway they may be either sprats (also known as brisling) or young herrings (sild).

Fresh sardines are delicious when grilled and are served in this way in many European sea-coast towns. To most people, however, sardines are more familiar in their canned form, packed in tomato juice or more commonly in olive or other oil; the bones are usually left in. Canned sardines packed in good-quality oil improve in flavour if left to mature in the can for about two years. The bones eventually become soft enough to eat with the fish and they then form a good source of calcium. Sardines are also good sources of protein, fat, iodine and vitamins A and D. They are more nutritious than white fish, but not so easily digested.

Sardines are mainly used for savouries of all kinds, from tiny cocktail titbits and appetizers to such snacks as grilled sardines on toast; they are also popular in hors d'œuvre and salads and as a sandwich filling.

SARSAPARILLA

A flavouring made from the dried roots of a tropical American plant; it was formerly used to make a refreshing still cold drink and is now used to flavour carbonated ones.

SATSUMA

(See Tangerine entry.)

SAUCE

A sauce is used to flavour, coat or accompany a dish and may also be used in the actual cooking to bind the ingredients together.

A sauce can make or mar a dish and must be carefully prepared. Use a clean, thick pan to prevent burning. Since the flavour depends largely on the liquid used, employ water only as a last resort; always keep some liquid back for last-minute adjustments, as it is easier to add more liquid to a sauce which is too thick than to thicken a too-thin one. Taste the sauce before serving and adjust the seasoning if necessary.

Types of Sauce

THIN SAUCES

These are made with unthickened liquids, common examples being mint sauce and thin gravy. These sauces are quite simple to make, but they must be well flavoured. (See individual entries for recipes.)

THICKENED SAUCES WITH A ROUX BASIS

This class includes a large number of the most frequently used sauces, which are really variations of the two main 'roux' sauces – white and brown. (See Roux entry.)

THICKENED BLENDED SAUCES

These are thickened by means of a starchy substance, which may be arrowroot, cornflour or custard powder. Arrowroot, when it is used with a clear liquid, gives a clear sauce, suitable for glazing flans, etc. (See Glaze entry.) Whichever type of flour is used, it is blended with the liquid (milk, stock, water or a mixture) and no fat is needed. For sweet sauces, fruit syrup or purée may be used and sugar is, of course, substituted for the seasoning.

SAUCES THICKENED WITH EGG

These can take the form of egg custard or Hollandaise sauce (see entries), but in both cases the whole egg or egg yolks are cooked for a short time until they thicken. They must not however be over-heated or the sauce curdles, i.e., the albumen hardens, shrinks and separates out from the liquid. To prevent this, the cooking temperature of egg sauces must always be kept below boiling point.

MISCELLANEOUS SAUCES

Many well-known accompaniments are not made according to any of the methods listed above – for example, rum butter, melted butter and flavouring butters, apple, gooseberry and bread sauces, horseradish cream, mayonnaise and aspic mayonnaise, some chocolate sauces, jam, marmalade and syrup sauces (which may be thickened or thin).

(See individual entries for recipes.)

SAUERKRAUT

This is cabbage which has been allowed to ferment in salt; it is a favourite dish on the Continent, especially when it is served with sausages. Sauerkraut may often be bought ready prepared in delicatessen shops and it is also obtainable in canned form.

Preparation and cooking: Fresh sauerkraut need only be washed in several cold waters to remove the brine.

Boil the sauerkraut in a very little water for about 30 minutes. To give additional flavour, add a few bacon rinds, a ham-bone or 1 to 2 tart apples (peeled, cored and sliced).

SAUSAGE

Meat mixed with fat, cereal or bread and seasonings, with suitable colouring and preservative, and packed into a special skin. The sausage skins used to be obtained from the entrails of pigs or oxen, but may now be a synthetic product. Their size, of course, determines the diameter of the sausage. After being filled the sausages are 'linked' by being twisted at the required intervals.

Regulations control the content and labelling of all sausages.

Ready-cooked sausages are obtainable in many varieties – for example, liver and breakfast sausages, salami and saveloys, some of which are smoked. A wide range is made in Continental countries and many of them are obtainable in delicatessen shops and supermarkets in this country. These cooked sausages are served sliced with appetizers or salads, in sandwiches and in savoury fillings, pies, patties, etc.

Uncooked sausages also may be either smoked (e.g. Vienna sausage) or unsmoked, like the ordinary butcher's pork and beef sausages. Pork sausages are regarded as having the better flavour. The smoked types are good served by themselves, but either type can be eaten with fried onion rings and mashed potatoes, with grilled tomatoes, with apple sauce and gravy, as part of a mixed grill, with spaghetti or macaroni cooked in tomato sauce or in savoury dishes, for instance, Toad-in-the-hole, or roast poultry. The sausage filling is sometimes removed from the skins for use in pies, rolls, forcemeat and other dishes. All uncooked sausages should be cooked and eaten as soon as possible after purchase; if it is necessary to store them for a short time, they should preferably be kept in a refrigerator.

Cooking: Sausages may be fried, grilled, baked or boiled. Extra fat is sometimes needed for frying and baking. Cook them slowly and turn them at frequent intervals to brown all sides.

They are also popular for barbecues and hot dogs.

Freezing: Sausages can be bought ready frozen or fresh ones can be stored in a freezer for up to 3 months. They can be thawed and cooked or cooked from frozen.

SAUSAGEMEAT

A mixture similar to that used for sausages, but not filled into skins. It is cheaper and more convenient to buy the meat in this form for sausage rolls, pies or stuffing.

SAUSAGE ROLLS

METRIC/IMPERIAL
200 g/7 oz shortcrust pastry, made with 200 g/7 oz
flour, etc.
225 g/8 oz sausagemeat
flour
milk to glaze.

Roll the pastry out thinly into an oblong, then cut it lengthwise into 2 strips. Divide the sausagemeat into 2 pieces, dust with flour, and form into 2 rolls the length of the pastry. Lay a roll of sausagemeat down the centre of each strip, brush down the edges of the pastry with a little milk, fold one side of the pastry over the sausagemeat and press the two edges firmly together. Seal the long edges together by flaking. Brush the length of the two rolls with milk, then cut each into slices 4 cm/ 1½ inches to 5 cm/2 inches long. Place on a baking sheet and bake in a moderately hot oven (200°C/400°F, Gas Mark 6) for 15 minutes; to cook the meat thoroughly, reduce the temperature to moderate (180°C/350°F, Gas Mark 4) and cook for a further 15 minutes.

Good sausage rolls can be made with bought puff pastry, fresh or frozen. Use a 215 g/7½ oz packet and allow it to reach room temperature (which will take about 2 hours) before rolling it out, then it will be easier to handle. Make the rolls as above, but heat the oven to moderate (180°C/350°F, Gas Mark 4) and bake a further 15 minutes.

SAUSAGE STUFFING

METRIC/IMPERIAL
1 large onion, skinned and chopped
0.5 kg/1 lb pork sausagemeat
2 × 5 ml spoons/2 teaspoons chopped parsley
1 × 5 ml spoon/1 teaspoon dried mixed herbs
25 g/1 oz fresh white breadcrumbs
salt
pepper

Mix all the ingredients together.

Use with chicken, or turkey, adapting the quantities as necessary. This stuffing is sufficient for a 4 kg/9 lb to 4.5 kg/10 lb oven-ready turkey.

SAUTER (SAUTÉ)

Food cooked in fat without being browned. The word is derived from the French sauter, to jump, and suggests the action of tossing the food in the hot fat.

The vegetables used in making soups, stews and sauces are often sautéed to improve their flavour without spoiling the colour of the finished dish. Sauté potatoes are boiled, cut into slices and cooked in a little fat until lightly browned.

SAUTERNES

The sweet white wine from the vineyards in the Gironde, near the village of Sauternes. Château Yquem is the best of the Sauternes, which also include Bommes, Barsac, Preignacs and Fargues. Sauternes is not a highly alcoholic wine, the average alcoholic content being 10 per cent. It may accompany fish, poultry and white meat, but is particularly suitable to serve with the sweet course of a meal.

SAVARIN

A rich yeast mixture baked in a ring mould; it is served soaked with a rum syrup and accompanied by cream or fruit salad. The sweet was named after Brillat-Savarin, a famous gastronomic writer of the eighteenth century.

SAVELOY

A short, thick sausage made from salted pork, lightly seasoned and coloured red with saltpetre. Saveloys are dried, smoked and sold ready cooked. They are served skinned and sliced as an appetizer or savoury.

SAVORY

Two types of plant go by this name. Summer savory is an annual which grows to about 30 cm/ 12 inches in height and has pointed leaves, with a flavour resembling thyme, but milder and more fragrant. The winter variety is perennial and grows like thyme. Both can be used either fresh or dried for flavouring salads, soups, stews, stuffing, etc.

SAVOURY

This term is applied to three different kinds of food: (1) the titbits eaten with the fingers, which are often known as cocktail savouries; (2) the highly seasoned type of dish, frequently hot, which is served after the sweet course and before the dessert at a formal dinner; (3) a more substantial dish which can form the main course of a simple lunch, high tea, supper or a snack meal.

Cocktail and After-dinner Savouries

Cocktail savouries should stimulate rather than satisfy appetite, so they should be small and piquant: they should also be easy to eat in the fingers, with nothing that will fall off or smear the hands; some titbits, such as tiny hot sausages, are better served on cocktail sticks.

The following list includes some of the most popular cold and hot cocktail titbits.

Olives, radishes, celery, stuffed prunes, salted nuts, potato crisps, fried chipolata sausages, canapés, haddock and other savoury balls, savoury rolls, boats and bouchées, cheese straws and cheese Dartois biscuits. A number of those suggested as after-dinner savouries (see below), may be served as cocktail snacks, if made very small; see also Canapé and Croûte entries.

After-dinner savouries should be small and particularly well made, flavoured and garnished. Cheese is a favourite ingredient for many of these dishes; other popular savouries are made with smoked or preserved fish (such as haddock and sardines), shellfish, foie gras, tongue, bacon and ham, chicken, veal and sweetbreads. Olives, gherkins, anchovies and similar piquant or salty ingredients are often added to heighten the flavour.

Both after-dinner and cocktail savouries may be presented in various ways. One of the most usual methods is to spread a savoury mixture on a base of toast, fried bread, plain biscuit, crispbread or pastry. Mushrooms, anchovies and sardines, cheese, etc., can all be used in this way, also mixtures such as chopped celery and mayonnaise, chutney and cheese, shrimps and butter, cream cheese garnished with asparagus tips, chopped prunes and mayonnaise, apple and cream cheese, scrambled egg, and cress.

Another method is to serve the savoury mixture in cases such as bouchées, croustades (see individual entries), tartlets and boats made of cheese or other pastry; hard-boiled eggs with the yolk removed and the centre filled with a savoury paste (which may include the sieved egg yolk); small tomatoes, celery sticks and chicory with a savoury filling; thick slices of beetroot or cucumber, hollowed out into a cup shape; soaked prunes with the stones removed and replaced by a savoury cream filling. Other savouries can be served in scallop shells, individual ramekins, cassolettes or small soufflé dishes.

The filling for savouries served in cases may consist of meat, fish, poultry, game, cheese, vegetables, etc., usually bound and given 'body' by a cooked sauce, macaroni, semolina, rice or breadcrumbs. Pickles, chutney, etc., may be added. Here are a few examples:

Fried mushrooms, mixed with fried rice, tomato ketchup, seasoning and grated cheese; asparagus tips and hollandaise sauce; minced cooked poultry, mushroom, bacon and tongue mixed with béchamel or plain white sauce; shrimps, breadcrumbs and anchovy sauce, with sliced stuffed olives as garnish; scrambled eggs with chopped capers, topped with pieces of fried herring roe.

Savoury Dishes, Snacks, etc.

This third group is large and almost anything which is fairly quickly prepared and satisfying can come under this head. Spaghetti, cheese and other food on toast, sandwiches and rolls, salads and vegetable dishes are typical examples. (See individual entries.)

SAVOY BISCUITS

Small sponge fingers, used particularly for making such sweets as Charlotte Russe.

SCALDING

The process of pouring boiling water over food in order to clean it, to loosen hairs (e.g. from a joint of pork) or to skin it (e.g. tomatoes, peaches). The food must not be left in boiling water, or it will begin to cook.

The term also means the process of heating milk almost to boiling point, to retard souring.

SCALLION

An onion which has developed no bulb – frequently used in Chinese and Eastern Cookery.

Shallots or spring onions can be used as a substitute for scallions.

SCALLOP

A shellfish of delicate flavour which makes excellent eating. Scallops should be used only when they are very fresh and in full season, from October to March; they are at their best in January and February. The roe should then be a bright orange colour and the flesh very white. They are generally sold opened but still attached to the deep part of the shell with the 'beard' removed. Scallops are also available frozen.

Preparation and cooking: The simplest method of cooking scallops is to simmer them in salted water, court bouillon or milk until tender, drain, dry and serve in their shells in Mornay sauce, garnished with chopped parsley. A white sauce can be made from the milk if used.

For fried scallops, either boil them first, or soak them for 30 minutes in a mixture of salad oil and lemon juice, seasoned with pepper and salt; dip in egg and breadcrumbs or batter and fry in the usual way.

SCALLOPED DISHES

Food (often previously cooked) baked in a scallop shell or similar small container; it is usually combined with a creamy sauce, topped with breadcrumbs and surrounded by a border of piped potato.

SCALLOP, TO

A way of decorating the double edge of the pastry covering of a pie. Make horizontal cuts with a knife close together round the edge of the pie, giving a flaked effect.

Now, using the back of the knife, pull the edge up vertically at regular intervals to form scallops. These should be close together for a sweet pie and wider apart for a savoury one.

SCAMPI

Very large prawns, native to the Adriatic. They are very similar to Dublin Bay prawns. Scampi are delicious when fried in egg and breadcrumbs and served with hollandaise or tartare sauce and a crisp green salad.

SCARLET RUNNER

(See Beans entry.)

SCHNAPPS (ALSO SCHIEDAM)

(See Hollands entry.)

369

SCHNITZEL

An Austrian name for a thin slice of meat, usually veal, which is egged, crumbed and fried. (See Veal entry for Wiener Schnitzel.)

SCONE

A light, plain cake, quickly made and containing very little fat, which is baked in a very hot oven or cooked on a girdle, and is usually eaten split open and spread with butter or filling. Scones can be eaten hot or cold, as a tea-time dish, with morning coffee, or as a base for open savouries for cocktail or supper parties. It is sometimes used as a base for pizzas. They are best eaten fresh, but can be kept in a cake tin for a day, when they may be re-heated in the oven or toasted. Scones also freeze very well for up to 3 months.

Oven Scones

These can be made with a variety of flours and other ingredients such as mashed potato, etc. When a plain flour is used, raising agent is added in the form of cream of tartar plus bicarbonate of soda or a baking powder. The liquid may be fresh or soured milk or buttermilk and may be diluted with water or mixed with golden syrup; eggs may be used with any of these liquids. Salt and sugar are added as required and the scones may if desired be flavoured with dried fruit, ginger, cheese or mixed herbs (fresh or dried).

OVEN SCONES

METRIC/IMPERIAL
225 g/8 oz self raising flour
1 × 2.5 ml spoon/ ½ teaspoon salt
1 × 5 ml spoon/1 teaspoon baking powder
25–50 g/1–2 oz butter or margarine
150 ml/¼ pint milk
beaten egg or milk to glaze, optional

Preheat a baking sheet in the oven. Sift the flour, salt and baking powder together then rub in the fat until the mixture resembles fine breadcrumbs. Make a well in the centre and stir in enough milk to give a fairly soft dough. Turn it on to a floured board, knead very lightly if necessary to remove any cracks, then roll out lightly to about 1.5 cm/¾ inch thick, or pat it out with the hand. Cut into 10 to 12 rounds with a 5 cm/2 inch cutter (dipped in flour) or cut into triangles with a sharp knife. Place on the baking sheet, brush if you wish with beaten egg or milk and bake towards the top of a hot oven (230°C/450°F, Gas Mark 8) for 8 to 10 minutes, until brown and well risen. Cool the scones on a rack. Serve split and buttered.

ALTERNATIVE RAISING AGENTS
If plain flour and baking powder are used instead of self raising flour, allow 1 × 15 ml spoon/1 tablespoon baking powder to 225 g/8 oz flour and sift them together twice before using. If you use cream of tartar and bicarbonate of soda in place of baking powder allow 1 × 5 ml spoon/1 teaspoon cream of tartar and 1 × 2.5 ml spoon/ ½ teaspoon bicarbonate of soda to 225 g/8 oz plain flour with ordinary milk or 1 × 2.5 ml spoon/ ½ teaspoon bicarbonate of soda and 1 × 2.5 ml spoon/ ½ teaspoon cream of tartar with soured milk.

EVERYDAY FRUIT SCONES
Add 50 g/2 oz currants, sultanas, stoned raisins or chopped dates (or a mixture of fruit) to the dry ingredients in the basic recipe.

RICH AFTERNOON TEA SCONES
Follow the basic recipe, adding 1–2 × 15 ml spoons/1–2 tablespoons caster sugar to the dry ingredients and using 1 beaten egg with 5 × 15 ml spoons/5 tablespoons water or milk in place of 150 ml/¼ pint milk; 50 g/2 oz dried fruit may also be included.

WHOLEMEAL SCONE ROUND

METRIC/IMPERIAL
3 × 5 ml spoons/3 teaspoons baking powder
pinch of salt
50 g/2 oz plain flour
50 g/2 oz caster sugar
175 g/6 oz plain wholemeal flour
50 g/2 oz butter or block margarine
about 150 ml/¼ pint milk

Preheat a baking sheet. Sift together the baking powder, salt and plain flour into a bowl. Add the sugar and the wholemeal flour. Lightly rub in the fat, then mix to a soft but manageable dough with the milk. Knead lightly on a floured surface. Shape into a flat 15 cm/6 inch round and mark with the back of a floured knife into six triangles. Place on the baking sheet and bake at once in a hot oven (230°C/450°F, Gas Mark 8) for about 15 minutes. Serve warm, split and buttered.

NOTE
If you wish to use self-raising wholemeal flour, reduce the amount of baking powder in the recipe to 1 × 5 ml spoon/1 teaspoon.

TREACLE SCONES

METRIC/IMPERIAL
225 g/8 oz self-raising flour
1 × 5 ml spoon/1 teaspoon baking powder
1 × 5 ml spoon/1 teaspoon mixed spice
pinch of salt
25–50 g/1–2 oz butter or block margarine
25 g/1 oz sugar
1 × 15 ml spoon/1 tablespoon black treacle
about 150 ml/¼ pint milk

Preheat a baking sheet. Sift together the flour, baking powder, spice and salt. Rub in the fat until the mixture resembles fine breadcrumbs. Add the sugar. Warm the treacle and mix with the milk, then use to make a light, manageable dough. Roll out to about 1.5 cm/¾ inch thick and stamp out into 6 cm/2½ inch rounds. Brush with milk, place on the baking sheet and bake in a hot oven (230°C/450°F, Gas Mark 8), for 10 to 15 minutes.

Serve split and spread with butter.

Girdle and Drop Scones

Girdle scones have similar ingredients to the oven type, but are cooked on a hot girdle, electric hot-plate or thick iron pan. Girdle scones are best when served warm and spread thickly with butter.

Drop scones, which are thin, light and spongy, are also known by the name of Scotch pancakes; they are made from a type of batter mixture. Drop scones are served hot or cold, with butter and syrup or jam. Though northern in origin, they are now equally popular in the south of England.

(For preparation of girdle see Girdle Cookery entry.)

SCOTCH PANCAKES OR DROP SCONES

METRIC/IMPERIAL
100 g/4 oz self raising flour
2 × 15 ml spoons/2 tablespoons caster sugar
1 egg, beaten
125–150 ml/about ¼ pint milk

Mix the flour and sugar. Make a well in the centre and stir in the egg, with enough of the milk to make a batter of the consistency of thick cream. The mixing should be done as quickly and lightly as possible – do not beat. If a thin pancake is wanted add slightly more milk.

Drop the mixture in spoonfuls on to a hot, lightly greased girdle, hot plate or heavy based frying pan; for round pancakes, drop it from the point of the spoon, for oval ones, from the side. Keep the girdle at a steady heat and when bubbles rise to the surface of the pancakes and burst – after 2 to 3 minutes – turn the cake over, using a palette knife. Continue cooking until golden brown on the other side – a further 2 to 3 minutes. Place the finished pancakes on a clean tea towel, cover with another towel and place on a rack to cool. (This keeps in the steam and the pancakes do not become dry). Serve with butter or with whipped cream and jam. Makes about 15 to 18 pancakes.

For richer drop scones, add about 25 g/1 oz fat, either rubbing it into the flour or adding it melted with the eggs and milk. If you wish, 50 g/2 oz sultanas may be added. If you prefer, use 100 g/4 oz plain flour, 1 × 2.5 ml spoon/½ teaspoon bicarbonate of soda and 1 × 5 ml spoon/1 teaspoon cream of tartar instead of the self raising flour.

SCORING

To make shallow cuts in the surface of food in order to improve its flavour and appearance or to help it cook more quickly. Thus fish has a better flavour if scored before being marinated or soused; the crackling of pork is scored before roasting to prevent its pulling the joint out of shape and to facilitate carving.

SCOTCH BROTH

(See Broth entry.)

SCOTCH BUN (BLACK BUN)

This spiced plum cake with a pastry crust, also known as Black Bun, is eaten at Hogmanay, New Year's Eve. It is made several months (sometimes even a year) beforehand, so that it has time to mature.

SCOTCH OR BLACK BUN FOR HOGMANAY

(New Year's Eve)

METRIC/IMPERIAL
FOR THE PASTRY
225 g/8 oz plain flour
pinch of salt
100 g/4 oz butter
beaten egg to glaze

FOR THE FILLING
225 g/8 oz plain flour
1 × 5 ml spoon/1 teaspoon ground cinnamon
1 × 5 ml spoon/1 teaspoon ground ginger
1 × 5 ml spoon/1 teaspoon ground allspice
1 × 5 ml spoon/1 teaspoon cream of tartar
1 × 5 ml spoon/1 teaspoon bicarbonate of soda
450 g/1 lb stoned raisins
450 g/1 lb currants
50 g/2 oz chopped mixed peel
100 g/4 oz nibbed almonds
100 g/4 oz brown sugar
1 egg
150 ml/¼ pint whisky
about 4 × 15 ml spoons/4 tablespoons milk

Grease a 20 cm/8 inch cake tin. Make the pastry in the usual way. Take two-thirds of it and roll out into a round about 35 cm/14 inches in diameter. Line the tin with it, making sure the pastry comes above the top of the sides of the cake tin and distributing the fullness evenly round the sides.

For the filling, sift the flour, spice, cream of tartar and bicarbonate of soda into a large bowl and mix in the raisins, currants, peel, almonds and sugar. Add the egg, whisky and milk and stir till the mixture is evenly moistened. Pack it into the pastry case and fold the top of the pastry over. Roll

371

out the remaining dough to a 20 cm/8 inch round. Moisten the edges of the pastry case, put on the lid and seal the edges firmly together. With a skewer make 4 or 5 holes right down to the bottom of the cake, then prick all over the top with a fork and brush with beaten egg. Bake in a moderate oven (180°C/350°F, Gas Mark 4) for 2½ to 3 hours; cover with brown paper if the pastry becomes too brown. Turn out to cool on a wire rack.

This cake should be made several weeks or even months before it is to be eaten, so that it may mature and mellow.

SCOTCH EGG

(See Egg entry.)

SCOTCH KALE (KAIL)

A thick broth or soup, resembling pot-au-feu, containing shredded cabbage.

SCOTCH PANCAKE

(See Drop Scone in Scone entry.)

SCOTCH WHISKY

The most popular spirit distilled from grain. It is made from malted barley and blended with an unmalted grain spirit. The different brands depend on the part of Scotland from which the malt whisky comes. Both the malt whisky and the plain grain spirit must, by law, be matured for 3 years before being blended. The blending is very important and has to be carefully carried out to produce a whisky of the same flavour and colour each year.

SCOTCH WOODCOCK

Toast spread with anchovy paste and topped with scrambled egg.

SEA PIE

This is not, as the name might suggest, a pie made of fish, but a beef stew with a suet-crust 'lid' cooked on the top. Cook the stew in a casserole for 1½ hours, then put a layer of suet-crust on top of the casserole, replace the lid and continue cooking for a further hour, or until the meat is tender. Serve in the casserole.

SEAKALE

A vegetable with a stalk somewhat like celery. Like celery, seakale is banked up with earth to keep it white, as it develops a strong and bitter taste when exposed to light. It is very important to use seakale as soon as possible after it is cut and while it is still white and crisp: when it has become limp and discoloured it is not worth cooking.

Preparation and cooking: Separate the stalks and wash and brush them lightly in cold water; then tie them in small bundles, or cut into small pieces, about 7.5 cm/1½ inches long. Have ready a saucepan of boiling salted water – just sufficient to cover the seakale – to which has been added the juice of ½ a lemon, to help to preserve the colour of the seakale. Cook until tender (about 30 to 35 minutes), then drain, reserving some of the liquid for the sauce, if required. The seakale may be re-heated in a white or hollandaise sauce and garnished with croûtons, or served on toast; alternatively, it may be served cold, with vinaigrette or mayonnaise sauce. Seakale may also be braised or served au gratin.

SEARING

To brown meat quickly in a little fat before grilling or roasting it. The term is sometimes used when vegetables are browned in fat before being used in soup or sauce-making.

SEASONING

This term usually refers to salt and pepper, but it may mean any herb or condiment, etc., added to improve the flavour of a savoury dish. Seasoning can be varied to suit individual tastes, but it should be used in moderation, for the sake of those who dislike highly seasoned food.

SEAWEED

Many types of seaweed are eaten in different parts of the world and in Iceland and other countries where fresh vegetables are scarce during the winter months, they form an important part of the diet, for seaweed has a good mineral content. In some parts of Great Britain such types as dulse, laver or sloke are eaten by themselves or used in cooking. The seaweed known as Carrageen Moss (see entry) may be used instead of gelatine to set jellies and creams. Sea oxeye and sea sandwort are often pickled or salted like sauerkraut. Other types, e.g., tangle stem, are burnt for kelp, which is a source of iodine.

To cook: Wash the seaweed very well in several changes of water, then simmer it in milk or water for 2 to 3 hours, until tender; the flavour is better if milk is used. Drain, and serve tossed in butter and seasonings.

Alginates
Carbohydrates derived from seaweeds. They have the property of forming jellies, and are used by

food manufacturers to improve the texture or consistency of such things as ready-prepared soups, jellies, ice cream and meat and fish pastes. Thus agar-agar, derived from the treated stems of the *gelidium algae*, is mainly used as a stabilizer for emulsions and in jellies and creams, while carrageen, from *Chondrus crispus*, is used as a thickening agent.

SEED CAKE

A type of Madeira cake (see entry), flavoured with caraway seeds and lemon rind or essence. Allow 2 × 5 ml spoons/2 teaspoons seeds for a cake made with 225 g/8 oz flour.

SELF-RAISING FLOUR

(See Flour entry.)

SELTZER

An effervescing mineral water, originally exported from the German town of Nieder Selters, and now widely imitated in manufactured table waters.

SEMOLINA

This is made from the endosperm of wheat, ground into small granules of various size. It supplies vegetable protein, carbohydrate and thiamine; when combined with milk it makes a useful food, especially for children and invalids. Semolina is used for making gnocchi (see entry), for thickening soups (use 25 g/1 oz to about 600 ml/1 pint liquid and blend with a little milk before adding), for making milk puddings, moulds and fruit whips; it is sometimes included in biscuits to give a 'nutty' texture. Finely ground semolina gives a smoother texture to moulds and puddings, but the granular texture of the coarser variety is useful for gnocchi and for biscuits.

SEMOLINA PUDDING

METRIC/IMPERIAL
600 ml/1 pint milk
knob of butter
4 × 15 ml spoons/4 tablespoons semolina
50 g/2 oz sugar

Heat the milk and butter and sprinkle on the semolina. Continue to heat until the milk boils and the mixture thickens, and cook for a further 2 to 3 minutes, until the grain is clear, stirring all the time. Remove from the heat and stir in the sugar. Pour the pudding into a greased ovenproof dish and bake in a moderately hot oven (200°C/400°F, Gas Mark 6) for about 30 minutes, till lightly browned. (Or serve as it is without baking, allowing up to 15 minutes' cooking in the pan).

VARIATIONS
1. Add the grated rind of an orange or lemon to the milk.
2. Pour the cooked pudding on to a layer of jam or stewed fruit before baking it as above.

SESAME

A herbaceous plant widely grown in the East. The seeds are used in cakes and confectionery and the oil expressed from them serves as a flavouring for both sweet and savoury dishes.

SEVILLE ORANGE

A type of Spanish orange which is too bitter to be eaten as dessert, but is used for making marmalade, wines and cordials; it can also be used for sauces and relishes, especially those to be served with duck. (See Marmalade entry.)

SHAD

A European white fish of reasonably good flavour, belonging to the herring family. Like the salmon, it migrates from the sea to the rivers for spawning, and is caught during the winter months only. There are several types, varying in length from about 30 cm/1 foot to 1 metre/3¼ feet.

Shad may be boiled, but is better grilled or baked, either plain or stuffed. When baked it is served with anchovy, hollandaise or other piquant sauce. Shad may also be pickled, like herrings.

SHADDOCK

A large rather coarse and bitter citrus fruit with a thick, bitter rind. The grapefruit (see entry) is one of the smaller, finer varieties of shaddock. It is sometimes known as a pomelo.

SHALLOT

A member of the onion family; each plant has a cluster of small bulbs. Some people consider that shallots have a better flavour than onions, and their smell does not cling so tenaciously. They may be used for flavouring in the same way as onions, the green tops being chopped and used for salads and soups, and the bulb in stews and other savoury dishes. Shallots are very suitable for pickling, on account of their flavour and small size. (See Onion and Pickling entries.)

SHALLOW FRYING

(See Frying entry.)

SHA–SHE **SHANDY GAFF**

A mixture of equal quantities of ale and ginger beer. Sometimes ginger ale, grapefruit or lemon mineral water is substituted for the ginger beer.

SHARK'S FIN

The fins of a type of shark found in the Indian Ocean and used to make a soup which is regarded in the East as a great delicacy.

SHELLFISH

The name given to all edible crustacea (fish which have shells). The best known types are clams, cockles, crabs, crawfish, crayfish, limpets, lobsters, mussels, oysters, prawns, Dublin Bay prawns, scallops, shrimps, whelks and winkles. Shellfish should only be bought in season and when quite fresh; if they have to be kept before use, it is better to buy them alive and kill them shortly before eating. The food value of shellfish lies chiefly in their protein content; they contribute useful amounts of the B vitamins and mineral salts. (See individual entries.)

SHEPHERD'S PIE

A dish consisting of well-flavoured cooked meat, usually minced but sometimes sliced, with a 'crust' of mashed potato, which is baked long enough to re-heat and brown the potatoes. If leftover potatoes are used, they should be mashed while still hot. Some people say that only lamb or mutton should be used in a shepherd's pie.

SHEPHERD'S PIE

METRIC/IMPERIAL
1 kg/2 lb potatoes
4 × 15 ml spoons/4 tablespoons milk
25 g/1 oz butter
pepper
salt
1–2 onions
dripping
0.5 kg/1 lb minced cold meat
stock
2 × 5 ml spoons/2 teaspoons chopped parsley
1 × 2.5 ml spoon/½ teaspoon mixed herbs

Boil, strain and mash the potatoes and stir in the milk, fat, pepper and salt. Chop or slice the onion and fry it in a little dripping. Mix the meat with a little stock, pepper, salt, parsley and herbs. Place this prepared meat mixture over the base of a pie dish and cover with the creamed potato, piling it up in the centre and marking it with a fork. Bake in a moderately hot oven (220°C/400°F, Gas Mark 6)

for 20 to 30 minutes. If necessary, put the pie under a slow grill to brown the top.

SHERBET

Originally an Oriental cooling drink made of fruit juice. In this country the name denotes (1) a powder, usually bought by children, used to make an effervescent drink and sometimes incorporated in boiled sweets; (2) a mixture of sweetened fruit juice and beaten egg whites, frozen to make a kind of ice.

In the frozen sherbets, milk is sometimes used instead of water, cream is sometimes included and gelatine is added in some recipes. As the acidity of the fruit varies, it is important to taste the sherbet mixture before freezing it and to add more sugar if required. (See Sorbet entry.)

ORANGE SHERBET

METRIC/IMPERIAL
225 g/8 oz sugar
150 ml/¼ pint water
600 ml/1 pint orange pulp and juice
2 × 15 ml spoons/2 tablespoons lemon juice
150 ml/¼ pint double cream
1 egg white

Boil the sugar and water for 10 minutes, skim and cool. Cut some oranges in halves crosswise and carefully remove the pulp and juice, discarding the seeds and hard centres. Measure the quantity required, add the lemon juice and combine with the cold syrup. Freeze the mixture until it is of a soft creamy consistency. Whip the cream and whip the egg white also until stiff, then fold both into the sherbet. Freeze until stiff enough to serve.

SHERRY

Sherry is made in Jerez in Andalusia, Spain from white grapes (Palomino) which are machine pressed and run off into casks. Fermentation takes place in the cask with ample air space between wine and bung. The sherry yeasts form a crust (flor) on the wine which protects it from the air. This flor feeds upon the alcohol but does not weaken the wine, since water evaporates through the wood of the cask more rapidly than the spirit. After fermentation is complete any residual sugar is consumed by the flor, meaning that sherries with a yeast flor crust are always dry.

All sherries are blended wines, the system being unique. The wines, maturing in casks are stacked in tiers, each row representing the produce of a year. The bottom row contains wines that have been passed through a solera system of blending and the top casks hold the 'new' wines. Wines from the bottom casks (6 to 7 years old) are run off and used to top up the casks above. A continuing blending process and standard quality is achieved by this process. The wine is then fined, using egg whites, and may be blended again to achieve standard quality for particular exports.

Sherries are classified according to the way they develop.

(a) Palmas: driest, used for amontillado and fino sherries.

(b) Cortados: full bodied, more alcoholic and used for oloroso sherries.

(c) Rayas: coarser wines which may be used for finos or olorosos depending on development.

The types are:
1. Finos – pale dry wines
2. Olorosos – sweetish and dark
3. Amontillados – older, stronger finos
4. Amorosos – pale, sweet wines
5. Brown sherry – dark and sweet

Sherry is served as an apéritif and with soup; the dark brown sweet type is also served with dessert. Cooking sherry is used widely in sauces, soups, trifles, etc.; the cheaper continental types (e.g., Cyprus) and the Commonwealth wines are useful for this purpose.

SHORTBREAD

A thick crisp cake of 'short', biscuit-like texture, which is particularly associated with Scotland, but is widely popular. It has a high proportion of butter to flour, therefore no liquid is required to bind the mixture. The dough is pressed into wooden or earthenware moulds to shape it, then turned on to a baking sheet. Shortbread keeps well if stored in an air-tight tin. It will also freeze.

SHORTBREAD

METRIC/IMPERIAL
150 g/5 oz plain flour
3 × 15 ml spoons/3 tablespoons rice flour
50 g/2 oz caster sugar
100 g/4 oz butter or block margarine

Grease a baking sheet. Sift the flours and add the sugar. Work in the butter with your fingertips – keep it in one piece and gradually work in the dry ingredients. Knead well and pack into a rice-floured shortbread mould or an 18 cm/7 inch sandwich tin. If using a mould, turn out on to the baking sheet and prick well. Bake in a moderate oven (160°C/325°F, Gas Mark 3) until firm and golden – about 45 minutes. Turn out if necessary. When cool, dredge with sugar. Serve cut into wedges.

NOTE
The rice flour is a traditional ingredient of shortbread, but it can be omitted, in which case use 175 g/6 oz plain flour.

SHORTCAKE

This is a sweet of American origin, consisting of a rich type of scone, with a filling of fruit and cream. Small individual shortcakes can also be served.

STRAWBERRY SHORTCAKE

METRIC/IMPERIAL
225 g/8 oz self raising flour
1 × 5 ml spoon/1 teaspoon baking powder
pinch of salt
75 g/3 oz butter or margarine
75 g/3 oz sugar
1 egg, beaten
1–2 × 15 ml spoons/1–2 tablespoons milk, optional
350–450 g/¾–1 lb strawberries
3–4 × 15 ml spoons/3–4 tablespoons caster sugar for filling
150 ml/¼ pint carton double or whipping cream

Grease a deep 20 cm/8 inch sandwich tin. Sift the flour, baking powder and salt together and rub in the fat until the mixture resembles fine breadcrumbs; stir in the sugar. Add the egg a little at a time to the rubbed-in mixture until this begins to bind together; use a little milk as well if necessary. Knead the mixture lightly into a smooth, light, manageable dough.

Turn the dough on to a floured board, form into a round and roll out until it is 20 cm/8 inches across. Press it evenly into the tin and bake in a moderately hot oven (190°C/375°F, Gas Mark 5) for 20 minutes, or until golden and firm. Turn the cake out of the tin on to a cooling tray.

Hull and wash the strawberries and drain them well. Keep about a dozen berries whole for decorating and crush the rest with a fork in a basin, sprinkling with 2–3 × 15 ml spoons/2–3 tablespoons of the caster sugar. Whisk the cream and stir in the remaining sugar. When the cake is nearly or just cold, split, spread with half of the cream and all the crushed fruit and replace the top. Pile the remaining cream on the top of the cake and decorate with whole berries.

SHORTCRUST PASTRY

(See Pastry entry.)

SHORTENING

The fat used in a dough, cake mixture, etc., is so named because it makes the mixture 'short', or tender. Such fats and oils as butter, dripping, lard, margarine, suet and nut oils all come under this heading.

Fats differ in their shortening powers; generally speaking, the more 'workable' the fat, the greater its shortening power; thus lard is good for the

375

purpose, but oils lack workability and must therefore be used somewhat differently to obtain good results.

(See Fats and Oil entries, also the individual entries for the different fats and oils; see also Cake and Pastry entries.)

SHREDDING

To slice a food such as cheese or raw vegetables into very fine pieces, which often curl as they are cut. To shred use a sharp knife or a coarse grater.

SHREWSBURY BISCUITS

(See Biscuit entry.)

SHRIMP

A very small shellfish, of the same family as the crayfish and the prawn, in season all the year round. There are several different varieties, the brown and the pink being the most familiar. The brown shrimp, which is very plentiful, is of a translucent grey colour when caught, but it becomes reddish-brown when boiled. The rose or pink shrimp, which is caught in deeper waters, has a more delicate flavour. Shrimps can be obtained frozen, potted and canned. They can also be bought ready cooked.

Shrimps are served as appetizers with bread and butter; they are also useful for garnishing, for flavouring a sauce to be served with fish and for adding to savouries and salads. Both dried and fresh shrimps are a very common ingredient in Oriental cookery. Shrimp paste is one of the more common spreads.

Cooking and serving: For those who catch their own shrimps, the process of boiling them is quite simple. Allow enough water to cover the shrimps well and add 25 g/1 oz salt to every 1.2 litres/2 pints of water. Bring the water to the boil, place the shrimps in a frying basket and plunge them in the water. Boil for about 6 minutes, or until the colour changes. Drain the shrimps and spread out to cool. They may be served either in their shells or picked, with bread and butter.

SHRUB

A bottled cordial, made of different fruits, spirits and sugar, which used to be popular.

SIEVING

To rub or press food (e.g., cooked vegetables) through a sieve; a wooden spoon is used to force it through. (See Purée entry.)

SILD

A small type of herring, caught in large quantities off the coast of Norway and exported in tinned form. They are used like sardines.

SILVER BEET (SEAKALE BEET)

(See Swiss Chard entry.)

SILVERSIDE

(See Beef entry.)

SIMMERING

To keep a liquid just below boiling point (i.e., at approximately 96°C or 205°F). First bring the liquid to the boil, then adjust the heat so that the surface of the liquid is kept just moving or 'shivering' – bubbling indicates that the temperature is too high.

Simmering is the method used for many dishes which require long, slow cooking, such as stews.

SIMNEL CAKE

A fruit cake with a layer of almond paste on top and sometimes another baked inside the cake. Originally this cake was baked for Mothering Sunday, in the days when many girls went into service and Mothering Sunday was the one day in the year they were allowed home. It is now more usual to have Simnel cake at Easter.

SIMNEL CAKE

METRIC/IMPERIAL
575 g/1¼ lb bought almond paste
350 g/12 oz currants
100 g/4 oz sultanas
75 g/3 oz mixed candied peel, chopped
225 g/8 oz plain flour
pinch of salt
1 × 5 ml spoon/1 teaspoon ground cinnamon
1 × 5 ml spoon/1 teaspoon ground nutmeg
175 g/6 oz butter or margarine
175 g/6 oz caster sugar
3 eggs, beaten
milk to mix
apricot jam or beaten egg to use under almond paste
glacé icing, optional

Line an 18 cm/7 inch cake tin. Divide the almond paste into three; take one portion and roll it out to a round the size of the cake tin. Using the remaining ingredients and following the method for Christmas cake, make up the mixture. Put half of it into the prepared tin, smooth and cover with the round of almond paste. Put the remaining cake mixture on top. Bake in a moderate oven (160°C/325°F,

Gas Mark 3) for about 1 hour, lower the heat to cool (150°C/300°F, Gas Mark 2) and bake for 3 hours, until the cake is golden brown and firm to the touch. Allow to cool in the tin.

Take another third of the almond paste and roll out to a round the size of the tin; make small balls from the remaining third – eleven is the traditional number. Brush the top of the cake with apricot jam or beaten egg, cover with the round of paste and place the small balls round the edge. Brush the paste with any remaining egg or jam and brown under the grill. The top of the cake may then be coated with glacé icing, made by mixing 3 × 15 ml spoons/3 tablespoons sifted icing sugar with a little cold water until it will coat the back of the spoon. Decorate the cake with a tiny model chicken or a few coloured sugar eggs.

SINGEING

(See Poultry entry.)

SINGING HINNIE

A type of girdle cake traditionally associated with Northumberland. It is made from a currant scone mixture shaped into a large round and cooked on a girdle. It is usually cut in half, buttered and eaten while hot.

SINGIN' HINNY

This Northumbrian favourite hisses when turned – hence the name.

METRIC/IMPERIAL
350 g/12 oz plain flour
50 g/2 oz ground rice
50 g/2 oz sugar
1 × 5 ml spoon/1 teaspoon salt
2 × 5 ml spoons/2 teaspoons baking powder
25 g/1 oz lard
75 g/3 oz currants
150 ml/¼ pint milk
150 ml/¼ pint single cream

Preheat a girdle. Mix together the flour, ground rice, sugar, salt and baking powder. Rub in the lard. Mix in the currants, then stir in the milk and cream. Roll out the dough into a 20 cm/8 inch round. Prick with a fork and cook slowly (about 20 minutes on each side) on the griddle until golden brown. To turn Singin' hinny over, place a baking sheet on top, reverse on to the baking sheet then slide 'hinny' back on to the griddle. Carefully split and serve buttered, cut in wedges, while still warm.

SIPPET

(See Croûton entry.)

SIRLOIN

(See Beef entry.)

SKATE

A coarse white fish with a large proportion of bone, in season from September to April. It is sold cut into pieces and slashed, the thickest pieces, taken from the middle cuts, being the best to buy; if large it is sometimes filleted. Skate is usually fried or baked in milk flavoured with bay leaf and a little nutmeg and served with a piquant sauce.

Preparation: Wash the fish well in salted water, skin it and remove the bones at each side. Cut into pieces, or fillet if large enough.

SKATE TOLEDO

METRIC/IMPERIAL
25g/1 oz butter
1 clove garlic, optional
1 large onion, cut into rings
1 large green pepper, thinly sliced
175 g/6 oz long grain rice
400 ml/¾ pint chicken stock
4 large tomatoes, skinned and chopped
black pepper
2 wings of skate
seasoned flour
chopped parsley

Melt the butter in a frying pan and add the crushed clove of garlic if used. Add the onion and pepper and cook gently without browning for about 5 minutes. Stir in the rice and chicken stock. Simmer steadily, stirring occasionally, until the rice is cooked and all the liquid absorbed, 15 to 20 minutes. Just before the rice is cooked stir in the chopped tomatoes. Season well with freshly ground black pepper.

While the rice is cooking wash and dry the fish and cut each wing into two or three pieces. Coat thoroughly in seasoned flour.

Heat 1 cm/½ inch of cooking oil in a frying pan and fry the fish quickly on both sides until pale golden brown, about 5 minutes. Drain on kitchen paper.

Pile the rice in the centre of a serving dish surrounded by the fish and sprinkle with freshly chopped parsley.

SLIMMING DIETS

Obesity (overweight) is becoming an increasing problem for people of all ages. This is partly due to our lifestyle today which includes the popularity of sedentary entertainment, increasing use of cars and labour saving gadgets, yet there is no reduction in food intake. Furthermore, advertising and food

377

promotions are becoming more attractive and tempting, especially for the energy-rich snack foods eaten between meals. The problem usually arises from eating more than the body requires to keep healthy, and this amount varies from person to person.

If only a small amount of weight needs to be lost just reducing the intake of food will help, but it is important to cut out the carbohydrate foods such as sugar, sweets, cakes, pastries, fried foods, etc., rather than protein foods (meat, fish, eggs, cheese). If a large amount of weight needs to be lost it is advisable to consult a doctor and/or one of the very good slimming organisations which have branches all over the country.

Overweight can be caused by physical disorders in which case no diet should be undertaken without medical supervision.

SLING

A toddy made with gin and fruit.

SLIPCOTE

A soft cheese produced at Wissenden. It is made up into little cheeses which are placed between cabbage leaves for a week or two to ripen. When ripe, its skin or coat becomes loose and slips off – hence its name.

SLIVOWITZ (SLIVOVICA)

A Hungarian brandy made from a particularly large, sweet type of plum.

SLOE

The wild plum or fruit of the blackthorn. Sloes are small, with a purple skin and very tart yellow flesh. They are used with other fruit to make jellies and are also made into liqueurs and cordials such as sloe gin, one of the most popular of English liqueurs.

SLOW COOKERS

An electric casserole which has been developed from a similar American product. The British models consist of a deep earthenware dish with a lid. Around the sides of the dish an electric element is wound and then the whole thing is surrounded by an outer casing. A control rocker switch gives either a high or low setting (120 to 170 watts, depending on the make and 60 watt respectively). A detachable mains or a cooker designed so that an earthenware dish is removable makes it possible to serve direct from the casserole. The capacity varies with the make and ranges from 1.8 litres/3 pints to 3.5 litres/6 pints.

The cookers can be left on the low setting all day without worry of the food spoiling. At this temperature the liquid will not boil. Also, water condensing inside the lid runs down to form a liquid seal around the lid rim so there is no loss from evaporation.

The cookers are particularly suitable for foods that require long, slow cooking such as stews, pot roasts, boiled bacon, etc. as the meat becomes tender, holds its shape well with virtually no shrinkage. However, it is necessary to sauté meat and vegetables on a stove before putting into a slow cooker. The cookers can also be used for cooking sponge puddings, milk puddings, soups, vegetables and fruit. As it is a very different method of cooking certain adjustments have to be made. Instructions and recipe booklets are supplied by the manufacturer with each cooker.

The main advantage of the cooker is the large fuel savings which can be as much as 40 per cent. However, this has to be offset by the initial cost of the slow cooker so it should be used regularly to make it a worthwhile buy. (See Haybox Cookery entry.)

SMELT

A small, delicately flavoured fish, from 10 cm/ 4 inches to 30 cm/12 inches long, closely allied to the salmon family. Smelts are in season from September to April, after which time they go up the rivers to spawn, in the same way as salmon.

Preparation and cooking: Pull out the gills, when the entrails should also come out if the fish is lightly squeezed. Wipe and dry well, but avoid washing and cook immediately. Frying is the usual method – roll the fish in seasoned flour, egg and crumb and fry in hot fat. Serve garnished with fried parsley and accompanied by hollandaise, tomato or shrimp sauce.

SMOKED HADDOCK, SALMON

(See Haddock and Salmon entries.)

SMOKING

The process of preserving meat and fish by drying them in the smoke of a wood fire. It is essential to use a wood fire and sawdust is usually thrown over it to create dense smoke. The flavour given to the food depends on the variety of wood employed: juniper, oak, beech, etc., all give their own special flavour. Some old houses had chimneys specially constructed for smoking; in others a special outhouse was used.

A new form of home-smoker is now available for use domestically. It is particularly suitable for fish, poultry, meat and cheese. Food smoked in this way is for immediate consumption and not for preservation.

378

SMÖRGÅSBORD

In Sweden and to a lesser extent in the rest of Scandinavia this is the traditional way of serving food. It resembles a buffet meal or cold table and can be either an appetizer course or a full meal.

No matter how elaborate it may be, a Smörgåsbord starts with bread and butter and herring dishes, accompanied by boiled potatoes and followed by one or two small piquant dishes. The plates are then changed and egg dishes are served, with salads, cold meats, perhaps some dishes in aspic and finally (for a fairly elaborate meal) perhaps some hot dishes such as kidneys or meat balls; then come rye bread, cheese and coffee.

SMØRREBRØD

Danish open sandwiches, consisting of an oblong slice of bread, generously buttered, topped with meat, fish or cheese (often combined with egg or salad ingredients) and attractively garnished. They may be served for lunch, high tea or supper and are very suitable for informal entertaining. Provided you have a reasonable supply of bread and some tins of meat, fish, etc., in the store-cupboard, smørrebrød can also be produced at short notice for unexpected guests.

In Denmark, rye bread is traditionally used, but other firm-textured types can, of course, be substituted. Cut the slices into pieces about 10 × 5 cm/4 × 2 inches and butter really well, right up to the edges – this not only adds to the flavour, but also holds the topping in place. Use a generous amount of topping – the smørrebrød are normally eaten with knife and fork, not in the fingers. To serve with cocktails or as a buffet party snack, make them half the size (the Danes call these titbits *Snittere*).

When serving smørrebrød at a party, allow about 3 per person of the ordinary-sized ones and follow the Danish order, offering the fish ones first, then the meat ones and finally cheese smørrebrød. They are best arranged on large, flat dishes, platters or trays; if possible, have cake or fish slices to act as servers. After preparing the trays of smørrebrød, cover with a slightly damp cloth or greaseproof paper and keep in a cool place until required. The Danes serve chilled Schnapps or lager with them, with perhaps a liqueur to accompany the cheese smørrebrød.

Smørrebrød Ingredients

The choice of ingredients is almost unlimited, but here are some of the most popular:

MEAT
Ham (fresh or canned), roast beef, pork, etc., pork luncheon meat, chopped pork, spiced pork roll, salami, tongue (fresh or canned), bacon, liver sausage and pâté. The slices of meat are often rolled.

FISH
Herrings (spiced or pickled), mackerel fillets, slices of cold cooked white fish, smoked salmon, shrimps, etc., caviare.

CHEESE
Almost any type that lends itself to easy slicing or spreading can be used, including the veined kinds such as Danish Blue. If the slices are sufficiently pliable, they are often folded like meat slices, to look more appealing.

OTHER INGREDIENTS AND GARNISHES
Lettuce leaves, cress, watercress, sliced hard-boiled egg, egg strips, sliced cucumber, tomato, radish, gherkin, beetroot, green pepper, etc., potato and Russian salads, cooked peas, button mushrooms, sprigs of parsley or other mild herbs, onion rings, radish roses, twists of tomato, lemon, cucumber, orange, etc., horseradish cream, mayonnaise, apple sauce and fried apple slices (particularly with bacon), meat jelly, cooked prunes, stoned grapes, sliced stuffed olives, halved walnuts.

To make egg strips: Mix 4 eggs with 300 ml/ ½ pint milk, beat well, strain and season. Cook slowly over hot water until set and when cold cut into strips. Alternatively, scramble eggs in the usual way and press them lightly while cooking.

Meat jelly: This is made by making up some aspic jelly in the usual way, including a little meat extract and gravy browning for extra flavour and colour.

SIMPLE SMØRREBRØD TOPPINGS
Chopped pork, potato salad, watercress, sliced tomato
Crisp-grilled bacon with scrambled egg
Tongue with Russian salad and a tomato twist
Salami with onion rings
Pork luncheon meat, sweet pickle, sliced cucumber
Liver pâté with sliced gherkin and a beetroot twist.

Four Party Smørrebrød

LUNCHEON MEAT WITH HORSERADISH
Arrange on each slice of bread 2 to 3 folded slices of pork luncheon meat. Add 2 × 5 ml spoons/2 teaspoons horseradish cream (horseradish sauce mixed with a little double cream) and top with a twist of fresh orange and a stoned cooked prune, one half each side of the orange.

TONGUE AND RUSSIAN SALAD
On each piece of bread arrange 3 small thinly cut slices of tongue, folding them to give height. Top with 2 × 5 ml spoons/2 teaspoons of Russian salad and add tomato and cucumber twists.

CHEESE AND BACON
First grill some streaky bacon rashers until crisp

379

and allow them to cool. Arrange across each slice of bread alternate rashers and slices of Samsoe cheese. Garnish with cooked button mushrooms and watercress.

CAVIARE AND EGG

Put 4 to 6 slices of hard-boiled egg on each piece of bread. Pipe a little mayonnaise on the centre of each ring and on this press 1 × 5 ml spoon/1 teaspoon caviare; garnish with a parsley sprig.

SNAIL, EDIBLE (ESCARGOT)

A cultivated variety of snail, most esteemed in France; the best are said to be those fed upon vine leaves. Snails have a good flavour (thought by some people to resemble that of oysters), but little food value. After being cleaned and boiled for 5 minutes, the snails are taken from the shells, the intestine is removed and the flesh is stewed with herbs, etc., before being returned to the shells for serving. They may also be fried or prepared in various other ways. Snails may be bought in cans, ready prepared and often accompanied by cleaned shells ready for serving.

SNAILS À LA BOURGUIGNONNE

METRIC/IMPERIAL
1 can snails (about 20)
300 ml/½ pint white wine
1 onion stuck with cloves
2 cloves garlic, skinned and crushed
150 ml/¼ pint brandy
bouquet garni
salt
butter

FOR GARLIC BUTTER
100 g/4 oz softened butter
½ shallot, skinned and finely chopped
1 clove garlic, skinned and crushed
1–2 × 5 ml spoons/1–2 teaspoons chopped parsley
good pinch of mixed spice
salt
pepper

Remove the snails from the can and place in a pan with the rest of the ingredients. Simmer gently for 1 hour, remove from the heat and allow to cool in the liquor. Meanwhile, mix the ingredients for the garlic butter, blending well. Put a snail into each shell, fill up with butter and put the shells in an ovenproof dish. Bake them in a hot oven (230°C/450°F, Gas Mark 8) for 10 minutes.

NOTE

If shells are not provided with the can of snails, simmer the snails as before, put them in an ovenproof dish, place the butter over and round them and bake as above.

SNAPDRAGON

A dish which is the basis of a traditional Christmas game. A quantity of raisins is placed in a broad shallow bowl or platter, some brandy or other spirit is poured over and ignited, then the members of the party try to snatch the fruit from the flaming mass.

SNIPE

A small bird with a long bill and striped plumage, in season from August 15th to March 15th. Snipe should be eaten really fresh, so make sure when buying them that the bill is dry and feet supple. (See Game entry for cooking.)

SNOEK

A fish related to the mackerel, the tuna and the swordfish, which is found in South African waters, in Australian waters, where it is known as barracouta, and off the coast of Chile, where it is called sierra. The fish grows to about 1.2 metres/ 4 feet in length and may weigh up to some 8 kg/18 lb. Canned snoek is available in this country but is not very popular.

SNOW

The name given to a mixture of sweetened fruit pulp and egg whites; it may be coloured and is usually accompanied by biscuits or sponge fingers; alternatively, it may be served on a bed of sponge cake previously soaked in a little fruit juice. Apples, apricots and prunes are excellent for use in this way. A similar sweet may be made with gelatine. It is particularly suitable to serve to invalids, the elderly and babies.

APPLE SNOW

METRIC/IMPERIAL
0.5 kg/1 lb cooking apples, peeled, cored and chopped
2 × 15 ml spoons/2 tablespoons water
2 × 5 ml spoons/2 teaspoons lemon juice
25–50 g/1–2 oz granulated sugar
green food colouring, optional
2 eggs, separated

Place apples, water, lemon juice and sugar in a saucepan and cook, covered, over a medium heat until the fruit is thick and pulpy. Pass it through a nylon sieve. In a basin combine the apple purée, a few drops of green colouring and the egg yolks. Beat well and allow to cool. Stiffly whisk the egg whites then fold them into the apple purée until well blended. Turn the purée into individual glasses and chill before serving decorated with cream or grated chocolate.

NOTE
300 ml/½ pint bottled or frozen unsweetened apple purée can be used as an alternative.

SODA BREAD

In this Irish type of bread the raising agent is bicarbonate of soda combined with buttermilk.

SODA BREAD

METRIC/IMPERIAL
450 g/1 lb plain flour
2 × 5 ml spoons/2 teaspoons bicarbonate of soda
2 × 5 ml spoons/2 teaspoons cream of tartar
1 × 5 ml spoon/1 teaspoon salt
25–50 g/1–2 oz lard
about 300 ml/½ pint soured milk or buttermilk

Grease and flour a baking sheet. Sift together the dry ingredients twice. Rub in the lard. Mix to a soft but manageable dough with the liquid: the amount required will depend on the absorbency of the flour. Shape into an 18 cm/7 inch round and mark into triangles. Place on the baking sheet and bake in a hot oven (220°C/425°F, Gas Mark 7) for about 30 minutes. Eat while fresh.

SODA WATER

Water aerated with carbon dioxide and sold in bottles or syphons. Soda water also contains a little bicarbonate of soda, the proportion varying in different makes. It is alkaline and may help to neutralize the acidity of the gastric juice. The chief value of soda water, however, is to add sparkle and therefore to accentuate the flavour of certain drinks such as claret cup and lemon squash.

Syphons and containers of the gas can be bought for producing soda water at home.

SODIUM GLUTAMATE (MONOSODIUM GLUTAMATE)

This is the sodium salt of the amino acid called glutamic acid – an almost tasteless substance which constitutes part of the casein of milk. It brings out the flavour of other foods, especially those of a savoury type, and is now often added to manufactured meat, fish and savoury products; fruit and sweet dishes are less suitable for this treatment. The amount required is very small – about 1 in 3,000 parts. Preparations for home use are sold under such names as Ac'cent.

SOFT DRINKS

Non-alcoholic bottled or canned drinks, ready to drink or requiring dilution. They include carbonated beverages such as various tonic waters, fizzy lemonades and herbal infusions, as well as still beverages which are ready to drink and the squashes and the comminuted fruit drinks. Squashes are made from fruit juice with added flavouring and colouring, saccharine and sugar. Comminuted drinks are made from the whole fruit, crushed, strained and then flavoured and coloured. Legislation specifies the composition of soft drinks including semi-sweet, diabetic and low calorie drinks. They should also be clearly labelled to show the contents.

None of these drinks has much food value. There is a very little sugar – frequently glucose – but this has no particular benefit for the healthy person, although it may be important to the seriously ill. In this connection, the word 'glucose' has in fact tended to become a gimmick. The amount of fruit used in soft drinks is very small indeed and unless extra Vitamin C is added, is of no particular value.

SOLE

Next to the turbot, the sole is considered the finest of all the flat fish. Its flesh is firm and delicate, with a delicious flavour. It is very easily digested and so is often given to invalids and convalescents. The real sole, called the Dover sole, is easily recognised by its dark brownish-grey back skin. Lemon sole is broader and its back is a reddish-brown colour. The lemon, witch and Torbay sole are not considered to have such a fine flavour as the true Dover sole. When fresh, soles are shiny and firm to the touch. Those without roes are superior in flavour. Sole is in season all the year round.

Soles are cooked by any of the usual methods, particularly frying and grilling. Fillets of sole are delicious steamed, baked or poached and served with a rich, well-flavoured sauce – cream, white wine, mushroom or a similar type.

SOLE MEUNIÈRE

METRIC/IMPERIAL
1 large sole, whole or filleted
salt
pepper
flour
butter
lemon
chopped parsley

Season the sole with pepper and salt, flour it lightly on both sides and fry it in butter until the fish is cooked and golden-brown on both sides. Serve on a hot dish, sprinkled with lemon juice and parsley, then pour on some lightly browned melted butter.

SORBET

Originally an iced Turkish drink (the name being

381

derived from the same origin as sherbet). The modern sorbet is a soft water ice, flavoured with either fruit or liqueur and sometimes containing whisked egg white. A sorbet was previously served at a formal dinner before the roast, to clear the palate but nowadays it is more often served at informal meals as part of the sweet course, combined with diced fruit or fruit salad. Sorbets are too soft to mould and are served in goblets or glasses.

SORBITOL

A sugar substitute which is tolerated by diabetics and can be used in their diet in place of sugar. However, it does have a high energy value, so it is not suitable for slimming diets.

SORGHUM

(See Millet entry.)

SORREL

A wild plant with sharply pointed leaves and red flowers. It is not used much in England but is very popular in France, where a cultivated variety is sometimes grown in gardens. Sorrel has a strongly acid taste and can be used in small quantities to add flavour to lettuce and other salads, sauces and certain savoury dishes. It may also be cooked like spinach and made into a purée for serving with poached eggs, sweetbreads and some meat dishes, or it can be mixed with spinach to improve its flavour. Sorrel should be picked when young and fresh.

SOUBISE SAUCE

A velvety onion sauce made by mixing 300 ml/ ½ pint cooked puréed onions with 300 ml/ ½ pint thick Béchamel sauce and 2 × 15 ml spoons/ 2 tablespoons cream. It can be served with any egg or vegetable dish and is a traditional accompaniment for cutlets.

SOUFFLÉ

A fluffy dish, either sweet or savoury, which is lightened by the addition of stiffly beaten egg whites. Success in making a soufflé depends largely on the adequate whisking of the egg whites and their very light but thorough incorporation into the flour or other mixture. There are two types of soufflé, one served hot and the other cold.

Hot Soufflés

These are based on a panada and may be steamed or baked, but in either case they should be served very hot and eaten at once, as they rapidly sink. Use an ovenproof china or glass mould or a tin.

BAKED
Prepare the tin or mould by greasing it well with clarified butter or a tasteless cooking fat. Grease a round of greaseproof paper to fit the base and put in position. Tie a double band of greased greaseproof paper firmly round the tin so that it stands 7.5 cm/3 inches above the top – this will protect the sides of the soufflé as it rises. Fill the prepared tin about two-thirds full and bake in a moderate oven (180°C/350°F, Gas Mark 4) for about 30 minutes, until well risen and golden-brown. Try to avoid opening the oven door until the soufflé is cooked. Remove paper band and serve immediately, in the dish.

Baked soufflés can also be cooked in individual moulds and are prepared in the same way; individual soufflés will take 15 to 20 minutes to cook.

STEAMED
Fill the tin only half-full, to allow for rising. Cover the top with a round of greased paper to prevent water dripping on to the surface. Steam gently in a steamer or in a saucepan of hot water. (If a saucepan is used, place the tin on a scone cutter or inverted saucer to raise it slightly). Cook until firm to the touch, ¾ to 1 hour. Remove the paper band, turn the soufflé out on to a hot dish, remove the round of paper from the top and serve at once.

Cold Soufflés

These are set with gelatine, the exact quantity varying according to circumstances – in very cold weather or when the soufflé can be set in a refrigerator, it may be necessary to use a smaller amount of gelatine. The usual method is to whisk together the egg yolks, sugar and flavouring (e.g., fruit juice, coffee or chocolate) over hot water until the mixture is thick and creamy – the warmth melts the sugar and air can then be whisked in more easily. (Do not overheat the mixture, for if it gets too hot, the egg cooks and the inclusion of air then becomes impossible.) The dissolved gelatine is then added and the mixture allowed to cool to 'setting point' (that is, when the mixture begins to set around the edges). Stir occasionally to ensure that all the ingredients are evenly distributed. The cream (if used) is whipped to the same consistency as the mixture and then folded in. The egg whites must be beaten very stiffly and are folded in at the last moment.

Preparing and filling the dish: A cold soufflé should be prepared so that when served it appears to have risen like a hot one. A straight-sided china or glass soufflé case is used; for these recipes it should be 5 cm/2 inches to 7.5 cm/3 inches deep; individual dishes are also available.

The dishes are prepared as follows: cut a strip of firm paper long enough to go round the case, overlapping slightly and deep enough to reach from the bottom of the dish to about 5 cm/2 inches above the top. Place it round the outside of the dish so that it fits exactly and pin it firmly in position or tie it with string. Take care to see that the paper forms a true circle, not an oval, otherwise the soufflé will not have a symmetrical appearance when finished.

Prepare the mixture according to the recipe and pour it at once into the soufflé case or cases, filling to 2.5 cm/1 inch to 5 cm/2 inches above the rim. Put in a refrigerator or cold larder to set.

Serving a cold soufflé: Remove the string or the pins very carefully and take off the paper. To do this, hold a knife which has been dipped in boiling water against the paper – this will melt the mixture slightly and enable the paper to be removed easily, leaving a smooth edge. Decorate the top with some suitable decoration, such as piped cream, glacé cherries, angelica, almonds, pistachios, etc.

The side of the soufflé mixture which stands above the dish may be decorated with chopped walnuts, ratafia crumbs, and so on. Press the finely chopped nuts or crumbs on to the mixture with a broad-bladed knife, letting any loose crumbs fall away. Repeat the process until the side is covered evenly all over.

CHEESE AND RICE SOUFFLÉ

METRIC/IMPERIAL
50 g/2 oz long grain rice
225 g/8 oz can tomatoes, drained
25 g/1 oz butter
4 × 15 ml spoons/4 tablespoons flour
300 ml/½ pint milk
175 g/6 oz cheese, grated
3 eggs, separated
salt
pepper

Cook the rice in the usual way until just soft. Put the tomatoes into a greased 1.2 litre/2 pint soufflé dish or well greased large ovenproof dish. Melt the fat, stir in the flour and cook for 2 to 3 minutes. Remove the pan from the heat and gradually stir in the milk. Bring to the boil, stirring all the time and when the sauce has thickened, remove from the heat, stir in the cooked rice, cheese, egg yolks and seasoning to taste. Finally whisk the egg whites stiffly and fold in lightly. Pour over the tomatoes and bake in a moderate oven (180°C/350°F, Gas Mark 4) for about 50 minutes until well risen.

VARIATION
1 small sliced onion and 3 to 4 chopped rashers of bacon can be sautéed lightly and used with or instead of the tomatoes.

SOUFFLÉ AU CHOCOLAT

METRIC/IMPERIAL
75–100 g/3–4 oz chocolate dots
2 × 15 ml spoons/2 tablespoons water
450 ml/¾ pint milk
50 g/2 oz caster sugar
4 × 15 ml spoons/4 tablespoons plain flour
knob of butter
3 egg yolks
4 egg whites
icing sugar

Butter an 18 cm/7 inch, 1.75 litre/3 pint soufflé dish. Put the chocolate dots in a basin with the water and melt them over a pan of boiling water. Heat the milk, reserving a little, with the sugar and pour on to the melted chocolate. Blend the flour to a smooth paste with the remaining milk, and stir in the chocolate mixture. Return to the pan, stir over a moderate heat until boiling, then cook for 2 minutes, stirring occasionally. Add the butter, in small pieces, then leave until lukewarm. Beat in the yolks, then fold in the stiffly whisked whites. Turn the mixture into the soufflé dish. Bake in a moderate oven (180°C/350°F, Gas Mark 4) for about 45 minutes, until well risen and firm to the touch. Dust with icing sugar before serving.

SOUFFLÉ MILANAISE

(Lemon)

METRIC/IMPERIAL
grated rind of 3 lemons
6 × 15 ml spoons/6 tablespoons lemon juice
100 g/4 oz caster sugar
4 egg yolks
3 × 15 ml spoons/3 tablespoons cold water
1 × 15 ml spoon/1 tablespoon powdered gelatine
175 ml/6 fl oz carton double cream, chilled
4 egg whites

TO DECORATE
150 ml/¼ pint carton double cream
angelica leaves, mimosa balls

Prepare a 13.5 cm/5½ inch, 900 ml/1½ pint soufflé dish. Place it on a baking sheet for easier handling. Finely grate the lemon rind free of white pith into a large deep bowl, add the juice, sugar and egg yolks. Place the bowl over a saucepan of hot (but not fast boiling) water and whisk the ingredients until pale in colour and of the consistency to coat the back of a wooden spoon, about 10 minutes. Remove the bowl from the heat and whisk from time to time while the mixture cools.

Spoon the measured cold water into a cup or small basin. Sprinkle the gelatine across the surface of the water. Stand the basin in a pan with water to come half way up, and heat the water until the gelatine has completely dissolved. Remove the basin from the water and cool it a little. When combining dissolved gelatine with a soufflé mixture, it is wise to add a few spoonfuls of the cool but not cold mixture to the gelatine (they should be the same temperature). Then whisk this into the rest of the mixture. By doing so, you will prevent any risk of 'roping' – a lumpy texture occurring. Chill until the mixture is the consistency of unbeaten egg white or until the edge shows signs of setting. As the mixture cools, scrape the bowl down with a rubber spatula to keep an even texture. If at this stage the egg is insufficiently set, the soufflé may separate out later, leaving a heavy jellied layer in the base.

Whip the chilled cream until it just holds its shape, but is still light and floppy. Whisk the whites until they are stiff but not dry-looking. Fold the cream through the lemon mixture using a large metal spoon in a figure-of-eight movement. Then when no cream is visible, fold in the egg whites a little at a time. Keep the mixture light, and stop folding as soon as the egg whites are evenly combined. Turn the mixture into the prepared dish and leave to set – minimum time about 3 hours in the refrigerator. If it is to be left overnight, place a piece of plastic film across the top of the paper collar to prevent a skin forming.

To serve, take the soufflé from the refrigerator about an hour before required. To remove the paper collar, first remove the fastening, then place a small knife between the folded paper and, with your other hand, gently pull the collar away with slight pressure from the knife against the soufflé edge. Very little soufflé mixture should adhere to the paper. Whip the cream for the decoration until it just holds its shape. Spoon it into a fabric forcing bag fitted with a small star vegetable nozzle, and pipe a series of shells round the edge. Finish with angelica leaf shapes and mimosa balls.

SOUP

Soup, which is usually served as the first course of a luncheon or dinner, not only stimulates the appetite for the food that follows but also adds some food value of its own.

Soups are infinitely varied in flavour, texture, appearance and nutritive value, but the majority of them may be divided into the thin soups (consommés and broths) and the thick soups (purées, thickened brown and white soups), the bisques (fish soups) and fruit soups. The choice of soup depends very much on the other dishes to be served. When the soup is intended merely as an appetizer to precede a substantial meal, choose a clear (consommé) type. If the main course is light, the soup may well be thick and nourishing. A soup may even form the main course, in which case it should be a broth or thick type, with plenty of vegetables and perhaps a garnish such as cheese

dumplings. The majority of soups are served hot, but in summer weather an iced soup is often appreciated. For luncheon or dinner parties, it is usual to allow 150 ml/¼ pint soup per person, but for family meals 200 ml/⅓ pint per person is more usual.

Most soups have a basis of meat or vegetables, or a combination of these with cereals, but bisques or fish soups are well known in some parts of the world and fruit soups are frequently served on the Continent, especially in Scandinavia. Stock made from white or brown meat, fish or vegetables (see Stock entry) forms the best foundation for most soups, but milk, water or a mixture may also be used.

Well-flavoured soups can be quickly made by using the many varieties of canned, condensed, packet and cube soups which are now available, particularly if they are mixed or diluted with milk or with chicken, meat or vegetable stock. Two soups of different flavours can be combined, while dehydrated or frozen vegetables or other ingredients can be added to give more variety, flavour and texture.

Serving soup: Soup may be ladled out at table into hot plates, soup cups or bowls, or it may be set at each person's place in a dish, from which it is poured into a plate. An appropriate garnish adds greatly to the appearance, flavour and often the nutritive value of a soup. In general, the more substantial garnishes are used with thickened soups and the lighter types with thin consommés and the more delicate cream soups.

CONSOMMÉS
These are made from a good stock and are cleared with egg shells and whites to give an appetizingly transparent liquid, which must be quite free of fat. Serve them either very hot or as iced jelly; garnish with Julienne strips or asparagus tips, etc., and hand round Melba toast, crisp rolls or bread sticks.

BROTHS
A broth is a substantial soup with meat cooked in it, though the meat is often removed and served separately. Strictly speaking, broths are thickened only by the vegetables cooked in them, but pearl barley is often added to the more substantial types such as Scotch broth.

PURÉES
Meat or vegetable stock, milk or water can all be used for these soups, which are thickened chiefly by the sieved or puréed vegetables, though it is usual to add a liaison of a starchy substance, egg or occasionally blood (as in hare soup).

Soup Garnishes

BACON
Cut into small strips or dice and fry lightly.

SAUSAGES AND SAUSAGEMEAT

Leftover cooked sausages, cut into rounds or small strips, go well with vegetable soups such as pea, onion or celery; they should be heated through in the soup just before it is served. Raw sausagemeat may also be used; roll into pieces about the size of a marble, coat with flour and either grill or fry, or poach in the soup for 10 to 15 minutes.

CHEESE

Grate the cheese (preferably Parmesan or dry Gruyère) and if desired mix it with either chopped parsley or watercress; hand it separately or sprinkle it on the soup just before serving.

CHEESE OR HERB DUMPLINGS

(See Dumpling entry.)

FRIED OR TOASTED CROÛTONS

(See Croûton entry.)

MACARONI, SPAGHETTI, NOODLES, SHELLS

These are good with minestrone or any thin soup. Break into short lengths, if necessary, and add to the soup about 30 minutes before serving.

RICE

Add dry boiled rice and freshly chopped parsley or chives just before serving the soup. Rice may also take the place of barley in mutton broth.

MUSHROOMS

Cut into thin slices and fry. When using button mushrooms leave whole.

ONIONS AND LEEKS

Slice into rings or chop finely and fry.

OTHER VEGETABLES

Cut raw carrot, turnip, etc., into 'matchsticks' or small balls, shred cabbage and slice celery and cook them separately for 10 minutes in some stock. Another method is to tie them in muslin and cook them in the soup. Sprinkle the pieces into the individual soup plates or cups before serving. Alternatively, frozen mixed vegetables may be added 5 to 10 minutes before serving.

CREAM OF TOMATO SOUP

METRIC/IMPERIAL
1 stick of celery, scrubbed and chopped
1 carrot, pared and sliced
1 small onion, skinned and chopped
1 rasher of bacon, rinded, boned and finely chopped
25 g/1 oz butter
2 × 15 ml spoons/2 tablespoons flour
0.75 kg/1½ lb tomatoes, quartered
600 ml/1 pint white or brown stock
bouquet garni
salt and pepper
pinch of sugar
2 × 15 ml spoons/2 tablespoons cream
chopped chervil, basil or parsley to garnish

Lightly fry the celery, carrot, onion and bacon in the butter for 5 minutes, until soft but not coloured. Sprinkle in the flour and stir. Add the quartered tomatoes, stock and bouquet garni, cover and cook gently for about 30 minutes, until soft. Remove the bouquet garni and sieve the soup or purée it in an electric blender and sieve to remove the seeds. Return it to the pan with the seasonings, add the cream and re-heat, but do not let it boil. Garnish with freshly chopped chervil or basil, when in season – otherwise use chopped parsley.

If the tomatoes lack flavour, add a little tomato purée. Canned tomatoes can be used to replace the fresh ones; drain off the liquor and make it up to 600 ml/1 pint with stock. When fresh celery is not available, use a few flakes of dried celery.

Thickened Soups

These are made of meat or vegetable stock, milk or water and may contain meat, fish, vegetables, etc. The thickening consists of a cereal of some sort or eggs. Thickened soups may be either brown or white – see the typical recipes below.

OX-TAIL SOUP

METRIC/IMPERIAL
1 ox-tail, jointed
25 g/1 oz butter
2 onions, skinned and chopped
1 carrot, pared and sliced
2 sticks of celery, trimmed and sliced
2 litres/3½ pints brown stock
25 g/1 oz lean ham or bacon, chopped
bouquet garni
salt
pepper
3 × 15 ml spoons/3 tablespoons flour
a little port, optional
a squeeze of lemon juice
celery leaves to garnish, optional

Wash and dry the ox-tail and trim off any excess fat. Fry the pieces of ox-tail in the butter with the vegetables for 5 minutes, until evenly browned. Just cover with the stock and bring to the boil. Add the chopped ham or bacon, bouquet garni and seasoning. Cover the saucepan and simmer gently for about 4 hours, or until the tail meat is tender. As ox-tail is very fatty, it is necessary to skim the soup occasionally with a metal spoon. Strain the soup, remove the meat from the bones and cut it up neatly. Return the meat and strained liquor to the pan and re-heat. Blend the flour and a little water or port to a smooth cream. Stir in a little of the hot liquid and add the mixture to the pan. Bring to the boil, stirring until it thickens, and cook for about 5 minutes. Add a squeeze of lemon juice and seasoning to taste before serving. If wished, serve garnished with celery leaves.

385

This 'hearty' soup can be made into a meal in itself by adding some small dumplings, putting them in 20 minutes before the end of the cooking time.

BISQUE
These thickened fish soups are usually made from shellfish. (See Bisque entry.)

FRUIT SOUPS
The basis of these soups is diluted fruit juice or a purée of rhubarb, gooseberries, red-currants, raspberries, oranges, lemons, etc.; this is slightly thickened with arrowroot, cornflour, potato flour or sago meal and sweetened to taste. A little white wine may be added and sometimes a touch of spice.

Before serving, the soup may be either poured on to one or two egg yolks, or a spoonful of whipped cream may be put on the top of each plateful. Fruit soups are often served with diced bread which has been baked until brown with a little butter and sugar, or with chopped nuts.

CREAM OF LEMON SOUP

METRIC/IMPERIAL
25 g/1 oz butter or margarine
100 g/4 oz onions, skinned and sliced
100 g/4 oz carrots, pared and sliced
1 litre/1¾ pints turkey or chicken stock
1 large lemon
1 bouquet garni
1 × 15 ml spoon/1 tablespoon arrowroot
salt
freshly ground black pepper
150 ml/¼ pint carton single cream

Melt the butter in a large saucepan. Add the sliced vegetables and cook gently until tender, stirring frequently. Pour over the stock, bring to the boil, reduce the heat and simmer. Using a vegetable peeler, thinly pare the rind from the lemon. Pour boiling water over the rind and leave for 1 minute; drain. Add the rind, juice of the lemon and bouquet garni to the pan contents. Cover and cook for 1 hour or until the vegetables are really soft. Remove the bouquet garni. Purée the soup a little at a time in an electric blender. In a clean pan, blend the arrowroot with a little of the soup then add the remainder, stirring. Bring to the boil, stirring. Adjust seasoning before adding the cream. Reheat but do not boil.

COCK-A-LEEKIE

METRIC/IMPERIAL
1 boiling fowl about 1 kg/2¼ lb
1 litre/1¾ pints stock
4 leeks, cleaned and sliced
salt

pepper
6 prunes, optional

Cover the fowl with stock or water and add the leeks and seasoning. Bring to the boil, cover and simmer for 3½ hours, until tender. Remove the chicken from the stock, carve off the meat and cut it into fairly large pieces. Serve the soup with the chicken pieces in it, or serve the soup on its own, with the chicken as a main course.

If prunes are used, soak them overnight in cold water, halve and stone them and add to the stock 30 minutes before the end of the cooking.

GOLDEN VEGETABLE SOUP

METRIC/IMPERIAL
175 g/6 oz potatoes
175 g/6 oz turnips
175 g/6 oz carrots
175 g/6 oz onion
175 g/6 oz celery
900 ml/1½ pints unseasoned bone or chicken stock
salt
freshly ground black pepper
bouquet garni
25 g/1 oz butter or margarine
Parmesan cheese, celery leaves for garnish

Peel the potatoes, turnips and carrots. Skin the onions and finely chop, finely slice the celery. Grate the potatoes, turnips and carrots into a large pan, add the onion, celery and stock together with 5 ml spoon/1 teaspoon salt, pepper and a bouquet garni. Bring to the boil, reduce the heat, cover and simmer for about 1 hour. Adjust the seasoning, add the butter and when melted serve the soup with a dusting of grated Parmesan cheese and snipped celery leaves.

WINTER HOTCHPOTCH

METRIC/IMPERIAL
225 g/8 oz Jerusalem artichokes
450 g/1 lb carrots, pared
225 g/8 oz turnips, peeled
2 onions, skinned, or 2 leeks, cleaned
2–3 sticks of celery, trimmed
½ small cabbage, washed
1 rasher of bacon, rinded and chopped
75 g/3 oz dripping or butter
bouquet garni
brown stock or water
salt
pepper
100 g/4 oz macaroni, in small pieces
chopped parsley
grated cheese

Peel the artichokes, cut them into slices and then strips and keep in water to which 2 × 5 ml spoons/2 teaspoons lemon juice has been added to prevent discoloration. Cut the rest of the vegetables (except the cabbage) into fairly small pieces. Fry the bacon lightly, add the fat and when it is melted, fry the vegetables (except the cabbage) for about 10 minutes, until soft but not coloured. Add the bouquet garni and enough stock or water to cover. Season well, cover and simmer for ¾ to 1 hour. Add the cabbage and macaroni and cook for a further 20 to 30 minutes, adding more liquid as required. When all the ingredients are soft, remove the bouquet garni and re-season if necessary. Serve sprinkled with fresh chopped parsley and grated cheese.

If preferred, the cabbage can be shredded and added just before serving, instead of being cooked in the soup; this gives a pleasant crispness.

SOYA

The soya bean, the most nutritious of all the bean family, is grown chiefly in the Far East, in America and in Germany. Over a hundred varieties are known, some early, some late; the colour of the beans may be green, yellow or brown. Unlike other beans, the soya contains very little starch. The protein is far superior in kind and quality to that of other vegetable foods and the fat content is about 20 per cent; soya contains calcium, iron, thiamine, also some riboflavin and nicotinic acid. It is a very important item in countries where food is short.

Soya beans may be cooked like haricot beans, but require a longer time. However, on account of their slightly bitter flavour, they are probably best eaten in the form of soya flour, which when properly manufactured has a less pronounced taste. Soya mixed with other flour in the proportion of 25 g/1 oz to every 200 g/7 oz flour in the making of pastry, cakes, puddings, biscuits, etc., gives extra nourishment. The flour can be used to give a creamy texture to soups, sauces and custards and is also sometimes employed in the manufacture of sausagemeat.

Soya bean curd is made from cooked and fermented beans and is used to supplement meat and fish in Eastern countries. (See Textured Vegetable Protein entry.)

Soya (Soy) Sauce
A dark brown, pungent sauce made from soya beans, very widely used in Eastern cookery as a flavouring and seasoning.

SPAGHETTI

Spaghetti is made from an Italian paste, which is formed into long 'strings'. (The word literally means 'little threads'). It is cooked as for macaroni.

A common method of serving spaghetti is to eat it with tomato, meat or cheese sauce. It is a staple food in Italy eaten with a spoon and fork. It may also be broken up and added to soups and used in making croquettes and other made-up dishes. (See Pasta entry.)

SPEARMINT

(See Mint entry.)

SPICE

The general term covering a wide variety of aromatic seasonings which are used to flavour both savoury and sweet dishes. They are usually derived from woody shrubs found in the tropics. Spices were formerly used to disguise putrefaction in the days before canning, dehydration and freezing could be successfully used to preserve foods. The use of curry powder in India is one example. Spices are sold both individually or in combination (e.g., as mixed spice and curry powder). The best flavour is obtained from freshly ground spices, so they should be bought in small quantities.

Spices stimulate the appetite, but should be used with moderation, as too much produces an unpleasant flavour. They should be avoided by those suffering from 'acid stomach'.

The following list gives the spices most commonly used in this country (in many cases fuller details are given under the individual names): allspice, aniseed, cardamom, cassia, cayenne, chillies, cinnamon, cloves, coriander, cubeb, cumin, curry powder, fenugreek, ginger, mustard, nutmeg, pepper and saffron.

SPINACH

An annual or perennial plant with succulent green leaves. Spinach should be picked young and eaten as soon as possible after picking; it is then a good source of vitamin C and an excellent source of vitamin A. It also contains a good percentage of calcium and iron, but probably neither of these is available to the body, because they form insoluble salts with the oxalic acid also present.

Preparation and cooking: Allow 225 g/8 oz spinach per person. Wash well in several waters, to remove all grit, and strip off any coarse stalks. Pack it into a saucepan with only the water that clings to it, heat gently and cook until it is tender, 10 to 15 minutes. Drain it thoroughly, and re-heat with a knob of butter and a sprinkling of salt and pepper. Alternatively, the spinach may be sieved, and 1–2 × 15 ml spoons/1–2 tablespoons of white sauce, cream or soured cream may be added. Re-heat before serving.

Creamed spinach can form a bed for poached eggs, slices of hard-boiled egg, or scrambled egg and chopped bacon. Snippets of fried bread make a suitable garnish. Spinach may also be added to soups, in which case it is best shredded and added 10 minutes before serving. Sorrel and spinach may be cooked together and served creamed, while young spinach leaves can be served in salads.

SPIRIT

Beverages made from an alcoholic bearing liquid, the result being of a high alcoholic content. The five main spirits of the world are Brandy, Whisky, Gin, Vodka and Rum (see individual entries).

A great deal of skill is required to make a good distillation although in principle it is quite simple. Alcohol vaporizes at 78.3°C and water at 100°C, so to drive off the alcohol a temperature between these is applied to the alcoholic wash. The required flavourings are also driven off, leaving the water behind.

The strength of alcohol in the spirit is indicated by the proof. British proof is represented by the figure 100 and pure alcohol is represented by the figure 175.25/175. British proof spirit therefore contains 57 per cent pure alcohol. Note that proof spirit is not the same as pure alcohol. In Britain the majority of spirits are sold at 70 British proof/30° under proof meaning that they contain 40 per cent pure alcohol by volume. Excise duty is calculated on so much per proof gallon. Eventually this system is to be superseded by that used on the Continent. Alcoholic strength is coded by stating the percentage of pure alcohol in a spirit which is a more logical method.

The American proof system is similar to the British except that pure alcohol is represented by the figure 200, therefore the figure on the label only has to be halved to obtain the actual alcoholic strength.

Food can be both preserved and flavoured with spirits; thus fruit is often preserved in brandy or gin, while rum, whisky or brandy may be added to such things as rich cakes and mincemeat. Spirits can also be used in savoury dishes.

SPIT-ROASTING

Originally meat was always roasted by turning it on a spit in front of an open fire. Meat cooked in a modern oven, although referred to as a roast, is really baked. However, a rotary spit, worked by an electric motor or a clockwork mechanism, can now be fitted to many cookers. The spit can be situated inside the oven or made into an eye-level fitment, usually combined with the ordinary grill.

This method of cooking is very successful for good cuts of meat, rabbit, poultry and game. It ensures very even cooking and an excellent flavour, as the meat is basted by its own juice. (See Rôtisserie entry.)

SPLIT

A type of yeast bun made in the West Country which is split open and served with cream or butter and jam. The term can also refer to a liquid measure of 250 ml/8 fl oz or the slang for a half bottle of aerated water.

DEVONSHIRE SPLITS

METRIC/IMPERIAL
15 g/½ oz fresh yeast
about 300 ml/½ pint tepid milk
450 g/1 lb strong plain flour
1 × 5 ml spoon/1 teaspoon salt
50 g/2 oz butter
2 × 15 ml spoons/2 tablespoons sugar

TO SERVE
jam and Devonshire or whipped cream
icing sugar

Grease a baking sheet. Blend the yeast with half the milk. Mix the flour and salt, warm the butter and sugar in the remaining milk and when at blood heat, stir into a well in the centre of the flour with the yeast liquid. Beat to an elastic dough, turn it out on to a floured surface and knead until smooth. Place in a bowl and cover with oiled polythene. Allow to rise until doubled in size, then turn it on to a lightly floured surface and divide into fourteen to sixteen pieces. Knead each lightly into a ball, place on a greased baking sheet and flatten slightly with the hand. Put to rise in a warm place for about 20 minutes and bake in a hot oven (220°C/425°F, Gas Mark 7) for 15 to 20 minutes. Turn out on to a wire rack. Before serving split them and spread one half with jam and Devonshire or whipped cream, sandwich together again and sprinkle the tops with icing sugar.

Traditionally Devonshire splits are cut across the top of the bun and then filled with cream and a thick fruit preserve.

SPLIT PEAS

(See Pea entry.)

SPONGE CAKE

A light cake, made of eggs, sugar, flour and flavouring and mixed by the whisking method. (For Genoese sponge (which contains fat) and for Victoria sponge (which is made by the creaming method) see individual entries.)

SPOTTED DICK (SPOTTED DOG)

A favourite type of steamed or boiled suet pudding containing currants, sultanas or other dried fruit and shaped in a roll.

SPOTTED DICK

METRIC/IMPERIAL
75 g/3 oz self raising flour
pinch of salt
75 g/3 oz fresh breadcrumbs
75 g/3 oz shredded suet
50 g/2 oz caster sugar
175 g/6 oz currants
about 4–6 × 15 ml spoons/4–6 tablespoons milk

Half-fill a steamer with water and put on to boil. Mix together the flour, salt, breadcrumbs, suet, sugar and currants in a bowl. Make a well in the centre and add enough milk to give a fairly soft dough. Form into a roll on a well floured board, wrap loosely in greased greaseproof paper and then in foil, sealing the ends well.

Steam over rapidly boiling water for 1½ to 2 hours. Unwrap the pudding, put in a hot dish and serve with custard or with a sweet white sauce flavoured with cinnamon or grated lemon rind. Alternatively, make the mixture of a soft dropping consistency and steam it for 1½ to 2 hours in a greased 900 ml/1½ pint pudding basin.

SPRAT

A small silvery fish, of the herring family, in season from November to March, and sold both fresh and smoked. Norwegian sprats are canned under the name of brisling. As the bones are eaten they are a good source of calcium. They also supply protein, fat, vitamins A, B₁ and D, riboflavine and nicotinic acid.

Preparation and cooking: Allow 225 g/8 oz sprats per person. Clean them well and draw them through the gills, then wipe them dry and flour them. Run a skewer through the gills of several fish and grill them until nicely browned. Remove from the skewer and serve very hot, with lemon or with mustard sauce and brown bread and butter.

SPRING GREENS

Fresh young cabbage, in season during May and June. (See Cabbage entry.)

SPRING ONION

A small type of onion with a green or white outer skin, grown for use in salads.

Wash the onions, remove the outer skin, and serve them whole in salads, or chopped and sprinkled over green salad, tomato salad, etc. They can also be used for flavouring savoury dishes. (See Onion entry.)

SPROUT, SPROUT TOPS

(See Brussels Sprouts, Cabbage entries)

SPRUCE BEER

A drink which is popular along the Western coast of Canada. It is made without barley, the branches, cones and bark of black spruce being boiled for several hours, then put into a cask with molasses, hops and yeast and allowed to ferment.

SQUAB

A young pigeon.

Squab Pie is a West-country dish made of meat, apples and onions.

SQUASH, FRUIT

A drink made with sweetened fruit pulp. (See Soft Drinks entry.) Various types of squash are sold ready prepared in concentrated form. There are legal requirements for their composition. Contents must also be shown on the label in order of quantity.

SQUASH (VEGETABLE)

The term used in the USA for gourd-like fruits, such as the vegetable marrow. There are many types, some edible and some inedible but used for decorative purposes.

STARCH

Starch is a carbohydrate of a more complicated type than sugar. When it is digested, it is broken down into sugar before being absorbed by the body.

It is found in most vegetables and fruits – in very small quantities in green vegetables and most fruits and in quite large quantities in root vegetables, peas, beans and cereals such as wheat and rice. It does not occur in animal tissues. In a raw state starch is insoluble in water so most foods containing starch are cooked to allow the grains to swell and gelatinize.

In general, starch is the biggest source of energy in the human diet throughout the world.

STEAK

A piece of meat cut from the fillet, rump, sirloin or any other lean and meaty part of the animal. Thick sections of a fish such as cod or salmon are sometimes called steaks. Unless otherwise qualified, however, the word is usually taken to mean beefsteak. The chief types cooked by grilling or frying are listed below. Stewing steak is cooked by stewing or braising. (See Stewing entry.)

RUMP
This has a very good flavour but is not always very tender. The 'point' is considered the best part.

FILLET

The undercut of sirloin. It is very tender, but has not as much flavour as rump. The fillet is often cut and shaped into small rounds known as tournedos.

PORTERHOUSE (CHATEAUBRIAND AND CONTREFILET).

A thick steak, on the bone, cut from the middle ribs and usually incorporating the fillet.

T-BONE STEAK

A steak cut from the sirloin, containing a T-shaped bone.

ENTRECÔTE

A steak without bone, cut normally from the sirloin and sometimes the ribs.

Cooking and serving steaks: Steak is usually fried or grilled and served with its own juice made into a thin gravy and with some or all of the following: Béarnaise sauce, maître d'hôtel butter, grilled tomatoes and mushrooms, crisp fried onion rings, sauté or chipped potatoes, green salad.

Steak which is not of the finest quality may be marinated before cooking.

Cooking times for steaks (in minutes)

Thickness	Rare	Medium Rare	Well-done
2 cm/¾ inch	5	9 to 10	12 to 15
2.5 cm/1 inch	6 to 7	10	15
3.5 cm/1½ inch	10	12 to 14	18 to 20

PLANKED STEAK

Grill a thick steak for 7 minutes and then transfer it to a wooden steak plank (a grooved wooden board with a well at one end to catch the juices). Surround it with a border of creamed potato and bake in a hot oven (230°C/450°F, Gas Mark 8) until done – 10 to 15 minutes. Spread with butter, sprinkle with parsley and garnish with vegetables.

VIENNA STEAK

Cakes of minced beef flavoured with onions, herbs and ketchup and cooked in a covered frying pan.

STEAMING

An economical method of cooking food in the steam from boiling water. It has the advantage of retaining mineral salts and the water-soluble vitamins B and C, which are apt to be dissolved out when food is boiled in water. Steamed food also keeps a better shape and often a better flavour. Disadvantages are that food may take longer to cook and the room can become filled with steam.

There are several ways of steaming, according to the equipment available. The chief points to remember are that the steamer must not be

allowed to boil dry, which ruins the steamer and burns the food, and the water must not go off the boil, which results in puddings being 'sad' and vegetables, etc., not being cooked properly.

Methods of Steaming

1. In a steamer with a perforated base placed over an ordinary saucepan. The steamer must fit the saucepan well, otherwise the latter quickly boils dry. Soups or a vegetable can be cooked in the bottom of the steamer, a pudding with some vegetables round it can go in the top and if required fish can be steamed on a plate on top of the steamer.
2. In a tiered steamer; this is an extremely useful utensil, but care must be taken to see that the steam enters all compartments and the regulator knobs should be checked each time it is used. Different dishes can be cooked in each tier without any fear of flavours becoming mixed.
3. In a large basin or mould standing in a pan of boiling water. The water should reach half-way up the basin or mould. For a delicate dish, such as a soufflé, the container should be placed on an upturned saucer, pastry cutter or tin, to protect the base from the direct heat.
4. In a compartmented steamer-saucepan. These pans are sold with several compartments fitted into the saucepan, and are useful for small families. The method is the same as above.
5. In a chafing dish.
6. By cooking with steam under pressure. The great advantage of this method is that food which normally takes hours can be cooked in a very short time. (See Pressure Cookery entry.)

MEAT

Any joint of meat can be steamed. Allow twice as long as for boiling. Soak salted meat for 3 hours beforehand.

POULTRY

The time depends very much on the size and age of the bird. A good way of cooking an old fowl is to steam it until it is tender, then to brown it in a hot oven (220°C/425°F, Gas Mark 7) for 30 minutes to 45 minutes.

PUDDINGS

To keep out the moisture caused by condensation, cover the pudding with a double thickness of greased greaseproof paper or a cloth dipped in hot water and floured. A basin cover or string should be tied round the basin, so that it may be easily lifted out of the steamer.

Suet puddings need 3 hours or longer. Sponge puddings in small dariole moulds cook in 20 to 30 minutes; larger puddings take 1½ to 2 hours, according to the size. Allow plenty of room in the basin for the pudding to rise.

CUSTARDS

The water should be only just boiling for these, as they curdle if the temperature becomes too high. Remove as soon as they are set.

(See individual entries for methods of steaming vegetables and fish.)

STEEPING

The process of pouring hot or cold water over food and leaving it to stand, either to soften it or to extract its flavour and colour.

STERILIZATION

The process of freeing food (and utensils) from living organisms. It is often confused with boiling, but in true sterilization the temperature varies according to the food: some bacteria form heat-resisting spores which need to be brought to a temperature of 125°C/257°F (i.e. above boiling point), or a longer time at a lower temperature, to kill them. The time required also varies, according to the food, the method of sterilization and the kind of bacteria likely to be present.

The simplest way of sterilizing utensils is to use one of the chemical liquids or tablets sold at chemists. These are dissolved in the correct amount of water. Instructions should be carefully followed to ensure proper sterilization.

STERILIZED MILK

(See Milk entry.)

STERLET

A small sturgeon; the swimming bladder is used to make isinglass, the flesh is highly prized and the roe yields the finest-quality caviare.

STEWING

A method of cooking by moist heat in a small amount of liquid which is kept at simmering point. Long, slow cooking ensures that flavours are well blended and that tough cuts of meat are made tender. Food can be cooked in a pan on top of the cooker or in a casserole in the oven; both should have tight fitting lids to reduce the loss of liquid from evaporation. The new slow cookers are particularly suitable for stewing as the food cooks at a very low temperature for several hours. (See Slow Cookers entry.)

STEWED FRUIT
(See Fruit and Dried Fruit entries.)

Meat Stews

BROWN
For this type the meat, vegetables and flour are fried before stewing. Stewing steak is commonly used for brown stew, but other meats such as ox-tail, kidney and liver may be used.

WHITE
Mutton, veal or rabbit is generally used for white stews and the meat and vegetables are not fried first. Irish stew is an example of a thin white stew, while a fricassée (see entry) is a thickened white stew.

Suitable meats for stewing

BEEF
Shoulder steak, chuck steak, shin beef, brisket, top rib, ox-tail.

VEAL
Knuckle, breast, shoulder, neck.

MUTTON
Middle and scrag end of mutton, breast.

Kidney, liver, heart, tripe.

The cheaper and coarser the meat, the longer it takes to cook. Most types of stew require at least 2 hours and some varieties such as ox-tail and brisket, may take 3 or even 4 hours. Herbs, spices and vegetables should be added in moderation to give flavour and interest to the dish.

BROWN STEW

METRIC/IMPERIAL
0.75 kg/1 ½ lb stewing steak
2 × 15 ml spoons/2 tablespoons fat or oil
2 onions, skinned and sliced
2 carrots, pared and sliced
4 × 15 ml spoons/4 tablespoons flour
900 ml/1 ½ pints stock
salt
pepper
bouquet garni

Cut the meat into 1 cm/ ½ inch cubes. Heat the fat or oil in a frying pan and fry the onions and carrots until browned. Remove from the pan and fry the meat until browned. Put the meat and vegetables in a casserole. Add the flour to the fat remaining in the pan, stir well and add the stock gradually; bring to the boil, season and add to the casserole, with the bouquet garni. Cover and cook in a moderate oven (160°C/325°F, Gas Mark 3) for about 2 hours.

Remove the bouquet garni before serving.

IRISH STEW

METRIC/IMPERIAL
8 middle neck chops
1 kg/2 lb potatoes, peeled and sliced

391

2 large onions, skinned and sliced
salt
pepper
chopped parsley

Trim some of the fat from the chops. Place alternate layers of vegetables and meat in a saucepan, seasoning with salt and pepper and finishing with a layer of potatoes. Add sufficient water to half cover. Cover with a lid and simmer very slowly for 3 hours. Serve sprinkled with chopped parsley.

Alternatively, cook the stew in a casserole in a moderately hot oven (190°C/375°F, Gas Mark 5) for 2½ to 3 hours.

If you use scrag end of neck for Irish stew it makes an economical dish.

STILTON CHEESE

Regarded as the 'King of English cheeses'. The blue veined variety has a soft close texture when ripe: the blue veins are a penicillin mould which is allowed to grow in the cheese. These give the cheese a very strong flavour. Stilton gained its name not because it was made in the village of Stilton, Rutland, but because this is where it was first sold. It is now only made in Melton Mowbray in Leicestershire, Dovedale in Derbyshire and parts of Nottinghamshire.

It used to be considered fashionable to scoop Stilton out from the centre of the cheese with a spoon or cheese scoop then pour port into the cheese to stop it hardening. This should be discouraged as it is extravagant and wasteful. A more suitable way to serve the whole or half cheese is to cut down the cheese 2.5 cm/1 inch to 5 cm/2 inch and take wedges all round on this level. There is a saying 'cut high, cut low, cut level', the advice being to draw the knife flat across the face of the cheese leaving it, if possible, more level than before. Stilton cheese can be bought in wedges by weight. It is also available prepacked in clingfilm.

There is also a white Stilton cheese which does not contain the blue veins. This is a mild crumbly cheese.

STIRABOUT

The Irish equivalent of porridge.

STOCK

The liquid produced when meat, bones or vegetables are simmered with herbs and flavourings in water for several hours. Stock forms the basis of soups, sauces, stews and many savoury dishes, giving a far better flavour than when plain water is used. It has no food value apart from some minerals.

MEAT OR BONE STOCK
Any meat (especially such cuts as shin of beef and knuckle of veal) and any bones, whether fresh or already cooked, can be used to make stock. Place the bones (and the meat, if used) in a saucepan with a few flavouring vegetables (e.g., carrot, onion, celery and a small amount of turnip), and add a few peppercorns, a clove, a blade of mace, a bay leaf, a pinch of mixed herbs, bring to the boil, cover and simmer for 2 to 3 hours.

Green vegetables and starchy foods should not normally be included, as they cause the stock to sour rapidly. If they are added, the stock should be used at once.

If the bones or scraps of meat are fatty, the liquid should be strained off after cooking and allowed to cool, so that the fat may be removed before the stock is used.

If the stock is not used at once, boil up the pot each day, adding any extra bones or vegetables and more water as required; empty the pot after 3 to 4 days and start afresh. The bones are sometimes used for a second lot of stock.

VEGETABLE STOCK
This is made in the same way as meat stock using a selection of vegetables such as carrots, onion, swede, turnip, celery and peppers, but is simmered for a shorter time and it must be used up quickly. A few bacon rinds help to give flavour and richness.

FISH STOCK
Use the bones and skin from fresh or cooked fish, with flavouring vegetables, herbs and spices, and make as above, simmering for 1 to 1½ hours. Fish stock should be used the day it is made.

BOUILLON CUBES
These provide an easy way of making stock. There are several flavours available including beef, chicken, onion and curry.

STOCKFISH

Cod which has been dried (in the air), but not salted.

STOUT

A beer made with a dark malt. It is thus darker (and sweeter) than ale.

STRAWBERRY

A low-growing plant that is now cultivated all over the world. The wild strawberry fruit is delicious, but smaller than the cultivated varieties. Strawberries are a good source of vitamin C.

Large, perfect berries can be washed, left unhulled, served with sugar and eaten in the fingers. When cream is served as an accompaniment, the fruit is hulled beforehand. Strawberries may also be included in fruit salads and fruit cocktails; when puréed, they make delicious creams and ices and form the filling for the ever-popular strawberry shortcake. Strawberries are not often used in cooked sweets, as they lose their shape, colour and flavour, nor do they bottle very successfully. Frozen strawberries are available for use when fresh ones are out of season, but they do not freeze well as they lose flavour and become watery when thawed. If strawberries are to be frozen at home they should be of very good quality, or preferably make them into a purée.

Strawberries make a well-flavoured jam, but as they are not rich in pectin it is often necessary to add lemon, red-currant or gooseberry juice, pectin extract or tartaric or citric acid, to help the jam to set. These additions affect the flavour, and the truest strawberry taste is obtained when the jam is made with only a little added acid.

STRAWBERRY JAM

METRIC/IMPERIAL
1.5 kg/3 ½ lb strawberries
3 × 15 ml spoons/3 tablespoons lemon juice
1.5 kg/3 ½ lb sugar

Hull and wash the strawberries, put in a pan with the lemon juice and simmer gently in their own juice for 20 to 30 minutes until really soft. Add the sugar, stir until dissolved and boil rapidly until setting point is reached. Allow to cool for 15 to 20 minutes then pot and cover in the usual way. *Makes about 2.25 kg/5 lb.*

STRAWBERRY TOMATO

Another name for Cape Gooseberry. (See Cape Gooseberry entry.)

STRUDEL

A form of pastry, very popular in Austria, Germany and central Europe generally. It is made from a soft dough which is stretched out by hand until paper-thin, covered with one of a variety of fillings (e.g., apple, black cherries, nuts, poppy seeds, cheese and vegetables) and rolled like a Swiss roll.

APFEL STRUDEL

METRIC/IMPERIAL
225 g/8 oz plain flour
1 × 2.5 ml spoon/ ½ teaspoon salt
1 egg, slightly beaten
2 × 15 ml spoons/2 tablespoons oil
4 × 15 ml spoons/4 tablespoons lukewarm water
3 × 15 ml spoons/3 tablespoons seedless raisins

3 × 15 ml spoons/3 tablespoons currants
75 g/3 oz caster sugar
1 × 2.5 ml spoon/ ½ teaspoon ground cinnamon
1 kg/2¼ lb cooking apples, peeled and grated
3 × 15 ml spoons/3 tablespoons melted butter
100 g/4 oz ground almonds
icing sugar

Put the flour and salt in a large bowl, make a well in the centre and pour in the egg and oil. Add the water gradually, stirring with a fork to make a soft, sticky dough. Work the dough in the bowl until it leaves the sides, turn it out on to a lightly floured surface and knead for 15 minutes. Form into a ball, place on a cloth and cover with a warmed bowl. Leave to 'rest' in a warm place for an hour.

Mix thoroughly the raisins, currants, sugar, cinnamon and apples.

Warm the rolling pin. Spread a clean old cotton tablecloth on the table and sprinkle lightly with 1–2 × 15 ml spoons/1–2 tablespoons flour. Place the dough on the cloth and roll out into a rectangle about 3 mm/ ⅛ inch thick, lifting and turning it to prevent its sticking to the cloth. Gently stretch the dough, working from the centre to the outside and using the backs of the hands, until it is paper-thin. Trim the edges to form a rectangle about 68 by 60 cm/27 by 24 inches. Leave to dry and 'rest' for 15 minutes.

Arrange the dough with one of the long sides towards you, brush it with melted butter and sprinkle with ground almonds. Spread the apple mixture over the dough, leaving a 5 cm/2 inch border uncovered all round the edge. Fold these pastry edges over the apple mixture, towards the centre. Lift the corners of the cloth nearest to you up and over the pastry, causing the strudel to roll up, but stop after each turn, to pat it into shape and to keep the roll even. Form the roll into a horse-shoe shape, brush it with melted butter and slide it on to a lightly buttered baking sheet. Bake in a moderately hot oven (190°C/375°F, Gas Mark 5) for about 40 minutes or until golden brown. Dust with icing sugar and serve hot or cold, with cream.

STUFFING

A savoury mixture used to give flavour (and sometimes shape) to a dish. It may be placed in the body cavities (as with poultry), laid flat between two portions, spread on fillets before they are rolled, or mixed with minced meat, etc., as in galantines, to increase the bulk. It is also used to stuff vegetables to serve as an accompaniment or main dish. White breadcrumbs, chopped vegetables, minced meat, pounded fish, rice, etc., are used as a base; vegetables, herbs, spices and essences, etc., are used for flavouring; and eggs, stock, gravy, sauce, milk or mayonnaise bind the ingredients together; some fat is also necessary, in the form of suet, melted butter, margarine, dripping or cream.

(See individual entries, e.g., Chestnut, Fish, Sage and Onion and Sausagemeat Stuffing and Forcemeat.)

STURGEON

A large shark-like fish, with an average weight of about 27 kg/60 lb, which is caught in northern river estuaries and is in season from August to March. It is not very common in Great Britain and by a mediaeval decree all English sturgeon are regarded as royal property; the custom nowadays is for the first sturgeon caught each season to be offered to the Sovereign.

Sturgeon is expensive, but its firm, white flesh is delicious if suitably prepared and cooked. When bought, it should have veins of a bluish colour – not brown, which indicates that the fish is stale. Sturgeon needs to be hung for 3 to 4 days before eating and it is then marinated for 12 to 24 hours in oil and white wine or vinegar. It may be cooked in various ways and is particularly good when roasted and stuffed.

The hard roes of the sturgeon caught in the estuaries of the Danube and the rivers flowing into the Caspian Sea are prepared in a special way and known as caviare (see Caviare entry). The air bladder of the sturgeon is used to make isinglass (see Isinglass entry).

SUCCOTASH

An American dish made from sweetcorn kernels and green or lima beans. The dish is said to be borrowed from the Narrangansett Indians.

SUCROSE

Common sugar (a chemical combination of glucose and fructose), as obtained from both sugar cane and sugar beet. When cooked with acid, sucrose is split into glucose and fructose; the former is less sweet and the latter sweeter than sucrose.

SUET

The fat around the kidneys and loins of sheep and bullocks. It is bought either from the butcher, in the form of solid lumps of fat, or from the grocer, packeted in the form of tiny shreds, ready for use. If bought in the piece, it must be prepared as follows: clean it of all pieces of meat and skin, then chop or grate it as finely as possible, adding a little flour; if it is not convenient to chop it immediately, it will keep for several days provided it is freed of skin, etc., and covered completely with flour.

Suet is used in stuffings and mincemeat, in steamed suet puddings (including Christmas puddings) and in suetcrust pastry.

Suet Puddings

A number of popular sweet and savoury puddings are made either with suet-crust pastry (see Pastry entry) or with a somewhat wetter, slacker mixture, which is steamed or boiled in a pudding basin or cloth.

STEAMED SUET PUDDING

METRIC/IMPERIAL
175 g/6 oz self raising flour
pinch of salt
75 g/3 oz shredded suet
50 g/2 oz caster sugar
about 150 ml/¼ pint milk

Half-fill a steamer or large saucepan with water and put on to boil. Grease a 900 ml/1½ pint pudding basin. Mix the flour, salt, suet and sugar. Make a well in the centre and add enough milk to give a soft dropping consistency. Put into the greased basin, cover with greased greaseproof paper or foil and secure with string. Steam over rapidly boiling water for 1½ to 2 hours. Serve with a jam, golden syrup, custard sauce or fruit sauce.

VARIATIONS
For a lighter pudding use 75 g/3 oz self raising flour and 75 g/3 oz fresh white breadcrumbs. For a richer pudding, use 1 beaten egg and 6 × 15 ml spoons/6 tablespoons milk instead of the 150 ml/¼ pint milk.

Jam: Put 2 × 15 ml spoons/2 tablespoons red jam in the bottom of the greased pudding basin before adding the mixture.

Apple: Add to the dry ingredients 225 g/8 oz cooking apples, peeled and finely chopped or grated. Serve the pudding with a sweet white sauce flavoured with a pinch of ground nutmeg or ground cinnamon.

Date: Add to the dry ingredients 100 g/4 oz chopped dates and the grated rind of a lemon; reduce the sugar to 2 × 15 ml spoons/2 tablespoons.

Apricot: Add to the dry ingredients 50 g/2 oz chopped dried apricots. 100 g/4 oz apple, peeled and finely chopped and the grated rind of 1 lemon or orange.

Rich fig: Add to the dry ingredients 100 g/4 oz chopped dried figs, 25 to 50 g/1 to 2 oz chopped blanched almonds and the grated rind of 1 lemon. Mix to a soft dropping consistency with 2 beaten eggs and 2 × 15 ml spoons/2 tablespoons sherry or milk. Serve hot, with lemon sauce or custard passed separately.

MINCEMEAT ROLY-POLY

METRIC/IMPERIAL
175 g/6 oz suetcrust pastry
4–6 × 15 ml spoons/4–6 tablespoons mincemeat
a little milk

Half-fill a steamer with water and put it on to boil.
　Grease a piece of foil 23 × 33 cm/9 × 13 inches.
Make the suetcrust pastry and roll it out to an
oblong about 23 × 28 cm/9 × 11 inches. Spread the
mincemeat on the pastry, leaving 5 mm/¼ inch
clear along each edge. Brush the edges with milk
and roll the pastry up evenly, starting from one
short side. Place the roll on the greased foil and
wrap the foil round the roll loosely, to allow room
for expansion, but seal the edges very well. Steam
the roly-poly over rapidly boiling water for 1½ to
2 hours. When it is cooked, remove it from the foil
and serve with custard.

APPLE SUET PUDDING

METRIC/IMPERIAL
200 g/7 oz suetcrust pastry
450 g/1 lb cooking apples, peeled, cored and sliced
100 g/4 oz sugar

Half-fill a steamer or large saucepan with water
and put it on to boil. Grease a 900 ml/1½ pint
pudding basin. Make the pastry and roll out into a
round 2.5 cm/1 inch or larger all round than the top
of the basin. Cut a quarter out of the round; with
the remaining portion line the pudding basin,
damping the cut edges, overlapping them and
pressing well to seal. Fill the basin with the sliced
apples and sugar in alternate layers. Roll out the
remaining pastry to make a lid, damp the edges of
the pastry in the basin and cover with the lid,
pressing the edges well together. Cover with
greased greaseproof paper and steam for 2½
hours.

VARIATION
Use different fruits, such as rhubarb, plums, damsons (increasing the sugar to 175 g/6 oz), blackberries combined with apples, or black-currants,
prepared as for stewing. When the softer fruits are
used steam for only 2 hours.

Steaming Times for Puddings

Small puddings: cooked in individual basins or
dariole moulds: 30 minutes to 1 hour.

Large puddings: 2 to 3 hours, according to size.

Christmas puddings: Steam for a total of about 13
hours.

Meat puddings: 3 to 4 hours, if meat is uncooked.
　A suet pudding improves with extra cooking,
but the result will be unpalatable if it is cooked for
too short a time. (See Pressure Cookery entry.)

SUGAR

A crystalline, sweet-tasting substance obtained
from various plants. The type normally used in the
home is sucrose, derived both from sugar cane,
grown in tropical and sub-tropical countries, and
from sugar beet, a root crop grown commercially
in the UK; contrary to some people's impression,
beet and cane sugar are of equal value. Other
sources of sugar of various kinds are maple trees,
sorghum (Chinese cane), millet, maize, certain
varieties of palm trees and malted substances.

Types of Sugar

SUCROSE
This is contained in sweet fruits and in roots such
as carrots, as well as in sugar cane and beet, which
give a product that is chemically the same.

GLUCOSE
Contained in honey, grapes, and sweetcorn.

FRUCTOSE
Contained in fruit juices and honey.

LACTOSE
Contained in milk.

MALTOSE
Formed during the germination of grain. (See
individual sugar entries.)

Food Value of Sugar
Sugar is a good source of energy and is easily and
speedily digested. However, it should not be taken
in place of more valuable foods.
　If eaten to excess it may lead to obesity. Whether
sugar has a bad effect on the teeth is a highly
controversial question, but it is known that when
sugar has been rationed the incidence of dental
decay has decreased, so many people consider it is
proven that it does affect the teeth.

Commercially Prepared Sugars
These are varieties of cane and beet sugar which are
all the same in structure.

Granulated: A refined white sugar with coarse
granules. It is used for most sweetening purposes,
and is the most economical sugar.

Caster: A fine white sugar mostly used in cakes and
puddings.

Lump, loaf, cube: Refined white sugar which is
compressed into cubes for convenient table use.

Preserving sugar: Specially made for jams, jellies etc.
It has large crystals which dissolve slowly and
produce less scum than granulated sugar.

Icing: White sugar which is ground to a fine powder. It is used for making icings, sorbets, ice
creams and meringues.

Barbados: A 'moist' dark brown, soft sugar with a characteristic flavour. It is often used to mask the flavour in dishes requiring bicarbonate of soda.

Demerara: Honey-coloured crystals; a sugar for table use.

Sand (soft): A pale brown sugar with a 'sandy' texture which is used for cooking.

Sugar candy (coffee sugar): Brown sugar with large crystals which are made by crystallizing the sugar at a certain temperature. Used for coffee. It dissolves slowly enabling the true flavour of coffee to be savoured first.

Maple sugar: Extracted from the sap of the maple tree, has a characteristic flavour. In sweetening power it is similar to cane and beet sugar.

Malt sugar: Found in the malting of cereals, etc.

Artificial honey: Ordinary sugar chemically inverted and consequently it has not the same flavour as the bee or true honey, which is a natural form of invert sugar less sweet than cane sugar and with a scent and flavour due to the flowers visited by the bees.

Treacle, molasses and golden syrup: These by-products arising during the refining of sugar are viscous liquids, consisting of an unrefined solution of sugar in water. Their sweetening power is about one-third less than that of sugar.

Uses of Sugar

Sugar sweetens food and is an essential ingredient in all cakes and in puddings made with a cake mixture. Combined with either fat or eggs in rich cakes, it helps to hold air; in rubbed-in mixtures it makes the cake lighter in texture.

Sugar is also useful as a preservative (e.g., in jam-making), since bacteria and moulds find it difficult to live in highly concentrated sugar solutions such as those found in jam, 60 to 70 per cent.

Sugar-boiling

This process is the basis of most sweet-making, and is also employed in some icings and for making caramels. The sugar is first dissolved in water and brought to the boil. At this stage the thermometer will register 100°C/212°F and the mixture will remain at this temperature until enough water has been evaporated to produce syrup consistency. Then the temperature will start to rise, continuing as more water evaporates. The syrup first becomes very thick but pale, darkening gradually, until finally, at 177°C/350°F it becomes dark brown. At this stage it is known as burnt sugar and being no longer sweet, it can be used for darkening gravy.

A sugar-boiling thermometer and if possible a saccharometer are desirable for this work, but for simple sweets it is possible to use instead the homely tests described below.

The list gives the various stages between boiling point and caramel, with their special names and the method of testing. Although definite temperatures are quoted for the different stages, the sugar passes almost imperceptibly from one stage to the next.

SMOOTH
(102°C to 104°C; 214°F to 220°F). The mixture begins to look syrupy. To test, dip the fingers in water, then in the syrup; the thumb slides smoothly over the fingers, but the sugar clings to the finger. Used for crystallizing purposes.

THREAD
(110°C to 112°C; 230°C to 234°F). Boil the solution for 2 to 3 minutes. Dip the fingers into cold water, dip them in the syrup, then back again into cold water; press the finger and thumb together, pull them apart and a fine thread will be observed. Used for making spun sugar.

SOFT BALL
(113°C to 118°C; 235°F to 245°F). When a drop of the syrup is put into very cold water it forms a soft ball; at 113°C/235°F the soft ball flattens on removal from water, but the higher the temperature, the firmer the ball, till it reaches the Firm Ball stage. Used for making fondants and fudge.

HARD BALL
(118°C to 129°C; 245°F to 265°F). The syrup, when dropped into cold water, forms a ball which is hard enough to hold its shape, but is still plastic. Used for making caramels and marshmallow.

SOFT CRACK
(132°C to 143°C; 270°F to 290°F). The syrup, when dropped into cold water, separates into threads which are hard but not brittle. Used for toffees.

HARD CRACK
(149°C to 154°C; 300°F to 310°F). When a drop of the syrup is put into cold water, it separates into threads which are hard and brittle. Used for hard toffees and rocks.

CARAMEL
(154°C/310°F). Shown by the syrup becoming golden-brown. Used for making praline and caramels, also for flavouring caramel custard, etc. (See Sweets entry.)

Crystallization

The technique of dissolving and boiling sugar needs great care, as the syrup has a tendency to re-crystallize if not handled correctly.

The chief causes are: 1. agitation of the mixture by stirring or beating, and 2. the presence of any solid particles such as sugar crystals or grit in the syrup while boiling.

To obtain a clear syrup, therefore, the pan must

be perfectly clean and the sugar must be completely dissolved before the mixture is allowed to boil. Should any crystals form on the sides of the pan after boiling has begun, they should be brushed down with a clean pastry brush dipped in cold water. Also, there must be no stirring or agitation of the mixture, but a wooden spatula can be used to tap the grains of sugar on to the bottom of the pan while dissolving, to hasten the process. Once the sugar is dissolved and the syrup has been brought to the boil, it can be heated rapidly to the exact temperature stated in the recipe and at once removed from the heat, so that the temperature does not rise any higher.

LEMON OR ORANGE SUGAR FOR TEA

Rub cubes of loaf sugar on every side against the rind of a scrubbed orange or lemon. Store in a glass jar with a tightly fitting lid and use to sweeten tea.

COLOURED SUGAR CAKE DECORATION

Spread some granulated sugar out on greaseproof paper, sprinkle a few drops of the desired food colouring over it, mix very thoroughly, so that the sugar is evenly tinted, then spread out and allow to dry before using.

SUGAR PEAS (MANGE-TOUT)

(See Peas entry.)

SULTANA

The fruit of a seedless species of grape vine, which is grown in many regions, principally Greece, Crete, Australia, South Africa and California. Originally sultanas came only from Turkey, being shipped from the port of Smyrna.

The best sultanas are pale yellow, with such thin skins that they are almost transparent; the inferior grades have many dark fruits mixed with the light. Sultanas have a pleasant fruity flavour and are used extensively in cakes, steamed puddings, milk puddings, mincemeat, pickles, curries, etc.

The chief nutritional value of sultanas is represented by the iron they contain and the energy provided by the sugar. They also contain calcium, thiamine and vitamin A. They are available cleaned and packed.

To clean sultanas: (See Dried Fruit entry.)

SUMMER PUDDING

A cold sweet made with bread or sponge cake as a case. The centre is filled with stewed fruit, sharp-flavoured ones such as red-currants, raspberries and loganberries being best.

SUMMER PUDDING

METRIC/IMPERIAL
2 × 15 ml spoons/2 tablespoons water
150 g/5 oz sugar
0.5 kg/1 lb raspberries and red-currants
100 g/4 oz bread, thinly sliced
whipped cream or cold custard sauce

Put the water and sugar together and bring to the boil, add the fruit and stew carefully until tender. Line a pudding basin with the bread, pour in the stewed fruit and cover with thin slices of bread: the basin should be full. Place a saucer with a weight on it on top of the pudding and leave for several hours. Turn out and serve decorated with cream.

SUNDAE

An ice cream, usually served in an ice cup, shallow dish (either glass or metal) or a tall glass, with a sweet sauce, syrup or marshmallow whip poured over it and a decoration of fresh or crystallized fruit, nuts or grated chocolate and whipped cream.

Some suitable sauces are given below.

STRAWBERRY SAUCE

Boil 50 g/2 oz sugar with 150 ml/¼ pint water until they form a syrup and add 225 g/8 oz crushed strawberries. Remove the pan from the heat ad chill very thoroughly before using.

RASPBERRY SAUCE

Make as for strawberry sauce. If canned fruit is used, replace the water by the liquid from the can and use sugar only if required. The mixture may be rubbed through a fine hair sieve to remove the seeds.

CHOCOLATE SAUCE

Melt 50 g/2 oz plain chocolate and 15 g/½ oz butter in a basin over hot water, then remove from the heat and stir in 1 × 15 ml spoon/1 tablespoon milk and 1 × 5 ml spoon/1 teaspoon vanilla essence. Use hot or cold.

CARAMEL SAUCE

Melt 1 × 15 ml spoon/1 tablespoon brown sugar, 1 × 15 ml spoon/1 tablespoon golden syrup and 25 g/1 oz butter in a strong pan and boil for 1 minute. Add 1 × 15 ml spoon/1 tablespoon milk and serve hot. If desired, add 15 g/½ oz to 25 g/1 oz chopped walnuts or the grated rind of ½ a lemon.

SUNFLOWER OIL

An oil extracted from sunflower seeds. It is used in

cooking in many Continental countries and in India. It has recently been introduced into this country and is used in salad dressings and for frying.

SUPRÊME

A white sauce made like a Velouté sauce, with a base of well-reduced chicken stock; cream, butter or egg yolks may be added just before the sauce is served. (See Menu Glossary entry.)

SWAN

Swans, which are known as royal birds, are seldom eaten nowadays, except on special occasions, and even then it is usually young cygnets which are served, as they provide the best meat. The breast only is eaten, the flavour somewhat resembling that of goose. Swans are served at the annual Swan Feast held by the Vintners' Company.

A cygnet is skinned like rabbit and after being cleaned, is stuffed with pork and herb forcemeat, covered by pastry (see Venison entry) and cooked in a moderately hot oven (190°C/375°F, Gas Mark 5) for about 10 minutes per 0.5 kg/lb. The pastry is then removed and the bird browned for 15 minutes.

SWEDE (SWEDISH TURNIP)

A large root vegetable with yellow flesh and tough skin, obtainable from late autumn to spring. Swedes can be served as a separate vegetable and used in soups or in savoury dishes combined with bacon or cheese.

Preparation and cooking: Swedes should be peeled thickly, so that all the tough outer skin is removed. They may be sliced, diced or cut into fancy shapes. Keep them covered with water, and cook as soon after peeling as possible. Boil till tender in a little salted water with the lid on, about 30 to 60 minutes (according to size and age). Drain and mash with a little salt, pepper, grated nutmeg and a knob of butter. Alternatively roast them as follows: Cut in chunks or fingers and cook round the joint, or in a separate tin with dripping, allowing 1 to 1¼ hours, according to the size of the pieces. Serve round the joint.

SWEET CICELY

An aromatic herb with a sweet flavour resembling aniseed. The herb looks a little like parsley and grows wild in the North of England. It can be used in salad dressings, herb butter, soups, cream sweets, fruit salad and trifles. It also adds sweetness to sharp fruits such as rhubarb and apple.

SWEET CORN

(See Maize and Corn on the Cob entries.)

SWEET POTATO

This plant (which is no relation to the ordinary potato) is a native of South America, but is now cultivated in other parts of the world with a similar climate. The tubers have a tender, sweet and slightly perfumed flesh and are usually served as an accompaniment to meat, but may also be eaten as a sweet. They are available in this country especially in the larger towns and cities where there is a large immigrant population. They are also imported in canned form: these canned sweet potatoes may be mashed with butter and milk, sweetened and flavoured with spice, etc., then used as a filling for a pie or tart, or they may be heated and served with roast meat.

The chief food value of sweet potatoes lies in their starch content and sugar; they also contain vitamin C and some B vitamins.

Sweet potatoes may be baked in their jackets and served with a knob of butter, or any of the following suggestions:

Soured cream.
Grated cheese and chopped onion.
Hot meat sauce.
Spicy tomato sauce.
Honey.

SWEETBREAD

The culinary term for the glands in the throat and near the heart of the lamb, calf or bullock.

The most delicate sweetbreads are lambs', but these are rather more expensive than the other kinds. Bullocks' sweetbreads are cheap, but inclined to be coarse and require long, slow cooking, about 3 to 4 hours, to make them really tender. Between the two extremes are calves' sweetbreads, which are very good. Both heart and throat sweetbreads can be bought, the heart sweetbread (pancreas) being the better, as it has fewer membranes and is a nicer shape.

In addition to their protein content, sweetbreads contribute a little fat and thiamine.

To prepare sweetbreads: Use very fresh; wash and soak in cold water for several hours, changing the water as it becomes discoloured. Blanch by covering with cold water with a few drops of lemon juice added, bring slowly to boiling point and boil for 5 minutes. Drain, put in cold water and pull off any fat and skin that will come away easily. Use as required; sweetbreads may be cooked in various ways and we give a couple of typical recipes.

CREAMED SWEETBREADS

METRIC/IMPERIAL
450 g/ 1 lb sweetbreads, prepared as for fried
   sweetbreads
½ onion, skinned and chopped
1 carrot, pared and chopped
few parsley stalks
½ bayleaf
salt
pepper
40 g/1½ oz butter
4 × 15 ml spoons/4 tablespoons flour
300 ml/½ pint milk
squeeze of lemon juice
chopped parsley to garnish

Put the sweetbreads, vegetables, herbs and seasoning in a pan with water to cover and simmer gently
until tender – 45 minutes to 1 hour. Drain and keep
hot, retaining 300 ml/½ pint of the cooking liquid.
Melt the butter, stir in the flour and cook for 2 to 3
minutes. Remove the pan from the heat and
gradually stir in the sweetbread liquid and the
milk. Bring to the boil and continue to stir until it
thickens, season well and add a few drops of lemon
juice. Reheat the sweetbreads in the sauce and
serve sprinkled with parsley.

FRIED SWEETBREADS

Allow 0.5 kg/1 lb lambs' or calves' sweetbreads for
4 people. Soak them for about 3 to 4 hours in cold
water, drain and put into a pan. Cover them with
water and the juice of ½ a lemon, bring slowly to
the boil, then simmer for 5 minutes. Drain and
leave in cold water until they are firm and cold,
then strip off any stringy tissues.

Press the sweetbreads well between kitchen
paper, slice and dip into beaten egg and crumbs.
Cut a few rashers of streaky bacon into strips and
fry lightly until just crisp; drain and keep hot, then
fry the sweetbreads in the same fat until golden.
Toss the bacon and sweetbreads together and serve
at once, with tartare or tomato sauce.

SWEETS

Although this can mean the sweet or dessert course
of a meal, it is also the name given to all types of
confectionery and candy, e.g., boiled sweets, jellies, creams, chocolates and toffees. It is rather
difficult to classify confectionery into exact
groups, as there is inevitably a good deal of overlap, but generally speaking the main types made at
home are: fondants and creams, both cooked and
uncooked; marzipan; fudge; toffee, butterscotch
and barley sugar; caramel, and nougat; and a mis-
cellaneous group including marshmallows, jellies,
Turkish delight and truffles. These sweets can be
made very successfully at home in small quantities,

but boiled sweets and chocolates are not really
suitable for the amateur to tackle.

A selection of recipes is given here for sweets in
each main group. (For sugar-boiling, see Sugar
entry.)

Fondants and Creams
These soft, creamy sweets can be given particularly pretty colourings and an unlimited variety of
fancy shapes. To make an assortment of different
fondants divide the mixture into portions and
flavour and colour them, using, for instance,
lemon, raspberry, violet, orange, coffee and peppermint flavourings, with appropriate colours.

Roll the fondant out on a slab, dredging this
lightly with icing sugar to prevent sticking. To
shape the sweets, cut the fondant into triangles,
etc., with a knife or tiny cutters or mould it by
hand. More elaborate shapes are obtained by melting the fondant over hot water and running it into
starch moulds, rubber mats or cream rings. The
fondants may be decorated with nuts, glacé fruit,
crystallized flowers, etc.

(See basic recipes for unboiled and boiled fondant in Fondant entry.)

Marzipan Sweets
The quickly made unboiled almond paste or marzipan may be used for the simpler sweets, but for
those which require moulding it is better to use a
boiled paste, as this is less likely to become oily or
crack when handled. (For recipes see Almond
Paste entry.)

MARZIPAN CANDIES
Make up some unboiled almond paste, adding
sufficient egg white to make it bind to a soft but
dry paste. Divide into portions, colour as desired,
roll out, place one layer on another and cut into
small squares, triangles, etc., or roll up Swiss roll
fashion and then slice.

Marzipan may be used to stuff stoned dessert
dates or it may be kneaded with chopped nuts or
glacé cherries and shaped into balls.

MARZIPAN FRUITS, ETC.
To make fruit and vegetables, take balls of boiled
almond paste, plain or coloured, and mould them
into the desired shapes with the fingers. Using a
small paint brush and edible vegetable colourings,
tint them all over or touch them up, as necessary.
Finish off as follows:

Oranges and other citrus fruit: To obtain a pitted
surface, roll the fruit lightly on the finest part of a
grater. Use a clove stuck into the 'orange' to suggest a calyx.

Strawberries and raspberries: Roll them in fine sugar
to give the bumpy surface

Apples and pears: Use a clove, or part only of its
stalk, to suggest the calyx.

399

Potatoes: Dust with a little chocolate powder.

Flowers: To make flowers, roll out the almond paste thinly and cut it into rounds, using a 1 cm/½ inch to 1.5 cm/¾ inch cutter. Mould these rounds into leaves or petals and fix them together to form flowers. Leave until quite dry, then touch them up with a little colouring, applied with a small brush.

Fudge

VANILLA FUDGE

METRIC/IMPERIAL
450 g/1 lb granulated sugar
50 g/2 oz butter
150 ml/¼ pint evaporated milk
150 ml/¼ pint milk
few drops of vanilla essence

Grease a tin 15 cm/6 inch square.

Put the sugar, butter and milks into a 2.75 litre/5 pint heavy-based pan and heat gently until the sugar has dissolved and the fat melted. Bring to the boil and boil steadily to 116°C/240°F (soft ball stage), stirring occasionally. Remove the pan from the heat, place on a cool surface, add the essence and beat until the mixture becomes thick and creamy and 'grains' – i.e. until minute crystals form. Pour it immediately into the tin. Leave until nearly cold and mark into squares with a sharp knife, using a sawing motion. When it is firm, cut into squares.

Toffees, Butterscotch, etc.

When making toffee, follow these general rules:
1. Use a large pan and oil the sides, as toffee is inclined to boil over.
2. Do not stir (unless the recipe specially states stirring is necessary).
3. Move the sugar-boiling thermometer from time to time, as toffee may stick to the bulb and give an inaccurate reading. If no thermometer is available, test the temperature by dropping a little syrup into a cup of cold water; it will be at the right temperature when it becomes brittle and snaps easily.
4. Keep the heat very low after the toffee has reached a temperature of 127°C/260°F.
5. When the required temperature is reached, pour the mixture out quickly.
6. Cool the toffee at an even temperature and when it is luke-warm mark out in squares with an oiled knife.
7. Rub the toffee with absorbent paper, to remove surplus oil, then wrap them individually in waxed papers.

'PULLED SWEETS'

If toffee and similar boiled sugar mixtures are 'pulled' while still warm and pliable, they acquire an attractive satiny, silvery appearance.

A toffee mixture may also be used to make lollipops.

TREACLE TOFFEE

METRIC/IMPERIAL
450 g/1 lb demerara sugar
150 ml/¼ pint water
75 g/3 oz butter
a pinch of cream of tartar
100 g/4 oz black treacle
100 g/4 oz golden syrup

Butter a tin 30 cm by 10 cm/12 inch by 4 inch or an 18 cm/7 inch square tin. Dissolve the sugar and water in a 2.25 litre/4 pint heavy-based pan over a low heat. Add the remaining ingredients and bring to the boil. Boil to 132°C/270°F, (soft crack stage). Pour into the tin, cool for 5 minutes, then mark into squares and leave to set. When cold, break into squares and wrap in waxed paper.

NOUGAT

METRIC/IMPERIAL
rice paper
75 g/3 oz honey
3 egg whites
50 g/2 oz glacé cherries, chopped
25 g/1 oz angelica, chopped
150 g/5 oz almonds, chopped
350 g/12 oz sugar
150 ml/¼ pint water
50 g/2 oz glucose
vanilla essence

Damp the inside of a tin 30 cm by 10 cm/12 inch by 4 inch or an 18 cm/7 inch square tin and line it with rice paper. Melt the honey in a basin over hot water, add the stiffly beaten egg whites and continue to beat until the mixture is pale and thick. Add the cherries and angelica to the almonds. Dissolve the sugar in the water in a small heavy-based saucepan. Add the glucose and boil to 118°C/245°F to 129°C/265°F (hard ball stage). Pour this syrup on to the honey mixture, add the vanilla essence and continue beating over hot water until a little of the mixture forms a hard ball when tested in cold water. This may take 30 to 40 minutes, but is very important if the nougat is to set firmly. Add the fruit and nuts and put the mixture into the tin. Cover with rice paper, put some weights on top and leave until quite cold. Cut into pieces and wrap in waxed paper.

TURKISH DELIGHT

METRIC/IMPERIAL
450 g/1 lb granulated sugar
900 ml/1½ pints water
a pinch of tartaric acid
75 g/3 oz cornflour

200 g/7 oz icing sugar
50 g/2 oz honey
few drops lemon extract
few drops rose water
pink colouring
icing sugar for dredging

Butter a tin 30 cm by 10 cm/12 inch by 4 inch.

Put the sugar and 150 ml/¼ pint of the water into a saucepan. Dissolve the sugar without boiling and bring to a temperature of 116°C/240°F (soft ball stage). Add the tartaric acid and leave on one side for the short time required to blend the cornflour. Mix the cornflour and icing sugar with a little of the remaining cold water. Boil the rest of the water, then pour on to the blended cornflour and sugar, stirring hard to prevent lumps forming. Return to the saucepan, boil and beat vigorously until clear and thick. Add the syrup gradually, beating meanwhile over the heat. Continue to boil for 20 to 30 minutes: the time of boiling must not be shortened, as it is essential that the character of the starch be changed by the prolonged boiling with acid. At the end of 30 minutes the mixture should be of a very pale straw colour and transparent. Add the honey and flavourings and blend thoroughly.

Pour half the contents of the pan into a buttered tin, colour the remainder pale rose pink and pour it on top of the mixture already in the tin. Stand it aside until quite cold. Dip a sharp knife into icing sugar, cut the mixture into neat pieces and toss in icing sugar.

Cover with greaseproof paper and leave standing in the sugar for at least 24 hours. Pack in boxes in a generous quantity of icing sugar to prevent the sweets from sticking together.

COFFEE WALNUT FUDGE

METRIC/IMPERIAL
700 g/1 ½ lb granulated sugar
300 ml/ ½ pint evaporated milk
150 ml/¼ pint water
100 g/4 oz butter
1.5 × 15 ml spoons/1 ½ tablespoons instant coffee
50 g/2 oz walnuts, chopped

Grease a tin 20 cm/8 inch square. Put the sugar, milk, water and butter into 3.4 litre/6 pint heavy-based saucepan. Blend the coffee with 15 ml/1 tablespoon water and add to the pan. Stir over a low heat until the sugar has dissolved. Boil gently to 116°C/240°F (soft ball stage); stir to prevent sticking. Remove from the heat, place the pan on a cool surface, add the nuts and beat with a wooden spoon until thick, creamy and beginning to 'grain'. Pour into the tin and leave until nearly cold; mark into squares. When firm, cut with a sharpe knife. Makes about 900 g/2 lbs.

CHOCOLATE TRUFFLES

SWE

METRIC/IMPERIAL
75 g/3 oz chocolate
1 egg yolk
15 g/ ½ oz butter
1 × 15 ml spoon/1 tablespoon whipped cream
1 × 15 ml spoon/1 tablespoon rum
chocolate vermicelli

Melt the chocolate over hot water, without allowing it to become hot. Add the egg yolk, butter, cream and rum and beat till thick and pasty. Using two teaspoons, form the mixture into balls and roll these in the vermicelli.

COCONUT ICE

METRIC/IMPERIAL
450 g/1 lb granulated sugar
150 ml/¼ pint milk
150 g/5 oz desiccated coconut
colouring

Oil or butter a tin 20 cm by 15 cm/8 inch by 6 inch. Dissolve the sugar in the milk over a low heat. Bring to the boil and boil gently for about 10 minutes, or until a temperature of 116°C/240°F (soft ball stage) is reached. Remove from the heat and stir in the coconut. Pour half the mixture quickly into the tin. Colour the second half and pour quickly over the first layer. Leave until half set, mark into bars and cut or break when cold.

CHOCOLATE FUDGE

METRIC/IMPERIAL
450 g/1 lb granulated sugar
150 ml/¼ pint milk
150 g/5 oz butter
100 g/4 oz plain chocolate
50 g/2 oz honey

Grease a tin 20 cm by 15 cm/8 inch by 6 inch.

Place all the ingredients into a 2.8 litre/5 pint heavy-based saucepan. Stir over a low heat until the sugar has dissolved. Bring to the boil and boil to 116°C/240°F (soft ball stage). Remove from the heat, stand the pan on a cool surface for 5 minutes, then beat the mixture until thick, creamy and beginning to 'grain'. Pour into the tin, mark into squares when nearly set and cut when firm. Makes about 700 g/1 ½ lbs.

MARSHMALLOW FUDGE
Add 225g/ ½ lb chopped marshmallows to the mixture before beating; continue as above.

FRUIT AND NUT FUDGE
Add 50 g/2 oz chopped nuts and 50 g/2 oz seedless raisins; continue as above.

DATE FUDGE
Replace the 150 ml/¼ pint milk by 150 ml/¼ pint water and add 75 g/3 oz finely chopped dates.

SWISS CHARD

This vegetable is also known as Spinach Beet or Seakale Beet. The green part of the leaves should be prepared and cooked as spinach and the mid-ribs as celery.

SWISS ROLL

A sponge cake which is spread with jam, cream or some other filling and then rolled up. It is usually served cold as a cake, but it also makes an excellent pudding if served hot, covered with hot coffee, chocolate or fruit sauce. Swiss roll may also be made into a trifle, or sliced to serve as a base for 'poached eggs,' made of half a peach, glazed with jam and surrounded with cream.

Make a 3-egg sponge (see Cake entry for method) and bake in a greased and lined Swiss roll tin in a hot oven (220°C/425°F, Gas Mark 7) for 8 to 10 minutes. Place a sheet of greaseproof paper on a cloth which has been dipped in hot water and tightly wrung and sprinkle the paper liberally with caster sugar. Turn the cake out on to the paper, remove the paper lining and trim off the edges of the sponge as quickly as possible, using a sharp knife. Spread the sponge with warm jam, taking care not to let this go too near the edges, and make a cut halfway through the thickness of the sponge, about 2.5 cm/1 inch from one end. Roll it up with the aid of the paper, making the first turn firmly (so that the whole cake rolls evenly and is a good shape), but rolling more lightly after this. Dredge with sugar and cool on a rack.

CHOCOLATE SWISS ROLL

Replace 1 × 15 ml spoon/1 tablespoon of the flour by 1 × 15 ml spoon/1 tablespoon cocoa. To add a cream filling turn out the cooked sponge and trim as above, but do not spread with filling immediately. Cover the sponge with a sheet of greaseproof paper and roll up loosely. When the cake is cold, unroll, remove the paper, spread with cream or butter icing and re-roll.

SUITABLE FILLINGS
Jam, jelly or marmalade
Butter icing, coloured and flavoured to taste

Confectioner's custard or whipped cream
Fresh fruit (puréed if necessary) with cream.

SYLLABUB

An old English sweet, traditionally made by gently pouring fresh milk, in a thin stream over wine, cider or ale, resulting in a frothy mixture which was sweetened to taste and flavoured with spices and spirit. Alternatively, cream was whisked with wine, sugar and grated lemon rind until frothy; as the froth formed, it was skimmed off, to be served piled on ratafia (small almond flavoured) biscuits.

SYLLABUB MADE WITH WINE

METRIC/IMPERIAL
2 egg whites
100 g/4 oz caster sugar
juice of ½ lemon
150 ml/¼ pint sweet white wine
300 ml/½ pint carton double cream, whipped
crystallized lemon slices

Whisk the egg whites stiffly and fold in the sugar, lemon juice, wine and cream. Pour the mixture into individual glasses and chill for several hours before serving. Decorate with the lemon slices. The mixture will separate out as it stands.

SYRUP

A solution of sugar dissolved in water and concentrated by being heated; the syrup is often flavoured with fruit juice or essence. The chief uses of syrup in cookery are for sweetening such things as cold beverages, stewed fruit and fruit salad, for preserving, glacéing, candying and crystallizing fruit and for making sweets. A recipe for the syrup used for cold fruit drinks is given below.

The term syrup also denotes the uncrystallizable fluid separated from sugar-cane juice in the process of refining molasses. (See Golden Syrup and Treacle entries.)

STOCK SYRUP FOR COLD DRINKS

Put 0.5 kg/1 lb sugar and 300 ml/½ pint water into a saucepan, dissolve over a gentle heat, bring to a temperature of 104°C/220°F, cool and bottle. Use as required for sweetening fruit cups, etc.

TABASCO

A very hot, red sauce made from a kind of capsicum (pepper), originally grown in Mexico.

TAMARIND

The fruit of a tropical tree grown in the East and West Indies and similar regions. The leaves and flowers are eaten as a vegetable, while the acid, juicy pulp found in the pods is used to make preserves, sauces and chutneys and figures largely in Eastern curries and other dishes. The seeds are ground into a meal and baked as cakes. In this country tamarind is known chiefly as an ingredient in chutney.

TAMMY

To squeeze a sauce through a fine woollen cloth to strain it and make it glossy.

TANGELO

(See Ugli entry.)

TANGERINE

A small, very sweet type of orange, with a skin which is easily removed. They are available in this country during the winter months.

Tangerines are usually served as dessert, but may also be used in making fruit salads, cakes, etc. the small, brightly coloured sections are useful for decorating sweets and gâteaux: to remove the pith from them, dip the sections quickly into boiling water and scrape them with a knife.

Tangerines can be made into very good marmalade, provided extra pectin or lemon juice is added to ensure a good set. The peel may be preserved like that of oranges (see Crystallized, Candied and Glacé Fruit entry).

There are several other citrus fruits somewhat resembling tangerines, the ones most likely to be seen on sale in this country being given below. The South Africa *naartje* is also a form of tangerine.

CLEMENTINE
A form of tangerine grown in North Africa. It has closer rind, more like that of an orange, is practically seedless and not quite so sweet as the ordinary tangerine.

MANDARIN
Also known as the clove or noble orange. Mandarins were originally grown in China, but are now cultivated in Spain, Italy, Malta and Algeria. They are small and flat in shape, with a thin, tender rind which is easily separated from the flesh. They are slightly larger, sweeter and darker in colour than the ordinary tangerine.

SATSUMA
A particularly prized form of mandarin grown in Spain.

ORTANIQUE, KUMQUAT AND UGLI
These are related to tangerines. (See individual entries.)

TANGLEBERRY

A type of huckleberry or blueberry grown in the U.S.A. They are dark blue and very sweet, with a pleasant, sharp flavour. Like all these berries, they are good in pies and puddings, as well as for dessert.

TANSY

A herb with bitter, aromatic leaves. It was widely used in earlier centuries, traditionally at Easter time. A 'tansy' was a baked egg custard flavoured with tansy leaves.

TAPIOCA

This cereal is obtained from the roots of the cassava plant (see Cassava entry), which grows in hot countries like Central and South America, Malaya and the East and West Indies. Tapioca is sold in different forms, the most common being flakes (large, irregularly shaped pieces) and 'pearls', which cook more quickly.

403

Tapioca contains very little protein and consists almost entirely of starch. Its chief uses are for making milk puddings and moulds (see Milk Puddings entry) and for thickening soups; allow 40 g/1 ½ oz to 50 g/2 oz pearl tapioca to 600 ml/ 1 pint of liquid.

TARO

Taro tubers (also known as coco yams) are a staple article of diet in the Pacific islands; they can be boiled or baked or made into a kind of bread. Taro must be well-cooked or fermented to break down the poisons it contains.

TARRAGON

An aromatic herb which is similar to wormwood. This herb has long, narrow leaves which have a mild licorice-type flavour. There are two varieties, Russian and French; the latter is more delicate in flavour and is the one grown for culinary purposes. It is used in tarragon vinegar which the French use for mixing mustard. It combines well with chicken and fish and is the correct flavouring for sauce 'tartare'.

TART, TARTLET

A large or small open pastry case with a filling such as fruit, jam, lemon curd, golden syrup, cake mixture, custard, etc. The term is often used interchangeably with 'pie' or 'flan'.

Tarts are usually made of shortcrust or flan pastry. For a plate 20 cm/8 inches to 23 cm/9 inches in diameter, pastry made from 100 g/4 oz flour (and other ingredients in proportion) will be sufficient, when it is rolled to a thickness of 3 mm/ ⅛ inch.

The filling is usually cooked in the pastry case, as for treacle (syrup) and Bakewell tarts, but in the case of a custard tart, the pastry may be baked blind for a short time before the filling is added.

Metal, enamel or fireproof glass or china plates, sandwich tins and flan rings may all be used for tarts and patty tins of various sizes for tartlets.

TART BAKED AFTER FILLING

Make the pastry and roll it out into a round rather larger than the pie plate or dish to be used. Fit the pastry evenly and neatly on the plate, taking care not to pull or stretch it and making sure that there are no air bubbles underneath. Trim round the plate with a sharp knife and decorate the edge as desired. Place on a baking sheet. Add the filling and bake in a hot oven (220°C/425°F, Gas Mark 7) for about 10 minutes, to set the pastry; then lower the heat according to the recipe and bake until the filling is cooked.

LATTICED TART

This is an attractive way of finishing tarts filled with jam, mincemeat, etc. For a 20 cm/8 inch pie plate about 150 g/5 oz to 175 g/6 oz pastry will be required. Line the plate with the pastry, reserving about one-third of it for the decoration. Spread the jam or other filling over the pastry. Cut strips of pastry 5 mm/¼ inch wide and arrange them lattice fashion over the filling. Moisten the edge of the tart with water, then lay a strip of pastry the width of the rim all the way round, covering the ends of the criss-cross strips, press down and decorate as desired. Glaze the pastry and bake in a hot oven (220°C/425°F, Gas Mark 7) for 15 to 20 minutes.

SMALL TARTLET CASES

Roll the pastry out about 3 mm/⅛ inch thick and cut into rounds with a floured cutter a size larger than the patty tins to be used, to allow for the depth of the tin. Line the tins evenly and neatly with the pastry, pressing it gently with the thumbs against the sides. Put in the filling or bake the cases blind, as directed in the particular recipe; in the latter case the bottom of the tartlets should be pricked with a fork to prevent their rising.

TARTARE SAUCE

A mayonnaise sauce flavoured with herbs, chopped capers and gherkins, etc., which is served with fish, salads and such vegetables as globe artichokes.

TARTARE SAUCE

METRIC/IMPERIAL
150 ml/¼ pint mayonnaise
1 × 5 ml spoon/1 teaspoon chopped fresh tarragon or chives
2 × 5 ml spoons/2 teaspoons chopped capers
2 × 5 ml spoons/2 teaspoons chopped gherkins
2 × 5 ml spoons/2 teaspoons chopped parsley
1 × 15 ml spoon/1 tablespoon lemon juice or tarragon vinegar

Mix all the ingredients together, then leave the sauce to stand for at least 1 hour before serving, to allow the flavours to blend. Serve with fish.

TARTARIC ACID

A colourless, crystalline compound, occurring in various plants, especially in unripe grapes. For domestic purposes its acid salt, potassium tartrate or cream of tartar, is more commonly used. This is a common ingredient in baking powder and self-raising flour and is combined with bicarbonate of soda to form a raising agent for domestic use; it is also used in sweet-making and occasionally to replace lemon juice in jam-making (to assist the setting of preserves made from fruits which are deficient in acid).

Tartaric acid, which is used commercially as a raising agent, has twice the strength of cream of tartar.

TEA

A tropical evergreen shrub: the dried leaves are used to make a drink which is an infusion with boiling water. Various types and quality of tea depend on differences in soil, climate and firing produce. It is grown in China, Pakistan, India, Sri Lanka and Japan and was first introduced into this country in the seventeenth century.

There are many varieties or grades of tea, but these are not classified on quality but on the size of the leaf. Those made from broken leaves are strong quick-brewing teas. 'Dust' is a trade term for small particle leaves. These are not used alone but are blended with other leaves. Most teas now consist of blends.

Tea as such has little food value, though when served with milk and sugar it acquires the food values of these substances. A good infusion of tea, properly made, contains little tannin, but tea that has been standing a long time will have an excessive amount of tannin extracted and this may be harmful if drunk in large amounts.

Types of Tea
There are several types of tea available:

GREEN TEA
Mainly produced in China. The leaf is steamed and dried quickly without being allowed to ferment and this preserves the green colour. Green tea has a much more astringent taste than black tea and a liking for it is an acquired taste.

BROWN TEA
After being picked, the leaves are partially fermented before drying. Tea made from these leaves is pale brown in colour, with a characteristic flavour. Oolong teas are examples of this type.

BLACK TEA
For this, the most popular type of tea in England, the leaves are fermented before drying; the brew made from black tea is darkish-brown and has a slightly astringent flavour.

The majority of black tea imported into the U.K. comes from India and Sri Lanka. Almost all of it is blended in this country and sold in branded packs. It is also possible to buy 'pure' teas from Sri Lanka, Assam and Darjeeling. The teas are usually blended to suit the average taste and water supply, but some firms specialize in making up teas to suit the water of a particular district. Tea bags and powdered instant tea are also available.

CHINA TEAS
These are black, green or oolong and usually blended, but occasionally an unblended China tea is sold, e.g., Keemun and Lapsang Soochong. The tea keeps very well and gives a light-coloured infusion with an aromatic odour, sometimes scented with dried jasmine flowers or oil of bergamot.

Choosing and Storing Tea
Most teas now sold in this country are ready-packed, so one cannot see the actual leaves when buying. Points to remember when trying a new brand are that a good tea is made up of small, well-rolled leaves and has a pleasing aroma, while a poor one has a large percentage of dust and stalk.

Since tea readily absorbs moisture, it must be kept tightly covered in a cool, dry place. The packets should be put in an airtight tin and not be opened till required; empty the contents into a small tea caddy with a tightly fitting lid. A measuring spoon should be kept in the caddy.

Making Tea
1. Boil some freshly drawn water. (Soft water makes a darker tea, but many people do not consider the flavour is so good as that of tea made with hard water).
2. Warm the pot and add the tea. The quantity varies according to the type and blend – more is required with China tea than with Indian, for example; an average amount is 2×5 ml spoons/ 2 teaspoons tea to 450 ml/¾ pint of water.
3. Make the tea as soon as the kettle boils or the water will go 'flat' and spoil the taste of the brew. Take the hot teapot to the kettle and pour the boiling water on to the leaves, then cover the pot to keep it warm.
4. Allow the infusion to stand for 3 minutes in the case of ordinary Indian teas, 5 to 6 minutes for China or high-grade Indian tea.

Serving Tea
Tea should be served really hot. Milk is usually served with black tea, but lemon can be offered as an alternative. Sugar should also be offered for those who prefer a sweet tea.

High grade teas are usually served with lemon, and China teas may be served with a syrup flavoured with mint, lemon or orange.

RUSSIAN TEA

Half-fill glasses with strong China tea, adding hot water and slices of lemon as required. Jam or rum may replace the lemon, if preferred.

AUSTRIAN TEA

This also requires very strong tea; pour a little into the glass, then fill up with warm milk.

ICED TEA

Prepare some China tea, strain it and pour into a tumbler part-filled with crushed ice. Add sugar and a slice of lemon and re-chill before serving – the quicker the chilling, the better the flavour and the clearer the tea. Alternatively, add orange juice and garnish with sliced orange and a mint leaf.

TEACAKE

A flat, round cake made with a yeast dough.
Teacakes are split, often toasted and served with butter.

YORKSHIRE TEACAKES

METRIC/IMPERIAL
*25 g/1 oz fresh yeast or 1 × 15 ml spoon/1 tablespoon
    dried yeast and 1 × 5 ml spoon/1 teaspoon sugar*
300–450 ml/½–¾ pint tepid milk or milk and water
450 g/1 lb strong plain flour
1 × 5 ml spoon/1 teaspoon salt
50 g/2 oz butter or lard
2 × 15 ml spoons/2 tablespoons sugar
100 g/4 oz currants
2 × 15 ml spoons/2 tablespoons cut mixed peel
sugar and milk glaze

Blend the fresh yeast with half the milk. For dried yeast, dissolve the sugar in half the milk, sprinkle the yeast over and leave until frothy. Mix the flour and salt, rub in the fat and stir in the sugar, currants and peel. Add the yeast liquid and sufficient of the remaining liquid to give a fairly soft dough. Beat well, turn it on to a floured board and knead until smooth. Allow to rise in a warm place, about 23°C/75°F until doubled in size, turn on to a lightly floured board and divide into 4 to 6 large or 12 smaller pieces. Knead lightly into rounds and put on a greased baking sheet. Allow to rise for 15 to 20 minutes and bake in a hot oven (220°C/425°F, Gas Mark 7) for 15 to 30 minutes, according to size. When the cakes are cooked, brush with a glaze made by dissolving 1 × 15 ml spoon/1 tablespoon sugar in 1 × 15 ml spoon/1 tablespoon milk and return them to the oven for a further 1 to 2 minutes for the glaze to dry.
To serve: Split teacakes and spread with butter and a fruit preserve or toast and just serve with butter.

TEAL

One of the smaller wild ducks, averaging about 36 cm/14 inches in length. Teal, which is highly prized, is in season from September to February and is at its best at Christmas. One bird per person is served. It is usually roasted in a moderate oven (180°C/350°F, Gas Mark 4) for 25 to 30 minutes

and served garnished with watercress and slices of lemon.

TEASEED OIL

An oil extracted from the seeds of a plant of the tea family. It is cheaper than olive oil and is used commercially to replace olive oil in salad dressings and for frying.

TEFF

A plant with very small grains about the size of a pin head which grows in Abyssinia, where a bread made of meal ground from these grains is the staple article of diet.

TEMPERATURES FOR COOKING

Accurate temperatures are essential to ensure good results in cooking – even a perfectly mixed cake, for example, can be spoilt by being baked at the wrong temperature.

Oven Temperatures
The ovens of most modern electric and gas cookers are thermostatically controlled; once the thermostat has been set, the oven heat will not rise above the selected temperature.

In the case of thermostatically controlled electric ovens, it is usually found that the thermostat scale is marked either in Celcius or degrees Fahrenheit, or in serial numbers (1, 2, 3, etc.), which correspond to the temperatures.

Oven heats in the recipes in this book are described by such terms as 'Cool', 'Hot', etc., with the corresponding temperatures and the oven settings used in most modern cookers; the table below shows the various equivalents. If in doubt about settings for your own cooker you can ask advice from your electricity or gas showrooms; they will also come and test the oven temperatures.

OVEN TEMPERATURE GUIDE

Oven	Electric setting		Gas Mark
	°C	°F	
Very cool	110	225	¼
	120	250	½
Cool	140	275	1
	150	300	2
Moderate	160	325	3
	180	350	4
Moderately hot	190	375	5
	200	400	6
Hot	220	425	7
	230	450	8
Very hot	240	475	9

WATER-BASED LIQUIDS		
Boiling	100°C	212°F
Simmering (approximately)	96°C	205°F
Blood heat (also called tepid and luke-warm) (approximately)	37°C	98°F
Freezing point	0°C	32°F

Temperatures for Sugar-boiling, Preserving, Frying

To judge these, it is best to use a sugar-boiling thermometer. (See the individual entries and recipes for the exact temperatures required.)

TENCH

This small fish is a member of the widespread carp family, inhabiting English and Continental rivers. To counteract its muddy flavour rub it well with salt and leave for a while, then clean and wash it and soak in salted water for 2 to 3 hours before cooking. Frying and grilling are the most suitable methods.

TEQUILA

A Mexican spirit distilled from pulque, a kind of beer.

TERRAPIN

A small turtle of North America, the flesh of which is considered a great delicacy.

TERRINE

An earthenware cooking dish and hence the potted meat, rabbit, game, fowl or fish cooked (and often served) in the dish. (See Pâté entry.)

LIVER TERRINE

METRIC/IMPERIAL
450 g/1 lb pig's liver
100 g/4 oz fat bacon
4 eggs, beaten
1 clove garlic, skinned and crushed
150 ml/¼ pint thick white sauce
salt
pepper
12 rashers streaky bacon, rinded

Mince the liver and fat bacon finely, then put the mixture through the mincer again and finally sieve it, to ensure a really smooth result. (Alternatively, purée in a blender, a little at a time with beaten egg.) Mix it with the beaten eggs, crushed garlic, sauce and seasoning to taste. Line a 1 litre/2 pint terrine dish with bacon rashers, fill up with the liver mixture and place in a dish containing enough cold water to come half-way up the sides of the terrine. Bake in a moderate oven (160°C/325°F, Gas Mark 3) for 2 hours. Cover the top of the liver mixture with greaseproof paper or foil. Press evenly and leave for 24 hours in a cold place before serving. Serve cold and sliced, with toast and butter and crisp lettuce.

DUCK TERRINE WITH ORANGE

METRIC/IMPERIAL
2 kg/4½ lb oven-ready duck
450 g/1 lb belly pork
225 g/8 oz pork fat
1 orange
225 g/8 oz onion, skinned and finely chopped
1 clove garlic, crushed
4 × 15 ml spoons/4 tablespoons red wine
2 × 15 ml spoons/2 tablespoons chopped parsley
1 × 5 ml spoon/1 teaspoon ground mace
1 × 5 ml spoon/1 teaspoon salt
pepper, pinch of
1 orange for garnish

Cut away the skin and fat layer from the duck and remove the flesh – about 700 g/1½ lb. Remove the rind and any bones from the belly pork. Pass all the meat and pork fat twice throught a fine mincer. Grate the rind from the orange. Remove all pith and membrane, collecting any juice and cut the flesh into small dice.

Combine the minced meats, orange rind, chopped orange and any juice, and all remaining ingredients, except the garnish. Press the pâté into an earthenware terrine, pie or soufflé dish. Cover with foil; put in a moderate oven (180°C/350°F, Gas Mark 4) for about 3 hours.

Strain off the juices and skin off the surface fat. Reduce these to a glaze and pour the juices over the pâté. Cover and weight down. Refrigerate until cold.

Peel the remaining orange. Slice it thinly and use half slices to garnish the dish.

TERRINE OF HARE

METRIC/IMPERIAL
1 good hare
larding bacon

MARINADE
1 × 15 ml spoon/1 tablespoon redcurrant jelly
75 ml/3 fl oz each of mushroom sauce, port and wine vinegar
1 × 5 ml spoon/1 teaspoon mixed herbs
1 medium onion, skinned and chopped
salt
pepper

225 g/8 oz fat or streaky pork (approx.)
finely chopped herbs (basil or thyme, marjoram)

a small glass of sherry or port
a good pinch of ground mace
salt
freshly ground black pepper
175 g/6 oz tongue, cut in a thick slice
2 bay leaves
flour and water paste
good jellied stock, made from bones of hare and
    trimmings of pork
gelatine if necessary

Choose a terrine or earthenware casserole. Remove the fillets from the back of the hare, lard them with the bacon, and put them into the marinade. Set on one side for a day or leave overnight.

Take all the meat from the rest of the hare, weigh it and take equal quantity of fat or streaky pork. Mince them twice together, then turn into a mortar and pound well, adding the herbs, wine, mace, salt and freshly ground pepper to flavour well.

Cut the tongue into thick long strips. Lay these with the hare fillets in the terrine, then spread the farce over them. Press the bay leaves on the top, cover with the lid and seal down with a flour and water paste. Stand the terrine in a bain-marie and cook in a slow to moderate oven about 1½ hours. Remove the lid, press with a good paper-covered weight and leave until the next day. Fill up with a good jellied stock (strengthened with gelatine if necessary) made from the bones of the hare and trimmings of the pork.

If the terrine is to be kept for any length of time, run clarified butter or melted lard over the top, and do not add any extra liquid.

Keep in a cool place or refrigerator and serve in the dish.

If no terrine is available make in a deep pie dish and cover the top with a lid of paste. When cooked remove the crust, press and finish as above.

THIAMINE

One of the B vitamins. (See Vitamin entries.)

TEXTURED VEGETABLE PROTEIN (TVP)

Sometimes called Textured Soya Protein (TSP). It is a protein food resembling meat; made by taking protein from plants (especially soya beans) and converting them into a meat type product. This is more efficient than feeding the plants to animals that are eventually eaten, as this only results in 10 to 12 per cent of vegetable protein being converted into animal protein. When fortified with iron, thiamine, riboflavin and Vitamin B12, textured vegetable protein can be used instead of meat; it also has the advantage of being a food acceptable to vegetarians.

There are two main types of TVP available:
1. Extruded. Soya protein is pressed then extruded. Steam is then flashed off leaving an expanded and relatively dry, textured product.
2. Spun. The protein is dissolved and given alkaline treatment. It is then passed through spinnerets, giving fibres which are placed in a precipitation bath consisting of a salt mixture. The fibres coagulate and are then pressed into blocks, coloured and flavoured.

Chunks of textured vegetable protein tend to have a slightly chewy texture, and are best used in conjunction with other meats. In a granular or flaked form it blends better and is useful as a meat extender, generally in the proportion of 25 per cent TVP to 75 per cent meat. For replacement value 25 g/1 oz TVP is equal to 100 g/4 oz fresh mince. TVP is often added to meat pies, beefburgers etc. to reduce the cost. However, this must be indicated on the label. In catering establishments where food is produced in large quantities a percentage of TVP is often added to meat dishes to enable costs to be kept down.

(See also Soya entry.)

THICKENING

Any substance added to sauces, soups, etc., to give them a thicker consistency and to bind them. (In most sauces, of course, the thickening or liaison is an integral part of the mixture, e.g., the flour used in many sauces and the butter used in Hollandaise and Béarnaise sauce.) A thickening also ensures a smooth texture and holds heavy ingredients (whether sieved or not) in suspension – failing a liaison, such ingredients as lentils would separate out from a soup and settle at the bottom.

THICKENING FOR SAUCES
See sauces entry.

THICKENING FOR SOUPS
Flour, rice flour, cornflour, potato flour, sago, tapioca, semolina, egg and cream are all used.

THICKENING FOR STEWS, ETC.
Flour, potato flour and cornflour can be used in the proportion of 25 g/1 oz thickening agent to 600 ml/1 pint of stock. Blood (see below) is used in meat dishes such as jugged hare.

How to Add Thickenings and Liaisons

FLOURS AND OTHER POWDERED CEREALS
For soups or stews, mix smoothly with a little cold liquid, then add just before serving and boil for at least 5 minutes, stirring all the time.

(For Sauces see Sauce entry.)

SMALL GRAIN, E.G., SAGO, TAPIOCA
These must be added 15 to 20 minutes before serving and cooked until quite transparent.

EGG

The richer white soups and sauces may be thickened by eggs or egg yolks beaten up with a little cream, milk or white stock. Just before serving, add 2–3 × 15 ml spoons/2–3 tablespoons of the hot but not boiling sauce or soup to the beaten egg mixture, then stir this into the contents of the pan (which should not be quite boiling). Cook and stir for a few minutes by the side of the heat, in order to coagulate the egg albumen and form the liaison, but do not boil or the egg will tend to curdle.

BUERRE MANIÉ (BUTTER AND FLOUR)

This provides a quick method of thickening the liquor in which meat, fish, vegetables, etc., have been cooked; it is used particularly in hotel and restaurant cookery. Knead together 75 g/3 oz plain flour and 100 g/4 oz butter; add this a small piece at a time to the hot liquid, whisking all the time, then bring to boiling point; repeat until the sauce, gravy or soup reaches the desired consistency.

BLOOD

This must be added after the dish has cooked. The coagulation of the proteins in the blood which causes the desired thickening takes place well below boiling point, at temperatures up to 80°C/176°F; if the mixture is allowed to boil after the blood is added, it takes on a curdled appearance.

THYME

A garden herb with a characteristic flavour, which is used in soups, sauces, stews, etc; the variety known as lemon thyme is excellent for veal stuffing.

Thyme should be used sparingly, as it easily overpowers other flavourings as it has a strong pungent flavour.

TIFFIN

Anglo-Indian term for a light mid-day meal not used very much nowadays.

TIMBALE

A round mould with straight or sloping sides made from fireproof china or tinned copper used for moulding meat or fish mixtures. Moulds for hot timbale are lined with macaroni, potato, pastry or raspings and cold moulds are usually lined with aspic and decorated. Dishes cooked in the mould usually take on the name 'timbale'. They are a good way of using left over meat, fish, vegetables etc.

TINNED FOOD

(See Canned Food entry.)

TIPSY CAKE

A tall sponge cake made into a trifle, but reassembled into its original shape and decorated with split blanched almonds. The wine and fruit juice with which it is soaked often cause it to topple sideways in the serving dish in a drunken fashion – hence the name.

TISANE

French name for a medicinal tea or infusion, made with such herbs and flavourings as camomile, lime blossoms, lemon balm, fennel seeds, etc.

TOAD-IN-THE-HOLE

A dish made by cooking sausages or chopped cooked meat in a Yorkshire pudding batter.

TOAD-IN-THE-HOLE

METRIC/IMPERIAL
100 g/4 oz plain flour
1 × 2.5 ml spoon/ ½ teaspoon salt
1 egg
300 ml/ ½ pint milk and water
0.5 kg/1 lb skinless sausages

Sift the flour and salt into a bowl. Add the egg and half the liquid. Gradually stir in the flour and beat until smooth; stir in the remaining liquid. Grease a shallow ovenproof dish or Yorkshire pudding tin, put in the sausages and pour in the batter. Bake in a hot oven (220°C/425°F, Gas Mark 7) for 40 to 45 minutes, or until the batter is well risen and golden brown.

TOAST

Bread browned on each side under a grill, in an electric toaster or in front of an open fire.

Toast may be buttered immediately on removal from the heat and placed in a covered dish to keep warm, but this uses more butter and it is less digestible than dry toast served with separate butter.

Fingers of hot buttered toast can be spread with savoury pastes such as anchovy, foie gras, etc. The popular cinnamon toast is made by spreading it with a mixture of equal quantities of cinnamon and sugar and then returning it to the grill to melt the sugar.

Fingers, rounds, diamonds and other shapes of toast are often used as bases for cocktail savouries.

TOAST MELBA

This light, crisp toast can be served instead of rolls.
Cut slices of bread 3 mm/ ⅛ inch thick and toast them slowly on both sides, so that they become

very crisp; or they can be dried slowly in the oven until crisp and gold in colour. Alternatively, cut 5 mm/¼ inch slices, toast them on each side, split them through the middle and toast the uncooked surfaces.

TODDY

A drink made with rum or whisky, hot water, sugar and lemon. In tropical countries the word is also used for the sap of various palm trees and for the fermented drinks made from them.

TOFFEE

A toffee is made from a simple sugar mixture boiled in a high temperature 138°C/280°F to 154°C/310°F. The majority of toffees contain butter, but some are made merely from sugar and water, with flavouring and sometimes colouring.
(See Sweets entry for recipes.)

TOHEROA

A shellfish found in the sand of certain beaches in New Zealand. It is very scarce and the greenish-coloured soup made from it is a highly prized delicacy.

TOKAY

The best-known Hungarian wine. The highest grades, known as *Essencia* and *Aszu*, are sweet and rich; they keep longer than any other wine and may be served with dessert or as a liqueur. They should be stored for some years before using.

Other grades of Tokay are drier and not in the same class, being more like ordinary table wines. The word *puttonys* applied to Tokay indicates the amount of over-ripe grapes used in the making; the higher the number of *puttonys*, the richer the wine.

TOM COLLINS

A drink made of gin, lemon or lime juice, sugar and cracked ice shaken together and served with soda water.

TOMATO

The soft, pulpy fruit of a trailing plant of South American origin, which is now widely grown in many parts of the world. There are many varieties of tomatoes, ranging from the size of small cherries to that of a large orange and in colour from red to orange and yellow. Since tomatoes can be grown both outdoors and in hot-houses and as large quantities are imported from such places as the Canary Islands, they are in season in this country all the year round, being cheapest in the late summer and early autumn.

Tomatoes are a useful source of vitamin A and C, the vitamin C content being about half that of citrus fruit. Those grown outdoors and allowed to ripen on the plant contain a higher proportion of vitamins than do the varieties grown indoors.

The characteristic flavour of tomatoes is best enjoyed when they are picked ripe and eaten raw as a salad vegetable, but they are very useful in cookery, making soups and many light savoury dishes (e.g., stuffed tomatoes) and forming a good flavouring for such things as stews and cheese dishes, while the juice makes a refreshing drink. Grilled, baked or fried tomatoes make a colourful garnish for hot dishes and raw tomatoes can be used in various ways for decoration. (See Garnish entry.)

In addition to the recipes given here, others will be found under such entries as Salad, Soup and so on.

Ripening and storing tomatoes: Tomatoes are best ripened on the plants, but if necessary they can be ripened indoors in one of the following ways:
1. Wrap them in paper and place in a drawer or a covered box.
2. Hang them up in trusses in a sunny window.
3. In the case of large quantities, pack them in a box, with sawdust to separate each tomato from its neighbours. (Only tomatoes that have begun to turn colour should be stored in this way.)

Preserving tomatoes: As they are available all the year round preservation is usually only carried out if there is an abundance of tomatoes. Both red and green tomatoes can be used for sauces and chutneys. Firm, ripe, red tomatoes can be bottled whole and less good ones can be made into purées or juice. Whole tomatoes do not freeze well as they become watery when thawed but they can be used for cooking. They are most useful if frozen as a purée or juice. The tomatoes should be skinned and simmered in their own juice for 5 minutes until soft. Sieve or liquidize and pack as required. For juice, season with salt 1 × 5 ml spoon/1 teaspoon to each 1.2 litres/2 pints.
(See Bottling, Chutney, Ketchup entries etc.)

TOMATO STUFFING

METRIC/IMPERIAL
2 large tomatoes, skinned and chopped
½ red pepper, seeded and finely chopped
½ clove garlic, skinned and crushed
3 × 15 ml spoons/3 tablespoons fresh white
  breadcrumbs
knob of butter, melted
salt
pepper

Mix the ingredients together and bind with the

juice from tomatoes and the melted butter. Season well.

Use instead of veal forcemeat for baked stuffed liver.

TOMATO COLESLAW

METRIC/IMPERIAL
450 g/1 lb crisp green eating apples
juice of 1 lemon
450 g/1 lb white cabbage
75 g/3 oz seedless raisins
300 ml/½ pint thick mayonnaise
450 g/1 lb tomatoes
salt
freshly ground black pepper

Wipe the apples. Core and dice them, leaving the skin on. Put the apple in a basin with the lemon juice and toss lightly to coat the pieces evenly with the juice. Finely shred the cabbage. In a large bowl, combine the cabbage with the raisins, mayonnaise and drained apple. Season well. Place two-thirds of the cabbage mixture in a deep serving dish, levelling the surface. Slice the tomatoes crosswise, season and place half in a layer over the slaw. Cover with remaining cabbage mixture, making a cone shape in the centre. Arrange a circle of over-lapping tomatoes around the top edge. Keep in a cool place.
Note If the slaw is made in advance, omit the apple and add before serving.

BACON-TOPPED TOMATOES

METRIC/IMPERIAL
450 g/1 lb tomatoes
1 onion, skinned
100 g/4 oz streaky bacon
salt
pepper
2 × 5 ml spoons/2 teaspoons chopped parsley

Skin the tomatoes, cut them into slices and arrange in a shallow ovenproof dish. Chop the onion very finely. Rind and mince the bacon and fry lightly. Season the tomatoes and sprinkle with the onion and bacon. Bake in a moderate oven at (180°C/350°F, Gas Mark 4) for 10 to 15 minutes. Garnish with the chopped parsley before serving.

TONGUE

The tongues of sheep, oxen, calves and pigs may be cooked in various ways and served either hot or cold. Pickled tongues take only half the normal time to cook, and are usually bought from the butcher, but we give below directions for pickling them at home. Tongues may also be bought ready cooked in tins or glasses. Hot tongue is generally served with a sauce such as Cumberland, mush-room or tomato, or it may be mixed with chicken, etc., in bouchées. Cold tongue is usually glazed with aspic and served with salad.

Like all meats, tongue is principally a protein food, with some minerals and B vitamins.

PICKLED TONGUE

Choose a tongue with as smooth a skin as possible; wash it very thoroughly, scraping it well and cutting off any gristle at the root end. Rinse in cold water and dry, then rub it over with coarse salt and leave it overnight.

Prepare a pickling liquid with the following ingredients:

METRIC/IMPERIAL
0.5 kg/1 lb cooking salt
25 g/1 oz saltpetre
175 g/6 oz brown sugar
4.5 litres/1 gallon water

Boil for 5 minutes, keeping the surface well skimmed, then strain and leave until cold. Pour the pickle over the tongue, completely covering it, allow to cool and leave for 7 to 10 days.

BOILED TONGUE

Soak the tongue in water for about 1 hour or overnight if it has been pickled. Wash it and skewer into shape, put into a large pan with some lukewarm water and bring slowly to the boil, skimming carefully. Add seasoning (omitting the salt for a pickled tongue), a few peppercorns and a few cut-up root vegetables for flavouring, then simmer very gently until tender (see table below). When the tongue is sufficiently cooked, the small bones in the root will come away quite easily.

Sheep's tongues	1½ to 2 hours
Calves' tongues	1½ to 2 hours
Ox-tongue (fresh)	4½ to 6 hours
Ox-tongue (pickled)	2½ to 3 hours

When the tongue is cooked, remove it from the pan and plunge it into cold water, so that the skin will come off more easily. Skin it very carefully and remove any bones and the remaining gristle from the root.

To serve hot: After skinning, cover the tongue with greased paper and put in the oven for a few minutes to re-heat, then glaze it or sprinkle with bread-crumbs. Garnish with slices of lemon and parsley sprigs. Serve with a brown sauce.

To serve cold: Roll the tongue while still hot into a round cake tin, fitting it in tightly. In the case of small tongues, several should be pressed together in one tin. Add a little jellied stock, put a weighted cover on top and leave to set for some hours. Serve garnished with parsley.

Another method is to trim and truss the skinned tongue into shape on a board, holding it down with fine skewers. When it is cold, cover it with glaze or brush it with melted aspic jelly and leave until quite cold to set. Serve with a paper frill round the root of the tongue and accompanied by a suitable garnish.

Cut into thin slices and serve with a crisp open salad and new boiled potatoes

TORTE

The name given to an open tart or rich cake-type mixture baked in a pastry case. An Austrian 'torte' called 'Linzertorte' is a flan case of rich spiced pastry filled with raspberry jam then topped with latticed strips of pastry. A 'torte' can include other ingredients such as nuts, fruit, chocolate and cream. In France savoury mixtures are often used as the filling for a rich savoury base. The richness is offset by serving with a green salad.

LINZERTORTE

METRIC/IMPERIAL
150 g/5 oz plain flour
1 × 2.5 ml spoon/½ teaspoon ground cinnamon
75 g/3 oz butter
50 g/2 oz caster sugar
50 g/2 oz ground almonds
grated rind of 1 lemon
2 egg yolks
1 × 15 ml spoon/1 tablespoon lemon juice
350 g/¾ lb raspberry jam
whipped double cream for serving

Sift the flour and cinnamon into a bowl and rub in the butter. Add the sugar, ground almonds and the lemon rind. Beat the egg yolks and add with the lemon juice to the flour, to make a stiff dough. Knead lightly and leave in a cool place for 30 minutes. Roll out two-thirds of the pastry and use to line a 20 cm/8 inch fluted flan ring on a baking sheet. Fill with raspberry jam. Roll out the remaining pastry and cut into 1 cm/½ inch strips. Use to make a lattice design over the jam.

Bake in the oven at (190°C/375°F, Gas Mark 5) for 25 to 35 minutes. Allow to cool, remove from the flan ring, and serve with whipped cream.

Note Fresh or frozen raspberries can be used in place of the jam: reduce 450 g/1 lb raspberries with 1 × 15 ml spoon/1 tablespoon water, a knob of butter and a little sugar to taste to a thick purée. Cool before serving.

TORTILLA

A kind of thin pancake eaten throughout Mexico, which is made from a dough of *maza* flour (corn kernels cooked with slaked lime, dried and ground). The pancakes are shaped and flattened by hand and cooked on both sides on a hot griddle until dry. Tortillas are served sprinkled with salt and rolled into a cylinder; if they are filled with beans, meat and a spicy sauce before rolling they are called Tacos.

TORTILLA (POTATO OMELETTE)

METRIC/IMPERIAL
300 ml/½ pint oil
0.5 kg/1 lb potatoes, peeled and sliced
½ onion, skinned and chopped
4 eggs
salt
freshly ground pepper

Heat the oil and fry the potato slices until lightly browned, then drain well on absorbent paper. Pour off the oil from the pan, leaving only 1 × 15 ml spoon/1 tablespoon. Sauté the onion until clear. Return the potatoes to the pan. Beat the eggs with salt and pepper and pour over the vegetables. Cook over a gentle heat and complete the cooking of the top under the grill to brown the top lightly.

TOURNEDOS

(See Steak entry.)

TOURTE

French name for a round, shallow tart (rather like a flan case), made of puff pastry, which can be filled with a savoury or sweet mixture.

TRAGACANTH, GUM

(See Gum entry.)

TRANSPARENT ICING

A very thin icing which is used to give a professional finish to royal-iced cakes. The surface of the royal icing should be very smooth, and if necessary should be shaved or scraped down with a sharp knife and brushed well with a clean, soft brush before the transparent icing is applied.

TRANSPARENT ICING

METRIC/IMPERIAL
450 g/1 lb loaf sugar
300 ml/½ pint water
a little lemon juice

Boil the sugar and water together and continue heating until the temperature reaches 107°C/225°F. Whilst it is boiling, remove any scum that rises on the sugar and brush the sides of the pan with a little cold water. When the required temperature is reached, pour the syrup into a clean basin, stir in a little lemon juice and beat well, until the icing thickens and looks opaque; then pour it over the cake, taking care to cover the entire surface.

TREACLE

The sticky fluid remaining after sugar cane has been processed. Black treacle, which contains more of the harmless impurities than light treacle (golden syrup), has a somewhat bitter taste, but it gives a good flavour and colour to treacle tart, gingerbread and rich fruit cakes. (See entries on Suet Puddings, Scones, Sweets, etc., for recipes using treacle; for the method of weighing treacle for cooking purposes, see Weights and Measures. See Golden Syrup entry.)

Treacle is a good source of energy and it contains useful amounts of calcium and iron. It has considerable sweetening power, though less than sugar, weight for weight, owing to the higher proportion of water which it contains.

TREACLE TART

METRIC/IMPERIAL
100 g/4 oz shortcrust pastry
6 × 15 ml spoons/6 tablespoons golden syrup
50 g/2 oz fresh white breadcrumbs
grated rind of ½ lemon

Roll out the pastry and line a shallow 18 cm/7 inch pie plate. Mix together the golden syrup, breadcrumbs and lemon rind. Spread the mixture in the pastry case, keeping the border free. Make cuts down the border at 2.5 cm/1 inch intervals and fold over each strip to form a triangle. Cook in a hot oven (220°C/425°F, Gas Mark 7) for about 20 minutes or until golden brown. Serve hot or cold.

TREE TOMATO

A fruit found in South America and New Zealand, which resembles the tomato but is egg-shaped; it contains many pips. Tree tomatoes are either much appreciated or heartily disliked.

TRIFLE

A cold sweet made with a basis of sponge cake soaked in a liquid such as sherry or fruit juice, then covered with custard sauce and whipped cream and decorated. Trifles for a party can be quite elaborately decorated with such things as glacé fruit, angelica, almonds, sweets, small silver balls, ratafias, grated chocolate and whipped cream. They may be made either in a large glass dish or in individual glasses or dishes.

Variations on the traditional trifle can be made with the use of convenience foods such as instant desserts and canned fruit.

SHERRY TRIFLE

METRIC/IMPERIAL
8 trifle sponge cakes
jam
150 ml/¼ pint medium sherry
6 macaroons, crushed
450 ml/¾ pint custard
300 ml/10 fl oz carton double cream, whipped
sugar and flavouring
glacé cherries, angelica and cream to decorate

Split the sponge cakes, spread them with jam and arrange in a glass dish, then pour the sherry over and leave to soak for 30 minutes. Sprinkle the macaroons over the sponge cakes and pour on the warm, not hot, custard. Cover the dish with a plate to prevent a skin forming and leave until cold. Sweeten and flavour the cream to taste and spread most of it over the custard. Decorate with the rest of the cream, piped, the cherries and angelica (or with ratafias, almonds, etc.). Fruit juice such as orange may replace some or all of the sherry, if you prefer.

TRIPE

Part of the stomach lining of the ox or cow, sold cleaned and usually parboiled. Tripe is pale cream in colour and in texture may be like a blanket or honeycomb, depending on whether it is from the first or second stomach. It is, like all meats, a protein food and contains a little fat, some minerals and some B vitamins.

Preparation and cooking: If the tripe has not already been cleaned and blanched, treat it as follows: Wash it in several changes of warm water, scraping it thoroughly and removing any discoloured parts and fat, cover with cold water, bring to the boil, then rinse. Repeat one or more times, until the tripe has a pleasant smell. Now put it in cold water, bring to the boil and simmer for 6 to 7 hours, then leave overnight in the water in which it was cooked. It is at this stage that tripe is usually sold in shops.

After blanching, tripe needs to be simmered in milk and water until tender, usually a further 1 to 1½ hours. It can be served plain with boiled onions, or the liquid can be made into a white sauce, which can be flavoured with tomato ketchup, mushrooms, capers, etc.

Blanket tripe is excellent if it is cooked, cut into small pieces, dipped in batter and fried; serve it with chips, fried onions or mushrooms and French mustard or Tartare sauce.

Tripe is also used extensively in Chinese cookery and often served cold in a hot sauce.

TROUT

There are three European varieties of this fish –

413

salmon trout, lake trout and river trout (in addition to the various American types, including rainbow trout).

Trout require clean, well-oxygenated water to survive. In recent years techniques have been developed for rearing trout on fish farms. They can then be released into natural lakes, etc. or reared to sell for table use.

Salmon trout, also known as sea trout, frequent all the countries bordering the Atlantic, from Spain northwards, and are in season from March to August; they are cooked in the same way as salmon. Lake trout are also treated like salmon.

River trout, although smaller than the other two types, are much prized for their delicate flavour; they are found in rivers and mountain streams all over Europe and are in season from March to early September, but are best from April to August. Their colour varies from silvery-white to dark grey and they may have red, brown or black spots.

River trout have such a fine flavour that they are best cooked very simply, either grilled or egg-and-crumbed and fried. They may also be smoked or boiled.

TROUT AND ALMONDS

METRIC/IMPERIAL
4 trout, about 100–150 g/4–5 oz each
seasoned flour
175 g/6 oz butter
50 g/2 oz blanched almonds, cut in slivers
juice of ½ lemon

Clean the fish, but leave the heads on. Wash and wipe them and coat with seasoned flour. Melt 100 g/4 oz butter in a frying pan and fry the fish in it two at a time, turning them once, until they are tender and golden on both sides, 12 to 15 minutes. Drain and keep them warm on a serving dish. Clean out the pan and melt the remaining butter; add the almonds and heat until lightly browned, add a squeeze of lemon juice and pour over the fish. Serve at once, with lemon

TROUT IN CREAM

METRIC/IMPERIAL
4 trout
juice of lemon
1 × 15 ml spoon/1 tablespoon chopped chives
1 × 15 ml spoon/1 tablespoon chopped parsley
142 ml/5 fl oz carton single cream
2 × 15 ml spoons/2 tablespoons white breadcrumbs
a little melted butter

Have the fish cleaned (the heads can be left on or removed). Wash and wipe the fish, lay them in a greased shallow ovenproof dish and sprinkle with lemon juice, herbs and about 1 × 15 ml spoon/1 tablespoon water. Cover with foil and bake in a

moderate oven (180°C/350°F, Gas Mark 4) for 10 to 15 minutes, or until tender. Heat the cream gently and pour it over the fish, sprinkle with the breadcrumbs and melted butter and brown under a hot grill. Serve at once.

TRUFFLE

An edible fungus which is much esteemed for flavour and garnish. It grows underground usually under oak or nut trees. As the fungi have a characteristic smell they are located with the help of pigs and dogs.

French black truffles are one of the finest and most famous and are found in Périgord; they also take on this name. Another famous truffle is a white one found in Piedmont, Italy. Truffles are available in the UK in cans.

TRUFFLE, CHOCOLATE

(See Sweets entry.)

TUNNY (TUNA)

A fish found in warm seas, such as the Mediterranean. It is blue-grey above and silver below and grows up to 3 metres/10 feet in length.

Fresh tunny, when obtainable, may be grilled or boiled and served with a suitable sauce.

Canned tunny, usually prepared in oil, is imported from various parts of the world and may be used as an appetizer or in salads and cooked dishes. When used as an appetizer, it is simply drained, cut into slices, arranged on a dish and garnished with chopped parsley and capers.

TURBOT

A large flatfish. The best ones are said to be those from the Dogger Bank, but they are also found off the coasts of Holland, Norway and the British Isles. Turbots are in season all the year round, but are at their best between March and August. They have a firm, creamy-white flesh with a characteristic and delicious flavour and are reckoned to be the finest of the flatfish. Because they are so big – they may weigh up to 22.5 kg/50 lb – they are usually sold cut into slices or cutlets; when possible, choose thick cuts, which are easier to handle and cook and tend to have a better flavour. Turbot has a useful protein content.

To cook: Small fish may be baked whole after the head and tail have been removed, and the steaks or fillets from larger fish are equally good cooked in this way. Put the turbot in a greased oven-proof dish, sprinkle with seasoning and grated nutmeg and cover it with milk, milk and water or white wine. Bake in a moderate oven (180°C/350°F, Gas

Mark 4); steaks need about 20 to 30 minutes; whole fish take longer, according to their size. Serve with a sauce made from the fish liquor, flavoured with anchovy essence or shrimps and tinted pink.

Fillets of turbot may be fried by dipping them in seasoned flour and cooking them gently in butter. Serve with lobster, shrimp or anchovy sauce and fried parsley.

Turbot can also be steamed, grilled or poached.

TURKEY

A large farmyard bird of American origin which has become popular in Europe on account of its excellent flavour and its size. In this country the black-plumed Norfolk turkeys are considered especially fine and the Cambridge, which has variegated plumage, is another well-known type. The birds are killed at 6 to 9 months.

At one time turkeys were only available at Christmas but they are now in the shops throughout the year. The majority are sold plucked, drawn and trussed, sealed in polythene and frozen. Small turkeys of about 2.25 kg/5 lb can be bought but they are available in various weights up to 9 kg/20 lb or more. Portions of turkey are also available. Boned and rolled cooked turkey can be bought and these joints are particularly useful for buffet or picnic meals.

Fresh turkey is available from butcher shops and a good one can be recognized by the whiteness of its skin and broad, plump breast. The hen bird tends to be more tender than the cock and has less bone.

In the U.S.A. roast turkey is the traditional Thanksgiving Day dish, while in this country it has become one of the most popular birds for the Christmas dinner. It is also served for special occasions, Bank holidays and Easter meals.

Left over turkey meat can be made into many interesting savoury dishes. Fricassée, bouchée fillings, galantines and pies are some of the more usual recipes.

Preparation: If freshly killed, a turkey should be kept for at least 3 days before cooking, being hung up to bleed. The bird is then plucked and drawn in the usual manner. (See Poultry entry.)

If frozen, the bird must be allowed to thaw out before cooking. Leave it for 2 to 3 days in a refrigerator, removing it a little while before cooking, for the flesh to reach room temperature; allow 20 to 30 hours in a cool larder, or about 18 hours in a warm kitchen. It is better to over- rather than underestimate thawing times as it is important that the bird is completely thawed before cooking. When the bird has thawed, remove the bag of giblets which is always packed in the body cavity. The giblets can be boiled with vegetables and flavourings to make stock for the gravy.

ROAST TURKEY

The stuffing for roast turkey may be veal forcemeat, chestnut or sausage stuffing and should be placed in the body cavity at the breast end.

Sew and truss the turkey, after making it as plump and even in shape as possible. Before cooking, spread the bird with softened dripping or butter; the breast may also be covered with strips of fat bacon. If you are going to cook it by the quick method (see below), you will obtain the best results by wrapping the bird in aluminium foil to prevent the flesh drying and the skin hardening. Foil is not recommended for the slow method, as it tends to give a steamed rather than a roast bird.

Roast either by the slow method in a moderate oven (160°C/325°F, Gas Mark 3) or by the quick method in a hot oven (230°C/450°F, Gas Mark 8), for times listed.

Unless the bird is cooked in foil, baste it regularly, turning it round once to ensure even browning. Foil, if used, should be unwrapped for the last 30 minutes, so that the bird may be well basted and then left to become crisp and golden.

Roasting Times for Turkey

Weight	Hours – slow method	Hours – quick method
2.75 kg/6 lb to 3.6 kg/8 lb	3 to 3½	2¼ to 2½
3.6 kg/8 lb to 4.5 kg/10 lb	3½ to 3¾	2½ to 2¾
4.5 kg/10 lb to 5.4 kg/12 lb	3¾ to 4	2¾
5.4 kg/12 lb to 6.3 kg/14 lb	4 to 4¼	3
6.3 kg/14 lb to 7.3 kg/16 lb	4¼ to 4½	3 to 3¼
7.3 kg/16 lb to 8.2 kg/18 lb	4½ to 4¾	3¼ to 3½
9 kg/20 lb to 10 kg/22 lb	4¾ to 5	3½ to 3¾

GARNISH
Small sausages, forcemeat balls, rolls of bacon and watercress may be used to garnish the turkey. Serve it with brown gravy and bread sauce; cranberry or some other sharp sauce can also be served. Sliced tongue or ham is a favourite accompaniment.

To carve a turkey: (See Carving entry.)

TURKEY CACCIATORA

METRIC/IMPERIAL
1 small onion, skinned and chopped
1 clove garlic, skinned and chopped
1 carrot, pared and thinly sliced
1 bayleaf
olive or cooking oil

415

120 g/4½ oz can tomato juice
salt
pepper
225 g/½ lb cooked turkey, cut into cubes
1 × 15 ml spoon/1 tablespoon flour
pinch of dried basil and pinch of ground allspice,
    mixed
2 × 15 ml spoons/2 tablespoons red wine
112 g/4 oz packet frozen peas

A delicious way of using up turkey leftovers.

Cook the onion, garlic, carrot and bayleaf in 2 × 15 ml spoons/2 tablespoons oil for about 10 minutes. Add the tomato juice and season with salt and pepper, then simmer for 20 minutes. Remove the bayleaf. Coat the cubed turkey with flour, basil and allspice. Fry it gently in a little more oil. Pour the tomato sauce over the turkey, add the wine and peas and simmer for 10 minutes. Serve poured over a bed of cooked macaroni.

TURKISH DELIGHT

A popular jelly-type sweet. The genuine Turkish delight sold in the East is made with dextrin or dextrinized flour and is flavoured and perfumed with flower essences, but a fair substitute can be made by using either gelatine or cornflour. (For recipe see Sweets entry.)

TURMERIC

An East Indian plant of the ginger family. The roots, when dried and ground, have an aromatic, slightly bitter flavour. The powder is orange-yellow in colour and is used as a food colouring. Turmeric adds the yellow colour to curry powder and mustard pickles and to prepared mustard.

TURNIP

A root vegetable with a thick skin and white or yellow flesh. Turnips are obtainable all the year round, as they may be stored in sand, straw or clamps. They have a strong, sweet flavour and only a little is required for flavouring stews, soups, etc. Turnips contain a small amount of vitamin C.

Preparation and cooking: Peel thickly to remove the outer layer of skin and put under water to prevent discoloration. Young turnips are left whole, but the older ones should be sliced or diced, or they may be cut into matchstick pieces or balls for use as a garnish.

Cook as for other roots (see Vegetable entry). If turnips are used whole, strain them and toss in butter or a little top of the milk, with added seasoning, or serve in white sauce.

TURNIP TOPS

This pleasant-flavoured green vegetable is pre-

pared and cooked like cabbage. Turnip tops are a good source of vitamins C and A.

TURNOVER

A large or small piece of pastry, folded over on itself and containing a filling of fruit, mincemeat, jam or some savoury mixture.

JAM TURNOVERS

Cut some thinly rolled puff pastry into squares and spread one half of each with jam to within about 1 cm/½ inch of the edge of the pastry. Brush the edges with water, fold the other half of the pastry over and seal the edges tightly. Flake the edges with a knife and scallop them boldly. Brush the top of each turnover with water and sprinkle with sugar. Bake in a hot oven (220°C/425°F, Gas Mark 7) for 15 to 20 minutes.

Serve hot with a custard sauce or cold on their own or with fresh cream.

APPLE TURNOVERS

METRIC/IMPERIAL
375 g/13 oz packet puff pasty – thawed
25–50 g/1–2 oz caster sugar
2 × 5 ml spoons/2 teaspoons arrowroot
0.5 kg/1 lb cooking apples
egg white and granulated sugar to glaze

Roll out pastry to a rectangle 25 cm/10 inches by 38 cm/15 inches. Cut out six 13 cm/5 inch squares. Mix caster sugar and arrowroot together. Peel, core and slice apples and cook until just tender with caster sugar mixture. Allow to cool. Divide apple between pastry squares. Dampen edges, fold over to make triangular shapes and seal well. Chill for at least 2 hours. Bake in a hot oven (220°C/425°F, Gas Mark 7) for 20 minutes. Remove from oven, brush with egg white and sprinkle with sugar. Return to oven for 5 to 10 minutes. Serve warm.

TURTLE

Various types of salt-water turtles are found in the warmer seas of the world and other types inhabit the rivers and lakes of the New World.

Turtles vary in size and the so-called Green Turtle from the South Atlantic, which is used to make the famous turtle soup, may weigh several hundred pounds. The soup must be made from freshly killed turtles, so for this reason and because the method of making the soup is very complex, it is out of the question except for commercial firms or for the skilled staff catering for special functions.

Ready-made turtle soup may be bought in bottles or cans and a version may be made from canned or diced turtle. The soup should be served accompanied by forcemeat balls.

UDDER

Cow's udder, which is an easily digested and delicious meat, is prepared like escalopes of veal.

UGLI (TANGELO)

A hybrid citrus fruit produced by crossing a grape-fruit with a tangerine. It has loose, tough, rather thick skin of greenish yellow and is about the size of a grapefruit, but in shape is more elongated at the stem end. The taste is pleasantly sweet.

UMBLES

The edible entrails of a deer or other animal, which used to be made into a pie – hence the expression 'to eat (h)umble pie'.

UNLEAVENED BREAD

Bread made with flour, but with no raising agent. A good example of unleavened bread are Matzos.

UPSIDE-DOWN CAKE (PUDDING)

This is made by lining a baking tin or dish with fruit and placing a sponge mixture over it, so that when the cake or pudding is cooked and turned out, the decoration will be on top. Fruits such as apricots, prunes, peaches, pineapple, etc., are especially suitable for this purpose, as they keep their shape well. Fresh, bottled or canned fruit can be used. To give variety, the sponge mixture may be flavoured with ginger, chocolate, lemon, etc. When it is served as a pudding it should be accompanied by a sauce made from the fruit juice, thickened with arrowroot, or by cream.

PINEAPPLE UPSIDE-DOWN PUDDING

METRIC/IMPERIAL
50 g/2 oz butter
50 g/2 oz brown sugar
225 g/8 oz can pineapple rings, drained
100 g/4 oz butter or margarine
100 g/4 oz caster sugar
2 eggs, beaten
175 g/6 oz self raising flour
2–3 × 15 ml spoons/2–3 tablespoons pineapple juice or milk

Grease an 18 cm/7 inch round cake tin. Cream together the butter and brown sugar and spread it over the bottom of the tin. Alternatively, use 2–3 × 15 ml spoons/2–3 tablespoons golden syrup. Arrange the rings of pineapple on this layer in the bottom of the tin. Cream together the remaining fat and sugar until pale and fluffy. Add the beaten egg a little at a time and beat well after each addition. Fold in the flour, adding some pineapple juice or milk to give a dropping consistency, and spread on top of the pineapple rings. Bake in a moderate oven (180°C/350°F, Gas Mark 4) for about 45 minutes. Invert on to a dish and serve with a pineapple sauce made by thickening the remaining juice with a little cornflour.

CHOCOLATE PEAR UPSIDE-DOWN PUDDING
Use canned pear halves instead of pineapple. Substitute 25 g/1 oz cocoa powder for 25 g/1 oz flour in the sponge mixture.

RHUBARB GINGER UPSIDE-DOWN PUDDING
Cut 225 g/8 oz to 350 g/12 oz trimmed rhubarb into 2.5 cm/1 inch lengths (or peel, core and thinly slice 2 cooking apples). Arrange the fruit over the layer of creamed fat and sugar or syrup. Make up the cake mixture, using soft brown sugar instead of white, and sift 1–2 × 5 ml spoons/1–2 teaspoons powdered ginger with the flour.

USQUEBAUGH

The Celtic form of the word whisky – literally meaning 'Water of Life' (c.f., the French eau-de-vie). It is also the name of an Irish liqueur made of whisky or brandy, spices, etc., infused overnight.

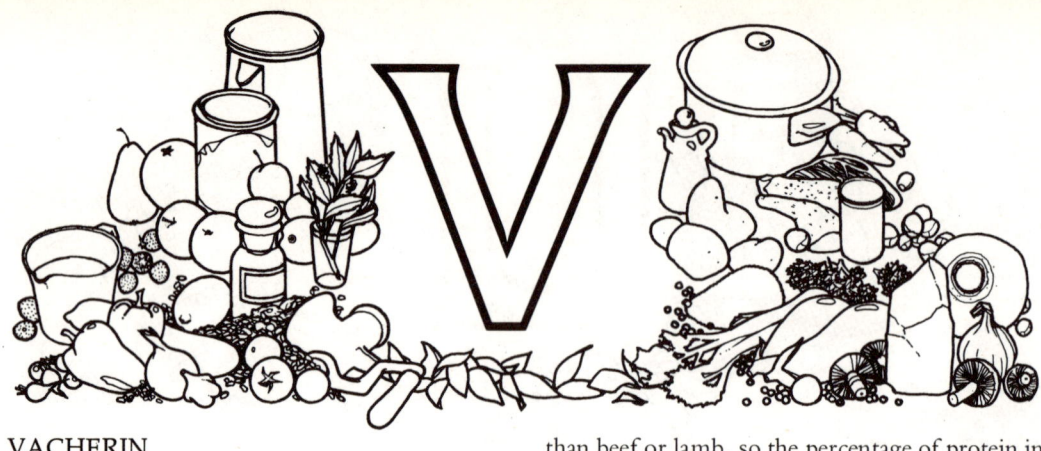

VACHERIN

A fairly elaborate sweet, consisting of a 'basket' made of meringue or macaroon mixture built up in rings on a pastry base, which is filled with cream or ice cream and fruit. It is also the name of a Jura cheese; a soft runny cheese with a firm rind, usually served with cream.

VAN DER HUM

A South African liqueur, flavoured with the South African tangerine or 'naartje'.

VANILLA

A flavouring made from the seed pods of a climbing plant of the orchid family, grown in Mexico and other tropical countries. When pods are fermented they turn brown and become covered with crystals of vanillin. When buying whole pods, see that these crystals are present and see also that the pods are not split for more than about one-third of their length.

A small piece of vanilla pod may be infused in the milk used for puddings, etc. Sugar may be flavoured by mixing ground pods with it in the proportion of 4 pods to 0.5 kg/1 lb or by placing a whole pod in the jar. Store the flavoured sugar in a jar with a tightly fitting lid and use as required for cakes, etc.

Vanilla Essence

This is made by soaking vanilla pods in alcohol or spirit of wine to extract the flavour; brown colouring is usually added. Vanilla essence is more variable in flavour than the pods, but is a more convenient form to use and quite satisfactory if a reliable brand is chosen. The synthetic 'vanilla essence' is based on oil of cloves. (See Essence entry.)

VEAL

The term applied to the meat of a calf about 2½ to 3 months old. (For Beef, see individual entry.) The flesh is pink and close-textured and contains less fat than beef or lamb, so the percentage of protein in veal is higher and its energy value lower than that of red meats. It contains some thiamine, iron, riboflavine and calcium.

Fillet of veal, which comes from the leg, is the most suitable cut for frying. Chops usually come from the chump end of the fillet and cutlets from best end of neck or loin. As veal comes from such a young animal, most joints are tender enough to be roasted, though breast and scrag are best braised or stewed. Since the meat is lean, frying in fat or roasting in added fat are very suitable methods of cooking and bacon or ham is often used as an accompaniment or garnish for veal.

Veal has not such a pronounced flavour as red meat and therefore needs a well-flavoured sauce or gravy as an accompaniment. It combines well with bacon, tomatoes, mushrooms, etc., in casserole dishes, while veal and ham pie is a popular cold buffet dish.

Cuts of Veal and How to Treat Them

Shoulder (bladebone)	Roast or stew
Loin	Roast
Loin (when cut into chops)	Fry or grill
Neck (scrag)	Stew
Best end of neck	Roast
Best end of neck (when cut into cutlets)	Fry or grill
Fillet (i.e., top of leg) in the piece	Roast
Fillet (i.e., top of leg) if sliced	Fry or fricassée
Knuckle	Stew or boil
Breast	Stew or braise
Breast (if boned, stuffed and rolled)	Roast, stew or braise

ROAST VEAL

Prepare the meat in the usual way. If the joint is to be stuffed, bone it, using a sharp-pointed knife, and wipe it well, insert some of the stuffing and tie the joint. Season and place in a roasting tin with the fat side uppermost and the dripping under the joint. If the meat is very lean, put some fat or fat bacon on top of it. Make any remaining stuffing into balls and place them round the meat.

Veal has a better flavour if roasted in a closed tin or in foil, although the appearance may not be quite so good. For the quick method allow 25 minutes per 0.5 kg/lb plus 25 minutes, for joints with bone; 30 minutes per 0.5 kg/lb plus 30 minutes for boned joints. When cooking by the slow method allow 40 minutes per 0.5 kg/lb plus 40 minutes.

VEAL ESCALOPES

When cooking escalopes by any of the methods described below it is not advisable to have more than 2 in the pan at once as they are difficult to turn over.

FRIED ESCALOPES

Allow 1 escalope per person and get the butcher to beat it until really thin. Rub each piece over with a cut lemon and sprinkle lightly with salt and black pepper. Coat with beaten egg and fresh white breadcrumbs, patting them on well. Melt 50 g/2 oz butter in a large frying pan and fry the veal gently (about 5 minutes on each side). Drain well on kitchen paper and serve with wedges of lemon and a green salad. Or if you wish, serve with vegetables and a tomato sauce.

ESCALOPES WITH PARMESAN CHEESE

Prepare and coat the escalopes as above, then fry gently in butter for about 3 minutes on each side or until just tender. Cover each escalope with a thin slice of cooked ham and 1 × 15 ml spoon/1 tablespoon grated Parmesan cheese. Spoon a little of the butter over the cheese, cover the pan with a lid or large plate and cook for a further 2 to 3 minutes, until the cheese just melts. Serve immediately with sauté or boiled potatoes, a crisp salad or a green vegetable.

ESCALOPES WITH MARSALA AND CHEESE

Coat each escalope with seasoned flour and fry gently in 50 g/2 oz butter until just tender and golden (3 minutes on each side). Stir into the pan 2–3 × 15 ml spoons/2–3 tablespoons Marsala (or sherry or Madeira) and sprinkle each escalope with 1 × 15 ml spoon/1 tablespoon grated Parmesan cheese. Spoon some of the butter-wine mixture over, cover the pan with a lid or plate and cook gently for a further 2 to 3 minutes, until the cheese just melts. Serve with sauté potatoes and a crisp salad of watercress, lettuce and chicory.

WIENER SCHNITZEL

Basically this famous Viennese dish is the same as veal escalope – that is, a large piece of fillet, beaten, dipped in flour, in beaten egg and finally in white breadcrumbs, then fried in deep fat. Schnitzels are traditionally served quite simply with a wedge of lemon, although a more elaborate garnish of sliced hard-boiled egg, olives and anchovies may be used.

BLANQUETTE OF VEAL

METRIC/IMPERIAL
0.5 kg/1 lb veal, cut up
2 onions
a bouquet garni
white stock or water
65 g/2½ oz butter
50 g/2 oz plain flour
2 egg yolks
2 × 15 ml spoons/2 tablespoons cream
juice of 1 lemon
chopped ham, lemon fans and chopped parsley to garnish

Put the veal, onions and bouquet garni in a stewpan with enough liquid to cover and simmer very gently until tender – 1½ hours. Strain and keep the meat hot. Make a sauce with the butter, flour and 600 ml/1 pint of the stock. Cook well, then add the egg yolks, beaten with the cream and lemon juice, and reheat carefully, but do not re-boil. Pour over the veal and garnish with the chopped ham, lemon fans and chopped parsley.

VEAL FRICASSÉE

METRIC/IMPERIAL
225 g/8 oz back bacon, cut in 2 thick rashers
0.75 kg/1½ lb stewing veal, cubed
50 g/2 oz butter
1 × 15 ml spoon/1 tablespoon oil
½ small onion, skinned and finely chopped
300 ml/½ pint white stock or water
salt
pepper
2 × 15 ml spoons/2 tablespoons flour
1–2 × 15 ml spoons/1–2 tablespoons lemon juice

A good standby for all occasions. Add your own personal touch with herbs, or use half stock and half dry white wine for cooking. Alternatively, use half the stated amount of stock for cooking and replace the other half by milk, added at the end.

Rind the bacon, trim off any excess fat and cut into pieces the same size as the veal. Fry the veal and bacon very lightly in 25 g/1 oz butter and the oil, but do not colour. Lift them out and place in a 1.75 litre/3 pint casserole. Fry the onion in the remaining fat until transparent but not brown and add to the veal. Pour the stock over the meat, season, cover and cook in a moderate oven (180°C/350°F, Gas Mark 4) for 1½ hours, or until tender. Strain off the liquor and keep the veal and bacon hot in the casserole. Melt the remaining butter, stir in the flour and cook for 2 to 3 minutes. Gradually stir in the strained liquor, bring to the boil and boil for 2 to 3 minutes, stirring all the time. Add the lemon juice and re-check the seasoning. Pour the sauce over the veal.

ROAST VEAL WITH BEER

METRIC/IMPERIAL
1.5 kg/3 lb loin of veal
50 g/2 oz dripping or lard
salt and pepper
2–3 carrots, pared and sliced
2–3 onions, skinned and sliced
300 ml/½ pint beer
1 bayleaf
2 cloves
1 × 15 ml spoon/1 tablespoon flour

Spread the meat thickly with the dripping or lard and put it in a meat tin; season with salt and pepper. Add the carrots and onions, and roast in a hot oven (220°C/425°F, Gas Mark 7) for 30 minutes. Pour the beer over the meat, add the bayleaf and cloves and return to the oven. Reduce heat to 190°C/375°F, Gas Mark 5 and cook the meat until tender, basting frequently – allow 30 minutes per 450 g/1 lb. When the meat is cooked place it on a serving dish. Blend the flour with the juices in the tin, heat until boiling, then strain over the meat.

OSSO BUCCO

METRIC/IMPERIAL
1 kg/2¼ lb shin of veal
salt and pepper
50 g/2 oz butter
1 medium sized onion, skinned and finely chopped
1 carrot, pared and thinly sliced
1 stalk of celery, scrubbed and thinly sliced
150 ml/¼ pint dry white wine
1 × 15 ml spoon/1 tablespoon flour
400 ml/¾ pint stock
225 g/½ lb tomatoes, skinned and chopped
pinch of dried rosemary
1 × 15 ml spoon/1 tablespoon chopped parsley to
    garnish
grated rind of ½ lemon

Ask your butcher to saw the veal into 5 cm/2 inch pieces. Season with salt and pepper. Melt the butter, brown the veal all over and remove from the pan. Add a little more butter if necessary and fry the onion, carrot and celery until they are golden brown. Drain off any excess fat, return the meat to the pan and add the wine. Cover and simmer gently for 20 minutes. Blend the flour with a little

stock to a smooth cream, add the remainder of the stock and add to the meat. Add the tomatoes and rosemary, cover tightly and continue to simmer for a further 1½ hours, or until the meat is tender. Arrange in a deep serving dish and sprinkle with a mixture of parsley and lemon rind. Serve with risotto and a dressed green salad.

VEAL CHOPS EN PAPILLOTE

METRIC/IMPERIAL
8 veal chops
4 × 15 ml spoons/4 tablespoons oil
2 × 15 ml spoons/2 tablespoons chopped parsley
2 × 15 ml spoons/2 tablespoons chopped onion
2 × 15 ml spoons/2 tablespoons chopped chives
100 g/4 oz mushrooms, sliced
butter
salt
pepper

Marinate the chops in the oil for 12 hours. Mix the parsley, onion and chives with the mushrooms. Cut 8 pieces of kitchen parchment paper or foil, each large enough to wrap a chop completely, spread with butter and sprinkle with the herb and mushroom mixture. Place a chop on each paper, cover with another layer of the herb mixture, season well and wrap up firmly. Bake in a moderately hot oven (200°C/400°F, Gas Mark 6) for 20 minutes, until tender. Serve the chops still in the papers.

VEGETABLE

Vegetables may roughly be classified as follows:
1. Roots and tubers, e.g., carrot, beetroot, salsify, radish, potato, Jerusalem artichoke, celeriac, parsnip.
2. Bulbs, stalks or stems, and buds, e.g., onion, seakale, leek, celery, asparagus, chicory, aubergine, fennel, kohlrabi.
3. Leaves and flowers, e.g., cabbage, lettuce, sorrel, spinach, watercress, cauliflower, broccoli, globe artichoke, sprouts, endive.
4. Pods and seeds, e.g., French and runner beans, broad bean, pea.
5. Fruit, e.g., tomato, cucumber, marrow, courgette, avocado.
6. Dried pulse vegetables, e.g., peas, beans, lentils.
7. Seaweed, e.g., Carrageen moss.
    Details of each vegetable will be found under the appropriate entry or under such collective entries as Pulses and Root Vegetables.

Food value

Vegetables are an essential part of a normal diet, since they provide vitamins and mineral salts, a good deal of roughage (cellulose) and, in the case of pulses, some protein and carbohydrates. They are also important as they help to made a meal look attractive and appetizing.

VITAMINS AND MINERALS
Vegetables provide vitamins A and C in important quantities. The amounts vary considerably, depending on the kind of vegetable, the season and the soil in which they grow. Carrots, for example, supply very large amounts of vitamin A, beetroot none at all; Brussels sprouts supply vitamin C, lettuce very little; the new season's potatoes contain far more vitamin C than old ones.

Minerals principally calcium and iron, are also present in vegetables in variable amounts.

It is now considered more satisfactory to recommend one or two helpings of vegetables each day, including as wide a variety as possible, rather than to worry about the composition of individual vegetables.

Canned, frozen and dehydrated vegetables retain their vitamin and mineral content, apart from a slight loss of vitamin C. Dried vegetables such as lentils and split peas contain no vitamin C.

PROTEIN, CARBOHYDRATE, FAT AND WATER CONTENT
Tubers, pods and seeds and pulses provide the largest amount of protein; although this is not as good as animal protein, it is extremely useful. The energy value of vegetables, except for roots, which contain carbohydrates, is low. Generally speaking, vegetables (with few exceptions, e.g., avocado pears) contain no fat. However, when they are roasted or fried, they acquire extra energy value from the fat used.

Vegetables contain 76 to 90 per cent water.

Choosing and Storing Vegetables
Green vegetables should be fresh, crisp and green – not yellow. Roots and tubers should feel firm. Most vegetables do not store well, so they should be bought frequently in small quantities. They are best kept in a cool dark place.

POTATOES
Store in a cool dark place, but are best eaten soon after lifting.

ROOT VEGETABLES
Large quantities may be stored in sand; when brought into the house they should be wrapped in newspaper, to prevent evaporation.

GREEN VEGETABLES
Should be put in a rack. Lettuce and other salads keep for a time in a salad box or covered basin, but keep best in a refrigerator, in the vegetable rack or in a plastic box or bag. Parsley, mint, watercress and cucumber, if not placed in a refrigerator, should be kept with the stalks in water.

Preparation and Cooking
All vegetables should be prepared as near to the

time of cooking as possible, to retain their flavour and vitamin C content.

GREEN VEGETABLES
Separate the leaves (except for sprouts, cauliflower and globe artichokes, which are left whole) and discard the tougher parts or discoloured outer leaves. Wash quickly, soaking the leaves only if they are contaminated by flies or grubs – in this case, leave in salted water for about 15 minutes. Cut up if necessary, using a sharp knife to prevent bruising the leaves. Place at once in a pan containing about 2.5 cm/1 inch to 5 cm/2 inches of fast-boiling salted water. Cover with a tight-fitting lid, bring back to the boil as quickly as possible and boil for 15 to 20 minutes. When cooked, the vegetables should be really green and just tender. Bicarbonate of soda should not be added to greens during cooking, for although it gives a good green colour, it destroys vitamin C.

ROOTS AND TUBERS
These should be washed if dirty and scraped or thinly peeled (except for turnips, which must be thickly peeled, and beetroot, which must not be peeled or cut at all before cooking). Cut into even-sized pieces, put in a pan and just cover with salted water. Bring to the boil and simmer until tender, allowing 20 to 30 minutes, depending on the vegetables.

PODS AND SEEDS
French and runner beans, if young, should be washed and left whole; if old, remove the strings on each side, then slice the pods. Peas and broad beans should be shelled. To cook, place in boiling salted water and simmer for about 20 to 30 minutes, until tender. A sprig of mint and a little sugar added to the cooking liquid improve the flavour of peas.

STEMS AND SHOOTS
They should be scrubbed and the leaves and base of the stems cut off. Asparagus is prepared by scraping off the lower leaves and trimming the base of the stems. During the preparation, celery and asparagus should be placed in water containing lemon juice to prevent discoloration. To cook asparagus, tie in bundles with muslin or a piece of bandage and simmer in salted water containing some lemon juice for about 20 minutes.

DRIED PEAS, BEANS AND LENTILS
Wash, then (except in the case of lentils) soak overnight with 1 × 5 ml spoon/1 teaspoon bicarbonate of soda to 0.5 kg/1 lb of pulses. Drain well, cover with fresh water and simmer for 1 to 1½ hours. (See Beans entry.)

Other Methods of Cooking
STEAMING
Potatoes, if steamed until just cooked, will retain

more of their vitamin C content than do boiled ones. Greens, however, discolour badly and lose more of their vitamin C content than do boiled ones. To prepare vegetables, scrub them and peel (except potatoes); if very large, cut into even-sized pieces. Allow up to half as long again cooking time as is needed for boiling.

PRESSURE COOKING
A useful quick method of cooking all but green vegetables; the short cooking time reduces the loss of nutritive value to a minimum, but thiamine and vitamin C are partially lost. (See Pressure Cooking entry.)

ROASTING
Adds flavour and produces an attractive crisp finish, but there is a greater loss of vitamin C than with boiling.

Potatoes, also carrots, turnips and parsnips, roast well round the joint, or may be cooked in fat in a separate tin. Peel or scrape the vegetables and boil them for 5 minutes in a little salted water (which can be saved to make gravy). Place them in hot fat and cook for 1 to 1½ hours, turning them over and basting once or twice during the cooking. If the meat is being cooked by the slow method, put the vegetables at the top of the oven to brown for the last 30 minutes.

FRYING
This method is particularly suitable for potatoes. Small cubes of marrow and flowerets of cauliflower are delicious sautéed in butter or margarine, while small portions of such vegetables as cauliflower and cucumber may also be dipped in batter and fried. (See Fritter entry.)

BAKING
Potatoes can be baked in their skins or jackets (see Potato entry), this method avoids waste in preparation and conserves much of the mineral and vitamin content.

BRAISING
This is a good method for such vegetables as carrots, celery, onions, etc. (See Braising entry for cooking details.)

Serving Vegetables
The cooked vegetables should be drained well and served immediately, while the flavour and food value are at their best. (It is better to re-heat them rather than to keep them hot for a long time.) The serving dishes should be hot and the vegetables arranged attractively, tossed in butter when appropriate and garnished with chopped parsley, paprika or a suitable sauce which is added just before serving. Cold cooked vegetables can be served as part of a side salad.

Two or more vegetables should be served with each main meal. Salads go well with hot dishes as

well as cold and can also be served as a separate course.

Preserving Vegetables
(See Freezing, Pickling, Bottling and Drying entries; see also Dehydrated Foods and Frozen Foods entries.)

VEGETABLE MARROW
A late summer vegetable of the Gourd family. It is rather watery and is best cooked in a casserole with butter or stuffed and baked.
(See Marrow entry.)

VEGETARIAN DIET
A true vegetarian diet, as the name suggests, should consist of vegetables and fruit only. Such followers are known as vegans; most followers of the régime interpret it as a non-flesh diet and permit themselves milk, cheese and often eggs, and strictly speaking are lacto-vegetarians. The diet is bulky (especially the strict version), and it is therefore particularly suitable for those who are overweight. It is, however, likely to cause flatulence and it is not suitable for people troubled with this condition. It may also be deficient in protein. Generally speaking, a lacto-vegetarian diet can be quite satisfactory if the person planning it has sufficient dietetic knowledge to keep it well balanced.

VELOUTÉ
A rich white sauce made with a foundation of white stock, which is used as the basis of many more elaborate sauces such as Allemande, Mousseline, etc. The liquid used may be veal, chicken or fish stock, according to the dish in question.

VELOUTÉ SAUCE
METRIC/IMPERIAL
knob of butter
about 2 × 15 ml spoons/2 tablespoons flour
450 ml/¾ pint chicken or other light stock
2–3 × 15 ml spoons/2–3 tablespoons single cream
few drops of lemon juice
salt
pepper

Melt the butter, stir in the flour and cook gently, stirring well, until the mixture is pale fawn colour. Stir in the stock gradually, bring to the boil, stirring all the time, and simmer until slightly reduced and syrupy. Remove from the heat and add the cream, lemon juice and seasoning.
Serve with poultry, fish or veal.

Velouté Soup is a thick soup of creamy consistency.

VENISON

The flesh of a deer. Buck venison, which is considered superior to that of the doe, is in season from October to December only.

The fat of venison should be a clear creamy-white and the flesh dark red; the meat should be hung for about 14 days before being eaten, so that it becomes slightly 'high' and the flavour is at its best. Test it at intervals by running a skewer through the haunch; so long as the skewer has no unpleasant smell when withdrawn, the meat is in good condition.

Venison is usually cut into the haunch, fillet, loin, neck and breast. Slow methods of cooking are better for neck and breast. But other joints roast or fry well, the haunch being the prime cut. When frying venison, treat it like beefsteak, but allow more fat.

ROAST VENISON

The best joint for roasting is the haunch, but the loin, neck and fillet may also be cooked in this way. It is best to cover the joint with a paste made by mixing flour and water to a stiff dough (allowing about 1.5 kg/3 lb flour to a haunch) and rolling it out to 1 cm/½ inch thickness. Venison requires a good deal of fat in the cooking. Roast in a moderate oven (180°C/350°F, Gas Mark 4), allowing 25 minutes to the 0.5 kg/1 lb. About 20 minutes before the cooking is completed, remove the paste, dredge the joint with flour and return it to the oven. It should be accompanied by a thick gravy and by gooseberry, redcurrant or cranberry jelly.

VERBENA

A herb with a faint lemon flavour, which used to be used for making a herb tea.

VERJUICE

The juice of unripe grapes, apples or crabapples. It was at one time used in sauces, etc., instead of lemon juice or vinegar.

VERMICELLI

An Italian pasta which is forced through very small holes and dried; the resulting fine 'strings' (the Italian word literally means 'little worms') are used in soups and for making milk puddings. (See Pasta entry.)

VERMOUTH

A drink with a white wine basis, fortified with spirit and flavoured with herbs and other substances; the name is derived from the German word for wormwood, which gives vermouth its characteristic flavour. French vermouth is dry and lighter coloured, the Italian type sweeter and darker. Vermouth is used in making various cocktails and is often served mixed with an equal quantity of gin. (See Cocktail entry.)

VESOP

A concentrated vegetable extract used in Chinese and other Eastern cookery.

VICHY CARROTS

Young carrots, lightly scraped and cooked in water and butter until all the liquid has evaporated and the carrots are glazed with the butter. Originally Vichy water was used as the cooking liquid – hence the name.

À la vichy indicates that carrots have been used in a dish or form a large part of its garnish.

VICHY WATER

A mineral table water from one of the springs at Vichy in France. Types other than Celestin should be taken only on doctor's orders.

VICHYSSOISE

A cold leek and potato cream soup introduced by Diat, Chef des Cuisines of the Ritz-Carlton Hotel, New York.

CRÈME VICHYSSOISE

METRIC/IMPERIAL
4 leeks, cleaned and sliced
1 onion, skinned and sliced
50 g/2 oz butter
1 litre/1¾ pints white stock
2 potatoes, peeled and thinly sliced
salt
pepper
200 ml/7 fl oz cream
chopped chives to garnish

Lightly fry the leeks and onion in the butter for about 10 minutes, until soft but not coloured. Add the stock and potatoes. Season, cover and cook until the vegetables are soft. Sieve the soup or purée it in an electric blender, stir in the cream, with more seasoning if necessary, and chill thoroughly for at least 2 hours. Sprinkle with chives before serving.

VICTORIA SPONGE SANDWICH

This popular type of cake is made with a creamed mixture based on equal amounts of flour, sugar and fat; the fat enables it to keep moist longer than the fatless or 'true' sponge.

VIC–VIN VICTORIA SANDWICH CAKE

METRIC/IMPERIAL
100 g/4 oz butter or margarine
100 g/4 oz caster sugar
2 eggs, beaten
100 g/4 oz self-raising flour
2 × 15 ml spoons/2 tablespoons jam
caster sugar to dredge

Grease two 18 cm/7 inch sandwich tins and line the base of each with a round of greased greaseproof paper. Cream the fat and sugar until pale and fluffy. Add the egg a little at a time, beating well after each addition. Fold in half the flour, using a metal spoon, then fold in the rest. Place half the mixture in each tin and level it with a knife. Bake both cakes on the same shelf of a moderately hot oven (190°C/375°F, Gas Mark 5) for about 20 minutes, or until they are well risen, golden, firm to the touch and beginning to shrink away from the sides of the tins. Turn out and cool on a wire rack.

When the cakes are cool, sandwich them together with jam and sprinkle the top with caster sugar.

CHOCOLATE SANDWICH CAKE
Replace 3 × 15 ml spoons/3 tablespoons of flour by 3 × 15 ml spoons/3 tablespoons of cocoa. Sandwich together with vanilla or chocolate butter cream. For a more moist cake blend the cocoa with water to give a thick paste. Beat into the creamed ingredients.

ORANGE OR LEMON SANDWICH CAKE
Add the finely grated rind of one orange or lemon to the mixture. Sandwich the cakes together with orange or lemon curd or orange or lemon butter cream. Use some of the juice from the fruit to make glacé icing.

COFFEE SANDWICH CAKE
Add 2 × 5 ml spoons/2 teaspoons instant coffee dissolved in a little warm water to the creamed mixture with the egg. Or use 2 × 5 ml spoons/2 teaspoons coffee essence.

VIEILLE CURE, LA

A sweet French liqueur, of high alcoholic strength, brown in colour and with a distinctive aromatic flavour.

VIENNA STEAK

(See Steak entry.)

VINAIGRETTE SAUCE

(See Salad Dressing entry.)

VINE

(See Grape and Wine entries.)

VINE LEAVES

The young leaves of the vine are much used in Greek and Turkish cooking. They are usually wrapped round a stuffing which may include meat and rice, then cooked in a sauce.

The Greek dish is known as Dolmades and the Turkish as Dolmas. (See Dolmas entry.)

DOLMADES

METRIC/IMPERIAL
1 can vine leaves
3 × 15 ml spoons/3 tablespoons lard or cooking oil
450 g/1 lb cooked lean meat, minced
1–2 onions, skinned and chopped
2 × 15 ml spoons/2 tablespoons cooked long grain rice
chopped parsley
a little tomato sauce
salt
pepper
juice of 1 lemon

Dip the vine leaves in boiling water for 1 to 2 minutes and leave to drain while the stuffing is prepared. Put 2 × 15 ml spoons/2 tablespoons of the lard or oil in a frying pan with the meat, onions, rice, parsley, tomato sauce and seasoning, mix well and fry. Add the lemon juice and put a small portion in the centre of each vine leaf; roll up and parcel envelope fashion. Secure if necessary with fine string or skewers. Put in a saucepan with the remaining fat or oil, a little more tomato sauce and a little water. Cook over a low heat until the sauce is well reduced.

VINEGAR

The liquid resulting from the alcoholic and later acetous fermentation of various grains and fruit. The process may be started by introducing 'vinegar plant' or 'mother of vinegar', a gelatinous mass of the bacteria which cause the fermentation. The by-products formed during fermentation give the characteristic flavour to vinegar and make it easily distinguishable from the coloured and flavoured acetic acid sometimes sold as vinegar (see Acetic Acid entry). Vinegar may be made from different substances, which give it varied flavours. In the United Kingdom it is made from malted grains; in France wine is employed, while in the United States cider apples are used. Vinegar can also be made from other substances such as sugar.

Strictly speaking, wine vinegar is the only type that has a right to the name. Either red or white grapes can be used and occasionally dried raisins,

424

though the last-named give an inferior vinegar.

Vinegar is used as a condiment in piquant sauces and salad dressings, for sousing foods like herrings and mackerel, for pickling and for marinating meat, etc. It is sometimes used with baking soda as a raising agent in cake and pudding mixtures. White wine vinegar, which is colourless, is used in white sauces. Vinegar flavoured with herbs or spices is used for some sauces, especially hot-flavoured ones.

TARRAGON, CHILLI OR CAYENNE VINEGAR

To 1.2 litres/2 pints vinegar allow 600 ml/1 pint tarragon leaves, 50 g/2 oz chillies or 25 g/1 oz cayenne pepper. Let the flavouring ingredient soak in the vinegar for 2 to 3 weeks, shaking the mixture occasionally, then strain and bottle the vinegar.

Wine vinegar is best for use with tarragon, but malt vinegar may equally well be used with chillies or cayenne.

Pickling or spiced vinegar: See Pickling entry.

VINTAGE

The word is translated from the French 'vendage' which means 'grape harvest'. Although there is a vintage each year the term is usually used as 'vintage year' meaning that the wines made in that year are of excellent quality.

They are made from one grape harvest which is exceptionally good. Individual wine growers may decide when a year can be termed a 'vintage year' or it may be a trade association decision.

The greatest vintages are usually small harvests as the fewer the grapes on a vine the more flavour there is in each grape. Vintages vary considerably in quality and style, therefore vintage charts can only be a generalization.

VITAMINS

Chemical substances required in small amounts to keep a body healthy by regulating the metabolic processes. They are found in foodstuffs, therefore in a good mixed diet an adequate amount will be supplied to the body.

Vitamins were discovered at the beginning of the twentieth century. Until this time it was believed the only essential nutrients were pure proteins, fats, carbohydrates and some inorganic elements.

Vitamins exist in more than one chemical form, but overall they are either fat soluble or water soluble. The former consists of vitamins A, D, E and K, and the latter, the vitamin B complex of thiamin (B_1), riboflavine (B_2), nicotinic acid (niacin), folic acid, vitamins B_6, B_{12}, biotin and

pantothenic acid. Vitamin C is also water soluble but always occurs in different foods from the B-vitamins.

If there is an absence or insufficient supply of vitamins in the diet, general and specific symptoms will result. General symptoms include a feeling of malaise and a restriction in the growth of children. If fat soluble vitamins are taken in excess the accumulation in the body can be dangerous, but an excess of water soluble vitamins has little effect as most is eliminated in the urine.

Vitamin A

A deficiency causes the mucous membranes to dry up and a vulnerability to infection (particularly in the eyes, where it causes defective vision in dim light); children do not grow and their teeth do not develop satisfactorily. Vitamin A is stored in the liver, which, in normal individuals contains enough to last for one to two years. Deficiency is most frequently found in Asia, and, rarely, in breast-fed babies when the mother has an insufficient supply.

Vitamin A is present in fish oils and offal (especially liver), and also in butter, eggs, vitaminized margarine, cheese, sardines, salmon, herrings and milk. Carotene, which is converted into vitamin A in the body, is present in carrots, green vegetables, apricots and tomatoes and to a lesser extent in other fruits; carotene, however, is less well utilized by the body than vitamin A and the 'activity' is usually assessed by dividing the carotene figures by three.

Vitamin A is fat soluble, and cooking has no effect on it. Taken in very large amounts it can cause poisoning as the effects are cumulative. Most cases of vitamin A poisoning recorded are children who have been given large amounts of fish liver oil.

The B Group of Vitamins

This consists of several vitamins which frequently occur together in food and were therefore mistaken in the early days for a single vitamin. Their functions are similar and are concerned with releasing energy from food in the body. The more important ones are:

Thiamine (Vitamin B_1 or aneurin)
Riboflavine (Vitamin B_2)
Nicotinic acid (Niacin)

Less important ones are:

Pyridoxine (Vitamin B_6)
Pantothenic acid
Biotin
Cyanocobalamin (Vitamin B_{12})

These B vitamins are widely distributed in foods and are therefore unlikely to be deficient in this country.

THIAMINE
The various actions and reactions which result in

the conversion of carbohydrates into energy are assisted by the presence of this vitamin. The amount of thiamine needed is affected by the amount of fat taken in the diet and the power of the individual to synthesize it in the intestines.

A deficiency of thiamine leads to such symptoms as tiring easily, irritability, nervousness, headaches, sleeplessness and loss of weight. Stiffness and cramp in the legs may be present, also palpitation and breathlessness, when the heart is affected; loss of appetite, indigestion and constipation are other possible symptoms. An acute deficiency of thiamine rarely seen in this country, leads to beri-beri.

Liver and edible food yeast, wheat germ and pork are rich sources. Bacon and other meat, potatoes, eggs and milk also contain useful amounts; peas, beans, lentils, spinach and cabbage contribute a little to the diet.

Prolonged cooking and the use of alkalis destroy the vitamin and since it is soluble in water, it is easily washed out. Meat loses about 5 per cent when roasted or grilled, 20 per cent when boiled, stewed or fried. In bread-making, about 15 per cent of the vitamin in flour is destroyed and in cake-making about 25 per cent.

RIBOFLAVINE

The function of this vitamin also is to form a link in the chain of processes through which the body obtains energy from food nutrients. When insufficient riboflavine is provided by the diet, cracks and sores appear on the skin at the corners of the mouth and the tongue becomes sore and red; the growth of children is checked.

Riboflavine cannot be stored in the body, so a regular intake is necessary. It is widely distributed in food, the richest sources being dried brewer's yeast, liver, meat extract, cheese, eggs, peanuts, beef, wholemeal bread, milk and fish.

NICOTINIC ACID (NIACIN)

One of the B vitamins chiefly concerned with the utilization of starch and sugars in the body. It is found in meat, offal, fish, yeast, meat and yeast extracts, potatoes and flour and milk. It is soluble in water and heat-stable. Little loss is likely to occur with ordinary methods of cooking. A deficiency of nicotinic acid causes pellagra, the classical picture being dermatitis, diarrhoea and dementia. The condition is almost unknown in this country.

Note: This vitamin should not be confused with the nicotine found in tobacco.

Vitamin C (Ascorbic Acid)

An important factor in making use of food in the body and in the formation of the intracellular 'cement' substance – collagen – found in human tissues.

Deficiency of this vitamin leads to proneness to catch infections, slow healing of wounds, poor teeth and bones, inflamed gums, poor circulation and anaemia and in acute stages to scurvy.

Good fruit sources of vitamin C are blackcurrants, oranges, grapefruit, lemon, rose hip syrup and strawberries. The best vegetable sources are sprouts, turnip tops, kale, cabbage, cauliflower, spinach, potatoes (new), tomatoes and watercress. Other fruits and vegetables also contribute a little. (See entries.)

Vitamin C is lost during storage and cooking. Generally speaking, the degree of wilting in a vegetable is an indication of its vitamin loss. Grating, shredding or mashing increases the vitamin C loss and a good deal is lost if vegetable cooking water is not used. Approximately 50 per cent of the vitamin is lost in boiling potatoes, 60 to 75 per cent in boiling green vegetables. The loss is greater with steaming, while pressure cooking compares favourably with ordinary methods. The loss is lessened if potatoes are boiled in their skins (about 15 per cent loss) or baked in their skins (20 per cent loss). Frying causes about 30 per cent loss.

Vitamin D

Needed to help absorb calcium from the food to keep the bones and teeth strong and healthy; a deficiency will lead to tooth decay and rickets. It is obtained from sunlight and food (particularly fish liver oil, milk, liver and egg yolks). In excess it can cause kidney stones and other deposits in the body, and care should be taken in giving fish liver oils and other fortified foods.

Vitamin E

An anti-sterility vitamin which has been used with success in rats; since corresponding deficiencies are not found in humans, its worth is unproven.

Vitamin K

A deficiency is extremely rare in a balanced diet and causes abnormal clotting of the blood. It is found in vegetables, peas and cereals. It can also be synthesized by intestinal bacteria.

VODKA

The Russian national drink, a strong, fiery, colourless, spirituous liquor distilled mainly from wheat, though rye or potatoes can also be used. Vodka is not coloured or matured. Apart from its use in Russia as an apéritif and elsewhere as a liqueur, it serves as the base of various cocktails.

Vodka is becoming more popular in the West and is frequently served in a similar way to gin.

VOL-AU-VENT

A case made of very light, rich puff pastry filled

with cut-up meat, poultry, game or fish in a richly flavoured sauce. A vol-au-vent may be served as an entrée or main dish or at a buffet meal.

CHICKEN VOL-AU-VENT

METRIC/IMPERIAL
225 g/8 oz puff pastry
beaten egg
175 g/6 oz diced cooked chicken
300 ml/½ pint well-flavoured coating sauce
mushrooms, cress and parsley to garnish

Roll out the pastry about 2.5 cm/1 inch thick, place it on a greased baking sheet and cut it into a large round or oval. (Try not to cut nearer than 1 cm/½ inch to the edge of the slab of pastry.) With a smaller cutter or a knife mark a circle or oval within the larger one to form a lid, cutting about halfway through the pastry. Make scallops on the outside edge with the back of a knife and brush the top with beaten egg. Bake in a very hot oven (230°C/450°F, Gas Mark 8) for about 30 to 35 minutes, covering the case with greaseproof paper when it is sufficiently brown. Remove the lid, scoop out any soft pastry inside and dry out the case in the oven for a further 5 to 10 minutes.

Stir the chicken into the sauce and fill the vol-au-vent. Garnish and serve hot.

WAFER

A very thin, crisp, sweetened biscuit, served with ice cream, etc. In addition to the conventional oblong, various fancy shapes are made. Smaller wafer biscuits are produced sandwiched together with a sweet or savoury cream filling.

WAFFLE

A crisp, golden-brown type of pancake, with deep indentations, made by baking a batter mixture in a special waffle iron, which cooks on both sides. The irons may be made for use over a gas jet or electric ring or they may be electrically heated. Waffles which are quickly prepared, may be eaten either as a sweet or as a savoury.

PLAIN WAFFLES

METRIC/IMPERIAL
100 g/4 oz self-raising flour
a pinch of salt
1 × 15 ml spoon/1 tablespoon caster sugar
1 egg, separated
2 × 15 ml spoons/2 tablespoons butter, melted
150 ml/¼ pint milk
1 × 2.5 ml spoon/½ teaspoon vanilla essence, optional

Mix the dry ingredients together in a bowl. Add the egg yolk, melted butter, milk and essence and beat to give a smooth coating batter. Whisk the egg white stiffly and fold into the batter. Heat the waffle iron. Pour enough batter into the iron to run over the surface. Close the iron over the mixture and leave for 2 to 3 minutes to cook, turning the iron if using a non-electric type, until crisp and golden brown. Serve with butter and golden syrup or maple syrup.

SPICE WAFFLES

Add 1 × 2.5 ml spoon/ ½ teaspoon ground mixed spice to the dry ingredients.

To preserve their crispness, waffles should be served immediately, after the addition of any spread or filling.

SWEET ACCOMPANIMENTS
Butter and sugar; jam and cream; golden syrup; maple syrup; syrup and ginger; ice cream; fresh or stewed fruit.

SAVOURY ACCOMPANIMENTS
Grilled or fried sausage, bacon, kidney, liver, tomatoes, mushrooms, minced meat or melted cheese. If finely chopped or grated, such flavourings as bacon, kidney, mushrooms or cheese may be added to the actual batter before the egg white is folded in.

WALNUT

The fruit of the walnut tree, many varieties of which are grown all over the world. The thin-shelled nuts are used for dessert, while the coarser types are crushed for the oil, which can be used in place of olive oil. English walnuts seldom ripen really well, owing to the climate, so they are often picked green towards the end of July, before the shell has formed, and are preserved as described under Pickling entry.

The walnut is a good source of vegetable protein and of fat and it contains small amounts of the B vitamins.

Walnuts can be used in the main dish of a meal, in salads and in nut roasts for vegetarians. They are, however, more commonly used as dessert and in cakes, puddings and sweets, either as an ingredient or as a decoration.

CHICKEN WITH WALNUTS

METRIC/IMPERIAL
1.5 kg/3¼ lb oven-ready chicken
1 large carrot, pared
1 onion, skinned
1 bayleaf
salt
pepper

WALNUT SAUCE
50 g/2 oz butter
175 g/6 oz walnut halves
225 g/8 oz onions, skinned and sliced

300 ml/½ pint natural yogurt
1 × 1.25 ml spoon/¼ teaspoon paprika
150 ml/¼ pint chicken stock

Place the chicken in a large saucepan and cover with cold water. Cut the carrot and onion into thick slices and add to the pan, together with the bayleaf and some salt and pepper. Bring to the boil, then cover, reduce the heat and simmer for 1½ hours. Leave the bird to cool in the stock for 1 hour. Remove and discard the skin from the chicken. Cut the chicken meat into largish pieces.

Heat the butter in a frying pan, add 50 g/2 oz of the walnut halves and fry gently until light golden brown, then remove from the pan. Add the onions and sauté until soft, but do not allow to brown; add the yogurt, paprika and chicken stock. Place the remaining walnuts in an electric blender until finely ground (or put through a Mouli grater), then add to the sauce. Add the walnut halves and the chicken, heat through and check the seasoning. Serve with buttered courgettes.

WASSAIL BOWL

A kind of spiced ale formerly served on Christmas Eve.

WATER

Water is essential to life. It is the largest constituent of all animal and plant life. It makes up two-thirds by weight of the human body.

Pure water is a colourless, tasteless and odourless liquid. At normal atmospheric pressure it boils at 100°C/212°F and freezes at 0°C/32°F. Most water contains dissolved gases, minerals and minute particles of dust. 'Hard' water is due to the presence of soluble calcium and magnesium salts, not present in 'soft' water.

Clean water is taken very much for granted in this country. The basic supplies are treated by filtering and other methods to make them safe.

Water is used in large quantities for drinking, cooking, other domestic uses and for industrial purposes.

Part of its value to life is due to the fact that it will dissolve many substances; it is not chemically changed, but it acts as a vehicle in the body for oxygen and food and for removing waste products. It is also involved in many other processes. Without water the body cannot survive for more than a few days.

Water is continually being lost from the body and must be replaced by the intake of liquid and food. The principal source, of course, is drinking water and other drinks. Normally about 1.2 litres/2 pints per day are required in a temperate climate. This is easily provided by, for example, 300 ml/½ pint milk, one glass of water and four

cups of tea, so it is clear that most of us drink more than this amount in a day.

The next most important amount comes from food, which also consists largely of water. This applies not only to such obvious things as gravy and custard – vegetables and fruit are largely water (up to 90 per cent for some of them) and even cheese, meat, bread and other apparently solid foods supply quite an appreciable amount of water.

A small amount of water is formed in the body itself through the breakdown of protein, fat and carbohydrates.

There is no evidence to show that it is harmful to drink with meals. In fact, it increases the secretion of digestive juices and softens the food.

WATER BISCUIT

A thin, crisp, plain biscuit, usually served with butter and cheese.

WATER CHESTNUT

Small tubers, related to the myrtle, eaten in China and other parts of the East. They are similar in appearance and flavour to ordinary chestnuts. They are available in cans in this country.

WATERCRESS

A plant with small green leaves, sometimes tinged with brown, which grows in water. Commercially grown watercress is now available all the year round. The leaves have a pleasant, slightly hot peppery taste and are excellent as an accompaniment to fish, game or grilled food, in a salad or sandwiches or made into a soup.

When eaten in large quantities, watercress is a useful source of vitamins A and C, also of iron and calcium.

Preparation and serving: Pick off the thick stalks and any tough or yellow leaves. Wash well in salted water, rinse and drain.

Watercress served as a salad may be left plain or tossed in French dressing; a sprinkling of chopped onion is sometimes added. For sandwiches it can be used either alone or mixed with cheese, tomato, yeast extract, etc. Sprigs or bunches of watercress may be used to garnish dishes and single leaves may be floated on the top of creamed soups.

CHEESE AND WATERCRESS SOUFFLÉ

METRIC/IMPERIAL
25 g/1 oz butter
1.5 × 15 ml spoons/1½ tablespoons flour
1 × 1.25 ml spoon/¼ teaspoon mustard
1 × 1.25 ml spoon/¼ teaspoon curry powder

429

150 ml/¼ pint milk
½ bunch watercress, washed
3 eggs, separated
100 g/4 oz Gouda cheese, grated
1 × 15 ml spoon/1 tablespoon snipped chives
salt
pepper

Melt the butter and stir in the flour, mustard and curry powder. Cook 2 to 3 minutes then gradually stir in the milk. Cook for a further 2 to 3 minutes.

Discard the coarse stems from the watercress and chop the leaves. Beat the egg yolks into the sauce, then stir in the cheese, watercress and chives. Season to taste.

Whisk the egg whites stiffly and fold them through the mixture. Turn the mixture into a buttered 15 cm/6 inch 1.2 litre/2 pint soufflé dish and bake in a moderate oven at (180°C/350°F, Gas Mark 4) for 30 to 35 minutes until well risen and golden. Serve at once.

WATER ICE

A refreshing frozen sweet, made from a sugar syrup flavoured with fruit juice or purée. Water ices are best made in an ice cream machine, but they can be made in a refrigerator if the mixture is stirred frequently during the freezing, although there will be a certain amount of crystallization. Two especially delicious types of water ice are made by adding stiffly beaten egg white or by flavouring with a liqueur. (See Sherbet and Sorbet entries.)

LEMON WATER ICE

METRIC/IMPERIAL
225 g/8 oz caster sugar
600 ml/1 pint water
rind and juice of 3 lemons
1 egg white, whisked

Dissolve the sugar in the water over a low heat, add the thinly pared lemon rind and boil gently for 10 minutes; leave to cool. Add the lemon juice and strain the mixture into the freezing container and leave to half-freeze to a mushy consistency. Turn the mixture into a bowl, fold in the egg white, mixing thoroughly, replace in the container and re-freeze.

ORANGE WATER ICE

METRIC/IMPERIAL
100 g/4 oz caster sugar
300 ml/½ pint water
1 × 15 ml spoon/1 tablespoon lemon juice
grated rind of 1 orange
grated rind of 1 lemon

juice of 3 oranges and 1 lemon, mixed (about 300 ml/ ½ pint)
1 egg white, whisked

Dissolve the sugar in the water over a low heat, bring to the boil and boil gently for 10 minutes. Add 1 × 15 ml spoon/1 tablespoon lemon juice. Put the grated fruit rinds in a basin, pour the boiling syrup over and leave until cold. Add the mixed fruit juices and strain into the freezing container. Freeze to a mushy consistency. Turn the mixture into a bowl; fold in the egg white, mixing thoroughly, replace in the container and freeze.

Other flavours of water ices (e.g. raspberry, strawberry) can be made by adding 300 ml/½ pint fruit purée and the juice of ½ a lemon to 300 ml/ ½ pint of the syrup; continue as above.

REDCURRANT WATER ICE

METRIC/IMPERIAL
0.5 kg/1 lb sugar
450 ml/¾ pint water
450 ml/¾ pint redcurrant juice
25 g/1 oz gelatine

Dissolve the sugar in the water over a low heat. Bring to boil and boil for 5 minutes. Strain and add redcurrant juice, reserving 3 × 15 ml spoons/3 tablespoons. Soak gelatine in reserved juice, then dissolve over a gentle heat and stir into liquid. Allow to cool.

Pour into a well chilled tray, put into freezer, and leave for 30 minutes. Turn into a bowl and beat. Return to tray and freeze for 40 to 50 minutes.

WATER MELON

(See Melon entry.)

WATERLESS COOKERY

A waterless cooker consists of a heavy aluminium pan with a tightly-fitting lid; this means that there is little evaporation and only the minimum amount of cooking liquid is needed – hence the name.

The food is placed in containers and the pan (on its base plate) is put on the stove. There is a steam vent in the lid to prevent a build-up of pressure in the pan, so although in the moist methods of cooking steam is produced and indeed helps to cook the food, it is not under pressure as in a pressure cooker. The pan can be used for pot-roasting, stewing, and braising, and for steaming and bottling. Complete meals can also be cooked all at once, thus saving space, fuel and washing-up. The fact that such a small amount of liquid is used helps to retain the soluble constituents of the foods.

WATERZOIE (BELGIAN); WATERZOETJE (DUTCH)

In Brussels this is a dish of boiled chicken and white wine served in a creamy white sauce containing Julienne strips of mixed vegetables. Elsewhere in Belgium and Holland it consists of a mixed fish stew containing Julienne strips of vegetables. It is usually eaten like soup.

WEDDING CAKE

The traditional rich fruit cake, with one, two or more tiers, covered with almond paste and decorated with royal icing, which is served at the wedding reception. The bride makes the first cut and the rest of the cutting up is then usually done in the background. The top tier of a wedding cake is often saved for the first christening, for the cake is rich enough to keep if wrapped well.

WEDDING CAKE

(Quantities sufficient for a cake of three round tiers, baked in tins measuring 30 cm/12 inches, 23 cm/9 inches and 15 cm/6 inches in diameter.)

METRIC/IMPERIAL
2.5 kg/5 ½ lb currants
900 g/2 lb sultanas
900 g/2 lb raisins
450 g/1 lb sweet almonds
675 g/1 ½ lb glacé cherries
450 g/1 lb mixed peel
1 lemon
1.5 kg/3 ½ lb plain flour
4–5 × 5 ml spoons/4–5 teaspoons ground cinnamon
2.5 × 5 ml spoons/2 ½ teaspoons ground mace
a pinch of salt
1.5 kg/3 lb butter or margarine
1.5 kg/3 lb sugar
24 eggs
200 ml/⅓ pint brandy or rum

Grease the tins and line with a double thickness of greased greaseproof paper. Wash and pick the dried fruit, stone the raisins, blanch and chop the almonds, cut the glacé cherries in half, chop the mixed peel, grate the lemon rind and strain the juice. Sieve the flour, spices and salt into a large mixing basin. Stir in the prepared fruit, almonds, etc. Cream the fat and sugar until pale in colour, then add the eggs, beating each one in separately; should the mixture curdle, stir in a little of the flour. Fold in the dry ingredients, stirring in the brandy or rum and lemon juice gradually. Pour the mixture into the prepared tins and bake in a cool oven (150°C/300°F, Gas Mark 2) reducing to very cool (120°C/250°F, Gas Mark ½) after 1 hour. Allow 3 to 3½ hours for the 15 cm/6 inch tin, 4½ to 5 hours for the 23 cm/9 inch tin and 7½ to 8

hours for the 30 cm/12 inch tin. When the cakes are cold, wrap them in fresh greaseproof paper and store for 2 to 3 weeks, thus allowing them to mature slightly before covering them with almond paste and royal icing. The table below shows the quantities of icing required for cakes of various sizes. (See Icings and Piping entries.)

Icing Quantities

These quantities are approximate. The amount of royal icing quoted should be enough to give two coats plus simple decoration.

Size of Cake	Almond Paste
13 cm/5 inch round	225 g/½ lb
13 cm/5 inch square	225 g/½ lb
15 cm/6 inch round	350 g/¾ lb
15 cm/6 inch square	350 g/¾ lb
18 cm/7 inch round	450 g/1 lb
18 cm/7 inch square	450 g/1 lb
20 cm/8 inch round	675 g/1½ lb
20 cm/8 inch square	800 g/1¾ lb
23 cm/9 inch round	800 g/1¾ lb
23 cm/9 inch square	900 g/2 lb
25 cm/10 inch round	900 g/2 lb
25 cm/10 inch square	1 kg/2¼ lb
28 cm/11 inch round	1.25 kg/2½ lb
28 cm/11 inch square	1.25 kg/2¾ lb
30 cm/12 inch round	1.25 kg/2¾ lb
30 cm/12 inch square	1.5 kg/3 lb
33 cm/13 inch round	1.5 kg/3¼ lb
33 cm/13 inch square	1.5 kg/3½ lb

Size of Cake	Royal Icing
13 cm/5 inch round	350 g/¾ lb
13 cm/5 inch square	350 g/¾ lb
15 cm/6 inch round	450 g/1 lb
15 cm/6 inch square	450 g/1 lb
18 cm/7 inch round	450 g/1 lb
18 cm/7 inch square	675 g/1½ lb
20 cm/8 inch round	800 g/1¾ lb
20 cm/8 inch square	900 g/2 lb
23 cm/9 inch round	900 g/2 lb
23 cm/9 inch square	1 kg/2¼ lb
25 cm/10 inch round	1 kg/2¼ lb
25 cm/10 inch square	1.25 kg/2½ lb
28 cm/11 inch round	1.25 kg/2¾ lb
28 cm/11 inch square	1.5 kg/3 lb
30 cm/12 inch round	1.5 kg/3¼ lb
30 cm/12 inch square	1.5 kg/3½ lb
33 cm/13 inch round	1.75 kg/3¾ lb
33 cm/13 inch square	1.75 kg/4 lb

WEIGHTS AND MEASURES

It is essential that the quantities of ingredients required for any recipe should be measured and at Good Housekeeping Institute we consider that

431

weighing is the most reliable method for all but the smallest quantities. In the recipes in this and other Good Housekeeping books, therefore, quantities are stated by weight wherever practical. With the changeover to metric, quantities are given in imperial and metric. It is important that only one or the other followed.

(See Metrication, Measures and American Measures entries.)

Handy Measures

If you have no scales or if you wish to measure out only a small weight of some ingredients, you can follow this table, using an average-sized tablespoon or 15 ml metric spoon.

25 g/1 oz (approx)	15 ml spoons/Tablespoonfuls
Breadcrumbs	3
Cheddar cheese, grated	3
Cocoa	3
Butter, margarine, lard, (soft enough to press into bowl of spoon)	2
Cornflour, custard powder	3
Flour, unsifted	3
Gelatine, powdered	2½
Oatmeal, medium	2½
Oats, rolled	3½
Rice	2
Semolina, ground rice	2½
Sugar (granulated)	2
Syrup, treacle	1½
Sultanas, currants	2
Salt	1¾
Ground almonds	3½

WELSH ONION

A plant with a leek-like bulb and tubular leaves. It is hardy and easy to grow and pieces may be broken off as required without disturbing the main plant. It is used like onion or leek for flavouring.

WELSH RAREBIT

Melted cheese on toast. Welsh rarebits are often served as a savoury and when eaten with tomatoes or similar vegetable they can make a nourishing main course for a light meal.

WELSH RAREBIT

METRIC/IMPERIAL
225 g/8 oz Cheddar cheese, grated
25 g/1 oz butter
1 × 5 ml spoon/1 teaspoon dry mustard
salt
pepper
4 × 15 ml spoons/4 tablespoons brown ale
toast

Place all the ingredients in a thick-based pan and heat very gently until a creamy mixture is obtained. Pour over the toast and put under a hot grill until golden and bubbling.

Serve with grilled tomatoes and watercress garnish.

BUCK RAREBIT

This is Welsh rarebit topped with a poached egg.
Serve as for Welsh rarebit.

WENSLEYDALE CHEESE

It is generally thought that the recipe for Wensleydale cheese originated from the one made by monks of the Jervaulx Abbey in Yorkshire during the eleventh century. At this time the cheese was made from ewes' milk, but it is now made from cows' milk; it is a white, mild cheese with a clean taste. It is ready to eat after being lightly pressed and matured for three weeks.

A small amount of blue Wensleydale is made but it is not easily available. It has an appearance very similar to blue Stilton and has a very strong flavour.

WHALE OIL

Oil extracted from the whale. At one time it was much used in the manufacture of oils and margarine, but it is now rarely used.

WHEAT

The grain that is grown in most parts of the world to provide flour for human consumption and also to some extent for use in cattle-feeding and in manufacturing processes.

There are two main groups of wheat, hard wheat which is rich in gluten and soft wheat which is richer in starch. The two varieties are blended according to availability and requirement.

The nutritional value of wheat is similar to that of barley, oats and rye, though it varies somewhat with different varieties and in different climates. Although the protein of wheat is not so valuable as animal protein, it is nevertheless a body-building food and 0.5 kg/1 lb of bread contains about a third of the daily protein requirements; wheat products also contain varying amounts of B vitamins, calcium and iron.

(See Bread and Flour entries.)

Wheat Germ
The part of the grain that actually gives rise to the new plant; it is a rich source of vitamins of the B group. The germ is largely removed during the milling of white flour, but it can be obtained as a commercial preparation and eaten sprinkled on cereals, yogurt etc.

WHEATMEAL

(See Flour and Bread entries.)

WHELK

A small fish with a conical twisted shell. Whelks are cooked and eaten like winkles.

WHEY

The watery liquid which separates from the curd when milk is clotted, as during the making of cheese. It contains lactose, a trace of easily digested protein (lactalbumin) and calcium.

Whey is little used in human diet, but can be fed to pigs.

WHIPPING, WHISKING

The process of beating egg whites, cream, etc., until thick and stiff. A whisk of some kind is usually employed, though some people prefer a fork. An electric mixer may also be used – follow the manufacturers' directions.

WHISKY, WHISKEY

The alcoholic spirit distilled from the fermented grain of cereals, chiefly barley, rye and maize. The best known type is distilled in Scotland, but whisky is also made in Ireland (where the spelling whiskey is preferred). The Canadian and American types are made from rye or maize. Liqueur whiskies are good quality spirits well matured, while Drambuie is a liqueur made from Scotch whisky and heather honey.

The quality of whisky depends on the grain used, the process followed in its manufacture, the time allowed for maturing and the blending. Distillers usually aim at achieving by blending a more or less standard spirit, so that people will know what to expect when they ask for a certain brand.

Whisky is drunk neat or with water or soda water; rye whisky is often drunk with ginger ale.

The quantity of water, soda or ginger ale added depends, of course, on personal taste. Whisky is also used as a basis of some mixed drinks such as Manhattan Cocktail, etc. (See Cocktail entry.) Whisky Sling is made by adding 200 ml/⅓ pint boiling water to 150 ml/¼ pint whisky and sprinkling a little grated nutmeg on top.

WHITE PUDDING

In different parts of the country and at different times this name has been applied to a variety of farmhouse sausages. Probably the commonest type is made at pig-killing time from the cooked brain, tongue, lights, heart, kidneys, etc., mixed with cooked pearl barley or oatmeal (or breadcrumbs), seasoned and flavoured to taste. The puddings are fried and eaten hot.

WHITE WINE

(See Wine entry.)

WHITE WINE CUP

METRIC/IMPERIAL
crushed ice
3 bottles white wine
¾ bottle dry sherry
4 × 15 ml spoons/4 tablespoons curaçao
4 'splits' tonic water
3 slices of cucumber, a slice of apple and a sprig of borage per jug

Mix all the ingredients together in one or more jugs and chill before serving. Makes about 3.5 litres/6½ pints.

WHITEBAIT

These tiny silvery fish, the young of the herring and the sprat, are in season from March to early September. Whitebait are served fried, accompanied by lemon and brown bread and butter. Being cooked in fat, they are a good source of energy and vitamin D is probably present in an appreciable amount; as the bones are eaten, whitebait also forms an excellent source of calcium. The fish must be eaten very fresh.

Wash the fish well, dry in a cloth and toss them in seasoned flour; heat some deep fat until a blue smoke rises. Put the whitebait into a frying basket, adding a few at a time to avoid lowering the temperature of the fat, and fry for 2 to 3 minutes, then drain well. When all the whitebait have been fried, return them to the basket (which can be filled up this time) and fry quickly for 3 minutes, to make them crisp. Drain well, sprinkle with salt and serve at once. Lemon wedges are usually served with whitebait.

WHITING

A fish about 25 cm/10 inches in length, with a grey back and silver underside. It is sometimes mistaken for a small haddock, but can be distinguished by the fact that it has no dark marks on the back. It is in season from March to August. As whiting does not possess a great deal of flavour, it needs to be accompanied by a good sauce, though when in prime condition it can be fried and simply served with lemon. Whiting is an easily digested fish and is therefore useful for those on light diets. It has a good protein content and supplies some vitamin D.

Preparation: Trim fins and tail and remove the guts

433

by slitting along the belly of the fish. Remove the eyes if the head is to be kept on, or else remove the entire head. Skin as described under Fish.

BAKED WHITING

Prepare the fish, removing the heads, and arrange in a fireproof dish, head to tail. Pour over some milk, milk and fish stock or white wine, season and sprinkle in 1×5 ml spoon/1 teaspoon herbs. Bake in a moderate oven (180°C/350°F, Gas Mark 4) for 20 minutes. Make an egg, shrimp, tomato anchovy or hollandaise sauce with the liquid; this sauce may be poured over the fish, if they have been skinned; otherwise serve it separately.

FRIED WHITING

Prepare and skin the whiting, then pull the tail through the eye sockets. Coat with egg and bread-crumbs and fry in a frying basket in hot fat (see Frying entry); handle carefully, as whiting breaks easily. Serve with fried parsley and lemon slices and serve hollandaise, shrimp or anchovy sauce separately.

WHOLEMEAL

(See Flour and Bread entries.)

WIDGEON

A small bird of the wild duck family, in season from 1st September to 28th February. It is plucked, drawn and trussed like a duck, but is cooked for only about 20 to 25 minutes in a hot oven (220°C/425°F, Gas Mark 7). Widgeon should be served with a rich gravy flavoured with red-currant jelly or port wine. Carve as for game. Orange salad, watercress and lemon should be served as accompaniments.

WIENER SCHNITZEL

(See Veal entry.)

WILD BOAR

The flesh of the young animal, up to one year of age, is considered excellent, and in countries on the Continent where boars are hunted a number of recipes have been evolved. The meat needs to be marinated first and can then be cooked like pork.

WILD DUCK

There are many varieties of wild duck but those mostly eaten in this country are mallard, widgeon, pintail and teal. The permitted time for shooting is between 1st September and 31st January and some-

times until 20th February.

The widgeon is said to have the best flavour but opinions differ. This bird feeds on short, sweet grass and keeps away from the sea. It is at its best in October and November whereas the mallard is best in November and December. The pintail is widely found in Britain and Western Europe, but is considered inferior to widgeon. Teal is the bird most commonly seen in shops and is at its best just before Christmas.

Wild duck has a fishy flavour which can be unpleasant. This can be reduced by marinating the bird in a strong liquid after being rubbed inside and out with a half lemon dipped in salt; or by placing a raw potato, and onion or apple inside the body during cooking.

The wild duck is lean, unlike the domesticated duck, therefore slices of fat should be used to bard it during cooking. The flavour is improved by the addition of red wine in basting and slight under-cooking; this also makes the meat more tender. The flavour is again improved by flaming with gin, whisky or brandy. It is important that wild duck is cooked within twenty-four hours of shooting, unless it has been bled, as it is likely to produce poisonous bacteria.

Wild duck is suitable for roasting.

WINE

The product of the alcoholic fermentation of fresh or dried grapes (raisins) or grape juice. There are also other types of wine made from fruits, vegetables and flowers.

The yeasts which are present on the skins of the grapes convert the glucose (grape sugar) into alcohol and carbon dioxide (the latter produces the bubbles during the fermentation). The length of the fermentation period varies – a short fermentation of 4 to 5 days gives a finer wine, more delicate in flavour; a longer period of 10 to 15 days gives a stronger, darker wine. After the first wine is drawn off, the residue can be pressed to produce slightly less alcoholic wines – called wines of the second (or third) pressing.

Dry wines are made by allowing complete fermentation leaving very little sugar; to make a sweet wine fermentation is halted to retain more natural sugar. However, for some of the poorer sweet wines sugar or sweet wine concentrate is added. The best sweet wines are made from over-ripe grapes containing sweet juice which kills the yeast before fermentation is complete.

Wine is produced from both white and black grapes, but more usually from the black ones. The skins of black grapes, if left in during the fermentation, turn the wine red; if the skins are removed at an early stage the wine is a rose or pink. White wine is made from the juice only of white or black grapes.

The flavour of the wine depends on the species of grape, the weather and the soil they are grown in and also on the degree and method of fermentation.

Wine is produced in many countries, but the best known exporting regions are France, Spain, Germany, Italy, Portugal, the Balkan countries, Algeria, Australia and South Africa.

Grapes

GAMAY
Makes first class wine when grown on granite; used in Beaujolais and also in California to make rosé.

SEMILLON
This grape rots in warmth and humidity, producing luscious wines; it is used extensively in Australia.

CHENIN BLANC
Used to make Vouvray and other wines from Anjou and Touraine. It ages well because of a high acid content. Successful in California.

RIESLING
The classic German grape which is also planted in Australia, South Africa, Chile and California.

CHARDONNAY
The grape of white burgundy and champagne. It gives a firm, full, strong wine; also used in Bulgaria and northern California.

MUSCAT
Either black or white grapes used to make a sweet wine (except in Alsace and Bulgaria). Muscat wines are made all over the world.

PINOT NOIR
The grape of the Côte d'Or, used to make champagne. The best red wine grape.

GRENACHE
A sweet grape, usually blended with others. It is used for dessert wines.

CABERNET SAUVIGNON
A small tough grape which gives distinction to the wines of Bordeaux. It is often blended.

SAUVIGNON BLANC
The chief white grape of Bordeaux. It makes a clean, light wine or it can be blended.

Some of the best known wines are as follows:

French Wines

BORDEAUX, RED
Claret is the greatest red wine in the world, comparable only to red Burgundy and available in much larger quantities. The four chief districts in France where these wines are produced are Médoc, St. Émilion, Graves, Entre-deux-Mers and Pomerol.

BORDEAUX, WHITE
The chief types are called after the regions, Graves (although the white Graves are not so good as the red); Sauternes (excellent sweet white wines) and Entre-deux-Mers (not so distinguished as the other two).

(See Bordeaux Wine entry.)

BURGUNDY, RED
This is made in a small strip of land called the Côte d'Or. The wine is slightly sweeter than claret.

BURGUNDY, WHITE
These districts produce wines named after them: Meursault and Montrachet, Chablis and Pouilly-Fuissé. Meursault and Montrachet are supposed to be the best white Burgundies. Chablis is the driest in flavour. Pouilly-Fuissé is the most plentiful and therefore the cheapest.

BEAUJOLAIS
A red wine, produced on the fringe of the Burgundy district; it has not the highly esteemed reputation of Burgundy or Bordeaux and is therefore much cheaper.

RHONE, LOIRE AND ALSACE
These regions also produce various wines, some of them very good but without the reputation of the foregoing.

CHAMPAGNE
Comes from the Champagne district between Rheims and Epernay. A secondary fermentation takes place in the bottle, forming carbon dioxide which dissolves in the wine. A sediment also forms, which is removed very carefully with the cork. A dose of sweetened wine is added, a new cork inserted and wired down. All this takes place about five years after the wine was started.

In all good wine countries other sparkling wines can be made by the *Méthode Champenoise*, but the makers are not allowed to use the name 'Champagne.'

Italian Wines
Chianti, in the wickered bottles, is the best known. Both red and white types are produced. There are also Barolo (which is perhaps the finest Italian Wine), Valpolicella, Orvieto, Soave and many others.

Spanish Wines
Spain is generally known for its sherry, but there are many other good Spanish wines, perhaps the best known being Rioja. Spanish wines are suitable for drinking and cooking and are available at a comparatively low price. Sherry is a non-vintage wine, fortified with brandy. It improves with age. The two basic types are Fino, pale and dry, and Oloroso, darker and mixed with a sweeter wine.

(See Sherry entry.)

German Wines

Hock is a general name covering the Rhine wines, including the districts Rheingau, Rheinhesse, Palatinate and Nahe. They are generally good wines and the labelling regulations are strict. Liebfraumilch is a name that can be applied to almost any German wine. It usually indicates a medium dry Rhineland wine.

Moselle is produced along the Moselle valley. It has a pleasant, fresh taste and a low alcoholic strength which makes it an attractive, refreshing drink for the summer and as part of a wine cup or punch.

Miscellaneous

VERMOUTH
A popular apéritif made in France and Italy; it is a non-vintage wine blended from three or four types, slightly fortified with brandy and finally flavoured with herbs. The fortifying gives it a strength of about 30° which is not much less than that of sherry and port.

PORT
Made in Portugal, up the river from Oporto. It is a fortified wine, like sherry. (See Sherry entry.)

Choice of Wine

This depends very much on personal tastes, of course, but certain major rules will prove helpful.

Before a meal: Serve dry sherry, Dubonnet, chilled Champagne.

With appetizers: Serve white Moselle, Alsace, Chablis or Graves.

With soup: Serve dry sherry or Madeira.

With fish, veal, chicken, turkey (i.e., white meats): Serve a full white wine, chilled – e.g., white Burgundy, Hock.

With beef, lamb and mutton: A fairly light red wine such as Beaujolais or red Graves.

With duck, goose, pork and game: A fuller red wine such as Burgundy or Claret.

With sweets: Serve Sauternes, Champagne, Anjou or Palatinate Hock.

With cheese and dessert: A sweet or fuller sherry, port or Madeira.

With (or after) coffee: Serve brandy, liqueurs.

In these days it is unusual to serve different wines for each course. Often an apéritif is followed by sherry with the soup, a wine with the main dish and a liqueur with the coffee. A dry wine is best before rather than after a sweet wine and a light wine before a heavier one.

Buying Wine

Always study the label: vintage wine bears a date and is expected to mature well, because it is the product of a year when climatic conditions were good and the wine is therefore of the best quality. Unfortunately, there is some bad wine made in vintage years but there is also some good wine in non-vintage years, so the date serves only as a general guide to the buyer. Furthermore, even a superb wine can be ruined by bad storage, too much shaking in transit, bad bottling, etc. The only safe course, therefore is to deal with a trustworthy merchant.

However, here is a guide to recent vintage years:

RED BORDEAUX (CLARET)
1973, 1971, 1970, 1969, 1967, 1966, 1964, 1962, 1961, 1960, 1959.

WHITE BORDEAUX
1971, 1970, 1969, 1967, 1966, 1962, 1961, 1959.

RED BURGUNDY
1974, 1972, 1971, 1970, 1969, 1966, 1964, 1962, 1961, 1959.

ALSACE
1971, 1970, 1969, 1967, 1966, 1964, 1961.

RHONE
1973, 1972, 1971, 1970, 1969, 1967, 1966, 1965, 1962, 1961, 1959.

MOSEL
1973, 1971, 1969, 1967, 1966, 1964.

HOCK
1971, 1970, 1969, 1967, 1966, 1964.

CHAMPAGNE
1969, 1967, 1966, 1964, 1962, 1961.

PORT
1972, 1970, 1967, 1966, 1963, 1960, 1958, 1955, 1950, 1948, 1945.

Cheaper Wines

Here is a guideline to some of the cheaper wines available. These can often be purchased in larger bottle or flagons.

RED	
Light Claret	Médoc
Full Claret	Algerian red
Soft Burgundy	Beaujolais or Cyprus red
Full Burgundy	Spanish Burgundy
ROSÉ	
Dry	Anjou Rosé
Medium	Bordeaux or Portuguese Rosé
WHITE	
Light dry	Alsatian Sylvaner
Full Dry	Mâcon Blanc
Medium Dry	Jugoslav Riesling
	Entre-deux-Mers
	Cyprus white
Medium Sweet	Premières Côtes de Bordeaux
	Spanish Sauternes

Storage of Wine

Wine should be stored in a dry, dark cellar or cupboard at a constant temperature, with the bottles lying on their sides – this keeps the corks damp so that they do not shrink and let in air. The bottles should be rested on shelves or racks, so that they need not be disturbed as movement does not improve the wine.

Serving Wine

It is important to serve wine at the correct temperature or the individual characteristics will be lost. Red wine should be served at about 18°C/65°F (Cambré). At this temperature it will become aromatic, but if allowed to become warmer the alcohol will start to vaporize. Red wine should be left to stand in a warm room for several hours before serving rather than be subjected to heat.

It is easier to serve white or rosé wines perfectly as they usually only require refrigeration for one hour. A quicker method is to place the bottle in a bucket of cold water and ice. The ideal temperature for serving white wine is 8°C/45°F to 10°C/50°F; at this temperature it has a scent and piquancy. The wine should not be allowed to become icy or frozen as flavour will be lost.

Wine is often decanted before serving; this is important with old wines containing sediment, but younger wines can also benefit. Once in a decanter the oxygen helps to develop the scent and flavour of a young wine. Wines are sometimes decanted for aesthetic reasons.

The wine glasses should be carefully chosen, for they can add greatly to the enjoyment of good wine by enabling one to appreciate its colour and bouquet. Connoisseurs usually prefer colourless glasses although coloured stems may enhance the colour of the wine. Many different shapes in various sizes are made for serving different wines, but the more usual ones are shown in the list below; it is unusual nowadays to have a large number of wine glasses.

Sherry: A fairly small, long-sided glass
Burgundy, Claret and white wines: A large, bowl-shaped glass.
Hock and Moselle: A long-stemmed glass with a fairly small cup-shaped bowl. Hock glasses usually have tinted stems.
Champagne and sparkling wines: A fairly large tulip-shaped glass or a tall thin 'flute' is favoured.
Port: A glass similar to that used for sherry but larger.
Brandy and liqueurs: A small glass although it has become fashionable to serve brandy in a bowl-shaped glass.

WINE VINEGAR

(See Vinegar entry.)

Home wine-making is becoming increasingly popular. Most people probably make wine because it is cheaper than buying it, but it is also a creative hobby. It can be linked with growing fruits and vegetables to use as a base for wines; or for those who live in the country, flowers and wild fruits can be picked while out walking.

There are many books and magazines giving information about home wine-making; also courses and practical instruction are held in many areas around the country. There are also wine clubs and circles where people can discuss and learn more about their hobby.

When first starting wine-making it is best to begin with just one or two wines for the first year, making them in half-gallon or gallon quantities, (2.4 or 4.5 litre). (The half-gallon amount is ideal for trying out a new recipe.)

Most wines will take up to one year to reach maturity, so any sampling done after the first month or so may not be pleasant. When the wines are ready for drinking, treat them with respect – while they do not usually exceed 14 per cent (by volume) of alcohol, they have a definite 'kick' and should not be taken in unlimited quantities.

If repeating a recipe, remember that the acid and sugar content of fruit can vary from year to year, according to climatic conditions, so the results may not be identical. Homemade wine cannot be sold without complying with the Excise laws.

The Ingredients

FRUITS AND VEGETABLES

Fruits used for wine-making must be as perfect and freshly gathered as possible, ripe but not over-ripe. The exception is windfall apples which even if bruised can be used for cider. Grape concentrates can be bought with instructions how to make various types of alcoholic wines. Canned or pulped fruits, jams, jellies and juices can also be used for making wine. Vegetables should be sound, but root ones such as beet and parsnip should be 'old' and mature, since the older roots contain less starch – a high proportion of this tends to slow down the clearing process and give the wine a slightly earthy flavour. Flowers should be fresh and gathered when dry.

Preparation: Use a stainless steel knife for cutting up. Fruit is often crushed, while root vegetables are cooked beforehand, and the strained juice used. As a rule, fruit and flowers are placed in a large container and hot or cold water (according to the recipe) is poured over. (See individual recipes.)

YEAST

This is the most important ingredient in making wine. There are thousands of different varieties of yeast but the type best used in wine making is

437

called saccharomyces elipsoideus as it is elliptical in shape. It is best not to use bakers' yeast in wine making but to choose a good wine yeast for the following reasons:

1. Wine yeast gives the wine a good flavour.
2. After fermentation wine yeast sinks to the bottom of the jar and packs closely together, allowing the clear wine to be easily syphoned off.
3. The yeast can resist a higher concentration of sulphur dioxide (used for sterilizing wine).
4. Wine yeast only needs oxygen for reproduction unlike most moulds and fungi which require air.
5. Wine yeast can tolerate higher levels of alcohol than other yeasts.

General purpose wine yeasts are available from specialist wine shops and chemists with a home-brewing section.

NUTRIENT
An additional food, in the form of nitrogen, for the yeast. It enables the yeast to develop well and creates enzymes to cause fermentation. Nutrient can be added in crystal or tablet form.

SUGAR
Granulated sugar is the most suitable for wine-making as it is easiest to handle and cheapest to buy. Sugar is a combination of fructose and glucose, but before fermentation can begin they have to be split; this is usually done by an enzyme secreted by the yeast; boiling the sugar with an acid has the same effect. 1 kg/2 lb sugar can be boiled in 600 ml/1 pint water and 1 × 5 ml spoon/1 teaspoon citric acid for twenty minutes to give 1.2 litres/ 2 pints inverted (split) sugar.

Sometimes all the sugar in a recipe is added at once, but this may result in a too sweet wine if the yeast is killed before sufficient alcohol has been produced. Therefore it is advisable to add a little at a time and use a hydrometer to measure the sugar level. (See note on hydrometer.) More alcohol is usually produced by using this method.

Brown sugars can be used in strong-flavoured red wines but as they tend to give a caramel flavour they are not suitable for delicate light white wines.

ACID
This is required by the yeast to help it thrive and develop within the wine. Some fruits used in wine making are rich in acid, therefore no addition is necessary. The commonest acids used in wine making are:

Citric Acid: found in oranges, lemons, etc. (aids rapid fermentation).

Tartaric Acid: found in grapes (reduces acidity in wine).

Malic Acid: found in apples (aids flavour).

The type of wine being made determines the acid used but it is sometimes a good idea to add a blend of all three.

TANNIN
This is found naturally in grape skins, stones and stalks; also in pear, apple, elderberry, damson, plum and blackberry skins. Tannin gives a bite to wine and should be added if the must does not contain it. To 4.5 litres/1 gallon add 1 × 2.5 ml spoon/ ½ teaspoon grape tannin powder. As tannin is found in tea some recipes include it as an ingredient.

PECTOLASE
An enzyme which destroys pectin contained in the fruit. This improves the flavour and aids the extraction of juice. The enzyme is particularly important if stone fruits are used such as apricot, peach or plum. It should be added before the sugar and is most effective in a warm must. For 4.5 litres/1 gallon add 1 × 5 ml spoon/1 teaspoon pectolase, except for fruits rich in pectin when 1 × 15 ml spoon/1 tablespoon is required.

SULPHITE
Used in the form of sodium metabisulphite or Camden tablets to prevent the growth of bacteria and moulds in the must and finished wine. Sulphite is also used as an anti-oxidant with fruit that goes brown through oxidation. As the fruit is cut it is placed in a sulphite solution which prevents discolouring and helps to preserve the flavour.

Sulphite can also be used to correct some of the wine ailments.

The Equipment
The equipment for wine-making can be bought from specialist wine shops, some chemists and some of the larger supermarkets. It is not necessary to have everything in the following list but with experience the range can be increased. The items are listed in the order they are used.

1. Plastic bucket with a lid (9 litre/2 gallon is the smallest to consider). Larger plastic dustbins can also be used. Alternatives are a large earthenware crock that has been glazed or an oak tub. However, these are heavy and the tub is difficult to keep clean.
2. Fruit crusher: This is only necessary if wines are frequently made from fresh fruits. A piece of oak or boxwood on a long handle can be used.
3. Fruit press: This is only really necessary for large quantities of fruit. A juice extractor makes a useful alternative. For small quantities a nylon straining bag can be used once the fruit has softened in liquid.
4. Plastic funnels: 12.5 cm/5 inch diameter for filling jars and 6 cm/2 ½ inch diameter for filling bottles.
5. Hydrometer: Essential for the keen wine-maker; very useful for controlling the sweetness and content of wine. A trial jar is useful but a milk bottle can be used if carefully sterilized.

6. Fermentation jars: 4.5 litre/1 gallon glass demijohns are widely available from chemists and specialist shops.

7. Air locks and bored corks: These should fit the top of the jars. Although glass airlocks show the activity of the fermentation best they break easily. The plastic airlocks are just as effective and cost less. A plug of cotton wool can be used if there are no airlocks available.

8. Syphon: A rubber or plastic tube.

9. Storage jars: Glass demijohns can be used. Earthenware jars have the advantage of keeping out the light and help to stabilize the temperature.

Old wine casks can be used for larger quantities of wine (never use vinegar casks). High density polythene vessels are only suitable for short periods.

10. Wine bottles: Old wine bottles can be collected or bottles can be bought from wine departments. Never use spirit bottles or screw top bottles as they are thin and dangerous. Furthermore they do not look right for wine.

11. Bottle brush: This is useful to clean bottles and jars thoroughly.

12. Wine corks: Straight ones are better than cork stoppers as they are longer. This enables the bottles to be stored on their sides which keeps the corks more moist and tight fitting.

13. Hand corking machine: This is useful for straight corks.

14. Elastic or foil bottle caps: These give the wine a professional appearance.

15. Wine labels: These are important for giving information about the wine such as the content and the date. The labels also improve the appearance of the bottles.

16. Wine rack: This is useful, as it enables wine to be stored correctly on its side.

STERILIZING EQUIPMENT
It is very important to keep all the equipment clean and sterile. Sulphite is best used for this (also mentioned under ingredients), in the form of Campden tablets or sodium metabisulphite crystals.

Dissolve 1 Campden tablet and a few grains of citric acid in 600 ml/1 pint cold water. (Use 3 tablets if citric acid is omitted.) Sulphur dioxide is given off which acts as a sterilizing agent. Hot water should not be used as the gas will be released too quickly and not be effective. The equipment should be left in the solution for 6 minutes to kill all bacteria etc. It is still necessary to wash it beforehand.

Once sterilized the equipment should be rinsed thoroughly with cold water.

USE OF THE HYDROMETER
This is used to measure the weight of other liquids relative to the same volume of water. If a quantity of water contains sugar it will be heavier than plain water. The difference between the two is known as specific gravity. If water is read as 1.000 the specific gravity of other liquids can be calculated.

With tables, which are available in more detailed wine books, the amount of sugar required for a certain alcoholic content can be calculated.

Stages in Wine-making
These notes must be used in conjunction with the particular recipe. Specialist books are available for more detailed instruction.

1. Prepare the yeast as required. Yeast can be added to the must without preparation but fermentation will be quicker if it is activated first. This can be done by making a starter bottle.

For 4.5 litres/1 gallon wine, place 300 ml/½ pint tepid boiled water in a sterilized bottle or jar. Dissolve 25 g/1 oz sugar and ⅙ nutrient tablet in the liquid; add the juice of half an orange and the yeast. Shake the bottle and place a cotton wool bung in the top or cover with polythene. Leave in a warm place for up to 48 hours.

2. Prepare the fruit or other main ingredients, then weigh or measure and cover with water or cook as required. If a Campden tablet is to be used, add it to the unfermented mixture (often called 'must') at this stage. Pectolase, tannin acid and nutrient can be added at this stage. Cover and leave for the required time; do not store near anything strong smelling.

3. Add the sugar (or part of it). Add the yeast and leave to ferment on the pulp.

4. Strain off the juice using a nylon bag; pour the mixture through a sterilized funnel into the fermentation jar or other containers, filling it up to the top. (If more sugar is to be added, leave a gap.) Insert a bung and leave till the frothing subsides, then take out the bung and insert a sterilized cork, complete with airlock, pressing down well. Label with content and date.

5. Leave the wine to ferment in a fairly warm place at a temperature of approx. 16°C/60°F to 18°C/65°F. If the room temperature is too low, put the brew in an airing cupboard or greenhouse, but take care not to overheat it. The fermentation may continue for up to six months.

6. When fermentation appears to be complete, that is when bubbles cease to rise, give the jar a twist to see if any more bubbles appear, then leave the brew to rest for a further few days.

Alternatively test with a hydrometer.

7. Rack (syphon) off the wine into a clean demijohn leaving the sediment behind. Cork lightly and leave for two months. Rack again and leave for four months before syphoning into individual wine bottles; cork, seal and label.

8. Leave the wine to mature. If possible, put the bottles on slats or in a wine rack which will allow the air to circulate around them; they should be laid on their sides so that the corks remain moist and airtight. Store at about 10°C/50°F. The usual time

is six to nine months. Never lie bottles on their sides if there is any indication that fermentation has not stopped.

Blending Wine

You can get some interesting and often delicious results by blending two or more homemade wines; the process is also helpful if you find that one particular wine is too sweet, for this can be offset by blending it with a dry one.

The wines must be fully matured and in the bottled state. Decide which one you wish to predominate, take about half a tumbler of this, then add the other wine (or wines) gently, by the 5 ml spoonful/teaspoonful, until you get a flavour that really pleases you. Note the proportions, so that you can repeat the effect on a larger scale.

MAKING SPARKLING WINES

Sweet sparkling wines can be rather tricky for beginners and require fuller instructions than can be given here.

For dry sparkling wines, follow any desired recipe for still wine, then add champagne yeast and syrup before racking into clean champagne bottles.

Use strong wine bottles with hollow bases, and 'champagne corks'.

General Notes for Wine-making

1. All equipment, especially straining cloths and fermenting vessels, must be carefully sterilized; this is best done just before the ingredients are ready for straining; bottles for the final bottling should be done shortly before use.
2. The brew must be kept closely covered before and during fermentation to prevent any airborne contamination – fruit flies, for instance, can turn the wine to vinegar. Failing lidded vessels, place a rack across and cover this with sterilized muslin or sheet polythene.
3. The brew must be kept at a constant temperature.
4. Label each brew at every stage.
5. Do not be impatient – generally speaking, a wine should mature for a year.
6. All the following recipes are based on the general method and are intended for use with a 4.5 litre/1 gallon fermenting jar. (If you have any surplus liquid, it may be kept for topping up if required – store it in a small bottle stoppered with cotton wool.)

ELDERFLOWER OR DANDELION WINE

METRIC/IMPERIAL
1.2 litres/2 pints elderflower florets or 4.5 litres/
1 gallon dandelion heads.
2 oranges
1 lemon
4 cloves or 2 pieces root ginger

4.5 litres/1 gallon boiling water
1.5 kg/3 ½ lb Demerara or granulated sugar
25 g/1 oz fresh baker's yeast or 1 tablet wine yeast
450 g/1 lb raisins, scalded and chopped

Collect the blooms when fully open but not turning brown. (A large polythene bag is ideal for putting them in whilst picking.) Shake the elderflower florets into a bowl and measure, tightly packed, or strip the dandelion flower petals from the green calyx. Put in a polythene bucket or polythene bowl, add the fruit juices and spice, pour the boiling water over and leave for 3 days, stirring each day. Follow Stages in Wine-making, stages 3 to 8, adding prepared raisins to the liquid in the fermentation jar.

WHITE GRAPE WINE

METRIC/IMPERIAL
2.25 kg/5 lb seedless grapes
4.5 litres/1 gallon water
1.25 kg/2 ½ lb white sugar

Strip the grapes from their stalks and leaves, crush them, cover with hot boiled water and leave for 4 to 5 days. Follow the Stages in Wine-making guide through stages 3 to 8 inclusive.

RED GRAPE WINE

METRIC/IMPERIAL
2.75 kg/6 lb black grapes
4.5 litres/1 gallon cold water
1.5 kg/3 lb white sugar

Remove the stalks and any faulty grapes, then mash the rest with your hands or use a wooden spatula or other suitable instrument, but do not crush the pips, as they contain an oil which would spoil the wine. Cover the fruit with cold water and add 450 g/1 lb sugar. Cover and leave for 8 days, stirring daily. Add the rest of the sugar, then, still keeping the mash covered, allow it to ferment on the skins for a further 10 days, stirring daily. Strain. Follow the Stages in Wine-making guide, stages 5 to 8 inclusive.

PEACH WINE

METRIC/IMPERIAL
2.25 kg/5 lb yellow peaches
1.25 kg/2 ½ lb granulated sugar
4.5 litres/1 gallon boiling water
1 lemon
2 oranges
1 tablet wine yeast

Halve and stone the peaches, then cut in quarters. Put the fruit in a polythene bucket or bowl with the sugar and cover with boiling water. Thinly peel the rind off the lemon and the oranges (do not include the pith); squeeze out the juice and discard the 'caps'. Add the peel and juice to the peaches, cover and leave for 3 days, stirring each day. Add the prepared yeast, then cover and leave to ferment on the fruit for 1 week, stirring occasionally. Follow the Stages in Wine-making guide stages 3 to 8.

RHUBARB WINE

METRIC/IMPERIAL
2.25 kg/5 lb rhubarb stalks without leaves (picked in May)
4.5 litres/1 gallon cold boiled water
1.5 kg/3½ lb granulated sugar
15 g/½ oz baker's yeast or 1 tablet wine yeast.

Wipe the rhubarb, cut in pieces and crush with a wooden rolling-pin or mallet. Cover with water and leave covered for 4 days, stirring each day. Follow Stages in Wine-making, steps 3 to 8.

A port-type wine may be made later in the season. When blackberries are in season and fully ripe, measure 1.5 kg/3 lb put into a saucepan with 600 ml/1 pint water, bring to the boil and simmer till tender (about 10 minutes), then strain. Cool and add to the rhubarb wine, which by then will have reached the end of its fermentation stage. Store for 4 to 5 months before the final bottling. Cork loosely for the first two weeks after adding the blackberry juice.

WINKLE (PERIWINKLE)

A small black shellfish. To prepare winkles, wash them well in several waters to remove the sand and boil for 20 minutes in salted water.

WITCH

A kind of flounder caught in the Atlantic.

WOOD PIGEON

(See Pigeon entry.)

WOODCOCK

A small wild bird with mottled plumage, long bill and large eyes. The young birds are best and can be recognized by the fact that the feathers beneath the wing are like down, the spurs are short and round, the flight feathers are rounded and the feet supple. Woodcock are in season from October 1st (September 1st in Scotland) to January 31st and at their best from October to November.

Preparation and Roasting: Allow one bird per person. Woodcock should be plucked very carefully, as the skins are very tender. The head is left on and they are not drawn. Turn the head round, thrusting the beak through the legs and body. Arrange the birds on a trivet with bacon over the breasts, put a little dripping on each bird and place in a tin, each bird on a square of toast (which catches the trail). Roast in a moderately hot oven (190°C/375°F, Gas Mark 5) for 15 to 25 minutes. Serve on the toast, garnished with watercress and lemon. A rich brown gravy should be made in the roasting tin to serve with the birds.

WORCESTERSHIRE SAUCE

A proprietary piquant sauce, thin in consistency and spicy in flavour.

WORMWOOD

Name given to various wild plants that were used for medicinal tisanes, herb-flavoured liqueurs and absinth. Its use is now forbidden as it has been proved to cause blindness.

YAM

The fleshy edible tuber of a tropical climbing plant; it somewhat resembles a sweet potato. A starch product, similar to arrowroot, is extracted from the yam.

YEAST

A microscopic single-celled plant which grows rapidly in favourable conditions. There are many different varieties but all have similar characteristics and properties. As yeast grows it produces ferments which are capable of breaking down starch and sugars, converting them into carbon dioxide and alcohol. It is the production of carbon dioxide gas in bread making which causes the dough to rise, while the by-products that are formed during the working of the yeast ferments that give the bread its special flavour. A different type of yeast is used in beer and wine making. This has a higher alcoholic tolerance than other yeasts.

Carbohydrates, air, water and warmth, in suitable proportions, are all necessary for the rapid growth of yeast. A certain amount of sugar enables it to grow quickly, though too much shrinks the cells and prevents budding. Too much salt and fat also slow down the budding process. All liquids used for yeast mixtures should be lukewarm, as cold retards the growth, and excess heat kills the yeast plant. (This happens of course, when the bread is put in the oven, but by that time the yeast has done its work.)

Yeast is a source of all the B vitamins, and is sometimes prescribed medically, either in its natural form or as one of the manufactured yeast extracts.

Types of Yeast

MOIST, COMPRESSED
This is the yeast usually supplied by bakers and grocers and the type referred to in most English recipes. When it is fresh, yeast in this form cuts cleanly, but it keeps fresh for only 2 to 3 days, after which it crumbles easily, becomes darker in colour and has a stale smell. It is best to buy just enough yeast for immediate use, but if it has to be stored for a few days, keep in a paper bag wrapped in a damp cloth or place it, well wrapped up, in the refrigerator. It can, however, be stored in a freezer for up to one year.

BAKERS' YEAST, DRIED
This is a granular type sold in cans or packets. There are different varieties and the manufacturers' instructions should be followed. When using dried yeast in a recipe specifying fresh yeast, allow half the quantity of the dried type. To add it to the other ingredients, dissolve 1×5 ml spoon/1 teaspoon sugar in a cup of liquid taken from the amount stated in the recipe; it should be warm (43°C/110°F); sprinkle the dried yeast on top, leave in a warm place for 10 minutes or until frothy, then mix with the dry ingredients and the remaining liquid to make a dough.

Dried yeast can also be obtained in tablet form for medical purposes.

BREWERS' YEAST
This semi-liquid yeast is not now commonly used, but it can sometimes be bought from the brewers. 150 ml/¼ pint of good strong yeast or 200 ml/⅓ pint of a weaker type will raise 3 kg/7 lb of flour; 2×15 ml spoons/2 tablespoons brewers' yeast are equivalent to 25 g/1 oz of compressed yeast. The yeast can be made stronger by adding 1×5 ml spoon/1 teaspoon sugar to 300 ml/½ pint of the liquid and leaving it for 3 to 4 hours. To 'de-bitter' the yeast before use, cover it with cold water and set it aside for a day, then pour off the water and the thick yeast will remain. Brewers' yeast is also available in dried form.

Quantities for Making Bread and Buns
The following table shows the amount of moist compressed yeast required to raise various quantities of flour:

15 g/½ oz yeast	0.5 kg/1 lb flour
25 g/1 oz yeast	1.5 kg/3½ lb flour
50 g/2 oz yeast	3 kg/7 lb flour
500 g/20 oz yeast	1 sack (127 kg/280 lb) flour

The above quantities apply to bread mixtures in

which no fat is used. For the enriched mixtures more yeast is required, since fat retards the growth of the yeast. With a rich bun type of mixture any extra sugar, fruit and fat are best added after the first proving, to give the yeast a better chance to grow, so producing a lighter dough. Sometimes a separate sponge is made using the yeast and some of the flour. This is left aside till it becomes full of bubbles and is then added to the rest of the ingredients.

RECIPES FOR USING YEAST
(See Bread, Bun and Roll entries.)

YEAST EXTRACT

This product, which is made by treating yeast with acid, is rich in the B vitamins.

Yeast extracts resemble meat extracts, with which they are often confused, the main difference being that they contain the nitrogenous substance called adenine, while the meat extracts contain the nitrogenous substances creatine and creatinine. They can be used to flavour soups, stews, etc., and as a sandwich spread.

YERBA MATÉ

A South American shrub, the leaves of which are dried and used to make a drink called Paraguay tea. The natives prepare it by putting the leaves in a hollowed out gourd and pouring on boiling water. A small tube, like a metal straw, is used to suck up the tea.

YOGURT

Yogurt is thought to have originated among the nomadic tribes of Eastern Europe. Traditionally it was a drink, made by allowing the natural milk flora to ferment the lactose (milk sugar) to lactic acid. A very sour yogurt results without refrigeration to limit acid production.

In this country yogurt is manufactured on a large scale under very strict hygienic conditions. Pasteurized milk is inoculated with a specific bacterial culture and incubated under controlled conditions to produce yogurt of the desired flavour and consistency.

Unless pasteurized after preparation, all yogurt contains 'live' bacteria which remain dormant when kept at a low temperature. If it is stored at room temperature or above, the bacteria become active and produce more acid which impairs the flavour of the yogurt. It also causes the yogurt to separate and the bacteria are eventually killed. Yogurt should therefore be kept under refrigeration and should not be purchased if the sell by date stamp on the lid has expired.

Manufacture of Yogurt

Yogurt is made from a skimmed milk base to which extra skimmed milk powder is added; this gives a total of 12 to 16 per cent milk solids.

The milk is pasteurized and cooked to 38°C/100°F, then inoculated with bacteria cultures, Lactobacillus bulgaricus and Streptococcus thermophilus. During incubation at 43°C/109°F some of the lactose is fermented to lactic acid. When the acidity reaches the point of precipitating the casein (milk protein) the yogurt is rapidly cooled to 4.5°C/40°F. If the yogurt is to be flavoured before packaging, fruit in the form of a syrup is added.

TYPES OF YOGURT

Fat free yogurt	contains less than 0.5 per cent milk fat
Low fat yogurt	contains maximum of 1.5 per cent milk fat

Ready frozen yogurts are available. A stabilizer may have been added to prevent separation on thawing, but usually there is sufficient sugar to prevent this happening.

Yogurt in the Diet

As it contains skimmed milk, yogurt has a very good food value. It is a good source of protein, due to the addition of extra milk solids, calcium and riboflavine. As most yogurt contains very little fat it does not supply much vitamin A and D; some brands of yogurt now have these vitamins added to make good the loss.

Yogurt is a very good food to take in place of milk which can be important if children will not drink the latter. Yogurt can also be given to babies once weaning commences.

Use of Yogurt

Most yogurt is eaten straight from the carton and sometimes with fruit, but it can be used in many recipes to give a refreshing piquant flavour.

Natural yogurt can be added to many savoury dishes such as chilled soups, cheese sauce, savoury flans, cheese scones, goulash, stroganoff, salad dressing; or made into a topping for savoury dishes by mixing 150 ml/5 fl oz yogurt with 1 egg (beaten).

Natural or fruit yogurts can be added to custards, rice puddings, blancmanges, jellies, fruit fools and cereals. Mix 1 carton of fruit yogurt with 150 ml/¼ pint cold milk to make a milk shake.

When adding yogurt to hot dishes it is important to add it towards the end of cooking and just heat through gently. If the liquid boils the yogurt will cause curdling and separation.

Making Yogurt at Home

There are several yogurt making appliances on the

443

1. Heat milk then blend yogurt and milk together. Place in a vacuum flask.

2. Turn into a basin and cool quickly in a second bowl containing cold water.

3. Flavour yogurt with sugar, honey, fruit syrups or fruits as desired.

market but it can quite easily be made in a large vacuum flask (a wide necked one is best).

1. Sterilize equipment to be used by immersing in boiling water or by using a commercial sterilizing solution. (Saucepan, spoons, small bowl, vacuum flask, thermometer.)

2. Heat 600 ml/1 pint sterilized or UHT milk to 43°C/110°F which is approximately blood heat. If pasteurized milk is used it should be boiled and cooled to this temperature.

3. Blend 1 × 15 ml spoon/1 tablespoon of fresh natural yogurt with a little of the milk in a bowl and mix into the remainder. Pour into the pre-warmed vacuum flask, seal and leave for seven hours.

4. Turn into a basin and cool the yogurt quickly by standing it in a bowl of cold water and whisking the yogurt.

5. Cover the basin and place in the refrigerator for four hours to allow the yogurt to thicken further.

6. The yogurt can be flavoured with sugar, honey, jam, fruit syrup or fruits as desired.

It will keep in a refrigerator for 4 to 5 days.

YORK HAM

(See Ham entry.)

YORKSHIRE PUDDING

A batter pudding traditionally eaten with roast beef. In Yorkshire it is usually served separately,

before the meat, accompanied by some of the hot beef gravy, but in much of the rest of the country the pudding is served with the meat. It may be cooked either in a separate tin, or round or under the joint. If preferred, the mixture can be made up as small individual puddings or popovers. (See Popover entry.)

Prepare the mixture as in Batter entry. Put 1 × 15 ml spoon/1 tablespoon dripping from the roast meat into a Yorkshire pudding tin or shallow fireproof dish. When it is really hot, pour in the batter and bake in a hot oven (220°C/425°F, Gas Mark 7) for about 40 minutes. Serve cut in squares, as an accompaniment to roast beef, etc.

YORKSHIRE RAREBIT

A Welsh rarebit topped with boiled bacon and an egg.

YUCCA

A plant grown in America. The fruit is roasted and the young stalks eaten like asparagus. (See Cassava entry.)

YULE LOG

A traditional Christmas cake, consisting of a Swiss roll filled and coated with chocolate and vanilla butter cream and decorated to represent a log of wood, using a fork to give the effect of bark.

ZABAGLIONE

An Italian sweet, a frothy mixture of wine (usually Marsala), egg yolks and sugar, beaten over a gentle heat until thick; it is served hot in glasses. The sauce called Sabayon (see Sabayon entry) is a variation of Zabaglione.

ZABAGLIONE

METRIC/IMPERIAL
6 egg yolks
50 g/2 oz caster sugar
5 × 15 ml spoons/5 tablespoons Marsala

Place beaten egg yolks, sugar, and Marsala in a deep basin over a pan of hot, but not boiling, water. Whisk continuously until thick and creamy. Pour at once into small glasses and serve immediately with macaroons or sponge fingers. If liked, a little fruit may be placed at the bottom of the glasses before adding the zabaglione mixture – pineapple goes particularly well.

ZAKUSKA

The Russian form of appetizer. It consists of many types of caviare, blinis (savoury pancakes), smoked sausages, cold meats, pickled fish and tvoroinki (cheese dumplings).

ZEST

The thin, oily outer skin of citrus fruits. In cookery, it means a thin shaving of orange or lemon peel or the coloured part of the peel, often rubbed off on to lumps of sugar

ZUCCHINI

Italian name for courgettes (see Courgette entry).

ZWIEBACK

A small type of rusk, usually bought ready-made, to serve with cocktails, sherry, etc.

COLOUR PLATES

DICTIONARY OF COOKING TERMS

(*Note:* A few entries, which needed to be treated at greater length, such as Baking Blind, Egg-and-Crumbing and Piping, are included in the main part of the Encyclopedia; see also the Menu Glossary which follows on page 451–455.)

Barding: To cover the breast of a bird with slices of fat before roasting it, to prevent the flesh from drying up.

Basting: To ladle hot fat (or liquid) over meat, poultry, etc., at intervals while it is baking or roasting, in order to improve the texture, flavour and appearance. A long-handled spoon is usually employed for the purpose.

Basting is not necessary for fatty joints, especially if the fat side can be placed uppermost.

Beating: To agitate an ingredient or a mixture by vigorously turning it over and over with an upward motion, in order to introduce air; a spoon, fork, whisk or electric mixer may be used.

To beat raw meat is to hit it briskly all over the surface with a rolling pin or something similar for the purpose of breaking down the fibres and making the meat more tender when cooked.

Binding: To add a liquid, egg or melted fat to a mixture to hold it together.

Blanching: To treat food with boiling water, in order to whiten it, to preserve its natural colour, to loosen its skin, to remove a flavour which is too acid, rank or otherwise too strong, or (in the case of vegetables which are to be bottled, etc.) to kill unwanted enzymes.

The two usual ways of blanching food are:
1. To plunge it into boiling water – use this method for tomatoes and nuts which are to be skinned and parsley which is to be dried.
2. To bring it to the boil in the water – used to whiten sweetbreads or veal or to reduce the saltiness of such things as pickled meat or kippers, before cooking them in a fresh lot of water or stock.

Blending: To mix flour, cornflour, rice flour and similar ground cereals to a smooth paste with a cold liquid (milk, water or stock), before a boiling liquid is added, in the preparation of soups, stews, puddings, gravies, etc., to prevent the cereal from forming lumps. Use a wooden spoon and add the liquid by degrees, stirring all the time. Experience will soon show the right amount of liquid to use – too little makes hard lumps which are almost impossible to disperse and too much causes smaller, softer lumps which are also difficult to smooth out.

Brining: To immerse food (mainly meat or fish which is to be pickled and vegetables which are to be preserved) in a salt-and-water solution: see Pickling entry.

Browning: To give a dish (usually already cooked) an appetizing golden-brown colour by placing it under the grill or in a hot oven for a short time.

Chining: To sever the rib bones from the backbone by sawing through the ribs close to the spine. Joints such as loin or neck of lamb, mutton, veal or pork are best chined, instead of merely being chopped through the backbone, as this makes them easier to carve into convenient-sized chops or cutlets.

Chopping: To divide food into very small pieces. The ingredient is placed on a chopping board and a very sharp knife is used with a quick up-and-down action.

Clarifying: To clear or purify. The term is used mainly to denote the freeing of fat from water, meat juices, salt, etc., so that it may be used for frying, pastry-making and so on.

The process of clearing jellies and consommés is also sometimes called clarifying.

See the Fats, Consommé and Jelly entries.

Coddling: A method of soft-boiling eggs. They are put into boiling water; the pan is then removed from the heat and allowed to stand with the eggs in it for 8 to 10 minutes.

Coring: To remove the central membranes, pips, etc., from apples, pears and so on, either by quartering the fruit and cutting out the core or by using a special apple-corer on the whole fruit. Also to remove the central membrane from kidneys.

Creaming: The beating together of fat and sugar to resemble whipped cream in colour and texture. This method of mixing is used for cakes and puddings with a high proportion of fat.

Put the fat and sugar into a bowl and mix them with a wooden spoon. (The bowl may be slightly warmed to make the process easier.) Now beat the fat and sugar hard until the mixture is light and creamy.

Notes: Caster sugar creams more easily than granulated. If the fat should oil through overheating, allow it to cool and then beat well. Do not cream mixtures until they are required – they will harden on standing. If using an electric mixer, follow the maker's instructions.

Crimping: This word has three meanings in cookery:

1. To slash a large fish at intervals to make it easier for the heat to penetrate the flesh.

2. To trim cucumber or similar foods in such a way that the slices appear to be "deckled."

3. To decorate the double edge of a pie or tart or the edge of shortbread by pinching it at regular intervals with the fingers, giving a fluted effect.

Cutting-and-Folding: Another name for folding-in – see Folding-in.

Cutting-in: To combine one ingredient (usually fat) with others, by means of a knife used with a repeated downward cutting motion.

Draining: The two main methods of removing surplus liquid or fat from foods are by means of a sieve or colander or by placing them on crumpled absorbent kitchen paper.

Drawing: See Poultry entry.

Dredging: The action of sprinkling food lightly and evenly with flour, sugar, etc. Fish and meat are often dredged with flour before frying, while cakes, biscuits, pancakes, etc., may be sprinkled with fine sugar to improve their appearance. A pierced container of metal or plastic (known as a dredger) is usually used.

Dressing Food: To prepare for cooking or serving in such a way that the food looks as attractive as possible. The term sometimes denotes a special method of preparation, as in dressed crab.

Dropping Consistency: The term used to describe the texture of a cake or pudding mixture before cooking. To test it, well fill a spoon with the mixture, hold the spoon on its side above a basin and count slowly – the mixture should drop in about 5 seconds without your having to jerk the spoon.

Filtering: To strain a liquid through a special fine filter, as when making coffee, or through a cloth, as when making jelly preserves.

Flamber: French term meaning to coat such foods as pancakes or Christmas pudding with a spirit, which is then ignited. The word also means to singe poultry before cooking – see Poultry entry.

Flouring: To dredge flour over the surface of a food in order to dry it or coat it for frying, or to sprinkle flour over a pastry board before use.

Folding-in (sometimes called Cutting-and-Folding): A method of combining a whisked mixture with other ingredients so that it retains its lightness; it is used for mixing meringues, soufflés and certain cake mixtures. A typical example is folding dry flour into a whisked sponge cake mixture. First sift the flour on top of the whisked mixture. Now, using a large metal spoon, take up a spoonful of the sponge mixture from the bottom of the bowl, drawing the spoon across the base, then fold it over the top, enclosing the dry flour in between. Repeat until all the flour is incorporated, occasionally cutting through the mixture with the spoon held at right angles to the direction of the folding.

Important points to remember are that the mixture must be folded very lightly and that it must not be agitated more than is absolutely necessary, because with every movement some of the air bubbles are broken down. It is not practicable to carry out this process using an electric mixer.

Frosting: A way of decorating the rim of a glass in which a cold drink is to be served. Coat the edge with whipped egg white, dip it into caster sugar and allow to dry.

For fruit decorated in a similar way, see the Frosted Fruit entry; for the cake icings called Frostings, see individual entry.

Frothing: To dredge the surface of roast joints and birds with flour and then baste them, in order to give an attractive brown finish.

Glaze: Anything used to give a glossy surface to a sweet or savoury food.

Grating: To shave foods such as cheese and vegetables into small shreds.

Foodstuffs to be grated must be firm and cheese should be first allowed to harden.

Food in grated form is often prescribed for invalids and babies, as it is more digestible; it is particularly important to serve it at once.

Some foodstuffs deteriorate in value when they are grated and thus exposed to the air, so such things as root vegetables for salads, etc., should be grated only just before serving.

Grinding: The process of reducing hard foodstuffs such as nuts and coffee beans to small particles by means of a food mill, grinder or electric liquidizer.

Gutting: To clean out the inside of a fish, removing all the entrails.

Hanging: See Meat, Poultry and Game entries.

Infusing: To extract the flavour from such things as spices by steeping them in a liquid, as when preparing milk to make Béchamel or bread sauce. Tea, coffee and lemonade are also infusions. The usual method of making an infusion is to pour on boiling liquid, cover and leave to stand in a warm place without further cooking or heating.

Kibbling: To grind or chop coarsely.

Kneading: The process used for combining a mixture which is too stiff to stir. Gather it into a ball and place on a board. If it is inclined to stick, first dust the board with flour; if the dough is of a soft type, flour the hands well. Pastry and scone doughs, etc., are kneaded lightly, the outside edges being brought into the centre of the mixture with the finger-tips. Bread dough, which must be kneaded to distribute the yeast and gas evenly throughout the mixture, needs firmer treatment. The easiest way to deal with it is to pull out the dough with the right hand, then fold it back over itself and push it away with the ball of the hand; give a quarter-turn and repeat the process.

Larding: To insert small strips of fat bacon into the flesh of game birds or meat before cooking, to prevent it from drying out when roasted. A special larding needle is used for the purpose.

Lukewarm: Moderately warm, i.e. about blood heat (approx. 38°C/100°F).

Masking: To cover or coat a cooked meat or similar dish with savoury jelly, glaze or sauce; also to coat the inside of a mould with jelly.

Melting: To convert a solid into liquid by gentle heating. Some foods, such as chocolate, need very careful handling and are best melted over warm water.

Mincing: To chop or cut into small pieces with a knife or, more commonly, in a mincing machine or electric mixer.

Mirepoix: A mixture of carrots, celery and onion, often including some ham or bacon, which are cut into large pieces, sautéed in fat and used as a bed on which to braise meat.

Mulling: To warm, spice and sweeten ale, cider or wine.

Parboiling: To part-boil. The food is boiled in the normal way, but for only half the time, until somewhat softened, and is then finished by some other method.

Parching: To brown in dry heat.

Paring: To peel or trim.

Paunching: To remove the entrails of rabbits, hares, etc. See Hare entry.

Planking: To cook (and usually to serve) meat or fish on a special wooden board. The plank should be of well-seasoned hardwood, oblong or oval in shape. It is heated in the oven, then oiled with olive oil or melted butter and the meat or fish is placed on it, dabbed with pieces of butter or bacon and cooked in a hot oven or under a grill (provided it can be placed at a safe distance from the heat).

Poaching: To simmer a food such as fish very gently in milk, water or other liquid. See Fish and Egg entries.

Purée: Fruit, vegetable, meat or fish which has been pounded or sieved (usually after cooking) to give a smooth, finely divided pulp. A soup made by sieving vegetables with a liquor in which they were cooked is also called a purée.

The thickness of the purée depends on the amount of liquid present before sieving; a purée of cooked green peas or potatoes, for example, is very stiff and can be piped for decoration. Tomato purée, on the other hand, is soft and runny and usually requires thickening before it can be used. When making a fruit purée for gelatine sweets, fools, etc., it is advisable to use very little water for stewing the fruit, otherwise the purée will be too thin.

The food is usually sieved while still warm; in the case of meat and fish, the bones and gristle must first be removed and the flesh can then be pounded in a mortar.

A wire sieve may be used for vegetables and meat, but a nylon or hair one is better for fruit, to avoid discoloration and a metallic taste.

Reducing: The process of boiling a mixture (especially when making a sauce, soup or syrup) in an uncovered pan to evaporate surplus liquid and give a more concentrated result.

Rendering: To extract fat from meat trimmings (see Fats entry for details).

Refreshing: A process used by French cooks when preparing vegetables. After the vegetables have been cooked, cold water is poured over them to preserve the colour; they are then reheated before being served.

Rubbing in: A method of incorporating fat into flour, used in making shortcrust pastry, plain cakes and so on, where a short texture is required. First cut the fat into small pieces in the flour, then rub fat and flour between the thumbs and finger-tips. Lift the hands well above the bowl, allowing the mixture to fall back into the bowl – this helps to keep it cool. Continue until the mixture is even throughout and resembles fine breadcrumbs: to test this, shake the bowl, when any large lumps remaining will be seen on the surface, while dry flour will collect at the bottom of the bowl.

1. Never try to rub in more than half as much fat as flour.

449

2. Have the fat cold and firm.

3. Do not cut short the rubbing-in process – it must be done thoroughly to ensure a short and even texture.

Sauté: Food cooked in fat without being browned. The word is derived from the French *sauter*, to jump, and suggests the action of tossing the food in the hot fat.

The vegetables used in making soups, stews and sauces are often sautéed to improve their flavour without spoiling the colour of the finished dish. Sauté potatoes are boiled, cut into slices and cooked in a little fat until lightly browned.

Scalding: The process of pouring boiling water over food in order to clean it, to loosen hairs (e.g., from a joint of pork) or to skin it (e.g., tomatoes, peaches). The food must not be left in boiling water, or it will begin to cook.

The term also means the process of heating milk almost to boiling point, to retard souring.

Scalloped Dishes: Food (often previously cooked) baked in a scallop shell or similar small container: it is usually combined with a creamy sauce, topped with breadcrumbs and surrounded by a border of piped potato.

Scalloping: A way of decorating the double edge of the pastry covering of a pie. Make horizontal cuts with a knife close together round the edge of the pie, giving a flaked effect. Now, using the back of the knife, pull the edge up vertically at regular intervals to form scallops. These should be close together for a sweet pie and wider apart for a savoury one.

Scoring: To make shallow cuts in the surface of food in order to improve its flavour or appearance or to help it cook more quickly. Thus fish has a better flavour if scored before being marinated or soused; the crackling of pork is scored before roasting to prevent its pulling the joint out of shape and to facilitate carving.

Searing: To brown meat quickly in a little fat before grilling or roasting it. The term is some-times used when vegetables are browned in fat before being used in soup- or sauce-making.

Shirring: To bake food (usually eggs) in a small shallow container or ramekin dish.

Shredding: To slice a food such as cheese or raw vegetables into very fine pieces, which often curl as they are cut. A sharp knife or a coarse grater is used.

Sieving: To rub or press food (e.g., cooked vegetables) through a sieve; a wooden spoon is used to force it through; see Purée entry.

Sifting: To sift is to shake flour and similar dry ingredients through a sieve. If more than one ingredient is being used, they should be mixed before sifting.

Simmering: To keep a liquid just below boiling point (i.e., at approx. 96°C/205°F). First bring the liquid to the boil, then adjust the heat so that the surface of the liquid is kept just moving or shivering – bubbling indicates that the temperature is too high.

Simmering is the method used for many dishes which require long, slow cooking, such as stews.

Singeing: To pass a plucked bird quickly over a flame to burn off the down. See Poultry entry.

Skimming: To take fat off the surface of stock, gravy, stews, etc., or scum from other foods, e.g. jams, while they are cooking. A torn piece of kitchen paper or a metal spoon may be used.

Steeping: The process of pouring hot or cold water over food and leaving it to stand, either to soften it or to extract its flavour and colour.

Tammy: To squeeze a sauce through a fine woollen cloth to strain it and make it glossy.

Tepid: See Lukewarm.

Whipping, Whisking: The process of beating egg whites, cream, etc., until thick and stiff. A whisk of some kind is usually employed, though some people prefer a fork. An electric mixer may also be used – follow the manufacturer's directions.

MENU GLOSSARY

In this alphabetical glossary we aim at including the French and other phrases most likely to be seen in restaurant and hotel menus. While it is easy enough to look up the name of foodstuffs such as *agneau* (lamb), it is not so easy to discover from a dictionary or phrase-book that *Sauté d'Agneau à l'hongroise*, for example, will have a cream and paprika sauce.

For ease of reference we give first those terms — usually describing a method of preparation or a garnish — which in formal menus are mostly preceded by the words *à la, au* or *en*, but listing them according to the first letter of the main word. These are followed by the names of particular types of dish such as *brandade* and adjectives often applied to food, such as *brûlé*.

Part I

À l'Allemande: Applied to dishes finished or garnished with such German specialities as sauerkraut, smoked sausage, pickled pork, potato dumplings or noodles tossed in butter. Also means dishes served with Allemande sauce.

À l'Alsacienne: With a fairly elaborate garnish, the best known variation probably being smoked sausages, ham and peas.

À l'Américaine: Denotes various methods of preparing meat, game, fish, vegetables and eggs, the best known example being Homard à l'Américaine, where the sauce has a basis of tomato, onion and herbs, cooked in wine or brandy.

À l'Ancienne: Literally, old-style. Usually means a dish with a mixed garnish, consisting of beans, cooked lettuce and hard-boiled egg.

À l'Andalouse: Applied to a variety of recipes, but often involving the use of tomatoes and rice.

À l'Anglaise: Plainly cooked, usually boiled in stock or water.

À l'Archiduc: Applies to many dishes, usually seasoned with paprika and blended with cream.

À l'Aurore: Dishes served with tomato-flavoured aurore sauce or items of a yellow colour, often dome shaped, suggesting the rising sun.

Au Beurre: Cooked or served with butter.

À la Bigarade: With orange or orange sauce.

Au Blanc: White or with white sauce.

Au Bleu: Fish such as trout, cooked immediately after they are caught by simmering in white wine with herbs, or in water containing salt and vinegar.

À la Bonne Femme: (See main entry, under Bonne Femme).

À la Bordelaise: Incorporating a wine sauce, cèpes, or a garnish of artichokes and potatoes.

En Bordure: With a border of cooked vegetables.

À la Bourgeoise: 'Family style', homely but appetizing cookery. Also means garnished with small carrots and onions and with diced lean bacon.

À la Bourgogne (Bourguignonne): With a garnish incorporating mushrooms, small onions and grilled bacon and cooked or served in red wine sauce.

À la Bretonne: Usually implies a garnish of haricot beans or bean purée. There is also a Bretonne sauce, used with eggs and fish, which includes onions or leeks and white wine.

En Broche (Brochette): Roasted or grilled on a spit or skewer.

À la Cardinal: With a scarlet effect, as when a fish dish is served with a coral or lobster sauce dusted with paprika or cayenne.

À la Carte: In a restaurant, food prepared or served to order and not part of a set (table d'hôte) meal.

(À la) Catalane: With a garnish of aubergine and rice.

À la Chantilly: Including or accompanied by vanilla-flavoured sweetened whipped cream.

À la Chasseur: Hunter's style. With a garnish of mushrooms cooked with shallots and white wine.

En Cocotte: Cooked and served in a small (or occasionally a large) casserole.

451

À la Colbert: Name given to two well-known dishes; for Sole Colbert see Sole entry. Consommé à la Colbert is garnished with small poached eggs.

(À la) Condé: Usually denotes the presence of rice. Also the name of a type of pâtisserie.

En Coquille: Served in the shell, or made to resemble a shell.

(À la) Crécy: Made or garnished with carrots.

À la Créole: Usually includes rice with – in the case of savoury dishes – a garnish or sauce of red peppers and tomatoes. For sweet dishes, orange, banana, pineapple or rum are often included.

En Croûte: Game, entrées and savouries, etc., served on a shaped slice of bread or pastry, which is toasted, fried or baked.

En Daube: Braised or stewed.

À la Diable (Diablé): Devilled or highly spiced.

À la Diéppoise: Sea water fish garnished with crayfish tails and mussels and served with a white wine sauce.

À la Dubarry: A rich cauliflower soup or a cauliflower garnish.

À la Duchesse: Rich creamed potato, either made into fancy shapes, or used as a topping; also Béchamel sauce with tongue and mushrooms.

À la Financière: Meat or poultry in a rich brown Madeira sauce containing mushrooms and truffles, or with a garnish of cocks' combs, cocks' kidneys, truffles, olives and mushrooms.

À la Flamande: Served with a garnish of braised vegetables and bacon or small pork sausages.

À la Florentine: Fish or eggs served with spinach.

À la Forestière: Meat or poultry with a garnish of mushrooms, ham or bacon and fried potatoes.

Au Four: Cooked in the oven.

Au Gras: Cooked and dressed with rich gravy or sauce.

Au Gratin: Sprinkled with breadcrumbs and/or grated cheese and then browned. (Note: although in England the phrase has come to suggest a cheese topping, this is not necessarily implied by the French word, which merely means that the dish has a thin brown top crust formed by grilling or by heating in a hot oven.)

À la Hollandaise: With Hollandaise sauce (see recipe entry).

À l'Hongroise: Cooked in a cream sauce seasoned with paprika.

À l'Huile: With olive oil or olive oil dressing.

À l'Impératrice: Name given to various dishes and cakes, the best known being Riz (rice) à l'Impératrice.

À l'Impériale: Dishes with a rich garnish of foie gras, truffles, cocks' combs and kidneys.

À l'Indienne: Generally applied to Indian-type dishes including curry or chutney and often served with rice.

À l'Italienne: Generally applied to dishes made partly or wholly of pasta and often with cheese and tomato flavouring.

À la Jardinière: Prepared or served with a variety of vegetables.

À la Julienne: See main entry, under Julienne.

Au Jus: Served with the natural juices or gravy.

Au Kari: Curried.

À la King: Served in a rich cream sauce (often flavoured with sherry) and including mushrooms and green peppers.

À la Lyonnaise: With fried shredded onion as a principal ingredient.

À la Madrilène: Flavoured with tomato.

Au Maigre: Without meat and therefore suitable for Lent or a fast day.

À la Maître d'Hôtel: With maître d'hôtel or parsley butter (see main entry).

À la Marinière: For Moules Marinière see Mussels entry. The term is also applied to fish dishes cooked in white wine and garnished with mussels.

À la Maryland: With a butter and cream sauce, often containing wine. Maryland Chicken has a garnish of sweet corn fritters and fried bananas.

À la Meunière: Fish dredged with flour, fried in butter and served with this butter and chopped parsley.

À la Milanaise: Garnished with spaghetti, tomato sauce and ham or tongue. Also food dipped in egg and a mixture of breadcrumbs and cheese, then fried.

À la Minute: Quickly cooked, e.g. grills, omelettes.

À la Mode: Beef braised in the classic way; also (in America) fruit or other sweet pie served with ice cream.

À la Montmorency: Name of various sweet dishes and cakes which include cherries.

À la Mornay: Coated with cheese (Mornay) sauce. (See Sauce entry.)

À la Nantua: Garnished (or in some cases made) with crayfish.

À la Napolitaine: With a garnish of spaghetti, cheese and tomato sauce.

Au Naturel: Plain, uncooked (e.g. oysters) or very simply cooked.

À la Nesselrode: Implies the use of chestnuts.

À la Niçoise: As a garnish for meat, implies use of tomatoes, olives and French beans; as a soup, garnished with tomato, flageolets and diced potato; as a sauce, concentrated tomato purée blended with demi-glace.

À la Normande: Containing apples; or, in the case of fish, served with Normande sauce and garnished with shrimps, truffles, crayfish or mussels.

À l'Orientale: Fish, eggs, vegetables, cooked with tomatoes and flavoured with garlic and often with saffron.

En Papillote: Made or served in a paper case.

À la Parisienne: A garnish which varies considerably, but always includes pommes de terre à la parisienne.

À la Parmesan: Including grated Parmesan cheese.

À la Paysanne: Peasant or simple country style. Meat or poultry, usually braised and accompanied by a garnish or mixed vegetables, bacon, etc.

À la Périgueux (à la Périgord, à la Périgourdine): Made or served with truffles and sometimes foie gras.

À la Polonaise: Used for a variety of dishes; often implies presence of soured cream, beetroot and red cabbage.

À la Portugaise: Most dishes with this title include tomato, onion or garlic.

À la Poulette: Usually means a sort of fricassée of cooked meat or poultry in rich white sauce, garnished with onions or garlic.

À la Provençale: Containing olive oil, garlic and often tomatoes.

À la Princesse: With a garnish of asparagus tips and truffles or noisette potatoes.

À la Printanière: Spring style, i.e. containing or garnished with small, young vegetables.

À la Reine: Implies that the dish is based on chicken.

À la Richelieu: Made with Richelieu sauce (a rich brown Madeira sauce) or garnished with mushrooms, artichoke bottoms, or stuffed tomatoes, etc. The name is also given to other dishes, such as a sweet pastry.

À la Royale: Applied to a variety of methods of cooking and serving. Consommé royale is garnished with tiny savoury custard shapes.

À la St. Germain: Indicates the use of green peas.

À la Soubise: Flavoured with onion or garnished with onion purée.

Table d'Hôte: A meal consisting of a certain number of courses at a fixed price; there is usually some choice of dishes within each course.

453

En Tasse: In a cup, especially of soups, etc.

Au Vert-pré: Garnished with watercress and straw potatoes and often served with maître d'hôtel butter; also, coated with green mayonnaise.

À la Vichy: Implies the use of carrots.

À la Vinaigrette: With a dressing of oil, vinegar and herbs.

À la Walewska: Fish with a lobster sauce and garnish.

Part II

Aiguillette: A thin strip or slice of cooked poultry, meat or fish.

Aillade: Name given to various sauces and accompaniments for salads, all strongly flavoured with garlic.

Ballottine: A kind of galantine, usually served hot but sometimes cold, made of meat, poultry, game or fish, boned, stuffed and rolled into a bundle. The word is also used for small balls of meat or poultry.

Barquette: Small boat-shaped pastry cases, used for both savoury and sweet mixtures.

Brandade: A dish based on salt cod, flavoured with garlic, which is popular in Southern France.

Brûlé: Literally, 'burnt' – in other words, the food is grilled or otherwise heated sufficiently to give it a good brown colour, as in Crème Brûlée.

Brunoise: A mixture of diced or shredded vegetables used as base for a soup or sauce or as a garnish.

Émincé: Cut in thin slices or shredded.

Estouffade (also Estouffat, Étuve): Meat cooked very slowly in very little liquid, i.e., braised or casseroled.

Frappé: Iced, frozen or chilled.

Friandises: A variety of small sweets, preserved fruits, etc., served as petits fours or desserts.

Frit: Fried; *Friture*, fried food.

Glacé: This can mean either (1) iced or frozen; or (2) having a smooth, glossy surface or glaze, whether savoury or sweet.

Haché: Minced or chopped.

Hachis: Mince of hash; food cut up finely.

Maison: In the style of the particular restaurant.

Matelote: A rich, well seasoned fish stew made with red or white wine.

Mignardise: Small and dainty made-up dishes.

Mignon: Small, dainty, e.g., small portions of fillet of beef.

Navarin: A ragoût of mutton and either potatoes and onions or mixed spring vegetables.

Noisette: A small, round, individual portion or slice of meat.

Pâte: Paste, dough, batter, pastry.

Pâté: A pie made with pastry or a terrine made in a pie dish, baked and served cold.

Paupiette: A small, thinly cut piece of meat wrapped round a filling of forcemeat, covered with a bacon rasher and braised; similar fillets of fish are rolled round a piece of potato (which is later removed) and then fried; the hollow left when the potato is removed is filled with a rich white sauce.

Plat du Jour: The main dish of the day at a restaurant.

Poêlé: Braised, pot-roasted.

Pré-Salé: Name given to mutton and lamb raised on salt marshes; the meat is considered especially well flavoured.

Rafraîchi: Chilled.

Recherché: Choice, rare, dainty.

Renversé: Turned out, as of a cream or jelly.

Rissolé: Baked or fried and well-browned.

Roulade: Meat roll or galantine.

Rubané: Built up of ribbon-like layers.

Soubise: Purée of rice and onions, or onions only.

Suprême: The best or most delicate part, e.g. breast of chicken. (See also Suprême Sauce entry.)

SHOPPING AND CATERING GUIDE

Given below are the approximate quantities per head per meal to allow for family catering; they will serve as a guide to anyone who is catering for the first time. (For quantities for entertaining see Party entry.)

MEAT

With bone	100 g/4 oz–175 g/6 oz
Boneless	75 g/3 oz–100 g/4 oz
For made-up dishes	50 g/2 oz–75 g/3 oz

FISH

With much bone	175 g/6 oz–225 g/8 oz
Little or no bone	75 g/3 oz–100 g/4 oz
For made-up dishes	50 g/2 oz–75 g/3 oz

VEGETABLES *(weight as purchased)*

Artichokes (Jerusalem)	175 g/6 oz
Beans (broad)	225 g/8 oz–350 g/12 oz
Beans (runner)	175 g/6 oz
Beans (butter or haricot)	50 g/2 oz
Beetroot (as a vegetable)	100 g/4 oz–175 g/6 oz
Brussels sprouts	175 g/6 oz
Cabbage	225 g/8 oz
Carrots	100 g/4 oz–175 g/6 oz
Celeriac	100 g/4 oz–175 g/6 oz
Celery	1 large head for 4–5 persons
Curly kale	175 g/6 oz–225 g/8 oz
Greens (spring)	225 g/8 oz
Onions (as a main vegetable)	175 g/6 oz
Parsnips	175 g/6 oz
Peas (green)	225 g/8 oz
Peas (dried)	50 g/2 oz
Potatoes	175 g/6 oz–225 g/8 oz
Savoy	175 g/6 oz–225 g/8 oz

Seakale	100 g/4 oz
Spinach	225 g/8 oz–350 g/12 oz
Swedes	225 g/8 oz
Turnips	225 g/8 oz
Turnip tops	225 g/8 oz

PUDDINGS

Sponge, suet puddings	40 g/1 ½ oz flour, etc.
Pastry (for pies, puddings)	40 g/1 ½ oz flour, etc.
Milk puddings	150 ml/¼ pint milk, etc.
Batter (Yorkshire pudding)	25 g/1 oz flour
Junket	150 ml/¼ pint milk
Fruit (pies, puddings, stewed)	100 g/4 oz of fruit
Custard, as sauce	60 ml/2 fl oz milk

CEREALS

Rice (for curry, etc.)	25 g/1 oz–40 g/1 ½ oz
Macaroni	25 g/1 oz–40 g/1 ½ oz
Oatmeal (for porridge)	25 g/1 oz–40 g/1 ½ oz

BEVERAGES

Coffee (breakfast)	75 g/3 oz per 4 people
Coffee (after-dinner)	40 g/1 ½ oz per 4 people
Milk (in tea)	300 ml/½ pint per 4 people
Tea	1 × 5 ml spoon/1 teaspoon per person

MISCELLANEOUS

Soup	150 ml/¼ pint–200 ml/⅓ pint
Sauces and gravies	60 ml/2 fl oz

When using recipes in this book, please note:

As a general rule, the quantities given make 4 average servings.

All spoonfuls are measures *level*, not rounded or heaped.

In quoting oven heats we have followed the gas settings approved by the gas council and gas appliance manufacturers, together with the nearest equivalent electric oven setting and corresponding Centigrade/Fahrenheit temperature.

Please see also the entry on Recipes, also such basic entries as Flour, Raising Agents and so on.